Hello

GIVE ME LIBERTY!

AN AMERICAN HISTORY

Brief Sixth High School Edition

★

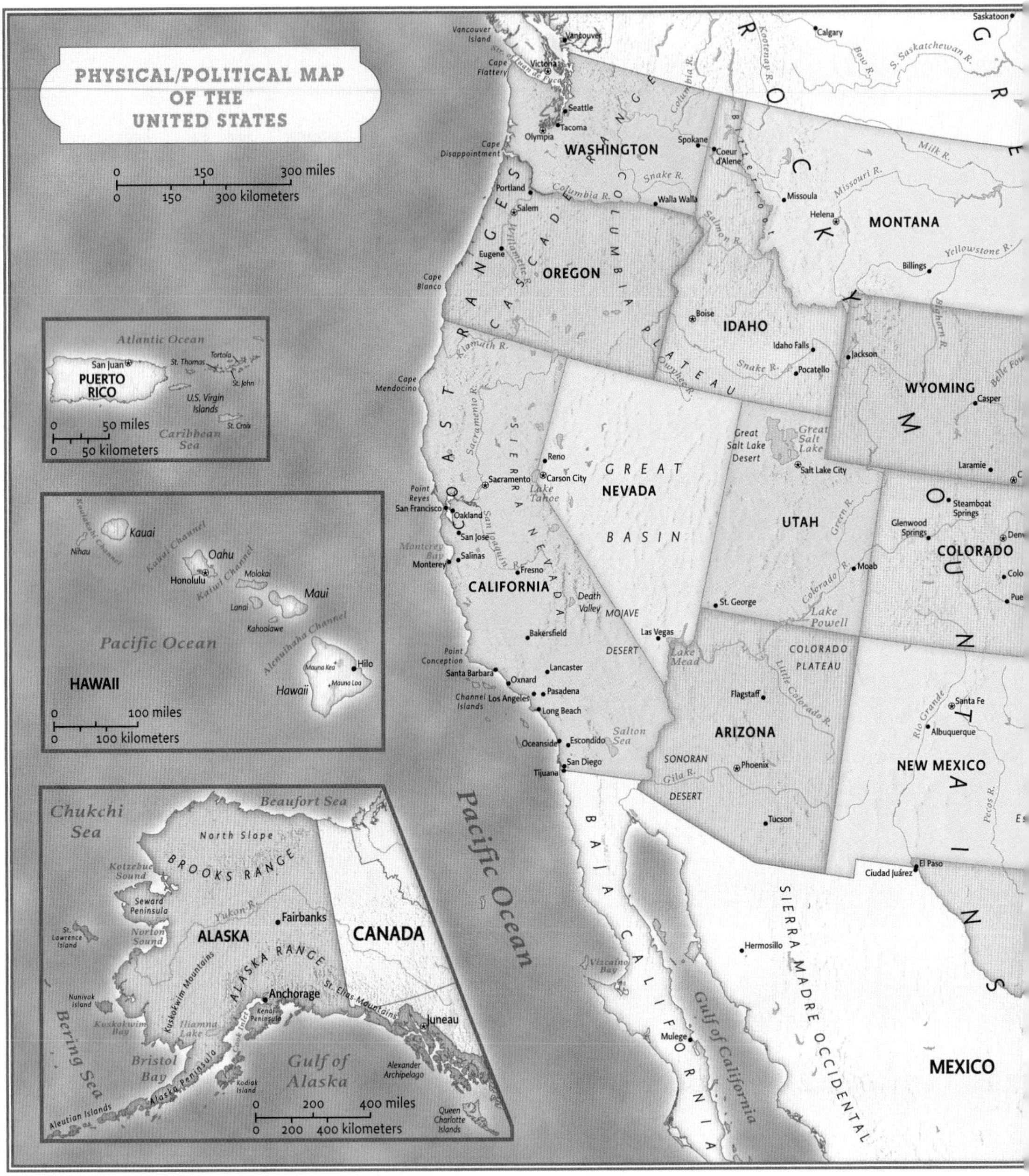
PHYSICAL/POLITICAL MAP OF THE UNITED STATES
0 150 300 miles
0 150 300 kilometers
Atlantic Ocean
San Juan
PUERTO RICO
St. Thomas
Tortola
St. John
U.S. Virgin Islands
St. Croix
Caribbean Sea
50 miles
50 kilometers
Kauai
Niihau
Kaulakahi Channel
Kauai Channel
Oahu
Honolulu
Kaiwi Channel
Molokai
Maui
Lanai
Kahoolawe
Alenuihaha Channel
Pacific Ocean
HAWAII
Hilo
Mauna Kea
Mauna Loa
Hawaii
100 miles
100 kilometers
Chukchi Sea
Beaufort Sea
North Slope
BROOKS RANGE
Kotzebue Sound
Seward Peninsula
Yukon R.
Fairbanks
St. Lawrence Island
Norton Sound
ALASKA
CANADA
Kuskokwim Mountains
ALASKA RANGE
Anchorage
St. Elias Mountains
Juneau
Nunivak Island
Kuskokwim Bay
Iliamna Lake
Kenai Peninsula
Cook Inlet
Bering Sea
Bristol Bay
Alaska Peninsula
Gulf of Alaska
Alexander Archipelago
Kodiak Island
Aleutian Islands
200 400 miles
200 400 kilometers
Queen Charlotte Islands
Pacific Ocean
Vancouver Island
Vancouver
Victoria
Str. of Juan de Fuca
Cape Flattery
Seattle
Tacoma
Olympia
Cape Disappointment
WASHINGTON
Spokane
Coeur d'Alene
Columbia R.
Kootenay R.
Calgary
Bow R.
S. Saskatchewan R.
Saskatoon
Milk R.
Missouri R.
Snake R.
Walla Walla
Portland
Salem
Willamette R.
Eugene
OREGON
Cape Blanco
Missoula
Helena
MONTANA
Yellowstone R.
Billings
Salmon R.
Boise
IDAHO
Idaho Falls
Pocatello
Jackson
Bighorn R.
WYOMING
Casper
Belle Fourche
Owyhee R.
Snake R.
Klamath R.
Cape Mendocino
Sacramento R.
Great Salt Lake
Great Salt Lake Desert
Salt Lake City
Reno
Carson City
Sacramento
Lake Tahoe
GREAT BASIN
NEVADA
Laramie
Point Reyes
San Francisco
Oakland
San Jose
Steamboat Springs
Glenwood Springs
UTAH
Green R.
COLORADO
Monterey Bay
Salinas
Monterey
San Joaquin R.
Fresno
CALIFORNIA
Colorado R.
Moab
Death Valley
MOJAVE DESERT
St. George
Lake Powell
Bakersfield
Las Vegas
Lake Mead
COLORADO PLATEAU
Point Conception
Santa Barbara
Oxnard
Lancaster
Channel Islands
Los Angeles
Pasadena
Long Beach
Flagstaff
Little Colorado R.
Santa Fe
Rio Grande
Albuquerque
Salton Sea
Oceanside
Escondido
San Diego
Tijuana
ARIZONA
SONORAN DESERT
Gila R.
Phoenix
NEW MEXICO
Tucson
Pecos R.
El Paso
Ciudad Juárez
COAST RANGES
CASCADE RANGE
COLUMBIA PLATEAU
SIERRA NEVADA
BITTERROOT
GREAT
ROCKY MOUNTAINS
BAJA CALIFORNIA
Vizcaíno Bay
Gulf of California
Mulegé
Hermosillo
SIERRA MADRE OCCIDENTAL
MEXICO

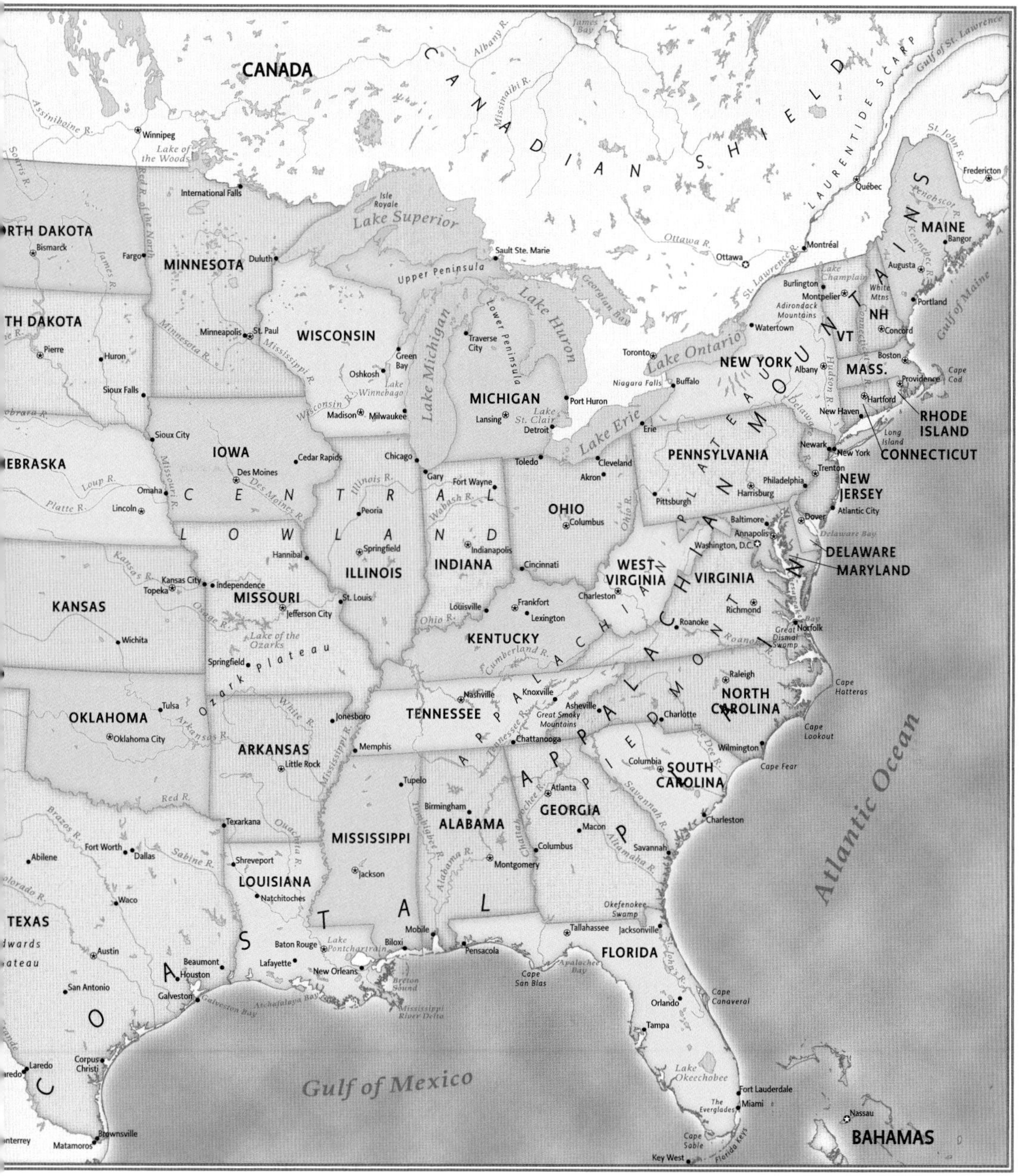
CANADA
CANADIAN SHIELD
LAURENTIDE SCARP
Gulf of St. Lawrence
James Bay
Albany R.
Missinaibi R.
Assiniboine R.
Winnipeg
Lake of the Woods
Souris R.
Red R. of the North
International Falls
Isle Royale
Lake Superior
Ottawa R.
Ottawa
Montréal
Québec
Fredericton
St. John R.
Sault Ste. Marie
Upper Peninsula
Lower Peninsula
Georgian Bay
Lake Huron
Lake Michigan
Lake Ontario
Lake Erie
Lake St. Clair
St. Lawrence R.
Lake Champlain
Adirondack Mountains
White Mtns
Penobscot R.
Kennebec R.
Gulf of Maine
APPALACHIAN MOUNTAINS
APPALACHIAN PLATEAU
PIEDMONT
CENTRAL LOWLAND
COASTAL PLAIN
Ozark plateau
NORTH DAKOTA
SOUTH DAKOTA
NEBRASKA
KANSAS
OKLAHOMA
TEXAS
MINNESOTA
IOWA
MISSOURI
ARKANSAS
LOUISIANA
WISCONSIN
ILLINOIS
MICHIGAN
INDIANA
OHIO
KENTUCKY
TENNESSEE
MISSISSIPPI
ALABAMA
GEORGIA
FLORIDA
SOUTH CAROLINA
NORTH CAROLINA
VIRGINIA
WEST VIRGINIA
PENNSYLVANIA
NEW YORK
VT
NH
MAINE
MASS.
RHODE ISLAND
CONNECTICUT
NEW JERSEY
DELAWARE
MARYLAND
BAHAMAS
Bismarck
Fargo
James R.
Pierre
Huron
Sioux Falls
Sioux City
Omaha
Lincoln
Loup R.
Platte R.
Niobrara R.
Duluth
Minneapolis
St. Paul
Minnesota R.
Mississippi R.
Green Bay
Oshkosh
Lake Winnebago
Wisconsin R.
Madison
Milwaukee
Traverse City
Lansing
Detroit
Port Huron
Toronto
Niagara Falls
Buffalo
Watertown
Burlington
Montpelier
Augusta
Bangor
Portland
Concord
Boston
Albany
Hudson R.
Connecticut R.
Delaware R.
Providence
Hartford
New Haven
Cape Cod
Long Island
Newark
New York
Trenton
Philadelphia
Harrisburg
Pittsburgh
Erie
Cleveland
Akron
Toledo
Chicago
Gary
Fort Wayne
Cedar Rapids
Des Moines
Des Moines R.
Missouri R.
Illinois R.
Wabash R.
Peoria
Springfield
Indianapolis
Columbus
Ohio R.
Cincinnati
Hannibal
Kansas City
Independence
Topeka
Kansas R.
St. Louis
Jefferson City
Osage R.
Lake of the Ozarks
Wichita
Springfield
Louisville
Frankfort
Lexington
Charleston
Cumberland R.
Baltimore
Annapolis
Dover
Atlantic City
Delaware Bay
Washington, D.C.
Richmond
Roanoke
Roanoke R.
Chesapeake Bay
Norfolk
Great Dismal Swamp
Raleigh
Cape Hatteras
Cape Lookout
Cape Fear
Wilmington
Charlotte
Asheville
Knoxville
Nashville
Great Smoky Mountains
Chattanooga
Tennessee R.
Tulsa
Arkansas R.
Oklahoma City
White R.
Jonesboro
Memphis
Little Rock
Red R.
Tupelo
Birmingham
Atlanta
Columbia
Savannah R.
Charleston
Macon
Columbus
Savannah
Altamaha R.
Chattahoochee R.
Alabama R.
Tombigbee R.
Montgomery
Jackson
Texarkana
Ouachita R.
Shreveport
Natchitoches
Sabine R.
Brazos R.
Fort Worth
Dallas
Abilene
Waco
Colorado R.
Edwards Plateau
Austin
San Antonio
Beaumont
Houston
Galveston
Galveston Bay
Baton Rouge
Lafayette
Lake Pontchartrain
New Orleans
Breton Sound
Atchafalaya Bay
Mississippi River Delta
Biloxi
Mobile
Pensacola
Tallahassee
Apalachee Bay
Cape San Blas
Jacksonville
Okefenokee Swamp
St. Johns R.
Cape Canaveral
Orlando
Tampa
Lake Okeechobee
Fort Lauderdale
Miami
The Everglades
Cape Sable
Key West
Florida Keys
Nassau
Laredo
Corpus Christi
Brownsville
Matamoros
Monterrey
Gulf of Mexico
Atlantic Ocean

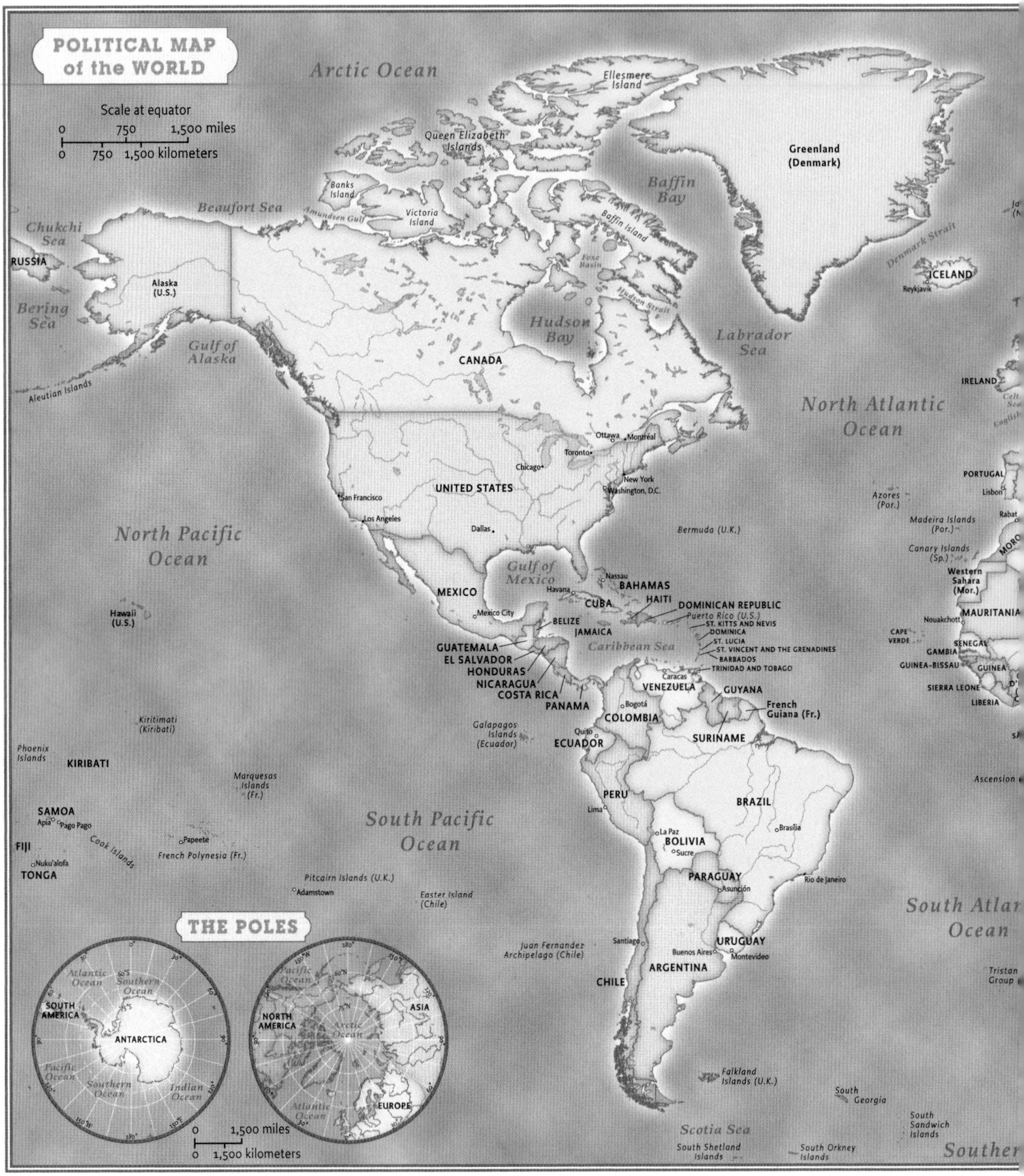
POLITICAL MAP of the WORLD
Scale at equator
0 750 1,500 miles
0 750 1,500 kilometers
Arctic Ocean
Ellesmere Island
Queen Elizabeth Islands
Greenland (Denmark)
Baffin Bay
Banks Island
Victoria Island
Amundsen Gulf
Beaufort Sea
Baffin Island
Foxe Basin
Denmark Strait
ICELAND
Reykjavik
Chukchi Sea
RUSSIA
Alaska (U.S.)
Bering Sea
Hudson Strait
Hudson Bay
Labrador Sea
Gulf of Alaska
CANADA
Aleutian Islands
IRELAND
North Atlantic Ocean
Ottawa
Montréal
Toronto
Chicago
New York
Washington, D.C.
PORTUGAL
Lisbon
San Francisco
UNITED STATES
Azores (Por.)
Los Angeles
Madeira Islands (Por.)
Rabat
Dallas
Bermuda (U.K.)
North Pacific Ocean
Canary Islands (Sp.)
Gulf of Mexico
Nassau
Western Sahara (Mor.)
BAHAMAS
MEXICO
Havana
CUBA
HAITI
DOMINICAN REPUBLIC
Puerto Rico (U.S.)
ST. KITTS AND NEVIS
DOMINICA
ST. LUCIA
ST. VINCENT AND THE GRENADINES
BARBADOS
TRINIDAD AND TOBAGO
Hawaii (U.S.)
Mexico City
BELIZE
JAMAICA
MAURITANIA
Nouakchott
CAPE VERDE
SENEGAL
GAMBIA
GUINEA-BISSAU
GUINEA
SIERRA LEONE
LIBERIA
GUATEMALA
EL SALVADOR
HONDURAS
NICARAGUA
COSTA RICA
PANAMA
Caribbean Sea
Caracas
VENEZUELA
GUYANA
French Guiana (Fr.)
Bogotá
COLOMBIA
SURINAME
Kiritimati (Kiribati)
Galapagos Islands (Ecuador)
Quito
ECUADOR
Phoenix Islands
KIRIBATI
Marquesas Islands (Fr.)
Ascension
PERU
BRAZIL
Lima
SAMOA
Apia
Pago Pago
South Pacific Ocean
La Paz
BOLIVIA
Sucre
Brasília
FIJI
Cook Islands
Papeete
French Polynesia (Fr.)
Nuku'alofa
TONGA
PARAGUAY
Asunción
Rio de Janeiro
Pitcairn Islands (U.K.)
Adamstown
Easter Island (Chile)
South Atlantic Ocean
THE POLES
Juan Fernandez Archipelago (Chile)
Santiago
URUGUAY
Buenos Aires
Montevideo
ARGENTINA
CHILE
Tristan Group
Atlantic Ocean
Southern Ocean
SOUTH AMERICA
ANTARCTICA
Pacific Ocean
Indian Ocean
Pacific Ocean
NORTH AMERICA
ASIA
Arctic Ocean
Atlantic Ocean
EUROPE
Falkland Islands (U.K.)
South Georgia
South Sandwich Islands
0 1,500 miles
0 1,500 kilometers
Scotia Sea
South Shetland Islands
South Orkney Islands

Arctic Ocean
Franz Josef Land
Severnaya Zemlya
Svalbard (Norway)
Novaya Zemlya
Kara Sea
Barents Sea
Laptev Sea
New Siberian Islands
East Siberian Sea
Wrangel Island
RUSSIA
FINLAND
SWEDEN
Oslo
Stockholm
ESTONIA
LATVIA
LITHUANIA
RUS.
Moscow
Berlin
POLAND
BELARUS
CZECH REP.
SLOVAKIA
UKRAINE
AUSTRIA
HUNGARY
MOLDOVA
ROMANIA
CROATIA
B.H.
SERBIA
BULGARIA
ITALY
Rome
MONT.
MAC.
ALBANIA
GREECE
Black Sea
GEORGIA
ARMENIA
AZERBAIJAN
TURKEY
Caspian Sea
Bering Sea
Sea of Okhotsk
Aleutian Islands
Lake Baikal
Astana
KAZAKHSTAN
Aral Sea
Lake Balkhash
Ulan Bator
MONGOLIA
Kuril Islands
NORTH KOREA
UZBEKISTAN
KYRGYZSTAN
TURKMENISTAN
TAJIKISTAN
Beijing
Seoul
SOUTH KOREA
Sea of Japan
JAPAN
Tokyo
North Pacific Ocean
CYPRUS
LEBANON
ISRAEL
SYRIA
IRAQ
Tehran
IRAN
Kabul
AFGHANISTAN
Islamabad
CHINA
Yellow Sea
Tripoli
Cairo
JORDAN
LIBYA
EGYPT
KUWAIT
BAHRAIN
QATAR
SAUDI ARABIA
UNITED ARAB EMIRATES
Persian Gulf
Muscat
OMAN
Red Sea
PAKISTAN
New Delhi
Kathmandu
NEPAL
BHUTAN
Thimphu
BANGLADESH
Dhaka
East China Sea
TAIWAN
INDIA
MYANMAR
LAOS
South China Sea
Philippine Sea
Northern Mariana Islands (U.S.)
CHAD
Khartoum
SUDAN
ERITREA
YEMEN
Arabian Sea
Bay of Bengal
THAILAND
Manila
N'Djamena
Gulf of Aden
DJIBOUTI
Socotra (Yemen)
Andaman Islands (India)
VIETNAM
CAMBODIA
Gulf of Thailand
PHILIPPINES
Guam (U.S.)
MARSHALL ISLANDS
CENTRAL AFRICAN REP.
Adis Ababa
ETHIOPIA
SRI LANKA
PALAU
FEDERATED STATES OF MICRONESIA
SOMALIA
BRUNEI
MALDIVES
MALAYSIA
Celebes Sea
UGANDA
KENYA
Mogadishu
SINGAPORE
Nairobi
RWANDA
CONGO
DEMOCRATIC REP. OF CONGO
BURUNDI
SEYCHELLES
Chagos Archipelago (U.K.)
Sumatra
Borneo
NAURU
KIRIBATI
TANZANIA
Dar es Salaam
Jakarta
Java Sea
INDONESIA
PAPUA NEW GUINEA
SOLOMON ISLANDS
Luanda
Diego Garcia
Java
EAST TIMOR
Arafura Sea
Timor
Timor Sea
TUVALU
ANGOLA
COMOROS
ZAMBIA
MALAWI
MOZAMBIQUE
Coral Sea
Indian Ocean
Mozambique Channel
FIJI
ZIMBABWE
VANUATU
Antananarivo
NAMIBIA
MAURITIUS
MADAGASCAR
BOTSWANA
Windhoek
Gaborone
Réunion (Fr.)
New Caledonia (Fr.)
South Pacific Ocean
Pretoria
Johannesburg
SWAZILAND
AUSTRALIA
Maseru
SOUTH AFRICA
LESOTHO
Norfolk Island (Aus.)
Kermadec Islands (N.Z.)
Cape Town
Sydney
Canberra, A.C.T.
Tasman Sea
Great Australian Bight
North Island
NEW ZEALAND
Tasmania
South Island
Prince Edward Islands (So. Africa)
Crozet Islands
French Southern and Antarctic Lands (Fr.)
Kerguélen Islands
Heard Island and McDonald Islands (Aus.)
Southern Ocean

E PLURIBUS UNUM
LIBERTY
CONSTITUTION & LAWS

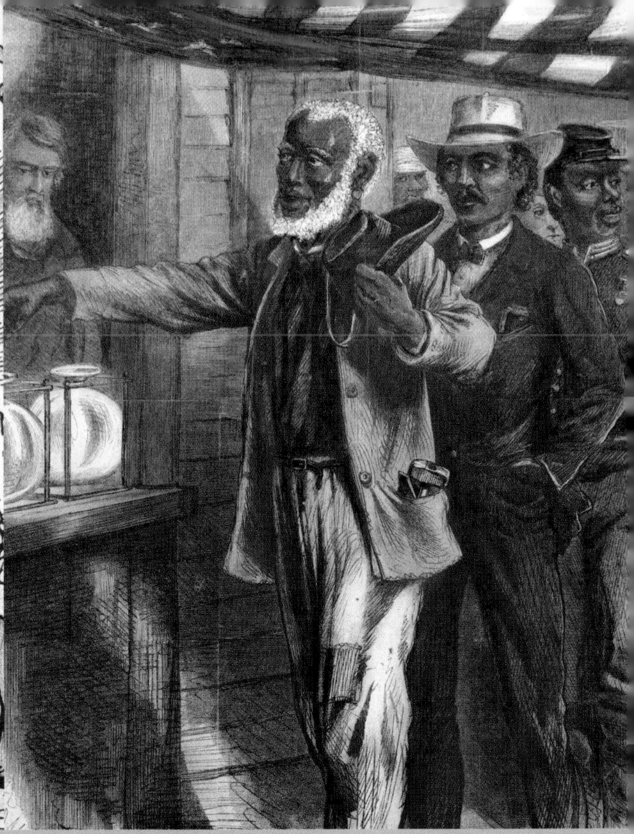

SOLD
by WHITE & POLLARD
GROCER
FRUITS
AND
VEGETABLES
I AM AN AMERIC

GIVE ME LIBERTY!

AN AMERICAN HISTORY

Brief Sixth High School Edition

ERIC FONER

W. W. NORTON & COMPANY
NEW YORK • LONDON

For my mother, Liza Foner (1909–2005), an accomplished artist who lived through most of the twentieth century and into the twenty-first

W. W. Norton & Company has been independent since its founding in 1923, when William Warder Norton and Mary D. Herter Norton first published lectures delivered at the People's Institute, the adult education division of New York City's Cooper Union. The firm soon expanded its program beyond the Institute, publishing books by celebrated academics from America and abroad. By midcentury, the two major pillars of Norton's publishing program—trade books and college texts—were firmly established. In the 1950s, the Norton family transferred control of the company to its employees, and today—with a staff of five hundred and hundreds of trade, college, and professional titles published each year—W. W. Norton & Company stands as the largest and oldest publishing house owned wholly by its employees.

Printed in Canada

Director of High School Publishing: Jenna Bookin Barry
Editor: Steve Forman
Project Editor: Maura Gaughan
Assistant Editor: Lily Gellman
Editorial Assistant: Anna Goodlett
Managing Editor, College: Marian Johnson
Associate Managing Editor: Melissa Atkin
Production Manager: Sean Mintus
Media Editor: Carson Russell
Associate Media Editors: Sarah Rose Aquilina and Alexander Lee
Media Project Editor: Rachel Mayer
Assistant Media Editor: Alexandra Malakhoff
Managing Editor, College Digital Media: Kim Yi
High School Marketing and Market Development Manager: Christina Magoulis
Ebook Production Manager: Danielle Lehmann
Marketing Manager, History: Sarah England Bartley
Design Director: Rubina Yeh
Designer: Chin-yee Lai / Lisa Buckley
Director of College Permissions: Megan Schindel
College Permissions Manager: Bethany Salminen
Photo Editor: Stephanie Romeo
Composition: Six Red Marbles
Illustrations: Mapping Specialists, Ltd.
Manufacturing: Transcontinental

Permission to use copyrighted material is included on page A-67.

The Library of Congress has cataloged an earlier edition as follows:

Names: Foner, Eric, 1943- author.
Title: Give me liberty! : an American history / Eric Foner.
Description: Sixth edition. | New York : W.W. Norton & Company, 2019. | Includes index.
Identifiers: LCCN 2019031048 | **ISBN 9780393675627 (hardcover)**
Subjects: LCSH: United States—History—Textbooks.
Classification: LCC E178 .F66 2019 | DDC 973—dc23
LC record available at https://lccn.loc.gov/2019031048

ISBN this edition: 978-0-393-41859-0

W. W. Norton & Company, Inc., 500 Fifth Avenue, New York, NY 10110
wwnorton.com
W. W. Norton & Company Ltd., 15 Carlisle Street, London W1D 3BS

3 4 5 6 7 8 9 0

ABOUT THE AUTHOR

★

ERIC FONER is DeWitt Clinton Professor Emeritus of History at Columbia University, where he earned his B.A. and Ph.D. In his teaching and scholarship, he focuses on the Civil War and Reconstruction, slavery, and nineteenth-century America. Professor Foner's publications include *Free Soil, Free Labor, Free Men: The Ideology of the Republican Party before the Civil War*; *Tom Paine and Revolutionary America*; *Nothing but Freedom: Emancipation and Its Legacy*; *Reconstruction: America's Unfinished Revolution, 1863–1877*; *The Story of American Freedom*; and *Forever Free: The Story of Emancipation and Reconstruction.* His history of Reconstruction won the *Los Angeles Times* Book Award for History, the Bancroft Prize, and the Parkman Prize. He has served as president of the Organization of American Historians and the American Historical Association. In 2006 he received the Presidential Award for Outstanding Teaching from Columbia University. His most recent books are *The Fiery Trial: Abraham Lincoln and American Slavery*, winner of the Bancroft and Lincoln Prizes and the Pulitzer Prize for History, *Gateway to Freedom: The Hidden History of the Underground Railroad*, winner of the New York Historical Society Book Prize, and *The Second Founding: How the Civil War and Reconstruction Remade the Constitution.*

CONTENTS

D. Martin di Loiola

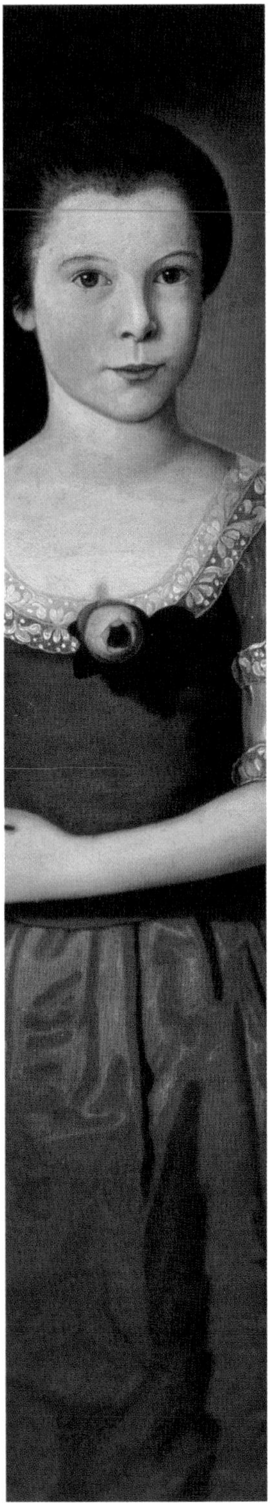

5. THE AMERICAN REVOLUTION, 1763–1783 ... 138

6. THE REVOLUTION WITHIN ... 167

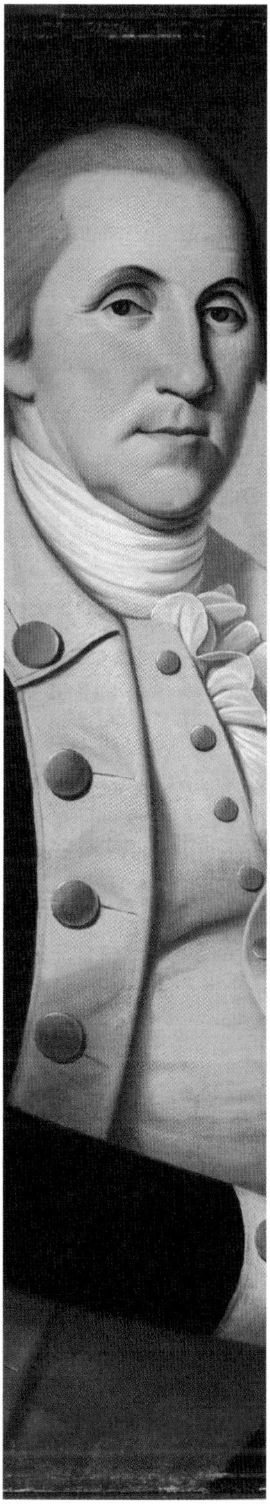

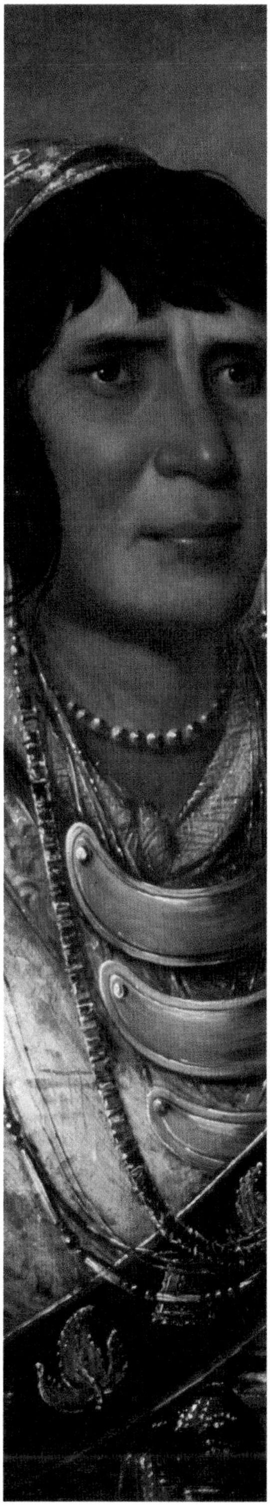

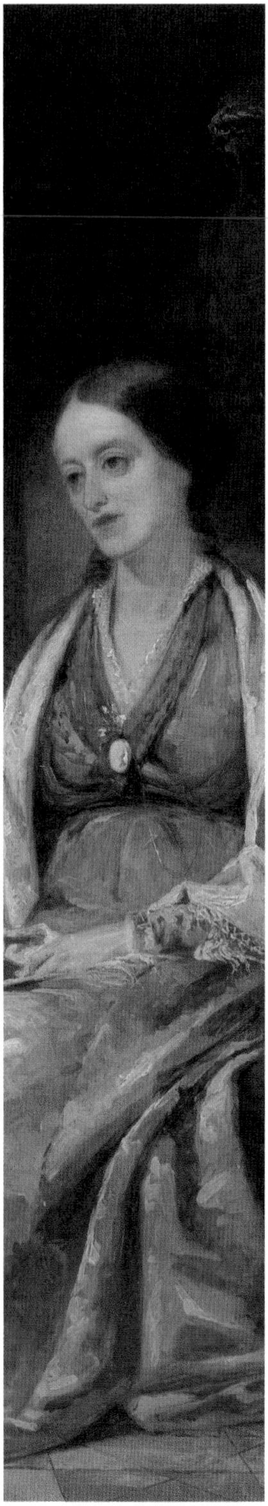

12. AN AGE OF REFORM, 1820–1840 ... 334

13. A HOUSE DIVIDED, 1840–1861 ... 360

14. A NEW BIRTH OF FREEDOM: THE CIVIL WAR, 1861–1865 ... 395

15. "WHAT IS FREEDOM?": RECONSTRUCTION, 1865–1877 ... 435

16. AMERICA'S GILDED AGE, 1870–1890 ... 469

ILDING, New York, April 6th, 1901.
ght, 1901, by Keppler & Schwarzmann.
WORLD POWER
NAVY
BIA'S EASTER BONNET.

18. THE PROGRESSIVE ERA, 1900–1916 ... 540

19. SAFE FOR DEMOCRACY: THE UNITED STATES AND WORLD WAR I, 1916–1920 ... 572

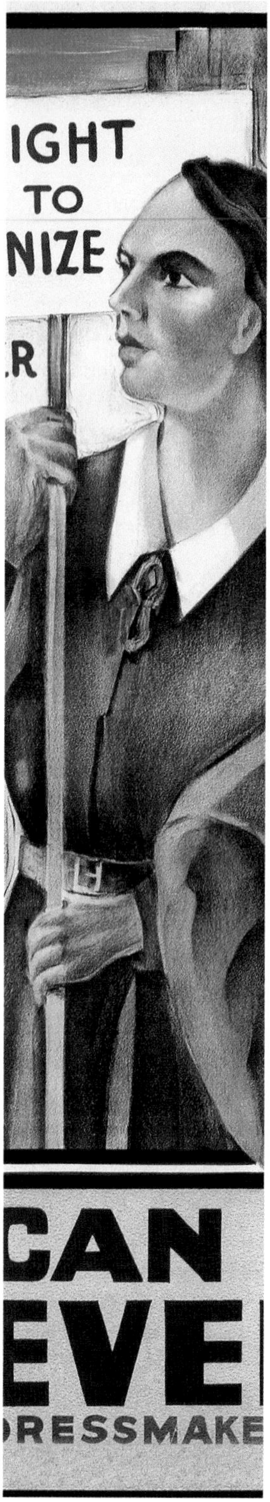
IGHT
TO
NIZE
CAN
EVE
RESSMAKE

USA
207

28. A DIVIDED NATION ... 880

APPENDIX

MAPS

CHAPTER 14

CHAPTER 15

CHAPTER 16

CHAPTER 17

CHAPTER 18

CHAPTER 19

CHAPTER 20

CHAPTER 21

CHAPTER 22

CHAPTER 23

CHAPTER 24

CHAPTER 25

CHAPTER 26

CHAPTER 27

CHAPTER 28

TABLES AND FIGURES

CHAPTER 27

CHAPTER 28

PREFACE

Give Me Liberty! An American History is a survey of American history from the earliest days of European exploration and conquest of the New World to the first decades of the twenty-first century. It offers students a clear, concise narrative whose central theme is the changing contours of American freedom.

I am extremely gratified by the response to the first five editions of *Give Me Liberty!*, which have been used in U.S. history classes at many hundreds of high schools throughout the country. The comments I have received from instructors and students encourage me to think that *Give Me Liberty!* has worked well in their classrooms. Their comments have also included many valuable suggestions for revisions, which I greatly appreciate. These have ranged from corrections of typographical and factual errors to thoughts about subjects that needed more extensive treatment. In making revisions for this Sixth Edition, I have tried to take these suggestions into account. I have also incorporated the findings and insights of new scholarship that has appeared since the original edition was written.

The most significant changes in this Sixth Edition involve heightened emphasis on a question as old as the republic and as current as today's newspapers: Who is an American?

Difference and commonality are both intrinsic parts of the American experience. Our national creed emphasizes democracy and freedom as universal rights, but these rights have frequently been limited to particular groups of people. The United States has long prided itself on being an "asylum for mankind," as Thomas Paine put it in *Common Sense*, his great pamphlet calling for American independence. Yet we as a people have long been divided by clashing definitions of "Americanness." The first Naturalization Act, adopted in 1790, limited the right to become a citizen when immigrating from abroad to white persons. And the right to vote was long denied to many Americans because of race, gender, property holding, a criminal record, or other reasons. Today, in debates over immigration and voting rights, the question of "Who is an American?" continues to roil our society.

In a nation resting, rhetorically at least, on the ideal of equality, the boundaries of inclusion and exclusion take on extreme significance. The greater the rights of American citizenship, the more important the definition of belonging. Groups like African-Americans and women, shut out from full equality from the beginning of the nation's history, have struggled to gain recognition as full and equal members of the society. The definition of citizenship itself and the rights that come with it have been subject to intense debate throughout American history. And the cry of "second-class citizenship" has provided a powerful language of social protest for those who feel themselves excluded. To be sure, not all groups have made demands for inclusion. In the colonial era and for much of the history of the American nation, many Native Americans have demanded recognition of their own national sovereignty.

There is stronger coverage of this theme throughout the book, and it is reinforced by a new primary-source feature, "Who Is an American?" The sixteen such features, distributed fairly evenly throughout the text, address the nature of American identity, the definition of citizenship, and controversies over inclusion and exclusion. These documents range from J. Hector St. John de Crèvecoeur's reflections on Americanness toward the end of the War of Independence and the Declaration of Sentiments of the Seneca Falls Convention to Frederick Douglass's great speech of 1869 in defense of Chinese immigration, "The Composite Nation," and Mary Church Terrell's poignant complaint about being treated as a stranger in her own country.

In the body of the text itself, the major additions that illuminate the history of this theme are as follows:

Chapter 3 contains a new discussion of the formation in colonial America of a British identity linked to a sense of difference from "others"—French and Spanish Catholics, Africans, and Native Americans. Chapter 4 discusses the development of a pan-Indian identity transcending the traditional rivalries between separate Native American nations. In Chapter 7, I have added an examination of how the U.S. Constitution deals with citizenship and how the lack of a clear definition made disagreement about its boundaries inevitable. A new subsection in Chapter 12 deals with claims by African-Americans before the Civil War to "birthright citizenship," the principle that anyone born in the country, regardless of race, national origin, or other characteristics, is entitled to full and equal citizenship. Chapter 15 expands the existing discussion of the constitutional amendments of the Reconstruction era to examine how they redrew the definition and boundaries of American citizenship.

In Chapter 17, I have expanded the section on the movement to restrict immigration. Chapter 18 contains a new discussion of Theodore Roosevelt's understanding of "Americanism" and whom it excluded. Chapter 19 examines the "science" of eugenics, which proposed various ways to "improve" the quality of the American population. Chapter 23 contains a new subsection on how the Cold War and the effort to root out "subversion" affected definitions of loyalty, disloyalty, and American identity. Immigration reform during the administration of Ronald Reagan receives additional attention in Chapter 26. Finally, Chapter 28 discusses the heated debates over immigration that helped elect Donald Trump in 2016, and how his administration in its first two years addressed the issue.

Other revisions, not directly related to the "Who Is an American?" theme, include a reorganization of the chapter on the Gilded Age (16) to give it greater clarity, a new subsection in Chapter 17 discussing the political and philosophical school known as pragmatism, and significant changes in Chapter 26 to take advantage of recent scholarship on modern conservatism. The final chapter (28) has been updated to discuss the election of 2016 and the first two years of the administration of Donald Trump. I have also added a number of new selections to Voices of Freedom to sharpen the juxtaposition of divergent concepts of freedom at particular moments in American history. And this edition contains many new images—paintings, photographs, broadsides, lithographs, and others.

Americans have always had a divided attitude toward history. On the one hand, they tend to be remarkably future-oriented, dismissing events of even the recent past as "ancient history" and sometimes seeing history as a burden to be overcome, a prison from which to escape. On the other hand, like many other peoples, Americans have always looked to history for a sense of personal or group identity and of national cohesiveness. This is why so many Americans devote time and energy to tracing their family trees and why they visit historical museums and National Park Service historical sites in ever-increasing numbers. My hope is that this book will convince readers with all degrees of interest that history does matter to them.

The novelist and essayist James Baldwin once observed that history "does not refer merely, or even principally, to the past. On the contrary, the great force of history comes from the fact that we carry it within us, . . . [that] history is literally present in all that we do." As Baldwin recognized, the force of history is evident in our own world. Especially in a political democracy like the United States, whose government is designed to rest on the consent of informed citizens, knowledge of the past is essential—not only for those of us whose profession is the teaching and writing of history, but for everyone. History, to be sure, does not offer simple lessons or immediate answers to current questions. Knowing the history of immigration to the United States, and all of the tensions, turmoil, and aspirations associated with it, for example, does not tell us what current immigration policy ought to be. But without that knowledge, we have no way of understanding which approaches have worked and which have not—essential information for the formulation of future public policy.

History, it has been said, is what the present chooses to remember about the past. Rather than a fixed collection of facts, or a group of interpretations that cannot be challenged, our understanding of history is constantly changing. There is nothing unusual in the fact that each generation rewrites history to meet its own needs, or that scholars disagree among themselves on basic questions like the causes of the Civil War or the reasons for the Great Depression. Precisely because each generation asks different questions of the past, each generation formulates different answers. The past thirty years have witnessed a remarkable expansion of the scope of historical study. The experiences of groups neglected by earlier scholars, including women, African-Americans, working people, and others, have received unprecedented attention from historians. New subfields—social history, cultural history, and family history among them—have taken their place alongside traditional political and diplomatic history.

Give Me Liberty! draws on this voluminous historical literature to present an up-to-date and inclusive account of the American past, paying due attention to the experience of diverse groups of Americans while in no way neglecting the events and processes Americans have experienced in common. It devotes serious attention to political, social, cultural, and economic history, and to their interconnections. The narrative brings together major events and prominent leaders with the many groups of ordinary people who make up American society. *Give Me Liberty!* has a rich cast of characters, from Thomas Jefferson to campaigners for woman suffrage, from Franklin D. Roosevelt to former slaves seeking to breathe meaning into emancipation during and after the Civil War.

Aimed at an audience of students with little or no detailed knowledge of American history, *Give Me Liberty!* guides readers through the complexities of the subject without overwhelming them with excessive detail. The unifying theme of freedom that runs through the text gives shape to the narrative and integrates the numerous strands that make up the American experience. This approach builds on that of my earlier book, *The Story of American Freedom* (1998), although *Give Me Liberty!* places events and personalities in the foreground and is more geared to the structure of the introductory survey course.

Freedom, and the battles to define its meaning, have long been central to my own scholarship and undergraduate teaching, which focuses on the nineteenth century and especially the era of the Civil War and Reconstruction (1850–1877). This was a time when the future of slavery tore the nation apart and emancipation produced a national debate over what rights the former slaves, and all Americans, should enjoy as free citizens. I have found that attention to clashing definitions of freedom and the struggles of different groups to achieve freedom as they understood it offers a way of making sense of the bitter battles and vast transformations of that pivotal era. I believe that the same is true for American history as a whole.

No idea is more fundamental to Americans' sense of themselves as individuals and as a nation than freedom. The central term in our political language, freedom—or liberty, with which it is almost always used interchangeably—is deeply embedded in the record of our history and the language of everyday life. The Declaration of Independence lists liberty among mankind's inalienable rights; the Constitution announces its purpose as securing liberty's blessings. The United States fought the Civil War to bring about a new birth of freedom, World War II for the Four Freedoms, and the Cold War to defend the Free World. Americans' love of liberty has been represented by liberty poles, liberty caps, and statues of liberty, and acted out by burning stamps and burning draft cards, by running away from slavery, and by demonstrating for the right to vote. "Every man in the street, white, black, red, or yellow," wrote the educator and statesman Ralph Bunche in 1940, "knows that this is 'the land of the free' . . . 'the cradle of liberty.'"

The very universality of the idea of freedom, however, can be misleading. Freedom is not a fixed, timeless category with a single unchanging definition. Indeed, the history of the United States is, in part, a story of debates, disagreements, and struggles over freedom. Crises like the American Revolution, the Civil War, and the Cold War have permanently transformed the idea of freedom. So too have demands by various groups of Americans to enjoy greater freedom. The meaning of freedom has been constructed not only in congressional debates and political treatises, but on plantations and picket lines, in parlors and even bedrooms.

Over the course of our history, American freedom has been both a reality and a mythic ideal—a living truth for millions of Americans, a cruel mockery for others. For some, freedom has been what some scholars call a "habit of the heart," an ideal so taken for granted that it is lived out but rarely analyzed. For others, freedom is not a birthright but a distant goal that has inspired great sacrifice.

Give Me Liberty! draws attention to three dimensions of freedom that have been critical in American history: (1) the *meanings* of freedom; (2) the *social conditions* that make freedom possible; and (3) the *boundaries* of freedom that determine who is entitled to enjoy freedom and who is not. All have changed over time.

In the era of the American Revolution, for example, freedom was primarily a set of rights enjoyed in public activity—the right of a community to be governed by laws to which its representatives had consented and of individuals to engage in religious worship without governmental interference. In the nineteenth century, freedom came to be closely identified with each person's opportunity to develop to the fullest his or her innate talents. In the twentieth, the "ability to choose," in both public and private life, became perhaps the dominant understanding of freedom. This development was encouraged by the explosive growth of the consumer marketplace (a development that receives considerable attention in *Give Me Liberty!*), which offered Americans an unprecedented array of goods with which to satisfy their needs and desires. During the 1960s, a crucial chapter in the history of American freedom, the idea of personal freedom was extended into virtually every realm, from attire and "lifestyle" to relations between the sexes. Thus, over time, more and more areas of life have been drawn into Americans' debates about the meaning of freedom.

A second important dimension of freedom focuses on the social conditions necessary to allow freedom to flourish. What kinds of economic institutions and relationships best encourage individual freedom? In the colonial era and for more than a century after independence, the answer centered on economic autonomy, enshrined in the glorification of the independent small producer—the farmer, skilled craftsman, or shopkeeper—who did not have to depend on another person for his livelihood. As the industrial economy matured, new conceptions of economic freedom came to the fore: "liberty of contract" in the Gilded Age, "industrial freedom" (a say in corporate decision-making) in the Progressive era, economic security during the New Deal, and, more recently, the ability to enjoy mass consumption within a market economy.

The boundaries of freedom, the third dimension of this theme, have inspired some of the most intense struggles in American history. Although founded on the premise that liberty is an entitlement of all humanity, the United States for much of its history deprived many of its own people of freedom. Non-whites have rarely enjoyed the same access to freedom as white Americans. The belief in equal opportunity as the birthright of all Americans has coexisted with persistent efforts to limit freedom by race, gender, and class and in other ways.

Less obvious, perhaps, is the fact that one person's freedom has frequently been linked to another's servitude. In the colonial era and nineteenth century, expanding freedom for many Americans rested on the lack of freedom—slavery, indentured servitude, the subordinate position of women—for others. By the same token, it has been through battles at the boundaries—the efforts of racial minorities, women, and others to secure greater freedom—that the meaning and experience of freedom have been deepened and the concept extended into new realms.

Time and again in American history, freedom has been transformed by the demands of excluded groups for inclusion. The idea of freedom as a universal birthright owes much both to abolitionists who sought to extend the blessings of liberty to blacks and to immigrant groups who insisted on full recognition as American citizens. The principle of equal protection of the law without regard to race, which became a central element of American freedom, arose from the antislavery struggle and the Civil War and was reinvigorated by the civil rights revolution of the 1960s, which called itself the "freedom movement." The battle for the right of free speech by labor radicals and birth-control advocates in the first part of the twentieth century helped to make civil liberties an essential element of freedom for all Americans.

Although concentrating on events within the United States, *Give Me Liberty!* also situates American history in the context of developments in other parts of the world. Many of the forces that shaped American history, including the international migration of peoples, the development of slavery, the spread of democracy, and the expansion of capitalism, were worldwide processes not confined to the United States. Today, American ideas, culture, and economic and military power exert unprecedented influence throughout the world. But beginning with the earliest days of settlement, when European empires competed to colonize North America and enrich themselves from its trade, American history cannot be understood in isolation from its global setting.

Freedom is the oldest of clichés and the most modern of aspirations. At various times in our history, it has served as the rallying cry of the powerless and as a justification of the status quo. Freedom helps to bind our culture together and exposes the contradictions between what America claims to be and what it sometimes has been. American history is not a narrative of continual progress toward greater and greater freedom. As the abolitionist Thomas Wentworth Higginson noted after the Civil War, "revolutions may go backward." Though freedom can be achieved, it may also be taken away. This happened, for example, when the equal rights granted to former slaves immediately after the Civil War were essentially nullified during the era of segregation. As was said in the eighteenth century, the price of freedom is eternal vigilance.

In the early twenty-first century, freedom continues to play a central role in American political and social life and thought. It is invoked by individuals and groups of all kinds, from critics of economic globalization to those who seek to secure American freedom at home and export it abroad. I hope that *Give Me Liberty!* will offer beginning students a clear account of the course of American history, and of its central theme, freedom, which today remains as varied, contentious, and ever-changing as America itself. And I hope that it also enables students to understand the connections between past and current events, the historical context and antecedents of the social, political, cultural, and economic issues that the American people confront today.

Acknowledgments

All works of history are, to a considerable extent, collaborative books, in that every writer builds on the research and writing of previous scholars. This is especially true of a textbook that covers the entire American experience, over more than five centuries. My greatest debt is to the innumerable historians on whose work I have drawn in preparing this volume. The Suggested Reading list at the end of each chapter offers only a brief introduction to the vast body of historical scholarship that has influenced and informed this book. More specifically, however, I wish to thank the following scholars, who offered valuable comments, criticisms, and suggestions after generously reading portions of this work or using it in their classes.

Jennifer Hudson Allen, Brookhaven College
Joel Benson, Northwest Missouri State University
Lori Bramson, Clark College

Andrea Brinton-Sanches, Cedar Valley College
Monica L. Butler, Motlow State Community College
Tonia Compton, Columbia College
Adam Costanzo, Texas A&M University
Carl Creasman Jr., Valencia College
Ashley Cruseturner, McLennan Community College
Richard Driver, Northwest Vista College
Laura Dunn, Eastern Florida State College
Kathleen DuVal, University of North Carolina, Chapel Hill
Blake Ellis, Lone Star College—CyFair
Carla Falkner, Northeast Mississippi Community College
Robert Glen Findley, Odessa College
Amy L. Fluker, University of Mississippi
Van Forsyth, Clark College
Yvonne Frear, San Jacinto College
Beverly Gage, Yale University
Michael A. Gonzalez, El Paso Community College
Aram Goudsouzian, University of Memphis
Michael Harkins, Harper College
Peter D. Haro, San Diego City College
Sandra Harvey, Lone Star College—CyFair
Robert Hines, Palo Alto College
Traci Hodgson, Chemeketa Community College
Tamora Hoskisson, Salt Lake Community College
William Jackson, Salt Lake Community College
Alfred H. Jones, State College of Florida
Junko Isono Kato, Waseda University
David Kiracofe, Tidewater Community College
Jeremy Lehman, McLennan Community College
Brad Lookingbill, Columbia College
Jennifer Macias, Salt Lake Community College
Scott P. Marler, University of Memphis
Thomas Massey, Cape Fear Community College
Derek Maxfield, Genesee Community College
Lisa McGirr, Harvard University
Marianne McKnight, Salt Lake Community College
Jonson Miller, Drexel University
Ted Moore, Salt Lake Community College
Laura Murphy, Dutchess Community College
Nathan Perl-Rosenthal, University of Southern California
Christopher Phelps, University of Nottingham
Robert Pierce, Foothills College
Ernst Pinjing, Minot State University
Harvey N. Plaunt, El Paso Community College
Steve Porter, University of Cincinnati

John Putman, San Diego State University
R. Lynn Rainard, Tidewater Community College, Chesapeake Campus
Janet Rankin, Sierra College
Nicole Ribianszky, Georgia Gwinnett College
Nancy Marie Robertson, Indiana University—Purdue University Indianapolis
Anderson Rouse, University of North Carolina, Greensboro
Horacio Salinas Jr., Laredo Community College
John Shaw, Portland Community College
Christina Snyder, Pennsylvania State University
Wendy Soltz, Purdue University Fort Wayne
Danielle Swiontek, Santa Barbara Community College
Chris Tingle, Northwest Mississippi Community College
Richard M. Trimble, Ocean County College
Alan Vangroll, Central Texas College
Karine Walther, Georgetown University
Eddie Weller, San Jacinto College
Ashli White, Miami University
Andrew Wiese, San Diego State University
Matthew Zembo, Hudson Valley Community College

I am particularly grateful to my colleagues in the Columbia University Department of History: Pablo Piccato, for his advice on Latin American history; Evan Haefeli and Ellen Baker, who read and made many suggestions for improvements in their areas of expertise (colonial America and the history of the West, respectively); and Sarah Phillips, who offered advice on treating the history of the environment.

I am also deeply indebted to the graduate students at Columbia University's Department of History who helped with this project. For this edition, Michael "Mookie" Kideckel offered invaluable assistance in gathering material related to borderlands and Western history and on citizenship and identity for the current one. For previous editions, Theresa Ventura assisted in locating material for new sections placing American history in a global context, April Holm did the same for new coverage of the history of American religion and debates over religious freedom, James Delbourgo conducted research for the chapters on the colonial era, and Beverly Gage did the same for the twentieth century. In addition, Daniel Freund provided all-around research assistance. Victoria Cain did a superb job of locating images. I also want to thank my colleagues Elizabeth Blackmar and the late Alan Brinkley for offering advice and encouragement throughout the writing of this book. I am also grateful to the numerous students who, while using the textbook, pointed out to me errors or omissions that I have corrected.

Many thanks to Joshua Brown, director of the American Social History Project, whose website, History Matters, lists innumerable online resources for the study of American history. Thanks also to the instructors who helped build our robust digital resource and ancillary package. InQuizitive for History was revised by Cornelia Lambert (University of North Georgia), Jodie Steeley (Fresno City College), Jen Murray (Oklahoma State University), and Joel Tannenbaum (Community College of Philadelphia). The Coursepack Quizzes and Instructor's Manual were thoroughly updated by Jason Newman (Cosumnes River College). Allison Faber (Texas A&M University) revised the Lecture PowerPoint slides. And our Test Bank was revised to include new questions authored by Robert O'Brien (Lone Star College—CyFair), Emily Pecora, and Carolina Zumaglini, with accuracy checking help from Matt Zembo (Hudson Valley Community College) and Jim Dudlo (Brookhaven College).

At W. W. Norton & Company, Steve Forman was an ideal editor—patient, encouraging, and always ready to offer sage advice. I would also like to thank Steve's assistant editor Lily Gellman for her indispensable and always cheerful help on all aspects of the project; Ellen Lohman and Annie Beck for their careful copyediting and proofreading work; Stephanie Romeo and Donna Ranieri for their resourceful attention to the illustrations program; Leah Clark, Ted Szczepanski, and Debra Morton-Hoyt for splendid work on the covers for the Sixth Edition; Jennifer Barnhardt and Maura Gaughan for keeping the many threads of the project aligned and then tying them together; Sean Mintus for his efficiency and care in book production; Carson Russell for orchestrating the rich media package that accompanies the textbook and his colleagues Sarah Rose Aquilina and Alexandra Malakhoff; Sarah England Bartley, Steve Dunn, and Mike Wright for their alert reads of the U.S. survey market and their hard work in helping establish *Give Me Liberty!* within it; and Drake McFeely, Roby Harrington, and Julia Reidhead for maintaining Norton as an independent, employee-owned publisher dedicated to excellence in its work.

Many students may have heard stories of how publishing companies alter the language and content of textbooks in an attempt to maximize sales and avoid alienating any potential reader. In this case, I can honestly say that W. W. Norton allowed me a free hand in writing the book and, apart from the usual editorial corrections, did not try to influence its content at all. For this I thank them, while I accept full responsibility for the interpretations presented and for any errors the book may contain. Since no book of this length can be entirely free of mistakes, I welcome readers to send me corrections at ef17@columbia.edu.

My greatest debt, as always, is to my family—my wife, Lynn Garafola, for her good-natured support while I was preoccupied by a project that consumed more than its fair share of my time and energy, and my daughter, Daria, who while a ninth and tenth grader read every chapter of the First Edition as it was written, for a modest payment, and offered invaluable suggestions about improving the book's clarity, logic, and grammar.

Eric Foner
New York City
March 2019

GIVE ME LIBERTY! DIGITAL RESOURCES FOR STUDENTS AND INSTRUCTORS

W. W. Norton offers a robust digital package to support teaching and learning with *Give Me Liberty!* These resources are designed to make students more effective textbook readers, while at the same time developing their critical thinking and history skills.

RESOURCES FOR STUDENTS

All resources are available at digital.wwnorton.com/givemeliberty6brhs with the access card at the front of this text.

NORTON INQUIZITIVE

InQuizitive is Norton's award-winning adaptive learning tool that enhances students' understanding of the key big-picture themes and objectives from each chapter using a series of highly visual and gamelike activities. The new Sixth Edition includes over 20 percent new or revised questions, including primary source document excerpts, maps and historical images from the text, interactive visual content, and new "Who Is an American?" videos featuring Eric Foner.

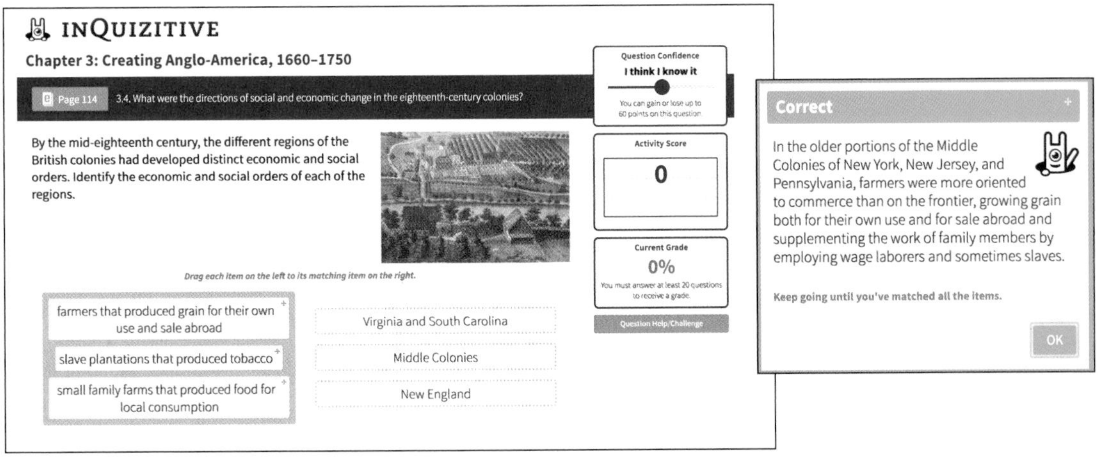

HISTORY SKILLS TUTORIALS

The History Skills Tutorials are interactive, online modules that provide students a framework for analyzing primary source documents, images, and maps. New to the Sixth Edition is a fourth tutorial, Analyzing Secondary Sources. All tutorials begin with author videos modeling the analysis process followed by interactive assessments that challenge students to apply what they have learned.

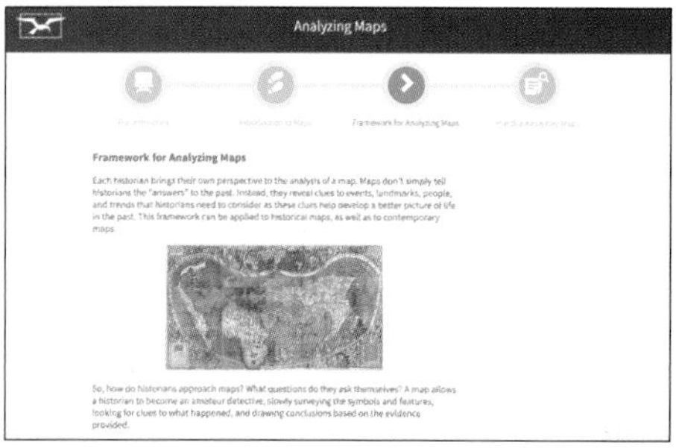

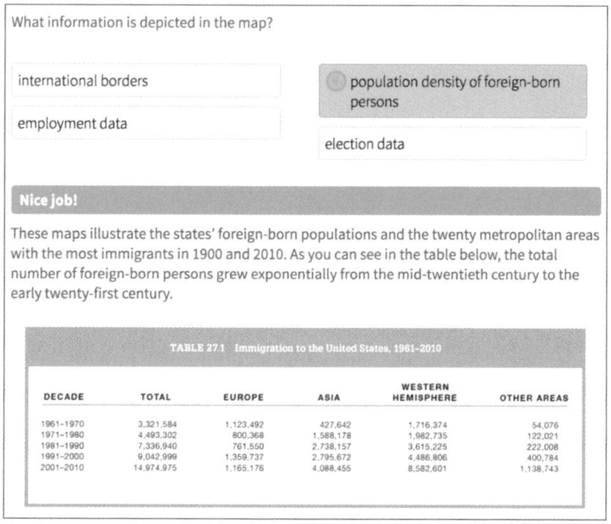

TABLE 27.1 Immigration to the United States, 1961–2010

DECADE	TOTAL	EUROPE	ASIA	WESTERN HEMISPHERE	OTHER AREAS
1961–1970	3,321,584	1,123,492	427,642	1,716,374	54,076
1971–1980	4,493,302	800,368	1,588,178	1,982,735	122,021
1981–1990	7,336,940	761,550	2,738,157	3,615,225	222,008
1991–2000	9,042,999	1,359,737	2,795,672	4,486,806	400,784
2001–2010	14,974,975	1,165,176	4,088,455	8,582,601	1,138,743

AUTHOR VIDEOS

In addition to the hundreds of author videos available through the ebook, student site, and InQuizitive, a new collection of videos featuring Eric Foner give students an in-depth look into the "Who Is an American?" book feature, and the issues of inclusion and exclusion as they have played out in American history. All videos are available with transcripts and closed captioning.

STUDENT SITE

The online Student Site offers additional resources for students to use outside of class. Resources include author videos in which Eric Foner explains the essential developments of each chapter, interactive iMaps study tools, and a comprehensive Online Reader with hundreds of additional primary sources, both textual and visual.

EBOOK

Norton Ebooks give students and instructors an enhanced reading experience. Students are able to have an active reading experience and can take notes, bookmark, search, highlight, and even read offline. Instructors can add notes for students to see as they read the text. Features in *Give Me Liberty!* include enlargeable maps and art, embedded author videos that further explain key developments in the chapter, and pop-up key term definitions that give students useful context as they read. Norton Ebooks can be viewed on—and synced among—all computers and mobile devices.

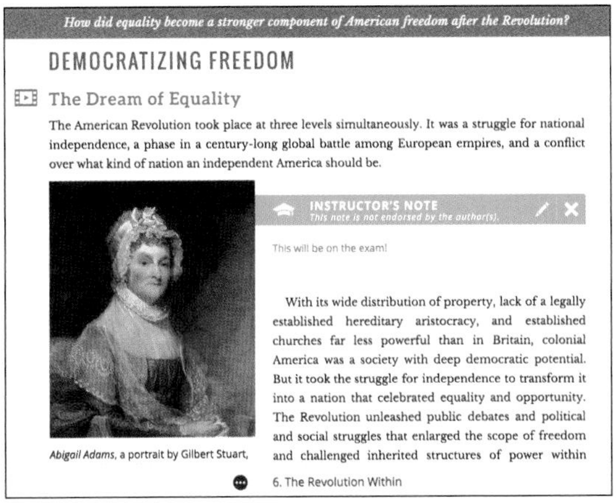

RESOURCES FOR INSTRUCTORS

All resources are available through wwnorton.com/instructors.

RESOURCES FOR YOUR LMS

Easily add high-quality Norton digital resources to your online, hybrid, or lecture course. Get started building your course with our easy-to-use coursepack files; all activities can be accessed right within your existing learning management system, and many components are customizable. Resources include InQuizitive, History Skills Tutorials, chapter outlines, review quizzes, flashcards, all of the resources from the Student Site, and more.

TEST BANK

The Test Bank features 30 percent new or revised questions, with more than 4,000 questions total—including multiple choice, true/false, matching, short answer, and essay questions—aligned with the chapter's Focus Questions. Classified according to level of difficulty and Bloom's Taxonomy, they provide multiple avenues for comprehension and skill assessment.

INSTRUCTOR'S MANUAL

The Instructor's Manual contains detailed Chapter Summaries, Chapter Outlines, Suggested Discussion Questions, Supplemental Web, Visual, and Print Resources, and new Interactive Instructor Activities.

LECTURE AND ART POWERPOINT SLIDES

The Lecture PowerPoints combine chapter review, art, and maps. Key topics to cover in class are sequentially arranged to follow the book, and new, robust lecture scripts, bulleted teaching points, and discussion questions fill the Notes section of each slide.

AP® RESOURCES

For instructors using the Brief Sixth High School Edition in the AP® classroom, we offer instructor materials written by master teachers with deep knowledge of the AP® course. A Correlation Chart aligns the content of this textbook to the key concepts and learning objectives of the AP® Curriculum Framework. A Course Planning and Pacing Guide provides specific lessons and activities for each of the course's nine periods. An AP® U.S. History Test Bank, featuring over 2,000 questions, includes every AP® question type as well as content mastery questions to test student understanding.

CHAPTER 1

A NEW WORLD

★

7000 BCE	Agriculture developed in Mexico and Andes
900–1200 CE	Hopi and Zuni tribes build planned towns
1200	Cahokia city-empire along the Mississippi
1400s	Iroquois League established
1434	Portuguese explore sub-Saharan African Coast
1487	Bartolomeu Dias reaches the Cape of Good Hope
1492	*Reconquista* of Spain
	Columbus's first voyage to the Americas
1498	Vasco da Gama sails to the Indian Ocean
1500	Pedro Cabral claims Brazil for Portugal
1502	First African slaves transported to the Caribbean islands
1517	Martin Luther's *Ninety-Five Theses*
1519	Hernán Cortés arrives in Mexico
1528	Las Casas's *History of the Indies*
1530s	Pizarro's conquest of Peru
1542	Spain promulgates the New Laws
1608	Champlain establishes Quebec
1609	Hudson claims New Netherland
1610	Santa Fe established
1680	Pueblo Revolt

Painted in 1718 by an unknown indigenous artist in modern-day Peru, *The Marriage of Captain Martin de Loyola to Beatriz Nusta* depicts the wedding, in 1572, of a daughter of the last ruler of the Inca empire and a nephew of Ignatius de Loyola, founder of the Jesuit order. With Inca royalty seated at the top left and Catholic saints in the center foreground, the work aims to legitimize Spain's colonial rule by assimilating into it the pre-conquest history of the Americas.

FOCUS QUESTIONS

- *What were the major patterns of Native American life in North America before Europeans arrived?*
- *How did Indian and European ideas of freedom differ on the eve of contact?*
- *What impelled European explorers to look west across the Atlantic?*
- *What happened when the peoples of the Americas came in contact with Europeans?*
- *What were the chief features of the Spanish empire in America?*
- *What were the chief features of the French and Dutch empires in North America?*

"The discovery of America," the British writer Adam Smith announced in his celebrated work *The Wealth of Nations* (1776), was one of "the two greatest and most important events recorded in the history of mankind." Historians no longer use the word "discovery" to describe the European exploration, conquest, and colonization of a hemisphere already home to millions of people. But there can be no doubt that when Christopher Columbus made landfall in the West Indian islands in 1492, he set in motion some of the most pivotal developments in human history. Immense changes soon followed in both the Old and New Worlds; the consequences of these changes are still with us today.

Human communities have interacted since the dawn of civilization. No society represents a single culture or people. For centuries before the conquest of the Americas, Europeans had intersected with Muslim populations in North Africa and Eurasia; indeed, the very idea of Europe as a distinct community arose out of such encounters. But since the voyages of Columbus, the interconnection of cultures and peoples has taken place on a global scale. The peoples of the American continents and Europe, previously unaware of each other's existence, were thrown into continuous interaction. Crops new to each hemisphere crossed the Atlantic, reshaping diets and transforming the natural environment. Because of centuries of lack of contact with peoples on other continents, the inhabitants of North and South America had developed no immunity to the germs that also accompanied the colonizers. As a result, they suffered a series of devastating epidemics, the greatest population catastrophe in human history. Within a decade of Columbus's voyage, a fourth continent—Africa—found itself drawn into the new transatlantic system of trade and population movement. In Africa, Europeans found a supply of unfree labor that enabled them to exploit the fertile lands of the Western Hemisphere. Indeed, of approximately 10 million men, women, and children who crossed from the Old World to the New between 1492 and 1820, the vast majority, about 7.7 million, were African slaves.

From the vantage point of 1776, the year the United States declared itself an independent nation, it seemed to Adam Smith that the "discovery" of America had produced both great "benefits" and great "misfortunes." To the nations of western Europe, the development of American colonies brought an era of "splendor and glory." Smith also noted, however, that to the "natives" of the Americas, the years since 1492 had been ones of "dreadful misfortunes" and "every sort of injustice." And for millions of Africans, the settlement of America meant a descent into the abyss of slavery.

Long before Columbus sailed, Europeans had dreamed of a land of abundance, riches, and ease beyond the western horizon. Europeans envisioned America as a religious refuge, a society of equals, a source of power and glory. They searched for golden cities and fountains of eternal youth. Some of these dreams would indeed be fulfilled. To many European settlers, America offered a far greater chance to own land and worship as they pleased than existed in Europe, with its rigid, unequal social order and official churches. Yet the New World also became the site of many forms of unfree labor, including indentured servitude, forced labor, and one of the most brutal and unjust systems, plantation slavery. The conquest and settlement of the Western Hemisphere opened new chapters in the long histories of both freedom and slavery.

THE FIRST AMERICANS

The Settling of the Americas

Origins of settlement in the Americas

The residents of the Americas were no more a single group than Europeans or Africans. They spoke hundreds of different languages and lived in numerous kinds of societies. Most, however, were descended from bands of hunters and fishers who had crossed the Bering Strait via a land bridge at various times between 15,000 and 60,000 years ago—the exact dates are hotly debated by archaeologists.

The New World was new to Europeans but an ancient homeland to those who already lived there. The hemisphere had witnessed many changes during its human history. First, the early inhabitants and their descendants spread across the two continents, reaching the tip of South America perhaps 11,000 years ago. As the climate warmed, they faced a food crisis as the immense animals they hunted, including woolly mammoths and giant bison, became extinct. Around 9,000 years ago, at the same time that agriculture was being developed in the Near East, it also emerged in modern-day Mexico and the Andes, and then spread to other parts of the Americas, making settled civilizations possible.

Emergence of agriculture

Indian Societies of the Americas

Roads, irrigation systems, and trade networks

When Europeans arrived, North and South America contained cities, roads, irrigation systems, extensive trade networks, and large structures such as pyramid-temples whose beauty still inspires wonder. With a population close to 250,000, **Tenochtitlán**, the capital of the **Aztec** empire in what is now Mexico, was one of the world's largest cities. Farther south lay the Inca kingdom, centered in modern-day Peru. Its population of

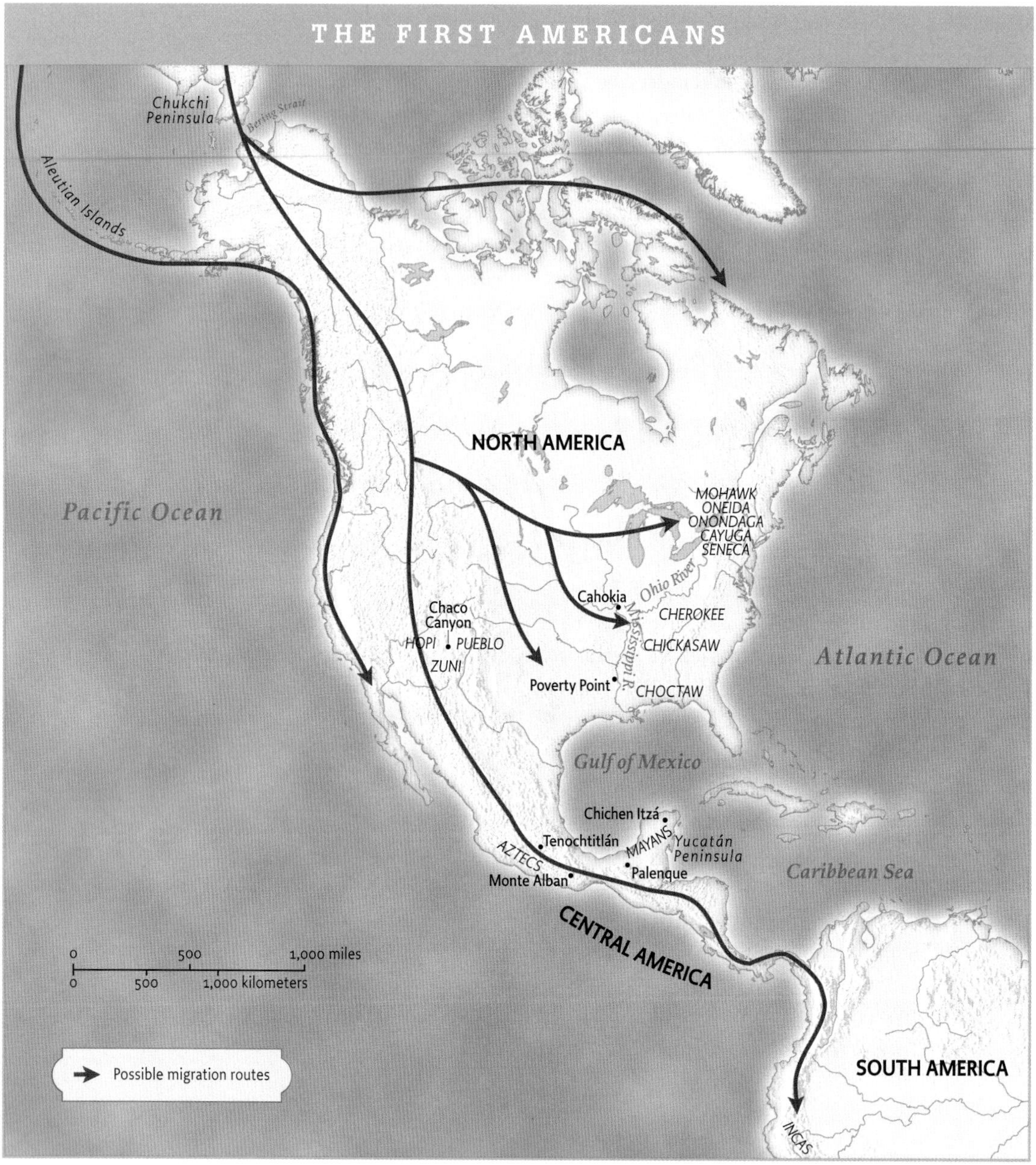

A map illustrating the probable routes by which the first Americans settled the Western Hemisphere at various times between 15,000 and 60,000 years ago.

A modern visualization of Cahokia in the Mississippi River Valley, the largest Native American urban center in what is now the United States.

perhaps 12 million was linked by a complex system of roads and bridges that extended 2,000 miles along the Andes mountain chain.

Indian civilizations in North America had not developed the scale, grandeur, or centralized organization of the Aztec and Inca societies to their south. North American Indians lacked the technologies Europeans had mastered, such as metal tools and machines, gunpowder, and the scientific knowledge necessary for long-distance navigation. Their "backwardness" became a central justification for European conquest. But Indian societies had perfected techniques of farming, hunting, and fishing, developed structures of political power and religious belief, and engaged in far-reaching networks of trade and communication.

Justification for conquest

Mound Builders of the Mississippi River Valley

Remarkable physical remains still exist from some of the early civilizations in North America. Around 3,500 years ago, before Egyptians built the pyramids, Native Americans constructed a large community centered on a series of giant semicircular mounds on a bluff overlooking the Mississippi River in present-day Louisiana. Known today as Poverty Point, it was a commercial and governmental center whose residents established trade routes throughout the Mississippi and Ohio River valleys.

More than a thousand years before Columbus sailed, Indians of the Ohio River valley, called "mound builders" by eighteenth-century settlers who encountered the large earthen burial mounds they created, traded across half the continent. After their decline, another culture flourished in the Mississippi River valley, centered on the city of Cahokia

Cahokia

near present-day St. Louis, a fortified community with between 10,000 and 30,000 inhabitants in the year 1200. It stood as the largest settled community in what is now the United States until surpassed in population by New York and Philadelphia around 1800. The remains can still be visited today.

A modern aerial photograph of the ruins of Pueblo Bonita, in Chaco Canyon in present-day New Mexico. The rectangular structures are the foundations of dwellings, and the circular ones are *kivas*, or places of religious worship.

Western Indians

In the arid northeastern area of present-day Arizona, the Hopi and Zuni and their ancestors engaged in settled village life for over 3,000 years. During the peak of the region's culture, between the years 900 and 1200, these peoples built great planned towns with large multiple-family dwellings in local canyons, constructed dams and canals to gather and distribute water, and conducted trade with groups as far away as central Mexico and the Mississippi valley. The largest of their structures, Pueblo Bonita, in Chaco Canyon, New Mexico, stood five stories high and had over 600 rooms. Not until the 1880s was a dwelling of comparable size constructed in the United States.

Pueblo Indians

After the decline of these communities, probably because of drought, survivors moved to the south and east, where they established villages and perfected the techniques of desert farming. These were the people Spanish explorers called the Pueblo Indians (because they lived in small villages, or *pueblos*, when the Spanish first encountered them in the sixteenth century). On the Pacific coast, another densely populated region, hundreds of distinct groups resided in independent villages and lived primarily by fishing, hunting sea mammals, and gathering wild plants and nuts.

Indians of Eastern North America

In eastern North America, hundreds of tribes inhabited towns and villages scattered from the Gulf of Mexico to present-day Canada. They lived on corn, squash, and beans, supplemented by fishing and hunting deer, turkeys, and other animals. Indian trade routes crisscrossed the eastern part of the continent. Tribes frequently warred with one another to obtain goods, seize captives, or take revenge for the killing of relatives. They conducted diplomacy and made peace. Little in the way of centralized authority existed until, in the fifteenth century, various leagues or confederations emerged in an effort to bring order to local regions. In the Southeast, the Choctaw, Cherokee, and

Chickasaw each united dozens of towns in loose alliances. In present-day New York and Pennsylvania, five Iroquois peoples—the Mohawk, Oneida, Cayuga, Seneca, and Onondaga—formed a **Great League of Peace**, bringing a period of stability to the area.

Diversity of Native American society

The most striking feature of Native American society at the time Europeans arrived was its sheer diversity. Each group had its own political system and set of religious beliefs, and North America was home to literally hundreds of mutually unintelligible languages. Indians did not think of themselves as a single people, an idea invented by Europeans and only many years later adopted by Indians themselves. Indian identity centered on the immediate social group—a tribe, village, chiefdom, or confederacy. When Europeans first arrived, many Indians saw them as simply one group among many. The sharp dichotomy between Indians and "white" persons did not emerge until later in the colonial era.

Native American Religion

Nonetheless, the diverse Indian societies of North America did share certain common characteristics. Their lives were steeped in religious ceremonies often directly related to farming and hunting. Spiritual power, they believed, suffused the world, and sacred spirits could be found in all kinds of living and inanimate things—animals, plants, trees, water,

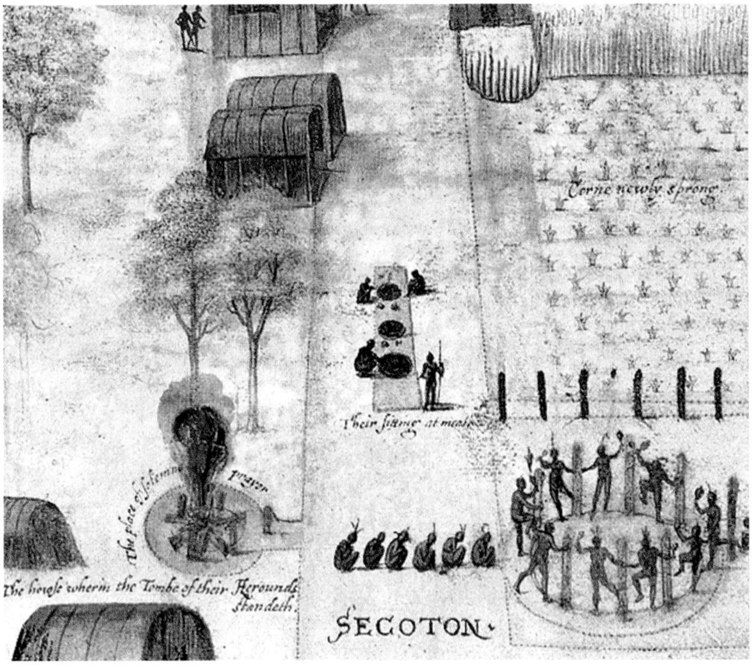

The Village of Secoton, by John White, an English artist who spent a year on the Outer Banks of North Carolina in 1585–1586 as part of an expedition sponsored by Sir Walter Raleigh. A central street links houses surrounded by fields of corn. In the lower part, dancing Indians take part in a religious ceremony.

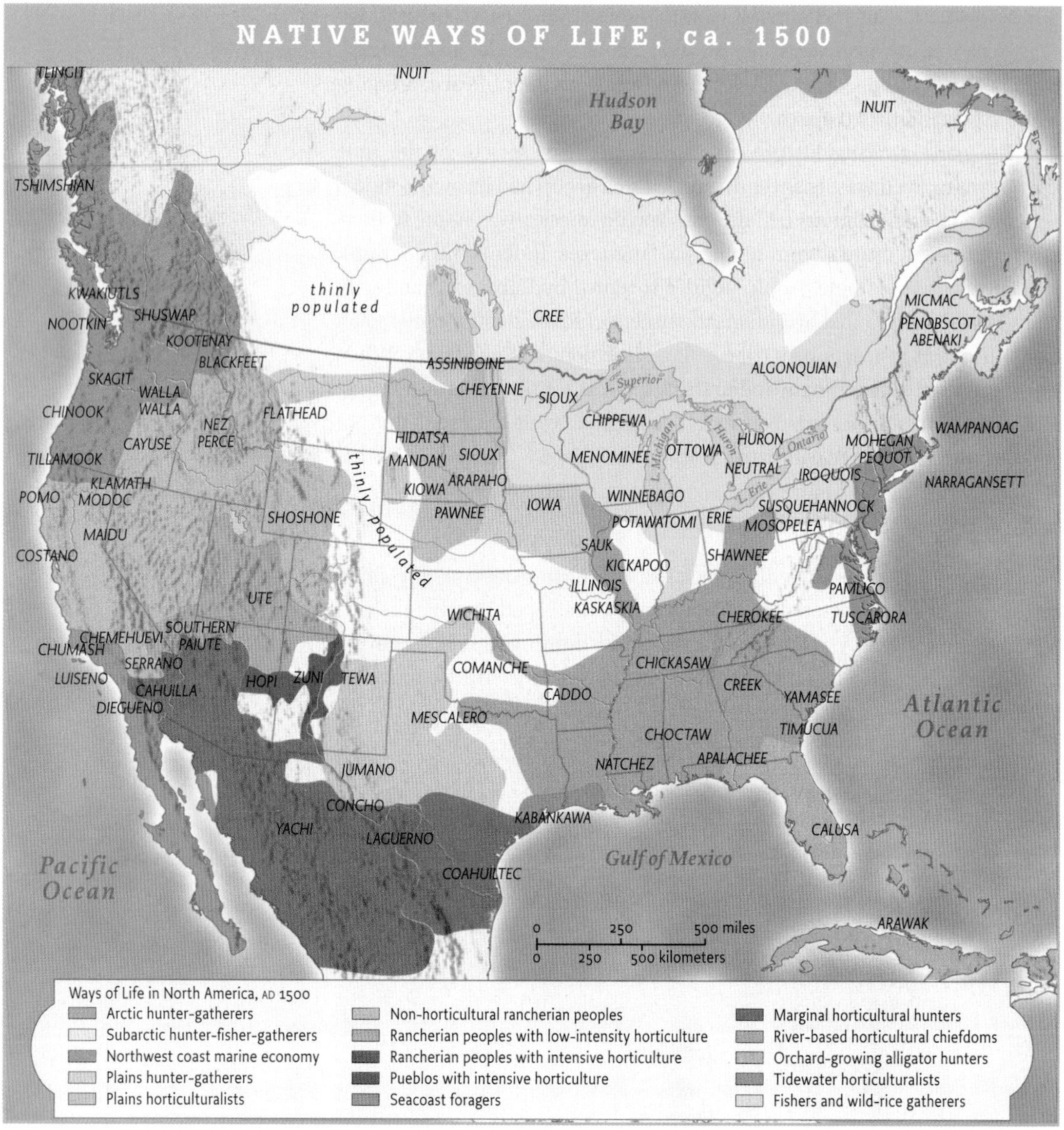

The native population of North America at the time of first contact with Europeans consisted of numerous tribes with their own languages, religious beliefs, and economic and social structures. This map suggests the numerous ways of life existing at the time.

Rituals

and wind. Through religious ceremonies, they aimed to harness the aid of powerful supernatural forces to serve human interests. Indian villages also held elaborate religious rites, participation in which helped to define the boundaries of community membership. In all Indian societies, those who seemed to possess special abilities to invoke supernatural powers—shamans, medicine men, and other religious leaders—held positions of respect and authority.

In some respects, Indian religion was not that different from popular spiritual beliefs in Europe. Most Indians held that a single Creator stood atop the spiritual hierarchy. Nonetheless, nearly all Europeans arriving in the New World quickly concluded that Indians were in dire need of being converted to a true, Christian faith.

Land and Property

Generally, village leaders assigned plots of land to individual families to use for a season or more, and tribes claimed specific areas for hunting. Unclaimed land remained free for anyone to use. Families "owned" the right to use land, but they did not own the land itself. Indians saw land as a common resource, not an economic commodity. There was no market in real estate before the coming of Europeans.

Land as a common resource

Nor were Indians devoted to the accumulation of wealth and material goods. Especially east of the Mississippi River, where villages moved every few years when soil or game became depleted, acquiring numerous possessions made little sense. However, status certainly mattered in Indian societies. Tribal leaders tended to come from a small number of families, and chiefs lived more splendidly than average members of society. But their reputation often rested on their willingness to share goods with others rather than hoarding them for themselves.

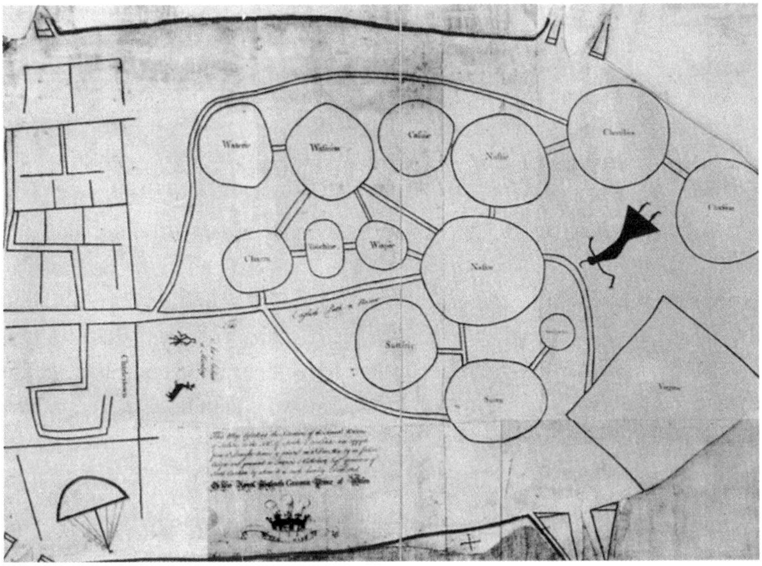

A Catawba map illustrates the differences between Indian and European conceptions of landed property. The map depicts not possession of a specific territory, but trade and diplomatic connections between various native groups and with the colony of Virginia, represented by the rectangle on the lower right. The map, inscribed on deerskin, was originally presented by Indian chiefs to Governor Francis Nicholson of South Carolina in 1721. This copy, the only version that survives, was made by the governor for the authorities in London. It added English labels that conveyed what the Indians had related orally with the gift.

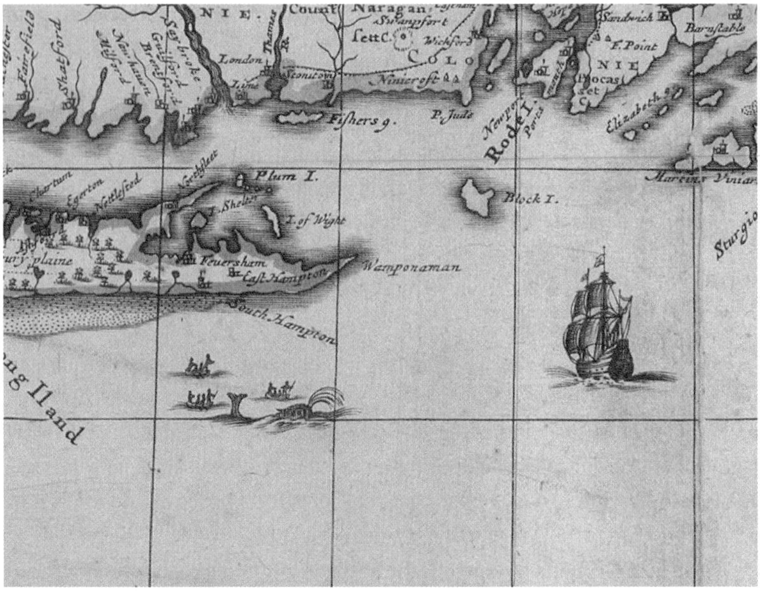

A detail from a seventeenth-century map of English North America shows Native Americans hunting whales off of Long Island.

Gift giving

Generosity was among the most valued social qualities, and gift giving was essential to Indian society. Trade, for example, meant more than a commercial transaction—it was accompanied by elaborate ceremonies of gift exchange that bound different groups in webs of mutual obligation. "There are no beggars among them," reported the English colonial leader Roger Williams of New England's Indians.

Gender Relations

Matrilineal societies

The system of gender relations in most Indian societies also differed markedly from that of Europe. Membership in a family defined women's lives, but they openly engaged in premarital sexual relations and could even choose to divorce their husbands. Most, although not all, Indian societies were matrilineal—that is, centered on clans or kinship groups in which children became members of the mother's family, not the father's. Under English law, a married man controlled the family's property and a wife had no independent legal identity. In contrast, Indian women owned dwellings and tools, and a husband generally moved to live with the family of his wife. Because men were frequently away on the hunt, women took responsibility not only for household duties but for most agricultural work as well.

European Views of the Indians

Indian women planting crops while men break the sod. An engraving by Theodor de Bry, based on a painting by Jacques Le Moyne de Morgues. Morgues was part of an expedition of French Huguenots to Florida in 1564; he escaped when the Spanish destroyed the outpost in the following year.

Europeans tended to view Indians in extreme terms. They were regarded either as "noble savages," gentle, friendly, and superior in some ways to Europeans, or as uncivilized barbarians. Over time, however, negative images of Indians came to overshadow positive ones. Early European descriptions of North American Indians as barbaric centered on three areas—religion, land use, and gender relations. Whatever their country of origin, European newcomers concluded that Indians lacked genuine religion, or in fact worshiped the devil. Whereas the Indians saw nature as a world of spirits and souls, the Europeans viewed it as a collection of potential commodities, a source of economic opportunity.

Europeans invoked the Indians' distinctive pattern of land use and ideas about property to answer the awkward question raised by a British minister at an early stage of England's colonization: "By what right or warrant can we enter into the land of these Savages, take away their rightful inheritance from them, and plant ourselves in their places?" While the Spanish claimed title to land in America by right of conquest and papal authority, the English, French, and Dutch came to rely on the idea that Indians had not actually "used" the land and thus had no claim to it. Despite the Indians' highly developed agriculture and well-established towns, Europeans frequently described them as nomads without settled communities.

In the Indians' gender division of labor and matrilineal family structures, Europeans saw weak men and mistreated women. Hunting and fishing, the primary occupations of Indian men, were considered leisure activities in much of Europe, not "real" work. Because Indian women worked in the fields, Europeans often described them as lacking freedom. Europeans insisted that by subduing the Indians, they were actually bringing them freedom—the freedom of true religion, private property, and the liberation of both men and women from uncivilized and unchristian gender roles.

A seventeenth-century engraving by a French Jesuit priest illustrates many Europeans' view of Indian religion. A demon hovers over an Iroquois longhouse, suggesting that Indians worship the devil.

INDIAN FREEDOM, EUROPEAN FREEDOM

Indian Freedom

Although many Europeans initially saw Indians as embodying freedom, most colonizers quickly concluded that the notion of "freedom" was alien to Indian societies. European settlers reached this conclusion in part because

Indians did not appear to live under established governments or fixed laws, followed their own—not European—definitions of authority, and lacked the kind of order and discipline common in European society. Indians also did not define freedom as individual autonomy or tie it to the ownership of property—two attributes important to Europeans.

Freedom in the group

What were the Indians' ideas of freedom? The modern notion of freedom as personal independence had little meaning in most Indian societies, but individuals were expected to think for themselves and did not always have to go along with collective decision making. Far more important than individual autonomy were kinship ties, the ability to follow one's spiritual values, and the well-being and security of one's community. In Indian culture, group autonomy and self-determination, and the mutual obligations that came with a sense of belonging and connectedness, took precedence over individual freedom. Ironically, the coming of Europeans, armed with their own language of liberty, would make freedom a preoccupation of American Indians, as part and parcel of the very process by which they were reduced to dependence on the colonizers.

Christian Liberty

On the eve of colonization, Europeans held numerous ideas of freedom. Some were as old as the city-states of ancient Greece, others arose during the political struggles of the early modern era. Some laid the foundations for modern conceptions of freedom, others are quite unfamiliar today. Freedom was not a single idea but a collection of distinct rights and privileges, many enjoyed by only a small portion of the population.

Freedom as a spiritual condition

One conception common throughout Europe understood freedom less as a political or social status than as a moral or spiritual condition. Freedom meant abandoning the life of sin to embrace the teachings of Christ. "Christian Liberty," however, had no connection to later ideas of religious toleration, a notion that scarcely existed anywhere on the eve of colonization. In the premodern world, religion was not simply a matter of spiritual doctrines and practices, but systems of belief that permeated every aspect of people's lives. Religious beliefs were therefore inseparable from what would later be considered "secular" matters, such as who enjoyed basic rights. A person's religion was closely tied to his or her economic, political, and social position.

Every nation in Europe had an established church that decreed what forms of religious worship and belief were acceptable. Dissenters faced persecution by the state as well as condemnation by church authorities. Religious uniformity was thought to be essential to public order; the modern idea that a person's religious beliefs and practices are a matter of private choice, not legal obligation, was almost unknown.

Freedom and Authority

In its secular form, the equating of liberty with devotion to a higher authority suggested that freedom meant obedience to law. The identification of freedom with the rule of law did not, though, mean that all subjects of the crown enjoyed the same degree of freedom. Early modern European societies were extremely hierarchical, with marked gradations of social status ranging from the king and hereditary aristocracy down to the urban and rural poor. Inequality was built into virtually every social relationship.

Hierarchy in the family

Within families, men exercised authority over their wives and children. According to the legal doctrine known as "coverture," when a woman married she surrendered her legal identity, which became "covered" by that of her husband. She could not own property or sign contracts in her own name, control her wages if she worked, write a separate will, or, except in the rarest of circumstances, go to court seeking a divorce. The husband had the exclusive right to his wife's "company," including domestic labor and sexual relations.

Everywhere in Europe, family life depended on male dominance and female submission. Indeed, political writers of the sixteenth century explicitly compared the king's authority over his subjects with the husband's over his family. Both were ordained by God.

Liberty and Liberties

Hierarchy in society

In this hierarchical society, liberty came from knowing one's social place and fulfilling the duties appropriate to one's rank. Most men lacked the freedom that came with economic independence. Property qualifications and other restrictions limited the electorate to a minuscule part of the adult male population. The law required strict obedience of employees, and breaches of labor contracts carried criminal penalties.

European ideas of freedom still bore the imprint of the Middle Ages, when "liberties" meant formal, specific privileges such as self-government, exemption from taxation, or the right to practice a particular trade, granted to individuals or groups by contract, royal decree, or purchase. Only those who enjoyed the "freedom of the city," for example, could engage in certain economic activities. Numerous modern civil liberties did not exist. The law decreed acceptable forms of religious worship. The government regularly suppressed publications it did not like, and criticism of authority could

Limited civil liberties

lead to imprisonment. Nonetheless, every European country that colonized the New World claimed to be spreading freedom—for its own population and for Native Americans.

THE EXPANSION OF EUROPE

Sea route to the East

It is fitting that the second epochal event that Adam Smith linked to Columbus's voyage of 1492 was the discovery by Portuguese navigators of a sea route from Europe to Asia around the southern tip of Africa. The European conquest of America began as an offshoot of the quest for a sea route to India, China, and the islands of the East Indies, the source of the silk, tea, spices, porcelain, and other luxury goods on which international trade in the early modern era centered. For centuries, this commerce had been conducted across land, from China and South Asia to the Middle East and the Mediterranean region. Profit and piety—the desire to eliminate Islamic middlemen and win control of the lucrative trade for Christian western Europe—combined to inspire the quest for a direct route to Asia.

Chinese and Portuguese Navigation

Zheng He's voyages

At the beginning of the fifteenth century, one might have predicted that China would establish the world's first global empire. Between 1405 and 1433, Admiral Zheng He led seven large naval expeditions in the Indian Ocean. The first convoy consisted of 62 ships that were larger than those of any European nation, along with 225 support vessels and more than 25,000 men. On his sixth voyage, Zheng explored the coast of East Africa. Had his ships continued westward, they could easily have reached North and South America. But as a wealthy land-based empire, China did not feel the need for overseas expansion, and after 1433 the government ended support for long-distance maritime expeditions.

New techniques of sailing and navigation

It fell to Portugal, far removed from the overland route to Asia, to begin exploring the Atlantic. Taking advantage of new long-distance ships known as **caravels** and new navigational devices such as the compass and quadrant, the Portuguese showed that it was possible to sail down the coast of Africa and return to Portugal. Until 1434, no European sailor had seen the coast of Africa below the Sahara. But in that year, a Portuguese ship brought a sprig of rosemary from West Africa, proof that one could sail beyond the desert and return.

Little by little, Portuguese ships moved farther down the coast. In 1485, they reached Benin, an imposing city whose craftsmen produced bronze sculptures that still inspire admiration for their artistic beauty and superb casting techniques. The Portuguese established fortified trading

THE OLD WORLD ON THE EVE OF AMERICAN COLONIZATION, ca. 1500

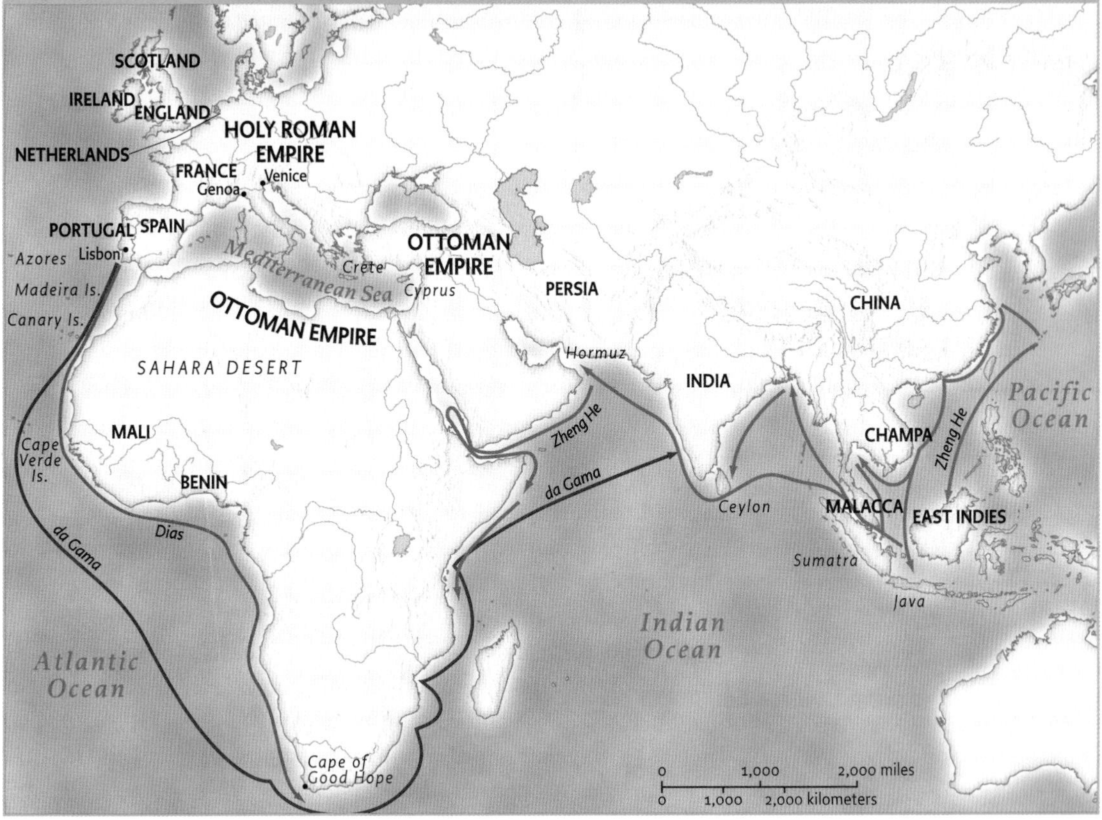

In the fifteenth century, the world known to Europeans was limited to Europe, parts of Africa, and Asia. Explorers from Portugal sought to find a sea route to the East in order to circumvent the Italian city-states and Middle Eastern rulers who controlled the overland trade.

posts on the western coast of Africa. The profits reaped by these Portuguese "factories"—so named because merchants were known as "factors"—inspired other European powers to follow in their footsteps.

Portugal also began to colonize Madeira, the Azores, and the Canary and Cape Verde Islands, which lie in the Atlantic off the African coast. The Portuguese established plantations on the Atlantic islands, eventually replacing the native populations with thousands of slaves shipped from Africa—an ominous precedent for the New World.

Freedom and Slavery in Africa

Slavery in Africa long predated the coming of Europeans. Traditionally, African slaves tended to be criminals, debtors, and captives in war. They worked within the households of their owners and had well-defined rights, such as possessing property and marrying free persons. It was not uncommon for African slaves to acquire their freedom. Slavery was one of several forms of labor, not the basis of the economy as it would become in large parts of the New World. The coming of the Portuguese, soon followed by traders from other European nations, accelerated the buying and selling of slaves within Africa. At least 100,000 African slaves were transported to Spain and Portugal between 1450 and 1500.

Having reached West Africa, Portuguese mariners pushed their explorations ever southward along the coast. Bartholomeu Dias reached the Cape of Good Hope at the continent's southern tip in 1487. In 1498, Vasco da Gama sailed around it to India, demonstrating the feasibility of a sea route to the East. With a population of under 1 million, Portugal established a vast trading empire, with bases in India, southern China, and Indonesia. But six years before da Gama's voyage, Christopher Columbus had, he believed, discovered a new route to China and India by sailing west.

The Voyages of Columbus

A seasoned mariner and fearless explorer from Genoa, a major port in northern Italy, Columbus had for years sailed the Mediterranean and North Atlantic, studying ocean currents and wind patterns. Like nearly all navigators of the time, Columbus knew the earth was round. But he drastically underestimated its size. He believed that by sailing westward he could relatively quickly cross the Atlantic and reach Asia. No one in Europe knew that two giant continents lay 3,000 miles to the west. The Vikings, to be sure, had sailed from Greenland to Newfoundland around the year 1000 and established a settlement, Vinland. But this outpost was abandoned after a few years and had been forgotten, except in Norse legends.

Columbus's Landfall, an engraving from *La lettera dell'isole* (Letter from the Islands). This 1493 pamphlet reproduced, in the form of a poem, Columbus's first letter describing his voyage of the previous year. Under the watchful eye of King Ferdinand of Spain, Columbus and his men land on a Caribbean island, while local Indians flee.

For Columbus, as for other figures of the time, religious and commercial motives reinforced one another. Along with developing trade with the East, he hoped to convert Asians to Christianity and enlist them in a crusade to redeem Jerusalem from Muslim control.

Columbus sought financial support throughout Europe for the planned voyage. He relied on a number of sources for his estimate of the size of the globe, including Marco Polo's account of his visit by land to China in the thirteenth century and, as a devout Catholic, the Bible. Eventually, King Ferdinand and Queen Isabella of Spain agreed to become sponsors. Their marriage in 1469 had united the warring kingdoms of Aragon and Castile. In 1492, they completed the ***reconquista***—the "reconquest" of Spain from the Moors, African Muslims who had occupied part of the Iberian Peninsula for centuries. With Spain's territory united, Ferdinand and Isabella—like the rulers of the Italian city-states—were anxious to circumvent the Muslim stranglehold on eastern trade. It is not surprising, then, that Columbus set sail with royal letters of introduction to Asian rulers, authorizing him to negotiate trade agreements.

CONTACT

Columbus in the New World

On October 12, 1492, after only thirty-three days of sailing from the Canary Islands, where he had stopped to resupply his three ships, Columbus and his expedition arrived at the Bahamas. Soon afterward, he encountered the far larger islands of Hispaniola (today the site of Haiti and the Dominican Republic) and Cuba. When one of his ships ran aground, he abandoned it and left thirty-eight men behind on Hispaniola. But he found room to bring ten inhabitants of the island back to Spain for conversion to Christianity.

In the following year, 1493, Columbus returned with seventeen ships and more than 1,000 men to explore the area and establish a Spanish outpost. Columbus's settlement on the island of Hispaniola, which he named La Isabella, failed, but in 1502 another Spanish explorer, Nicolás de Ovando, arrived with 2,500 men and established a permanent base, the first center of the Spanish empire in America. Columbus went to his grave believing that he had discovered a westward route to Asia. The explorations of another Italian, Amerigo Vespucci, along the coast of South America between 1499 and 1502 made plain that a continent entirely unknown to Europeans had been encountered. The New World would come to bear not Columbus's name but one based on Vespucci's—America. Vespucci also realized that the native inhabitants were distinct peoples, not residents of the East Indies as Columbus had believed, although the name "Indians," applied to them by Columbus, has endured to this day.

Exploration and Conquest

Thanks to Johannes Gutenberg's invention of the printing press in the 1430s, news of Columbus's achievement traveled quickly, at least among the educated minority in

Engravings, from the *Florentine Codex*, of the forces of Cortés marching on Tenochtitlán and assaulting the city with cannon fire. The difference in military technology between the Spanish and Aztecs is evident. Indians who allied with Cortés had helped him build vessels and carry them in pieces over mountains to the city. The codex (a volume formed by stitching together manuscript pages) was prepared under the supervision of a Spanish missionary in sixteenth-century Mexico.

VOYAGES OF DISCOVERY

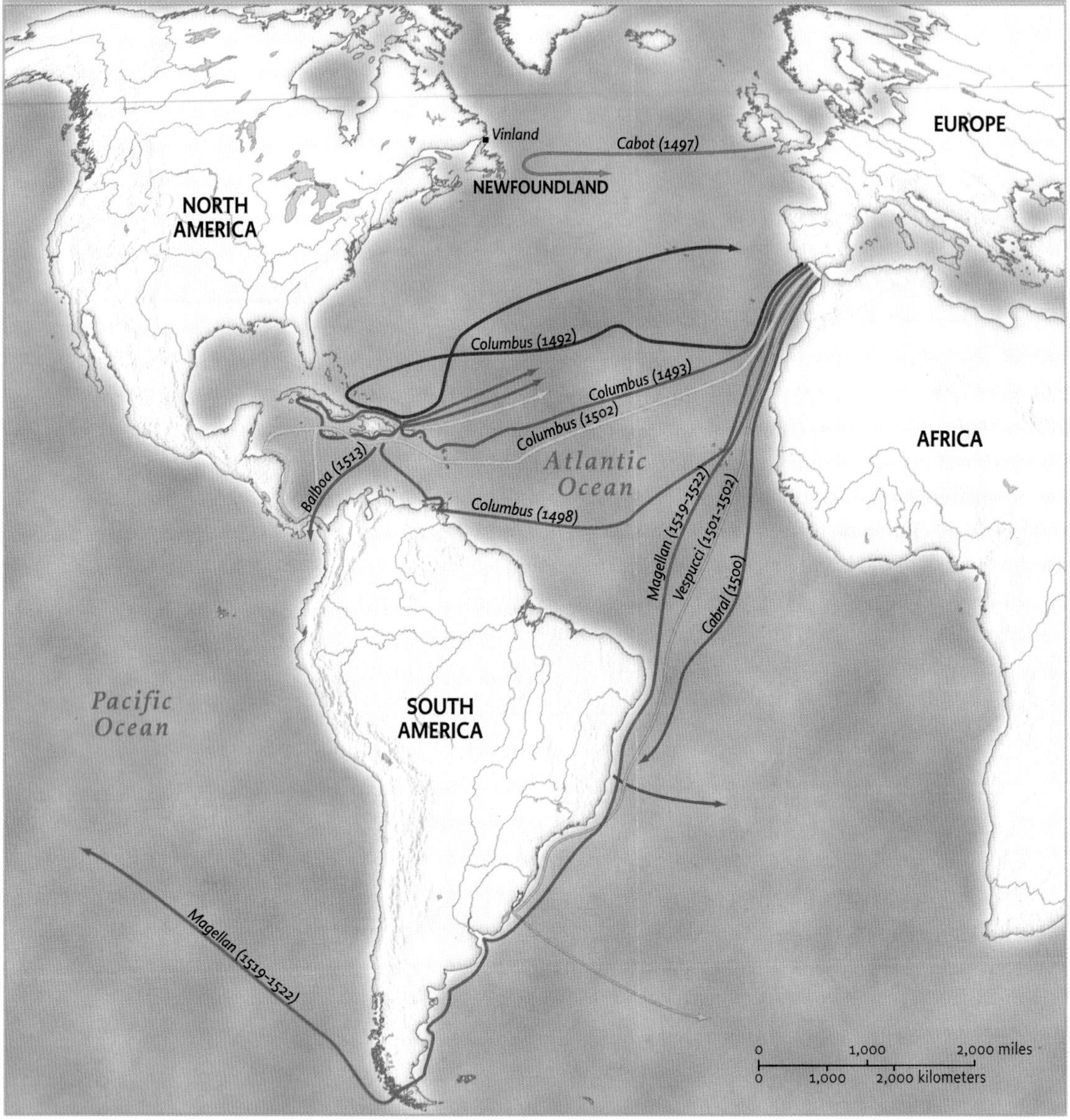

Christopher Columbus's first Atlantic crossing, in 1492, was soon followed by voyages of discovery by English, Portuguese, Spanish, and Italian explorers.

Europe. Other explorers were inspired to follow in his wake. John Cabot, a Genoese merchant who had settled in England, reached Newfoundland in 1497. Soon, scores of fishing boats from France, Spain, and England were active in the region. Pedro Cabral claimed Brazil for Portugal in 1500.

Spreading Catholicism

But the Spanish took the lead in exploration and conquest. Inspired by a search for wealth, national glory, and the desire to spread Catholicism, Spanish ***conquistadores***, often accompanied by religious missionaries and carrying flags emblazoned with the sign of the cross, radiated outward from Hispaniola. In 1513, Vasco Núñez de Balboa trekked across the isthmus of Panama and became the first European to gaze upon the Pacific Ocean. Between 1519 and 1522, Ferdinand Magellan led the first expedition to sail around the world, encountering Pacific islands and peoples previously unknown to Europe.

The first explorer to encounter a major American civilization was Hernán Cortés, who in 1519 arrived at Tenochtitlán, the nerve center of the Aztec empire, whose wealth and power rested on domination of numerous subordinate peoples nearby. The Aztecs were violent warriors who engaged in the ritual sacrifice of captives and others, sometimes thousands at a time. This practice thoroughly alienated their neighbors.

Hernán Cortés and Francisco Pizarro

With only a few hundred European men, Cortés conquered the Aztec city, relying on superior military technology such as iron weapons and gunpowder. He shrewdly enlisted the aid of some of the Aztecs' subject peoples, who supplied him with thousands of warriors, without whose aid he could not have succeeded. His most powerful ally, however, was disease—a smallpox epidemic that devastated Aztec society. A few years later, Francisco Pizarro conquered the great Inca kingdom centered in modern-day Peru. Pizarro's tactics were typical of the *conquistadores*. He captured the Incan king, demanded and received a ransom, and then killed the king anyway. Soon, treasure fleets carrying cargoes of gold and silver from the mines of Mexico and Peru were traversing the Atlantic to enrich the Spanish crown.

TABLE 1.1 Estimated Regional Populations: The Americas, ca. 1500

North America	3,800,000
Mexico	17,200,000
Central America	5,625,000
Hispaniola	1,000,000
The Caribbean	3,000,000
The Andes	15,700,000
South America	8,620,000
Total	54,945,000

The Demographic Disaster

The transatlantic flow of goods and people is sometimes called the **Columbian Exchange**. Plants, animals, and cultures that had evolved independently on separate continents were now thrown together. Products introduced to Europe from the Americas included corn, tomatoes, potatoes, peanuts, and

TABLE 1.2 Estimated Regional Populations: The World, ca. 1500

India	110,000,000
China	103,000,000
Other Asia	55,400,000
Western Europe	57,200,000
The Americas	55,000,000
Russia and Eastern Europe	34,000,000
Sub-Saharan Africa	38,300,000
Japan	15,400,000
World Total	467,300,000

tobacco, while people from the Old World brought wheat, rice, sugarcane, horses, cattle, pigs, and sheep to the New. But Europeans also carried germs previously unknown in the Americas.

No one knows exactly how many people lived in the Americas at the time of Columbus's voyages—current estimates range between 50 and 90 million, most of whom lived in Central and South America. In 1492, the Indian population within what are now the borders of the United States was between 2 and 5 million. The Indian populations of the Americas suffered a catastrophic decline because of contact with Europeans. Never having encountered diseases like smallpox, influenza, and measles, Indians had not developed antibodies to fight them. The result was devastating. The population of Mexico would fall by more than 90 percent in the sixteenth century, from perhaps 20 million to under 2 million. As for the area that now forms the United States, its Native American population fell continuously. It reached its lowest point around 1900, at only 250,000.

Overall, the death of perhaps 80 million people—close to one-fifth of humankind—in the first century and a half after contact with Europeans represents the greatest loss of life in human history. The causes were numerous—not only disease but other consequences of European colonization, including wars using advanced military technology, enslavement, forced conversion to Christianity, and destruction of long-established communities. All these enabled Europeans to conquer the Americas.

Young Woman with a Harpsichord, a colorful painting from Mexico in the early 1700s, depicts an upper-class woman. Her dress, jewelry, fan, the cross around her neck, and the musical instrument all emphasize that while she lives in the colonies she embodies the latest in European fashion and culture.

THE SPANISH EMPIRE

By the middle of the sixteenth century, Spain had established an immense empire that reached from Europe to the Americas and Asia. The Atlantic and Pacific oceans, once barriers separating different parts of the world, now became highways for the exchange of goods and the movement of people. Spanish galleons carried gold and silver from Mexico and Peru eastward to Spain and westward to Manila in the Philippines and on to China.

Stretching from the Andes Mountains of South America through present-day Mexico and the Caribbean and eventually into Florida and the southwestern United States, Spain's empire exceeded in size the Roman empire of the ancient world. Its center was Mexico City, a magnificent capital built on the ruins of the Aztec city of Tenochtitlán that boasted churches, hospitals, monasteries, government buildings, and the New World's first university. Unlike the English and French New World empires, Spanish America was essentially an urban civilization. For centuries, its great cities, notably Mexico City, Quito, and Lima, far outshone any urban centers in North America and most of those in Europe.

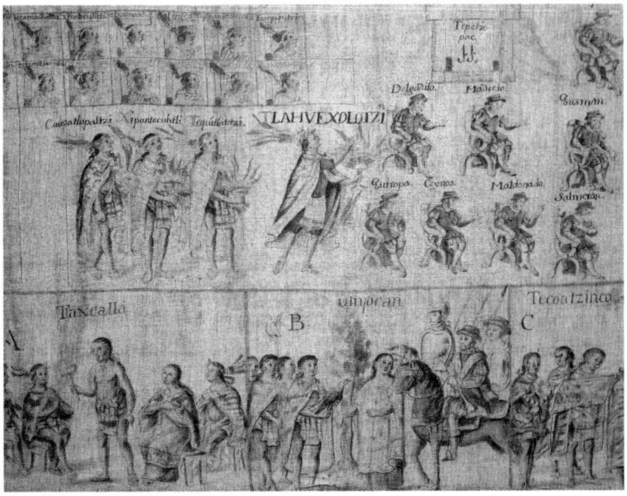

An image from the *Tlaxcala Codex*, which chronicles events in a region of central Mexico in the sixteenth century. Aztec warriors dressed in eagle and jaguar costumes dance before Spanish officials and priests.

Governing Spanish America

At least in theory, the government of Spanish America reflected the absolutism of the newly unified nation at home. Authority originated with the king and flowed downward through the Council of the Indies—the main body in Spain for colonial administration—and then to viceroys in Mexico and Peru and other local officials in America. The Catholic Church also played a significant role in the administration of Spanish colonies, frequently exerting its authority on matters of faith, morals, and treatment of the Indians.

Successive kings kept elected assemblies out of Spain's New World empire. Royal officials were generally appointees from Spain, rather than *criollos*, or **creoles**, as persons born in the colonies of European ancestry were called. But as Spain's power declined in Europe beginning in the seventeenth century, the local elite came to enjoy more and more effective authority over colonial affairs.

Colonists and Indians in Spanish America

Despite the decline in the native population, Spanish America remained populous enough that, with the exception of the West Indies and a few cities, large-scale importations of African slaves were unnecessary. Instead, the Spanish forced tens of thousands of Indians to work in gold and silver mines, which supplied the empire's wealth, and on large-scale farms, or ***haciendas***, controlled by Spanish landlords. In Spanish America, unlike other New World empires, Indians performed most of the labor.

Social mobility in Spanish America

The opportunity for social advancement drew numerous colonists from Spain—225,000 in the sixteenth century and a total of 750,000 in the three centuries of Spain's colonial rule. Eventually, a significant number came in families, but at first the large majority were young, single men, many of them laborers, craftsmen, and soldiers. Many also came as government officials, priests, professionals, and minor aristocrats, all ready to direct the manual work of Indians, since living without having to labor was a sign of noble status. The most successful of these colonists enjoyed lives of luxury similar to those of the upper classes at home.

Unlike in the later British empire, Indian inhabitants always outnumbered European colonists and their descendants in Spanish America, and large areas remained effectively under Indian control for many years. Spanish authorities granted Indians certain rights within colonial society and looked forward to their eventual assimilation. The Spanish crown ordered wives of colonists to join them in America and demanded that single men marry. But with the population of Spanish women remaining low, the intermixing of the colonial and Indian peoples soon began. As early as 1514, the Spanish government formally approved of such marriages, partly as a way of bringing Christianity to the native population. By 1600, ***mestizos*** (persons of mixed origin) made up a large part of the urban population of Spanish America. Over time, Spanish America evolved into a hybrid culture, part Spanish, part Indian, and in some areas part African, but with a single official faith, language, and governmental system.

A hybrid culture

Justifications for Conquest

The Europeans who crossed the Atlantic in the wake of Columbus's voyage had immense confidence in the superiority of their own cultures to those they encountered in America. They expected these societies to abandon their own beliefs and traditions and embrace those of the newcomers. Failure to do so reinforced the conviction that these people were uncivilized "heathens" (non-Christians). In addition, Europeans brought with them a long history of using violence to subdue their foes and a missionary zeal to spread the benefits of their own civilization to others, while reaping the benefits of empire. Spain was no exception.

Religious motivation

To further legitimize Spain's claim to rule the New World, a year after Columbus's first voyage Pope Alexander VI divided the non-Christian world between Spain and Portugal. The line was subsequently adjusted to give Portugal control of Brazil, with the remainder of the Western Hemisphere falling under Spanish authority. Its missionary purpose in colonization was already familiar because of the long holy war against Islam within Spain itself and Spain's 1492 order that all Muslims and Jews had to convert to Catholicism or leave the country. But missionary zeal was powerfully reinforced in the sixteenth century, when the Protestant Reformation divided the Catholic Church. In 1517, Martin Luther, a German priest, posted

Spanish *conquistadores* murdering Indians at Cuzco, in Peru. The Dutch-born engraver Theodor de Bry and his sons illustrated ten volumes about New World exploration published between 1590 and 1618. A Protestant, de Bry created vivid images that helped to spread the Black Legend of Spain as a uniquely cruel colonizer.

his ***Ninety-Five Theses***, which accused the church of worldliness and corruption. Luther wanted to cleanse the church of abuses such as the sale of indulgences (official dispensations forgiving sins). He insisted that all believers should read the Bible for themselves, rather than relying on priests to interpret it for them. His call for reform led to the rise of new Protestant churches independent of Rome and plunged Europe into more than a century of religious and political strife.

Converting Indians

Spain, the most powerful bastion of orthodox Catholicism, redoubled its efforts to convert the Indians to the "true faith." Spain insisted that the primary goal of colonization was to save the Indians from heathenism and prevent them from falling under the sway of Protestantism. Religious orders established missions throughout the empire, and over time millions of Indians were converted to Catholicism. On the other hand, Spanish rule, especially in its initial period, decimated the Indian population and subjected Indians to brutal labor conditions. The *conquistadores* and subsequent governors, who required conquered peoples to acknowledge the Catholic Church and provide gold and silver, saw no contradiction between serving God and enriching themselves. Others, however, did.

As early as 1537, Pope Paul III, who hoped to see Indians become devout subjects of Catholic monarchs, outlawed Indians' enslavement (an edict never extended to apply to Africans). Fifteen years later, the Dominican priest **Bartolomé de Las Casas** published an account of the decimation of the Indian population with the compelling title *A Very Brief Account of the Destruction of the Indies.*

Spain's "strange cruelties"

Las Casas's writings denounced Spain for causing the death of millions of innocent people and for denying Indians their freedom. He narrated in shocking detail the "strange cruelties" carried out by "the Christians," including the burning alive of men, women, and children and the imposition of forced labor. "The entire human race is one," he proclaimed, and while he continued to believe that Spain had a right to rule in America, largely on religious grounds, he called for Indians to enjoy "all guarantees of liberty and justice" from the moment they became subjects of Spain. Las Casas also suggested, however, that importing slaves from Africa would help to protect the Indians from exploitation.

Reforming the Empire

Indian labor

Largely because of Las Casas's efforts, Spain in 1542 promulgated the New Laws, commanding that Indians no longer be enslaved. In 1550, Spain abolished the *encomienda* system, under which the first settlers had been granted authority over conquered Indian lands with the right to extract forced labor from the native inhabitants. In its place, the government established the ***repartimiento* system**, whereby residents of Indian villages remained legally free and entitled to wages, but were still required to perform a fixed amount of labor each year. The Indians were not slaves—they had access to land, were paid wages, and could not be bought and sold. But since the requirement that they work for the Spanish remained the essence of the system, it still allowed for many abuses by Spanish landlords and by priests who required Indians to toil on mission lands as part of the conversion process.

Over time, Spain's brutal treatment of Indians improved somewhat. The Spanish established their domination not just through violence and disease but by bringing education, medical care, and European goods, and because many Indians embraced Christianity. But Las Casas's writings, translated almost immediately into several European languages, contributed to the spread of the **Black Legend**—the image of Spain as a uniquely brutal and exploitative colonizer. This image would provide a potent justification for other European powers to challenge Spain's predominance in the New World.

Exploring North America

New colonies

While the Spanish empire centered on Mexico, Peru, and the West Indies, the hope of finding a new kingdom of gold soon led Spanish explorers into new territory. In 1508, Spain established the first permanent colony in what is now the United States. That first colony was not, as many people believe, at Jamestown, Virginia, or St. Augustine, Florida, but on the island of Puerto Rico, now a U.S. "commonwealth." Unlike many other European settlements that followed it, Puerto Rico had gold; Juan Ponce de León, who

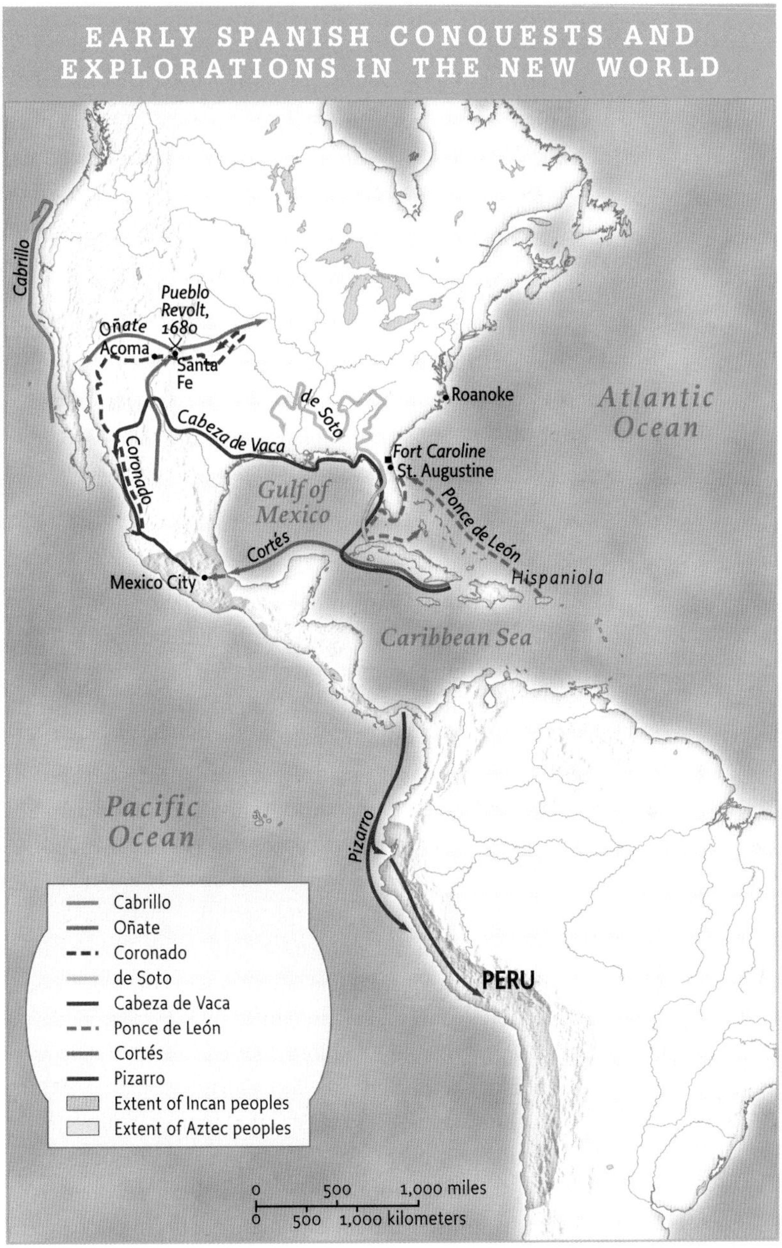

By around 1600, New Spain had become a vast empire stretching from the modern-day American Southwest through Mexico and Central America and into the former Inca kingdom in South America. This map shows early Spanish exploration, especially in the present-day United States, Mexico, and Peru.

led the colony, sent a considerable amount to Spain, while keeping some for himself. In 1513, Ponce embarked for Florida, in search of wealth, slaves, and a fountain of eternal youth, only to be repelled by local Indians.

In the late 1530s and 1540s, Juan Rodriguez Cabrillo explored the Pacific coast as far north as present-day Oregon, and expeditions led by Hernando de Soto, Cabeza de Vaca, Francisco Vásquez de Coronado, and others marched through the Gulf region and the Southwest, fruitlessly searching for another Mexico or Peru. These expeditions, really mobile communities with hundreds of adventurers, priests, potential settlers, slaves, and livestock, spread disease and devastation among Indian communities. De Soto's was particularly brutal. His men tortured, raped, and enslaved countless Indians and transmitted deadly diseases. When Europeans in the seventeenth century returned to colonize the area traversed by de Soto's party, little remained of the societies he had encountered.

Hernando De Soto

Spain in Florida and the Southwest

Nonetheless, these explorations established Spain's claim to a large part of what is now the American South and Southwest. The first region to be colonized within the present-day United States was Florida. Spain hoped to establish a military base there to combat pirates who threatened the treasure fleet that each year sailed from Havana for Europe loaded with gold and silver from Mexico and Peru. Spain also wanted to forestall French incursions in the area. In 1565, Philip II of Spain authorized the nobleman Pedro Menéndez de Avilés to lead a colonizing expedition to Florida. Menéndez destroyed a small outpost at Fort Caroline, which a group of Huguenots (French Protestants) had established in 1562 near present-day Jacksonville. Menéndez and his men went on to establish Spanish forts on St. Simons Island, Georgia, and at St. Augustine, Florida. The latter remains the oldest site in the continental United States continuously inhabited by European settlers and their descendants. In general, though, Florida failed to attract settlers, remaining an isolated military settlement, in effect a fortified outpost of Cuba. As late as 1763, Spanish Florida had only 4,000 inhabitants of European descent.

Florida as military base

Spain took even longer to begin the colonization of the American Southwest. It was not until 1598 that Juan de Oñate led a group of 400 soldiers, colonists, and missionaries north from Mexico to establish a permanent settlement. While searching for fabled deposits of precious metals, Oñate's nephew and fourteen soldiers were killed by inhabitants of Acoma, the "sky city" located on a high bluff in present-day New Mexico.

Juan de Oñate in New Mexico

Oñate decided to teach the local Indians a lesson. After a two-day siege, his forces scaled the seemingly impregnable heights and destroyed Acoma, killing more than 800 of its 1,500 or so inhabitants, including 300 women. Of the 600 Indians captured, the women and children were consigned to servitude in Spanish families, while adult men were punished by the cutting off of one foot. Oñate's message was plain—any Indians who resisted Spanish authority would be crushed. In 1606, however, Oñate was ordered home and punished for his treatment of New Mexico's Indians. In 1610, Spain established the capital of New Mexico at Santa Fe, the first permanent European settlement in the Southwest.

St. Anthony and the Infant Jesus, painted on a tanned buffalo hide by a Franciscan priest in New Mexico in the early eighteenth century. This was not long after the Spanish reconquered the area, from which they had been driven by the Pueblo Revolt.

The Pueblo Revolt

In 1680, New Mexico's small and vulnerable colonist population numbered fewer than 3,000. Relations between the Pueblo Indians and colonial authorities had deteriorated throughout the seventeenth century, as governors, settlers, and missionaries sought to exploit the labor of an Indian population that declined from about 60,000 in 1600 to some 17,000 eighty years later. Franciscan friars worked relentlessly to convert Indians to Catholicism, often using intimidation and violence. As the Inquisition—the persecution of non-Catholics—became more and more intense in Spain, so did the friars' efforts to stamp out traditional religious ceremonies in New Mexico. At the same time, the Spanish assumed that the Indians could never unite against the colonizers. In August 1680, they were proven wrong.

Little is known about the life of Popé, who became the main organizer of an uprising that aimed to drive the Spanish from the colony and restore the Indians' traditional autonomy. Under Popé's leadership, New Mexico's Indians joined in a coordinated uprising. Ironically, because the Pueblos spoke six different languages, Spanish became the revolt's "lingua franca" (a common means of communication among persons of different linguistic backgrounds). Some 2,000 warriors destroyed isolated farms and missions, killing 400 colonists, including 21 Franciscan missionaries. Most of the Spanish survivors, accompanied by several hundred Christian Indians, made their way south out of New Mexico. Within a few weeks, a century of colonization in the area had been destroyed.

The **Pueblo Revolt** was the most complete victory for Native Americans over Europeans and the only wholesale expulsion of settlers in the history of North America. Cooperation among the Pueblo peoples, however, soon evaporated. By the end of the 1680s, warfare had broken out among several villages, even as Apache and Navajo raids continued. Popé died around 1690. In 1692, the Spanish launched an invasion that reconquered New Mexico.

VOICES OF FREEDOM

From Bartolomé de Las Casas, *History of the Indies* (1528)

Las Casas was the Dominican priest who condemned the treatment of Indians in the Spanish empire. His widely disseminated *History of the Indies* helped to establish the Black Legend of Spanish cruelty.

The Indians [of Hispaniola] were totally deprived of their freedom and were put in the harshest, fiercest, most horrible servitude and captivity which no one who has not seen it can understand. Even beasts enjoy more freedom when they are allowed to graze in the fields. But our Spaniards gave no such opportunity to Indians and truly considered them perpetual slaves, since the Indians had not the free will to dispose of their persons but instead were disposed of according to Spanish greed and cruelty, not as men in captivity but as beasts tied to a rope to prevent free movement. When they were allowed to go home, they often found it deserted and had no other recourse than to go out into the woods to find food and to die. When they fell ill, which was very frequently because they are a delicate people unaccustomed to such work, the Spaniards did not believe them and pitilessly called them lazy dogs and kicked and beat them; and when illness was apparent they sent them home as useless. . . . They would go then, falling into the first stream and dying there in desperation; others would hold on longer but very few ever made it home. I sometimes came upon dead bodies on my way, and upon others who were gasping and moaning in their death agony, repeating "Hungry, hungry." And this was the freedom, the good treatment and the Christianity the Indians received.

About eight years passed under [Spanish rule] and this disorder had time to grow; no one gave it a thought and the multitude of people who originally lived on the island . . . was consumed at such a rate that in these eight years 90 per cent had perished. From here this sweeping plague went to San Juan, Jamaica, Cuba and the continent, spreading destruction over the whole hemisphere.

From "Declaration of Josephe" (December 19, 1681)

Josephe was a Spanish-speaking Indian questioned by a royal attorney in Mexico City investigating the Pueblo Revolt. The revolt of the Indian population, in 1680, temporarily drove Spanish settlers from present-day New Mexico.

Asked what causes or motives the said Indian rebels had for renouncing the law of God and obedience to his Majesty, and for committing so many of crimes, [he answered] the causes they have were alleged ill treatment and injuries received from [Spanish authorities], because they beat them, took away what they had, and made them work without pay. Thus he replies.

Asked if he has learned if it has come to his notice during the time that he has been here the reason why the apostates burned the images, churches, and things pertaining to divine worship, making a mockery and a trophy of them, killing the priests and doing the other things they did, he said that he knows and had heard it generally stated that while they were besieging the villa the rebellious traitors burned the church and shouted in loud voices, "Now the God of the Spaniards, who was their father, is dead, and Santa Maria, who was their mother, and the saints, who were pieces of rotten wood," saying that only their own god lived. Thus they ordered all the temples and images, crosses and rosaries burned, and their function being over, they all went to bathe in the rivers, saying that they thereby washed away the water of baptism. For their churches, they placed on the four sides and in the center of the plaza some small circular enclosures of stone where they went to offer flour, feathers, and the seed of maguey [a local plant], maize, and tobacco, and performed other superstitious rites, giving the children to understand that they must all do this in the future. The captains and the chiefs ordered that the names of Jesus and Mary should nowhere be uttered. . . . He has seen many houses of idolatry which they have built, dancing the dance of the cachina [part of a traditional Indian religious ceremony], which this declarant has also danced. Thus he replies to the question.

QUESTIONS

1. *Why does Las Casas, after describing the ill treatment of Indians, write, "And this was the freedom, the good treatment and the Christianity the Indians received"?*
2. *What role did religion play in the Pueblo Revolt?*
3. *What ideas of freedom are apparent in the two documents?*

Some communities welcomed them back as a source of military protection. But Spain had learned a lesson. In the eighteenth century, colonial authorities adopted a more tolerant attitude toward traditional religious practices and made fewer demands on Indian labor.

THE FRENCH AND DUTCH EMPIRES

If the Black Legend inspired a sense of superiority among Spain's European rivals, the precious metals that poured from the New World into the Spanish treasury aroused the desire to match Spain's success. The establishment of Spain's American empire transformed the balance of power in the world economy. The Atlantic replaced the overland route to Asia as the major axis of global trade. During the seventeenth century, the French, Dutch, and English established colonies in North America. England's mainland colonies, to be discussed in the next chapter, consisted of agricultural settlements with growing populations whose hunger for land produced incessant conflict with native peoples. New France and New Netherland were primarily commercial ventures that never attracted large numbers of colonists. Because French and Dutch settlements were more dependent than the English on Indians as trading partners and military allies, Native Americans exercised more power and enjoyed more freedom in their relations with these settlements.

Shifts in global trade

French Colonization

The first of Spain's major European rivals to embark on New World explorations was France. The explorer Samuel de Champlain, sponsored by a French fur-trading company, founded Quebec in 1608. In 1673, the Jesuit priest Jacques Marquette and the fur trader Louis Joliet located the Mississippi River, and by 1681 René-Robert Cavelier, Sieur de La Salle, had descended to the Gulf of Mexico, claiming the entire Mississippi River valley for France. New France eventually formed a giant arc along the St. Lawrence, Mississippi, and Ohio rivers.

Settlement in New France

By 1700, the number of white inhabitants of New France had risen to only 19,000. With a far larger population than England, France sent many fewer emigrants to the Western Hemisphere. The government at home feared that significant emigration would undermine France's role as a European great power and might compromise its effort to establish trade and good relations with the Indians. Unfavorable reports about America circulated widely in France. Canada was widely depicted as an icebox, a land of savage Indians, a dumping ground for criminals. Most French who left their homes during these years preferred to settle in the Netherlands, Spain, or the West Indies. The revocation in 1685 of the Edict of Nantes,

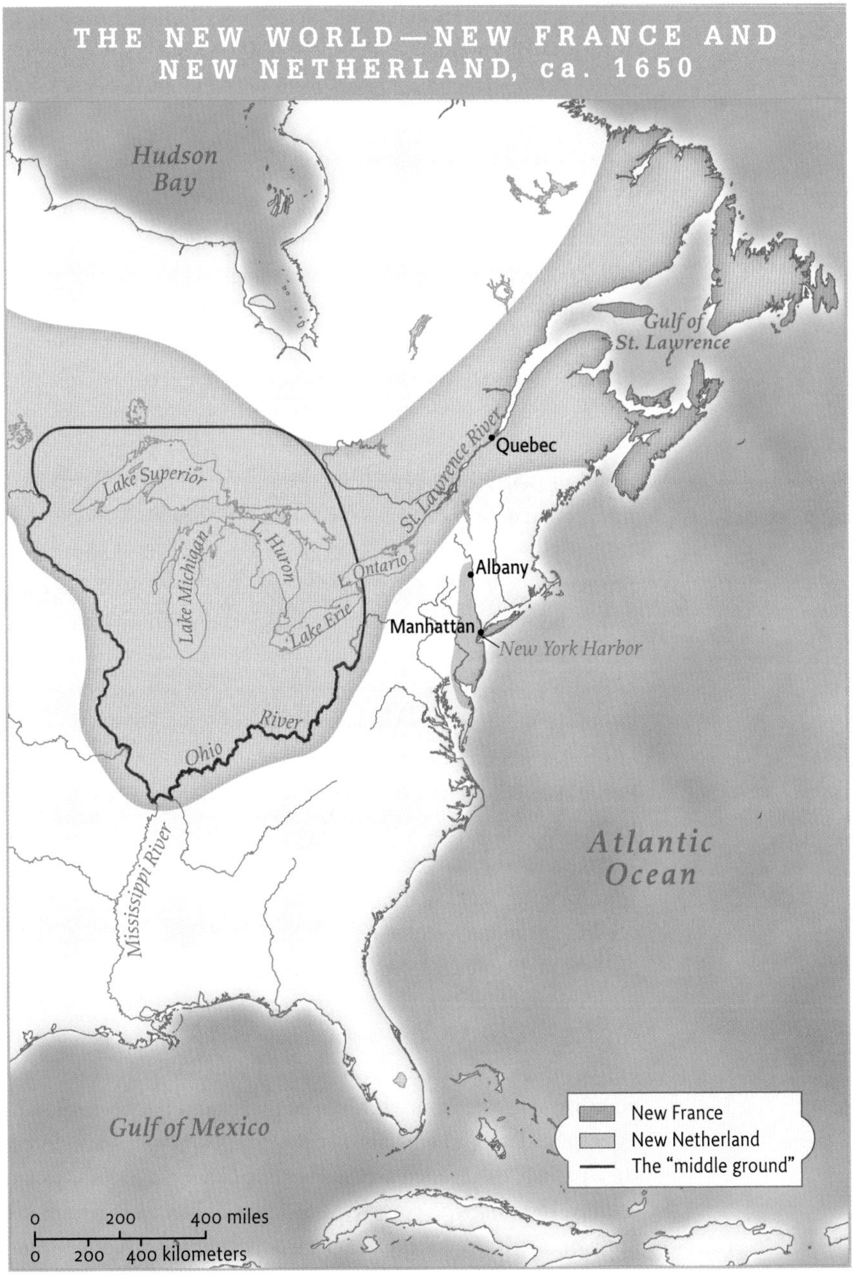
THE NEW WORLD—NEW FRANCE AND NEW NETHERLAND, ca. 1650
Hudson Bay
Gulf of St. Lawrence
St. Lawrence River
Quebec
Lake Superior
Lake Michigan
L. Huron
L. Ontario
Lake Erie
Albany
Manhattan
New York Harbor
Ohio River
Mississippi River
Atlantic Ocean
Gulf of Mexico
New France
New Netherland
The "middle ground"
0 200 400 miles
0 200 400 kilometers

New France and New Netherland.

which had extended religious toleration to French Protestants, led well over 100,000 Huguenots to flee their country. But they were not welcome in New France, which the crown desired to remain an outpost of Catholicism.

New France and the Indians

Alliances with Indians

With its small white population and emphasis on the fur trade rather than agricultural settlement, the viability of New France depended on friendly relations with local Indians. The French prided themselves on adopting a more humane policy than their imperial rivals. "Only our nation," declared one French writer, "knows the secret of winning the Indians' affection." The French worked out a complex series of military, commercial, and diplomatic connections, the most enduring alliances between Indians and settlers in colonial North America. Samuel de Champlain, the intrepid explorer who dominated the early history of New France, denied that Native Americans were intellectually or culturally inferior to Europeans. Although he occasionally engaged in wars with local Indians, he dreamed of creating a colony based on mutual respect between diverse peoples. The Jesuits, a missionary religious order, did seek, with some success, to convert Indians to Catholicism. Unlike Spanish missionaries in early New Mexico, they allowed Christian Indians to retain a high degree of independence and much of their traditional social structure, and they did not seek to suppress all traditional religious practices.

Jesuits

Like other colonists throughout North America, however, the French brought striking changes in Indian life. Contact with Europeans was inevitably followed by the spread of disease. Participation in the fur trade drew natives into the burgeoning Atlantic economy, introducing new goods and transforming hunting from a search for food into a quest for marketable commodities. Indians were soon swept into the rivalries among European empires.

The middle ground

As in the Spanish empire, New France witnessed considerable cultural exchange and intermixing between colonial and native populations. On the "middle ground" of the Great Lakes region in French America, Indians and whites encountered each other for many years on a basis of relative equality. And ***métis***, or children of marriages between Indian women and French traders and officials, became guides, traders, and interpreters. Like the Spanish, the French seemed willing to accept Indians as part of colonial society. Indians who converted to Catholicism were promised full citizenship. In fact, however, it was far rarer for natives to adopt French ways than for French settlers to become attracted to the "free" life of the Indians.

Movement between societies

The Dutch Empire

In 1609, Henry Hudson, an Englishman employed by the Dutch East India Company, sailed into New York Harbor searching for a Northwest Passage to Asia. Hudson and his crew became the first Europeans to sail up the

This engraving, which appears in Samuel de Champlain's 1613 account of his voyages, is the only likeness of the explorer from his own time. Champlain, wearing European armor and brandishing an arquebus (an advanced weapon of the period), stands at the center of this pitched battle between his Indian allies and the hostile Iroquois.

river that now bears his name. Hudson did not find a route to Asia, but he did encounter abundant fur-bearing animals and Native Americans more than willing to trade furs for European goods. He claimed the area for the Netherlands, and his voyage planted the seeds of what would eventually become a great metropolis, New York City. In 1624, the Dutch West India Company, which had been awarded a monopoly of Dutch trade with America, settled colonists on Manhattan Island.

Henry Hudson

These ventures formed one small part in the rise of the Dutch overseas empire. In the early seventeenth century, the Netherlands dominated international commerce, and Amsterdam was Europe's foremost shipping and banking center. The small nation had entered a golden age of rapidly accumulating wealth and stunning achievements in painting, philosophy, and the sciences. With a population of only 2 million, the Netherlands established a far-flung empire that reached from Indonesia to South Africa and the Caribbean and temporarily wrested control of Brazil from Portugal.

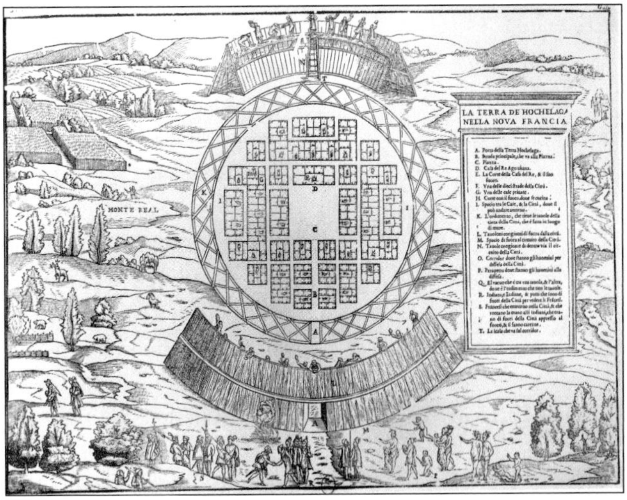

An engraving of the Huron town Hochelaga, site of modern-day Montreal, from a book about voyages of discovery by Giovanni Battista Ramusio, an Italian geographer, published in 1556.

Dutch Freedom

The Dutch prided themselves on their devotion to liberty. Indeed, in the early seventeenth century they enjoyed two freedoms not recognized elsewhere in Europe—freedom of the press and of private religious practice. Amsterdam became a haven for persecuted Protestants from all over Europe and for Jews as well.

New Netherland

Despite the Dutch reputation for cherishing freedom, New Netherland was hardly governed democratically. New Amsterdam, the main population center, was essentially a fortified military outpost controlled by appointees of the West India Company. Although the governor called on prominent citizens for advice from time to time, neither an elected assembly nor a town council, the basic unit of government at home, was established.

"Half-freedom"

In other ways, however, the colonists enjoyed more liberty than their counterparts elsewhere in North America. Even their slaves possessed rights. Some enjoyed "half-freedom"—they were required to pay an annual fee to the company and work for it when called upon, but they were given land to support their families. Settlers employed slaves on family farms or for household or craft labor, not on large plantations as in the West Indies.

Women's rights

Women in the Dutch settlement enjoyed far more independence than in other colonies. According to Dutch law, married women retained their separate legal identity. They could go to court, borrow money, and own property. Men were used to sharing property with their wives.

New Netherland attracted a remarkably diverse population. As early as the 1630s, at least eighteen languages were said to be spoken in New Amsterdam, whose residents included not only Dutch settlers but also Africans, Belgians, English, French, Germans, Irish, and Scandinavians.

The Dutch and Religious Toleration

The Dutch long prided themselves on being uniquely tolerant in religious matters compared to other European nations and their empires. It would be wrong, however, to attribute modern ideas of religious freedom to either the Dutch government and company at home or the rulers of New Netherland. Both Holland and New Netherland had an official religion, the Dutch Reformed Church, one of the Protestant national churches to emerge from the Reformation. The Dutch commitment to freedom of conscience extended to religious devotion exercised in private, not public worship in nonestablished churches.

Denial of religious freedom

When Jews, Quakers, Lutherans, and others demanded the right to practice their religion openly, Governor Petrus Stuyvesant adamantly refused, seeing such diversity as a threat to a godly, prosperous order. Twenty-three Jews arrived in New Amsterdam in 1654 from Brazil and the Caribbean. Referring to them as "members of a deceitful race," Stuyvesant ordered the newcomers to leave. But the company overruled him, noting that Jews at home had invested "a large amount of capital" in its shares.

Religious pluralism

Nonetheless, it is true that the Dutch dealt with religious pluralism in ways quite different from the practices common in other New World empires. Religious dissent was tolerated as long as it did not involve open

Coastal Native Americans were adept mariners. This detail from the earliest known engraving of New Amsterdam (1627) depicts Dutch and Indian boats in the harbor.

and public worship. No one in New Netherland was forced to attend the official church, nor was anyone executed for holding the wrong religious beliefs (as would happen in Puritan New England).

Settling New Netherland

During the seventeenth century, the Netherlands sent 1 million people overseas (many of them recent immigrants who were not in fact Dutch) to populate and govern their far-flung colonies. Very few, however, made North America their destination. By the mid-1660s, the European population of New Netherland numbered only 9,000. New Netherland remained a tiny backwater in the Dutch empire. So did an even smaller outpost near present-day Wilmington, Delaware, established in 1638 by a group of Dutch merchants. To circumvent the West India Company's trade monopoly, they claimed to be operating under the Swedish flag and called their settlement New Sweden. Only 300 settlers were living there when New Netherland seized the colony in 1655.

Sparse European settlement in New Netherland

New Netherland and the Indians

The Dutch came to North America to trade, not to conquer. Mindful of the Black Legend of Spanish cruelty, the Dutch determined to treat the native inhabitants more humanely. Having won their own independence from Spain after the longest and bloodiest war of sixteenth-century Europe, many Dutch identified with American Indians as fellow victims of Spanish oppression.

Dutch treatment of American Indians

From the beginning, Dutch authorities recognized Indian sovereignty over the land and forbade settlement in any area until it had been

The seal of New Netherland, adopted by the Dutch West India Company in 1630, suggests the centrality of the fur trade to the colony's prospects. Surrounding the beaver is *wampum*, a string of beads used by Indians in religious rituals and as currency.

purchased. But they also required tribes to make payments to colonial authorities. Near the coast, where most newcomers settled, New Netherland was hardly free of conflict with the Indians. With the powerful Iroquois Confederacy of the upper Hudson Valley, however, the Dutch established friendly commercial and diplomatic relations.

Borderlands and Empire in Early America

A **borderland**, according to one historian, is "a meeting place of peoples where geographical and cultural borders are not clearly defined." Numerous such places came into existence during the era of European conquest and settlement, including the "middle ground" of the Great Lakes region in New France. Boundaries between empires, and between colonists and native peoples, shifted constantly, overlapping claims to authority abounded, and hybrid cultures developed. As Europeans consolidated their control in some areas, the power of native peoples weakened. But at the edges of empire, power was always unstable, and overlapping cultural interactions at the local level defied any single pattern. European conquest was not a simple story of expanding domination over either empty space or powerless peoples, but of a continual struggle to establish authority. The Spanish, French, and Dutch empires fought each other for dominance in various parts of the continent, and Indians often wielded both economic and political power, pitting European empires against each other. Despite laws restricting commerce between empires, traders challenged boundaries, traversing lands claimed by both Europeans and Indians. People of European and Indian descent married and exchanged cultural attributes.

Shared features of the Spanish, French, and Dutch empires

Thus, before the planting of English colonies in North America, other European nations had established various kinds of settlements in the New World. Despite their differences, the Spanish, French, and Dutch empires shared certain features. All brought Christianity, new forms of technology and learning, new legal systems and family relations, and new forms of economic enterprise and wealth creation. They also brought savage warfare and widespread disease. These empires were aware of one another's existence. They studied and borrowed from one another, each lauding itself as superior to the others.

From the outset, dreams of freedom—for Indians, for settlers, for the entire world through the spread of Christianity—inspired and justified colonization. It would be no different when, at the beginning of the seventeenth century, England entered the struggle for empire in North America.

CHAPTER REVIEW AND ONLINE RESOURCES

REVIEW QUESTIONS

1. *Describe why the "discovery" of America was one of the "most important events recorded in the history of mankind," according to Adam Smith.*

2. *Describe the different global economies that Europeans participated in or created during the European age of expansion.*

3. *One of the most striking features of Indian societies at the time of the encounter with Europeans was their diversity. Support this statement with several examples.*

4. *Compare and contrast European values and ways of life with those of the Indians. Consider addressing religion, views about ownership of land, gender relations, and notions of freedom.*

5. *What were the main factors fueling the European age of expansion?*

6. *Compare the different economic and political systems of Spain, Portugal, the Netherlands, and France in the age of expansion.*

7. *Compare the political, economic, and religious motivations behind the French and Dutch empires with those of New Spain.*

8. *How would European settlers explain their superiority to Native Americans and justify both the conquest of native lands and terminating their freedom?*

9. *Why did Native Americans exercise more power in their relations with the Dutch and French than with the English?*

KEY TERMS

Tenochtitlán (p. 3)
Aztec (p. 3)
Great League of Peace (p. 7)
caravels (p. 14)
reconquista (p. 16)
conquistadores (p. 19)
Columbian Exchange (p. 19)
creoles (p. 21)
haciendas (p. 21)
mestizos (p. 22)
Ninety-Five Theses (p. 23)
Bartolomé de Las Casas (p. 23)
repartimiento system (p. 24)
Black Legend (p. 24)
Pueblo Revolt (p. 27)
métis (p. 32)
borderland (p. 36)

Go to INQUIZITIVE

To see what you know—and learn what you've missed—with personalized feedback along the way.

Visit the ***Give Me Liberty!* Student Site** for primary source documents and images, interactive maps, author videos featuring Eric Foner, and more.

1215	Magna Carta
1584	Hakluyt's *A Discourse Concerning Western Planting*
1585	Roanoke Island settlement
1607	Jamestown established
1619	First Africans arrive in Virginia
1619	House of Burgesses convenes
1620	Pilgrims found Plymouth
1622	Uprising led by Opechancanough against Virginia
1624	Virginia becomes first royal colony
1630s	Great Migration to New England
1630	Massachusetts Bay Colony founded
1632	Maryland founded
1636	Roger Williams banished from Massachusetts to Rhode Island
1637	Anne Hutchinson placed on trial in Massachusetts
1636–1637	Pequot War
1639	Fundamental Orders of Connecticut
1641	Body of Liberties
1642–1651	English Civil War
1649	Maryland adopts an Act Concerning Religion
1662	Puritans' Half-Way Covenant
1691	Virginia outlaws English–Indian marriages

CHAPTER 2

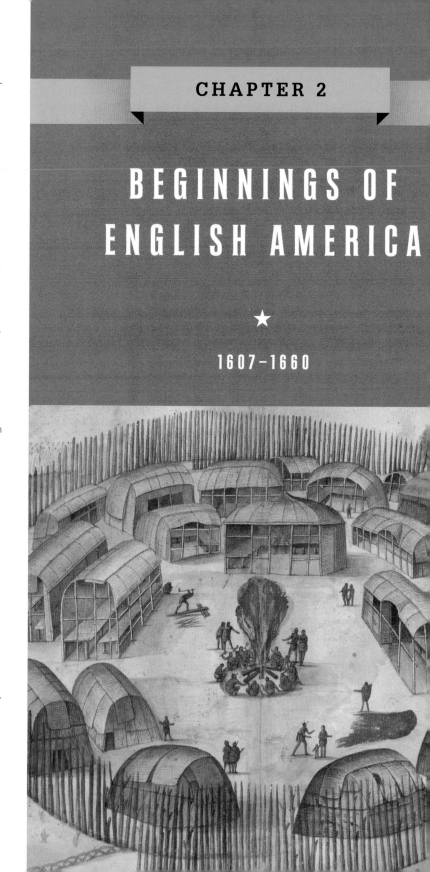

BEGINNINGS OF ENGLISH AMERICA

★

1607–1660

The artist John White spent a year on the Outer Banks of North Carolina in 1785–86 as part of an expedition sponsored by Sir Walter Raleigh. In this drawing, he depicts an Indian village surrounded by a stockade.

On April 26, 1607, three small ships carrying colonists from England sailed into the mouth of Chesapeake Bay. After exploring the area for a little over two weeks, they chose a site sixty miles inland on the James River for their settlement, hoping to protect themselves from marauding Spanish warships. Here they established Jamestown (named for the king of England) as the capital of the colony of Virginia (named for his predecessor, Elizabeth I, the "virgin queen"). But despite these bows to royal authority, the voyage was sponsored not by the English government, which in 1607 was hard-pressed for funds, but by the **Virginia Company**, a private business organization whose shareholders included merchants, aristocrats, and members of Parliament, and to which the queen had given her blessing before her death in 1603.

When the three ships returned home, 104 settlers remained in Virginia. All were men, for the Virginia Company had more interest in searching for gold and in other ways exploiting the area's natural resources than in establishing a functioning society. Nevertheless, Jamestown became the first permanent English settlement in the area that is now the United States. The settlers were the first of tens of thousands of Europeans who crossed the Atlantic during the seventeenth century to live and work in North America. They led the way for new empires that mobilized labor and economic resources, reshaped societies throughout the Atlantic world, and shifted the balance of power at home from Spain and Portugal to the nations of northwestern Europe.

English North America in the seventeenth century was a place where entrepreneurs sought to make fortunes, religious minorities hoped to worship without governmental interference and to create societies based on biblical teachings, and aristocrats dreamed of re-creating a vanished world of feudalism. For ordinary men and women, emigration offered an escape from lives of deprivation and inequality. "No man," wrote John Smith, an early leader of Jamestown, "will go from [England] to have less freedom" in America. The settlers of English America came to enjoy greater rights than colonists of other empires, including the power to choose members of elected assemblies, protections of the common law such as the right to trial by jury, and access to land, the key to economic independence. In some colonies, though by no means all, colonists enjoyed considerably more religious freedom than existed in Europe.

Many degrees of freedom coexisted in seventeenth-century North America, from the slave, stripped completely of liberty, to the independent landowner, who enjoyed a full range of rights. The settlers' success, however, rested on depriving Native Americans of their land and, in some colonies, on importing large numbers of African slaves as laborers. Freedom and lack of freedom expanded together in seventeenth-century America.

FOCUS QUESTIONS

- *What were the main contours of English colonization in the seventeenth century?*
- *What challenges did the early English settlers face?*
- *How did Virginia and Maryland develop in their early years?*
- *What made the English settlement of New England distinctive?*
- *What were the main sources of discord in early New England?*
- *How did the English Civil War affect the colonies in America?*

Mary I, the queen who tried to restore Catholicism in England, as painted in 1554 by Antonis Mor, a Dutch artist who made numerous portraits of European royalty. He depicts her as a woman of firm determination. During her brief reign (1553–1558), nearly 300 Protestants were burned at the stake.

ENGLAND AND THE NEW WORLD

Unifying the English Nation

As the case of Spain suggests, early empire building was, in large part, an extension of the consolidation of national power in Europe. But during the sixteenth century, England was a second-rate power wracked by internal disunity. Henry VIII, crowned in 1509, launched the Reformation in England. When the Pope refused to annul his marriage to Catherine of Aragon, Henry severed the nation from the Catholic Church. In its place he established the Church of England, or **Anglican Church**, with himself at the head. Decades of religious strife followed, as did considerable persecution of Catholics under Henry's successor, Edward VI. In 1553, Edward's half sister Mary became queen. She temporarily restored Catholicism as the state religion and executed a number of Protestants. Mary's successor, Elizabeth I (reigned 1558–1603), restored the Anglican ascendancy and executed more than 100 Catholic priests.

England and Ireland

Subduing Ireland

England's long struggle to conquer and pacify Ireland, which lasted well into the seventeenth century, absorbed money and energy that might have been directed toward the New World. In subduing Ireland, whose Catholic population was deemed a threat to the stability of Protestant rule in England, the government employed a variety of approaches, including military conquest, the slaughter of civilians, the seizure of land and introduction of English economic practices, and the dispatch of large numbers of settlers. Rather than seeking to absorb the Irish into English society, the English excluded the native population from a territory of settlement known as the Pale, where the colonists created their own social order.

The methods used in Ireland anticipated policies England would undertake in America. Some sixteenth-century English writers directly compared the allegedly barbaric "wild Irish" with American Indians.

England and North America

Not until the reign of Elizabeth I did the English turn their attention to North America, although sailors and adventurers still showed more interest in raiding Spanish cities and treasure fleets in the Caribbean than establishing settlements. The government granted charters (grants of exclusive rights and privileges) to Sir Humphrey Gilbert and Sir Walter

Raleigh, authorizing them to establish colonies in North America at their own expense.

With little or no support from the crown, both ventures failed. Gilbert, who had earned a reputation for brutality in the Irish wars by murdering civilians and burning their crops, established a short-lived settlement on Newfoundland in 1582. Three years later, Raleigh dispatched a fleet of five ships with some 100 colonists to set up a base on Roanoke Island, off the North Carolina coast. But the colonists, mostly young men under military leadership, abandoned the venture in 1586 and returned to England. A second group of 100 settlers, composed of families who hoped to establish a permanent colony, was dispatched that year. Their fate remains a mystery. When a ship bearing supplies arrived in 1590, the sailors found the **Roanoke colony** abandoned. Raleigh, by now nearly bankrupt, lost his enthusiasm for colonization. To establish a successful colony, it seemed clear, would require more planning and economic resources than any individual could provide.

The Roanoke colony

Spreading Protestantism

As in the case of Spain, national glory, profit, and religious mission merged in early English thinking about the New World. The Reformation heightened the English government's sense of Catholic Spain as its mortal enemy

The Armada Portrait of Queen Elizabeth I, by the artist George Gower, commemorates the defeat of the Spanish Armada in 1588 and appears to link it with English colonization of the New World. England's victorious navy is visible through the window, while the queen's hand rests on a globe, with her fingers pointing to the coast of North America.

(a belief reinforced in 1588 when a Spanish naval armada unsuccessfully attempted to invade the British Isles). By the late sixteenth century, anti-Catholicism had become deeply ingrained in English popular culture.

Although atrocities were hardly confined to any one nation—as England's own conduct in Ireland demonstrated—the idea that the empire of Catholic Spain was uniquely murderous and tyrannical enabled the English to describe their own imperial ambitions in the language of freedom. In *A Discourse Concerning Western Planting*, written in 1584, the Protestant minister and scholar Richard Hakluyt listed twenty-three reasons that Queen Elizabeth I should support the establishment of colonies. Among them was the idea that English settlements would form part of a divine mission to rescue the New World and its inhabitants from the influence of Catholicism and tyranny.

Richard Hakluyt

But bringing freedom to Indians was hardly the only motivation Hakluyt and other writers advanced. National power and glory, they argued, could be achieved through colonization. England, a relatively minor power at the end of the sixteenth century, could come to rival great nations like Spain and France.

Yet another motivation was that colonists could enrich the mother country and themselves by providing English consumers with goods now supplied by foreigners and opening a new market for English products. Unlike early adventurers such as Raleigh, who thought of wealth in terms of deposits of gold, Hakluyt insisted that trade would be the basis of England's empire.

The Social Crisis

Equally important, America could be a refuge for England's "surplus" population, benefiting mother country and emigrants alike. The late sixteenth century was a time of social crisis in England, with economic growth unable to keep pace with the needs of a population that grew from 3 million in 1550 to about 4 million in 1600. In the sixteenth and seventeenth centuries, landlords sought profits by raising sheep for the expanding trade in wool and introducing more modern farming practices such as crop rotation. They evicted small farmers and fenced off "commons" previously open to all.

Population growth

While many landlords, farmers, and town merchants benefited from the **enclosure movement**, as this process was called, thousands of persons were uprooted from the land. Many flooded into England's cities. Others, denounced by authorities as rogues, vagabonds, and vagrants, wandered the roads in search of work. "All our towns," wrote the Puritan leader John Winthrop in 1629, shortly before leaving England for Massachusetts, "complain of the burden of poor people and strive by all means to rid any such as they have." England, he added somberly, "grows weary of her inhabitants."

From poverty to emigration

For years, the government struggled to deal with this social crisis, sometimes resorting to extreme measures, such as whipping or hanging the unemployed or forcing them to accept any job offered to them. Another solution was to encourage the unruly poor to leave for the New World. As colonists, they could become productive citizens, contributing to the nation's wealth.

Masterless Men

Although authorities saw wandering or unemployed "masterless men" as a danger to society, popular attitudes viewed economic dependence as lack of freedom. Only those who controlled their own labor could be regarded as truly free. Indeed, popular tales and ballads romanticized the very vagabonds, highwaymen, and even beggars denounced by the propertied and powerful, since despite their poverty they at least enjoyed freedom from wage work.

The New World as a land of opportunity

The image of the New World as a unique place of opportunity, where the English laboring classes could regain economic independence by acquiring land and where even criminals would enjoy a second chance, was deeply rooted from the earliest days of settlement. John Smith had scarcely landed in Virginia in 1607 when he wrote that in America "every man may be the master and owner of his own labor and land." The main lure for emigrants from England to the New World was not so much riches in gold and silver as the promise of independence that followed from owning land. Economic freedom and the possibility of passing it on to one's children attracted the largest number of English colonists.

A pamphlet published in 1609 promoting emigration to Virginia.

THE COMING OF THE ENGLISH

English Emigrants

Seventeenth-century North America was an unstable and dangerous environment. Diseases decimated Indian and settler populations alike. Without sustained immigration, most settlements would have collapsed. With a population of between 4 million and 5 million, about half that of Spain and a quarter of that of France, England produced a far larger number of men, women, and children willing to brave the dangers of emigration to the New World. In large part, this was because economic conditions in England were so bad.

Between 1607 and 1700, more than half a million people left England. North America was not the destination of the majority of these emigrants. Approximately 180,000 settled in Ireland, and about the same number migrated to the West Indies, where the introduction of sugar cultivation promised riches for those who could obtain land. Nonetheless, the population of England's mainland colonies quickly outstripped that of their rivals. The Chesapeake area, where the tobacco-producing colonies of Virginia and Maryland developed a constant demand for cheap labor, received about 120,000 settlers. New England attracted 21,000 immigrants, nearly all of them arriving before 1640. In the second part of the seventeenth century, the Middle Colonies (New York, New Jersey, and Pennsylvania) attracted about 23,000 settlers. Although the arrivals to New England and the Middle Colonies included many families, the majority of newcomers were young, single men from the bottom rungs of English society, who had little to lose by emigrating.

Demographics of colonists

Indentured Servants

Settlers who could pay for their own passage—government officials, clergymen, merchants, artisans, landowning farmers, and members of the lesser nobility—arrived in America as free persons. Most quickly acquired land. In the seventeenth century, however, nearly two-thirds of English settlers came as **indentured servants**, who voluntarily surrendered their freedom for a specified time (usually five to seven years) in exchange for passage to America.

Slavery and indentured servitude

Like slaves, servants could be bought and sold, could not marry without the permission of their owner, were subject to physical punishment, and saw their obligation to labor enforced by the courts. But, unlike slaves, servants could look forward to a release from bondage. Assuming they survived their period of labor, servants would receive a payment known as "freedom dues" and become free members of society.

Given the high death rate, many servants did not live to the end of their terms. Many servants found the reality of life in the New World less appealing than they had anticipated. Employers constantly complained of servants running away, not working diligently, or being unruly, all manifestations of what one commentator called their "fondness for freedom."

Land and Liberty

Landownership as the basis of liberty

Land, English settlers believed, was the basis of liberty. Owning land gave men control over their own labor and, in most colonies, the right to vote. The promise of immediate access to land lured free settlers, and freedom dues that included land persuaded potential immigrants to sign contracts as indentured servants. Land in America also became a way for the king to reward relatives and allies. Each colony was launched with a huge grant of land from the crown, either to a company or to a private individual known as a proprietor. Some grants, if taken literally, stretched from the Atlantic Ocean to the Pacific.

Without labor, however, land would have little value. Since immigrants did not come to America intending to work the land of others (except temporarily in the case of indentured servants), the very abundance of "free" land eventually led many property owners to turn to slaves as a workforce.

Englishmen and Indians

Land in North America, of course, was already occupied. And the arrival of English settlers presented the native inhabitants of eastern North America with the greatest crisis in their history. Unlike the Spanish, English colonists were chiefly interested in displacing the Indians and settling on their land, not intermarrying with them, organizing their labor, or making them subjects of the crown. The English exchanged goods with the native population, and Indians often traveled through colonial settlements. Fur traders on the frontiers of settlement sometimes married Indian women, partly as a way of gaining access to native societies and the kin networks essential to economic relationships. Most English settlers, however, remained obstinately separate from their Indian neighbors.

Despite their insistence that Indians had no real claim to the land since they did not cultivate or improve it, most colonial authorities acquired land by purchase, often in treaties forced upon Indians after they had suffered military defeat. To keep the peace, some colonial governments tried to prevent the private seizure or purchase of Indian lands, or they declared certain areas off-limits to settlers. But these measures were rarely enforced and ultimately proved ineffective. New settlers and freed servants sought land for themselves, and those who established families in America needed land for their children.

The seventeenth century was marked by recurrent warfare between colonists and Indians. These conflicts generated a strong feeling of superiority among the colonists and left them

The only known contemporary portrait of a New England Indian, this 1681 painting by an unknown artist was long thought to represent Ninigret II, a leader of the Narragansetts of Rhode Island. It has been more recently identified as Robin Cassacinamon, an influential Pequot leader and friend of John Winthrop II, a governor of colonial Connecticut, who originally owned the painting. Apart from the wampum beads around his neck, everything the Indian wears is of English manufacture.

intent on maintaining the real and imagined boundaries separating the two peoples. Over time the English displaced the original inhabitants more thoroughly than any other European empire.

The Transformation of Indian Life

Many eastern Indians initially welcomed the newcomers, or at least their goods, which they appreciated for their practical advantages. Items like woven cloth, metal kettles, iron axes, fishhooks, hoes, and guns were quickly integrated into Indian life. Indians also displayed a great desire for goods like colorful glass beads and copper ornaments that could be incorporated into their religious ceremonies.

Changes in Indian farming, hunting, and cooking practices

As Indians became integrated into the Atlantic economy, subtle changes took place in Indian life. European metal goods changed their farming, hunting, and cooking practices. Men devoted more time to hunting beaver for fur trading. Later observers would describe this trade as one in which Indians exchanged valuable commodities like furs and animal skins for worthless European trinkets. In fact, both Europeans and Indians gave up goods they had in abundance in exchange for items in short supply in their own society. But as the colonists achieved military superiority over the Indians, the profits of trade mostly flowed to colonial and European merchants.

Environmental changes

As settlers fenced in more and more land and introduced new crops and livestock, the natural environment changed in ways that undermined

Another drawing by the artist John White shows seventeen male and female Secotan Indians dancing around a circle of posts in a religious ritual in modern-day North Carolina. White was a careful observer of their clothing and body markings and the objects used in the ceremony.

traditional Indian agriculture and hunting. Pigs and cattle roamed freely, trampling Indian cornfields and gardens. The need for wood to build and heat homes and export to England depleted forests on which Indians relied for hunting. The rapid expansion of the fur trade diminished the population of beaver and other animals. In short, Indians' lives were powerfully altered by the changes set in motion in 1607 when English colonists landed at Jamestown.

SETTLING THE CHESAPEAKE

The Jamestown Colony

The early history of Jamestown was, to say the least, not promising. The colony's leadership changed repeatedly, its inhabitants suffered an extraordinarily high death rate, and, with the Virginia Company seeking a quick profit, supplies from England proved inadequate. The first settlers were "a quarrelsome band of gentlemen and servants." They included few farmers and laborers and numerous sons of English gentry who preferred to prospect for gold rather than farm.

Disease and lack of food took a heavy toll. By the end of the first year, the original population of 104 had fallen by half. New arrivals (including the first two women, who landed in 1608) brought the numbers up to 400 in 1609, but by 1610, after a winter long remembered as the "starving time," only 65 settlers remained alive. At one point, the survivors abandoned Jamestown and sailed for England, only to be intercepted and persuaded to return to Virginia by ships carrying a new governor, 250 colonists, and supplies.

Only rigorous military discipline held the colony together. **John Smith**, one of the colony's first leaders, imposed a regime of forced labor on company lands. "He that will not work, shall not eat," Smith declared.

By 1640, English settlement in the Chesapeake had spread well beyond the initial colony at Jamestown, as tobacco planters sought fertile land near navigable waterways.

ENGLISH SETTLEMENT IN THE CHESAPEAKE, ca. 1640

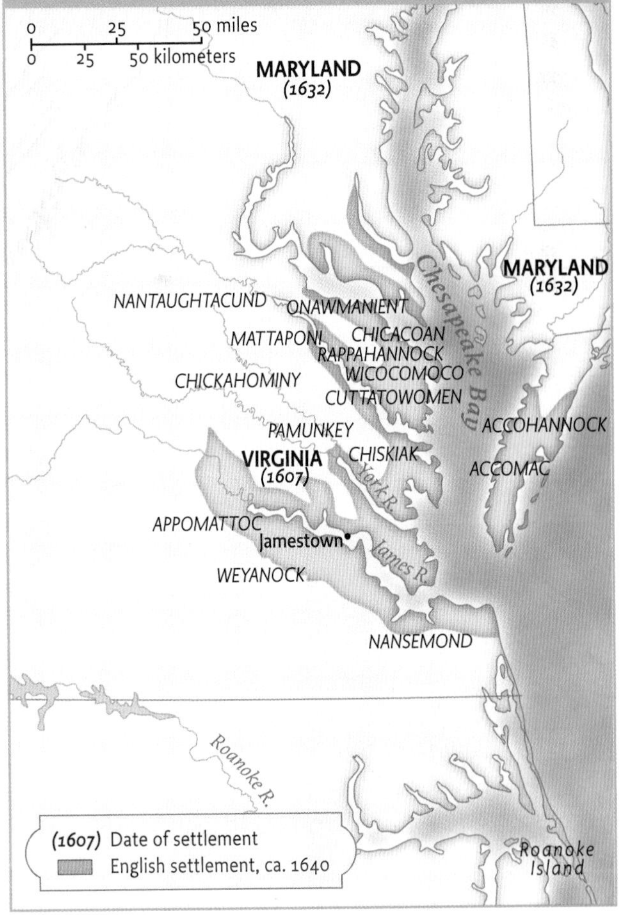

Powhatan, the most prominent Indian leader in the original area of English settlement in Virginia. This image, showing Powhatan and his court, was engraved on John Smith's map of Virginia and included in Smith's *General History of Virginia*, published in 1624.

Smith's autocratic mode of governing alienated many of the colonists. After being injured in an accidental gunpowder explosion in 1609, he was forced to return to England. But his immediate successors continued his iron rule.

The Virginia Company slowly realized that for the colony to survive it would have to abandon the search for gold, grow its own food, and find a marketable commodity. It would also have to attract more settlers. With this end in view, it announced new policies in 1618. Instead of retaining all the land for itself, the company introduced the **headright system**, awarding fifty acres of land to any colonist who paid for his own or another's passage. Thus, anyone who brought in a sizable number of servants would immediately acquire a large estate. In place of the governor's militaristic regime, a "charter of grants and liberties" was issued, including the establishment of a **House of Burgesses**. When it convened in 1619, this became the first elected assembly in colonial America. Also in 1619, the first twenty Africans arrived in Virginia on a Dutch vessel. These events laid the foundation for a society that would one day be dominated economically and politically by slaveowning planters.

Powhatan and Pocahontas

When the English arrived at Jamestown, they landed in an area inhabited by some 15,000 to 25,000 Indians living in numerous small agricultural villages. Most acknowledged the rule of Wahunsonacock, a shrewd and forceful leader who had recently consolidated his authority over the region and collected tribute from some thirty subordinate tribes. Called Powhatan by the settlers after the Indian word for both his tribe and his title of paramount chief, he quickly realized the advantages of trade with the newcomers.

In the first two years of Jamestown's existence, relations with Indians were mostly peaceful and based on a fairly equal give-and-take. At one point, Smith was captured by the Indians and threatened with execution by Powhatan, only to be rescued by Pocahontas, reputedly the favorite among his many children by dozens of wives. The incident has come down in legend as an example of a rebellious, love-struck teenager defying her father. In fact, it was probably part of an elaborate ceremony designed by Powhatan to demonstrate his power over the colonists and incorporate them into his realm. Pocahontas subsequently became an intermediary between the two peoples, bringing food and messages to Jamestown. In 1614, she married the English colonist John Rolfe. Two years later, she accompanied her husband to England, where she caused a sensation in the court of James I as a symbol of Anglo-Indian harmony and missionary success. But she succumbed to disease in 1617. Her father died the following year.

The only portrait of Pocahontas during her lifetime was engraved by Simon van de Passe in England in 1616. This is a later copy by an unknown artist. After converting to Christianity, she took the name Rebecca.

The Uprising of 1622

Once it became clear that the English were interested in establishing a permanent and constantly expanding colony, not a trading post, conflict with local Indians was inevitable. In 1622, Powhatan's brother and successor, Opechancanough, led a brilliantly planned surprise attack that in a single day wiped out one-quarter of Virginia's settler population of 1,200. The surviving 900 colonists organized themselves into military bands, which then massacred scores of Indians and devastated their villages. By going to war, declared Governor Francis Wyatt, the Indians had forfeited any claim to the land. Virginia's policy, he continued, must now be nothing less than the "expulsion of the savages to gain the free range of the country."

Opechancanough

The unsuccessful **Uprising of 1622** fundamentally shifted the balance of power in the colony. The settlers' supremacy was reinforced in 1644 when a last desperate rebellion led by Opechancanough, now said to be 100 years old, was crushed after causing the deaths of some 500 colonists. Virginia forced a treaty on the surviving coastal Indians, who now numbered fewer than 2,000, that acknowledged their subordination to the government at Jamestown and required them to move to tribal reservations to the west and not enter areas of European settlement without permission. Settlers spreading inland into the Virginia countryside continued to seize Indian lands.

The destruction caused by the Uprising of 1622 was the last in a series of blows suffered by the Virginia Company. Two years later, it surrendered its charter and Virginia became the first royal colony, its governor now appointed by the crown. Investors had not turned a profit, and although the company had sent 6,000 settlers to Virginia, its white population numbered only 1,200 when the king assumed control. The government in London for years paid little attention to Virginia. Henceforth, the local elite, not a faraway company, controlled the colony's development. And that elite was growing rapidly in wealth and power thanks to the cultivation of a crop introduced from the West Indies by John Rolfe—tobacco.

The first royal colony

A Tobacco Colony

King James I considered tobacco "harmful to the brain and dangerous to the lungs" and issued a spirited warning against its use. But increasing numbers of Europeans enjoyed smoking and believed the tobacco plant had medicinal benefits. Tobacco became Virginia's substitute for gold. It enriched an emerging class of tobacco planters, as well as members of the colonial government who assigned good land to themselves. The crown

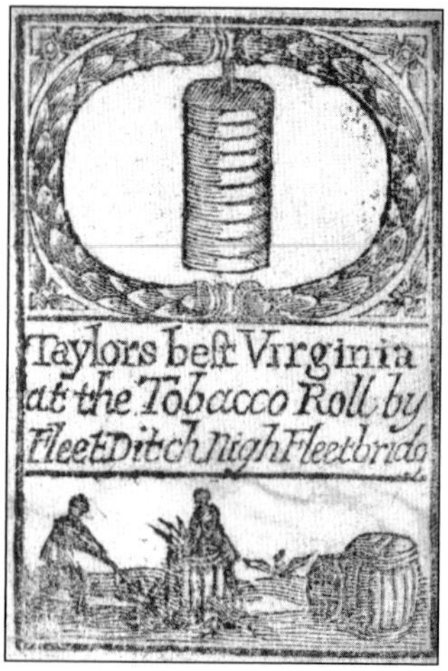

An advertisement for tobacco includes images of slaves handling barrels and tobacco plants.

profited from customs duties (taxes on tobacco that entered or left the kingdom). The spread of tobacco farming produced a dispersed society with few towns and inspired a frenzied scramble for land. By the middle of the seventeenth century, a new influx of immigrants with ample financial resources—sons of merchants and English gentlemen—had taken advantage of the headright system and governmental connections to acquire large estates along navigable rivers. They established themselves as the colony's social and political elite.

The expansion of tobacco cultivation also led to an increased demand for field labor, met for most of the seventeenth century by young, male indentured servants. Despite harsh conditions of work in the tobacco fields, a persistently high death rate, and laws mandating punishments from whipping to an extension of service for those who ran away or were unruly, the abundance of land continued to attract migrants. Of the 120,000 English immigrants who entered the Chesapeake region during the seventeenth century, three-quarters came as servants. Virginia's white society increasingly came to resemble that of England, with a wealthy landed gentry at the top; a group of small farmers, mostly former indentured servants who had managed to acquire land, in the middle; and an army of poor laborers—servants and landless former indentured servants—at the bottom.

Women and the Family

Virginia, however, lacked one essential element of English society—stable family life. Given the demand for male servants to work in the tobacco fields, men in the Chesapeake outnumbered women for most of the seventeenth century by four or five to one. The vast majority of women who immigrated to the region came as indentured servants. Since they usually had to complete their terms of service before marrying, they did not begin to form families until their mid-twenties. The high death rate, unequal ratio between the sexes, and late age of marriage retarded population growth.

Slow population growth

In the colonies as in England, a married woman possessed certain rights before the law, including a claim to **dower rights** of one-third of her husband's property in the event that he died before she did. When the widow died, however, the property passed to the husband's male heirs. (English law was far less generous than in Spain, where a woman could hold independently any property inherited from her parents, and a man and wife owned jointly all the wealth accumulated during a marriage.)

Women's lives

Social conditions in the colonies, however, opened the door to roles women rarely assumed in England. A widow or one of the few women who never married could sometimes take advantage of her legal status as a *feme sole* (a "woman alone," who enjoyed an independent legal iden-

Processing tobacco was as labor intensive as caring for the plant in the fields. Here slaves and female indentured servants work with the crop after it has been harvested.

tity denied to married women) to make contracts and conduct business. Margaret Brent, who arrived in the Chesapeake in 1638, acquired land, managed her own plantation, and acted as a lawyer in court. But because most women came to Virginia as indentured servants, they could look forward only to a life of hard labor in the tobacco fields and early death.

The Maryland Experiment

The second Chesapeake colony, Maryland, followed a similar course of development. As in Virginia, tobacco came to dominate the economy and tobacco planters the society. But in other ways, Maryland's history was strikingly different.

Proprietary colony

Maryland was established in 1632 as a proprietary colony, that is, a grant of land and governmental authority to a single individual. This was Cecilius Calvert, the son of a recently deceased favorite of King Charles I. The charter granted him "full, free, and absolute power," including control of trade and the right to initiate all legislation, with an elected assembly confined to approving or disapproving his proposals. Although Calvert disliked representative institutions, the charter guaranteed to colonists "all privileges, franchises, and liberties" of Englishmen. While these were not spelled out, they undoubtedly included the idea of a government limited by the law. Here was a recipe for conflict, and Maryland had more than its share during the seventeenth century.

Religion in Maryland

Further aggravating instability in the colony was the fact that Calvert, a Catholic, envisioned Maryland as a refuge for his persecuted coreligionists, especially the younger sons of Catholic gentry who had few economic or political prospects in England. In Maryland, he hoped, Protestants and Catholics could live in a harmony unknown in Europe. Most appointed officials were Catholic, including relatives of the proprietor. But Protestants always formed a majority of the settlers. Most, as in Virginia, came as indentured servants.

Maryland as a refuge for persecuted Catholics

As in Virginia, the death rate remained very high. Almost 70 percent of male settlers in Maryland died before reaching the age of fifty, and half the children born in the colony did not live to adulthood. But at least initially, Maryland seems to have offered servants greater opportunity for landownership than Virginia. Unlike in the older colony, freedom dues in Maryland included fifty acres of land. As tobacco planters engrossed the best land later in the century, however, the prospects for landless men diminished.

THE NEW ENGLAND WAY

The Rise of Puritanism

As Virginia and Maryland evolved toward societies dominated by a small aristocracy ruling over numerous bound laborers, a very different social order emerged in seventeenth-century New England. The early history of that region is intimately connected to the religious movement known as "Puritanism," which arose in England late in the sixteenth century. The term was initially coined by opponents to ridicule those not satisfied with the progress of the Protestant Reformation in England. **Puritans** differed among themselves on many issues. But all shared the conviction that the Church of England retained too many elements of Catholicism in its religious rituals and doctrines. Puritans saw elaborate church ceremonies, the rule that priests could not marry, and ornate church decorations as vestiges of "popery." Many rejected the Catholic structure of religious authority descending from a pope or king to archbishops, bishops, and priests. Only independent local congregations, they believed, should choose clergymen and determine modes of worship. These Puritans were called "Congregationalists."

Puritanism and the Protestant Reformation in England

Puritans considered religious belief a complex and demanding matter and urged believers to seek the truth by reading the Bible and listening to sermons by educated ministers, rather than devoting themselves to sacraments administered by priests and to what Puritans considered formulaic prayers. The sermon was the central rite of Puritan practice. In the course of a lifetime, according to one estimate, the average Puritan listened to some 7,000 sermons. In their religious beliefs, Puritans followed the ideas of the French-born Swiss theologian John Calvin. The world, Calvin taught, was divided between the elect and the damned, but no one knew who was destined to be saved, which had already been determined by God. Nevertheless, leading a good life and prospering economically might be indications of God's grace, whereas idleness and immoral behavior were sure signs of damnation.

John Calvin

Moral Liberty

Puritanism was characterized by a zeal that alienated many who held differing religious views. A minority of Puritans (such as those who settled in Plymouth Colony) became separatists, abandoning the Church of England entirely to form their own independent churches. Most, however, hoped to purify the church from within. But in the 1620s and 1630s, as Charles I seemed to be moving toward a restoration of Catholic ceremonies and the Church of England dismissed Puritan ministers and censored their writings, many Puritans decided to emigrate. When Puritans emigrated to New England, they hoped to escape what they believed to be the religious and worldly corruptions of English society. They would establish a "city set upon a hill," a Bible Commonwealth whose influence would flow back across the Atlantic and rescue England from godlessness and social decay.

"City set upon a hill"

Like so many other immigrants to America, Puritans came in search of liberty, especially the right to worship and govern themselves in what they deemed a truly Christian manner. Freedom certainly did not mean unrestrained action, improper religious practices, or sinful behavior, of which, Puritans thought, there were far too many examples in England. In a 1645 speech to the Massachusetts legislature explaining the Puritan conception of freedom, **John Winthrop**, the colony's governor, distinguished sharply between two kinds of liberty. "Natural" liberty, or acting without restraint, suggested "a liberty to do evil." This was the false idea of freedom supposedly adopted by the Irish, Indians, and bad Christians generally. Genuine "moral" liberty meant "a liberty to that only which is good." It was quite compatible with severe restraints on speech, religion, and personal behavior. True freedom, Winthrop insisted, depended on "subjection to authority," both religious and secular; otherwise, anarchy was sure to follow. To Puritans, liberty meant that the elect had a right

"Natural liberty" and "moral liberty"

to establish churches and govern society, not that others could challenge their beliefs or authority.

The Pilgrims at Plymouth

The Mayflower

The first Puritans to arrive in America were a group of separatists known as the **Pilgrims**. They had already fled to the Netherlands in 1608. A decade later, fearing that their children were being corrupted by the surrounding culture, they decided to emigrate to Virginia. In September 1620, the *Mayflower*, carrying 150 settlers and crew (among them many non-Puritans), embarked from England. Blown off course, they landed not in Virginia but hundreds of miles to the north, on Cape Cod. Here the 102 who survived the journey established the colony of Plymouth. Before landing, the Pilgrim leaders drew up the **Mayflower Compact**, in which the forty-one adult men going ashore agreed to obey "just and equal laws" enacted by representatives of their own choosing. This was the first written frame of government in what is now the United States. Men not normally signatories to such documents—printers, carpenters, even indentured servants—were among those who affixed their names. (This was over 200 years before most working-class men were allowed to vote in Great Britain.)

The Pilgrims arrived in an area whose native population had recently been decimated by smallpox. They established Plymouth on the site of an abandoned Indian village whose fields had been cleared before the

An early seventeenth-century engraving shows the English explorer Bartholomew Gosnold encountering Native Americans. Gosnold landed at Cape Cod in 1602 and then established a small outpost on nearby Cuttyhunk Island. The region's Indians had much experience with Europeans before Pilgrims settled there.

epidemic and were ready for cultivation. Nonetheless, the settlers arrived six weeks before winter without food or farm animals. Half died during the first winter. The remaining colonists survived only through the help of local Indians. In the autumn of 1621, the Pilgrims invited their Indian allies to a harvest feast celebrating their survival, the first Thanksgiving.

The Pilgrims hoped to establish a society based on the lives of the early Christian saints. Their government rested on the principle of consent, and voting was not restricted to church members. All land was held in common until 1627, when it was divided among the settlers. Plymouth survived as an independent colony until 1691, but it was soon overshadowed by Massachusetts Bay to its north.

Seal of the Massachusetts Bay Colony. The Indian's scanty attire suggests a lack of civilization. His statement "Come Over and Help Us," based on an incident in the Bible, illustrates the English conviction that they were liberating the native population, rather than exploiting them as other empires had.

The Great Migration

Chartered in 1629, the Massachusetts Bay Company was founded by a group of London merchants who hoped to further the Puritan cause and turn a profit through trade with the Indians. The first five ships sailed from England in 1629, and by 1642 some 21,000 Puritans had immigrated to Massachusetts, a flow of population long remembered as the **Great Migration**. After 1640, migration to New England virtually ceased, and in some years more colonists left the region than arrived. Nonetheless, the Great Migration established the basis for a stable and thriving society.

A migration of families

In many ways, the settling of New England was unique. Although servants represented about one-quarter of the Great Migration, most settlers arrived in Massachusetts in families. Compared with colonists in Virginia and Maryland, they were older and more prosperous, and the number of men and women more equally balanced. Because of the even sex ratio and New England's healthier climate, the population grew rapidly, doubling every twenty-seven years. By 1700 New England's white population of 91,000 outnumbered that of both the Chesapeake and the West Indies.

The Puritan Family

Male authority in the household

Whatever their differences with other Englishmen on religious matters, Puritans shared with the larger society a belief in male authority within the household as well as an adherence to the common-law tradition that severely limited married women's legal and economic rights. Male authority was especially vital because in a farming society without large numbers of slaves or servants, control over the labor of one's family was essential to a man's economic success.

To be sure, Puritans deemed women to be the spiritual equals of men, and women were allowed to become full church members. Although

The Savage Family, a 1779 painting by the New England artist Edward Savage, depicts several generations of a typically numerous Puritan family.

all ministers were men, the Puritan belief in the ability of believers to interpret the Bible opened the door for some women to claim positions of religious leadership. The ideal Puritan marriage was based on reciprocal affection and companionship, and divorce was legal. Yet within the household, the husband's authority was virtually absolute.

Family and society

The family was the foundation of strong communities, and unmarried adults seemed a danger to the social fabric. The typical New England woman married at twenty-two, a younger age than her English counterparts, and gave birth seven times. Because New England was a far healthier environment than the Chesapeake, more children survived infancy. Thus, much of a woman's adult life was devoted to bearing and rearing children.

Government and Society in Massachusetts

The New England town

Since Puritans feared excessive individualism and lack of social unity, the leaders of Massachusetts organized the colony in self-governing towns. Groups of settlers received a land grant from the colony's government and then subdivided it, with residents awarded house lots in a central area and land on the outskirts for farming. Much land remained in commons, either for collective use or to be divided among later settlers or the sons of the town's founders. Each town had its own Congregational Church. Each, according to a law of 1647, was required to establish a school, since the ability to read the Bible was central to Puritan belief. To train an educated ministry, Harvard College was established in 1636 (nearly a century after the Royal University of Mexico, founded in 1551), and two years later the first printing press in English America was established in Cambridge.

The Massachusetts Bay Charter

Wishing to rule the colony without outside interference and to prevent non-Puritans from influencing decision making, the eight shareholders of the Massachusetts Bay Company emigrated to America, taking the charter with them and transforming a commercial document into a form of government. In 1634, a group of deputies elected by freemen (landowning church members) was added to form a single ruling body, the General Court. Ten years later, company officers and elected deputies were divided into two legislative houses. Unlike Virginia, whose governors were appointed first by a faraway company and, after 1624, by the crown, or Maryland, where authority rested with a single proprietor, the freemen of Massachusetts elected their governor.

The principle of consent was central to Puritanism. Churches were formed by voluntary agreement among members, who elected the minister. No important church decision was made without the agreement of the male members. Towns governed themselves, and local officials, delegates to the General Court, and the colonial governor were all elected.

Church membership

Puritans, however, were hardly believers in equality. Church membership, a status that carried great prestige and power, was a restrictive category. Anyone could worship at a church, but to be a full member

An embroidered banner depicting the main building at Harvard, the first college established in the English colonies. It was probably made by a Massachusetts woman for a husband or son who attended Harvard.

required demonstrating that one had experienced divine grace and could be considered a "visible saint," usually by testifying about a conversion experience. Voting in colony-wide elections was limited to men who had been accepted as full church members. Puritan democracy was for those within the circle of church membership; those outside the boundary occupied a secondary place in the Bible Commonwealth.

Church and State in Puritan Massachusetts

The Body of Liberties

Seventeenth-century New England was a hierarchical society in which socially prominent families were assigned the best land and the most desirable seats in church. Ordinary settlers were addressed as "goodman" and "goodwife," while the better sort were called "gentleman" and "lady" or "master" and "mistress." When the General Court in 1641 issued a Body of Liberties outlining the rights and responsibilities of Massachusetts colonists, it adopted the traditional understanding of liberties as privileges that derived from one's place in the social order. While some liberties applied to all inhabitants, there were separate lists of rights for freemen, women, children, and servants. The Body of Liberties also allowed for slavery. The first African slave appears in the records of Massachusetts Bay in 1640.

Massachusetts forbade ministers to hold office so as not to interfere with their spiritual responsibilities. But the law required each town to establish a church and to levy a tax to support the minister. Massachusetts prescribed the death penalty for, among other things, worshiping "any god, but the lord god," practicing witchcraft, or committing blasphemy.

Religious uniformity

Like many others in the seventeenth century, Puritans believed that religious uniformity was essential to social order. Puritans did not believe in religious toleration—there was one truth, and their faith embodied it. Religious liberty meant the liberty to practice this truth. But the principle of autonomy for local congregations soon clashed with the desire for religious uniformity.

NEW ENGLANDERS DIVIDED

Modern ideas of individualism, privacy, and personal freedom would have struck Puritans as quite strange. They considered too much emphasis on the "self" dangerous to social harmony and community stability. In the closely knit towns of New England, residents carefully monitored one another's behavior and chastised or expelled those who violated communal norms. Towns banished individuals for such offenses as criticiz-

ENGLISH SETTLEMENT IN NEW ENGLAND, ca. 1640

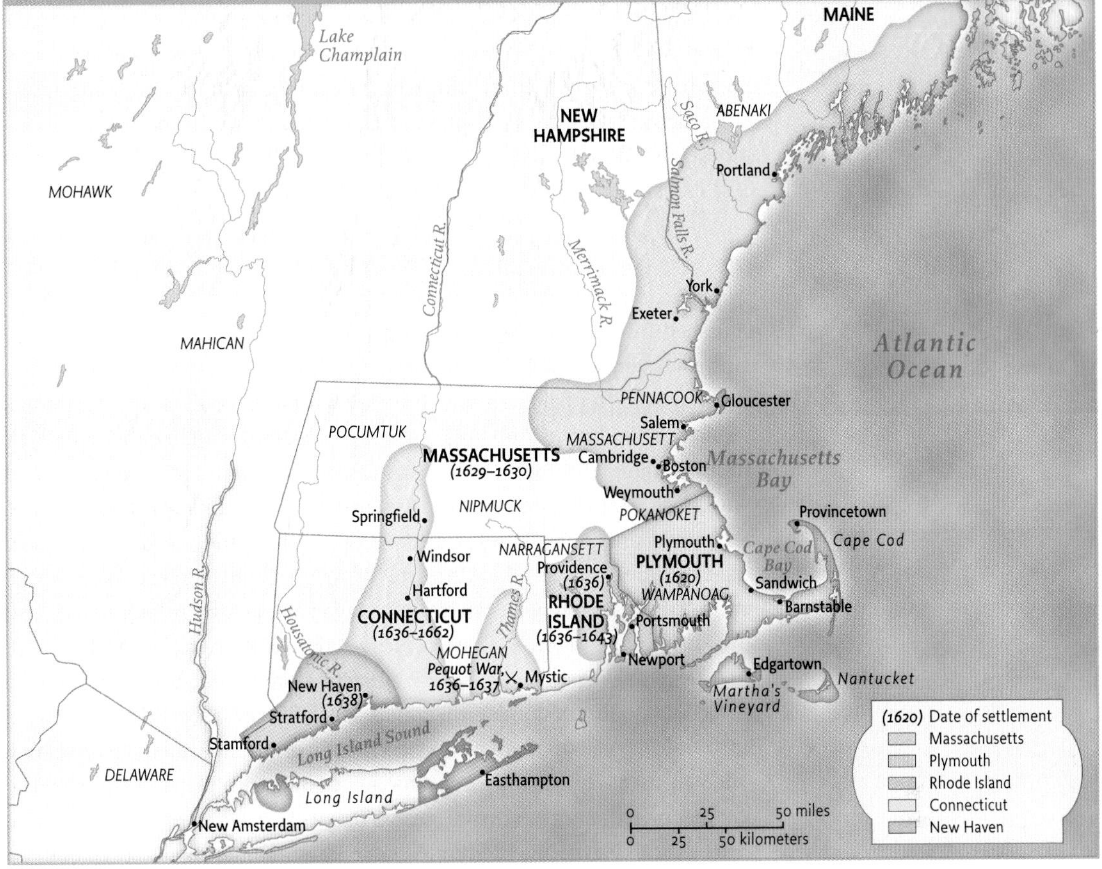

By the mid-seventeenth century, English settlement in New England had spread well inland and up and down the Atlantic coast.

ing the church or government, complaining about the colony in letters home to England, or, in the case of one individual, Abigail Gifford, being "a very burdensome woman." Tolerance of difference was not high on the list of Puritan values.

Roger Williams

Differences of opinion about how to organize a Bible Commonwealth, however, emerged almost from the founding of Massachusetts. With its emphasis on individual interpretation of the Bible, Puritanism contained the seeds of its own fragmentation. The first sustained criticism of the existing order came from the young minister Roger Williams, who arrived in Massachusetts in 1631 and soon began to insist that its congregations withdraw from the Church of England and that church and state be separated. Williams believed that any law-abiding citizen should be allowed to practice whatever form of religion he chose.

Williams aimed to strengthen religion, not weaken it. The embrace of government, he insisted, corrupted the purity of Christian faith and drew believers into endless religious wars like those that racked Europe. Furthermore, Williams rejected the conviction that Puritans were an elect people on a divine mission to spread the true faith. Williams denied that God had singled out any group as special favorites.

Roger Williams, New England's most prominent advocate of religious toleration.

Rhode Island and Connecticut

Banished from Massachusetts in 1636, Williams and his followers moved south, where they established the colony of Rhode Island, which eventually received a charter from London. Rhode Island became a beacon of religious freedom. It had no established church, no religious qualifications for voting until the eighteenth century, and no requirement that citizens attend church. It became a haven for **Dissenters** (Protestants who belonged to denominations other than the established church) and Jews persecuted in other colonies. Rhode Island's frame of government was also more democratic. The assembly was elected twice a year, the governor annually, and town meetings were held more frequently than elsewhere in New England.

Connecticut

Religious disagreements in Massachusetts generated other colonies as well. In 1636, the minister Thomas Hooker established a settlement at Hartford. Its system of government, embodied in the Fundamental Orders of 1639, was modeled on that of Massachusetts—with the significant exception that men did not have to be church members to vote. Quite different was the colony of New Haven, founded in 1638 by immigrants who wanted an even closer connection between church and state. In 1662, Hartford and New Haven received a royal charter that united them as the colony of Connecticut.

The Trial of Anne Hutchinson

Hutchinson's criticisms of Puritan leaders

Another threat to the Puritan establishment, because of both her gender and her influential following, was Anne Hutchinson. A midwife and the daughter of a clergyman, Hutchinson, wrote John Winthrop, was "a woman of a ready wit and bold spirit." Hutchinson began holding meetings in her home, where she led discussions of religious issues among men and women, including a number of prominent merchants and public officials. In Hutchinson's view, salvation was God's direct gift to the elect and could not be earned by good works, devotional practices, or other human effort. Most Puritans shared this belief. What set Hutchinson apart was her charge that nearly all the ministers in Massachusetts were guilty of faulty preaching for distinguishing "saints" from the damned on the basis of activities such as church attendance and moral behavior rather than an inner state of grace.

Critics denounced Hutchinson for Antinomianism (a term for putting one's own judgment or faith above both human law and the teachings of the church). In 1637, she was tried in civil court for sedition (expressing opinions dangerous to authority). An articulate woman, Hutchinson ably debated her university-educated accusers during her trial. But when she said God spoke to her directly rather than through ministers or the Bible, she violated Puritan doctrine and sealed her own fate. Such a claim, the colony's leaders felt, posed a threat to organized churches—and, indeed, to all authority. Hutchinson and a number of her followers were banished.

Hutchinson's trial

Anne Hutchinson lived in New England for only eight years, but she left her mark on the region's religious culture. As in the case of Roger Williams, her career showed how the Puritan belief in individual interpretation of the Bible could easily lead to criticism of the religious and political establishment. It would take many years before religious toleration—which violated the Puritans' understanding of "moral liberty" and social harmony—came to Massachusetts.

Significance of Anne Hutchinson

Puritans and Indians

Along with disruptive religious controversies, New England, like other colonies, had to deal with the difficult problem of relations with Indians. The native population of New England numbered perhaps 100,000 when the Puritans arrived. But because of recent epidemics, the migrants encountered fewer Indians near the coast than in other parts of eastern North America. In areas of European settlement, colonists quickly outnumbered the native population. Some settlers, notably Roger Williams, sought to treat the Indians with justice. Williams insisted that the king had no right to grant land already belonging to someone else. No town, said Williams, should be established before its site had been purchased. John Winthrop, on the other hand, believed uncultivated land could legitimately be taken. Although he recognized the benefits of buying land rather than simply seizing it, he insisted that such purchases require Indians to submit to English authority and pay tribute to the colonists.

Treating Indians with justice

To New England's leaders, the Indians represented both savagery and temptation. They enjoyed freedom but of the wrong kind—what Winthrop condemned as undisciplined "natural liberty." Puritans feared that Indian society might attract colonists who lacked the proper moral fiber. In 1642, the Connecticut General Court set a penalty of three years at hard labor for any colonist who abandoned "godly society" to live

VOICES OF FREEDOM

From "The Trial of Anne Hutchinson" (1637)

Anne Hutchinson began holding religious meetings in her home in Massachusetts in 1634. She attracted followers who believed that most ministers were not adhering strictly to Puritan theology. In 1637, she was placed on trial for sedition. In her defense, she claimed to be inspired by a revelation from God, a violation of Puritan beliefs. The examination of Hutchinson is a classic example of the clash between established power and individual conscience.

GOV. JOHN WINTHROP: Mrs. Hutchinson, you are called here as one of those that have troubled the peace of the commonwealth and the churches here; you are known to be a woman that hath had a great share in the promoting and divulging of those opinions that are the cause of this trouble, . . . and you have maintained a meeting and an assembly in your house that hath been condemned by the general assembly as a thing not tolerable nor comely on the sight of God nor fitting for your sex. . . .

MRS. ANNE HUTCHINSON: That's matter of conscience, Sir.

GOV. JOHN WINTHROP: Your conscience you must keep, or it must be kept for you. . . . Your course is not to be suffered for. Besides we find such a course as this to be greatly prejudicial to the state. . . . And besides that it will not well stand with the commonwealth that families should be neglected for so many neighbors and dames and so much time spent. We see no rule of God for this. We see not that any should have authority to set up any other exercises besides what authority hath already set up. . . .

MRS. ANNE HUTCHINSON: I bless the Lord, he hath let me see which was the clear ministry and which the wrong. . . . Now if you do condemn me for speaking what in my conscience I know to be truth I must commit myself unto the Lord.

MR. NOWEL (ASSISTANT TO THE COURT): How do you know that was the spirit?

MRS. ANNE HUTCHINSON: By an immediate revelation.

DEP. GOV. THOMAS DUDLEY: How! An immediate revelation. . . .

GOV. JOHN WINTHROP: Mrs. Hutchinson, the sentence of the court you hear is that you are banished from out of our jurisdiction as being a woman not fit for our society, and are to be imprisoned till the court shall send you away.

From John Winthrop, Speech to the Massachusetts General Court (July 3, 1645)

John Winthrop, governor of the Massachusetts Bay Colony, describes two very different definitions of liberty in this speech.

The great questions that have troubled the country, are about the authority of the magistrates and the liberty of the people. . . . Concerning liberty, I observe a great mistake in the country about that. There is a twofold liberty, natural (I mean as our nature is now corrupt) and civil or federal. The first is common to man with beasts and other creatures. By this, man, as he stands in relation to man simply, hath liberty to do what he lists; it is a liberty to do evil as well as to [do] good. This liberty is incompatible and inconsistent with authority, and cannot endure the least restraint of the most just authority. The exercise and maintaining of this liberty makes men grow more evil, and in time to be worse than brute beasts. . . . This is that great enemy of truth and peace, that wild beast, which all the ordinances of God are bent against, to restrain and subdue it.

The other kind of liberty I call civil or federal, it may also be termed moral. . . . This liberty is the proper end and object of authority, and cannot subsist without it; and it is a liberty to that only which is good, just, and honest. . . . This liberty is maintained and exercised in a way of subjection to authority; it is of the same kind of liberty wherewith Christ hath made us free. The woman's own choice makes . . . a man her husband; yet being so chosen, he is her lord, and she is to be subject to him, yet in a way of liberty, not of bondage; and a true wife accounts her subjection her honor and freedom, and would not think her condition safe and free, but in her subjection to her husband's authority. Such is the liberty of the church under the authority of Christ.

QUESTIONS

1. *To what extent does Hutchinson's being a woman play a part in the accusations against her?*
2. *Why does Winthrop consider "natural" liberty dangerous?*
3. *How do Hutchinson and Winthrop differ in their understanding of religious liberty?*

with the Indians. To counteract the attraction of Indian life, the leaders of New England also encouraged the publication of **captivity narratives** by those captured by Indians. The most popular was *The Sovereignty and Goodness of God* by Mary Rowlandson, who was seized with other settlers and held for three months until ransomed during an Indian war in the 1670s. Rowlandson acknowledged that she had been well treated and suffered "not the least abuse or unchastity," but her book's overriding theme was her determination to return to Christian society.

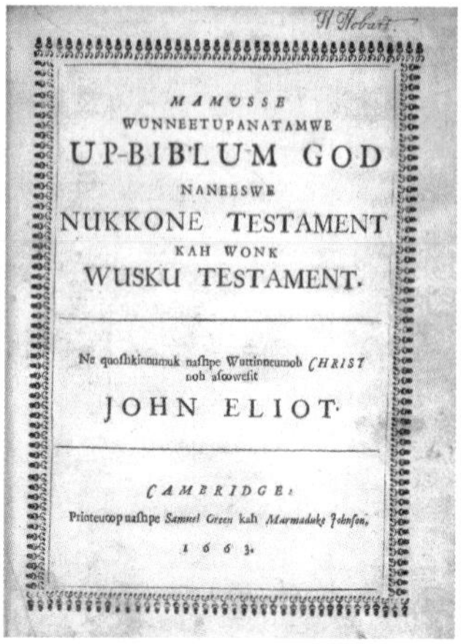

MAMUSSE
WUNNEETUPANATAMWE
UP-BIBLUM GOD
NANEESWE
NUKKONE TESTAMENT
KAH WONK
WUSKU TESTAMENT.

Ne quoshkinnumuk nashpe Wuttinneumoh CHRIST
noh asoowesit
JOHN ELIOT.

CAMBRIDGE:
Printeuoop nashpe Samuel Green kah Marmaduke Johnson.
1663.

The title page of a translation of the Bible into the Massachusett Indian language, published by John Eliot in 1663.

Puritans announced that they intended to bring Christian faith to the Indians, but they did nothing in the first two decades of settlement to accomplish this. They generally saw Indians as an obstacle to be pushed aside.

The Pequot War

Indians in New England lacked a paramount chief like Powhatan in Virginia. Coastal Indian tribes, their numbers severely reduced by disease, initially sought to forge alliances with the newcomers to enhance their own position against inland rivals. But as the white population expanded and new towns proliferated, conflict with the region's Indians became unavoidable. The turning point came in 1637 when a fur trader was killed by Pequots—a powerful tribe who controlled southern New England's fur trade and exacted tribute from other Indians. A force of Connecticut and Massachusetts soldiers, augmented by Narragansett allies, surrounded the main Pequot fortified village at Mystic and set it ablaze, killing those who tried to escape. Over 500 men, women, and children lost their lives in the massacre. By the end of the **Pequot War** a few months later, most of the Pequots had been exterminated or sold into Caribbean slavery. The treaty that restored peace decreed that their name be wiped from the historical record.

Massacre at Mystic

The colonists' ferocity shocked their Indian allies, who considered European military practices barbaric. But to most Puritans, the defeat of a "barbarous nation" by "the sword of the Lord" offered further proof that Indians were unworthy of sharing New England with the visible saints of the church.

The New England Economy

Economic motivation for emigrants

The leaders of the New England colonies prided themselves on the idea that religion was the primary motivation for emigration. But economic motives were hardly unimportant. One promotional pamphlet of the 1620s spoke of New England as a place "where religion and profit jump together."

Most Puritans came from the middle ranks of society and paid for their family's passage rather than indenturing themselves to labor. They sought in New England not only religious liberty but also economic

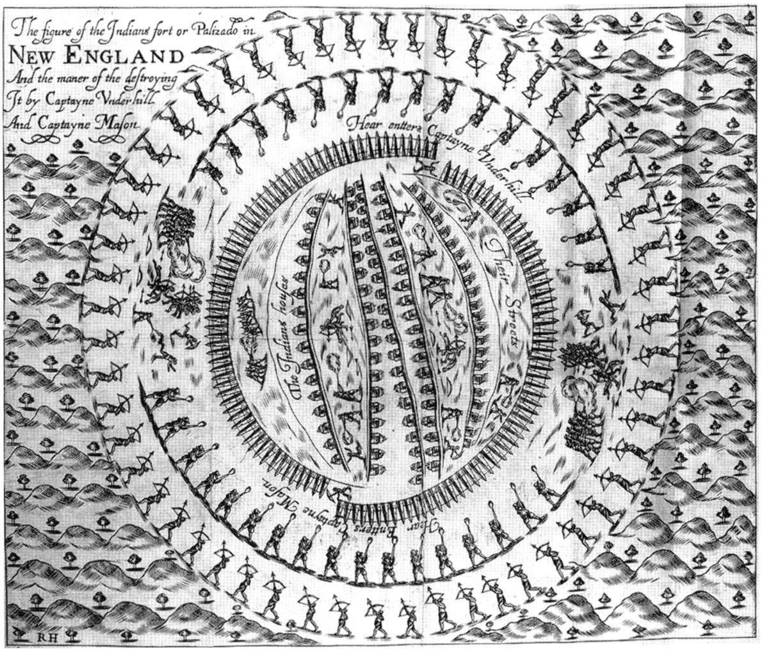

An engraving from John Underhill's *News from America*, published in London in 1638, shows the destruction of the Pequot village on the Mystic River in 1637. The colonial forces, firing guns, are aided by Indian allies with bows and arrows.

advancement—if not riches, then at least a "competency," the economic independence that came with secure landownership or craft status.

Fish and timber exports

Lacking a marketable staple like sugar or tobacco, New Englanders turned to fishing and timber for exports. With very few slaves in seventeenth-century New England, most households relied on the labor of their own members, including women in the home and children in the fields. Sons remained unmarried into their mid-twenties, when they could expect to receive land from their fathers, from local authorities, or by moving to a new town.

The Merchant Elite

Social inequalities

Per capita wealth in New England lagged far behind that of the Chesapeake, but it was much more equally distributed. A majority of New England families owned their own land, the foundation for a comfortable independence. Nonetheless, as in the Chesapeake, economic development produced some social inequalities. For example, on completing their terms, indentured servants rarely achieved full church membership or received grants of land. Most became disenfranchised wage earners.

New England assumed a growing role within the British empire based on trade. As early as the 1640s, New England merchants shipped and marketed the staples of other colonies to markets in Europe and Africa. They

Mrs. Elizabeth Freake and Baby Mary. Painted by an anonymous artist in the 1670s, this portrait depicts the wife and daughter of John Freake, a prominent Boston merchant and lawyer. To illustrate the family's wealth, Mrs. Freake wears a triple strand of pearls, a garnet bracelet, and a gold ring, and her child wears a yellow silk dress.

engaged in a particularly profitable trade with the West Indies, whose growing slave plantations they supplied with fish, timber, and agricultural produce gathered at home. Especially in Boston, a powerful class of merchants arose who challenged some key Puritan policies, including the subordination of economic activity to the common good. As early as the 1630s, when the General Court established limits on prices and wages and gave a small group of merchants a monopoly on imports from Europe, others protested. Some left Boston to establish a new town at Portsmouth, in the region eventually chartered as the royal colony of New Hampshire. Others remained to fight, with increasing success, for the right to conduct business as they pleased. By the 1640s, Massachusetts had repealed many of its early economic regulations. Eventually, the Puritan experiment would evolve into a merchant-dominated colonial government.

Some Puritan leaders were understandably worried about their society's growing commercialization. By 1650, less than half the population of Boston had become full church members, which forced Puritan leaders to deal with the religious status of the third generation. Should they uphold the rigorous admission standards of the Congregational Church, thus limiting its size? Or should they make admission easier and remain connected to more people? The **Half-Way Covenant** of 1662 tried to address this problem by allowing for the baptism of and a kind of "half-way" membership for grandchildren of those who arrived during the Great Migration. But church membership continued to stagnate.

"Jeremiads"

By the 1660s and 1670s, ministers were regularly castigating the people for selfishness and a "great backsliding" from the colony's original purposes. These warnings, called "jeremiads" after the ancient Hebrew prophet Jeremiah, interpreted crop failures and disease as signs of divine disapproval and warned of further punishment to come if New Englanders did not mend their ways. Yet hard work and commercial success had always been central Puritan values. In this sense, the commercialization of New England was as much a fulfillment of the Puritan mission in America as a betrayal.

RELIGION, POLITICS, AND FREEDOM

The Rights of Englishmen

Even as English emigrants began the settlement of colonies in North America, England itself became enmeshed in political and religious conflict, in which ideas of liberty played a central role. By 1600, the traditional definition of "liberties" as a set of privileges confined to one or another social group still persisted, but alongside it had arisen the idea that certain

The execution of Charles I in 1649, a central event of the English Civil War.

"rights of Englishmen" applied to all within the kingdom. This tradition rested on the Magna Carta (or Great Charter) of 1215. An agreement between King John and a group of barons, the Magna Carta listed a series of "liberties" granted by the king to "all the free men of our realm," a restricted group at the time, since many residents of England were serfs. The liberties mentioned in the Magna Carta included protection against arbitrary imprisonment and the seizure of one's property without due process of law.

The Magna Carta

Over time, the document came to be seen as embodying the idea of "**English liberty**"—that the king was subject to the rule of law, and that all persons should enjoy security of person and property. These rights were embodied in the common law, whose provisions, such as habeas corpus (a protection against being imprisoned without a legal charge), the right to face one's accuser, and trial by jury came to apply to all free subjects of the English crown. As serfdom slowly disappeared, the number of Englishmen considered "freeborn," and therefore entitled to these rights, expanded enormously. The belief in freedom as the common heritage of all Englishmen and the conception of the British empire as the world's guardian of liberty helped to legitimize English colonization in the Western Hemisphere and to cast imperial wars against Catholic France and Spain as struggles between freedom and tyranny.

Rights of "freeborns"

The English Civil War

At the beginning of the seventeenth century, when English immigrants began arriving in the New World, "freedom" still played only a minor role in England's political debates. But the political upheavals of that century elevated the notion of "English freedom" to a central place. The struggle for political supremacy between Parliament and the Stuart monarchs James I and Charles I culminated in the English Civil War of the 1640s and early 1650s.

Meeting of the General Council of the Army at Putney, scene of the debate in 1647 over liberty and democracy between Levellers and more conservative army officers.

The leaders of the House of Commons (the elective body that, along with the hereditary aristocrats of the House of Lords, made up the English Parliament) accused the Stuart kings of endangering liberty by imposing taxes without parliamentary consent, imprisoning political foes, and leading the nation back toward Catholicism. Civil war broke out in 1642, resulting in a victory for the forces of Parliament. In 1649, Charles I was beheaded, the monarchy abolished, and England declared "a Commonwealth and Free State"—a nation governed by the will of the people. Oliver Cromwell, the head of the victorious Parliamentary army, ruled for almost a decade after the execution of the king. In 1660, the monarchy was restored and Charles II assumed the throne. But by then, the breakdown of authority had stimulated intense discussions of liberty, authority, and what it meant to be a "freeborn Englishman."

England's Debate over Freedom

The idea of freedom suddenly took on new and expanded meanings between 1640 and 1660. The writer John Milton called for freedom of speech and of the press. New religious sects sprang up, demanding religious toleration for all Protestants as well as the end of public financing and special privileges for the Anglican Church. The Levellers, history's first democratic political movement, proposed a written constitution, the Agreement of the People, which began by proclaiming "at how high a rate we value our just freedom," and went on to list inalienable rights Parliament could not infringe upon. Although "democracy" was still widely equated with anarchy, the document proposed to abolish the monarchy and House of Lords and to greatly expand the right to vote.

The Diggers

The Levellers offered a glimpse of the modern definition of freedom as a universal entitlement in a society based on equal rights, not a function of social class. Another new group, the Diggers, went even further, hoping to give freedom an economic underpinning through the common ownership of land. Gerard Winstanley, the Diggers' leader, said that true freedom applied equally "to the poor as well as the rich"; all were entitled to "a comfortable livelihood in this their own land." Some of the ideas of liberty that flourished during the 1640s and 1650s would be carried to America by English immigrants.

The Civil War and English America

The Civil War, accompanied by vigorous discussions of the rights of freeborn Englishmen, inevitably reverberated in England's colonies, dividing them from one another and internally. Most New Englanders sided with

WHO IS AN AMERICAN?

From Henry Care, *English Liberties, Or, The Free-Born Subject's Inheritance* (1680).

Before the United States existed as an independent nation, settlers in Britain's North American colonies shared a sense of identity linked with the idea that liberty was a unique possession of Englishmen. Care was a British journalist and writer on politics. His book was an influential example of how seventeenth-century identities rested, in part, on negative images of other nations. Well into the eighteenth century, it was widely reprinted in the colonies as well as the mother country.

The Constitution of our English government (the best in the world) is no arbitrary tyranny like the Turkish Grand Seignior's, or the French Kings, whose wills (or rather lusts) dispose of the lives and fortunes of their unhappy subjects; nor an Oligarchy where the great men (like fish in the ocean) prey upon, and live by devouring the lesser at their pleasure. Nor yet a Democracy or popular State, much less an Anarchy, where all confusedly are hail fellows well met, but a most excellently mixt or qualified Monarchy, where the King is vested with large prerogatives sufficient to support majesty; and restrained only from power of doing himself and his people harm, which would be contrary to the end of all government, . . . the nobility adorned with privileges to be a screen to majesty, and a refreshing shade to their inferiors, and the commonality, too, so guarded in their persons and properties by the fence of law, [which] renders them Freemen, not Slaves.

In France and other nations the mere will of the prince is law, his word takes off any . . . head, imposes taxes, or seizes any man's estate, when, how, and as often as he wishes. . . . But in England, the law is both the measure and the bond of every subject's duty and allegiance, each man having a fixed fundamental right born with him as to the freedom of his person and property in his estate, which he cannot be deprived of, but either by his consent, or some crime for which the law has imposed . . . a penalty. . . .

This original happy frame of government is truly and properly called an Englishman's liberty, a privilege not to [be] exempt from the law, but to be freed in person and estate, from arbitrary violence and oppression.

QUESTIONS

1. *Why does Care consider the English system of "balanced" government the best in the world?*
2. *How does his view of other countries affect his pride in being English?*

Parliament in the Civil War of the 1640s. Some returned to England to join the Parliamentary army or take up pulpits to help create a godly commonwealth at home. But Puritan leaders were increasingly uncomfortable as the idea of religious toleration for Protestants gained favor in England.

The Quakers

Meanwhile, a number of followers of Anne Hutchinson became Quakers, one of the sects that sprang up in England during the Civil War. Quakers held that the spirit of God dwelled within every individual, not just the elect, and that this "inner light," rather than the Bible or teachings of the clergy, offered the surest guidance in spiritual matters. When Quakers appeared in Massachusetts, colonial officials had them whipped, fined, and banished. In 1659 and 1660, four Quakers who returned from exile were hanged. When Charles II, after the restoration of the monarchy in 1660, reaffirmed the Massachusetts charter, he ordered the colony to recognize the "liberty of conscience" of all Protestants.

In Maryland, the combination of the religious and political battles of the Civil War, homegrown conflict between Catholic and Protestant settlers, and anti-proprietary feeling produced a violent civil war within the colony, later recalled as the "plundering time." Indeed, Maryland in the 1640s verged on total anarchy, with a pro-Parliament force assaulting those loyal to Charles I.

Religious freedom in Maryland

After years of struggle between the Protestant planter class and the Catholic elite, Maryland in 1649 adopted an **Act Concerning Religion (or Maryland Toleration Act)**, which institutionalized the principle of toleration that had prevailed from the colony's beginning. All Christians were guaranteed the "free exercise" of religion. Although the Act did not grant this right to non-Christians, it did, over time, bring some political stability to Maryland. The law was also a milestone in the history of religious freedom in colonial America.

England's colonial expansion

By the middle of the seventeenth century, several English colonies existed along the Atlantic coast of North America. Established as part of an ad hoc process rather than arising under any coherent national plan, they differed enormously in economic, political, and social structure. The seeds had been planted, in the Chesapeake, for the development of plantation societies based on unfree labor, and in New England, for settlements centered on small towns and family farms. Throughout the colonies, many residents enjoyed freedoms they had not possessed at home, especially access to land and the right to worship as they desired. Others found themselves confined to unfree labor for many years or an entire lifetime.

The next century would be a time of crisis and consolidation as the population expanded, social conflicts intensified, and Britain moved to exert greater control over its flourishing North American colonies.

CHAPTER REVIEW AND ONLINE RESOURCES

REVIEW QUESTIONS

1. *Compare and contrast settlement patterns, treatment of Indians, and religion of the Spanish and English in the Americas.*
2. *For English settlers, land was the basis of independence and liberty. Explain the reasoning behind that concept and how it differed from the Indians' conception of land.*
3. *Describe the factors promoting and limiting religious freedom in the New England and Chesapeake colonies.*
4. *Describe who chose to emigrate to North America from England in the seventeenth century and explain their reasons.*
5. *In what ways did the economy, government, and household structure differ in New England and the Chesapeake colonies?*
6. *The English believed that, unlike the Spanish, their motives for colonization were pure, and that the growth of empire and freedom would always go hand in hand. How did the expansion of the British empire affect the freedoms of Native Americans, the Irish, and even many English citizens?*
7. *Considering politics, social tensions, and debates over the meaning of liberty, how do the events and aftermath of the English Civil War demonstrate that the English colonies in North America were part of a larger Atlantic community?*
8. *How did the tobacco economy draw the Chesapeake colonies into the greater Atlantic World?*
9. *How did the idea of freedom help legitimize English colonization?*

KEY TERMS

Virginia Company (p. 39)
Anglican Church (p. 40)
Roanoke colony (p. 41)
enclosure movement (p. 42)
indentured servants (p. 44)
John Smith (p. 47)
headright system (p. 48)
House of Burgesses (p. 48)
Uprising of 1622 (p. 49)
dower rights (p. 50)
Puritans (p. 52)
John Winthrop (p. 53)
Pilgrims (p. 54)
Mayflower Compact (p. 54)
Great Migration (p. 55)
Dissenters (p. 60)
captivity narratives (p. 64)
Pequot War (p. 64)
Half-Way Covenant (p. 66)
English liberty (p. 67)
Act Concerning Religion (or Maryland Toleration Act) (p. 70)

Go to INQUIZITIVE

To see what you know—and learn what you've missed—with personalized feedback along the way.

Visit the ***Give Me Liberty!* Student Site** for primary source documents and images, interactive maps, author videos featuring Eric Foner, and more.

1651	First Navigation Act issued by Parliament
1664	English seize New Netherland, which becomes New York
1670	First English settlers arrive in Carolina
1675	Lords of Trade established
1675–1676	King Philip's War
1676	Bacon's Rebellion
1677	Covenant Chain alliance
1681	William Penn granted Pennsylvania
1682	Charter of Liberty drafted by Penn
1683	Charter of Liberties and Privileges drafted by New York assembly
1686–1689	Dominion of New England
1688	Glorious Revolution in England
1689	Parliament enacts a Bill of Rights
	Maryland Protestant Association revolts
	Leisler's Rebellion
	Parliament passes Toleration Act
1691	Plymouth colony absorbed into Massachusetts
1692	Salem witch trials
1705	Virginia passes slave code
1715–1717	Yamasee uprising
1737	Walking Purchase

CHAPTER 3

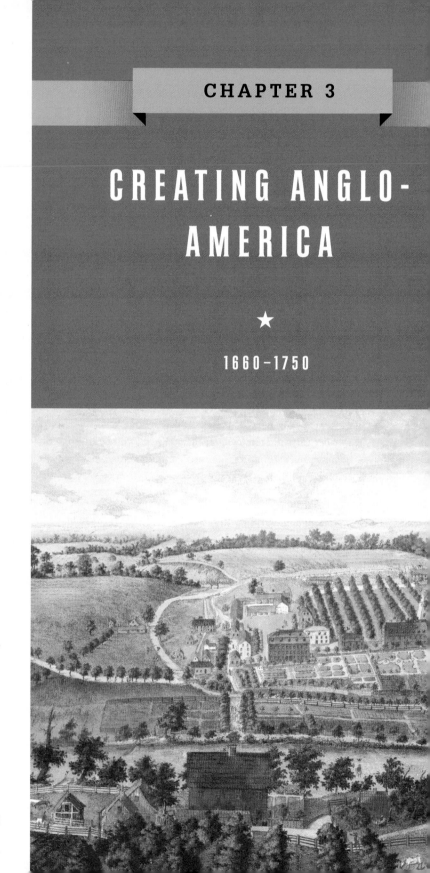

CREATING ANGLO-AMERICA

★

1660–1750

A View of Bethlehem, One of the Brethren's Principal Settlements in Pennsylvania, a lithograph produced in London in 1757, depicts a prosperous Moravian community, one of numerous settlements established by religious groups who emigrated from Europe to Britain's American colonies. In the left foreground, with a roof made of tiles from a local workshop, is the Crown Inn, which stood for over a century until razed to make way for a railroad. To its right is a large barn, with animals grazing nearby.

In the last quarter of the seventeenth century, a series of crises rocked the European colonies of North America. Social and political tensions boiled over in sometimes ruthless conflicts between rich and poor, free and slave, settler and Indian, and members of different religious groups. At the same time, struggles within and between European empires echoed in the colonies.

The bloodiest and most bitter conflict occurred in southern New England, where in 1675 an Indian alliance launched attacks on farms and settlements that were encroaching on Indian lands. It was the most dramatic and violent warfare in the region in the entire seventeenth century.

New Englanders described the Wampanoag leader **Metacom** (known to the colonists as King Philip) as the uprising's mastermind, although in fact most tribes fought under their own leaders. By 1676, Indian forces had attacked nearly half of New England's ninety towns. Twelve in Massachusetts were destroyed. As refugees fled eastward, the line of settlement was pushed back almost to the Atlantic coast. Some 1,000 settlers, out of a population of 52,000, and 3,000 of New England's 20,000 Indians perished in the fighting.

In mid-1676, the tide of battle turned and a ferocious counterattack broke the Indians' power once and for all. Although the uprising united numerous tribes, others remained loyal to the colonists. The role of the Iroquois in providing essential military aid to the colonists helped to solidify their developing alliance with the government of New York. Together, colonial and Indian forces inflicted devastating punishment on the rebels. Metacom was executed, Indian villages were destroyed, and captives were killed or sold into slavery in the West Indies. Both sides committed atrocities in this merciless conflict, but in its aftermath the image of Indians as bloodthirsty savages became firmly entrenched in the New England mind.

In the long run, **King Philip's War** produced a broadening of freedom for white New Englanders by expanding their access to land. But this freedom rested on the final dispossession of the region's Indians.

FOCUS QUESTIONS

- *How did the English empire in America expand in the mid-seventeenth century?*
- *How was slavery established in the Western Atlantic world?*
- *What major social and political crises rocked the colonies in the late seventeenth century?*
- *What were the directions of social and economic change in the eighteenth-century colonies?*
- *How did patterns of class and gender roles change in eighteenth-century America?*

GLOBAL COMPETITION AND THE EXPANSION OF ENGLAND'S EMPIRE

The Mercantilist System

By the middle of the seventeenth century, it was apparent that the colonies could be an important source of wealth for England. According to the prevailing theory known as **mercantilism**, governments should regulate economic activity so as to promote national power. They should encourage manufacturing and commerce by special bounties, monopolies, and other measures. Above all, trade should be controlled so that more gold and silver flowed into countries than left them. That is, exports of goods, which generated revenue from abroad, should exceed imports, which required paying foreigners for their products. In the mercantilist outlook, the role of colonies was to serve the interests of the mother country by producing marketable raw materials and importing manufactured goods from home. "Foreign trade," declared an influential work written in 1664 by a London merchant, formed the basis of "England's treasure." Commerce, not territorial plunder, was the foundation of empire.

The role of colonies

Parliament in 1651 passed the first **Navigation Act**, which aimed to wrest control of world trade from the Dutch, whose merchants profited from free trade with all parts of the world and all existing empires. Additional measures followed in 1660 and 1663. According to the Navigation laws, certain "enumerated" goods—essentially, the most valuable colonial products, such as tobacco and sugar—had to be transported in English ships and sold initially in English ports, although they could then be re-exported to foreign markets. Similarly, most European goods imported into the colonies had to be shipped through England, where customs duties were paid. This enabled English merchants, manufacturers, shipbuilders, and sailors to reap the benefits of colonial trade, and the government to enjoy added income from taxes. As members of the empire, American colonies would profit as well, since their ships were considered English. Indeed, the Navigation Acts stimulated the rise of New England's shipbuilding industry.

"Enumerated" goods

The Conquest of New Netherland

The restoration of the English monarchy when Charles II assumed the throne in 1660 sparked a new period of colonial expansion. The government chartered new trading ventures, notably the Royal African Company, which was given a monopoly of the slave trade. Within a generation, the number of English colonies in North America doubled.

Colonial expansion

First to come under English control was New Netherland, seized in 1664 during an Anglo-Dutch war that also saw England gain control of Dutch trading posts in Africa. Charles II awarded the colony to his younger brother James, the duke of York, with "full and absolute power" to govern as he pleased. (Hence the colony's name became New York.) English rule transformed this minor military base into an important imperial outpost, a seaport trading with the Caribbean and Europe, and a launching pad for military operations against the French. New York's European population, around 9,000 when the English assumed control, rose to 20,000 by 1685.

English rule in New York

EASTERN NORTH AMERICA IN THE SEVENTEENTH AND EARLY EIGHTEENTH CENTURIES

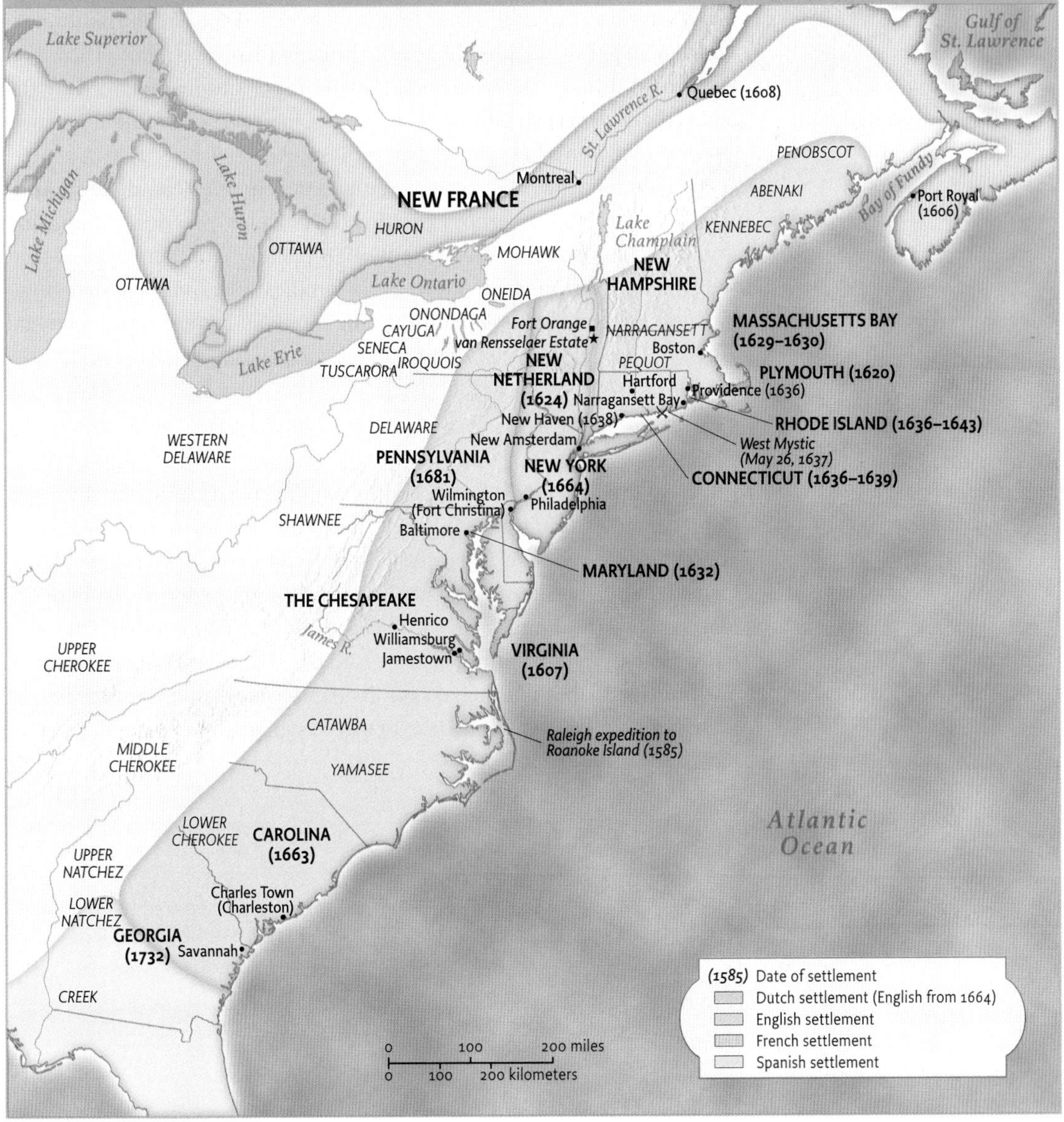

By the early eighteenth century, numerous English colonies populated eastern North America, while the French had established their own presence to the north and west.

English rule expanded the freedom of some New Yorkers, while reducing that of others. The terms of surrender guaranteed that the English would respect the religious beliefs and property holdings of the colony's many ethnic communities. But English law ended the Dutch tradition by which married women conducted business in their own name. There had been many female traders in New Amsterdam, but few remained by the end of the seventeenth century. The English, in a reversal of Dutch practice, also expelled free blacks from many skilled jobs.

English rule and blacks

Others benefited enormously from English rule. The duke of York and his appointed governors continued the Dutch practice of awarding immense land grants to favorites. By 1700, nearly 2 million acres of land were owned by only five New York families who intermarried regularly, exerted considerable political influence, and formed one of colonial America's most tightly knit landed elites.

New York and the Indians

Initially, English rule also strengthened the position of the Iroquois Confederacy of upstate New York. Sir Edmund Andros, who had been appointed governor of New York after fighting the French in the Caribbean, formed an alliance known as the **Covenant Chain**, in which the imperial ambitions of the English and Indians reinforced one another. The Five (later Six) Iroquois Nations assisted Andros in clearing parts of New York of rival tribes and helped the British in attacks on the French and their Indian allies. Andros, for his part, recognized the Iroquois claim to

The Iroquois Nations

An engraving representing the Grand Council of the Iroquois Nations of the area of present-day upstate New York. From a book about American Indians published in Paris by a Jesuit missionary, who depicts the Indians in the attire of ancient Romans. Note the prevalence of wampum belts in the image, in the foreground and in the hand and at the feet of the central figure. Wampum was used to certify treaties and other transactions.

authority over Indian communities in the vast area stretching to the Ohio River. But beginning in the 1680s, Indians around the Great Lakes and Ohio Valley regrouped and with French aid attacked the Iroquois, pushing them to the east. By the end of the century, the Iroquois Nations adopted a policy of careful neutrality, seeking to play the European empires off one another while continuing to profit from the fur trade.

The Charter of Liberties

Many New York colonists, meanwhile, began to complain that they were being denied the "liberties of Englishmen," especially the right to consent to taxation. In 1683, the duke of York agreed to call an elected assembly, whose first act was to draft a Charter of Liberties and Privileges. The charter required that elections be held every three years among male property owners and the freemen of New York City; it also reaffirmed traditional English rights such as trial by jury and security of property, as well as religious toleration for all Protestants.

English rights

The Founding of Carolina

For more than three decades after the establishment of Maryland in 1632, no new English settlement was planted in North America. Then, in 1663, Charles II awarded to eight proprietors the right to establish a colony to the north of Florida, as a barrier to Spanish expansion. Not until 1670 did the first settlers arrive to found Carolina. In its early years, Carolina was the "colony of a colony," an offshoot of the tiny island of Barbados. In the mid-seventeenth century, Barbados was the Caribbean's richest plantation economy, but a shortage of available land led wealthy planters to seek opportunities in Carolina for their sons. At first, Carolinians armed friendly Indians, employing them on raids into Spanish Florida, and enslaved others, shipping them to other mainland colonies and the West Indies. Between 1670 and 1720, the number of Indian slaves exported from Charleston was larger than the number of African slaves imported. In 1715, the Yamasee and Creek rebelled, but the **Yamasee uprising** was crushed, and most of the remaining Indians were enslaved or driven out of the colony into Spanish Florida.

Carolina as a barrier to Spanish expansion

The Fundamental Constitutions of Carolina, issued by the proprietors in 1669, proposed to establish a feudal society with a hereditary nobility, serfs, and slaves. Needing to attract settlers quickly, however, the proprietors also provided for an elected assembly and religious toleration—by now recognized as essential to enticing migrants to North America. They also instituted a generous headright system, offering 150 acres for each

The Fundamental Constitutions of Carolina

member of an arriving family (in the case of indentured servants, of course, the land went to the employer) and 100 acres to male servants who completed their terms.

Rights of slaveholders

The proprietors instituted a rigorous legal code that promised slaveowners "absolute power and authority" over their human property and included imported slaves in the headright system. This allowed any persons who settled in Carolina and brought with them slaves instantly to acquire large new landholdings. In its early days, however, the economy centered on cattle raising and trade with local Indians. Carolina grew slowly until planters discovered the staple—rice—that would make them the wealthiest elite in English North America and their colony an epicenter of mainland slavery.

The Holy Experiment

William Penn

The last English colony to be established in the seventeenth century was Pennsylvania in 1681. The proprietor, William Penn, envisioned it as a place where those facing religious persecution in Europe could enjoy spiritual freedom, and colonists and Indians would coexist in harmony.

A devout member of the **Society of Friends (Quakers)**, Penn was particularly concerned with establishing a refuge for his coreligionists, who faced increasing persecution in England. He had already assisted a group of English Quakers in purchasing half of what became the colony of New Jersey from Lord John Berkeley, who had received a land grant from the duke of York. Penn was largely responsible for the frame of government announced in 1677, the West Jersey Concessions, which created an elected assembly with a broad suffrage and established religious liberty.

A Quaker Meeting, a painting by an unidentified British artist, dating from the late eighteenth or early nineteenth century. It illustrates the prominent place of women in Quaker gatherings.

Like the Puritans, Penn considered his colony a "holy experiment," but of a different kind—"a free colony for all mankind that should go hither." He hoped that Pennsylvania could be governed according to Quaker principles, among them the equality of all persons (including women, blacks, and Indians) before God and the primacy of the individual conscience. To Quakers, liberty was a universal entitlement, not the possession of any single people—a position that would eventually make them the first group of whites to repudiate slavery. Penn also treated Indians with a consideration unique in the colonial experience, purchasing land before reselling it to colonists and offering refuge to tribes driven out of other colonies by warfare. Since Quakers were pacifists who came to America unarmed and did not even organize a militia until the 1740s, peace with the native population was essential.

Penn and religious liberty

Religious freedom was Penn's most fundamental principle. His Charter of Liberty, approved by the assembly in 1682, offered "Christian liberty" to all who affirmed a belief in God and did not use their freedom to promote "licentiousness." There was no established church in Pennsylvania, and attendance at religious services was entirely voluntary, although Jews were barred from office by a required oath affirming belief in the divinity of Jesus Christ. At the same time, the Quakers upheld a strict code of personal morality. Penn's Frame of Government prohibited swearing, drunkenness, and adultery. Not religious uniformity but a virtuous citizenry would be the foundation of Penn's social order.

Land in Pennsylvania

Pennsylvania's elected government

Given the power to determine the colony's form of government, Penn established an appointed council to originate legislation and an assembly elected by male taxpayers and "freemen" (owners of 100 acres of land for free immigrants and 50 acres for former indentured servants). These rules made a majority of the male population eligible to vote. Penn owned all the colony's land and sold it to settlers at low prices, which helped the colony prosper. Pennsylvania's religious toleration, healthy climate, and inexpensive land, along with Penn's aggressive efforts to publicize the colony's advantages, soon attracted immigrants from all over western Europe.

Freedoms in Pennsylvania

Ironically, the freedoms Pennsylvania offered to European immigrants contributed to the deterioration of freedom for others. The colony's successful efforts to attract settlers would eventually come into conflict with Penn's benevolent Indian policy. And the opening of Pennsylvania caused fewer indentured servants to choose Virginia and Maryland, a development that did much to shift those colonies toward reliance on slave labor.

ORIGINS OF AMERICAN SLAVERY

The turn to slavery

The incessant demand for workers spurred by the spread of tobacco cultivation eventually led Chesapeake planters to turn to the transatlantic trade in slaves. Compared with indentured servants, slaves offered planters many advantages. As Africans, they could not claim the protections of English common law. Slaves' terms of service never expired, and they therefore did not become a population of unruly landless men. Their children were slaves, and their skin color made it more difficult for them to escape into the surrounding society. African men, moreover, unlike their Native American counterparts, were accustomed to intensive agricultural labor, and they had encountered many diseases known in Europe and developed resistance to them, so were less likely to succumb to epidemics.

Englishmen and Africans

English views of alien peoples

The English had long viewed alien peoples with disdain, including the Irish, Native Americans, and Africans. They described these strangers in remarkably similar language as savage, pagan, and uncivilized. "Race"—the idea that humanity is divided into well-defined groups associated with skin color—is a modern concept that had not fully developed in the seventeenth century. Nor had "racism"—an ideology based on the belief that some races are inherently superior to others and entitled to rule over them.

Nonetheless, anti-black stereotypes flourished in seventeenth-century England. Africans were seen as so alien—in color, religion, and social practices—that they were "enslavable" in a way that poor Englishmen were not. Most English also deemed Indians to be uncivilized. But the Indian population declined so rapidly, and it was so easy for Indians, familiar with the countryside, to run away, that Indian slavery never became viable in the Atlantic colonies.

Slavery in History

Slavery has existed for nearly the entire span of human history. It was central to the societies of ancient Greece and Rome. In the Mediterranean world, a slave trade in Slavic peoples survived into the fifteenth century. (The English word "slavery" derives from "Slav.") In West Africa, as noted in Chapter 1, slavery and a slave trade predated the coming of Europeans, and small-scale slavery existed among Native Americans. But slavery in nearly all these instances differed greatly from the institution that developed in the New World.

In the Americas, slavery was based on the **plantation**, an agricultural enterprise that brought together large numbers of workers under the control of a single owner. This imbalance magnified the possibility of slave resistance and made it necessary to police the system rigidly. Labor on slave

In *Free Women of Color with Their Children and Servants in a Landscape*, Agostino Brunias, an Italian artist who was sent to the West Indies by the British government in the 1760s to paint the local population, portrays an outing of fashionable free women with their children and slaves, some dressed in livery. Although the scene depicted is in the Caribbean, the work resembles numerous paintings of the leisure activities of the well-to-do in Britain. The painting reflects the three-race system that developed in the British Caribbean—the free women are light-skinned but not white. The woman at the center looks directly at the viewer, emphasizing her aristocratic bearing.

plantations was far more demanding than the household slavery common in Africa, and the death rate among slaves much higher. In the New World, slavery would come to be associated with race, a concept that drew a permanent line between whites and blacks.

Slavery in the West Indies

A sense of Africans as alien and inferior made their enslavement by the English possible. But prejudice by itself did not create North American slavery. For this institution to take root, planters and government authorities had to be convinced that importing African slaves was the best way to solve their persistent shortage of labor. During the seventeenth century, the shipping of slaves from Africa to the New World became a major international business. By 1600, huge sugar plantations worked by slaves from Africa had made their appearance in Brazil, a colony of Portugal. In the seventeenth century, England, Holland, Denmark, and France joined Spain as owners of West Indian islands.

Sugar plantations

With the Indian population having been wiped out by disease, and with the white indentured servants unwilling to do the back-breaking, monotonous work of sugar cultivation, the massive importation of slaves from Africa began. On Barbados, for example, the slave population increased from 20,000 to more than 80,000 between 1660 and 1670. By the end of the seventeenth century, huge sugar plantations manned by hundreds of slaves dominated the West Indian economy, and on most of the islands the African population far outnumbered that of European origin.

Sugar was the first crop to be mass-marketed to consumers in Europe. Before its emergence, international trade consisted largely of precious metals like gold and silver, and luxury goods aimed at an elite market, like the spices and silks imported from Asia. Sugar was by far the most important product of the British, French, and Portuguese empires, and New World sugar plantations produced immense profits. Saint Domingue, today's Haiti, was the jewel of the French empire. In 1660, Barbados generated more trade than all the other English colonies combined.

Compared with its rapid introduction in Brazil and the West Indies, slavery developed slowly in North America. Slaves cost more than indentured servants, and the high death rate among tobacco workers

Cutting Sugar Cane, an engraving from *Ten Views in Antigua*, published in 1823. Male and female slaves harvest and load the sugar crop while an overseer on horseback addresses a slave. During the eighteenth century, sugar was the chief crop produced by Western Hemisphere slaves.

Slow development in North America

made it economically unappealing to pay for a lifetime of labor. As late as 1680, there were only 4,500 blacks in the Chesapeake, a little over 5 percent of the region's population. The most important social distinction in the seventeenth-century Chesapeake was not between black and white but between the white plantation owners who dominated politics and society and everybody else—small farmers, indentured servants, and slaves.

Slavery and the Law

English and Spanish empires on slavery

Centuries before the voyages of Columbus, Spain had enacted a series of laws granting slaves certain rights relating to marriage, the holding of property, and access to freedom. These laws were transferred to Spain's American empire. They were often violated but nonetheless gave slaves opportunities to claim rights under the law. The law of slavery in English North America would become far more repressive than in the Spanish empire, especially on the all-important question of whether avenues existed by which slaves could obtain freedom.

For much of the seventeenth century, however, the legal status of Chesapeake blacks remained ambiguous and the line between slavery and freedom more permeable than it would later become. The first Africans, twenty in all, arrived in Virginia in 1619. Although the first black arrivals were almost certainly treated as slaves, it appears that at least some managed to become free after serving a term of years. To be sure, racial distinctions were enacted into law from the outset. As early as the 1620s, the law barred blacks from serving in the Virginia militia. In 1643, a poll tax (a tax levied on individuals) was imposed on African but not white women. In both Virginia and Maryland, however, free blacks could sue and testify in court, and some even managed to acquire land and purchase white servants or African slaves. Blacks and whites labored side by side in the tobacco fields, sometimes ran away together, and established intimate relationships.

Rights of the free blacks

The Rise of Chesapeake Slavery

Not until the 1660s did the laws of Virginia and Maryland refer explicitly to slavery. As tobacco planting spread and the demand for labor increased, the condition of black and white servants diverged sharply. Authorities sought to improve the status of white servants, hoping to counteract the widespread impression in England that Virginia was a death trap. At the same time, access to freedom for blacks receded.

Legal changes in the 1660s

A Virginia law of 1662 provided that in the case of a child one of whose parents was free and one slave, the status of the offspring followed that of the mother. (This provision not only reversed the European practice of defining a child's status through the father but also made the sexual abuse of slave women profitable for slaveholders, since any children that resulted remained the owner's property.) In 1667, the Virginia House of Burgesses decreed that religious conversion did not release a slave from bondage. Thus, Christians could own other Christians as slaves. Authorities also defined all offspring of interracial relationships as illegitimate. By 1680, even though the black population was still small, notions of racial difference were well entrenched in the law. In British North America, unlike the Spanish empire, no distinctive mulatto, or mixed-race, class existed; the law treated everyone with African ancestry as black.

Black slavery

Bacon's Rebellion: Land and Labor in Virginia

Virginia's shift from white indentured servants to African slaves as the main plantation labor force was accelerated by one of the most dramatic confrontations of this era, **Bacon's Rebellion** of 1676. Governor William Berkeley had for thirty years run a corrupt regime in alliance with an inner circle of the colony's wealthiest tobacco planters. He rewarded his followers with land grants and lucrative offices. But as tobacco farming spread inland, planters connected with the governor engrossed the best lands, leaving freed servants (a growing population, since Virginia's death rate was finally falling) with no options but to work as tenants or to move to the frontier. By the 1670s, poverty among whites had reached levels reminiscent of England. In addition, the right to vote, previously enjoyed by all adult men, was confined to landowners in 1670. Governor Berkeley maintained peaceful relations with Virginia's remaining native population. His refusal to allow white settlement in areas reserved for Indians angered many land-hungry colonists.

Sir William Berkeley, governor of colonial Virginia, 1641–1652 and 1660–1677, in a portrait by Sir Peter Lely. Berkeley's authoritarian rule helped to spark Bacon's Rebellion.

Long-simmering social tensions coupled with widespread resentment against the injustices of the Berkeley regime erupted in Bacon's Rebellion. In 1676, after a minor confrontation between Indians and colonists on Virginia's western frontier, settlers demanded that the governor authorize the extermination or removal of the colony's Indians, to open more land for whites. When Berkeley refused, a series of Indian massacres quickly grew into a full-fledged rebellion.

To some extent, Bacon's Rebellion was a conflict within the Virginia elite—between Berkeley's men and the backers of Nathaniel Bacon, a wealthy and ambitious planter who disdained Berkeley's cronies. But

VOICES OF FREEDOM

Maryland Act Concerning Negroes and Other Slaves (1664)

Like Virginia, Maryland in the 1660s enacted laws to clarify questions arising from the growing importance of slavery. This law made all black servants in the colony slaves for life, and required any white woman who married a slave to serve her husband's owner until the slave's death.

Be it enacted by the Right Honorable the Lord Proprietary by the advice and consent of the upper and lower house of this present General Assembly, that all Negroes or other slaves already within the province, and all Negroes and other slaves to be hereafter imported into the province, shall serve durante vita [for life]. And all children born of any Negro or other slave shall be slaves as their fathers were, for the term of their lives.

And forasmuch as divers freeborn English women, forgetful of their free condition and to the disgrace of our nation, marry Negro slaves, by which also divers suits may arise touching the issue [children] of such women, and a great damage befalls the masters of such Negroes for prevention whereof, for deterring such freeborn women from such shameful matches. Be it further enacted by the authority, advice, and consent aforesaid, that whatsoever freeborn woman shall marry any slave from and after the last day of this present Assembly shall serve the master of such slave during the life of her husband. And that all the issue of such freeborn women so married shall be slaves as their fathers were. And be it further enacted, that all the issues of English or other freeborn women that have already married Negroes shall serve the masters of their parents till they be thirty years of age and no longer.

From Letter by a Female Indentured Servant (September 22, 1756)

Only a minority of emigrants from Europe to British North America were fully free. Indentured servants were men and women who surrendered their freedom for a specified period of time in exchange for passage to America. The letter by Elizabeth Springs from Maryland to her father in England expresses complaints voiced by many indentured servants.

Honored Father,

My being forever banished from your sight, will I hope pardon the boldness I now take of troubling you with these. My long silence has been purely owing to my undutifulness to you, and well knowing I had offended in the highest degree, put a tie on my tongue and pen, for fear I should be extinct from your good graces and add a further trouble to you. . . .

O Dear Father, believe what I am going to relate the words of truth and sincerity and balance my former bad conduct [to] my sufferings here, and then I am sure you'll pity your distressed daughter. What we unfortunate English people suffer here is beyond the probability of you in England to conceive. Let it suffice that I am one of the unhappy number, am toiling almost day and night, and very often in the horse's drudgery, . . . and then tied up and whipped to that degree that you now serve an animal. Scarce any thing but Indian corn and salt to eat and that even begrudged nay many Negroes are better used, almost naked no shoes nor stockings to wear, and the comfort after slaving during master's pleasure, what rest we can get is to wrap ourselves up in a blanket and lie upon the ground. This is the deplorable condition your poor Betty endures, and now I beg if you have any bowels of compassion left show it by sending me some relief. Clothing is the principal thing wanting, which if you should condescend to, may easily send them to me by any of the ships bound to Baltimore town, Patapsco River, Maryland. And give me leave to conclude in duty to you and uncles and aunts, and respect to all friends. . . . Elizabeth Sprigs.

QUESTIONS

1. *What does the Maryland law tell us about how the consolidation of slavery affected ideas about racial difference?*
2. *Why does Elizabeth Sprigs compare her condition unfavorably to that of blacks?*
3. *What do these documents suggest about the limits of freedom in early colonial America?*

Bacon's supporters

Bacon's call for the removal of all Indians from the colony, a reduction of taxes at a time of economic recession, and an end to rule by "grandees" rapidly gained support from small farmers, landless men, indentured servants, and even some Africans. The bulk of his army consisted of discontented men who had recently been servants.

Bacon promised freedom (including access to Indian lands) to all who joined his ranks. In 1676, Bacon gathered an armed force for an unauthorized and indiscriminate campaign against those he called the governor's "protected and darling Indians." He marched on Jamestown, burning it to the ground. The governor fled, and Bacon became the ruler of Virginia. Only the arrival of a squadron of warships from England restored order.

Effects of Bacon's Rebellion

The specter of a civil war among whites greatly frightened Virginia's ruling elite, who took dramatic steps to consolidate their power and improve their image after Bacon's death in October 1676. They restored property qualifications for voting, which Bacon had rescinded, and reduced taxes. They also adopted a more aggressive Indian policy, opening western areas to small farmers, many of whom prospered from a rise in tobacco prices after 1680. To avert the further growth of a rebellious population of landless former indentured servants, Virginia's authorities accelerated the shift to slaves (who would never become free) on the tobacco plantations.

A Slave Society

The spread of slavery

Between 1680 and 1700, slave labor began to supplant indentured servitude on Chesapeake plantations. Bacon's Rebellion contributed to this development, but so did other factors. As the death rate began to fall, it became more economical to purchase a laborer for life. Moreover, the Royal Africa Company's monopoly on the English slave trade ended, thus opening the door to other traders and reducing the price of imported African slaves.

Slave code of 1705

By 1700, blacks constituted more than 10 percent of Virginia's population. Fifty years later, they made up nearly half. Recognizing the growing importance of slavery, the House of Burgesses in 1705 enacted a new slave code. Slaves were property, completely subject to the will of their masters and, more generally, of the white community. They could be bought and sold, leased, fought over in court, and passed on to one's descendants. Henceforth, blacks and whites were tried in separate courts. No black, free or slave, could own arms, strike a white man, or employ a white servant. Virginia had changed from a "society with slaves," in which slavery was one system of labor among others, to a "slave society," where slavery stood at the center of the economic process.

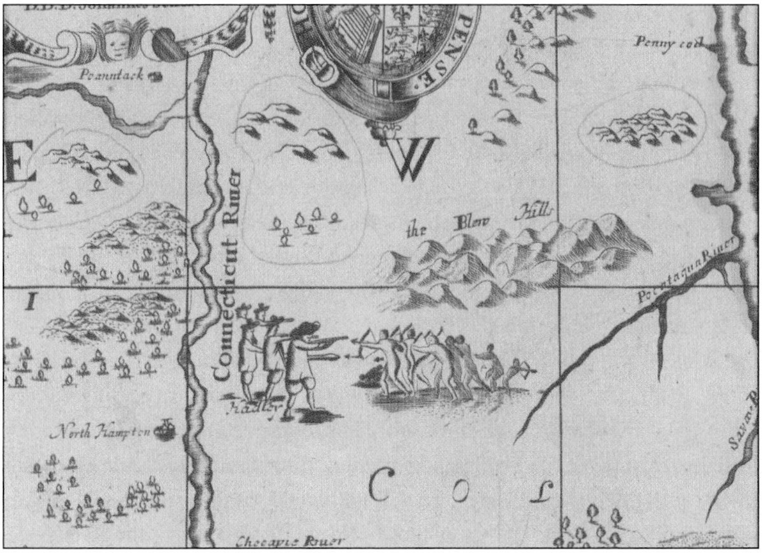

A scene from King Philip's War, included on a 1675 map of New England.

Throughout history, slaves have run away and in other ways resisted bondage. Colonial newspapers were filled with advertisements for runaway slaves. These notices described the appearance and skills of the fugitive and included such comments as "He has great notions of freedom."

Runaway slaves

COLONIES IN CRISIS

King Philip's War of 1675–1676 and Bacon's Rebellion the following year coincided with disturbances in other colonies. In Maryland, where the proprietor, Lord Baltimore, in 1670 suddenly restricted the right to vote to owners of fifty acres of land or a certain amount of personal property, a Protestant uprising unsuccessfully sought to oust his government and restore the suffrage for all freemen. In several colonies, increasing settlement on the frontier led to resistance by alarmed Indians. The Pueblo Revolt of 1680 (discussed in Chapter 1) indicated that the crisis of colonial authority was not confined to the British empire.

Uprisings

The Glorious Revolution

Turmoil in England also reverberated in the colonies. In 1688, the long struggle for domination of English government between Parliament and the crown reached its culmination in the **Glorious Revolution**, which established parliamentary supremacy once and for all and secured the

Parliamentary supremacy

Protestant succession to the throne. When Charles II died in 1685, he was succeeded by his brother James II (formerly the duke of York), a practicing Catholic and a believer that kings ruled by divine right. In 1687, James decreed religious toleration for both Protestant Dissenters and Catholics. The following year, the birth of James's son raised the alarming prospect of a Catholic succession. A group of English aristocrats invited the Dutch nobleman William of Orange, the husband of James's Protestant daughter Mary, to assume the throne in the name of English liberties. As the landed elite and leaders of the Anglican Church rallied to William's cause, James II fled and the revolution was complete.

Unlike the broad social upheaval that marked the English Civil War of the 1640s, the Glorious Revolution was in effect a coup engineered by a group of aristocrats in alliance with an ambitious Dutch prince. But the overthrow of James II entrenched more firmly than ever the notion that liberty was the birthright of all Englishmen and that the king was subject to the rule of law. To justify the ouster of James II, Parliament in 1689 enacted an **English Bill of Rights**, which listed parliamentary powers such as control over taxation as well as rights of individuals, including trial by jury. In the same year, the Toleration Act allowed Protestant Dissenters (but not Catholics) to worship freely, although only Anglicans could hold public office.

Liberty as the birthright of all Englishmen

As always, British politics were mirrored in the American colonies. After the Glorious Revolution, Protestant domination was secured in most of the colonies, while Catholics and Dissenters suffered various forms of discrimination. Throughout English America the Glorious Revolution powerfully reinforced among the colonists the sense of sharing a proud legacy of freedom and Protestantism with the mother country.

Effects of the Glorious Revolution

The Glorious Revolution in America

The Glorious Revolution exposed fault lines in colonial society and offered local elites an opportunity to regain authority that had recently been challenged. Until the mid-1670s, the North American colonies had essentially governed themselves, with little interference from England. Governor Berkeley ran Virginia as he saw fit; proprietors in New York, Maryland, and Carolina governed in any fashion they could persuade colonists to accept; and New England colonies elected their own officials and openly flouted trade regulations. In 1675, however, England established the **Lords of Trade** to oversee colonial affairs. Three years later, the Lords questioned the Massachusetts government about its compliance with the Navigation Acts. They received the surprising reply that since the colony had no representatives in Parliament, the acts did not apply to it unless the Massachusetts General Court approved.

English oversight

English authority and colonial autonomy

In the 1680s, England moved to reduce colonial autonomy. Shortly before his death, James II between 1686 and 1689 combined Connecticut, Plymouth, Massachusetts, New Hampshire, Rhode Island, New York, and East and West Jersey into a single super-colony, the **Dominion of New England**. It was ruled by the former New York governor Sir Edmund Andros, who did not have to answer to an elected assembly. These events reinforced the impression that James II was an enemy of freedom.

Rebellions in American colonies

In 1689, news of the overthrow of James II triggered rebellions in several American colonies. In April, the Boston militia seized and jailed Edmund Andros and other officials, whereupon the New England colonies reestablished the governments abolished when the Dominion of New England was created. In May, a rebel militia headed by Captain Jacob Leisler established a Committee of Safety and took control of New York. Two months later, Maryland's Protestant Association overthrew the government of the colony's Catholic proprietor, Lord Baltimore.

All of these new regimes claimed to have acted in the name of English liberties and looked to London for approval. But the degrees of success of these coups varied markedly. Concluding that Lord Baltimore had mismanaged the Maryland colony, William revoked his charter (although the proprietor retained his land and rents) and established a new, Protestant-dominated government. In 1715, after the Baltimore family had converted to Anglicanism, proprietary power was restored. But the events of 1689 transformed the ruling group in Maryland and put an end to the colony's unique history of religious toleration.

Turmoil in New York

The outcome in New York was far different. Although it was not his intention, Jacob Leisler's regime divided the colony along ethnic and economic lines. Members of the Dutch majority reclaimed local power after more than two decades of English rule, while bands of rebels ransacked the homes of wealthy New Yorkers. William refused to recognize Leisler's authority and dispatched a new governor, backed by troops. Many of Leisler's followers were imprisoned, and he himself was executed. For generations, the rivalry between Leisler and anti-Leisler parties polarized New York politics.

Political change in Massachusetts

The New England colonies, after deposing Governor Andros, lobbied hard in London for the restoration of their original charters. Most were successful, but Massachusetts was not. In 1691, the crown issued a new charter that absorbed Plymouth into Massachusetts and transformed the political structure of the Bible Commonwealth. Town government remained intact, but henceforth property ownership, not church membership, would be the requirement to vote in elections for the General Court. The governor was now appointed in London rather than elected. Massachusetts became a royal colony, the majority of whose voters were no longer Puritan "saints." Moreover, it was required to abide by the **English Toleration Act** of 1690—that is, to allow all Protestants to worship freely.

These events produced an atmosphere of considerable tension in Massachusetts, exacerbated by raids by French troops and their Indian allies on the northern New England frontier. The advent of religious toleration heightened anxieties among the Puritan clergy, who considered other Protestant denominations a form of heresy. Indeed, not a few Puritans thought they saw the hand of Satan in the events of 1690 and 1691.

The Salem Witch Trials

Belief in witchcraft

Belief in magic, astrology, and witchcraft was widespread in seventeenth-century Europe and America, existing alongside the religious beliefs sanctioned by the clergy and churches. Witches were individuals, usually women, who were accused of having entered into a pact with the devil to obtain supernatural powers, which they used to harm others or to interfere with natural processes. When a child was stillborn or crops failed, many believed that witchcraft was at work.

In Europe and the colonies, witchcraft was punishable by execution. It is estimated that between the years 1400 and 1800, more than 50,000 people were executed in Europe after being convicted of witchcraft. Witches were, from time to time, hanged in seventeenth-century New England. Most were women beyond childbearing age who were outspoken, economically independent, or estranged from their husbands, or who in other ways violated traditional gender norms.

Until 1692, the prosecution of witches had been sporadic. But in that year, a series of trials and executions took place in Salem, Massachusetts, that made its name to this day a byword for fanaticism and persecution. The **Salem witch trials** began when several young girls began to suffer fits and nightmares, attributed by their elders to witchcraft. Soon, three "witches" had been named, including Tituba, an Indian from the Caribbean who was a slave in the home of one of the girls. Since the only way to avoid prosecution was to confess and name others, accusations of witchcraft began to snowball. By the middle of 1692, hundreds of residents of Salem had come forward to accuse their neighbors. Although many of the accused confessed to save their lives, fourteen women and five men were hanged, protesting their innocence to the end.

An engraving from Ralph Gardiner's *England's Grievance Discovered*, published in 1655, depicts women hanged as witches in England. The letters identify local officials: A is the hangman, B the town crier, C the sheriff, and D a magistrate.

As accusations and executions multiplied, it became clear that something was seriously wrong with the colony's system of justice. The governor of Massachusetts dissolved the Salem court and ordered the remaining prisoners released. The events in Salem discredited the tradition of prosecuting witches and encouraged prominent colonists to seek scientific explanations for natural events such as comets and illnesses, rather than attribute them to magic.

THE GROWTH OF COLONIAL AMERICA

As stability returned after the crises of the late seventeenth century, English North America experienced an era of remarkable growth. Between 1700 and 1770, crude backwoods settlements became bustling provincial capitals. The hazards of disease among colonists diminished, agricultural settlement pressed westward, and hundreds of thousands of newcomers arrived from the Old World. Thanks to a high birthrate and continuing immigration, the population of England's mainland colonies, 265,000 in 1700, grew nearly tenfold, to over 2.3 million seventy years later. (It is worth noting, however, that because of the decline suffered by the Indians, the North American population was considerably lower in 1770 than it had been in 1492.)

Population increase

A Diverse Population

Probably the most striking characteristic of colonial American society in the eighteenth century was its sheer diversity. In 1700, the colonies were essentially English outposts. In the eighteenth century, African and non-English European arrivals skyrocketed, while the number emigrating from England declined.

African and non-English arrivals surge

About 40 percent of European immigrants to the colonies during the eighteenth century continued to arrive as bound laborers who had temporarily sacrificed their freedom to make the voyage to the New World. But as the colonial economy prospered, poor indentured migrants were increasingly joined by professionals and skilled craftsmen—teachers, ministers, weavers, carpenters—whom England could ill afford to lose. This brought to an end official efforts to promote English emigration.

End of official English emigration efforts

Nevertheless, the government in London remained convinced that colonial development enhanced the nation's power and wealth. To bolster the Chesapeake labor force, nearly 50,000 convicts were sent to work in the tobacco fields. Officials also encouraged Protestant immigration from

TABLE 3.1 Origins and Status of Migrants to British North American Colonies, 1700–1775

	TOTAL	SLAVES	INDENTURED SERVANTS	CONVICTS	FREE
Africa	278,400	278,400	—	—	—
Ireland	108,600	—	39,000	17,500	52,100
Germany	84,500	—	30,000	—	54,500
England/Wales	73,100	—	27,200	32,500	13,400
Scotland	35,300	—	7,400	2,200	25,700
Other	5,900	—	—	—	5,900
Total	585,800	278,400	103,600	52,200	151,600

the non-English parts of the British Isles and from the European continent, promising newcomers access to land and the right to worship freely.

Among eighteenth-century migrants from the British Isles, the 70,000 English newcomers were considerably outnumbered by 145,000 from Scotland and Ulster, the northern part of Ireland, where many Scots had settled as part of England's effort to subdue the island. Mostly Presbyterians, they added significantly to religious diversity in North America.

The German Migration

Germans the largest group of newcomers from Europe

Germans, 85,000 in all, formed the largest group of newcomers from the European continent. In the eighteenth century, Germany was divided into numerous small states, each with a ruling prince who determined the official religion. Those who found themselves worshiping the "wrong" religion—Lutherans in Catholic areas, Catholics in Lutheran areas, and everywhere, followers of small Protestant sects such as Mennonites, Moravians, and Dunkers—faced persecution. Many decided to emigrate. Other migrants were motivated by persistent agricultural crises and the difficulty of acquiring land.

German settlements

English and Dutch merchants created a well-organized system whereby **redemptioners** (as indentured families were called) received passage in exchange for a promise to work off their debt in America. Most settled in frontier areas—rural New York, western Pennsylvania, and the southern backcountry—where they formed tightly knit farming communities in which German remained the dominant language.

EUROPEAN SETTLEMENT AND ETHNIC DIVERSITY ON THE ATLANTIC COAST OF NORTH AMERICA, 1760

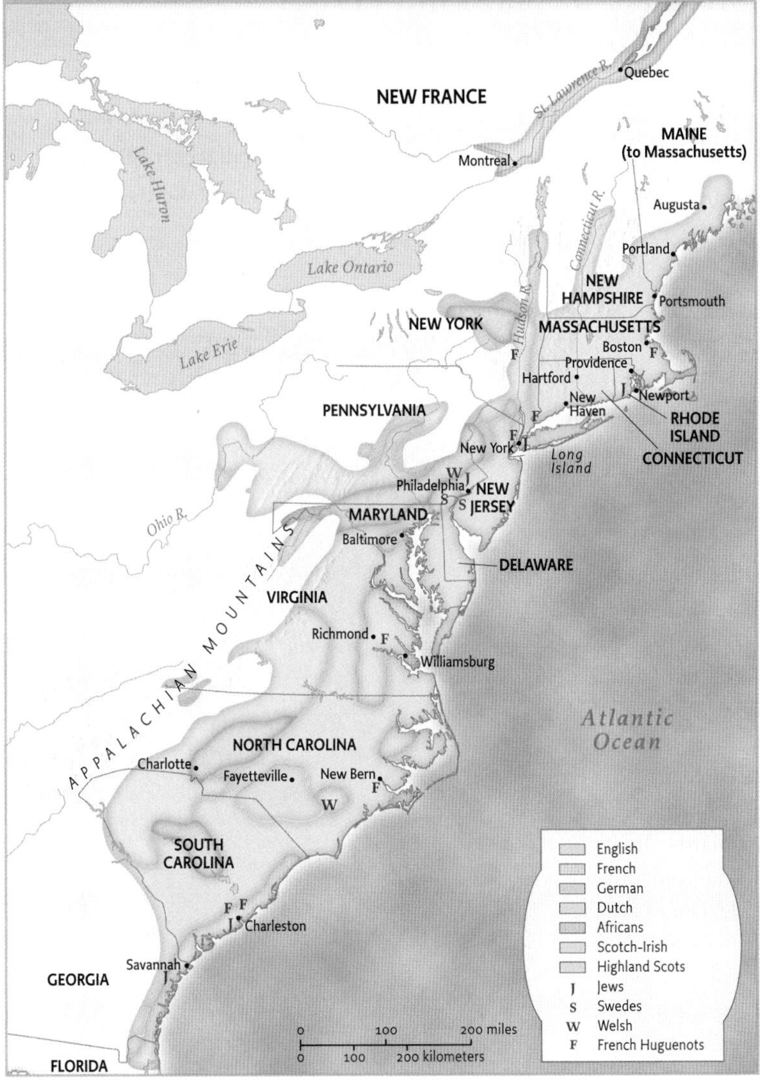

Among the most striking features of eighteenth-century colonial society was the racial and ethnic diversity of the population (except in New England). This resulted from increased immigration from the non-English parts of the British Isles and from mainland Europe, as well as the rapid expansion of the slave trade from Africa.

Religious Diversity

Eighteenth-century British America was not a "melting pot" of cultures. Ethnic groups tended to live and worship in relatively homogeneous communities. But outside of New England, which received few immigrants and retained its overwhelmingly English ethnic character, American society

American society more diverse than Britain

WHO IS AN AMERICAN?

From Benjamin Franklin, *Observations Concerning the Increase of Mankind* (1751)

Only a minority of immigrants from Europe to British North America in the eighteenth century came from the British Isles. Some prominent colonists found the growing diversity of the population quite disturbing. Benjamin Franklin was particularly troubled by the large influx of newcomers from Germany into Pennsylvania in the mid-eighteenth century.

Why should the Palatine [German] boors be suffered to swarm into our settlements, and by herding together establish their language and manners to the exclusion of ours? Why should Pennsylvania, founded by the English, become a Colony of *Aliens*, who will shortly be so numerous as to Germanize us instead of our Anglifying them, and will never adopt our language or customs, any more than they can acquire our complexion?

Which leads me to add one remark: That the number of purely white people in the world is proportionably very small. All Africa is black or tawny. Asia chiefly tawny. America (exclusive of the newcomers) wholly so. And in Europe, the Spaniards, Italians, French, Russians and Swedes, are generally of what we call a swarthy complexion; as are the Germans also, the Saxons only excepted, who with the English, make the principal body of white people on the face of the earth. I could wish their numbers were increased. And while we are, as I may call it, *scouring* our planet, by clearing America of woods, and so making this side of our globe reflect a brighter light to the eyes of inhabitants in Mars or Venus, why should we . . . darken its people? Why increase the sons of Africa, by planting them in America, where we have so fair an opportunity, by excluding all Blacks and Tawneys, of increasing the lovely White and Red? But perhaps I am partial to the complexion of my country, for such kind of partiality is natural to mankind.

QUESTIONS

1. *What is Franklin's objection to the growing German presence?*
2. *What does Franklin's characterization of the complexions of various groups suggest about the reliability of his perceptions of non-English peoples?*

had a far more diverse population than Britain. Nowhere was this more evident than in the practice of religion.

Apart from New Jersey (formed from East and West Jersey in 1702), Rhode Island, and Pennsylvania, the colonies did not adhere to a modern separation of church and state. Nearly every colony levied taxes to pay the salaries of ministers of an established church, and most barred Catholics and Jews from voting and holding public office. But increasingly, de facto toleration among Protestant denominations flourished. By the mid-eighteenth century, dissenting Protestants in most colonies had gained the right to worship as they pleased and own their churches, although many places still barred them from holding public office and taxed them to support the official church. A visitor to Pennsylvania in 1750 described the colony's religious diversity: "We find there Lutherans, Reformed, Catholics, Quakers, Menonists or Anabaptists, Herrnhuters or Moravian Brethren, Pietists, Seventh Day Baptists, Dunkers, Presbyterians, . . . Jews, Mohammedans, Pagans."

Protestants

Indian Life in Transition

The tide of newcomers, who equated liberty with secure possession of land, threatened to engulf the surviving Indian populations. By the eighteenth century, Indian societies that had existed for centuries had disappeared, the victims of disease and warfare, and the communities that remained were well integrated into the British imperial system. Indeed, Indian warriors did much of the fighting in the century's imperial wars. Few Indians chose to live among whites rather than in their own communities. But they had become well accustomed to using European products such as knives, hatchets, needles, kettles, and firearms. Alcohol introduced by traders created social chaos in many Indian communities. One Cherokee told the governor of South Carolina in 1753, "The clothes we wear, we cannot make ourselves. . . . We use their ammunition with which we kill deer. . . . Every necessary thing we must have from the white people."

Indians and European empire

While traders saw in Indian villages potential profits and British officials saw allies against France and Spain, farmers and planters viewed Indians as little more than an obstacle to their desire for land. They expected Indians to give way to white settlers. In Pennsylvania, for example, the flood of German and Scotch-Irish settlers into the backcountry upset the relatively peaceful Indian–white relations constructed by William Penn. The infamous **Walking Purchase** of 1737 brought the fraudulent dealing so common in other colonies to Pennsylvania. The Lenni Lanape Indians agreed to cede a tract of land bounded by the distance a man could walk in thirty-six hours. To their amazement, Governor James Logan hired a team of swift runners, who marked out an area far in excess of

America was often depicted as a Native American in the colonial era, as in this print from the first half of the eighteenth century.

William Penn's Treaty with the Indians. Penn's grandson, Thomas, the proprietor of Pennsylvania, commissioned this romanticized painting from the artist Benjamin West in 1771, by which time harmony between Indians and colonists had long since turned to hostility. In the nineteenth century, many reproductions of this image circulated, reminding Americans that Indians had once been central figures in their history.

what the Indians had anticipated. By 1760, when Pennsylvania's population, a mere 20,000 in 1700, had grown to 220,000, Indian-colonist relations, initially the most harmonious in British North America, had become poisoned by suspicion and hostility.

Regional Diversity

By the mid-eighteenth century, the different regions of the British colonies had developed distinct economic and social orders. Small farms tilled by family labor and geared primarily to production for local consumption predominated in New England and the new settlements of the **backcountry** (the area stretching from central Pennsylvania southward through the Shenandoah Valley of Virginia and into upland North and South Carolina). The backcountry was the most rapidly growing region in North America. By the eve of the American Revolution, it contained one-quarter of Virginia's population and half of South Carolina's. Most were farm families raising grain and livestock.

In the older portions of the Middle Colonies of New York, New Jersey, and Pennsylvania, farmers were more oriented to commerce than on the frontier. They grew grain both for their own use and for sale abroad and supplemented the work of family members by employing wage laborers, tenants, and in some instances slaves. With its fertile soil, favorable climate, initially peaceful Indian relations, generous governmental land distribution policy, and rivers that facilitated long-distance trading, Pennsylvania came to be known as "the best poor man's country." Ordinary colonists there enjoyed a standard of living unimaginable in Europe.

The Consumer Revolution

Inexpensive consumer goods

During the eighteenth century, Great Britain eclipsed the Dutch as the leading producer and trader of inexpensive consumer goods, including colonial products like coffee and tea, and such manufactured goods as linen, metalware, pins, ribbons, glassware, ceramics, and clothing. Trade integrated the British empire. The American colonies shared in the era's consumer revolution. In port cities and small inland towns, shops proliferated and American newspapers were filled with advertisements for British goods.

Consumerism in a modern sense—the mass production, advertising, and sale of consumer goods—did not exist in colonial America. Nonetheless, even modest farmers and artisans owned books, ceramic plates, metal cutlery, and items made of imported silk and cotton. Tea, once a luxury enjoyed only by the wealthy, became virtually a necessity of life.

Colonial Cities

Colonial cities like Boston, New York, Philadelphia, and Charleston were quite small by the standards of Europe or Spanish America. In 1700, when the population of Mexico City stood at 100,000, Boston had 6,000 residents and New York 4,500.

The rise of port cities

English American cities were mainly gathering places for agricultural goods and for imported items to be distributed to the countryside. Nonetheless, the expansion of trade encouraged the rise of port cities, home to a growing population of colonial merchants and artisans (skilled craftsmen) as well as an increasing number of poor. In 1770, with some 30,000 inhabitants, Philadelphia was "the capital of the New World," at least its British component, and, after London and Liverpool, the empire's third busiest port. The financial, commercial, and cultural center of British America, Philadelphia founded its growth on economic integration with the rich agricultural region nearby. Philadelphia merchants organized the collection of farm goods, supplied rural storekeepers, and extended credit to consumers. They exported flour, bread, and meat to the West Indies and Europe.

The city was also home to a large population of furniture makers, jewelers, and silversmiths serving wealthier citizens, and hundreds of lesser artisans like weavers, blacksmiths, coopers, and construction workers. The typical artisan owned his own tools and labored in a small workshop, often his home, assisted by family members and young journeymen and apprentices learning the trade. The artisan's skill gave him a far greater degree of economic freedom than those dependent on others for a livelihood.

American craftsmen and the expanding consumer market

Despite the influx of British goods, American craftsmen benefited from the expanding consumer market. Most journeymen enjoyed a reasonable chance of rising to the status of master and establishing workshops of their own.

An Atlantic World

Trade in the Atlantic world

People, ideas, and goods flowed back and forth across the Atlantic, knitting together the empire and its diverse populations and creating webs of interdependence among the European empires. As trade expanded, the North American and West Indian colonies became the major overseas market for British manufactured goods. Although most colonial output was consumed at home, North Americans shipped farm products to Britain, the West Indies, and, with the exception of goods like tobacco "enumerated" under the Navigation Acts, outside the empire. Virtually the entire Chesapeake tobacco crop was marketed in Britain, with most of it then re-exported to Europe by British merchants. Most of the bread and flour exported from the colonies was destined for the West Indies. African slaves there grew sugar that could be distilled into rum, a product increasingly popular among both North American colonists and Indians, who obtained it by trading furs and deerskins that were then shipped to Europe. The mainland colonies carried on a flourishing trade in fish and grains with southern Europe. Ships built in New England made up one-third of the British empire's trading fleet.

Membership in the empire had many advantages for the colonists. Most Americans did not complain about British regulation of their trade because commerce enriched the colonies as well as the mother country and lax enforcement of the Navigation Acts allowed smuggling to flourish. In a dangerous world, moreover, the Royal Navy protected American shipping. Eighteenth-century English America drew closer to, and in some ways became more similar to, the mother country across the Atlantic.

This portrait of Jane Beekman—daughter of James Beekman, one of the wealthiest colonists—was painted by the artist John Durand in 1767. It is unusual in depicting a young girl with a book (a collection, in Latin, of the works of the Renaissance scholar Erasmus), rather than simply emphasizing fashionable attire. The Beekman family was of Dutch and French Huguenot heritage, and both cultures emphasized the importance of education, including education for women.

SOCIAL CLASSES IN THE COLONIES

The Colonial Elite

Most free Americans benefited from economic growth, but as colonial society matured an elite emerged that, while neither as powerful nor as wealthy as the aristocracy of England, increasingly dominated politics and society. In New England and the Middle Colonies, expanding trade made possible the emergence of a powerful upper class of merchants, often linked by family or commercial ties to great trading firms in London. By 1750, the Chesapeake and Lower South were dominated by slave plantations producing **staple crops**, especially tobacco and rice, for the world market. Here great planters accumulated enormous wealth. The colonial elite also included the rulers of proprietary colonies like Pennsylvania and Maryland.

America had no titled aristocracy as in Britain. But throughout British America, men of prominence controlled colonial government. In Virginia, the upper class was so tightly knit and intermarried so often that the colony was said to be governed by a "cousinocracy." Nearly every Virginian of note achieved prominence through family connections. Thomas Jefferson's grandfather was a justice of the peace (an important local official), militia captain, and sheriff, and his father a member of the House of Burgesses. George Washington's father, grandfather, and great-grandfather had been justices of the peace. The Virginia gentry used its control of provincial government to gain possession of large tracts of land as western areas opened for settlement.

The richest group of mainland colonists were South Carolina planters. Like their Virginia counterparts, South Carolina grandees lived a lavish lifestyle amid imported furniture, fine wines, silk clothing, and other items from England. Their wealth enabled them to spend much of their time enjoying the social life of Charleston, the only real urban center south of Philadelphia and the richest city in British North America.

Robert "King" Carter of Virginia, painted by an unknown artist around 1720. Carter was one of the wealthiest and most influential men in the colonies. At his death he owned 300,000 acres of land and over 700 slaves. He served twice as Speaker of the House of Burgesses and once as governor. He is dressed in the attire of an English gentleman.

New World Cultures

Before the American Revolution, there was no real "American" identity. In the seventeenth century, the term "Americans" tended to be used to describe Indians rather than colonists. Europeans often depicted the colonies pictorially with an image of a Native American. Many European immigrants maintained traditions, including the use of languages other than English, from their home countries. Some cultures mixed more than others: intermarriage with other groups was more common among Huguenots (French Protestants) than among Jews, for example. Those from the British Isles sought to create a dominant "English" identity in the New World. This involved convincing Britons that the colonists were like themselves.

Many in Great Britain, however, saw the colonists as a collection of convicts, religious dissidents, and impoverished servants. This, in turn, inspired many colonists to assert a claim to Britishness more strongly. They insisted that British identity meant allegiance to certain values, among them free commerce and "English liberty." Yet many colonists saw some people, including American Indians and Africans, as unable to wield the responsibilities of liberty due to their place of birth, culture, or inborn traits. They must be ruled over, not take part in governance.

British identity in the colonies was defined, in part, in opposition to others, including Spanish and French Catholics, Africans, and Native Americans. As early as the late sixteenth century, in his writings on colonization, Richard Hakluyt wrote that there was "no greater glory" than "to conquer the barbarian, to recall the savage and the pagan to civility, to

Fashionably dressed twelve-year-old Ralph Izard, painted in 1754 by Jeremiah Theus, just before Izard's departure to receive an education in England. The boy had recently inherited a large plantation in South Carolina, upon the death of his parents.

draw the ignorant within the orbit of reason, and to fill with reverence for divinity the godless and the ungodly." But since most Indians preferred to maintain their own cultures and religions, the colonists did not include them in a collective colonial identity. This was a major difference with the Spanish and French New World Empires, where, as noted in Chapter 1, intermarriage and culture exchange between settlers and Indians were far more common.

Anglicization

For much of the eighteenth century, the American colonies had more regular trade and communications with Britain than among themselves. Rather than thinking of themselves as distinctively American, they became more and more English—a process historians call "Anglicization."

Wealthy Americans tried to model their lives on British etiquette and behavior. Somewhat resentful at living in provincial isolation—"at the end of the world," as one Virginia aristocrat put it—they sought to demonstrate their status and legitimacy by importing the latest London fashions and literature, sending their sons to Britain for education, and building homes equipped with fashionable furnishings modeled on the country estates and town houses of the English gentry.

Throughout the colonies, elites emulated what they saw as England's balanced, stable social order. Liberty, in their eyes, meant, in part, the power to rule—the right of those blessed with wealth and prominence to dominate others. They viewed society as a hierarchical structure in which some men were endowed with greater talents than others and were destined to govern. Each place in the hierarchy carried with it different responsibilities, and one's status was revealed in dress, manners, and the splendor of one's home. On both sides of the Atlantic, elites viewed work as something reserved for common folk and slaves. Freedom from labor was the mark of the gentleman.

Poverty in the Colonies

At the other end of the social scale, poverty emerged as a visible feature of eighteenth-century colonial life. Although not considered by most colonists part of their society, the growing number of slaves lived in impoverished conditions. Among free Americans, poverty was hardly as widespread as in Britain, where in the early part of the century between one-quarter and one-half of the people regularly required public assistance. But as the colonial population expanded, access to land diminished rapidly, especially in long-settled areas, forcing many propertyless males to seek work in their region's cities or in other colonies. In colonial cities, the number of propertyless wage earners subsisting at the poverty line steadily increased. Taking the colonies as a whole, half of the wealth at mid-century was concentrated in the hands of the richest 10 percent of the population.

Increase in poverty in eighteenth-century colonies

Attitudes and policies toward poverty in colonial America mirrored British precedents. The better-off colonists generally viewed the poor as lazy, shiftless, and responsible for their own plight. To minimize the burden on taxpayers, poor persons were frequently set to labor in workhouses, where they produced goods that reimbursed authorities for part of their upkeep.

The Middle Ranks

The large majority of free Americans lived between the extremes of wealth and poverty. Along with racial and ethnic diversity, what distinguished the mainland colonies from Europe was the wide distribution of land and the economic autonomy of most ordinary free families. Altogether, perhaps two-thirds of the free male population were farmers who owned their own land.

By the eighteenth century, colonial farm families viewed landownership almost as a right, the social precondition of freedom. They strongly resented efforts, whether by Native Americans, great landlords, or colonial governments, to limit their access to land. A dislike of personal dependence and an understanding of freedom as not relying on others for a livelihood sank deep roots in British North America.

Women and the Household Economy

In the household economy of eighteenth-century America, the family was the center of economic life. The independence of the small farmer depended in considerable measure on the labor of dependent women and children. "He that hath an industrious family shall soon be rich," declared one colonial saying, and the high birthrate in part reflected the need for as many hands as possible on colonial farms.

This portrait of the Cheney family by an unknown late-eighteenth-century artist illustrates the high birthrate in colonial America and suggests how many years of a woman's life were spent bearing and raising children.

As the population grew and the death rate declined, family life stabilized and more marriages became lifetime commitments. Free women were expected to devote their lives to being good wives and mothers. As colonial society became more structured, opportunities that had existed for women in the early period receded. In Connecticut, for example, the courts were informal and unorganized in the seventeenth century, and women often represented themselves. In the eighteenth century, it became necessary to hire a lawyer as one's spokesman in court. Women, barred from practicing as attorneys, disappeared from judicial proceedings. Because of the desperate need for labor in the seventeenth century, men and women both did various kinds of work. In the eighteenth century, the division of labor along gender lines solidified. Women's work was clearly defined, including cooking, cleaning, sewing, making butter, and assisting with agricultural chores. Even as the consumer revolution reduced the demands on many women by making available store-bought goods previously produced at home, women's work seemed to increase. Lower infant mortality meant more time spent in child care and domestic chores.

Division of labor along gender lines

North America at Mid-Century

By the mid-eighteenth century, the area that would become the United States was home to a remarkable diversity of peoples and different kinds of social organization, from Pueblo villages of the Southwest to tobacco plantations of the Chesapeake, towns and small farms of New England, and fur-trading outposts of the northern and western frontier. Elites tied to imperial centers of power dominated the political and economic life of nearly every colony. But large numbers of colonists enjoyed far greater opportunities for freedom—access to the vote, prospects of acquiring land, the right to worship as they pleased, and an escape from oppressive government—than existed in Europe. The colonies' economic growth contributed to a high birthrate, long life expectancy, and expanding demand for consumer goods.

Opportunities for freedom

Yet many others found themselves confined to the partial freedom of indentured servitude or to the complete absence of freedom in slavery. Both timeless longings for freedom and new and unprecedented forms of unfreedom had been essential to the North American colonies' remarkable development.

Freedom and unfreedom

CHAPTER REVIEW AND ONLINE RESOURCES

REVIEW QUESTIONS

1. *Both the Puritans and William Penn viewed their colonies as "holy experiments." How did they differ?*
2. *The textbook states, "Prejudice by itself did not create North American slavery." Examine the economic forces, events, and laws that shaped the experiences of enslaved people.*
3. *How did English leaders understand the place and role of the American colonies in England's empire?*
4. *How did King Philip's War, Bacon's Rebellion, and the Salem witch trials illustrate a widespread crisis in British North America in the late seventeenth century?*
5. *The social structure of the eighteenth-century colonies was growing more open for some but not for others. Consider the statement with respect to men and women, whites and blacks, and rich and poor.*
6. *By the end of the seventeenth century, commerce was the foundation of empire and the leading cause of competition between European empires. Explain how the North American colonies were directly linked to Atlantic commerce by laws and trade.*
7. *If you traveled from New England to the South, how would you describe the diversity you saw between the different colonies?*
8. *What impact did the family's being the center of economic life have on gender relations and the roles of women?*
9. *Why did the colonists identify themselves as British through the mid-eighteenth century?*

KEY TERMS

Metacom (p. 73)
King Philip's War (p. 73)
mercantilism (p. 73)
Navigation Act (p. 74)
Covenant Chain (p. 76)
Yamasee uprising (p. 77)
Society of Friends (Quakers) (p. 78)
plantation (p. 80)
Bacon's Rebellion (p. 83)
Glorious Revolution (p. 87)
English Bill of Rights (p. 88)
Lords of Trade (p. 88)
Dominion of New England (p. 89)
English Toleration Act (p. 90)
Salem witch trials (p. 90)
redemptioners (p. 92)
Walking Purchase (p. 95)
backcountry (p. 96)
staple crops (p. 98)

Go to INQUIZITIVE

To see what you know—and learn what you've missed—with personalized feedback along the way.

Visit the ***Give Me Liberty!* Student Site** for primary source documents and images, interactive maps, author videos featuring Eric Foner, and more.

1689	Locke's *Two Treatises of Government* published
1707	Act of Union creating Great Britain
1712	Slave uprising in New York City
1718	French establish New Orleans
1728	*Pennsylvania Gazette* established
1730s	Beginnings of the Great Awakening
1732	Georgia colony founded
1735	John Peter Zenger tried for libel
1739	Stono Rebellion
1741	Rumors of slave revolt in New York
1749	Virginia awards land to the Ohio Company
1756–1763	Seven Years' War
1754	Albany Plan of Union proposed
1763	Pontiac's Rebellion
	Proclamation of 1763
1764	Paxton Boys march on Philadelphia
1769	Father Serra establishes first mission in California
1789	*The Interesting Narrative of the Life of Olaudah Equiano* published

CHAPTER 4

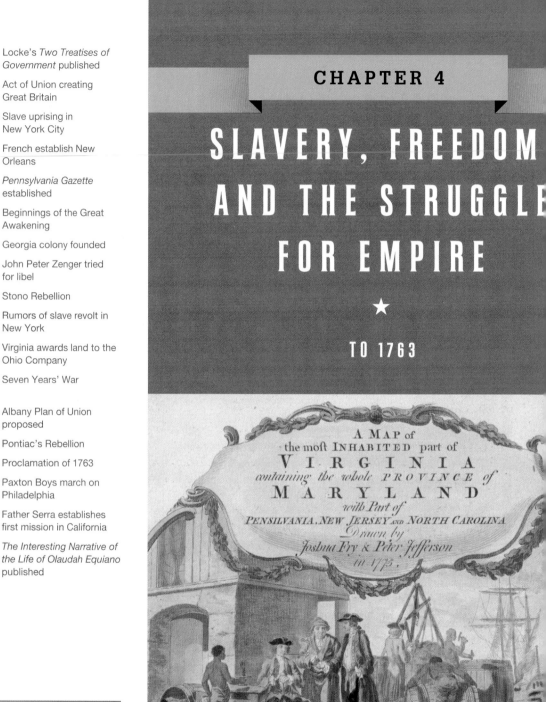

SLAVERY, FREEDOM AND THE STRUGGLE FOR EMPIRE

★

TO 1763

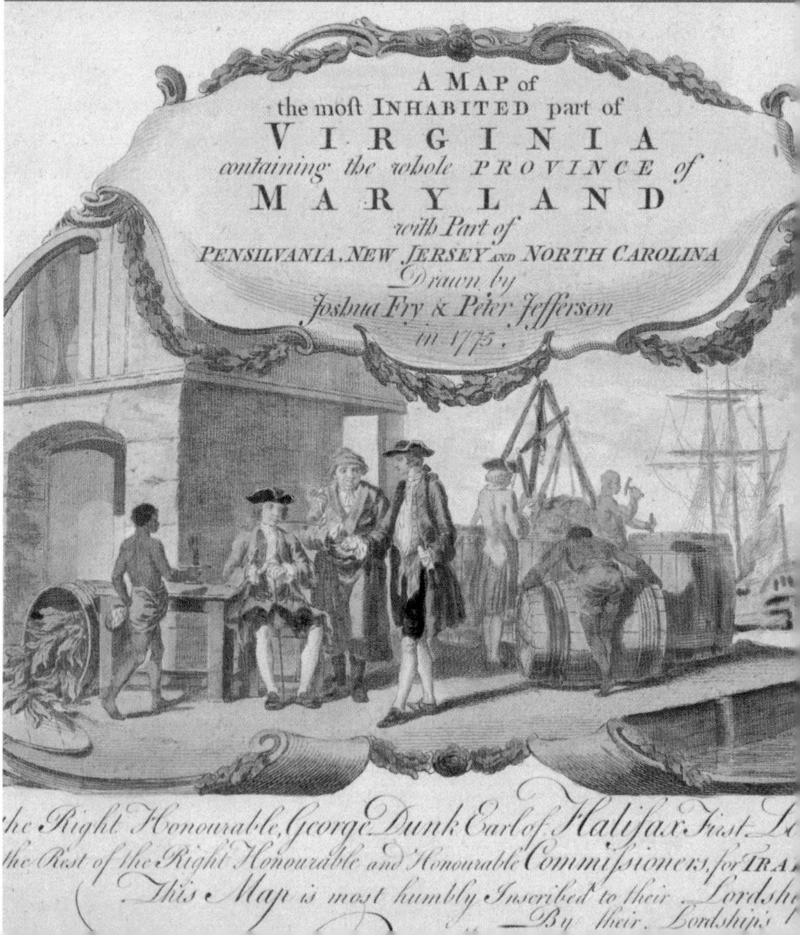

A MAP of
the most INHABITED part of
VIRGINIA
containing the whole PROVINCE of
MARYLAND
with Part of
PENSILVANIA, NEW JERSEY AND NORTH CAROLINA
Drawn by
Joshua Fry & Peter Jefferson
in 1775.
Right Honourable, George Dunk Earl of Halifax
the Rest of the Right Honourable and Honourable Commissioners, for
This Map is most humbly Inscribed to their
By their

A detail from a 1768 map of Virginia and Maryland depicts a tobacco wharf. A planter negotiates with a merchant or sea captain, while slaves go about their work.

Sometime in the mid-1750s, Olaudah Equiano, the eleven-year-old son of a West African village chief, was kidnapped by slave traders. He soon found himself on a ship headed for Barbados. Equiano was sold to a plantation owner in Virginia and then purchased by a British sea captain, who renamed him Gustavus Vassa. While still a slave, he enrolled in a school in England where he learned to read and write, and then enlisted in the Royal Navy. In 1763, however, Equiano was sold once again and returned to the Caribbean. Three years later, he purchased his freedom. He went on to experience shipwrecks, a colonizing venture in Central America, and even an expedition to the Arctic Circle. Equiano eventually settled in London, and in 1789 he published *The Interesting Narrative of the Life of Olaudah Equiano, or Gustavus Vassa, the African*, which he described as a "history of neither a saint, a hero, nor a tyrant," but of a victim of slavery who through luck or fate ended up more fortunate than most of his people. He condemned the idea that Africans were inferior to Europeans and therefore deserved to be slaves. The book became the era's most widely read account by a slave of his own experiences. Equiano died in 1797.

Recent scholars have suggested that Equiano may have been born in the New World rather than Africa. In either case, while his life was no doubt unusual, it illuminates broad patterns of eighteenth-century American history. As noted in the previous chapter, this was a period of sustained development for British North America. Compared with England and Scotland—united to create Great Britain by the Act of Union of 1707—the colonies were growing much more rapidly.

Ideas, people, and goods flowed back and forth across the ocean. Even as the colonies' populations became more diverse, they were increasingly integrated into the British empire. Their laws and political institutions were extensions of those of Britain, their ideas about society and culture reflected British values, their economies were geared to serving the empire's needs.

Equiano's life also underscores the greatest irony in the history of the eighteenth century—the simultaneous expansion of freedom and slavery. This was the era when the idea of the "freeborn Englishman" became powerfully entrenched in the outlook of both colonists and Britons. More than any other principle, liberty was seen as what made the British empire distinct. Yet the eighteenth century was also the height of the Atlantic slave trade, a commerce increasingly dominated by British merchants and ships. Slavery existed in every colony of British North America. And unlike Equiano, very few slaves were fortunate enough to gain their freedom.

FOCUS QUESTIONS

- *How did African slavery differ regionally in eighteenth-century North America?*
- *What factors led to distinct African-American cultures in the eighteenth century?*
- *What were the meanings of British liberty in the eighteenth century?*
- *What concepts and institutions dominated colonial politics in the eighteenth century?*
- *How did the Great Awakening challenge the religious and social structure of British North America?*
- *How did the Spanish and French empires in America develop in the eighteenth century?*
- *What was the impact of the Seven Years' War on imperial and Indian–white relations?*

The frontispiece of Olaudah Equiano's account of his life, the best-known narrative by an eighteenth-century slave. The portrait of Equiano in European dress and holding a Bible challenges stereotypes of blacks as "savages" incapable of becoming civilized.

SLAVERY AND EMPIRE

Of the Africans transported to the New World between 1492 and 1820, more than half arrived between 1700 and 1800. The **Atlantic slave trade** would later be condemned by statesmen and general opinion as a crime against humanity. But in the eighteenth century, it was a regularized business in which European merchants, African traders, and American planters engaged in complex bargaining over human lives, all with the expectation of securing a profit. The slave trade was a vital part of world commerce.

In the British empire of the eighteenth century, free laborers working for wages were atypical and slavery was the norm. The first mass consumer goods in international trade were produced by slaves—sugar, rice, coffee, and tobacco. The rising demand for these products fueled the rapid growth of the Atlantic slave trade.

Atlantic Trade

In the eighteenth century, the Caribbean remained the commercial focus of the British empire and the major producer of revenue for the crown. A series of triangular trading routes crisscrossed the Atlantic, carrying British manufactured goods to Africa and the colonies, colonial products to Europe, and slaves from Africa to the New World. Most colonial vessels, however, went back and forth between cities like New York, Charleston, and Savannah, and to ports in the Caribbean. Merchants in New York, Massachusetts, and Rhode Island participated actively in the slave trade, shipping slaves from Africa to the Caribbean or southern colonies. The slave economies of the West Indies were the largest market for fish, grain, livestock, and lumber exported from New England and the Middle Colonies. In Britain itself, the profits from slavery and the slave trade stimulated the rise of ports such as Liverpool and Bristol and the growth of banking, shipbuilding, and insurance. They also helped to finance the early industrial revolution.

Entrenchment of slavery

With slavery so central to Atlantic commerce, it should not be surprising that for large numbers of free colonists and Europeans, freedom meant in part the power and right to enslave others. And as slavery became more and more entrenched, so too, as the Quaker abolitionist John Woolman commented in 1762, did "the idea of slavery being connected with the black color, and liberty with the white."

Africa and the Slave Trade

A few African societies, like Benin for a time, opted out of the Atlantic slave trade, hoping to avoid the disruptions it inevitably caused. But most African

ATLANTIC TRADING ROUTES

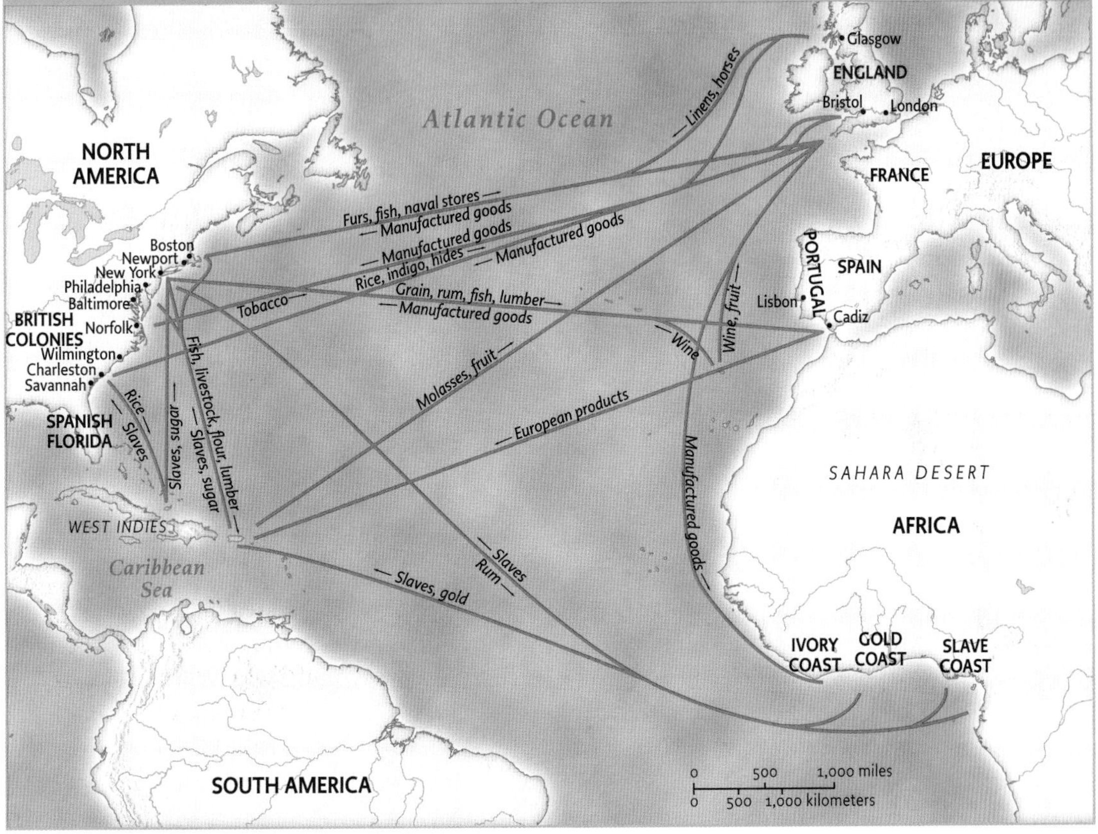

A series of trading routes crisscrossed the Atlantic, bringing manufactured goods to Africa and Britain's American colonies, slaves to the New World, and colonial products to Europe.

rulers took part, and they proved quite adept at playing the Europeans off against one another, collecting taxes from foreign merchants, and keeping the capture and sale of slaves under their own control. Few Europeans ventured inland from the coast. Traders remained in their "factories" and purchased slaves brought to them by African rulers and dealers.

From a minor institution, slavery grew to become more and more central to West African society, a source of wealth for African merchants and of power for newly emerging African kingdoms. But the loss every year of tens of thousands of men and women in the prime of their lives to the slave trade weakened and distorted West Africa's society and economy.

The Middle Passage

For slaves, the voyage across the Atlantic—known as the **Middle Passage** because it was the second, or middle, leg in the triangular trading routes linking Europe, Africa, and America—was a harrowing experience. Men,

THE SLAVE TRADE IN THE ATLANTIC WORLD, 1460–1770

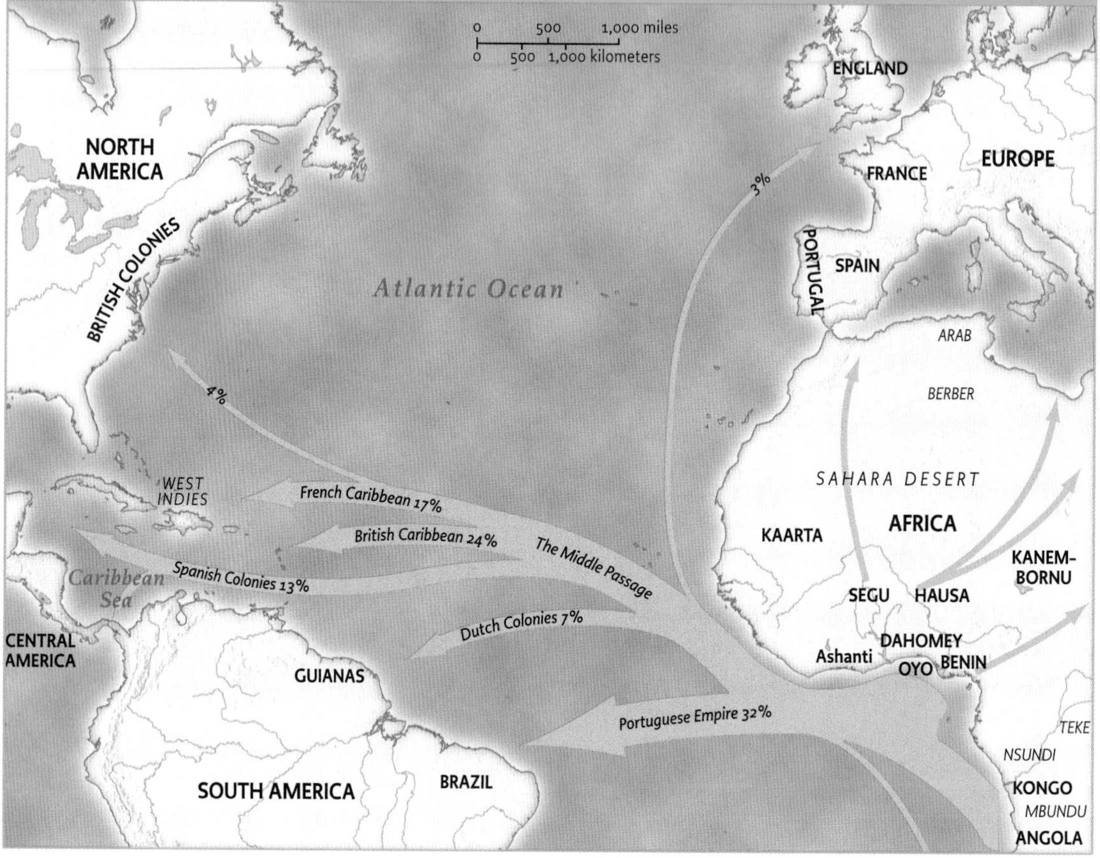

The Atlantic slave trade expanded rapidly in the eighteenth century. The mainland colonies received only a tiny proportion of the Africans brought to the New World, most of whom were transported to Brazil and the West Indies.

women, and children were crammed aboard vessels as tightly as possible to maximize profits. Equiano, who later described "the shrieks of the women and the groans of the dying," survived the Middle Passage, but many Africans did not. Diseases such as measles and smallpox spread rapidly, and about one slave in five perished before reaching the New World. Ship captains were known to throw the sick overboard in order to prevent the spread of epidemics.

Slave population

Only a small proportion (less than 5 percent) of slaves carried to the New World were destined for mainland North America. The vast majority landed in Brazil or the West Indies, where the high death rate on the sugar plantations led to a constant demand for new slave imports. Overall, the area that was to become the United States imported between 400,000 and 600,000 slaves. By 1770, due to the natural reproduction of the slave

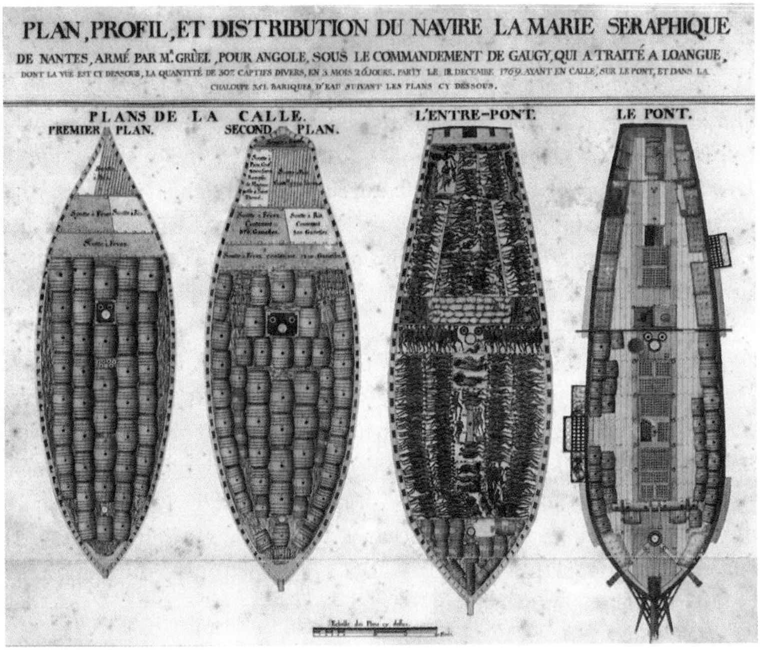

This image, made by a sailor in 1769 for the ship's owner, a merchant in Nantes, France, depicts the interior of a slave-trading vessel, the *Marie-Séraphique*. The cargo carried in barrels, generally guns, cloth, and metal goods, was to be traded for slaves. The third image from the left depicts the conditions under which slaves endured the Middle Passage across the Atlantic. The ship carried over 300 slaves. The broadside also included a calculation of the profit of the voyage.

population, around one-fifth of the estimated 2.3 million persons (not including Indians) living in the English colonies of North America were Africans and their descendants.

Chesapeake Slavery

Tobacco-based plantation slavery

By the mid-eighteenth century, three distinct slave systems were well entrenched in Britain's mainland colonies: tobacco-based plantation slavery in the Chesapeake, rice-based plantation slavery in South Carolina and Georgia, and nonplantation slavery in New England and the Middle Colonies. The largest and oldest of these was the plantation system of the Chesapeake, where more than 270,000 slaves resided in 1770, nearly half of the region's population. Virginia and Maryland were as closely tied to Britain as any other colonies, and their economies were models of mercantilist policy (described in Chapter 3).

Types of slave labor

As Virginia expanded westward, so did slavery. By the eve of the American Revolution, the center of gravity of slavery in the colony had shifted from the Tidewater (the region along the coast) to the Piedmont farther inland. Most Chesapeake slaves, male and female, worked in the tobacco fields, but thousands labored as teamsters, as boatmen, and in skilled crafts. Numerous slave women became cooks, seamstresses, dairy maids, and personal servants. Slavery was common on small farms as well as plantations; nearly half of Virginia's white families owned at least one slave in 1770.

Hierarchy of Chesapeake society

Slavery transformed Chesapeake society into an elaborate hierarchy of degrees of freedom. At the top stood large planters, below them numerous lesser planters and landowning yeomen, and at the bottom a large population of convicts, indentured servants, tenant farmers, and slaves. Violence lay at the heart of the slave system. Even a planter like Landon Carter, who prided himself on his concern for the well-being of his slaves, noted casually in his diary, "They have been severely whipped day by day."

Race as a line of social division

Race took on more and more importance as a line of social division. Whites increasingly considered free blacks dangerous and undesirable. Free blacks lost the right to employ white servants and to bear arms, were subjected to special taxes, and could be punished for striking a white person, regardless of the cause. In 1723, Virginia revoked the voting privileges of property-owning free blacks. Because Virginia law required that freed slaves be sent out of the colony, free blacks remained only a tiny part of the population—less than 4 percent in 1750.

The Rice Kingdom

As in early Virginia, frontier conditions allowed leeway to South Carolina's small population of African-born slaves, who farmed, tended livestock, and were initially allowed to serve in the militia to fight the Spanish and Indians. And as in Virginia, the introduction of a marketable staple crop, in this case rice, led directly to economic development, the large-scale importation of slaves, and a growing divide between white and black. In the 1740s, another staple, indigo (a crop used in producing blue dye), was developed. Like rice, indigo required large-scale cultivation and was grown by slaves.

Staple crops

Large-scale rice plantations

Since rice production requires considerable capital investment to drain swamps and create irrigation systems, it is economically advantageous for rice plantations to be as large as possible. Thus, South Carolina planters owned far more land and slaves than their counterparts in Virginia. Moreover, since mosquitoes bearing malaria (a disease to which Africans had developed partial immunity) flourished in the watery rice fields, planters tended to leave plantations under the control of overseers and the slaves themselves.

The task system

In the Chesapeake, field slaves worked in groups under constant supervision. Under the "task" system that developed in eighteenth-century South Carolina, individual slaves were assigned daily jobs, the completion of which allowed them time for leisure or to cultivate crops of their own.

In 1762, one rice district had a population of only 76 white males among 1,000 slaves. By 1770, the number of South Carolina slaves had reached 75,000, well over half the colony's population.

The Georgia Experiment

James Oglethorpe

Rice cultivation also spread into Georgia. The colony was founded in 1732 by a group of philanthropists led by James Oglethorpe, a wealthy reformer who sought to improve conditions for imprisoned debtors and abolish slavery. Oglethorpe hoped to establish a haven where the "worthy poor" of England could enjoy economic opportunity. The government in London supported the creation of Georgia to protect South Carolina against the Spanish and their Indian allies in Florida.

Initially, the proprietors banned liquor and slaves, leading to continual battles with settlers, who desired both. By the 1740s, Georgia offered the spectacle of colonists pleading for the "English liberty" of self-government so that they could enact laws introducing slavery. In 1751, the proprietors surrendered the colony to the crown. The colonists quickly won the right to an elected assembly, which met in Savannah. It repealed the ban on slavery (and liquor), as well as an early measure that had limited landholdings to 500 acres. Georgia became a miniature version of South Carolina. By 1770, as many as 15,000 slaves labored on its coastal rice plantations.

TABLE 4.1 Slave Population as Percentage of Total Population of Original Thirteen Colonies, 1770

COLONY	SLAVE POPULATION	PERCENTAGE
Virginia	187,600	42%
South Carolina	75,168	61
North Carolina	69,600	35
Maryland	63,818	32
New York	19,062	12
Georgia	15,000	45
New Jersey	8,220	7
Connecticut	5,698	3
Pennsylvania	5,561	2
Massachusetts	4,754	2
Rhode Island	3,761	6
Delaware	1,836	5
New Hampshire	654	1

Slavery in the North

Unlike in the plantation regions, slavery was less central to the economies of New England and the Middle Colonies, where small farms predominated. Slaves made up only a small percentage of these colonies' populations, and it was unusual for families to own more than one or two slaves. Nonetheless, slavery was not marginal to northern colonial life. Slaves worked as farm hands, in artisan shops, as stevedores loading and unloading ships, and as personal servants. With slaves so small a part of the population that they seemed to pose no threat to the white majority, laws were

A portrait of Ayuba Diallo, a Muslim merchant in Senegal who became a victim of the slave trade in 1731 and was transported to Maryland. He escaped in 1733 and with the help of wealthy patrons regained his freedom. Because of Diallo's unusual talents—he knew both English and Arabic and could relate the Koran from memory—he became a celebrity in England, which he visited in 1733. He sat for two portraits by the noted artist William Hoare. This is the earliest known painting of an African who experienced slavery in Britain's North American colonies. Diallo returned to his homeland in 1734.

less harsh than in the South. In New England, where in 1770 the 15,000 slaves represented less than 3 percent of the region's population, slave marriages were recognized in law; the severe physical punishment of slaves was prohibited; and slaves could bring suits in court, testify against whites, and own property and pass it on to their children—rights unknown in the South.

Slavery had been present in New York from the earliest days of Dutch settlement. As New York City's role in the slave trade expanded, so did slavery in the city. In 1746, its 2,440 slaves amounted to one-fifth of the city's total population. Most were domestic workers, but slaves worked in all sectors of the economy. In 1770, about 27,000 slaves lived in New York and New Jersey, 10 percent of their total population. Slavery was also a significant presence in Philadelphia, although the institution stagnated after 1750 as artisans and merchants relied increasingly on wage laborers, whose numbers were augmented by population growth and the completion of the terms of indentured servants.

SLAVE CULTURES AND SLAVE RESISTANCE

Becoming African-American

The nearly 300,000 Africans brought to the mainland colonies during the eighteenth century were not a single people. They came from different cultures, spoke different languages, and practiced many religions. Slavery threw together individuals who would never otherwise have encountered one another and who had never considered their color or residence on a single continent a source of identity or unity. Their bond was not kinship, language, or even "race," but slavery itself. By the nineteenth century, slaves no longer identified themselves as Ibo, Ashanti, Yoruba, and so on, but as African-Americans. In music, art, folklore, language, and religion, their cultural expressions emerged as a synthesis of African traditions, European elements, and new conditions in America.

Slave imports

For most of the eighteenth century, the majority of American slaves were African by birth. Advertisements seeking information about runaways often described them by African origin ("young Gambia Negro," "new Banbara Negro fellow"). Indeed, during the eighteenth century, black life in the colonies was "re-Africanized" as the earlier Creoles (slaves born in the New World) came to be outnumbered by large-scale importations from Africa.

African Religion in Colonial America

The Old Plantation, a late-eighteenth-century watercolor, depicts slaves dancing in a plantation's slave quarters, perhaps at a wedding. The musical instruments and pottery are African in origin, while much of the clothing is of European manufacture, indicating the mixing of African and white cultures among the era's slaves. The artist has been identified as John Rose, owner of a rice plantation near Beaufort, South Carolina.

No experience was more wrenching for African slaves in the colonies than the transition from traditional religions to Christianity. Although African religions varied as much as those on other continents, they shared some elements, especially belief in the presence of spiritual forces in nature and a close relationship between the sacred and secular worlds. In the religions of West Africa, the region from which most slaves brought to British North America originated, there was no hard and fast distinction between the secular and spiritual worlds. Nature was suffused with spirits, and the dead could influence the living.

Although some slaves came to the colonies familiar with Christianity or Islam, the majority of North American slaves practiced traditional African religions (which many Europeans deemed superstition or even witchcraft) well into the eighteenth century. When they did adopt Christian practices, many slaves merged them with traditional beliefs, adding the Christian God to their own pantheon of lesser spirits, whom they continued to worship.

African-American Cultures

By the mid-eighteenth century, the three slave systems in British North America had produced distinct African-American cultures. In the Chesapeake, because of a more healthful climate, the slave population began to reproduce itself by 1740. Because of the small size of most plantations and the large number of white **yeoman farmers**, slaves here were continuously exposed to white culture. They soon learned English, and many were swept up in the religious revivals known as the Great Awakening, discussed later in this chapter.

In South Carolina and Georgia, two very different black societies emerged. On the rice plantations, slaves lived in extremely harsh conditions and had a low birthrate throughout the eighteenth century, making rice production dependent on continued slave imports from Africa. The slaves seldom came into contact with whites. They constructed African-style houses, chose African names for their children, and spoke Gullah, a language that mixed various African roots and was unintelligible to most whites. In Charleston and Savannah, however, the experience of slaves who labored as servants or skilled workers was quite different. They assimilated more quickly into Euro-American culture, and sexual liaisons between white owners and slave women produced the beginning of a class of free mulattos.

In the northern colonies, where slaves represented a smaller part of the population, a distinctive African-American culture developed more slowly. Living in close proximity to whites, slaves enjoyed more mobility and access to the mainstream of life than their counterparts farther south. But they had fewer opportunities to create stable family life or a cohesive community.

This portrait of William Duguid, a Boston textile merchant, was painted in 1773 by Prince Demah Barnes. It depicts Duguid wearing imported clothing with an elaborate floral pattern. What makes the painting unique, however, is that Barnes was a slave, whose owner, a Massachusetts merchant, encouraged what he called Barnes's "natural genius" and took him on a brief visit to London for training. Still a slave, Barnes enlisted in the Massachusetts militia in 1777 after his Loyalist owners fled the state. He died of smallpox in 1778.

Resistance to Slavery

The common threads that linked these regional African-American cultures were the experience of slavery and the desire for freedom. Throughout the eighteenth century, blacks risked their lives in efforts to resist enslavement. Colonial newspapers, especially in the southern colonies, were filled with advertisements for runaway slaves. In South Carolina and Georgia, they fled to Florida, to uninhabited coastal and river swamps, or to Charleston and Savannah, where they could pass for free. In the Chesapeake and Middle Colonies, fugitive slaves tended to be familiar with white culture and therefore, as one advertisement put it, could "pretend to be free."

Slave rebellions

What Edward Trelawny, the colonial governor of Jamaica, called "a dangerous spirit of liberty" was widespread among the New World's slaves. The eighteenth century's first slave uprising occurred in New York City in 1712, when a group of slaves set fire to houses on the outskirts of the city and killed the first nine whites who arrived on the scene. During the 1730s and 1740s, continuous warfare involving European empires and Indians opened the door to slave resistance. In 1731, a slave rebellion in Louisiana, where the French and the Natchez Indians were at war, temporarily halted efforts to introduce the plantation system in that region.

Slaves seized the opportunity for rebellion offered by the War of Jenkins' Ear, which pitted England against Spain. In September 1739, a group of South Carolina slaves, most of them recently arrived from Kongo where some had been soldiers, seized a store containing numerous weapons at the town of Stono. Beating drums to attract followers, the armed band marched southward toward Florida, burning houses and barns, killing whites they encountered, and shouting "Liberty." The **Stono Rebellion** took the lives of more than two dozen whites and as many as 200 slaves. Some slaves managed to reach Florida, where in 1740 they were armed by the Spanish to help repel an attack by a force from Georgia.

In 1741, a panic (which some observers compared to the fear of witches in Salem in the 1690s) swept New York City. Rumors spread that slaves, with some white allies, planned to burn part of the city, seize weapons, and either turn New York over to Spain or murder the white population. More than 150 blacks and 20 whites were arrested, and 34 alleged conspirators, including 4 white persons, were executed. Historians still disagree as to how extensive the plot was or whether it existed at all. In eighteenth-century America, dreams of freedom knew no racial boundary.

RUN AWAY

THE 18th Inſtant at Night from the Subſcriber, in the City of New-York, four Negro Men, Viz. LESTER, about 40 Years of Age, had on a white Flannel Jacket and Drawers, Duck Trowſers and Home-ſpun Shirt. CÆSAR, about 18 Years of Age, cloth-ed in the ſame Manner. ISAAC, aged 17 Years cloathed in the ſame Manner, except that his Breeches were Leather; and MINGO, 15 Years of Age, with the the ſame Clothing as the 2 firſt, all of them of a middling Size, Whoever delivers either of the ſaid Negroes to the Subſcriber, ſhall receive TWENTY SHILLINGS Reward for each beſide all reaſon-able Charges. If any perſon can give Intelligence of their being harbour'd, a reward of TEN POUNDS will be paid upon conviction of the Offender. All Maſters of Veſſels and others are forewarn'd not to Tranſport them from the City, as I am reſolved to proſecute as far as the Law will allow. WILLIAM BULL.

N. B. If the Negroes return, they ſhall be pardon'd. 88

An advertisement seeking the return of four runaway slaves from New York City.

AN EMPIRE OF FREEDOM

British Patriotism

Despite the centrality of slavery to its empire, eighteenth-century Great Britain prided itself on being the world's most advanced and freest nation. It was not only the era's greatest naval and commercial power but also the home of a complex governmental system, with a powerful Parliament representing the interests of a self-confident landed aristocracy and merchant class. For much of the eighteenth century, Britain found itself at war with France, which had replaced Spain as its major continental rival. This situation led to a large military, high taxes, and the creation of the Bank of England to help finance the conflicts. For both Britons and colonists, war helped to sharpen a sense of national identity against foreign foes.

British power

British patriotic sentiment became more assertive as the eighteenth century progressed. Symbols of British identity proliferated: the songs "God Save the King" and "Rule, Britannia," and even the modern rules of cricket, the national sport. Especially in contrast to France, Britain saw itself as a realm of widespread prosperity, individual liberty, the rule of law, and the Protestant faith. Wealth, religion, and freedom went together.

British identity

The British Constitution

Central to this sense of British identity was the concept of liberty. Eighteenth-century Britons believed power and liberty to be natural antagonists. To mediate between them, advocates of British freedom

British liberty

A 1770 engraving from the *Boston Gazette* by Paul Revere illustrates the association of British patriotism and liberty. Britannia sits with a liberty cap and her national shield, and releases a bird from a cage.

celebrated the rule of law, the right to live under legislation to which one's representatives had consented, restraints on the arbitrary exercise of political authority, and rights such as trial by jury enshrined in the common law. Until the 1770s, most colonists believed themselves to be part of the freest political system mankind had ever known.

These ideas sank deep roots not only within the "political nation"—those who voted, held office, and engaged in structured political debate—but also far more broadly in British and colonial society. Ordinary persons challenged efforts by merchants to raise the cost of bread above the traditional "just price" and the Royal Navy's practice of "impressment"—kidnapping poor men on the streets for maritime service.

Republican Liberty

Liberty was central to two sets of political ideas that flourished in the Anglo-American world. One is termed by scholars **republicanism**, which celebrated active participation in public life by economically independent citizens as the essence of liberty. Republicans assumed that only property-owning citizens possessed "virtue"—defined in the eighteenth century not simply as a personal moral quality but as the willingness to subordinate self-interest to the pursuit of the public good.

Moral and economic ideas of liberty

In eighteenth-century Britain, this body of thought about freedom was most closely associated with a group of critics known as the "Country Party" because much of their support arose from the landed gentry. In Britain, Country Party writings had little impact, but they were eagerly devoured in the American colonies, whose elites were attracted to the emphasis on the political role of the independent landowner and their warnings against the tendency of political power to infringe on liberty.

The "Country Party"

Liberal Freedom

The second set of eighteenth-century political ideas celebrating freedom came to be known as **liberalism** (although its meaning was quite different from what the word suggests today). Whereas republican liberty had a public and social quality, liberalism was essentially individual and private. The leading philosopher of liberalism was John Locke, whose *Two Treatises of*

Locke's treatises

Government, written around 1680, had limited influence in his own lifetime but became extremely well known in the next century. Government, he wrote, was formed by a mutual agreement among equals (the parties being male heads of households, not all persons). In this "social contract," men surrendered a part of their right to govern themselves in order to enjoy the benefits of the rule of law. They retained, however, their natural rights, whose existence predated the establishment of political authority. Protecting the security of life, liberty, and property required shielding a realm of private life and personal concerns—including family relations, religious preferences, and economic activity—from interference by the state. During the eighteenth century, Lockean ideas—individual rights, the consent of the governed, the right of rebellion against unjust or oppressive government—would become familiar on both sides of the Atlantic.

Like other Britons, Locke spoke of liberty as a universal right yet seemed to exclude many persons from its full benefits. The free individual in liberal thought was essentially the propertied white man. Nonetheless, by proclaiming that all individuals possess natural rights that no government may violate, Lockean liberalism opened the door to the poor, women, and even slaves to challenge limitations on their own freedom.

In the eighteenth century, republicanism and liberalism often reinforced each other. Both political outlooks could inspire a commitment to constitutional government and restraints on despotic power. Both emphasized the security of property as a foundation of freedom. Both traditions were transported to eighteenth-century America and would eventually help to divide the empire.

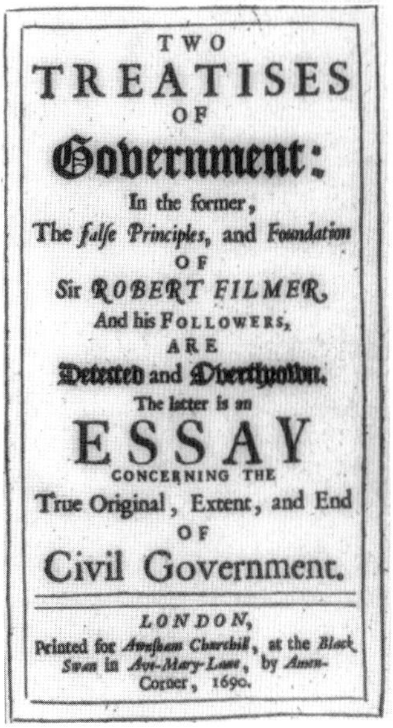
TWO
TREATISES
OF
Government:
In the former,
The false Principles, and Foundation
OF
Sir ROBERT FILMER,
And his FOLLOWERS,
ARE
Detected and Overthrown.
The latter is an
ESSAY
CONCERNING THE
True Original, Extent, and End
OF
Civil Government.
LONDON,
Printed for Awnsham Churchill, at the Black Swan in Ave-Mary-Lane, by Amen-Corner, 1690.

The title page of John Locke's *Two Treatises of Government*, which traced the origins of government to an original state of nature and insisted that political authorities must not abridge mankind's natural rights.

THE PUBLIC SPHERE

Colonial politics for most of the eighteenth century was considerably less tempestuous than in the seventeenth, with its bitter struggles for power and frequent armed uprisings. Political stability in Britain coupled with the maturation of local elites in America made for more tranquil government.

The Right to Vote

In many respects, politics in eighteenth-century America had a more democratic quality than in Great Britain. Suffrage requirements varied from colony to colony, but as in Britain the linchpin of voting laws was the property qualification. Its purpose was to ensure that men who possessed an economic stake in society and the independence of judgment that

Property and the vote

supposedly went with it determined the policies of the government. Slaves, servants, tenants, adult sons living in the homes of their parents, the poor, and women all lacked a "will of their own" and were therefore ineligible to vote. The wide distribution of property in the colonies, however, meant that a far higher percentage of the population enjoyed voting rights than in the Old World. It is estimated that between 50 and 80 percent of adult white men could vote in eighteenth-century colonial America, as opposed to fewer than 5 percent in Britain.

Limits on voting

Colonial politics, however, was hardly democratic in a modern sense. Voting was almost everywhere considered a male prerogative. In some colonies, Jews, Catholics, and Protestant Dissenters like Baptists and Quakers could not vote. Propertied free blacks, who enjoyed the franchise in Virginia, South Carolina, and Georgia in the early days of settlement, lost that right during the eighteenth century. In the northern colonies, although the law did not bar blacks from voting, local custom often did. Native Americans were generally prohibited from voting.

Political Cultures

Appointive office

Despite the broad electorate among white men, "the people" existed only on election day. Between elections, members of colonial assemblies remained out of touch with their constituents. Strongly competitive elections were the norm only in the Middle Colonies. Considerable power in colonial politics rested with those who held appointive, not elective, office. Governors and councils were appointed by the crown in the nine royal colonies and by the proprietors of Pennsylvania and Maryland. Moreover, laws passed by colonial assemblies could be vetoed by governors or in London. In New England, most town officers were elected, but local officials in other colonies were appointed by the governor or by powerful officials in London.

Qualifications for voting and office

Property qualifications for officeholding were far higher than for voting. In South Carolina, for example, nearly every free adult white male could meet the voting qualification of fifty acres of land or payment of twenty shillings in taxes, but to sit in the assembly one had to own 500 acres of land and ten slaves or town property worth £1,000. As a result, throughout the eighteenth century nearly all of South Carolina's legislators were planters or wealthy merchants.

Democracy and deference

In some colonies, an ingrained tradition of "deference"—the assumption among ordinary people that wealth, education, and social prominence carried a right to public office—sharply limited effective choice in elections. Virginia politics, for example, combined political democracy for white men with the tradition that voters should choose among candidates from the gentry. Aspirants for public office actively sought to ingratiate themselves with ordinary voters, distributing food and liquor freely at the courthouse where balloting took place. In Thomas Jefferson's first campaign for the House of Burgesses in 1768, his expenses included hiring two men "for bringing up rum" to the polling place. Even in New England, with its larger number of elective positions, town leaders were generally the largest property holders.

The Rise of the Assemblies

Colonial governors

In the seventeenth century, the governor was the focal point of political authority, and colonial assemblies were weak bodies that met infrequently. But preoccupied with events in Europe and imperial rivalries, successive British governments during the first half of the eighteenth century adopted a policy of **salutary neglect**, leaving the colonies largely to govern themselves. As economic development enhanced the power of American elites, the assemblies they dominated became more and more assertive. Their leaders insisted that assemblies possessed the same rights and powers in local affairs as the House of Commons enjoyed in Britain. The most successful governors were those who accommodated the rising power of the assemblies and used their appointive powers and control of land grants to win allies among assembly members.

Conflicts between governors and assemblies

Many of the conflicts between governors and elected assemblies stemmed from the colonies' economic growth. To deal with the scarcity of gold and silver coins, the only legal form of currency, some colonies printed paper money, although this was strongly opposed by the governors, authorities in London, and British merchants who did not wish to be paid in what they considered worthless paper. Numerous battles also took place over land policy (sometimes involving divergent attitudes toward

This 1765 engraving depicting an election in Pennsylvania suggests the intensity of political debate in the Middle Colonies, as well as the social composition of the electorate. Those shown arguing outside the Old Court House in Philadelphia include physicians (with wigs and gold-topped canes), ministers, and lawyers. A line of men wait on the steps to vote.

the remaining Indian population) and the level of rents charged to farmers on land owned by the crown or proprietors.

In their negotiations and conflicts with royal governors, leaders of the assemblies drew on the writings of the English Country Party, whose emphasis on the constant tension between liberty and political power and the dangers of executive influence over the legislature made sense of their own experience. Of the European settlements in North America, only the British colonies possessed any considerable degree of popular participation in government.

Popular participation in British colonial government

Politics in Public

The language of liberty reverberated outside the relatively narrow world of elective and legislative politics. The "political nation" was dominated by the American gentry, whose members addressed each other in letters, speeches, newspaper articles, and pamphlets filled with references to classical learning. But especially in colonial cities, the eighteenth century witnessed a considerable expansion of the "public sphere"—the world of political organization independent of the government, where an informed citizenry openly discussed questions that had previously been the preserve of officials.

The public sphere

In Boston, New York, and Philadelphia, clubs proliferated where literary, philosophical, scientific, and political issues were debated. Such groups were generally composed of men of property, but some drew ordinary citizens into discussions of public affairs. Colonial taverns and coffeehouses also became important sites for political debates. In Philadelphia, one clergyman commented, "the poorest laborer thinks himself entitled to deliver his sentiments in matters of religion or politics with as much freedom as the gentleman or scholar."

Taverns and coffeehouses

The Colonial Press

Neither the Spanish possessions of Florida and New Mexico nor New France possessed a printing press, although missionaries had established one in Mexico City in the 1530s. In British North America, however, the press expanded rapidly during the eighteenth century. So did the number of political broadsides and pamphlets published, especially at election time. By the eve of the American Revolution, some three-quarters of the free adult male population in the colonies (and more than one-third of the women) could read and write, and a majority of American families owned at least one book. Circulating libraries appeared in many colonial cities and towns, making possible a wider dissemination of knowledge at

Literacy in colonial America

a time when books were still expensive. The first, the Library Company of Philadelphia, was established by Benjamin Franklin in 1731.

Newspapers

The first continuously published colonial newspaper, the *Boston News-Letter*, appeared in 1704. There were twenty-five colonial newspapers by 1765, mostly weeklies with small circulations—an average of 600 sales per issue. Probably the best-edited was the *Pennsylvania Gazette*, established in 1728 in Philadelphia and purchased the following year by Benjamin Franklin. At its peak, the *Gazette* attracted 2,000 subscribers. By the 1730s, political commentary was widespread in the American press.

Freedom of Expression and Its Limits

Freedom of speech

The public sphere thrived on the free exchange of ideas. But freedom of expression was not generally considered one of the ancient rights of Englishmen. The phrase "freedom of speech" originated in Britain during the sixteenth century. A right of legislators, not ordinary citizens, it referred to the ability of members of Parliament to express their views without fear of reprisal, on the grounds that only in this way could they effectively represent the people. Outside of Parliament, free speech had no legal protection. A subject could be beheaded for accusing the king of failing to hold "true" religious beliefs, and language from swearing to criticism of the government exposed a person to criminal penalties.

Freedom of the press

As for freedom of the press, governments on both sides of the Atlantic viewed this as extremely dangerous. Until 1695, when a British law requiring the licensing of printed works before publication lapsed, no newspaper, book, or pamphlet could legally be printed without a government license. After 1695, the government could not censor newspapers, books, and pamphlets before they appeared in print, but it continued to try to manage the press by direct payments to publishers and journalists. Authors and publishers could still be prosecuted for "seditious libel"—a crime that included defaming government officials—or punished for contempt.

Elected assemblies, not governors, most frequently discouraged freedom of the press in colonial America. Dozens of publishers were hauled before assemblies and forced to apologize for comments regarding one or another member. Colonial newspapers vigorously defended freedom of the press as a central component of liberty, insisting that the citizenry had a right to monitor the workings of government and subject public officials to criticism. But since government printing contracts were crucial for economic success, few newspapers attacked colonial governments unless financially supported by an opposition faction.

John Peter Zenger

The Trial of Zenger

The most famous colonial court case involving freedom of the press demonstrated that popular sentiment opposed prosecutions for criticism of public officials. This was the 1735 trial of John Peter Zenger, a German-born printer who had immigrated to New York as a youth. Financed by wealthy opponents of Governor William Cosby, Zenger's newspaper, the *Weekly Journal*, lambasted the governor for corruption, influence peddling, and "tyranny." New York's council ordered four issues burned and had Zenger himself arrested and tried for seditious libel. Zenger's attorney, Andrew Hamilton, urged the jury to judge not the publisher but the governor. If they decided that Zenger's charges were correct, they must acquit him, and, Hamilton proclaimed, "every man who prefers freedom to a life of slavery will bless you."

Zenger was found not guilty. The case sent a warning to prosecutors that libel cases might be very difficult to win, especially in the superheated atmosphere of New York politics. The outcome demonstrated that the idea of free expression was becoming ingrained in the popular imagination.

Benjamin West's depiction of Benjamin Franklin, painted in 1816, twenty-six years after his subject's death, emphasizes his scientific work rather than his political career. Franklin conducted pioneering experiments in 1752 that demonstrated the electrical nature of lightning. West shows him seated on clouds, surrounded by angelic assistants.

The American Enlightenment

During the eighteenth century, many educated Americans began to be influenced by the outlook of the European **Enlightenment**. This philosophical movement, which originated among French thinkers and soon spread to Britain, sought to apply the scientific method of careful investigation based on research and experiment to political and social life. Enlightenment ideas crisscrossed the Atlantic along with goods and people. Enlightenment thinkers insisted that every human institution, authority, and tradition be judged before the bar of reason. The self-educated Benjamin Franklin's wide range of activities—establishing a newspaper, debating club, and library; publishing the widely circulated *Poor Richard's Almanack*; and conducting experiments to demonstrate that lightning is a form of electricity—exemplified the

Enlightenment spirit and made him probably the best-known American in the eighteenth-century world.

Enlightenment thinkers hoped that "reason," not religious enthusiasm, could govern human life. During the eighteenth century, many prominent Americans moved toward the position called Arminianism, which taught that reason alone was capable of establishing the essentials of religion. Others adopted **Deism**, a belief that God essentially withdrew after creating the world, leaving it to function according to scientific laws without divine intervention. Belief in miracles, in the revealed truth of the Bible, and in the innate sinfulness of mankind were viewed by Arminians, Deists, and others as outdated superstitions that should be abandoned in the modern age.

Deism

In the seventeenth century, the English scientist Isaac Newton had revealed the natural laws that governed the physical universe. Here, Deists believed, was the purest evidence of God's handiwork. Deists concluded that the best form of religious devotion was to study the workings of nature, rather than to worship in organized churches or appeal to divine grace for salvation. By the late colonial era, a small but influential group of leading Americans, including Benjamin Franklin and Thomas Jefferson, could be classified as Deists.

THE GREAT AWAKENING

Like freedom of the press, religion was another realm where the actual experience of liberty outstripped its legal recognition. Religion remained central to eighteenth-century American life. Sermons, theological treatises, and copies of the Bible were by far the largest category of material produced by colonial printers.

Religious Revivals

Many ministers were concerned that westward expansion, commercial development, the growth of Enlightenment rationalism, and lack of individual engagement in church services were undermining religious devotion. These fears helped to inspire the revivals that swept through the colonies beginning in the 1730s. Known as the **Great Awakening**, the revivals were less a coordinated movement than a series of local events united by a commitment to a "religion of the heart," a more emotional and personal Christianity than that offered by existing churches.

A more personal Christianity

Religious fundamentalism

The eighteenth century witnessed a resurgence of religious fundamentalism in many parts of the world, in part a response to the rationalism of the Enlightenment and a desire for greater religious purity. In the Middle East and Central Asia, where Islam was widespread, followers of a form of the religion known as Wahabbism called for a return to the practices of the religion's early days. Methodism and other forms of enthusiastic religion were flourishing in Europe. Like other intellectual currents of the time, the Great Awakening was a transatlantic movement.

Jonathan Edwards

During the 1720s and 1730s, the New Jersey Dutch Reformed clergyman Theodore Frelinghuysen, his Presbyterian neighbors William and Gilbert Tennent, and the Massachusetts Congregationalist minister Jonathan Edwards pioneered an intensely emotional style of preaching. Edwards's famous sermon *Sinners in the Hands of an Angry God* portrayed sinful man as a "loathsome insect" suspended over a bottomless pit of eternal fire by a slender thread that might break at any moment. Only a "new birth"—immediately acknowledging one's sins and pleading for divine grace—could save men and women from eternal damnation.

The Preaching of Whitefield

George Whitefield, the English evangelist who helped to spark the Great Awakening in the colonies. Painted around 1742 by John Wollaston, who had immigrated from England to the colonies, the work depicts Whitefield's powerful effect on male and female listeners. It also illustrates Whitefield's eye problem, which led critics to dub him "Dr. Squintum."

More than any other individual, the English minister George Whitefield, who declared "the whole world his parish," sparked the Great Awakening. For two years after his arrival in America in 1739, Whitefield brought his highly emotional brand of preaching to colonies from Georgia to New England. God, Whitefield proclaimed, was merciful. Rather than being predestined for damnation, men and women could save themselves by repenting of their sins. Whitefield appealed to the passions of his listeners, powerfully sketching the boundless joy of salvation and the horrors of damnation.

Tens of thousands of colonists flocked to Whitefield's sermons, which were widely reported in the American press, making him a celebrity and helping to establish the revivals as the first major intercolonial event in North American history. In Whitefield's footsteps, a host of traveling preachers or "evangelists" (meaning, literally, bearers of good news) held revivalist meetings, often to the alarm of established ministers.

The Awakening's Impact

By the time they subsided in the 1760s, the revivals had changed the religious configuration of the colonies and enlarged the boundaries of liberty. Whitefield inspired the emergence of numerous Dissenting churches. Congregations split into factions headed by Old Lights (traditionalists) and New Lights (revivalists), and new churches proliferated—Baptist, Methodist, Presbyterian, and others. Many of these new churches began to criticize the colonial practice of levying taxes to support an established church; they defended religious freedom as one of the natural rights government must not restrict.

The Great Awakening threw into question many forms of authority and inspired criticism of aspects of colonial society. Revivalist preachers frequently criticized commercial society, insisting that believers should make salvation, not profit, "the one business of their lives." Preaching to the small farmers of the southern backcountry, Baptist and Methodist revivalists criticized the worldliness of wealthy planters and attacked as sinful activities such as gambling, horse racing, and lavish entertainments on the Sabbath. A few preachers explicitly condemned slavery. Especially in the Chesapeake, the revivals brought numerous slaves into the Christian fold, an important step in their acculturation as African-Americans.

Critique of commercial society

The revivals encouraged many colonists to trust their own views rather than those of established elites. In listening to the sermons of self-educated preachers, forming Bible study groups, and engaging in intense religious discussions, ordinary colonists asserted the right to independent judgment. Although the revivalists' aim was spiritual salvation, the independent frame of mind they encouraged would have significant political consequences.

A rare map by a Comanche artist depicts the Battle of Sierra Blanca of July 30, 1787, between Comanche and Apache warriors in modern-day New Mexico. It was presented to the Spanish governor, who had recently formed an alliance with the Comanche. The battle was a resounding victory for the Comanche, who suffered only one dead and four wounded, while killing four Apache and capturing thirty-five. The letters on the map refer to an accompanying key, including A: the Comanche commander; B: Comanche warriors; D: Apache prisoners; and E: 16 captured horses—an indication of the importance of horses to southwestern Indians by this time.

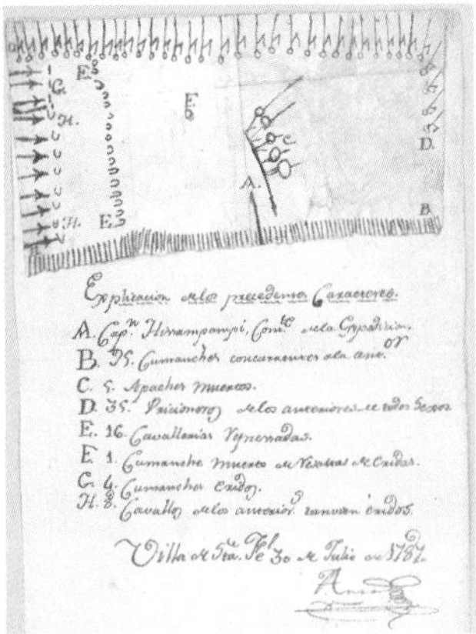

IMPERIAL RIVALRIES

Spanish North America

The rapid growth of Britain's North American colonies took place at a time of increased jockeying for power among European empires. But the colonies of England's rivals, although covering immense territories, remained thinly populated and far weaker economically. The Spanish empire encompassed an area that stretched from the Pacific coast and New Mexico into the Great Plains and eastward through Texas and Florida. After 1763, it also included Louisiana, which Spain obtained from France. On paper a vast territorial empire, Spanish North America actually consisted of a few isolated urban clusters, most prominently St. Augustine in Florida, San Antonio in Texas, and Santa Fe and Albuquerque in New Mexico.

In the second half of the century, the Spanish government made a concerted effort to reinvigorate its empire north of the Rio Grande River. It sought to stabilize relations with Indians, especially the nomadic Comanche and Apache, who controlled much of the land claimed by Spain

This illustration of friars preaching, from an eighteenth-century work by the missionary Pablo de Beaumont, depicts demons dispatched by the devil as an ever-present threat to the missionaries' efforts to convert Native Americans.

and whose raids on mines and ranches, settled Indian communities, and each other wreaked havoc. Spain was also alarmed by the growing number of French merchants who made their way into the region from Louisiana.

During the reigns of Carlos II and Carlos III, Spanish reformers, like other Enlightenment figures, hoped that applying scientific methods to society would bring about progress, but at the same time they aimed to preserve the absolutist monarchy and Spain's American empire. Reformers condemned Spain's past treatment of Indians and called for more humane policies. They pointed out that despite the Black Legend of unique Spanish cruelty, Indians comprised well over half of the inhabitants of New Spain, but now amounted to less than 6 percent of the population of the mainland English colonies. But no coherent policy was adopted. In 1776, Spain put the region, previously governed from Mexico City, under a local military commander, who used a combination of coercion, gifts, and trade to woo unconquered Indians. These tactics to some extent strengthened Spain's hold on the northern part of its American empire, but did not succeed in eliminating Indian power in the area.

Spain's problem stemmed in large part from the small size of the settler population. New Mexico in 1765 had only 20,000 inhabitants, with Pueblo Indians slightly outnumbering persons of European descent. Although ranching expanded, the economy of New Mexico essentially rested on trading with and extracting labor from the surviving Indian population. Moreover, the manpower demands of wars in Europe made it impossible for the Spanish government to meet local military commanders' requests for more troops. The powerful Comanche and Apache continued to dominate large parts of northern New Spain.

Texas colonization

Similar problems existed in Texas. Spain began the colonization of Texas at the beginning of the eighteenth century, partly as a buffer to prevent French commercial influence, then spreading in the Mississippi Valley, from intruding into New Mexico. The Spanish established complexes consisting of religious missions and *presidios* (military outposts) at Los Adaes, La Bahía, and San Antonio. But the region attracted few settlers. Texas had only 1,200 Spanish colonists in 1760. Florida stagnated as well.

The Spanish in California

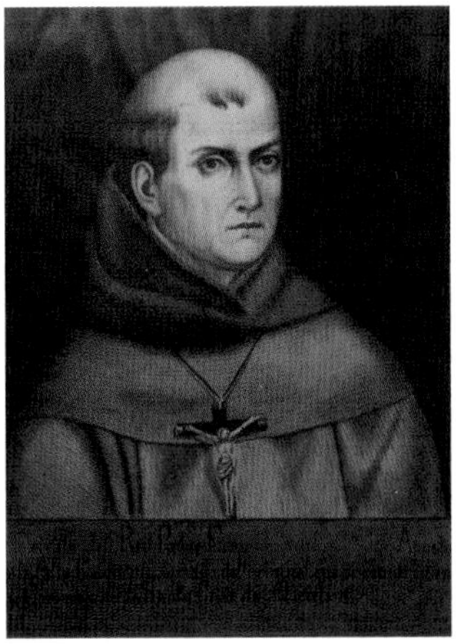

Although painted in the twentieth century, this portrait of Father Junípero Serra is based on one that dates from the eighteenth century, when Serra conducted missionary work in present-day California.

The clash of empires also took place on the Pacific Coast. In the mid-eighteenth century, empire builders in Moscow dreamed of challenging the Spanish for control of the region's fur trade, minerals, and ports. Russian traders established a series of forts in Alaska and then moved southward toward modern-day California. As late as 1812, Russians founded Fort Ross, only 100 miles north of San Francisco.

Even though only a small number of Russians actually appeared in California, the alarmed Spanish in 1769 launched the "Sacred Experiment" to take control of the coast north of San Diego to prevent its occupation by foreigners. In 1774, Juan Bautista de Anza, an explorer and military officer, led an expedition that discovered a usable overland route to California from northern Mexico. But a Native American uprising in 1781 wrested control of the overland route from the Spanish. Given the distance and difficulties of communication, authorities in Mexico City decided to establish missions in California, run by the Franciscan religious order, rather than sending colonists. The friars would set up ranching and farming activities and convert Indians into loyal Spaniards.

A string of Spanish missions and *presidios* soon dotted the California coastline, from San Diego to Los Angeles, Santa Barbara, Monterey, San Francisco, and Sonoma. Born on the Spanish Mediterranean island of Mallorca, **Father Junípero Serra** became one of the most controversial figures in California's early history. He founded the first California mission, in San Diego, in 1769 and administered the mission network until his death in 1784. Serra was widely praised in Spain for converting thousands of Indians to Christianity. In 2015, he was elevated to sainthood by the Catholic Church. But forced labor and disease took a heavy toll among Indians who lived at the missions Serra directed. Many ran away, and the friars responded with whippings and imprisonment. "Naturally we want our liberty," one fugitive from the missions remarked.

California missions

Present-day California was a densely populated area, with a native population of perhaps 250,000 when Spanish settlement began. But as in other regions, the coming of soldiers and missionaries proved a disaster for the Indians. More than any other Spanish colony, California was a mission frontier. These outposts served simultaneously as religious institutions and centers of government and labor. Father Serra and other missionaries hoped to convert the natives to Christianity and settled farming, although Serra accommodated native traditions such as dancing and traditional healing. The missions also relied on forced Indian labor to grow grain, work in orchards and vineyards, and tend cattle. By 1821, when Mexico won its independence from Spain, California's native population had declined by

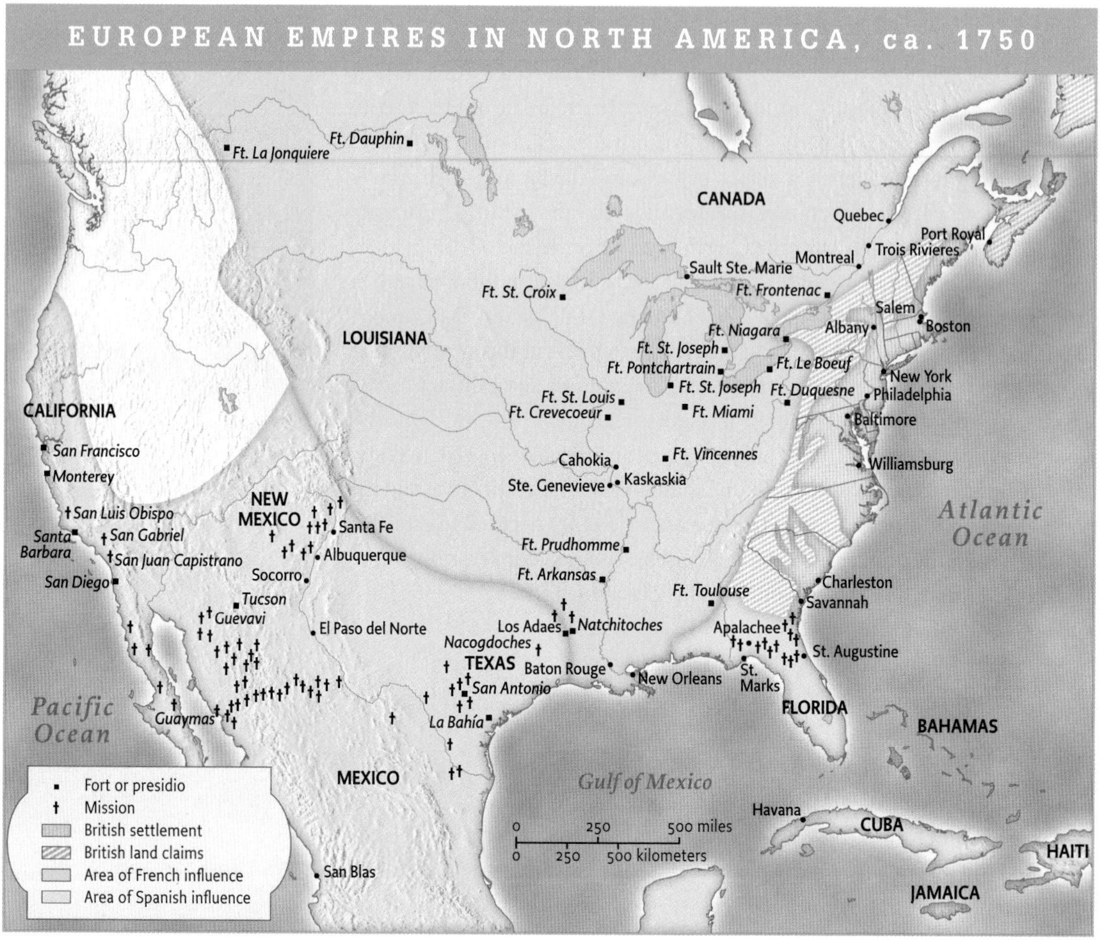

Three great empires—the British, French, and Spanish—competed for influence in North America for much of the eighteenth century.

more than one-third. But the area had not attracted Spanish settlers. When Spanish rule came to an end in 1821, twenty missions were operating, with an average population of over 1,000 Indians, but *Californios* (California residents of Spanish descent) numbered only 3,200.

The French Empire

French expansion

Indians retained far more power in Spanish North America than in areas of English settlement. The same was true when it came to a greater rival to British power in North America—as well as in Europe and the Caribbean—France. During the eighteenth century, the population and economy of Canada expanded. At the same time, French traders pushed into the Mississippi River valley southward from the Great Lakes and northward from Mobile, founded in 1702, and New Orleans, established in 1718. In the St. Lawrence River valley of French Canada, prosperous farming communities developed. By 1750, the area had a population of about 55,000 colonists. Another 10,000 (about half Europeans, half African-American slaves) resided in Louisiana.

French and British empires

Nonetheless, the population of French North America continued to be dwarfed by the British colonies. Prejudice against emigration to North America remained widespread in France because many there viewed the French colony as a place of cruel exile for criminals and social outcasts. Nonetheless, by claiming control of a large arc of territory and by establishing close trading and military relations with many Indian tribes, the French empire posed a real challenge to the British. French forts and trading posts ringed the British colonies. The French were a presence on the New England and New York frontiers and in western Pennsylvania.

BATTLE FOR THE CONTINENT

The Ohio Valley

For much of the eighteenth century, the western frontier of British North America was the flashpoint of imperial rivalries. The Ohio Valley became caught up in a complex struggle for power involving the French, British, rival Indian communities, and settlers and land companies pursuing their own interests. On this **middle ground**, a borderland between the French and British empires and Indian sovereignty, villages sprang up where members of numerous tribes lived side by side, along with European traders and the occasional missionary.

By the mid-eighteenth century, Indians had learned that direct military confrontation with Europeans meant suicide, and that an alliance with a single European power exposed them to danger from others. The Indians of the Ohio Valley sought (with some success) to play the British and French empires off against one another and to control the lucrative commerce with whites. The Iroquois were masters of balance-of-power diplomacy.

In 1750, few white settlers inhabited the Ohio Valley. The area was known more by rumor than by observation, and contemporary maps bore little resemblance to the actual geography. Nonetheless, many prominent colonists dreamed of establishing a new "empire" in what was then the West. Many others saw the West as a place where they could easily acquire land, and the freedom that went with it. In 1749, the government of Virginia awarded an immense land grant—half

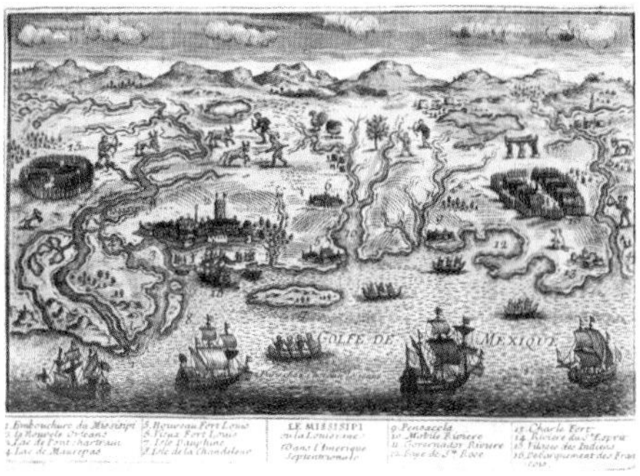

This hand-colored engraving from around 1720 depicts the mouth of the Mississippi River and the city of New Orleans, then quite small. On the left and right are Native American villages surrounded by stockades.

The Ohio Company

a million acres—to the Ohio Company. The company's members included the colony's royal governor, Robert Dinwiddie, and the cream of Virginia society—Lees, Carters, and the young George Washington. The land grant sparked the French to bolster their presence in the region. It was the Ohio Company's demand for French recognition of its land claims that inaugurated the **Seven Years' War** (known in the colonies as the **French and Indian War**), the first of the century's imperial wars to begin in the colonies and the first to result in a decisive victory for one combatant. It permanently altered the global balance of power.

The Seven Years' War

The world's leading empire

Only in the eighteenth century, after numerous wars against its great rivals France and Spain, did Britain emerge as the world's leading empire and its center of trade and banking. By the 1750s, British possessions and trade reached around the globe. The existence of global empires implied that warfare among them would also be global.

Attempts to dislodge the French

What became a worldwide struggle for imperial domination began in 1754 with British efforts to dislodge the French from forts in western Pennsylvania. In the previous year, George Washington, then only twenty-one years old, had been dispatched by the colony's governor on an unsuccessful mission to persuade French soldiers to abandon a fort they were building on lands claimed by the Ohio Company. In 1754, Washington returned to the area with two companies of soldiers. After an ill-considered attack on a larger French and Indian force, resulting in the loss of one-third of his men, Washington was forced to surrender. Soon afterward, an expedition led by General Edward Braddock against Fort Duquesne (today's Pittsburgh) was ambushed by French and Indian forces, leaving Braddock and two-thirds of his 3,000 soldiers dead or wounded.

For two years, the war went against the British. The southern backcountry was ablaze with fighting among British forces, colonists, and Indians. Inhumanity flourished on all sides. Indians killed hundreds of colonists in western Pennsylvania and pushed the line of settlement all the way back to Carlisle, only 100 miles west of Philadelphia. In Nova Scotia, the British rounded up 5,000 local French residents, called Acadians, confiscated their land, and expelled them from the region, selling their farms to settlers from New England. Some of those expelled ended up as far away as Louisiana, where their descendants came to be known as Cajuns.

Benjamin Franklin produced this famous cartoon in 1754, calling on Britain's North American colonies to unite against the French.

As the British government under Secretary of State William Pitt, who took office in 1757, raised huge sums of money and poured men and naval forces into the war, the tide of battle turned. By 1759, Britain—with colonial and Indian soldiers playing a major role—had captured the pivotal French outposts Forts Duquesne, Ticonderoga (north of Albany), and Louisbourg on Cape Breton Island, which guarded the mouth of the St. Lawrence River. In September of that year, a French army was defeated on the Plains of Abraham near Quebec. British forces also seized nearly all the islands in the French Caribbean and established control of India.

A World Transformed

The global balance of power

Britain's victory fundamentally reshaped the world balance of power. In the Peace of Paris in 1763, France ceded Canada to Britain, receiving back in return the sugar islands of Guadeloupe and Martinique (far more lucrative colonies from the point of view of French authorities). Spain ceded Florida to Britain in exchange for the return of the Philippines and Cuba (seized by the British during the war). Spain also acquired from France the vast Louisiana colony. France's 200-year-old North American empire had come to an end. The entire continent east of the Mississippi River was now in British hands.

The costs of war

Eighteenth-century warfare, conducted on land and sea across the globe, was enormously expensive. The Seven Years' War put strains on all the participants. The war's cost produced a financial crisis in France that almost three decades later would help to spark the French Revolution. The British would try to recoup part of the cost of war by increasing taxes on their American colonies.

New Indian Identities

Pan-Indian identity

Among other consequences, the Seven Years' War helped lay the foundation for the emergence of a distinct Native American identity. American Indians had traditionally identified most strongly along lines of kinship, shared language, and common geographical residence, including towns and confederacies. Like early colonists, they did not have well-formed ideas about nation and race. The violence directed against Indians by soldiers and settlers during the war led many Indian leaders to envision both stronger allegiance to tribal "nationhood" and pan-Indian identity more broadly. A religious movement that emerged during the Seven Years' War saw different prophets urge Indians toward a sense of themselves based on shared conflict with Anglo-America. Some even developed racial theories, arguing that Indians, whites, and Africans constituted the primary division of peoples in North America. Not all Indians, however, embraced this message. Many rejected the idea of a single Native American identity. Serious debates took place among Indians about the best way to secure their individual and collective independence.

EASTERN NORTH AMERICA AFTER THE PEACE OF PARIS, 1763

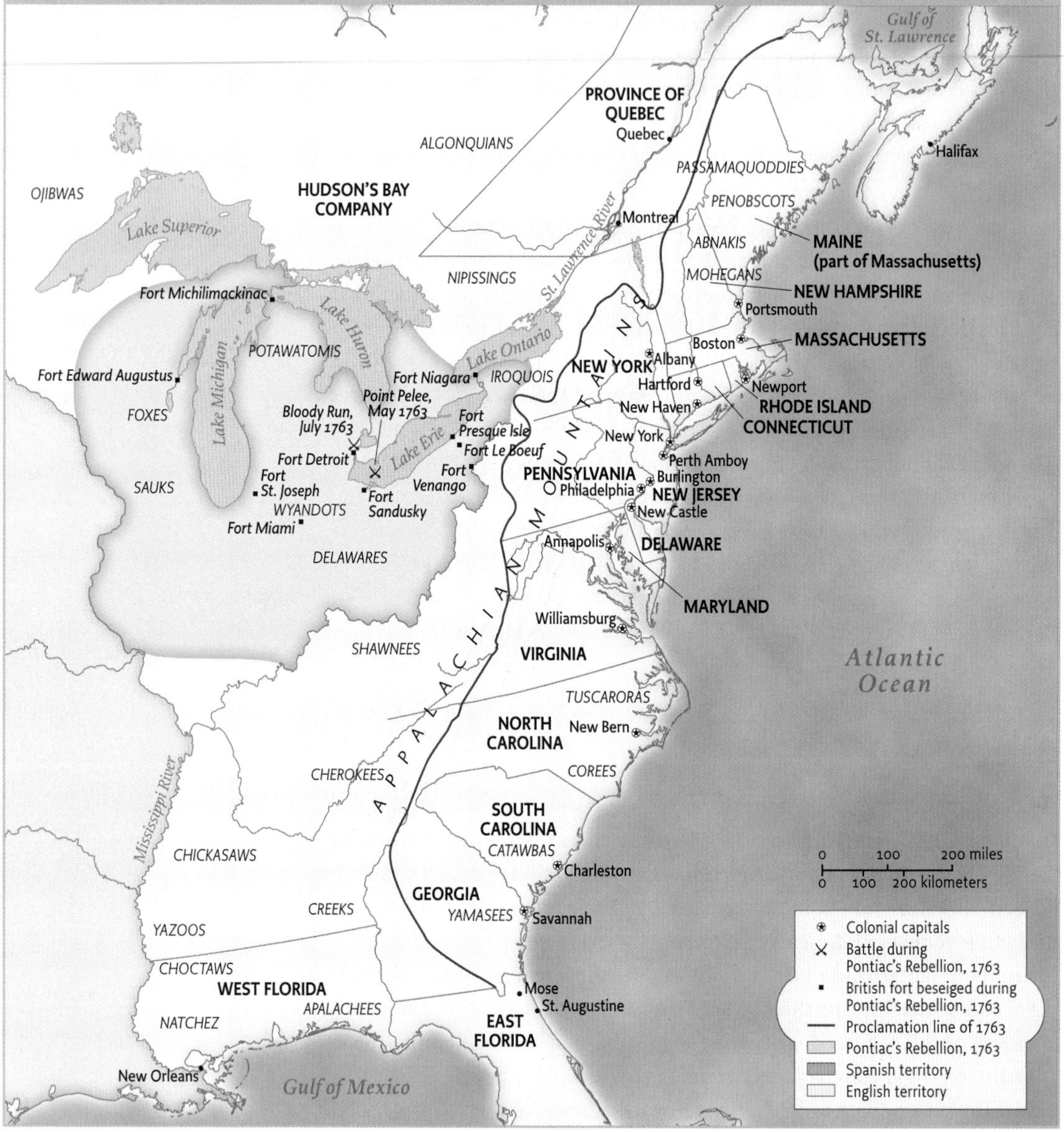

The Peace of Paris, which ended the Seven Years' War, left all of North America east of the Mississippi in British hands, ending the French presence on the continent.

Throughout eastern North America, the abrupt departure of the French in the aftermath of the Seven Years' War eliminated the balance-of-power diplomacy that had enabled groups like the Iroquois to maintain a significant degree of autonomy. Without consulting them, the French had ceded land Indians claimed as their own to British control. The Treaty of Paris left Indians more dependent than ever on the British and ushered in a period of confusion over land claims, control of the fur trade, and tribal relations in general.

Effect on Indians

In 1763, in the wake of the French defeat, Indians of the Ohio Valley and Great Lakes launched a revolt against British rule. Although known among the colonists as **Pontiac's Rebellion** after an Ottawa war leader, the rebellion owed at least as much to the teachings of **Neolin**, a Delaware religious prophet. During a religious vision, the Master of Life instructed Neolin that his people must reject European technology, free themselves from commercial ties with whites and dependence on alcohol, clothe themselves in the garb of their ancestors, and drive the British from their territory (although friendly French inhabitants could remain). Neolin combined this message with the relatively new idea of pan-Indian identity. All Indians, he preached, were a single people, and only through cooperation could they regain their lost independence.

Neolin's message

The Proclamation Line

In the spring and summer of 1763, Ottawas, Hurons, and other Indians besieged Detroit, then a major British military outpost, seized nine other forts, and killed hundreds of white settlers who had intruded onto Indian lands. British forces soon launched a counterattack, and over the next few years the tribes one by one made peace. But the uprising inspired the government in London to issue the **Proclamation of 1763**, prohibiting further colonial settlement west of the Appalachian Mountains. These lands were reserved exclusively for Indians. Moreover, the proclamation banned the sale of Native American lands to private individuals.

Proclamation of 1763

The British aim was less to protect the Indians than to stabilize the situation on the colonial frontier and to avoid being dragged into an endless series of border conflicts. But the proclamation enraged both settlers and speculators hoping to take advantage of the expulsion of the French to consolidate their claims to western lands. They ignored the new policy. George Washington himself ordered his agents to buy up as much Indian land as possible, while keeping the transactions "a profound secret" because of their illegality. Failing to offer a viable solution to the question of westward expansion, the Proclamation of 1763 ended up further exacerbating settler–Indian relations.

VOICES OF FREEDOM

From Scarouyady, Speech to Pennsylvania Provincial Council (1756)

The outbreak of the Seven Years' War inflamed relations between Native Americans and white settlers in the Pennsylvania backcountry. Scarouyady, an Oneida leader who wished to maintain harmony, told the colony's leaders that he approved of war against hostile tribes and hoped that a fort could be built to protect friendly Indians and keep armed whites in check. But the middle ground was rapidly disappearing.

You have . . . tried all amicable means with [the Delaware Indians] and with the Six Nations, but as all have proved ineffectual, you do right to strike them. You have had a great deal of patience; other people on losing a single man, would have armed and drove off the foe; but you have sat still while numbers of your people have been and now are murdered. . . . Your enemies have got great advantage by your inactivity; show them you are men.

You told us that you must now build a Fort at Shamokin; we are glad to hear it; it is a good thing. . . . The Fort at Shamokin is not a thing of little consequence; it is of the greatest importance to us as well as you. Your people are foolish; for want of this Fort, the Indians, who are your friends, can be of no service to you, having no place to go to where they can promise themselves protection. They cannot be called together; they can do nothing for you; they are not secure any where. At present your people cannot distinguish foes from friends; they think every Indian is against them; they blame us all without distinction, because they see nobody appear for them; the common people to a man entertain this notion, and insult us wherever we go. We bear their ill usage, though very irksome; but all this will be set right when you have built the Fort, and you will see that we in particular are sincere, and many others will come to your assistance. We desire when the fort is built, you will put into the command of so important a place some of your people; grave, solid, and sensible men, who are in repute amongst you, and in whom we can place a Confidence. . . . Do yourselves and us Justice, and bring your Enemies to a due Sense of themselves, and to offer just Terms, and then, and not till then, think of a Peace. This is our Advice.

From Pontiac, Speeches (1762 and 1763)

Pontiac was a leader of the pan-Indian resistance to English rule known as Pontiac's Rebellion, which followed the end of the Seven Years' War. Neolin was a Delaware religious prophet who helped to inspire the rebellion.

Englishmen, although you have conquered the French, you have not yet conquered us! We are not your slaves. These lakes, these woods, and mountains were left to us by our ancestors. They are our inheritance; and we will part with them to none. Your nation supposes that we, like the white people, cannot live without bread and pork and beef! But you ought to know that He, the Great Spirit and Master of Life, has provided food for us in these spacious lakes, and on these woody mountains.

[The Master of Life has said to Neolin:]

I am the Maker of heaven and earth, the trees, lakes, rivers, and all else. I am the Maker of all mankind; and because I love you, you must do my will. The land on which you live I have made for you and not for others. Why do you suffer the white man to dwell among you? My children, you have forgotten the customs and traditions of your forefathers. Why do you not clothe yourselves in skins, as they did, use bows and arrows and the stone-pointed lances, which they used? You have bought guns, knives, kettles and blankets from the white man until you can no longer do without them; and what is worse, you have drunk the poison firewater, which turns you into fools. Fling all these things away; live as your wise forefathers did before you. And as for these English—these dogs dressed in red, who have come to rob you of your hunting-grounds, and drive away the game—you must lift the hatchet against them. Wipe them from the face of the earth, and then you will win my favor back again, and once more be happy and prosperous.

QUESTIONS

1. *What aspects of white behavior does Scarouyady object to?*
2. *What elements of Indian life does Neolin criticize most strongly?*
3. *How do Scarouyady and Pontiac differ in the ways they address white audiences?*

Pennsylvania and the Indians

The Seven Years' War not only redrew the map of the world but produced dramatic changes within the American colonies as well. In Pennsylvania, the conflict shattered the decades-old rule of the Quaker elite and dealt the final blow to the colony's policy of accommodation with the Indians. During the war, with the frontier ablaze with battles between settlers and French and Indian warriors, western Pennsylvanians demanded that colonial authorities adopt a more aggressive stance. When the governor declared war on hostile Delawares, raised a militia, and offered a bounty for Indian scalps, many of the assembly's pacifist Quakers resigned their seats, effectively ending their control of Pennsylvania politics.

Frontier tensions

In December 1763, while Pontiac's Rebellion still raged, a party of fifty armed men, mostly Scotch-Irish farmers from the vicinity of the Pennsylvania town of Paxton, destroyed the Indian village of Conestoga and then marched on Philadelphia, intending to attack Moravian Indians who resided near the city. The governor ordered the expulsion of much of the Indian population. By the 1760s, Pennsylvania's Holy Experiment was at an end and with it William Penn's promise of "true friendship and amity" between colonists and the native population.

The town of Paxton

Colonial Identities

Before the war, the colonies had been largely isolated from one another. Outside of New England, more Americans probably traveled to England than from one colony to another. The **Albany Plan of Union** of 1754, drafted by Benjamin Franklin at the outbreak of the Seven Years' War, envisioned the creation of a Grand Council composed of delegates from each colony, with the power to levy taxes and deal with Indian relations and the common defense. Rejected by the colonial assemblies, whose powers Franklin's proposal would curtail, the plan was never sent to London for approval.

Participation in the Seven Years' War created greater bonds among the colonies. But the war also strengthened colonists' pride in being members of the British empire. It has been said that Americans were never more British than in 1763. The defeat of the Catholic French reinforced the equation of British nationality, Protestantism, and freedom.

The war and American identity

But soon, the American colonists would come to believe that membership in the empire jeopardized their liberty. When they did, they set out on a road that led to independence.

CHAPTER REVIEW AND ONLINE RESOURCES

REVIEW QUESTIONS

1. *How did Great Britain's position in North America change relative to the other European powers during the first three-quarters of the eighteenth century?*
2. *How did the ideas of republicanism and liberalism differ in eighteenth-century British North America?*
3. *Three distinct slave systems were well entrenched in Britain's mainland colonies. Describe the main characteristics of each system.*
4. *How and why did the colonists' sense of a collective British identity change during the years before 1764?*
5. *What ideas generated by the American Enlightenment and the Great Awakening prompted challenges to religious, social, and political authorities in the British colonies?*
6. *How were colonial merchants in British America involved in the Atlantic economy, and what was the role of the slave trade in that economy?*
7. *We often consider the impact of the slave trade only on the United States, but its impact extended much further. How did it affect West African nations and society, other regions of the New World, and the nations of Europe?*
8. *How was an African-American collective identity created in these years, and what role did slave rebellions play in that process?*
9. *How did a distinct Native American identity start to emerge after the Seven Years' War?*

KEY TERMS

Atlantic slave trade (p. 106)
Middle Passage (p. 107)
yeoman farmers (p. 113)
Stono Rebellion (p. 114)
republicanism (p. 116)
liberalism (p. 116)
salutary neglect (p. 119)
Enlightenment (p. 122)
Deism (p. 123)
Great Awakening (p. 123)
Father Junípero Serra (p. 127)
middle ground (p. 129)
Seven Years' War (p. 130)
French and Indian War (p. 130)
Pontiac's Rebellion (p. 133)
Neolin (p. 133)
Proclamation of 1763 (p. 133)
Albany Plan of Union (p. 136)

Go to INQUIZITIVE

To see what you know—and learn what you've missed—with personalized feedback along the way.

Visit the ***Give Me Liberty!* Student Site** for primary source documents and images, interactive maps, author videos featuring Eric Foner, and more.

CHAPTER 5

THE AMERICAN REVOLUTION

★

1763–1783

1760	George III assumes the British throne
1764	Sugar Act
1765	Stamp Act
	Sons of Liberty organized
	Stamp Act Congress
1767	Townshend Acts
1768	British troops stationed in Boston
1770	Boston Massacre
1773	Tea Act
	Boston Tea Party
1774	Intolerable Acts
	First Continental Congress convenes
1775	Battles at Lexington and Concord
	Lord Dunmore's proclamation
1776	Thomas Paine's *Common Sense*
	Declaration of Independence
	Battle of Trenton
1777	Battle of Saratoga
1778	Treaty of Amity and Commerce with France
1781	Cornwallis surrenders at Yorktown
1783	Treaty of Paris

A French engraving depicts New Yorkers tearing down the statue of King George III in July 1776, after the approval of the Declaration of Independence. Slaves are doing the work, while whites look on. The statue was later melted down to make bullets for the Continental army.

On the night of August 26, 1765, a violent crowd of Bostonians assaulted the elegant home of Thomas Hutchinson, chief justice and lieutenant governor of Massachusetts. Hutchinson and his family barely had time to escape before the crowd broke down the front door and proceeded to destroy or carry off most of their possessions, including paintings, furniture, silverware, and notes for a history of Massachusetts Hutchinson was writing. By the time the crowd departed, only the outer walls of the home remained standing.

The immediate cause of the riot was the **Stamp Act**, a recently enacted British tax that many colonists felt violated their liberty. Only a few days earlier, Hutchinson had helped to disperse a crowd attacking a building owned by his relative Andrew Oliver, a merchant who had been appointed to help administer the new law. Both crowds were led by Ebenezer Mackintosh, a shoemaker who enjoyed a wide following among Boston's working people.

The riot of August 26 was one small episode in a series of events that launched a half-century of popular protest and political upheaval throughout the Western world. The momentous era that came to be called the Age of Revolution began in British North America, spread to Europe and the Caribbean, and culminated in the Latin American wars for independence. In all these struggles, "Liberty" emerged as the foremost rallying cry for popular discontent. Rarely has the idea played so central a role in political debate and social upheaval.

If the attack on Hutchinson's home demonstrated the depths of feeling aroused by Britain's efforts to impose greater control over its empire, it also revealed that revolution is a dynamic process whose consequences no one can anticipate. The crowd's fury expressed resentments against the rich and powerful quite different from colonial leaders' objections to Parliament's attempt to tax the colonies. The Stamp Act crisis inaugurated not only a struggle for colonial liberty in relation to Great Britain but also a multisided battle to define and extend liberty within the new nation.

FOCUS QUESTIONS

- *What were the roots and significance of the Stamp Act controversy?*
- *What key events sharpened the divisions between Britain and the colonists in the late 1760s and early 1770s?*
- *What key events marked the move toward American independence?*
- *How were American forces able to prevail in the Revolutionary War?*

THE CRISIS BEGINS

Consolidating the Empire

When George III assumed the throne of Great Britain in 1760, no one on either side of the Atlantic imagined that within two decades Britain's American colonies would separate from the empire. Having treated the colonists as allies during the Seven Years' War, Britain reverted in the mid-1760s to seeing them as subordinates whose main role was to enrich

According to the doctrine of "virtual representation," the House of Commons represented all residents of the British empire, whether or not they could vote for members. In this 1775 cartoon criticizing the idea, a blinded Britannia, on the far right, stumbles into a pit. Next to her, two colonists complain of being robbed by British taxation. In the background, according to an accompanying explanation of the cartoon, stand the "Catholic" city of Quebec and the "Protestant town of Boston," the latter in flames.

the mother country. During this period, the government in London concerned itself with the colonies in unprecedented ways, hoping to make British rule more efficient and systematic and to raise funds to help pay for the war and to finance the empire. Nearly all British political leaders supported the new laws that so enraged the colonists. To fight the Seven Years' War, Britain had borrowed from banks and individual investors more than £150 million (the equivalent of tens of trillions of dollars in today's money). It seemed only reasonable that the colonies should help pay this national debt, foot part of the bill for continued British protection, and stop cheating the treasury by violating the Navigation Acts.

Nearly all Britons, moreover, believed that Parliament represented the entire empire and had a right to legislate for it. Millions of Britons, including the residents of major cities like Manchester and Birmingham, had no representatives in Parliament. But according to the widely accepted theory of **virtual representation**—which held that each member represented the empire, not just his own district—the interests of all who lived under the British crown were supposedly taken into account. When Americans began to insist that because they were unrepresented in Parliament, the British government could not tax the colonies, they won little support in the mother country.

The British government had already alarmed many colonists by issuing **writs of assistance** to combat smuggling. These were general search warrants that allowed customs officials to search anywhere they chose for smuggled goods. In a celebrated court case in Boston in 1761, the lawyer James Otis insisted that the writs were "an instrument of arbitrary power, destructive to English liberty, and the fundamental principles of the [British] Constitution," and that Parliament therefore had no right to authorize them. ("American independence was then and there born," the Boston lawyer John Adams later remarked—a considerable exaggeration.)

Outrage in the colonies

Many colonists were also outraged by the Proclamation of 1763 (mentioned in the previous chapter), which barred further settlement on lands west of the Appalachian Mountains.

Taxing the Colonies

The Sugar Act of 1764

In 1764, the **Sugar Act**, introduced by Prime Minister George Grenville, reduced the existing tax on molasses imported into North America from the French West Indies from six pence to three pence per gallon. But the act also established a new machinery to end widespread smuggling by colonial merchants. And to counteract the tendency of colonial juries to acquit merchants charged with violating trade regulations, it strengthened the admiralty courts, where accused smugglers could be judged without benefit of a jury trial. Thus, colonists saw the measure not as a welcome reduction in taxation but as an attempt to get them to pay a levy they would otherwise have evaded. At the same time, the Currency Act reaffirmed the earlier ban on colonial assemblies' issuing paper as "legal tender"—that is, money that individuals are required to accept in payment of debts.

The Stamp Act of 1765

The Sugar Act was an effort to strengthen the long-established (and long-evaded) Navigation Acts. The Stamp Act of 1765 was a new departure in imperial policy. For the first time, Parliament attempted to raise money from direct taxes in the colonies rather than through the regulation of trade. The act required that all sorts of printed material produced in the colonies—such as newspapers, books, court documents, commercial papers, land deeds, and almanacs—carry a stamp purchased from authorities. Its purpose was to help finance the operations of the empire, including the cost of stationing British troops in North America, without seeking revenue from colonial assemblies.

Whereas the Sugar Act had mainly affected residents of colonial ports, the Stamp Act managed to offend virtually every free colonist—rich and poor, farmers, artisans, and merchants. It was especially resented by members of the public sphere who wrote, published, and read books and newspapers and followed political affairs. The prospect of a British army permanently stationed on American soil also alarmed many colonists. And by imposing the stamp tax without colonial consent, Parliament directly challenged the authority of local elites who, through the assemblies they controlled, had established their power over the raising and spending of money. They were ready to defend this authority in the name of liberty.

Opposition to the Stamp Act

Opposition to the Stamp Act was the first great drama of the revolutionary era and the first major split between colonists and Great Britain over the meaning of freedom. Nearly all colonial political leaders opposed the act. They invoked the rights of the freeborn Englishman, which, they insisted, colonists should also enjoy. Liberty, they insisted, could not be secure where property was "taken away without consent."

Taxation and Representation

At stake were clashing ideas of the British empire itself. American leaders viewed the empire as an association of equals in which free inhabitants overseas enjoyed the same rights as Britons at home. Colonists in other

This teapot protesting the Stamp Act was produced in England and marketed in colonial America, illustrating the close political and economic connections between the two.

outposts of the empire, such as India, the West Indies, and Canada, echoed this outlook. All, in the name of liberty, claimed the right to govern their own affairs. The British government and its appointed representatives in America, by contrast, saw the empire as a system of unequal parts in which different principles governed different areas, and all were subject to the authority of Parliament. To surrender the right to tax the colonies would set a dangerous precedent for the empire as a whole.

Some opponents of the Stamp Act distinguished between "internal" taxes like the stamp duty, which they claimed Parliament had no right to impose, and revenue legitimately raised through the regulation of trade. But more and more colonists insisted that Britain had no right to tax them at all, since Americans were unrepresented in the House of Commons. **"No taxation without representation"** became their rallying cry. Virginia's House of Burgesses approved four resolutions offered by the fiery orator Patrick Henry. They insisted that the colonists enjoyed the same "liberties, privileges, franchises, and immunities" as residents of the mother country and that the right to consent to taxation was a cornerstone of "British freedom." (The House rejected as too radical three other resolutions, including Henry's call for outright resistance to unlawful taxation, but these were also reprinted in colonial newspapers.)

Stamp Act repeal

In October 1765, the Stamp Act Congress, with twenty-seven delegates from nine colonies, including some of the most prominent men in America, met in New York and endorsed Virginia's position. Its resolutions began by affirming the "allegiance" of all colonists to the "Crown of Great Britain" and their "due subordination" to Parliament. But they went on to insist that the right to consent to taxation was "essential to the freedom of a people." Soon, merchants throughout the colonies agreed to boycott British goods until Parliament repealed the Stamp Act. This was the first major cooperative action among Britain's mainland colonies. By seeking to impose uniformity on the colonies rather than dealing with them individually as in the past, Parliament had inadvertently united America.

The Stamp Act crisis, however, did not lead inevitably to revolution. Nearly all the British colonies in the Western Hemisphere protested the tax, but only about half eventually decided to strike for independence. At this point, most colonists continued to believe that their liberties and material interests were safer inside the British empire than outside it.

Liberty and Resistance

No word was more frequently invoked by critics of the Stamp Act than "liberty." Throughout the colonies, opponents of the new tax staged mock funerals in which liberty's coffin was carried to a burial ground, only to have the occupant miraculously revived at the last moment, whereupon the assembled crowd repaired to a tavern to celebrate. As the crisis continued, symbols of liberty proliferated. A large elm tree came to be known as the Liberty Tree. Its image soon appeared in prints and pamphlets throughout the colonies.

The Liberty Tree

Colonial leaders resolved to prevent the new law's implementation, and by and large they succeeded. Even before the passage of the Stamp Act, a **Committee of Correspondence** in Boston communicated with other colonies to encourage opposition to the Sugar and Currency Acts. Now, such committees sprang up in other colonies, exchanging ideas and information about resistance. Initiated by colonial elites, the movement against the Stamp Act quickly drew in a far broader range of Americans. The act, wrote John Adams, had inspired "the people, even to the lowest ranks," to become "more attentive to their liberties, more inquisitive about them, and more determined to defend them, than they were ever before known."

Organized resistance

Opponents of the Stamp Act, however, did not rely solely on debate. Even before the law went into effect, crowds forced those chosen to administer it to resign and destroyed shipments of stamps. In 1765, New York City residents were organized by the newly created **Sons of Liberty**, who led protest processions, posted notices reading "Liberty, Property, and No Stamps," and enforced the boycott of British imports.

Stunned by the ferocity of American resistance and pressured by London merchants and manufacturers who did not wish to lose their American markets, the British government retreated. In 1766, Parliament repealed the Stamp Act. But this concession was accompanied by the Declaratory Act, which rejected Americans' claims that only their elected representatives could levy taxes. Parliament, proclaimed this measure, possessed the power to pass laws for "the colonies and people of America . . . in all cases whatsoever." Since the debt-ridden British government continued to need money raised in the colonies, passage of the Declaratory Act promised further conflict.

The Declaratory Act

The Regulators

The Stamp Act crisis was not the only example of violent social turmoil during the 1760s. Many colonies experienced contentious internal divisions as well. As population moved westward, the conflicting land claims of settlers, speculators, colonial governments, and Indians sparked fierce disputes. As in the Stamp Act crisis, "Liberty" was the rallying cry, but in this case liberty had less to do with imperial policy than with secure possession of land.

Beginning in the mid-1760s, a group of wealthy residents of the South Carolina backcountry calling themselves **Regulators** protested the under-representation of western settlements in the colony's assembly and the legislators' failure to establish local governments that could regularize land titles and suppress bands of outlaws.

Backcountry tensions

A parallel movement in North Carolina mobilized small farmers, who refused to pay taxes, kidnapped local officials, assaulted the homes of land speculators, merchants, and lawyers, and disrupted court proceedings. Here, the complaint was not a lack of government, but corrupt county authorities. Demanding the democratization of local government, the Regulators condemned the "rich and powerful" (the colony's elite) who used their political authority to prosper at the expense of "poor industrious" farmers. At their peak, the Regulators numbered around 8,000 armed farmers. The region remained in turmoil until 1771, when, in the "battle of Alamance," the farmers were suppressed by the colony's militia.

Social divisions and politics

The emerging rift between Britain and America eventually superimposed itself on conflicts within the colonies. But the social divisions revealed in the Stamp Act riots and backcountry uprisings made some members of the colonial elite fear that opposition to British measures might unleash turmoil at home. As a result, they were more reluctant to challenge British authority when the next imperial crisis arose.

THE ROAD TO REVOLUTION

The Townshend Crisis

In 1767, the government in London decided to impose a new set of taxes on Americans, known as the **Townshend Acts**. They were devised by the Chancellor of the Exchequer (the cabinet's chief financial minister), Charles Townshend. In opposing the Stamp Act, some colonists had seemed to suggest that they would not object if Britain raised revenue by regulating trade. Taking them at their word, Townshend persuaded Parliament to impose new taxes on goods imported into the colonies and to create a new board of customs commissioners to collect them and suppress smuggling. Although many merchants objected to the new enforcement procedures, opposition to the Townshend duties developed more slowly than in the case of the Stamp Act. Leaders in several colonies nonetheless decided in 1768 to reimpose the ban on importing British goods.

Homespun clothing as resistance

Reliance on American rather than British goods, on homespun clothing rather than imported finery, became a symbol of American resistance. It also reflected, as the colonists saw it, a virtuous spirit of self-sacrifice as compared with the self-indulgence and luxury many Americans were coming to associate with Britain. Women who spun and wove at home so as not to purchase British goods were hailed as Daughters of Liberty.

Nonimportation

The idea of using homemade rather than imported goods especially appealed to Chesapeake planters, who found themselves owing increasing amounts of money to British merchants. Nonimportation, wrote George Washington, gave "the extravagant man" an opportunity to "retrench his expenses" by reducing the purchase of British luxuries, without having to advertise to his neighbors that he might be in financial distress.

Urban artisans, who welcomed an end to competition from imported British manufactured goods, strongly supported the boycott. Philadelphia and New York merchants at first were reluctant to take part, although they eventually agreed to go along. As had happened during the Stamp Act crisis, the streets of American cities filled with popular protests against the duties imposed by Parliament. Extralegal local committees attempted to enforce the boycott of British goods.

The Boston Massacre

Royal troops in Boston

Boston once again became the focal point of conflict. Royal troops had been stationed in the city in 1768 after rioting that followed the British seizure of the ship *Liberty* for violating trade regulations. The soldiers, who competed for jobs on Boston's waterfront with the city's laborers, became more and more unpopular. On March 5, 1770, a fight between a snowball-throwing crowd and British troops escalated into an armed confrontation that left five Bostonians dead. One of those who fell in what came to be called the **Boston Massacre** was **Crispus Attucks,** a sailor of mixed Indian-African-white ancestry. The commanding officer and eight soldiers were put on trial in Massachusetts. Ably defended by John Adams, who viewed lower-class crowd actions as a dangerous method of opposing British policies, seven were found not guilty, while two were convicted of manslaughter. But Paul Revere, a member of the Boston Sons of Liberty and a silversmith and engraver, helped to stir up indignation against the British army by producing a widely circulated (and quite inaccurate) print of the Boston Massacre depicting a line of British soldiers firing into an unarmed crowd.

By 1770, as merchants' profits shriveled and many members of the colonial elite found they could not do without British goods, the

The Boston Massacre. Less than a month after the Boston Massacre of 1770, in which five colonists died, Paul Revere produced this engraving of the event. Although it inaccurately depicts what was actually a disorganized brawl between residents of Boston and British soldiers, this image became one of the most influential pieces of political propaganda of the revolutionary era.

nonimportation movement was collapsing. British merchants, who wished to remove a possible source of future interruption of trade, pressed for repeal of the Townshend duties. When the British ministry agreed, leaving in place only a tax on tea, and agreed to remove troops from Boston, American merchants quickly abandoned the boycott.

Once again, an immediate crisis had been resolved. Nonetheless, many Americans concluded that Britain was succumbing to the same pattern of political corruption and decline of liberty that afflicted other countries. In addition, rumors circulated in the colonies that the Anglican Church in England planned to send bishops to America. Among members of other Protestant denominations, the rumors—strongly denied in London—sparked fears that bishops would establish religious courts like those that had once persecuted Dissenters.

The Tea Act

The next crisis underscored how powerfully events in other parts of Britain's global empire affected the American colonies. The East India Company, a giant trading monopoly, effectively governed recently acquired British possessions in India. Numerous British merchants, bankers, and other individuals had invested heavily in its stock. A classic speculative bubble ensued, with the price of stock in the company rising sharply and then collapsing. To rescue the company and its investors, the British government decided to help it market its enormous holdings of Chinese tea in North America.

To further stimulate its sales and bail out the East India Company, the British government, now headed by Frederick Lord North, offered the company a series of rebates and tax exemptions. These enabled it to dump low-priced tea on the American market, undercutting both established merchants and smugglers.

The tax on tea was not new. But many colonists insisted that to pay it on this large new body of imports would acknowledge Britain's right to tax the colonies. As tea shipments arrived, resistance developed in the major ports. On December 16, 1773, a group of colonists disguised as Indians boarded three ships at anchor in Boston Harbor and threw more than 300 chests of tea into the water. The event became known as the **Boston Tea Party**. The loss to the East India Company was around £10,000 (the equivalent of more than $4 million today).

An Attempt to Land a Bishop in America, an engraving from a London magazine published in 1769. A crowd of New Englanders prevents a ship carrying a bishop dispatched by the Church of England from landing. The crowd carries the works of political philosopher John Locke and a banner proclaiming "Liberty and Freedom of Conscience," and hurls the writings of Protestant theologian John Calvin at the bishop.

The Intolerable Acts

The British government, declared Lord North, must now demonstrate "whether we have, or have not, any authority in that country." Its response to the Boston Tea Party was swift and decisive. Parliament closed the port of Boston to all trade until the tea was paid for. It radically altered the Massachusetts Charter of 1691 by curtailing town meetings and authorizing the governor to appoint members to the council—positions previously filled by election. Parliament also empowered military commanders to lodge soldiers in private homes. These measures, called the Coercive or **Intolerable Acts** by Americans, united the colonies in opposition to what was widely seen as a direct threat to their political freedom.

At almost the same time, Parliament passed the Quebec Act. This extended the southern boundary of that Canadian province to the Ohio River and granted legal toleration to the Roman Catholic Church in Canada. The act not only threw into question land claims in the Ohio country but also persuaded many colonists that the government in London was conspiring to strengthen Catholicism—dreaded by most Protestants—in its American empire.

THE COMING OF INDEPENDENCE

The Continental Congress

Opposition to the Intolerable Acts now spread to small towns and rural areas that had not participated actively in previous resistance. In September 1774, in the town of Worcester, Massachusetts, 4,600 militiamen from thirty-seven towns (half the adult male population of the entire county) lined both sides of Main Street as the British-appointed officials walked between them. That month, a convention of delegates from Massachusetts towns approved a series of resolutions (called the Suffolk Resolves for the county in which Boston is located) that urged Americans to refuse obedience to the new laws, withhold taxes, and prepare for war.

Suffolk Resolves

To coordinate resistance to the Intolerable Acts, a **Continental Congress** convened in Philadelphia, bringing together the most prominent political leaders of twelve mainland colonies (Georgia did not take part). From Massachusetts came the "brace of Adamses"—John and his more radical cousin Samuel. Virginia's seven delegates included George Washington, Richard Henry Lee, and the renowned orator Patrick Henry. "The distinctions between Virginians, Pennsylvanians, New Yorkers, and New Englanders," Henry declared, "are no more. I am not a Virginian, but an American." In March 1775, Henry concluded a speech urging a Virginia convention to begin military preparations with a legendary credo: "Give me liberty, or give me death!"

Leaders of the Congress

The Continental Association

Before it adjourned at the end of October 1774, the Congress endorsed the Suffolk Resolves and adopted the Continental Association, which called for an almost complete halt to trade with Great Britain and the West Indies (at South Carolina's insistence, exports of rice to Europe were exempted). Congress authorized local Committees of Safety to implement its mandates and to take action against "enemies of American liberty," including businessmen who tried to profit from the sudden scarcity of goods.

The Committees of Safety

The Committees of Safety began the process of transferring effective political power from established governments whose authority derived from Great Britain to extralegal grassroots bodies reflecting the will of the people. By early 1775, some 7,000 men were serving on local committees throughout the colonies, a vast expansion of the "political nation." The committees became training grounds where small farmers, city artisans, propertyless laborers, and others who had heretofore had little role in government discussed political issues and exercised political power. When the New York assembly refused to endorse the Association, local committees continued to enforce it anyway.

The Sweets of Liberty

By 1775, talk of liberty pervaded the colonies. The past few years had witnessed an endless parade of pamphlets with titles like *A Chariot of Liberty* and *Oration on the Beauties of Liberty*. (The latter, a sermon delivered in Boston by Joseph Allen in 1772, became the most popular public address of the years before independence.) Sober men spoke longingly of the "sweets of liberty." Commented a British immigrant who arrived in Maryland early in 1775: "They are all liberty mad."

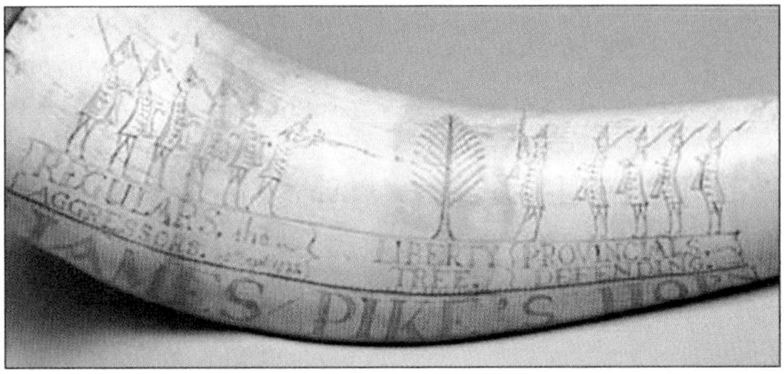

In March 1776, James Pike, a soldier in the Massachusetts militia, carved this scene on his powder horn to commemorate the battles of Lexington and Concord. At the center stands the Liberty Tree.

As the crisis deepened, Americans increasingly based their claims not simply on the historical rights of Englishmen but on the more abstract language of natural rights and universal freedom. The First Continental Congress defended its actions by appealing to the "principles of the English constitution," the "liberties of free and natural-born subjects within the realm of England," and the "immutable law of nature." John Locke's theory of natural rights offered a powerful justification for colonial resistance, as did Thomas Jefferson in *A Summary View of the Rights of British America*, written in 1774. Americans, Jefferson declared, were "a free people claiming their rights, as derived from the laws of nature, and not as the gift of their chief magistrate."

The Outbreak of War

By the time the Second Continental Congress convened in May 1775, war had broken out between British soldiers and armed citizens of Massachusetts. On April 19, a force of British soldiers marched from Boston toward the nearby town of Concord to seize arms being stockpiled there. Riders from Boston, among them Paul Revere, warned local leaders of the troops' approach. Militiamen took up arms and tried to resist the British advance. Skirmishes between Americans and British soldiers took place, known as the **Battles of Lexington and Concord**. By the time the British retreated to the safety of Boston, some forty-nine Americans and seventy-three members of the Royal Army lay dead.

Lexington and Concord

What the philosopher Ralph Waldo Emerson would later call "the shot heard 'round the world" began the American War of Independence. In May 1775, Ethan Allen and the Green Mountain Boys from Vermont, together with militiamen from Connecticut led by Benedict Arnold, surrounded Fort Ticonderoga in New York and forced it to surrender. The following winter, Henry Knox, George Washington's commander of artillery, arranged for some of the Ticonderoga cannon to be dragged hundreds of miles to the east to reinforce the siege of Boston, where British forces were ensconced. On June 17, 1775, two months after Lexington and Concord, the British had dislodged colonial militiamen from Breed's Hill, although only at a heavy cost in casualties. (The battle came to be named the **Battle of Bunker Hill**, after the nearby Bunker Hill.) But the arrival of American cannon in March 1776 and their entrenchment above the city made the British position in Boston untenable. The British army under the command of Sir William Howe was forced to abandon the city. Before leaving, Howe's forces cut down the original Liberty Tree.

The Second Continental Congress

Meanwhile, the Second Continental Congress authorized the raising of a **Continental army**, printed money to pay for it, and appointed George Washington its commander. In response, Britain declared the colonies in a state of rebellion, dispatched thousands of troops, and ordered the closing of all colonial ports.

Independence?

By the end of 1775, the breach with Britain seemed irreparable. But many colonists shied away from the idea of independence. Pride in membership in the British empire was still strong, and many political leaders, especially in colonies that had experienced internal turmoil, feared that a complete break with the mother country might unleash further conflict.

The Dunmore proclamation

Such fears affected how colonial leaders responded to the idea of independence. The elites of Massachusetts and Virginia, who felt supremely confident of their ability to retain authority at home, tended to support a break with Britain. Southern leaders not only were highly protective of their political liberty but also were outraged by a proclamation issued in November 1775 by Lord Dunmore, the British governor and military commander in Virginia. **Lord Dunmore's proclamation** offered freedom to any slave who escaped to his lines and bore arms for the king.

Fear of domestic turmoil

In New York and Pennsylvania, however, the diversity of the population made it difficult to work out a consensus on how far to go in resisting British measures. Many established leaders drew back from further resistance. Joseph Galloway, a Pennsylvania leader and delegate to the Second Continental Congress who worked to devise a compromise between British and colonial positions, warned that independence would be accompanied by constant disputes within America. He even predicted a war between the northern and southern colonies.

Common Sense

As 1776 dawned, America presented the unusual spectacle of colonists at war against the British empire but still pleading for their rights within it. Ironically, it was a recent emigrant from England, not a colonist from a family long established on American soil, who grasped the inner logic of the situation and offered a vision of the broad significance of American independence. Thomas Paine had emigrated to Philadelphia late in 1774. He quickly became associated with a group of advocates of the American cause, including John Adams and Dr. Benjamin Rush, a leading Philadelphia physician. It was Rush who suggested to Paine that he write a pamphlet supporting American independence.

Paine on monarchy and aristocracy

Common Sense appeared in January 1776. The pamphlet began not with a recital of colonial grievances but with an attack on the "so much boasted Constitution of England" and the principles of hereditary rule and monarchical government. Rather than being the most perfect system of government in the world, Paine wrote, the English monarchy was headed by "the royal brute of England," and the English constitution was composed in large part of "the base remains of two ancient tyrannies . . . monarchical tyranny in the person of the king [and] aristocratical tyranny in the persons of the peers."

Turning to independence, Paine drew on the colonists' experiences to make his case. "There is something absurd," he wrote, "in supposing a Continent to be perpetually governed by an island." With independence, moreover, the colonies could for the first time trade freely with the entire world and insulate themselves from involvement in the endless imperial wars of Europe. Membership in the British empire, Paine insisted, was a burden to the colonies, not a benefit.

Toward the close of the pamphlet, Paine moved beyond practical considerations to outline a breathtaking vision of the historical importance of the American Revolution. "The cause of America," he proclaimed in stirring language, "is in great measure, the cause of all mankind." The new nation would become the home of freedom, "an asylum for mankind."

Few of Paine's ideas were original. What made *Common Sense* unique was his mode of expressing them and the audience he addressed. Previous political writings had generally been directed toward the educated elite. Paine, however, pioneered a new style of political writing, one designed to expand dramatically the public sphere where political discussion took place. He wrote clearly and directly, and he avoided the complex language and Latin phrases common in pamphlets aimed at educated readers. *Common Sense* quickly became one of the most successful and influential pamphlets in the history of political writing, selling, by Paine's estimate, some 150,000 copies. Paine directed that his share of the profits be used to buy supplies for the Continental army.

In the spring of 1776, scores of American communities adopted resolutions calling for a separation from Britain. Only six months elapsed between the appearance of *Common Sense* and the decision by the Second Continental Congress to sever the colonies' ties with Great Britain.

The cover of *Common Sense*, Thomas Paine's influential pamphlet denouncing the idea of hereditary rule and calling for American independence.

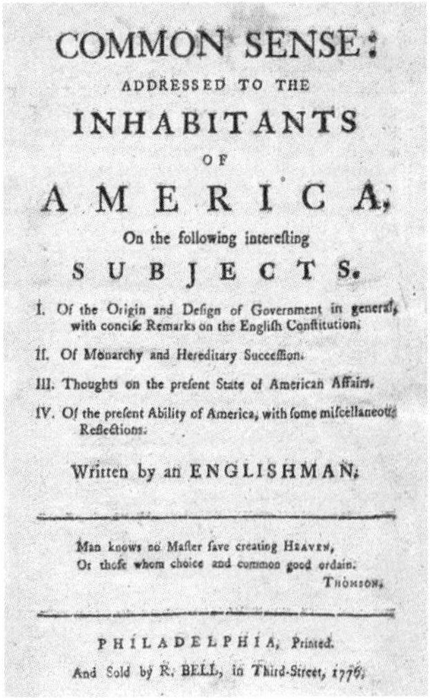

COMMON SENSE;
ADDRESSED TO THE
INHABITANTS
OF
AMERICA,
On the following intereſting
SUBJECTS.

I. Of the Origin and Deſign of Government in general, with conciſe Remarks on the Engliſh Conſtitution.

II. Of Monarchy and Hereditary Succeſſion.

III. Thoughts on the preſent State of American Affairs.

IV. Of the preſent Ability of America, with ſome miſcellaneous Reflections.

Written by an ENGLISHMAN.

Man knows no Maſter ſave creating HEAVEN,
Or thoſe whom choice and common good ordain.
THOMSON.

PHILADELPHIA, Printed.
And Sold by R. BELL, in Third-Street, 1776.

The Declaration of Independence

On July 2, 1776, the Congress formally declared the United States an independent nation. Two days later, it approved the **Declaration of Independence**, written by Thomas Jefferson and revised by the Congress before approval. (See the Appendix for the full text.) Most of the Declaration consists of a lengthy list of grievances directed against King George III, ranging from quartering troops in colonial homes to imposing taxes without the colonists' consent. One clause in Jefferson's draft, which condemned the inhumanity of the slave trade and criticized the king for overturning colonial laws that sought to restrict the importation of slaves, was deleted by the Congress at the insistence of Georgia and South Carolina.

Colonial grievances

The Declaration's enduring impact came not from the complaints against George III but from Jefferson's preamble, especially the second paragraph, which begins, "We hold these truths to be self-evident, that all men are created equal, that they are endowed by their Creator with certain unalienable Rights, that among these are Life, Liberty, and the pursuit of Happiness." By "unalienable rights," Jefferson meant rights so basic, so rooted in human nature itself, that no government could take them away.

Jefferson's preamble

Jefferson then went on to justify the breach with Britain. Government, he wrote, derives its powers from "the consent of the governed." When a government threatens its subjects' natural rights, the people have the authority "to alter or to abolish it." The Declaration of Independence is ultimately an assertion of the right of revolution.

The Declaration also changed forever the meaning of American freedom. It completed the shift from the rights of Englishmen to the rights of mankind as the object of American independence. No longer a set of specific rights, no longer a privilege to be enjoyed by a corporate body or people in certain social circumstances, liberty had become a universal entitlement.

The Declaration and American freedom

When Jefferson substituted the "pursuit of happiness" for property in the familiar triad that opens the Declaration, he tied the new nation's star to an open-ended, democratic process whereby individuals develop their own potential and seek to realize their own life goals. Individual self-fulfillment, unimpeded by government, would become a central element of American freedom. Tradition would no longer rule the present, and Americans could shape their society as they saw fit.

An Asylum for Mankind

A distinctive definition of nationality resting on American freedom was born in the Revolution. From the beginning, the idea of "American exceptionalism"—the belief that the United States has a special mission to be a refuge from tyranny, a symbol of freedom, and a model for the rest of the world—has occupied a central place in American nationalism. The new nation declared itself, in the words of Virginia leader James Madison, the "workshop of liberty to the Civilized World." Unburdened by the institutions—monarchy, aristocracy, hereditary privilege—that oppressed the peoples of the Old World, America and America alone was the place where the principle of universal freedom could take root. This was why Jefferson addressed the Declaration to "the opinions of mankind," not just the colonists themselves or Great Britain.

America as a Symbol of Liberty, a 1775 engraving from the cover of the *Pennsylvania Magazine*, edited by Thomas Paine soon after his arrival in America. The shield displays the colony's coat of arms. The female figure holding a liberty cap is surrounded by weaponry of the patriotic struggle, including a cartridge box marked "liberty," hanging from a tree (*right*).

First to add his name to the Declaration of Independence was the Massachusetts merchant John Hancock, president of the Second Continental Congress, with a signature so large, he declared, according to legend, that King George III could read it without his spectacles.

The Global Declaration of Independence

Even apart from the Declaration of Independence, 1776 was a momentous year in North America. Spain established Mission Dolores, the first European settlement at San Francisco, in an effort to block Russian advances on the Pacific coast. In San Diego, local Indians rebelled, unsuccessfully, against Spanish rule. The Lakota Sioux, migrating westward from Minnesota, settled in the Black Hills of North Dakota, their homeland for the next century. All these places and peoples would eventually become part of the United States, but, of course, no one knew this in 1776.

Meanwhile, the struggle for independence reverberated around the globe. The American colonists were less concerned with securing human rights for all mankind than with winning international recognition in their struggle for independence from Britain. But Jefferson hoped that this rebellion would become "the signal of arousing men to burst the chains . . . and to assume the blessings and security of self-government." The Declaration quickly appeared in French and German translations, although not, at first, in Spanish, since the government feared it would inspire dangerous ideas among the peoples of Spain's American empire.

Legacy of the Declaration

In the years since 1776, numerous anticolonial movements have modeled their own declarations of independence on America's. Today more than half the countries in the world, in places as far-flung as China (issued

VOICES OF FREEDOM

From Samuel Seabury, *An Alarm to the Legislature of the Province in New-York* (1775)

An Anglican minister and graduate of Yale College, Samuel Seabury was a devoted Loyalist who in 1774 and 1775 published several pamphlets opposing the revolutionary movement. He remained in the United States after the War of Independence and became the new nation's first Episcopal bishop.

The unhappy contention we have entered into with our parent state, would inevitably be attended with many disagreeable circumstances, with many and great inconveniences to us, even were it conducted on our part, with propriety and moderation. What then must be the case, when all proper and moderate measures are rejected? . . . When every scheme that tends to peace, is branded with ignominy; as being the machination of slavery! When nothing is called FREEDOM but SEDITION! Nothing LIBERTY but REBELLION! . . .

A Committee, chosen in a tumultuous, illegal manner, usurped the most despotic authority over the province. They entered into contracts, compacts, combinations, treaties of alliance, with the other colonies, without any power from the legislature of the province. They agreed with the other Colonies to send Delegates to meet in convention at Philadelphia, to determine upon the rights and liberties of the good people of this province.

The state to which the Grand Congress, and the subordinate Committees, have reduced the colonies, is really deplorable. They have introduced a system of the most oppressive tyranny that can possibly be imagined;—a tyranny, not only over the actions, but over the words, thoughts, and minds, of the good people of this province. People have been threatened with the vengeance of a mob, for speaking in support of order and good government. . . .

Behold, Gentlemen, behold the wretched state to which we are reduced! A foreign power is brought in to govern this province. Laws made at Philadelphia, by factious men from New-England, New-Jersey, Pennsylvania, Maryland, Virginia, and the Carolinas, are imposed upon us by the most imperious menaces. Money is levied upon us without the consent of our representatives. . . . Mobs and riots are encouraged, in order to force submission to the tyranny of the Congress.

From Thomas Paine, *Common Sense* (1776)

A recent emigrant from England, Thomas Paine in January 1776 published *Common Sense*, a highly influential pamphlet that in stirring language made the case for American independence.

In the following pages I offer nothing more than simple facts, plain arguments, and common sense. . . .

Male and female are the distinctions of nature, good and bad the distinctions of heaven; but how a race of men came into the world so exalted above the rest, and distinguished like some new species, is worth enquiring into, and whether they are the means of happiness or of misery to mankind. . . . One of the strongest *natural* proofs of the folly of hereditary right in kings, is, that nature disapproves it, otherwise she would not so frequently turn it into ridicule, by giving mankind an *ass for a lion*. . . .

The sun never shined on a cause of greater worth. 'Tis not the affair of a city, a country, a province, or a kingdom, but of a continent—of at least one eighth part of the habitable globe. 'Tis not the concern of a day, a year, or an age; posterity are virtually involved in the context, and will be more or less affected, even to the end of time, by the proceedings now. Now is the seed time of continental union, faith and honor. . . .

I challenge the warmest advocate for reconciliation to show a single advantage that this continent can reap by being connected with Great Britain. . . . But the injuries and disadvantages which we sustain by that connection, are without number. . . . Any submission to, or dependence on, Great Britain, tends directly to involve this Continent in European wars and quarrels, and set us at variance with nations who would otherwise seek our friendship, and against whom we have neither anger nor complaint.

O ye that love mankind! Ye that dare oppose, not only the tyranny, but the tyrant, stand forth! Every spot of the old world is overrun with oppression. Freedom hath been hunted round the globe. Asia, and Africa, have long expelled her. Europe regards her like a stranger, and England hath given her warning to depart. O! Receive the fugitive, and prepare in time an asylum for mankind.

QUESTIONS

1. *Why does Seabury believe the Continental Congress and local committees are undermining Americans' liberties?*
2. *What does Paine see as the global significance of the American struggle for independence?*
3. *How do the two writers differ in their view of the main threats to American freedom?*

after the revolution of 1911) and Vietnam (1945), have such declarations, though few of them include a list, like Jefferson's, of the rights of citizens that their governments cannot abridge.

The will of "the people"

But even more than the specific language of the Declaration, the principle that legitimate political authority rests on the will of "the people" has been adopted around the world. The idea that "the people" possess rights was quickly internationalized. Slaves in the Caribbean, colonial subjects in India, and indigenous inhabitants of Latin America could all speak this language, to the dismay of those who exercised power over them.

SECURING INDEPENDENCE

The Balance of Power

The Yankee Doodle Intrenchments near Boston, a 1776 British cartoon depicting the American revolutionaries as unimposing citizen soldiers egged on—according to the accompanying text—by a thieving commander and a reckless Puritan minister. The British greatly underestimated Americans' fighting ability in the War of Independence. One member of Parliament in 1775 claimed the colonists "were neither soldiers, nor could be made so," as they were naturally cowardly and "incapable of any sort of order or discipline."

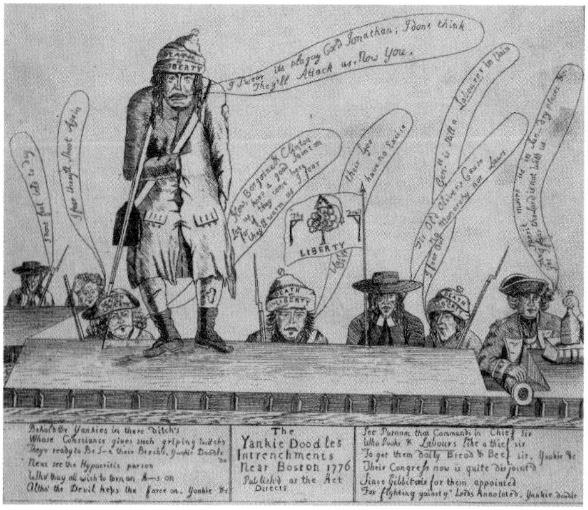

Declaring Americans independent was one thing; winning independence another. The newly created American army confronted the greatest military power on earth. Viewing the Americans as traitors, Britain resolved to crush the rebellion. On the surface, the balance of power seemed heavily weighted in Britain's favor. It had a well-trained army (supplemented by hired soldiers from German states such as Hesse), the world's most powerful navy, and experienced military commanders. Americans had to rely on local militias and an inadequately equipped Continental army.

On the other hand, American soldiers were fighting on their own soil for a cause that inspired devotion and sacrifice. During the eight years of war from 1775 to 1783, some 200,000 men bore arms in the American army (whose soldiers were volunteers) and militias (where service was required of every able-bodied man unless he provided a substitute). The patriots suffered dearly for the cause. Of the colonies' free white male population aged sixteen to forty-five, one in twenty died in the War of Independence, the equivalent of nearly 2 million deaths in today's population. But so long as the Americans maintained an army in the field, the idea of independence remained alive no matter how much territory the British occupied.

Despite British power, to conquer the thirteen colonies would be an enormous and expensive task, and it was not at all certain that the public at home wished to pay the additional taxes that a lengthy war would require. Moreover, European rivals, notably France, welcomed the prospect of a British defeat. If the Americans could forge an alliance with France, a world power second only to Britain, it would go a long way toward equalizing the balance of forces.

American Foot Soldiers, Yorktown Campaign, a 1781 watercolor by a French officer, includes a black soldier from the First Rhode Island Regiment, an all-black unit of 250 men.

Blacks in the Revolution

To American slaves, the War of Independence offered an unprecedented opportunity to seize their own freedom. Many pursued this goal by fighting in one of the opposing armies. At the war's outset, George Washington refused to accept black recruits. But he changed his mind after Lord Dunmore's 1775 proclamation, which offered freedom to slaves who joined the British cause. Some 5,000 blacks enlisted in state militias and the Continental army and navy. Since individuals drafted into the militia were allowed to provide a substitute, slaves suddenly gained considerable bargaining power. Not a few acquired their freedom by agreeing to serve in place of an owner or his son. In 1778, Rhode Island formed a black regiment and promised freedom to slaves who enlisted, while compensating the owners for their loss of property. Blacks who fought under George Washington and in other state militias did so in racially integrated companies (although invariably under white officers). They were the last black American soldiers to do so officially until the Korean War.

Except for South Carolina and Georgia, the southern colonies also enrolled free blacks and slaves to fight. They were not explicitly promised freedom, but many received it individually after the war ended.

Dunmore's regiment

Fighting on the side of the British also offered opportunities for freedom. Before his forces were expelled from Virginia, 800 or more slaves had escaped from their owners to join Lord Dunmore's Ethiopian Regiment, wearing, according to legend, uniforms that bore the motto "Liberty to Slaves." Other escaped slaves served the Royal Army as spies, guided their troops through swamps, and worked as military cooks, laundresses, and construction workers. George Washington himself saw seventeen of his slaves flee to the British, some of whom signed up to fight the colonists. "There is not a man of them, but would leave us, if they believed they could make their escape," his cousin Lund Washington reported. "Liberty is sweet."

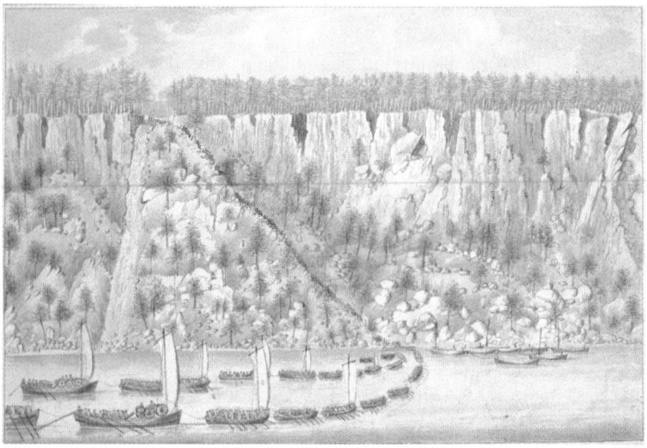

British ships landing sailors on the New Jersey side of the Hudson River in November 1776. They quickly scaled the palisades and began pursuing George Washington's retreating army.

The First Years of the War

Had the British commander, Sir William Howe, prosecuted the war more vigorously at the outset, he might have nipped the rebellion in the bud by destroying Washington's army. But although Washington suffered numerous defeats in the first years of the war, he generally avoided direct confrontations with the British and managed to keep his army intact. Having abandoned Boston, Howe attacked New York City in the summer of 1776. Washington's army had likewise moved from Massachusetts to Brooklyn to defend the city. Howe pushed American forces back and almost cut off Washington's retreat across the East River.

Battles of New Jersey

Howe pursued the American army but never managed to inflict a decisive defeat. Demoralized by successive failures, however, many American soldiers simply went home. Once 28,000 men, Washington's army dwindled to fewer than 3,000. To restore morale and regain the initiative, he launched successful surprise attacks on **Hessian** soldiers at Trenton, New Jersey, on December 26, 1776, and on a British force at Princeton on January 3, 1777. Shortly before crossing the Delaware River to attack the Hessians, Washington had Thomas Paine's inspiring essay *The American Crisis* read to his troops. "These are the times that try men's souls," Paine wrote. "The summer soldier and the sunshine patriot will, in this crisis, shrink from the service of their country; but he that stands it *now*, deserves the love and thanks of man and woman."

The Battle of Saratoga

Howe and Burgoyne

In the summer of 1777, a second British army, led by General John Burgoyne, advanced south from Canada, hoping to link up with Howe and isolate New England. But in July, Howe instead moved his forces from New York City to attack Philadelphia. In September, the Continental Congress fled to Lancaster in central Pennsylvania, and Howe occupied the City of Brotherly Love. Not having been informed of Burgoyne's plans, Howe had unintentionally abandoned him. American forces blocked Burgoyne's way, surrounded his army, and on October 17, 1777, forced him to surrender at the **Battle of Saratoga**. The victory provided a significant boost to American morale.

During the winter of 1777–1778, the British army, now commanded by Sir Henry Clinton, was quartered in Philadelphia. (In the Revolution,

THE REVOLUTIONARY WAR IN NEW ENGLAND AND THE MIDDLE STATES, 1775–1781

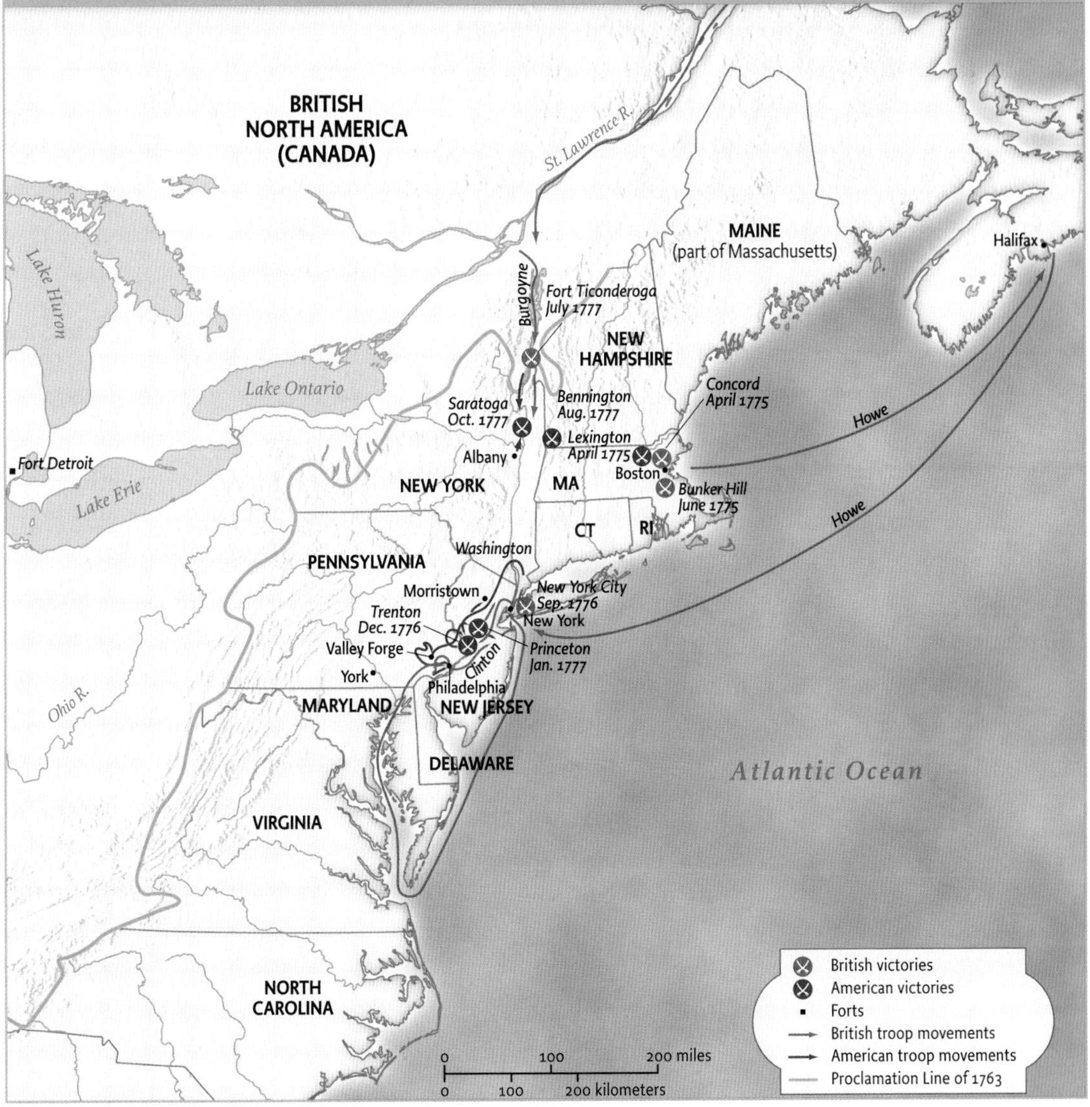

Key battles in New England and the middle states during the War of Independence included Lexington and Concord, which began the armed conflict; the campaign in New York and New Jersey; and Saratoga, sometimes called the turning point of the war.

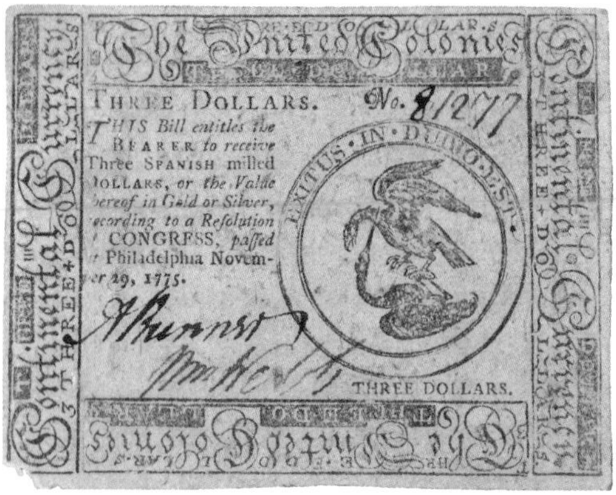

Benjamin Franklin designed this three-dollar bill for the new nation. It depicts an eagle fighting a crane with a Latin motto meaning "the outcome is in doubt."

as in most eighteenth-century wars, fighting came to a halt during the winter.) Meanwhile, Washington's army remained encamped at Valley Forge, where they suffered terribly from the frigid weather. Men who had other options simply went home. By the end of that difficult winter, recent immigrants and African-Americans made up half the soldiers at Valley Forge, and most of the rest were landless or unskilled laborers.

But Saratoga helped to persuade the French that American victory was possible. In 1778, American diplomats led by Benjamin Franklin concluded a Treaty of Amity and Commerce in which France recognized the United States and agreed to supply military assistance. Soon afterward, Spain also joined the war on the American side. French assistance would play a decisive part in the war's end. At the outset, however, the French fleet showed more interest in attacking British outposts in the West Indies than in directly aiding the Americans. Nonetheless, French and Spanish entry transformed the War of Independence into a global conflict. By putting the British on the defensive in places ranging from Gibraltar to the West Indies, it greatly complicated their military prospects.

The War in the Borderlands

In the trans-Appalachian West, the war took on the character of a borderlands conflict as much as a struggle for independence. Here, where British authority remained weak even after the expulsion of the French in the Seven Years' War and Indians enjoyed considerable authority, the patriots' victory marked a decisive shift of power away from native tribes and toward white settlers.

Indian lands in the West

Despite the Proclamation of 1763, discussed in Chapter 4, colonists had continued to move westward during the 1760s and early 1770s, leading Indian tribes to complain of intrusions on their land. Lord Dunmore, Virginia's royal governor, observed in 1772 that he had found it impossible "to restrain the Americans. . . . They do not conceive that government has any right to forbid their taking possession of a vast tract of country" or to force them to honor treaties with Indians.

Many patriot leaders, including George Washington, Patrick Henry, and Thomas Jefferson, were deeply involved in western land speculation. Washington himself had acquired more than 60,000 acres of land in western Pennsylvania after the Seven Years' War by purchasing land vouchers (a form of soldiers' wages) from his men at discount rates.

About 200,000 Native Americans lived east of the Mississippi River in 1790. Like white Americans, Indians divided in allegiance during the

War of Independence. Indians chose the side they felt would advance their own ideas of liberty. Some, like the Stockbridge tribe in Massachusetts, suffered heavy losses fighting the British. Many tribes tried to maintain neutrality, only to see themselves break into pro-American and pro-British factions. Most of the Iroquois nations sided with the British, but the Oneida joined the Americans. Despite strenuous efforts to avoid conflict, members of the Iroquois Confederacy for the first time faced each other in battle. (After the war, the Oneida submitted to Congress claims for losses suffered during the war, including sheep, hogs, kettles, frying pans, plows, and pewter plates—evidence of how fully they had been integrated into the market economy.) In the South, younger Cherokee leaders joined the British while older chiefs tended to favor the Americans.

Choosing sides

Among the grievances listed by Jefferson in the Declaration of Independence was Britain's enlisting "savages" to fight on its side. But in the war that raged throughout the western frontier, savagery was not confined to either combatant. In the Ohio country, the British encouraged Indian allies to burn frontier farms and settlements. For their part, otherwise humane patriot leaders ignored the traditional rules of warfare when it came to Indians. William Henry Drayton, a leader of the patriot cause in South Carolina and the state's chief justice in 1776, advised officers marching against the Cherokees to "cut up every Indian cornfield, burn every Indian town," and enslave all Indian captives. Three years later, Washington dispatched an expedition, led by General John Sullivan, against hostile Iroquois, with the aim of "the total destruction and devastation of their settlements and the capture of as many prisoners of every age and sex as possible." After his campaign ended, Sullivan reported that he had burned forty Indian towns, destroyed thousands of bushels of corn, and uprooted a vast number of fruit trees and vegetable gardens. Many Iroquois communities faced starvation. The destruction of the "middle ground" would not be completed until after the War of 1812, but it received a major impetus from American independence.

Savage warfare

The War in the South

In 1778, the focus of the war shifted to the South. Here the British hoped to exploit the social tensions between backcountry farmers and wealthy planters that had surfaced in the Regulator movements, to enlist the support of the numerous colonists in the region who remained loyal to the crown, and to disrupt the economy by encouraging slaves to escape. In December 1778, British forces occupied Savannah, Georgia. In May 1780, Clinton captured Charleston, South Carolina, and with it an American army of 5,000 men.

British occupation in the South

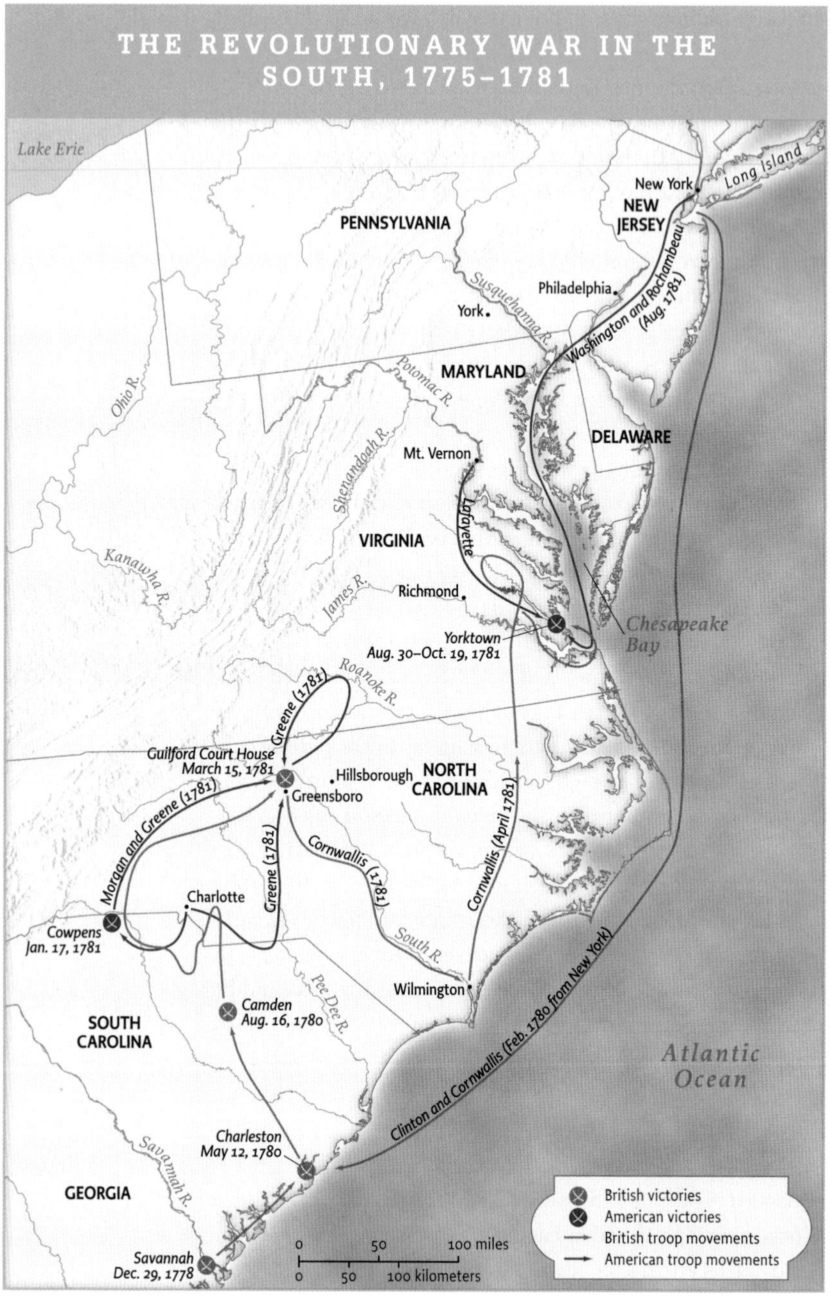

After 1777, the focus of the War of Independence shifted to the South, where it culminated in 1781 with the British defeat at Yorktown.

The year 1780 was arguably the low point of the struggle for independence. Congress was essentially bankrupt, and the army went months without being paid. The British seemed successful in playing on social conflicts within the colonies, as thousands of southern Loyalists joined up with British forces (fourteen regiments from Savannah alone) and tens of thousands of slaves sought freedom by fleeing to British lines. In August, Lord Charles Cornwallis routed an American army at Camden, South Carolina. The following month one of Washington's ablest commanders, **Benedict Arnold**, defected and almost succeeded in turning over to the British the important fort at West Point on the Hudson River.

THE HORSE AMERICA, throwing his Master.

A British cartoon from 1779, *The Horse America Throwing His Master*, lampoons King George III for being unable to keep control of the colonies. In the background, a French officer carries a flag adorned with the fleur-de-lis, a symbol of that country, the colonists' ally. Powerful satirical attacks on public authorities, including the king, were commonplace in eighteenth-century Britain.

But the British failed to turn these advantages into victory. British commanders were unable to consolidate their hold on the South. Wherever their forces went, American militias harassed them. A bloody civil war engulfed North and South Carolina and Georgia, with patriot and Loyalist militias inflicting retribution on each other and plundering the farms of their opponents' supporters.

Victory at Last

Yorktown

In January 1781, American forces under Daniel Morgan dealt a crushing defeat to British forces at Cowpens, South Carolina. Two months later, at Guilford Courthouse, North Carolina, General Nathanael Greene, while conducting a campaign of strategic retreats, inflicted heavy losses on Cornwallis, the British commander in the South. Cornwallis moved into Virginia and encamped at Yorktown, located on a peninsula that juts into Chesapeake Bay. Brilliantly recognizing the opportunity to surround Cornwallis, Washington rushed his forces, augmented by French troops under the Marquis de Lafayette, to block a British escape by land. Meanwhile, a French fleet controlled the mouth of the Chesapeake, preventing supplies and reinforcements from reaching Cornwallis's army.

Imperial rivalries had helped to create the American colonies. Now, the rivalry of European empires helped to secure American independence. Taking land and sea forces together, more Frenchmen than Americans participated in the decisive **Battle of Yorktown**. On October 19, 1781, Cornwallis surrendered his army of 8,000 men. When the news reached London, public support for the war evaporated and peace negotiations soon began.

Two years later, in September 1783, American and British negotiators concluded the **Treaty of Paris**. The American delegation—John Adams,

NORTH AMERICA, 1783

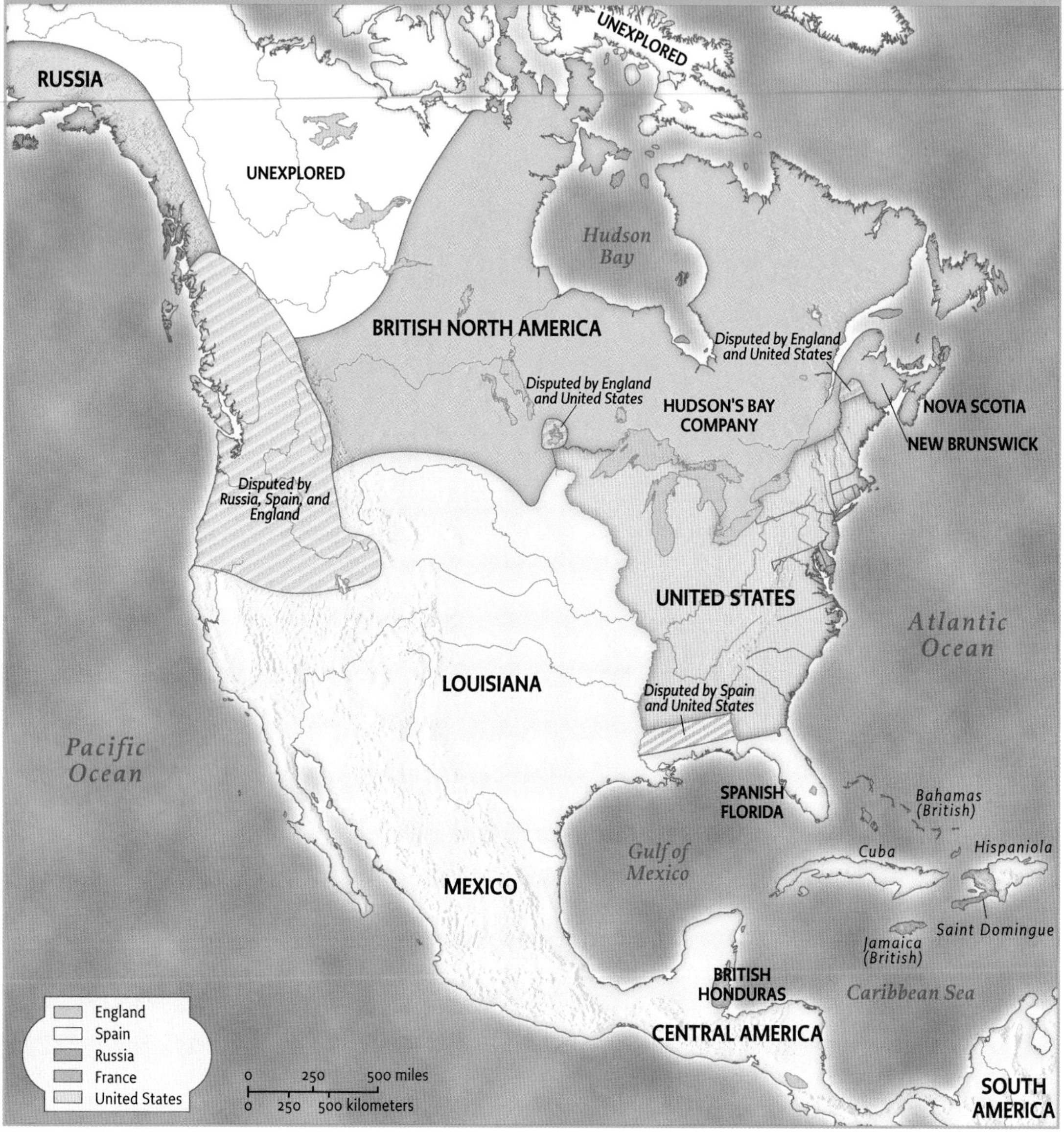

The newly independent United States occupied only a small part of the North American continent in 1783.

Benjamin Franklin, and John Jay—achieved one of the greatest diplomatic triumphs in the country's history. They not only won recognition of American independence but also gained control of the entire region between Canada and Florida east of the Mississippi River and the right of Americans to fish in Atlantic waters off of Canada (a matter of considerable importance to New Englanders). At British insistence, the Americans agreed that colonists who had remained loyal to the mother country would not suffer persecution and that Loyalists' property that had been seized by local and state governments would be restored.

Territorial gains

Until independence, the thirteen colonies had formed part of Britain's American empire, along with Canada and the West Indies. But Canada rebuffed repeated calls to join the War of Independence, and leaders of the West Indies, fearful of slave uprisings, also remained loyal to the crown. With the Treaty of Paris, the United States of America became the Western Hemisphere's first independent nation. Its boundaries reflected not so much the long-standing unity of a geographical region, but the circumstances of its birth.

CHAPTER REVIEW AND ONLINE RESOURCES

REVIEW QUESTIONS

1. *How important was the Stamp Act crisis in bringing about the American Revolution?*

2. *Patrick Henry proclaimed that he was not a Virginian, but rather an American. What unified the colonists and what divided them at the time of the Revolution?*

3. *Discuss the ramifications of using slaves in the British and Continental armies. Why did the British authorize the use of slaves? Why did the Americans? How did the slaves benefit?*

4. *Why did the colonists reach the conclusion that membership in the empire threatened their freedoms, rather than guaranteed them?*

5. *How did new ideas of liberty contribute to tensions between the social classes in the American colonies?*

6. *Why did people in other countries believe that the American Revolution (or the Declaration of Independence) was important to them or their own countries?*

7. *Summarize the difference of opinion between British officials and colonial leaders over the issues of taxation and representation.*

8. *How did the actions of the British authorities help to unite the American colonists during the 1760s and 1770s?*

KEY TERMS

Stamp Act (p. 139)
virtual representation (p. 140)
writs of assistance (p. 140)
Sugar Act (p. 140)
"no taxation without representation" (p. 142)
Committee of Correspondence (p. 143)
Sons of Liberty (p. 143)
Regulators (p. 144)
Townshend Acts (p. 144)
Boston Massacre (p. 145)
Crispus Attucks (p. 145)
Boston Tea Party (p. 147)
Intolerable Acts (p. 147)
Continental Congress (p. 148)
Battles of Lexington and Concord (p. 149)
Battle of Bunker Hill (p. 150)
Continental army (p. 150)
Lord Dunmore's proclamation (p. 150)
Common Sense (p. 151)
Declaration of Independence (p. 152)
Hessian (p. 158)
Battle of Saratoga (p. 158)
Benedict Arnold (p. 163)
Battle of Yorktown (p. 163)
Treaty of Paris (p. 163)

Go to INQUIZITIVE

To see what you know—and learn what you've missed—with personalized feedback along the way.

Visit the ***Give Me Liberty!* Student Site** for primary source documents and images, interactive maps, author videos featuring Eric Foner, and more.

CHAPTER 6

THE REVOLUTION WITHIN

★

1700	Samuel Sewall's *The Selling of Joseph*, first antislavery tract in America
1770s	Freedom petitions presented by slaves to New England courts and legislatures
1776	Adam Smith's *The Wealth of Nations*
	John Adams's *Thoughts on Government*
1777	Vermont state constitution bans slavery
1779	Thomas Jefferson writes Bill for Establishing Religious Freedom
	Philipsburg Proclamation
1782	Deborah Sampson enlists in Continental army

Liberty Displaying the Arts and Sciences. This 1792 painting by Samuel Jennings is one of the few visual images of the early republic explicitly linking slavery with tyranny and liberty with abolition. The female figure offers books to newly freed slaves. Other forms of knowledge depicted include a globe and an artist's palette. Beneath her left foot lies a broken chain. In the background, freed slaves enjoy some leisure time. By this time, allegorical representations of America as a woman in classical clothing, with a cap of liberty, had mostly replaced America as a Native American.

FOCUS QUESTIONS

- *How did equality become a stronger component of American freedom after the Revolution?*
- *How did the expansion of religious liberty after the Revolution reflect the new American ideal of freedom?*
- *How did the definition of economic freedom change after the Revolution, and who benefited from the changes?*
- *How did the Revolution diminish the freedoms of both Loyalists and Native Americans?*
- *What was the impact of the Revolution on slavery?*
- *How did the Revolution affect the status of women?*

Born in Massachusetts in 1744, Abigail Adams became one of the revolutionary era's most articulate and influential women. At a time when educational opportunities for girls were extremely limited, she taught herself by reading books in the library of her father, a Congregational minister. In 1764, she married John Adams. During the War of Independence, with her husband away in Philadelphia and Europe serving the American cause, she stayed behind at their Massachusetts home, raising their four children and managing the family's farm. The letters they exchanged form one of the most remarkable correspondences in American history. A keen observer of public affairs, she kept her husband informed of events in Massachusetts and offered opinions on political matters. Later, when Adams served as president, he relied on her for advice more than on members of his cabinet.

In March 1776, a few months before the Second Continental Congress declared American independence, Abigail Adams wrote her best-known letter to her husband. She began by commenting indirectly on the evils of slavery. How strong, she wondered, could the "passion for Liberty" be among those "accustomed to deprive their fellow citizens of theirs"? She went on to urge Congress, when it drew up a "Code of Laws" for the new republic, to "remember the ladies." All men, she warned, "would be tyrants if they could."

It was the leaders of colonial society who initiated resistance to British taxation. But as Abigail Adams's letter illustrates, the struggle for American liberty emboldened other colonists to demand more liberty for themselves. At a time when so many Americans—slaves, indentured servants, women, Indians, apprentices, propertyless men—were denied full freedom, the struggle against Britain threw into question many forms of authority and inequality.

Abigail Adams accepted the prevailing belief that a woman's primary responsibility was to her family. But she resented the "absolute power" husbands exercised over their wives. Her letter is widely remembered today. Less familiar is John Adams's response, which illuminated how the Revolution had unleashed challenges to all sorts of inherited ideas of deference and authority: "We have been told that our struggle has loosened the bands of government everywhere; that children and apprentices were disobedient; that schools and colleges were grown turbulent; that Indians slighted their guardians, and negroes grew insolent to their masters." To John Adams, this upheaval, including his wife's claim to greater freedom, was an affront to the natural order of things. To others, it formed the essence of the American Revolution.

DEMOCRATIZING FREEDOM

The Dream of Equality

Abigail Adams, a portrait by Gilbert Stuart, painted over several years beginning in 1800. Stuart told a friend that, as a young woman, Adams must have been a "perfect Venus."

The American Revolution took place at three levels simultaneously. It was a struggle for national independence, a phase in a century-long global battle among European empires, and a conflict over what kind of nation an independent America should be.

The Revolution unleashed public debates and political and social struggles that enlarged the scope of freedom and challenged inherited structures of power within America. In rejecting the crown and the principle of hereditary aristocracy, many Americans also rejected the society of privilege, patronage, and fixed status that these institutions embodied. The idea of liberty became a revolutionary rallying cry, a standard by which to judge and challenge homegrown institutions as well as imperial ones.

The Revolution and equality

Jefferson's seemingly straightforward assertion in the Declaration of Independence that "all men are created equal" announced a radical principle whose full implications no one could anticipate. In both Britain and its colonies, a well-ordered society was widely thought to depend on obedience to authority—the power of rulers over their subjects, husbands over wives, parents over children, employers over servants and apprentices, slaveholders over slaves. Inequality had been fundamental to the colonial social order; the Revolution challenged it in many ways. Henceforth, American freedom would be forever linked with the idea of equality—equality before the law, equality in political rights, equality of economic opportunity, and, for some, equality of condition. "Whenever I use the words *freedom* or *rights*," wrote Thomas Paine, "I desire to be understood to mean a perfect equality of them. . . . The floor of Freedom is as level as water."

Expanding the Political Nation

Political participation

In political, social, and religious life, previously marginalized groups challenged the domination by a privileged few. In the end, the Revolution did not undo the obedience to which male heads of household were entitled from their wives and children, and, at least in the southern states, their slaves. For free men, however, the democratization of freedom was dramatic. Nowhere was this more evident than in challenges to the traditional limitation of political participation to those who owned property.

Democracy

In the political thought of the eighteenth century, "democracy" had several meanings. One, derived from the writings of Aristotle, defined democracy as a system in which the entire people governed directly.

However, this was thought to mean mob rule. In the wake of the American Revolution, the term came into wider use to express the popular aspirations for greater equality inspired by the struggle for independence.

The public and politics

Throughout the colonies, election campaigns became freewheeling debates on the fundamentals of government. Universal male suffrage, religious toleration, and even the abolition of slavery were discussed not only by the educated elite but also by artisans, small farmers, and laborers, now emerging as a self-conscious element in politics. In many colonies-turned-states, members of the militia demanded the right to elect all their officers and to vote for public officials whether or not they met age and property qualifications. They thereby established the tradition that service in the army enabled excluded groups to stake a claim to full citizenship.

The Revolution in Pennsylvania

The Revolution's radical potential was more evident in Pennsylvania than in any other state. Nearly the entire prewar elite opposed independence, fearing that severing the tie with Britain would lead to rule by the "rabble" and to attacks on property. The vacuum of political leadership opened the door for the rise of a new pro-independence grouping, based on the artisan and lower-class communities of Philadelphia, and organized in extralegal committees and the local militia.

Staunch advocates of equality, Pennsylvania's radical leaders particularly attacked property qualifications for voting. "God gave mankind freedom by nature," declared the anonymous author of the pamphlet *The People the Best Governors,* "and made every man equal to his neighbors." The people, therefore, were "the best guardians of their own liberties," and every free man should be eligible to vote and hold office. Three months after independence, Pennsylvania adopted a new state constitution that sought to institutionalize democracy by concentrating power in a one-house legislature elected annually by all men over age twenty-one who paid taxes. It abolished the office of governor, dispensed with property qualifications for officeholding, and provided that schools with low fees be established in every county. It also included clauses guaranteeing "freedom of speech, and of writing," and religious liberty.

A pewter mug, made by William Will, an important craftsman in Philadelphia, in the late 1770s, depicts Captain Peter Ickes, a Pennsylvania militia officer, with the popular slogan "Liberty or Death."

The New Constitutions

Like Pennsylvania, every state adopted a new constitution in the aftermath of independence. Nearly all Americans now agreed that their governments must be **republics**, meaning that their authority rested on the consent of the governed, and that there would be no king or hereditary aristocracy.

In part to counteract what he saw as Pennsylvania's excessive radicalism, John Adams in 1776 published *Thoughts on Government*, which insisted that the new constitutions should create balanced governments whose structure would reflect the division of society between the wealthy (represented in the upper house) and ordinary men (who would control the lower). A powerful governor and judiciary would ensure that neither class infringed on the liberty of the other. Adams's call for two-house legislatures was followed by every state except Pennsylvania, Georgia, and Vermont. But only his own state, Massachusetts, gave the governor an effective veto over laws passed by the legislature. Americans had long resented efforts by appointed governors to challenge the power of colonial assemblies. They preferred power to rest with the legislature.

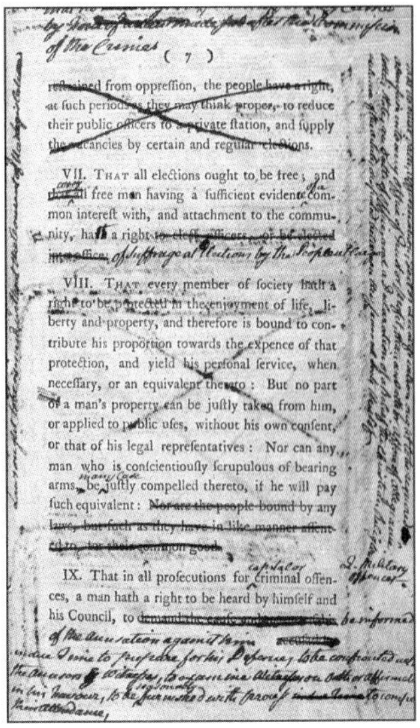

(7)

restrained from oppression, the people have a right, at such periods as they may think proper, to reduce their public officers to a private station, and supply the vacancies by certain and regular elections.

VII. THAT all elections ought to be free; and that all free men having a sufficient evident common interest with, and attachment to the community, have a right to elect officers, or be elected into office.

VIII. THAT every member of society hath a right to be protected in the enjoyment of life, liberty and property, and therefore is bound to contribute his proportion towards the expence of that protection, and yield his personal service, when necessary, or an equivalent thereto: But no part of a man's property can be justly taken from him, or applied to public uses, without his own consent, or that of his legal representatives: Nor can any man who is conscientiously scrupulous of bearing arms, be justly compelled thereto, if he will pay such equivalent: Nor are the people bound by any laws, but such as they have in like manner assented to, for their common good.

IX. That in all prosecutions for criminal offences, a man hath a right to be heard by himself and his Council, to

John Dickinson's copy of the Pennsylvania constitution of 1776, with handwritten proposals for changes. Dickinson, one of the more conservative advocates of independence, felt the new state constitution was far too democratic. He crossed out a provision that all "free men" should be eligible to hold office, and another declaring the people not bound by laws that did not promote "the common good."

The Right to Vote

The issue of requirements for voting and officeholding proved far more contentious. To John Adams, as conservative on the internal affairs of America as he had been radical on independence, freedom and equality were opposites. Men without property, he believed, had no "judgment of their own," and the removal of property qualifications, therefore, would "confound and destroy all distinctions, and prostrate all ranks to one common level."

Democracy gained the least ground in the southern states, whose highly deferential political traditions enabled the landed gentry to retain their control of political affairs. In Virginia and South Carolina, the new constitutions retained property qualifications for voting and authorized the gentry-dominated legislature to choose the governor.

The most democratic new constitutions moved much of the way toward the idea of voting as an entitlement rather than a privilege, but they generally stopped short of universal **suffrage**, even for free men. Pennsylvania's constitution no longer required ownership of property, but it retained the taxpaying qualification. As a result, it enfranchised nearly all of the state's free male population but still barred a small number, mainly paupers and domestic servants, from voting. Nonetheless, even with the taxpaying requirement, it was a dramatic departure from the colonial practice of restricting the suffrage to those who could claim to be economically independent. It elevated "personal liberty," in the words of one essayist, to a position more important than property ownership in defining the boundaries of the political nation.

Freedom and the right to vote

By the 1780s, except in Virginia, Maryland, and New York, a large majority of the adult white male population could meet voting requirements. New Jersey's new state constitution of 1776 granted the suffrage to all "inhabitants" who met a property qualification. Until the state added the word "male" (along with "white") in 1807, property-owning women, mostly widows, did cast ballots. In the popular language of politics, if not in law, freedom and an individual's right to vote had become interchangeable. Who should vote remains controversial to this day.

TOWARD RELIGIOUS TOLERATION

Religious pluralism

As remarkable as the expansion of political freedom was the Revolution's impact on American religion. Religious toleration, declared one Virginia patriot, was part of "the common cause of Freedom." We have already seen that Rhode Island and Pennsylvania had long made a practice of toleration. But freedom of worship before the Revolution arose more from the reality of religious pluralism than from a well-developed theory of religious liberty. Most colonies supported religious institutions with public funds and discriminated in voting and officeholding against Catholics, Jews, and even dissenting Protestants. On the very eve of independence, Baptists who refused to pay taxes to support local Congregational ministers were still being jailed in Massachusetts. "While our country are pleading so high for liberty," the victims complained, "yet they are denying of it to their neighbors."

Catholic Americans

The War of Independence weakened the deep tradition of American anti-Catholicism. When the Second Continental Congress decided on an ill-fated invasion of Canada, it invited the inhabitants of predominantly Catholic Quebec to join in the struggle against Britain, assuring them

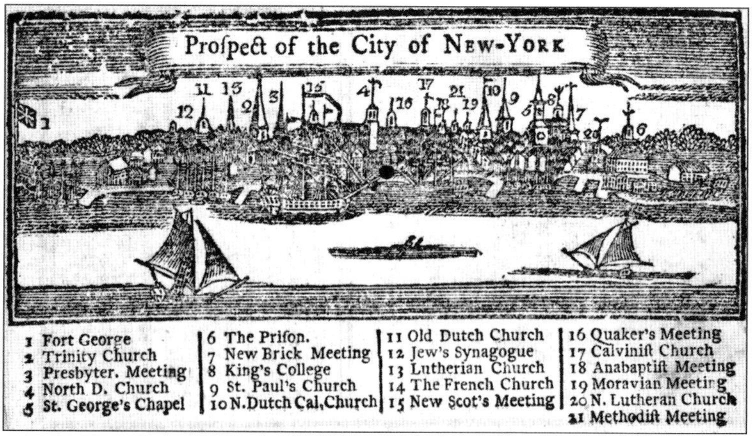

A 1771 image of New York City lists some of the numerous churches visible from the New Jersey shore, illustrating the diversity of religions practiced in the city.

that Protestants and Catholics could readily cooperate. In 1778, the United States formed an alliance with France, a Catholic nation. The indispensable assistance provided by France to American victory strengthened the idea that Catholics had a role to play in the newly independent nation. This was a marked departure from the traditional notion that the full rights of Englishmen applied only to Protestants. When America's first Roman Catholic bishop, John Carroll of Maryland, visited Boston in 1791, he received a cordial welcome.

In Side of the Old Lutheran Church in 1800, York, Pa. A watercolor by a local artist depicts the interior of one of the numerous churches that flourished after independence. While the choir sings, a man chases a dog out of the building and another man stokes the stove. The institutionalization of religious liberty was one of the most important results of the American Revolution.

Separating Church and State

Many of the leaders of the Revolution considered it essential for the new nation to shield itself from the unruly passions and violent conflicts that religious differences had inspired during the past three centuries. Men like Thomas Jefferson, John Adams, James Madison, and Alexander Hamilton viewed religious doctrines through the Enlightenment lens of rationalism and skepticism. They believed in a benevolent Creator but not in supernatural interventions into the affairs of men.

The drive to separate church and state brought together Deists like Jefferson, who hoped to erect a "wall of separation" that would free politics and the exercise of the intellect from religious control, with members of evangelical sects, who sought to protect religion from the corrupting embrace of government.

Disestablishing churches

The movement toward religious freedom received a major impetus during the revolutionary era. Throughout the new nation, states disestablished their established churches—that is, deprived them of public funding and special legal privileges—although in some cases they appropriated money for the general support of Protestant denominations. The seven state constitutions that began with declarations of rights all declared a commitment to "the free exercise of religion."

Limits to religious freedom

To be sure, every state but New York—whose constitution of 1777 established complete religious liberty—kept intact colonial provisions barring Jews from voting and holding public office. Massachusetts retained its Congregationalist establishment well into the nineteenth century. It would not end public financial support for religious institutions until

1833. Throughout the country, however, Catholics gained the right to worship without persecution.

Jefferson and Religious Liberty

In Virginia, Thomas Jefferson drew up a **Bill for Establishing Religious Freedom**, which was introduced in the House of Burgesses in 1779 and adopted, after considerable controversy, in 1786. Jefferson's bill, whose preamble declared that God "hath created the mind free," eliminated religious requirements for voting and officeholding and government financial support for churches, and barred the state from "forcing" individuals to adopt one or another religious outlook. Late in life, Jefferson would list this measure, along with the Declaration of Independence and the founding of the University of Virginia, as the three accomplishments (leaving out his two terms as president) for which he wished to be remembered.

Definition of "rights"

Religious liberty became the model for the revolutionary generation's definition of "rights" as private matters that must be protected from governmental interference. In an overwhelmingly Christian (though not necessarily churchgoing) nation, the separation of church and state drew a sharp line between public authority and a realm defined as "private." It also offered a new justification for the idea of the United States as a beacon of liberty. In successfully opposing a Virginia tax for the general support of Christian churches, James Madison insisted that one reason for the complete separation of church and state was to reinforce the principle that the new nation offered "asylum to the persecuted and oppressed of every nation and religion."

Religious denominations

The Revolution did not end the influence of religion on American society—quite the reverse. Thanks to religious freedom, the early republic witnessed an amazing proliferation of religious denominations. The most well-established churches—Anglican, Presbyterian, and Congregationalist—found themselves constantly challenged by upstarts like Free-Will Baptists and Universalists. Today, even as debate continues over the proper relationship between spiritual and political authority, more than 1,300 religions are practiced in the United States.

Christian Republicanism

Despite the separation of church and state, colonial leaders were not hostile to religion. Indeed, religious and secular language merged in the struggle for independence, producing an outlook scholars have called Christian Republicanism. Proponents of evangelical religion and of republican government both believed that in the absence of some kind of moral restraint (provided by religion and government), human nature was likely to succumb to corruption and vice. Samuel Adams, for example, believed the new nation would become a "Christian Sparta," in which Christianity and personal self-discipline underpinned both personal and national progress. American religious leaders interpreted the American Revolution as a divinely sanctioned event, part of God's plan to promote the development of a good society. Rather than being so sinful that it would have to be destroyed before Christ returned, as many ministers had previously preached, the world, the Revolution demonstrated, could be perfected.

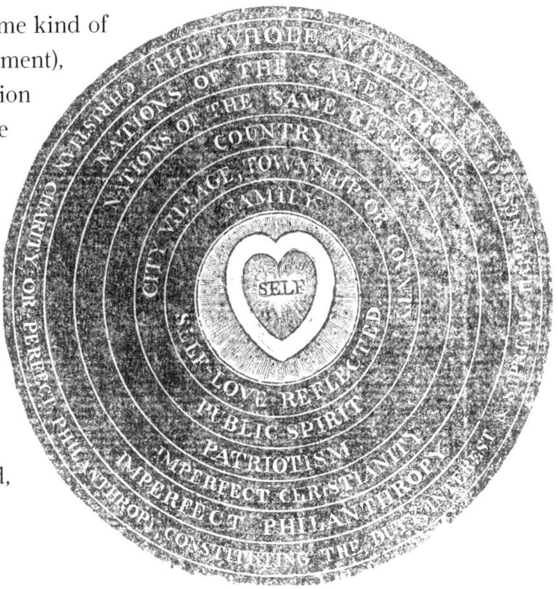

Circle of the Social and Benevolent Affections, an engraving in *The Columbian Magazine*, 1789, illustrates various admirable qualities radiating outward from the virtuous citizen, including love for one's family, community, nation, and all humanity. Affection only for those of the same religion or "colour" is labeled "imperfect."

A Virtuous Citizenry

Patriot leaders worried about the character of future citizens, especially how to encourage the quality of "virtue," the ability to sacrifice self-interest for the public good. Some, like Jefferson, John Adams, and Benjamin Rush, put forward plans for the establishment of free, state-supported public schools. These would instruct future citizens in what Adams called "the principles of freedom," equipping them for participation in the now-expanded public sphere and for the wise election of representatives. A broad diffusion of knowledge was essential for a government based on the will of the people to survive. No nation, Jefferson wrote, could "expect to be ignorant and free."

DEFINING ECONOMIC FREEDOM

Toward Free Labor

Unfree labor

In economic as well as political and religious affairs, the Revolution rewrote the definition of freedom. In colonial America, slavery was one part of a broad spectrum of kinds of unfree labor. In the generation after independence, with the rapid decline of indentured servitude and apprenticeship and the transformation of paid domestic service into an occupation for blacks and white females, the halfway houses between slavery and freedom disappeared, at least for white men.

The lack of freedom inherent in apprenticeship and servitude increasingly came to be seen as incompatible with republican citizenship. In 1784, a group of "respectable" New Yorkers released a newly arrived shipload of indentured servants on the grounds that their status was "contrary to . . . the idea of liberty this country has so happily established." By 1800, indentured servitude had all but disappeared from the United States. This development sharpened the distinction between freedom and slavery, and between a northern economy relying on what would come to be called "free labor" (that is, working for wages or owning a farm or shop) and a southern economy ever more heavily dependent on the labor of slaves.

Decline in indentured servitude

The Soul of a Republic

Americans of the revolutionary generation were preoccupied with the social conditions of freedom. Could a republic survive with a sizable dependent class of citizens? "A general and tolerably equal distribution of landed property," proclaimed the educator and newspaper editor Noah Webster, "is the whole basis of national freedom." "Equality," he added, was "the very soul of a republic." At the Revolution's radical edge, some patriots believed that government had a responsibility to limit accumulations of property in the name of equality. To most free Americans, however, "equality" meant equal opportunity, rather than equality of condition. Many leaders of the Revolution nevertheless assumed that in the exceptional circumstances of the New World, with its vast areas of available land and large population of independent farmers and artisans, the natural workings of society would produce justice, liberty, and equality.

Equal opportunity rather than equality of condition

Like many other Americans of his generation, Thomas Jefferson believed that to lack economic resources was to lack freedom. Among his achievements included laws passed by Virginia abolishing entail

View from Bushongo Tavern, an engraving from *The Columbian Magazine*, 1788, depicts the landscape of York County, Pennsylvania, exemplifying the kind of rural independence many Americans thought essential to freedom.

(the limitation of inheritance to a specified line of heirs to keep an estate within a family) and primogeniture (the practice of passing a family's land entirely to the eldest son). These measures, he believed, would help to prevent the rise of a "future aristocracy."

Abolishing entail and primogeniture

The Politics of Inflation

The Revolution thrust to the forefront of politics debates over whether local and national authorities should take steps to bolster household independence and protect Americans' livelihoods by limiting price increases. To finance the war, Congress issued hundreds of millions of dollars in paper money. Coupled with wartime disruption of agriculture and trade and the hoarding of goods by some Americans hoping to profit from shortages, this produced an enormous **inflation** as prices rapidly rose.

Responses to wartime inflation

Between 1776 and 1779, more than thirty incidents took place in which crowds confronted merchants accused of holding scarce goods off the market. Often, they seized stocks of food and sold them at the traditional "just price," a form of protest common in eighteenth-century England. In one such incident, a crowd of 100 Massachusetts women accused an "eminent, wealthy, stingy merchant" of hoarding coffee, opened his warehouse, and carted off the goods. "A large concourse of men," wrote Abigail Adams, "stood amazed, silent spectators of the whole transaction."

The Debate over Free Trade

In 1779, with inflation totally out of control (in one month, prices in Philadelphia jumped 45 percent), Congress urged states to adopt measures to fix wages and prices. This request reflected the belief that the task of republican government was to promote the public good, not individuals' self-interest. But when a Committee of Safety tried to enforce price controls, it met spirited opposition from merchants and other advocates of a free market.

Against the traditional view that men should sacrifice for the public good, believers in **free trade** argued that economic development arose from economic self-interest. Adam Smith's great treatise on economics, ***The Wealth of Nations***, published in England in 1776, was beginning to become known in the United States. Smith's argument that the "invisible hand" of the free market directed economic life more effectively and fairly than governmental intervention offered intellectual justification for those who believed that the economy should be left to regulate itself.

Smith's "invisible hand"

Advocates of independence had envisioned America, released from the British Navigation Acts, trading freely with all the world.

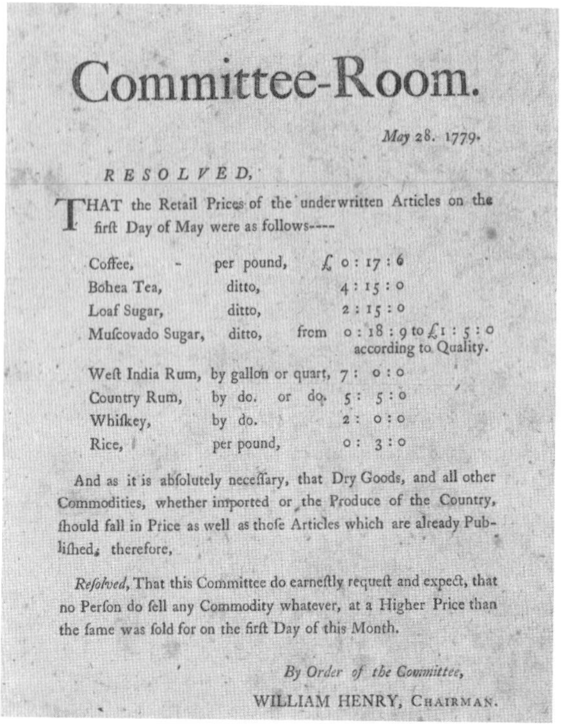

Committee-Room.

May 28. 1779.

RESOLVED,

THAT the Retail Prices of the underwritten Articles on the firſt Day of May were as follows----

Coffee, -	per pound,		£ 0 : 17 : 6
Bohea Tea,	ditto,		4 : 15 : 0
Loaf Sugar,	ditto,		2 : 15 : 0
Muſcovado Sugar,	ditto,	from	0 : 18 : 9 to £1 : 5 : 0 according to Quality.
Weſt India Rum,	by gallon or quart,		7 : 0 : 0
Country Rum,	by do. or do.		5 : 5 : 0
Whiſkey,	by do.		2 : 0 : 0
Rice,	per pound,		0 : 3 : 0

And as it is abſolutely neceſſary, that Dry Goods, and all other Commodities, whether imported or the Produce of the Country, ſhould fall in Price as well as thoſe Articles which are already Publiſhed; therefore,

Reſolved, That this Committee do earneſtly requeſt and expect, that no Perſon do ſell any Commodity whatever, at a Higher Price than the ſame was ſold for on the firſt Day of this Month.

By Order of the Committee,
WILLIAM HENRY, CHAIRMAN.

A broadside printed by the extralegal Philadelphia price control committee, setting the retail prices of various goods. Advocates of a free market strongly opposed the committee's efforts.

Opponents of price controls advocated free trade at home as well. "Natural liberty" would regulate prices. Here were two competing conceptions of economic freedom—one based on the traditional view that the interests of the community took precedence over the property rights of individuals, the other insisting that unregulated economic freedom would produce social harmony and public gain. After 1779, state and federal efforts to regulate prices ceased. But the clash between these two visions of economic freedom would continue long after independence had been achieved.

THE LIMITS OF LIBERTY

Colonial Loyalists

Not all Americans shared in the democratization of freedom brought on by the American Revolution. **Loyalists**—those who retained their allegiance to the crown—experienced the conflict and its aftermath as a loss of liberty. Many leading Loyalists had supported American resistance in the 1760s but drew back at the prospect of independence and war. Altogether, an estimated 20 to 25 percent of free Americans remained loyal to the British, and nearly 20,000 fought on their side.

There were Loyalists in every colony, but they were most numerous in New York, Pennsylvania, and the backcountry of the Carolinas and Georgia. Some were wealthy men whose livelihoods depended on close working relationships with Britain—lawyers, merchants, Anglican ministers, and imperial officials. Many feared anarchy in the event of an American victory.

Social bases of loyalism

The struggle for independence heightened existing tensions between ethnic groups and social classes within the colonies. Some Loyalist ethnic minorities, like Highland Scots in North Carolina, feared that local majorities would infringe on their cultural autonomy. In the South, many backcountry farmers who had long resented the domination of public affairs by wealthy planters sided with the British, as did numerous slaves, who hoped an American defeat would bring them freedom.

The Loyalists' Plight

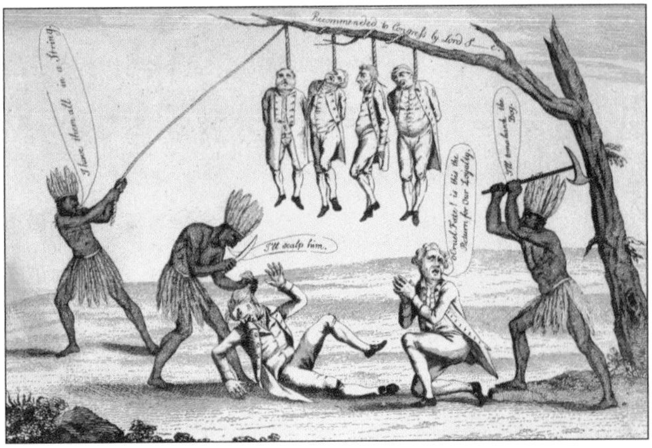

A 1780 British cartoon commenting on the "cruel fate" of American Loyalists. Pro-independence colonists are likened to savage Indians.

The War of Independence was in some respects a civil war among Americans. The new state governments, or crowds of patriots, suppressed newspapers thought to be loyal to Britain. Pennsylvania arrested and seized the property of Quakers, Mennonites, and Moravians—pacifist denominations who refused to bear arms because of their religious beliefs. With the approval of Congress, many states required residents to take oaths of allegiance to the new nation. Those who refused were denied the right to vote and in many cases forced into exile. Some wealthy Loyalists saw their land confiscated and sold at auction.

When the war ended, as many as 60,000 Loyalists were banished from the United States or emigrated voluntarily—mostly to Britain, Canada, or the West Indies—rather than live in an independent United States. But for those who remained, hostility proved to be short-lived. In the Treaty of Paris of 1783, as noted in Chapter 5, Americans pledged to end the persecution of Loyalists by state and local governments and to restore property seized during the war. Loyalists who did not leave the country were quickly reintegrated into American society, although confiscated Loyalist property was not returned.

White Freedom, Indian Freedom

Dispossession of Indian lands

Independence created governments democratically accountable to voters who coveted Indian land. But liberty for whites meant loss of liberty for Indians. Independence offered the opportunity to complete the process of dispossessing Indians of their rich lands in upstate New York, the Ohio Valley, and the southern backcountry. The only hope for the Indians, Jefferson wrote, lay in their "removal beyond the Mississippi."

The Treaty of Paris and Indian peoples

American independence, a group of visiting Indians told the Spanish governor of St. Louis, was "the greatest blow that could have been dealt us." The Treaty of Paris marked the culmination of a century in which the balance of power in eastern North America shifted away from the Indians and toward white Americans. In the treaty, the British abandoned their Indian allies, agreeing to recognize American sovereignty over the entire region east of the Mississippi River, completely ignoring the Indian presence. In

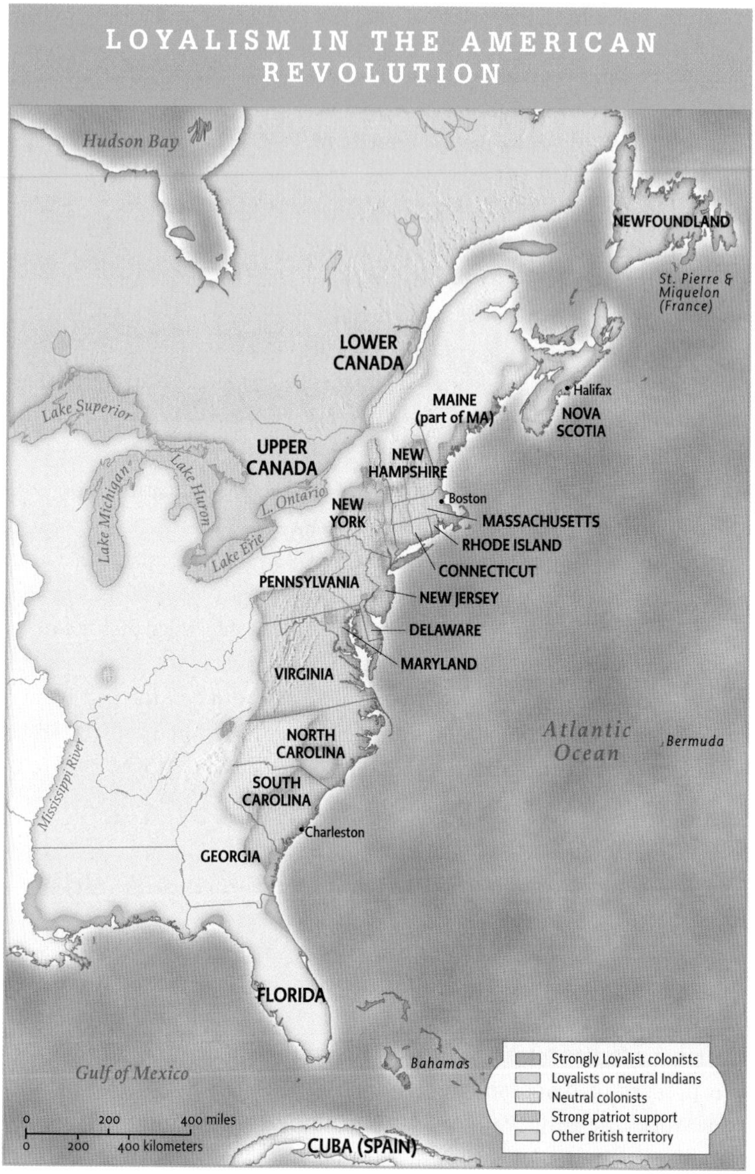

The Revolutionary War was, in some ways, a civil war within the colonies. There were Loyalists in every colony; they were most numerous in New York and North and South Carolina.

the end there seemed to be no permanent place for the descendants of the continent's native population in a new nation bent on creating an empire in the West.

SLAVERY AND THE REVOLUTION

Although Indians experienced American independence as a real threat to their own liberty, African-Americans saw in the ideals of the Revolution and the reality of war an opportunity to claim freedom. When the United States declared its independence in 1776, the slave population had grown to 500,000, about one-fifth of the new nation's inhabitants.

The Language of Slavery and Freedom

The meaning of slavery

Slavery played a central part in the language of revolution. Apart from "liberty," it was the word most frequently invoked in the era's legal and political literature. In debates over British rule, slavery was primarily a political category, shorthand for the denial of one's personal and political rights by arbitrary government. Those who lacked a voice in public affairs, declared a 1769 petition demanding an expansion of the right to vote in Britain, were "enslaved."

The presence of hundreds of thousands of slaves powerfully affected the meaning of freedom for the leaders of the American Revolution. In a famous speech to Parliament warning against attempts to intimidate the colonies, the British statesman Edmund Burke suggested that familiarity with slavery made colonial leaders unusually sensitive to threats to their own liberties. Where freedom was a privilege, not a common right, he observed, "those who are free are by far the most proud and jealous of their freedom." On the other hand, many British observers could not resist pointing out the colonists' apparent hypocrisy. "How is it," asked Dr. Samuel Johnson, "that we hear the loudest yelps for liberty from the drivers of negroes?"

Advertisement for newly arrived slaves, in a Savannah newspaper, 1774. Even as colonists defended their own liberty against the British, the buying and selling of slaves continued.

Obstacles to Abolition

The contradiction between freedom and slavery seems so self-evident that it is difficult today to appreciate the power of the obstacles to **abolition**. At the time of the Revolution, slavery was already an old institution in America. It existed in every colony and formed the basis of the economy and social structure from Maryland southward. Virtually every founding father owned slaves at one point in his life, including not only southern planters but also northern merchants, lawyers, and farmers. (John Adams and Tom Paine were notable exceptions.) Thomas Jefferson owned more than 100 slaves when he wrote of mankind's unalienable right to liberty, and everything he cherished in his own manner of life, from lavish entertainments to the leisure that made possible the pursuit of arts and sciences, ultimately rested on slave labor.

Slavery amid freedom

Some patriots, in fact, argued that slavery for blacks made freedom possible for whites. Owning slaves offered a route to the economic autonomy widely deemed necessary for genuine freedom, a point driven home by a 1780 Virginia law that rewarded veterans of the War of Independence with 300 acres of land—and a slave.

The Cause of General Liberty

Freedom as universal

Nonetheless, by imparting so absolute a value to liberty and defining freedom as a universal entitlement rather than a set of rights specific to a particular place or people, the Revolution inevitably raised questions about the status of slavery in the new nation. Before independence, there had

Excelsior (Latin for "Ever Upward"), a large oil painting by an unknown artist, is probably an early representation of the coat of arms of New York, adopted in 1778 as one part of the transition from colony to state. It contains numerous symbols of liberty, independence, and optimism for the future including a cap of liberty, the sunrise, an eagle atop a world globe, Justice with her scales, and an olive branch of peace.

been little public discussion of the institution, even though enlightened opinion in the Atlantic world had come to view slavery as morally wrong and economically inefficient, a relic of a barbarous past.

Samuel Sewall, a Boston merchant, published *The Selling of Joseph* in 1700, the first antislavery tract printed in America. All "the sons of Adam," Sewall insisted, were entitled to "have equal right unto liberty." During the course of the eighteenth century, antislavery sentiments had spread among Pennsylvania's Quakers, whose belief that all persons possessed the divine "inner light" made them particularly receptive.

Antislavery sentiments

But it was during the revolutionary era that slavery for the first time became a focus of public debate. The Pennsylvania patriot Benjamin Rush in 1773 called on "advocates for American liberty" to "espouse the cause of . . . general liberty" and warned that slavery was one of those "national crimes" that one day would bring "national punishment."

Petitions for Freedom

The Revolution inspired widespread hopes that slavery could be removed from American life. Most dramatically, slaves themselves appreciated that by defining freedom as a universal right, the leaders of the Revolution had devised a weapon that could be used against their own bondage. The language of liberty echoed in slave communities, North and South. The most insistent advocates of freedom as a universal entitlement were African-Americans, who demanded that the leaders of the struggle for independence live up to their self-proclaimed creed.

The first concrete steps toward emancipation in revolutionary America were **freedom petitions**—arguments for liberty presented to New England's courts and legislatures in the early 1770s by enslaved African-Americans. How, one such petition asked, could America "seek release from English tyranny and not seek the same for disadvantaged Africans in her midst?" The turmoil of war offered other avenues to freedom. Many slaves ran away from their masters and tried to pass as freeborn. The number of fugitive-slave advertisements in colonial newspapers rose dramatically in the 1770s and 1780s. As one owner put it in accounting for his slave Jim's escape, "I believe he has nothing in view but freedom."

A portrait of the poet Phillis Wheatley (1753–1784).

In 1776, the year of American independence, **Lemuel Haynes**, a black member of the Massachusetts militia and later a celebrated minister, urged Americans to "extend" their conception of freedom. If liberty were truly "an innate principle" for all mankind, Haynes insisted, "even an African [had] as equally good a right to his liberty in common with Englishmen." Like Haynes, many black writers and leaders sought to make white Americans understand slavery as a concrete reality—the denial of all the essential elements of freedom—not a metaphor for lack of political representation, as many whites used the word.

Most slaves of the revolutionary era were only one or two generations removed from Africa. They did not need the ideology of the Revolution to persuade them that freedom was a birthright—their experience and that of their parents and grandparents suggested as much. "My love of freedom," wrote the black poet Phillis Wheatley in 1783, arose from the "cruel fate" of being "snatch'd from Afric's" shore. Yet when blacks invoked the Revolution's ideology of liberty to demand their own rights and defined freedom as a universal entitlement, they demonstrated how American they had become.

British Emancipators

As noted in the previous chapter, some 5,000 slaves fought for American independence, and many thereby gained their freedom. Yet far more slaves obtained liberty from the British. Lord Dunmore's proclamation of 1775, and the Philipsburg Proclamation of General Henry Clinton issued four years later, offered sanctuary to slaves, except those owned by Loyalists, who escaped to British lines. All told, tens of thousands of slaves, including one-quarter of all the slaves in South Carolina and one-third of those in Georgia, deserted their owners and fled to British lines. This was by far the largest exodus from the plantations until the outbreak of the Civil War.

Miss Breme Jones, a late eighteenth-century watercolor depicting a South Carolina slave. The inscription on the left, based on a passage from John Milton's *Paradise Lost*, reads: "Grave in her steps / Heaven in her eyes / And all her movement / Dignity and Love." The work was commissioned by Jones's owner John Rose, possibly as recognition of how she helped him raise his two small children after the death of his wife.

Some of these escaped slaves were recaptured as the tide of battle turned in the patriots' favor. But at the war's end, more than 15,000 black men, women, and children accompanied the British out of the country. They ended up in Nova Scotia, England, and Sierra Leone, a settlement for former slaves from the United States established by the British on the coast of West Africa. Some were re-enslaved in the West Indies.

The issue of compensation for the slaves who departed with the British poisoned relations between Britain and the new United States for decades to come. Finally, in 1827, Britain agreed to make payments to 1,100 Americans who claimed they had been improperly deprived of their slave property.

Voluntary Emancipations

For a brief moment, the revolutionary upheaval appeared to threaten the continued existence of slavery. During the War of Independence, nearly every state prohibited or discouraged the further importation of

Voluntary emancipations in the South

slaves from Africa. The war left much of the plantation South in ruins. During the 1780s and 1790s, a considerable number of slaveholders, especially in Virginia and Maryland, voluntarily emancipated their slaves. In 1796, for example, Richard Randolph, a member of a prominent Virginia family, drafted a will that condemned slavery as an "infamous practice," provided for the freedom of about ninety slaves, and set aside part of his land for them to own. Farther south, however, voluntary emancipation never got under way. Even during the war, when South Carolina needed more troops, the colony's leaders rejected the idea of emancipating some blacks to aid in the fight against the British. They would rather lose the war than lose their slaves.

Abolition in the North

Legislation against slavery

Between 1777 (when Vermont drew up a constitution that banned slavery) and 1804 (when New Jersey acted), every state north of Maryland took steps toward emancipation, the first time in recorded history that legislative power had been invoked to eradicate slavery. But even here, where slavery was not central to the economy, the method of abolition reflected how property rights impeded emancipation. Generally, abolition laws did not free living slaves. Instead, they provided for the liberty of any child born in the future to a slave mother, but only after he or she had served the mother's master until adulthood as compensation for the owner's future economic loss.

Slow process of abolition

Because of these legal provisions, abolition in the North was a slow, drawn-out process. The first national census, in 1790, recorded 21,000 slaves still living in New York and 11,000 in New Jersey. New Yorker John Jay, chief justice of the United States, owned five slaves in 1800. As late as 1830, the census revealed that there were still 3,500 slaves in the North.

This engraving depicts a parade welcoming George Washington and the Continental army into New York City on November 25, 1783, shortly after British forces evacuated the city, which they had occupied for almost the entire War of Independence. Women take part in the celebration alongside men. But the crowd is shown as entirely white—even though many blacks and some Native Americans resided in the city.

VOICES OF FREEDOM

From Abigail Adams to John Adams, Braintree, Mass. (March 31, 1776)

From their home in Massachusetts, Abigail Adams maintained a lively correspondence with her husband while he was in Philadelphia serving in the Continental Congress. In this letter, she suggests some of the limits of the patriots' commitment to liberty.

I wish you would write me a letter half as long as I write you, and tell me if you may where your fleet have gone? What sort of defense Virginia can make against our common enemy? Whether it is so situated as to make an able defense? . . . I have sometimes been ready to think that the passion for Liberty cannot be equally strong in the breasts of those who have been accustomed to deprive their fellow creatures of theirs. Of this I am certain, that it is not founded upon that generous and Christian principle of doing to others as we would that others should do unto us. . . .

I long to hear that you have declared an independency, and by the way in the new Code of Laws which I suppose it will be necessary for you to make I desire you would Remember the Ladies, and be more generous and favorable to them than your ancestors. Do not put such unlimited power into the hands of the husbands. Remember all men would be tyrants if they could. If particular care and attention is not paid to the Ladies we are determined to foment a Rebellion, and will not hold ourselves bound by any such laws in which we have no voice, or representation.

That your sex are naturally tyrannical is a truth so thoroughly established as to admit of no dispute, but such of you as wish to be happy willingly give up the harsh title of Master for the more tender and endearing one of Friend. Why then, not put it out of the power of the vicious and the lawless to use us with cruelty and indignity with impunity? Men of sense in all ages abhor those customs which treat us only as the vassals of your sex. Regard us then as beings placed by providence under your protection and in imitation of the Supreme Being make use of that power only for our happiness.

From Petitions of Slaves to the Massachusetts Legislature (1773 and 1777)

Many slaves saw the struggle for independence as an opportunity to assert their own claims to freedom. Among the first efforts toward abolition were petitions by Massachusetts slaves to their legislature.

The efforts made by the legislative of this province in their last sessions to free themselves from slavery, gave us, who are in that deplorable state, a high degree of satisfaction. We expect great things from men who have made such a noble stand against the designs of their *fellow-men* to enslave them. We cannot but wish and hope Sir, that you will have the same grand object, we mean civil and religious liberty, in view in your next session. The divine spirit of *freedom*, seems to fire every breast on this continent. . . .

* * *

Your petitioners apprehend that they have in common with all other men a natural and unalienable right to that freedom which the great parent of the universe hath bestowed equally on all mankind and which they have never forfeited by any compact or agreement whatever but [they] were unjustly dragged by the hand of cruel power from their dearest friends and . . . from a populous, pleasant, and plentiful country and in violation of laws of nature and of nations and in defiance of all the tender feelings of humanity brought here . . . to be sold like beast[s] of burden . . . among a people professing the mild religion of Jesus. . . .

In imitation of the laudable example of the good people of these states your petitioners have long and patiently waited the event of petition after petition by them presented to the legislative body. . . . They cannot but express their astonishment that it has never been considered that every principle from which America has acted in the course of their unhappy difficulties with Great Britain pleads stronger than a thousand arguments in favor of your petitioners [and their desire] to be restored to the enjoyment of that which is the natural right of all men.

QUESTIONS

1. *What does Abigail Adams have in mind when she refers to the "unlimited power" husbands exercise over their wives?*
2. *How do the slaves employ the principles of the Revolution for their own aims?*
3. *What do these documents suggest about the boundaries of freedom in the era of the American Revolution?*

A photograph from around 1851 of Caesar, who had been a slave in New York State until the institution was finally ended in 1827.

Free Black Communities

All in all, the Revolution had a contradictory impact on American slavery and, therefore, on American freedom. Gradual as it was, the abolition of slavery in the North drew a line across the new nation, creating the dangerous division between free and slave states. Abolition in the North, voluntary manumissions in the Upper South, and the escape of thousands from bondage created, for the first time in American history, a sizable population of **free blacks** (many of whose members took new family names like Freeman or Freeland).

On the eve of independence, virtually every black person in America had been a slave. Now, free communities, with their own churches, schools, and leaders, came into existence. They formed a standing challenge to the logic of slavery, a haven for fugitives, and a springboard for further efforts at abolition. From 1776 to 1810, the number of free blacks residing in the United States grew from 10,000 to nearly 200,000, and many free black men, especially in the North, enjoyed the right to vote under new state constitutions.

Nonetheless, the stark fact is that slavery survived the War of Independence and, thanks to the natural increase of the slave population, continued to grow. The national census of 1790 revealed that despite all those who had become free through state laws, voluntary emancipation, and escape, the number of slaves in the United States had grown to 700,000—200,000 more than in 1776.

A woodcut widely reprinted during the War of Independence shows Hannah Snell, who allegedly joined the British army in 1745 disguised as a man. It suggests that women could take up arms in their country's cause.

DAUGHTERS OF LIBERTY

Revolutionary Women

The revolutionary generation included numerous women who contributed to the struggle for independence. Deborah Sampson, the daughter of a poor Massachusetts farmer, disguised herself as a man and in 1782, at age twenty-one, enlisted in the Continental army. Ultimately, her commanding officer learned her secret but kept it to himself, and she was honorably discharged at the end of the war. Years later, Congress awarded her a soldier's pension. Other patriotic women participated in crowd actions against unscrupulous merchants, raised funds to assist soldiers, contributed homespun goods to the army, and passed along information about British army movements.

Within American households, women participated in the political discussions unleashed by independence. "Was not every fireside," John Adams later recalled, "a theater of politics?" Gender formed a boundary limiting those entitled to the full blessings of American freedom. The principle of **coverture** (described in Chapter 1) remained intact in the new nation. The husband still held legal authority over the person, property, and choices of his wife. Despite the expansion of democracy, politics remained overwhelmingly a male realm.

For men, political freedom meant the right to self-government, the power to consent to the individuals and political arrangements that ruled over them. For women, however, the marriage contract superseded the social contract. A woman's relationship to the larger society was mediated through her relationship with her husband. In both law and social reality, women lacked the essential qualification of political participation—autonomy based on ownership of property or control of one's own person. Overall, the republican citizen was, by definition, male.

Portrait of John and Elizabeth Lloyd Cadwalader and Their Daughter Anne. This 1772 portrait of a prominent Philadelphia businessman and his family by the American artist Charles Willson Peale illustrates the emerging ideal of the "companionate" marriage, which is based on affection rather than male authority.

Republican Motherhood

According to the ideology of **republican motherhood** that emerged as a result of independence, women played an indispensable role by training future citizens. Even though republican motherhood ruled out direct female involvement in politics, it encouraged the expansion of educational opportunities for women, so that they could impart political wisdom to their children. Women, wrote Benjamin Rush, needed to have a "suitable education," to enable them to "instruct their sons in the principles of liberty and government."

The idea of republican motherhood reinforced the trend, already evident in the eighteenth century, toward the idea of "companionate" marriage, a voluntary union held together by affection and mutual dependency rather than male authority. In her letter to John Adams quoted above, Abigail Adams recommended that men should willingly give up "the harsh title of Master for the more tender and endearing one of Friend."

The structure of family life itself was altered by the Revolution. In colonial America, those living within the household often included indentured servants, apprentices, and slaves. After independence, southern slaves remained, rhetorically at least, members of the owner's "family." In the North, however, with the rapid decline of various forms of indentured servitude and apprenticeship, a more modern definition of the household as consisting of parents and their children took hold. Hired workers, whether domestic servants or farm laborers, were not considered part of the family.

Keep Within the Compass, a late eighteenth-century engraving, illustrates the happiness of a "virtuous woman" if she remains within the world of home and family and some of the "troubles" awaiting her if she ventures outside. The woman appears in a space marked off by a compass, an instrument for drawing a circle.

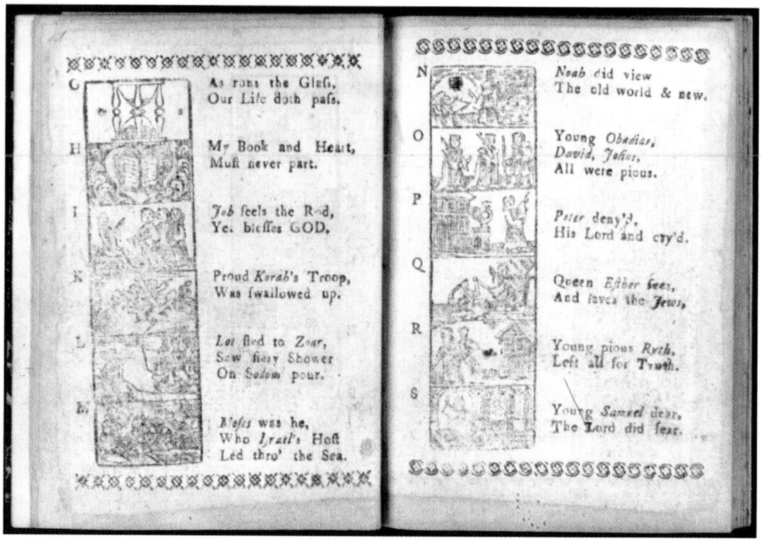
G As runs the Glaſs,
Our Life doth paſs.
H My Book and Heart,
Muſt never part.
I Job feels the Rod,
Yet bleſſes GOD.
K Proud Korah's Troop,
Was ſwallowed up.
L Lot fled to Zoar,
Saw fiery Shower
On Sodom pour.
M Moſes was he,
Who Iſrael's Hoſt
Led thro' the Sea.
N Noah did view
The old world & new.
O Young Obadias,
David, Joſias,
All were pious.
P Peter deny'd,
His Lord and cry'd.
Q Queen Eſther ſues,
And ſaves the Jews,
R Young pious Ruth,
Left all for Truth.
S Young Samuel dear,
The Lord did fear.

Two pages from *The New England Primer*, first published in Boston around 1690 and reissued in numerous editions throughout the eighteenth century. The book taught the alphabet to young children by referring to moral principles and stories from the Bible. Schoolbooks of the era emphasized both learning and religious devotion.

The Arduous Struggle for Liberty

The Revolution changed the life of virtually every American. As a result of the long struggle against British rule, the public sphere, and with it the right to vote, expanded markedly. Bound labor among whites declined dramatically, religious groups enjoyed greater liberty, blacks mounted a challenge to slavery in which many won their freedom, and women in some ways enjoyed a higher status. On the other hand, for Indians, many Loyalists, and the majority of slaves, American independence meant a deprivation of freedom.

The winds of change were sweeping across the Atlantic world. The year 1776 saw not only Paine's *Common Sense* and Jefferson's Declaration but also the publication in England of Adam Smith's *Wealth of Nations*, which attacked the British policy of closely regulating trade, and Jeremy Bentham's *Fragment on Government*, which criticized the nature of British government. Moreover, the ideals of the American Revolution helped to inspire countless subsequent struggles for social equality and national independence, from the French Revolution, which exploded in 1789, to the uprising that overthrew the slave system in Haiti in the 1790s, to the Latin American wars for independence in the early nineteenth century, and numerous struggles of colonial peoples for nationhood in the twentieth. But within the new republic, the debate over who should enjoy the blessings of liberty would continue long after independence had been achieved.

CHAPTER REVIEW AND ONLINE RESOURCES

REVIEW QUESTIONS

1. *For the lower classes, colonial society had been based on inequality, deference, and obedience. How did the American Revolution challenge that social order?*
2. *Why did the Revolution cause more radical changes in Pennsylvania than elsewhere, and how was this radicalism demonstrated in the new state constitution?*
3. *How did ideas of political freedom affect people's ideas about economic rights and relationships?*
4. *What role did the founders foresee for religion in American government and society?*
5. *What was the impact of the American Revolution on Native Americans?*
6. *What were the most important features of the new state constitutions?*
7. *How did popular views of property rights prevent slaves from enjoying all the freedoms of the social contract?*
8. *How did revolutionary America see both improvements and limitations in women's roles and rights?*

KEY TERMS

republics (p. 170)
suffrage (p. 171)
Bill for Establishing Religious Freedom (p. 174)
inflation (p. 177)
free trade (p. 177)
The Wealth of Nations (p. 177)
Loyalists (p. 178)
abolition (p. 181)
freedom petitions (p. 183)
Lemuel Haynes (p. 183)
free blacks (p. 188)
coverture (p. 189)
republican motherhood (p. 189)

Go to INQUIZITIVE

To see what you know—and learn what you've missed—with personalized feedback along the way.

Visit the ***Give Me Liberty!*** **Student Site** for primary source documents and images, interactive maps, author videos featuring Eric Foner, and more.

1777	Articles of Confederation drafted
1781	Articles of Confederation ratified
1782	*Letters from an American Farmer*
1783	Treaty of Paris
1784–1785	Land Ordinances approved
1785	Jefferson's *Notes on the State of Virginia*
1786–1787	Shays's Rebellion
1787	Constitutional Convention
	Northwest Ordinance of 1787
1788	*The Federalist*
	Constitution ratified
1790	Naturalization Act
	First national census
1791	Little Turtle defeats Arthur St. Clair's forces
	Bill of Rights ratified
1794	Little Turtle defeated at Battle of Fallen Timbers
1795	Treaty of Greenville
1808	Congress prohibits the slave trade

CHAPTER 7

FOUNDING A NATION

★

1783–1791

The Federal Ship Hamilton, an engraving depicting the centerpiece of the Grand Federal Procession in New York City in 1788 that celebrated the ratification of the Constitution. The ship carried over thirty seamen and fired several thirteen-gun salutes during the parade, one for each state. Alexander Hamilton was one of the era's key nationalists and an author of *The Federalist*, which made the argument for ratification.

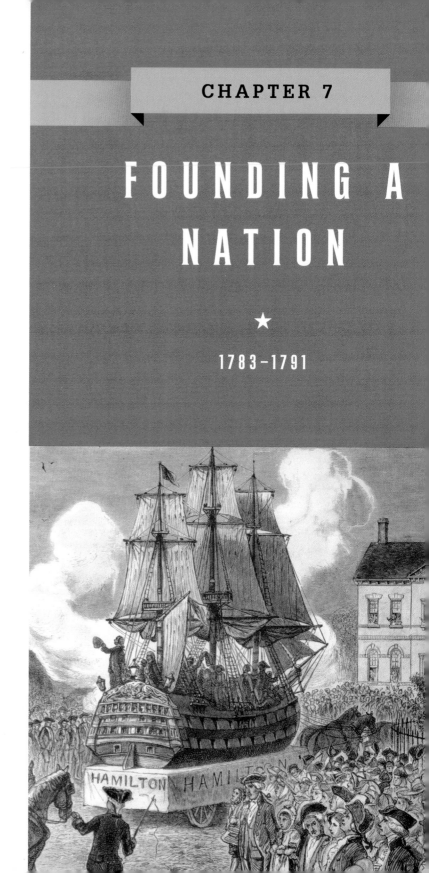

During June and July of 1788, civic leaders in cities up and down the Atlantic coast organized colorful pageants to celebrate the ratification of the U.S. Constitution. For one day, Benjamin Rush commented of Philadelphia's parade, social class "forgot its claims," as thousands of marchers—rich and poor, businessman and apprentice—joined in a common public ceremony. The parades testified to the strong popular support for the Constitution in the nation's cities. Elaborate banners and floats gave voice to the hopes inspired by the new structure of government. "May commerce flourish and industry be rewarded," declared Philadelphia's mariners and shipbuilders.

Throughout the era of the Revolution, Americans spoke of their nation as a "rising empire." Whereas Europe's empires were governed by force, America's would be different. In Jefferson's phrase, it would be "an empire of liberty," bound together by a common devotion to the principles of the Declaration of Independence. Already, the United States exceeded in size Great Britain, Spain, and France combined. As a new nation, it possessed many advantages, including physical isolation from the Old World (a significant asset between 1789 and 1815, when European powers were almost constantly at war), a youthful population certain to grow much larger, and a broad distribution of property ownership and literacy among white citizens.

On the other hand, the nation's prospects at the time of independence were not entirely promising. Control of its vast territory was by no means secure. Nearly all of the 3.9 million Americans recorded in the first national census of 1790 lived near the Atlantic coast. Large areas west of the Appalachian Mountains remained in Indian hands. The British retained military posts on American territory near the Great Lakes.

Away from navigable waterways, communication and transportation were primitive. The population consisted of numerous ethnic and religious groups and some 700,000 slaves, making unity difficult to achieve. No republican government had ever been established over so vast a territory or with so diverse a population. "We have no Americans in America," commented John Adams. It would take time for consciousness of a common nationality to sink deep roots.

Profound questions needed to be answered. What course of development should the United States follow? How could the competing claims of local self-government, sectional interests, and national authority be balanced? Who should be considered full-fledged members of the American people, entitled to the blessings of liberty? These issues became the focus of heated debate as the first generation of Americans sought to consolidate their new republic.

FOCUS QUESTIONS

- *What were the achievements and problems of the Confederation government?*
- *What major compromises molded the final content of the Constitution?*
- *How did Anti-Federalist concerns raised during the ratification process lead to the creation of the Bill of Rights?*
- *How did the definition of citizenship in the new republic exclude Native Americans and African-Americans?*

AMERICA UNDER THE CONFEDERATION

The Articles of Confederation

The first written constitution of the United States was the **Articles of Confederation**, drafted by Congress in 1777 and ratified by the states four years later. The Articles sought to balance the need for national coordination of the War of Independence with widespread fear that centralized political power posed a danger to liberty. It explicitly declared the new national government to be a "perpetual union." But it resembled less a blueprint for a common government than a treaty for mutual defense. Under the Articles, the thirteen states retained their individual "sovereignty, freedom, and independence." The national government consisted of a one-house Congress, in which each state, no matter how large or populous, cast a single vote. There was no president to enforce the laws and no judiciary to interpret them. Major decisions required the approval of nine states rather than a simple majority.

Limitations of the Articles

The only powers specifically granted to the national government by the Articles of Confederation were those essential to the struggle for independence—declaring war, conducting foreign affairs, and making treaties with other governments. Congress had no real financial resources. It could coin money but lacked the power to levy taxes or regulate commerce. Its revenue came mainly from contributions by the individual states. To amend the Articles required the unanimous consent of the states, a formidable obstacle to change.

Accomplishments under the Articles

But Congress in the 1780s did not lack for accomplishments. The most important was establishing national control over land to the west of the thirteen states and devising rules for its settlement. Citing their original royal charters, which granted territory running all the way to the "South Sea" (the Pacific Ocean), states such as Virginia, the Carolinas, and Connecticut claimed immense tracts of western land. Land speculators, politicians, and prospective settlers from states with clearly defined boundaries insisted that such land must belong to the nation at large. Only after the land-rich states, in the interest of national unity, ceded their western claims to the central government did the Articles win ratification.

Congress, Settlers, and the West

Establishing rules for the settlement of this national domain—the area controlled by the federal government, stretching from the western boundaries of existing states to the Mississippi River—was critical. Although some Americans spoke of it as if it were empty, over 100,000 Indians inhabited the region. Congress took the position that by aiding the British, Indians had forfeited the right to their lands. But little distinction was made among tribes that had sided with the enemy, aided the patriots, or played no part in the war at all. At peace conferences at Fort Stanwix, New York, in 1784 and Fort McIntosh near Pittsburgh the following year, American representatives demanded and received large surrenders of Indian land north of the Ohio River. Similar treaties soon followed with the Cherokee, Choctaw, and Chickasaw tribes in the South.

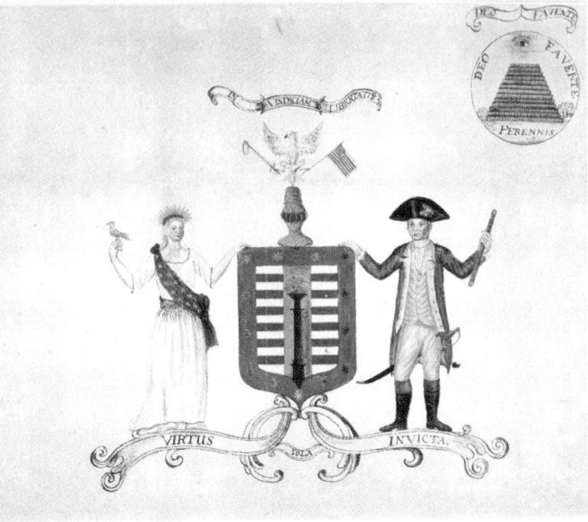

A design for the Great Seal of the United States produced by a committee of Congress in 1782 includes symbols of liberty, war, and peace, a shield with thirteen stars, and an eagle, all below a Latin phrase meaning "In Defense of Liberty." On the reverse (illustrated at upper right) is an unfinished pyramid with thirteen steps and the Eye of Providence.

When it came to disposing of western land and regulating its settlement, the Confederation government faced conflicting pressures. Many leaders believed that the economic health of the new republic required that farmers have access to land in the West. But they also saw land sales as a potential source of revenue.

The arrival of peace triggered a large population movement from settled parts of the original states into frontier areas like upstate New York and across the Appalachian Mountains into Kentucky and Tennessee. To settlers, the right to take possession of western lands was an essential element of American freedom. When a group of Ohioans petitioned Congress in 1785, assailing landlords and speculators who monopolized available acreage and asking that preference in land ownership be given to "actual settlements," their motto was "Grant us Liberty."

Frontier fears

At the same time, however, like British colonial officials before them, many leaders of the new nation feared that an unregulated flow of population across the Appalachian Mountains would provoke constant warfare with Indians. Moreover, they viewed frontier settlers as disorderly and lacking in proper respect for authority.

The Land Ordinances

Western settlement and self-government

A series of measures approved by Congress during the 1780s defined the terms by which western land would be marketed and settled. Drafted by Thomas Jefferson, the **Ordinance of 1784** established stages of self-government for the West. The region would be divided into districts initially governed by Congress and eventually admitted to the Union as member states. By a single vote, Congress rejected a clause that would have prohibited slavery throughout the West. A second resolution, the **Ordinance of 1785**, regulated land sales in the region north of the Ohio

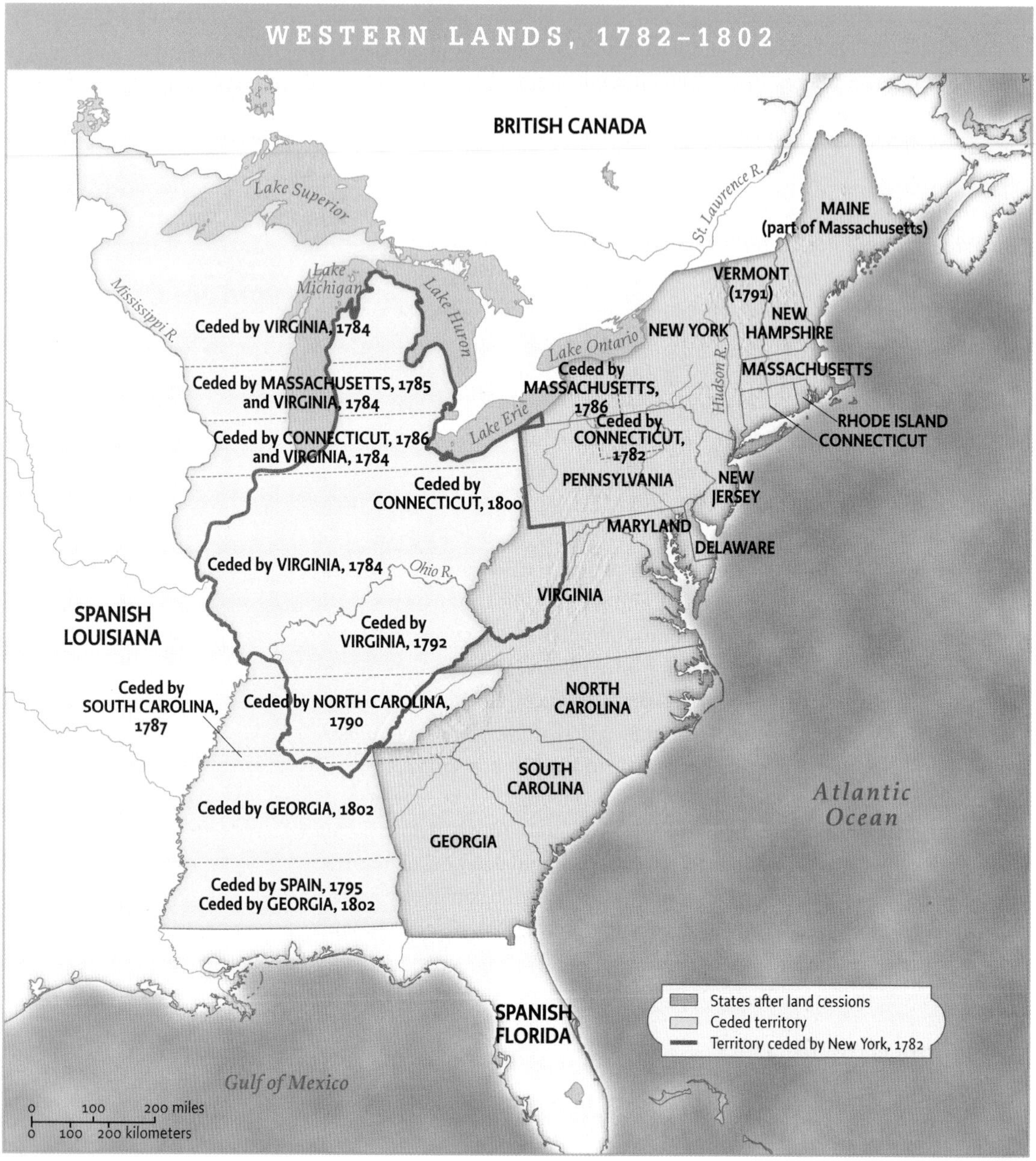

The creation of a nationally controlled public domain from western land ceded by the states was one of the main achievements of the federal government under the Articles of Confederation.

River, which came to be known as the Old Northwest. Land would be surveyed by the government and then sold in "sections" of a square mile (640 acres) at $1 per acre. In each township, one section would be set aside to provide funds for public education.

Price of land

Like the British before them, American officials found it difficult to regulate the thirst for new land. The minimum purchase price of $640, however, put public land out of the financial reach of most settlers. They generally ended up buying smaller parcels from speculators and land companies. For many years, actual and prospective settlers pressed for a reduction in the price of government-owned land, a movement that did not end until the Homestead Act of 1862 offered free land in the public domain.

Territorial expansion and self-government

A final measure, the **Northwest Ordinance of 1787**, called for the eventual establishment of from three to five states north of the Ohio River and east of the Mississippi. Thus was enacted the basic principle of what Jefferson called the **empire of liberty**—rather than ruling over the West as a colonial power, the United States would admit the area's population as equal members of the political system. Territorial expansion and self-government would grow together.

Slavery prohibited

The Northwest Ordinance pledged that "the utmost good faith" would be observed toward local Indians and that their land would not be taken without consent. "It will cost much less," one congressman noted, "to conciliate the good opinion of the Indians than to pay men for destroying them." But national land policy assumed that whether through purchase, treaties, or voluntary removal, the Indian presence would soon disappear. The ordinance also prohibited slavery in the Old Northwest, a provision that would have far-reaching consequences when the sectional conflict between North and South developed. But for years, owners brought slaves into the area, claiming that they had voluntarily signed long-term labor contracts.

The Confederation's Weaknesses

Whatever the achievements of the Confederation government, in the eyes of many influential Americans they were outweighed by its failings. Both the national government and the country at large faced worsening economic problems. To finance the War of Independence, Congress had borrowed large sums of money by selling interest-bearing bonds and paying soldiers and suppliers in notes to be redeemed in the future. Lacking a secure source of revenue, it found itself unable to pay either interest or the debts themselves. With the United States now outside the British empire, American ships were barred from trading with the West

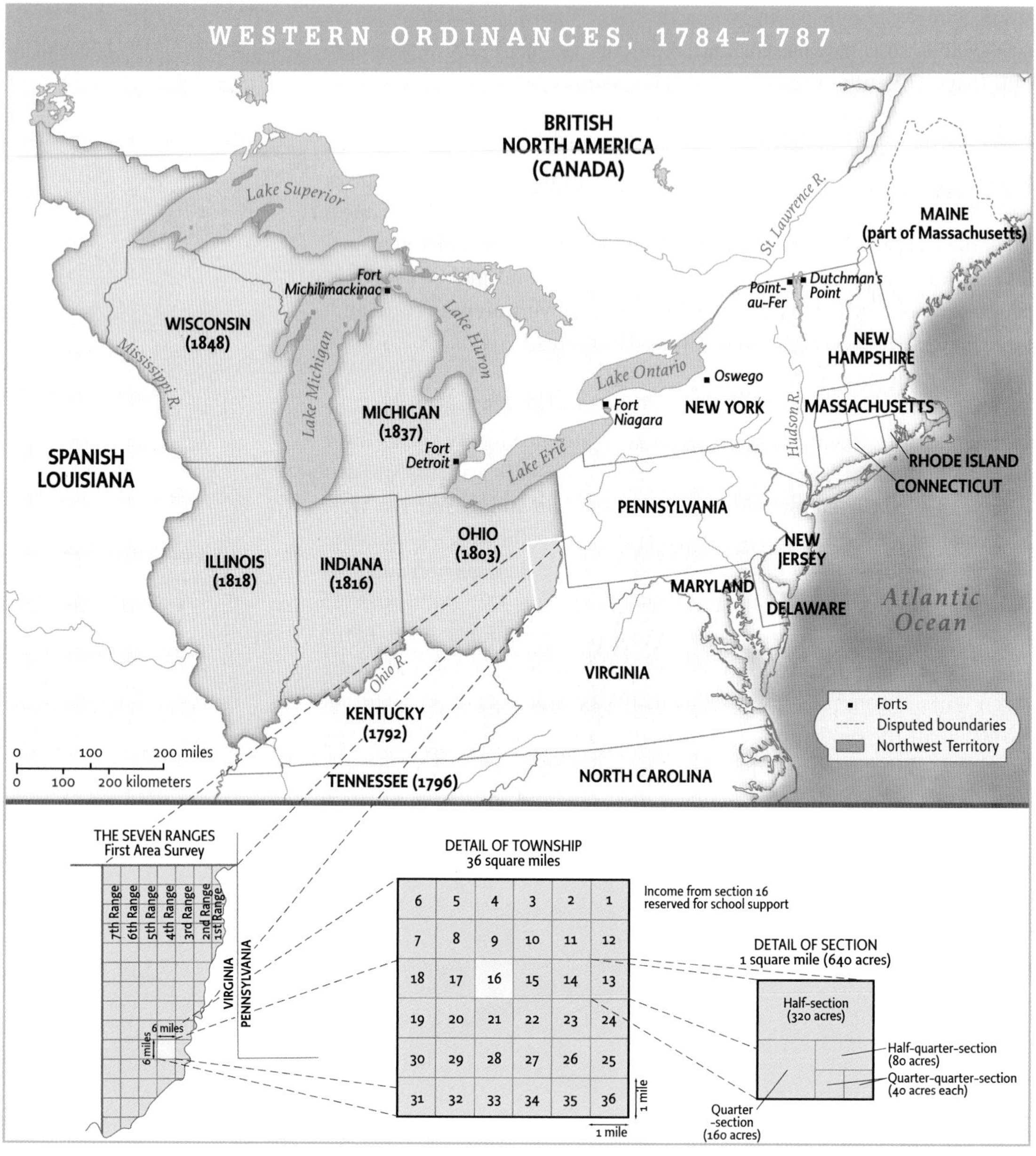

A series of ordinances in the 1780s provided for both the surveying and sale of lands in the public domain north of the Ohio River and the eventual admission of states carved from the area as equal members of the Union.

Indies. Imported goods, however, flooded the market, undercutting the business of many craftsmen, driving down wages, and draining money out of the country.

Some American businessmen looked for new areas with which to trade. In 1784, the *Empress of China* set sail for Canton, the first ship to do so flying the American flag. It carried furs, wine, Spanish silver dollars, and American ginseng. It returned the following year with silk, tea, and Chinese porcelain. The investors turned a large profit. The voyage demonstrated the feasibility of trade with Asia, but for the moment, this could not compensate for the loss of nearby markets in the British West Indies.

A Bankruptcy Scene. Creditors repossess the belongings of a family unable to pay its debts, while a woman weeps in the background. Popular fears of bankruptcy led several states during the 1780s to pass laws postponing the collection of debts.

With Congress unable to act, the states adopted their own economic policies. Several imposed tariff duties on goods imported from abroad. In order to increase the amount of currency in circulation and make it easier for individuals to pay their debts, several states printed large sums of paper money. Others enacted laws postponing debt collection. Creditors considered such measures attacks on their property rights.

Shays's Rebellion

Uprising in Massachusetts

In late 1786 and early 1787, crowds of debt-ridden farmers closed the courts in western Massachusetts to prevent the seizure of their land for failure to pay taxes. The uprising came to be known as **Shays's Rebellion**, a name affixed to it by its opponents, after Daniel Shays, one of the leaders and a veteran of the War of Independence. The participants in Shays's Rebellion modeled their tactics on the crowd activities of the 1760s and 1770s and employed liberty trees and liberty poles as symbols of their cause. They received no sympathy from Governor James Bowdoin, who dispatched an army headed by the former Revolutionary War general Benjamin Lincoln. The rebels were dispersed in January 1787.

Observing Shays's Rebellion from Paris where he was serving as ambassador, Thomas Jefferson refused to be alarmed. "A little rebellion now and then is a good thing," he wrote to a friend. "The tree of liberty must be refreshed from time to time with the blood of patriots and tyrants." But the uprising was the culmination of a series of events in the 1780s that persuaded an influential group of Americans that the national government must be strengthened so that it could develop uniform economic policies and protect property owners from infringements on their rights by local majorities.

"Abuses of liberty"

Among proponents of stronger national authority, liberty had lost some of its luster. The danger to individual rights, they came to believe, now arose not from a tyrannical central government, but from the people themselves. "Liberty," declared James Madison, "may be endangered by the abuses of liberty as well as the abuses of power." To put it another way, private liberty, especially the secure enjoyment of property rights, could be endangered by public liberty—unchecked power in the hands of the people.

James Madison, "father of the Constitution," in a miniature portrait painted by Charles Willson Peale in 1783. Madison was only thirty-six years old when the Constitutional Convention met.

Nationalists of the 1780s

Madison, a diminutive Virginian and the lifelong disciple and ally of Thomas Jefferson, thought deeply about the nature of political freedom. He was among the group of talented and well-organized men who spearheaded the movement for a stronger national government. Another was Alexander Hamilton, who had come to North America from the West Indies as a youth. Hamilton was perhaps the most vigorous proponent of an "energetic" government that would enable the new nation to become a powerful commercial and diplomatic presence in world affairs. Men like Madison and Hamilton were nation builders. They came to believe during the 1780s that the country's future greatness depended on enhancing national authority.

The concerns voiced by critics of the Articles found a sympathetic hearing among men who had developed a national consciousness during the Revolution. Nationalists included army officers, members of Congress accustomed to working with individuals from different states, and diplomats who represented the country abroad. Influential economic interests also desired a stronger national government. Among these were bondholders who despaired of being paid so long as Congress lacked a source of revenue, urban artisans seeking tariff protection from foreign imports, merchants desiring access to British markets, and all those who feared that the states were seriously interfering with property rights.

Alexander Hamilton, another youthful leader of the nationalists of the 1780s, was born in the West Indies in 1755. This life-size portrait was commissioned by five New York merchants and painted by John Trumbull in 1792, when Hamilton was Secretary of the Treasury.

In September 1786, delegates from six states met at Annapolis, Maryland, to consider ways for better regulating interstate and international commerce. The delegates proposed another gathering, in Philadelphia, to amend the Articles of Confederation. Every state except Rhode Island, which had gone the furthest in developing its own debtor-relief and trade policies, sent delegates to the Philadelphia convention. When they assembled in May 1787, they decided to scrap the Articles of Confederation entirely and draft a new constitution for the United States.

A NEW CONSTITUTION

The fifty-five men who gathered for the **Constitutional Convention** included some of the most prominent Americans. Thomas Jefferson and John Adams, serving as diplomats in Europe, did not take part. But among the delegates were George Washington (whose willingness to serve as presiding officer was an enormous asset) and Benjamin Franklin (now eighty-one years old). John Adams described the convention as a gathering of men of "ability, weight, and experience." He might have added, "and wealth." They earned their livings as lawyers, merchants, planters, and large farmers. Nearly half, including a number of Northerners, owned slaves. Washington owned over two hundred, three of whom he brought to Philadelphia.

Elite convention delegates

At a time when fewer than one-tenth of 1 percent of Americans attended college, more than half the delegates had college educations. Their shared social status and political experiences bolstered their common belief in the need to strengthen national authority and curb what one called "the excesses of democracy." To ensure free and candid debate, the deliberations took place in private. Madison, who believed the outcome would have great consequences for "the cause of liberty throughout the world," took careful notes. They were not published, however, until 1840, four years after he became the last delegate to pass away.

The Structure of Government

Legislature, executive, and national judiciary

It quickly became apparent that the delegates agreed on many points. The new constitution would create a legislature, an executive, and a national judiciary. Congress would have the power to raise money without relying on the states. States would be prohibited from infringing on the rights of property. And the government would represent the people. Most delegates hoped to find a middle ground between the despotism of monarchy and aristocracy and what they considered the excesses of popular self-government. "We had been too democratic," observed George Mason of Virginia, but he warned against the danger of going to "the opposite extreme." The key to stable, effective republican government was finding a way to balance the competing claims of liberty and power.

Competing interests

Differences quickly emerged over the proper balance between the federal and state governments and between the interests of large and small states. Early in the proceedings, Madison presented what came to be called the **Virginia Plan**. It proposed the creation of a two-house legislature with a state's population determining its representation in each. Smaller states, fearing that populous Virginia, Massachusetts, and Pennsylvania would dominate the new government, rallied behind the **New Jersey Plan**.

This called for a single-house Congress in which each state cast one vote, as under the Articles of Confederation. In the end, a compromise was reached—a two-house Congress consisting of a Senate in which each state had two members, and a House of Representatives apportioned according to population. Senators would be chosen by state legislatures for six-year terms. They were thus insulated from sudden shifts in public opinion. Representatives were to be elected every two years directly by the people.

The Limits of Democracy

Under the Articles of Confederation, no national official had been chosen by popular vote. Thus, the mode of choosing the House of Representatives signaled an expansion of democracy. The Constitution, moreover, imposed neither property nor religious qualifications for voting.

Less-than-democratic structure

Overall, however, the new structure of government was less than democratic. The delegates sought to shield the national government from the popular enthusiasms that had alarmed them during the 1780s and to ensure that the right kind of men held office. The delegates assumed that the Senate would be composed of each state's most distinguished citizens. They made the House of Representatives quite small (initially 65 members, at a time when the Massachusetts assembly had 200), on the assumption that only prominent individuals could win election in large districts.

Nor did the delegates provide for direct election of either federal judges or the president. Members of the Supreme Court would be appointed by the president for life terms. The president would be chosen either by members of an electoral college or by the House of Representatives. A state's electors would be chosen either by its legislature or by popular vote.

This portrait of George Washington, painted in the early 1790s by Charles Peale Polk, is based on one executed in 1787 by Polk's uncle, Charles Willson Peale. It depicts Washington as he looked when he presided over the Constitutional Convention in Philadelphia.

The actual system of election seemed a recipe for confusion. Each elector was to cast votes for two candidates for president, with the second-place finisher becoming vice president. If no candidate received a majority of the electoral ballots—as the delegates seem to have assumed would normally be the case—the president would be chosen from among the top three finishers by the House of Representatives, with each state casting one vote. The Senate would then elect the vice president. The delegates devised this extremely cumbersome system of indirect election because they did not trust ordinary voters to choose the president and vice president directly.

The Division and Separation of Powers

Hammered out in four months of discussion and compromise, the Constitution is a document of only 4,000 words that provides only the briefest outline of the new structure of government. (See the Appendix for the full text.) It embodies two basic political principles—**federalism**, sometimes called the **division of powers**, and the system of **checks and balances** between the different branches of the national government, also known as the **separation of powers**.

Federalism

"Federalism" refers to the relationship between the national government and the states. Compared with the Articles of Confederation, the Constitution significantly strengthened national authority. It charged the president with enforcing the law and commanding the military. It empowered Congress to levy taxes, borrow money, regulate commerce, declare war, deal with foreign nations and Indians, and promote the "general welfare." The Constitution also included strong provisions to prevent the states from infringing on property rights. They were barred from issuing paper money, impairing contracts, interfering with interstate commerce, and levying their own import or export duties. On the other hand, most day-to-day affairs of government, from education to law enforcement, remained in the hands of the states. This principle of divided sovereignty was a recipe for debate, which continues to this day, over the balance of power between the national government and the states.

Checks and balances

The separation of powers, or the system of checks and balances, refers to the way the Constitution seeks to prevent any branch of the national government from dominating the other two. To prevent an accumulation of power dangerous to liberty, authority within the government is diffused and balanced against itself. Congress enacts laws, but the president can veto them, and a two-thirds majority is required to pass legislation over his objection. Federal judges are nominated by the president and approved by the Senate, but to ensure their independence, the judges then serve for life. The president can be impeached by the House and removed from office by the Senate for "high crimes and misdemeanors."

The Debate over Slavery

The structure of government was not the only source of debate at the Constitutional Convention. As Madison recorded, "the institution of slavery and its implications" divided the delegates at many sessions.

The words "slave" and "slavery" do not appear in the original Constitution—a concession to the sensibilities of delegates who feared they would "contaminate the glorious fabric of American liberty." Nonetheless, the document contained strong protections for slavery. It prohibited Congress from abolishing the importation of slaves from abroad for twenty years. It required states to return to their owners fugitives from bondage.

This advertisement by a slave-trading company appeared in a Richmond, Virginia, newspaper only a few months after the signing of the Constitution. The company seeks to buy 100 slaves to sell to purchasers in states farther south. Slavery was a major subject of debate at the Constitutional Convention.

WANTED,
ONE HUNDRED
NEGROES,
From 12 to 30 years old, for which a good price will be given.
THEY are to be sent out of the state, therefore we shall not be particular respecting the character of any of them—Hearty and well made is all that is necessary.
Moses Austin & Co.
Richmond, Dec. 15, 1787.

And the **three-fifths clause** provided that three-fifths of the slave population would be counted in determining each state's representation in the House of Representatives and its electoral votes for president.

South Carolina's influence

South Carolina's delegates had come to Philadelphia determined to defend slavery, and they had a powerful impact on the final document. They originated the fugitive slave clause and the electoral college. They insisted on strict limits on the power of Congress to levy taxes within the states, fearing future efforts to raise revenue by taxing slave property. Gouverneur Morris, one of Pennsylvania's delegates, declared that he was being forced to decide between offending the southern states and doing injustice to "human nature." For the sake of national unity, he said, he would choose the latter.

Nonetheless, the Constitution did provide a basis for later antislavery political movements. Many of the framers, including slaveholders from the Upper South, hoped that the institution would eventually die out, and they successfully resisted efforts to place an explicit national recognition of property in human beings in the document. Slavery remained an institution created by state, not national, law. This opened the door to efforts to bar slavery in places of national jurisdiction, especially the western territories.

Slavery in the Constitution

The Constitution's slavery clauses were compromises, efforts to find a middle ground between the institution's critics and defenders. Taken together, however, they embedded slavery more deeply than ever in American life and politics. The slave trade clause allowed a commerce condemned by civilized society—one that had been suspended during the War of Independence—to continue until 1808. On January 1, 1808, the first day that Congress was allowed under the Constitution, it prohibited the further importation of slaves. But in the interim, partly to replace slaves who had escaped to the British and partly to provide labor for the expansion of slavery to fertile land away from the coast, some 170,000 Africans were brought to the new nation as slaves.

Slave trade clause

The fugitive slave clause accorded slave laws "extraterritoriality"—that is, the condition of bondage remained attached to a person even if he or she escaped to a state where slavery had been abolished. Nonetheless, the clause was strikingly ambiguous. It did not say who was responsible for apprehending a fugitive slave or what judicial procedures would be employed to return him or her to bondage. As time went on, these questions would become a major source of conflict between the North and the South. And the three-fifths clause allowed the white South to exercise far greater power in national affairs than

Fugitive slave clause

Three-fifths clause

the size of its free population warranted. Of the first sixteen presidential elections, between 1788 and 1848, all but four placed a southern slaveholder in the White House.

Threat to slavery

Nevertheless, some slaveholders detected a potential threat buried in the Constitution. Patrick Henry, who condemned slavery but feared abolition, warned that, in time of war, the new government might take steps to arm and liberate the slaves. "May Congress not say," he asked, "that every black man must fight?" What Henry could not anticipate was that the war that eventually destroyed slavery would be launched by the South itself to protect the institution.

The Final Document

The Preamble

Gouverneur Morris put the finishing touches on the final draft of the new Constitution, trying to make it, he explained, "as clear as our language would permit." For the original preamble, which began, "We the people of the States of New Hampshire, Massachusetts," etc., he substituted the far more powerful "We the people of the United States." He added a statement of the Constitution's purposes, including to "establish justice," promote "the general welfare," and "secure the blessings of liberty"—things the Articles of Confederation, in the eyes of most of the delegates, had failed to accomplish.

The last session of the Constitutional Convention took place on September 17, 1787. Benjamin Franklin urged the delegates to put aside individual objections and approve the document, whatever its imperfections.

The Signing of the Constitution, by mid-nineteenth-century American artist Thomas Prichard Rossiter, depicts the conclusion of the Constitutional Convention of 1787. Among the founding fathers depicted are James Wilson, signing the document at the table in the center, and George Washington, presiding from the dais with an image of the sun behind him.

Of the forty-five delegates who remained in Philadelphia, thirty-nine signed the Constitution. It was then sent to the states for ratification.

The Constitution created a new framework for American development. It made possible a national economic market. It created national political institutions, reduced the powers of the states, and sought to place limits on popular democracy. The ratification process, however, unleashed a nationwide debate over the best means of preserving American freedom.

THE RATIFICATION DEBATE AND THE ORIGIN OF THE BILL OF RIGHTS

The Federalist

For ratification: Alexander Hamilton, James Madison, John Jay

Even though the Constitution provided that it would go into effect when nine states, not all thirteen as required by the Articles of Confederation, had given their approval, ratification was by no means certain. Each state held an election for delegates to a special ratifying convention. A fierce public battle ensued, producing hundreds of pamphlets and newspaper articles and spirited campaigns to elect delegates. To generate support, Hamilton, Madison, and John Jay composed a series of eighty-five essays

This satirical engraving by Amos Doolittle depicts some of the issues in the debate over the ratification of the Constitution. The wagon in the center is carrying Connecticut and sinking into the mud under the weight of debts and paper money as "Federals" and "Antifederals" try to pull it out. Federals call for the state to "comply with Congress" (that is, to pay money requisitioned by the national government); the Antifederals reply, "Tax luxury" and "Success to Shays," a reference to Shays's Rebellion. Underneath the three merchant ships is a phrase criticizing the tariffs that states were imposing on imports from one another (which the Constitution prohibited).

that appeared in newspapers under the pen name Publius and were gathered as a book, ***The Federalist***, in 1788. Today, the essays are regarded as among the most important American contributions to political thought. At the time, however, they were only one part of a much larger national debate over ratification.

Protecting American liberties

Again and again, Hamilton and Madison repeated that rather than posing a danger to Americans' liberties, the Constitution in fact protected them. Any government, Hamilton insisted, could become oppressive, but with its checks and balances and division of power, the Constitution made political tyranny almost impossible. At the New York ratifying convention, Hamilton assured the delegates that the Constitution had created "the perfect balance between liberty and power."

"Extend the Sphere"

Madison's Federalist nos. 10 and 51

Madison, too, emphasized how the Constitution was structured to prevent abuses of authority. But in several essays, especially *Federalist* nos. 10 and 51, he moved beyond such assurances to develop a strikingly new vision of the relationship between government and society in the United States. Madison identified the essential dilemma, as he saw it, of the new republic—government must be based on the will of the people, yet the people had shown themselves susceptible to dangerous enthusiasms. The problem of balancing democracy and respect for property would only grow in the years ahead because, he warned, economic development would inevitably increase the numbers of poor. What was to prevent them from using their political power to secure "a more equal distribution" of wealth by seizing the property of the rich?

The answer, Madison explained, lay not simply in the way power balanced power in the structure of government, but in the nation's size and diversity. Previous republics had existed only in small territories—the Dutch republic or the Italian city-states of the Renaissance. But, argued Madison, the very size of the United States was a source of stability, not, as many feared, weakness. "Extend the sphere," he wrote. In a nation as large as the United States, so many distinct interests—economic, regional, and political—would arise that no single one would ever be able to take over the government and oppress the rest.

Madison's writings did much to shape the early nation's understanding of its new political institutions. In arguing that the size of the republic helped to secure Americans' rights, they reinforced the tradition that saw continuous westward expansion as essential to freedom.

In this late eighteenth-century engraving, Americans celebrate the signing of the Constitution beneath a temple of liberty.

The Anti-Federalists

Opponents of ratification, called **Anti-Federalists**, insisted that the Constitution shifted the balance between liberty and power too far in the direction of the latter. Anti-Federalists lacked the coherent leadership of the Constitution's defenders. They included state politicians fearful of seeing their influence diminish, among them such revolutionary heroes as Samuel Adams, John Hancock, and Patrick Henry. Small farmers, many of whom supported the state debtor-relief measures of the 1780s that the Constitution's supporters deplored, also saw no need for a stronger central government. Some opponents of the Constitution denounced the document's protections for slavery; others warned that the powers of Congress were so broad that it might enact a law for abolition.

Against ratification: Samuel Adams, John Hancock, Patrick Henry

Anti-Federalists repeatedly predicted that the new government would fall under the sway of merchants, creditors, and others hostile to the interests of ordinary Americans. Popular self-government, they claimed, flourished best in small communities, where rulers and ruled interacted daily. The result of the Constitution, warned Melancton Smith of New York, a member of Congress under the Articles of Confederation, would be domination of the "common people" by the "well-born."

Rule by the "well-born"

"Liberty" was the Anti-Federalists' watchword. America's happiness, they insisted, "arises from the freedom of our institutions and the limited nature of our government," both threatened by the new Constitution. To the vision of the United States as an energetic great power, Anti-Federalists counterposed a way of life grounded in local, democratic institutions. Anti-Federalists also pointed to the Constitution's lack of a **Bill of Rights**, which left unprotected rights such as trial by jury and freedom of speech and the press.

Social bases of support and opposition

In general, pro-Constitution sentiment flourished in the nation's cities and in rural areas closely tied to the commercial marketplace. The Constitution's most energetic supporters were men of substantial property. But what George Bryan of Pennsylvania, a supporter of ratification, called the "golden phantom" of prosperity also swung urban artisans, laborers, and sailors behind the movement for a government that would use its "energy and power" to revive the depressed economy. Anti-Federalism drew its support from small farmers in more isolated rural areas such as the Hudson Valley of New York, western Massachusetts, and the southern backcountry.

In the end, the supporters' energy and organization, coupled with their domination of the colonial press, carried the day. Ninety-two news-

Banner of the Society of Pewterers. A banner carried by one of the many artisan groups that took part in New York City's Grand Federal Procession of 1788 celebrating the ratification of the Constitution. The banner depicts artisans at work in their shop and some of their products. The words "Solid and Pure," and the inscription at the upper right, link the quality of their pewter to their opinion of the new frame of government and hopes for the future. The inscription reads:

The Federal Plan Most Solid and Secure / Americans Their Freedom Will Endure / All Arts Shall Flourish in Columbia's Land / And All Her Sons Join as One Social Band

papers and magazines existed in the United States in 1787. Of these, only twelve published a significant number of Anti-Federalist pieces. Madison also won support for the new Constitution by promising that the first Congress would enact a Bill of Rights. By mid-1788, the required nine states had ratified. Only Rhode Island and North Carolina voted against ratification, and they subsequently had little choice but to join the new government. Anti-Federalism died. But as with other movements in American history that did not immediately achieve their goals—for example, the Populists of the late nineteenth century—some of the Anti-Federalists' ideas eventually entered the political mainstream. To this day, their belief that a too-powerful central government is a threat to liberty continues to influence American political culture.

The Bill of Rights

Ironically, the parts of the Constitution Americans most value today—the freedoms of speech, the press, and religion; protection against unjust criminal procedures; equality before the law—were not in the original document. All of these but the last (which was enshrined in the Fourteenth Amendment after the Civil War) were contained in the first ten amendments, known as the Bill of Rights. Madison believed a Bill of Rights "redundant or pointless." "Parchment barriers" to the abuse of authority, he observed, would prove least effective when most needed. Madison's prediction would be amply borne out at future times of popular hysteria, such as during the Red Scare following World War I and the McCarthy era of the 1950s, when all branches of government joined in trampling on freedom of expression.

Nevertheless, every new state constitution contained some kind of declaration of citizens' rights, and large numbers of Americans—Federalist and Anti-Federalist alike—believed the new national Constitution should also have one. Madison presented to Congress a series of amendments that became the basis of the Bill of Rights, which was ratified by the states in 1791. The First Amendment prohibited Congress from legislating with regard to

First Amendment rights

VOICES OF FREEDOM

From David Ramsay, *The History of the American Revolution* (1789)

A member of the Continental Congress from South Carolina, David Ramsay published his history of the Revolution the year after the Constitution was ratified. In this excerpt, he lauds the principles of representative government and the right of future amendment, embodied in the state constitutions and adopted in the national one, as unique American political principles and the best ways of securing liberty.

The world has not hitherto exhibited so fair an opportunity for promoting social happiness. It is hoped for the honor of human nature, that the result will prove the fallacy of those theories that mankind are incapable of self government. The ancients, not knowing the doctrine of representation, were apt in their public meetings to run into confusion, but in America this mode of taking the sense of the people, is so well understood, and so completely reduced to system, that its most populous states are often peaceably convened in an assembly of deputies, not too large for orderly deliberation, and yet representing the whole in equal proportion. These popular branches of legislature are miniature pictures of the community, and from their mode of election are likely to be influenced by the same interests and feelings with the people whom they represent. . . .

In no age before, and in no other country, did man ever possess an election of the kind of government, under which he would choose to live. The constituent parts of the ancient free governments were thrown together by accident. The freedom of modern European governments was, for the most part, obtained by concessions, or liberality of monarchs, or military leaders. In America alone, reason and liberty concurred in the formation of constitutions. . . . In one thing they were all perfect. They left the people in the power of altering and amending them, whenever they pleased. In this happy peculiarity they placed the science of politics on a footing with the other sciences, by opening it to improvements from experience, and the discoveries of future ages. By means of this power of amending American constitutions, the friends of mankind have fondly hoped that oppression will one day be no more.

From James Winthrop, Anti-Federalist Essay Signed "Agrippa" (1787)

A local official in Middlesex, Massachusetts, James Winthrop published sixteen public letters between November 1787 and February 1788 opposing ratification of the Constitution.

It is the opinion of the ablest writers on the subject, that no extensive empire can be governed upon republican principles, and that such a government will degenerate into a despotism, unless it be made up of a confederacy of smaller states, each having the full powers of internal regulation. This is precisely the principle which has hitherto preserved our freedom. No instance can be found of any free government of considerable extent which has been supported upon any other plan. Large and consolidated empires may indeed dazzle the eyes of a distant spectator with their splendor, but if examined more nearly are always found to be full of misery. . . . It is under such tyranny that the Spanish provinces languish, and such would be our misfortune and degradation, if we should submit to have the concerns of the whole empire managed by one empire. To promote the happiness of the people it is necessary that there should be local laws; and it is necessary that those laws should be made by the representatives of those who are immediately subject to [them]. . . .

It is impossible for one code of laws to suit Georgia and Massachusetts. They must, therefore, legislate for themselves. Yet there is, I believe, not one point of legislation that is not surrendered in the proposed plan. Questions of every kind respecting property are determinable in a continental court, and so are all kinds of criminal causes. The continental legislature has, therefore, a right to make rules in all cases. . . . No rights are reserved to the citizens. . . . This new system is, therefore, a consolidation of all the states into one large mass, however diverse the parts may be of which it is composed. . . .

A bill of rights . . . serves to secure the minority against the usurpation and tyranny of the majority. . . . The experience of all mankind has proved the prevalence of a disposition to use power wantonly. It is therefore as necessary to defend an individual against the majority in a republic as against the king in a monarchy.

QUESTIONS

1. *Why does Ramsay feel that the power to amend the Constitution is so important a political innovation?*
2. *Why does Winthrop believe that a Bill of Rights is essential in the Constitution?*
3. *How do Ramsay and Winthrop differ concerning how the principle of representation operates in the United States?*

RATIFICATION OF THE CONSTITUTION

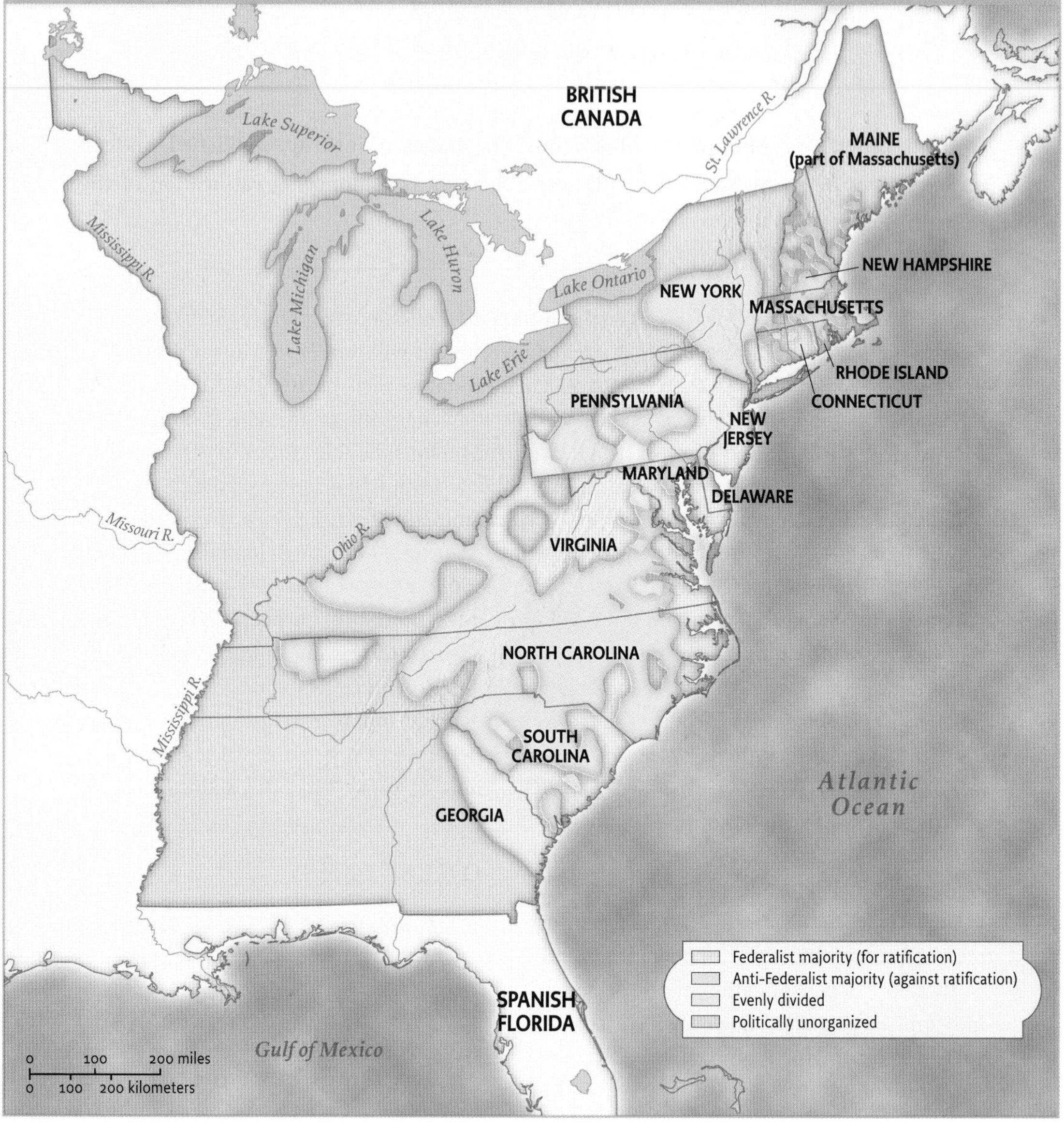

Federalists—those who supported the new Constitution—tended to be concentrated in cities and nearby rural areas, whereas backcountry farmers were more likely to oppose the new frame of government.

religion or infringing on freedom of speech, freedom of the press, or the right of assembly. The Second upheld the people's right to "keep and bear arms" in conjunction with "a well-regulated militia." Others prohibited abuses such as arrests without warrants and forcing a person accused of a crime to testify against himself, and reaffirmed the right to trial by jury.

Constitutional recognition of religious freedom

Although the roots and even the specific language of some parts of the Bill of Rights lay far back in English history, other provisions reflected the changes in American life brought about by the Revolution. The most remarkable of these was constitutional recognition of religious freedom. Unlike the Declaration of Independence, which invokes the blessing of divine providence, the Constitution is a purely secular document that contains no reference to God and bars religious tests for federal officeholders. The First Amendment prohibits the federal government from legislating on the subject of religion—a complete departure from British and colonial precedent. Under the Constitution it was and remains possible, as one critic complained, for "a papist, a Mohomatan, a deist, yea an atheist" to become president of the United States. Madison was so adamant about separating church and state that he even opposed the appointment of chaplains to serve Congress and the military.

Legacy of the Bill of Rights

The Bill of Rights aroused little enthusiasm on ratification and for decades was all but ignored. Not until the twentieth century would it come to be revered as an indispensable expression of American freedom. Nonetheless, the Bill of Rights subtly affected the language of liberty. Applying only to the federal government, not the states, it reinforced the idea that concentrated national power posed the greatest threat to freedom. And it contributed to the long process whereby freedom came to be discussed in the vocabulary of rights.

Among the most important rights were freedom of speech and the press, vital building blocks of a democratic public sphere. Once an entitlement of members of Parliament and colonial assemblies, free speech came to be seen as a basic right of citizenship.

"WE THE PEOPLE"

Who Belongs? The Constitution and American Citizenship

A nation, in one scholar's famous phrase, is more than a political entity or a specific piece of territory—it is also "an imagined political community," whose borders are as much intellectual as geographic. The creation of the United States required creating "Americans," that is, people who considered themselves members of the new nation, not simply of individual states. But who qualified as an American citizen? The Constitution did not say.

In British law, the American colonists, like persons in Great Britain, were "subjects" of the crown, entitled to protection and required to provide allegiance and, if male, to take up arms when called upon by the government. Independence transformed British subjecthood into American citizenship but did little to clarify its definition and rights. The word "citizen" appears several times in the Constitution, but no definition is given. One provision, known as the "comity" clause, prohibits states from discriminating between the "privileges and immunities" of their own citizens and those of other states. In other words, a person who moves from New York to Illinois must enjoy the same rights as those already in Illinois. This language assumes that the rights of citizens are determined by the states, not the federal government.

"Citizen"

The Constitution does require the president to be a "natural born citizen," that is, a person born in the country. This suggests, but does not explicitly state, that citizenship derives either from birth in the United States or, for immigrants from abroad (ineligible to become president), from a "naturalization" process. On occasion, the federal government created American citizens by purchasing the land on which they lived, for example, the Louisiana Territory acquired from France in 1803, or via conquest, as in the Mexican-American War. In both cases, residents of territory acquired by the United States could choose to become American citizens if they so desired (although whether this applied to Native Americans living under tribal sovereignty remained unclear).

Derivation of citizenship

Despite the enormous prestige that the idea of citizenship acquired in the first half of the nineteenth century, there was no commonly agreed-upon understanding of the rights that went with it or the role of the federal government in defining and guaranteeing those rights. Whites, male and female, born in the United States were commonly assumed to be citizens, but white women lacked basic rights enjoyed by men. Slaves were not American citizens, nor were Indians, but the status of free black Americans born in the United States remained highly controversial. Blacks voted in elections that chose delegates to the state conventions that ratified the Constitution. In the 1790s, the federal government issued certificates affirming the citizenship of black sailors, to prevent them from being seized by the British and "impressed" into the Royal Navy. Yet as time went on, the slave states placed increasingly severe restrictions on the lives of free blacks and refused to recognize them as citizens. Some northern states did, however, and all of the northern states accorded African-Americans basic rights such as property ownership, trial by jury, and the ability to hold public meetings, publish newspapers, and establish their own churches. But nowhere did they enjoy full equality before the law. One judge referred to free blacks as "quasi citizens." Not until the Reconstruction era that followed the Civil War was a clear statement added to the Constitution that affirmed the principle of "birthright citizenship"—that anyone born in the United States, no matter his or her race, language, religion, national origin, or the legal situation of one's parents, is an American citizen and is entitled to the equal protection of the laws.

"Birthright citizenship"

National Identity

The Constitution opens with the words "We the People." Although one might assume that the "people" of the United States included all those living within the nation's borders, the text made clear that this was not the case. The Constitution identifies three populations inhabiting the United States: Indians, treated as members of independent tribes and not part of the American body politic; "other persons"—that is, slaves; and the "people." Only the third were entitled to American freedom.

Exclusion of Indians and slaves

Indians in the New Nation

The early republic's policies toward Indians and African-Americans illustrate the conflicting principles that shaped American nationality. American leaders agreed that the West should not be left in Indian hands, but they disagreed about the Indians' ultimate fate. The government hoped to encourage the westward expansion of white settlement, which implied one of three things: the removal of the Indian population to lands even farther west, their total disappearance, or their incorporation into white "civilization" with the expectation that they might one day become part of American society.

Political status of Indian tribes

Indian tribes had no representation in the new government. The treaty system gave them a unique status within the American political system. But despite this recognition of their sovereignty, treaties were essentially ways of transferring land from Indians to the federal government or the states.

Open warfare continued in the Ohio Valley after ratification. In 1791, Little Turtle, leader of the Miami Confederacy, inflicted a humiliating defeat on American forces led by Arthur St. Clair, the American governor of the Northwest Territory. With 630 dead, this was the costliest loss ever suffered by the U.S. Army at the hands of Indians. In 1794, 3,000 American troops under Anthony Wayne defeated Little Turtle's forces at the Battle of Fallen Timbers. This led directly to the **Treaty of Greenville** of 1795, in which twelve Indian tribes ceded most of Ohio and Indiana to the federal government. The treaty also established the **annuity system**—yearly grants of federal money to Indian tribes that institutionalized continuing government influence in tribal affairs and gave outsiders considerable control over Indian life.

The signing of the Treaty of Greenville of 1795, painted by an unknown member of General Anthony Wayne's staff. In the treaty, a group of tribes ceded most of the area of the current states of Ohio and Indiana, along with the site that became the city of Chicago, to the United States.

Many prominent figures, however, rejected the idea that Indians were innately inferior to white Americans. Thomas Jefferson believed that Indians merely lived at a less advanced stage of civilization. Indians could become full-fledged members of the republic by abandoning communal landholding and hunting in favor of small-scale farming.

To pursue the goal of assimilation, Congress in the 1790s authorized President Washington to distribute agricultural tools and livestock to Indian men and spinning wheels and looms to Indian women. To whites, the adoption of American gender norms, with men working the land and women tending to their homes, would be a crucial sign that the Indians were becoming "civilized." But the American notion of civilization required so great a transformation of Indian life that most tribes rejected it. To Indians, freedom meant retaining tribal autonomy and identity, including the ability to travel widely in search of game. "Since our acquaintance with our brother white people," declared a Mohawk speaker at a 1796 treaty council, "that which we call freedom and liberty, becomes an entire stranger to us." There was no room for Indians who desired to retain their traditional way of life in the American empire of liberty.

Blacks and the Republic

By 1790, the 700,000 African-Americans far exceeded the Indian population within the United States. The status of free blacks was somewhat indeterminate. The North's **gradual emancipation** acts assumed that former slaves would remain in the country, not be colonized abroad. During the era of the Revolution, free blacks enjoyed at least some of the legal rights accorded to whites, including, in most states, the right to vote. The large majority of blacks, of course, were slaves, and slavery rendered them all but invisible to those imagining the American community.

Naturalization Act of 1790

Many white Americans excluded blacks from their conception of the American people. The Constitution empowered Congress to create a uniform system by which immigrants became citizens, and the Naturalization Act of 1790 offered the first legislative definition of American nationality. With no debate, Congress restricted the process of becoming a citizen from abroad to "free white persons." The word "white" in this act excluded a large majority of the world's population from emigrating to the "asylum for

WHO IS AN AMERICAN?

From J. Hector St. John de Crèvecoeur, *Letters from an American Farmer* (1782)

In the era of the Revolution, many foreigners celebrated the United States as not only an independent nation but a new society, in which individuals could enjoy opportunities unknown in the Old World and where a new nationality was being forged from the diverse populations of Europe. No one promoted this image of America more enthusiastically than J. Hector St. John de Crèvecoeur, a Frenchman who had settled in New York, married the daughter of a prominent landowner, and later returned to Europe and wrote about his experiences in America.

[The European who comes to the United States] beholds fair cities, substantial villages, extensive fields, an immense country filled with decent houses, good roads, orchards, meadows, and bridges, where an hundred years ago all was wild, woody and uncultivated. . . . A modern society offers itself to his contemplation, different from what he had hitherto seen. It is not composed, as in Europe, of great lords who possess every thing and of a herd of people who have nothing. Here are no aristocratical families, no courts, no kings, no bishops, no ecclesiastical dominion. . . . We have no princes, for whom we toil, starve, and bleed: we are the most perfect society now existing in the world. Here man is free; as he ought to be. . . .

The next wish of this traveler will be to know whence came all these people? They are a mixture of English, Scotch, Irish, French, Dutch, Germans, and Swedes. From this promiscuous breed, that race now called Americans have arisen. . . . In this great American asylum, the poor of Europe have by some means met together. . . . Urged by a variety of motives, here they came. . . .

What then is the American, this new man? He is either an European, or the descendant of an European, hence that strange mixture of blood, which you will find in no other country. . . . He is an American, who leaving behind him all his ancient prejudices and manners, receives new ones from the new mode of life he has embraced, the new government he obeys, and the new rank he holds. . . . Here individuals of all nations are melted into a new race of men.

QUESTIONS

1. *What characteristics of American life does Crèvecoeur believe unite people of different origins in the United States into one people?*
2. *What aspects of society, and what parts of the American people, are left out of his description?*

TABLE 7.1 Total Population and Black Population of the United States, 1790

STATE	TOTAL POPULATION	SLAVES	FREE BLACKS
New England:			
New Hampshire	141,899	158	630
Vermont*	85,341	0	271
Massachusetts	378,556	0	5,369
Connecticut	237,655	2,764	2,771
Rhode Island	69,112	948	3,484
Maine**	96,643	0	536
Middle States:			
New York	340,241	21,324	4,682
New Jersey	184,139	11,423	2,762
Pennsylvania	433,611	3,737	6,531
South:			
Delaware	59,096	8,887	3,899
Maryland	319,728	103,036	8,043
Virginia	747,610	292,627	12,866
North Carolina	395,005	100,572	5,041
South Carolina	249,073	107,094	1,801
Georgia	82,548	29,264	398
Kentucky*	73,677	12,430	114
Tennessee*	35,691	3,417	361
Total	3,929,625	697,624	59,557

*Vermont, Kentucky, and Tennessee were territories that had not yet been admitted as states.

**Maine was part of Massachusetts in 1790.

mankind" and partaking in the blessings of American freedom. For eighty years, no non-white immigrant could become a naturalized citizen. Africans were allowed to do so in 1870, but not until the 1940s did persons of Asian origin become eligible. (Native Americans were granted American citizenship in 1924.)

Jefferson, Slavery, and Race

Man's liberty, John Locke had written, flowed from "his having reason." To deny liberty to those who were not considered rational beings did not seem to be a contradiction. White Americans increasingly viewed blacks as permanently deficient in the qualities that made freedom possible—the capacity for self-control, reason, and devotion to the larger community. These were the characteristics that Jefferson, in a famous comparison of the races in his book ***Notes on the State of Virginia***, published in 1785, claimed blacks lacked, partly due to natural incapacity and partly because the bitter experience of slavery had (quite understandably, he felt) rendered them disloyal to the nation.

Jefferson was obsessed with the connection between heredity and environment, race and intelligence. His belief that individuals' abilities and achievements are shaped by social conditions inclined him to hope that no group was fixed permanently in a status of inferiority. In the case of blacks, however, he could not avoid the "suspicion" that nature had permanently deprived them of the qualities that made republican citizenship possible. Benjamin Banneker, a free African-American from Maryland who had taught himself the principles of mathematics, sent Jefferson a copy of an astronomical almanac he had published, along with a plea for the abolition of slavery. Jefferson replied, "Nobody wishes more than I do to see such proofs as you exhibit, that nature has given to our black brethren, talents equal to the other colors of men." To his friend Joel Barlow, however, Jefferson suggested that a white person must have helped Banneker with his calculations.

"Nothing is more certainly written in the book of fate," wrote Jefferson, "than that these people are to be free." Yet he felt that America should have a homogeneous citizenry with common experiences, values, and inborn abilities. These contradictions in Jefferson reflected the divided mind of his generation. Some prominent Virginians assumed that blacks could become part of the American nation. Edward Coles, an early governor of Illinois, brought his slaves from Virginia, freed them, and settled them on farms. Washington, who died in 1799, provided in his will that his 277 slaves would become free after the death of his wife, Martha. Believing the slave trade immoral, Jefferson tried to avoid selling slaves to pay off his mounting debts. But his will provided for the freedom of only five, all relatives of his slave Sally Hemings, with whom he appears to have fathered one or more children.

This portrait from around 1825 depicts Euphemia Toussaint, the New York–born niece of Pierre Toussaint, a slave who had been brought to the city by his owner from the French colony Saint Domingue (modern-day Haiti) around 1787. Toussaint gained his freedom in 1807 and renamed himself in honor of the leader of the Haitian Revolution of the 1790s. He became a successful hairdresser and contributor to various charities in the city. Born in 1815, Euphemia died at the age of fourteen.

Principles of Freedom

Even as the decline of apprenticeship and indentured servitude narrowed the gradations of freedom among the white population, the Revolution widened the divide between free Americans and those who remained in slavery. Race, one among many kinds of legal and social inequality in colonial America, now emerged as a convenient justification for the existence of slavery in a land that claimed to be committed to freedom. Blacks' "natural faculties," Alexander Hamilton noted in 1779, were "probably as good as ours." But the existence of slavery, he added, "makes us fancy many things that are founded neither in reason nor experience."

"We the people" increasingly meant only white Americans. "Principles of freedom, which embrace only half mankind, are only half systems," declared the anonymous author of a Fourth of July speech in Hartford, Connecticut, in 1800. "Declaration of Independence," he wondered, "where art thou now?" The answer came from a Richmond newspaper: "Tell us not of principles. Those principles have been annihilated by the existence of slavery among us."

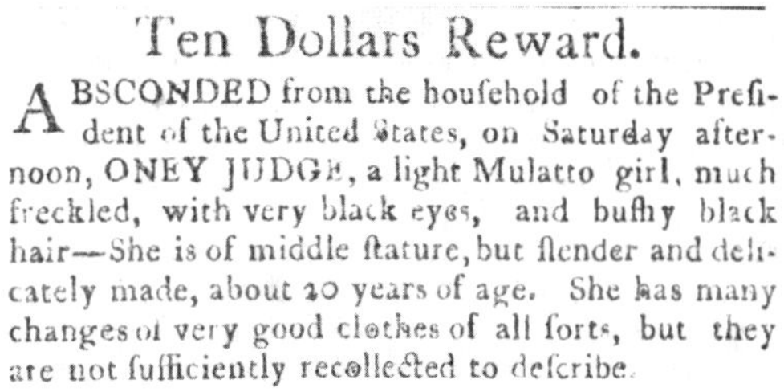

Ten Dollars Reward.

ABSCONDED from the houfehold of the Prefident of the United States, on Saturday afternoon, ONEY JUDGE, a light Mulatto girl, much freckled, with very black eyes, and bufhy black hair—She is of middle ftature, but flender and delicately made, about 20 years of age. She has many changes of very good clothes of all forts, but they are not fufficiently recollected to defcribe.

An advertisement seeking the return of Ona Judge, a domestic slave of Martha Washington, who escaped in 1796 while the family was in Philadelphia, where George Washington served as president. She made her way to New Hampshire, and evaded efforts to recapture her.

CHAPTER REVIEW AND ONLINE RESOURCES

REVIEW QUESTIONS

1. *How did the limited central government created by the Articles of Confederation reflect the issues behind the Revolution and fears for individual liberties?*

2. *What were the ideas and motivations that pushed Americans to expand west?*

3. *What events and ideas led to the belief in 1786 and 1787 that the Articles of Confederation were not working well?*

4. *The Constitution has been described as a "bundle of compromises." Which compromises were the most significant in shaping the direction of the new nation and why?*

5. *What were the major arguments in support of the Constitution given by the Federalists?*

6. *What were the major arguments against the Constitution put forth by the Anti-Federalists?*

7. *How did the Constitution address the status of American slavery?*

8. *How did the Constitution address the question of who is an American citizen?*

9. *How did the idea of citizenship change in the first half of the nineteenth century?*

KEY TERMS

Articles of Confederation (p. 194)
Ordinance of 1784 (p. 195)
Ordinance of 1785 (p. 195)
Northwest Ordinance of 1787 (p. 197)
empire of liberty (p. 197)
Shays's Rebellion (p. 199)
Constitutional Convention (p. 201)
Virginia Plan (p. 201)
New Jersey Plan (p. 201)
federalism (p. 203)
division of powers (p. 203)
checks and balances (p. 203)
separation of powers (p. 203)
three-fifths clause (p. 204)
The Federalist (p. 207)
Anti-Federalists (p. 208)
Bill of Rights (p. 208)
Treaty of Greenville (p. 215)
annuity system (p. 216)
gradual emancipation (p. 216)
Notes on the State of Virginia (p. 218)

Go to INQUIZITIVE

To see what you know—and learn what you've missed—with personalized feedback along the way.

Visit the ***Give Me Liberty!* Student Site** for primary source documents and images, interactive maps, author videos featuring Eric Foner, and more.

CHAPTER 8

SECURING THE REPUBLIC

★

1791–1815

1789	Inauguration of George Washington
	French Revolution begins
1791	First Bank of the United States
	Hamilton's Report on Manufactures
1791–1804	Haitian Revolution
1791	Thomas Paine's *The Rights of Man*
1792	Mary Wollstonecraft's *A Vindication of the Rights of Woman*
1793	First federal fugitive slave law
1794	Whiskey Rebellion
	Jay's Treaty
1797	Inauguration of John Adams
1798	XYZ affair
	Alien and Sedition Acts
1800	Gabriel's Rebellion
1801	Inauguration of Thomas Jefferson
1801–1805	First Barbary War
1803	Louisiana Purchase
1804–1806	Lewis and Clark expedition
1809	Inauguration of James Madison
1812–1814	War of 1812
1814	Treaty of Ghent
	Hartford Convention

New Orleans in 1803, at the time of the Louisiana Purchase. The painting shows a view of the city from a nearby plantation. The town houses of merchants and plantation owners line the broad promenade along the waterfront. At the lower center, a slave goes about his work. An eagle holds aloft a banner that suggests the heady optimism of the young republic: Under My Wings Every Thing Prospers.

FOCUS QUESTIONS

- *What issues made the politics of the 1790s so divisive?*
- *How did competing views of freedom and global events promote the political divisions of the 1790s?*
- *What were the achievements and failures of Jefferson's presidency?*
- *What were the causes and significant results of the War of 1812?*

On April 30, 1789, in New York City, the nation's temporary capital, George Washington became the first president under the new Constitution. All sixty-nine electors had awarded him their votes. Dressed in a plain suit of "superfine American broad cloth" rather than European finery, Washington took the oath of office on the balcony of Federal Hall before a large crowd that reacted with "loud and repeated shouts" of approval. He then retreated inside to deliver his inaugural address before members of Congress and other dignitaries.

Washington's speech expressed the revolutionary generation's conviction that it had embarked on an experiment of enormous historical importance, whose outcome was by no means certain. "The preservation of the sacred fire of liberty and the destiny of the republican model of government," Washington proclaimed, depended on the success of the American experiment in self-government.

American leaders believed that maintaining political harmony was crucial to this success. They were especially anxious to avoid the emergence of organized political parties, which had already appeared in several states. Parties were considered divisive and disloyal. "They serve to organize faction," Washington would later declare, and to substitute the aims of "a small but artful" minority for the "will of the nation." The Constitution makes no mention of political parties, and the original method of electing the president assumes that candidates would run as individuals, not on a party ticket (otherwise, the second-place finisher would not have become vice president). Nonetheless, national political parties quickly arose. Originating in Congress, they soon spread to the general populace. Instead of harmony, the 1790s became, in the words of one historian, an "age of passion." Political rhetoric became inflamed because the stakes seemed so high—nothing less than the legacy of the Revolution, the new nation's future, and the survival of American freedom.

POLITICS IN AN AGE OF PASSION

Washington's first administration

President Washington provided a much-needed symbol of national unity. He brought into his cabinet some of the new nation's most prominent political leaders, including Thomas Jefferson as secretary of state and Alexander Hamilton to head the Treasury Department. He also appointed a Supreme Court of six members, headed by John Jay of New York. But harmonious government proved short-lived.

Hamilton's Program

Liberty and Washington, painted by an unknown artist around 1800, depicts a female figure of liberty placing a wreath on a bust of the first president. She carries an American flag and stands on a royal crown, which has been thrown to the ground. In the background is a liberty cap. Washington had died in 1799 and was now immortalized as a symbol of freedom, independence, and national pride.

Political divisions first surfaced over the financial plan developed by Hamilton in 1790 and 1791. His immediate aims were to establish the nation's financial stability, bring to the government's support the country's most powerful financial interests, and encourage economic development. His long-term purpose was to make the United States a major commercial and military power. The goal of national greatness, he believed, could never be realized if the government suffered from the same weaknesses as under the Articles of Confederation.

Hamilton's program had five parts. The first step was to establish the new nation's credit-worthiness—that is, to create conditions under which persons would loan money to the government by purchasing its bonds, confident that they would be repaid. Hamilton proposed that the federal government assume responsibility for paying off at its full face value the national debt inherited from the War of Independence, as well as outstanding debts of the states. Second, he called for the creation of a new national debt. The old debts would be replaced by new interest-bearing bonds issued to the government's creditors. This would give men of economic substance a stake in promoting the new nation's stability, because the stronger and more economically secure the federal government, the more likely it would be to pay its debts.

The third part of Hamilton's program called for the creation of a **Bank of the United States**, modeled on the Bank of England, to serve as the nation's main financial agent. A private corporation rather than a branch of the government, it would hold public funds, issue bank notes that would serve as currency, and make loans to the government when necessary, all the while returning a tidy profit to its stockholders. Fourth, to raise revenue, Hamilton proposed a tax on producers of whiskey. Finally, in a Report on Manufactures delivered to Congress in December 1791, Hamilton called for the imposition of a tariff (a tax on imported foreign goods) and government subsidies to encourage the development of factories that could manufacture products currently purchased from abroad.

The Emergence of Opposition

Support for Hamilton's plan

Hamilton's vision of a powerful commercial republic won strong support from American financiers, manufacturers, and merchants. But it alarmed those who believed the new nation's destiny lay in charting a different path of development. Hamilton's plans hinged on close ties with Britain, America's main trading partner. To James Madison and Thomas Jefferson, the future lay in westward expansion, not connections with Europe. Their goal was a republic of independent farmers marketing grain, tobacco, and other products freely to the entire world. Jefferson and Madison quickly concluded that the greatest threat to American freedom lay in the alliance of a powerful central government with an emerging class of commercial capitalists, such as Hamilton appeared to envision.

Opposition to Hamilton's plan

To Jefferson, Hamilton's system "flowed from principles adverse to liberty, and was calculated to undermine and demolish the republic." Hamilton's plans for a standing army seemed to his critics a bold threat to freedom. The national bank and assumption of state debts, they feared, would introduce into American politics the same corruption that had undermined British liberty, and enrich the wealthy at the expense of ordinary Americans. During the 1780s, speculators had bought up at great discounts (often only a few cents on the dollar) government bonds and paper notes that had been used to pay those who fought in the Revolution or supplied the army. Under Hamilton's plan, speculators would reap a windfall by being paid at face value while the original holders received nothing. Because transportation was so poor, moreover, many backcountry farmers were used to distilling their grain harvest into whiskey, which could then be carried more easily to market. Hamilton's whiskey tax seemed to single them out unfairly in order to enrich bondholders.

The Jefferson–Hamilton Bargain

At first, opposition to Hamilton's program arose almost entirely from the South, the region that had the least interest in manufacturing development. It also had fewer holders of federal bonds than the Middle States and New England. Because Hamilton insisted that all his plans were authorized by the Constitution's broad "general welfare" clause, many southerners who had supported the new Constitution now became "strict constructionists," who insisted that the federal government could exercise only powers specifically listed in the document. Jefferson believed the new national bank unconstitutional, because the right of Congress to create a bank was not mentioned in the Constitution.

"Strict constructionists"

Opposition in Congress threatened the enactment of Hamilton's plans. Behind-the-scenes negotiations followed. They culminated at a famous dinner in 1790 at which Jefferson brokered an agreement whereby southerners accepted Hamilton's fiscal program (with the exception of subsidies to manufacturers) in exchange for the establishment of the permanent national capital on the Potomac River between Maryland and Virginia. Major Pierre-Charles L'Enfant, a French-born veteran of the War of Independence, designed a grandiose plan for

A bargain struck

The national capital

the "federal city" modeled on the great urban centers of Europe, with wide boulevards, parks, and fountains. When it came to constructing public buildings in the nation's new capital, most of the labor was performed by slaves.

The Impact of the French Revolution

War between France and Great Britain

Political divisions deepened in response to events in Europe. When it began in 1789, nearly all Americans welcomed the French Revolution, inspired in part by the example of their own rebellion. But in 1793, the revolution took a more radical turn with the execution of King Louis XVI along with numerous aristocrats and other foes of the new government, and war broke out between France and Great Britain.

Events in France became a source of bitter conflict in America. Jefferson and his followers believed that despite its excesses the revolution marked a historic victory for the idea of popular self-government, which must be defended at all costs. Enthusiasm for France inspired a rebirth of symbols of liberty. Liberty poles and caps reappeared on the streets of American towns and cities. To Washington, Hamilton, and their supporters, however, the revolution raised the specter of anarchy.

The rivalry between Britain and France did much to shape early American politics. The "permanent" alliance between France and the United States, which dated to 1778, complicated the situation. No one advocated that the United States should become involved in the European war, and Washington in April 1793 issued a proclamation of American neutrality. Meanwhile, the British seized hundreds of American ships trading with the French West Indies and resumed the hated practice of **impressment**—kidnapping sailors, including American citizens of British origin, to serve in their navy. Sent to London to present objections, while still serving as chief justice, John Jay negotiated an agreement in 1794 that produced the greatest public controversy of Washington's presidency. **Jay's Treaty** contained no British concessions on impressment or the rights of American shipping. Britain did agree to abandon outposts on the western frontier, which it was supposed to have done in 1783. Critics of the administration charged that it aligned the United States with monarchical Britain in its conflict with republican France. Jay's Treaty sharpened political divisions in the United States and led directly to the formation of an organized opposition party.

In the 1790s, the French Revolution set Great Britain and France on the path to war. Yet British merchants, aware of the enthusiasm for revolutionary France in the United States, produced items for sale to Americans that celebrated the bonds between "the two great republics." This pitcher is adorned with the flags of the two countries and a cap of liberty.

A 1794 painting by the Baltimore artist and sign painter Frederick Kemmelmeyer depicting President George Washington as commander-in-chief of the army dispatched to put down the Whiskey Rebellion.

Political Parties

By the mid-1790s, two increasingly coherent parties had appeared in Congress, calling themselves **Federalists and Republicans**. (The latter had no connection with today's Republican Party, which was founded in the 1850s.) Both parties laid claim to the language of liberty, and each accused its opponent of engaging in a conspiracy to destroy it.

The Federalists, supporters of the Washington administration, favored Hamilton's economic program and close ties with Britain. Prosperous merchants, farmers, lawyers, and established political leaders (especially outside the South) tended to support the Federalists. Their outlook was generally elitist, reflecting the traditional eighteenth-century view of society as a fixed hierarchy and of public office as reserved for men of economic substance—the "rich, the able, and the well-born," as Hamilton put it. Freedom, Federalists insisted, did not mean the right to stand up in opposition to the government. Federalists feared that the "spirit of liberty" unleashed by the American Revolution was degenerating into anarchy and "licentiousness."

The Federalists may have been the only major party in American history forthrightly to proclaim democracy and freedom dangerous in the hands of ordinary citizens. The **Whiskey Rebellion** of 1794, which broke out when backcountry Pennsylvania farmers sought to block collection of the new tax on distilled spirits, reinforced this conviction. The "rebels" invoked the symbols of 1776, displaying banners reading "Liberty or Death." But Washington dispatched 13,000 militiamen to western Pennsylvania (a larger force than he had commanded during the Revolution). He accompanied them part of the way, the only time in American history that a president has actually commanded an army in the field. The "rebels" offered no resistance.

Venerate the Plough, a medal of the Philadelphia Society for the Promotion of Agriculture, 1786. Americans such as Jefferson and Madison believed that farmers were the most virtuous citizens and therefore agriculture must remain the foundation of American life.

The Republican Party

Republicans, led by Madison and Jefferson, were more sympathetic to France than the Federalists and had more faith in democratic self-government. They drew their support from an unusual alliance of wealthy southern planters and ordinary farmers throughout the country. Enthusiasm for the French Revolution increasingly drew urban artisans into Republican ranks as well. Republicans were far more critical than the

Federalists of social and economic inequality, and more accepting of broad democratic participation as essential to freedom.

Political language became more and more heated. Federalists denounced Republicans as French agents, anarchists, and traitors. Republicans called their opponents monarchists. Each charged the other with betraying the principles of American freedom. Washington himself received mounting abuse. When he left office, a Republican newspaper declared that his name had become synonymous with "political iniquity" and "legalized corruption."

A print shop in the early republic. The increasing number of newspapers played a major role in the expansion of the public sphere.

An Expanding Public Sphere

The debates of the 1790s produced not only one of the most intense periods of partisan warfare in American history but also an enduring expansion of the public sphere and with it the democratic content of American freedom. More and more citizens attended political meetings and became avid readers of pamphlets and newspapers. The establishment of nearly 1,000 post offices made possible the wider circulation of personal letters and printed materials. The era witnessed the rapid growth of the American press—the number of newspapers rose from around 100 to 260 during the 1790s, and reached nearly 400 by 1810.

Inspired by the Jacobin clubs of Paris, supporters of the French Revolution and critics of the Washington administration in 1793 and 1794 formed nearly fifty **Democratic-Republican societies**. The Republican press publicized their meetings, replete with toasts to French and American liberty. Federalists saw the societies as another example of how liberty was getting out of hand. The government, not "self-created societies," declared the president, was the authentic voice of the American people. Forced to justify their existence, the societies developed a defense of the right of the people to debate political issues and organize to affect public policy. To the societies, political liberty meant not simply voting in elections but constant involvement in public affairs. Blamed by Federalists for helping to inspire the Whiskey Rebellion, the societies disappeared by the end of 1795.

This piece of needlework woven in 1808 by twenty-year-old Lucina Hudson of South Hadley, Massachusetts, depicts a young woman holding an American flag topped by a liberty cap. "Liberty needlework" was quite popular in the early nineteenth century.

VOICES OF FREEDOM

From Judith Sargent Murray, "On the Equality of the Sexes" (1790)

A prominent writer of plays, novels, and poetry, Judith Sargent Murray of Massachusetts was one of the first women to demand equal educational opportunities for women.

Is it upon mature consideration we adopt the idea, that nature is thus partial in her distributions? Is it indeed a fact, that she hath yielded to one half of the human species so unquestionable a mental superiority? I know that to both sexes elevated understandings, and the reverse, are common. But, suffer me to ask, in what the minds of females are so notoriously deficient, or unequal. . . .

Are we deficient in reason? We can only reason from what we know, and if an opportunity of acquiring knowledge hath been denied us, the inferiority of our sex cannot fairly be deduced from thence. . . . Will it be said that the judgment of a male of two years old, is more sage than that of a female's of the same age? I believe the reverse is generally observed to be true. But from that period what partiality! How is the one exalted, and the other depressed, by the contrary modes of education which are adopted! The one is taught to aspire, and the other is early confined and limited. As their years increase, the sister must be wholly domesticated, while the brother is led by the hand through all the flowery paths of science. Grant that their minds are by nature equal, yet who shall wonder at the *apparent* superiority. . . . At length arrived at womanhood, the uncultivated fair one feels a void, which the employments allotted her are by no means capable of filling. . . . She herself is most unhappy; she feels the want of a cultivated mind. . . . Should it . . . be vociferated, "Your domestic employments are sufficient"—I would calmly ask, is it reasonable, that a candidate for immortality, for the joys of heaven, an intelligent being, who is to spend an eternity in contemplating the works of Deity, should at present be so degraded, as to be allowed no other ideas, than those which are suggested by the mechanism of a pudding, or the sewing the seams of a garment? . . .

Yes, ye lordly, ye haughty sex, our souls are by nature *equal* to yours.

From Address of the Democratic-Republican Society of Pennsylvania (December 18, 1794)

The creation of around fifty Democratic-Republican societies in 1793 and 1794 reflected the expansion of the public sphere. The Pennsylvania society issued an address defending itself against critics who questioned its right to criticize the administration of George Washington.

The principles and proceedings of our Association have lately been caluminated [tarred by malicious falsehoods]. We should think ourselves unworthy to be ranked as Freemen, if awed by the name of any man, however he may command the public gratitude for past services, we could suffer in silence so sacred a right, so important a principle, as the freedom of opinion to be infringed, by attack on Societies which stand on that constitutional basis.

Freedom of thought, and a free communication of opinions by speech through the medium of the press, are the safeguards of our Liberties. . . . By the freedom of opinion, cannot be meant the right of thinking merely; for of this right the greatest Tyrant cannot deprive his meanest slave; but, it is freedom in the communication of sentiments [by] speech or through the press. This liberty is an imprescriptable [unlimitable] right, independent of any Constitution or social compact; it is as complete a right as that which any man has to the enjoyment of his life. These principles are eternal—they are recognized by our Constitution; and that nation is already enslaved that does not acknowledge their truth. . . .

If freedom of opinion, in the sense we understand it, is the right of every Citizen, by what mode of reasoning can that right be denied to an assemblage of Citizens? . . . The Society are free to declare that they never were more strongly impressed with . . . the importance of associations . . . than at the present time. The germ of an odious Aristocracy is planted among us—it has taken root. . . . Let us remain firm in attachment to principles. . . . Let us be particularly watchful to preserve inviolate the freedom of opinion, assured that it is the most effectual weapon for the protection of our liberty.

QUESTIONS

1. *How does Murray answer the argument that offering education to women will lead them to neglect their "domestic employments"?*
2. *Why does the Democratic-Republican Society insist on the centrality of "free communication of opinions" in preserving American liberty?*
3. *How do these documents reflect expanding ideas about who should enjoy the freedom to express one's ideas in the early republic?*

But much of their organization and outlook was absorbed into the emerging Republican Party. They helped to legitimize the right of "any portion of the people," regardless of station in life, to express political opinions and take an active role in public life.

An engraving from *The Lady's Magazine and Repository of Entertaining Knowledge*, published in Philadelphia in 1792. A woman identified as the "Genius of the Ladies Magazine" kneels before Liberty, presenting a petition for the "Rights of Women." In the foreground are symbols of the arts, science, and literature—knowledge that should be available to women as well as men.

The Rights of Women

The democratic ferment of the 1790s inspired renewed discussion about women's rights. In 1792, Mary Wollstonecraft published in England her extraordinary pamphlet *A Vindication of the Rights of Woman*. Wollstonecraft did not directly challenge traditional gender roles. Her call for greater access to education and to paid employment for women rested on the idea that this would enable single women to support themselves and married women to perform more capably as wives and mothers. But she did "drop a hint," as she put it, that women "ought to have representation" in government. Within two years, American editions of Wollstonecraft's work had appeared, signaling new opportunities for women in the public sphere. Increasing numbers began expressing their thoughts in print. **Judith Sargent Murray**, one of the era's most accomplished American women, wrote essays for the *Massachusetts Magazine* under the pen name "The Gleaner."

Women were contributing new ideas, but were they part of the new body politic? There was nothing explicitly limiting the rights in the Constitution to men. The Constitution's use of the word "he" to describe officeholders, however, reflected the widespread assumption that politics was a realm for men. The time had not yet come for a broad assault on gender inequality.

The men who wrote the Constitution did not envision the active and continuing involvement of ordinary citizens in affairs of state. But the rise of political parties seeking to mobilize voters in hotly contested elections, the emergence of the "self-created societies," the stirrings of women's political consciousness, and even armed uprisings such as the Whiskey Rebellion broadened and deepened the democratization of public life set in motion by the American Revolution.

THE ADAMS PRESIDENCY

In 1792, Washington won unanimous reelection in the electoral college. Four years later, he decided to retire from public life, in part to establish the precedent that the presidency is not a life office. In his Farewell Address (mostly drafted by Hamilton and published in the newspapers rather than delivered orally; see the Appendix for excerpts from the speech), Washington defended his administration against criticism, warned against the party spirit, and advised his countrymen to steer clear of international power politics by avoiding "permanent alliances with any portion of the foreign world."

The Election of 1796

The first contested presidential election

George Washington's departure unleashed fierce party competition over the choice of his successor. In this, the first contested presidential election, two tickets presented themselves: John Adams, with Thomas Pinckney of South Carolina for vice president, representing the Federalists, and Thomas Jefferson, with Aaron Burr of New York, for the Republicans. Adams received seventy-one electoral votes to Jefferson's sixty-eight. Because of factionalism among the Federalists, Pinckney received only fifty-nine votes, so Jefferson, the leader of the opposition party, became vice president. Voting fell almost entirely along sectional lines: Adams carried New England, New York, and New Jersey, while Jefferson swept the South, along with Pennsylvania.

In 1797, John Adams assumed leadership of a divided nation. His presidency was beset by crises. On the international front, the country was nearly dragged into the ongoing European war. As a neutral nation, the United States claimed the right to trade nonmilitary goods with both Britain and France, but both countries seized American ships with impunity. In 1797, American diplomats were sent to Paris to negotiate a treaty to replace the old alliance of 1778. French officials presented them with a demand for bribes before negotiations could proceed. When Adams made public the envoys' dispatches, the French officials were designated by the last three letters of the alphabet. This **XYZ affair** poisoned America's relations with its former ally. By 1798, the United States and France were engaged in a "quasi-war" at sea. But despite pressure from Hamilton, who desired a declaration of war, Adams in 1800 negotiated peace with France.

XYZ affair

Adams was less cautious in domestic affairs. Unrest continued in many rural areas. In 1799, farmers in southeastern Pennsylvania obstructed the assessment of a tax on land and houses that Congress had imposed to help fund an expanded army and navy. A crowd led by John Fries, a local militia leader and auctioneer, released arrested men from prison. The army arrested Fries for treason and proceeded to terrorize his supporters, tear down liberty poles, and whip Republican newspaper editors.

The "Reign of Witches"

But the greatest crisis of the Adams administration arose over the **Alien and Sedition Acts** of 1798. Confronted with mounting opposition, some of it voiced by immigrant pamphleteers and editors, Federalists moved to silence their critics. A new Naturalization Act extended from five to fourteen years the residency requirement for immigrants seeking American citizenship. The Alien Act allowed the deportation of persons from abroad deemed "dangerous" by federal authorities. The Sedition Act (which was set to expire in 1801, by which time Adams hoped to have been reelected) authorized the prosecution of virtually any public assembly or publication critical of the government. The new law meant that opposition editors could be jailed for almost any political comment they printed.

Matthew Lyon

The passage of these measures launched what Jefferson—recalling events in Salem, Massachusetts, a century earlier—termed a "reign of witches." Eighteen individuals, including several Republican newspaper editors, were charged under the Sedition Act. Ten were convicted of spreading "false, scandalous, and malicious" information about the government. Matthew Lyon, a member of Congress from Vermont and editor of a Republican newspaper, *The Scourge of Aristocracy*, received a sentence of four months in prison and a fine of $1,000. In Massachusetts, authorities indicted several men for erecting a liberty pole bearing the inscription "No Stamp Act, no Sedition, no Alien Bill, no Land Tax; Downfall to the Tyrants of America."

The Virginia and Kentucky Resolutions

Opposition to the Sedition Act

The Sedition Act thrust freedom of expression to the center of discussions of American liberty. Madison and Jefferson mobilized opposition, drafting resolutions adopted by the Virginia and Kentucky legislatures. The **Virginia and Kentucky resolutions** attacked the Sedition Act as an unconstitutional violation of the First Amendment. Virginia's, written by Madison, called on the federal courts to protect free speech. The original version of Jefferson's Kentucky resolution went further, asserting that states could nullify laws of Congress that violated the Constitution—that is, states could unilaterally prevent the enforcement of such laws within their borders. The legislature deleted this passage.

"Freedom of discussion"

No other state endorsed the Virginia and Kentucky resolutions. Many Americans, including many Republicans, were horrified by the idea of state action that might endanger the Union. But the "crisis of freedom" of the late 1790s strongly reinforced the idea that "freedom of discussion" was an indispensable attribute of American liberty and of democratic government. Free speech, as the Massachusetts Federalist Harrison Gray Otis noted, had become the people's "darling privilege."

The "Revolution of 1800"

"Jefferson and Liberty" became the watchword of the Republican campaign of 1800. By this time, Republicans had developed effective techniques for mobilizing voters, such as printing pamphlets, handbills, and newspapers and holding mass meetings to promote their cause. The Federalists, who viewed politics as an activity for a small group of elite men, found it difficult to match their opponents' mobilization. Nonetheless, they still dominated New England and enjoyed considerable support in the Middle Atlantic states. Jefferson triumphed, with seventy-three electoral votes to Adams's sixty-five.

Detail of an 1800 campaign banner, with a portrait of Thomas Jefferson and the words "John Adams is no more."

Before assuming office, Jefferson was forced to weather an unusual constitutional crisis. Each party arranged to have an elector throw away one of his two votes for president, so that its presidential candidate would come out a vote ahead of the vice presidential. But the designated Republican elector failed to do so. As a result, both Jefferson and his running mate, Aaron Burr, received seventy-three electoral votes. With no candidate having a majority, the election was thrown into the House of Representatives that had been elected in 1798, where the Federalists enjoyed a slight majority. For thirty-five ballots, neither man received a majority of the votes. Finally, Hamilton intervened. He disliked Jefferson but believed him enough of a statesman to recognize that the Federalist financial system could not be dismantled.

Hamilton's support for Jefferson tipped the balance. To avoid a repetition of the crisis, Congress and the states soon adopted the Twelfth Amendment to the Constitution, requiring electors to cast separate votes for president and vice president. The election of 1800 also set in motion a chain of events that culminated four years later when Burr killed Hamilton in a duel.

The events of the 1790s demonstrated that a majority of Americans believed ordinary people had a right to play an active role in politics, express their opinions freely, and contest the policies of their government. To their credit, Federalists never considered resistance to the election result. Adams's acceptance of defeat established the vital precedent of a peaceful transfer of power from a defeated party to its successor.

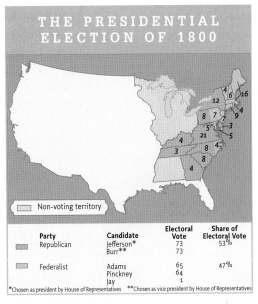

THE PRESIDENTIAL ELECTION OF 1800

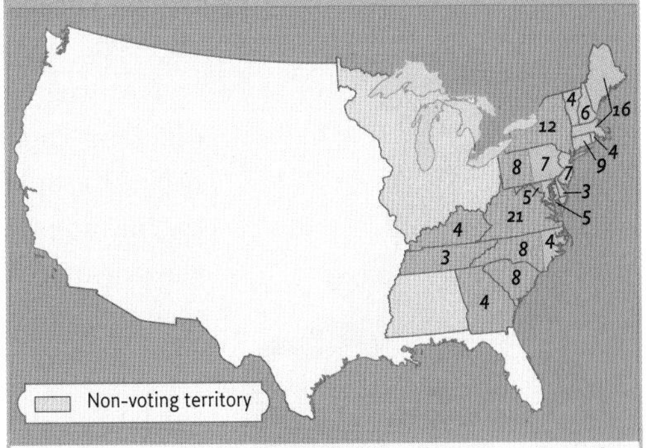

Party	Candidate	Electoral Vote	Share of Electoral Vote
Republican	Jefferson*	73	53%
	Burr**	73	
Federalist	Adams	65	47%
	Pinckney	64	
	Jay	1	

*Chosen as president by House of Representatives **Chosen as vice president by House of Representatives

Slavery and Politics

Lurking behind the political battles of the 1790s lay the divisive issue of slavery. Jefferson, after all, received every one of the South's forty-one electoral votes. He always referred to his victory as the **Revolution of 1800** and saw it not simply as a party success but as a vindication of American freedom. Yet the triumph of "Jefferson and Liberty" would not have been possible without slavery. Had

Slavery's role in Jefferson's election

three-fifths of the slaves not been counted in apportionment of electoral votes among the states, John Adams would have been reelected in 1800.

Franklin and abolition

The issue of slavery would not disappear. The very first Congress under the new Constitution received petitions calling for emancipation. One bore the weighty signature of Benjamin Franklin, who in 1787 had agreed to serve as president of the Pennsylvania Abolition Society. The blessings of liberty, Franklin's petition insisted, should be available "without distinction of color to all descriptions of people." Congress avoided the issue of emancipation. But in 1793, to implement the Constitution's fugitive slave clause, it enacted a law providing for local officials to facilitate the return of escaped slaves.

The Haitian Revolution

Events during the 1790s underscored how powerfully slavery defined and distorted American freedom. The same Jeffersonians who hailed the French Revolution as a step in the universal progress of liberty reacted in horror at the slave revolution that began in 1791 in Saint Domingue, the jewel of the French overseas empire situated not far from the southern coast of the United States. Toussaint L'Ouverture, an educated slave on a sugar plantation, forged the rebellious slaves into an army able to defeat British forces seeking to seize the island and then an expedition hoping to reestablish French authority. The slave uprising led to the establishment of Haiti as an independent nation in 1804.

Toussaint L'Ouverture, leader of the slave revolution in Saint Domingue (modern-day Haiti). Painted in 1800 as part of a series of portraits of French military leaders, it depicts him as a courageous general.

Although much of the country was left in ruins by years of warfare, the **Haitian Revolution** affirmed the universality of the revolutionary era's creed of liberty. It inspired hopes for freedom among slaves in the United States. Throughout the nineteenth century, black Americans would celebrate the winning of Haitian independence.

Among white Americans, the response to the Haitian Revolution was different. Thousands of refugees from Haiti poured into the United States, fleeing the upheaval. Many spread tales of the massacres of slaveowners and the burning of their plantations, which reinforced white Americans' fears of slave insurrection at home. When Jefferson became president, he sought to quarantine and destroy the hemisphere's second independent republic.

Gabriel's Rebellion

The momentous year of 1800 witnessed not only the "revolution" of Jefferson's election but also an attempted real one, a plot by slaves in Virginia to gain their freedom. It was organized by a Richmond blacksmith,

Gabriel, and his brothers Solomon, also a blacksmith, and Martin, a slave preacher. The conspirators planned to march on the city from surrounding plantations. They would kill some white inhabitants and hold the rest, including Governor James Monroe, hostage until their demand for the abolition of slavery was met. The plot was soon discovered and the leaders arrested. Twenty-six slaves, including Gabriel, were hanged and dozens more transported out of the state.

The black community in Richmond

Blacks in 1800 made up half of Richmond's population. One-fifth were free. A black community had emerged in the 1780s and 1790s, and **Gabriel's Rebellion** was rooted in its institutions. In cities like Richmond, many skilled slave craftsmen, including Gabriel himself, could read and write and enjoyed the privilege of hiring themselves out to employers—that is, negotiating their own labor arrangements, with their owner receiving their "wages." Their relative autonomy helps account for slave artisans' prominent role in the conspiracy.

Tightening control over blacks in Virginia

Like other Virginians, the participants in the conspiracy spoke the language of liberty forged in the American Revolution and reinvigorated during the 1790s. "We have as much right," one conspirator declared, "to fight for our liberty as any men." After the rebellion, however, the Virginia legislature tightened controls over the black population—making it illegal for them to congregate on Sundays without white supervision—and severely restricted the possibility that masters could voluntarily free their slaves. Any slave freed after 1806 was required to leave Virginia or be sold back into slavery. The door to manumission, thrown open during the American Revolution, had been slammed shut.

JEFFERSON IN POWER

The first president to begin his term in Washington, D.C., Jefferson assumed office on March 4, 1801. The city, with its unpaved streets, impoverished residents, and unfinished public buildings, scarcely resembled L'Enfant's grand plan. At one point, part of the roof of the Capitol collapsed, narrowly missing the vice president.

Jefferson's inauguration

Jefferson's inaugural address was conciliatory toward his opponents. "Every difference of opinion," he declared, "is not a difference of principle. . . . We are all Republicans, we are all Federalists." He went on to expound the policies his administration would follow—economy in government, unrestricted trade, freedom of religion and the press, friendship to all nations but "entangling alliances" with none. America, "the world's best hope," would flourish if a limited government allowed its citizens to be "free to regulate their own pursuits."

Dismantling the Federalist system

Jefferson hoped to dismantle as much of the Federalist system as possible. Among his first acts as president was to pardon all those imprisoned under the Sedition Act. During his eight years as president, he reduced the number of government employees and slashed the army and navy. He abolished all taxes except the tariff, including the hated tax on whiskey, and paid off part of the national debt. His policies ensured that the United States would not become a centralized state on a European model, as Hamilton had envisioned.

Judicial Review

The Marshall court

Nonetheless, as Hamilton predicted, it proved impossible to uproot national authority entirely. Jefferson distrusted the unelected judiciary. But during his presidency, and for many years thereafter, the Federalist John Marshall headed the Supreme Court. A strong believer in national supremacy, Marshall established the Court's power to review laws of Congress and the states.

The first landmark decision of the Marshall Court came in 1803, in the case of ***Marbury v. Madison***. On the eve of leaving office, Adams had appointed a number of justices of the peace for the District of Columbia. Madison, Jefferson's secretary of state, refused to issue commissions (the official documents entitling them to assume their posts) to these "midnight judges." Four, including William Marbury, sued for their offices. Marshall's decision declared unconstitutional the section of the Judiciary Act of 1789 that allowed the courts to order executive officials to deliver judges' commissions. It exceeded the power of Congress as outlined in the Constitution and was therefore void. Marbury, in other words, may have been entitled to his commission, but the Court had no power under the Constitution to order Madison to deliver it. The Supreme Court had assumed the right to determine whether an act of Congress violates the Constitution—a power known as "judicial review."

John Marshall, who served as Chief Justice from 1801 to 1835, in an 1810 portrait by Cephas Thompson.

Seven years later, in *Fletcher v. Peck*, the Court extended judicial review to state laws. In 1794, four land companies had paid nearly every member of the state legislature, Georgia's two U.S. senators, and a number of federal judges to secure their right to purchase land in present-day Alabama and Mississippi claimed by Georgia. Two years later, many of the corrupt lawmakers were defeated for reelection, and the new legislature rescinded the land grant and subsequent sales. Whatever the circumstances of the legislature's initial action, Marshall declared, the Constitution prohibited Georgia from taking any action that impaired a contract. Therefore, the individual purchasers could keep their land, and the legislature could not repeal the original grant.

The Louisiana Purchase

But the greatest irony of Jefferson's presidency involved his greatest achievement, the **Louisiana Purchase** of 1803. This resulted not from astute American diplomacy but because the rebellious slaves of Saint Domingue defeated forces sent by the ruler of France, Napoleon Bonaparte, to reconquer the island. Moreover, to take advantage of the sudden opportunity to purchase Louisiana, Jefferson had to abandon his conviction that the federal government was limited to powers specifically mentioned in the Constitution, because the document said nothing about buying territory from a foreign power.

Jefferson's ideological compromise

This vast Louisiana Territory, which stretched from the Gulf of Mexico to Canada and from the Mississippi River to the Rocky Mountains, had been ceded by France to Spain in 1762 as part of the reshuffling of colonial possessions at the end of the Seven Years' War. France secretly reacquired it in 1800. Soon after taking office, Jefferson learned of the arrangement. He had long been concerned about American access to the port of New Orleans, which lay within Louisiana at the mouth of the Mississippi River. The right to trade through New Orleans, essential to western farmers, had been acknowledged in the Treaty of San Lorenzo (also known as Pinckney's Treaty) of 1795 between the United States and Spain. But Jefferson feared that the far more powerful French might try to interfere with American commerce. Needing money for military campaigns in Europe and with his dreams of American empire in ruins because of his inability to reestablish control over Saint Domingue, Napoleon offered to sell the entire Louisiana Territory. The cost, $15 million (the equivalent of perhaps $250 million in today's money), made the Louisiana Purchase one of history's greatest real estate bargains.

Reasons for the Louisiana Purchase

In a stroke, Jefferson had doubled the size of the United States. Jefferson admitted that he had "done an act beyond the Constitution." But he believed the benefits justified his transgression. Farmers, Jefferson had written, were "the chosen people of God," and the country would remain "virtuous" as long as it was "chiefly agricultural." Now, Jefferson believed, he had ensured the agrarian character of the United States and its political stability for centuries to come.

Effects of the Purchase

Lewis and Clark

Within a year of the purchase, Jefferson dispatched an expedition led by Meriwether Lewis and William Clark, two Virginia-born veterans of Indian wars in the Ohio Valley, to explore the new territory. Their objectives were both scientific and commercial—to study the area's plants, animal life, and geography, and to discover how the region could be exploited economically.

Scientific and commercial objectives

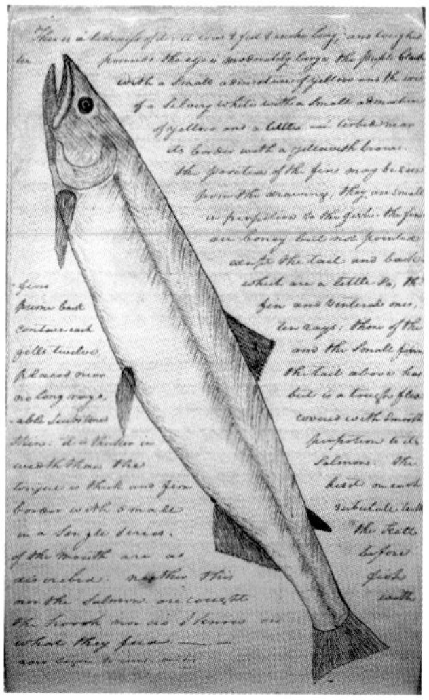

A page from William Clark's journal of the Lewis and Clark expedition, depicting a salmon. Among their tasks was to record information about the West's plants, animal life, and geography.

Jefferson hoped the **Lewis and Clark expedition** would establish trading relations with western Indians and locate a water route to the Pacific Ocean.

In the spring of 1804, Lewis and Clark's fifty-member "corps of discovery" set out from St. Louis on the most famous exploring party in American history. They were accompanied by a fifteen-year-old Shoshone Indian woman, Sacajawea, the wife of a French fur trader, who served as their guide and interpreter. After crossing the Rocky Mountains, the expedition reached the Pacific Ocean in present-day Oregon. They returned in 1806, bringing an immense amount of information about the region as well as numerous plant and animal specimens. The success of their journey helped to strengthen the idea that American territory was destined to reach all the way to the Pacific.

Incorporating Louisiana

The only part of the Louisiana Purchase with a significant non-Indian population in 1803 was the region around New Orleans. When the United States took control, the city had around 8,000 inhabitants, including nearly 3,000 slaves and 1,300 free persons of color. Incorporating this diverse population into the United States was by no means easy. French and Spanish law accorded free blacks, many of whom were the offspring of unions between white military officers and slave women, nearly all the rights of white citizens. Moreover, Spain made it easy for slaves to obtain their freedom through purchase or voluntary emancipation by the owners.

Louisiana slavery

The treaty that transferred Louisiana to the United States promised that all free inhabitants would enjoy "the rights, advantages, and immunities of citizens." Spanish and French civil codes, unlike British and American law, recognized women as co-owners of family property. Under American rule, Louisiana retained this principle of "community property" within marriage. But free blacks suffered a steady decline in status. And the local legislature soon adopted one of the most sweeping slave codes in the South. Louisiana's slaves had enjoyed far more freedom under the rule of tyrannical Spain than as part of the liberty-loving United States.

The Barbary Wars

The first war fought by the U.S.

Jefferson hoped to avoid foreign entanglements, but he found it impossible as president to avoid being drawn into the continuing wars of Europe. Even as he sought to limit the power of the national government, foreign relations compelled him to expand it. The first war fought by the United States was to protect American commerce in a dangerous world.

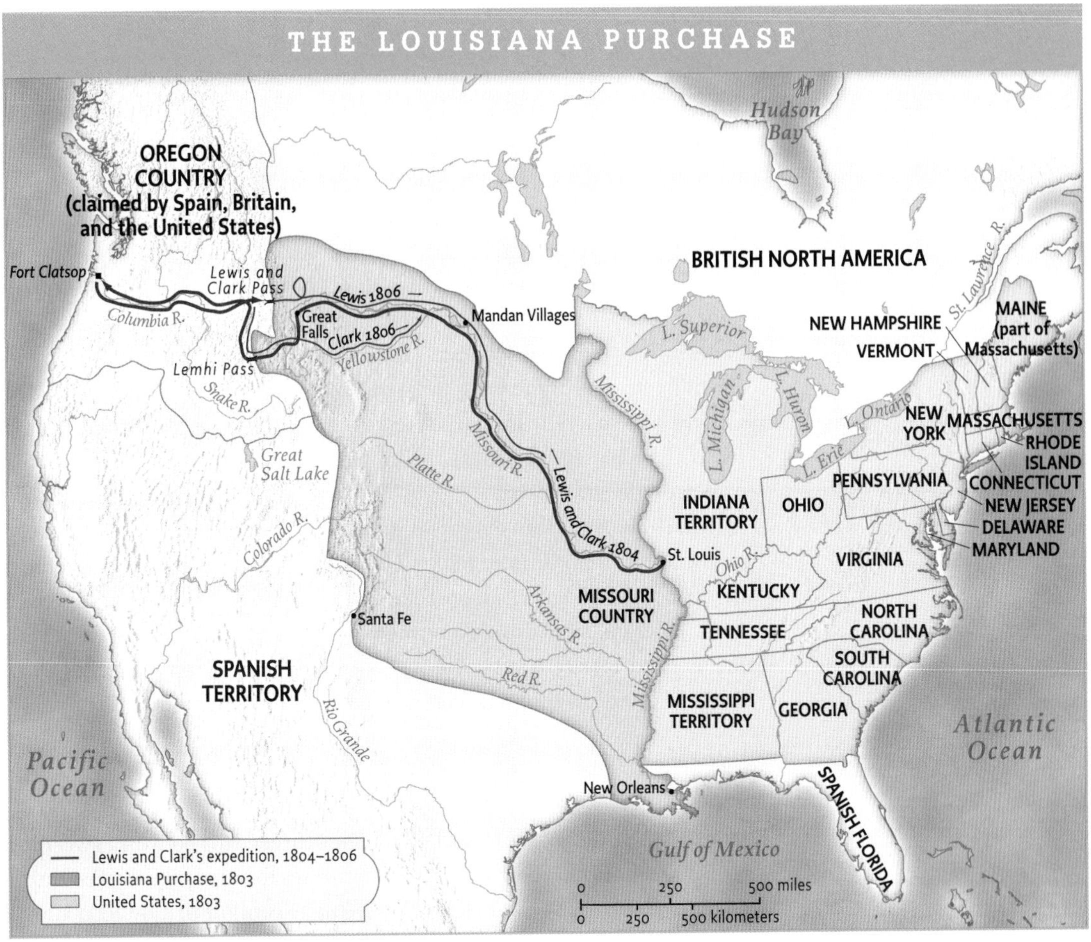

The Louisiana Purchase of 1803 doubled the land area of the United States.

Defending American shipping

The Barbary states on the northern coast of Africa had long preyed on shipping in the Mediterranean and Atlantic, receiving tribute from several countries, including the United States, to protect their vessels. In 1801, Jefferson refused demands for increased payments, and the pasha of Tripoli, in modern-day Libya, declared war on the United States. The naval conflict lasted until 1804, when an American squadron won a victory at Tripoli harbor (a victory commemorated in the official hymn of the Marine Corps, which mentions fighting on "the shores of Tripoli").

The **Barbary Wars** were the new nation's first encounter with the Islamic world. In the 1790s, as part of an attempt to establish peaceful relations, the federal government declared that the United States was "not, in any sense, founded on the Christian religion." But the conflicts helped to establish a long-lasting pattern in which many Americans viewed Muslims as an exotic people whose way of life did not adhere to Western standards.

The Embargo

Blockades by Britain and France

Far more serious in its impact on the United States was warfare between Britain and France, which resumed in 1803 after a brief lull. By 1806, each combatant had declared the other under blockade, seeking to deny trade with America to its rival. The Royal Navy resumed the practice of impressment. By the end of 1807, it had seized more than 6,000 American sailors (claiming they were British citizens and deserters).

To Jefferson, the economic health of the United States required freedom of trade with which no foreign government had a right to interfere. American farmers needed access to markets in Europe and the Caribbean. Deciding to use trade as a weapon, in December 1807 he persuaded Congress to enact the **Embargo Act**, a ban on all American vessels sailing for foreign ports. For a believer in limited government, this was an amazing exercise of federal power.

Effects of the Embargo

In 1808, American exports plummeted by 80 percent. Unfortunately, neither Britain nor France took much notice. But the Embargo devastated the economies of American port cities. Just before his term ended, in March 1809, Jefferson signed the Non-Intercourse Act, banning trade only with Britain and France but providing that if either side rescinded its edicts against American shipping, commerce with that country would resume.

Madison and Pressure for War

Jefferson left office at the lowest point of his career. He had won a sweeping reelection in 1804, receiving 162 electoral votes to only 14 for the Federalist candidate, Charles C. Pinckney. With the exception of Connecticut, he even carried the Federalist stronghold of New England. Four years later, his handpicked successor, James Madison, also won an easy victory. The Embargo, however, failed to achieve its aims and was increasingly violated by American shippers. In 1810, Madison adopted a new policy.

Macon's Bill No. 2

Congress enacted a measure known as Macon's Bill No. 2, which allowed trade to resume but provided that if either France or Britain ceased interfering with American rights, the president could reimpose an embargo on the other. With little to lose, since Britain controlled the seas, the French emperor Napoleon announced that he had repealed his decrees against neutral shipping. But the British continued to attack American vessels. In the spring of 1812, Madison reimposed the embargo on trade with Britain.

Meanwhile, a group of younger congressmen, mostly from the West, were calling for war with Britain. Known as the War Hawks, this new generation of political leaders had come of age after the winning of independence and were ardent nationalists. Their leaders included Henry Clay of Kentucky, elected Speaker of the House of Representatives in 1810, and John

C. Calhoun of South Carolina. The War Hawks spoke passionately of defending the national honor against British insults, but they also had more practical goals in mind, notably the annexation of Canada and the conquest of Florida, a haven for fugitive slaves owned by Britain's ally Spain. Members of Congress also spoke of the necessity of upholding the principle of free trade and liberating the United States once and for all from European infringements on its independence.

War Party at Fort Douglas, a watercolor by the Swiss-born Canadian artist Peter Rindisbacher. Painted in 1823, it depicts an incident during the War of 1812 when Indian allies of Great Britain fired rifles into the air to greet their commander, Captain Andrew Bulger, pictured on the far right.

THE "SECOND WAR OF INDEPENDENCE"

The growing crisis between the United States and Britain took place against the background of deteriorating Indian relations in the West, which also helped propel the United States down the road to war. Jefferson had long favored the removal beyond the Mississippi River of Indian tribes that refused to cooperate in "civilizing" themselves. He encouraged traders to lend money to Indians, in the hope that accumulating debt would force them to sell some of their holdings west of the Appalachian Mountains, thus freeing up more land for "our increasing numbers." On the other hand, the government continued President Washington's policy of promoting settled farming among the Indians.

The Indian Response

By 1800, nearly 400,000 American settlers lived west of the Appalachian Mountains. They far outnumbered the remaining Indians, whose seemingly irreversible decline in power led some to rethink their opposition to assimilation. Among the Creek and Cherokee, a group led by men of mixed Indian-white ancestry like Major Ridge and John Ross enthusiastically endorsed the federal policy of promoting "civilization." Many had established businesses as traders and slaveowning farmers with the help of their white fathers. Their views, in turn, infuriated "nativists," who strongly opposed assimilation.

An "age of prophecy"

The period from 1800 to 1812 was an "age of prophecy" among the Indians, as many tribal leaders sought to revitalize Native American life. A militant message was expounded by two Shawnee brothers,

WHO IS AN AMERICAN?

From Tecumseh, Speech to the Osage (1810)

While some Native Americans claimed rights as Americans, others asserted a pan-Indian identity, insisting that all Indian nations shared a common set of values and a common future of freedom and autonomy rather than assimilation or removal. The Shawnee leader Tecumseh sought to rally Indians to unite as one people. This speech, to Osage Indians, was recorded by John P. Hunter, who had been held captive by the Osage since childhood.

Brothers—We all belong to one family; we are all children of the Great Spirit; we walk in the same path; slake our thirst at the same spring; and now affairs of the greatest concern lead us to smoke the pipe around the same council fire!

Brothers—we are friends; we must assist each other to bear our burdens. The blood of many of our fathers and brothers has run like water on the ground, to satisfy the avarice of the white men. We, ourselves, are threatened with a great evil; nothing will pacify them but the destruction of all the red men.

Brothers—The white men are not friends to the Indians: at first, they only asked for land sufficient for a wigwam; now, nothing will satisfy them but the whole of our hunting grounds, from the rising to the setting sun. . . .

Brothers—My people are brave and numerous; but the white people are too strong for them alone. I wish you to take up the tomahawk with them. If we all unite, we will cause the rivers to stain the great waters with their blood.

Brothers—if you do not unite with us, they will first destroy us, and then you will fall an easy prey to them. They have destroyed many nations of red men because they were not united. . . . They wish to make us enemies, that they may sweep over and desolate our hunting grounds, like devastating winds, or rushing waters.

Brothers—Our Great Father over the great waters [the king of England] is angry with the white people, our enemies. He will send his brave warriors against them; he will send us rifles, and whatever else we want—he is our friend, and we are his children.

Brothers—We must be united; we must smoke the same pipe; we must fight each other's battles; and more than all, we must love the Great Spirit; he is for us; he will destroy our enemies, and make his red children happy.

QUESTIONS

1. *How does Tecumseh's understanding of national identity compare with that of most white Americans of his era?*
2. *Why does he claim that the king of England is the Indians' ally, and what does this suggest about his attitudes toward white people?*

Tecumseh and Tenskwatawa. Tecumseh was a chief who had refused to sign the Treaty of Greenville in 1795, and Tenskwatawa was a religious prophet who called for complete separation from whites, the revival of traditional Indian culture, and resistance to federal policies. White people, Tenskwatawa preached, were the source of all evil in the world, and Indians should abandon American alcohol, clothing, food, and manufactured goods. His followers gathered at Prophetstown, located in Indiana.

Tecumseh meanwhile traversed the Mississippi Valley, pressing the argument that the alternative to Indian resistance was extermination. He repudiated chiefs who had sold land to the federal government: "Sell a country! Why not sell the air, the great sea, as well as the earth? Did not the Great Spirit make them all for the use of his children?" In 1810, Tecumseh called for attacks on American frontier settlements. In November 1811, while he was absent, American forces under William Henry Harrison destroyed Prophetstown in the Battle of Tippecanoe.

Tenskwatawa (the Prophet), in a portrait by the American artist Charles Bird King, who painted numerous Indian leaders.

The War of 1812

In 1795, James Madison had written that war is the greatest enemy of "true liberty." Nonetheless, Madison became a war president. Reports that the British were encouraging Tecumseh's efforts contributed to the coming of the **War of 1812**. In June 1812, with assaults on American shipping continuing, Madison asked Congress for a declaration of war. American nationality, the president declared, was at stake—would Americans remain "an independent people" or become "colonists and vassals" of Great Britain? The vote revealed a deeply divided country. Both Federalists and Republicans representing the states from New Jersey northward, where most of the mercantile and financial resources of the country were concentrated, voted against war. The South and West were strongly in favor. The bill passed the House by a vote of 79–49 and the Senate by 19–13. It was the first time the United States declared war on another country, and it was approved by the smallest margin of any declaration of war in American history.

In retrospect, it seems remarkably foolhardy for a disunited and militarily unprepared nation to go to war with one of the world's two major powers. Fortunately for the United States, Great Britain at the outset was preoccupied with the struggle in Europe. But it easily repelled two feeble American invasions of Canada and imposed a blockade that all but destroyed American commerce. In 1814, having finally defeated Napoleon,

An engraving depicting the burning of Washington, D.C., by the British during the War of 1812, from an 1817 book by the antislavery Philadelphia physician Jesse Torrey. Torrey suggests that the event is divine punishment for the practice of slave trading in the nation's capital. The image includes children among the group of chained slaves at the right, to emphasize the breakup of slave families. At the top is a heavenly image of liberty.

Britain invaded the United States. Its forces seized Washington, D.C., and burned the Capitol and the White House, while the government fled for safety.

Americans did enjoy a few military successes. In August 1812, the American frigate *Constitution* defeated the British warship *Guerriere*. Commodore Oliver H. Perry defeated a British naval force in September 1813 on Lake Erie. In the following year, a British assault on Baltimore was repulsed when **Fort McHenry** at the entrance to the harbor withstood a British bombardment. This was the occasion when Francis Scott Key composed "The Star-Spangled Banner," an ode to the "land of the free and home of the brave" that became the national anthem during the 1930s.

Fighting the British and the Indians

Like the War of Independence, the War of 1812 was a two-front struggle—against the British and against the Indians. The war produced significant victories over western Indians who sided with the British. In 1813, pan-Indian forces led by Tecumseh (who had been commissioned a general in the British army) were defeated, and he himself was killed, at the Battle of the Thames, near Detroit, by an American force led by William Henry Harrison. In March 1814, an army of Americans and pro-assimilation Cherokees and Creeks under the command of Andrew Jackson defeated hostile Creeks known as the Red Sticks at the Battle of Horseshoe Bend in Alabama, killing more than 800. Jackson dictated terms of surrender that required the Indians, hostile and friendly alike, to cede more than half their land, over 23 million acres in all, to the federal government.

Jackson then proceeded to New Orleans, where he engineered the war's greatest American victory, fighting off a British invasion in January 1815. Although a slaveholder, Jackson recruited the city's free men of color into his forces, appealing to them as "sons of freedom" and promising them the same pay and land bounties as white recruits.

Treaty of Ghent

With neither side wishing to continue the conflict, the United States and Britain signed the Treaty of Ghent, ending the war. Although the treaty was signed in December 1814, ships carrying news of the agreement did not reach America until after the **Battle of New Orleans** had been fought. The treaty restored the previous status quo. No territory changed hands, nor did any provisions relate to impressment or neutral shipping rights.

The War's Aftermath

A number of contemporaries called the War of 1812 the Second War of Independence. Jackson's victory at New Orleans not only made him a national hero but also became a celebrated example of the ability of virtuous citizens of a republic to defeat the forces of despotic Europe.

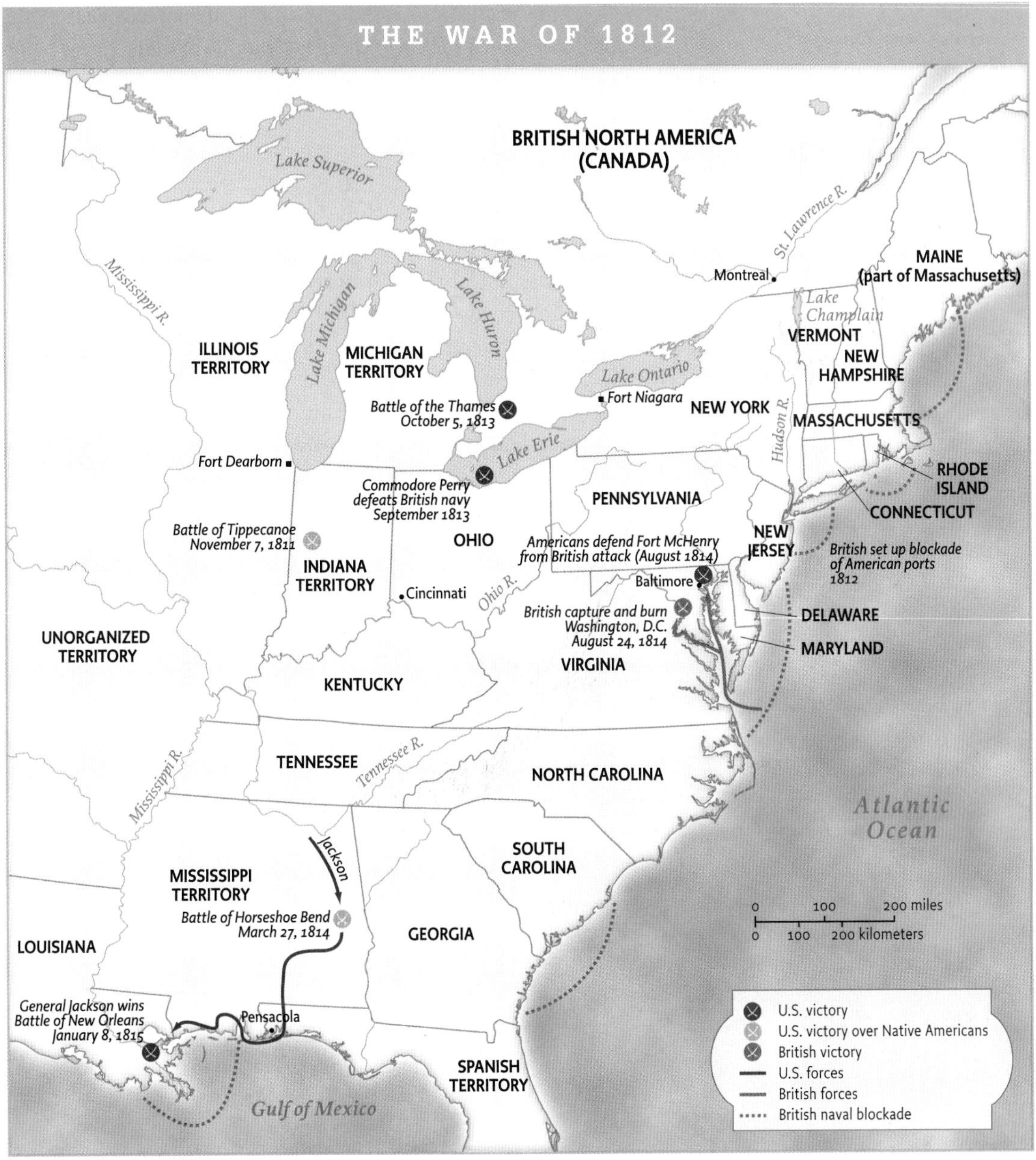

Although the British burned the nation's capital, the War of 1812 essentially was a military draw.

American control east of the Mississippi

Moreover, the war completed the conquest of the area east of the Mississippi River, which had begun during the Revolution. Never again would the British or Indians pose a threat to American control of this vast region. In its aftermath, white settlers poured into Indiana, Michigan, Alabama, and Mississippi.

The War of 1812 and the Canadian Borderland

The War of 1812 had a profound impact along the border between the United States and Canada, further solidifying it as a dividing line. Much of the fighting took place in the long-contested region near Detroit and on the Great Lakes. A great deal of trade had developed between Vermont and Quebec, and across the lakes, which became a flourishing smuggling business during Jefferson's embargo. When war broke out, Canadians began to see American traders as spies. The unsuccessful American attacks on Canada during the war (some led by Irish immigrants resentful at British rule over their country of birth) strengthened anti-Americanism even among Canadians not connected to revolutionary-era Loyalists. To be sure, as in so many borderland regions, many people had family ties on both sides and the exchange of goods and ideas continued after the war ended. But for both Canadians and Americans, the war reaffirmed a sense of national identity, and both came to see the conflict as a struggle for freedom—for the United States, freedom from dependence on Great Britain; for Canada, freedom from domination by the United States.

This colorful painting by the artist John Archibald Woodside from around the time of the War of 1812 contains numerous symbols of freedom, among them the goddess of liberty with her liberty cap, a broken chain at the sailor's feet, the fallen crown (under his left foot), a broken royal scepter, and the sailor himself, because English interference with American shipping was one of the war's causes.

Britain's defeat of Napoleon inaugurated a long period of peace in Europe. With diplomatic affairs playing less and less of a role in American public life, Americans' sense of separateness from the Old World grew ever stronger.

The End of the Federalist Party

Jefferson and Madison succeeded in one major political aim—the elimination of the Federalist Party. At first, the war led to a revival of Federalist fortunes. With antiwar sentiment at its peak in 1812, Madison was reelected by the relatively narrow margin of 128 electoral votes to 89 over his Federalist opponent, DeWitt Clinton of New York. But then came a self-inflicted blow. In December 1814, a group of New England Federalists gathered at Hartford, Connecticut, to give voice to their party's long-standing grievances, especially the domination of the federal government by Virginia presidents and their region's declining influence as new western states entered the Union. The **Hartford Convention** did not call for secession or disunion. But it affirmed the right of a state to "interpose" its authority if the federal government violated the Constitution.

Demise of the Federalists

The Hartford Convention had barely adjourned before Jackson electrified the nation with his victory at New Orleans. In speeches and sermons, political and religious leaders alike proclaimed that Jackson's triumph revealed, once again, that a divine hand oversaw America's destiny. The Federalists could not free themselves from the charge of lacking patriotism. Within a few years, their party no longer existed. Yet in their dying moments Federalists had raised an issue—southern domination of the national government—that would long outlive their political party. And the country stood on the verge of a profound economic and social transformation that strengthened the very forces of commercial development that Federalists had welcomed and many Republicans feared.

CHAPTER REVIEW AND ONLINE RESOURCES

REVIEW QUESTIONS

1. *Identify the major parts of Hamilton's financial plan, who supported these proposals, and why they aroused such passionate opposition.*
2. *How did the French Revolution and the ensuing global struggle between Great Britain and France shape early American politics?*
3. *How did the United States become involved in foreign affairs in this period?*
4. *How did the expansion of the public sphere and a new language of rights offer opportunities to women?*
5. *What caused the demise of the Federalists?*
6. *What impact did the Haitian Revolution have on the United States?*
7. *How did the Louisiana Purchase affect the situation of Native Americans in that region?*
8. *Whose status was changed the most by the War of 1812—that of Great Britain, the United States, or Native Americans?*

KEY TERMS

Bank of the United States (p. 223)
impressment (p. 225)
Jay's Treaty (p. 225)
Federalists and Republicans (p. 226)
Whiskey Rebellion (p. 226)
Democratic-Republican societies (p. 227)
Judith Sargent Murray (p. 230)
XYZ affair (p. 231)
Alien and Sedition Acts (p. 231)
Virginia and Kentucky resolutions (p. 232)
Revolution of 1800 (p. 233)
Haitian Revolution (p. 234)
Gabriel's Rebellion (p. 235)
Marbury v. Madison (p. 236)
Louisiana Purchase (p. 237)
Lewis and Clark expedition (p. 238)
Barbary Wars (p. 239)
Embargo Act (p. 240)
Tecumseh and Tenskwatawa (p. 243)
War of 1812 (p. 243)
Fort McHenry (p. 244)
Battle of New Orleans (p. 244)
Hartford Convention (p. 247)

Go to INQUIZITIVE

To see what you know—and learn what you've missed—with personalized feedback along the way.

Visit the ***Give Me Liberty!*** **Student Site** for primary source documents and images, interactive maps, author videos featuring Eric Foner, and more.

CHAPTER 9

THE MARKET REVOLUTION

★

1800–1840

1793	Eli Whitney's cotton gin
1790s–1830s	Second Great Awakening
1806	Congress approves funds for the National Road
1807	Robert Fulton's steamboat
1814	Waltham textile factory
1819	*Dartmouth College v. Woodward*
	Adams-Onís Treaty with Spain
1825	Erie Canal opens
1831	Cyrus McCormick's reaper
1837	John Deere's steel plow
	Depression begins
1844	Telegraph put into commercial operation
1845	John O'Sullivan coins phrase "manifest destiny"
1845–1851	Ireland's Great Famine
1854	Henry David Thoreau's *Walden*

A painting from 1850 of the steamboat *Reindeer*, by the artist John Bard. Steamboats, able to travel against the current on rivers and across the Great Lakes, played an essential role in opening large parts of the nation's interior to commercial agriculture, an essential component of the market revolution.

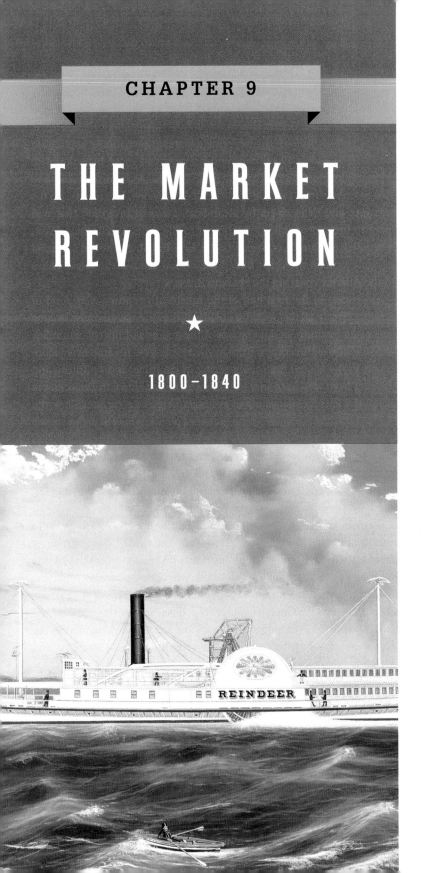

FOCUS QUESTIONS

- *What were the main elements of the market revolution?*
- *How did the market revolution spark social change?*
- *How did the meanings of American freedom change in this period?*
- *How did the market revolution affect the lives of workers, women, and African-Americans?*

In 1824, the Marquis de Lafayette visited the United States. Nearly fifty years had passed since, as a youth of twenty, the French nobleman fought at Washington's side in the War of Independence. Since 1784, when he last journeyed to the United States, the nation's population had tripled to nearly 12 million, its land area had more than doubled, and its political institutions had thrived. The thirteen states of 1784 had grown to twenty-four, and Lafayette visited every one. He traveled up the Mississippi and Ohio rivers by steamboat, a recent invention that was helping to bring economic development to the trans-Appalachian West, and crossed upstate New York via the Erie Canal, the world's longest man-made waterway, which linked the region around the Great Lakes with the Atlantic coast via the Hudson River.

Americans in the first half of the nineteenth century were fond of describing liberty as the defining quality of their new nation, the unique genius of its institutions. Likenesses of the goddess of liberty, a familiar figure in eighteenth-century British visual imagery, became even more common in the United States, appearing in paintings and sculpture and on folk art from weather vanes to quilts and tavern signs. In *Democracy in America*, the French historian and politician Alexis de Tocqueville wrote of the "holy cult of freedom" he encountered on his own visit to the United States during the early 1830s. "For fifty years," he wrote, "the inhabitants of the United States have been repeatedly and constantly told that they are the only religious, enlightened, and free people. They . . . have an immensely high opinion of themselves and are not far from believing that they form a species apart from the rest of the human race."

Even as Lafayette, Tocqueville, and numerous other visitors from abroad toured the United States, however, Americans' understandings of freedom were changing. Three historical processes unleashed by the Revolution accelerated after the War of 1812: the spread of market relations, the westward movement of the population, and the rise of a vigorous political democracy. (The first two will be discussed in this chapter, the third in Chapter 10.) All helped to reshape the idea of freedom, identifying it ever more closely with economic opportunity, physical mobility, and participation in a vibrantly democratic political system.

But American freedom also continued to be shaped by the presence of slavery. Lafayette, who had purchased a plantation in the West Indies and freed its slaves, once wrote, "I would never have drawn my sword in the cause of America if I could have conceived that thereby I was founding a land of slavery." Yet slavery was moving westward with the young republic. Half a century after the winning of independence, the coexistence of liberty and slavery, and their simultaneous expansion, remained the central contradiction of American life.

A NEW ECONOMY

An economic transformation

In the first half of the nineteenth century, an economic transformation known to historians as the market revolution swept over the United States. Its catalyst was a series of innovations in transportation and communication. The market revolution was an acceleration of developments already under way in the colonial era. As noted in previous chapters, southern planters were selling the products of slave labor in the international market as early as the seventeenth century. By the eighteenth, many colonists had been drawn into Britain's commercial empire. Consumer goods like sugar and tea and market-oriented tactics like the boycott of British goods had been central to the political battles leading up to independence.

Nonetheless, as Americans moved across the Appalachian Mountains and into interior regions of the states along the Atlantic coast, they found themselves more and more isolated from markets. In 1800, American farm families produced at home most of what they needed, from clothing to farm implements. What they could not make themselves, they obtained by bartering with their neighbors or purchasing from local stores and from rural craftsmen like blacksmiths and shoemakers. Those farmers not located near cities or navigable waterways found it almost impossible to market their produce. Many Americans devoted their energies to solving the technological problems that inhibited commerce within the country.

Roads and Steamboats

In the first half of the nineteenth century, in rapid succession, the steamboat, canal, railroad, and telegraph wrenched America out of its economic past. These innovations opened new land to settlement, lowered transportation costs, and made it far easier for economic enterprises to sell their products. They linked farmers to national and world markets and made them major consumers of manufactured goods. Americans, wrote Tocqueville, had "annihilated space and time."

In 1806, Congress authorized the construction of the paved National Road from Cumberland, Maryland, to the Old Northwest. It reached Wheeling, on the Ohio River, in 1818 and by 1838 extended to Illinois, where it ended. But it was improved water transportation

A watercolor from 1829 depicts the Erie Canal five years after it opened. Boats carrying passengers and goods traverse the waterway, along whose banks farms and villages have sprung up.

A view of New York City, in 1849, by the noted lithographer Nathaniel Currier. Steamships and sailing vessels of various sizes crowd the harbor of the nation's largest city and busiest port.

that most dramatically increased the speed and lowered the expense of commerce.

Advantages of the steamboat

Robert Fulton, a Pennsylvania-born artist and engineer, had experimented with **steamboat** designs while living in France during the 1790s. But not until 1807, when Fulton's ship the *Clermont* navigated the Hudson River from New York City to Albany, was the steamboat's technological and commercial feasibility demonstrated. The invention made possible upstream commerce (that is, travel against the current) on the country's major rivers as well as rapid transport across the Great Lakes and, eventually, the Atlantic Ocean. By 1811, the first steamboat had been introduced on the Mississippi River; twenty years later some 200 plied its waters.

The Erie Canal

Connecting New York City and the Old Northwest

The completion in 1825 of the 363-mile **Erie Canal** across upstate New York (a remarkable feat of engineering at a time when America's next-largest canal was only twenty-eight miles long) allowed goods to flow between the Great Lakes and New York City. Almost instantaneously, the canal attracted an influx of farmers migrating from New England, giving birth to cities like Buffalo, Rochester, and Syracuse along its path.

New York governor DeWitt Clinton, who oversaw the construction of the state-financed canal, predicted that it would make New York City "the granary of the world, the emporium of commerce, the seat of manufactures, the focus of great moneyed operations." And, indeed, the canal gave

THE MARKET REVOLUTION: ROADS AND CANALS, 1840

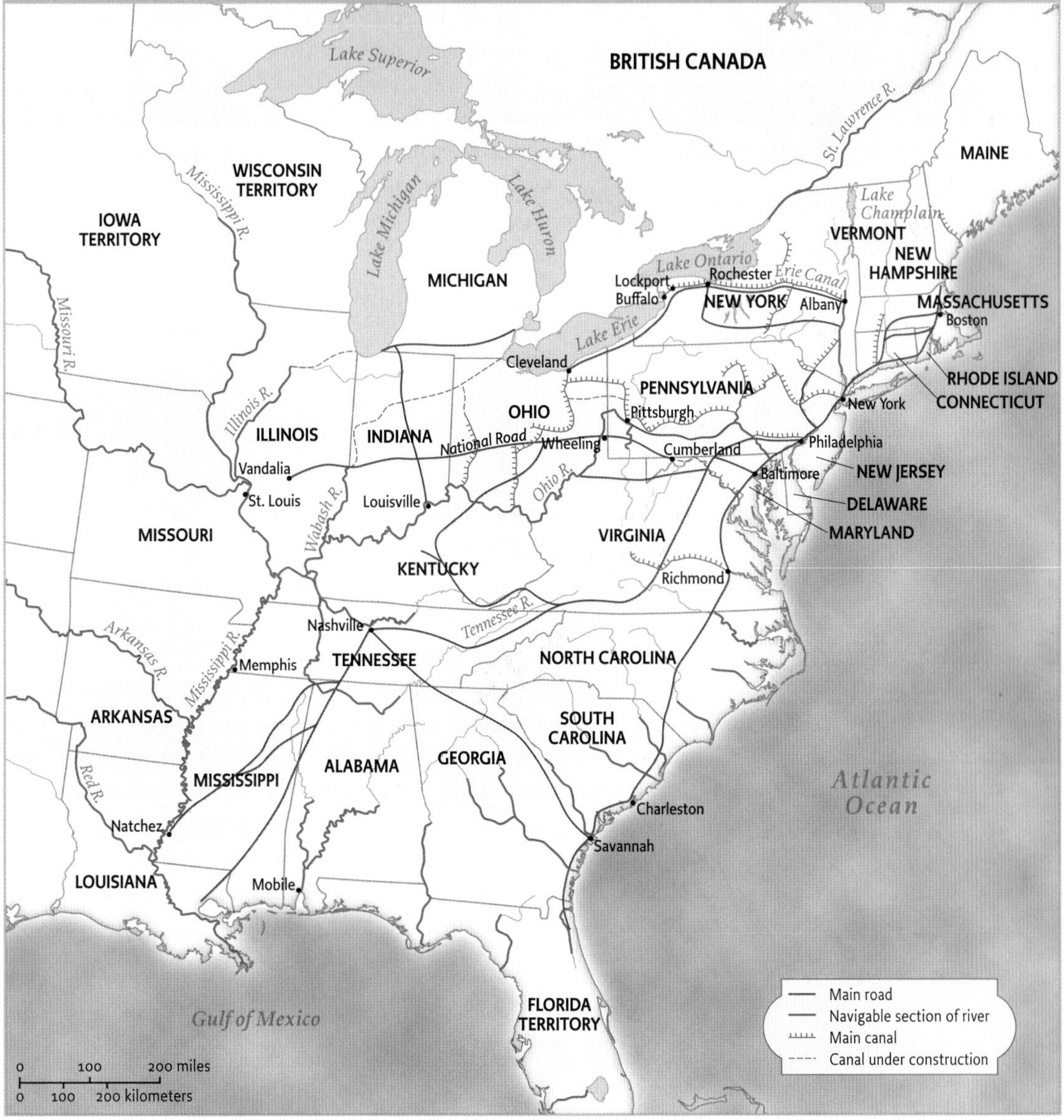

The improvement of existing roads and building of new roads and canals sharply reduced transportation times and costs and stimulated the growth of the market economy.

This "diploma" issued in the 1850s by the Delaware County (Pennsylvania) Society for the Promotion of Agriculture, Horticulture, Manufactures, and the Mechanic and Household Arts depicts scenes of an integrated diversified economy, including farming, manufacturing, and household labor. Farmers plow and reap the fields and transport produce; women work at sewing machines and a power loom; a ship is under construction; and a water-powered factory is also visible.

New York City primacy over competing ports in access to trade with the Old Northwest. In its financing by the state government, the Erie Canal typified the developing transportation infrastructure.

The completion of the Erie Canal set off a scramble among other states to match New York's success. Several borrowed so much money to finance elaborate programs of canal construction that they went bankrupt during the economic depression that began in 1837. By then, however, more than 3,000 miles of canals had been built, creating a network linking the Atlantic states with the Ohio and Mississippi Valleys and drastically reducing the cost of transportation.

Railroads and the Telegraph

Canals connected existing waterways. The railroad opened vast new areas of the American interior to settlement, while stimulating the mining of coal for fuel and the manufacture of iron for locomotives and rails. Work on the Baltimore and Ohio, the nation's first commercial railroad, began in 1828. By 1860, the railroad network had grown to 30,000 miles, more than the total in the rest of the world combined.

At the same time, the telegraph made possible instantaneous communication throughout the nation. The device was invented during the 1830s by Samuel F. B. Morse, an artist and amateur scientist living in New York City, and was put into commercial operation in 1844. Within sixteen years, some 50,000 miles of telegraph wire had been strung. Initially, the telegraph was a service for businesses, and especially newspapers, rather than individuals. It helped speed the flow of information and brought uniformity to prices throughout the country.

The Rise of the West

Migration west

Improvements in transportation and communication made possible the rise of the West as a powerful, self-conscious region of the new nation. Between 1790 and 1840, some 4.5 million people crossed the Appalachian Mountains—more than the entire U.S. population at the time of Washington's first inauguration. Most of this migration took place after the War of 1812, which unleashed a flood of land-hungry settlers moving from eastern states. In the six years following the end of the war in 1815, six new states entered the Union (Indiana, Illinois, Missouri, Alabama, Mississippi, and Maine—the last an eastern frontier for New England).

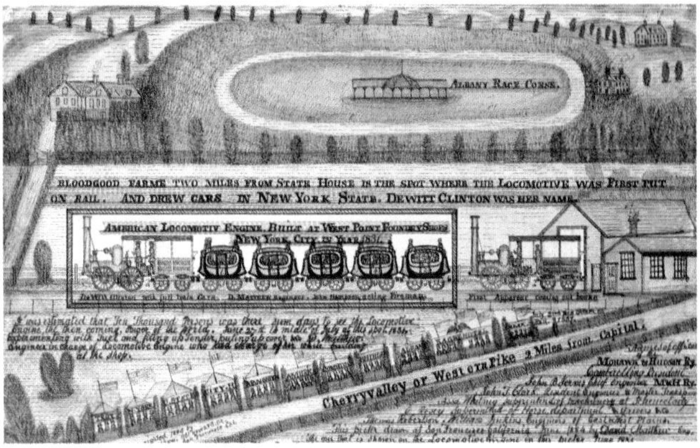

An 1884 watercolor, *Locomotive DeWitt Clinton*, recalls the early days of rail travel. The train is driven by a steam-powered locomotive and the cars strongly resemble horse-drawn stagecoaches.

Few Americans moved west as lone pioneers. More frequently, people traveled in groups and, once they arrived in the West, cooperated with each other to clear land, build houses and barns, and establish communities. One stream of migration, including both small farmers and planters with their slaves, flowed out of the South to create the new Cotton Kingdom of Alabama, Mississippi, Louisiana, and Arkansas. Many farm families from the Upper South crossed into southern Ohio, Indiana, and Illinois. A third population stream moved from New England across New York to the Upper Northwest—northern Ohio, Indiana, and Illinois, and Michigan and Wisconsin.

Some western migrants became "squatters," setting up farms on unoccupied land without a clear legal title. Those who purchased land acquired it either from the federal government, at the price, after 1820, of $1.25 per acre payable in cash or from land speculators on long-term credit. The West became the home of regional cultures very much like those the migrants had left behind. Upstate New York and the Upper Northwest resembled New England, with its small towns, churches, and schools, while the Lower South replicated the plantation-based society of the southern Atlantic states.

Expansion across national boundaries

National boundaries made little difference to territorial expansion—in Florida, and later in Texas and Oregon, American settlers rushed in to claim land under the jurisdiction of foreign countries (Spain, Mexico, and Britain) or Indian tribes, confident that American sovereignty would soon follow in their wake. In 1810, American residents of West Florida rebelled and seized Baton Rouge, and the United States soon annexed the area. The drive for the acquisition of East Florida was spurred by Georgia and Alabama planters who wished to eliminate a refuge for fugitive slaves and hostile Seminole Indians. Andrew Jackson led troops into the area in 1818. While on foreign soil, he created an international crisis by executing two British traders and a number of Indian chiefs. Although Jackson withdrew, Spain, aware that it could not defend the territory, sold it to the United States in the Adams-Onís Treaty of 1819 negotiated by John Quincy Adams.

Adams-Onís Treaty of 1819

Successive censuses told the remarkable story of western growth. In 1840, by which time the government had sold to settlers and land companies nearly 43 million acres of land, 7 million Americans—two-fifths of

TRAVEL TIMES FROM NEW YORK CITY IN 1800 AND 1830

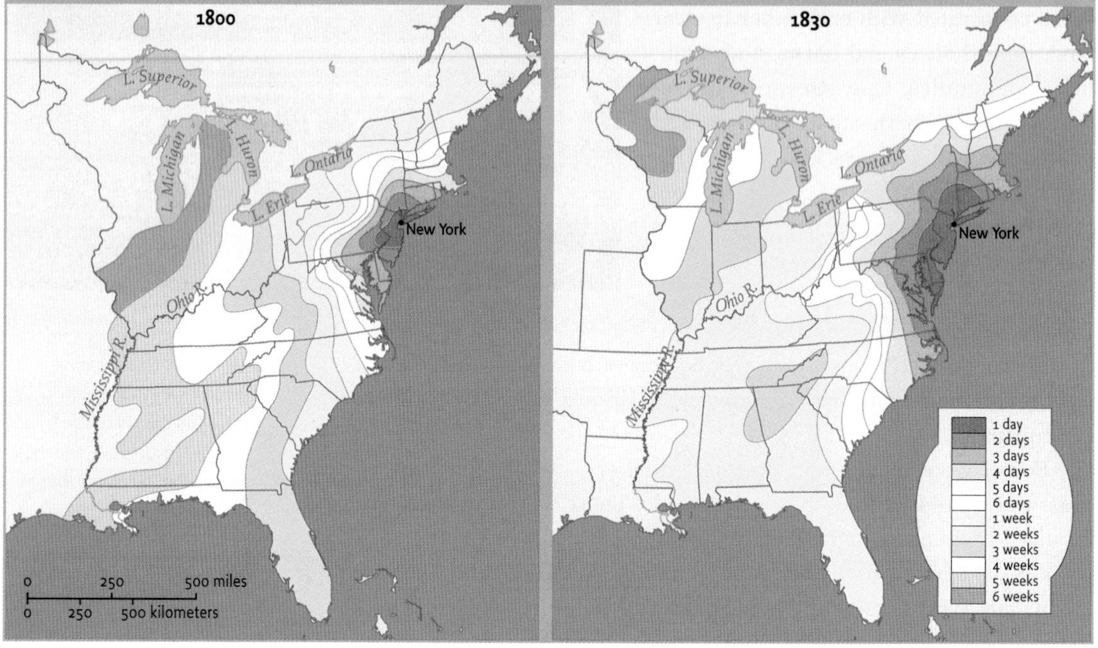

These maps illustrate how the transportation revolution of the early nineteenth century made possible much more rapid travel within the United States.

the total population—lived beyond the Appalachian Mountains. Between 1810 and 1830, Ohio's population grew from 231,000 to more than 900,000. It reached nearly 2 million in 1850, when it ranked third among all the states. The careers of the era's leading public figures reflected the westward movement. Andrew Jackson, Henry Clay, and many other statesmen were born in states along the Atlantic coast but made their mark in politics after moving west.

An Internal Borderland

Before the War of 1812, the Old Northwest was a prime example of a borderland, a meeting-ground of Native Americans and various people of English, French, and American descent, where cultural boundaries remained unstable and political authority uncertain. The American victory over the British and Indians erased any doubt over who would control the region. But a new, internal borderland region quickly developed.

Ohio River as boundary

Because the Northwest Ordinance of 1787 prohibited slavery in the Old Northwest, the Ohio River came to mark a boundary between free and slave societies. But for many years it was easier for people and goods to travel between the slave state Kentucky and the southern counties of Ohio, Indiana, and Illinois than to the northern parts of those states. The region stretching northward from the Ohio River retained much of the cultural flavor of the Upper South. Its food, speech, settlement pat terns, family ties, and economic relations had more in common with Kentucky and Tennessee than with the northern counties of their own states, soon to be settled by New Englanders. Until the 1850s, farmers in the southern counties of Ohio, Indiana, and Illinois were far more likely to ship their produce southward via the Ohio and Mississippi Rivers than northward or to the East. The large concentration of people of southern ancestry would make Indiana and Illinois key political battlegrounds as the slavery controversy developed.

TABLE 9.1 Population Growth of Selected Western States, 1810–1850 (Excluding Indians)

STATE	1810	1830	1850
Alabama	9,000	310,000	772,000
Illinois	12,000	157,000	851,000
Indiana	25,000	343,000	988,000
Louisiana	77,000	216,000	518,000
Mississippi	31,000	137,000	607,000
Missouri	20,000	140,000	682,000
Ohio	231,000	938,000	1,980,000

The Cotton Kingdom

Although the market revolution and westward expansion occurred simultaneously in the North and the South, their combined effects heightened the nation's sectional divisions. In some ways, the most dynamic feature of the American economy in the first thirty years of the nineteenth century was the rise of the **Cotton Kingdom**. The early industrial revolution, which began in England and soon spread to parts of the North, centered on factories producing cotton textiles with water-powered spinning and weaving machinery. These factories generated an immense demand for cotton, a crop the Lower South was particularly suited to growing because of its climate and soil fertility. Until 1793, the marketing of cotton had been slowed by the laborious task of removing seeds from the plant itself. But in that year, Eli Whitney, a Yale graduate working in Georgia as a private tutor, invented the **cotton gin**. A fairly simple device consisting of rollers and brushes, the gin quickly separated the seed from the cotton. Coupled with rising demand for cotton and the opening of new lands in the West, Whitney's invention revolutionized American slavery, an institution that many Americans had expected to die out because its major crop, tobacco, exhausted the soil.

Cotton and industry

Whitney's cotton gin

After the War of 1812, the federal government moved to consolidate American control over the Deep South, forcing defeated Indians to cede land, encouraging white settlement, and acquiring Florida. Settlers from

THE MARKET REVOLUTION: THE SPREAD OF COTTON CULTIVATION, 1820–1840

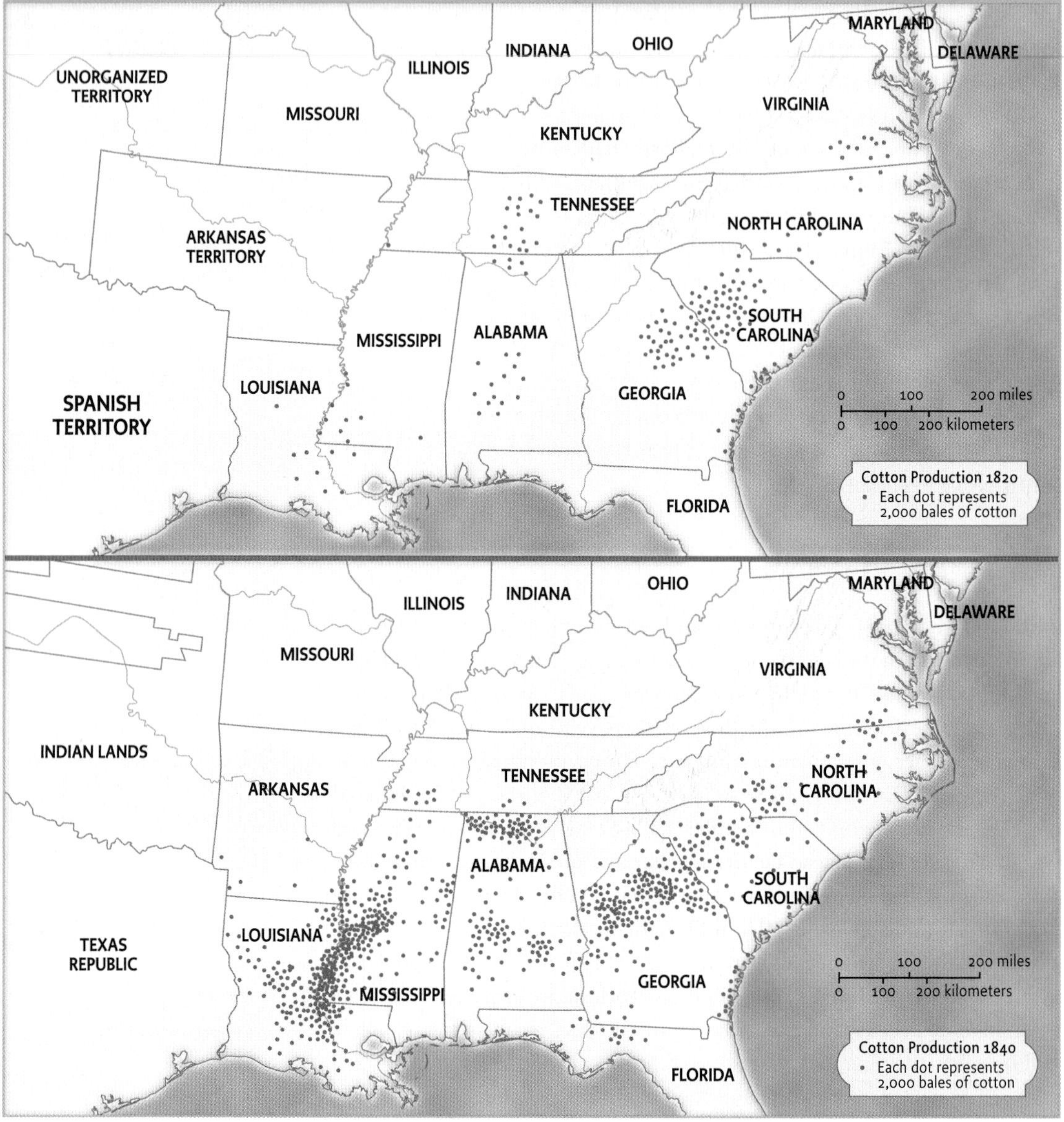

Maps of cotton production graphically illustrate the rise of the Cotton Kingdom stretching from South Carolina to Louisiana.

the older southern states flooded into the region. Planters monopolized the most fertile land, whereas poorer farmers were generally confined to less productive and less accessible areas in the "hill country" and piney woods. After Congress prohibited the Atlantic slave trade in 1808, a massive trade in slaves developed within the United States, supplying the labor force required by the new Cotton Kingdom.

Monopolization of fertile land

Slave trading became a well-organized business, with firms gathering slaves in Maryland, Virginia, and South Carolina and shipping them to markets in Mobile, Natchez, and New Orleans. Slave coffles—groups chained to one another on forced marches to the Lower South—became a common sight. Indeed, historians estimate that around 1 million slaves were shifted from the older slave states to the Lower South between 1800 and 1860. A source of greater freedom for many whites, the westward movement meant to African-Americans the destruction of family ties, the breakup of long-standing communities, and receding opportunities for liberty.

In 1793, when Whitney designed his invention, the United States produced 5 million pounds of cotton. By 1820, the crop had grown to nearly 170 million pounds.

MARKET SOCIETY

Since cotton was produced solely for sale in national and international markets, the South was in some ways the most commercially oriented region of the United States. Yet rather than spurring economic change, the South's expansion westward simply reproduced the agrarian, slave-based social order of the older states. The region remained overwhelmingly rural. In 1860, roughly 80 percent of southerners worked the land—the same proportion as in 1800.

Commercial Farmers

In the North, however, the market revolution and westward expansion set in motion changes that transformed the region into an integrated economy of commercial farms and manufacturing cities. As the Old Northwest became a more settled society, bound by a web of transportation and credit to eastern centers of commerce and banking, farmers found themselves drawn into the new market economy. They increasingly concentrated on growing crops and raising livestock for sale, while purchasing at stores goods previously produced at home.

Western farmers found in the growing cities of the East a market for their produce and a source of credit. Loans originating with eastern banks and insurance companies financed the acquisition of land and supplies and, in the 1840s and 1850s, the purchase of fertilizer and new agricultural machinery to expand production. The steel plow, invented by John Deere in 1837 and mass-produced by the 1850s, made possible the rapid subduing of the western prairies. The reaper, a horse-drawn machine that greatly increased the amount of wheat a farmer could harvest, was invented by Cyrus McCormick in 1831 and produced in large quantities soon afterward. Eastern farmers, unable to grow wheat and corn as cheaply as their western counterparts, increasingly concentrated on producing dairy products, fruits, and vegetables for nearby urban centers.

Technology and western farming

The Growth of Cities

From the beginning, cities formed part of the western frontier. Cincinnati was known as **Porkopolis**, after its slaughterhouses, where hundreds of thousands of pigs were butchered each year and processed for shipment to eastern consumers of meat. The greatest of all the western cities was Chicago. In the early 1830s, it was a tiny settlement on the shore of Lake Michigan. By 1860, thanks to the railroad, Chicago had become the nation's fourth-largest city, where farm products from throughout the Northwest were gathered to be sent east.

Western cities

Like rural areas, urban centers witnessed dramatic changes due to the market revolution. Urban merchants, bankers, and master craftsmen took advantage of the economic opportunities created by the expanding market among commercial farmers. The drive among these businessmen to increase production and reduce labor costs fundamentally altered the nature of work. Traditionally, skilled artisans had manufactured goods at home, where they controlled the pace and intensity of their own labor. Now, entrepreneurs gathered artisans into large workshops in order to oversee their work and subdivide their tasks. Craftsmen who traditionally produced an entire pair of shoes or piece of furniture saw the labor process broken down into numerous steps requiring far less skill and training. They found themselves subjected to constant supervision by their employers and relentless pressure for greater output and lower wages.

A trade card depicts the interior of a chair-manufacturing workshop in New York City. The owner stands at the center, dressed quite differently from his employees. The men are using traditional hand tools; furniture manufacturing had not yet been mechanized.

The Factory System

In some industries, most notably textiles, the factory superseded traditional craft production altogether. Factories gathered large groups of workers under central supervision and replaced hand tools with power-driven machinery. Samuel Slater, an immigrant from England, established America's first factory in 1790 at Pawtucket, Rhode Island. Since British law made it illegal to export the plans for industrial machinery, Slater, a skilled mechanic, built from memory a power-driven spinning jenny, one of the key inventions of the early industrial revolution.

A painting of Cincinnati, self-styled Queen City of the West, from 1835. Steamboats line the Ohio River waterfront.

Spinning factories such as Slater's produced yarn, which was then sent to traditional hand-loom weavers and farm families to be woven into cloth. This "outwork" system, in which rural men and women earned money by taking in jobs from factories, typified early industrialization. Eventually, however, the entire manufacturing process in textiles, shoes, and many other products was brought under a single factory roof.

The cutoff of British imports because of the Embargo of 1807 and the War of 1812 stimulated the establishment of the first large-scale American factory utilizing power looms for weaving cotton cloth. This was constructed in 1814 at Waltham, Massachusetts, by a group of merchants who came to be called the Boston Associates. In the 1820s, they expanded their enterprise by creating an entirely new factory town (incorporated as the city of Lowell in 1836) on the Merrimack River, twenty-seven miles from Boston. Here they built a group of modern textile factories that brought together all phases of production from the spinning of thread to the weaving and finishing of cloth.

The earliest factories, including those at Pawtucket, Waltham, and Lowell, were located along the "fall line," where waterfalls and river rapids could be harnessed to provide power for spinning and weaving machinery. By the 1840s, steam power made it possible for factory owners to locate in towns like New Bedford that were nearer to the coast, and in large cities like Philadelphia and Chicago with their immense local markets. In 1850, manufacturers produced in factories not only textiles but also a wide variety of other goods, including tools, firearms, shoes, clocks, ironware, and agricultural machinery. What came to be called the **American system of manufactures** relied on the mass production of interchangeable parts that could be rapidly assembled into standardized finished products. More impressive, in a way, than factory production was the wide dispersion of mechanical skills throughout northern society. Every town, it seemed, had its sawmill, paper mill, iron works, shoemaker, hatmaker, tailor, and a host of other such small enterprises.

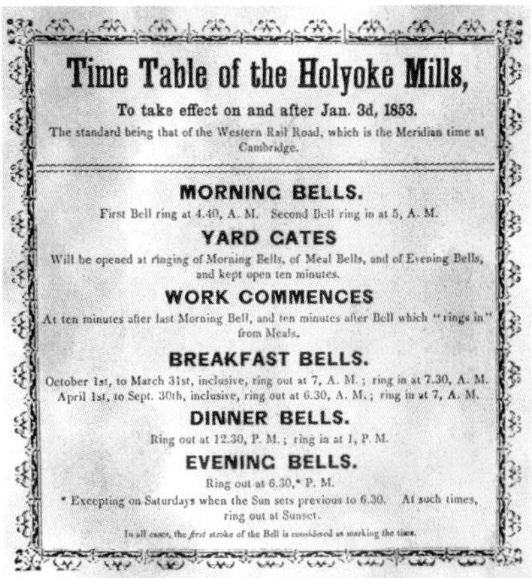

Time Table of the Holyoke Mills,

To take effect on and after Jan. 3d, 1853.

The standard being that of the Western Rail Road, which is the Meridian time at Cambridge.

MORNING BELLS.

First Bell ring at 4.40, A. M. Second Bell ring in at 5, A. M.

YARD GATES

Will be opened at ringing of Morning Bells, of Meal Bells, and of Evening Bells, and kept open ten minutes.

WORK COMMENCES

At ten minutes after last Morning Bell, and ten minutes after Bell which "rings in" from Meals.

BREAKFAST BELLS.

October 1st, to March 31st, inclusive, ring out at 7, A. M.; ring in at 7.30, A. M.
April 1st, to Sept. 30th, inclusive, ring out at 6.30, A. M.; ring in at 7, A. M.

DINNER BELLS.

Ring out at 12.30, P. M.; ring in at 1, P. M.

EVENING BELLS.

Ring out at 6.30,* P. M.

* Excepting on Saturdays when the Sun sets previous to 6.30. At such times, ring out at Sunset.

In all cases, the *first* stroke of the Bell is considered as marking the time.

A broadside from 1853 illustrates the long hours of work (from 5 AM to 6:30 PM with brief breaks for meals) in the textile mills of Holyoke, Massachusetts. Factory labor was strictly regulated by the clock.

Women at work tending machines in the Lowell textile mills.

The "Mill Girls"

Although some factories employed entire families, the early New England textile mills relied largely on female and child labor. At Lowell, the most famous center of early textile manufacturing, young unmarried women from Yankee farm families dominated the workforce that tended the spinning machines. To persuade parents to allow their daughters to leave home to work in the mills, Lowell owners set up boarding houses with strict rules regulating personal behavior. They also established lecture halls and churches to occupy the women's free time.

This was the first time in history that large numbers of women left their homes to participate in the public world. Many **mill girls** complained about low wages and long hours. Others valued the opportunity to earn money independently at a time when few other jobs were open to women. But these women did not become a permanent class of factory workers. They typically remained in the factories for only a few years, after which they left to return home, marry, or move west.

The Growth of Immigration

Economic expansion fueled a demand for labor, which was met, in part, by increased immigration from abroad. Between 1790 and 1830, immigrants contributed only marginally to American population growth. But between 1840 and 1860, over 4 million people (more than the entire population in 1790) entered the United States, the majority from Ireland and Germany. About 90 percent headed for the northern states, where job opportunities were most abundant and the new arrivals would not have to compete with slave labor. In 1860, the 814,000 residents of New York City, the major port of entry, included more than 384,000 immigrants, and one-third of the population of Wisconsin was foreign-born.

TABLE 9.2 Total Number of Immigrants by Five-Year Period

YEARS	NUMBER OF IMMIGRANTS
1841–1845	430,000
1846–1850	1,283,000
1851–1855	1,748,000
1856–1860	850,000

Numerous factors inspired this massive flow of population across the Atlantic. In Europe, the modernization of agriculture and the industrial revolution disrupted centuries-old patterns of life, pushing peasants off the land and eliminating the jobs of traditional craft workers. The introduction of the oceangoing steamship and the railroad made long-distance travel more practical. Moreover, America's political and religious freedoms attracted Europeans, including political refugees from the failed revolutions of 1848, who chafed under the continent's repressive governments and rigid social hierarchies.

The largest number of immigrants, however, were refugees from disaster—Irish men and women fleeing the Great Famine of

COTTON MILLS, 1820s

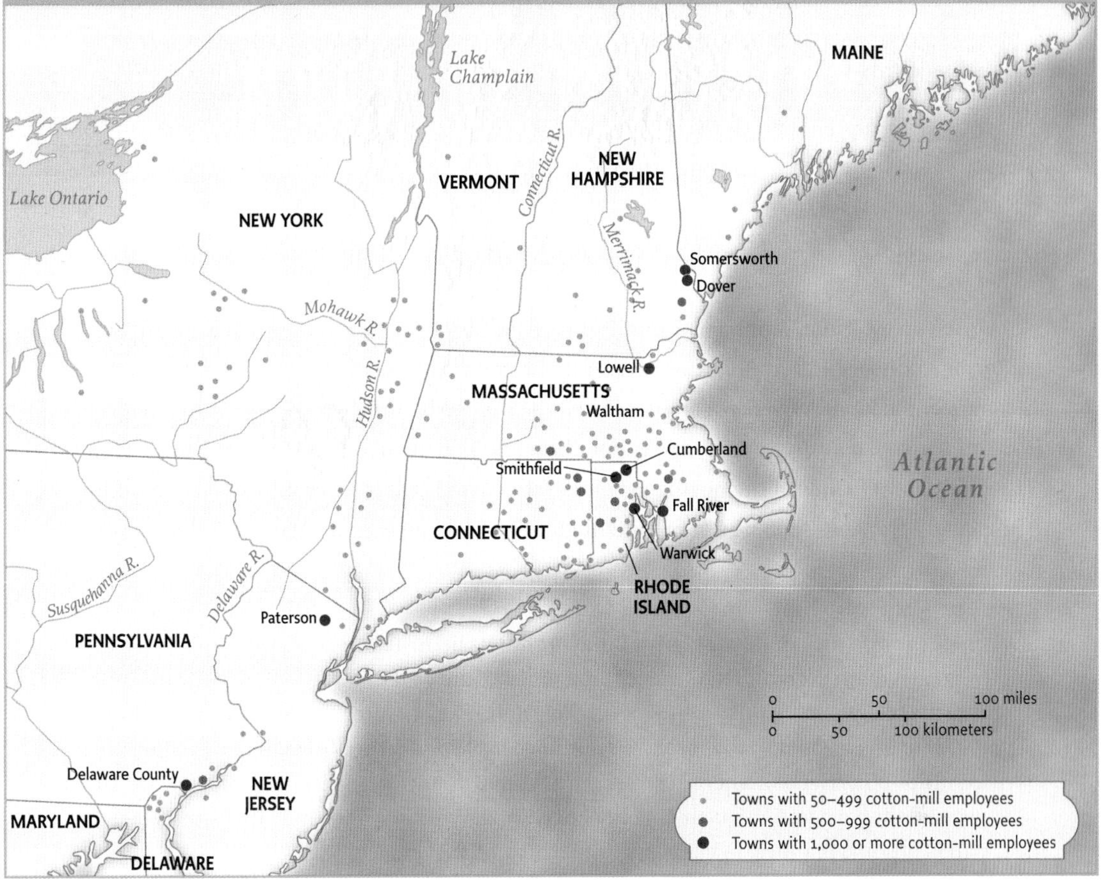

The early industrial revolution was concentrated in New England, where factories producing textiles from raw cotton sprang up along the region's many rivers, taking advantage of water power to drive their machinery.

1845–1851, when a blight destroyed the potato crop on which the island's diet relied. An estimated 1 million persons starved to death and another million emigrated in those years, most of them to the United States. Lacking industrial skills and capital, these impoverished agricultural laborers and small farmers ended up filling the low-wage unskilled jobs native-born Americans sought to avoid. Male Irish immigrants built America's railroads, dug canals, and worked as common laborers, servants, longshoremen, and factory operatives. Irish women frequently went to work as servants in the homes of native-born Americans, although some preferred factory work to domestic service. By the end of the 1850s, the Lowell textile mills had largely replaced Yankee farm women with immigrant Irish families. Four-fifths of Irish immigrants remained in the Northeast.

VOICES OF FREEDOM

From Sarah Bagley, untitled essay in *Voice of Industry* (1845)

Born to a New Hampshire farm family in 1806, Sarah Bagley came to Lowell in 1837 after her father suffered financial reverses. She soon became one of the most outspoken leaders of the labor movement among the city's "mill girls." In 1845 she became the editor of the *Voice of Industry*, which spoke for the male and female labor movement of New England. Her critique of the northern labor system was similar to arguments advanced by proslavery thinkers such as George Fitzhugh (discussed in Chapter 11).

Whenever I raise the point that it is immoral to shut us up in a close room twelve hours a day in the most monotonous and tedious of employment, I am told that we have come to the mills voluntarily and we can leave when we will. Voluntary! Let us look a little at this remarkable form of human freedom. Do we from mere choice leave our fathers' dwellings, the firesides where all of our friends, where too our earliest and fondest recollections cluster, for the factory and the corporation's boarding house? . . . A slave too goes voluntarily to his task, but his will is in some manner quickened by the whip of the overseer.

The whip which brings us to Lowell is NECESSITY. We must have money; a father's debts are to be paid, an aged mother to be sup ported, a brother's ambition to be aided, and so the factories are supplied. Is this to act from free will? . . . Is any one such a fool as to suppose that out of six thousand factory girls of Lowell, sixty would be there if they could help it? Everybody knows that it is necessity alone, in some form or other, that takes us to Lowell and keeps us there. Is this freedom? To my mind it is slavery quite as really as any in Turkey or Carolina. It matters little as to the fact of slavery, whether the slave be compelled to his task by the whip of the over-seer or the wages of the Lowell Corporation. In either case it is not free will, leading the laborer to work, but an outward necessity that puts free will out of the question.

From Letter of Margaret McCarthy to Her Family (1850)

Between 1840 and 1860, over 4 million people (more than the entire population of 1790) entered the United States, the majority from Ireland and Germany. Many sent money home to help family members join them, a process today sometimes called chain migration. In this letter, Margaret McCarthy, a young immigrant writing from New York City, offers advice to her family in Ireland.

My dear father I must only say that this is a good place and a good country for if one place does not suit a man he can go to another and can very easy please himself. . . . [But] I would advise no one to come to America that would not have some money after landing here that [will] enable them to go west in case they would get no work to do here. But any man or woman without a family are fools that would not venture and come to this plentiful country where no man or woman ever hungered or ever will. . . .

Come you all together courageously and bid adieu to that lovely place the land of our birth. . . . But alas I am now told it's the gulf of misery, oppression, degradation and ruin. . . . This, my dear father induces me to remit to you in this letter 20 dollars. . . . Dan Keliher tells me that you knew more of house carpentry than he did himself and he can earn from twelve to fourteen shilling a day and he also tells me that Florence will do very well and that Michael can get a place right off. . . . It is not for slavery I want you to come here no its for affording my brothers and sisters and I an opportunity of showing our kindness and gratitude and coming on your senior days . . . [so] that you my dear father and mother could walk about leisurely and independently . . . .

Oh how happy I feel [that] the Lord had not it destined for me to get married . . . at home [and] after a few months he and I may be an encumbrance on you or perhaps in the poor house.

QUESTIONS

1. *Why does Sarah Bagley compare the situation of female factory workers with slavery?*
2. *What aspirations seem to be uppermost in Margaret McCarthy's mind?*
3. *What do these documents suggest about how Americans of different backgrounds experienced and responded to economic conditions during the first half of the nineteenth century?*

A lithograph by an anonymous artist depicts the city of Lowell, Massachusetts, an early center of textile manufacturing, around 1850. Factories line the banks of the Merrimack River, which provided power for spinning machines and power looms. By this time, the original workforce of young New England women was being replaced by Irish immigrant families.

The second-largest group of immigrants, Germans, included a considerably larger number of skilled craftsmen than the Irish. Germans also settled in tightly knit neighborhoods in eastern cities, but many were able to move to the West, where they established themselves as craftsmen, shopkeepers, and farmers. The "German triangle," as the cities of Cincinnati, St. Louis, and Milwaukee were sometimes called, attracted large German populations.

Some 40,000 Scandinavians also emigrated to the United States in these years, most of whom settled on farms in the Old Northwest.

FIGURE 9.1 Sources of Immigration, 1850

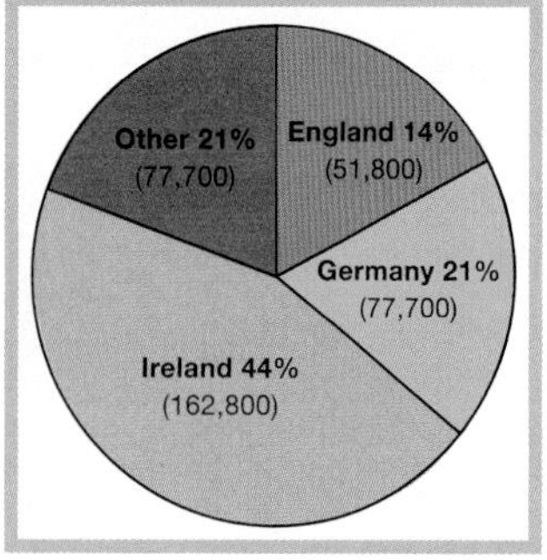

The Rise of Nativism

The idea of the United States as a refuge for those seeking economic opportunity or as an escape from oppression has always coexisted with suspicion of and hostility to foreign newcomers. American history has witnessed periods of intense anxiety over immigration. The Alien Act of 1798 reflected fear of immigrants with radical political views. During the early twentieth century, as will be discussed below, there was widespread hostility to the "new immigration" from southern and eastern Europe. In the early twenty-first century, the question of how many persons should be allowed to enter the United States, and under what circumstances, remains a volatile political issue.

Archbishop John Hughes of New York City made the Catholic Church a more assertive institution. He condemned the use of the Protestant King James Bible in the city's public schools, pressed Catholic parents to send their children to an expanding network of parochial schools, and sought

Riot in Philadelphia, an 1844 lithograph, depicts street battles between nativists and Irish Catholics that left fifteen persons dead. The violence originated in a dispute over the use of the Protestant King James Bible in the city's public schools.

government funding to pay for them. He aggressively sought to win converts from Protestantism.

In the eyes of many Protestants, the newly assertive activities of the Catholic Church raised anew the question of national identity—the question, Who is an American, and its close relative, what kinds of immigrants should the country welcome. Catholicism, they feared, threatened American institutions and American freedom. In 1834, Lyman Beecher, a prominent Presbyterian minister (and father of the religious leader Henry Ward Beecher and the writers Harriet Beecher Stowe and Catharine Beecher), delivered a sermon in Boston, soon published as "A Plea for the West." Beecher warned that Catholics were seeking to dominate the American West, where the future of Christianity in the world would be worked out. His sermon inspired a mob to burn a Catholic convent in the city.

Nativist stereotypes

The Irish influx of the 1840s and 1850s thoroughly alarmed many native-born Americans. Those who feared the impact of immigration on American political and social life were called "nativists." They blamed immigrants for urban crime, political corruption, and a fondness for intoxicating liquor, and accused them of undercutting native-born skilled laborers by working for starvation wages. Stereotypes similar to those directed at blacks flourished regarding the Irish as well—seen as childlike, lazy, and slaves of their passions, they were said to be unsuited for republican freedom.

Nativism would not become a national political movement until the 1850s, as we will see in Chapter 13. But in the 1840s, nativism found expression both in the streets and at the ballot box. New York City and Philadelphia witnessed violent anti-immigrant, anti-Catholic riots.

The Transformation of Law

Corporations

American law increasingly supported the efforts of entrepreneurs to participate in the market revolution, while shielding them from interference by local governments and liability for some of the less desirable results of economic growth. The corporate form of business organization became central to the new market economy. A corporate firm enjoys special privileges and powers granted in a charter from the government, among them that investors and directors are not personally liable for the company's debts. Unlike companies owned by an individual, family, or limited partnership, in other words, a corporation can fail without ruining its directors and stockholders.

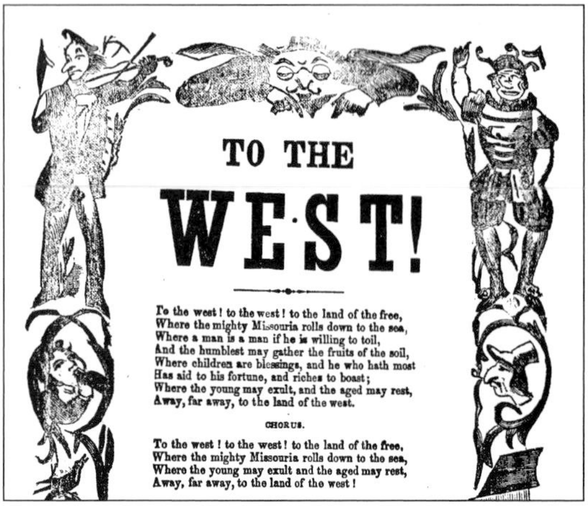

A song written in 1845 offers a satire of the widely held image of the West as "the land of the free," a place where the "humblest" American can achieve economic success. The pictures surrounding the text offer a somewhat different image of westerners, and the verses go on to complain about illness and hardship. But the opening words reflect the ways in which Americans have always viewed the West.

Many Americans distrusted corporate charters as a form of government-granted special privilege. But the courts upheld their validity, while opposing efforts by established firms to limit competition from newcomers. In ***Dartmouth College v. Woodward*** (1819), John Marshall's Supreme Court defined corporate charters issued by state legislatures as contracts, which future lawmakers could not alter or rescind. Five years later, in ***Gibbons v. Ogden***, the Court struck down a monopoly the New York legislature had granted for steamboat navigation. And in 1837, with Roger B. Taney now the chief justice, the Court ruled that the Massachusetts legislature did not infringe the charter of an existing company that had constructed a bridge over the Charles River when it empowered a second company to build a competing bridge. The community, Taney declared, had a legitimate interest in promoting transportation and prosperity.

THE FREE INDIVIDUAL

By the 1830s, the market revolution and westward expansion had produced a society that amazed European visitors: energetic, materialistic, and seemingly in constant motion. Alexis de Tocqueville was struck by Americans' restless energy and apparent lack of attachment to place. "No sooner do you set foot on American soil," he observed, "than you find yourself in a sort of tumult. All around you, everything is on the move."

The West and Freedom

Westward expansion and the market revolution reinforced some older ideas of freedom and helped to create new ones. American freedom, for example, had long been linked with the availability of land in the West. A New York journalist, John L. O'Sullivan, first employed the phrase "**manifest destiny**," meaning that the United States had a divinely appointed mission, so obvious as to be beyond dispute, to occupy all of North America. Americans, he proclaimed, had a far better title to western lands than could be provided by any international treaty, right of discovery, or long-term settlement.

O'Sullivan wrote these words in 1845, but the essential idea was familiar much earlier. Many Americans believed that the settlement and economic exploitation of the West would prevent the United States from following the path of Europe and becoming a society with fixed social classes and a large group of wage-earning poor. In the West, where land was more readily available and oppressive factory labor far less common than in the East, there continued to be the chance to achieve economic independence, the social condition of freedom. In national myth and ideology, the West would long remain, as the writer Wallace Stegner later put it, "the last home of the freeborn American."

Westward expansion and freedom

The Transcendentalists

The restless, competitive world of the market revolution strongly encouraged the identification of American freedom with the absence of restraints on self-directed individuals seeking economic advancement and personal development. The "one important revolution" of the day, the philosopher Ralph Waldo Emerson wrote in the 1830s, was "the new value of the private man." In Emerson's definition, rather than a preexisting set of rights or privileges, freedom was an open-ended process of self-realization by which individuals could remake themselves and their own lives.

Emerson was perhaps the most prominent member of a group of New England intellectuals known as the **transcendentalists**, who insisted on the primacy of individual judgment over existing social traditions and institutions. Emerson's Concord, Massachusetts, neighbor, the writer Henry David Thoreau, echoed his call for individual self-reliance. "Any man more right than his neighbors," Thoreau wrote, "is a majority of one."

In his own life, Thoreau illustrated Emerson's point about the primacy of individual conscience in matters political, social, and personal, and the need to find one's own way rather than following the crowd. Thoreau became persuaded that modern society stifled individual judgment by making men "tools of their tools," trapped in stultifying jobs by their obsession with acquiring wealth. Even in "this comparatively free country," he wrote, most persons were so preoccupied with material things that they had no time to contemplate the beauties of nature.

To escape this fate, Thoreau retreated for two years to a cabin on Walden Pond near Concord, where he could enjoy the freedom of isolation from the "economical and moral tyranny" he believed ruled American society. He subsequently published *Walden* (1854), an account of his experiences and a critique of how the market revolution was, in his opinion, degrading both Americans' values and the natural environment. An area

The daguerreotype, an early form of photography, required the sitter to remain perfectly still for twenty seconds or longer, meaning that the subject usually looked rather stiff. Nonetheless, Henry David Thoreau, pictured here in 1856, wrote, "my friends think it is pretty good though better looking than I."

that had been covered with dense forest in his youth, he observed, had been so transformed by woodcutters and farmers that it was almost completely devoid of trees and wild animals. Thoreau appealed to Americans to "simplify" their lives rather than become obsessed with the accumulation of wealth. Genuine freedom, he insisted, lay within.

The Second Great Awakening

Religious revivals

The popular religious revivals that swept the country during the **Second Great Awakening** added a religious underpinning to the celebration of personal self-improvement, self-reliance, and self-determination. These revivals, which began at the turn of the century, were originally organized by established religious leaders alarmed by low levels of church attendance in the young republic (perhaps as few as 10 percent of white Americans regularly attended church during the 1790s). But they quickly expanded far beyond existing churches. They peaked in the 1820s and early 1830s, when the Reverend Charles Grandison Finney held months-long revival meetings in upstate New York and New York City. Like the evangelists (traveling preachers) of the first Great Awakening of the mid-eighteenth century discussed in Chapter 4, Finney warned of hell in vivid language while offering the promise of salvation to converts who abandoned their sinful ways.

The Second Great Awakening democratized American Christianity, making it a truly mass enterprise. At the time of independence, fewer than 2,000 Christian ministers preached in the United States. In 1845, they numbered 40,000. Evangelical denominations such as the Methodists and Baptists enjoyed explosive growth in membership, and smaller sects proliferated. By the 1840s, Methodism, with more than 1 million members, had become the country's largest denomination. At large camp meetings, especially prominent on the frontier, fiery revivalist preachers rejected the idea that man is a sinful creature with a preordained fate, promoting instead the doctrine of human free will. At these gatherings, rich and poor, male and female, and in some instances whites and blacks worshiped alongside one another and pledged to abandon worldly sins in favor of the godly life.

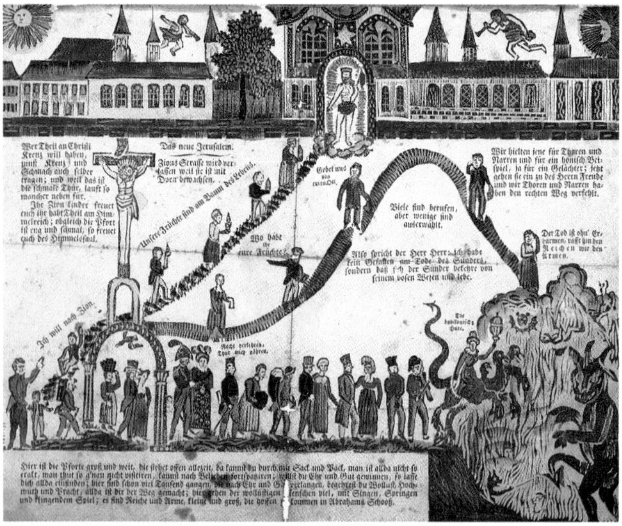

Das neue Jerusalem (The New Jerusalem), an early nineteenth-century watercolor, in German, illustrates the narrow gateway to heaven and the fate awaiting sinners in hell. These were common themes of preachers in the Second Great Awakening.

The Awakening's Impact

Even more than its predecessor of several decades earlier, the Second Great Awakening stressed the right of private judgment in spiritual matters and the possibility of universal salvation through faith and good works. Every person, Finney insisted, was a "moral free agent"—that is, a person free to choose between a Christian life and sin.

Mass religion

Revivalist ministers seized the opportunities offered by the market revolution to spread their message. They raised funds, embarked on lengthy preaching tours by canal, steamboat, and railroad, and flooded the country with mass-produced, inexpensive religious tracts. The revivals' opening of religion to mass participation and their message that ordinary Americans could shape their own spiritual destinies resonated with the spread of market values.

The Awakening and market society

To be sure, evangelical preachers can hardly be described as cheerleaders for a market society. They regularly railed against greed and indifference to the welfare of others as sins. Yet the revivals thrived in areas caught up in the rapid expansion of the market economy, such as the region of upstate New York along the path of the Erie Canal. Most of Finney's converts here came from the commercial and professional classes. Evangelical ministers promoted what might be called a controlled **individualism** as the essence of freedom. In stressing the importance of industry, sobriety, and self-discipline as examples of freely chosen moral behavior, evangelical preachers promoted the very qualities necessary for success in a market culture.

The Emergence of Mormonism

The end of governmental support for established churches promoted competition among religious groups that kept religion vibrant and promoted the emergence of new denominations. Among the most successful of the religions that sprang up was the **Church of Jesus Christ of Latter-Day Saints**, or Mormons, which hoped to create a Kingdom of God on earth. The Mormons were founded in the 1820s by Joseph Smith, a farmer in upstate New York who as a youth began to experience religious visions. He claimed to have been led by an angel to a set of golden plates covered with strange writing. Smith translated and published them as *The Book of Mormon*, after a fourth-century prophet.

The Book of Mormon

The Book of Mormon tells the story of three families who traveled from the ancient Middle East to the Americas, where they eventually evolved into Native American tribes. Jesus Christ plays a prominent role in the book, appearing to one of the family groups in the

In this 1846 photograph, the massive Mormon temple in Nauvoo, Illinois, towers over the ramshackle wooden buildings of this town along the Mississippi River.

Brigham Young

Western Hemisphere after his death and resurrection. The second coming of Christ would take place in the New World, where Smith was God's prophet.

Mormonism emerged in a center of the Second Great Awakening, upstate New York. The church founded by Smith shared some features with other Christian denominations including a focus on the family and community as the basis of social order and a rejection of alcohol. Gradually, however, Smith began to receive visions that led to more controversial doctrines, notably polygamy, which allows one man to have more than one wife. By the end of his life, Smith had married no fewer than thirty women. Along with the absolute authority Smith exercised over his followers, this doctrine outraged the Mormons' neighbors. Mobs drove Smith and his followers out of New York, Ohio, and Missouri before they settled in 1839 in Nauvoo, Illinois. There, five years later, Smith was arrested on the charge of inciting a riot that destroyed an anti-Mormon newspaper. While in jail awaiting trial, Smith was murdered by a group of intruders. In 1847, his successor as Mormon leader, Brigham Young, led more than 2,000 followers across the Great Plains and Rocky Mountains to the shores of the Great Salt Lake in present-day Utah. By 1852, the number of Mormons in various settlements in Utah reached 16,000. The Mormons' experience revealed the limits of religious toleration in nineteenth-century America but also the opportunities offered by religious pluralism. Today, Mormons constitute the fourth largest church in the United States, and *The Book of Mormon* has been translated into over 100 languages.

THE LIMITS OF PROSPERITY

Liberty and Prosperity

As the market revolution progressed, the right to compete for economic advancement became a touchstone of American freedom. Americans celebrated the opportunities open to the "self-made man," a term that came into use at this time. According to this idea, those who achieved success in America did so not as a result of hereditary privilege or government favoritism as in Europe, but through their own intelligence and hard work. The market revolution enriched numerous bankers, merchants, industrialists, and planters. It produced a new middle class—an army of clerks, accountants, and other office employees who staffed businesses in Boston, New York, and elsewhere. It created new opportunities for farmers who profited from the growing demand at home and abroad for American agricultural products, and for skilled craftsmen such as Thomas Rodgers, a machine builder who established a successful locomotive factory in Paterson, New Jersey. New opportunities for talented men opened in professions such as law, medicine, and teaching. By the early 1820s, there were an estimated 10,000 physicians in the United States.

Pat Lyon at the Forge, an 1826–1827 painting of a prosperous blacksmith. Proud of his accomplishments as a self-made man who had achieved success through hard work and skill rather than inheritance, Lyon asked the artist to paint him in his shop wearing his work clothes.

Race and Opportunity

The market revolution affected the lives of all Americans. But not all were positioned to take advantage of its benefits. Most blacks, of course, were slaves, but even free blacks found themselves excluded from the new economic opportunities. The 220,000 blacks living in the free states on the eve of the Civil War (less than 2 percent of the North's population) suffered discrimination in every phase of their lives. The majority of blacks lived in the poorest, unhealthiest sections of cities like New York, Philadelphia, and Cincinnati. And even these neighborhoods were subject to occasional violent assault by white mobs, like the armed bands that attacked blacks and destroyed their homes and businesses in Cincinnati in 1829.

Black institutions

Barred from schools and other public facilities, free blacks laboriously constructed their own institutional life, centered on mutual-aid and educational societies, as well as independent churches, most notably the African Methodist Episcopal Church. Richard Allen of Philadelphia, a Methodist preacher, had been spurred to found it after being forcibly removed from his former church for praying at the altar rail, a place reserved for whites.

Downward mobility of free blacks

Whereas many white Americans could look forward to a life of economic accumulation and individual advancement, large numbers of free blacks experienced downward mobility. At the time of abolition in the North, because of widespread slave ownership among eighteenth-century artisans, a considerable number of northern blacks possessed craft skills. But it became more and more difficult for blacks to utilize these skills once they became free. Although many white artisans criticized slavery, most viewed the freed slaves as low-wage competitors and sought to bar them from skilled employment.

Hostility from white craftsmen, however, was only one of many obstacles that kept blacks confined to the lowest ranks of the labor market. White employers refused to hire them in anything but menial positions, and white customers did not wish to be served by them. The result was a rapid decline in economic status until by mid-century, the vast majority of northern blacks labored for wages in unskilled jobs and as domestic servants. The state census of 1855 revealed 122 black barbers and 808 black servants in New York City, but only 1 lawyer and 6 doctors. Nor could free blacks take advantage of the opening of the West to improve their economic status, a central component of American freedom. Federal law barred them from access to public land, and by 1860 four states—Indiana, Illinois, Iowa, and Oregon—prohibited them from entering their territory altogether.

The Cult of Domesticity

Women, too, found many of the opportunities opened by the market revolution closed to them. As the household declined as a center of economic production, many women saw their traditional roles undermined by the availability of mass-produced goods previously made at home. Some women, as noted above, followed work as it moved from household to factory. Others embraced a new definition of femininity, which glorified not a woman's contribution to the family's economic well-being, but her ability to create a private environment shielded from the competitive tensions of the market economy. Woman's "place" was in the home, a site increasingly emptied of economically productive functions as work moved from the household to workshops and factories. Her role was to sustain nonmarket values like love, friendship, and mutual obligation, providing men with a shelter from the competitive marketplace.

The earlier ideology of "republican motherhood," which allowed women a kind of public role as mothers of future citizens, subtly evolved into the mid-nineteenth-century **cult of domesticity**. "In whatever situation of life a woman is placed from her cradle to her grave," declared *The Young Lady's Book*, one of numerous popular magazines addressed to female audiences of the 1820s and 1830s, "a spirit of obedience and submission, pliability of temper, and humility of mind, are required from her."

The Industrious Man, a lithograph from a book produced for children by the American Sunday School Union in the 1840s, depicts an ideal family scene. The father, a laborer, returns home carrying his lunch pail to find his wife and children awaiting him in a comfortable although hardly extravagant home. The scene exemplifies the idea of separate spheres according to which men worked outside the home and women's role was to fulfill their family responsibilities.

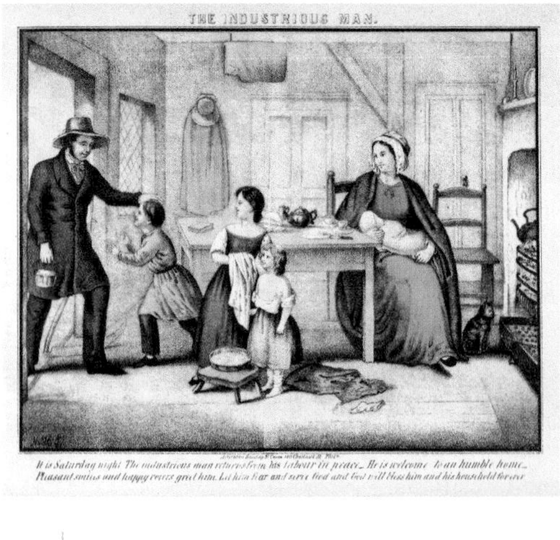

With more and more men leaving the home for work, women did exercise considerable power over personal affairs within the family. The rapid decline in the American birthrate during the nineteenth century (from an average of seven children per woman in 1800 to four in 1900) cannot be explained except by the conscious decision of millions of women to limit the number of children they bore. But the idea of domesticity minimized women's even indirect participation in the outside world. Men moved freely between the public and private "spheres"; women were supposed to remain cloistered in the private realm of the family.

This nineteenth-century wood sculpture of a woman at a spinning wheel depicts a form of labor practiced by millions of American women in their homes—despite the advent of machines that did the same work—producing thread or yarn from fibers such as wool and cotton.

Women and Work

Prevailing ideas concerning gender bore little relation to the experience of those women who worked for wages at least some time in their lives. They did so despite severe disadvantages. Women could not compete freely for employment, since only low-paying jobs were available to them. Married women still could not sign independent contracts or sue in their own names, and not until after the Civil War did they, not their husbands, control the wages they earned. Nonetheless, for poor city dwellers and farm families, the labor of all family members was essential to economic survival. Thousands of poor women found jobs as domestic servants, factory workers, and seamstresses.

For the expanding middle class, however, it became a badge of respectability for wives to remain at home, outside the disorderly new market economy, while husbands conducted business in their offices, shops, and factories. In larger cities, where families of different social classes had previously lived alongside one another, fashionable middle-class neighborhoods populated by merchants, factory owners, and professionals like lawyers and doctors began to develop. Work in middle-class homes was done by domestic servants, the largest employment category for women in nineteenth-century America. The freedom of the middle-class woman—defined in part as freedom from labor—rested on the employment of other women within her household.

Discussions of labor excluding women

Even though most women were anything but idle, in a market economy where labor increasingly meant work that created monetary value, it became more and more difficult to think of labor as encompassing anyone but men. Discussions of labor rarely mentioned housewives, domestic servants, and female outworkers, except as an indication of how the spread of capitalism was degrading men. The idea that the male head of household should command a **family wage** that enabled him to support his wife and children became a popular definition of social justice. It sank deep roots not only among middle-class Americans but among working-class men as well.

The Early Labor Movement

Although many Americans welcomed the market revolution, others felt threatened by its consequences. Surviving members of the revolutionary generation feared that the obsession with personal economic gain was undermining devotion to the public good.

"The Intelligence Office," an 1849 painting by the artist William Henry Burr, depicts a female employment office. The two women at the left are responding to an ad for a domestic worker printed in a New York City newspaper, which lies crumpled on the ground. The seated woman is the prospective employer, and in the middle is the agent who runs the office. Domestic work was the largest category of female employment throughout the nineteenth century.

Many Americans experienced the market revolution not as an enhancement of the power to shape their own lives, but as a loss of freedom. The period between the War of 1812 and 1840 witnessed a sharp economic downturn in 1819, a full-fledged depression starting in 1837, and numerous ups and downs in between, during which employment was irregular and numerous businesses failed. The economic transformation significantly widened the gap between wealthy merchants and industrialists on the one hand and impoverished factory workers, unskilled dockworkers, and seamstresses laboring at home on the other. In Massachusetts, the most industrialized state in the country, the richest 5 percent of the population owned more than half the wealth.

Alarmed at the erosion of traditional skills and the threat of being reduced to the status of dependent wage earners, skilled craftsmen in the late 1820s created the world's first Workingmen's Parties, short-lived political organizations that sought to mobilize lower-class support for candidates who would press for free public education, an end to imprisonment for debt, and legislation limiting work to ten hours per day. In the 1830s, a time of rapidly rising prices, union organization spread and strikes became commonplace. Along with demands for higher wages and shorter hours, the early labor movement called for free homesteads for settlers on public land and an end to the imprisonment of union leaders for conspiracy.

The "Liberty of Living"

Labor actions

But over and above these specific issues, workers' language of protest drew on older ideas of freedom linked to economic autonomy, public-spirited virtue, and social equality. The conviction of twenty New York tailors in 1835 under the common law of conspiracy for combining to seek higher wages inspired a public procession marking the "burial of liberty." Such actions and language were not confined to male workers. The young mill women of Lowell walked off their jobs in 1834 to protest a reduction in wages and again two years later when employers raised rents at their boardinghouses. They carried banners affirming their rights as "daughters of free men," and, addressing the factory owners, charged that "the oppressive hand of avarice [greed] would enslave us."

The Shoemakers' Strike in Lynn—Procession in the Midst of a Snow-Storm, of Eight Hundred Women Operatives, an engraving from *Frank Leslie's Illustrated Newspaper*, March 17, 1860. The striking women workers carry a banner comparing their condition to that of slaves.

Rooted in the traditions of the small producer and the identification of freedom with economic independence, labor's critique of the market economy directly challenged the idea that individual improvement—Emerson's "self-trust, self-reliance, self-control, self-culture"—offered an adequate response to social inequality. Orestes Brownson, in his influential essay "The Laboring Classes" (1840), argued that the solution to workers' problems did not require a more complete individualism. What was needed instead, he believed, was a "radical change [in] existing social arrangements" so as to produce "equality between man and man." Here lay the origins of the idea, which would become far more prominent in the late nineteenth and twentieth centuries, that economic security—a standard of life below which no person would fall—formed an essential part of American freedom.

Thus, the market revolution transformed and divided American society and its conceptions of freedom. It encouraged a new emphasis on individualism and physical mobility among white men while severely limiting the options available to women and African-Americans. It opened new opportunities for economic freedom for many Americans while leading others to fear that their traditional economic independence was being eroded. In a democratic society, it was inevitable that the debate over the market revolution and its consequences for freedom would be reflected in American politics.

CHAPTER REVIEW AND ONLINE RESOURCES

REVIEW QUESTIONS

1. *Identify the major transportation improvements in this period, and explain how they influenced the market economy.*
2. *How did state and local governments promote the national economy in this period?*
3. *How did the market economy and westward expansion entrench the institution of slavery?*
4. *How did westward expansion and the market revolution drive each other?*
5. *What role did immigrants play in the new market society?*
6. *How did changes in the law promote development in the economic system?*
7. *As it democratized American Christianity, the Second Great Awakening both took advantage of the market revolution and criticized its excesses. Explain.*
8. *How did the market revolution change women's work and family roles?*
9. *Give some examples of the rise of individualism in these years.*
10. *How did immigration and nativism address the question of who is an American?*

KEY TERMS

Go to INQUIZITIVE

To see what you know—and learn what you've missed—with personalized feedback along the way.

Visit the ***Give Me Liberty!* Student Site** for primary source documents and images, interactive maps, author videos featuring Eric Foner, and more.

CHAPTER 10

DEMOCRACY IN AMERICA

★

1815–1840

1811	Bank of the United States charter expires
1816	Second Bank of the United States established
1817	Inauguration of James Monroe
1819	Panic of 1819
	McCulloch v. Maryland
1820	Missouri Compromise
1823	Monroe Doctrine
1825	Inauguration of John Quincy Adams
1828	"Tariff of abominations"
1829	Inauguration of Andrew Jackson
1830	Indian Removal Act
1831	*Cherokee Nation v. Georgia*
1832	Nullification crisis
	Worcester v. Georgia
1833	Force Act
1835	Tocqueville's *Democracy in America*
1835–1842	Second Seminole War
1837	Inauguration of Martin Van Buren
1837–1843	Panic of 1837 and ensuing depression
1838–1839	Trail of Tears
1841	Inauguration of William Henry Harrison
	Dorr War

"Militia Training," an 1841 painting by the British-born artist James G. Clonney, depicts the Fourth of July celebration of an all-white militia company. Black dancers perform in the foreground while militia members socialize. A handful of women are also present.

FOCUS QUESTIONS

- *What were the social bases for the flourishing democracy of the early mid-nineteenth century?*
- *What efforts strengthened or hindered the economic integration of the nation?*
- *What were the major areas of conflict between nationalism and sectionalism?*
- *In what ways did Andrew Jackson embody the contradictions of democratic nationalism?*
- *How did the Bank War influence the economy and party competition?*

The inauguration of Andrew Jackson on March 4, 1829, made it clear that something had changed in American politics. The swearing-in of the president had previously been a small, dignified event. Jackson's inauguration attracted a crowd of some 20,000 people who poured into the White House after the ceremony, ruining furniture and breaking china and glassware in the crush. It was "the reign of King Mob," lamented Justice Joseph Story of the Supreme Court.

Jackson's career embodied the major developments of his era—the market revolution, the westward movement, the expansion of slavery, and the growth of democracy. He was a symbol of the self-made man. Unlike previous presidents, Jackson rose to prominence from a humble background, reflecting his era's democratic opportunities. Born in 1767 on the South Carolina frontier, he had been orphaned during the American Revolution. While still a youth, he served as a courier for patriotic forces during the War of Independence. His military campaigns against the British and Indians during the War of 1812 helped to consolidate American control over the Lower South, making possible the rise of the Cotton Kingdom. He himself acquired a large plantation in Tennessee. But more than anything else, to this generation of Americans Andrew Jackson symbolized one of the most crucial features of national life—the triumph of political democracy.

Americans pride themselves on being the world's oldest democracy. New Zealand, whose constitution of 1893 gave women and Maoris (the native population) the right to vote, may have a better claim. Europe, however, lagged far behind. Britain did not achieve universal male suffrage until the 1880s. France instituted it in 1793, abandoned it in 1799, reintroduced it in 1848, and abandoned it again a few years later. More to the point, perhaps, democracy became a central part of the definition of American nationality and the American idea of freedom.

THE TRIUMPH OF DEMOCRACY

Property and Democracy

The market revolution and territorial expansion were intimately connected with a third central element of American freedom—political democracy. The challenge to property qualifications for voting, begun during the American Revolution, reached its culmination in the early nineteenth century. Not a single state that entered the Union after the original thirteen required ownership of property to vote. In the older states, by 1860 all but one had ended property requirements for voting (though several continued to bar persons accepting poor relief, on the grounds that they lacked genuine independence). The personal independence necessary in the citizen now rested not on ownership of property but on ownership of one's self—a reflection of the era's individualism.

An anti-Jackson cartoon from 1832 portrays Andrew Jackson as an aspiring monarch, wielding the veto power while trampling on the Constitution.

The Dorr War

The lone exception to the trend toward democratization was Rhode Island, which required voters to own real estate valued at $134 or rent property for at least $7 per year. A center of factory production, Rhode Island had a steadily growing population of propertyless wage earners unable to vote. In October 1841, proponents of democratic reform organized a People's Convention, which drafted a new state constitution. It enfranchised all adult white men while eliminating entirely blacks (although in a subsequent referendum, blacks' right to vote was restored). When the reformers ratified their constitution in an extralegal referendum and proceeded to inaugurate Thomas Dorr, a prominent Rhode Island lawyer, as governor, President John Tyler dispatched federal troops to the state. The movement collapsed, and Dorr subsequently served nearly two years in prison for treason. **The Dorr War** demonstrated the passions aroused by the continuing exclusion of any group of white men from voting.

Tocqueville on Democracy

White male suffrage

By 1840, more than 90 percent of adult white men were eligible to vote. A flourishing democratic system had been consolidated. American politics was boisterous, highly partisan, and sometimes violent, and it engaged the energies of massive numbers of citizens. In a country that lacked more traditional bases of nationality—a powerful and menacing neighbor, historic ethnic, religious, or cultural unity—democratic political institutions came to define the nation's sense of its own identity.

Alexis de Tocqueville

Alexis de Tocqueville, the French writer who visited the United States in the early 1830s, returned home to produce ***Democracy in America***, a classic account of a society in the midst of a political transformation. Tocqueville had come to the United States to study prisons. But he soon realized that to understand America, he must understand democracy (which as a person of aristocratic background he rather disliked). His key insight was that democracy by this time meant far more than either the right to vote or a particular set of political institutions. It was a "habit of the heart," a culture that encouraged individual initiative, belief in equality, and an active public sphere populated by numerous voluntary

Democratic culture

Justice's Court in the Back Woods, an 1852 painting by Tompkins Harrison Matteson, depicts the expansion of the public sphere to include ordinary Americans. A court is in session in a local tavern. The justice of the peace, who presides, is a shoemaker who has set aside his tools but still wears his leather work apron. A lawyer appeals to the jury, composed of average (male) citizens. The case has to do with an assault. The plaintiff, his head bandaged, leans on the table at the right.

organizations that sought to improve society. Democracy, Tocqueville saw, had become an essential attribute of American freedom.

Popular sovereignty

As Tocqueville recognized, the idea that sovereignty belongs to the mass of ordinary citizens was a profound shift in political thought. The founders of the republic, who believed that government must rest on the consent of the governed, also sought to shield political authority from excessive influence by ordinary people (hence the Electoral College, Supreme Court, and other undemocratic features of the Constitution). Nonetheless, thanks to persistent pressure from those originally excluded from political participation, democracy—for white males—triumphed by the Age of Jackson.

The Information Revolution

The rise of the mass-circulation press

The market revolution and political democracy produced a large expansion of the public sphere and an explosion in printing sometimes called the "information revolution." The application of steam power to newspaper printing led to a great increase in output and the rise of the mass-circulation "penny press," priced at one cent per issue instead of the traditional six. Newspapers such as the *New York Sun* and *New York Herald* introduced a new style of journalism, appealing to a mass audience by emphasizing sensationalism, crime stories, and exposés of official misconduct. By 1840, according to one estimate, the total weekly circulation of newspapers in the United States, with a population of 17 million, exceeded that of Europe, with 233 million people.

Alternative journalism

The reduction in the cost of printing also made possible the appearance of "alternative" newspapers in the late 1820s and early 1830s, including

Freedom's Journal (the first black newspaper), *Philadelphia Mechanic's Advocate* and other labor publications, the abolitionist weekly *The Liberator*, and *Cherokee Phoenix*, the first Native American newspaper.

The Limits of Democracy

By the 1830s, the time of Andrew Jackson's presidency, the axiom that "the people" ruled had become a universally accepted part of American politics. Those who opposed this principle, wrote Tocqueville, "hide their heads." But the very centrality of democracy to the definition of both freedom and nationality made it all the more necessary to define the boundaries of the political nation. As older economic exclusions fell away, others survived and new ones were added.

"Universal suffrage"

The "principle of universal suffrage," declared the *United States Magazine and Democratic Review* in 1851, meant that "white males of age constituted the political nation." How could the word "universal" be reconciled with barring blacks and women from political participation? As democracy triumphed, the intellectual grounds for exclusion shifted from economic dependency to natural incapacity. Gender and racial differences were widely understood as part of a single, natural hierarchy of innate endowments. White males were considered inherently superior in character and abilities to non-whites and women. The debate over which people are and are not qualified to take part in American democracy has lasted well into the twenty-first century. Not until 1920 was the Constitution amended to require states to allow women to vote. The Voting Rights Act of 1965 swept away restrictions on black voting imposed by many southern states.

Democracy, gender, and race

A Racial Democracy

If the exclusion of women from political freedom continued a long-standing practice, the increasing identification of democracy and whiteness marked something of a departure. Blacks were increasingly considered a group apart. Racist imagery became the stock-in-trade of popular theatrical presentations like minstrel shows, in which white actors in blackface entertained the audience by portraying African-Americans as stupid, dishonest, and altogether ridiculous. With the exception of Herman Melville, who portrayed complex, sometimes heroic black characters in works like *Moby Dick* and *Benito Cereno* (the latter a fictionalized account of a shipboard slave rebellion), American authors either ignored blacks entirely or presented them as stereotypes—happy slaves prone to superstition or long-suffering but devout Christians. Meanwhile, the somewhat tentative thinking of the revolutionary era about the status of non-whites

Racist imagery

flowered into an elaborate ideology of racial superiority and inferiority, complete with "scientific" underpinnings. These developments affected the boundaries of the political nation.

Jim Crow, a piece of sheet music from 1829. Minstrel shows were a form of nineteenth-century entertainment in which white actors impersonated blacks. One of the most popular characters was Jim Crow, the happy, childlike plantation slave created by the performer Thomas D. Rice. Years later, "Jim Crow" would come to mean the laws and customs of southern segregation.

In the revolutionary era, only Virginia, South Carolina, and Georgia explicitly confined the vote to whites, although elsewhere, custom often made it difficult for free blacks to exercise the **franchise**. As late as 1800, no northern state barred blacks from voting. But every state that entered the Union after that year, with the single exception of Maine, limited the right to vote to white males. And, beginning with Kentucky in 1799 and Maryland two years later, several states that had allowed blacks to vote rescinded the privilege. By 1860, blacks could vote on the same basis as whites in only five New England states, which contained only 4 percent of the nation's free black population.

In effect, race had replaced class as the boundary between those American men who were entitled to enjoy political freedom and those who were not. Even as this focus on race limited America's political community as a whole, it helped to solidify a sense of national identity among the diverse groups of European origin. In a country where the right to vote had become central to the meaning of freedom, it is difficult to overstate the importance of the fact that white male immigrants could vote in some states almost from the moment they landed in America, whereas nearly all free blacks (and, of course, slaves), whose ancestors had lived in the country for centuries, could not vote at all.

NATIONALISM AND ITS DISCONTENTS

The American System

War of 1812 and American nationalism

The War of 1812, which the United States and Great Britain—the world's foremost military power—fought to a draw, inspired an outburst of nationalist pride. But the war also revealed how far the United States still was from being a truly integrated nation. With the Bank of the United States having gone out of existence when its charter expired in 1811, the country lacked a uniform currency and found it almost impossible to raise funds for the war effort. Given the primitive state of transportation, it proved very difficult to move men and goods around the country. One shipment of supplies from New England had taken seventy-five days to reach New Orleans. With the coming of peace, the manufacturing enterprises that sprang up while trade with Britain had been suspended faced intense competition from low-cost imported goods. A younger generation of Republicans, including Henry Clay and John C. Calhoun, who had led the call for war in 1812, believed these "infant industries" deserved national protection.

In his annual message (now known as the State of the Union address) to Congress in December 1815, President James Madison put forward a blueprint for government-promoted economic development that came to be known as the **American System**, a label coined by Henry Clay. The plan rested on three pillars: a new national bank, a tariff on imported manufactured goods to protect American industry, and federal financing of improved roads and canals. The last was particularly important to those worried about the dangers of disunity. "Let us bind the nation together, with a perfect system of roads and canals," John C. Calhoun implored Congress in 1815. "Let us conquer space."

An image from a broadside from the campaign of 1824, promoting the American System of government-sponsored economic development. The illustrations represent industry, commerce, and agriculture. The ship at the center is named the *John Quincy Adams*. Its flag, "No Colonial Subjection," suggests that without a balanced economy, the United States will remain economically dependent on Great Britain.

Congress enacted an internal improvements program drafted by Calhoun, only to be astonished when the president, on the eve of his retirement from office in March 1817, vetoed the bill. Since calling for its enactment, Madison had become convinced that allowing the national government to exercise powers not mentioned in the Constitution would prove dangerous to individual liberty and southern interests. The other two parts of his plan, however, became law. The **tariff of 1816** offered protection to goods that could be produced in the United States, especially cheap cotton textiles, while admitting tax-free those that could not be manufactured at home. Many southerners supported the tariff, believing that it would enable their region to develop a manufacturing base to rival New England's. And in 1816, a new Bank of the United States was created, with a twenty-year charter from Congress.

Bank of the United States

Banks and Money

The Second Bank of the United States soon became the focus of public resentment. Like its predecessor, it was a private, profit-making corporation that acted as the government's financial agent, issuing paper money, collecting taxes, and paying the government's debts. It was also charged with ensuring that paper money issued by local banks had real value. In the nineteenth century, paper money consisted of notes promising to pay the bearer on demand a specified amount of "specie" (gold or silver). Since banks often printed far more money than the specie in their vaults, the value of paper currency fluctuated wildly. The Bank of the United States was supposed to correct this problem by preventing the overissuance of money.

Regulating local banks

The Panic of 1819

Land boom

But instead of effectively regulating the currency and loans issued by local banks, the Bank of the United States participated in a speculative fever that swept the country after the end of the War of 1812. The resumption of trade with Europe created a huge overseas market for American cotton and grain. Coupled with the rapid expansion of settlement into the West, this stimulated demand for loans to purchase land, which local banks and branches of the Bank of the United States were only too happy to meet by printing more money. The land boom was especially acute in the South, where the Cotton Kingdom was expanding.

The economic bubble bursts

Early in 1819, as European demand for American farm products declined to normal levels, the economic bubble burst. The Bank of the United States, followed by state banks, began asking for payments from those to whom it had loaned money. Farmers and businessmen who could not repay declared bankruptcy, and unemployment rose in eastern cities.

The **Panic of 1819** lasted little more than a year, but it severely disrupted the political harmony of the previous years. To the consternation of creditors, many states, especially in the West, suspended the collection of debts. Kentucky went even further, establishing a state bank that flooded the state with paper money that creditors were required to accept in repayment of loans. This eased the burden on indebted farmers but injured those who had loaned them the money. Overall, the panic deepened many Americans' traditional distrust of banks. It undermined the reputation of the Second Bank of the United States, which was widely blamed for causing the panic. Several states retaliated against the national bank by taxing its local branches.

These tax laws produced another of John Marshall's landmark Supreme Court decisions, in the case of ***McCulloch v. Maryland*** (1819). Reasserting his broad interpretation of governmental powers, Marshall declared the Bank a legitimate exercise of congressional authority under the Constitution's clause that allowed Congress to pass "necessary and proper" laws. Marshall's interpretation of the Constitution directly contradicted the "strict construction" view that limited Congress to powers specifically granted in the Constitution.

The House of Representatives in 1822, in a painting by Samuel F. B. Morse (who also invented the telegraph). By this time, most adult white men could vote for members of the House, a far wider franchise than was known in Europe at the time.

The Missouri Controversy

In 1816, James Monroe handily defeated the Federalist candidate Rufus King, becoming the last of the Virginia presidents. By 1820,

THE MISSOURI COMPROMISE, 1820

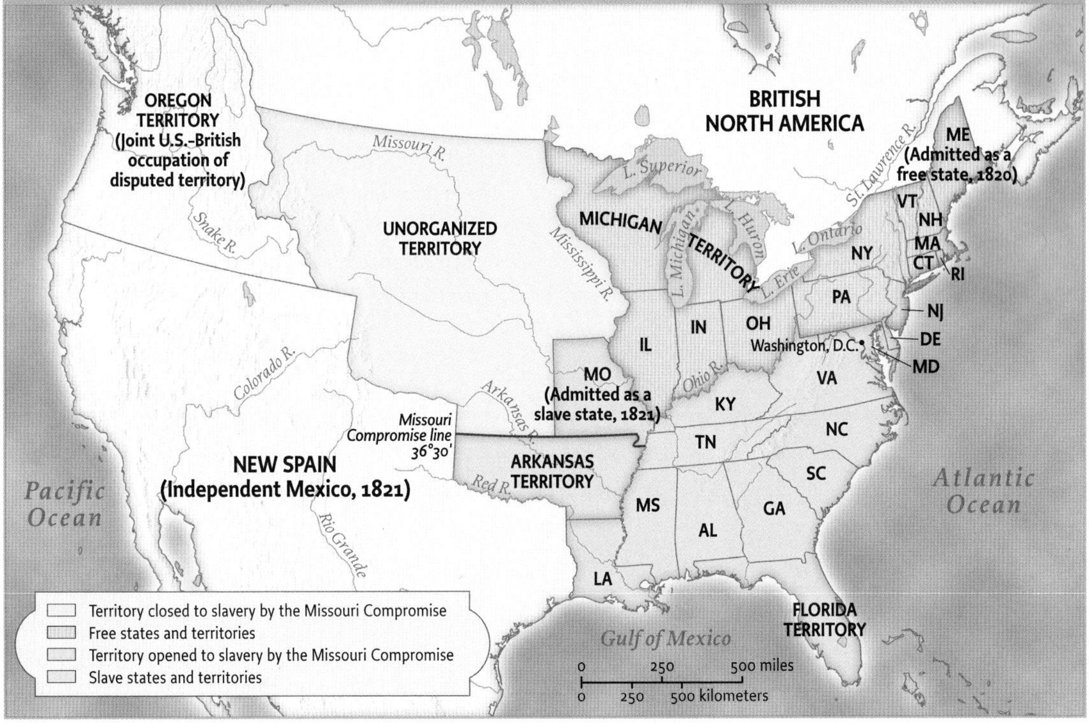

The Missouri Compromise temporarily settled the question of the expansion of slavery by dividing the Louisiana Purchase into free and slave areas.

the Federalists fielded electoral tickets in only two states, and Monroe carried the entire country. Monroe's two terms in office were years of one-party government, sometimes called the **Era of Good Feelings**. Plenty of bad feelings, however, surfaced during his presidency. In the absence of two-party competition, politics was organized along lines of competing sectional interests.

In 1819, Congress considered a request from Missouri, an area carved out of the Louisiana Purchase, to draft a constitution in preparation for admission to the Union as a state. Missouri's slave population already exceeded 10,000. James Tallmadge, a Republican congressman from New York, moved that the introduction of further slaves be prohibited and that children of those already in Missouri be freed at age twenty-five.

Tallmadge's proposal sparked two years of controversy, during which Republican unity shattered along sectional lines. His restriction passed the House, where most northern congressmen supported it over the objections of southern representatives. It died in the Senate, however. When Congress reconvened in 1820, Senator Jesse Thomas of Illinois proposed a compromise. Missouri would be authorized to draft a constitution without

Tallmadge's restriction. Maine, which prohibited slavery, would be admitted to the Union to maintain the sectional balance between free and slave states. And slavery would be prohibited in all remaining territory within the Louisiana Purchase north of latitude 36°30' (Missouri's southern boundary). Congress adopted Thomas's plan as the **Missouri Compromise**.

Westward expansion of slavery

The Missouri controversy raised for the first time what would prove to be a fatal issue—the westward expansion of slavery. The sectional division it revealed aroused widespread feelings of dismay. "This momentous question," wrote Jefferson, "like a fire bell in the night, awakened and filled me with terror. I considered it at once as the knell of the union." For the moment, however, the slavery issue faded once again from national debate.

NATION, SECTION, AND PARTY

The United States and the Latin American Wars of Independence

The new Latin American republics

Between 1810 and 1822, Spain's Latin American colonies rose in rebellion and established a series of independent nations, including Mexico, Venezuela, Ecuador, and Peru. By 1825, Spain's once vast American empire had been reduced to the islands of Cuba and Puerto Rico. The uprisings inspired a wave of sympathy in the United States. In 1822, the Monroe administration became the first government to extend diplomatic recognition to the new Latin American republics.

Parallels existed between the Spanish-American revolutions and the one that had given birth to the United States. In both cases, the crisis of empire was precipitated by programs launched by the imperial country aimed in large measure at making the colonies contribute more to its finances. As had happened in British North America, local elites demanded status and treatment equal to residents of the imperial power. The Spanish-American declarations of independence borrowed directly from that of the United States. The first, issued in 1811, declared that the "United Provinces" of Venezuela now enjoyed "among the sovereign nations of the earth the rank which the Supreme Being and nature has assigned us"—language strikingly similar to Jefferson's.

Latin American constitutions

In some ways, the new Latin American constitutions—adopted by seventeen different nations—were more democratic than that of the United States. Most sought to implement the transatlantic ideals of rights and freedom by creating a single national "people" out of the diverse populations that made up the Spanish empire. To do so, they extended the right to vote to Indians and free blacks. The Latin American wars of independence, in which black soldiers participated on both sides, also set in motion the gradual abolition of slavery. But the Latin American wars of independence lasted longer—sometimes more than a decade—and were more destructive than the one in the United States had been. As a result, it proved far more difficult for the new Latin American republics to achieve economic development than for the United States.

The Monroe Doctrine

John Quincy Adams

John Quincy Adams, who was serving as James Monroe's secretary of state, was devoted to consolidating the power of the national government at home and abroad. Adams feared that Spain would try to regain its Latin American colonies. In 1823, he drafted a section of the president's annual message to Congress that became known as the **Monroe Doctrine**. It expressed three principles. First, the United States would oppose any further efforts at colonization by European powers in the Americas. Second, the United States would abstain from involvement in the wars of Europe. Finally, Monroe warned European powers not to interfere with the newly independent states of Latin America.

America's diplomatic declaration of independence

The Monroe Doctrine is sometimes called America's diplomatic declaration of independence. For many decades, it remained a cornerstone of American foreign policy. Based on the assumption that the Old and New Worlds formed separate political and diplomatic systems, it claimed for the United States the role of dominant power in the Western Hemisphere.

The Election of 1824

Sectionalism and domestic politics

The Monroe Doctrine reflected a rising sense of American nationalism. But sectionalism seemed to rule domestic politics. As the election of 1824 approached, only Andrew Jackson could claim truly national support. Jackson's popularity rested not on any specific public policy—few voters knew his views—but on military victories over the British at the Battle of New Orleans, and over the Creek and Seminole Indians. Other candidates included John Quincy Adams, Secretary of the Treasury William H. Crawford of Georgia, and Henry Clay of Kentucky. Adams's support was concentrated in New England and, more generally, in the North, where Republican leaders insisted the time had come for the South to relinquish the presidency. Crawford represented the South's Old Republicans, who wanted the party to reaffirm the principles of states' rights and limited government. Clay was one of the era's most popular politicians, but his support in 1824 lay primarily in the West.

A split election

Jackson received 153,544 votes and carried states in all the regions outside of New England. But with four candidates in the field, none

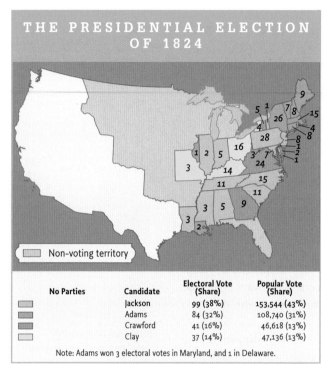

THE PRESIDENTIAL ELECTION OF 1824

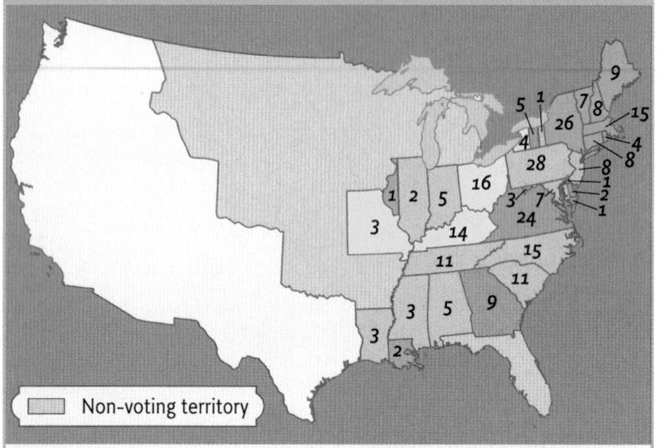

No Parties	Candidate	Electoral Vote (Share)	Popular Vote (Share)
	Jackson	99 (38%)	153,544 (43%)
	Adams	84 (32%)	108,740 (31%)
	Crawford	41 (16%)	46,618 (13%)
	Clay	37 (14%)	47,136 (13%)

Note: Adams won 3 electoral votes in Maryland, and 1 in Delaware.

received a majority of the electoral votes. As required by the Constitution, Clay, who finished fourth, was eliminated, and the choice among the other three fell to the House of Representatives. Sincerely believing Adams to be the most qualified candidate and the one most likely to promote the American System, and probably calculating that the election of Jackson, a westerner, would impede his own presidential ambitions, Clay gave his support to Adams, helping to elect him. He soon became secretary of state in Adams's cabinet. The charge that he had made a "corrupt bargain"—bartering critical votes in the presidential contest for a public office—clung to Clay for the rest of his career, making it all but impossible for him to reach the White House. The election of 1824 laid the groundwork for a new system of political parties. Supporters of Jackson and Crawford would soon unite in the Democratic Party. The alliance of Clay and Adams became the basis for the Whig Party of the 1830s.

John Quincy Adams in an 1843 daguerreotype.

The Nationalism of John Quincy Adams

John Quincy Adams enjoyed one of the most distinguished pre-presidential careers of any American president. The son of John Adams, he had witnessed the Battle of Bunker Hill at age eight and at fourteen had worked as private secretary and French interpreter for an American envoy in Europe. He had gone on to serve as ambassador to Prussia, the Netherlands, Britain, and Russia, and as a senator from Massachusetts.

Adams was not an engaging figure. He described himself as "a man of cold, austere, and foreboding manners." But he had a clear vision of national greatness. At home, he strongly supported the American System of government-sponsored economic development. Abroad, he hoped to encourage American commerce throughout the world and, as illustrated by his authorship of the Monroe Doctrine, enhance American influence in the Western Hemisphere. An ardent expansionist, Adams was certain that the United States would eventually, and peacefully, absorb Canada, Cuba, and at least part of Mexico.

"Liberty Is Power"

Adams held a view of federal power far more expansive than did most of his contemporaries. In his first message to Congress, in December 1825, he set forth a comprehensive program for an activist national state. "The spirit of improvement is abroad in the land," Adams announced, and the federal government should be its patron. He called for legislation promoting agriculture, commerce, manufacturing, and "the mechanical and elegant arts." His plans included the establishment of a national university, an astronomical observatory, and a naval academy. At a time when many Americans felt that governmental authority posed the greatest threat to freedom, Adams astonished many listeners with the bold statement "Liberty is power."

Adams's nationalism

Adams's proposals alarmed all believers in strict construction of the Constitution. His administration spent more on internal improvements than those of his five predecessors combined, and it enacted a steep increase in tariff rates in 1828. But the rest of Adams's ambitious ideas received little support in Congress.

Martin Van Buren and the Democratic Party

Adams's program handed his political rivals a powerful weapon. With individual liberty, states' rights, and limited government as their rallying cries, Jackson's supporters began to organize for the election of 1828 almost as soon as Adams assumed office. Martin Van Buren, a senator from New York, supervised the task. The clash between Adams and Van Buren demonstrated how democracy was changing the nature of American politics. Adams typified the old politics—he was the son of a president and, like Jefferson and Madison, a man of sterling intellectual accomplishments. Van Buren represented the new political era. The son of a tavern keeper, he was a talented party manager, not a person of great vision or intellect.

The new politics

But Van Buren did have a compelling idea. Rather than being dangerous and divisive, as the founding generation had believed, political parties, he insisted, were necessary and desirable. Party competition provided a check on those in power and offered voters a real choice in elections. And by bringing together political leaders from different regions in support of common candidates and principles, national parties could counteract the sectionalism that had reared its head during the 1820s. National political parties, Van Buren realized, formed a bond of unity in a divided nation. He set out to reconstruct the Jeffersonian political alliance between "the planters of the South and the plain republicans [the farmers and urban workers] of the North."

Political parties as desirable

VOICES OF FREEDOM

From The Memorial of the Non-Freeholders of the City of Richmond (1829)

By the 1820s, as political democracy expanded, only North Carolina, Rhode Island, and Virginia still required property qualifications for voting for white men. When Virginia held a constitutional convention in 1829–1830, "non-freeholders" of Richmond—men who did not possess enough property—petitioned for the right to vote. The major slaveholders who dominated Virginia politics resisted their demand; not until 1850 did the state eliminate the property qualification.

Your memorialists . . . belong to that class of citizens, who, not having the good fortune to possess a certain portion of land, are, for that cause only, debarred from the enjoyment of the right of suffrage. . . . Comprising a very large part, probably a majority of male citizens of mature age, they have been passed by, like aliens or slaves, as if . . . unworthy of a voice, in the measures involving their future political destiny. . . .

The existing regulation of the suffrage . . . creates an odious distinction between members of the same community; robs of all share, in the enactment of the laws, a large portion of the citizens, . . . and vests in a favored class, not in consideration of their public services, but of their private possessions, the highest of all privileges. . . . [We] cannot discern in the possession of land any evidence of peculiar merit, or superior title [to] moral or intellectual endowments. . . . Such possession no more proves him who has it, wiser or better, than it proves him taller or stronger, than him who has it not. . . .

Let us concede that the right of suffrage is a social right; that it must of necessity be regulated by society. . . . For obvious reasons, by almost universal consent, women and children, aliens and slaves, are excluded. . . . But the exclusion of these classes for reasons peculiarly applicable to them, is no argument for excluding others. . . .

They alone deserve to be called free, or have a guarantee for their rights, who participate in the formation of their political institutions, and in control of those who make and administer the law.

From Appeal of Forty Thousand Citizens Threatened with Disfranchisement (1838)

In many states, the expansion of political democracy for white men went hand in hand with the elimination of democratic participation for blacks. In 1837, a constitutional convention in Pennsylvania stripped black men of the right to vote. A large gathering in Philadelphia issued a protest to "fellow citizens" of Pennsylvania.

Fellow Citizens:—We appeal to you from the decision of the "Reform Convention," which has stripped us of a right peaceably enjoyed during forty-seven years under the Constitution of this commonwealth. We honor Pennsylvania and her noble institutions too much to part with our birthright, as her free citizens, without a struggle. To all her citizens the right of suffrage is valuable in proportion as she is free; but surely there are none who can so ill afford to spare it as ourselves. . . .

When a distinct class of the community, already sufficiently the objects of prejudice, are wholly, and for ever, disfranchised and excluded, to the remotest posterity, from the possibility of a voice in regard to the laws under which they are to live—it is the same thing as if their abode were transferred to the dominions of the Russian Autocrat, or of the Grand Turk. They have lost their check upon oppression, their wherewith to buy friends, their panoply of manhood; in short, they are thrown upon the mercy of a despotic majority. . . .

It was said in the Convention, that this government belongs to the Whites. We have already shown this to be false, as to the past. Those who established our present government designed it equally for all. It is for you to decide whether it shall be confined to the European complexion in future. Why should you exclude us from a fair participation in the benefits of the republic? . . . We put it to the conscience of every Pennsylvanian, whether there is, or ever has been, in the commonwealth, either a political party or religious sect which has less deserved than ourselves to be thus disfranchised. . . . If we are bad citizens let them apply the proper remedies. . . . Fair protection is all that we aspire to.

QUESTIONS

1. *What "obvious reasons" exclude women, children, noncitizens, and slaves from the right to vote?*
2. *How do the Philadelphia memorialists link their claims to the legacy of the American Revolution?*
3. *How similar are the definitions of political freedom in the two documents?*

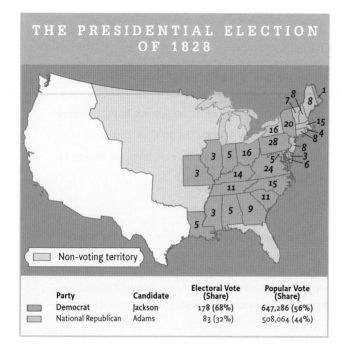

THE PRESIDENTIAL ELECTION OF 1828

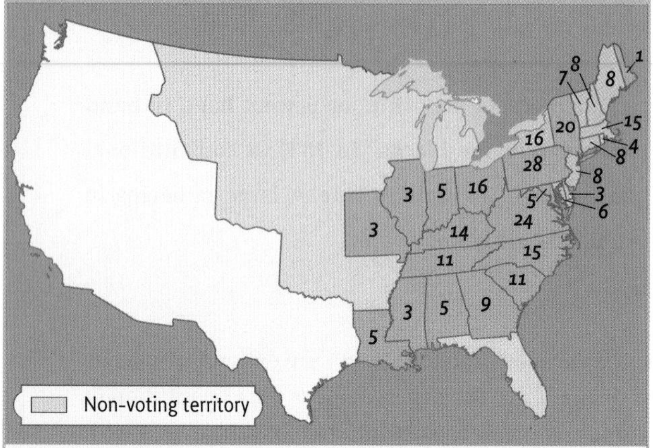

	Party	Candidate	Electoral Vote (Share)	Popular Vote (Share)
■	Democrat	Jackson	178 (68%)	647,286 (56%)
■	National Republican	Adams	83 (32%)	508,064 (44%)

The Election of 1828

By 1828, Van Buren had established the political apparatus of the Democratic Party, complete with local and state party units overseen by a national committee and a network of local newspapers devoted to the party and to the election of Andrew Jackson. Apart from a general commitment to limited government, Jackson's supporters made few campaign promises, relying on their candidate's popularity and the workings of party machinery to get out the vote. The 1828 election campaign was scurrilous. Jackson's supporters praised their candidate's frontier manliness and ridiculed Adams's intellectual attainments. ("Vote for Andrew Jackson who can fight, not John Quincy Adams who can write," declared one campaign slogan.) Jackson's opponents condemned him as a murderer for having executed army deserters and killing men in duels. They questioned the morality of his wife, Rachel, because she had married Jackson before her divorce from her first husband had become final.

Nearly 57 percent of the eligible electorate cast ballots, more than double the percentage four years earlier. Jackson won a resounding victory, carrying the entire South and West, along with Pennsylvania. His election was the first to demonstrate how the advent of universal white male voting, organized by national political parties, had transformed American politics. For better or worse, the United States had entered the Age of Jackson.

"The Old Democrat," a painting by Edward Hicks, illustrates the association of Andrew Jackson with nationalism and democracy.

THE AGE OF JACKSON

Andrew Jackson was a man of many contradictions. Although he had little formal education, Jackson was capable of genuine eloquence in his public statements. A self-proclaimed champion of the common man, he held a vision of democracy that excluded any role for Indians, whom he believed should be pushed west of the Mississippi River, and African-Americans, who should remain as slaves or be freed and sent abroad. A strong nationalist, Jackson nonetheless believed that the states, not Washington, D.C., should be the focal point of governmental activity.

The Party System

By the time of Jackson's presidency, politics had become more than a series of political contests—it was a spectacle, a form of mass entertainment, a part of Americans' daily lives. Every year witnessed elections to some office—local, state, or national—and millions took part in the parades and rallies organized by the parties. Politicians were popular heroes with mass followings and popular nicknames. Jackson was Old Hickory, Clay Harry of the West, and Van Buren the Little Magician (or, to his critics, the Sly Fox). Thousands of Americans willingly attended lengthy political orations and debates.

Politics and public life

Party machines, headed by professional politicians, reached into every neighborhood, especially in cities. They provided benefits like jobs to constituents and ensured that voters went to the polls on election day. Government posts, Jackson declared, should be open to the people, not reserved for a privileged class of permanent bureaucrats. He introduced the principle of rotation in office (called the **spoils system** by opponents) into national government, making loyalty to the party the main qualification for jobs like postmaster and customs official.

Professional politicians

Large national conventions where state leaders gathered to hammer out a platform now chose national candidates. Newspapers played a greater and greater role in politics. Every significant town, it seemed, had its Democratic and Whig papers whose job was not so much to report the news as to present the party's position on issues of the day. Jackson's Kitchen Cabinet—an informal group of advisers who helped to write his speeches and supervise communication between the White House and local party officials—mostly consisted of newspaper editors.

Role of newspapers

Democrats and Whigs

There was more to party politics, however, than spectacle and organization. Jacksonian politics revolved around issues spawned by the market revolution and the continuing tension between national and sectional loyalties.

Democrats on the issues

Democrats tended to be alarmed by the widening gap between social classes. They warned that "nonproducers"—bankers, merchants, and speculators—were seeking to use connections with government to enhance their wealth to the disadvantage of the "producing classes" of farmers, artisans, and laborers. They believed the government should adopt a hands-off attitude toward the economy and not award special favors to entrenched economic interests. This would enable ordinary Americans to test their abilities in the fair competition of the self-regulating market. The Democratic Party attracted aspiring entrepreneurs who resented government aid to established businessmen, as well as large numbers of farmers and city workingmen suspicious of new corporate enterprises. Poorer farming regions isolated from markets, like the lower Northwest and the southern backcountry, tended to vote Democratic.

Whigs on the issues

Whigs united behind the American System, believing that via a protective tariff, a national bank, and aid to internal improvements, the federal government could guide economic development. They were strongest in the Northeast, the most rapidly modernizing region of the country. Most established businessmen and bankers supported their program of government-promoted economic growth, as did farmers in regions near rivers, canals, and the Great Lakes, who benefited from economic changes or hoped to do so. The counties of upstate New York along the Erie Canal, for example, became a Whig stronghold, whereas more isolated rural communities tended to vote Democratic. Many slaveholders supported the Democrats, believing states' rights to be slavery's first line of defense. But like well-to-do merchants and industrialists in the North, the largest southern planters generally voted Whig.

Public and Private Freedom

The party battles of the Jacksonian era reflected the clash between "public" and "private" definitions of American freedom and their relationship to governmental power, a persistent tension in the nation's history. For Democrats, liberty was a set of private rights best secured by local governments and endangered by powerful national authority. "The limitation of power, in every branch of our government," wrote a Democratic newspaper in 1842, "is the only safeguard of liberty." During Jackson's presidency, Democrats reduced expenditures, lowered the tariff, killed the national bank, and refused pleas for federal aid to internal improvements. By 1835, Jackson even managed to pay off the national debt. As a result, states replaced the federal government as the country's main economic actors, planning systems of canals and roads and chartering banks and other corporations.

The Democrats: power a threat to liberty

Democrats, moreover, considered individual morality a private matter, not a public concern. They opposed attempts to impose a unified moral vision on society, such as "temperance" legislation, which restricted or outlawed the production and sale of liquor, and laws prohibiting various kinds of entertainment on Sundays. "In this country," declared the New York *Journal of Commerce* in 1848, "liberty is understood to be the *absence* of government from private affairs."

The Whigs: power allied with liberty

Whigs, for their part, insisted that liberty and power reinforced each other. An activist national government could enhance the realm of freedom. The government, Whigs believed, should create the conditions for balanced and regulated economic development, thereby promoting a prosperity in which all classes and regions would share.

Government and private life

Whigs, moreover, rejected the premise that the government must not interfere in private life. To function as free—that is, self-directed and self-disciplined—moral agents, individuals required certain character traits, which government could help to instill. Many evangelical Protestants supported the Whigs, convinced that via public education, the building of schools and asylums, temperance legislation, and the like, democratic governments could inculcate the "principles of morality." And during the Jacksonian era, popularly elected local authorities enacted numerous laws, ordinances, and regulations that tried to shape public morals by banning prostitution and the consumption of alcohol, and regulating other kinds of personal behavior.

Shaping public morals

South Carolina and Nullification

Andrew Jackson, it has been said, left office with many more principles than he came in with. Elected as a military hero backed by an efficient party machinery, he was soon forced to define his stance on public issues. Despite his commitment to states' rights, Jackson's first term was dominated by a battle to uphold the supremacy of federal over state law. The tariff of 1828, which raised taxes on imported manufactured goods made of wool as well as on raw materials such as iron, had aroused considerable opposition in the South, nowhere more than in South Carolina, where it was called the **tariff of abominations**. The state's leaders no longer believed it possible or desirable to compete with the North in industrial development. Insisting that the tariff on imported manufactured goods raised the prices paid by southern consumers to benefit the North, the legislature threatened to "nullify" it—that is, declare it null and void within their state.

The south and the "tariff of abominations"

The state with the largest proportion of slaves in its population (55 percent in 1830), South Carolina was controlled by a tightly knit group of large planters. They maintained their grip on power by a state constitution that gave plantation counties far greater representation in the legislature than their population warranted, as well as through high property qualifications for officeholders. Behind their economic complaints against the tariff lay the conviction that the federal government must be weakened lest it one day take action against slavery.

Calhoun's Political Theory

John C. Calhoun, who evolved from a nationalist into the most prominent spokesman for state sovereignty and the right of nullification, in an 1845 portrait by George P. A. Healy.

John C. Calhoun soon emerged as the leading theorist of nullification. As the South began to fall behind the rest of the country in population, Calhoun had evolved from the nationalist of 1812 into a powerful defender of southern sectionalism. Having been elected vice president in 1828, Calhoun at first remained behind the scenes, secretly drafting the ***Exposition and Protest*** in which the South Carolina legislature justified nullification. The national government, Calhoun insisted, had been created by an agreement, or compact, among sovereign states, each of which retained the right to prevent the enforcement within its borders of acts of Congress that exceeded the powers specifically spelled out in the Constitution.

Almost from the beginning of Jackson's first term, Calhoun's influence in the administration waned, while Secretary of State Martin Van Buren emerged as the president's closest adviser. One incident that helped set Jackson against Calhoun occurred a few weeks after the inauguration. Led by Calhoun's wife, Floride, Washington society women ostracized Peggy Eaton, the wife of Jackson's secretary of war, because she was the daughter of a Washington tavern keeper and, allegedly, a woman of "easy virtue." Jackson identified the criticism of Peggy Eaton with the abuse his own wife had suffered during the campaign of 1828.

Webster-Hayne debate

Far weightier matters soon divided Jackson and Calhoun. Debate over nullification raged in Washington. In a memorable exchange in the Senate in January 1830 that came to be known as the **Webster-Hayne debate**, Daniel Webster, a senator from Massachusetts, responded to South Carolina senator Robert Y. Hayne, a disciple of Calhoun. The people, not the states, declared Webster, created the Constitution, making the federal government sovereign. He called nullification illegal, unconstitutional, and treasonous. Webster's ending was widely hailed throughout the country—"Liberty *and* Union, now and forever, one and inseparable." A few weeks later, at a White House dinner, Jackson delivered a toast while fixing his gaze on Calhoun: "Our Federal Union—it must be preserved." Calhoun's reply came immediately: "The Union—next to our liberty most dear." By 1831, Calhoun had publicly emerged as the leading theorist of states' rights.

The Nullification Crisis

Nullification was not a purely sectional issue. South Carolina stood alone during the **nullification crisis**, and several southern states passed resolutions condemning its action. Nonetheless, the elaboration of the compact theory of the Constitution gave the South a well-developed political philosophy to which it would turn when sectional conflict became more intense.

Jackson's stance

To Jackson, nullification amounted to nothing less than disunion. He dismissed Calhoun's constitutional arguments out of hand: "Can anyone of common sense believe the absurdity, that a faction of any state, or a state, has a right to secede and destroy this union, and the liberty of the country with it?" The issue came to a head in 1832, when a new tariff was enacted. Despite a reduction in rates, South Carolina declared the tax on imported goods null and void in the state after the following February. In response, Jackson persuaded Congress to pass a Force Act authorizing him to use the army and navy to collect customs duties. To avert a confrontation, Henry Clay, with Calhoun's assistance, engineered the passage of a new tariff, in 1833, further reducing duties. South Carolina then rescinded the ordinance of nullification, although it proceeded to "nullify" the **Force Act**. Calhoun abandoned the Democratic Party for the Whigs, where, with Clay and Webster, he became part of a formidable trio of political leaders (even though the three agreed on virtually nothing except hostility toward Jackson).

South Carolina and the tariff of 1832

Indian Removal

The nullification crisis underscored Jackson's commitment to the sovereignty of the nation. His exclusion of Indians from the era's assertive democratic nationalism led to the final act in the centuries-long conflict between white Americans and Indians east of the Mississippi River. In the slave states, the onward march of cotton cultivation placed enormous pressure on remaining Indian holdings. One of the early laws of Jackson's administration, the **Indian Removal Act** of 1830, provided funds for uprooting the so-called Five Civilized Tribes—the Cherokee, Chickasaw, Choctaw, Creek, and Seminole—with a population of around 60,000 living in North Carolina, Georgia, Florida, Alabama, and Mississippi.

Indian Removal Act of 1830

Shift in Indian policy

The law marked a repudiation of the Jeffersonian idea that "civilized" Indians could be assimilated into the American population. These tribes had made great efforts to become everything republican citizens should be. The Cherokee had taken the lead, establishing schools, adopting written laws and a constitution modeled on that of the United States, and becoming successful farmers, many of whom owned slaves. But in his messages to Congress, Jackson repeatedly referred to them as "savages" and supported Georgia's effort to seize Cherokee land and nullify the tribe's laws.

In 1832, the "headmen and warriors of the Creek nation" sent a memorial to Congress that dwelled on the meaning of freedom and what they considered oppression by Alabama's lawmakers. "We never have been

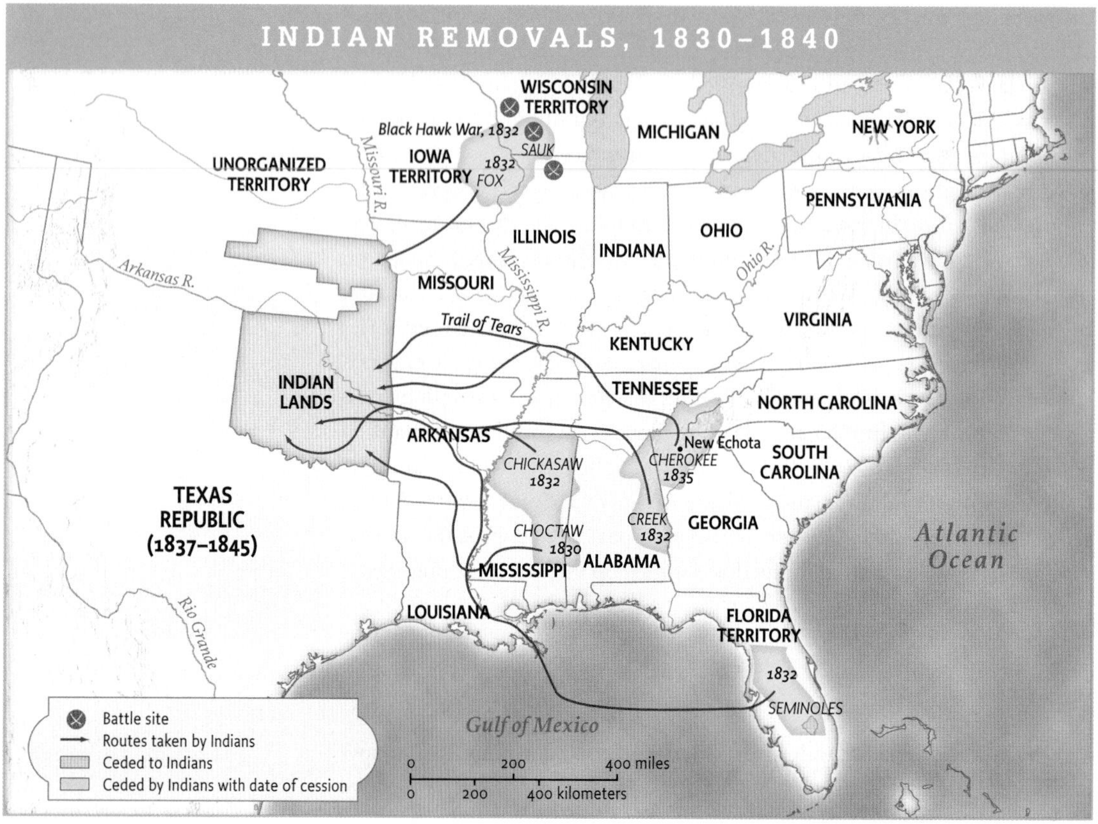

The removal of the so-called Five Civilized Tribes from the Southeast all but ended the Indian presence east of the Mississippi River.

slaves," they proclaimed, "we have been born free. As freemen we have assisted in fighting the battles of our white brethren." Yet now their people were being "subjected to the penalties of forfeiture" of their land. The Creeks were claiming a place in the nation's life, but unlike their white contemporaries, identification with their own "nation" came before identity as Americans. And freedom meant maintaining their cultural independence, which, in turn, required keeping possession of ancestral lands.

In good American fashion, Cherokee leaders went to court to protect their rights, guaranteed in treaties with the federal government. Their appeals forced the Supreme Court to clarify the unique status of American Indians.

The Supreme Court and the Indians

"Right of occupancy"

In a crucial case involving Indians in 1823, *Johnson v. M'Intosh*, the Court had proclaimed that Indians were not in fact owners of their land but merely had a "right of occupancy." Chief Justice John Marshall declared that from the early colonial era, Indians had lived as nomads and hunters, not farmers. Entirely inaccurate as history, the decision struck a serious blow against Indian efforts to retain their lands. In *Cherokee Nation v. Georgia* (1831), Marshall described Indians as "wards" of the federal government. They deserved paternal regard and protection, but they lacked the standing as citizens that would allow the Supreme Court to enforce their rights. The justices could not, therefore, block Georgia's effort to extend its jurisdiction over the tribe.

A lithograph from 1836 depicts Sequoia, with the alphabet of the Cherokee language that he developed. Because of their written language and constitution, the Cherokee were considered by many white Americans to be a "civilized tribe."

Marshall, however, believed strongly in the supremacy of the federal government over the states. In 1832, in ***Worcester v. Georgia***, the Court seemed to change its mind, holding that Indian nations were a distinct people with the right to maintain a separate political identity. They must be dealt with by the federal government, not the states, and Georgia's actions violated the Cherokees' treaties with Washington. Jackson, however, refused to recognize the validity of the *Worcester* ruling. "John Marshall has made his decision," he supposedly declared, "now let him enforce it."

With legal appeals exhausted, one faction of the tribe agreed to cede their lands, but the majority, led by John Ross, who had been elected "principal chief" under the Cherokee constitution, adopted a policy of passive resistance. Federal soldiers forcibly removed them during the presidency of Jackson's successor, Martin Van Buren. The army herded 18,000 Cherokee men, women, and children into stockades and then forced them to move west. At least one-quarter perished during the winter of 1838–1839 on the **Trail of Tears**, as the removal route from Georgia to present-day Oklahoma came to be called. (In the Cherokee language, it literally meant "the trail on which we cried.")

During the 1830s, most of the other southern tribes bowed to the inevitable and departed peacefully. But with the assistance of escaped slaves, the Seminoles of sparsely settled Florida resisted. In the Second Seminole War, which lasted from 1835 to 1842 (the first had preceded American acquisition of Florida in 1819), some 1,500 American soldiers and the same number of Seminoles were killed, and perhaps 3,000 Indians and 500 blacks were forced to move to the West. A small number of Seminoles managed to remain in Florida, a tiny remnant of the once sizable Indian population east of the Mississippi River.

John Mix Stanley painted Native Americans engaged in a buffalo hunt on the western prairies in 1845.

Removal of the Indians powerfully reinforced the racial definition of American nationhood and freedom. At the time of independence, Indians had been a familiar presence in many parts of the United States. But by 1840, in the eyes of most whites east of the Mississippi River, they were simply a curiosity, a relic of an earlier period of American history. Although Indians still dominated

The Last of the Race, by Tompkins Harrison Matteson, depicts a Native American family looking out at the Pacific Ocean, having been pushed westward by the inexorable tide of white settlement. Matteson, like Stanley, saw himself as recording a vanishing way of life.

the trans-Mississippi West, as American settlement pushed relentlessly westward it was clear that their days of freedom there also were numbered.

THE BANK WAR AND AFTER

Biddle's Bank

The central political struggle of the Age of Jackson was the president's war on the Bank of the United States. The Bank symbolized the hopes and fears inspired by the market revolution. The expansion of banking helped to finance the nation's economic development. But many Americans, including Jackson, distrusted bankers as "nonproducers" who contributed nothing to the nation's wealth but profited from the labor of others. The tendency of banks to overissue paper money, whose deterioration in value reduced the real income of wage earners, reinforced this conviction.

Distrust of banks

Heading the Bank was Nicholas Biddle of Pennsylvania, who during the 1820s had effectively used the institution's power to curb the overissuing of money by local banks and to create a stable currency throughout the nation. A snobbish, aristocratic Philadelphian, Biddle was as strong-willed as Jackson and as unwilling to back down in a fight. In 1832, he told a congressional committee that his Bank had the ability to "destroy" any state bank. He hastened to add that he had never "injured" any of them. But Democrats wondered whether any

Nicholas Biddle

The Downfall of Mother Bank, a Democratic cartoon celebrating the destruction of the Second Bank of the United States. President Andrew Jackson topples the building by brandishing his order removing federal funds from the Bank. Led by Nicholas Biddle, with the head of a demon, the Bank's corrupt supporters flee, among them Henry Clay, Daniel Webster, and newspaper editors allegedly paid by the institution.

institution, public or private, ought to possess such power. Many called it the Monster Bank, an illegitimate union of political authority and entrenched economic privilege. The issue of the Bank's future came to a head in 1832. Although the institution's charter would not expire until 1836, Biddle's allies persuaded Congress to approve a bill extending it for another twenty years. Jackson saw the tactic as a form of blackmail—if he did not sign the bill, the Bank would use its considerable resources to oppose his reelection.

Jackson's veto of the bank bill

Jackson's veto message is perhaps the central document of his presidency. In a democratic government, Jackson insisted, it was unacceptable for Congress to create a source of concentrated power and economic privilege unaccountable to the people. "It is to be regretted," he declared, "that the rich and powerful too often bend the acts of government to their selfish purposes." Exclusive privileges like the Bank's charter widened the gap between the wealthy and "the humble members of society—the farmers, mechanics, and laborers." Jackson presented himself as the defender of these "humble" Americans.

Enhancing the power of the presidency

The **Bank War** reflected how Jackson enhanced the power of the presidency during his eight years in office, proclaiming himself the symbolic representative of all the people. He was the first president to use the veto power as a major weapon and to appeal directly to the public for political support, over the head of Congress. Whigs denounced him for usurping the power of the legislature. But Jackson's effective appeal to democratic popular sentiments helped him win a sweeping reelection victory in 1832 over the Whig candidate, Henry Clay. His victory ensured the death of the Bank of the United States.

Pet Banks, the Economy, and the Panic of 1837

What, however, would take the Bank's place? Two very different groups applauded Jackson's veto—state bankers who wished to free themselves from Biddle's regulations and issue more paper currency (called **soft money**), **and hard money** advocates who opposed all banks and believed that gold and silver formed the only reliable currency. Not content to wait for the charter of the Bank of the United States to expire in 1836, Jackson authorized the removal of federal funds from its vaults and their deposit in select local banks. Not surprisingly, political and personal connections often determined the choice of these **pet banks**. Two secretaries of the Treasury refused to transfer federal money to the pet banks, since the law creating the Bank had specified that government funds could not be removed except for a good cause as communicated to Congress. Jackson finally appointed Attorney General Roger B. Taney, a loyal Maryland Democrat, to the Treasury post, and he carried out the order. When John Marshall died in 1835, Jackson rewarded Taney by appointing him chief justice.

Jackson's pet banks

Consequences of the removal of federal deposits

Without government deposits, the Bank of the United States lost its ability to regulate the activities of state banks. The value of bank notes in circulation rose from $10 million in 1833 to $149 million in 1837. As prices rose dramatically, "real wages"—the actual value of workers' pay—declined. Numerous labor unions emerged, which attempted to protect the earnings of urban workers. Meanwhile, speculators hastened to cash in on rising land prices. Using paper money, they bought up huge blocks of public land, which they resold to farmers or to eastern purchasers of lots in entirely nonexistent western towns.

The Specie Circular

Inevitably, the speculative boom collapsed. The government sold 20 million acres of federal land in 1836, ten times the amount sold in 1830, nearly all of it paid for in paper money, often of questionable value. In July 1836, the Jackson administration issued the Specie Circular, declaring that henceforth it would only accept gold and silver as payment for public land. At the same time, the Bank of England, increasingly suspicious about the value of American bank notes, demanded that American merchants pay their creditors in London in gold or silver. Then, an economic downturn in Britain dampened demand for American cotton, the country's major export.

Economic collapse

Taken together, these events triggered an economic collapse in the United States, the **Panic of 1837**, followed by a depression that lasted to 1843. Businesses throughout the country failed, and many farmers, unable to meet mortgage payments because of declining income, lost their land. Tens of thousands of urban workers saw their jobs disappear. The fledgling labor movement collapsed as strikes became impossible, given the surplus of unemployed labor.

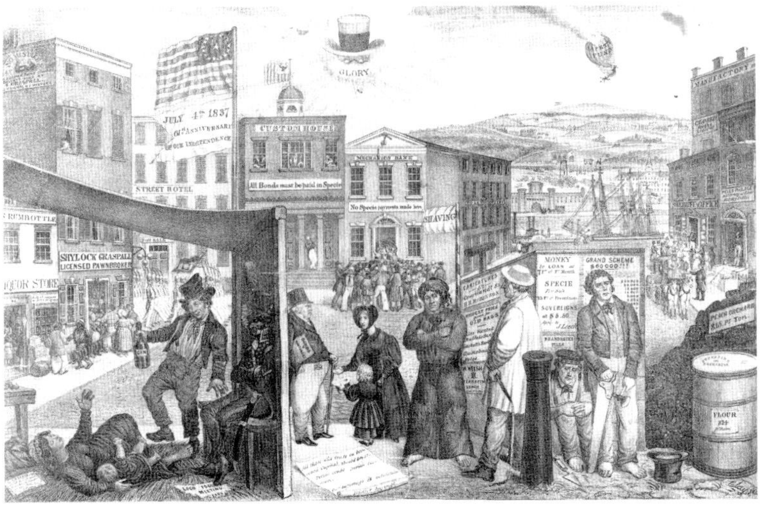

The Times, an 1837 engraving that blames Andrew Jackson's policies for the economic depression. The Custom House is idle, while next door a bank is mobbed by worried depositors. Beneath Jackson's hat, spectacles, and clay pipe (with the ironic word "glory"), images of hardship abound.

Van Buren in Office

The president forced to deal with the depression was Martin Van Buren, who had been elected in 1836 over three regional candidates put forward by the Whigs. Under Van Buren, the hard-money, anti-bank wing of the Democratic Party came to power. In 1837, the administration announced its intention to remove federal funds from the pet banks and hold them in the Treasury Department in Washington, under the control of government officials. Not until 1840 did Congress approve the new policy, known as the Independent Treasury, which completely separated the federal government from the nation's banking system. It would be repealed in 1841 when the Whigs returned to power, but it was reinstated under President James K. Polk in 1846.

The Independent Treasury

The Election of 1840

Despite his reputation as a political magician, Van Buren found that without Jackson's personal popularity he could not hold the Democratic coalition together. In 1840, he also discovered that his Whig opponents had mastered the political techniques he had helped to pioneer. Confronting an unprecedented opportunity for victory because of the continuing economic depression, the Whigs abandoned their most prominent leader, Henry Clay, and nominated William Henry Harrison. Harrison's main claim to fame was military success against the British and Indians during the War of 1812.

The party nominated Harrison without a platform. In a flood of publications, banners, parades, and mass meetings, they promoted him as

A political cartoon from the 1840 presidential campaign shows public opinion as the "almighty lever" of politics in a democracy. Under the gaze of the American eagle, "Loco-Foco" Democrats slide into an abyss, while the people are poised to lift William Henry Harrison, the Whig candidate, to victory.

the "log cabin" candidate, the champion of the common man. This tactic proved enormously effective, even though it bore little relationship to the actual life of the wealthy Harrison. His running mate was John Tyler, a states'-rights Democrat from Virginia who had joined the Whigs after the nullification crisis and did not follow Calhoun back to the Democrats. On almost every issue of political significance, Tyler held views totally opposed to those of other Whigs. But party leaders hoped he could expand their base in the South.

By 1840, the mass democratic politics of the Age of Jackson had absorbed the logic of the marketplace. Selling candidates and their images was as important as the positions for which they stood. With two highly organized parties competing throughout the country, voter turnout soared to 80 percent of those eligible. Harrison won a sweeping victory. "We have taught them how to conquer us," lamented a Democratic newspaper.

Whig success proved short-lived. Immediately on assuming office, Harrison contracted pneumonia. He died a month later, and John Tyler succeeded him. When the Whig majority in Congress tried to enact the American System into law, Tyler vetoed nearly every measure, including a new national bank and higher tariff. Most of the cabinet resigned, and his party repudiated him. Tyler's four years in office were nearly devoid of accomplishment. If the campaign that resulted in the election of Harrison demonstrated how a flourishing system of democratic politics had come into existence, Tyler's lack of success showed that political parties had become central to American government. Without a party behind him, a president could not govern. But a storm was now gathering that would test the stability of American democracy and the statesmanship of its political leaders and of the party system itself.

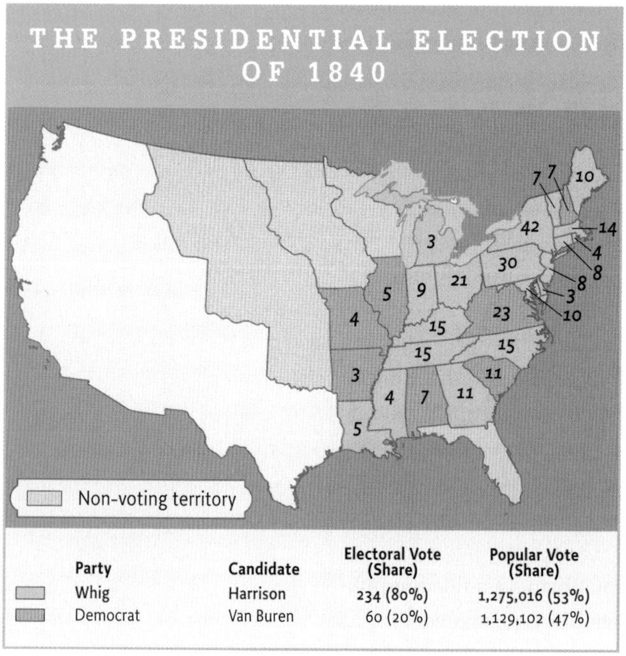

CHAPTER REVIEW AND ONLINE RESOURCES

REVIEW QUESTIONS

1. *What global changes prompted the Monroe Doctrine? What were its key provisions? How does it show America's growing international presence?*
2. *How did Andrew Jackson represent the major developments of the era: westward movement, the market revolution, and the expansion of democracy for some alongside the limits on it for others?*
3. *How did the expansion of white male democracy run counter to the ideals of the founders, who believed government should be sheltered from excessive influence by ordinary people?*
4. *What were the components of the American System, and how were they designed to promote the national economy under the guidance of the federal government?*
5. *How did the Missouri Compromise and the nullification crisis demonstrate increasing sectional competition and disagreements over slavery?*
6. *According to Martin Van Buren, why were political parties a desirable element of public life? What did he do to build the party system?*
7. *What rights did the Creek nation seek to confirm in its 1832 memorial to Congress?*
8. *What were the major economic, humanitarian, political, and social arguments for and against Indian Removal?*
9. *What were the key issues that divided the Democratic and Whig Parties? Where did each party stand on those issues?*
10. *Explain the causes and effects of the Panic of 1837.*

KEY TERMS

the Dorr War (p. 281)
Democracy in America (p. 281)
franchise (p. 284)
American System (p. 285)
tariff of 1816 (p. 285)
Panic of 1819 (p. 286)
McCulloch v. Maryland (p. 286)
Era of Good Feelings (p. 287)
Missouri Compromise (p. 288)
Monroe Doctrine (p. 289)
spoils system (p. 295)
tariff of abominations (p. 297)
Exposition and Protest (p. 298)
Webster-Hayne debate (p. 298)
nullification crisis (p. 298)
Force Act (p. 299)
Indian Removal Act (p. 299)
Worcester v. Georgia (p. 301)
Trail of Tears (p. 301)
Bank War (p. 303)
soft money and hard money (p. 304)
pet banks (p. 304)
Panic of 1837 (p. 304)

Go to INQUIZITIVE

To see what you know—and learn what you've missed—with personalized feedback along the way.

Visit the ***Give Me Liberty!* Student Site** for primary source documents and images, interactive maps, author videos featuring Eric Foner, and more.

1791–1804	Haitian Revolution
1800	Gabriel's Rebellion
1811	Slave revolt in Louisiana
1822	Denmark Vesey's slave conspiracy
1830s	States legislate against teaching slaves to read or write
1831	William Lloyd Garrison's *The Liberator* debuts
	Nat Turner's Rebellion
1831–1832	Slave revolt in Jamaica
1832	Virginia laws tighten the slave system
1833	Great Britain abolishes slavery within its empire
1838	Frederick Douglass escapes slavery
1839	Slaves take control of the *Amistad*
1841	Slave uprising on the *Creole*
1849	Harriet Tubman escapes slavery
1855	Trial of Celia

CHAPTER 11

THE PECULIAR INSTITUTION

★

This image of the Portuguese slave ship *Diligente* was painted by an officer on a British naval vessel in 1838. By this time, the *Diligente*'s voyage—with 600 slaves on board—was illegal. The international agreement outlawing the Atlantic slave trade was largely enforced by British ships.

In an age of "self-made" men, no American rose more dramatically from humble origins to national and international distinction than Frederick Douglass. Born into slavery in 1818, he became a major figure in the crusade for abolition, the drama of emancipation, and the effort during Reconstruction to give meaning to black freedom.

Douglass was the son of a slave mother and an unidentified white man, possibly his owner. As a youth in Maryland, he gazed out at the ships in Chesapeake Bay, seeing them as "freedom's swift-winged angels." In violation of Maryland law, Douglass learned to read and write, initially with the assistance of his owner's wife and then, after her husband forbade her to continue, with the help of local white children. "From that moment," he later wrote, he understood that knowledge was "the pathway from slavery to freedom." In 1838, having borrowed the free papers of a black sailor, he escaped to the North.

Frederick Douglass went on to become the most influential African-American of the nineteenth century and the nation's preeminent advocate of racial equality. He also published a widely read autobiography that offered an eloquent condemnation of slavery and racism. Indeed, his own accomplishments testified to the incorrectness of prevailing ideas about blacks' inborn inferiority. Douglass was also active in other reform movements, including the campaign for women's rights. Douglass argued that in their desire for freedom, the slaves were truer to the nation's underlying principles than the white Americans who annually celebrated the Fourth of July while allowing the continued existence of slavery.

FOCUS QUESTIONS

- *How did slavery shape social and economic relations in the Old South?*
- *What were the legal and material constraints on slaves' lives and work?*
- *How did a distinct slave culture emerge in the Old South?*
- *What were the major forms of resistance to slavery?*

THE OLD SOUTH

Mason-Dixon Line

When Frederick Douglass was born, slavery was already an old institution in America. Two centuries had passed since the first twenty Africans were landed in Virginia from a Dutch ship. After abolition in the North, slavery had become **the "peculiar institution"** of the South—that is, an institution unique to southern society. The Mason-Dixon Line, drawn by two surveyors in the eighteenth century to settle a boundary dispute between Maryland and Pennsylvania, eventually became the dividing line between slavery and freedom.

The expansion of slavery

Despite the hope of some of the founders that slavery might die out, in fact the institution survived the crisis of the American Revolution and rapidly expanded westward. On the eve of the Civil War, the slave population had risen to nearly 4 million, its high rate of natural increase more than making up for the prohibition in 1808 of further slave imports from Africa. In the South as a whole, slaves made up one-third of the total population, and in the cotton-producing states of the Lower South, around half. By the 1850s, slavery had crossed the Mississippi River and was expanding rapidly in Arkansas, Louisiana, and eastern Texas.

Cotton Is King

Rise of cotton

In the nineteenth century, cotton replaced sugar as the world's major crop produced by slave labor. And although slavery survived in Brazil and the Spanish and French Caribbean, its abolition in the British empire in 1833 made the United States indisputably the center of New World slavery.

Because the early industrial revolution centered on factories using cotton as the raw material to manufacture cloth, cotton became by far the most important commodity in international trade. And three-fourths of the world's cotton supply came from the southern United States. Textile manufacturers in places as far flung as Massachusetts, Lancashire in Great Britain, Normandy in France, and the suburbs of Moscow depended on a regular supply of American cotton.

Cotton sales earned the money from abroad that allowed the United States to pay for imported manufactured goods. On the eve of the Civil War, cotton accounted for well over half of the total value of American exports. In 1860, the economic investment represented by the slave population exceeded the value of the nation's factories, railroads, and banks combined.

Economic value of slavery

The Second Middle Passage

As noted in Chapter 9, to replace the slave trade from Africa, which had been prohibited by Congress in 1808, a massive trade in slaves developed within the United States. More than 2 million slaves were sold between 1820 and 1860, resulting in what came to be known as the **Second Middle Passage**. The main commercial districts of southern cities contained the offices of slave traders, complete with signs reading "Negro Sales" or "Negroes Bought Here." Auctions of slaves took place at public slave markets, as in New Orleans, or at courthouses. Southern newspapers carried advertisements

Texan Farm in Montgomery County, a drawing from 1843, depicts a cotton farm on the Texas frontier. The owner's house is at the center, flanked by slave cabins and, on the far right, a cotton gin and press. At this point, two years before its annexation by the United States, Texas was an independent republic.

In this painting from 1842, slaves—men, women, and children—accompany an oxcart carrying the week's cotton crop to New Orleans.

for slave sales, southern banks financed slave trading, southern ships and railroads carried slaves from buyers to sellers, and southern states and municipalities earned revenue by taxing the sale of slaves.

Slave trade in the South

Slavery and the Nation

Slavery shaped the lives of all Americans, white as well as black. It helped to determine where they lived, how they worked, and under what conditions they could exercise their freedoms of speech, assembly, and the press.

Northern merchants and manufacturers participated in the slave economy and shared in its profits. Money earned in the cotton trade helped to finance industrial development and internal improvements in the North. Northern ships carried cotton to New York and Europe, northern bankers financed cotton plantations, northern companies insured slave property, and northern factories turned cotton into cloth. New York City's rise to commercial prominence depended as much on the establishment of shipping lines that gathered the South's cotton and transported it to Europe as on the Erie Canal.

TABLE 11.1 Growth of the Slave Population

YEAR	SLAVE POPULATION
1790	697,624
1800	893,602
1810	1,191,362
1820	1,538,022
1830	2,009,043
1840	2,487,355
1850	3,204,313
1860	3,953,760

The Southern Economy

There was no single South before the Civil War. In the eight slave states of the Upper South, slaves and slaveowners made up a smaller percentage of the total population than in the seven Lower South states, which stretched from South Carolina west to Texas. The Upper South had major centers of industry in Baltimore, Richmond, and St. Louis, and its economy was more diversified than that of the Lower South, which was heavily dependent on cotton.

SLAVE POPULATION, 1860

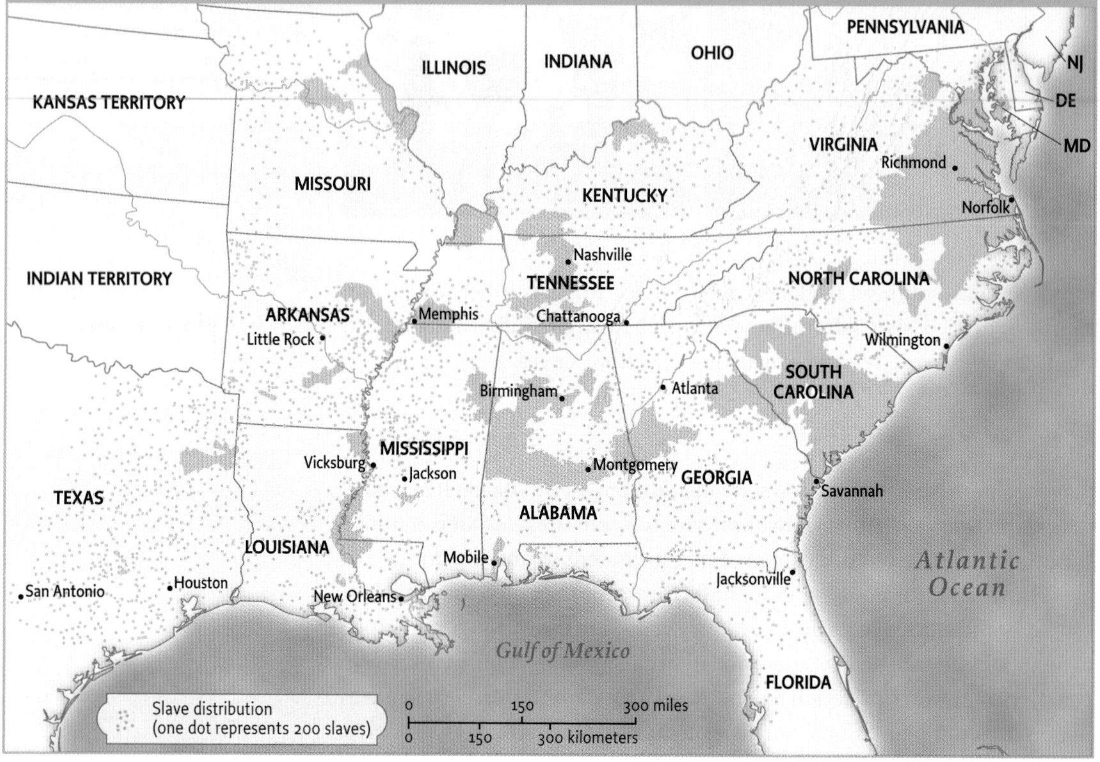

Rather than being evenly distributed throughout the South, the slave population was concentrated in areas with the most fertile soil and easiest access to national and international markets. By 1860, a significant percentage of the slave population had been transported from the Atlantic coast to the Lower South via the internal slave trade.

Not surprisingly, during the secession crisis of 1860–1861, the Lower South states were the first to leave the Union.

Nonetheless, slavery led the South down a very different path of economic development than the North's, limiting the growth of industry, discouraging immigrants from entering the region, and inhibiting technological progress. The South did not share in the urban growth experienced by the rest of the country. In the Cotton Kingdom, the only city of significant size was New Orleans. With a population of 168,000 in 1860, New Orleans ranked as the nation's sixth-largest city. As the gathering point for cotton grown along the Mississippi River and sugar from the plantations of southeastern Louisiana, it was the world's leading exporter of slave-grown crops.

In 1860, the South produced less than 10 percent of the nation's manufactured goods. Many northerners viewed slavery as an obstacle to American economic progress. But as New Orleans showed, slavery and economic growth could go hand in hand. In general, the southern economy was hardly stagnant, and slavery proved very profitable for most owners. The profits produced by slavery for the South and the nation as a whole

This 1860 view of New Orleans captures the size and scale of the cotton trade in the South's largest city. More than 3,500 steamboats arrived in New Orleans in 1860.

formed a powerful obstacle to abolition. Senator James Henry Hammond of South Carolina declared, "No power on earth dares to make war upon it. **Cotton is king**."

Plain Folk of the Old South

The foundation of the Old South's economy, slavery powerfully shaped race relations, politics, religion, and the law. Its influence was pervasive: "Nothing escaped," writes one historian, "nothing and no one." This was true despite the fact that the majority of white southerners—three out of four white families—owned no slaves. Many southern farmers lived outside the plantation belt in hilly areas unsuitable for cotton production. Using family labor, they raised livestock and grew food for their own use, purchasing relatively few goods at local stores. Unlike northern farmers, therefore, they did not provide a market for manufactured goods. This was one of the main reasons that the South did not develop an industrial base.

Some poorer whites resented the power and privileges of the great planters. Politicians such as Andrew Johnson of Tennessee and Joseph Brown of Georgia rose to power as self-proclaimed spokesmen of the common man against the "slavocracy." But most poor whites made their peace with the planters in whose hands economic and social power was concentrated. Racism, kinship ties, common participation in a democratic political culture, and regional loyalty in the face

An upcountry family, dressed in homespun, in Cedar Mountain, Virginia. Many white families in the pre–Civil War South were largely isolated from the market economy. This photograph was taken in 1862 but reflects the prewar way of life.

Planters and "plain folk"

of outside criticism all served to cement bonds between planters and the South's "plain folk." Like other white southerners, most small farmers believed their economic and personal freedom rested on slavery.

The Planter Class

Even among slaveholders, the planter was far from typical. In 1850, a majority of slaveholding families owned five or fewer slaves. Fewer than 40,000 families possessed the twenty or more slaves that qualified them as planters. Fewer than 2,000 families owned a hundred slaves or more. Nonetheless, the planter's values and aspirations dominated southern life. The plantation, wrote Frederick Douglass, was "a little nation by itself, with its own language, its own rules, regulations, and customs." These rules and customs set the tone for southern society.

Slave ownership and status

Ownership of slaves provided the route to wealth, status, and influence. Planters not only held the majority of slaves but also controlled the most fertile land, enjoyed the highest incomes, and dominated state and local offices and the leadership of both political parties. Slavery, of course, was a profit-making system, and slaveowners kept close watch on world prices for their products, invested in enterprises such as railroads and canals, and carefully supervised their plantations. Their wives—the "plantation mistresses" idealized in southern lore for femininity, beauty, and dependence on men—were hardly idle. They cared for sick slaves, directed the domestic servants, and supervised the entire plantation when their husbands were away. Of course, owners' sexual exploitation of slave women produced deep resentment among their wives, who sometimes took it out on the slaves themselves.

On the cotton frontier, many planters lived in crude log homes. But in the older slave states, and as settled society developed in the Lower South, they constructed elegant mansions adorned with white columns in the Greek Revival style of architecture.

Louisa, a slave woman, with her charge in an 1858 photograph. The slave had been purchased at age twenty-two at a slave auction in New Orleans to serve as a nursemaid. Because of a death in the white family, the child was her legal owner.

The Paternalist Ethos

The slave plantation was deeply embedded in the world market, and planters sought to accumulate land, slaves, and profits. However, planters' values glorified not the competitive capitalist marketplace but a hierarchical, agrarian society in which slaveholding gentlemen took personal responsibility for the physical and moral well-being of their dependents—women, children, and slaves.

This outlook, known as **paternalism** (from the Latin word for "father"), had been a feature of American slavery even in the eighteenth century. But it became more ingrained after the closing of the African slave trade in 1808, which narrowed the cultural gap between master and slave. Unlike the absentee planters of the West Indies, many of whom resided in Great Britain, southern slaveholders lived on their plantations and thus had year-round contact with their slaves.

The paternalist outlook both masked and justified the brutal reality of slavery. It enabled slaveowners to think of themselves as kind, responsible masters even as they bought and sold their human property—a practice at odds with the claim that slaves formed part of the master's "family."

A slave dealer's place of business in Alexandria, Virginia, then part of the District of Columbia, the nation's capital. The buying and selling of slaves was a regularized part of the southern economy, and such businesses were a common sight in every southern city. This building contained a "slave pen" that typically contained over 300 slaves being kept before their sale.

The Proslavery Argument

In the thirty years before the outbreak of the Civil War, even as northern criticism of the "peculiar institution" began to deepen, proslavery thought came to dominate southern public life. Even those who had no direct stake in slavery shared with planters a deep commitment to white supremacy. Indeed, racism—the belief that blacks were innately inferior to whites and unsuited for life in any condition other than slavery—formed one pillar of the **proslavery argument**. Most slaveholders also found legitimation for slavery in biblical passages such as the injunction that servants should obey their masters. Others argued that slavery was essential to human progress. Without slavery, they believed, planters would be unable to cultivate the arts, sciences, and other civilized pursuits.

White southerners thought slavery was "modern," in tune with the times. Despite British emancipation, other forms of unfree labor were spreading in the world. The products of slave labor, especially cotton, were essential to the nineteenth-century economy. Southern planters were hardly parochial. They took a deep interest in international affairs. They felt a community of interest with owners in Cuba and Brazil and used their power in the federal government to insist that American foreign policy promote the interests of slavery throughout the hemisphere.

Still other defenders of slavery insisted that the institution guaranteed equality for whites by preventing the growth of a class doomed to a life of unskilled labor. Like

TABLE 11.2 Slaveholding, 1850 (in Round Numbers)

NUMBER OF SLAVES OWNED	SLAVEHOLDERS
1	68,000
2–4	105,000
5–9	80,000
10–19	55,000
20–49	30,000
50–99	6,000
100–199	1,500
200+	250

SIZE OF SLAVEHOLDINGS, 1860

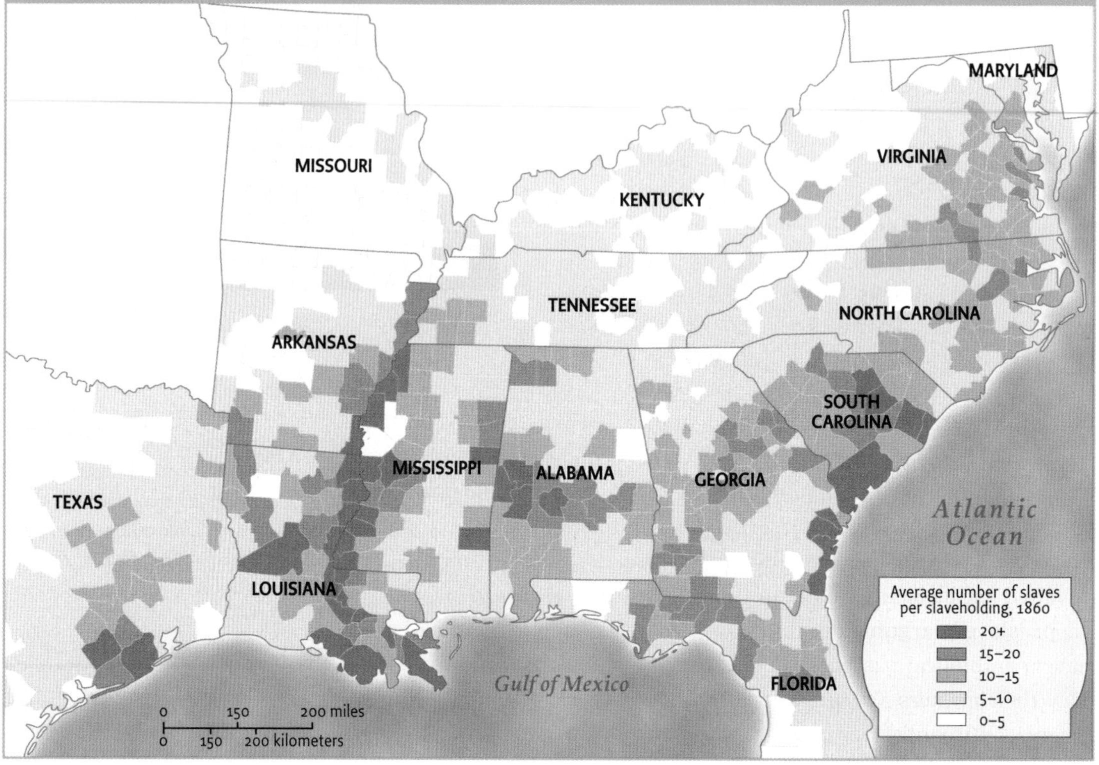

Most southern slaveholders owned fewer than five slaves. The largest plantations were concentrated in coastal South Carolina and along the Mississippi River.

northerners, they claimed to be committed to the ideal of freedom. Slavery for blacks, they declared, was the surest guarantee of "perfect equality" among whites, liberating them from the "low, menial" jobs such as factory labor and domestic service performed by wage laborers in the North.

Abolition in the Americas

American slaveowners were well aware of developments in slave systems elsewhere in the Western Hemisphere. They observed carefully the results of the wave of emancipations that swept the hemisphere in the first four decades of the century. In these years, slavery was abolished in most of Spanish America and in the British empire.

The experience of emancipation in other parts of the hemisphere strongly affected debates over slavery in the United States. Southern slave-owners judged the vitality of the Caribbean economy by how much sugar and other crops it produced for the world market. Since many former slaves preferred to grow food for their own families, defenders of slavery in the United States charged that British emancipation had been a failure.

Abolitionists disagreed, pointing to the rising standard of living of freed slaves, the spread of education among them, and other improvements in their lives. In a hemispheric perspective, slavery was a declining institution. At mid-century, significant New World slave systems remained only in Cuba, Puerto Rico, Brazil—and the United States.

A plate manufactured in England to celebrate emancipation in the British empire. After a brief period of apprenticeship, all slaves were freed on August 1, 1838. At the center, a family of former slaves celebrates outside their cabin.

Slavery and Liberty

Many white southerners declared themselves the true heirs of the American Revolution. They claimed to be inspired by "the same spirit of freedom and independence" that motivated the founding generation. Beginning in the 1830s, however, proslavery writers began to question the ideals of liberty, equality, and democracy so widely shared elsewhere in the nation. South Carolina, where a majority of white families owned slaves, became the home of an aggressive defense of slavery that repudiated the idea that freedom and equality were universal entitlements. The language of the Declaration of Independence—that all men were created equal and entitled to liberty—was "the most false and dangerous of all political errors," insisted John C. Calhoun.

The Virginia writer George Fitzhugh took the argument to its most radical conclusion. Far from being the natural condition of mankind, Fitzhugh wrote, "universal liberty" was the exception, an experiment carried on "for a little while" in "a corner of Europe" and the northern United States. Taking the world and its history as a whole, slavery, "without regard to race and color," was "the general, . . . normal, natural" basis of "civilized society."

Spreading defense of slavery

After 1830, southern writers, newspaper editors, politicians, and clergymen increasingly devoted themselves to spreading the defense of slavery. The majority of white southerners came to believe that freedom for whites rested on the power to command the labor of blacks. In the words of the Richmond *Enquirer*, "freedom is not possible without slavery."

LIFE UNDER SLAVERY

Slaves and the Law

Slaves as property

For slaves, the "peculiar institution" meant a life of incessant toil, brutal punishment, and the constant fear that their families would be destroyed by sale. Under the law, slaves were property. Although they had a few legal rights (all states made it illegal to kill a slave except in self-defense, and slaves accused of serious crimes were entitled to their day in court, before all-white judges and juries), these were haphazardly enforced. Slaves could be sold or leased by their owners at will and lacked any voice in the governments that ruled over them. They could not testify in court against a white person, sign contracts or acquire property, own firearms, hold meetings unless a white person was present, or leave the farm or plantation without the permission of their owner. By the 1830s, it was against the law to teach a slave to read or write.

Legal restrictions on slaves

Not all of these laws were rigorously enforced. Some members of slaveholding families taught slave children to read (although rather few, since well over 90 percent of the slave population was illiterate in 1860). It was quite common throughout the South for slaves to gather without white supervision at crossroads villages and country stores on Sunday, their day of rest.

The slave, declared a Louisiana law, "owes to his master . . . a respect without bounds, and an absolute obedience." No aspect of slaves' lives, from the choice of marriage partners to how they spent their free time, was immune from his interference. The entire system of southern justice, from the state militia and courts down to armed patrols in each locality, was designed to enforce the master's control over the persons and labor of his slaves.

In one famous case, a Missouri court considered the case of Celia, a slave who had killed her master in 1855 while resisting a sexual assault. State law deemed "any woman" in such circumstances to be acting in self-defense. But Celia, the court ruled, was not a "woman" in the eyes of the law. She was a slave, whose master had complete power over her person. The court sentenced her to death. However, since Celia was pregnant, her execution was postponed until the child was born, so as not to deprive her owner's heirs of their property rights.

A poster advertising the raffle of a horse and a slave, treated as equivalents, at a Missouri store.

Conditions of Slave Life

Compared with their counterparts in the West Indies and Brazil, American slaves enjoyed better diets, lower rates of infant mortality, and longer life expectancies. Many factors contributed to improving material conditions. Most of the South lies outside the geographical area where tropical diseases like malaria, yellow fever, and typhoid fever flourish, so health among all southerners was better than in the Caribbean. And with the price of slaves rising dramatically after the closing of the African slave trade, it made economic sense for owners to become concerned with the health and living conditions of their human property.

Slaves outside their cabin on a South Carolina plantation, probably photographed in the 1850s. They had brought their furniture outdoors to be included in the photo.

Although slaves in the United States enjoyed better material lives than elsewhere in the Western Hemisphere, they had far less access to freedom. In Brazil, it was not uncommon for an owner to free slaves as a form of celebration—on the occasion of a wedding in the owner's family, for example—or to allow slaves to purchase their freedom. In the nineteenth-century South, however, more and more states set limits on voluntary manumission, requiring that such acts be approved by the legislature. Few slave societies in history have so systematically closed off all avenues to freedom as the Old South.

Free Blacks in the Old South

The existence of slavery helped to define the status of those blacks who did enjoy freedom. On the eve of the Civil War, nearly half a million free blacks lived in the United States, a majority in the South. Most were the descendants of slaves freed by southern owners in the aftermath of the Revolution or by the gradual emancipation laws of the northern states. Their numbers were supplemented by slaves who had been voluntarily liberated by their masters, who had been allowed to purchase their freedom, or who succeeded in running away.

Restrictions on free blacks

When followed by "black" or "Negro," the word "free" took on an entirely new meaning. Free blacks in the South could legally own property and marry and, of course, could not be bought and sold. But many regulations restricting the lives of slaves also applied to them. Free blacks had no voice in selecting public officials. They were not allowed to testify in court against whites or serve on juries, and they had to carry at all times a certificate of freedom. Poor free blacks who required public assistance could be bound out to labor alongside slaves. By the 1850s, most southern states prohibited free blacks from entering their territory. A few states even moved to expel them altogether, offering the choice of enslavement or departure.

In New Orleans and Charleston, on the other hand, relatively prosperous free black communities developed, mostly composed of mixed-race descendants of unions between white men and slave women. Many free blacks in these cities acquired an education and worked as skilled craftsmen such as tailors, carpenters, and mechanics. They established churches for their communities and schools for their children. In the Upper South, where the large majority of southern free blacks lived, they generally worked for wages as farm laborers. Overall, in the words of Willis A. Hodges, a member of a free Virginia family that helped runaways reach the North, free blacks and slaves were "one man of sorrow."

Slave Labor

A system of labor

First and foremost, slavery was a system of labor; "from sunup to first dark," with only brief interruptions for meals, work occupied most of the slaves' time. Large plantations were diversified communities, where slaves performed all kinds of work. The 125 slaves on one plantation, for instance, included a butler, two waitresses, a nurse, a dairymaid, a gardener, ten carpenters, and two shoemakers. Other plantations counted among their slaves engineers, blacksmiths, and weavers, as well as domestic workers from cooks to coachmen.

The large majority of slaves—75 percent of women and nearly 90 percent of men, according to one study—worked in the fields. The precise organization of their labor varied according to the crop and the size of the holding. On small farms, the owner often toiled side by side with his slaves. The largest concentration of slaves, however, lived and worked on plantations in the Cotton Belt, where men, women, and children labored in gangs, often under the direction of an overseer and perhaps a slave "driver" who assisted him. Among slaves, overseers had a reputation for meting out brutal treatment.

In this undated photograph, men, women, and children pick cotton under the watchful eye of an overseer. Unlike sugarcane, cotton does not grow to a great height, allowing an overseer to supervise a large number of slaves.

The 150,000 slaves who worked in the sugar fields of southern Louisiana also labored in large gangs. Conditions here were among the harshest in the South, for the late fall harvest season required round-the-clock labor to cut and process the sugarcane before it spoiled. On the rice plantations of South Carolina and Georgia, the system of task labor, which had originated in the colonial era, prevailed. With few whites willing to venture into the malaria-infested swamps, slaves were assigned daily tasks and allowed to set their own pace of work. Once a slave's task had been completed, he or she could spend the rest of the day hunting, fishing, or cultivating garden crops.

Slavery in the Cities

Businessmen, merchants, lawyers, and civil servants owned slaves, and by 1860 some

200,000 worked in industry, especially in the ironworks and tobacco factories of the Upper South. Most city slaves were servants, cooks, and other domestic laborers. But owners sometimes allowed those with craft skills to "hire their own time." This meant that they could make work arrangements individually with employers, with most of the wages going to the slave's owner. Many urban slaves even lived on their own. But slaveholders increasingly became convinced that, as one wrote, the growing independence of skilled urban slaves "exerts a most injurious influence upon the relation of master and servant." For this reason, many owners in the 1850s sold city slaves to the countryside and sought replacements among skilled white labor.

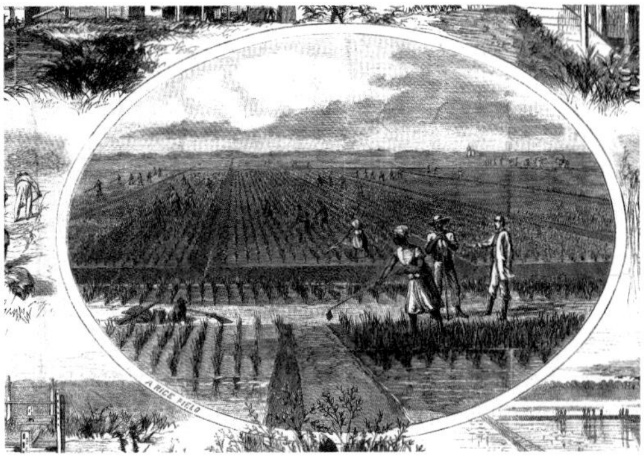

Detail from *Rice Culture on the Ogeechee*. Published in January 1867 in *Harper's Weekly*, this engraving illustrates work on a rice plantation divided into a checkerboard pattern by irrigation ditches. Although a white person is present, most slaves in the rice fields worked under the task system, without daily oversight.

Maintaining Order

Slaveowners employed a variety of means in their attempts to maintain order and discipline among their human property and persuade them to labor productively. At base, the system rested on force. Masters had almost complete discretion in inflicting punishment, and rare was the slave who went through his or her life without experiencing a whipping. Any infraction of plantation rules, no matter how minor, could be punished by the lash. One Georgia planter recorded in his journal that he had whipped a slave "for not bringing over milk for my coffee, being compelled to take it without."

Subtler means of control supplemented violence. Owners encouraged and exploited divisions among the slaves, especially between field hands and house servants. They created systems of incentives that rewarded good work with time off or even money payments. Probably the most powerful weapon wielded by slaveowners was the threat of sale, which separated slaves from their immediate families and from the communities that, despite overwhelming odds, African-Americans created on plantations throughout the South.

A Public Whipping of Slaves in Lexington, Missouri, in 1856, an illustration from the abolitionist publication *The Suppressed Book about Slavery*. Whipping was a common form of punishment for slaves.

SLAVE CULTURE

Slaves never abandoned their desire for freedom or their determination to resist total white control over their lives. In the face of grim realities, they succeeded in forging a

MAJOR CROPS OF THE SOUTH, 1860

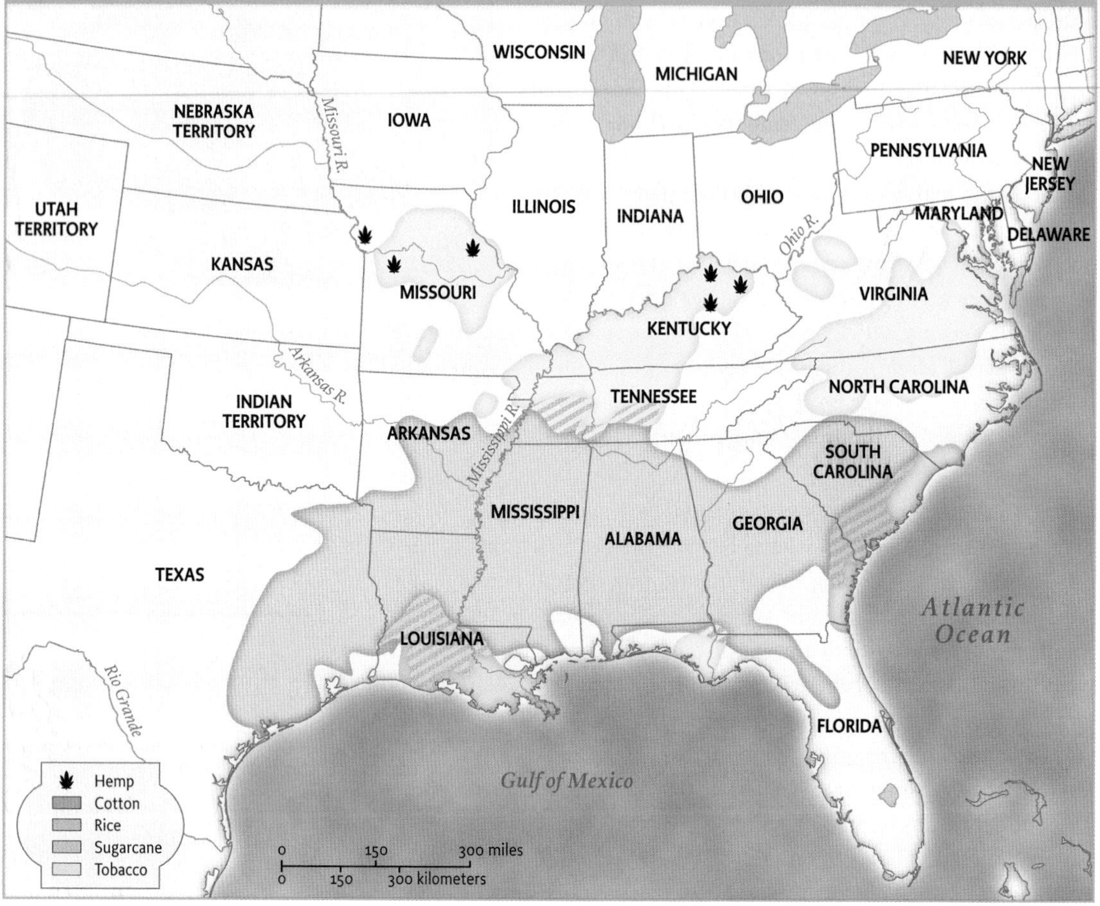

Cotton was the major agricultural crop of the South and, indeed, the nation, but slaves also grew rice, sugarcane, tobacco, and hemp.

semi-independent culture, centered on the family and church. This enabled them to survive the experience of bondage without surrendering their self-esteem and to pass from generation to generation a set of ideas and values fundamentally at odds with those of their masters.

Slave culture drew on the African heritage. African influences were evident in the slaves' music and dances, their style of religious worship, and the use of herbs by slave healers to combat disease. Slave culture was a new creation, shaped by African traditions and American values and experiences.

The Slave Family

At the center of the slave community stood the family. On the sugar plantations of the West Indies, the number of males far exceeded that of females, the workers lived in barracks-type buildings, and settled family life was nearly impossible. The United States, where the slave population grew from natural increase rather than continued importation from Africa, had an even male-female ratio, making the creation of families far more possible. To be sure, the law did not recognize the legality of slave marriages. The master had to consent before a man and woman could "jump over the broomstick" (the slaves' marriage ceremony), and families stood in constant danger of being broken up by sale.

Nonetheless, most adult slaves married, and their unions, when not disrupted by sale, typically lasted for a lifetime. To solidify a sense of family continuity, slaves frequently named children after cousins, uncles, grandparents, and other relatives. Because of constant sales, the slave community had a significantly higher number of female-headed households than among whites, as well as families in which grandparents, other relatives, or even non-kin assumed responsibility for raising children.

SALE OF ESTATES, PICTURES AND SLAVES IN THE ROTUNDA, NEW ORLEANS.

This 1842 engraving depicts an estate sale in New Orleans. At the center, a family of slaves is being sold. On the extreme right and left, auctioneers sell other property, including paintings.

The Threat of Sale

As noted above, the threat of sale, which disrupted family ties, was perhaps the most powerful disciplinary weapon slaveholders possessed. As the domestic slave trade expanded with the rise of the Cotton Kingdom, about one slave marriage in three in slave-selling states like Virginia was broken by sale. Many children were separated from their parents by sale.

Slave traders gave little attention to preserving family ties. A public notice, "Sale of Slaves and Stock," announced the 1852 auction of property belonging to a recently deceased Georgia planter. It listed thirty-six individuals ranging from an infant to a sixty-nine-year-old woman and ended with the proviso: "Slaves will be sold separate, or in lots, as best suits the purchaser." Sales like this were a human tragedy.

A broadside advertising the public sale of slaves, along with horses, mules, and cattle, after the death of their owner. The advertisement notes that the slaves will be sold individually or in groups "as best suits the purchaser," an indication that families were likely to be broken up. The prices are based on each slave's sex, age, and skill.

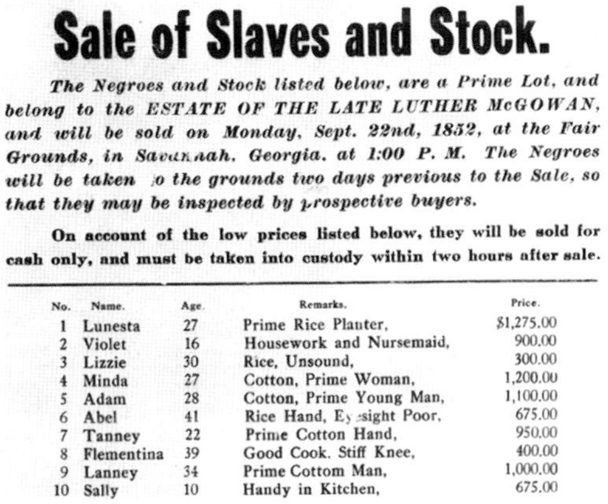

Sale of Slaves and Stock.

The Negroes and Stock listed below, are a Prime Lot, and belong to the ESTATE OF THE LATE LUTHER McGOWAN, and will be sold on Monday, Sept. 22nd, 1852, at the Fair Grounds, in Savannah, Georgia. at 1:00 P. M. The Negroes will be taken to the grounds two days previous to the Sale, so that they may be inspected by prospective buyers.

On account of the low prices listed below, they will be sold for cash only, and must be taken into custody within two hours after sale.

No.	Name.	Age.	Remarks.	Price.
1	Lunesta	27	Prime Rice Planter,	$1,275.00
2	Violet	16	Housework and Nursemaid,	900.00
3	Lizzie	30	Rice, Unsound,	300.00
4	Minda	27	Cotton, Prime Woman,	1,200.00
5	Adam	28	Cotton, Prime Young Man,	1,100.00
6	Abel	41	Rice Hand, Eyesight Poor,	675.00
7	Tanney	22	Prime Cotton Hand,	950.00
8	Flementina	39	Good Cook. Stiff Knee,	400.00
9	Lanney	34	Prime Cottom Man,	1,000.00
10	Sally	10	Handy in Kitchen,	675.00

Gender Roles among Slaves

In some ways, gender roles under slavery differed markedly from those in the larger society. Slave men and women experienced, in a sense, the equality of powerlessness. The nineteenth century's "cult of domesticity," which defined the home as a woman's proper sphere, did

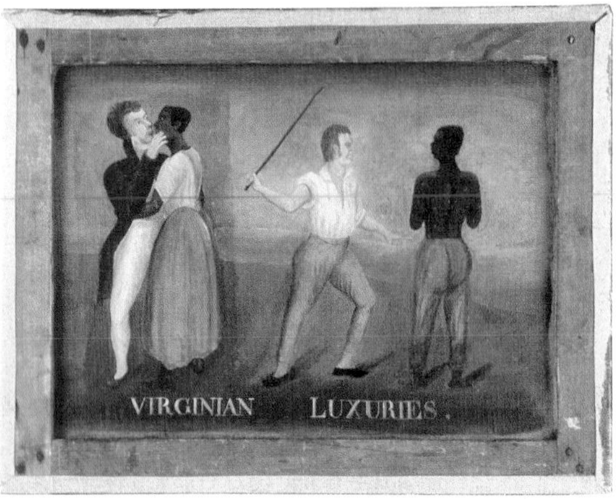

Virginian Luxuries. Originally painted on the back panel of a formal portrait, this image illustrates two "luxuries" of a Virginia slaveowner—the power to sexually abuse slave women and to whip slaves.

not apply to slave women, who regularly worked in the fields. Slave men could not act as the economic providers for their families. Nor could they protect their wives from physical or sexual abuse by owners and overseers (a frequent occurrence on many plantations) or determine when and under what conditions their children worked.

When slaves worked "on their own time," however, more conventional gender roles prevailed. Slave men chopped wood, hunted, and fished, while women washed, sewed, and assumed primary responsibility for the care of children. Some planters allowed their slaves small plots of land on which to grow food to supplement the rations provided by the owner; women usually took charge of these "garden plots."

Slave Religion

A distinctive version of Christianity also offered solace to slaves in the face of hardship and hope for liberation from bondage. Some blacks, free and slave, had taken part in the Great Awakening of the colonial era, and even more were swept into the South's Baptist and Methodist churches during the religious revivals of the late eighteenth and early nineteenth centuries. As one preacher recalled of the great camp meeting that drew thousands of worshipers to Cane Ridge, Kentucky, in 1801, no distinctions were made "as to age, sex, color, or anything of a temporary nature; old and young, male and female, black and white, had equal privilege to minister the light which they received, in whatever way the Spirit directed."

Even though the law prohibited slaves from gathering without a white person present, every plantation, it seemed, had its own black preacher. Usually the preacher was a "self-called" slave who possessed little or no formal education but whose rhetorical abilities and familiarity with the Bible made him one of the most respected members of the slave community. Especially in southern cities, slaves also worshiped in biracial congregations with white ministers, where they generally were required to sit in the back pews or in the balcony. Urban free blacks established their own churches, sometimes attended by slaves.

To masters, Christianity offered another means of social control. Many required slaves to

Plantation Burial, a painting from around 1860 by John Antrobus, an English artist who emigrated to New Orleans in 1850 and later married the daughter of a plantation owner. A slave preacher conducts a funeral service while black men, women, and children look on. This is a rare eyewitness depiction of black culture under slavery.

attend services conducted by white ministers, who preached that theft was immoral and that the Bible required servants to obey their masters. One slave later recalled being told in a white minister's sermon "how good God was in bringing us over to this country from dark and benighted Africa, and permitting us to listen to the sound of the gospel."

Transforming Christianity

In their own religious gatherings, slaves transformed the Christianity they had embraced, turning it to their own purposes. The biblical story of Exodus, for example, in which God chose Moses to lead the enslaved Jews of Egypt into a promised land of freedom, played a central role in black Christianity. Slaves identified themselves as a chosen people whom God in the fullness of time would deliver from bondage. At the same time, the figure of Jesus Christ represented to slaves a personal redeemer, one who truly cared for the oppressed. And in the slaves' eyes, the Christian message of brotherhood and the equality of all souls before the Creator offered an irrefutable indictment of the institution of slavery.

The Desire for Liberty

Despite their masters' elaborate ideology defending the South's "peculiar institution," slave culture rested on a conviction of the injustices of bondage and the desire for freedom. When slaves sang, "I'm bound for the land of Canaan," they meant not only relief from worldly woes in an afterlife but also escaping to the North or witnessing the breaking of slavery's chains.

Folk tales

Most slaves, however, fully understood the impossibility of directly confronting such an entrenched system. Their folk tales had no figures equivalent to Paul Bunyan, the powerful, larger-than-life backwoodsman popular in white folklore. Slaves' folklore, such as the Brer Rabbit stories, glorified the weak hare who outwitted stronger foes like the bear and fox, rather than challenging them outright. Their religious songs, or spirituals, spoke of lives of sorrow ("I've been 'buked and I've been scorned"), while holding out hope for ultimate liberation ("Didn't my Lord deliver Daniel?").

Neighborhood networks

Owners attempted to prevent slaves from learning about the larger world. But slaves created neighborhood networks that transmitted information between plantations. Skilled craftsmen, preachers, pilots on ships, and other privileged slaves spread news of local and national events. James Henry Hammond of South Carolina was "astonished and shocked" to find that his slaves understood the political views of the presidential candidates of 1844, Henry Clay and James K. Polk, and knew "most of what the abolitionists are doing."

Language of freedom

The world of most rural slaves was bounded by their local communities and kin. Nor could slaves remain indifferent to the currents of thought unleashed by the American Revolution or to the language of freedom in the society around them. "I am in a land of liberty," wrote Joseph Taper, a Virginia slave who escaped to Canada around 1840. "Man is as God intended he should be."

RESISTANCE TO SLAVERY

Revolts and resistance

Confronted with federal, state, and local authorities committed to preserving slavery, and outnumbered within the South as a whole by the white population, slaves could only rarely express their desire for freedom by outright rebellion. Compared with revolts in Brazil and the West Indies, which experienced numerous uprisings, involving hundreds or even thousands of slaves, revolts in the United States were smaller and less frequent. Resistance to slavery took many forms in the Old South, from individual acts of defiance to occasional uprisings. These actions posed a constant challenge to the slaveholders' self-image as benign paternalists and their belief that slaves were obedient subjects grateful for their owners' care.

Forms of Resistance

The most widespread expression of hostility to slavery was "day-to-day resistance" or "silent sabotage"—doing poor work, breaking tools, abusing animals, and in other ways disrupting the plantation routine. Then there was the theft of food, a form of resistance so common that one southern physician diagnosed it as a hereditary disease unique to blacks. Less frequent, but more dangerous, were serious crimes committed by slaves, including arson, poisoning, and armed assaults against individual whites.

Runaway slaves

Even more threatening to the stability of the slave system were slaves who ran away. Formidable obstacles confronted the prospective **fugitive slaves**. Patrols were constantly on the lookout for runaway slaves. Slaves had little or no knowledge of geography, apart from understanding that following the north star led to freedom. Not surprisingly, most of those who succeeded lived, like Frederick Douglass, in the Upper South, especially Maryland, Virginia, and Kentucky, which bordered on the free states. Douglass, who escaped at age twenty, was also typical in that the large majority of fugitives were young men. Most slave women were not willing to leave children behind, and taking them along on the arduous escape journey was nearly impossible.

Fugitive destinations

In the Lower South, fugitives tended to head for cities like New Orleans or Charleston, where they hoped to lose themselves in the free black community. Other escapees fled to remote areas like the Great Dismal Swamp of Virginia or the Florida Everglades, where the Seminole

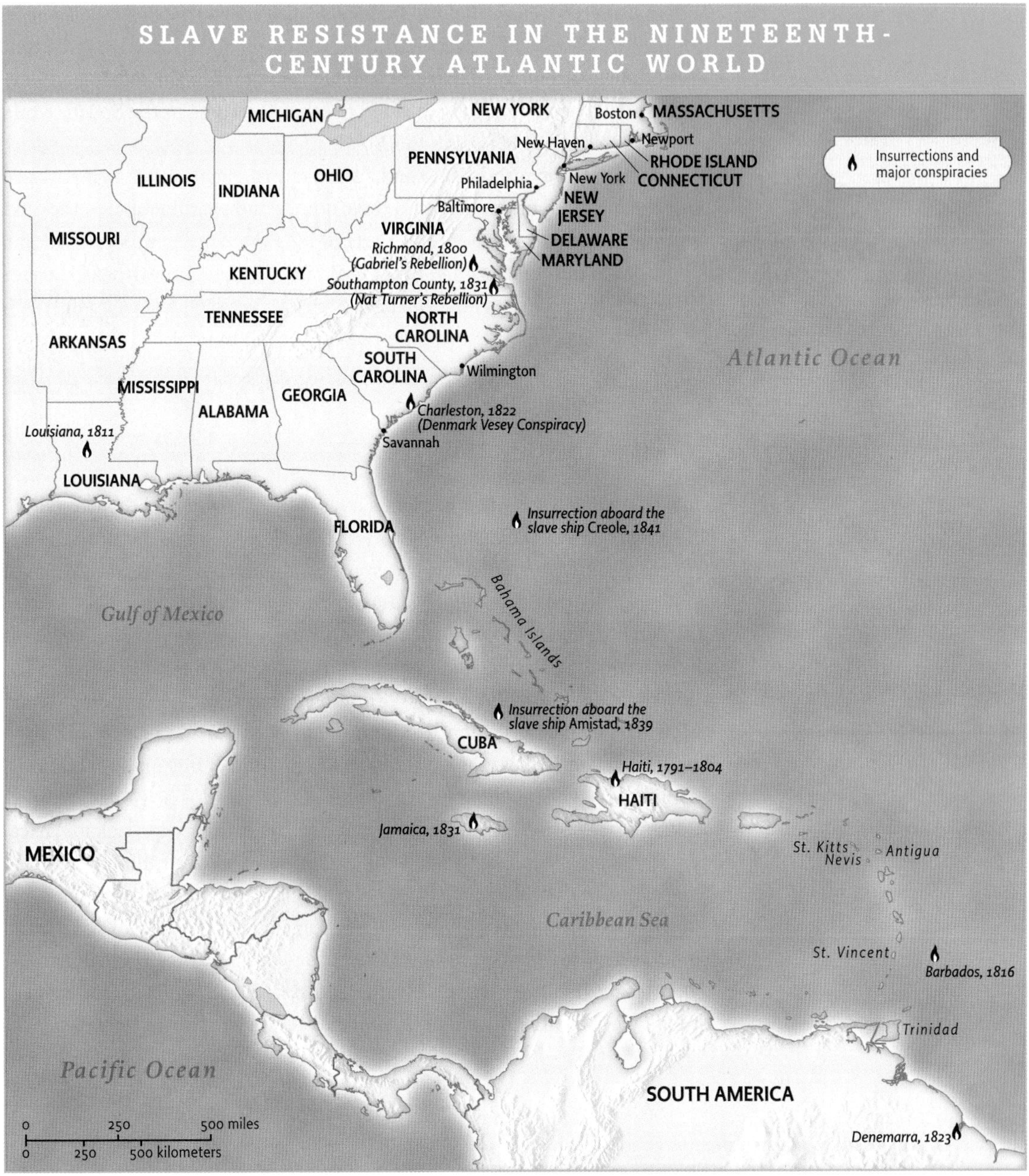

Instances of slave resistance occurred throughout the Western Hemisphere, on land and at sea. This map shows the location of major events in the nineteenth century.

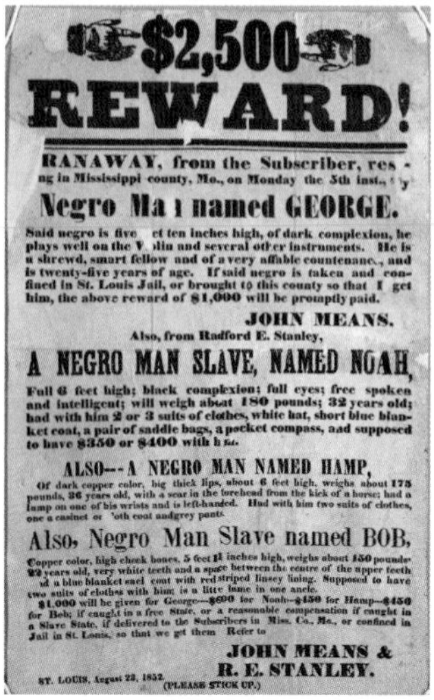

$2,500 REWARD!

RANAWAY, from the Subscriber, res- ng in Mississippi county, Mo., on Monday the 5th inst., [illegible]

Negro Ma[illegible] named GEORGE.

Said negro is five [illegible]et ten inches high, of dark complexion, he plays well on the V[illegible]lin and several other instruments. He is a shrewd, smart fellow and of a very affable countenanc[illegible], and is twenty-five years of age. If said negro is taken and confined in St. Louis Jail, or brought to this county so that I get him, the above reward of $1,000 will be promptly paid.

JOHN MEANS.

Also, from Radford E. Stanley,

A NEGRO MAN SLAVE, NAMED NOAH,

Full 6 feet high; black complexion; full eyes; free spoken and intelligent; will weigh about 180 pounds; 32 years old; had with him 2 or 3 suits of clothes, white hat, short blue blanket coat, a pair of saddle bags, a pocket compass, and supposed to have $350 or $400 with h[illegible].

ALSO--A NEGRO MAN NAMED HAMP,

Of dark copper color, big thick lips, about 6 feet high, weighs about 175 pounds, 36 years old, with a scar in the forehead from the kick of a horse; had a lump on one of his wrists and is left-handed. Had with him two suits of clothes, one a casinet or [illegible]oth coat and grey pants.

Also, Negro Man Slave named BOB,

Copper color, high cheek bones, 5 feet [illegible] inches high, weighs about 150 pounds, 22 years old, very white teeth and a space between the centre of the upper teeth [illegible] a blue blanket [illegible] coat with red striped linsey lining. Supposed to have two suits of clothes with him; is a little lame in one ancle.

$1,000 will be given for George—$600 for Noah—$450 for Hamp—$450 for Bob; if caught in a free State, or a reasonable compensation if caught in a Slave State, if delivered to the Subscribers in Miss. Co., Mo., or confined in Jail in St. Louis, so that we get them. Refer to

JOHN MEANS &
R. E. STANLEY.

ST. LOUIS, August 23, 1852.

(PLEASE STICK UP.)

The top part of a typical broadside offering a reward for the capture of four runaway slaves. This was distributed in Mississippi County, Missouri, in 1852. The high reward for George, $1,000, suggests that he is an extremely valued worker.

Indians offered refuge before they were forced to move west. Even in Tennessee, a study of newspaper advertisements for runaways finds that around 40 percent were thought to have remained in the local neighborhood and 30 percent to have headed to other locations in the South, while only 25 percent tried to reach the North.

The **Underground Railroad**, a loose organization of sympathetic abolitionists who hid fugitives in their homes and sent them on to the next "station," assisted some runaway slaves. A few courageous individuals made forays into the South to liberate slaves. The best known was **Harriet Tubman**. Born in Maryland in 1820, Tubman escaped to Philadelphia in 1849 and during the next decade risked her life by making some twenty trips back to her state of birth to lead relatives and other slaves to freedom.

The *Amistad*

In a few instances, large groups of slaves collectively seized their freedom. The most celebrated instance involved fifty-three slaves who in 1839 took control of **the *Amistad***, a ship transporting them from one port in Cuba to another, and tried to force the navigator to steer it to Africa. The *Amistad* wended its way up the Atlantic coast until an American vessel seized it off the coast of Long Island. President Martin Van Buren favored returning the slaves to Cuba. But abolitionists brought their case to the Supreme Court, where the former president John Quincy Adams argued that since they had been recently brought from Africa in violation of international treaties banning the slave trade, the captives should be freed. The Court accepted Adams's reasoning, and most of the captives made their way back to Africa.

Uprising on ship

The *Amistad* case had no legal bearing on slaves within the United States. But it may well have inspired a similar uprising in 1841, when 135 slaves being transported by sea from Norfolk, Virginia, to New Orleans seized control of the ship *Creole* and sailed for Nassau in the British Bahamas. Their leader had the evocative name Madison Washington. To the dismay of the Tyler administration, the British gave refuge to the *Creole* slaves.

Slave Revolts

Resistance to slavery occasionally moved beyond such individual and group acts of defiance to outright rebellion. The four largest conspiracies in American history occurred within the space of thirty-one years in the early nineteenth century. The first, organized by the Virginia slave Gabriel in 1800, was discussed in Chapter 8. It was followed eleven years later by an uprising on sugar plantations upriver from New Orleans. Some 500 men and women, armed with sugarcane knives, axes, clubs, and a few guns, marched toward the city, destroying property as they proceeded. The white population along the route fled in panic to New Orleans. Within two days, the militia and regular army troops met the rebels and dispersed them in a pitched battle, killing sixty-six.

The next major conspiracy was organized in 1822 by Denmark Vesey, a slave carpenter in Charleston, South Carolina, who had purchased his freedom after winning a local lottery. **Denmark Vesey's conspiracy** reflected the combination of American and African influences then circulating in the Atlantic world and coming together in black culture. "He studied the Bible a great deal," recalled one of his followers, "and tried to prove from it that slavery and bondage is against the Bible." Vesey also quoted the Declaration of Independence, pored over newspaper reports of the debates in Congress regarding the Missouri Compromise, and made pronouncements like "all men had equal rights, blacks as well as whites." And he read to his conspirators accounts of the successful slave revolution in Haiti. The African heritage was present in the person of Vesey's lieutenant Gullah Jack, a religious "conjurer" from Angola who claimed to be able to protect the rebels against injury or death. The plot was discovered before it could reach fruition.

As with many slave conspiracies, evidence about the Vesey plot is contradictory and disputed. Much of it comes from a series of trials in which the court operated in secret and failed to allow the accused to confront those who testified against them.

Cinque, a leader of the slave revolt on the *Amistad*, in an 1839 painting by Nathaniel Jocelyn, a prominent Connecticut artist.

Nat Turner's Rebellion

The best known of all slave rebels was Nat Turner, a slave preacher and religious mystic in Southampton County, Virginia, who came to believe that God had chosen him to lead a black uprising. Turner traveled widely in the county, conducting religious services. He told of seeing black and white angels fighting in the sky and the heavens running red with blood. Perhaps from a sense of irony, Turner initially chose July 4, 1831, for his rebellion, only to fall ill on the appointed day. On August 22, he and a handful of followers marched from farm to farm assaulting the white inhabitants. By the time the militia put down the uprising, about eighty slaves had joined Turner's band, and some sixty whites had been killed. Turner was subsequently captured and, with seventeen other rebels, condemned to die. Asked before his execution whether he regretted what he had done, Turner responded, "Was not Christ crucified?"

Nat Turner's Rebellion sent shock waves through the entire South. "A Nat Turner," one white Virginian warned, "might be in any family." In the panic that followed the revolt, hundreds of innocent slaves were whipped, and scores

In one of the most celebrated escapes of the antebellum years, Henry Brown, a slave in Richmond, had himself concealed in a crate and shipped to the antislavery office in Philadelphia. This lithograph from 1851 shows three white abolitionists, including J. Miller McKim, with a hatchet, as well as the African-American William Still, a leader of the underground railroad in the city, who holds the top of the crate as Brown emerges.

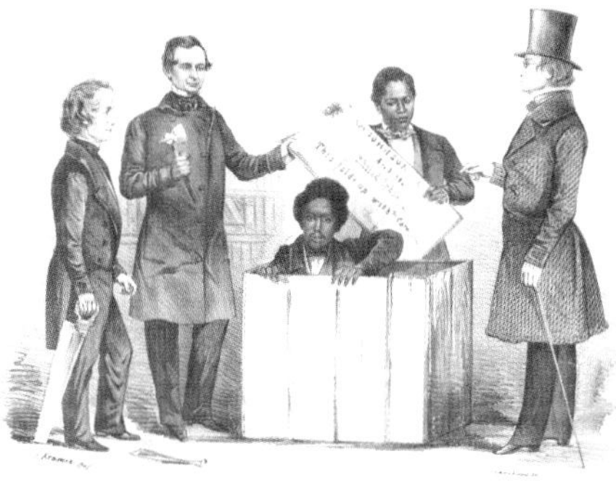

VOICES OF FREEDOM

From Letter by Joseph Taper to Joseph Long (1840)

No one knows how many slaves succeeded in escaping from bondage before the Civil War. Some settled in northern cities like Boston, Cincinnati, and New York. But because the Constitution required that fugitives be returned to slavery, many continued northward until they reached Canada.

One successful fugitive was Joseph Taper, a slave in Frederick County, Virginia, who in 1837 ran away to Pennsylvania with his wife and children. Two years later, learning that a "slave catcher" was in the neighborhood, the Tapers fled to Canada. In 1840, Taper wrote to a white acquaintance in Virginia recounting some of his experiences.

The biblical passage to which Taper refers reads: "And I will come near to you to judgment; and I will be a swift witness against the sorcerers, and against the adulterers, and against false swearers, and against those that oppress the hireling in his wages, the widow, and the fatherless, and that turn aside the stranger from his right, and fear not me, saith the Lord of hosts."

Dear sir,

I now take the opportunity to inform you that I am in a land of liberty, in good health. . . . Since I have been in the Queen's dominions I have been well contented, Yes well contented for Sure, man is as God intended he should be. That is, all are born free and equal. This is a wholesome law, not like the Southern laws which puts man made in the image of God, on level with brutes. O, what will become of the people, and where will they stand in the day of Judgment. Would that the 5th verse of the 3d chapter of Malachi were written as with the bar of iron, and the point of a diamond upon every oppressor's heart that they might repent of this evil, and let the oppressed go free. . . .

We have good schools, and all the colored population supplied with schools. My boy Edward who will be six years next January, is now reading, and I intend keeping him at school until he becomes a good scholar.

I have enjoyed more pleasure within one month here than in all my life in the land of bondage. . . . My wife and self are sitting by a good comfortable fire happy, knowing that there are none to molest [us] or make [us] afraid. God save Queen Victoria. The Lord bless her in this life, and crown her with glory in the world to come is my prayer,

Yours With much respect
most obt, Joseph Taper

From "Slavery and the Bible" (1850)

White southerners developed an elaborate set of arguments defending slavery in the period before the Civil War. One pillar of proslavery thought was the idea that the institution was sanctioned by the Bible, as in this essay from the influential southern magazine *De Bow's Review*.

A very large party in the United States believe that holding slaves is morally wrong; this party founds its belief upon precepts taught in the Bible, and takes that book as the standard of morality and religion.

. . . We think we can show, that the Bible teaches clearly and conclusively that the holding of slaves is right; and if so, no deduction from general principles can make it wrong, if that book is true. . . .

Slavery has existed in some form or under some name, in almost every country of the globe. It existed in every country known, even by name, to any one of the sacred writers, at the time of his writing; yet none of them condemns it in the slightest degree. Would this have been the case had it been wrong in itself? Would not some one of the host of sacred writers have spoken of this alleged crime, in such terms as to show, in a manner not to be misunderstood, that God wished all men to be equal?

Abraham, the chosen servant of God, had his bond servants, whose condition was similar to, or worse than, that of our slaves. He considered them as his property, to be bought and sold as any other property which he owned. . . .

We find . . . that both the Old and New Testaments speak of slavery—that they do not condemn the relation, but, on the contrary, expressly allow it or create it; and they give commands and exhortations, which are based upon its legality and propriety. It can not, then, be wrong.

QUESTIONS

1. *How does Taper's letter reverse the rhetoric, common among white Americans, which saw the United States as a land of freedom and the British empire as lacking in liberty?*
2. *Why does De Bow feel that it is important to show that the Bible sanctions slavery?*
3. *How do Taper and De Bow differ in their understanding of the relationship of slavery and Christianity?*

An engraving depicting Nat Turner's slave rebellion of 1831, from a book published soon after the revolt.

executed. For one last time, Virginia's leaders openly debated whether steps ought to be taken to do away with the "peculiar institution." But a proposal for gradual emancipation and the removal of the black population from the state failed to win legislative approval.

Instead of moving toward emancipation, the Virginia legislature of 1832 decided to fasten even more tightly the chains of bondage. New laws prohibited blacks, free or slave, from acting as preachers (a measure that proved impossible to enforce), strengthened the militia and patrol systems, banned free blacks from owning firearms, and prohibited teaching slaves to read. Other southern states followed suit.

A turning point

In some ways, 1831 marked a turning point for the Old South. In that year, Parliament debated a program for abolishing slavery throughout the British empire, underscoring the South's growing isolation. Turner's rebellion, following only a few months after the appearance in Boston of William Lloyd Garrison's abolitionist journal, *The Liberator*, suggested that American slavery faced enemies both within and outside the South. The proslavery argument increasingly permeated southern intellectual and political life, while dissenting opinions were suppressed. Some states made membership in an abolitionist society a criminal offense, while mobs drove critics of slavery from their homes. The South's "great reaction" produced one of the most thoroughgoing suppressions of freedom of speech in American history. Even as reform movements arose in the North that condemned slavery as contrary to Christianity and to basic American values, and national debate over the peculiar institution intensified, southern society closed in defense of slavery.

An intensifying debate

CHAPTER REVIEW AND ONLINE RESOURCES

REVIEW QUESTIONS

1. *Given that most northern states had abolished slavery by the 1830s, how is it useful to think of slavery as a national—rather than regional—economic and political system?*

2. *Although some poor southern whites resented the dominance of the "slavocracy," most supported the institution and accepted the power of the planter class. Why did the "plain folk" continue to support slavery?*

3. *How did the planters' paternalism serve to justify the system of slavery? How did it hide the reality of life for slaves?*

4. *Identify the basic elements of the proslavery defense and those points aimed especially at non-southern audiences.*

5. *In what sense did southern slaveholders consider themselves forward-looking?*

6. *Compare slaves in the Old South with those elsewhere in the world, focusing on health, diet, and opportunities for freedom.*

7. *Describe the difference between gang labor and task labor for slaves, and explain how slaves' tasks varied by region across the Old South.*

8. *How did enslaved people create community and a culture that allowed them to survive in an oppressive society?*

9. *Identify the different types of resistance to slavery. Which ones were the most common, the most effective, and the most demonstrative?*

KEY TERMS

the "peculiar institution" (p. 309)
Second Middle Passage (p. 310)
"Cotton is king" (p. 313)
paternalism (p. 314)
proslavery argument (p. 315)
fugitive slaves (p. 326)
Underground Railroad (p. 328)
Harriet Tubman (p. 328)
the *Amistad* (p. 328)
Denmark Vesey's conspiracy (p. 329)
Nat Turner's Rebellion (p. 329)

Go to INQUIZITIVE

To see what you know—and learn what you've missed—with personalized feedback along the way.

Visit the ***Give Me Liberty!* Student Site** for primary source documents and images, interactive maps, author videos featuring Eric Foner, and more.

CHAPTER 12

AN AGE OF REFORM

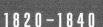

★

1820–1840

1816	American Colonization Society founded
1825	Owenite community established at New Harmony, Indiana
1826	American Temperance Society founded
1827	First U.S. black newspaper, *Freedom's Journal*, established
1829	David Walker's *An Appeal to the Coloured Citizens of the World*
1833	American Anti-Slavery Society founded
1836	Congress adopts the "gag rule"
1837	Elijah Lovejoy killed
1845	Margaret Fuller's *Woman in the Nineteenth Century*
1848	John Humphrey Noyes founds Oneida, New York
	Seneca Falls Convention held
1852	Harriet Beecher Stowe's *Uncle Tom's Cabin*
	Frederick Douglass's speech "What, to the Slave, Is the Fourth of July?"

A Woman's Rights Quilt. Made by an unknown woman only a few years after the Seneca Falls Convention of 1848, this quilt embodies an unusual form of political expression. It includes scenes visualizing a woman engaged in various activities that violated the era's cult of domesticity, and it illustrates some of the demands of the early women's rights movement. The individual blocks show a woman driving her own buggy and a banner advocating "woman rights," another dressing to go out while her husband remains at home wearing an apron, and a third addressing a public meeting with a mixed male-female audience.

FOCUS QUESTIONS

- *What were the major movements and goals of antebellum reform?*
- *What were the different varieties of abolitionism?*
- *How did abolitionism challenge barriers to racial equality and free speech?*
- *What were the diverse sources of the antebellum women's rights movement and its significance?*

Among the many Americans who devoted their lives to the crusade against slavery, few were as selfless or courageous as Abby Kelley. As a teacher in Lynn, Massachusetts, she joined the Female Anti-Slavery Society and, like thousands of other northern women, threw herself into the abolitionist movement. In 1838, Kelley began to give public speeches about slavery. Her first lecture outside of Lynn was literally a baptism of fire. Enraged by reports that abolitionists favored "amalgamation" of the races—that is, sexual relations between whites and blacks—residents of Philadelphia stormed the meeting hall and burned it to the ground.

For two decades, Kelley traveled throughout the North, speaking almost daily in churches, public halls, and antislavery homes on "the holy cause of human rights." Her career illustrated the interconnections of the era's reform movements. In addition to abolitionism, she was active in pacifist organizations—which opposed the use of force, including war, to settle disputes—and was a pioneer in the early struggle for women's rights. She forthrightly challenged her era's assumption that a woman's "place" was in the home. More than any other individual, remarked Lucy Stone, another women's rights advocate, Kelley "earned for us all the right of free speech."

Abby Kelley's private life was as unconventional as her public career. Happily married to the ardent abolitionist Stephen S. Foster, she gave birth to a daughter in 1847 but soon returned to lecturing. When criticized for not devoting herself to the care of her infant, Kelley replied: "I have done it for the sake of the mothers whose babies are sold away from them. The most precious legacy I can leave my child is a free country."

THE REFORM IMPULSE

Goals of reformers

"In the history of the world," wrote Ralph Waldo Emerson in 1841, "the doctrine of reform has never had such hope as at the present hour." Abolitionism was only one of this era's numerous efforts to improve American society. Americans established voluntary organizations that worked to prevent the manufacture and sale of liquor, end public entertainments and the delivery of the mail on Sunday, improve conditions in prisons, expand public education, uplift the condition of wage laborers, and reorganize society on the basis of cooperation rather than competitive individualism.

Nearly all these groups worked to convert public opinion to their cause. They sent out speakers, gathered signatures on petitions, and published pamphlets. Some reform movements, like restraining the consumption of liquor and alleviating the plight of the blind and insane, flourished throughout the nation. Others, including women's rights, labor

A rare photograph of an abolitionist meeting in New York State around 1850. Frederick Douglass is to the left of the woman at the center.

unionism, and educational reform, were weak or nonexistent in the South, where they were widely associated with antislavery sentiment. Reform was an international crusade. Peace, temperance, women's rights, and antislavery advocates regularly crisscrossed the Atlantic to promote their ideas.

Reformers adopted a wide variety of tactics to bring about social change. Some relied on "moral suasion" to convert people to their cause. Others, such as opponents of "demon rum," sought to use the power of the government to force sinners to change their ways. Some reformers decided to withdraw altogether from the larger society and establish their own cooperative settlements. They hoped to change American life by creating "heavens on earth," where they could demonstrate by example the superiority of a collective way of life.

Utopian Communities

Thomas More

About 100 reform communities were established in the decades before the Civil War. Historians call them "utopian" after Thomas More's sixteenth-century novel *Utopia*, an outline of a perfect society. (The word has also come to imply that such plans are impractical and impossible to realize.) Most communities arose from religious conviction, but others were inspired by the secular desire to counteract the social and economic changes set in motion by the market revolution.

Social harmony

Nearly all the communities set out to reorganize society on a cooperative basis, hoping to restore social harmony to a world of excessive individualism and to narrow the widening gap between rich and poor. Through their efforts, the words "socialism" and "communism," meaning a social organization in which productive property is owned by the community rather than private individuals, entered the language of politics. Most **utopian communities** also tried to find substitutes for conventional gender relations and marriage patterns. Some prohibited sexual relations between men and women altogether; others allowed them to change partners at will. But nearly all insisted that the abolition of private property must be accompanied by an end to men's "property" in women.

The Shakers

Religious communities attracted those who sought to find a retreat from a society permeated by sin. But the **Shakers**, the most successful of the

An engraving of a Shaker dance, drawn by Benson Lossing, an artist who visited a Shaker community and reported on life there for *Harper's Magazine* in 1857.

religious communities, also had a significant impact on the outside world. At their peak during the 1840s, cooperative Shaker settlements, which stretched from Maine to Kentucky, included more than 5,000 members.

Shaker beliefs

God, the Shakers believed, had a "dual" personality, both male and female, and thus the two sexes were spiritually equal. "Virgin purity" formed a pillar of the Shakers' faith. They completely abandoned traditional family life. Men and women lived separately in large dormitory-like structures and ate in communal dining rooms. They increased their numbers by attracting converts and adopting children from orphanages, rather than through natural increase. Although they rejected the individual accumulation of private property, the Shakers proved remarkably successful economically. They were among the first to market vegetable and flower seeds and herbal medicines commercially and to breed cattle for profit. Their beautifully crafted furniture is still widely admired today.

Oneida

John Humphrey Noyes

"Complex marriage"

Another influential and controversial community was **Oneida**, founded in 1848 in upstate New York by John Humphrey Noyes, the Vermont-born son of a U.S. congressman. In 1836, Noyes and his disciples formed a small community in Putney, Vermont. The community became notorious for what Noyes called "complex marriage," whereby any man could propose sexual relations to any woman, who had the right to reject or accept his invitation, which would then be registered in a public record book. The great danger was "exclusive affections," which, Noyes felt, destroyed social harmony.

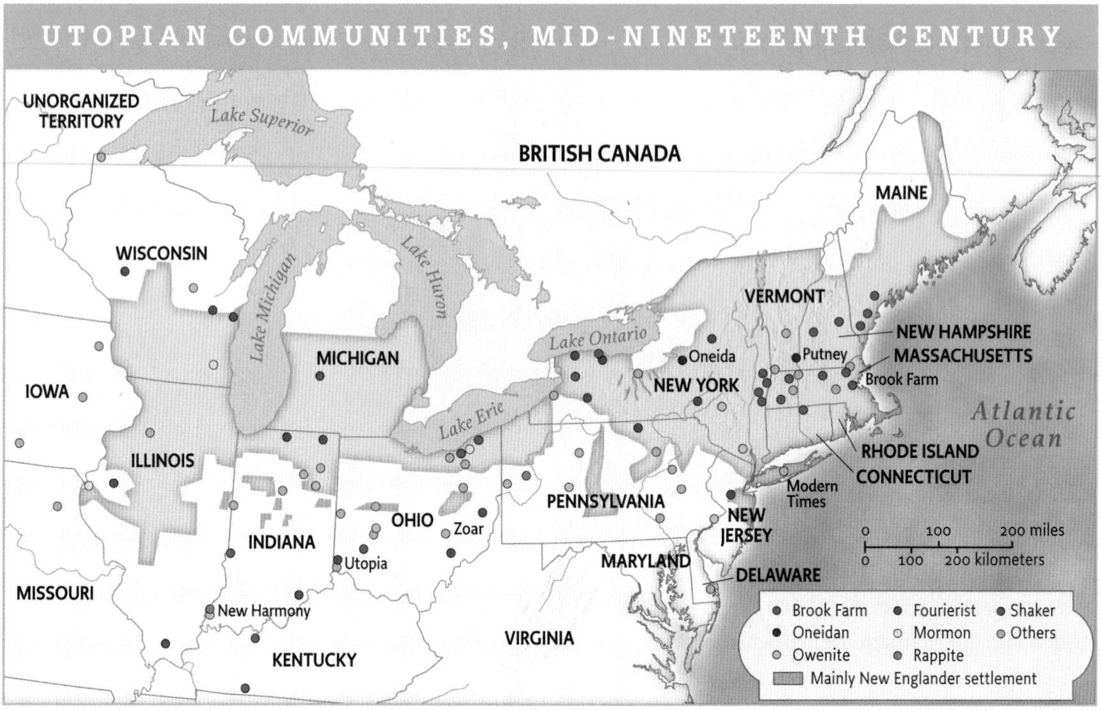

In the first half of the nineteenth century, dozens of utopian communities were established in the United States, where small groups of men and women attempted to establish a more perfect social order within the larger society.

After being indicted for adultery by local officials, Noyes in 1848 moved his community to Oneida, where it survived until 1881. Oneida was an extremely dictatorial environment. To become a member of the community, one had to demonstrate command of Noyes's religious teachings and live according to his rules.

Worldly Communities

Longevity of utopian communities

To outside observers, utopian communities like Oneida seemed cases of "voluntary slavery." But because of their members' selfless devotion to the teachings and rules laid down by their leader, spiritually oriented communities often achieved remarkable longevity. The Shakers survived well into the twentieth century. Communities with a more worldly orientation tended to be beset by internal divisions and therefore lasted for much shorter periods.

The most important secular communitarian (meaning a person who plans or lives in a cooperative community) was Robert Owen, a British factory owner. Appalled by the degradation of workers in the early industrial revolution, Owen created a model factory village at New Lanark, Scotland, which combined strict rules of work discipline with comfortable housing and free public education. Around 1815, its 1,500 employees made New Lanark the largest center of cotton manufacturing in the world. Owen promoted **communitarianism** as a peaceful means of ensuring that workers received the full value of their labor. In 1824, he purchased the Harmony community in Indiana—originally founded by the German Protestant religious leader George Rapp, who had emigrated to America with his followers at the beginning of the nineteenth century. Here, Owen established **New Harmony**, where he hoped to create a "new moral world."

In Owen's scheme, children would be removed at an early age from the care of their parents to be educated in schools where they would be trained to subordinate individual ambition to the common good. Owen also defended women's rights, especially access to education and the right to divorce. At New Harmony, he promised, women would no longer be "enslaved" to their husbands, and "false notions" about innate differences between the sexes would be abandoned.

Harmony eluded the residents of New Harmony. They squabbled about everything from the community's constitution to the distribution of property. Owen's settlement survived for only a few years, but it strongly influenced the labor movement, educational reformers, and women's rights advocates. Owen's vision resonated with the widely held American belief that a community of equals could be created in the New World.

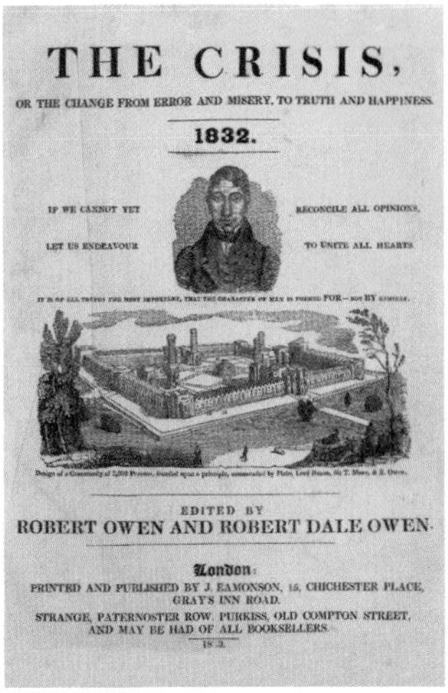
THE CRISIS,
OR THE CHANGE FROM ERROR AND MISERY, TO TRUTH AND HAPPINESS.
1832.
IF WE CANNOT YET RECONCILE ALL OPINIONS,
LET US ENDEAVOUR TO UNITE ALL HEARTS
EDITED BY
ROBERT OWEN AND ROBERT DALE OWEN.
London:
PRINTED AND PUBLISHED BY J. EAMONSON, 15, CHICHESTER PLACE, GRAY'S INN ROAD.
STRANGE, PATERNOSTER ROW. PURKISS, OLD COMPTON STREET, AND MAY BE HAD OF ALL BOOKSELLERS.

The Crisis, a publication by the communitarian Robert Owen and his son, Robert Dale Owen. The cover depicts Owen's vision of a planned socialist community.

Religion and Reform

Mainstream reform

Most Americans saw the ownership of property as the key to economic independence—and, therefore, to freedom—and marriage as the foundation of the social order. Few were likely to join communities that required them to surrender both. Far more typical of the reform impulse were movements that aimed at liberating men and women either from restraints external to themselves, such as slavery and war, or from forms of internal "servitude" like drinking, illiteracy, and a tendency toward criminality. Many of these reform movements drew their inspiration from the religious revivalism of the Second Great Awakening, discussed in Chapter 9. If, as the revivalist preachers maintained, God had created man as a "free moral agent," sinners could not only reform themselves but could also remake the world.

Temperance

The revivals popularized the outlook known as **perfectionism**, which saw both individuals and society at large as capable of indefinite improvement. Under the impact of the revivals, older reform efforts moved in a new, radical direction. Temperance (which literally means moderation in the consumption of liquor) was transformed into a crusade to eliminate drinking entirely, known as the **temperance movement**. Criticism of war became outright pacifism. And, as will be related below, critics of

A temperance banner from around 1850 depicts a young man torn between a woman in white, who illustrates female purity, and a temptress, who offers him a drink of liquor.

slavery now demanded not gradual emancipation but immediate and total abolition.

To members of the North's emerging middle-class culture, reform became a badge of respectability, an indication that individuals had taken control of their own lives and had become morally accountable. The American Temperance Society, founded in 1826, sought to redeem not only habitual drunkards but also the occasional drinker. It claimed by the 1830s to have persuaded hundreds of thousands of Americans to renounce liquor. By 1840, the consumption of alcohol per person had fallen to less than half the level of a decade earlier. (It had peaked in 1830 at seven gallons per person per year, compared with around two gallons today.)

Critics of Reform

Many Americans saw the reform impulse as an attack on their own freedom. Taverns were popular meeting places for workingmen, sites not only of drinking but also of political discussions, organizational meetings, and recreation. Drinking was a prominent feature of festive celebrations and events like militia gatherings. A "Liberty Loving Citizen" of Worcester, Massachusetts, wondered what gave one group of citizens the right to dictate to others how to conduct their personal lives.

Catholics on reform

American Catholics, their numbers growing because of Irish and German immigration, proved hostile to the reform impulse. Catholics understood freedom in ways quite different from how Protestant reformers did. They viewed sin as an inescapable burden of individuals and society. The perfectionist idea that evil could be banished from the world struck them as an affront to genuine religion, and they bitterly opposed what they saw as reformers' efforts to impose their own version of Protestant morality on their neighbors. Whereas reformers spoke of man as a free moral agent, Catholics tended to place less emphasis on individual independence and more on the importance of communities centered on family and church.

Reformers and Freedom

Tension between liberation and control

Reformers had to reconcile their desire to create moral order with their quest to enhance personal freedom. They did this through a vision of freedom that was liberating and controlling at the same time. On the one hand, reformers insisted that their goal was to enable Americans to enjoy genuine liberty. In a world in which personal freedom increasingly meant the opportunity to compete for economic gain and individual self-improvement, they spoke of liberating Americans from various forms of "slavery" that made it impossible to succeed—slavery to drink, to poverty, to sin.

On the other hand, reformers insisted that self-fulfillment came through self-discipline. Their definition of the free individual was the person who internalized the practice of self-control. In some ways, reformers believed, American society suffered from an excess of liberty—the anarchic "natural liberty" John Winthrop had warned against in the early days of Puritan Massachusetts, as opposed to the "Christian liberty" of the morally upright citizen.

Self-discipline

Many religious groups in the East worried that settlers in the West and immigrants from abroad lacked self-control and led lives of vice, exhibited by drinking, violations of the Sabbath, and lack of Protestant devotion. They formed the American Tract Society, the American Bible Society, and other groups that flooded eastern cities and the western frontier with copies of the gospel and pamphlets promoting religious virtue. Between 1825 and 1835, the pamphlets distributed by the Tract Society amounted to more than 500 million pages.

American Tract Society

The Invention of the Asylum

The tension between liberation and control in the era's reform movements was vividly evident in the proliferation of new institutions that reformers hoped could remake human beings into free, morally upright citizens. In colonial America, crime had mostly been punished by whipping, fines, or banishment. The poor received relief in their own homes, orphans lived with neighbors, and families took care of mentally ill members.

During the 1830s and 1840s, Americans embarked on a program of institution building—jails for criminals, poorhouses for the destitute, asylums for the insane, and orphanages for children without families. These institutions differed in many respects, but they shared with believers in "perfectionism" the idea that social ills once considered incurable could in fact be eliminated. Today, prisons and asylums have become overcrowded places where rehabilitating the inmates seems less important than simply holding them at bay, away from society. At the outset, however, these institutions were inspired by the conviction that those who passed through their doors could eventually be released to become productive, self-disciplined citizens.

Reform institutions

The Common School

The largest effort at institution building before the Civil War came in the movement to establish **common schools**—that is, tax-supported state school systems open to all children. In the early nineteenth century, most children were educated in locally supported schools, private academies, charity schools, or at home. Many had no access to learning at all. School reform reflected the numerous purposes that came together in the era's reform impulse. Horace Mann, a Massachusetts lawyer and Whig politician who served as director of the state's board of education, was the era's leading educational reformer. He hoped that universal public education could restore equality to a fractured society by bringing the children of all classes together in a common learning experience and equipping the less fortunate to advance in the social scale.

Horace Mann

With labor organizations, factory owners, and middle-class reformers all supporting the idea, every northern state by 1860 had established tax-supported school systems for its children. The common-school movement created the first real career opportunity for women, who quickly came to dominate the ranks of teachers. The South, where literate blacks were viewed as a danger to social order and planters had no desire to tax themselves to pay for education for poor white children, lagged far behind. This was one of many ways in which North and South seemed to be growing apart.

The rise of public education

THE CRUSADE AGAINST SLAVERY

Compared with drinking, Sabbath-breaking, and illiteracy, the greatest evil in American society at first appeared to attract the least attention from reformers. For many years, it seemed that the only Americans willing to challenge the existence of slavery were Quakers, slaves, and free blacks.

Colonization

Before the 1830s, those white Americans willing to contemplate an end to bondage almost always coupled calls for abolition with the "colonization" of freed slaves—their deportation to Africa, the Caribbean, or Central America. In 1816, proponents of this idea founded the **American Colonization Society**, which promoted the gradual abolition of slavery and the settlement of black Americans in Africa. It soon established Liberia on the coast of West Africa, an outpost of American influence whose capital, Monrovia, was named for President James Monroe.

Liberia

Colonization struck many observers as totally impractical. Nonetheless, numerous prominent political leaders of the Jacksonian era—including Henry Clay, John Marshall, and Jackson himself—supported the Colonization Society. Many colonizationists believed that slavery and

Supporters of colonization

racism were so deeply embedded in American life that blacks could never achieve equality if freed and allowed to remain in the country. Like Indian removal, colonization rested on the premise that America is fundamentally a white society.

In the decades before the Civil War, several thousand black Americans did emigrate to Liberia with the aid of the Colonization Society. Some were slaves emancipated by their owners on the condition that they depart, while others left voluntarily, motivated by a desire to spread Christianity in Africa or to enjoy rights denied them in the United States. Having experienced "the legal slavery of the South and the social slavery of the North," wrote one emigrant on leaving for Liberia, he knew he could "never be a free man in this country."

But most African-Americans adamantly opposed the idea of colonization. In fact, the formation of the American Colonization Society galvanized free blacks to claim their rights as Americans. Early in 1817, some 3,000 free blacks assembled in Philadelphia for the first national black convention. Their resolutions insisted that blacks were Americans, entitled to the same freedom and rights enjoyed by whites.

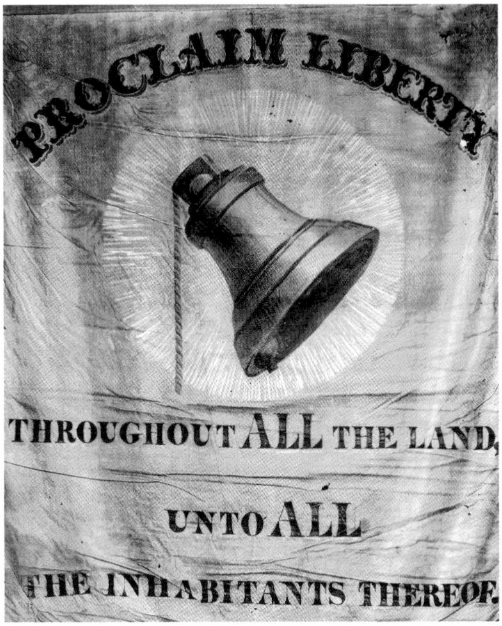

An abolitionist banner. Antislavery organizations adopted the Liberty Bell as a symbol of their campaign to extend freedom to black Americans. Previously, the bell, forged in Philadelphia in the eighteenth century, had simply been known as the Old State House Bell.

Militant Abolitionism

The abolitionist movement that arose in the 1830s differed profoundly from its genteel, conservative predecessor. Drawing on the religious conviction that slavery was an unparalleled sin and the secular one that it contradicted the values enshrined in the Declaration of Independence, a new generation of reformers rejected the traditional approach of gradual emancipation and demanded immediate abolition. Also unlike their predecessors, they directed explosive language against slavery and slaveholders and insisted that blacks, once free, should be incorporated as equal members of the republic rather than being deported. Perfecting American society, they insisted, meant rooting out not just slavery, but racism in all its forms.

David Walker

The first indication of the new spirit of abolitionism came in 1829 with the appearance of *An Appeal to the Coloured Citizens of the World* by David Walker, a free black who had been born in North Carolina and now operated a used-clothing store in Boston. A passionate indictment of slavery and racial prejudice, the *Appeal* warned whites that the nation faced divine punishment if it did not mend its sinful ways. Walker called on blacks to

William Lloyd Garrison, editor of *The Liberator* and one of the country's most prominent abolitionists, in an undated portrait by Edwin T. Billings.

take pride in the achievements of ancient African civilizations and to claim all their rights as Americans.

Walker died in mysterious circumstances in 1830. Not until the appearance in 1831 of *The Liberator*, William Lloyd Garrison's weekly journal published in Boston, did the new breed of abolitionism find a permanent voice. "I will be as harsh as truth," Garrison announced, "and as uncompromising as justice. On this subject, I do not wish to think, or speak, or write, with moderation. . . . I will not equivocate—I will not excuse—I will not retreat a single inch—and I will be heard."

And heard he was. Some of Garrison's ideas, such as his suggestion that the North abrogate the Constitution and dissolve the Union to end its complicity in the evil of slavery, were rejected by most abolitionists. But his call for the immediate abolition of slavery echoed throughout antislavery circles. Garrison's pamphlet *Thoughts on African Colonization* persuaded many foes of slavery that blacks must be recognized as part of American society, not viewed as aliens to be shipped overseas.

Spreading the Abolitionist Message

Pamphlets, broadsides, newspapers

Beginning with a handful of activists, the abolitionist movement expanded swiftly throughout the North. Antislavery leaders took advantage of the rapid development of print technology and the expansion of literacy due to common-school education to spread their message. Like radical pamphleteers of the American Revolution and evangelical ministers of the Second Great Awakening, they recognized the democratic potential in the production of printed material. Abolitionists seized on the recently invented steam printing press to produce millions of copies of pamphlets, newspapers, petitions, novels, and broadsides. Between the formation of the **American Anti-Slavery Society** in 1833 and the end of the decade, some 100,000 northerners joined local groups devoted to abolition. Most were ordinary citizens—farmers, shopkeepers, craftsmen, and laborers, along with a few prominent businessmen like the merchants Arthur and Lewis Tappan of New York.

Theodore Weld

If Garrison was the movement's most notable propagandist, Theodore Weld, a young minister who had been converted by the evangelical preacher Charles G. Finney, helped to create its mass constituency. A brilliant orator, Weld trained a band of speakers who brought the abolitionist message into the heart of the rural and small-town North. Their methods were those of the revivals—fervent preaching, calls for individuals to renounce their immoral ways—and their message was a simple one: slavery is a sin.

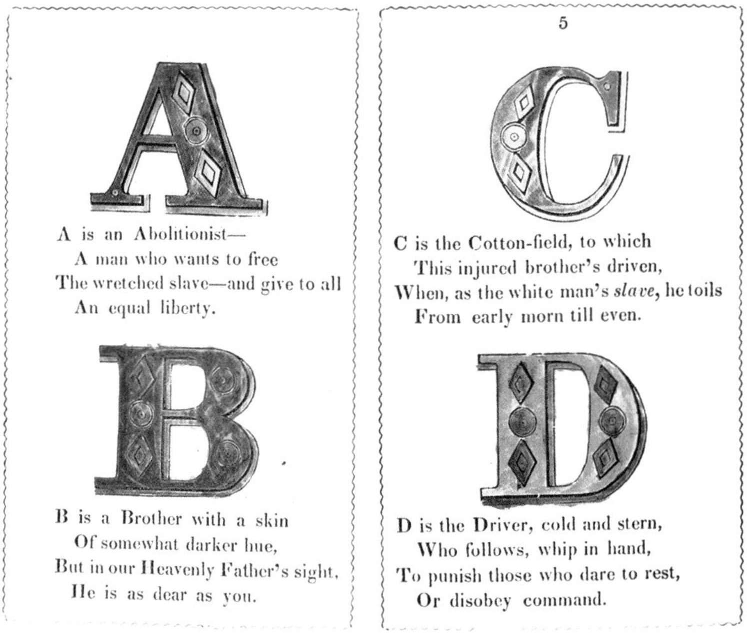

A is an Abolitionist—
A man who wants to free
The wretched slave—and give to all
An equal liberty.

B is a Brother with a skin
Of somewhat darker hue,
But in our Heavenly Father's sight,
He is as dear as you.

5

C is the Cotton-field, to which
This injured brother's driven,
When, as the white man's *slave*, he toils
From early morn till even.

D is the Driver, cold and stern,
Who follows, whip in hand,
To punish those who dare to rest,
Or disobey command.

Pages from an abolitionist book for children. Abolitionists sought to convince young and old of the evils of slavery.

Slavery and Moral Suasion

Many southerners feared that the abolitionists intended to spark a slave insurrection, a belief strengthened by the outbreak of Nat Turner's Rebellion a few months after *The Liberator* made its appearance. Yet not only was Garrison completely unknown to Turner, but nearly all abolitionists, despite their militant language, rejected violence as a means of ending slavery. Many were pacifists or "non-resistants," who believed that coercion should be eliminated from all human relationships and institutions. Their strategy was **moral suasion** and their arena the public sphere. Slaveholders must be convinced of the sinfulness of their ways, and the North of its complicity in the peculiar institution.

"Non-resistants"

Among the first to appreciate the key role of public opinion in a mass democracy, abolitionists focused their efforts not on infiltrating the existing political parties, but on awakening the nation to the moral evil of slavery. Their language was deliberately provocative, calculated to seize public attention. "Slavery," said Garrison, "will not be overthrown without excitement, without a most tremendous excitement." Abolitionists argued that the inherent, natural, and absolute right to personal liberty, regardless of race, took precedence over other forms of freedom, such as the right of citizens to accumulate and hold property or self-government by local political communities.

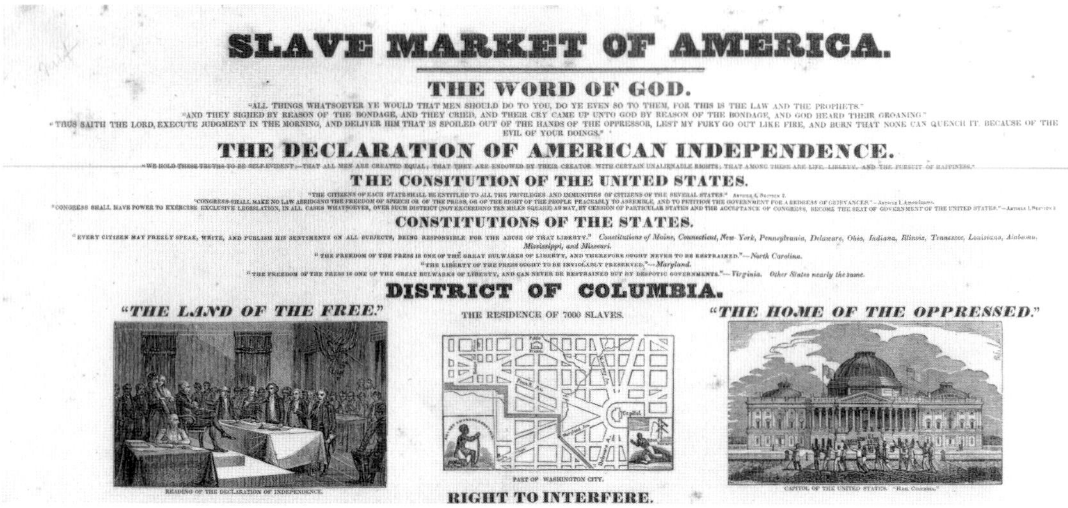

SLAVE MARKET OF AMERICA.
THE WORD OF GOD.
"ALL THINGS WHATSOEVER YE WOULD THAT MEN SHOULD DO TO YOU, DO YE EVEN SO TO THEM, FOR THIS IS THE LAW AND THE PROPHETS."
"AND THEY SIGHED BY REASON OF THE BONDAGE, AND THEY CRIED, AND THEIR CRY CAME UP UNTO GOD BY REASON OF THE BONDAGE, AND GOD HEARD THEIR GROANING."
"THUS SAITH THE LORD, EXECUTE JUDGMENT IN THE MORNING, AND DELIVER HIM THAT IS SPOILED OUT OF THE HANDS OF THE OPPRESSOR, LEST MY FURY GO OUT LIKE FIRE, AND BURN THAT NONE CAN QUENCH IT, BECAUSE OF THE EVIL OF YOUR DOINGS."
THE DECLARATION OF AMERICAN INDEPENDENCE.
THE CONSITUTION OF THE UNITED STATES.
CONSTITUTIONS OF THE STATES.
"THE FREEDOM OF THE PRESS IS ONE OF THE GREAT BULWARKS OF LIBERTY, AND THEREFORE OUGHT NEVER TO BE RESTRAINED."—North Carolina.
"THE LIBERTY OF THE PRESS OUGHT TO BE INVIOLABLY PRESERVED."—Maryland.
DISTRICT OF COLUMBIA.
"THE LAND OF THE FREE."
THE RESIDENCE OF 7000 SLAVES.
"THE HOME OF THE OPPRESSED."
RIGHT TO INTERFERE.

Slave Market of America, an engraving produced by the American Anti-Slavery Society in 1836, illustrates how abolitionists sought to identify their cause with American traditions, even as they mocked the nation's claim to be a "land of the free."

Birthright Citizenship

The crusade against slavery gave birth to a new understanding of citizenship and the rights it entailed, a new answer to the question, Who is an American? Long before the Civil War, abolitionists black and white developed a definition of national citizenship severed from the concept of race, with citizens' rights enforced by the federal government. Abolitionists campaigned for northern free blacks' right to vote, access to education, and equal treatment by transportation companies and public accommodations such as hotels and theaters. They put forward ideas that would be incorporated into the laws and Constitution after the Civil War: that any person born in the United States was entitled to American citizenship and that citizens should enjoy full equality, regardless of race.

"Colored citizens"

The antislavery conventions organized by free blacks promoted the principle of "birthright citizenship," commonly describing themselves as gatherings of "colored citizens." "Nothing could be plainer," declared the National Convention of Colored Citizens in 1843, "than that native free born men must be citizens." Black leaders insistently claimed the same civil and political rights as enjoyed by white citizens, as well as what they called "public rights," which encompassed equal access to businesses serving the public such as hotels, theaters, streetcars, steamships, and railroads, which regularly excluded blacks. Free blacks and their white allies used a variety of tactics to press for citizenship rights. They launched campaigns for the right to vote, sued streetcar companies that excluded black passengers, and challenged discriminatory laws in local, state, and federal courts. Their efforts were usually unsuccessful, but they did win a few victories, such as the repeal of Ohio's discriminatory Black Laws in

1849 and the racial integration of Boston's public schools in 1855. These campaigns helped to establish a new discourse of citizens' rights.

A New Vision of America

In a society in which the rights of citizenship had become more and more closely associated with whiteness, the antislavery movement sought to reinvigorate the idea of freedom as a truly universal entitlement. The origin of the idea of an American people unbounded by race lies not with the founders, who by and large made their peace with slavery, but with the abolitionists. The antislavery crusade viewed slaves and free blacks as members of the national community, a position summarized in the title of Lydia Maria Child's popular treatise of 1833, *An Appeal in Favor of That Class of Americans Called Africans.*

An American people unbounded by race

The crusade against slavery, wrote Angelina Grimké, who became a leading abolitionist speaker, was the nation's preeminent "school in which human rights are . . . investigated." Abolitionists debated the Constitution's relationship to slavery. William Lloyd Garrison burned the document, calling it a covenant with the devil; Frederick Douglass came to believe that it offered no national protection to slavery. But despite this difference of opinion, abolitionists developed an alternative, rights-oriented view of constitutional law, grounded in their universalistic understanding of liberty. Seeking to define the core rights to which all Americans were entitled—the meaning of freedom in concrete legal terms—abolitionists invented the concept of equality before the law regardless of race, one all but unknown in American life before the Civil War. Abolitionist literature also helped to expand the definition of cruelty. The graphic descriptions of the beatings, brandings, and other physical sufferings of the slaves helped to popularize the idea of bodily integrity as a basic right that slavery violated.

Abolitionism and the Constitution

Despite being denounced by their opponents as enemies of American principles, abolitionists consciously identified their movement with the revolutionary heritage. The Declaration of Independence was not as fundamental to public oratory in the early republic as it would later become. Abolitionists seized upon it, interpreting the document's preamble as a condemnation of slavery. The Liberty Bell, later one of the nation's most venerated emblems of freedom, did not achieve that status until abolitionists adopted it as a symbol and gave it its name as part of an effort to identify their principles with those of the founders. Of course, Americans of all regions and political beliefs claimed the Revolution's legacy. Abolitionists never represented more than a small part of the North's population. But as the slavery controversy intensified, the belief spread far beyond abolitionist circles that slavery contradicted the nation's heritage of freedom.

Abolitionism and the revolutionary heritage

BLACK AND WHITE ABOLITIONISM

Black Abolitionists

One of many popular lithographs illustrating scenes from Harriet Beecher Stowe's novel *Uncle Tom's Cabin*, the most widely read of all antislavery writings. This depicts the slave Eliza escaping with her child across the ice floes of the Ohio River.

Blacks played a leading role in the antislavery movement. Frederick Douglass was only one among many former slaves who published accounts of their lives in bondage; these works convinced thousands of northerners of the evils of slavery. Indeed, the most effective piece of antislavery literature of the entire period, Harriet Beecher Stowe's novel *Uncle Tom's Cabin*, was to some extent modeled on the autobiography of the fugitive slave Josiah Henson. Serialized in 1851 in a Washington antislavery newspaper and published as a book the following year, ***Uncle Tom's Cabin*** sold more than 1 million copies by 1854, and it also inspired numerous stage versions. By portraying slaves as sympathetic men and women, and as Christians at the mercy of slaveholders who split up families and set bloodhounds on innocent mothers and children, Stowe's melodrama gave the abolitionist message a powerful human appeal.

By the 1840s, black abolitionists sought an independent role within the movement, regularly holding their own conventions. The black abolitionist Henry Highland Garnet, who as a child had escaped from slavery in Maryland with his father, proclaimed at one such gathering in 1843 that slaves should rise in rebellion to throw off their shackles. His position was so at odds with the prevailing belief in moral suasion that the published proceedings entirely omitted the speech.

At every opportunity, black abolitionists rejected the nation's pretensions as a land of liberty. Free black communities in the North devised an alternative calendar of "freedom celebrations" centered on January 1, the date in 1808 on which the slave trade became illegal, and August 1, the anniversary of West Indian emancipation, rather than July 4. Even more persistently than their white counterparts, black abolitionists articulated the ideal of color-blind citizenship.

A photograph of Frederick Douglass, the fugitive slave who became a prominent abolitionist, taken between 1847 and 1852. As a fellow abolitionist noted at the time, "The very look and bearing of Douglass are an irresistible logic against the oppression of his race."

The greatest oration on American slavery and American freedom was delivered in Rochester in 1852 by Frederick Douglass. Speaking just after the annual Independence Day celebration, Douglass posed the question, "What, to the Slave, Is the Fourth of July?" He answered that Fourth of July festivities revealed the hypocrisy of a nation that proclaimed its belief in liberty yet daily committed "practices more shocking and bloody" than did any other country on earth. Like other abolitionists, however, Douglass also laid claim to the founders' legacy. The Revolution had left a "rich inheritance of justice, liberty, prosperity, and independence" from which subsequent generations had tragically strayed. Only by abolishing slavery and freeing the "great doctrines" of the Declaration of Independence from the "narrow bounds" of race could the United States recapture its original mission.

Gentlemen of Property and Standing

At first, abolitionism aroused violent hostility from northerners who feared that the movement threatened to disrupt the Union, interfere with profits wrested from slave labor, and overturn white supremacy. Led by "**gentlemen of property and standing**" (often merchants with close commercial ties to the South), mobs disrupted abolitionist meetings in northern cities.

Elijah P. Lovejoy

In 1837, antislavery editor Elijah P. Lovejoy became the movement's first martyr when he was killed by a mob in Alton, Illinois, while defending his press. In 1838, a mob in Philadelphia burned to the ground Pennsylvania Hall, which abolitionists had built to hold their meetings. Before starting the fire, however, the mob patriotically carried a portrait of George Washington to safety.

Burning abolitionist literature

Elsewhere, crowds of southerners, with the unspoken approval of Andrew Jackson's postmaster general, Amos Kendall, burned abolitionist literature that they had removed from the mails. In 1836, when abolitionists began to flood Washington with petitions calling for emancipation in the nation's capital, the House of Representatives adopted the notorious **gag rule**, which prohibited their consideration. The rule was repealed in 1844, thanks largely to the tireless opposition of former president John Quincy Adams, who from 1831 represented Massachusetts in the House.

Far from stemming the movement's growth, however, mob attacks and attempts to limit abolitionists' freedom of speech convinced many northerners that slavery was incompatible with the democratic liberties of white Americans. "We commenced the present struggle," announced

Destruction by Fire of Pennsylvania Hall, a lithograph depicting the burning of the abolitionist meeting hall by a Philadelphia mob in 1838.

Am I Not a Man and a Brother? The most common abolitionist depiction of a slave, this image not only presents African-Americans as unthreatening individuals seeking white assistance but also calls upon white Americans to recognize blacks as fellow men unjustly held in bondage.

abolitionist William Jay, "to obtain the freedom of the slave; we are compelled to continue it to preserve our own. We are now contending . . . for the liberty of speech, of the press, and of conscience."

The abolitionist movement now broadened its appeal so as to win the support of northerners who cared little about the rights of blacks but could be convinced that slavery endangered their own cherished freedoms. The gag rule aroused considerable resentment in the North. "If the government once begins to discriminate as to what is orthodox and what heterodox in opinion," wrote the *New York Evening Post*, hardly a supporter of abolitionism, "farewell, a long farewell to our freedom."

THE ORIGINS OF FEMINISM

The Rise of the Public Woman

"When the true history of the antislavery cause shall be written," Frederick Douglass later recalled, "women will occupy a large space in its pages." Much of the movement's grassroots strength derived from northern women, who joined by the thousands. Most were evangelical Protestants, New England Congregationalists, or Quakers convinced, as Martha Higginson of Vermont wrote, that slavery was "a disgrace in this land of Christian light and liberty."

Women and politics

The public sphere was open to women in ways government and party politics were not. Women's letters and diaries reveal a keen interest in political issues, from slavery to presidential campaigns. Long before they could vote, women circulated petitions, attended mass meetings, marched in political parades, delivered public lectures, and raised money for political causes. They became active in the temperance movement, the building of asylums, and other reform activities. **Dorothea Dix**, a Massachusetts schoolteacher, was the leading advocate of more humane treatment of the insane, who at the time generally were placed in jails alongside debtors and hardened criminals. Thanks to her efforts, twenty-eight states constructed mental hospitals before the Civil War.

Women and Free Speech

Abolitionism and women's rights

All these activities enabled women to carve out a place in the public sphere. But it was participation in abolitionism that inspired the early movement for women's rights. In working for the rights of the slave, not a few women developed a new understanding of their own subordinate status. The daughters of a prominent South Carolina slaveholder, Angelina and Sarah Grimké had been converted first to Quakerism and then to abolitionism while visiting Philadelphia. During the 1830s, they began to deliver popular lectures that offered a scathing condemnation of slavery from the perspective of those who had witnessed its evils firsthand.

The Grimké sisters

Outraged by the sight of females sacrificing all "modesty and delicacy" by appearing on the public lecture platform, a group of Massachusetts clergymen denounced the sisters. In reply, they forthrightly defended not only the right of women to take part in political debate but also their right to share the social and educational privileges enjoyed by men. "Since I engaged in the investigation of the rights of the slave," declared Angelina Grimké, "I have necessarily been led to a better understanding of my own." Her sister Sarah proceeded to publish *Letters on the Equality of the Sexes* (1838), a powerful call for equal rights for women. The book raised numerous issues familiar even today, including what later generations would call "equal pay for equal work." Why, Sarah Grimké wondered, did male teachers invariably receive higher wages than women, and a male tailor earn "two or three times as much" as a female counterpart "although the work done by each may be equally good?"

Letters on the Equality of the Sexes

Women's Rights

The Grimké sisters were the first to apply the abolitionist doctrine of universal freedom and equality to the status of women. Although they soon retired from the fray, unwilling to endure the intense criticism to which they were subjected, their writings helped to spark the movement for women's rights, which arose in the 1840s.

Elizabeth Cady Stanton and Lucretia Mott, the key organizers of the Seneca Falls Convention of 1848, were veterans of the antislavery crusade. In 1840, they had traveled to London as delegates to the World Anti-Slavery Convention, only to be barred from participating because of their sex. The Seneca Falls Convention, a gathering on behalf of women's rights held in the upstate New York town where Stanton lived, raised the issue of **woman suffrage** for the first time. Stanton, the principal author, modeled the Seneca Falls Declaration of Sentiments on the Declaration of Independence (see the Appendix for the full text). But the document added "women" to Jefferson's axiom "all men are created equal," and in place of a list of injustices committed by George III, it condemned the "injuries and usurpations on the part of man toward woman." The first was denying her the right to vote. As Stanton told the convention, only the vote would make woman "free as man is free," since in a democratic society, freedom was impossible without access to the ballot. The argument was simple and irrefutable: in the words of Lydia Maria Child, "either the theory of our government is *false*, or women have a right to vote."

The Seneca Falls Convention

The Declaration of Sentiments

WHO IS AN AMERICAN?

From Declaration of Sentiments of the Seneca Falls Convention (1848)

The Seneca Falls Convention is best known as the beginning of the seventy-year struggle for woman suffrage. Modeled on the Declaration of Independence and mainly written by Elizabeth Cady Stanton, the Declaration of Sentiments began by demanding the right to vote but went on to denounce numerous forms of inequality that prevented women from enjoying full participation in American life.

We hold these truths to be self-evident: that all men and women are created equal; that they are endowed by their Creator with certain inalienable rights; that among these are life, liberty, and the pursuit of happiness. . . .

The history of mankind is a history of repeated injuries and usurpations on the part of man toward woman, having in direct object the establishment of an absolute tyranny over her. To prove this, let facts be submitted to a candid world.

He has never permitted her to exercise her inalienable right to the elective franchise. . . .

He has made her, if married, in the eye of the law, civilly dead.

He has taken from her all right in property, even to the wages she earns. . . . In the covenant of marriage, she is compelled to promise obedience to her husband, he becoming, to all intents and purposes, her master—the law giving him power to deprive her of her liberty, and to administer chastisement. . . .

He has monopolized nearly all the profitable employments, and from those she is permitted to follow, she receives but a scanty remuneration. He closes against her all the avenues to wealth and distinction which he considers most honorable to himself. As a teacher of theology, medicine, or law, she is not known. He has denied her the facilities of obtaining a thorough education, all colleges being closed against her. . . .

He has endeavored, in every way that he could, to destroy her confidence in her own powers, to lessen her self-respect, and to make her willing to lead a dependent and abject life.

Now, in view of the unjust laws mentioned above, and because women do feel themselves aggrieved, oppressed, and fraudulently deprived of their most sacred rights, we insist that they have immediate admission to all the rights and privileges which belong to them as citizens of the United States.

QUESTIONS

1. *Other than denial of the right to vote, what are the key grievances of these women?*
2. *Why does the document model itself on the Declaration of Independence?*

Start of the struggle for suffrage

Seneca Falls marked the beginning of the seventy-year struggle for woman suffrage. The vote, however, was hardly the only issue raised at the convention. The Declaration of Sentiments condemned the entire structure of inequality that denied women access to education and employment, gave husbands control over the property and wages of their wives and custody of children in the event of divorce, deprived women of independent legal status after they married, and restricted them to the home as their "sphere of action." Equal rights became the rallying cry of the early movement for women's rights, and equal rights meant claiming access to all the prevailing definitions of freedom.

Feminism and Freedom

Like abolitionism, temperance, and other reforms, **feminism** was an international movement. Lacking broad backing at home, early feminists found allies abroad. "Women alone will say what freedom they want," declared an article in *The Free Woman*, a journal established in Paris in 1832.

Women, wrote Margaret Fuller, had the same right as men to develop their talents, to "grow . . . to live freely and unimpeded." The daughter of a Jeffersonian congressman, Fuller was educated at home. (She learned Latin before the age of six.) She became part of New England's transcendentalist circle (discussed in Chapter 9) and from 1840 to 1842 edited *The Dial*, a magazine that reflected the group's views. In 1844, Fuller became literary editor of the *New York Tribune*, the first woman to achieve so important a position in American journalism.

In *Woman in the Nineteenth Century*, published in 1845, Fuller sought to apply to women the transcendentalist idea that freedom meant a quest for personal development. "Every path" to self-fulfillment, she insisted, should be "open to woman as freely as to man." Fuller traveled to Europe as a correspondent for the *Tribune*, and there she married an Italian patriot. Along with her husband and baby, she died in a shipwreck in 1850 while returning to the United States.

The artist Thomas Hicks painted this portrait of the feminist writer and editor Margaret Fuller in 1848, two years before she died in a shipwreck as she was returning from a sojourn in Europe.

Women and Work

Women also demanded the right to participate in the market revolution. At an 1851 women's rights convention, the black abolitionist Sojourner Truth insisted that the movement devote attention to the plight of poor and working-class women and repudiate the idea that women were too delicate to engage in work outside the home. Born a slave in New York State around 1799, Truth did not obtain her freedom until slavery finally ended in the state in 1827. A listener at her 1851 speech (which was not recorded at the time) later recalled that Truth had spoken of her years of hard physical labor, flexed her arm to show her strength, and exclaimed, "And aren't I a woman?"

VOICES OF FREEDOM

From Angelina Grimké, Letter in *The Liberator* (August 2, 1837)

The daughters of a prominent South Carolina slaveholder, Angelina and Sarah Grimké became abolitionists after being sent to Philadelphia for education. In this article, Angelina Grimké explains how participation in the movement against slavery led her to a greater recognition of women's lack of basic freedoms.

Since I engaged in the investigation of the rights of the slave, I have necessarily been led to a better understanding of my own; for I have found the Anti-Slavery cause to be . . . the school in which human rights are more fully investigated, and better understood and taught, than in any other [reform] enterprise. . . . Here we are led to examine why human beings have any rights. It is because they are moral beings. . . . Now it naturally occurred to me, that if rights were founded in moral being, then the circumstance of sex could not give to man higher rights and responsibilities, than to woman. . . .

When I look at human beings as moral beings, all distinction in sex sinks to insignificance and nothingness; for I believe it regulates rights and responsibilities no more than the color of the skin or the eyes. My doctrine, then is, that whatever it is morally right for man to do, it is morally right for woman to do. . . . This regulation of duty by the mere circumstance of sex . . . has led to all that [numerous] train of evils flowing out of the anti-christian doctrine of masculine and feminine virtues. By this doctrine, man has been converted into the warrior, and clothed in sternness . . . whilst woman has been taught to lean upon an arm of flesh, to . . . be admired for her personal charms, and caressed and humored like a spoiled child, or converted into a mere drudge to suit the convenience of her lord and master. . . . It has robbed woman of . . . the right to think and speak and act on all great moral questions, just as men think and speak and act. . . .

The discussion of the wrongs of slavery has opened the way for the discussion of other rights, and the ultimate result will most certainly be . . . the letting of the oppressed of every grade and description go free.

From Catharine Beecher, *An Essay on Slavery and Abolitionism* (1837)

Most men, and many women, did not approve of women taking part in public debate. The prominent writer Catharine Beecher responded to the activities of the Grimké sisters by urging them to accept the fact that "heaven" had designated man "the superior" and woman "the subordinate."

I have . . . been informed, that you contemplate a tour, during the ensuing year, for the purpose of exerting your influence to form Abolition Societies among ladies of the non-slave-holding States. . . . The object I have in view, is to present some reasons why it seems unwise and inexpedient for ladies of the non-slave-holding States to unite themselves in Abolition Societies; and thus, at the same time, to exhibit the inexpediency of the course you propose to adopt. . . .

Heaven has appointed to one sex the superior, and to the other the subordinate station, and this without any reference to the character or conduct of either. It is therefore as much for the dignity as it is for the interest of females, in all respects to conform to the duties of this relation. . . . But while woman holds a subordinate relation in society to the other sex, it is not because it was designed that her duties or her influence should be any the less important, or all-pervading. But it was designed that the mode of gaining influence and of exercising power should be altogether different and peculiar. . . . Woman is to win every thing by peace and love; by making herself so much respected, esteemed and loved, that to yield to her opinions and to gratify her wishes, will be the free-will offering of the heart. But this is to be all accomplished in the domestic and social circle. . . . The moment woman begins to feel the promptings of ambition, or the thirst for power, her ægis of defence is gone. All the sacred protection of religion, all the generous promptings of chivalry, all the poetry of romantic gallantry, depend upon woman's retaining her place as dependent and defenceless, and making no claims, and maintaining no right but what are the gifts of honour, rectitude and love.

A woman may seek the aid of co-operation and combination among her own sex, to assist her in her appropriate offices of piety, charity, maternal and domestic duty; but whatever, in any measure, throws a woman into the attitude of a combatant, either for herself or others—whatever binds her in a party conflict—whatever obliges her in any way to exert coercive influences, throws her out of her appropriate sphere. . . . In this country, petitions to congress, in reference to the official duties of legislators, seem, IN ALL CASES, to fall entirely without the sphere of female duty. Men are the proper persons to make appeals to the rulers whom they appoint, and if their female friends, by arguments and persuasions, can induce them to petition, all the good that can be done by such measures will be secured.

QUESTIONS

1. *What consequences does Grimké believe follow from the idea of rights being founded in the individual's "moral being"?*
2. *How does Beecher believe women should exert power within American society?*
3. *How do the two definitions of women's freedom differ from one another?*

Amelia Bloomer and female attire

Although those who convened at Seneca Falls were predominantly from the middle class—no representatives of the growing number of "factory girls" and domestic servants took part—the participants rejected the identification of the home as woman's "sphere." During the 1850s, some feminists tried to popularize a new style of dress, devised by Amelia Bloomer, consisting of a loose-fitting tunic and trousers. The target of innumerable male jokes, the "bloomer" costume attempted to make a serious point—that the long dresses, tight corsets, and numerous petticoats considered to be appropriate female attire were so confining that they made it almost impossible for women to claim a place in the public sphere or to work outside the home.

The Slavery of Sex

Marriage and slavery

The dichotomy between freedom and slavery powerfully shaped early feminists' political language. Just as the idea of "wage slavery" enabled northern workers to challenge the inequalities of the market revolution, the concept of the "slavery of sex" empowered the women's movement to develop an all-encompassing critique of male authority and their own subordination. Feminists of the 1840s and 1850s pointed out that the law of marriage made nonsense of the description of the family as a "private" institution independent of public authority. When the abolitionists and women's rights activists Lucy Stone and Henry Blackwell married, they felt obliged to repudiate New York's laws that clothed the husband "with legal powers which . . . no man should possess." The analogy between free women and slaves gained prominence as it was swept up in the accelerating debate over slavery. For their part, southern defenders of slavery frequently linked slavery and marriage as natural and just forms of inequality. Eliminating the former institution, they charged, would threaten the latter.

Marriage was not, literally speaking, equivalent to slavery. The married woman, however, did not enjoy the fruits of her own labor—a central element of freedom. Beginning with Mississippi in 1839, numerous states enacted married women's property laws, shielding from a husband's creditors property brought into a marriage by his wife. Such laws initially aimed not to expand women's rights so much as to prevent families from losing their property during the depression that began in 1837. But in 1860, New York enacted a more far-reaching measure, allowing married women to sign contracts, buy and sell property, and keep their

Woman's Emancipation, a satirical engraving from *Harper's Monthly*, August 1851, illustrating the much-ridiculed "bloomer" costume.

own wages. In most states, however, property accumulated after marriage, as well as wages earned by the wife, still belonged to the husband.

"Social Freedom"

Self-ownership

Influenced by abolitionism, women's rights advocates turned another popular understanding of freedom—self-ownership, or control over one's own person—in an entirely new direction. The law of domestic relations presupposed the husband's right of sexual access to his wife and to inflict corporal punishment on her. Courts proved reluctant to intervene in cases of physical abuse so long as it was not "extreme" or "intolerable." "Women's Rights," declared a Boston meeting in 1859, included "freedom and equal rights in the family." The demand that women should enjoy the rights to regulate their own sexual activity and procreation and to be protected by the state against violence at the hands of their husbands challenged the notion that claims for justice, freedom, and individual rights should stop at the household's door.

Rights within the family

The issue of women's private freedom revealed underlying differences within the movement for women's rights. Belief in equality between the sexes and in the sexes' natural differences coexisted in antebellum feminist thought. Even as they entered the public sphere and thereby challenged some aspects of the era's "cult of domesticity" (discussed in Chapter 9), many early feminists accepted other elements. Allowing women a greater role in the public sphere, many female reformers argued, would bring their "inborn" maternal instincts to bear on public life, to the benefit of the entire society.

Women's private freedom

Even feminists critical of the existing institution of marriage generally refrained from raising in public the explosive issue of women's "private" freedom. Not until the twentieth century would the demand that freedom be extended to intimate aspects of life inspire a mass movement. But the dramatic fall in the birthrate over the course of the nineteenth century suggests that many women were quietly exercising "personal freedom" within their families.

The Abolitionist Schism

The role of women in abolitionism

Even in reform circles, the demand for a greater public role for women remained extremely controversial. Massachusetts physician Samuel Gridley Howe pioneered humane treatment of the blind and educational reform, and he was an ardent abolitionist. But Howe did not support his wife's participation in the movement for female suffrage, which, he complained, caused her to "neglect domestic relations." When abolitionism split into two wings in 1840, the immediate cause was a dispute over the proper role of women in antislavery work. Abby Kelley's election to the business committee of the

This image appeared on the cover of the sheet music for "Get Off the Track!," a song popularized by the Hutchinson singers, who performed antislavery songs. The trains *Immediate Emancipation* (with *The Liberator* as its front wheel) and *Liberty Party* pull into a railroad station. *The Herald of Freedom* and *American Standard* were antislavery newspapers. The song's lyrics praised William Lloyd Garrison and criticized various politicians, among them Henry Clay. The chorus went: "Roll it along! Through the nation / Freedom's car, Emancipation."

American Anti-Slavery Society sparked the formation of a rival abolitionist organization, the American and Foreign Anti-Slavery Society, which believed it wrong for a woman to occupy so prominent a position. The antislavery poet John Greenleaf Whittier compared Kelley to Eve, Delilah, and Helen of Troy, women who had sown the seeds of male destruction.

Behind the split lay the fear among some abolitionists that Garrison's radicalism on issues like women's rights, as well as his refusal to support the idea of abolitionists voting or running for public office, impeded the movement's growth. Determined to make abolitionism a political movement, the seceders formed the **Liberty Party**, which nominated James G. Birney as its candidate for president. He received only 7,000 votes (about one-third of 1 percent of the total). In 1840, antislavery northerners saw little wisdom in "throwing away" their ballots.

Achievements of feminism and abolitionism

While the achievement of most of their demands lay far in the future, the women's rights movement succeeded in making "the woman question" a permanent part of the transatlantic discussion of social reform. As for abolitionism, although it remained a significant presence in northern public life until emancipation was achieved, by 1840 the movement had accomplished its most important work. More than 1,000 local antislavery societies were now scattered throughout the North, representing a broad constituency awakened to the moral issue of slavery. The "great duty of freedom," Ralph Waldo Emerson had declared in 1837, was "to open our halls to discussion of this question." The abolitionists' greatest achievement lay in shattering the conspiracy of silence that had sought to preserve national unity by suppressing public debate over slavery.

CHAPTER REVIEW AND ONLINE RESOURCES

REVIEW QUESTIONS

1. *How did the utopian communities challenge existing ideas about property and marriage?*
2. *How did the supporters and opponents of temperance understand the meaning of freedom differently?*
3. *What were the similarities and differences between the common school and the institutions like asylums, orphanages, and prisons that were created by reformers?*
4. *Why did so many prominent white Americans, from both the North and South, support the colonization of freed slaves?*
5. *How was the abolition movement affected by other social and economic changes such as the rise in literacy, new print technology, and ideas associated with the market revolution?*
6. *How was racism evident even in the abolitionist movement? What steps did some abolitionists take to fight racism in American society?*
7. *How could antebellum women participate in the public sphere even though they were excluded from government and politics?*
8. *How did white women's participation in the abolitionist movement push them to a new understanding of their own rights and oppression?*
9. *How did advocates for women's rights in these years both accept and challenge existing gender beliefs and social roles?*
10. *To what degree was antebellum reform international in scope?*
11. *How did the antislavery movement give rise to a new understanding of citizenship and the rights it afforded?*

KEY TERMS

utopian communities (p. 336)
Shakers (p. 336)
Oneida (p. 337)
communitarianism (p. 339)
New Harmony (p. 339)
perfectionism (p. 339)
temperance movement (p. 339)
common school (p. 341)
American Colonization Society (p. 342)
American Anti-Slavery Society (p. 344)
moral suasion (p. 345)
Uncle Tom's Cabin (p. 348)
"gentlemen of property and standing" (p. 349)
gag rule (p. 349)
Dorothea Dix (p. 350)
woman suffrage (p. 351)
feminism (p. 353)
Liberty Party (p. 358)

Go to INQUIZITIVE

To see what you know—and learn what you've missed—with personalized feedback along the way.

Visit the ***Give Me Liberty!* Student Site** for primary source documents and images, interactive maps, author videos featuring Eric Foner, and more.

1820	Moses Austin receives Mexican land grant
1836	Texas independence from Mexico
1845	Inauguration of James Polk
	United States annexes Texas
1846–1848	Mexican War
1846	Wilmot Proviso
1848	Treaty of Guadalupe Hidalgo
	Gold discovered in California
	Free Soil Party organized
1849	Inauguration of Zachary Taylor
1850	Compromise of 1850
	Fugitive Slave Act
1853	Inauguration of Franklin Pierce
1854	Kansas-Nebraska Act
	Know-Nothing Party established
	Ostend Manifesto
	Republican Party organized
1856	"Bleeding Kansas"
1857	Inauguration of James Buchanan
	Dred Scott decision
1858	Lincoln-Douglas debates
1859	John Brown's raid on Harpers Ferry
1860	South Carolina secedes
1861	Inauguration of Abraham Lincoln
	Fort Sumter fired on

CHAPTER 13

A HOUSE DIVIDE

★

1840–1861

An 1835 painting of the federal arsenal at Harpers Ferry, Virginia (now West Virginia). John Brown's raid on Harpers Ferry in October 1859 helped to bring on the Civil War.

In 1855, Thomas Crawford, one of the era's most prominent American sculptors, was asked to design a statue to adorn the Capitol's dome, still under construction in Washington, D.C. He proposed a statue of Freedom, a female figure wearing a liberty cap. Secretary of War Jefferson Davis of Mississippi, one of the country's largest slaveholders, objected to Crawford's plan. Ancient Romans, he noted, regarded the cap as "the badge of the freed slave." Its use, he feared, might suggest that there was a connection between the slaves' longing for freedom and the liberty of freeborn Americans. Davis ordered the liberty cap replaced with a less controversial military symbol, a feathered helmet.

In 1863, the colossal Statue of Freedom was installed atop the Capitol, where it can still be seen today. By the time it was put in place, the country was immersed in the Civil War and Jefferson Davis had become president of the Confederate States of America. The dispute over the Statue of Freedom offers a small illustration of how, by the mid-1850s, nearly every public question was being swept up into the gathering storm over slavery.

FOCUS QUESTIONS

- *What were the major factors contributing to U.S. territorial expansion in the 1840s?*
- *Why did the expansion of slavery become the most divisive political issue in the 1840s and 1850s?*
- *What combination of issues and events fueled the creation of the Republican Party in the 1850s?*
- *What enabled Lincoln to emerge from the divisive party politics of the 1850s?*
- *What were the final steps on the road to secession?*

FRUITS OF MANIFEST DESTINY

Continental Expansion

In the 1840s, slavery moved to the center stage of American politics. It did so not in the moral language or with the immediatist program of

The original and final designs for Thomas Crawford's *Statue of Freedom* for the dome of the Capitol building. Secretary of War Jefferson Davis of Mississippi insisted that the liberty cap in the first design, a symbol of the emancipated slave in ancient Rome, be replaced.

abolitionism, but as a result of the nation's territorial expansion. Between 1840 and 1860, nearly 300,000 men, women, and children braved disease, starvation, the natural barrier of the Rocky Mountains, and occasional Indian attacks to travel overland to Oregon and California.

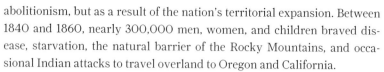

"Manifest destiny"

During most of the 1840s, the United States and Great Britain jointly administered Oregon, and Utah was part of Mexico. This did not stop Americans from settling in either region. National boundaries meant little to those who moved west. The 1840s witnessed an intensification of the old belief that God intended the American nation to reach all the way to the Pacific Ocean. As noted in Chapter 9, the term that became a shorthand for this expansionist spirit was "manifest destiny."

The Mexican Frontier: New Mexico and California

Mexican California

Settlement of Oregon did not directly raise the issue of slavery, although the prospect of new states in a region that did not seem hospitable to slavery alarmed some southerners. But the nation's acquisition of part of Mexico did. When Mexico achieved its independence from Spain in 1821, it was nearly as large as the United States, and its population of 6.5 million was about two-thirds that of its northern neighbor. However, Mexico's northern provinces—California, New Mexico, and Texas—were isolated and sparsely settled outposts surrounded by Indian country. California's non-Indian population in 1821, some 3,200 missionaries, soldiers, and settlers, was vastly outnumbered by about 20,000 Indians living and working on land owned by religious missions and by 150,000 members of unsubdued tribes in the interior. By 1840, California was already linked commercially with the United States, and New England ships were trading with the region. In 1846, Alfred Robinson, who had moved from Boston, published *Life in California*. "In this age of annexation," he wondered, "why not extend the 'area of freedom' by the annexation of California?"

A scene on a California ranch in 1849, with *Californios* (on horseback) and Native Americans at work.

The Texas Revolt

The first part of Mexico to be settled by significant numbers of Americans was Texas, whose non-Indian population of Spanish origin (called ***Tejanos***)

THE TRANS-MISSISSIPPI WEST, 1830s–1840s

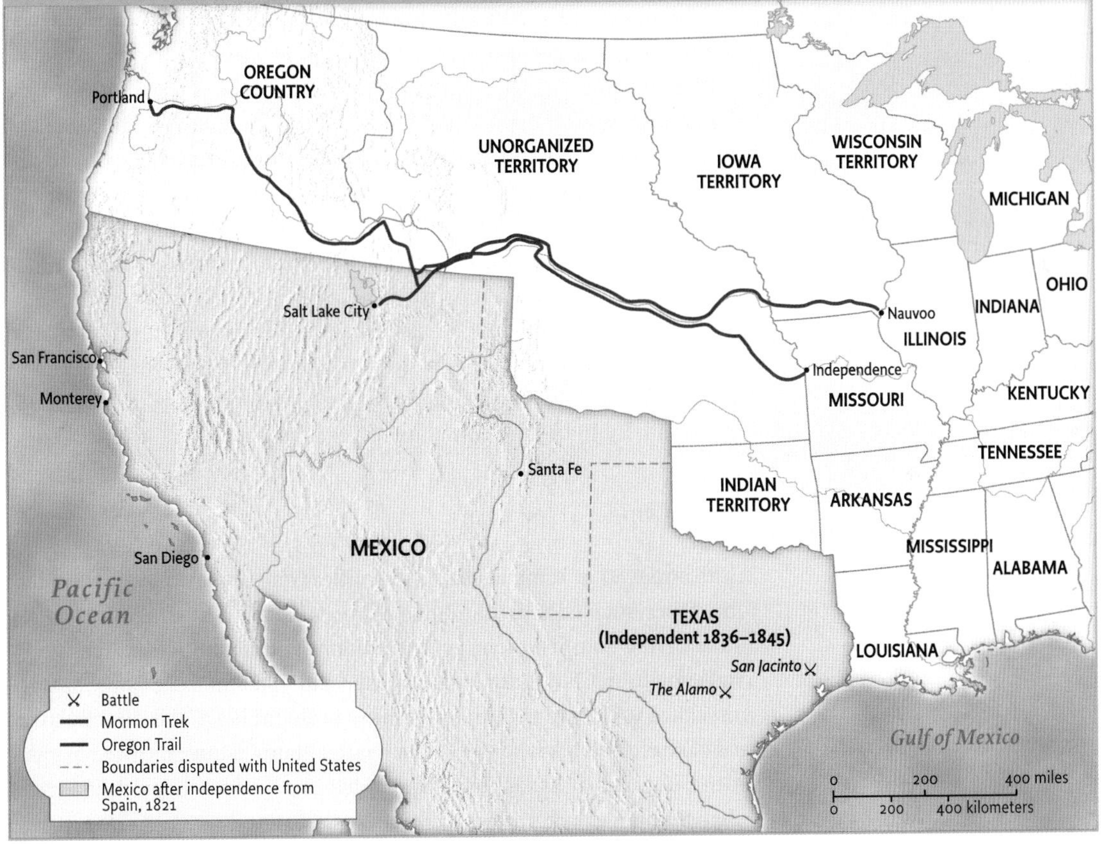

Westward migration in the early and mid-1840s took American settlers across Indian country into the Oregon Territory, ownership of which was disputed with Great Britain. The Mormons migrated west to Salt Lake City, then part of Mexico.

numbered only about 2,000 when Mexico became independent. In order to develop the region, the Spanish government had accepted an offer by Moses Austin, a Connecticut-born farmer, to colonize it with Americans. In 1820, Austin received a large land grant. He died soon afterward, and his son Stephen continued the plan, now in independent Mexico, reselling land in smaller plots to American settlers at twelve cents per acre.

Reasons for the Texas revolt

Alarmed that its grip on the area was weakening, the Mexican government in 1830 annulled existing land contracts and barred future emigration from the United States. Led by Stephen Austin, American settlers demanded greater autonomy within Mexico. Part of the area's tiny *Tejano* elite joined them. Mostly ranchers and large farmers, they had welcomed the economic boom that accompanied the settlers and had formed economic alliances with American traders. The issue of slavery further exacerbated matters. Mexico had abolished slavery, but local authorities allowed American settlers to bring slaves with them. Mexico's ruler,

General **Antonio López de Santa Anna**, sent an army in 1835 to impose central authority.

The appearance of Santa Anna's army sparked the chaotic **Texas revolt**. The rebels formed a provisional government that soon called for Texan independence. On March 6, 1836, Santa Anna's army stormed the Alamo, a mission compound in San Antonio, killing its 187 American and *Tejano* defenders. "Remember the Alamo" became the Texans' rallying cry. In April, forces under Sam Houston, a former governor of Tennessee, routed Santa Anna's army at the Battle of San Jacinto and forced him to recognize Texas independence. In 1837, the Texas Congress called for union with the United States. But fearing the political disputes certain to result from an attempt to add another slave state to the Union, President Martin Van Buren shelved the question. Settlers from the United States nonetheless poured into the region, many of them slaveowners taking up fertile cotton land. By 1845, the population of Texas reached nearly 150,000.

Battle of San Jacinto

The Election of 1844

The Tyler administration and Texas

Slavery and expansion

Texas annexation remained on the political back burner until President John Tyler revived it in the hope of rescuing his failed administration and securing southern support for renomination in 1844. In April 1844, a letter by John C. Calhoun, whom Tyler had appointed secretary of state, was leaked to the press. It linked the idea of absorbing Texas directly to the goal of strengthening slavery in the United States. Some southern leaders, indeed, hoped that Texas could be divided into several states, thus further enhancing the South's power in Congress. Late that month, Henry Clay and former president Van Buren, the prospective Whig and Democratic candidates for president and two of the party system's most venerable leaders, met at Clay's Kentucky plantation. They agreed to issue letters rejecting immediate annexation on the grounds that it might provoke war with Mexico.

Clay went on to receive the Whig nomination, but for Van Buren the letters proved to be a disaster. At the Democratic convention, southerners bent on annexation deserted Van Buren's cause, and he failed to receive the two-thirds majority necessary for nomination. The delegates then turned to the little-known James K. Polk, a former governor of Tennessee

The plaza in San Antonio not long after the United States annexed Texas in 1845.

whose main assets were his support for annexation and his close association with Andrew Jackson, still the party's most popular figure. To soothe injured feelings among northern Democrats over the rejection of Van Buren, the party platform called for not only the "reannexation" of Texas (implying that Texas had been part of the Louisiana Purchase and therefore had once belonged to the United States) but also the "reoccupation" of all of Oregon. "Fifty-four forty or fight"—American control of Oregon all the way to its northern boundary at north latitude 54°40'—became a popular campaign slogan.

Polk was the first "dark horse" candidate for president—that is, one whose nomination was completely unexpected. In the fall, he defeated Clay in an extremely close election. Polk's margin in the popular vote was less than 2 percent. Had not James G. Birney, running again as the Liberty Party candidate, received 16,000 votes in New York, mostly from antislavery Whigs, Clay would have been elected. In March 1845, only days before Polk's inauguration, Congress declared Texas part of the United States.

A campaign handkerchief from 1844 depicts the Whig candidate for president, Henry Clay, surrounded by images of national unity and the economic progress that, Whigs argued, would follow from the enactment of a protective tariff. Clay and his running mate, Theodore Frelinghuysen, were narrowly defeated by the Democrat James K. Polk.

The Road to War

James K. Polk may have been virtually unknown, but he assumed the presidency with a clearly defined set of goals: to reduce the tariff, reestablish the Independent Treasury system, settle the dispute over ownership of Oregon, and bring California into the Union. Congress soon enacted the

This 1853 watercolor by Sarah Ann Lillie Hardinge depicts a river crossing in Texas. Before bridges were built, a ferryman (in this case, a slave) brought people and goods across a river by pulling on a rope.

first two goals, and the third was accomplished in an agreement with Great Britain dividing Oregon at the forty-ninth parallel.

Acquiring California

Acquiring California proved more difficult. Polk dispatched an emissary to Mexico offering to purchase the region, but the Mexican government refused to negotiate. By the spring of 1846, Polk was planning for military action. In April, American soldiers under Zachary Taylor moved into the region between the Nueces River and the Rio Grande, land claimed by both countries on the disputed border between Texas and Mexico. This action made conflict with Mexican forces inevitable. When fighting broke out, Polk claimed that the Mexicans had "shed blood upon American soil" and called for a declaration of war.

The War and Its Critics

The **Mexican War** was the first American conflict to be fought primarily on foreign soil and the first in which American troops occupied a foreign capital. Inspired by the expansionist fervor of manifest destiny, a majority of Americans supported the war. But a significant minority in the North dissented, fearing that far from expanding the "great empire of liberty," the administration's real aim was to acquire new land for the expansion of slavery. Henry David Thoreau was jailed in Massachusetts in 1846 for refusing to pay taxes as a protest against the war. Defending his action, Thoreau wrote an important essay, "On Civil Disobedience," which inspired such later advocates of nonviolent resistance to unjust laws as Martin Luther King Jr.

"On Civil Disobedience"

Among the war's critics was Abraham Lincoln, who had been elected to Congress in 1846 from Illinois. Like many Whigs, Lincoln questioned whether the Mexicans had actually inflicted casualties on American soil, as Polk claimed. Lincoln's stance proved unpopular in Illinois. He had already agreed to serve only one term in Congress, but when Democrats captured his seat in 1848, many blamed the result on Lincoln's criticism of the war. Nonetheless, the concerns he raised regarding the president's power to "make war at pleasure" would continue to echo in the twentieth and twenty-first centuries.

Lincoln as war critic

Combat in Mexico

More than 60,000 volunteers enlisted and did most of the fighting. Combat took place on three fronts. In June 1846, a band of American insurrectionists proclaimed California freed from Mexican control and named Captain John C. Frémont, head of a small scientific expedition in the West, its ruler. Their aim was California's incorporation into the United States, but for the moment they adopted a flag depicting a large bear as the symbol of the area's independence. A month later, the U.S. Navy sailed into Monterey and San Francisco harbors, raised the American flag, and put an end to the "bear flag republic." At almost the same time, 1,600 American troops under General Stephen W. Kearney occupied Sante Fe without resistance and then set out for southern California, where they helped to put down a Mexican uprising against American rule.

War News from Mexico, an 1848 painting by Richard C. Woodville, shows how Americans received war news through the popular press.

The bulk of the fighting occurred in central Mexico. In February 1847, Taylor defeated Santa Anna's army at the Battle of Buena Vista. When the Mexican government still refused to negotiate, Polk ordered American forces under Winfield Scott to march inland from the port of Veracruz toward Mexico City. Scott's forces routed Mexican defenders and in September occupied the country's capital. In February 1848, the two governments agreed to the Treaty of Guadalupe Hidalgo, which confirmed the annexation of Texas and ceded California and present-day New Mexico, Arizona, Nevada, and Utah to the United States.

The Mexican War is only a footnote in most Americans' historical memory. Unlike for other wars, few public monuments celebrate the conflict. Mexicans, however, regard the war (or "the dismemberment," as it is called) as a central event of their national history and a source of resentment over a century and a half after it was fought.

The Mexican Cession

With the end of the Mexican War, the United States absorbed half a million square miles of Mexico's territory, one-third of that nation's total area. A region that for centuries had been united was suddenly split in two, dividing families and severing trade routes. An estimated 75,000 to 100,000 Spanish-speaking Mexicans and more than 150,000 Indians inhabited the land annexed from Mexico, known as the Mexican Cession. The Treaty of Guadalupe Hidalgo guaranteed to "male citizens" of the area "the free enjoyment of their liberty and property" and "all the rights" of Americans—a provision designed to protect the property of large Mexican landowners in California. Thus, in the first half of the nineteenth century, some residents of the area went from being Spaniards to Mexicans to Americans. Although not newcomers, they had to adjust to a new identity as if they were immigrants. As for Indians whose homelands and hunting grounds suddenly became part of the United States, the treaty referred to them only as "savage tribes" whom the United States must prevent from launching incursions into Mexico across the new border.

THE MEXICAN WAR, 1846–1848

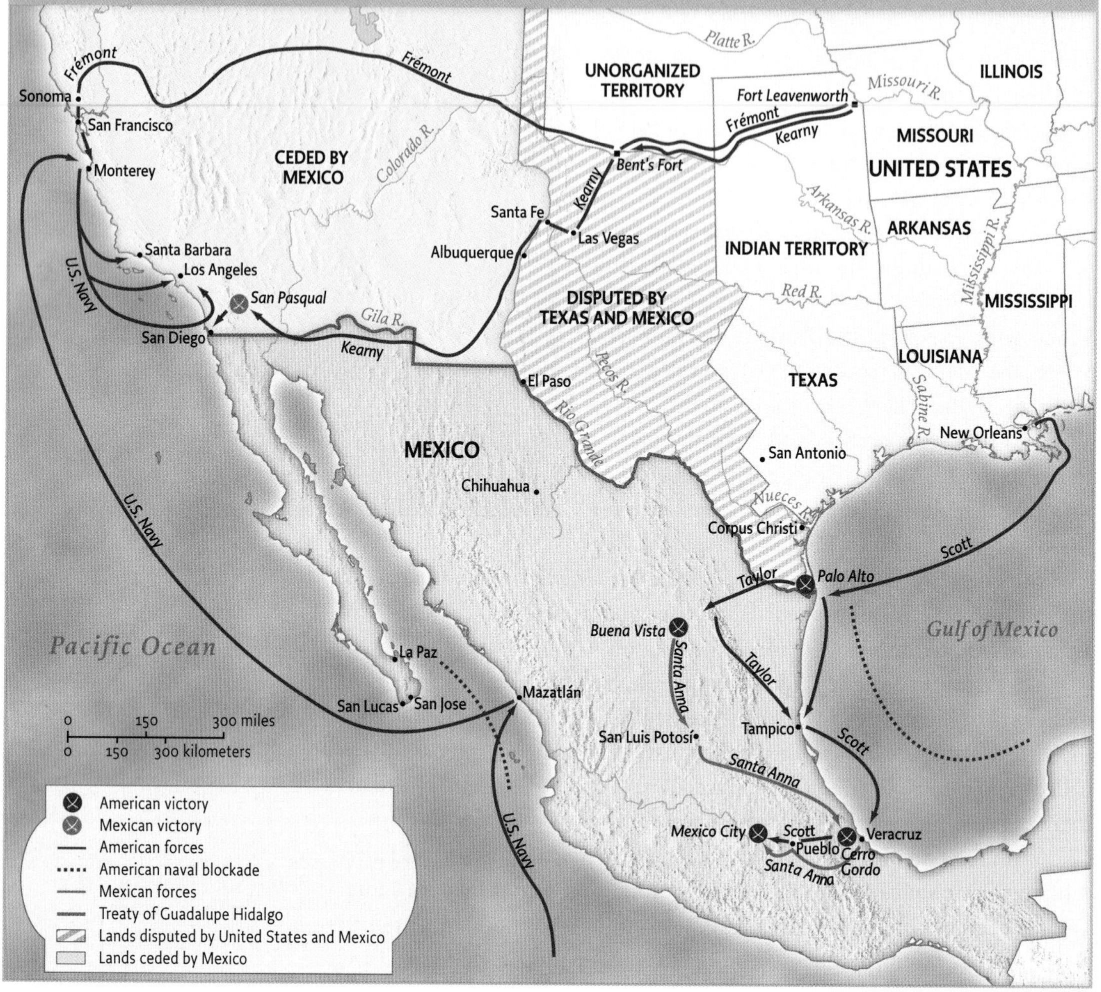

The Mexican War was the first in which an American army invaded another country and occupied its capital. As a result of the war, the United States acquired a vast new area in the modern-day Southwest.

The Texas Borderland

After achieving independence in 1836, Texas became a prime example of a western borderland. *Anglos* (white settlers from the East) and *Tejanos* had fought together to achieve independence, but soon relations between them soured. *Anglos* in search of land and resources expelled some Mexicans, including former allies, now suspected of loyalty to Mexico. Juan Seguín, a *Tejano*, had played an active role in the revolt and served for a time as mayor of San Antonio. In 1842, still mayor, he was driven from the town by vigilantes. He had become, he lamented, "a foreigner in my native land."

CONTINENTAL EXPANSION THROUGH 1853

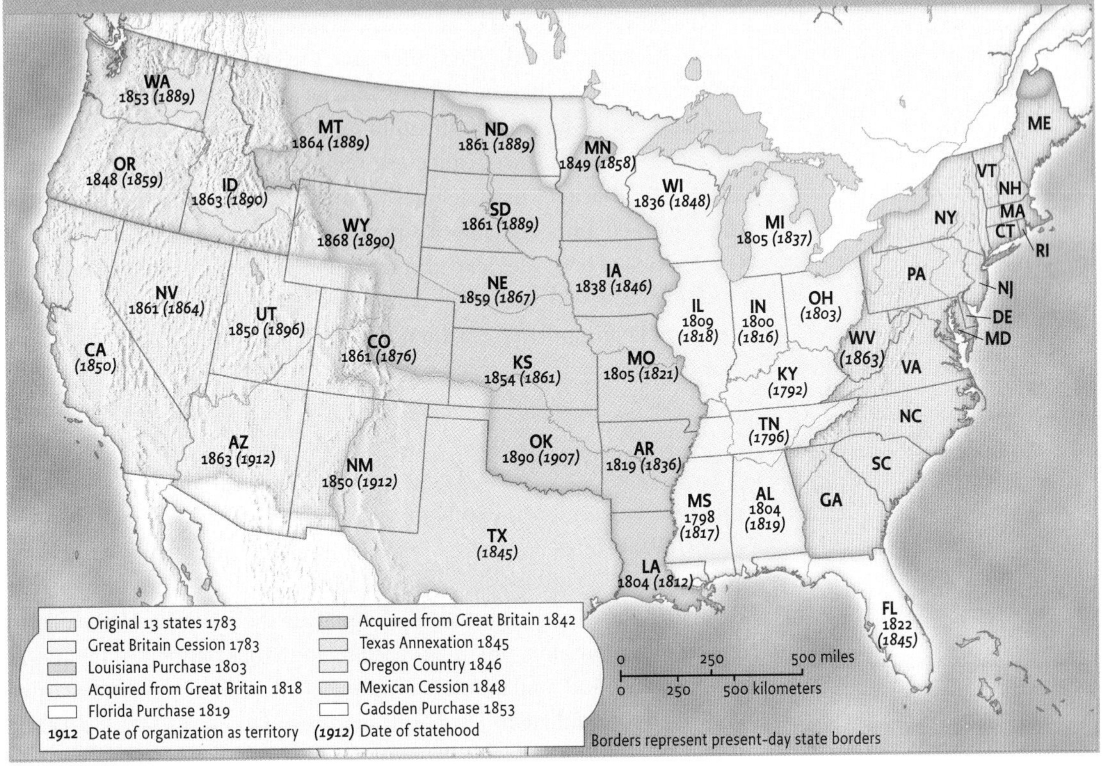

By 1853, with the Gadsden Purchase, the present boundaries of the United States in North America, with the exception of Alaska, had been created.

Increasingly, *Tejanos* were confined to unskilled agricultural or urban labor. Some *Tejanos* used their ambiguous identities to their own advantage. During the Civil War, some *Tejano* men avoided the Confederate draft by claiming to be citizens of Mexico.

Meanwhile, in southern Texas, the disputed territory between the Nueces River and the Rio Grande, claimed by both Texas and Mexico but actually controlled by Comanche Indians, became a site of continual conflict. Authority in the area remained contested until Texas became part of the much more powerful United States and even then, Comanche power would not be broken until the 1860s and 1870s.

Race and Manifest Destiny

During the 1840s, territorial expansion came to be seen as proof of the innate superiority of the "Anglo-Saxon race" (a mythical construct defined largely by its opposites: blacks, Indians, Hispanics, and Catholics). "*Race*," declared John L. O'Sullivan's *Democratic Review*, was the "key" to the "history of nations." Newspapers, magazines, and scholarly works popularized the link between American freedom and the supposedly innate liberty-loving qualities of Anglo-Saxon Protestants. Indeed, calls by some expansionists for the United States to annex all of Mexico failed in part because of fear that the nation could not assimilate its large non-white Catholic population, supposedly unfit for citizenship in a republic.

"Spanish" Mexicans as white

Local circumstances affected racial definitions in the former Mexican territories. Texas defined "Spanish" Mexicans, especially those who occupied important social positions, as white. The residents of New Mexico of both Mexican and Indian origin, on the other hand, were long deemed "too Mexican" for democratic self-government. With white migration lagging, Congress did not allow New Mexico to become a state until 1912.

Gold-Rush California

Sutter's mill

California had a non-Indian population of fewer than 15,000 when the Mexican War ended. For most of the 1840s, five times as many Americans emigrated to Oregon as to California. But this changed dramatically after January 1848, when gold was discovered in the foothills of the Sierra Nevada Mountains at a sawmill owned by the Swiss immigrant Johann A. Sutter. By ship and land, newcomers poured into California, in what came to be called the **gold rush**. The non-Indian population rose to 200,000 by 1852 and more than 360,000 eight years later.

A hand-colored engraving from the 1850s advertises the sale of a sixteen-year-old Southern California Native American woman. The price, listed in French, is a pound of gunpowder and a bottle of brandy. Slavery had been abolished in California law but persisted in some parts of the state.

California's gold-rush population was incredibly diverse. Experienced miners flooded in from Mexico and South America. Tens of thousands of Americans who had never seen a mine arrived from the East, and from overseas came Irish, Germans, Italians, and Australians. Nearly 25,000 Chinese landed between 1849 and 1852. Unlike the families who settled farming frontiers, most of the gold-rush migrants were young men. Women played many roles in western mining communities, running restaurants and boardinghouses and working as laundresses, cooks, and prostitutes. But as late as 1860, California's male population outnumbered females by nearly three to one.

As early surface mines quickly became exhausted, they gave way to underground mining that required a large investment of capital. This economic development worsened conflicts among California's many racial and ethnic groups engaged in fierce competition for gold. White miners organized extralegal groups that expelled "foreign miners"—Mexicans, Chileans, Chinese, French, and American Indians—from areas with gold. The state legislature imposed a tax of twenty dollars per month on foreign miners, driving many of them from the state.

For California's Indians, the gold rush and absorption into the United States proved to be disastrous. Gold seekers overran Indian communities. Miners, ranchers, and vigilantes murdered thousands of Indians. Determined to reduce the native population, state officials paid millions in bounties to private militias that launched attacks on the state's Indians. Although California was a free state, thousands of Indian children, declared orphans or vagrants by local courts, were bought and sold as slaves. By 1860, California's Indian population, nearly 150,000 when the Mexican War ended, had been reduced to around 30,000.

Opening Japan

The Mexican War ended with the United States in possession of the magnificent harbors of San Diego and San Francisco, long seen as jumping-off points for trade with the Far East. Between 1848 and 1860 American trade with China tripled. In the 1850s, the United States took the lead in opening Japan, a country that had closed itself to nearly all foreign contact for more than two centuries. In 1853 and 1854, American warships under the command of **Commodore Matthew Perry** (the younger brother of Oliver Perry, a hero of the War of 1812) sailed into Tokyo Harbor. Perry, who had been sent by President Millard Fillmore to negotiate a trade treaty, demanded that the Japanese deal with him. Alarmed by European intrusions into China and impressed by Perry's armaments as well as a musical pageant he presented that included a blackface minstrel show, Japanese leaders agreed to do so. In 1854, they opened two ports to American shipping. Japan soon launched a process of modernization that transformed it into the region's major military power.

Transportation of Cargo by Westerners at the Port of Yokohama, 1861, by the Japanese artist Utagawa Sadahide, depicts ships in port, including an American one on the left, eight years after Commodore Perry's first voyage to Japan.

A DOSE OF ARSENIC

Victory over Mexico added more than 1 million square miles to the United States—an area larger than the Louisiana Purchase. But the acquisition of this vast territory raised the fatal issue that would disrupt the political system and

Slavery in the West

plunge the nation into civil war—whether slavery should be allowed to expand into the West. Events soon confirmed Ralph Waldo Emerson's prediction that if the United States gobbled up part of Mexico, "it will be as the man who swallows arsenic. . . . Mexico will poison us."

Already, the bonds of union were fraying. In 1844 and 1845, the Methodists and Baptists, the two largest evangelical churches, divided into northern and southern branches. But it was the entrance of the slavery issue into the heart of American politics as the result of the Mexican War that eventually dissolved perhaps the strongest force for national unity—the two-party system.

The Wilmot Proviso

Party vs. section

Before 1846, the status of slavery in all parts of the United States had been settled, either by state law or by the Missouri Compromise, which determined slavery's status in the Louisiana Purchase. The acquisition of new land reopened the question of slavery's expansion. The divisive potential of this issue became clear in 1846, when Congressman David Wilmot of Pennsylvania proposed a resolution prohibiting slavery from all territory acquired from Mexico. Party lines crumbled as every northerner, Democrat and Whig alike, supported what came to be known as the **Wilmot Proviso**, while nearly all southerners opposed it. The measure passed the House, where the more populous North possessed a majority, but failed in the Senate, with its even balance of free and slave states.

"Popular Sovereignty

Effect on California's Indians

In 1848, opponents of slavery's expansion organized the **Free Soil Party** and nominated Martin Van Buren for president and Charles Francis Adams, the son of John Quincy Adams, as his running mate. Democrats nominated Lewis Cass of Michigan, who proposed that the decision on whether to allow slavery should be left to settlers in the new territories (an idea later given the name "popular sovereignty"). Van Buren was motivated in part by revenge against the South for jettisoning him in 1844. But his campaign struck a chord among northerners opposed to the expansion of slavery, and he polled some 300,000 votes, 14 percent of the northern total. Victory in 1848 went to the Whig candidate, Zachary Taylor, a hero of the Mexican War and a Louisiana sugar planter. But the fact that one former president and the son of another abandoned their parties to run on a Free Soil platform showed that antislavery sentiment had spread far beyond abolitionist ranks.

The Free Soil Appeal

The Free Soil position had a popular appeal in the North that far exceeded the abolitionists' demand for immediate emancipation and equal rights for blacks. Many northerners had long resented what they considered southern domination of the federal government. The idea of preventing the creation of new slave states appealed to those who favored policies, such as the protective tariff and government aid to internal improvements, that the majority of southern political leaders opposed.

Economic betterment

For thousands of northerners, moreover, the ability to move to the new western territories held out the promise of economic betterment. "Freedom of the soil," declared George Henry Evans, the editor of a pro-labor newspaper, offered the only alternative to permanent economic dependence for American workers.

The Free Soil platform of 1848

Such views merged easily with opposition to the expansion of slavery. If slave plantations were to occupy the fertile lands of the West, northern migration would be effectively blocked. The term "free soil" had a double meaning. The Free Soil platform of 1848 called both for barring slavery from western territories and for the federal government to provide free homesteads to settlers in the new territories. Unlike abolitionism, the "free soil" idea also appealed to the racism so widespread in northern society. Wilmot himself insisted that his controversial proviso was motivated to advance "the cause and rights of the free white man," in part by preventing him from having to compete with "black labor."

The view of southern leaders

To white southerners, the idea of barring slavery from territory acquired from Mexico seemed a violation of their equal rights as members of the Union. Just as northerners believed westward expansion essential to their economic well-being, southern leaders became convinced that slavery must expand or die. Moreover, the admission of new free states would overturn the delicate political balance between the sections and make the South a permanent minority. Southern interests would not be secure in a Union dominated by non-slaveholding states.

Crisis and Compromise

"Springtime of nations"

Developments in Europe

In world history, the year 1848 is remembered as the "springtime of nations," a time of democratic uprisings against the monarchies of Europe and demands by ethnic minorities for national independence. American principles of liberty and self-government appeared to be triumphing in the Old World. The Chartist movement in Great Britain organized massive demonstrations in support of democratic reforms. The French replaced their monarchy with a republic. Hungarians proclaimed their independence from Austrian rule. Patriots in Italy and Germany, both divided into numerous states, demanded national unification. But the revolutionary tide receded. Chartism faded away, Emperor Napoleon III soon restored the French monarchy, and revolts in Budapest, Rome, and other cities

Senator Daniel Webster of Massachusetts in a daguerreotype from 1850, the year his speech in support of the Compromise of 1850 contributed to its passage.

were crushed. Would their own experiment in self-government, some Americans wondered, suffer the same fate as the failed revolutions of Europe?

With the slavery issue appearing more and more ominous, established party leaders moved to resolve differences between the sections. In 1850, California asked to be admitted to the Union as a free state. Many southerners opposed the measure, fearing that it would upset the sectional balance in Congress. Senator Henry Clay offered a plan with four main provisions that came to be known as the **Compromise of 1850**. California would enter the Union as a free state. The slave trade, but not slavery itself, would be abolished in the nation's capital. A stringent new law would help southerners reclaim runaway slaves. And the status of slavery in the remaining territories acquired from Mexico would be left to the decision of the local white inhabitants. The United States would also agree to pay off the massive debt Texas had accumulated while independent.

The Great Debate

In the Senate debate on the Compromise, powerful leaders spoke for and against compromise. Daniel Webster of Massachusetts announced his willingness to abandon the Wilmot Proviso and accept a new fugitive slave law if this were the price of sectional peace. John C. Calhoun, again representing South Carolina, was too ill to speak. A colleague read his remarks rejecting the very idea of compromise. The North must yield, Calhoun insisted, or the Union could not survive. William H. Seward of New York also opposed compromise. To southerners' talk of their constitutional rights, Seward responded that a "higher law" than the Constitution condemned slavery—the law of morality. Here was the voice of abolitionism, now represented in the U.S. Senate.

President Zachary Taylor, like Andrew Jackson a southerner but a strong nationalist, insisted that all Congress needed to do was admit California to the Union. But Taylor died suddenly of an intestinal infection on July 9, 1850. His successor, Millard Fillmore of New York, threw his support to Clay's proposals. Fillmore helped to break the impasse in Congress and secure adoption of the Compromise of 1850.

This daguerreotype of Henry Clay, by the studio of the photographer Matthew Brady, was taken between 1850—when Clay became the chief author of the Compromise of 1850—and his death two years later.

The Fugitive Slave Issue

For one last time, political leaders had removed the dangerous slavery question from congressional debate. The new **Fugitive Slave Act**, however, made further controversy inevitable. The law allowed special federal commissioners to determine the fate of alleged fugitives without benefit of a jury trial or even testimony by the accused individual. It prohibited local authorities from interfering with the capture of fugitives and required individual citizens to assist in such capture when called upon by federal agents. Thus, southern leaders, usually strong defenders of states' rights and local autonomy, supported a measure that brought federal agents into communities throughout the North, armed with the power to override local law enforcement and judicial procedures to secure the return of runaway slaves. The security of slavery was more important to them than states'-rights consistency.

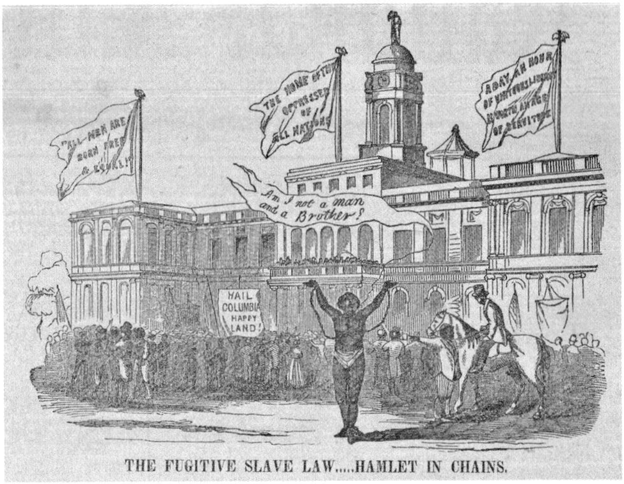

An engraving from the *National Anti-Slavery Standard*, October 17, 1850, depicts James Hamlet, the first person returned to slavery under the Fugitive Slave Act of 1850, in front of City Hall in New York. Flags fly from the building, emblazoned with popular American maxims violated by Hamlet's rendition. By the time this appeared in print, New Yorkers had raised the money to purchase Hamlet's freedom and he was back in the city.

During the 1850s, federal tribunals heard more than 300 cases throughout the free states and ordered 157 fugitives returned to the South, many at the government's expense. The law further widened sectional divisions and reinvigorated the Underground Railroad. In a series of dramatic confrontations, fugitives, aided by abolitionist allies, violently resisted recapture. A large crowd in 1851 rescued the escaped slave Jerry from jail in Syracuse, New York, and spirited him off to Canada. In the same year, an owner who attempted to recapture a fugitive was killed in Christiana, Pennsylvania.

Less dramatically, the men and women involved in the Underground Railroad redoubled their efforts to assist fugitives. Thanks to the consolidation of the railroad network in the North, it was now possible for escaping slaves who reached the free states to be placed on trains that would take them to safety in Canada in a day or two. In 1855 and 1856, Sydney Howard Gay, an abolitionist editor in New York City and a key Underground Railroad operative, recorded in a notebook the arrival of over 200 fugitives—men, women, and children—a majority of whom had been sent by train from Philadelphia. Gay dispatched them to upstate New York and Canada.

Fleeing to Canada

Overall, several thousand fugitives and freeborn blacks, worried that they might be swept up in the stringent provisions of the Fugitive Slave Act, fled to safety in Canada. The sight of so many refugees seeking liberty in a foreign land challenged the familiar image of the United States as an asylum for freedom.

Douglas and Popular Sovereignty

At least temporarily, the Compromise of 1850 seemed to restore sectional peace and party unity. In the 1852 presidential election, Democrat Franklin

Pierce won a sweeping victory over the Whig Winfield Scott on a platform that recognized the Compromise as a final settlement of the slavery controversy.

In 1854, the party system finally succumbed to the disruptive pressures of sectionalism. Early in that year, Illinois senator Stephen A. Douglas introduced a bill to provide territorial governments for Kansas and Nebraska, located within the Louisiana Purchase. A strong believer in western development, he hoped that a transcontinental railroad could be constructed through Kansas or Nebraska. Southerners in Congress, however, seemed adamant against allowing the organization of new free territories that might further upset the sectional balance. Douglas hoped to satisfy them by applying the principle of **popular sovereignty**, whereby the status of slavery would be determined by the votes of local settlers, not Congress. To Douglas, popular sovereignty embodied the idea of local self-government and offered a middle ground between the extremes of North and South.

The Kansas-Nebraska Act opened a vast area in the nation's heartland to the possible spread of slavery by repealing the Missouri Compromise and providing that settlers would determine the status of slavery in these territories.

THE KANSAS-NEBRASKA ACT, 1854

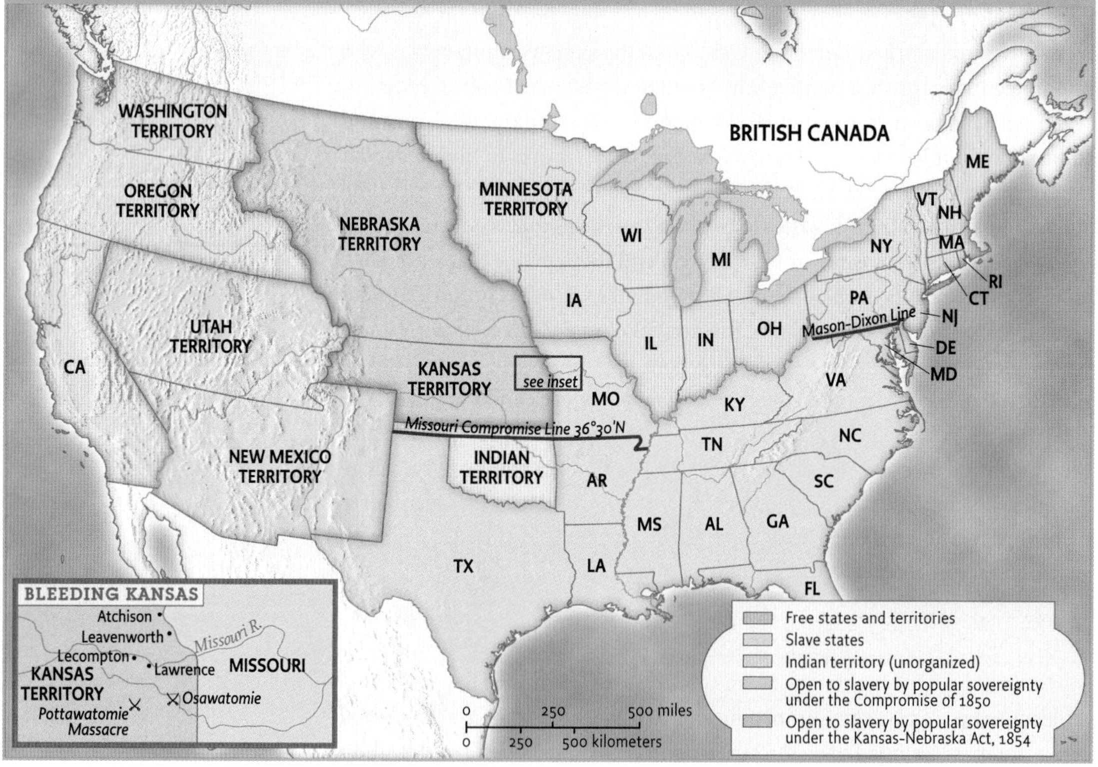

The Kansas-Nebraska Act

Unlike the lands taken from Mexico, Kansas and Nebraska lay in the nation's heartland, directly in the path of westward migration. Slavery, moreover, was prohibited there under the terms of the Missouri Compromise, which Douglas's bill would repeal. In response, a group of antislavery congressmen issued the *Appeal of the Independent Democrats*. It arraigned Douglas's bill as a "gross violation of a sacred pledge," part and parcel of "an atrocious plot" to convert free territory into a "dreary region of despotism, inhabited by masters and slaves." It helped to convince millions of northerners that southern leaders aimed at nothing less than extending their peculiar institution throughout the West.

Appeal of Independent Democrats

Thanks to Douglas's energetic leadership, the **Kansas-Nebraska Act** became law in 1854. But it shattered the Democratic Party's unity and sparked a profound reorganization of American politics. During the next two years, the Whig Party, unable to develop a unified response to the political crisis, collapsed. The South became solidly Democratic. Most northern Whigs, augmented by thousands of disgruntled Democrats, joined a new organization, the Republican Party, dedicated to preventing the further expansion of slavery.

The collapse of the Whig Party

THE RISE OF THE REPUBLICAN PARTY

The Northern Economy

The disruptive impact of slavery on the traditional parties was the immediate cause of political transformation in the mid-1850s. But the rise of the Republican Party also reflected underlying economic and social changes, notably the completion of the market revolution and the beginning of mass immigration from Europe.

The period from 1843 to 1857 witnessed explosive economic growth, especially in the North. The catalyst was the completion of the railroad network. From 5,000 miles in 1848, railroad track mileage grew to 30,000 by 1860, with most of the construction occurring in Ohio, Illinois, and other states of the Old Northwest. Four great trunk railroads now linked eastern cities with western farming and commercial centers. The railroads completed the reorientation of the Northwest's trade from the South to the East. As late as 1850, most western farmers still shipped their produce down the Mississippi River. Ten years later, however, railroads transported nearly all their crops to the East, at a fraction of the previous cost. Eastern industrialists marketed manufactured goods to the com-

The railroad network in the North

THE RAILROAD NETWORK, 1850s

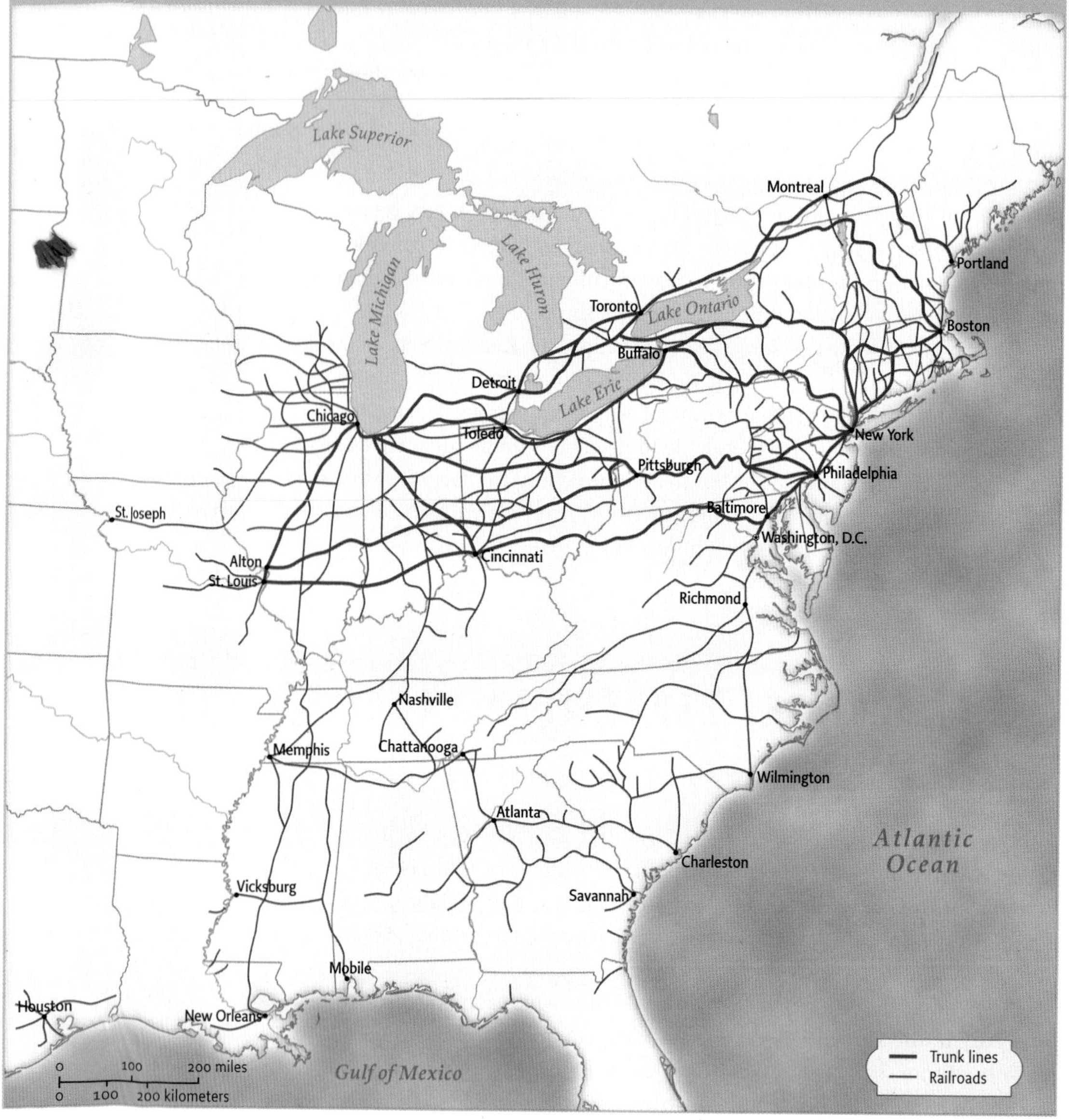

The rapid expansion of the railroad network in the 1850s linked the Northeast and Old Northwest in a web of commerce. The South's rail network was considerably less developed, accounting for only 30 percent of the nation's track mileage.

mercial farmers of the West, while residents of the region's growing cities consumed the food westerners produced. The economic integration of the Northwest and Northeast created the groundwork for their political unification in the Republican Party.

Integration of Northwest and Northeast

Although most northerners still lived in small towns and rural areas, the majority of the workforce no longer labored in agriculture. Two great areas of industrial production had arisen. One, along the Atlantic coast, stretched from Boston to Philadelphia and Baltimore. A second was centered on or near the Great Lakes, in inland cities like Buffalo, Cleveland, Pittsburgh, and Chicago. Driven by railroad expansion, coal mining and iron manufacturing were growing rapidly. Chicago, the Old Northwest's major rail center and the jumping-off place for settlers heading for the Great Plains, had become a complex manufacturing center. Although the southern economy was also growing and the continuing expansion of cotton production brought wealth to slaveholders, the South did not share in these broad economic changes.

Industrial manufacturing in the North

The Rise and Fall of the Know-Nothings

Nativism

Nativism—hostility to immigrants, especially Catholics—became a national political movement with the sudden appearance in 1854 of the American, or Know-Nothing, Party (so called because it began as a secret organization whose members, when asked about its existence, were supposed to respond, "I know nothing"). The **Know-Nothing Party** trumpeted its dedication to reserving political office for native-born Americans and to resisting the "aggressions" of the Catholic Church, such as its supposed

The Propagation Society—More Free than Welcome, an anti-Catholic cartoon from the 1850s, illustrates the nativist fear that the Catholic Church poses a threat to American society. Pope Pius IX, cross in hand, steps ashore from a boat that also holds five bishops. Addressing "Young America," who holds a Bible, he says that he has come to "take charge of your spiritual welfare." A bishop adds, "I cannot bear to see that boy, with that horrible book."

efforts to undermine public school systems. The Know-Nothings swept the 1854 state elections in Massachusetts, electing the governor, all of the state's congressmen, and nearly every member of the state legislature. In many states, nativists emerged as a major component of victorious "anti-Nebraska" coalitions of voters opposed to the Kansas-Nebraska Act. In the North, the Know-Nothings' appeal combined anti-Catholic and antislavery sentiment, with opposition to the sale of liquor often added to the equation.

Immigrant suffrage

Despite severe anti-Irish discrimination in jobs, housing, and education, however, it is remarkable how little came of demands that immigrants be barred from the political nation. All European immigrants benefited from being white. The newcomers had the good fortune to arrive after white male suffrage had become the norm and automatically received the right to vote.

The Free Labor Ideology

The Republican Party

By 1856, it was clear that the Republican Party—a coalition of antislavery Democrats, northern Whigs, Free Soilers, and Know-Nothings opposed to the further expansion of slavery—would become the major alternative to the Democratic Party in the North. The party's appeal rested on the idea of "free labor." In Republican hands, the antithesis between "free society" and "slave society" coalesced into a comprehensive worldview that glorified the North as the home of progress, opportunity, and freedom.

Slavery versus free labor

The defining quality of northern society, Republicans declared, was the opportunity it offered each laborer to move up to the status of landowning farmer or independent craftsman, thus achieving the economic independence essential to freedom. Slavery, by contrast, spawned a social order consisting of degraded slaves, poor whites with no hope of advancement, and idle aristocrats. If slavery were to spread into the West, northern free laborers would be barred, and their chances for social advancement severely diminished. Slavery, Republicans insisted, must be kept out of the territories so that free labor could flourish.

Republicans were not abolitionists—they focused on preventing the spread of slavery, not attacking it where it existed. Nonetheless, many party leaders viewed the nation's division into free and slave societies as an "irrepressible conflict," as Senator William H. Seward of New York put it in 1858, that eventually would have to be resolved.

"Bleeding Kansas" and the Election of 1856

Their free labor outlook, which resonated so effectively with deeply held northern values, helps to explain the Republicans' rapid rise to prominence.

But dramatic events also fueled the party's growth. When Kansas held elections in 1854 and 1855, hundreds of proslavery Missourians crossed the border to cast fraudulent ballots. President Franklin Pierce recognized the legitimacy of the resulting proslavery legislature. Settlers from free states soon established a rival government. A sporadic civil war broke out in Kansas in which some 200 persons eventually lost their lives. In one incident, in May 1856, a proslavery mob attacked the free-soil stronghold of Lawrence, burning public buildings and pillaging private homes.

SOUTHERN CHIVALRY — ARGUMENT VERSUS CLUB'S.

A contemporary print denounces South Carolina congressman Preston S. Brooks's assault on Massachusetts senator Charles Sumner in May 1856. The attack on the floor of the Senate was in retaliation for Sumner's speech accusing Senator Andrew P. Butler (Brooks's distant cousin) of having taken "the harlot slavery" as his mistress.

"**Bleeding Kansas**" seemed to discredit Douglas's policy of leaving the decision on slavery up to the local population, thus aiding the Republicans. The party also drew strength from an unprecedented incident in the halls of Congress. South Carolina representative Preston Brooks, wielding a gold-tipped cane, beat the antislavery senator Charles Sumner of Massachusetts unconscious.

In the election of 1856, the Republican Party chose as its candidate John C. Frémont and drafted a platform that strongly opposed the further expansion of slavery. Stung by the northern reaction to the Kansas-Nebraska Act, the Democrats nominated James Buchanan, who had been minister to Great Britain in 1854 and thus had no direct connection with that divisive measure. The Democratic platform endorsed the principle of popular sovereignty as the only viable solution to the slavery controversy. Meanwhile, the Know-Nothings presented ex-president Millard Fillmore as their candidate. Frémont outpolled Buchanan in the North, carrying eleven of sixteen free states—a remarkable achievement for an organization that had existed for only two years. But Buchanan won the entire South and the key northern states of Illinois, Indiana, and Pennsylvania, enough to ensure his victory. Fillmore carried only Maryland. The 1856 election returns made starkly clear that political parties had reoriented themselves along sectional lines. One major party had been destroyed, another was seriously weakened, and a new one had arisen, devoted entirely to the interests of the North.

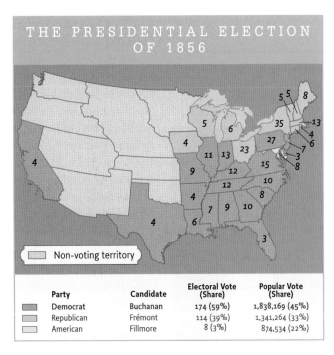

THE PRESIDENTIAL ELECTION OF 1856

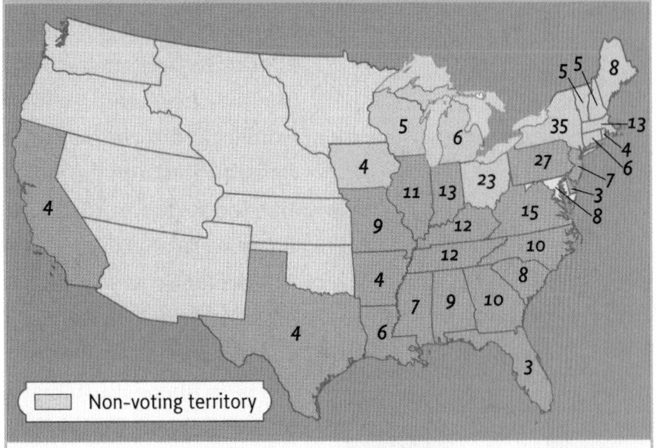

	Party	Candidate	Electoral Vote (Share)	Popular Vote (Share)
(Democrat)	Democrat	Buchanan	174 (59%)	1,838,169 (45%)
(Republican)	Republican	Frémont	114 (39%)	1,341,264 (33%)
(American)	American	Fillmore	8 (3%)	874,534 (22%)

THE EMERGENCE OF LINCOLN

The final collapse of the party system took place during the administration of a president who epitomized the old political order. Born during George Washington's presidency, James Buchanan had served in Pennsylvania's legislature, in both houses of Congress, and as secretary of state under James K. Polk. A staunch believer in the Union, he committed himself to pacifying inflamed sectional emotions. Few presidents have failed more disastrously in what they set out to accomplish.

The Dred Scott Decision

Even before his inauguration, Buchanan became aware of an impending Supreme Court decision that held out the hope of settling the slavery controversy once and for all. This was the case of ***Dred Scott v. Sandford***. During the 1830s, Scott had accompanied his owner, Dr. John Emerson of Missouri, to Illinois, where slavery had been prohibited by the Northwest Ordinance of 1787 and by state law, and to Wisconsin Territory, where it was barred by the Missouri Compromise. After returning to Missouri, Scott sued for his freedom, claiming that residence on free soil had made him free.

The Dred Scott decision, one of the most famous—or infamous—rulings in the long history of the Supreme Court, was announced in March 1857, two days after Buchanan's inauguration. Speaking for the majority, Chief Justice Roger B. Taney declared that only white persons could be citizens of the United States. The nation's founders, Taney insisted, believed that blacks "had no rights which the white man was bound to respect." Ironically, one reason for Taney's ruling was his robust understanding of what citizenship entailed. Being a citizen, he declared, meant freedom from legal discrimination and full enjoyment of the rights specified in the Constitution, among them the ability to travel anywhere in the country and the right "to keep and carry arms wherever they [citizens] went." These were not rights he thought black people, free or slave, should enjoy.

As for Scott's residence in Wisconsin, the ruling stated that Congress possessed no power under the Constitution to bar slavery from a territory. The Missouri Compromise, recently repealed by the Kansas-Nebraska Act, had been unconstitutional, and so was any measure interfering with southerners' right to bring slaves into the western territories. The decision in effect declared unconstitutional the Republican platform of restricting slavery's expansion. It also seemed to undermine Douglas's doctrine of popular sovereignty. For if Congress lacked the power to prohibit slavery in a territory, how could a territorial legislature created by Congress do so?

Dred Scott as painted in 1857, the year the Supreme Court ruled that he and his family must remain in slavery.

WHO IS AN AMERICAN?

From Opinion of the Court, Chief Justice Roger B. Taney, The Dred Scott Decision (1857)

In the Dred Scott decision, the Supreme Court attempted to resolve a divisive question: were free African-Americans citizens of the United States? The Court answered "no." For the majority, Chief Justice Roger B. Taney insisted that American citizenship was for white persons alone.

The words "people of the United States" and "citizens" are synonymous terms, and mean the same thing. They both describe the political body who, according to our republican institutions, form the sovereignty, and who hold the power and conduct the government through their representatives. They are what we familiarly call the "sovereign people," and every citizen is one of this people and a constituent member of this sovereignty. The question before us is, whether the class of persons described in the plea . . . compose a portion of this people, and are constituent members of this sovereignty? We think they are not, and that they are not included, and were not intended to be included, under the word "citizens" in the Constitution, and can therefore claim none of the rights and privileges which that instrument provides for and secures to citizens of the United States. On the contrary, they were at that time considered as a subordinate and inferior class of beings, who had been subjugated by the dominant race, and, whether emancipated or not, yet remained subject to their authority, and had no rights or privileges but such as those who held the power and the government might choose to grant them. . . .

They had for more than a century before been regarded as beings of an inferior order, and altogether unfit to associate with the white race, either in social or political relations; and so far inferior, that they had no rights which the white man was bound to respect. . . .

The general words [of the Declaration of Independence] would seem to embrace the whole human family, . . . but it is too clear for dispute, that the enslaved African race were not intended to be included. [The authors] perfectly understood the meaning of the language they used, and they knew that it would not in any part of the civilized world be supposed to embrace the Negro race.

QUESTIONS

1. *What evidence does Taney present that blacks were not considered citizens by the authors of the Declaration of Independence and the Constitution?*
2. *Why do you think he bases his argument on what he says were the intentions of the founders rather than the situation of free blacks in the 1850s?*

The Dred Scott decision caused a furor in the North and put the question of black citizenship on the national political agenda. James McCune Smith, a black physician, author, and antislavery activist, carefully dissected Taney's reasoning, citing legal precedents going back to "the annals of lofty Rome" to demonstrate that all free persons born in the United States, black as well as white, "must be citizens." Many Republicans also rejected Taney's reasoning. In a stinging dissent, Justice John McLean of Ohio insisted that regardless of race, "birth on the soil of a country both creates the duties and confers the rights of citizenship." Ohio's legislature adopted a resolution declaring that "every free person, born within the limits of any state of this Union, is a citizen thereof."

The Lecampton battle

Slavery, announced President Buchanan, henceforth existed in all the territories, "by virtue of the Constitution." In 1858, his administration attempted to admit Kansas as a slave state under the Lecompton Constitution, which had been drafted by a pro-southern convention and never submitted to a popular vote. Outraged by this violation of popular sovereignty, Douglas formed an unlikely alliance with congressional Republicans to block the attempt. The Lecompton battle convinced southern Democrats that they could not trust their party's most popular northern leader.

Lincoln and Slavery

Abraham Lincoln's nickname, "The Railsplitter," recalled his humble origins. An unknown artist created this larger-than-life portrait. The White House is visible in the distance. The painting is said to have been displayed during campaign rallies in 1860.

The depth of Americans' divisions over slavery was brought into sharp focus in 1858 in one of the most storied election campaigns in the nation's history. Seeking reelection to the Senate as both a champion of popular sovereignty and the man who had prevented the administration from forcing slavery on the people of Kansas, Douglas faced an unexpectedly strong challenge from Abraham Lincoln, then little known outside of Illinois. Born into a modest farm family in Kentucky in 1809, Lincoln had moved as a youth to frontier Indiana and then Illinois. He had served four terms as a Whig in the state legislature and one in Congress from 1847 to 1849.

Lincoln developed a critique of slavery and its expansion that gave voice to the central values of the emerging Republican Party and the millions of northerners whose loyalty it commanded. His speeches combined the moral fervor of the abolitionists with the respect for order and the Constitution of more conservative northerners.

"I want every man to have the chance," said Lincoln, "and I believe a black man is entitled to it, in which he *can* better his condition." Blacks might not be the equal of whites in all respects, but in their "natural right" to the fruits of their labor, they were "my equal and the equal of all others."

The Lincoln-Douglas Campaign

The campaign against Douglas, the North's preeminent political leader, created Lincoln's national reputation. Accepting his party's nomination for the Senate in June 1858, Lincoln announced, "A house divided against itself cannot stand. I believe this government cannot endure, permanently half *slave* and half *free*." Lincoln's point was not that civil war was imminent, but that Americans must choose between favoring and opposing slavery.

The **Lincoln-Douglas debates**, held in seven Illinois towns and attended by tens of thousands of listeners, remain classics of American political oratory. Clashing definitions of freedom lay at their heart. To Lincoln, freedom meant opposition to slavery. Douglas argued, on the other hand, that the essence of freedom lay in local self-government and individual self-determination. A large and diverse nation could only survive by respecting the right of each locality to determine its own institutions. In response to a question posed by Lincoln during the Freeport debate, Douglas insisted that popular sovereignty was not incompatible with the Dred Scott decision. Although territorial legislatures could no longer exclude slavery directly, he argued, if the people wished to keep slaveholders out, all they needed to do was refrain from giving the institution legal protection.

Abraham Lincoln in 1858, the year of the Lincoln-Douglas debates.

Lincoln shared many of the racial prejudices of his day. He opposed giving Illinois blacks the right to vote or serve on juries and spoke frequently of colonizing blacks overseas as the best solution to the problems of slavery and race. Yet, unlike Douglas, Lincoln did not use appeals to racism to garner votes. And he refused to exclude blacks from the human family. No less than whites, they were entitled to the inalienable rights of the Declaration of Independence, which applied to "all men, in all lands, everywhere," not merely to Europeans and their descendants.

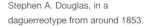

Stephen A. Douglas, in a daguerreotype from around 1853.

The 1858 Illinois election returns revealed a state sharply divided, like the nation itself. Southern Illinois, settled from the South, voted strongly Democratic, while the rapidly growing northern part of the state was firmly in the Republican column. Douglas was reelected. His victory was remarkable because elsewhere in the North Republicans swept to victory in 1858.

John Brown at Harpers Ferry

An armed assault by the abolitionist John Brown on the federal arsenal at **Harpers Ferry, Virginia**, further heightened sectional tensions. During the civil war in Kansas, Brown traveled to the territory. In May 1856, after the attack on Lawrence, he and a few followers murdered five proslavery settlers at Pottawatomie Creek. For the next two years, he traveled through the North and Canada, raising funds and enlisting followers for a war against slavery.

On October 16, 1859, with twenty-one men, five of them black, Brown seized Harpers Ferry. The plan made little military sense. Brown's band was soon surrounded and killed or captured by a detachment of federal soldiers headed by Colonel Robert E. Lee. Placed on trial for treason against the state of Virginia, Brown conducted himself with dignity and courage. When Virginia's governor, Henry A. Wise, spurned pleas for clemency and ordered Brown executed, he turned Brown into a martyr to much of the North.

To the South, the failure of Brown's assault seemed less significant than the adulation he seemed to arouse from much of the northern public. His raid and execution further widened the breach between the sections. Brown's last letter was a brief, prophetic statement: "I, John Brown, am quite certain that the crimes of this guilty land will never be purged away but with blood."

Two years after the end of the Civil War in 1867, the artist Thomas Satterwhite Noble, a veteran of the Confederate army, painted *John Brown's Blessing*, commemorating an apocryphal incident in which a slave woman presented her child to Brown as he was being led to the gallows. Two white children, accompanied by their black nurse, look on.

The Rise of Southern Nationalism

With the Republicans continuing to gain strength in the North, Democrats might have been expected to put a premium on party unity as the election of 1860 approached. By this time, however, a sizable group of southerners viewed their region's prospects as more favorable outside the Union than within it. To remain in the Union, secessionists argued, meant to accept "bondage" to the North. But an independent South could become the foundation of a slave empire ringing the Caribbean and embracing Cuba, other West Indian islands, Mexico, and parts of Central America.

More and more southerners were speaking openly of southward expansion. In 1854, Pierre Soulé of Louisiana, the

American ambassador to Spain, persuaded the ministers to Britain and France to join him in signing the Ostend Manifesto, which called on the United States to purchase or seize Cuba, where slavery was still legal, from Spain. Meanwhile, the military adventurer William Walker led a series of "filibustering" expeditions (the term derived from the Spanish word for pirate, *filibustero*) in Central America.

William Walker

By the late 1850s, southern leaders were bending every effort to strengthen the bonds of slavery. "Slavery is our king," declared a South Carolina politician in 1860. "Slavery is our truth, slavery is our divine right." By early 1860, seven states of the Lower South had gone on record demanding that the Democratic platform pledge to protect slavery in all the territories that had not yet been admitted to the Union as states. Virtually no northern politician could accept this position. For southern leaders to insist on it would guarantee the destruction of the Democratic Party as a national institution. But southern nationalists, known as "fire-eaters," hoped to split the party and the country and form an independent southern Confederacy.

The "fire-eaters"

The Election of 1860

When the Democratic convention met in April 1860, Douglas's supporters commanded a majority but not the two-thirds required for a presidential nomination. When the convention adopted a platform reaffirming the doctrine of popular sovereignty, delegates from the seven slave states of the Lower South walked out, and the gathering recessed in confusion. Six weeks later, it reconvened, replaced the bolters with Douglas supporters, and nominated him for president. In response, southern Democrats placed their own ticket in the field, headed by John C. Breckinridge of Kentucky. Breckinridge insisted that slavery must be protected in the western territories.

The Democratic Party, the last great bond of national unity, had been shattered. National conventions had traditionally been places where party

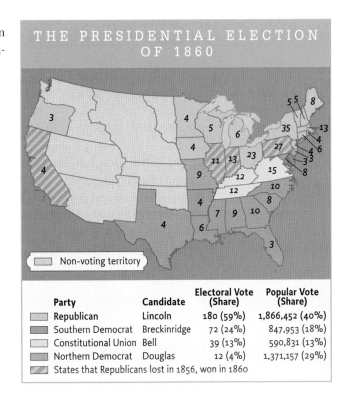

THE PRESIDENTIAL ELECTION OF 1860

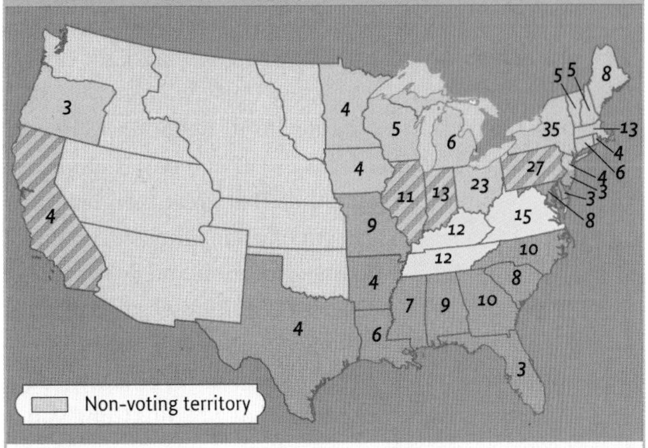

Party	Candidate	Electoral Vote (Share)	Popular Vote (Share)
Republican	Lincoln	180 (59%)	1,866,452 (40%)
Southern Democrat	Breckinridge	72 (24%)	847,953 (18%)
Constitutional Union	Bell	39 (13%)	590,831 (13%)
Northern Democrat	Douglas	12 (4%)	1,371,157 (29%)
States that Republicans lost in 1856, won in 1860			

VOICES OF FREEDOM

From William Lyman and Others, Letter to the *Middletown Sentinel and Witness* (1850)

The passage of the Fugitive Slave Act in 1850 raised in the most direct way the relationship between law and liberty. Six residents of Middletown, Connecticut, in a letter to the local newspaper, explained why they would not obey the new law.

The undersigned are friends of law. We reverence law. We are of the party of law and order... Even an imperfect law we will respect and bear with, till we can obtain its modification or repeal. But all is not law which calls itself law. When iniquity frames itself into law, the sacredness of law is gone. When an enactment, falsely calling itself law, is imposed upon us, which disgraces our country, which invades our conscience, which dishonors our religion, which is an outrage upon our sense of justice, we take our stand against the imposition.

The Fugitive Slave Law commands all good citizens to be slave catchers. Good citizens *cannot* be slave catchers, any more than light can be darkness. You tell us, the Union will be endangered if we oppose this law. We reply, that greater things than the Union will be endangered, if we submit to it: Conscience, Humanity, Self-respect are greater than the Union . . . . When our sense of decency is clean gone forever, we will turn slave catchers; till then, never. You tell us that great men made this law. If great men choose to disgrace themselves, choose to put off all manliness, and plunge all over into meanness and dishonor, it does not follow that small men should do so too. If Beacon Street [a chief commercial street in Boston] and Marshfield [Daniel Webster's estate] choose to turn slave catchers, let them. We farmers and working men choose to stay by our plows and mills . . . . We are not yet ready to give ourselves over to all manner of villainy. Be the consequence what it may, come fines, come imprisonment, come what will, this thing you call law *we will not obey.*

From Declaration of the Immediate Causes of Secession (1860)

In December 1860, South Carolina declared its secession from the Union. Like the American Revolutionaries of 1776, the legislature issued a document explaining to the world why the state had taken this step.

The non-slaveholding States . . . have assumed the right of deciding upon the propriety of our domestic institutions; and have denied the rights of property established in fifteen of the States and recognized by the Constitution; they have denounced as sinful the institution of slavery; they have permitted open establishment among them of societies, whose avowed object is to disturb the peace and to eloign [take away] the property of the citizens of other States. They have encouraged and assisted thousands of our slaves to leave their homes; and those who remain, have been incited by emissaries, books and pictures to servile insurrection.

For twenty-five years this agitation has been steadily increasing, until it has now secured to its aid the power of the common Government . . . . A geographical line has been drawn across the Union, and all the States north of that line have united in the election of a man to the high office of President of the United States, whose opinions and purposes are hostile to slavery. He is to be entrusted with the administration of the common Government, because he has declared that that "government cannot endure permanently half slave, half free," and that the public mind must rest in the belief that slavery is in the course of ultimate extinction. . . .

On the 4th of March next this party will take possession of the Government. It has announced that the South shall be excluded from the common territory, that the Judicial tribunal shall be made sectional, and that a war must be waged against slavery until it shall cease throughout the United States.

The guarantees of the Constitution will then no longer exist; the equal rights of the states will be lost. The slaveholding states will no longer have the power of self-government, or self-protection, and the federal government will have become their enemy.

QUESTIONS

1. *Whom do the Connecticut writers seem to blame for the Fugitive Slave Act?*
2. *What is the main motivation for South Carolina's secession?*
3. *What do these documents indicate about the rule of law in the nineteenth-century United States?*

managers, mindful of the need for unity in the fall campaign, reconciled their differences. But in 1860, neither northern nor southern Democrats were interested in conciliation. Southern Democrats no longer trusted their northern counterparts. Douglas's backers, for their part, would not accept a platform that doomed their party to certain defeat in the North.

Meanwhile, Republicans gathered in Chicago and chose Lincoln as their standard-bearer. The party platform denied the validity of the Dred Scott decision, reaffirmed Republicans' opposition to slavery's expansion, and added economic planks designed to appeal to a broad array of northern voters—free homesteads in the West, a protective tariff, and government aid in building a transcontinental railroad.

Two presidential campaigns

In effect, two presidential campaigns took place in 1860. In the North, Lincoln and Douglas were the combatants. In the South, the Republicans had no presence, and three candidates contested the election—Douglas, Breckinridge, and John Bell of Tennessee, the candidate of the hastily organized Constitutional Union Party. A haven for Unionist former Whigs, this new party adopted a platform consisting of a single pledge—to preserve "the Constitution as it is [that is, with slavery] and the Union as it was [without sectional discord]."

Sectional results

The most striking thing about the election returns was their sectional character. Lincoln carried all of the North except New Jersey, receiving 1.8 million popular votes (54 percent of the regional total and 40 percent of the national) and 180 electoral votes (a clear majority). Breckinridge captured most of the slave states, although Bell carried three Upper South states and about 40 percent of the southern vote as a whole. Douglas placed first only in Missouri, but he was the only candidate with significant support in all parts of the country. His failure to carry either section, however, suggested that a traditional political career based on devotion to the Union was no longer possible. Without a single vote in ten southern states, Lincoln was elected the nation's sixteenth president. But because of the North's superiority in population, Lincoln would still have carried the electoral college and thus been elected president even if the votes of his three opponents had all been cast for a single candidate.

THE IMPENDING CRISIS

The Secession Movement

Southern response to Lincoln's victory

In the eyes of many white southerners, Lincoln's victory placed their future at the mercy of a party avowedly hostile to their region's values and interests. Those advocating secession did not believe Lincoln's administration would take immediate steps against slavery in the states. But if, as seemed quite possible, the election of 1860 marked a fundamental shift in power, the beginning of a long period of Republican rule, who could say what the North's antislavery sentiment would demand in five years, or ten? Slaveowners, moreover, feared Republican efforts to extend their party into the South by appealing to non-slaveholders. Rather than accept permanent minority status, Lower South political leaders boldly struck for their region's independence.

In the months that followed Lincoln's election, seven states stretching from South Carolina to Texas seceded from the Union. These were the states of the Cotton Kingdom, where slaves represented a larger part of the total population than in the Upper South. First to secede was South Carolina, the state with the highest percentage of slaves in its population and a long history of political radicalism. On December 20, 1860, the legislature unanimously voted to leave the Union. Its *Declaration of the Immediate Causes of Secession* placed the issue of slavery squarely at the center of the crisis.

South Carolina

The Secession Crisis

As the Union unraveled, President Buchanan seemed paralyzed. He denied that a state could secede, but he also insisted that the federal government had no right to use force against it. Other political leaders struggled to find a formula to resolve the crisis. Senator John J. Crittenden of Kentucky, a slave state on the border between North and South, offered the most widely supported compromise plan of the secession winter. Embodied in a series of unamendable constitutional amendments, Crittenden's proposal would have guaranteed the future of slavery in the states where it existed and extended the Missouri Compromise line to the Pacific Ocean, dividing between slavery and free soil all territories "now held, or hereafter acquired." The seceding states rejected the compromise as too little, too late. But many in the Upper South and North saw it as a way to settle sectional differences and prevent civil war.

Crittenden's plan, however, foundered on the opposition of Abraham

An 1860 engraving of a mass meeting in Savannah, Georgia, shortly after Lincoln's election as president, which called for the state to secede from the Union. The banner on the obelisk at the center reads, "Our Motto Southern Rights, Equality of the States, Don't Tread on Me"—the last a slogan from the American Revolution.

Lincoln. Willing to conciliate the South on issues like the return of fugitive slaves, Lincoln took an unyielding stand against the expansion of slavery. "We have just carried an election," he wrote, "on principles fairly stated to the people. Now we are told in advance that the government shall be broken up unless we surrender to those we have beaten, before we take the offices. . . . If we surrender, it is the end of us and the end of the government."

The Confederate States of America

Before Lincoln assumed office on March 4, 1861, the seven seceding states formed the Confederate States of America, adopted a constitution, and chose as their president Jefferson Davis of Mississippi. With a few alterations—the president served a single six-year term; cabinet members, as in Britain, could sit in Congress—the Confederate constitution was modeled closely on that of the United States. It departed from the federal Constitution, however, in explicitly guaranteeing slave property both in the states and in any territories the new nation acquired. The "cornerstone" of the Confederacy, announced Davis's vice president, Alexander H. Stephens of Georgia, was "the great truth that the negro is not equal to the white man, that slavery, subordination to the superior race, is his natural and normal condition." Confederates were confident their new nation would thrive on the global stage. They looked forward to aggressively pursuing a pro-slavery foreign policy in the Caribbean and annexing new areas.

And the War Came

In his inaugural address, Lincoln tried to be conciliatory. He rejected the right of secession but denied any intention of interfering with slavery in the states. He said nothing of retaking the forts, arsenals, and customs houses the Confederacy had seized, although he did promise to "hold" remaining federal property in the seceding states. But Lincoln also issued a veiled warning: "In your hands, my dissatisfied fellow countrymen, and not in mine, is the momentous issue of civil war."

Inauguration of Mr. Lincoln, a photograph taken on March 4, 1861. The unfinished dome of the Capitol building symbolizes the precarious state of the Union at the time Lincoln assumed office.

In his first month as president, Lincoln walked a tightrope. He avoided any action that might drive more states from the Union, encouraged southern Unionists to assert themselves within the Confederacy, and sought to quiet a growing clamor

An Allegory of the North and the South, painted in 1858 by the Connecticut-born artist Luther Terry, offers a symbolic portrait of the United States on the eve of the Civil War. At the center is a female figure representing the nation and wearing a cap of liberty, with a horn of plenty at her feet. The figure of the South, on the left, is seated on a bale of cotton, with slaves visible in the fields behind her. The North, on the right, holds a book, *Useful Arts and Sciences*, and sits before a New England town with a church and a textile mill. The sectional harmony portrayed here would soon be replaced by bloody warfare.

in the North for forceful action against secession. Knowing that the risk of war existed, Lincoln strove to ensure that if hostilities did break out, the South, not the Union, would fire the first shot. And that is precisely what happened on April 12, 1861, at **Fort Sumter**, an enclave of Union control in the harbor of Charleston, South Carolina.

Fort Sumter

A few days earlier, Lincoln had notified South Carolina's governor that he intended to replenish the garrison's dwindling food supplies. Viewing Fort Sumter's presence as an affront to southern nationhood and perhaps hoping to force the wavering Upper South to join the Confederacy, Jefferson Davis ordered batteries to fire on the fort. On April 14, its commander surrendered. The following day, Lincoln proclaimed that an insurrection existed in the South and called for 75,000 troops to suppress it. Civil war had begun. Within weeks, Virginia, North Carolina, Tennessee, and Arkansas joined the Confederacy. "Both sides deprecated war," Lincoln later said, "but one of them would *make* war rather than let the nation survive; and the other would *accept* war rather than let it perish. And the war came."

The Union created by the founders lay in ruins. The struggle to rebuild it would bring about a new birth of American freedom.

CHAPTER REVIEW AND ONLINE RESOURCES

REVIEW QUESTIONS

1. *Explain the justifications for the doctrine of manifest destiny, including material and idealistic motivations.*
2. *Why did many Americans criticize the Mexican War? How did they see expansion as a threat to American liberties?*
3. *How did the concept of "race" develop by the mid-nineteenth century? How did it enter into the manifest destiny debate?*
4. *How did western expansion affect the sectional tensions between the North and South?*
5. *How did the market revolution contribute to the rise of the Republican Party? How did those economic and political factors serve to unite groups in the Northeast and in the Northwest, and why was that unity significant?*
6. *How did the Dred Scott decision spark new debates over citizenship for African-Americans?*
7. *Based on the Lincoln-Douglas debates, how did the two differ on the expansion of slavery, equal rights, and the role of the national government? Use examples of their words to illustrate your points.*
8. *Why did Stephen Douglas, among others, believe that "popular sovereignty" could resolve sectional divisions of the 1850s? Why did the idea not work out?*
9. *Explain how sectional voting patterns in the 1860 presidential election allowed southern "fire-eaters" to justify secession.*
10. *What do the California gold rush and the opening of Japan reveal about the United States' involvement in a global economic system?*

KEY TERMS

Tejanos (p. 362)
Antonio López de Santa Anna (p. 364)
Texas revolt (p. 364)
Mexican War (p. 366)
gold rush (p. 370)
Commodore Matthew Perry (p. 371)
Wilmot Proviso (p. 372)
Free Soil Party (p. 372)
Compromise of 1850 (p. 374)
Fugitive Slave Act (p. 374)
popular sovereignty (p. 376)
Kansas-Nebraska Act (p. 377)
Know-Nothing Party (p. 379)
"Bleeding Kansas" (p. 381)
Dred Scott v. Sandford (p. 382)
Lincoln-Douglas debates (p. 385)
Harpers Ferry, Virginia (p. 385)
Fort Sumter (p. 393)

Go to INQUIZITIVE

To see what you know—and learn what you've missed—with personalized feedback along the way.

Visit the ***Give Me Liberty!* Student Site** for primary source documents and images, interactive maps, author videos featuring Eric Foner, and more.

CHAPTER 14

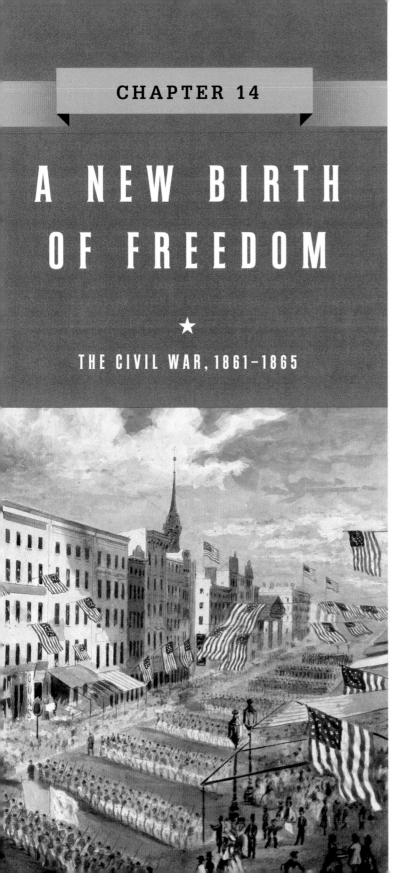

A NEW BIRTH OF FREEDOM

★

THE CIVIL WAR, 1861–1865

1861	Civil War begins at Fort Sumter
	First Battle of Bull Run
1862	Forts Henry and Donelson captured
	Monitor v. *Merrimac* sea battle
	Battle of Shiloh
	Confederacy institutes the draft
	Homestead Act
	Seven Days' Campaign
	Second Battle of Bull Run
	Union Pacific and Central Pacific chartered
	Morrill Act of 1862
	Battle at Antietam
1863	Emancipation Proclamation
	Siege of Vicksburg
	Battle at Gettysburg
	New York draft riots
	Lincoln introduces his Ten-Percent Plan
1864	General Grant begins a war of attrition
	Wade-Davis Bill
	General Sherman marches to the sea
1865	Thirteenth Amendment
	Union capture of Richmond
	General Lee surrenders to General Grant at Appomattox Courthouse
	Lincoln assassinated
1866	*Ex parte Milligan* ruling

Departure of the 7th Regiment, a lithograph from 1861 illustrating the departure of a unit of the New York State militia for service in the Civil War. A contemporary writer captured the exuberant spirit of the early days of the war: "New York was certainly raving mad with excitement. The ladies laughed, smiled, sighed, sobbed, and wept. The men cheered and shouted as never men cheered and shouted before."

FOCUS QUESTIONS

- *Why is the Civil War considered the first modern war?*
- *How did a war to preserve the Union become a war to end slavery?*
- *How did the Civil War transform the national economy and create a stronger nation-state?*
- *How did the war effort affect the society and economy of the Confederacy?*
- *What were the military and political turning points of the war?*
- *What were the most important wartime "rehearsals for Reconstruction"?*

Like hundreds of thousands of other Americans, Marcus M. Spiegel volunteered in 1861 to fight in the Civil War. Born into a Jewish family in Germany in 1829, Spiegel emigrated to Ohio, where he married the daughter of a local farmer. When the Civil War broke out, the nation's 150,000 Jews represented less than 1 percent of the total population. But Spiegel shared wholeheartedly in American patriotism. He went to war, he wrote to his brother-in-law, to defend "the flag that was ever ready to protect you and me and every one who sought its protection from oppression." He never wavered in his commitment to the "glorious cause" of preserving the Union and its heritage of freedom.

What one Pennsylvania recruit called "the magic word *Freedom*" shaped how many Union soldiers understood the conflict. But as the war progressed, prewar understandings of liberty gave way to something new. Millions of northerners who had not been abolitionists became convinced that preserving the Union required the destruction of slavery. Marcus Spiegel's changing views mirrored this transformation. Spiegel was an ardent Democrat. He shared the era's racist attitudes and thought Lincoln's Emancipation Proclamation a serious mistake. Yet as the Union army penetrated the heart of the Lower South, Spiegel became increasingly opposed to slavery. "Since I am here," he wrote to his wife from Louisiana in January 1864, "I have learned and seen . . . the horrors of slavery. . . . Never hereafter will I either speak or vote in favor of slavery."

Marcus Spiegel was killed in a minor engagement in Louisiana in May 1864, one of hundreds of thousands of Americans to perish in the Civil War.

THE FIRST MODERN WAR

The American Civil War is often called the first modern war. Never before had mass armies confronted each other on the battlefield with the deadly weapons created by the industrial revolution. The resulting casualties dwarfed anything in the American experience. Beginning as a battle of army versus army, the war became a conflict of society against society, in which the distinction between military and civilian targets often disappeared. In a war of this kind, the effectiveness of political leadership, the ability to mobilize economic resources, and a society's willingness to keep up the fight despite setbacks are as crucial to the outcome as success or failure on individual battlefields.

THE SECESSION OF SOUTHERN STATES, 1860–1861

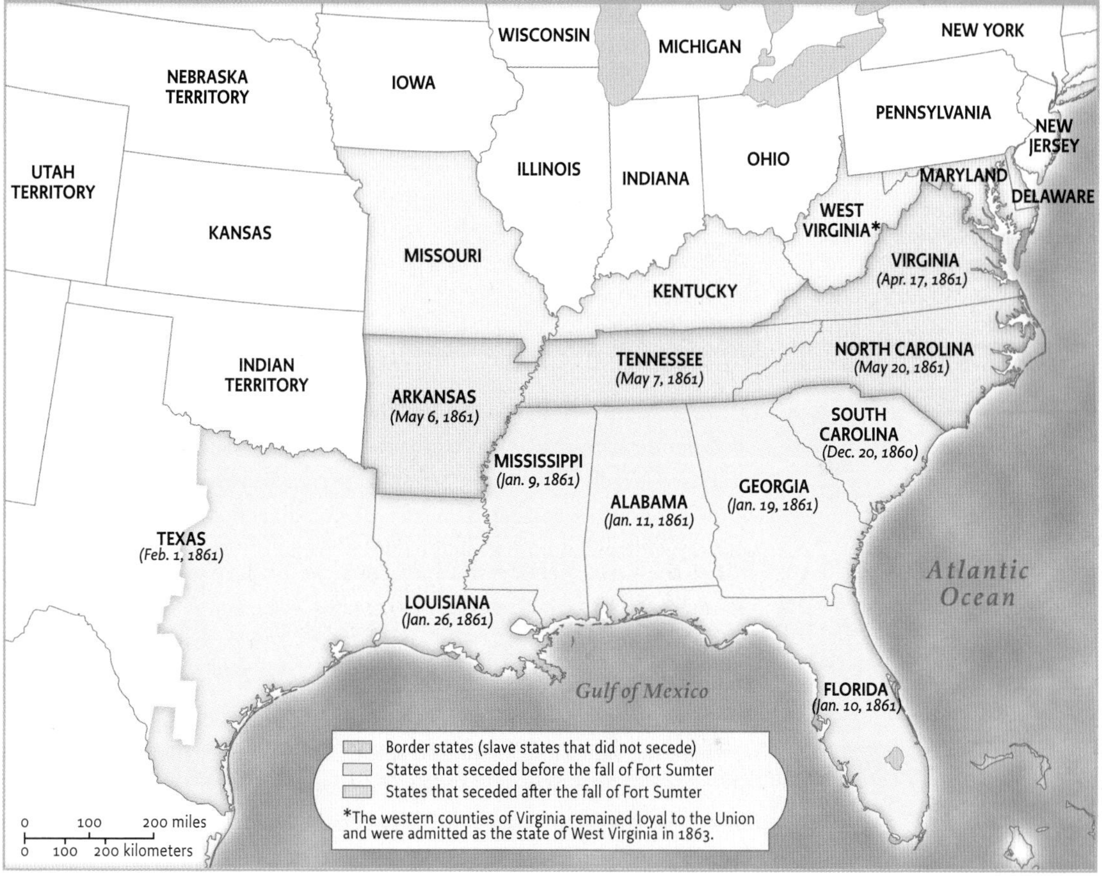

By the time secession ran its course, eleven slave states had left the Union.

The Two Combatants

Advantages of the North and South

Almost any comparison between Union and Confederacy seemed to favor the Union. The population of the North and the loyal border slave states numbered 22 million in 1860, whereas only 9 million persons lived in the Confederacy, 3.5 million of them slaves. In manufacturing, railroad mileage, and financial resources, the Union far outstripped its opponent. On the other hand, the Union confronted by far the greater task. To restore the shattered nation, it had to invade and conquer an area larger than western Europe. Moreover, Confederate soldiers were highly motivated fighters, defending their homes and families.

Patriotism

On both sides, the outbreak of war stirred powerful feelings of patriotism. Recruits rushed to enlist, expecting a short, glorious war. Later, as enthusiasm waned, both sides resorted to a draft. By 1865, more

Sergeant James W. Travis, Thirty-eighth Illinois Infantry, Union army, and Private Edwin Francis Jemison, Second Louisiana Regiment, Confederate army, two of the nearly 3 million Americans who fought in the Civil War. Before going off to war, many soldiers sat for photographs like these, reproduced on small cards called *cartes de visite*, which they distributed to friends and loved ones. Jemison was killed in the Battle of Malvern Hill in July 1862.

Soldiers North and South

than 2 million men had served in the Union army and 900,000 in the Confederate army. Each was a cross section of its society: the North's was composed largely of farm boys, shopkeepers, artisans, and urban workers, while the South's consisted mostly of non-slaveholding small farmers, with slaveowners dominating the officer corps.

The Technology of War

Ironclad ships

Neither the soldiers nor their officers were prepared for the way technology had transformed warfare. The Civil War was the first major conflict in which the railroad transported troops and supplies and the first to see railroad junctions such as Atlanta and Petersburg become major military objectives. The famous sea battle between the Union vessel *Monitor* and the Confederate *Merrimac* in 1862 was the first demonstration of the superiority of ironclads over wooden ships, revolutionizing naval warfare. The war saw the use of the telegraph for military communication, the introduction of observation balloons to view enemy lines, and even primitive hand grenades and submarines.

The rifle

Perhaps most important, a revolution in arms manufacturing had replaced the traditional musket, accurate at only a short range, with the more modern rifle, deadly at 600 yards or more because of its grooved (or "rifled") barrel. This development changed the nature of combat, emphasizing the importance of heavy fortifications and elaborate trenches and giving those on the defensive—usually southern armies—a significant advantage over attacking forces. The war of rifle and trench produced the appalling casualty statistics of Civil War battles. The most recent estimate of those who perished in the war—around 750,000 men—represents the equivalent, in terms of today's population, of more than 7 million. The death toll in the Civil War exceeds the total number of Americans who died in all the nation's other wars, from the Revolution to the wars in Iraq and Afghanistan.

Nor was either side ready for other aspects of modern warfare. Medical care remained primitive. Diseases such as measles, dysentery, malaria, and typhus swept through army camps, killing more men than did combat. The Civil War was the first war in which large numbers of Americans were captured by the enemy and held in dire conditions in military prisons. Some 50,000 men died in these prisons, victims of starvation and disease, including 13,000 Union soldiers at Andersonville, Georgia.

An eight-inch cannon, one of the weapons forged in the industrial revolution and deployed in the Civil War.

The Public and the War

Another modern feature of the Civil War was that both sides employed a vast propaganda effort to mobilize public opinion. In the Union, an outpouring of lithographs, souvenirs, sheet music, and pamphlets issued by patriotic organizations and the War Department reaffirmed northern values, tarred the Democratic Party with the brush of treason, and accused the South of numerous crimes against Union soldiers and loyal civilians. Comparable items appeared in the Confederacy.

War Spirit at Home, an 1866 painting by the New Jersey artist Lilly M. Spencer, depicts a family reading the news of the Union capture of Vicksburg in 1863. The household is now composed of women and children; the husband may be off in the army. While the children play as soldiers, the cross in the folds of the newspaper suggests a less celebratory reflection on the conflict. Newspapers brought news of the war into American homes.

FIGURE 14.1 Resources for War: Union versus Confederacy

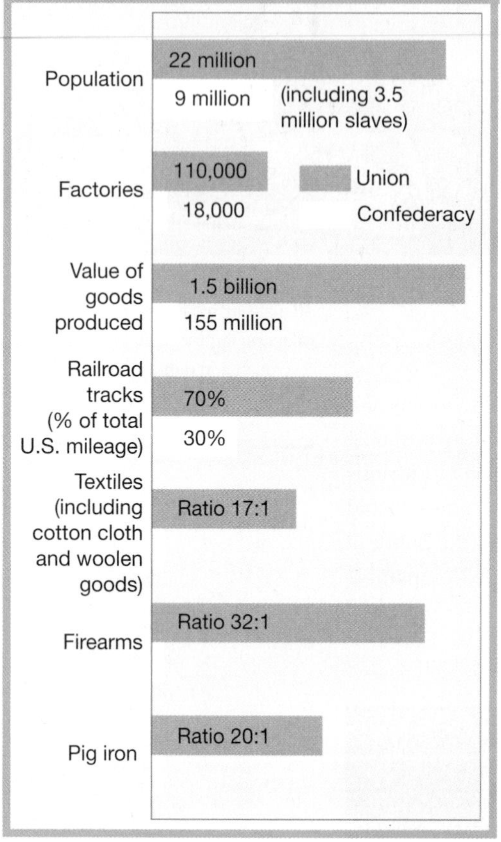

In nearly every resource for warfare, the Union enjoyed a distinct advantage. But this did not make Union victory inevitable; as in the War of Independence, the stronger side sometimes loses.

At the same time, the war's brutal realities were brought home with unprecedented immediacy to the public at large. War correspondents accompanied the armies, and newspapers reported the results of battles on the following day and quickly published long lists of casualties. The infant art of photography carried images of war into millions of American living rooms.

Mobilizing Resources

The outbreak of the war found both sides unprepared. In 1861, there was no national railroad gauge (the distance separating the two rails), so trains built for one line could not run on another. There was no national banking system, no tax system capable of raising the enormous funds needed to finance the war, and not even accurate maps of the southern states. Soon after the firing on Fort Sumter, Lincoln proclaimed a naval blockade of the South, part of the so-called Anaconda Plan, which aimed to strangle the South economically. But the navy, charged with patrolling the 3,500-mile coastline, consisted of only ninety vessels, fewer than half of them steam powered. Not until late in the war did the blockade become effective.

Then there was the problem of purchasing and distributing the food, weapons, and other supplies required by the soldiers. The Union army eventually became the best-fed and best-supplied military force in history. By the war's third year, on the other hand, southern armies were suffering from acute shortages of food, uniforms, and shoes.

Military Strategies

Southern strategy

Each side tried to find ways to maximize its advantages. Essentially, the Confederacy adopted a defensive strategy, with occasional thrusts into the North. General Robert E. Lee, the leading southern commander, was a brilliant battlefield tactician who felt confident of his ability to fend off attacks by larger Union forces. He hoped that a series of defeats would weaken the North's resolve and lead it eventually to abandon the conflict and recognize southern independence.

Lincoln's early generals initially concentrated on occupying southern territory and attempting to capture Richmond, the Confederate capital. They attacked sporadically and withdrew after a battle, thus sacrificing the

North's manpower superiority and allowing the South to concentrate its smaller forces when an engagement impended. Well before his generals, Lincoln realized that simply capturing and occupying territory would not win the war, and that defeating the South's armies, not capturing its capital, had to be the North's battlefield objective. And when he came to adopt the policy of emancipation, Lincoln acknowledged that to win the war, the Union must make the institution that lay at the economic and social foundation of southern life a military target.

Changing northern strategy

The War Begins

In the East, most of the war's fighting took place in a narrow corridor between Washington and Richmond—a distance of only 100 miles—as a succession of Union generals led the Army of the Potomac (as the main northern force in the East was called) toward the Confederate capital, only to be turned back by southern forces. The first significant engagement, the **first Battle of Bull Run**, took place in northern Virginia on July 21, 1861. It ended with the chaotic retreat of the Union soldiers, along with the sightseers and politicians who had come to watch the battle.

First Bull Run

In the wake of Bull Run, George B. McClellan, an army engineer who had recently won a minor engagement with Confederate troops in western Virginia, assumed command of the Union's Army of the Potomac. A brilliant organizer, McClellan succeeded in welding his men into a superb fighting force. He seemed reluctant, however, to commit them to battle, since he tended to overestimate the size of enemy forces. And as a Democrat, he hoped that compromise might end the war without large-scale loss of life or a weakening of slavery. Months of military inactivity followed.

McClellan

The War in the East, 1862

Not until the spring of 1862, after a growing clamor for action by Republican newspapers, members of Congress, and an increasingly impatient Lincoln, did McClellan lead his army of more than 100,000 men into Virginia. Here they confronted the smaller Army of Northern Virginia under the command of the Confederate general Joseph E. Johnston, and after he was wounded, Robert E. Lee. In the Seven Days' Campaign, a series of engagements in June 1862 on the peninsula south of Richmond, Lee blunted McClellan's attacks and forced him to withdraw to the vicinity of Washington, D.C. In August 1862, Lee again emerged victorious at the **second Battle of Bull Run** against Union forces under the command of General John Pope.

The Seven Days' Campaign

Successful on the defensive, Lee now launched an invasion of the North. At the **Battle of Antietam**, in Maryland, McClellan and the Army

THE CIVIL WAR IN THE EAST, 1861–1862

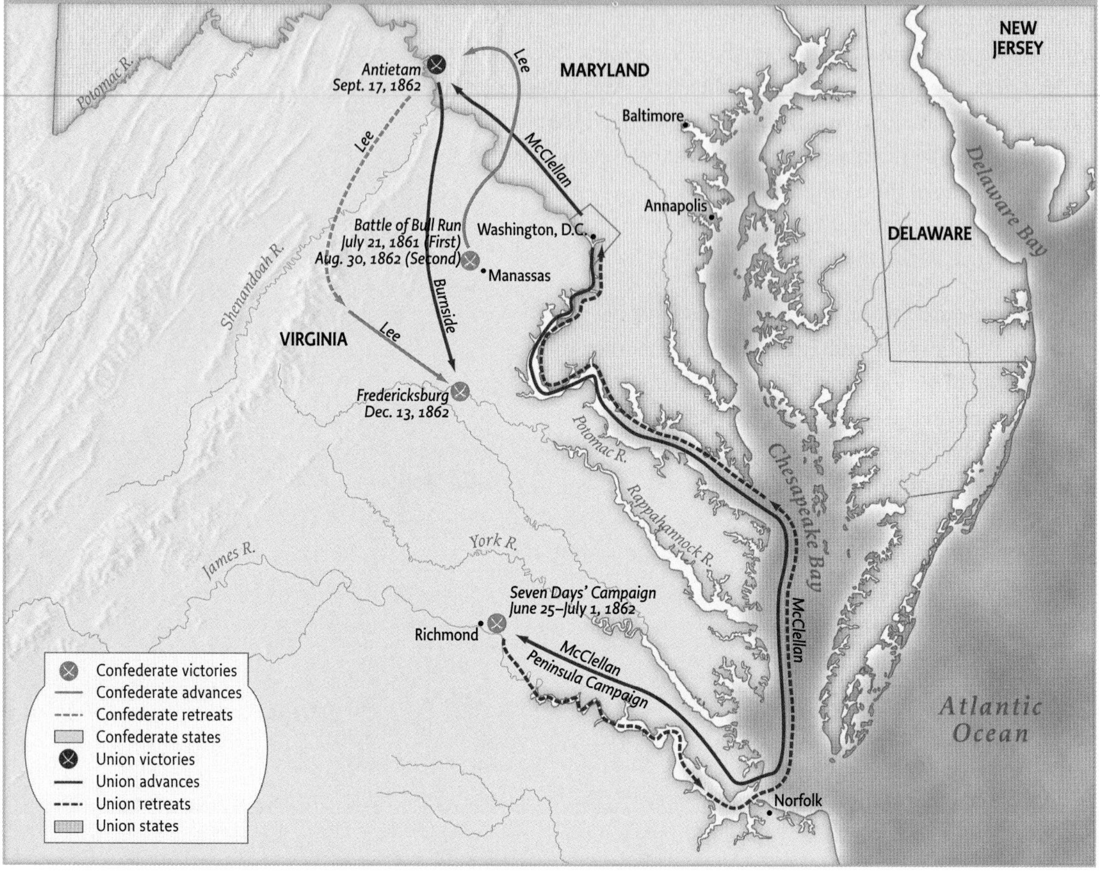

During the first two years of the war, most of the fighting took place in Virginia and Maryland.

of the Potomac repelled Lee's advance. In a single day of fighting, nearly 4,000 men were killed and 18,000 wounded (2,000 of whom later died of their injuries). More Americans died on September 17, 1862, when the Battle of Antietam was fought, than on any other day in the nation's history, including Pearl Harbor and D-Day in World War II and the terrorist attacks of September 11, 2001.

The War in the West

Emergence of Grant

While the Union accomplished little in the East in the first two years of the war, events in the West followed a different course. Here, the architect of early success was Ulysses S. Grant. A West Point graduate who had resigned from the army in 1854, Grant had been notably unsuccessful in civilian life. When the war broke out, he was working as a clerk in his

Union General George B. McClellan drilling his troops during the winter of 1861–1862, a painting by an unknown artist.

brother's leather store in Galena, Illinois. But after being commissioned as a colonel in an Illinois regiment, Grant quickly displayed the daring, the logical mind, and the grasp of strategy he would demonstrate throughout the war.

Union victories in the West

In February 1862, Grant won the Union's first significant victory when he captured Forts Henry and Donelson in Tennessee. In April, naval forces under Admiral David G. Farragut steamed into New Orleans, giving the Union control of the South's largest city and the rich sugar plantation parishes to its south and west. At the same time, Grant withstood a surprise Confederate attack at Shiloh, Tennessee. But Union momentum in the West then stalled.

THE COMING OF EMANCIPATION

Slavery and the War

War, it has been said, is the midwife of revolution. And the Civil War produced far-reaching changes in American life. The most dramatic of these was the destruction of slavery, the central institution of southern society. In numbers, scale, and the economic power of the institution of slavery, American emancipation dwarfed that of any other country (although far more people were liberated in 1861 when Czar Alexander II abolished serfdom in the Russian empire).

THE CIVIL WAR IN THE WEST, 1861–1862

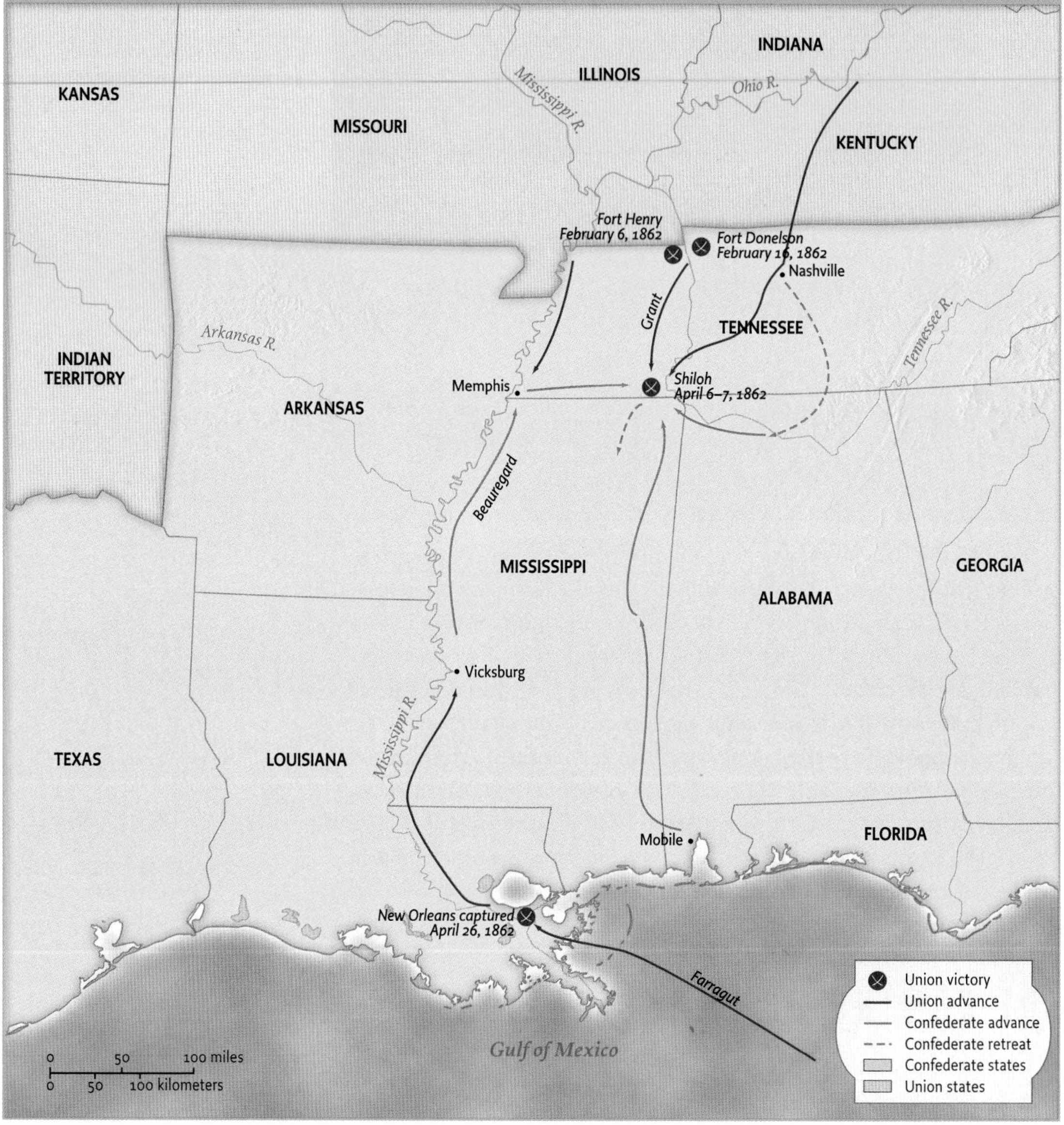

Most of the Union's victories in the first two years of the war occurred in the West, especially at Shiloh and New Orleans.

Lincoln initially insisted that slavery was irrelevant to the conflict. In the war's first year, his paramount concerns were to keep the border slave states—Delaware, Maryland, Kentucky, and Missouri—in the Union and to build the broadest base of support in the North for the war effort. Action against slavery, he feared, would drive the border, with its white population of 2.6 million and nearly 500,000 slaves, into the Confederacy and alienate conservative northerners.

A Civil War photograph depicts African-American men, women, and children who have escaped to Union lines in a mule-drawn covered wagon. The actions of fugitives like these helped propel the nation down the road to emancipation.

Thus, in the early days of the war, a nearly unanimous Congress adopted a resolution proposed by Senator John J. Crittenden of Kentucky, which affirmed that the Union had no intention of interfering with slavery. Northern military commanders even returned fugitive slaves to their owners, a policy that raised an outcry in antislavery circles. Yet as the Confederacy set slaves to work as military laborers and blacks began to escape to Union lines, the policy of ignoring slavery unraveled. By the end of 1861, the military had adopted the plan, begun in Virginia by General Benjamin F. Butler, of treating escaped blacks as contraband of war—that is, property of military value subject to confiscation. Butler's order added a word to the war's vocabulary. Escaping slaves ("**the contrabands**") were housed by the army in "contraband camps" and educated in new "contraband schools."

Meanwhile, slaves took actions that helped propel a reluctant white America down the road to emancipation. Well before Lincoln made emancipation a war aim, blacks, in the North and the South, were calling the conflict the "freedom war." In 1861 and 1862, as the federal army occupied Confederate territory, slaves by the thousands headed for Union lines. Unlike fugitives before the war, these runaways included large numbers of women and children, as entire families abandoned the plantations. Not a few passed along military intelligence and detailed knowledge of the South's terrain. In southern Louisiana, the arrival of the Union army in 1862 led slaves to sack plantation houses and refuse to work unless wages were paid. Slavery there, wrote a northern reporter, "is forever destroyed and worthless, no matter what Mr. Lincoln or anyone else may say on the subject."

Fortress Monroe, Virginia, a Union installation near Norfolk, where the process of emancipation began early in the Civil War when General Benjamin F. Butler refused to return runaway slaves to their owners.

Steps toward Emancipation

Fighting for emancipation

The most uncompromising opponents of slavery before the war, abolitionists and **Radical Republicans**, quickly concluded that the institution must become a target of the Union war effort. Outside of Congress, few pressed the case for emancipation more eloquently than Frederick Douglass. From the outset, he insisted that it was futile to "separate the freedom of the slave from the victory of the government."

Congressional policy against slavery

These appeals won increasing support in a Congress frustrated by lack of military success. In March 1862, Congress prohibited the army from returning fugitive slaves. Then came abolition in the District of Columbia (with monetary compensation for slaveholders) and the territories, followed in July by the Second Confiscation Act, which liberated slaves of disloyal owners in Union-occupied territory, as well as slaves who escaped to Union lines.

Lincoln's evolving policy

Throughout these months, Lincoln struggled to retain control of the emancipation issue. In August 1861, John C. Frémont, commanding Union forces in Missouri, a state racked by a bitter guerrilla war between pro-northern and pro-southern bands, decreed the freedom of its slaves. Fearful of the order's impact on the border states, Lincoln swiftly rescinded it. In November, the president proposed that the border states embark on a program of gradual emancipation with the federal government paying owners for their loss of property. He also revived the idea of colonization. In August 1862, Lincoln met at the White House with a delegation of black leaders and urged them to promote emigration from the United States. "You and we are different races," he declared. "It is better for us both to be separated." As late as December 1862, the president signed an agreement with a shady entrepreneur to settle former slaves on an island off the coast of Haiti.

Abe Lincoln's Last Card, an engraving from the British magazine *Punch*, October 18, 1862, portrays the Preliminary Emancipation Proclamation as the last move of a desperate gambler.

Lincoln's Decision

During the summer of 1862, Lincoln concluded that emancipation had become a political and military necessity. Many factors contributed to his decision—lack of military success, hope that emancipated slaves might help meet the army's growing manpower needs, changing northern public opinion, and the calculation that making slavery a target of the war effort would counteract sentiment in Britain for recognition of the Confederacy. But on the advice of

THE EMANCIPATION PROCLAMATION

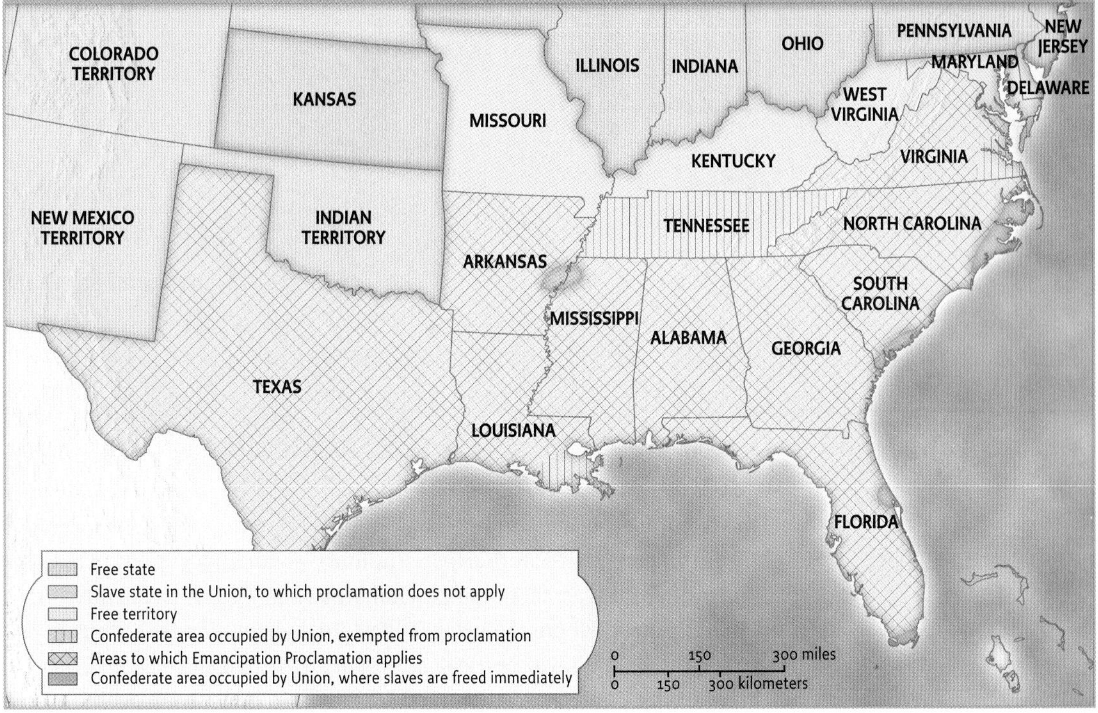

With the exception of a few areas, the Emancipation Proclamation applied only to slaves in parts of the Confederacy not under Union control on January 1, 1863. Lincoln did not "free the slaves" with a stroke of his pen, but the proclamation did change the nature of the Civil War.

Secretary of State William H. Seward, Lincoln delayed his announcement until after a Union victory, lest it seem an act of desperation. On September 22, 1862, five days after McClellan's army forced Lee to retreat at Antietam, Lincoln issued the Preliminary Emancipation Proclamation. It warned that unless the South laid down its arms by the end of 1862, he would decree abolition.

The initial northern reaction was not encouraging. In the fall elections of 1862, Democrats made opposition to emancipation the centerpiece of their campaign. The Republicans suffered sharp reverses. In his annual message to Congress, early in December, Lincoln tried to calm northerners' racial fears: "In giving freedom to the slave, we assure freedom to the free—honorable alike in what we give, and what we preserve."

The Emancipation Proclamation

On January 1, 1863, after greeting visitors at the annual White House New Year's reception, Lincoln retired to his study to sign the **Emancipation Proclamation**. The document did not liberate all the slaves—indeed, on

Freed Negroes Celebrating President Lincoln's Decree of Emancipation, a fanciful engraving from the French periodical *Le Monde Illustré*, March 21, 1863.

the day it was issued, it applied to very few. Because its legality derived from the president's authority as military commander-in-chief to combat the South's rebellion, the proclamation exempted areas firmly under Union control (where the war, in effect, had already ended). Thus, it did not apply to the loyal border slave states that had never seceded or to areas of the Confederacy occupied by Union soldiers, such as Tennessee and parts of Virginia and Louisiana. But the vast majority of the South's slaves—more than 3 million men, women, and children—it declared "henceforward shall be free." Since most of these slaves were still behind Confederate lines, however, their liberation would have to await Union victories.

A military proclamation

Responses to the proclamation

Despite its limitations, the proclamation set off scenes of jubilation among free blacks and abolitionists in the North and "contrabands" and slaves in the South. "Sound the loud timbrel o'er Egypt's dark sea," intoned a black preacher at a celebration in Boston. "Jehovah hath triumphed, his people are free." By making the Union army an agent of emancipation and wedding the goals of Union and abolition, the proclamation sounded the eventual death knell of slavery.

The proclamation's legacy

Not only did the Emancipation Proclamation alter the nature of the Civil War and the course of American history, but it also marked a turning point in Lincoln's own thinking. For the first time, it committed the government to enlisting black soldiers in the Union army. He would later refuse suggestions that he rescind or modify the proclamation in the interest of peace. Were he to do so, he told one visitor, "I should be damned in time and eternity."

Enlisting Black Troops

Of the proclamation's provisions, few were more radical in their implications than the enrollment of blacks into military service. Since sailor had been one of the few occupations open to free blacks before the war, Secretary of the Navy Gideon Welles had already allowed African-Americans to serve on Union warships. But at the outset, the administration feared that whites would not be willing to fight alongside blacks and that enlisting black soldiers would alienate the border slave states that remained in the Union.

By the end of the war, however, more than 180,000 black men had served in the Union army and 24,000 in the navy. One-third died in battle, or of wounds or disease. Some black units won considerable renown, among them the Fifty-fourth Massachusetts Volunteers, a company of free blacks from throughout the North commanded by Robert Gould Shaw, a young reformer from a prominent Boston family. The bravery of the Fifty-fourth in the July 1863 attack on Fort Wagner, South Carolina, where nearly half the unit, including Shaw, perished, helped to dispel widespread doubts about blacks' ability to withstand the pressures of the Civil War battlefield.

Most black soldiers were emancipated slaves who joined the army in the South. After Union forces in 1863 seized control of the rich plantation lands of the Mississippi Valley, General Lorenzo Thomas raised fifty regiments of black soldiers—some 76,000 men in all. Another large group hailed from the border states exempted from the Emancipation Proclamation, where enlistment was, for most of the war, the only route to freedom. Here black military service undermined slavery, for Congress expanded the Emancipation Proclamation to liberate the families of black soldiers.

A photograph of a black washerwoman for the Union army wearing a small American flag reflects how the war and emancipation led African-Americans to identify strongly with the nation.

This is the only known photograph of a black Union soldier with his family.

The Black Soldier

For black soldiers themselves, military service proved to be a liberating experience. Out of the army came many of the leaders of the Reconstruction era. At least 130 former soldiers served in political office after the Civil War. In time, the memory of black military service would fade from white America's collective memory. Of the hundreds of Civil War monuments that still dot the northern landscape, fewer than a dozen contain an image of a black soldier. But well into the twentieth century, it remained a point of

The illustration accompanying *The American Flag*, a piece of patriotic Civil War sheet music, exemplifies how the war united the ideals of liberty and nationhood.

pride in black families throughout the United States that their fathers and grandfathers had fought for freedom.

Within the army, however, black soldiers received treatment that was anything but equal to that of their white counterparts. Organized into segregated units under sometimes abusive white officers, they initially received lower pay (ten dollars per month, compared to sixteen dollars for white soldiers). They were disproportionately assigned to labor rather than combat, and they could not rise to the rank of commissioned officer until the very end of the war. In a notorious incident in 1864, 200 of 262 black soldiers died when southern troops under the command of Nathan B. Forrest overran Fort Pillow in Tennessee. Some of those who perished had been killed after surrendering.

Nonetheless, black soldiers played a crucial role not only in winning the Civil War but also in defining the war's consequences. Thanks in part to black military service, many Republicans in the last two years of the war came to believe that emancipation must bring with it equal protection of the laws regardless of race. One of the first acts of the federal government to recognize this principle was the granting of retroactive equal pay to black soldiers early in 1865.

The service of black soldiers affected Lincoln's own outlook. In 1864, Lincoln, who before the war had never supported suffrage for African-Americans, urged the governor of Union-occupied Louisiana to work for the partial enfranchisement of blacks, singling out soldiers as especially deserving. At some future time, he observed, they might again be called upon to "keep the *jewel of Liberty* in the family of freedom."

A songbook compiled and illustrated by a Union soldier includes "John Brown's Body," sung to the melody of a Methodist hymn.

THE SECOND AMERICAN REVOLUTION

The changing status of black Americans was only one dramatic example of what some historians call the **Second American Revolution**—the transformation of American government and society brought about by the Civil War.

Liberty, Union, and Nation

Never was freedom's contested nature more evident than during the Civil War. "We all declare for liberty," Lincoln observed in 1864, "but in using the same *word* we do not all mean the same *thing*." To the North, he continued, freedom meant for "each man" to enjoy "the product of his labor." To southern whites, it conveyed mastership—the power to do "as they please with other men, and the product of other men's labor." The Union's triumph consolidated the northern understanding of freedom as the national norm.

Nation building

But it was Lincoln himself who linked the conflict with the deepest beliefs of northern society. It is sometimes said that the American Civil War was part of a broader nineteenth-century process of nation building. Throughout the world, powerful, centralized nation-states developed in old countries, and new nations emerged where none had previously existed. The Civil War took place as modern states were consolidating their power and reducing local autonomy. Lincoln has been called the American equivalent of Giuseppe Mazzini or Otto von Bismarck, who during this same era created nation-states in Italy and Germany from disunited collections of principalities. But Lincoln's nation was different from those being constructed in Europe. They were based on the idea of unifying a particular people with a common ethnic, cultural, and linguistic heritage. To Lincoln, the American nation embodied, instead, a set of universal ideas, centered on political democracy and human liberty.

The Gettysburg Address

Lincoln summarized his conception of the war's meaning in November 1863 in brief remarks at the dedication of a military cemetery at the site of the war's greatest battle. The Gettysburg Address is considered his finest speech (see the Appendix for the full text). In less than three minutes, he identified the nation's mission with the principle that "all men are created equal," spoke of the war as bringing about a "new birth of freedom," and defined the essence of democratic government. The sacrifices of Union soldiers, he declared, would ensure that "government of the people, by the people, for the people, shall not perish from the earth."

The mobilization of the Union's resources for modern war brought into being a new American nation-state with greatly expanded powers and responsibilities. The United States remained a federal republic with sovereignty divided between the state and national governments. But the war forged a new national self-consciousness, reflected in the increasing use of the word "nation"—a unified political entity—in place of the older "Union" of separate states. In his inaugural address in 1861, Lincoln used the word "Union" twenty times, while making no mention of the "nation." By 1863, "Union" does not appear at all in the 269-word Gettysburg Address, while Lincoln referred five times to the "nation."

Lincoln and the Female Slave, by the free black artist David B. Bowser. Working in Philadelphia, Bowser painted flags for a number of black Civil War regiments. Lincoln confers freedom on a kneeling slave, an image that downplays blacks' role in their own emancipation.

The War and American Religion

The upsurge of patriotism, and of national power, was reflected in many aspects of American life. Even as the war produced unprecedented casualties, the northern Protestant clergy strove to provide it with a religious

The Sisters of Charity, an order of nuns, photographed with doctors and soldiers at a hospital in Philadelphia in 1863. Many of the wounded from the Battle of Gettysburg were sent here for treatment. The Catholic contribution to the Union war effort mitigated the nativist bias so prominent in the 1850s.

Religious justification

justification and to reassure their congregations that the dead had not died in vain. The religious press now devoted more space to military and political developments than to spiritual matters. In numerous wartime sermons, Christianity and patriotism were joined in a civic religion that saw the war as God's mechanism for ridding the United States of slavery and enabling it to become what it had never really been—a land of freedom. Of course, the southern clergy was equally convinced that the Confederate cause represented God's will.

Religious beliefs enabled Americans to cope with mass death. Coping with death, moreover, required unprecedented governmental action, from notifying next of kin to accounting for the dead and missing. Both the Union and Confederacy established elaborate systems for gathering statistics and maintaining records of dead and wounded soldiers, an effort supplemented by private philanthropic organizations. After the war ended, the federal government embarked on a program to locate and re-bury hundreds of thousands of Union soldiers in national military cemeteries. Between 1865 and 1871, the government reinterred more than 300,000 Union (but not Confederate) soldiers—including black soldiers, who were buried in segregated sections of military cemeteries.

A girl in mourning dress holds a framed photograph of her father, a cavalryman.

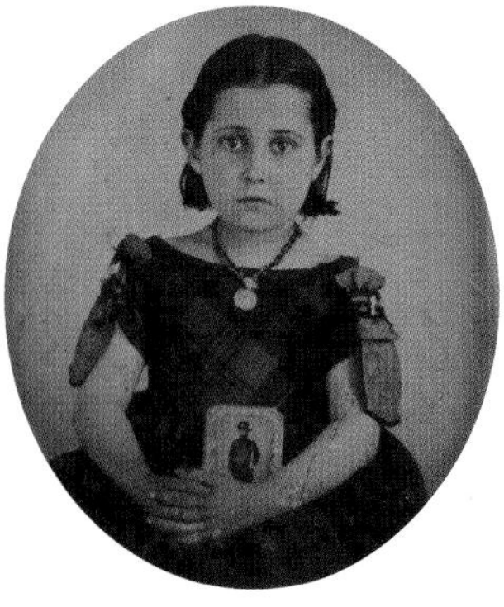

Liberty in Wartime

This intense new nationalism made criticism of the war effort—or of the policies of the Lincoln administration—seem to Republicans equivalent to treason. During the conflict, declared the Republican *New York Times*, "the safety of the nation is the supreme law." Arbitrary arrests numbered in the thousands. They included opposition newspaper editors, Democratic politicians, individuals who discouraged enlistment in the army, and ordinary civilians like the Chicago man briefly imprisoned for calling the president a "damned fool." With the Constitution unclear as to who possessed the power to suspend the writ of habeas corpus (thus allowing prisoners to be held without charge), Lincoln claimed the right under the presidential war powers and twice suspended the writ throughout the entire Union for those accused of "disloyal activities." Not until 1866, after the fighting had ended, did the Supreme Court, in the case ***Ex parte Milligan***, declare it unconstitutional to bring accused persons before military tribunals where civil courts were operating. The Constitution, declared Justice David Davis, is not suspended in wartime—it remains "a law for rulers and people, equally in time of war and peace."

Arbitrary arrests and the suspension of habeas corpus

Lincoln was not a despot. Most of those arrested were quickly released, the Democratic press continued to flourish, and contested elections were held throughout the war. But the policies of the Lincoln administration offered proof—to be repeated during later wars—of the fragility of civil liberties in the face of assertive patriotism and wartime demands for national unity.

Sheet music for two of the best-known patriotic songs written during the Civil War.

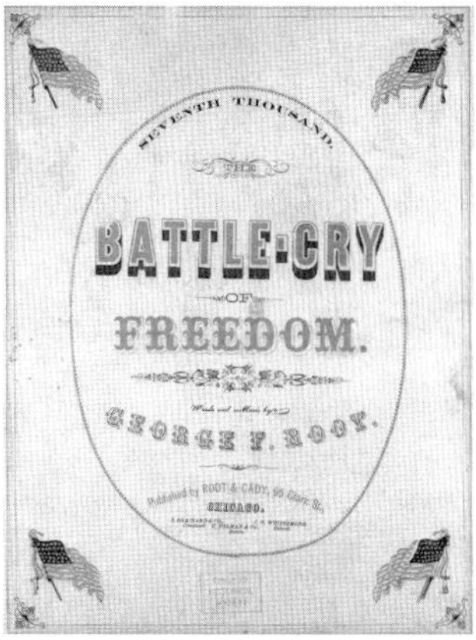

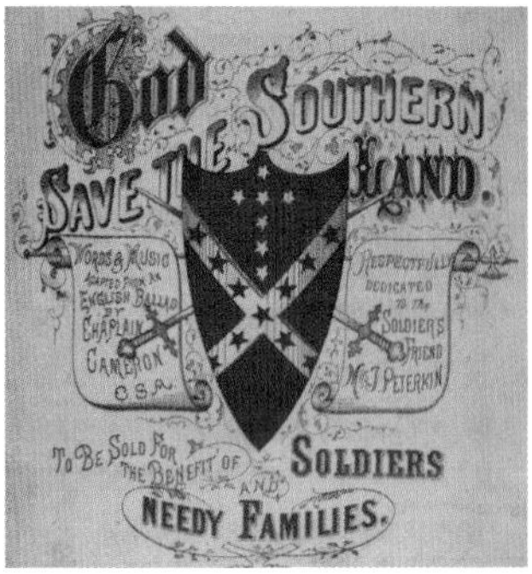

The North's Transformation

Even as he invoked traditional values, Lincoln presided over far-reaching changes in northern life. The effort to mobilize the resources of the Union greatly enhanced the power not only of the federal government but also of a rising class of capitalist entrepreneurs. Unlike the South, which suffered economic devastation, the North experienced the war as a time of prosperity.

Nourished by wartime inflation and government contracts, the profits of industry boomed. New England mills worked day and night to supply the army with blankets and uniforms, and Pennsylvania coal mines and ironworks rapidly expanded their production. Mechanization proceeded apace in many industries, especially those, such as boot and shoe production and meatpacking, that supplied the army's ever-increasing needs. Agriculture also flourished, for even as farm boys by the hundreds of thousands joined the army, the frontier of cultivation pushed westward, with machinery and immigrants replacing lost labor.

Government and the Economy

The new American nation-state that emerged during the Civil War was committed to rapid economic development. Congress adopted policies that promoted economic growth and permanently altered the nation's financial system. To spur agricultural development, the **Homestead Act**

Land grants

offered 160 acres of free public land to settlers in the West. It took effect on January 1, 1863, the same day as the Emancipation Proclamation, and like the proclamation, tried to implement a vision of freedom. By the 1930s, more than 400,000 families had acquired farms under its provisions. In addition, the Morrill Land Grant College Act, named for Justin S. Morrill of Vermont, who introduced the measure, assisted the states in establishing "agricultural and mechanic colleges."

Congress also made huge grants of money and land for internal improvements, including up to 100 million acres to the Union Pacific and Central Pacific, two companies chartered in 1862 and charged with building a railroad from the Missouri River to the Pacific coast. (These were the first corporate charters issued by the federal government since the Second Bank of the United States in 1816.) It required some 20,000 men to lay the tracks across prairies and mountains, a substantial number of them immigrant Chinese contract laborers, called "coolies" by many Americans. Hundreds of Chinese workers died blasting tunnels and building bridges through this treacherous terrain. When it was completed in 1869, the **transcontinental railroad**, which ran from Omaha, Nebraska, to San Francisco, reduced the time of a cross-country journey from four or five months to six days. It expanded the national market, facilitated the spread of settlement and investment in the West, and heralded the doom of the Plains Indians.

This photograph from 1861 depicts Native American volunteer soldiers being enrolled in the Union army. Indian soldiers were recruited well before the army admitted blacks.

The West and the War

Most accounts of the Civil War say little or nothing about the West. Yet the conflict engulfed Missouri, Kansas, and Indian Territory, and spread into the Southwest borderlands. The war divided western communities as residents flocked to both armies.

Since the beginning of the republic, the question of slavery had been tied up with the status of new western lands. Jefferson Davis had long been interested in the expansion of slavery into the Southwest. In pursuit of this goal, in October 1861, Confederate units from Texas launched an invasion of New Mexico (which Texans had long claimed as part of their state). They hoped to conquer the region as a gateway to acquisition of southern California and northern Mexico, a continuation of a southern version of manifest destiny, evidenced before the war in filibustering expeditions in the Caribbean. But the Confederates were defeated at Glorieta Pass in March 1862 by a small Union army contingent reinforced by volunteers from Colorado and California. With their retreat to Texas died the dream of a slave empire in the Far West.

A lithograph depicts the hanging of thirty-eight Sioux Indians in December 1862, the largest mass execution in American history.

The war had a profound impact on western Indians. One of Lincoln's first orders as president was to withdraw federal troops from the West so that they could protect Washington, D.C. Recognizing that this would make it impossible for the army to keep white interlopers from intruding on Indian land, as treaties required it to do, Indian leaders begged Lincoln to reverse this decision, but to no avail. Inevitably, conflict flared in the West between Native Americans and white settlers, with disastrous results. During the Civil War, the Sioux killed hundreds of white farmers in Minnesota before being subdued by the army. After a military court sentenced more than 300 Indians to death, Lincoln commuted the sentences of all but 38. But their hanging in December 1862 remains the largest official execution in American history.

In November 1864, Colorado militiamen attacked a group of around 700 Cheyennes and Arapahos camped along Sand Creek in Colorado. Led by Colonel John Chivington, an abolitionist and a former Methodist minister, the soldiers were bent on punishing Indians responsible for raids on nearby settlements. They failed to locate the hostile Indians, but chose to assault the peaceful encampment with rifles and artillery, killing more than 150 men, women, and children. The incident sparked intensified warfare on the southern plains, as Cheyennes and Arapahos retaliated with attacks of their own.

Union campaigns against Indians

The Union army also launched a series of campaigns in the Southwest against tribes like the Kiowas and Comanches, whose violent raids on ranches and settlements had been an essential, although disruptive, part of the borderlands economy, organized around trading and exchanging captives (usually women), livestock, and horses. The army also made war on the Navajo, who were more victims than perpetrators of these raids. Indian raiding parties had stolen more than 50,000 sheep from their settlements in 1860 alone. Union forces destroyed Navajo orchards and sheep and

Navajo's Long Walk

forced 8,000 people to move to a reservation set aside by the government. The **Navajo's Long Walk** became as central to their historical experience as the Trail of Tears to the Cherokee (see Chapter 10). Unlike the eastern Indians, however, the Navajo were eventually allowed to return to a portion of their lands. The wars against Native Americans, a small part of the violence that engulfed the nation during the Civil War, would continue for more than two decades after the sectional conflict ended.

Cherokee nation and slavery

Some tribes that owned slaves, like the Cherokee, sided with the Confederacy. After 1865, they were forced to cede much of their land to the federal government and to accept former slaves into the Cherokee nation and give them land (the only slaveowners required to do so). Their status remains a point of controversy to this day. The Cherokee constitution was recently amended to exclude descendants of slaves from citizenship, leading to lawsuits that have yet to be resolved.

A New Financial System

Financing the war

The need to pay for the war produced dramatic changes in financial policy. To raise money, the government increased the tariff to unprecedented heights (thus promoting the further growth of northern industry), imposed new taxes on the production and consumption of goods, and enacted the nation's first income tax. It also borrowed more than $2 billion by selling interest-bearing bonds, thus creating an immense national debt. And it printed more than $400 million worth of paper money, called "greenbacks," declared to be legal tender—that is, money that must be accepted for nearly all public and private payments and debts. To rationalize banking, Congress established a system of nationally chartered banks, which were required to purchase government bonds and were given the right to issue bank notes as currency.

"Captains of industry"

Numerous Americans who would take the lead in reshaping the nation's postwar economy created or consolidated their fortunes during the Civil War, among them the iron and steel entrepreneur Andrew Carnegie, the oil magnate John D. Rockefeller, the financiers Jay Gould and J. P. Morgan, and Philip D. Armour, who earned millions supplying beef to the Union army. These and other "captains of industry" managed to escape military service, sometimes by purchasing exemptions or hiring substitutes, as allowed by the draft law.

Taken together, the Union's economic policies vastly increased the power and size of the federal government. The federal budget for 1865 exceeded $1 billion—nearly twenty times that of 1860. With its new army of clerks, tax collectors, and other officials, the government became the nation's largest employer. And although much of this expansion proved

THE CIVIL WAR IN THE WESTERN TERRITORIES, 1862–1864

WASHINGTON TERRITORY
OREGON
IDAHO TERRITORY
MONTANA TERRITORY
Missouri River
Snake River
DAKOTA TERRITORY
MINNESOTA
Fort Ridgely, August 20–22, 1862
Mankato
CHEYENNE
ARAPAHO
NEVADA
UTAH TERRITORY
NEBRASKA TERRITORY
IOWA
San Francisco
CALIFORNIA
COLORADO TERRITORY
Colorado River
Sand Creek Massacre, November 29, 1864
KANSAS
MISSOURI
St. Louis
NAVAJO
ARAPAHO
Fort Defiance
Long Walk of the Navajo, 1864–66
Glorieta Pass, March 26–28, 1862
KIOWA
NEW MEXICO TERRITORY
Fort Sumner
INDIAN TERRITORY
ARKANSAS
Mississippi River
COMANCHE
Pacific Ocean
Rio Grande
LOUISIANA
TEXAS
Houston
Gulf of Mexico
Long Walk of the Navajo
Major Indian conflict
Union victory
Confederate states
Union states
Union territories
0 100 200 miles
0 100 200 kilometers

Filling Cartridges at the U.S. Arsenal of Watertown, Massachusetts, an engraving from *Harper's Weekly*, September 21, 1861. Both men and women were drawn to work in the booming war-related industries of the North.

temporary, the government would never return to its weak and fragmented condition of the prewar period.

Women and the War

For many northern women, the conflict opened new doors of opportunity. Women took advantage of the wartime labor shortage to move into jobs in factories and into certain largely male professions, particularly nursing. The expansion of the activities of the national government opened new jobs for women as clerks in government offices. Many of these wartime gains were short lived, but in white-collar government jobs, retail sales, and nursing, women found a permanent place in the workforce.

Hundreds of thousands of northern women took part in organizations that gathered money and medical supplies for soldiers and sent books, clothing, and food to freedmen. The U.S. Sanitary Commission emerged as a centralized national relief agency to coordinate donations on the northern home front. Although control at the national level remained in male hands, patriotic women did most of the grassroots work. Women played the leading role in organizing **Sanitary Fairs**—grand bazaars that displayed military banners, uniforms, and other relics of the war and sold goods to raise money for soldiers' aid.

Many men understood women's war work as an extension of their "natural" capacity for self-sacrifice. But the very act of volunteering for the war effort brought many northern women into the public sphere and offered them a taste of independence. From the ranks of this wartime mobilization came many of the leaders of the postwar movement for women's rights. Clara Barton organized supply lines and nursed wounded soldiers in northern Virginia. After the war, she became not only an advocate of woman suffrage but also, as president of the American National Red Cross, a strong proponent of the humane treatment of battlefield casualties.

Children at the Colored Orphan Asylum in New York City, photographed in 1862.

The Divided North

Despite Lincoln's political skills, the war and his administration's policies divided northern society. Republicans labeled those opposed to the war Copperheads, after a poisonous snake that strikes without warning. Mounting casualties and rapid societal changes divided the North. Disaffection was strongest among the large southern-born population of states like Ohio, Indiana, and Illinois and working-class Catholic immigrants in eastern cities.

As the war progressed, it heightened existing social tensions and created new ones. The growing power of the federal government challenged traditional notions of local autonomy. The Union's draft law, which allowed individuals to provide a substitute or buy their way out of the army, caused widespread indignation. Workers resented manufacturers and financiers who reaped large profits while their own real incomes dwindled because of inflation. The prospect of a sweeping change in the status of blacks called forth a racist reaction in many parts of the North. Throughout the war, the Democratic Party subjected Lincoln's policies to withering criticism, although it remained divided between "War Democrats," who supported the military effort while criticizing emancipation and the draft, and those who favored immediate peace.

Whimsical potholders expressing hope for a better life for emancipated slaves were sold at the Chicago Sanitary Fair of 1865 to raise money for soldiers' aid.

Rioting in New York City

On occasion, dissent degenerated into outright violence. In July 1863, the introduction of the draft provoked four days of rioting in New York City. The mob, composed largely of Irish immigrants, assaulted symbols of the new order being created by the war—draft offices, the mansions of wealthy Republicans, industrial establishments, and the city's black

THE RIOTS IN NEW YORK: DESTRUCTION OF THE COLOURED ORPHAN ASYLUM.

The burning of the Colored Orphan Asylum during the New York City draft riots of 1863. The children were evacuated before the mob destroyed the building.

population, many of whom fled to New Jersey or took refuge in Central Park. Only the arrival of Union troops quelled the uprising, but not before more than 100 persons had died.

THE CONFEDERATE NATION

Leadership and Government

Jefferson Davis

The man charged with the task of rallying public support for the Confederacy proved unequal to the task. Jefferson Davis moved to Mississippi as a youth, attended West Point, and acquired a large plantation. Aloof and stubborn, Davis lacked Lincoln's political flexibility and ability to communicate the war's meaning effectively to ordinary men and women.

Centralizing the South

Under Davis, the Confederate nation became far more centralized than the Old South had been. The government raised armies from scratch, took control of southern railroads, and built manufacturing plants. But it failed to find an effective way of utilizing the South's major economic resource, cotton. In the early part of the war, the administration tried to suppress cotton production, urging planters to grow food instead and banning cotton exports. This, it was hoped, would promote economic self-sufficiency and force Great Britain, whose textile mills could not operate without southern cotton, to intervene on the side of the Confederacy.

The international dimension

"**King Cotton diplomacy**" turned out to be ineffective. But the Confederate policy had far-reaching global consequences. Recognizing their overdependence on southern cotton, other nations moved to expand production. Britain promoted cultivation of the crop in Egypt and India, and Russia did the same in parts of Central Asia. As a result, the resumption of American cotton production after the war led directly to a worldwide crisis of overproduction that drove down the price of cotton, impoverishing farmers around the world.

The Inner Civil War

Social change in the South

As the war progressed, social change and internal turmoil engulfed much of the Confederacy. At the outset, most white southerners rallied to the Confederate cause. No less fervently than northern troops, southern soldiers spoke of their cause in the language of freedom. "We are fighting for our liberty," wrote one volunteer, without any sense of contradiction, "against tyrants of the North . . . who are determined to destroy slavery."

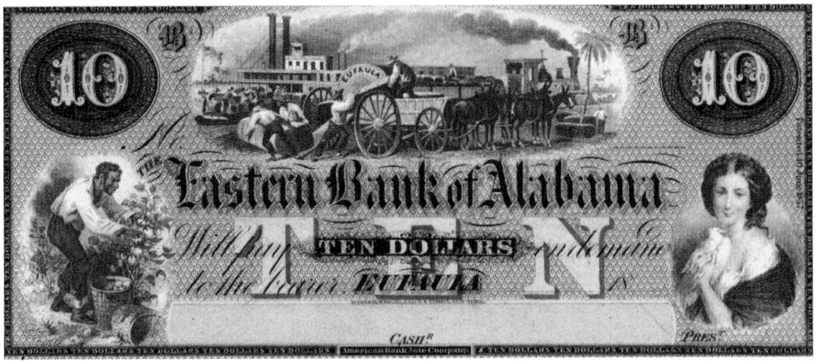

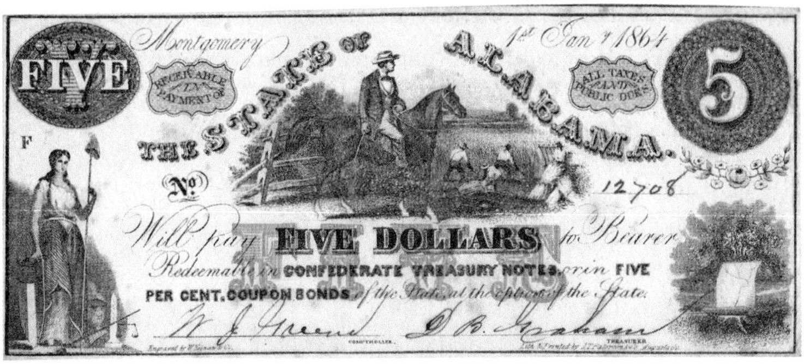

The centrality of slavery to the Confederacy is illustrated by the paper money issued by state governments and private banks, which frequently juxtaposed scenes of slaves at work with other revered images. The ten-dollar note of the Eastern Bank of Alabama depicts slaves working in the field and at a port, along with an idealized image of southern white womanhood. Alabama's five-dollar bill includes an overseer directing slaves in the field and a symbol of liberty.

"Twenty-negro" provision

But even as it waged a desperate struggle for independence, the South found itself increasingly divided. One grievance was the draft. Like the Union, the Confederacy allowed individuals to provide a substitute. Because of the accelerating disintegration of slavery, it also exempted one white male for every twenty slaves on a plantation (thus releasing many overseers and planters' sons from service). The "twenty-negro" provision convinced many yeomen that the struggle for southern independence had become "a rich man's war and a poor man's fight."

Economic Problems

Declining southern production

Economic deprivation also sparked disaffection. As the blockade tightened, areas of the Confederacy came under Union occupation, and production by slaves declined, shortages arose of essential commodities such as salt, corn, and meat. The war left countless farms, plantations, businesses, and railroads in ruins. The economic crisis, which stood in glaring contrast to the North's boom, was an unavoidable result of the war. But Confederate policies exaggerated its effects. War requires sacrifice, and civilian support for war depends, in part, on the belief that sacrifice is being fairly shared. Many non-slaveholders, however, became convinced that they were bearing an unfair share of the war's burdens.

VOICES OF FREEDOM

From Letter of Thomas F. Drayton (1861)

A South Carolina plantation owner and ardent supporter of secession, Thomas F. Drayton explained the Confederate cause in this letter to his brother Percival, an officer in the U.S. Navy, written from Charleston in April 1861, shortly after the firing on Fort Sumter. Drayton went on to serve as a brigadier general in the Confederate army.

My dear Percy

And so Sumter is at last ours, and this too without the loss of a *single* life upon either side. . . . Before this dispute is over however, I look for abundance of death & blood. . . .

You say I don't yet understand the position you have taken. I do fully, but certainly differ from you when you say that to side with us, would be "battling for slavery against freedom." On the contrary, by siding with us, you likewise defend yourselves at the North against a far greater danger than we are threatened with, which is the enslavement of the *whites*; for the tendency with you is towards consolidation & the abrogation of State rights. . . . All these evils & horrors will be laid to your doors, because you have encouraged . . . in the form of abolition lecturers, fanatical preachers, unscrupulous editors, selfish politicians; . . . and by voting for men . . . with the *avowed object* of abolishing slavery throughout the Southern States . . . who made a merit of John Brown's murderous invasion; set at defiance all fugitive slave laws, . . . and whose clergy denounced us indiscriminately as barbarians. . . .

We are fighting for home & liberty. Can the North say as much? Good night. And don't say again, that in siding for us, you would be defending slavery and fighting for what is abhorrent to your feelings & convictions. On the contrary, in fighting on our side, you will be battling for law & order & against abstract fanatical ideas which will certainly bring about vastly greater evils upon our race, then could possibly result from the perpetuation of slavery among us.

From Abraham Lincoln, Address at a Sanitary Fair, Baltimore (1864)

Abraham Lincoln's speech at a Sanitary Fair (a grand bazaar that raised money for the care of Union soldiers) offers a dramatic illustration of the contested meaning of freedom during the Civil War.

The world has never had a good definition of the word liberty, and the American people, just now, are much in want of one. We all declare for liberty; but in using the same *word* we do not all mean the same *thing*. With some the word liberty may mean for each man to do as he pleases with himself, and the product of his labor; while with others the same word may mean for some men to do as they please with other men, and the product of other men's labor. Here are two, not only different, but incompatible things, called by the same name—liberty. And it follows that each of the things is, by the respective parties, called by two different and incompatible names—liberty and tyranny.

The shepherd drives the wolf from the sheep's throat, for which the sheep thanks the shepherd as a *liberator*, while the wolf denounces him for the same act as the destroyer of liberty, especially as the sheep was a black one. Plainly the sheep and the wolf are not agreed upon a definition of the word liberty; and precisely the same difference prevails today among us human creatures, even in the North, and all professing to love liberty. Hence we behold the process by which thousands are daily passing from under the yoke of bondage, hailed by some as the advance of liberty, and bewailed by others as the destruction of all liberty. Recently, as it seems, the people of Maryland have been doing something to define liberty [abolishing slavery in the state]; and thanks to them that, in what they have done, the wolf's dictionary, has been repudiated.

QUESTIONS

1. *Why does Drayton deny that the Confederacy is fighting to defend slavery?*
2. *What does Lincoln identify as the essential difference between northern and southern definitions of freedom?*
3. *How do Drayton and Lincoln differ in their definitions of liberty and whether it applies to African-Americans?*

An engraving in the *New York Illustrated News* depicts the bread riot that took place in Mobile, Alabama, in the fall of 1863.

Like the Union, the Confederacy borrowed heavily to finance the war. Unlike federal lawmakers, however, the planter-dominated Confederate Congress proved unwilling to levy heavy taxes that planters would have to pay. It relied on paper money, of which it issued $1.5 billion, far more than the North's greenbacks. The Confederate Congress also authorized military officers to seize farm goods to supply the army, paying with increasingly worthless Confederate money. Small farmers deeply resented this practice, known as "impressment." Food riots broke out in many places, including Richmond, Virginia, and Mobile, Alabama, where in 1863 large crowds of women plundered army food supplies. As the war progressed, desertion became what one officer called a "crying evil" for the southern armies. By the war's end, more than 100,000 men had deserted, almost entirely from among "the poorest class of nonslaveholders whose labor is indispensable to the daily support of their families."

By 1864, organized peace movements had appeared in several southern states, and secret pro-Union societies such as the Heroes of America were actively promoting disaffection.

Women and the Confederacy

Wartime roles for women in the Confederacy

Even more than in the North, the war placed unprecedented burdens on southern white women. Left alone on farms and plantations, they were often forced to manage business affairs and discipline slaves, previously the responsibility of men. As in the North, women mobilized to support soldiers in the field and stepped out of their traditional "sphere" to run commercial establishments and work in arms factories. In Richmond, "government girls" staffed many of the clerkships in the new Confederate bureaucracy.

Women mobilizing for assistance

All Confederate women struggled to cope as their loved ones were drawn off into the army. The war led to the political mobilization, for the first time, of non-slaveholding white women. Lacking the aid of slave labor, they found that the absence of their husbands from their previously self-sufficient farms made it impossible to feed their families. They flooded Confederate authorities with petitions seeking assistance, not as charity but as a right. Politicians could not ignore the pleas of soldiers' wives, and state governments began to distribute supplies to needy families.

Painted in 1864 by the Virginia artist William D. Washington, *The Burial of Latané* depicts a common wartime scene. The deceased is Confederate cavalry officer William Latané. The work illustrates how women, children, and slaves predominated on the southern home front. The painting was displayed in Richmond accompanied by a bucket into which viewers were urged to deposit contributions to the southern cause.

Decline in morale among women

Southern women's self-sacrificing devotion to the cause became legendary. But as the war went on and the death toll mounted, increasing numbers of women came to believe that the goal of independence was not worth the cost. The growing disaffection of southern white women, conveyed in letters to loved ones at the front, contributed to the decline in civilian morale and encouraged desertion from the army.

Black Soldiers for the Confederacy

Southern debate over arming the slaves

The growing shortage of white manpower eventually led Confederate authorities to a decision no one could have foreseen when the war began: they authorized the arming of slaves to fight for the South. Many slaveholders fiercely resisted this idea, and initially, the Confederate Senate rejected it. Not until March 1865, after Robert E. Lee had endorsed the plan, did the Confederate Congress authorize the arming of slaves.

Employing blacks as laborers

The war ended before the recruitment of black soldiers actually began. But the Confederate army did employ numerous blacks, nearly all of them slaves, as laborers. This later led to some confusion over whether blacks actually fought for the Confederacy—apart from a handful who "passed" for white, none in fact did. But the South's decision to raise black troops illustrates how the war undermined not only slavery but also the proslavery ideology. Declared Howell Cobb, a Georgia planter and politician, "If slaves make good soldiers, our whole theory of slavery is wrong."

TURNING POINTS

Gettysburg and Vicksburg

Despite the accelerating demise of slavery and the decline of morale in the South, the war's outcome remained very much in doubt for much of its third and fourth years. In April 1863, "Fighting Joe" Hooker, who had succeeded Ambrose E. Burnside as the Union commander in the East, brought the Army of the Potomac into central Virginia to confront Lee. Outnumbered two to one, Lee repelled Hooker's attack at Chancellorsville, although he lost his ablest lieutenant, "Stonewall" Jackson, mistakenly killed by fire from his own soldiers.

Generals Robert E. Lee and Ulysses S. Grant, leaders of the opposing armies in the East, 1864–1865.

Lee now gambled on another invasion of the North, although his strategic objective remains unclear. Perhaps he believed a defeat on its own territory would destroy the morale of the northern army and public. In any event, the two armies, with Union soldiers now under the command of General George G. Meade, met at Gettysburg, Pennsylvania, on the first three days of July 1863. With 165,000 troops involved, the **Battle of Gettysburg** remains the largest battle ever fought on the North American continent. On July 3, Confederate forces, led by Major General George E. Pickett's crack division, marched across an open field toward Union forces. Withering artillery and rifle fire met the charge, and most of Pickett's soldiers never reached Union lines. Pickett's Charge was Lee's greatest blunder. His army retreated to Virginia, never again to set foot on northern soil.

On the same day that Lee began his retreat from Gettysburg, the Union achieved a significant victory in the West at the **Battle of Vicksburg**. Late in 1862, Grant had moved into Mississippi toward the city of Vicksburg. From its heights, defended by miles of trenches and earthworks, the Confederacy commanded the central Mississippi River. When direct attacks failed, Grant launched a siege. On July 4, 1863, Vicksburg surrendered, and with it John C. Pemberton's army of 30,000 men, a loss the Confederacy could ill afford. The entire Mississippi Valley now lay in Union hands.

1864

Nearly two years, however, would pass before the war ended. Brought east to take command of Union forces, Grant in 1864 began a war of attrition against Lee's army in Virginia. That is, he was willing to accept high numbers of casualties, knowing that the North could replace its manpower losses, whereas the South could not. Grant understood that to bring the North's manpower advantage into play, he must attack continuously "all along the line," thereby preventing the enemy from concentrating its forces or retreating to safety after an engagement.

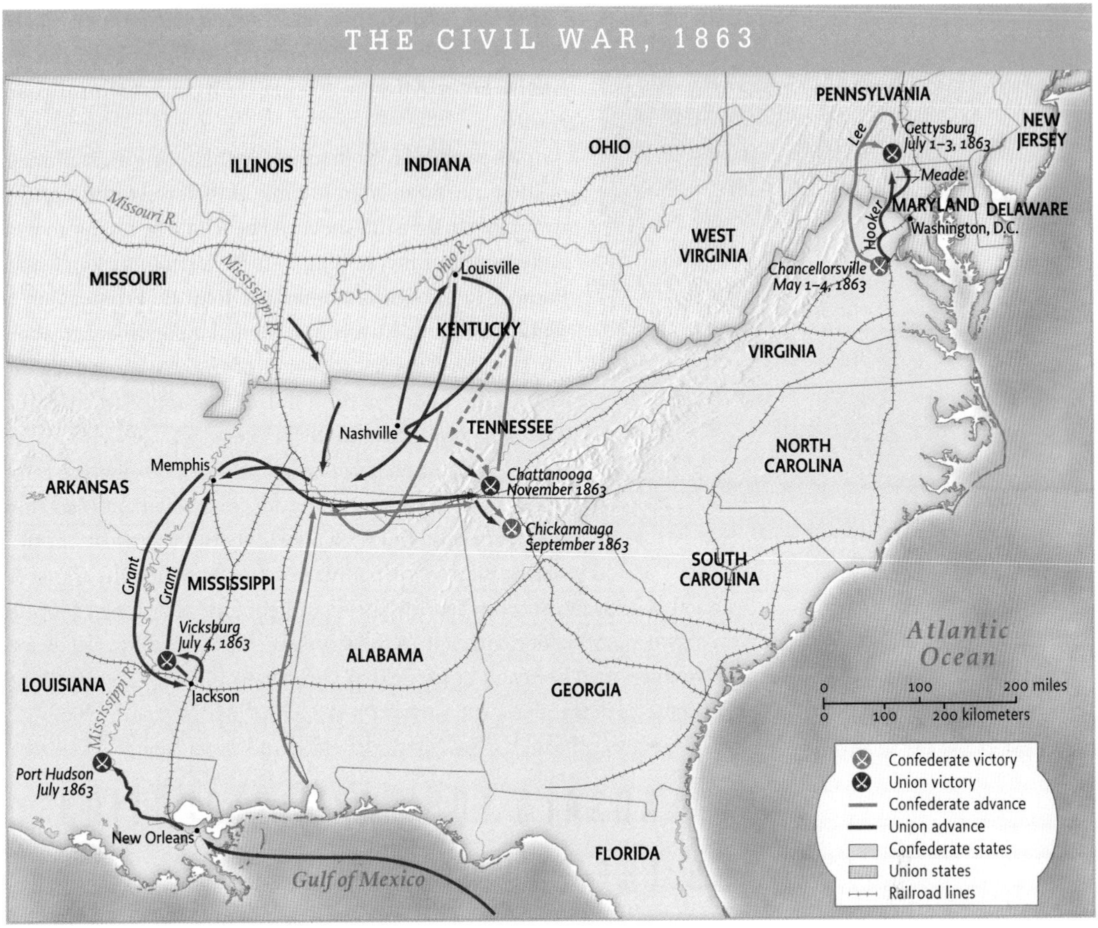

In July 1863, the Union won major victories at Gettysburg and Vicksburg.

In May 1864, the 115,000-man Army of the Potomac crossed the Rapidan River to do battle with Lee's forces in Virginia. At the end of six weeks of fighting, Grant's casualties stood at 60,000—almost the size of Lee's entire army—while Lee had lost 30,000 men. The sustained fighting in Virginia was a turning point in modern warfare. With daily combat and a fearsome casualty toll, it had far more in common with the trench warfare of World War I (discussed in Chapter 19) than the almost gentlemanly fighting with which the Civil War began.

Grant had become the only Union general to maintain the initiative against Lee, but at a cost that led critics to label him a "butcher of men." Victory still eluded him. Grant attempted to capture Petersburg, which controlled the railway link to Richmond, but Lee got to Petersburg first, and Grant settled in for a prolonged siege. Meanwhile, General William T. Sherman, who had moved his forces into Georgia from

General Grant's Council of War, an unusual candid photograph taken in Virginia in 1864 from the upper floor of a nearby church, shows Grant leaning over the shoulder of General George G. Meade to examine a map. Other generals and staff sit on pews removed from the church.

Tennessee, encountered dogged resistance from Confederate troops. Not until September 1864 did he finally enter Atlanta, seizing Georgia's main railroad center.

As casualty rolls mounted in the spring and summer of 1864, northern morale sank to its lowest point of the war. Lincoln for a time believed he would be unable to win reelection. In May, hoping to force Lincoln to step aside, Radical Republicans nominated John C. Frémont on a platform calling for a constitutional amendment to abolish slavery, federal protection of the freedmen's rights, and confiscation of the land of leading Confederates. The Democratic candidate for president, General George B. McClellan, was hampered from the outset of the campaign by a platform calling for an immediate cease-fire and peace conference—a plan that even war-weary northerners viewed as equivalent to surrender. In the end, Frémont withdrew, and buoyed by Sherman's capture of Atlanta, Lincoln won a sweeping victory. He captured every state but Kentucky, Delaware, and New Jersey. The result ensured that the war would continue until the Confederacy's defeat.

REHEARSALS FOR RECONSTRUCTION AND THE END OF THE WAR

A political cartoon from 1864 suggests the difficulty faced by the Democratic candidate, George B. McClellan, in reconciling the party's war and peace wings.

LITTLE MAC, IN HIS GREAT TWO HORSE ACT, IN THE PRESIDENTIAL CANVASS OF 1864.

As the war drew toward a close and more and more parts of the Confederacy came under Union control, federal authorities found themselves presiding over the transition from slavery to freedom. In South Carolina, Louisiana, and other parts of the South, debates took place over issues—access to land, control of labor, and the new structure of political power—that would reverberate in the postwar world.

The Sea Islands Experiment

The most famous "rehearsal for Reconstruction" took place on the Sea Islands just off the coast of South Carolina. The war was only a few months old when, in November 1861, the Union navy occupied the islands. Nearly the entire white population fled, leaving behind some 10,000 slaves. The navy was soon followed by other northerners—army officers, Treasury agents, prospective investors in cotton land, and a group known as Gideon's Band, which included black and white reformers and teachers committed to uplifting the freed slaves. Northern-born teachers like Charlotte Forten, a member of one of Philadelphia's most prominent black families, and Laura M. Towne, a white native of Pittsburgh, devoted themselves to teaching the freed blacks.

Gideon's Band

Forten and Towne

Many northerners believed that the transition from slave to free labor meant enabling blacks to work for wages in more humane conditions than under slavery. When the federal government put land on the islands up for sale, most was acquired not by former slaves but by northern investors bent on demonstrating the superiority of free wage labor and turning a tidy profit at the same time. By 1865, the **Sea Islands experiment** was widely held to be a success. But the experiment also bequeathed to postwar Reconstruction the contentious issue of whether landownership should accompany black freedom.

Wartime Reconstruction in the West

A very different rehearsal for Reconstruction, involving a far larger area and population than the Sea Islands, took place in Louisiana and the Mississippi Valley. After the capture of Vicksburg, the Union army established regulations for plantation labor. Military authorities insisted that the emancipated slaves must sign labor contracts with plantation owners who took an oath of loyalty. But, unlike before the war, the laborers would be paid wages and provided with education, physical punishment was prohibited, and their families were safe from disruption by sale.

Neither side was satisfied with the new labor system. Blacks resented having to resume working for whites and being forced to sign labor contracts. Planters complained that their workers were insubordinate. But only occasionally did army officers seek to implement a different vision of freedom. At Davis Bend, Mississippi, site of the cotton plantations of Jefferson Davis and his brother Joseph, the emancipated slaves saw the land divided among themselves. In addition, a system of government was established that allowed the former slaves to elect their own judges and sheriffs.

A school for freedpeople established in 1862 on St. Helena Island, South Carolina, by an aid association in Pennsylvania.

The Politics of Wartime Reconstruction

Lincoln's Ten-Percent Plan

As the Civil War progressed, the future political status of African-Americans emerged as a key dividing line in public debates. Events in Union-occupied Louisiana brought the issue to national attention. Hoping to establish a functioning civilian government in the state, Lincoln in 1863 announced his **Ten-Percent Plan of Reconstruction**. He essentially offered an amnesty and full restoration of rights, including property except for slaves, to nearly all white southerners who took an oath affirming loyalty to the Union and support for emancipation. When 10 percent of the voters of 1860 had taken the oath, they could elect a new state government, which would be required to abolish slavery. Lincoln's plan offered no role to blacks in shaping the post-slavery order.

Wade-Davis Bill

Another group now stepped onto the stage of politics—the free blacks of New Orleans, who saw the Union occupation as a golden opportunity to press for equality before the law and a role in government for themselves. Their complaints at being excluded under Lincoln's Reconstruction plan won a sympathetic hearing from Radical Republicans in Congress. By the summer of 1864, dissatisfaction with events in Louisiana helped to inspire the **Wade-Davis Bill**, named for two leading Republican members of Congress. This bill required a majority (not one-tenth) of white male southerners to pledge support for the Union before Reconstruction could begin in any state, and it guaranteed blacks equality before the law, although not the right to vote. The bill passed Congress only to die when Lincoln refused to sign it and Congress adjourned. As the war drew to a close, it was clear that although slavery was dead, no agreement existed as to what social and political system should take its place.

Victory at Last

General William T. Sherman, photographed in 1864.

After Lincoln's reelection, the war hastened to its conclusion. In November 1864, Sherman and his army of 60,000 set out from Atlanta on their March to the Sea. Cutting a sixty-mile-wide swath through the heart of Georgia, they destroyed railroads, buildings, and all the food and supplies they could not use. His aim, Sherman wrote, was "to whip the rebels, to humble their pride, to follow them to their innermost recesses, and make them fear and dread us." Here was modern war in all its destructiveness, even though few civilians were physically harmed. In January 1865, after capturing Savannah, Sherman moved into South Carolina, bringing even greater destruction.

On January 31, 1865, Congress approved the **Thirteenth Amendment**, which abolished slavery throughout the entire Union—and in so doing, introduced the word "slavery" into the Constitution for the first time. In

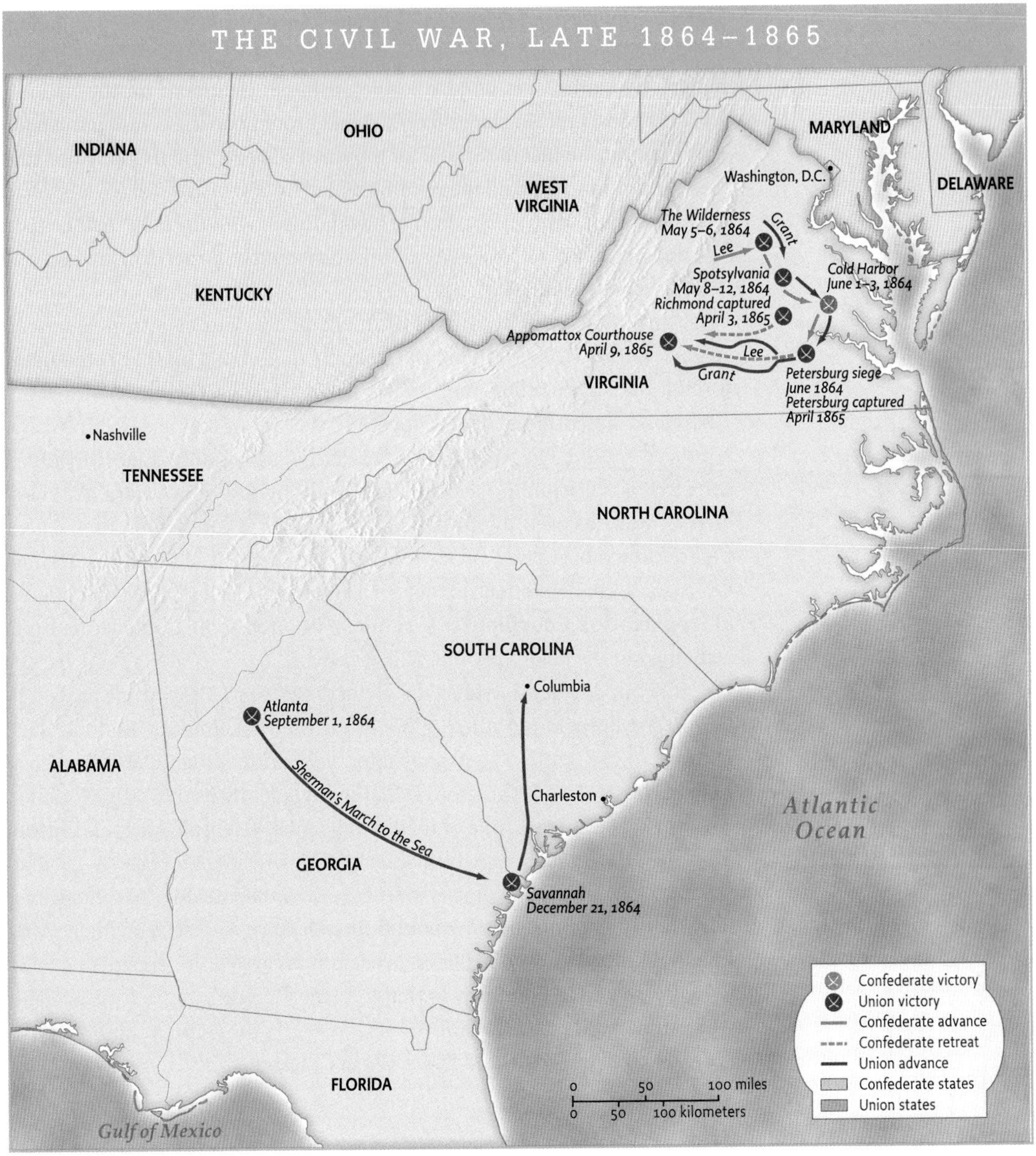

The military defeat of the Confederacy came in the East, with Sherman's March to the Sea, Grant's occupation of Richmond, and the surrender of Robert E. Lee's army.

March, in his second inaugural address, Lincoln called for reconciliation: "With malice toward none, with charity for all, . . . let us . . . bind up the nation's wounds." Yet he also leveled a harsh judgment on the nation's past. Perhaps, Lincoln suggested, God had brought on the war to punish the entire nation, not just the South, for the sin of slavery. And if God willed that the war continue until all the wealth created by 250 years of slave labor had been destroyed, and "every drop of blood drawn with the lash shall be paid by another drawn with the sword," this too would be an act of justice (see the Appendix for the full text).

Occupation at Richmond

April 1865 brought some of the most momentous events in American history. On April 2, Grant finally broke through Lee's lines at Petersburg, forcing the Army of Northern Virginia to abandon the city and leaving Richmond defenseless. The following day, Union soldiers occupied the southern capital. On April 4, heedless of his own safety, Lincoln walked the streets of Richmond accompanied only by a dozen sailors. At every step he was besieged by former slaves, some of whom fell on their knees before the embarrassed president, who urged them to remain standing. On April 9, realizing that further resistance was useless, Lee surrendered at **Appomattox Courthouse, Virginia**. Although some Confederate units remained in the field, the Civil War was over.

Surrender at Appomattox

Lincoln did not live to savor victory. On April 11, in what proved to be his last speech, he called publicly for the first time for limited black suffrage in the South. Three days later, while attending a performance at Ford's Theatre in Washington, D.C., the president was mortally wounded by John Wilkes Booth, one of the nation's most celebrated actors. Lincoln died the next morning. A train carried the president's body to its final resting place in Illinois on a winding 1,600-mile journey that illustrated how tightly the railroad now bound the northern states. Grieving crowds lined the train route, and solemn processions carried the president's body to lie in state in major cities so that mourners could pay their respects. It was estimated that 300,000 persons passed by the coffin in Philadelphia, 500,000 in New York, and 200,000 in Chicago.

A redesign of the American flag proposed in 1863 illustrates the linkage of nationalism and freedom that was solidified by the Civil War. The thirty-five stars forming the word "FREE" include the eleven Confederate states.

The War and the World

In 1877, soon after retiring as president, Ulysses S. Grant embarked with his wife on a two-year tour of the world. At almost every location, he was greeted as a modern-day hero. What did America in the aftermath of the Civil War represent to the world? In England, the son of the duke of Wellington greeted Grant as a military genius. In Newcastle, parading English workers hailed him as the man whose military prowess had saved the world's leading experiment in democratic government and as a "Hero of

Freedom." In Berlin, Otto von Bismarck, the chancellor of Germany, welcomed Grant as a nation-builder, who had accomplished on the battlefield something—national unity—that Bismarck was attempting to create for his own people.

Some of the more than 200,000 victorious soldiers who paraded in Washington on May 23 and 24, 1865, in the Grand Review of the Union Armies. In the background stands the Capitol, its dome, unfinished when the war began, now complete.

The War in American History

The Civil War laid the foundation for modern America, guaranteeing the Union's permanence, destroying slavery, and shifting power in the nation from the South to the North (and, more specifically, from slaveowning planters to northern capitalists). It dramatically increased the power of the federal government and accelerated the modernization of the northern economy. And it placed on the postwar agenda the challenge of defining and protecting African-American freedom. "Verily," as Frederick Douglass declared, "the work does not *end* with the abolition of slavery, but only *begins*."

Paradoxically, both sides lost something they had gone to war to defend. Slavery was the cornerstone of the Confederacy, but the war led inexorably to slavery's destruction. In the North, the war hastened the transformation of Lincoln's America—the world of free labor, of the small shop and independent farmer—into an industrial giant. Americans, in the words of the abolitionist Wendell Phillips, would "never again . . . see the republic in which we were born."

Winslow Homer's painting *The Veteran in a New Field*, completed in the fall of 1865, offers a reflection on the Civil War and its legacy. The former Union soldier, whose army jacket lies in the right corner, is at work cutting wheat. The scythe brings to mind the grim reaper, a symbol of death, perhaps a reference not only to war casualties but also to Lincoln's assassination. But the bountiful field suggests national regeneration.

CHAPTER REVIEW AND ONLINE RESOURCES

REVIEW QUESTIONS

1. *What made the American Civil War the first modern war?*
2. *How was the North's victory over the South tied to the different ways the market revolution had developed in the North and South?*
3. *Describe how President Lincoln's war aims evolved between 1861 and 1863, changing from simply preserving the Union to also ending slavery.*
4. *How did the actions of slaves themselves, northern military strategy, and the Emancipation Proclamation combine to end slavery?*
5. *What role did blacks play in winning the Civil War and in defining the war's consequences?*
6. *How did federal policies undertaken during the Civil War transform the United States into a stronger nation-state—economically, politically, and ideologically?*
7. *What was the impact of the Civil War on civil liberties?*
8. *Compare and contrast women's efforts in the North and South to support the war effort and their families.*
9. *In what ways did the outcome of the Civil War change the United States' status in the world?*

KEY TERMS

first Battle of Bull Run (p. 401)
second Battle of Bull Run (p. 401)
Battle of Antietam (p. 401)
"the contrabands" (p. 405)
Radical Republicans (p. 406)
Emancipation Proclamation (p. 407)
Second American Revolution (p. 410)
Ex parte Milligan (p. 413)
Homestead Act (p. 413)
transcontinental railroad (p. 414)
Navajo's Long Walk (p. 416)
Sanitary Fairs (p. 418)
"King Cotton diplomacy" (p. 420)
Battle of Gettysburg (p. 426)
Battle of Vicksburg (p. 426)
Sea Islands experiment (p. 429)
Ten-Percent Plan of Reconstruction (p. 430)
Wade-Davis Bill (p. 430)
Thirteenth Amendment (p. 430)
Appomattox Courthouse, Virginia (p. 432)

Go to INQUIZITIVE

To see what you know—and learn what you've missed—with personalized feedback along the way.

Visit the ***Give Me Liberty!*** **Student Site** for primary source documents and images, interactive maps, author videos featuring Eric Foner, and more.

CHAPTER 15

"WHAT IS FREEDOM?"

★

RECONSTRUCTION, 1865–1877

1865	Special Field Order 15
	Freedmen's Bureau established
	Lincoln assassinated; Andrew Johnson becomes president
1865–1867	Presidential Reconstruction
	Black Codes
1866	Civil Rights Bill
	Ku Klux Klan established
1867	Reconstruction Act of 1867
	Tenure of Office Act
1867–1877	Radical Reconstruction
1868	Impeachment and trial of President Johnson
	Fourteenth Amendment ratified
1869	Inauguration of Ulysses S. Grant
1870	Hiram Revels, first black U.S. senator
	Fifteenth Amendment ratified
1870–1871	Enforcement Acts
1872	Liberal Republicans established
1873	Colfax Massacre
	Slaughterhouse Cases
	National economic depression begins
1876	*United States v. Cruikshank*
1877	Bargain of 1877

The Shackle Broken—by the Genius of Freedom. This 1874 lithograph depicts Robert B. Elliott, a black congressman from South Carolina, delivering a celebrated speech supporting the bill that became the Civil Rights Act of 1875.

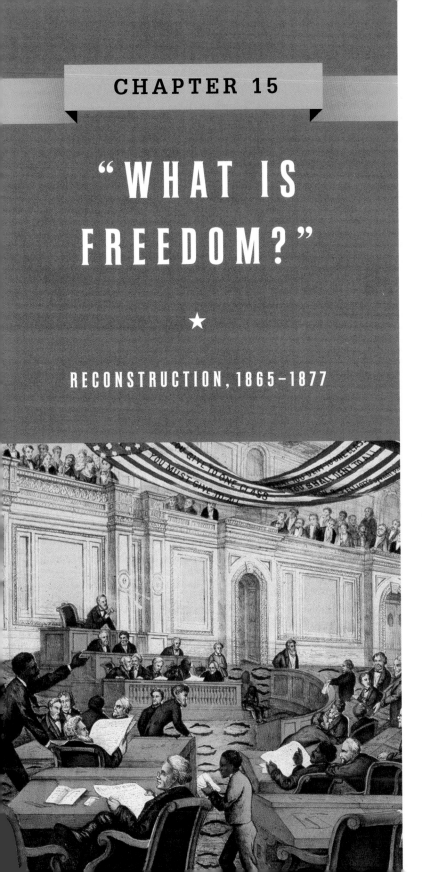

FOCUS QUESTIONS

- *What visions of freedom did the former slaves and slaveholders pursue in the postwar South?*
- *What were the competing visions of Reconstruction?*
- *What were the social and political effects of Radical Reconstruction in the South?*
- *What were the main factors, in both the North and South, for the overthrow of Reconstruction?*

On the evening of January 12, 1865, less than a month after Union forces captured Savannah, Georgia, twenty leaders of the city's black community gathered for a discussion with General William T. Sherman and Secretary of War Edwin M. Stanton. The conversation revealed that the black leaders brought out of slavery a clear definition of freedom. Asked what he understood by slavery, Garrison Frazier, a Baptist minister chosen as the group's spokesman, responded that it meant one person's "receiving by irresistible power the work of another man, and not by his consent." Freedom he defined as "placing us where we could reap the fruit of our own labor, and take care of ourselves." The way to accomplish this was "to have land, and turn it and till it by our own labor."

Sherman's meeting with the black leaders foreshadowed some of the radical changes that would take place during the era known as Reconstruction (meaning, literally, the rebuilding of the shattered nation). In the years following the Civil War, former slaves and their white allies, North and South, would seek to redefine the meaning and boundaries of American freedom and citizenship. Previously an entitlement of whites, these would be expanded to include black Americans. The laws and Constitution would be rewritten to guarantee African-Americans, for the first time in the nation's history, recognition as citizens and equality before the law. Black men would be granted the right to vote, ushering in a period of interracial democracy throughout the South. Black schools, churches, and other institutions would flourish, laying the foundation for the modern African-American community. Many of the advances of Reconstruction would prove temporary, swept away during a campaign of violence in the South and the North's retreat from the ideal of equality. But Reconstruction laid the foundation for future struggles to extend freedom to all Americans.

Four days after the meeting, Sherman responded to the black delegation by issuing Special Field Order 15. This set aside the Sea Islands and a large area along the South Carolina and Georgia coasts for the settlement of black families on forty-acre plots of land. He also offered them broken-down mules that the army could no longer use. In Sherman's order lay the origins of the phrase "forty acres and a mule," which would reverberate across the South in the next few years. Among the emancipated slaves, Sherman's order raised hopes that the end of slavery would be accompanied by the economic independence that they, like other Americans, believed essential to genuine freedom.

THE MEANING OF FREEDOM

"What is freedom?" asked Congressman James A. Garfield in 1865. "Is it the bare privilege of not being chained? If this is all, then freedom is a bitter mockery, a cruel delusion." Did freedom mean simply the absence of slavery, or did it imply other rights for the former slaves, and if so, which ones? Equal civil rights, the vote, ownership of property? During Reconstruction, freedom became a terrain of conflict, its substance open to different, often contradictory interpretations.

Conflicts over freedom

African-Americans' understanding of freedom was shaped by their experiences as slaves and their observation of the free society around them. To begin with, freedom meant escaping the numerous injustices of slavery—punishment by the lash, the separation of families, denial of access to education, the sexual exploitation of black women by their owners—and sharing in the rights and opportunities of American citizens. "If I cannot do like a white man," Henry Adams, an emancipated slave in Louisiana, told his former master in 1865, "I am not free."

Families in Freedom

With slavery dead, institutions that had existed before the war, like the black family, free blacks' churches and schools, and the secret slave church, were strengthened, expanded, and freed from white supervision. The family was central to the postemancipation black community. Former slaves made remarkable efforts to locate loved ones from whom they had been separated under slavery. One northern reporter in 1865 encountered a freedman who

Marriage of a Colored Soldier at Vicksburg, a sketch of a wedding ceremony by Alfred R. Waud soon after the end of the Civil War.

Five Generations of a Black Family, an 1862 photograph that suggests the power of family ties among emancipated slaves.

had walked more than 600 miles from Georgia to North Carolina, searching for the wife and children from whom he had been sold away before the war.

While freedom helped to stabilize family life, it also subtly altered relationships within the family. Immediately after the Civil War, planters complained that freedwomen had "withdrawn" from field labor and work as house servants. Many black women preferred to devote more time to their families than had been possible under slavery, and men considered it a badge of honor to see their wives remain at home. Eventually, the dire poverty of the black community would compel a far higher proportion of black women than white women to go to work for wages.

Church and School

At the same time, blacks abandoned white-controlled religious institutions to create churches of their own. On the eve of the Civil War, 42,000 black Methodists worshiped in biracial South Carolina churches; by the end of Reconstruction, only 600 remained. As the major institution independent of white control, the church played a central role in the black community. A place of worship, it also housed schools, social events, and political gatherings. Black ministers came to play a major role in politics. Some 250 held public office during Reconstruction.

Another striking example of the freedpeople's quest for individual and community improvement was their desire for education. The thirst for learning sprang from many sources—a desire to read the Bible, the need to prepare for the economic marketplace, and the opportunity, which arose in 1867, to take part in politics. Blacks of all ages flocked to the schools established by northern missionary societies, the Freedmen's Bureau, and groups of ex-slaves. Reconstruction also witnessed the creation of the nation's first black colleges, including Fisk University in Tennessee, Hampton Institute in Virginia, and Howard University in the nation's capital.

Mother and Daughter Reading, Mt. Meigs, Alabama, an 1890 photograph by Rudolph Eickemeyer. During Reconstruction and for years thereafter, former slaves exhibited a deep desire for education, and learning took place outside of school as well as within.

Political Freedom

In a society that had made political participation a core element of freedom, the right to vote inevitably became central to the former slaves' desire for empowerment and equality. As Frederick Douglass put it soon after the South's surrender in 1865, "Slavery is not abolished until the black man has the ballot." In a "monarchial government," Douglass explained, no "special" disgrace applied to those denied the right to vote. But in a

The First African Church, Richmond, as depicted in *Harper's Weekly*, June 27, 1874. The establishment of independent black churches was an enduring accomplishment of Reconstruction.

democracy, "where universal suffrage is the rule," excluding any group meant branding them with "the stigma of inferiority." Anything less than full citizenship, black spokesmen insisted, would betray the nation's democratic promise and the war's meaning.

Land, Labor, and Freedom

Freedom and landownership

Like those of rural people throughout the world, former slaves' ideas of freedom were directly related to landownership. On the land they would develop independent communities free of white control. Many former slaves insisted that through their unpaid labor, they had acquired a right to the land. "The property which they hold," declared an Alabama black convention, "was nearly all earned by the sweat of *our* brows." In some parts of the South, blacks in 1865 seized property, insisting that it belonged to them.

Freedom's meaning for former slaves

In its individual elements and much of its language, former slaves' definition of freedom resembled that of white Americans—self-ownership, family stability, religious liberty, political participation, and economic autonomy. But these elements combined to form a vision very much their own. For whites, freedom, no matter how defined, was a given, a birthright to be defended. For African-Americans, it was an open-ended process, a transformation of every aspect of their lives and of the society and culture that had sustained slavery in the first place. Although the freedpeople failed to achieve full freedom as they understood it, their definition did much to shape national debate during the turbulent era of Reconstruction.

Masters without Slaves

The southern white reaction to emancipation

Most white southerners reacted to military defeat and emancipation with dismay, not only because of the widespread devastation but also because

Two maps of the Barrow plantation illustrate the effects of emancipation on rural life in the South. In 1860, slaves lived in communal quarters near the owner's house. Twenty-one years later, former slaves working as sharecroppers lived scattered across the plantation and had their own church and school.

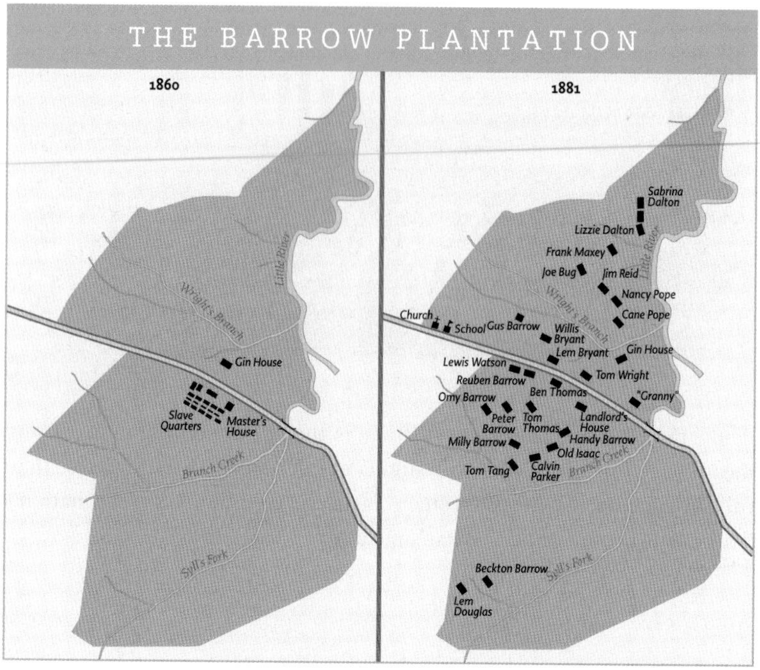

they must now submit to northern demands. "The demoralization is complete," wrote a Georgia girl. "We are whipped, there is no doubt about it." The appalling loss of life, a disaster without parallel in the American experience, affected all classes of southerners. Nearly 260,000 men died for the Confederacy—more than one-fifth of the South's adult male white population. The wholesale destruction of work animals, farm buildings, and machinery ensured that economic revival would be slow and painful. In 1870, the value of property in the South, not counting that represented by slaves, was 30 percent lower than before the war.

Confederate deaths

Planter families faced profound changes in the war's aftermath. Many lost not only their slaves but also their life savings, which they had patriotically invested in now-worthless Confederate bonds. Some, whose slaves departed the plantation, for the first time found themselves compelled to do physical labor.

Planters

Southern planters sought to implement an understanding of freedom quite different from that of the former slaves. As they struggled to accept the reality of emancipation, most planters defined black freedom in the narrowest manner. As journalist Sidney Andrews discovered late in 1865, "The whites seem wholly unable to comprehend that freedom for the negro means the same thing as freedom for them."

Narrow understanding of freedom

The Free Labor Vision

Along with former slaves and former masters, the victorious Republican North tried to implement its own vision of freedom. Central to its definition was the antebellum principle of free labor, now further strengthened as a definition of the good society by the Union's triumph. In the free labor vision of a reconstructed South, emancipated blacks, enjoying the same opportunities for advancement as northern workers, would labor more productively than they had as slaves. At the same time, northern capital and migrants would energize the economy. The South would eventually come to resemble the "free society" of the North, complete with public schools, small towns, and independent farmers.

Free labor and the good society

With planters seeking to establish a labor system as close to slavery as possible, and former slaves demanding economic autonomy and access to land, a long period of conflict over the organization and control of labor followed on plantations throughout the South. It fell to **the Freedmen's Bureau**, an agency established by Congress in March 1865, to attempt to establish a working free labor system.

The Freedmen's Bureau

Under the direction of O. O. Howard, a graduate of Bowdoin College in Maine and a veteran of the Civil War, the bureau took on responsibilities that can only be described as daunting. The bureau was an experiment in government social policy that seems to belong more comfortably to the New Deal of the 1930s or the Great Society of the 1960s (see Chapters 21 and 25, respectively) than to nineteenth-century America. Bureau agents were supposed to establish schools, provide aid to the poor and aged, settle disputes between whites and blacks and among the freedpeople, and secure for former slaves and white Unionists equal treatment before the courts. "It is not . . . in your power to fulfill one-tenth of the expectations of those who framed the Bureau," General William T. Sherman wrote to Howard. "I fear you have Hercules' task."

The bureau lasted from 1865 to 1870. Even at its peak, there were fewer than 1,000 agents in the entire South.

Winslow Homer's 1876 painting *A Visit from the Old Mistress* depicts an imaginary meeting between a southern white woman and her former slaves. Their stance and gaze suggest the tensions arising from the birth of a new social order. Despite the clear class difference suggested by their clothing, Homer places his subjects on an equal footing, yet maintains a space of separation between them. He exhibited the painting to acclaim at the Paris Universal Exposition in 1878.

The Freedmen's Bureau, an engraving from *Harper's Weekly*, July 25, 1868, depicts the bureau agent as a promoter of racial peace in the violent postwar South.

Nonetheless, the bureau's achievements in some areas, notably education and health care, were striking. By 1869, nearly 3,000 schools, serving more than 150,000 pupils in the South, reported to the bureau. Bureau agents also assumed control of hospitals established during the war and provided medical care to both black and white southerners.

The Failure of Land Reform

Andrew Johnson and land reform

One provision of the law establishing the bureau gave it the authority to divide abandoned and confiscated land into forty-acre plots for rental and eventual sale to the former slaves. In the summer of 1865, however, President Andrew Johnson, who had succeeded Lincoln, ordered nearly all land in federal hands returned to its former owners. A series of confrontations followed, notably in South Carolina and Georgia, where the army forcibly evicted blacks who had settled on "Sherman land." When O. O. Howard, head of the Freedmen's Bureau, traveled to the Sea Islands to inform blacks of the new policy, he was greeted with disbelief and protest. A committee of former slaves drew up petitions to Howard and President Johnson. Land, the freedmen insisted, was essential to the meaning of freedom. Without it, they declared, "we have not bettered our condition" from the days of slavery—"you will see, this is not the condition of really free men."

Because no land distribution took place, the vast majority of rural freedpeople remained poor and without property during Reconstruction. They had no alternative but to work on white-owned plantations, often for their former owners. Far from being able to rise in the social scale through hard work, black men were largely confined to farm work, unskilled labor, and service jobs, and black women to positions in private homes as cooks and maids. The failure of land reform produced a deep sense of betrayal that survived among the former slaves and their descendants long after the end of Reconstruction. "No sir," Mary Gaffney, an elderly ex-slave, recalled in the 1930s, "we were not given a thing but freedom."

A nursemaid and her charge, from a daguerreotype around 1865.

Out of the conflict on the plantations, new systems of labor emerged in the different regions of the South. **Sharecropping** came to dominate the Cotton Belt and much of the Tobacco Belt of Virginia and North Carolina. Sharecropping initially arose as a compromise between blacks' desire for land and planters' demand for labor discipline. The system allowed each black family to rent a part of a plantation, with the crop divided between worker and owner at the end of the year. Sharecropping guaranteed the planters a stable resident labor force. Former slaves preferred it to gang labor because it offered them the prospect of working without day-to-day white supervision. But as the years went on, sharecropping became more and more oppressive. Sharecroppers' economic opportunities were severely limited by a world market in which the price of farm products suffered a prolonged decline.

The White Farmer

The crop-lien system

The plight of the small farmer was not confined to blacks in the postwar South. Wartime devastation set in motion a train of events that permanently altered the independent way of life of white yeomen, leading to what they considered a loss of freedom. To obtain supplies from merchants, farmers were forced to take up the growing of cotton and pledge a part of the crop as collateral (property the creditor can seize if a debt is not paid). This system became known as the **crop lien**. Since interest rates were extremely high and the price of cotton fell steadily, many farmers found themselves still in debt after marketing their portion of the crop at year's end. They had no choice but to continue to plant cotton to obtain new loans. By the mid-1870s, white farmers, who cultivated only 10 percent of the South's cotton crop in 1860, were growing 40 percent, and many who had owned their land had fallen into dependency as sharecroppers who now rented land owned by others.

The burden of debt

Both black and white farmers found themselves caught in the sharecropping and crop-lien systems. The workings of sharecropping and the crop-lien system are illustrated by the case of Matt Brown, a Mississippi farmer who borrowed money each year from a local merchant. He began 1892 with a debt of $226 held over from the previous year. By 1893,

VOICES OF FREEDOM

From Petition of Committee in Behalf of the Freedmen to Andrew Johnson (1865)

In the summer of 1865, President Andrew Johnson ordered land that had been distributed to freed slaves in South Carolina and Georgia returned to its former owners. A committee of freedmen drafted a petition asking for the right to obtain land. Johnson did not, however, change his policy.

We the freedmen of Edisto Island, South Carolina, have learned from you through Major General O. O. Howard . . . with deep sorrow and painful hearts of the possibility of [the] government restoring these lands to the former owners. We are well aware of the many perplexing and trying questions that burden your mind, and therefore pray to god (the preserver of all, and who has through our late and beloved President [Lincoln's] proclamation and the war made us a free people) that he may guide you in making your decisions and give you that wisdom that cometh from above to settle these great and important questions for the best interests of the country and the colored race.

Here is where secession was born and nurtured. Here is where we have toiled nearly all our lives as slaves and treated like dumb driven cattle. This is our home, we have made these lands what they were, we are the only true and loyal people that were found in possession of these lands. We have been always ready to strike for liberty and humanity, yea to fight if need be to preserve this glorious Union. Shall not we who are freedmen and have always been true to this Union have the same rights as are enjoyed by others? . . . Are not our rights as a free people and good citizens of these United States to be considered before those who were found in rebellion against this good and just government? . . .

[Are] we who have been abused and oppressed for many long years not to be allowed the privilege of purchasing land but be subject to the will of these large land owners? God forbid. Land monopoly is injurious to the advancement of the course of freedom, and if government does not make some provision by which we as freedmen can obtain a homestead, we have not bettered our condition. . . .

We look to you . . . for protection and equal rights with the privilege of purchasing a homestead—a homestead right here in the heart of South Carolina.

From a Sharecropping Contract (1866)

Few former slaves were able to acquire land in the post–Civil War South. Most ended up as sharecroppers, working on white-owned land for a share of the crop at the end of the growing season. This contract, typical of thousands of others, originated in Tennessee. The laborers signed with an X, as they were illiterate.

Thomas J. Ross agrees to employ the Freedmen to plant and raise a crop on his Rosstown Plantation. . . . On the following Rules, Regulations and Remunerations.

The said Ross agrees to furnish the land to cultivate, and a sufficient number of mules & horses and feed them to make and house said crop and all necessary farming utensils to carry on the same and to give unto said Freedmen whose names appear below one half of all the cotton, corn and wheat that is raised on said place for the year 1866 after all the necessary expenses are deducted out that accrues on said crop. Outside of the Freedmen's labor in harvesting, carrying to market and selling the same the said Freedmen . . . covenant and agrees to and with said Thomas J. Ross that for and in consideration of one half of the crop before mentioned that they will plant, cultivate, and raise under the management control and Superintendence of said Ross, in good faith, a cotton, corn and oat crop under his management for the year 1866. And we the said Freedmen agrees to furnish ourselves & families in provisions, clothing, medicine and medical bills and all, and every kind of other expenses that we may incur on said plantation for the year 1866 free of charge to said Ross. Should the said Ross furnish us any of the above supplies or any other kind of expenses, during said year, [we] are to settle and pay him out of the net proceeds of our part of the crop the retail price of the county at time of sale or any price we may agree upon—The said Ross shall keep a regular book account, against each and every one or the head of every family to be adjusted and settled at the end of the year.

We furthermore bind ourselves to and with said Ross that we will do good work and labor ten hours a day on an average, winter and summer. . . . We further agree that we will lose all lost time, or pay at the rate of one dollar per day, rainy days excepted. In sickness and women lying in childbed are to lose the time and account for it to the other hands out of his or her part of the crop. . . .

We furthermore bind ourselves that we will obey the orders of said Ross in all things in carrying out and managing said crop for said year and be docked for disobedience . . . and are also responsible to said Ross if we carelessly, maliciously maltreat any of his stock for said year to said Ross for damages to be assessed out of our wages.

Samuel (X) Johnson, Thomas (X) Richard, Tinny (X) Fitch, Jessie (X) Simmons, Sophe (X) Pruden, Henry (X) Pruden, Frances (X) Pruden, Elijah (X) Smith.

QUESTIONS

1. *Why do the black petitioners believe that owning land is essential to the enjoyment of freedom?*
2. *In what ways does the contract limit the freedom of the laborers?*
3. *What do these documents suggest about competing definitions of black freedom in the aftermath of slavery?*

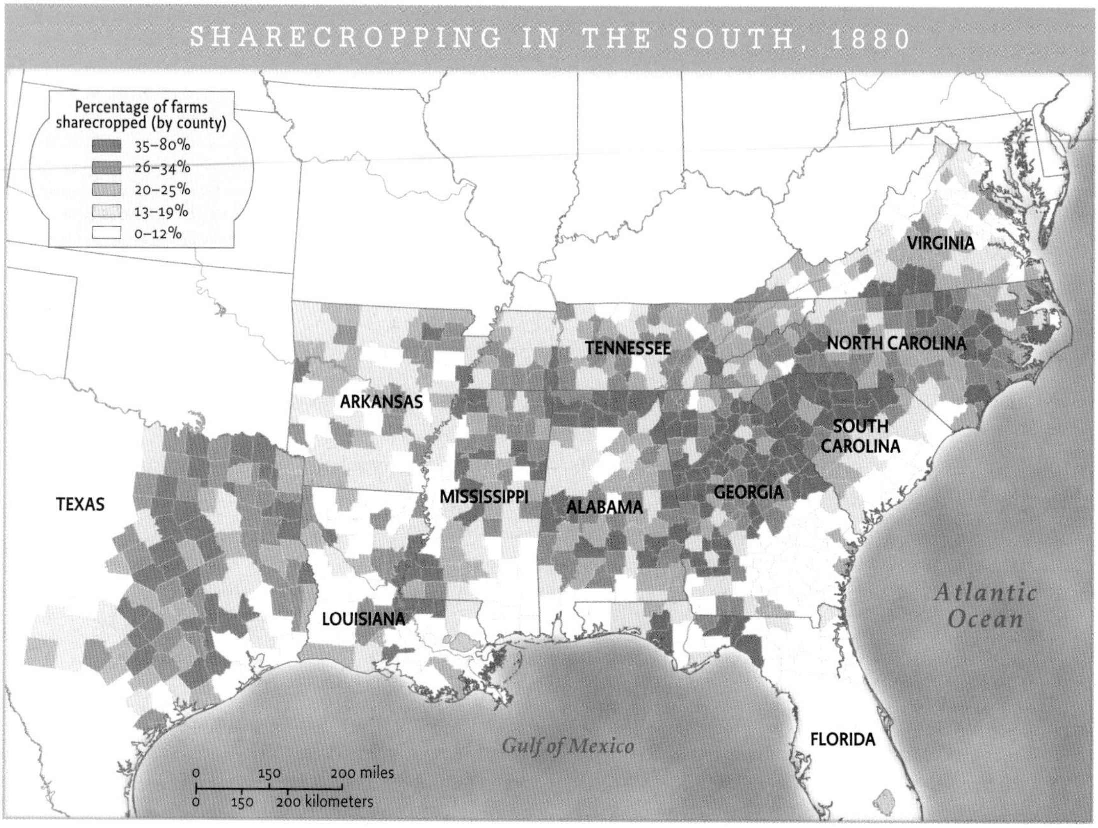

By 1880, sharecropping had become the dominant form of agricultural labor in large parts of the South. The system involved both white and black farmers.

although he produced cotton worth $171, Brown's debt had increased to $402, because he had borrowed $33 for food, $29 for clothing, $173 for supplies, and $112 for other items. Brown never succeeded in getting out of debt. He died in 1905; the last entry under his name in the merchant's account book is a coffin.

Growth of southern cities

Even as the rural South stagnated economically, southern cities experienced remarkable growth after the Civil War. As railroads penetrated the interior, they enabled merchants in market centers like Atlanta to trade directly with the North, bypassing coastal cities that had traditionally monopolized southern commerce. A new urban middle class of merchants, railroad promoters, and bankers reaped the benefits of the spread of cotton production in the postwar South.

Aftermath of Slavery

The United States, of course, was not the only society to confront the transition from slavery to freedom. Indeed, many parallels exist between the debates during Reconstruction and struggles that followed slavery in other parts of the Western Hemisphere over the same issues of land, control of labor, and political power. Planters elsewhere held the same stereotypical views of black laborers as were voiced by their counterparts in the United States—former slaves were supposedly lazy and lacking in ambition, and thought that freedom meant an absence of labor.

Chinese laborers at work on a Louisiana plantation during Reconstruction.

For their part, former slaves throughout the hemisphere tried to carve out as much independence as possible, both in their daily lives and in their labor. In many places, the plantations either fell to pieces, as in Haiti, or continued operating with a new labor force composed of indentured servants from India and China, as in Jamaica, Trinidad, and British Guiana. Southern planters in the United States brought in a few Chinese laborers in an attempt to replace freedmen, but since the federal government opposed such efforts, the Chinese remained only a tiny proportion of the southern workforce.

Emancipation and the right to vote

But if struggles over land and labor united its postemancipation experience with that of other societies, in one respect the United States was unique. Only in the United States were former slaves, within two years of the end of slavery, granted the right to vote and, thus, given a major share of political power. Few anticipated this development when the Civil War ended. It came about as the result of one of the greatest political crises of American history—the battle between President Andrew Johnson and Congress over Reconstruction. The struggle resulted in profound changes in the nature of citizenship, the structure of constitutional authority, and the meaning of American freedom.

THE MAKING OF RADICAL RECONSTRUCTION

Andrew Johnson

Johnson's background

To Lincoln's successor, Andrew Johnson, fell the task of overseeing the restoration of the Union. Born in poverty in North Carolina, as a youth Johnson worked as a tailor's apprentice. Becoming a successful politician after moving to Tennessee, Johnson identified himself as the champion of his state's "honest yeomen" and a foe of large planters, whom he described as a "bloated, corrupted aristocracy." A strong defender of the Union, he became the only senator from a seceding state to remain at his post in Washington, D.C., when the Civil War began. When northern forces occupied Tennessee, Abraham Lincoln named him military governor. In 1864, Republicans nominated him to run for vice president as a symbol of the party's hope of extending its organization into the South.

Outlook

In personality and outlook, Johnson proved unsuited for the responsibilities he shouldered after Lincoln's death. A lonely, stubborn man, he was intolerant of criticism and unable to compromise. He lacked Lincoln's political skills and keen sense of public opinion. Moreover, while Johnson had supported emancipation once Lincoln made it a goal of the war effort, he held deeply racist views. African-Americans, Johnson believed, had no role to play in Reconstruction.

The Failure of Presidential Reconstruction

Johnson's program

A little over a month after Lee's surrender at Appomattox, and with Congress out of session until December, Johnson in May 1865 outlined his plan for reuniting the nation. He issued a series of proclamations that began the period of Presidential Reconstruction (1865–1867). Johnson offered a pardon (which restored political and property rights, except for slaves) to nearly all white southerners who took an oath of allegiance to the Union. He excluded Confederate leaders and wealthy planters whose prewar property had been valued at more than $20,000. Most of those exempted, however, soon received individual pardons from the president. Johnson also appointed provisional governors and ordered them to call state conventions, elected by whites alone, that would establish loyal governments in the South. Apart from the requirement that they abolish slavery, repudiate secession, and refuse to pay the Confederate debt—all unavoidable consequences of southern defeat—he granted the new governments a free hand in managing local affairs.

Republicans against Johnson

The conduct of the southern governments elected under Johnson's program turned most of the Republican North against the president. By and large, white voters returned prominent Confederates and members of the old elite to power. Reports of violence directed against former slaves and northern visitors in the South further alarmed Republicans.

The Black Codes

Regulating former slaves

But what aroused the most opposition to Johnson's Reconstruction policy were the **Black Codes**, laws passed by the new southern governments that attempted to regulate the lives of the former slaves. These laws granted blacks certain rights, such as legalized marriage, ownership of property,

Selling a Freedman to Pay His Fine at Monticello, Florida, an engraving from *Frank Leslie's Illustrated Newspaper*, January 19, 1867. Under the Black Codes enacted by southern legislatures immediately after the Civil War, blacks convicted of "vagrancy"—often because they refused to sign contracts to work on plantations—were fined and, if unable to pay, auctioned off to work for the person who paid the fine.

and limited access to the courts. But they denied them the rights to testify against whites, to serve on juries or in state militias, or to vote. And in response to planters' demands that the freedpeople be required to work on the plantations, the Black Codes declared that those who failed to sign yearly labor contracts could be arrested and hired out to white landowners.

Reaction to Black Codes

Clearly, the death of slavery did not automatically mean the birth of freedom. But the Black Codes so completely violated free labor principles that they called forth a vigorous response from the Republican North. In general, few groups of rebels in history have been treated more leniently than the defeated Confederates. A handful of southern leaders were arrested, but most were quickly released. Only one was executed—Henry Wirz, the commander of Andersonville prison, where thousands of Union prisoners of war had died. Most of the Union army was swiftly demobilized. What motivated the North's turn against Johnson's policies was not a desire to "punish" the white South, but the inability of the South's political leaders to accept the reality of emancipation as evidenced by the Black Codes.

The Radical Republicans

When Congress assembled in December 1865, Johnson announced that with loyal governments functioning in all the southern states, the nation had been reunited. In response, Radical Republicans, who had grown increasingly disenchanted with Johnson during the summer and fall, called for the dissolution of these governments and the establishment of new ones with "rebels" excluded from power and black men guaranteed the right to vote.

Thaddeus Stevens, leader of the Radical Republicans in the House of Representatives during Reconstruction.

Radicals shared the conviction that Union victory created a golden opportunity to institutionalize the principle of equal rights for all, regardless of race.

The most prominent Radicals in Congress were Charles Sumner, a senator from Massachusetts, and Thaddeus Stevens, a lawyer and iron manufacturer who represented Pennsylvania in the House of Representatives. Before the Civil War, both had been outspoken foes of slavery and defenders of black rights. Stevens's most cherished aim was to confiscate the land of disloyal planters and divide it among former slaves and northern migrants to the South. But his plan to make "small independent landholders" of the former slaves proved too radical even for many of his Radical colleagues and failed to pass.

The Origins of Civil Rights

With the South unrepresented, Republicans enjoyed an overwhelming majority in Congress. Most Republicans were moderates, not Radicals. Moderates believed that Johnson's plan was flawed, but they desired to work with the president to modify it. They feared that neither northern nor southern whites would accept black suffrage. Moderates and Radicals joined in refusing to seat the southerners recently elected to Congress, but moderates broke with the Radicals by leaving the Johnson governments in place.

The Civil Rights Bill of 1866

Early in 1866, Senator Lyman Trumbull of Illinois proposed two bills that reflected the moderates' belief that Johnson's policy required modification. The first extended the life of the Freedmen's Bureau, which had originally been established for only one year. The second, the **Civil Rights Bill of 1866**, was described by one congressman as "one of the most important bills ever presented to the House for its action." It defined all persons born in the United States as citizens and spelled out rights they were to enjoy without regard to race. Equality before the law was central to the measure—no longer could states enact laws like the Black Codes discriminating between white and black citizens. So were free labor values. According to the law, no state could deprive any citizen of the right to make contracts, bring lawsuits, or enjoy equal protection of one's person and property. These, said Trumbull, were the "fundamental rights belonging to every man as a free man." The bill made no mention of the right to vote for blacks. In constitutional terms, the Civil Rights Bill represented the first attempt to define in law the essence of freedom.

To the surprise of Congress, Johnson vetoed both bills. Both, he said, would centralize power in the national government and deprive the states of the authority to regulate their own affairs. Moreover, he argued, blacks did not deserve the rights of citizenship. Congress failed by a single vote to muster the two-thirds majority necessary to override the veto of the Freedmen's Bureau Bill (although later in 1866, it did extend the bureau's life to 1870). But in April 1866, the Civil Rights Bill became the first major law in American history to be passed over a presidential veto.

President Andrew Johnson, in an 1868 lithograph by Currier and Ives. Because of Johnson's stubborn opposition to the congressional Reconstruction policy, one disgruntled citizen drew a crown on his head with the words, "I am King."

The Fourteenth Amendment

Congress now proceeded to adopt its own plan of Reconstruction. In June, it approved and sent to the states for ratification the **Fourteenth Amendment**, which placed in the Constitution the principle of birthright citizenship, except for Native Americans subject to tribal authority, and which empowered the federal government to protect the rights of all Americans. The amendment prohibited the states from abridging the "privileges or immunities" of citizens or denying any person the "equal protection of the laws." This broad language opened the door for future Congresses and the federal courts to breathe meaning into the guarantee of legal equality.

In a compromise between the radical and moderate positions on black suffrage, the amendment did not grant blacks the right to vote. But it did provide that if a state denied the vote to any group of men, that state's representation in Congress would be reduced. (This provision did not apply when states barred women from voting.) The abolition of slavery threatened to increase southern political power, since now all blacks, not merely three-fifths as in the case of slaves, would be counted in determining a state's representation in Congress. The Fourteenth Amendment offered the leaders of the white South a choice—allow black men to vote and keep their state's full representation in the House of Representatives, or limit the vote to whites and sacrifice part of their political power.

Significance of the fourteenth amendment

By writing into the Constitution the principle that equality before the law regardless of race is a fundamental right of all American citizens, the amendment made the most important change in that document since the adoption of the Bill of Rights.

The Reconstruction Act

Johnson's speaking tour

The Fourteenth Amendment became the central issue of the political campaign of 1866. Johnson embarked on a speaking tour of the North. Denouncing his critics, the president made wild accusations that the Radicals were plotting to assassinate him. His behavior further undermined public support for his policies, as did riots that broke out in Memphis and New Orleans, in which white policemen and citizens killed dozens of blacks.

In the northern congressional elections that fall, Republicans opposed to Johnson's policies won a sweeping victory. Nonetheless, at the president's urging, every southern state but Tennessee refused to ratify the Fourteenth Amendment. The intransigence of Johnson and the bulk of the white South pushed moderate Republicans toward the Radicals. In March 1867, over

A Democratic Party broadside from the election of 1866 in Pennsylvania uses racist imagery to argue that government assistance aids lazy former slaves at the expense of hardworking whites.

Johnson's veto, Congress adopted the **Reconstruction Act**, which temporarily divided the South into five military districts and called for the creation of new state governments, with black men given the right to vote. Thus began the period of Radical Reconstruction, which lasted until 1877.

Radical Reconstruction

Impeachment and the Election of Grant

In March 1867, Congress adopted the **Tenure of Office Act**, barring the president from removing certain officeholders, including cabinet members, without the consent of the Senate. Johnson considered this an unconstitutional restriction on his authority. In February 1868, he dismissed Secretary of War Edwin M. Stanton, an ally of the Radicals. The House of Representatives responded by approving articles of **impeachment**—that is, it presented charges against Johnson to the Senate, which had to decide whether to remove him from office.

First impeachment trial

That spring, for the first time in American history, a president was placed on trial before the Senate for "high crimes and misdemeanors." By this point, virtually all Republicans considered Johnson a failure as president. But some moderates feared that conviction would damage the constitutional separation of powers between Congress and the executive. Johnson's lawyers assured moderate Republicans that, if acquitted, he would stop interfering with Reconstruction policy. The final tally was 35-19 to convict Johnson, one vote short of the two-thirds necessary to remove him. Seven Republicans joined the Democrats in voting to acquit the president.

Reconstruction, an elaborate allegory of national reconciliation, equality, and progress, designed by Horatio Bateman and printed in 1867. The overall message is that Reconstruction, grounded in liberty and equality, will restore good will between the sections and races. The structure at the center symbolizes the federal government; it is being rebuilt as black and white men carry new pillars, representing the states, to support it. The old bases of some of the columns, called "Foundations of Slavery" are being replaced by new ones representing Liberty, Justice, and Education. Under the dome, former rivals shake hands, including Generals Grant and Lee, and Republican editor Horace Greeley and Jefferson Davis. Scenes surrounding it include a schoolyard, men and women voting, and Indians and whites sitting together. At the top are the heads of great figures of American history, as well as other historical characters including Joan of Arc, John Milton, and Jesus Christ. The eagle at the center carries a streamer reading: "All men are born free and equal."

A few days after the vote, Republicans nominated Ulysses S. Grant, the Union's most prominent military hero, as their candidate for president. Grant's Democratic opponent was Horatio Seymour, the former governor of New York. Reconstruction became the central issue of the bitterly fought 1868 campaign. Democrats denounced Reconstruction as unconstitutional and condemned black suffrage as a violation of America's political traditions. They appealed openly to racism. Seymour's running mate, Francis P. Blair Jr., charged Republicans with placing the South under the rule of "a semi-barbarous race" who longed to "subject the white women to their unbridled lust."

The Fifteenth Amendment

Grant won the election of 1868, although by a margin—300,000 of 6 million votes cast—that many Republicans found uncomfortably slim. The result led Congress to adopt the **Fifteenth Amendment**, which prohibited the federal and state governments from denying any citizen the right to vote because of race. Bitterly opposed by the Democratic Party, it was ratified in 1870.

Although the Fifteenth Amendment left the door open to suffrage restrictions not explicitly based on race—literacy tests, property qualifications, and poll taxes—and did not extend the right to vote to women, it marked the culmination of four decades of abolitionist agitation. "Nothing in all history," exclaimed veteran abolitionist William Lloyd Garrison,

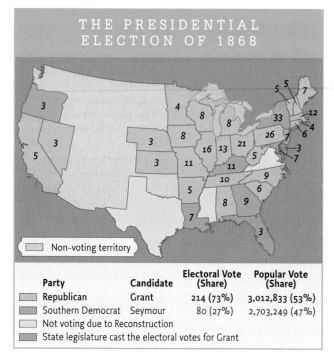

THE PRESIDENTIAL ELECTION OF 1868

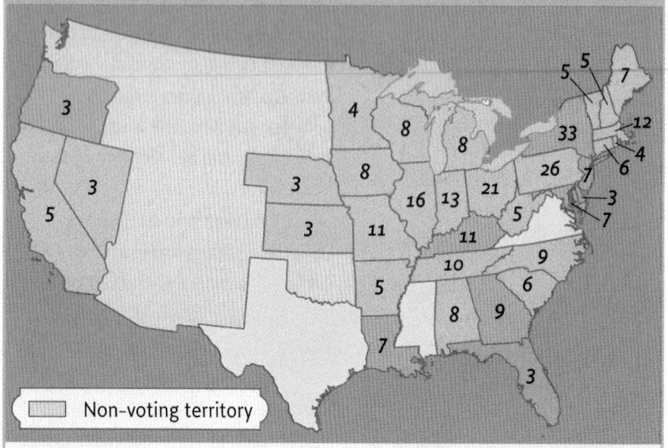

Party	Candidate	Electoral Vote (Share)	Popular Vote (Share)
Republican	Grant	214 (73%)	3,012,833 (53%)
Southern Democrat	Seymour	80 (27%)	2,703,249 (47%)
Not voting due to Reconstruction			
State legislature cast the electoral votes for Grant			

equaled "this wonderful, quiet, sudden transformation of four millions of human beings from . . . the auction-block to the ballot-box."

The Second Founding

The laws and amendments of Reconstruction reflected the intersection of two products of the Civil War era—a newly empowered national state, and the idea of a national citizenry enjoying equality before the law. What Republican leader Carl Schurz called the "great Constitutional revolution" of Reconstruction transformed the federal system and with it, the language of freedom so central to American political culture.

Race and citizenship

But the laws and amendments of Reconstruction repudiated the pre–Civil War idea that citizenship was an entitlement of whites alone. As one congressman noted, the amendments expanded the liberty of whites as well as blacks, including "the millions of people of foreign birth who will flock to our shores."

National power

The new amendments also transformed the relationship between the federal government and the states. The Bill of Rights had linked civil liberties to the autonomy of the states. Its language—"Congress shall make no law"—reflected the belief that concentrated national power posed the greatest threat to freedom. The authors of the Reconstruction amendments assumed that rights required national power to enforce them. Rather than a threat to liberty, the federal government, in Charles Sumner's words, had become "the custodian of freedom."

Constitutional significance

The Reconstruction amendments transformed the Constitution from a document primarily concerned with federal-state relations and the rights of property into a vehicle through which members of vulnerable minorities could stake a claim to freedom and seek protection against misconduct by all levels of government. In the twentieth century, many of the Supreme Court's most important decisions expanding the rights of American citizens were based on the Fourteenth Amendment, including the 1954 *Brown* ruling that outlawed school segregation and the decision in 2015 preventing states from discriminating against gay Americans in the right to marry.

Together with far-reaching congressional legislation meant to secure to former slaves access to the courts, ballot box, and public accommodations, and to protect them against violence, the Reconstruction amendments transferred much of the authority to define citizens' rights from the states to the nation. They were crucial in creating the world's first biracial democracy, in which people only a few years removed from slavery exercised significant political power. Introducing into the Constitution for the first time the words "equal protection of the law" and "the right to vote" (along with "male," to the outrage of the era's advocates of women's rights), the amendments both reflected and reinforced a new era of individual rights consciousness among Americans of all races and backgrounds. They forged a new constitutional relationship between individual Americans and the national government and created a new definition of citizenship.

Biracial democracy

Today, the legal doctrine of birthright citizenship sets the United States apart. Most countries, including every one in Europe, limit automatic access to citizenship via ethnicity, culture, or religion. Birthright citizenship remains an eloquent statement about the nature of American society, and a repudiation of a long history of equating citizenship with whiteness.

Birthright citizenship

So profound were these changes that the amendments are frequently seen not simply as an alteration of an existing structure but as a second founding, which created a fundamentally new document with a new definition of both the status of blacks and the rights of all Americans.

The Rights of Women

"The contest with the South that destroyed slavery," wrote the Philadelphia lawyer Sidney George Fisher in his diary, "has caused an immense increase in the popular passion for liberty and equality." But advocates of women's rights encountered the limits of the Reconstruction commitment to equality. Women activists saw Reconstruction as the moment to claim their own emancipation. The rewriting of the Constitution, declared suffrage leader Olympia Brown, offered the opportunity to sever the blessings of freedom from sex as well as race and to "bury the black man and the woman in the citizen."

Women and the limits of equality

Even Radical Republicans insisted that Reconstruction was the "Negro's hour" (the hour, that is, of the black male). The Fourteenth Amendment for the first time introduced the word "male" into the Constitution, in its clause penalizing a state for denying any group of men the right to vote. The Fifteenth Amendment outlawed discrimination in voting based on race but not gender. These measures produced a bitter split both between feminists and Radical Republicans, and within feminist circles. Some leaders, like Elizabeth Cady Stanton and Susan B. Anthony, denounced their former

WHO IS AN AMERICAN?

From Frederick Douglass, "The Composite Nation" (1869)

In a remarkable speech delivered in Boston, Frederick Douglass condemned anti-Asian discrimination and called for giving Chinese immigrants all the rights of other Americans, including the right to vote. Douglass's vision of a country made up of people of all races and national origins enjoying equal rights was too radical for the time, and remains controversial today.

We are a country of all extremes, ends and opposites; the most conspicuous example of composite nationality in the world. Our people defy all the ethnological and logical classifications. In races we range all the way from black to white, with intermediate shades which . . . no man can name a number. . . . Our land is capable of supporting one fifth of all the globe. Here, labor is abundant and here labor is better remunerated that anywhere else. All moral, social and geographical causes conspire to bring to us the peoples of all other over-populated countries.

Europe and Africa are already here, and the Indian was here before either. . . . Heretofore the policy of our government has been governed by race pride, rather than by wisdom. . . . Before the relations of [blacks and Indians] are satisfactorily settled, and in spite of all opposition, a new race is making its appearance within our borders, and claiming attention [the Chinese]. . . . Do you ask, if I favor such immigration. I answer *I would.* Would you have them naturalized, and have them invested with all the rights of American citizenship? *I would.* Would you allow them to hold office? *I would.* . . .

There are such things in the world as human rights. They rest upon no conventional foundation, but are external, universal, and indestructible. Among these, is the right of locomotion; the right of migration; the right which belongs to no particular race, but belongs alike to all. . . . We shall mold them all . . . into Americans; Indian and Celt, Negro and Saxon, Latin and Teuton, Mongolian and Caucasian, Jew and Gentile, all shall here bow to the same law, speak the same language, support the same government, enjoy the same liberty.

QUESTIONS

1. *What is Douglass's answer to the question, "Who is an American?"*
2. *Why does he believe that being able to move freely from one country to another should be considered a universal human right?*

abolitionist allies and moved to sever the women's rights movement from its earlier moorings in the antislavery tradition.

Thus, even as it rejected the racial definition of freedom that had emerged in the first half of the nineteenth century, Reconstruction left the gender boundary largely intact. When women tried to use the rewritten legal code and Constitution to claim equal rights, they found the courts unreceptive. Myra Bradwell invoked the idea of free labor in challenging an Illinois rule limiting the practice of law to men, but the Supreme Court in 1873 rebuffed her claim. Free labor principles, the justices declared, did not apply to women, since "the law of the Creator" had assigned them to "the domestic sphere."

Despite their limitations, the Fourteenth and Fifteenth Amendments and the Reconstruction Act of 1867 marked a radical departure in American history. The Reconstruction Act of 1867 inaugurated America's first real experiment in interracial democracy.

A Delegation of Advocates of Woman Suffrage Addressing the House Judiciary Committee, an engraving from *Frank Leslie's Illustrated Newspaper*, February 4, 1871. The group includes Elizabeth Cady Stanton, seated just to the right of the speaker, and Susan B. Anthony, at the table on the extreme right.

RADICAL RECONSTRUCTION IN THE SOUTH

"The Tocsin of Freedom"

Political action by African-Americans

Among the former slaves, the passage of the Reconstruction Act inspired an outburst of political organization. At mass political meetings—community gatherings attended by men, women, and children—African-Americans staked their claim to equal citizenship. Blacks, declared an Alabama meeting, deserved "exactly the same rights, privileges and immunities as are enjoyed by white men. We ask for nothing more and will be content with nothing less."

The Union League

Determined to exercise their new rights as citizens, thousands joined the Union League, an organization closely linked to the Republican Party, and the vast majority of eligible African-Americans registered to vote. James K. Green, a former slave in Hale County, Alabama, and a League organizer, went on to serve eight years in the Alabama legislature. In the 1880s, Green looked back on his political career. Before the war, he declared, "I was entirely ignorant; I knew nothing more than to obey my master; and there were thousands of us in the same attitude. . . . But the tocsin

Electioneering at the South, an engraving from *Harper's Weekly*, July 25, 1868, depicts a speaker at a political meeting in the rural South. Women as well as men took part in these grassroots gatherings.

[warning bell] of freedom sounded and knocked at the door and we walked out like free men and shouldered the responsibilities."

By 1870, all the former Confederate states had been readmitted to the Union, and in a region where the Republican Party had not existed before the war, nearly all were under Republican control. Their new state constitutions, drafted in 1868 and 1869 by the first public bodies in American history with substantial black representation, marked a considerable improvement over those they replaced. The constitutions established the region's first state-funded systems of free public education, and they created new penitentiaries, orphan asylums, and homes for the insane. They guaranteed equality of civil and political rights and abolished practices of the antebellum era such as whipping as a punishment for crime, property qualifications for officeholding, and imprisonment for debt. A few states initially barred former Confederates from voting, but this policy was quickly abandoned by the new state governments.

From the Plantation to the Senate, an 1883 lithograph celebrating African-American progress during Reconstruction. Among the black leaders pictured at the top are Reconstruction congressmen Benjamin S. Turner, Josiah T. Walls, and Joseph H. Rainey; Hiram Revels of Mississippi, the first African-American senator; religious leader Richard Allen; and abolitionists Frederick Douglass and William Wells Brown. At the center emancipated slaves work in the cotton fields, and below children attend school and a black family stands outside its home.

The Black Officeholder

Throughout Reconstruction, black voters provided the bulk of the Republican Party's support. But African-Americans did not control Reconstruction politics, as their opponents frequently charged. The highest offices remained almost entirely in white hands, and only in South Carolina, where blacks made up 60 percent of the population, did they form a majority of the legislature. Nonetheless, the fact that some 2,000 African-Americans held public office during Reconstruction marked a fundamental shift of power in the South and a radical departure in American government.

African-Americans were represented at every level of government. Fourteen were elected to the national House of Representatives. Two blacks served in the U.S. Senate during Reconstruction, both representing Mississippi. Hiram Revels, who had been born free in North Carolina, in 1870 became the first black senator in American history. The second, Blanche K. Bruce, a former slave, was elected in 1875. At state and local levels, the presence of black officeholders and their white allies made a real difference in southern life, ensuring that blacks accused of crimes would be tried before juries of their peers and enforcing fairness in such aspects of local government as road repair, tax assessment, and poor relief.

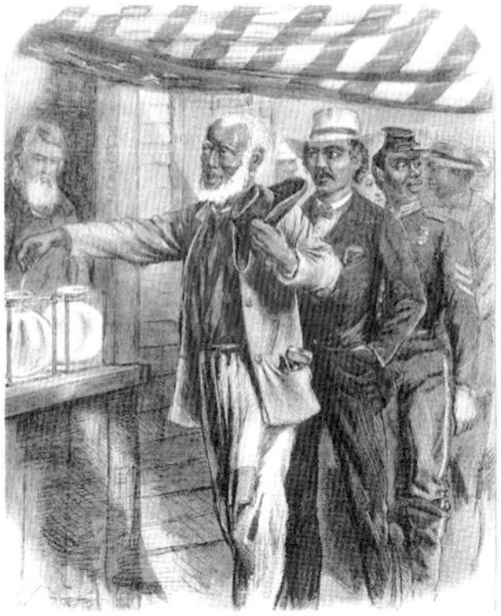

The First Vote, an engraving from *Harper's Weekly*, November 16, 1867, depicts the first biracial elections in southern history. The voters represent key sources of the black political leadership that emerged during Reconstruction—the artisan carrying his tools, the well-dressed city person (probably free before the war), and the soldier.

In South Carolina and Louisiana, homes of the South's wealthiest and best-educated free black communities, most prominent Reconstruction officeholders had never experienced slavery. In addition, a number of black Reconstruction officials, like Pennsylvania-born Jonathan J. Wright, who served on the South Carolina Supreme Court, had come from the North after the Civil War. The majority, however, were former slaves who had established their leadership in the black community by serving in the Union army; working as ministers, teachers, or skilled craftsmen; or engaging in Union League organizing.

Carpetbaggers and Scalawags

White northerners in the South

The new southern governments also brought to power new groups of whites. Many Reconstruction officials were northerners who for one reason or another made their homes in the South after the war. Their opponents dubbed them **carpetbaggers**, implying that they had packed all their belongings in a suitcase and left their homes in order to reap the spoils of office in the South. Some carpetbaggers were undoubtedly corrupt adventurers. The large majority, however, were former Union soldiers who decided to remain in the South when the war ended, before there was any prospect of going into politics.

Most white Republicans had been born in the South. Former Confederates reserved their greatest scorn for these **scalawags**, whom they considered traitors to their race and region. Some southern-born Republicans were men of stature and wealth, like James L. Alcorn, the owner of one of Mississippi's largest plantations and the state's first Republican governor. Most scalawags, however, were non-slaveholding white farmers from the southern upcountry. Many had been wartime Unionists, and they now cooperated with the Republicans in order to prevent "rebels" from returning to power.

A portrait of Hiram Revels, the first black U.S. senator, by Theodore Kaufmann, a German-born artist who immigrated to the United States in 1855. Lithograph copies sold widely in the North during Reconstruction. Frederick Douglass, commenting on the dignified image, noted that African-Americans "so often see ourselves described and painted as monkeys, that we think it a great piece of fortune to find an exception to this general rule."

Southern Republicans in Power

In view of the daunting challenges they faced, the remarkable thing is not that Reconstruction governments in some respects failed, but how much they did accomplish. Perhaps their greatest achievement lay in establishing the South's first state-supported public schools. The new educational systems served both black and white children, although generally in schools segregated by race. Only in New Orleans were the public schools integrated during Reconstruction, and only in South Carolina did the state university admit black students (elsewhere, separate colleges were established). The new governments also pioneered civil rights legislation. Their laws made it illegal for railroads, hotels, and other institutions to discriminate on the basis of race. Enforcement varied considerably from locality to locality, but Reconstruction established for the first time at the state level a standard of equal citizenship and a recognition of blacks' right to a share of public services.

Republican governments also took steps to strengthen the position of rural laborers and promote the South's economic recovery. They passed laws to ensure that agricultural laborers and sharecroppers had the first claim on harvested crops, rather than merchants to whom the landowner owed money. South Carolina created a state Land Commission, which by 1876 had settled 14,000 black families and a few poor whites on their own farms.

The Quest for Prosperity

Economic development during Reconstruction

Rather than on land distribution, however, the Reconstruction governments pinned their hopes for southern economic growth and opportunity for African-Americans and poor whites alike on regional economic development. Railroad construction, they believed, was the key to transforming the South into a society of booming factories, bustling towns, and diversified agriculture. Every state during Reconstruction helped to finance railroad construction, and through tax reductions and other incentives tried to attract northern manufacturers to invest in the region. The program had mixed results. Economic development in general remained weak.

To their supporters, the governments of Radical Reconstruction presented a complex pattern of disappointment and accomplishment. A revitalized southern economy failed to materialize, and most African-Americans remained locked in poverty. On the other hand, biracial democratic government, a thing unknown in American history, for the first time functioned effectively in many parts of the South. The conservative elite that had dominated southern government from colonial times to 1867

A group of black students and their teacher in a picture taken by an amateur photographer, probably a Union army veteran, while touring Civil War battlefields.

found itself excluded from political power, while poor whites, newcomers from the North, and former slaves cast ballots, sat on juries, and enacted and administered laws. It is a measure of how far change had progressed that the reaction against Reconstruction proved so extreme.

THE OVERTHROW OF RECONSTRUCTION

Reconstruction's Opponents

Sources of opposition

The South's traditional leaders—planters, merchants, and Democratic politicians—bitterly opposed the new governments. "Intelligence, virtue, and patriotism" in public life, declared a protest by prominent southern Democrats, had given way to "ignorance, stupidity, and vice." Corruption did exist during Reconstruction, but it was confined to no race, region, or party. The rapid growth of state budgets and the benefits to be gained from public aid led in some states to a scramble for influence that produced bribery, insider dealing, and a get-rich-quick atmosphere. Southern frauds, however, were dwarfed by those practiced in these years by the Whiskey Ring, which involved high officials of the Grant administration, and by New York's Tweed Ring, controlled by the Democrats, whose thefts ran into the tens of millions of dollars. (These are discussed in the next chapter.) The rising taxes needed to pay for schools and other new public facilities and to assist railroad development were another cause of opposition to Reconstruction. Many poor whites who had initially supported the Republican Party turned against it when it became clear that their economic situation was not improving.

The most basic reason for opposition to Reconstruction, however, was that most white southerners could not accept the idea of former slaves voting, holding office, and enjoying equality before the law. Opponents launched a campaign of violence in an effort to end Republican rule. Their actions posed a fundamental challenge both for Reconstruction governments in the South and for policymakers in Washington, D.C.

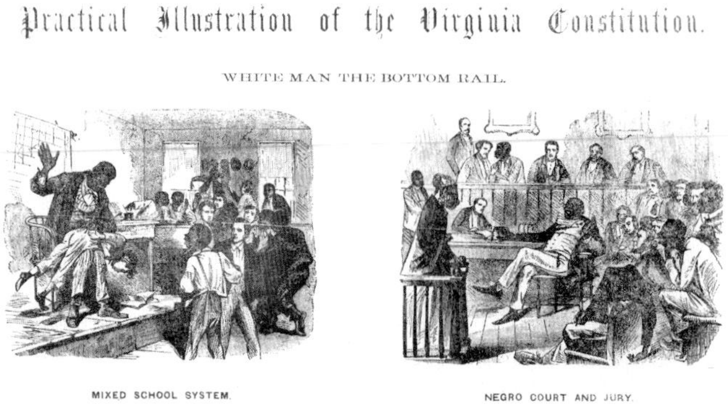

Practical Illustration of the Virginia Constitution.
WHITE MAN THE BOTTOM RAIL.
MIXED SCHOOL SYSTEM.
NEGRO COURT AND JURY.

A cartoon from around 1870 illustrates a key theme of the racist opposition to Reconstruction—that blacks had forced themselves upon whites and gained domination over them. A black schoolteacher inflicts punishment on a white student in an integrated classroom, and a racially mixed jury judges a white defendant.

"A Reign of Terror"

The Civil War ended in 1865, but violence remained widespread in large parts of the postwar South. In the early years of Reconstruction, violence was mostly local and unorganized. Blacks were assaulted and murdered for refusing to give way to whites on city sidewalks, using "insolent" language, challenging end-of-year contract settlements, and attempting to buy land. The violence that greeted the advent of Republican governments after 1867, however, was far more pervasive and more directly motivated by politics. In wide areas of the South, secret societies sprang up with the aim of preventing blacks from voting and destroying the organization of the Republican Party by assassinating local leaders and public officials.

A terrorist organization

The most notorious such organization was the **Ku Klux Klan**, which in effect served as a military arm of the Democratic Party in the South. The Klan was a terrorist organization. It committed some of the most brutal criminal acts in American history. In many counties throughout the South, it launched what one victim called a "reign of terror" against Republican leaders, black and white.

The Klan's victims included white Republicans, among them wartime Unionists and local officeholders, teachers, and party organizers. But African-Americans—local political leaders, those who managed to acquire land, and others who in one way or another defied the norms of white supremacy—bore the brunt of the violence. On occasion, violence escalated from assaults on individuals to mass terrorism and even local insurrections. The bloodiest act of violence during Reconstruction took place in Colfax, Louisiana, in 1873, where armed whites assaulted the town with a small cannon. Scores of former slaves were murdered, including fifty members of a black militia unit after they had surrendered.

In 1870 and 1871, Congress adopted three **Enforcement Acts**, outlawing terrorist societies and allowing the president to use the army against them. These laws continued the expansion of national authority during Reconstruction. In 1871, President Grant dispatched federal marshals, backed up by troops in some areas, to arrest hundreds of accused Klansmen. Many Klan leaders fled the South. After a series of well-publicized trials, the Klan went out of existence. In 1872, for the first time since before the Civil War, peace reigned in most of the former Confederacy.

A Prospective Scene in the City of Oaks, a cartoon in the September 1, 1868, issue of the *Independent Monitor*, a Democratic newspaper published in Tuscaloosa, Alabama. The cartoon sent a warning to the Reverend A. S. Lakin, who had moved from Ohio to become president of the University of Alabama, and Dr. N. B. Cloud, a southern-born Republican serving as Alabama's superintendent of public education. The Ku Klux Klan forced both men from their positions. While most of the Klan's victims were black, the two men pictured here are white.

The Liberal Republicans

Despite the Grant administration's effective response to Klan terrorism, the North's commitment to Reconstruction waned during the 1870s. Northerners increasingly felt that the South should be able to solve its own problems without constant interference from Washington. The federal government had freed the slaves, made them citizens, and given them the right to vote. Now, blacks should rely on their own resources, not demand further assistance.

In 1872, an influential group of Republicans, alienated by corruption within the Grant administration and believing that the growth of federal power during and after the war needed to be curtailed, formed their own party. They included Republican founders like Lyman Trumbull and prominent editors and journalists such as E. L. Godkin of *The Nation*. Calling themselves Liberal Republicans, they nominated Horace Greeley, editor of the *New York Tribune*, for president.

Horace Greeley

Democratic criticisms of Reconstruction found a receptive audience among the Liberals. As in the North, they became convinced, the "best men" of the South had been excluded from power while "ignorant" voters controlled politics, producing corruption and misgovernment. Greeley had spent most of his career, first as a Whig and then as a Republican, denouncing the Democratic Party. But with the Republican split presenting an opportunity to repair their political fortunes, Democratic leaders endorsed Greeley as their candidate. But many rank-and-file Democrats, unable to bring themselves to vote for Greeley, stayed at home on election day. As a result, Greeley suffered a devastating defeat by Grant, whose margin of more than 700,000 popular votes was the largest in a

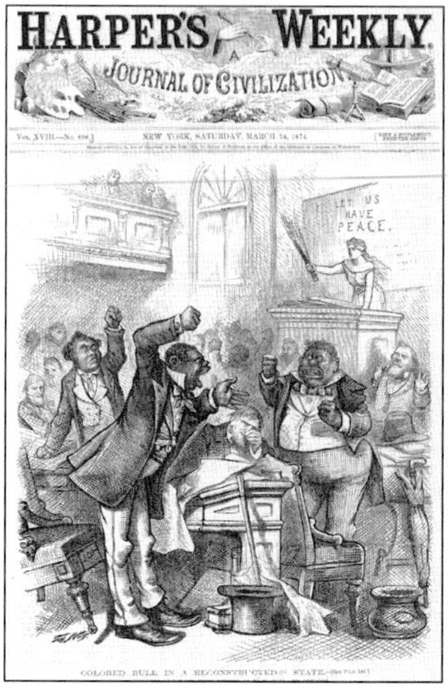

Changes in graphic artist Thomas Nast's depiction of blacks in *Harper's Weekly* mirrored the evolution of Republican sentiment in the North. *And Not This Man?*, August 5, 1865, shows the black soldier as an upstanding citizen deserving of the vote. *Colored Rule in a Reconstructed (?) State*, March 14, 1874, suggests that Reconstruction legislatures had become travesties of democratic government.

nineteenth-century presidential contest. But Greeley's campaign placed on the northern agenda the one issue on which the Liberal reformers and the Democrats could agree—a new policy toward the South.

A bankbook issued by the Freedman's Savings and Trust Company, a private corporation established by Congress to promote thrift among the former slaves. Black individuals, families, church groups, and civic organizations deposited nearly $2 million in branches scattered across the South. The bank failed in 1874 because of mismanagement, and thousands of depositors lost their savings.

The North's Retreat

The Liberal attack on Reconstruction, which continued after 1872, contributed to a resurgence of racism in the North. Journalist James S. Pike, a leading Greeley supporter, in 1874 published *The Prostrate State*, an influential account of a visit to South Carolina. The book depicted a state engulfed by political corruption and under the control of "a mass of black barbarism." Resurgent racism offered blacks' alleged incapacity as a convenient explanation for the "failure" of Reconstruction. The solution, for many, was to restore leading whites to political power.

Other factors also weakened northern support for Reconstruction. In 1873, the country plunged into a severe economic depression. Distracted by economic problems, Republicans were in no mood to devote further attention to the South. The depression dealt the South a severe blow and further weakened the prospect that Republicans could revitalize the region's economy. Democrats made substantial gains throughout the nation in the elections of 1874. For the first time since the Civil War, their party took control of the House of Representatives. Before the new Congress met, the old one enacted a final piece of Reconstruction legislation, the **Civil Rights Act of 1875**. This outlawed

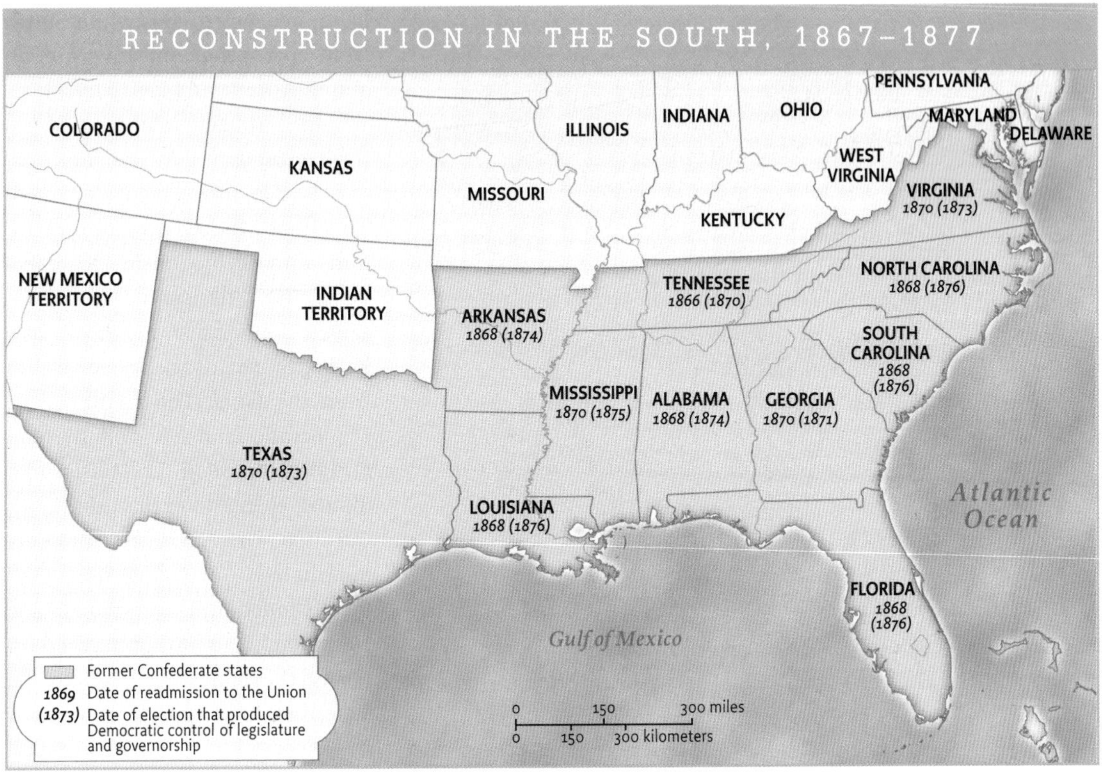

racial discrimination in places of public accommodation like hotels and theaters. But it was clear that the northern public was retreating from Reconstruction.

The Supreme Court and Reconstruction

The Supreme Court whittled away at the guarantees of black rights Congress had adopted. In the *Slaughterhouse Cases* (1873), the justices ruled that the Fourteenth Amendment had not altered traditional federalism. Most of the rights of citizens, it declared, remained under state control. Three years later, in *United States v. Cruikshank*, the Court gutted the Enforcement Acts by throwing out the convictions of some of those responsible for the Colfax Massacre of 1873.

The Triumph of the Redeemers

By the mid-1870s, Reconstruction was clearly on the defensive. Democrats had already regained control of states with substantial white voting majorities such as Tennessee, North Carolina, and Texas. The victorious Democrats called themselves **Redeemers**, since they claimed to have "redeemed" the white South from corruption, misgovernment, and northern and black control.

In those states where Reconstruction governments survived, violence again erupted. This time, the Grant administration showed no desire to intervene. In Mississippi, in 1875, armed Democrats destroyed ballot boxes and drove former slaves from the polls. The result was a Democratic landslide and the end of Reconstruction in Mississippi. Similar events took place in South Carolina in 1876. Democrats nominated for governor former Confederate general Wade Hampton. Hampton promised to respect the rights of all citizens of the state, but his supporters, inspired by Democratic tactics in Mississippi, launched a wave of intimidation. Democrats intended to carry the election, one planter told a black official, "if we have to wade in blood knee-deep."

"The Ignorant Vote," a famous cartoon by Thomas Nast in *Harper's Weekly*, December 9, 1876, equates blacks and Irish immigrants as unworthy of participation in democracy. It reflects a growing reaction against universal manhood suffrage in both North and South.

The Disputed Election and Bargain of 1877

Events in South Carolina directly affected the outcome of the presidential campaign of 1876. To succeed Grant, the Republicans nominated Governor Rutherford B. Hayes of Ohio. The Democrats chose as his opponent New York's governor, Samuel J. Tilden. By this time, only South Carolina, Florida, and Louisiana remained under Republican control in the South. The election turned out to be so close that whoever captured these states—which both parties claimed to have carried—would become the next president.

Unable to resolve the impasse on its own, Congress in January 1877 appointed a fifteen-member Electoral Commission, composed of senators, representatives, and Supreme Court justices. Republicans enjoyed an 8-7 majority on the commission, and to no one's surprise, the members decided by that margin that Hayes had carried the disputed southern states and had been elected president.

Even as the commission deliberated, however, behind-the-scenes negotiations took place between leaders of the two parties. Hayes's representatives agreed to recognize Democratic control of the entire South and to avoid further intervention in local affairs. For their part, Democrats promised not to dispute Hayes's right to office and to respect the civil and political rights of blacks.

Thus was concluded the **Bargain of 1877**. Hayes became president and quickly ordered federal troops to stop guarding the state houses in Louisiana and South Carolina, allowing Democratic claimants to become governors. (Contrary to legend, Hayes did not remove the last soldiers from the South—he simply ordered them to return to their barracks.) The triumphant southern Democrats failed to live up to their pledge to recognize blacks as equal citizens.

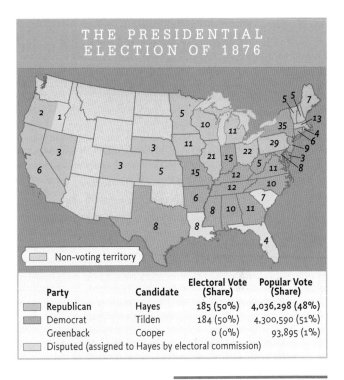

THE PRESIDENTIAL ELECTION OF 1876

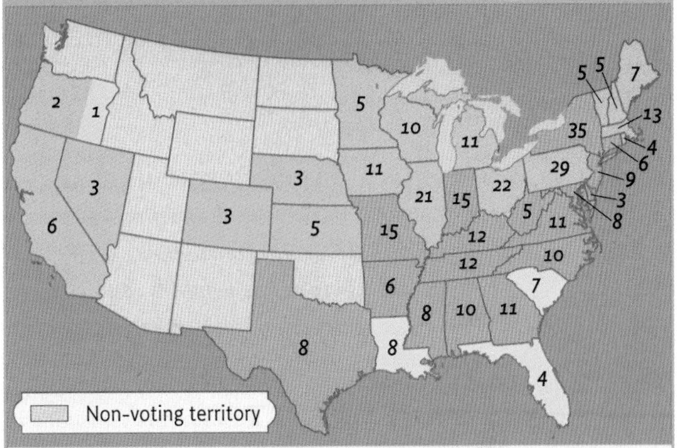

Party	Candidate	Electoral Vote (Share)	Popular Vote (Share)
Republican	Hayes	185 (50%)	4,036,298 (48%)
Democrat	Tilden	184 (50%)	4,300,590 (51%)
Greenback	Cooper	0 (0%)	93,895 (1%)
Disputed (assigned to Hayes by electoral commission)			

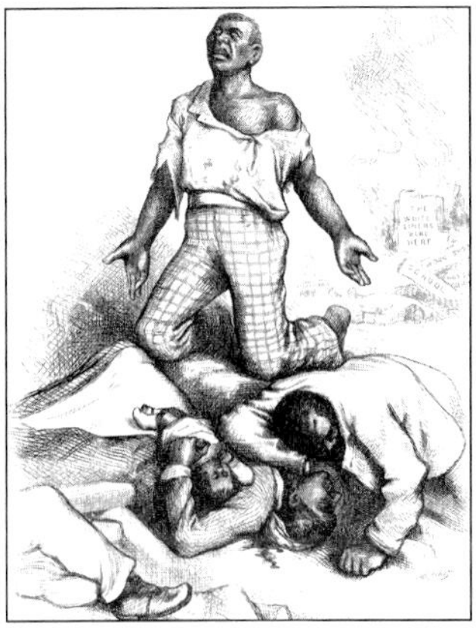

Is This a Republican Form of Government?, a cartoon by Thomas Nast in *Harper's Weekly*, September 2, 1876, illustrates his conviction that the overthrow of Reconstruction meant that the United States was not prepared to live up to its democratic ideals or protect the rights of black citizens threatened by violence.

The End of Reconstruction

As a historical process—the nation's adjustment to the destruction of slavery—Reconstruction continued well after 1877. Blacks continued to vote and, in some states, hold office into the 1890s. But as a distinct era of national history—when Republicans controlled much of the South, blacks exercised significant political power, and the federal government accepted the responsibility for protecting the fundamental rights of all American citizens—Reconstruction had come to an end. Despite its limitations, Reconstruction was a remarkable chapter in the story of American freedom. Nearly a century would pass before the nation again tried to bring equal rights to the descendants of slaves. The civil rights era of the 1950s and 1960s would sometimes be called the Second Reconstruction.

CHAPTER REVIEW AND ONLINE RESOURCES

REVIEW QUESTIONS

1. *In 1865, the former Confederate general Robert Richardson remarked that "the emancipated slaves own nothing, because nothing but freedom has been given to them." Explain whether this would be an accurate assessment of Reconstruction twelve years later.*
2. *The women's movement split into two separate national organizations in part because the Fifteenth Amendment did not give women the vote. Explain why the two groups split.*
3. *In what sense did the Reconstruction amendments mark a second founding of the United States?*
4. *What is birthright citizenship, and why is it important?*
5. *How did black families, churches, schools, and other institutions contribute to the development of African-American culture and political activism in this period?*
6. *Why did ownership of land and control of labor become major points of contention between former slaves and whites in the South?*
7. *By what methods did southern whites seek to limit African-American civil rights and liberties? How did the federal government respond?*
8. *How did the failure of land reform and continued poverty lead to new forms of servitude for both blacks and whites?*
9. *What caused the confrontation between President Johnson and Congress over Reconstruction policies?*
10. *What national issues and attitudes combined to bring an end to Reconstruction by 1877?*
11. *By 1877, how did the condition of former slaves in the United States compare with that of freedpeople around the globe?*

KEY TERMS

the Freedmen's Bureau (p. 441)
sharecropping (p. 443)
crop lien (p. 443)
Black Codes (p. 448)
Civil Rights Bill of 1866 (p. 450)
Fourteenth Amendment (p. 451)
Reconstruction Act (p. 452)
Tenure of Office Act (p. 452)
impeachment (p. 452)
Fifteenth Amendment (p. 453)
carpetbaggers (p. 459)
scalawags (p. 459)
Ku Klux Klan (p. 462)
Enforcement Acts (p. 463)
Civil Rights Act of 1875 (p. 464)
Redeemers (p. 465)
Bargain of 1877 (p. 466)

Go to INQUIZITIVE

To see what you know—and learn what you've missed—with personalized feedback along the way.

Visit the ***Give Me Liberty!* Student Site** for primary source documents and images, interactive maps, author videos featuring Eric Foner, and more.

CHAPTER 16

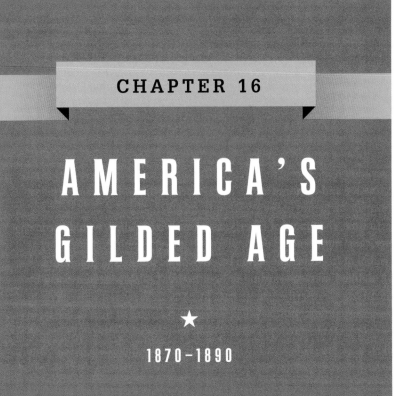

AMERICA'S GILDED AGE

★

1870–1890

1872	Crédit Mobilier Scandal
1873	Mark Twain and Charles Dudley Warner's *Gilded Age*
1876	Battle of the Little Bighorn
1877	Reconstruction ends
	Great Railroad Strike
1879	Henry George's *Progress and Poverty*
1883	Civil Service Act
	Railroads create time zones
1886	Knights of Labor's membership peaks
	Haymarket affair
1887	Interstate Commerce Commission created
	Dawes Act
1888	Edward Bellamy's *Looking Backward*
1890	Sherman Antitrust Act
	Jacob Riis's *How the Other Half Lives*
	Massacre at Wounded Knee
1894	Henry Demarest Lloyd's *Wealth against Commonwealth*
1895	*United States v. E. C. Knight Co.*
1899	Thorstein Veblen's *The Theory of the Leisure Class*
1905	*Lochner v. New York*

In *Palo Alto Spring* (1878), a portrait of upper-class life in Gilded Age America by the artist Thomas Hill, the family and friends of railroad magnate Leland Stanford (shown with a painting on his lap) gather at the Stanford farm in Palo Alto, California, today the site of Stanford University. The painting originally hung in the Stanfords' San Francisco mansion, which was destroyed by an earthquake in 1906.

FOCUS QUESTIONS

- *What factors combined to make the United States a mature industrial society after the Civil War?*
- *How did the economic development of the Gilded Age affect American freedom?*
- *How did reformers of the period approach the problems of an industrial society?*
- *How was the West transformed economically and socially in this period?*
- *Was the Gilded Age political system effective in meeting its goals?*

An immense crowd gathered in New York Harbor on October 28, 1886, for the dedication of *Liberty Enlightening the World*, a fitting symbol for a nation now wholly free. The idea for the statue originated in 1865 with Édouard de Laboulaye, a French educator and the author of several books on the United States, as a response to the assassination of Abraham Lincoln. Measuring more than 150 feet from torch to toe and standing atop a huge pedestal, the edifice was the tallest man-made structure in the Western Hemisphere.

In time, the Statue of Liberty, as it came to be called, would become Americans' most revered national icon. For over a century it has stood as a symbol of freedom. The statue has welcomed millions of immigrants—the "huddled masses yearning to breathe free" celebrated in a poem by Emma Lazarus inscribed on its base in 1903. In the years since its dedication, the statue's familiar image has been reproduced by folk artists in every conceivable medium and has been used by advertisers to promote everything from cigarettes and lawn mowers to war bonds. It has become a powerful international symbol as well.

Although the Civil War was over, the country in the late nineteenth century was racked by violence, by not only white supremacists in the South but also widespread labor conflict, warfare against Native Americans in the West, and political assassinations. Indeed, the year of the statue's dedication, 1886, also witnessed the "great upheaval," a wave of strikes and labor protests that touched every part of the nation. The 600 dignitaries (598 of them men) who gathered on what is now called Liberty Island for the dedication hoped the Statue of Liberty would inspire renewed devotion to the nation's political and economic system. But for all its grandeur, the statue could not conceal the deep social divisions and fears about the future of American freedom that accompanied the country's emergence as the world's leading industrial power. Crucial questions moved to the center stage of American public life during the 1870s and 1880s and remained there for decades to come: What are the social conditions that make freedom possible, and what role should the national government play in defining and protecting the liberty of its citizens?

THE SECOND INDUSTRIAL REVOLUTION

Roots of economic change

Between the end of the Civil War and the early twentieth century, the United States underwent one of the most rapid and profound economic revolutions any country has ever experienced. There were numerous causes for this explosive economic growth. The country enjoyed abundant natural resources, a growing supply of labor, an expanding market for manufactured goods, and the availability of capital for investment. In addition, the federal government actively promoted industrial and agricultural development. It enacted high tariffs that protected American industry from foreign competition, granted land to railroad companies to encourage construction, and used the army to remove Indians from western lands desired by farmers and mining companies.

Promoting development

The Industrial Economy

The rapid expansion of factory production, mining, and railroad construction in all parts of the country except the South signaled the transition from Lincoln's America—a world centered on the small farm and

A changing America

TABLE 16.1 Indicators of Economic Change, 1870–1920

	1870	1900	1920
Farms (millions)	2.7	5.7	6.4
Land in farms (million acres)	408	841	956
Wheat grown (million bushels)	254	599	843
Employment (millions)	14	28.5	44.5
In manufacturing (millions)	2.5	5.9	11.2
Percentage in workforce[a]			
Agricultural	52	38	27
Industry[b]	29	31	44
Trade, service, administration[c]	20	31	27
Railroad track (thousands of miles)	53	258	407
Steel produced (thousands of tons)	0.8	11.2	46
GNP (billions of dollars)	7.4	18.7	91.5
Per capita (in 1920 dollars)	371	707	920
Life expectancy at birth (years)	42	47	54

[a] Percentages are rounded and do not total 100
[b] Includes manufacturing, transportation, mining, construction
[c] Includes trade, finance, public administration

Forging the Shaft, a painting from the 1870s by the American artist John Ferguson Weir, depicts workers in a steel factory making a propeller shaft for an ocean liner. Weir illustrates both the dramatic power of the factory at a time when the United States was overtaking European countries in manufacturing, and the fact that industrial production still required hard physical labor.

artisan workshop—to a mature industrial society. By 1913, the United States produced one-third of the world's industrial output—more than Great Britain, France, and Germany combined. By 1880, for the first time, the U.S. Census Bureau found a majority of the workforce engaged in non-farming jobs.

The traditional dream of economic independence seemed obsolete. By 1890, two-thirds of Americans worked for wages, rather than owning a farm, business, or craft shop. Drawn to factories by the promise of employment, a new working class emerged in these years. Between 1870 and 1920, almost 11 million Americans moved from farm to city, and another 25 million immigrants arrived from overseas.

Most manufacturing now took place in industrial cities. The heartland of the second industrial revolution was the region around the Great Lakes, with its factories producing iron and steel, machinery, chemicals, and packaged foods. Pittsburgh had become the world's center of iron and steel manufacturing. Chicago, by 1900 the nation's second-largest city with 1.7 million inhabitants, was home to factories producing steel and farm machinery and giant stockyards where cattle were processed into meat products for shipment east in refrigerated rail cars.

A painting by Edward Moran captures the excitement at the unveiling of the Statue of Liberty in 1886.

THE RAILROAD NETWORK, 1880

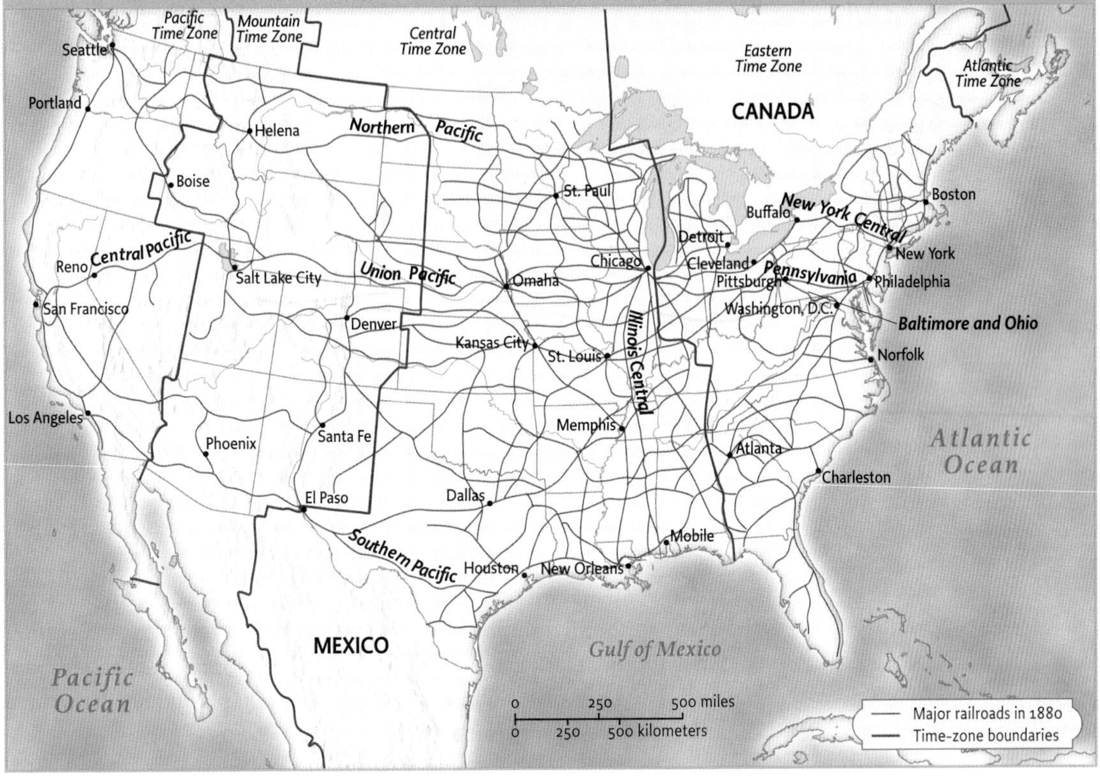

By 1880, the transnational rail network made possible the creation of a truly national market for goods.

Railroads and the National Market

The railroad made possible the second industrial revolution. Spurred by private investment and massive grants of land and money by federal, state, and local governments, the number of miles of railroad track in the United States tripled between 1860 and 1880 and tripled again by 1920, opening vast new areas to commercial farming and creating a truly national market for manufactured goods. The railroads even reorganized time itself. In 1883, the major companies divided the nation into the four time zones still in use today.

The rise of national brands

The growing population formed an ever-expanding market for the mass production, mass distribution, and mass marketing of goods, essential elements of a modern industrial economy. The spread of national brands like Ivory Soap and Quaker Oats symbolized the continuing integration of the economy. So did the growth of national chains, most prominently the Atlantic and Pacific Tea Company, better known as A & P grocery stores. Based in Chicago, the national mail-order firms

The Greatest Department Store on Earth, a cartoon from *Puck*, November 29, 1899, depicts Uncle Sam selling goods, mostly manufactured products, to the nations of the world. The search for markets overseas would be a recurring theme of twentieth-century American foreign policy.

Montgomery Ward and Sears, Roebuck & Co. sold clothing, jewelry, farm equipment, and numerous other goods to rural families throughout the country.

The Spirit of Innovation

A remarkable series of technological innovations spurred rapid communication and economic growth. The opening of the Atlantic cable in 1866 made it possible to send electronic telegraph messages instantaneously between the United States and Europe. During the 1870s and 1880s, the telephone, typewriter, and handheld camera came into use.

Scientific breakthroughs poured forth from research laboratories in Menlo Park and West Orange, New Jersey, created by the era's greatest inventor, Thomas A. Edison. During the course of his life, Edison helped to establish entirely new industries that transformed private life, public entertainment, and economic activity. Among Edison's innovations were the phonograph, lightbulb, motion picture, and a system for generating and distributing electric power. The spread of electricity was essential to industrial and urban growth, providing a more reliable and flexible source of power than water or steam.

Competition and Consolidation

Deflation

Economic growth was dramatic but highly volatile. The combination of a market flooded with goods and the federal monetary policies (discussed later in this chapter) that removed money from the national economy led to a relentless fall in prices. The world economy suffered prolonged downturns in the 1870s and 1890s.

Pools and trusts

Businesses engaged in ruthless competition. Railroads and other companies tried various means of bringing order to the chaotic marketplace. They formed "pools" that divided up markets between supposedly competing firms and fixed prices. They established **trusts**—legal devices whereby the affairs of several rival companies were managed by a single director. Such efforts to coordinate the economic activities of independent companies generally proved short-lived.

To avoid cutthroat competition, more and more corporations battled to control entire industries. Between 1897 and 1904, some 4,000 firms fell by the wayside or were gobbled up by others. By the time the wave of mergers had been completed, giant corporations like U.S. Steel (created by financier J. P. Morgan in 1901 by combining eight large steel companies into the first billion-dollar economic enterprise), Standard Oil, and International Harvester (a manufacturer of agricultural machinery) dominated major industries.

Giant corporations

The Rise of Andrew Carnegie

In an era without personal or corporate income taxes, some business leaders accumulated enormous fortunes and economic power. During the depression that began in 1873, Andrew Carnegie set out to establish a steel company that incorporated **vertical integration**—that is, one that controlled every phase of the business from raw materials to transportation, manufacturing, and distribution. By the 1890s, he dominated the steel industry and had accumulated a fortune worth hundreds of millions of dollars. Carnegie's complex of steel factories at Homestead, Pennsylvania, was the most technologically advanced in the world.

Believing that the rich had a moral obligation to promote the advancement of society, Carnegie denounced the "worship of money" and distributed much of his wealth to various philanthropies, especially the creation of public libraries in towns throughout the country. But he ran his companies with a dictatorial hand. His factories operated nonstop, with two twelve-hour shifts every day of the year except the Fourth of July.

Philanthropy

The Triumph of John D. Rockefeller

If any single name became a byword for enormous wealth, it was John D. Rockefeller, who began his working career as a clerk for a Cleveland merchant and rose to dominate the oil industry. He drove out rival firms through cutthroat competition, arranging secret deals with railroad companies, and fixing prices and production quotas. Rockefeller began with **horizontal expansion**—buying out competing oil refineries. Like Carnegie, he soon established a vertically integrated monopoly, which controlled the drilling, refining, storage, and distribution of oil. By the 1880s, his Standard Oil Company controlled 90 percent of the nation's oil industry. Like Carnegie, Rockefeller gave much of his fortune away, establishing foundations to promote education and medical research. And like Carnegie, he bitterly fought his employees' efforts to organize unions.

The Electricity Building at the Chicago World's Fair of 1893, painted by Childe Hassam. The electric lighting at the fair astonished visitors and illustrated how electricity was changing the visual landscape.

A cartoon in the satirical magazine *Puck*, February 7, 1883, shows robber barons Jay Gould, Cyrus Field, Russell Sage, and Cornelius Vanderbilt seated on a raft with their "millions," while workers from various occupations keep them afloat.

These and other industrial leaders inspired among ordinary Americans a combination of awe, admiration, and hostility. Depending on one's point of view, they were "captains of industry," whose energy and vision pushed the economy forward, or "**robber barons**," who wielded power without any accountability in an unregulated marketplace. Their dictatorial attitudes, unscrupulous methods, repressive labor policies, and exercise of power without any democratic control led to fears that they were undermining political and economic freedom. Concentrated wealth degraded the political process, declared Henry Demarest Lloyd in *Wealth against Commonwealth* (1894), an exposé of how Rockefeller's Standard Oil Company made a mockery of economic competition and political democracy by manipulating the market and bribing legislators. "Liberty and monopoly," Lloyd concluded, "cannot live together."

Liberty versus monopoly

Workers' Freedom in an Industrial Age

Remarkable as it was, the country's economic growth distributed its benefits very unevenly. For a minority of workers, the rapidly expanding industrial system created new forms of freedom. In some industries, skilled workers commanded high wages and exercised considerable control over the production process. A worker's economic independence now rested on technical skill rather than ownership of one's own shop and tools as in earlier times. Through their union, skilled iron- and steelworkers fixed output quotas and controlled the training of apprentices in the technique of iron rolling. These workers often knew more about the details of production than their employers did.

The music room of The Breakers, the opulent mansion of millionaire Cornelius Vanderbilt II in Newport, Rhode Island, an exclusive retreat for rich socialites of the Gilded Age.

For most workers, however, economic insecurity remained a basic fact of life. During the depressions of the 1870s and 1890s, millions of workers lost their jobs or were forced to accept reductions of pay. The "tramp" became a familiar figure on the social landscape as thousands of men took to the roads in search of work. Between 1880 and 1900, an average of 35,000 workers perished each year in factory and mine accidents, the highest rate in the industrial world. Much of the working class remained desperately poor and to survive needed income from all family members.

By 1890, the richest 1 percent of Americans received the same total income as the bottom half of the population and owned more property than the remaining 99 percent. Many of the wealthiest Americans consciously pursued an aristocratic lifestyle, building palatial homes, attending exclusive social clubs, schools, and colleges, holding fancy-dress balls,

The Gilded Age upper class: Mrs. Cornelia Ward Hall, wife of the millionaire John H. Hall, with her four children. All are dressed in expensive silk and lace.

Baxter Street Court, 1890, one of numerous photographs by Jacob Riis depicting living conditions in New York City's slums.

and marrying into each other's families. In 1899, the economist and social historian Thorstein Veblen published *The Theory of the Leisure Class*, a devastating critique of an upper-class culture focused on "conspicuous consumption"—that is, spending money not on needed or even desired goods, but simply to demonstrate the possession of wealth.

At the same time much of the working class lived in desperate conditions. Jacob Riis, in *How the Other Half Lives* (1890), offered a shocking account of living conditions among the urban poor, complete with photographs of apartments in dark, airless, overcrowded tenement houses.

FREEDOM IN THE GILDED AGE

The era from 1870 to 1890 is the only period of American history commonly known by a derogatory name—**the Gilded Age**, after the title of an 1873 novel by Mark Twain and Charles Dudley Warner. "Gilded" means covered with a layer of gold, but it also suggests that the glittering surface masks a core of little real value and is therefore deceptive. Twain and Warner were referring not only to the remarkable expansion of the economy in this period but also to the corruption caused by corporate dominance of politics and to the oppressive treatment of those left behind in the scramble for wealth. "Get rich, dishonestly if we can, honestly if we must," was the era's slogan, according to *The Gilded Age*.

Prayer Time in the Nursery, Five Points House of Industry, taken by Jacob Riis around 1889, offers a striking contrast to the bleak homes of New York City's poor families, depicted in many of his photographs.

The Social Problem

As the United States matured into an industrial economy, Americans struggled to make sense of the new social order. Debates over political economy engaged the attention of millions, reaching far beyond the tiny academic world into the public sphere inhabited by self-educated workingmen and farmers, reformers of all kinds, newspaper editors, and politicians. This broad public discussion produced thousands of books, pamphlets, and articles on such technical issues as land taxation and currency reform, as well as widespread debate over the social and ethical implications of economic change.

Social unrest

Many Americans sensed that something had gone wrong in the nation's social development. Talk of "better classes," "respectable classes," and "dangerous classes" dominated public discussion, and bitter labor strikes seemed to have become the rule. In 1881, the Massachusetts Bureau of Labor Statistics reported that virtually every worker it interviewed in Fall River, the nation's largest center of textile production, complained of overwork, poor housing, and tyrannical employers.

Freedom and equality disconnected

With factory workers living on the edge of poverty alongside a growing class of millionaires, it became increasingly difficult to view wage labor as a temporary resting place on the road to economic independence. Yet given the vast expansion of the nation's productive capacity, many Americans viewed the concentration of wealth as inevitable, natural, and justified by progress. By the turn of the century, advanced economics taught that wages were determined by the iron law of supply and demand and that wealth rightly flowed not to those who worked the hardest but to men with business skills and access to money. The close link between freedom and equality, forged in the Revolution and reinforced during the Civil War, appeared increasingly out of date.

Social Darwinism in America

Charles Darwin

The idea of the natural superiority of some groups to others, which before the Civil War had been invoked to justify slavery in an otherwise free society, now reemerged in the vocabulary of modern science to explain the success and failure of individuals and social classes. In 1859, the British scientist Charles Darwin published *On the Origin of Species*. One of the most influential works of science ever to appear, it expounded the theory of evolution whereby plant and animal species best suited to their environment took the place of those less able to adapt.

The misapplication of Darwin's theory of evolution

In a highly oversimplified form, language borrowed from Darwin, such as "natural selection," "the struggle for existence," and "the survival of the fittest," entered public discussion of social problems. According to what came to be called **Social Darwinism**, evolution was as natural a process in human society as in nature, and government must not interfere. Especially misguided, in this view, were efforts to uplift those at the bottom of the social order, such as laws regulating conditions of work or public assistance to the poor. The giant industrial corporation, Social Darwinists believed, had emerged because it was better adapted to its environment than earlier forms of enterprise. To restrict its operations by legislation would reduce society to a more primitive level.

Even the depressions of the 1870s and 1890s did not shake the widespread view that the poor were essentially responsible for their own fate. Failure to advance in society was widely thought to indicate a lack of character, an absence of self-reliance and determination in the face of adversity.

William Graham Sumner

The era's most influential Social Darwinist was Yale professor William Graham Sumner. For Sumner, freedom required frank acceptance of inequality. Society faced two and only two alternatives: "liberty, inequality, survival of the fittest; not-liberty, equality, survival of the unfittest." Government, Sumner believed, existed only to protect "the property of men and the honor of women," not to upset social arrangements decreed by nature.

Liberty of Contract and the Courts

The growing influence of Social Darwinism helped to popularize an idea that would be embraced by the business and professional classes in the last quarter of the nineteenth century—a "negative" definition of freedom as limited government and an unrestrained free market. Central to this social vision was the idea of contract. So long as labor relations were governed by contracts freely arrived at by independent individuals, neither the government nor unions had a right to interfere with working conditions, and Americans had no grounds to complain of a loss of freedom.

A new idea of free labor

Thus the principle of free labor, which originated as a celebration of the independent small producer in a society of broad equality and social harmony, was transformed into a defense of the unrestrained operations of the capitalist marketplace.

State and federal courts struck down state laws regulating economic enterprise as an interference with the right of the free laborer to choose his employment and working conditions, and of the entrepreneur to utilize his property as he saw fit. For decades, the courts viewed state regulation of business—especially laws establishing maximum hours of work and safe working conditions—as an insult to free labor.

The courts and economic freedom

The courts generally sided with business enterprises that complained of a loss of economic freedom. In 1885, the New York Court of Appeals invalidated a state law that prohibited the manufacture of cigars in tenement dwellings on the grounds that such legislation deprived the worker of

Women and work

the "liberty" to work "where he will." Although women still lacked political rights, they were increasingly understood to possess the same economic "liberty," defined in this way, as men. The Illinois Supreme Court in 1895 declared unconstitutional a state law that outlawed the production of garments in sweatshops and established a maximum forty-eight-hour workweek for women and children.

United States v. *E. C. Knight Co.*

In 1895 in *United States v. E. C. Knight Co.*, the U.S. Supreme Court ruled that the Sherman Antitrust Act of 1890, which barred combinations in restraint of trade, could not be used to break up a sugar refining monopoly because the Constitution empowered Congress to regulate commerce but not manufacturing. Their unwillingness to allow regulation of the economy, however, did not prevent the courts from acting to impede labor organization. The Sherman Act, intended to prevent business mergers that stifled competition, was used by judges primarily to issue injunctions prohibiting strikes on the grounds that they illegally interfered with the freedom of trade.

Lochner v. New York

In a 1905 case that became almost as notorious as *Dred Scott*, the Supreme Court in *Lochner v. New York* voided a state law establishing ten hours per day or sixty per week as the maximum hours of work for bakers. By this time, the Court was invoking "liberty" in ways that could easily seem absurd. In one case, it overturned as a violation of "personal liberty" a Kansas law prohibiting "yellow-dog" contracts, which made nonmembership in a union a condition of employment. In another, it struck down state laws requiring payment of coal miners in money rather than paper usable only at company-owned stores. Workers, observed mine union leader John P. Mitchell, could not but feel that "they are being guaranteed the liberties they do not want and denied the liberty that is of real value to them."

LABOR AND THE REPUBLIC

"The Overwhelming Labor Question"

Public debate divided along class lines

As Mitchell's remark suggests, public debate in the late nineteenth century, more than at almost any other moment in American history, divided along class lines. The shift from the slavery controversy to what one politician called "the overwhelming labor question" was dramatically illustrated in 1877, the year of both the end of Reconstruction and also the first national labor walkout—the **Great Railroad Strike**. When workers protesting a pay cut paralyzed rail traffic in much of the country, militia units tried to force them back to work. After troops fired on strikers in Pittsburgh, killing twenty people, workers responded by burning the city's railroad yards, destroying millions of dollars in property. General strikes paralyzed Chicago and St. Louis. The strike revealed both a strong sense of solidarity among workers and the close ties between the Republican Party and the new class of industrialists. President Rutherford B. Hayes, who a few months earlier had ordered federal troops in the South to end their involvement in local politics,

Railroad strikes

Ruins of the Pittsburgh Round House, a photograph published in the July 1895 issue of *Scribner's Magazine*, shows the widespread destruction of property during the Great Railroad Strike of July 1877.

ordered the army into the North. The workers, the president wrote in his diary, were "put down by force."

In the aftermath of 1877, the federal government constructed armories in major cities to ensure that troops would be on hand in the event of further labor difficulties. Henceforth, national power would be used not to protect beleaguered former slaves but to guarantee the rights of property.

The Knights of Labor and the "Conditions Essential to Liberty"

The 1880s witnessed a new wave of labor organizing. At its center stood the **Knights of Labor**, led by Terence V. Powderly. The Knights were the first group to try to organize unskilled workers as well as skilled ones, women alongside men, and blacks as well as whites (although even the Knights excluded the despised Asian immigrants on the West Coast). The group reached a peak membership of nearly 800,000 in 1886 and involved millions of workers in strikes, boycotts, political action, and educational and social activities.

Labor reformers of the Gilded Age put forward a wide array of programs, from the eight-hour day to public employment in hard times, currency reform, anarchism, socialism, and the creation of a vaguely defined "cooperative commonwealth." Labor raised the question whether meaningful freedom could exist in a situation of extreme economic inequality.

Middle-Class Reformers

Dissatisfaction with social conditions in the Gilded Age extended well beyond aggrieved workers. Alarmed by fear of class warfare and the growing power of concentrated capital, social thinkers offered numerous plans for change. In the last quarter of the century, more than 150 utopian or cataclysmic novels appeared, predicting that social conflict would end either in a new, harmonious social order or in total catastrophe.

The Great Labor Parade of September 1, from *Frank Leslie's Illustrated Newspaper*, September 13, 1884. A placard illustrates how the labor movement identified employers with the Slave Power of the pre–Civil War era.

Of the many books proposing more optimistic remedies for the unequal distribution of wealth, the most popular were *Progress and Poverty* (1879) by Henry George, *The Cooperative Commonwealth* (1884) by Laurence Gronlund, and Edward Bellamy's *Looking Backward* (1888). All three were among the century's greatest best-sellers, their extraordinary success testifying to what George called "a widespread consciousness . . . that there is something *radically* wrong in the present social organization." All three writers, though in very different ways, sought to reclaim an imagined golden age of social harmony and American freedom.

Progress and Poverty probably commanded more public attention than any book on economics in American history. Henry George began with a famous statement of "the problem" suggested by its title—the growth of "squalor and misery" alongside material progress. His solution was the **single tax**, which would replace other taxes with a levy on increases in the value of real estate. No one knows how many of Henry George's readers actually believed in this way of solving the nation's ills. But millions responded to his clear explanation of economic relationships and his stirring account of how the "social distress" long thought to be confined to the Old World had made its appearance in the New.

Henry George, author of *Progress and Poverty*.

The Cooperative Commonwealth

Quite different in outlook was *The Cooperative Commonwealth*, the first book to popularize socialist ideas for an American audience. Its author, Laurence Gronlund, was a lawyer who had emigrated from Denmark in 1867. Socialism—the belief that private control of economic enterprises should be replaced by public ownership in order to ensure a fairer distribution of the benefits of the wealth produced—became a major political force in western Europe in the late nineteenth century. In the United States, however, where access to private property was widely considered essential to individual freedom, socialist beliefs at this point were largely confined to immigrants, whose writings, frequently in foreign languages, attracted little attention.

Gronlund began the process of socialism's Americanization. Whereas Karl Marx, the nineteenth century's most influential socialist theorist, had predicted that socialism would come into being via a working-class revolution, Gronlund portrayed it as the end result of a process of peaceful evolution, not violent upheaval. He thus made socialism seem more acceptable to middle-class Americans who desired an end to class conflict and the restoration of social harmony.

Edward Bellamy, author of the utopian novel *Looking Backward*.

Not until the early twentieth century would socialism become a significant presence in American public life. As Gronlund himself noted, the most important result of *The Cooperative Commonwealth* was to prepare an audience for Edward Bellamy's *Looking Backward*, which promoted socialist ideas while "ignoring that name" (Bellamy wrote of nationalism, not socialism). In *Looking Backward*, his main character falls asleep in the late nineteenth century only to awaken in the year 2000, in a world where cooperation has replaced class strife, "excessive individualism," and cutthroat competition. Freedom, Bellamy insisted, was a social condition resting on interdependence, not autonomy.

The book inspired the creation of hundreds of nationalist clubs devoted to bringing into existence the world of 2000 and left a profound mark on a generation of reformers and intellectuals. Bellamy held out the hope of retaining the material abundance made possible by industrial capitalism while eliminating inequality.

Protestants and Moral Reform

"Christian lobby"

Mainstream Protestants played a major role in seeking to stamp out sin in the late nineteenth century. What one historian calls a "Christian lobby" promoted political solutions to what they saw as the moral problems raised by labor conflict and the growth of cities, and threats to religious faith by Darwinism and other scientific advances.

Legislation on morals

Unlike the pre-Civil War period, when "moral suasion" was the preferred approach of many reformers, powerful national organizations like the Woman's Christian Temperance Union, National Reform Association, and Reform Bureau now campaigned for federal legislation that would "Christianize the government" by outlawing sinful behavior. Among the proposed targets were the consumption of alcohol, gambling, prostitution, polygamy, and birth control. In a striking departure from the prewar situation, southerners joined in the campaign for federal regulation of individual behavior, something whites in the region had strongly opposed before the Civil War, fearing it could lead to action against slavery. The key role played by the white South in the campaign for moral legislation helped earn the region a reputation as the Bible Belt—a place where political action revolved around religious principles. Although efforts to enact a national law requiring businesses to close on Sunday failed, the Christian lobby's efforts set the stage for later legislation such as the Mann Act of 1910, banning the transportation of women across state lines for immoral purposes (an effort to suppress prostitution), and Prohibition.

The Bible Belt

A Social Gospel

Rauschenbusch and Gladden

Most of the era's Protestant preachers concentrated on attacking individual sins like drinking and Sabbath-breaking and saw nothing immoral about the pursuit of riches. But the outlines of what came to be called the **Social Gospel** were taking shape in the writings of Walter Rauschenbusch, a Baptist minister in New York City; Washington Gladden, a Congregational clergyman in Columbus, Ohio; and others. They insisted that freedom and spiritual self-development required an equalization of wealth and power and that unbridled competition mocked the Christian ideal of brotherhood.

Religion and social reform

The Social Gospel movement originated as an effort to reform Protestant churches by expanding their appeal in poor urban neighborhoods and making them more attentive to the era's social ills. The movement's adherents established missions and relief programs in urban areas that attempted to alleviate poverty, combat child labor, and encourage the construction of better working-class housing. Within American Catholicism as well, a group of priests and bishops emerged who attempted to alter the church's traditional hostility to movements for social reform and its isolation from contemporary currents of social thought. With most of its parishioners working men and women, they argued, the church should lend its support to the labor movement.

The Haymarket Affair

The first May Day

The year of the dedication of the Statue of Liberty, 1886, also witnessed an unprecedented upsurge in labor activity. On May 1, 1886, some 350,000 workers in cities across the country demonstrated for an eight-hour day. Having originated in the United States, May 1, or May Day as it came to be called, soon became an annual date of parades, picnics, and protests, celebrated around the world by organized labor.

Haymarket protests

The most dramatic events of 1886 took place in Chicago, a city with a large and vibrant labor movement that brought together native-born and immigrant workers, whose outlooks ranged from immigrant socialism and anarchism to American traditions of equality and anti-monopoly. On May 3, 1886, four strikers were killed by police. The next day, a rally was held in Haymarket Square to protest the killings. Near the end of the speeches, someone—whose identity has never been determined—threw a bomb into the crowd, killing a policeman. The panicked police opened fire, shooting several bystanders and a number of their own force. Soon after, police raided the offices of labor and radical groups and arrested their leaders. Employers took the opportunity presented by the **Haymarket affair** to paint the labor movement as a dangerous and un-American force, prone to violence and controlled by foreign-born radicals. Eight anarchists were charged with plotting and carrying out the bombing. Even though the evidence against them was extremely weak, a jury convicted the "Haymarket martyrs." Four were hanged, one committed suicide in prison, and the remaining three were imprisoned until John Peter Altgeld, a pro-labor governor of Illinois, commuted their sentences in 1893.

Albert Parsons

Most of the eight men accused of plotting the Haymarket bombing were foreign-born—five Germans and an English immigrant. One was of German descent. The last was Albert Parsons, a native of Alabama who had

In this pro-labor cartoon from 1888, a workingman rescues liberty from the stranglehold of monopolies and the pro-business major parties.

served in the Confederate army in the Civil War, married a black woman, and edited a Republican newspaper in Texas during Reconstruction. Having survived the Ku Klux Klan in Reconstruction Texas, Parsons perished on the Illinois gallows for a crime that he, like the other "Haymarket martyrs," did not commit. Lucy Parsons, Albert Parsons's wife, went on to become one of the era's most celebrated radical orators. She probably addressed more Americans than any other black speaker in the nineteenth century except Frederick Douglass.

Labor and Politics

The Haymarket affair took place amid an outburst of independent labor political activity. In Kansas City, for example, a coalition of black and Irish-American workers and middle-class voters elected Tom Hanna as mayor. He proceeded to side with unions rather than employers in industrial disputes.

Henry George's labor campaign

The most celebrated labor campaign took place in New York City, where in 1886, somewhat to his own surprise, Henry George found himself thrust into the role of labor's candidate for mayor. George's aim in running was to bring attention to the single tax on land. The labor leaders who organized the United Labor Party had more immediate goals in mind, especially stopping the courts from barring strikes and jailing unionists for conspiracy. A few days after the dedication of the Statue of Liberty, New Yorkers flocked to the polls to elect their mayor. Nearly 70,000 voted for George, who finished second, eclipsing the total of the Republican candidate, Theodore Roosevelt, and coming close to defeating Democrat Abram Hewitt.

The events of 1886 suggested that labor might be on the verge of establishing itself as a permanent political force. In fact, that year marked the high point of the Knights of Labor. Facing increasing employer hostility and linked by employers and the press to the violence and radicalism associated with the Haymarket events, the Knights soon declined. The major parties, moreover, proved remarkably resourceful in appealing to labor voters.

THE TRANSFORMATION OF THE WEST

Nowhere did capitalism penetrate more rapidly or dramatically than in the trans-Mississippi West, whose "vast, trackless spaces," as the poet Walt Whitman called them, were now absorbed into the expanding economy. At the close of the Civil War, the frontier of continuous white settlement did not extend far beyond the Mississippi River. To the west lay millions of acres of fertile and mineral-rich land roamed by giant herds of buffalo whose meat and hides provided food, clothing, and shelter for a population of more than 250,000 Indians.

The West as a place of opportunity

Ever since the beginning of colonial settlement in British North America, the West—a region whose definition shifted as the population expanded—had been seen as a place of opportunity for those seeking to improve their condition in life. From farmers moving into Ohio, Indiana, and Illinois in the decades after the American Revolution to prospectors who struck it rich in the California gold rush of the mid-nineteenth century, millions of Americans and immigrants from abroad found in the westward movement a path to economic opportunity. But the West was hardly a uniform paradise of small, independent farmers. Landlords, railroads, and mining companies in the West also utilized Mexican migrant and indentured labor, Chinese working on long-term contracts, and, until the end of the Civil War, African-American slaves.

A Diverse Region

The West, of course, was hardly a single area. West of the Mississippi River lay a variety of regions, all marked by remarkable physical beauty—the Great Plains, the Rocky Mountains, the desert of the Southwest, the Sierra Nevada, and the valleys and coastline of California and the Pacific Northwest. It would take many decades before individual settlers and corporate business enterprises penetrated all these areas. But the process was far advanced by the end of the nineteenth century.

The political and economic incorporation of the American West was part of a global process. In many parts of the world, indigenous inhabitants—the Zulu in South Africa, Aboriginal peoples in Australia, American Indians—were pushed aside (often after fierce resistance) as centralizing governments brought large interior regions under their control. In the United States, the incorporation of the West required the active intervention of the federal government, which acquired Indian land by war and treaty, administered land sales, regulated territorial politics, and distributed land and money to farmers, railroads, and mining companies.

Western states used land donated by the federal government, in accordance with the Morrill Land Grant Act passed during the Civil War, to establish public universities. And, of course, the abolition of slavery by the Thirteenth Amendment decided the long contest over whether the West would be a society based on free or slave labor.

Newly created western territories such as Arizona, Idaho, Montana, and the Dakotas remained under federal control far longer than had been

Having been granted millions of acres of land by the federal and state governments, railroads sought to encourage emigration to the West by both Americans and immigrants so that they could sell real estate to settlers. This brochure by the Chicago, Burlington & Quincy Railroad Company, circulated in Europe, advertises land in Nebraska in Danish.

the pattern in the East. Many easterners were wary of granting statehood to the territories until white and non-Mormon settlers counterbalanced the large Latino and Mormon populations.

In the twentieth century, the construction of federally financed irrigation systems and dams would open large areas to commercial farming. The West would become known (not least to its own inhabitants) as a place of rugged individualism and sturdy independence. But, ironically, without active governmental assistance, the region could never have been settled and developed.

Farming in the Trans-Mississippi West

Agricultural development

Even as sporadic Indian wars raged, settlers poured into the West. Territorial and state governments eager for population and railroad companies anxious to sell the immense tracts of land they had acquired from the government flooded European countries and eastern cities with promotional literature promising easy access to land. More land came into cultivation in the thirty years after the Civil War than in the previous two and a half centuries of American history. Hundreds of thousands of families acquired farms under the Homestead Act, and even more purchased land from speculators and from railroad companies. A new agricultural empire producing wheat and corn arose on the Middle Border (Minnesota, the Dakotas, Nebraska, and Kansas), whose population rose from 300,000 in 1860 to 5 million in 1900. The farmers were a diverse group, including native-born easterners, blacks escaping the post-Reconstruction South, and immigrants from Canada, Germany, Scandinavia, and Great Britain. In the late nineteenth century the most multicultural state in the Union was North Dakota.

The family of David Hilton on their Nebraska homestead in 1887. The Hiltons insisted on being photographed with their organ, away from the modest sod house in which they lived, to better represent their aspiration for prosperity.

Despite the promises of promotional pamphlets, farming on the Great Plains was not an easy task. Much of the burden fell on women. Farm families generally invested in the kinds of labor-saving machinery that would bring in cash, not machines that would ease women's burdens in the household (like the back-breaking task of doing laundry). A farm woman in Arizona described her morning chores in her diary: "Get up, turn out my chickens, draw a pail of water . . . make a fire, put potatoes to cook, brush and sweep half inch of dust off floor, feed three litters of chickens, then mix biscuits, get breakfast, milk, besides work in the house, and this morning had to go half mile after calves."

Despite the emergence of a few **bonanza farms** that covered thousands of acres and employed large numbers of agricultural wage workers, family farms still dominated the trans-Mississippi West. Even small farmers, however, became increasingly oriented to national and international markets, specializing in the production of single crops for sale in faraway places. At the same time, railroads brought factory-made goods to rural people, replacing items previously produced in farmers' homes. Farm families became more and more dependent on loans to purchase land, machinery, and industrial products, and increasingly vulnerable to the ups and downs of prices for agricultural goods in the world market. Agriculture reflected how the international economy was becoming more integrated. The combination of economic depressions and expanding agricultural production in places like Argentina, Australia, and the American West pushed prices of farm products steadily downward. Small farmers throughout the world suffered severe difficulties in the last quarter of the nineteenth century. Many joined the migration to cities within their countries or the increasing international migration of labor.

Agriculture and the international economy

The future of western farming ultimately lay with giant agricultural enterprises relying heavily on irrigation, chemicals, and machinery—investments far beyond the means of family farmers. A preview of the agricultural future was already evident in California, where, as far back as Spanish and Mexican days, landownership had been concentrated in large units. In the late nineteenth century, California's giant fruit and vegetable farms, owned by corporations like the Southern Pacific Railroad, were tilled not by agricultural laborers who could expect to acquire land of their own, but by migrant laborers from China, the Philippines, Japan, and Mexico, who tramped from place to place following the ripening crops. In the 1870s, California's "wheat barons," who owned ranches of 30,000 or more acres, shipped their grain from San Francisco all the way to Great Britain, while large-scale growers in the new "Orange Empire" of the southern part of the state sent fruit east by rail, packaged in crates bedecked with images of an Edenic landscape filled with lush orchards.

The Cowboy and the Corporate West

The two decades following the Civil War also witnessed the golden age of the cattle kingdom. The Kansas Pacific Railroad's stations at Abilene, Dodge City, and Wichita, Kansas, became destinations for the fabled drives of millions of cattle from Texas. A collection of white, Mexican, and black men who conducted the cattle drives, the cowboys became symbols

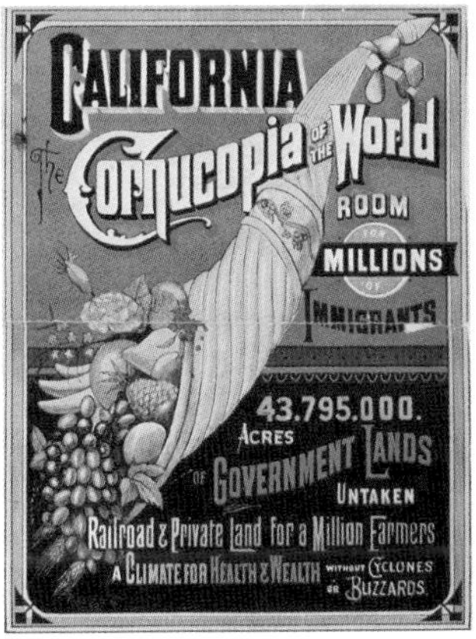

In the late 1800s, California tried to attract immigrants by advertising its pleasant climate and the availability of land, although large-scale corporate farms were coming to dominate the state's agriculture.

A family festival in San Juan, a town in southern California, around 1880. Long after the area was annexed to the United States, the Spanish-speaking residents continued their traditional religious and cultural practices.

of a life of freedom on the open range. Their exploits would later serve as the theme of many a Hollywood movie, and their clothing inspired fashions that remain popular today. But there was nothing romantic about the life of the cowboys, most of whom were low-paid wage workers. (Texas cowboys even went on strike for higher pay in 1883.) The days of the long-distance cattle drive ended in the mid-1880s, as farmers enclosed more and more of the open range with barbed-wire fences, making it difficult to graze cattle on the grasslands of the Great Plains, and two terrible winters destroyed millions of cattle. When the industry recuperated, it was reorganized in large, enclosed ranches close to rail connections.

The West was more than a farming empire. By 1890, a higher percentage of its population lived in cities than was the case in other regions. Large corporate enterprises appeared throughout the West. Western mining, from Michigan iron ore and copper to gold and silver in California, Nevada, and Colorado, fell under the sway of companies that mobilized eastern and European investment to introduce advanced technology. Gold and silver rushes took place in the Dakotas in 1876, Idaho in 1883, Colorado in the 1890s, and Alaska at the end of the century.

The Chinese Presence

Chinese immigration

Chinese immigration, which had begun at the time of the California gold rush, continued in the postwar years. Before the Civil War, nearly all Chinese newcomers had been unattached men, brought in by labor contractors to work in western gold fields, railroad construction, and factories. In the early 1870s, entire Chinese families began to immigrate.

A photograph of Denver, Colorado, in the early 1890s. Although generally thought of as a region of rural pioneers, the West, like the East, experienced rapid urbanization.

THE INDUSTRIAL WEST

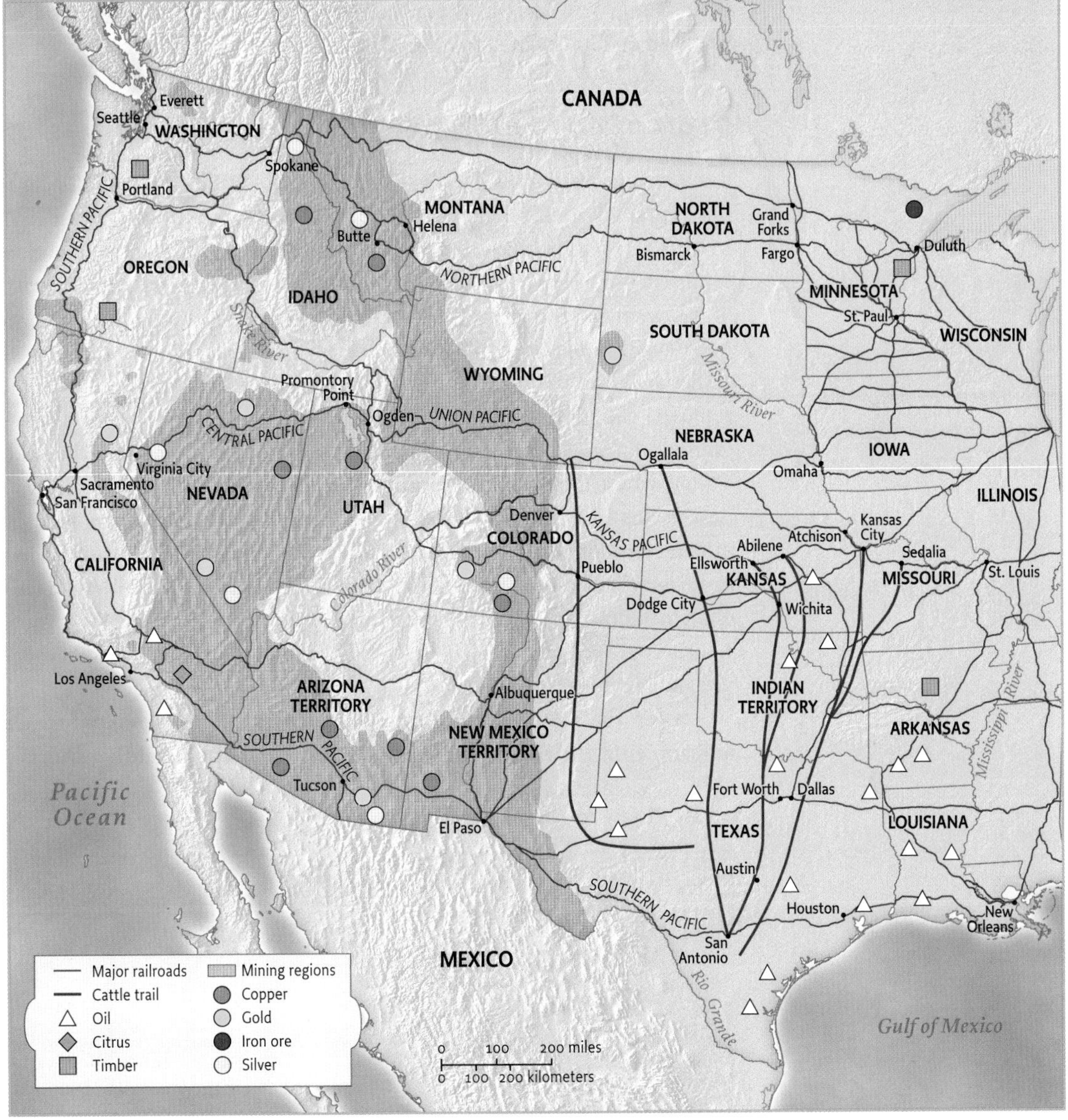

By 1880, 105,000 persons of Chinese descent lived in the United States. Three-quarters lived in California, where Chinese made up over half of the state's farm workers. But Chinese immigrants could be found in mines in Idaho, Colorado, and Nevada, as domestic workers in urban households, and in factories producing cigars, clothing, and shoes in western cities.

Many men had wives and children in China, and like members of other immigrant groups, they kept in touch by sending letters and money to their families at home and reading magazines aimed at emigrants that reported on local events in China.

Conflict on the Mormon Frontier

The Mormons had moved to the Great Salt Lake Valley in the 1840s, hoping to practice their religion free of the persecution they had encountered in the East. They envisioned their community in Utah as the foundation of a great empire they called Deseret. Given the widespread unpopularity of Mormon polygamy and the close connection of church and state in Mormon theology, conflict with the growing numbers of non-Mormon settlers moving west became inevitable. When President James Buchanan removed the Mormon leader Brigham Young as Utah's territorial governor and Young refused to comply, federal troops entered the Salt Lake Valley, where they remained until the beginning of the Civil War. In 1857, during this time of tension, a group of Mormons attacked a wagon train of non-Mormon settlers traveling through Utah toward California. What came to be called the Mountain Meadows Massacre resulted in the death of all the adults and older children in the wagon train—over 100 persons. Nearly twenty years later, one leader of the assault was convicted of murder and executed.

Deseret

Mountain Meadows Massacre

After the Civil War, Mormon leaders sought to avoid further antagonizing the federal government. In the 1880s, Utah banned the

Albert Bierstadt's 1863 painting *The Rocky Mountains, Lander's Peak* depicts Indians as an integral part of the majestic landscape of the West.

This pencil-and-crayon drawing by a Cheyenne Indian from the 1880s depicts a Native American fighting two black members of the U.S. military. After the Civil War, black soldiers, whose presence was resented by many whites, in the North as well as the South, were reassigned to the West.

practice of polygamy, a prohibition written into the state constitution as a requirement before Utah gained admission as a state in 1896.

The Subjugation of the Plains Indians

The new West and the Plains Indians

The transcontinental railroad, a symbol of the reunited nation, brought tens of thousands of newcomers to the West and stimulated the expansion of farming, mining, and other enterprises. The incorporation of the West into the national economy spelled the doom of the Plains Indians and their world. Their lives had already undergone profound transformations. In the eighteenth century, the spread of horses, originally introduced by the Spanish, led to a wholesale shift from farming and hunting on foot to mounted hunting of buffalo.

Most migrants on the Oregon and California Trails before the Civil War encountered little hostility from Indians, often trading with them for food and supplies. But as settlers encroached on Indian lands, bloody conflict between the army and Plains tribes began in the 1850s and continued for decades.

Short-lived "peace policy"

In 1869, President Ulysses S. Grant announced a new "peace policy" in the West, but warfare soon resumed. Drawing on methods used to defeat the Confederacy, Civil War generals like Philip H. Sheridan set out to destroy the foundations of the Indian economy—villages, horses, and especially the buffalo. Hunting by mounted Indians had already reduced the buffalo population—estimated at 30 million in 1800—but it was army campaigns and the depredations of hunters seeking buffalo hides that rendered the vast herds all but extinct.

The buffalo

"Let Me Be a Free Man"

The army's relentless attacks broke the power of one tribe after another. In 1877, troops commanded by former Freedmen's Bureau

Chief Joseph of the Nez Percé, in a photograph possibly taken in Washington, D.C., in 1879, when he was part of an Indian delegation to the nation's capital.

commissioner O. O. Howard pursued the Nez Percé Indians and their leader Chief Joseph on a 1,700-mile chase across the Far West. The Nez Percé (whose name was given to them by Lewis and Clark in 1805 and means "pierced nose" in French) were seeking to escape to Canada after fights with settlers who had encroached on tribal lands in Oregon and Idaho. After four months, Howard forced the Indians to surrender, and they were removed to Oklahoma and later to a reservation in Washington Territory. Until his death in 1904, Joseph would unsuccessfully petition successive presidents for his people's right to return to their beloved Oregon homeland.

Indians occasionally managed to inflict costly delay and even defeat on army units. The most famous Indian victory took place in June 1876 at the **Battle of the Little Bighorn**, when General George A. Custer and his entire command of 250 men perished. The Sioux and Cheyenne warriors, led by Sitting Bull and Crazy Horse, were defending tribal land in the Black Hills of the Dakota Territory. Eventually the Sioux were worn down, partly because of the decimation of the buffalo, and relinquished their claim to the Black Hills.

Remaking Indian Life

"The life my people want is a life of freedom," Sitting Bull declared. The Indian idea of freedom, however, which centered on preserving their cultural and political autonomy and control of ancestral lands, conflicted with the interests and values of most white Americans.

The Bureau of Indian Affairs

In 1871, Congress eliminated the treaty system that dated back to the revolutionary era, by which the federal government negotiated agreements with Indians as if they were independent nations. The federal government also pressed forward with its assault on Indian culture. The Bureau of Indian Affairs established boarding schools where Indian children, removed from the "negative" influences of their parents and tribes, were dressed in non-Indian clothes, given new names, and educated in white ways.

The Dawes Act

The crucial step in attacking "tribalism" came in 1887 with the passage of the **Dawes Act**, named for Senator Henry L. Dawes of Massachusetts, chair of the Senate's Indian Affairs Committee. The act broke up the land of nearly all tribes into small parcels to be distributed to Indian families, with the remainder auctioned off to white purchasers. Indians who accepted the farms and "adopted the habits of civilized life" would become full-fledged American citizens. The policy proved to be a disaster, leading to the loss of much tribal land and the erosion of Indian cultural tradi-

This photograph depicts Lakota, Cheyenne, and Arapaho leaders who visited the White House in 1877.

tions. When the government made 2 million acres of Indian land available in Oklahoma, 50,000 white settlers poured into the territory to claim farms on the single day of April 22, 1889. Further land rushes followed in the 1890s. In the half century after the passage of the Dawes Act, Indians lost 86 million of the 138 million acres of land in their possession in 1887. Overall, according to one estimate, between 1776 and today, via the "right of discovery," treaties, executive orders, court decisions, and outright theft, the United States has acquired over 1.5 billion acres of land from Native Americans, an area twenty-five times as large as Great Britain.

Loss of tribal land

Are Native Americans American?

Many laws and treaties in the nineteenth century offered Indians the right to become American citizens if they left the tribal setting and assimilated into American society. But tribal identity was the one thing nearly every Indian wished to maintain, and very few took advantage of these offers. Thus, few Native Americans were recognized as American citizens. Western courts ruled that the rights guaranteed in the Civil Rights Act of 1866 and the Fourteenth and Fifteenth Amendments did not apply to them. In one of its most controversial rulings, *Elk v. Wilkins* (1884), the Supreme Court agreed.

Elk v. Wilkins

Between Two Worlds, a drawing produced in the 1870s by the Kiowa warrior Wohaw when he was a prisoner in Fort Marion, Florida. Wohaw depicts himself being torn between his traditional way of life, represented by the buffalo, and the culture whites were trying to force him to accept, symbolized by the steer and tiny farmhouse. Wohaw later returned to the West and served in the U.S. Army.

John Elk was born in Indian Territory (in present-day Oklahoma), but gave up his tribal affiliation and moved to Omaha, where he worked and paid taxes. He tried, unsuccessfully, to claim American citizenship and register to vote. The Supreme Court rejected his appeal. It questioned whether any Indian had achieved the degree of "civilization" required of American citizens.

By 1900, roughly 53,000 Indians had become American citizens by accepting land allotments under the Dawes Act. The following year, Congress granted citizenship to 100,000 residents of Indian Territory. The remainder would have to wait until 1919 (for those who fought in World War I). In that year there were around 300,000 Indians in the United States, of whom 125,000 were not citizens. Finally, in 1924, Congress extended citizenship to all Native Americans. But their right to cast ballots remained contested. As late as 1948, Arizona and New Mexico did not allow Indians to vote.

The Ghost Dance and Wounded Knee

Some Indians sought solace in the **Ghost Dance**, a religious revitalization campaign. Its leaders foretold a day when whites would disappear, the buffalo would return, and Indians could once again practice their ancestral customs "free from misery, death, and disease." Large numbers of Indians gathered for days of singing, dancing, and religious observances. Fearing a general uprising, the government sent troops to the reservations. On December 29, 1890, soldiers opened fire on Ghost Dancers encamped near Wounded Knee Creek in South Dakota, killing between 150 and 200 Indians, mostly women and children. The **Wounded Knee massacre** was widely applauded in the press. An Army Court of Inquiry essentially exonerated the troops and their commander, and twenty soldiers were

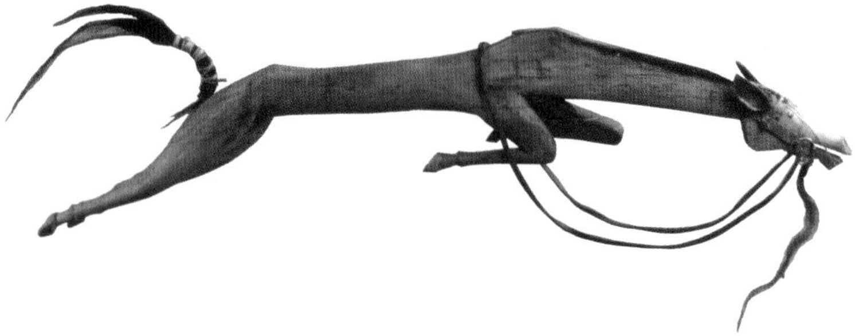

One of the masterpieces of Native American art, this three-foot-long wood sculpture carved by a Lakota Sioux artist around 1870 honors a dead or wounded horse. It has a horsehair mane and tail and leather reins and bridle, and there are holes representing bullet wounds on the torso and red paint representing blood. The horse may be leaping from life to death.

later awarded the Medal of Honor, a recognition of exceptional heroism in battle, for their actions at Wounded Knee.

Although violent skirmishes from Oklahoma to Minnesota in the early twentieth century showed that small-scale Indian resistance continued, the Wounded Knee massacre marked the end of four centuries of armed conflict between the continent's native population and European settlers and their descendants. By 1900, the Indian population had fallen to 250,000, the lowest point in American history. Of that number, roughly 53,000 had become American citizens by accepting land allotments under the Dawes Act. The following year, Congress granted citizenship to 100,000 residents of Indian Territory (in present-day Oklahoma). The remainder would have to wait until 1919 (for those who fought in World War I) and 1924, when Congress made all Indians American citizens.

Settler Societies and Global Wests

The conquest of the American West was part of a global process whereby settlers moved boldly into the interior of regions in temperate climates around the world, bringing their familiar crops and livestock and establishing mining and other industries. Countries such as Argentina, Australia, Canada, and New Zealand, as well as the United States, are often called "settler societies," because immigrants from overseas quickly outnumbered and displaced the original inhabitants—unlike in India and most parts of colonial Africa, where fewer Europeans ventured and those who did relied on the labor of the indigenous inhabitants.

In many settler societies, native peoples were subjected to cultural reconstruction similar to policies in the United States. In Australia, the government gathered the Aboriginal populations—their numbers devastated by disease—in "reserves" reminiscent of American Indian reservations. Australia went further than the United States in the forced assimilation of surviving Aboriginal peoples. The government removed large numbers of children from their families to be adopted by whites—a policy abandoned only in the 1970s.

William "Buffalo Bill" Cody and the Native American leader Sitting Bull, who both appeared in Buffalo Bill's Wild West Show, which brought a romantic image of the West to audiences in the East and Europe.

Myth, Reality, and the Wild West

The West has long played many roles in Americans' national self-consciousness. It has been imagined as a place of individual freedom and unbridled opportunity for

VOICES OF FREEDOM

From Speech of Chief Joseph of the Nez Percé Indians, in Washington, D.C. (1879)

Chief Joseph, leader of the Nez Percé Indians, led his people on a 1,700-mile trek through the Far West in 1877 in an unsuccessful effort to escape to Canada. Two years later, he addressed an audience in Washington, D.C. that included President Rutherford B. Hayes, appealing for the freedom and equal rights enshrined in the law after the Civil War.

I have heard talk and talk, but nothing is done. Good words do not last long unless they amount to something. Words do not pay for my dead people. They do not pay for my country, now overrun by white men.... Good words will not get my people a home where they can live in peace and take care of themselves. I am tired of talk that comes to nothing. It makes my heart sick when I remember all the ... broken promises....

If the white man wants to live in peace with the Indian he can live in peace. There need be no trouble. Treat all men alike. Give them the same law. Give them all an even chance to live and grow. All men were made by the same Great Spirit Chief. They are all brothers. The earth is the mother of all people, and all people should have equal rights upon it. You might as well expect the rivers to run backward as that any man who was born a free man should be contented when penned up and denied liberty to go where he pleases....

When I think of our condition my heart is heavy. I see men of my race treated as outlaws and driven from country to country, or shot down like animals. I know that my race must change. We cannot hold our own with the white men as we are. We only ask an even chance to live as other men live....

Let me be a free man—free to travel, free to stop, free to work, free to trade where I choose, free to choose my own teachers, free to follow the religion of my fathers, free to think and talk and act for myself—and I will obey every law, or submit to the penalty.

From Letter by Saum Song Bo, *American Missionary* (October 1885)

During the 1880s, Chinese-Americans were subjected to discrimination in every phase of their lives. In 1882, Congress temporarily barred further immigration from China. In 1885, when funds were being raised to build a pedestal for the Statue of Liberty, Saum Song Bo, a Chinese-American writer, contrasted the celebration of liberty with the treatment of the Chinese.

A paper was presented to me yesterday for inspection, and I found it to be specially drawn up for subscription among my countrymen toward the Pedestal Fund of the . . . Statue of Liberty. . . . But the word liberty makes me think of the fact that this country is the land of liberty for men of all nations except the Chinese. I consider it as an insult to us Chinese to call on us to contribute toward building in this land a pedestal for a statue of Liberty. That statue represents Liberty holding a torch which lights the passage of those of all nations who come into this country. But are the Chinese allowed to come? As for the Chinese who are here, are they allowed to enjoy liberty as men of all other nationalities enjoy it? Are they allowed to go about everywhere free from the insults, abuses, assaults, wrongs, and injuries from which men of other nationalities are free? . . .

And this statue of Liberty is a gift from another people who do not love liberty for the Chinese. [To] the Annamese and Tonquinese Chinese [colonial subjects of the French empire in Indochina], . . . liberty is as dear as to the French. What right have the French to deprive them of their liberty?

Whether this statute against the Chinese or the statue to Liberty will be the most lasting monument to tell future ages of the liberty and greatness of this country, will be known only to future generations.

QUESTIONS

1. *What are Chief Joseph's complaints about the treatment of his people?*
2. *Why does Saum Song Bo believe that the Chinese do not enjoy liberty in the United States?*
3. *What are the similarities and differences in the definition of freedom in the two documents?*

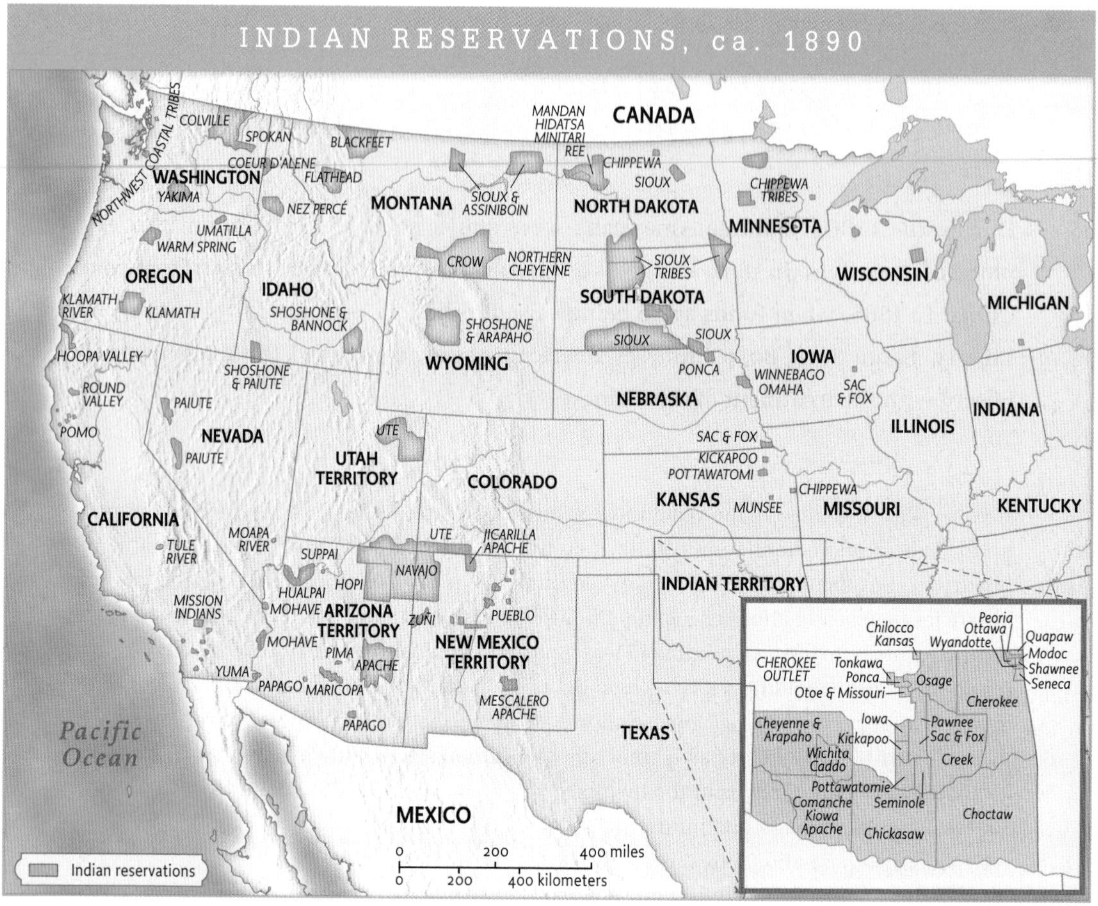

By 1890, the vast majority of the remaining Indian population had been removed to reservations scattered across the western states.

those dissatisfied with their lives in the East and as a future empire that would dominate the continent and the world. Even as farms, mines, and cities spread over the landscape in the post–Civil War years, a new image of the West began to circulate—the Wild West, a lawless place ruled by cowboys and Indians (two groups by this time vastly outnumbered by other westerners), and marked by gunfights, cattle drives, and stagecoach robberies.

The image of a violent yet romantic frontier world would later become a staple of Hollywood movies. In the late nineteenth century, it was disseminated in vaudeville shows that achieved immense popularity. Although not the first, William "Buffalo Bill" Cody was the most important popularizer of this idea of the West. Buffalo Bill's Wild West Show included reenactments of battles with Indians (including Custer's Last Stand), buffalo hunts, Indian rituals, and feats by the sharpshooter Annie Oakley. The image of the Wild

West also circulated in cheap popular books known as dime novels and sensational journalistic accounts.

The real West

Theater audiences and readers found fantasies of adventure in observing western violence from a safe distance and marveled at the skills of horseback riding, roping, and shooting on display. They imagined the West as a timeless place immune to the corruption of civilization, which offered a striking contrast to the increasingly sedentary lives of men in eastern cities. The real West—for example, the struggles of farm families—played no role in this depiction. The West's multiracial, multiethnic population also disappeared, although different groups added their own elements to the mythical West. Mexican-Americans, for example, made a folk hero of Gregorio Cortez, a Texas outlaw renowned for his ability to outwit pursuers.

POLITICS IN A GILDED AGE

The Corruption of Politics

As they had earlier in the nineteenth century, Americans during the Gilded Age saw their nation as an island of political democracy in a world still dominated by undemocratic governments. In Europe, only France and Switzerland enjoyed universal male suffrage. Even in Britain, most of the working class could not vote until the passage of the Reform Act of 1884.

Corporations' influence

Nonetheless, the power of the new corporations, seemingly immune to democratic control, raised disturbing questions for the American understanding of political freedom as popular self-government. In 1873, the chief justice of the Wisconsin Supreme Court warned that a "new and dark power" threatened American democracy. "Which shall rule," he asked,

The Bosses of the Senate, a cartoon from *Puck*, January 23, 1889, shows well-fed monopolists towering over the obedient senators. Above them, a sign rewrites the closing words of Lincoln's Gettysburg Address: "This is the Senate of the Monopolists, by the Monopolists, and for the Monopolists."

"wealth or man; which shall lead, money or intellect; who shall fill public stations, educated and patriotic freemen, or the feudal slaves of corporate capital?" Political corruption was rife. In Pennsylvania's legislature, the "third house" of railroad lobbyists was said to enjoy as much influence as the elected chambers. In the West, many lawmakers held stock or directorships in lumber companies and railroads that received public aid.

New York's Tweed Ring

Urban politics fell under the sway of corrupt political machines like New York's Tweed Ring, which plundered the city of tens of millions of dollars. "Boss" William M. Tweed's organization reached into every neighborhood. He won support from the city's immigrant poor by fashioning a kind of private welfare system that provided food, fuel, and jobs in hard times. A combination of political reformers and businessmen tired of paying tribute to the ring ousted Tweed in the early 1870s, although he remained popular among the city's poor, who considered him an urban Robin Hood.

The Crédit Mobilier scandal

At the national level, the most notorious example of corruption came to light during Grant's presidency. This was Crédit Mobilier, a corporation formed by an inner ring of Union Pacific Railroad stockholders to oversee the line's government-assisted construction. Essentially, it enabled the participants to sign contracts with themselves, at an exorbitant profit, to build the new line. The arrangement was protected by the distribution of stock to influential politicians.

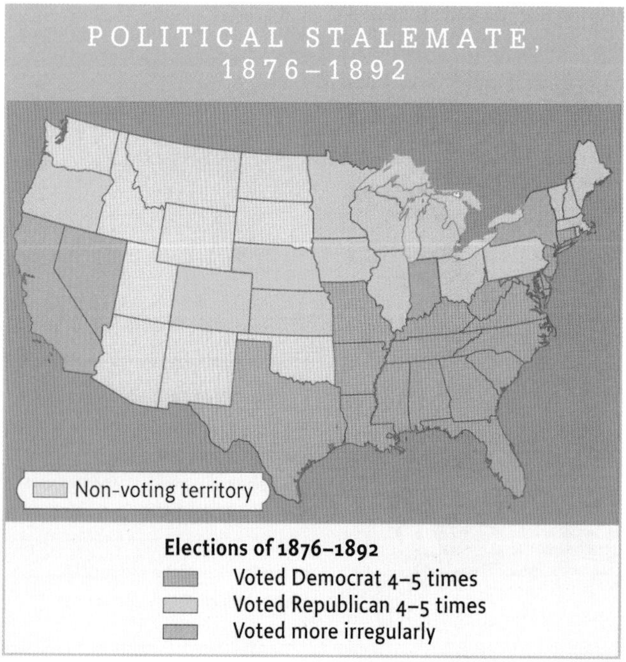

The Politics of Dead Center

In national elections, party politics bore the powerful imprint of the Civil War. Republicans controlled the industrial North and Midwest and the agrarian West and were particularly strong among members of revivalist churches, Protestant immigrants, and blacks. Organizations of Union veterans formed a bulwark of Republican support. Every Republican candidate for president from 1868 to 1900 except James G. Blaine had fought in the Union army. By 1893, a lavish system of pensions for Union soldiers and their widows and children consumed more than 40 percent of the federal budget. Democrats, after 1877, dominated the South and did well among Catholic voters, especially Irish-Americans, in the nation's cities.

The parties were closely divided. In three of the five presidential elections between 1876 and 1892, the margin separating the major candidates was less than 1 percent of the popular vote. Twice, in 1876 and 1888, the candidate with an electoral-college majority trailed in the popular ballot. Only for brief periods did the same party control the White House and both houses of Congress. More than once, Congress found itself paralyzed as important bills shuttled back and forth between House and Senate, and special sessions to complete legislation became necessary. Gilded Age presidents made little effort to mobilize public opinion or extend executive leadership.

In some ways, though, American democracy in the Gilded Age seemed remarkably healthy. Elections were closely contested, party loyalty was intense, and 80 percent or more of eligible voters turned out to cast ballots.

This political cartoon from the 1884 presidential campaign depicts Republican nominee James G. Blaine as a champion of a high tariff that would protect American workers from cheap foreign labor. Blaine's attire is a reference to a nominating speech at the 1876 Republican convention by Robert G. Ingersoll, who referred to the candidate as a "plumed knight."

Government and the Economy

The nation's political structure, however, proved ill equipped to deal with the problems created by the economy's rapid growth. Despite its expanded scope and powers arising from the Civil War, the federal government remained remarkably small by modern standards. The federal workforce in 1880 numbered 100,000 (today, it exceeds 2.5 million).

Nationally, both parties came under the control of powerful political managers with close ties to business interests. Republicans strongly supported a high tariff to protect American industry, and throughout the 1870s they pursued a fiscal policy based on reducing federal spending, repaying much of the national debt, and withdrawing greenbacks—the paper money issued by the Union during the Civil War—from circulation. Democrats opposed the high tariff, but the party's national leadership remained closely linked to New York bankers and financiers and resisted demands from debt-ridden agricultural areas for an increase in the money supply. In 1879, for the first time since the war, the United States returned to the **gold standard**—that is, paper currency became exchangeable for gold at a fixed rate.

Favoring easterners

Republican economic policies strongly favored the interests of eastern industrialists and bankers. These policies worked to the disadvantage of southern and western farmers, who had to pay a premium for manufactured goods while the prices they received for their produce steadily declined.

Reform Legislation

Civil Service Act of 1883

Gilded Age national politics did not entirely lack accomplishments. Inspired in part by President Garfield's assassination by a disappointed office seeker, the **Civil Service Act of 1883** created a merit system for federal employees, with appointment via competitive examinations rather than political influence. Although it applied at first to only 10 percent of government workers, the act marked the first step in establishing a professional civil service and removing officeholding from the hands of political machines. (However, since funds raised from political appointees had helped to finance the political parties, civil service reform had the unintended result of increasing politicians' dependence on donations from business interests.)

Regulating economic activity

In 1887, in response to public outcries against railroad practices, Congress established the **Interstate Commerce Commission** (ICC) to ensure that the rates railroads charged farmers and merchants to transport their goods were "reasonable" and did not offer more favorable treatment to some shippers. The ICC was the first federal agency intended to regulate economic activity, but since it lacked the power to establish rates on its own—it could only sue companies in court—it had little impact on railroad practices. Three years later, Congress passed the **Sherman Antitrust Act**, which banned all combinations and practices that restrained free trade. But the language was so vague that the act proved almost impossible to enforce. Weak as they were, these laws helped to establish the precedent that the national government could regulate the economy to promote the public good.

Political Conflict in the States

At the state and local levels, the Gilded Age was an era of political ferment and conflict over the proper uses of governmental authority. In the immediate aftermath of the Civil War, state governments in the North, like those in the Reconstruction South, greatly expanded their responsibility for public health, welfare, and education, and cities invested heavily in public works such as park construction and improved water and gas services.

Criticism of railroad companies

The policies of railroad companies produced a growing chorus of protest, especially in the West. Farmers and local merchants complained of excessively high freight rates, discrimination in favor of large producers and shippers, and high fees charged by railroad-controlled grain warehouses. Critics of the railroads came together in the Patrons of Husbandry, or Grange (1867), which moved to establish cooperatives for storing and marketing farm output in the hope of forcing the carriers "to take our produce at a fair price."

In the early twentieth century, reformers would turn to new ways of addressing the social conditions of freedom and new means of increasing ordinary Americans' political and economic liberty. But before this, in the 1890s, the nation would face its gravest crisis since the Civil War, and the boundaries of freedom would once again be redrawn.

CHAPTER REVIEW AND ONLINE RESOURCES

REVIEW QUESTIONS

1. *The American economy thrived because of federal involvement, not the lack of it. How did the federal government actively promote industrial and agricultural development in this period?*
2. *Why were railroads so important to America's second industrial revolution? What events demonstrate their influence on society and politics as well as the economy?*
3. *Why did organized efforts of farmers, workers, and local reformers largely fail to achieve substantive change in the Gilded Age?*
4. *How do the ideas of Henry George, Edward Bellamy, and other authors conflict with Social Darwinism?*
5. *How did social reformers such as Edward Bellamy, Henry George, and advocates of the Social Gospel movement conceive of liberty and freedom differently than the proponents of the liberty of contract ideal and laissez-faire?*
6. *In what ways did the West provide a "safety valve" for the problems in the industrial East? In what ways did it reveal some of the same problems?*
7. *Describe the involvement of American family farmers in the global economy after 1870 and its effects on their independence.*
8. *How did American political leaders seek to remake Native Americans and change the ways they lived?*
9. *What were some of the obstacles that made it difficult for Native Americans to claim American citizenship in the nineteenth century?*

KEY TERMS

trusts (p. 474)
vertical integration (p. 475)
horizontal expansion (p. 475)
robber barons (p. 476)
the Gilded Age (p. 478)
Social Darwinism (p. 479)
Great Railroad Strike (p. 481)
Knights of Labor (p. 482)
single tax (p. 483)
Social Gospel (p. 484)
Haymarket affair (p. 485)
bonanza farms (p. 489)
Battle of the Little Bighorn (p. 494)
Dawes Act (p. 494)
Ghost Dance (p. 496)
Wounded Knee massacre (p. 496)
gold standard (p. 503)
Civil Service Act of 1883 (p. 503)
Interstate Commerce Commission (p. 504)
Sherman Antitrust Act (p. 504)

Go to INQUIZITIVE

To see what you know—and learn what you've missed—with personalized feedback along the way.

Visit the ***Give Me Liberty!* Student Site** for primary source documents and images, interactive maps, author videos featuring Eric Foner, and more.

1867	Alaska purchased
1874	Woman's Christian Temperance Union founded
1879–1880	Kansas Exodus
1882	Chinese Exclusion Act
1883	*Civil Rights Cases*
1886	American Federation of Labor established
1890	National American Woman Suffrage Association organized
	Alfred T. Mahan's *The Influence of Sea Power upon History*
1892	Homestead Strike
	Populist Party organized
1893	Hawaii's Queen Liliuokalani overthrown
	Economic depression begins
1894	Coxey's Army marches to Washington
	Pullman Strike
	Immigration Restriction League established
1895	Booker T. Washington's Atlanta speech
1896	*Plessy v. Ferguson*
	The National Association of Colored Women established
1897	William McKinley inaugurated president
1898	Spanish-American War
1899–1903	Philippine War
1900	Gold Standard Act
1901–1904	Insular Cases

CHAPTER 17

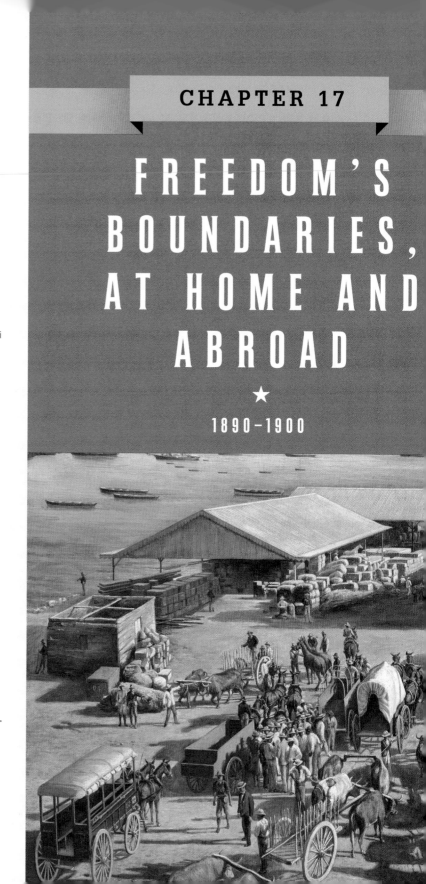

FREEDOM'S BOUNDARIES, AT HOME AND ABROAD

★

1890–1900

American Landing in Ponce, 1898, by the Spanish artist Manuel Cuyàs Agulló, depicts the seizure of one of the largest cities on Puerto Rico, a key moment in the conquest of the island during the Spanish-American War. American warships lie just offshore from the port.

One of the most popular songs of 1892 bore the title "Father Was Killed by a Pinkerton Man." It was inspired by an incident during a bitter strike at Andrew Carnegie's steelworks at Homestead, Pennsylvania, the nineteenth century's most widely publicized confrontation between labor and capital.

Homestead's twelve steel mills were the most profitable and technologically advanced in the world. The union contract gave the Amalgamated Association a considerable say in their operation, including the right to approve the hiring of new workers and to regulate the pace of work. In 1892, Carnegie and Henry Clay Frick, his local supervisor, decided to operate the plant on a nonunion basis. Henceforth, only workers who agreed not to join the union could work at Homestead. In response, the workers blockaded the steelworks and mobilized support from the local community. The battle memorialized in song took place on July 6, 1892, when armed strikers confronted 300 private policemen from the Pinkerton Detective Agency. Seven workers and three Pinkerton agents were killed, and the Pinkertons were forced to retreat. Four days later, the governor of Pennsylvania dispatched 8,000 militiamen to open the complex on management's terms. In the end, the Amalgamated Association was destroyed.

Homestead demonstrated that neither a powerful union nor public opinion could influence the conduct of the largest corporations. Moreover, two American ideas of freedom collided at Homestead—the employers' definition, based on the idea that property rights, unrestrained by union rules or public regulation, sustained the public good; and the workers' conception, which stressed economic security and independence from what they considered the "tyranny" of employers. During the 1890s, many Americans came to believe that they were being denied economic independence and democratic self-government, long central to the popular understanding of freedom.

Millions of farmers joined the Populist movement in an attempt to reverse their declining economic prospects and to rescue the government from what they saw as control by powerful corporate interests. The 1890s witnessed the imposition of a new racial system in the South that locked African-Americans into the status of second-class citizenship, denying them many of the freedoms white Americans took for granted. Increasing immigration produced heated debates over whether the country should reconsider its traditional self-definition as a refuge for foreigners seeking greater freedom on American shores. At the end of the 1890s, in the Spanish-American War, the United States for the first time acquired overseas possessions and found itself ruling over subject peoples from Puerto Rico to the Philippines. Was the democratic

FOCUS QUESTIONS

- *What were the origins and the significance of Populism?*
- *How did the liberties of blacks after 1877 give way to legal segregation across the South?*
- *In what ways did the boundaries of American freedom grow narrower in this period?*
- *How did the United States emerge as an imperial power in the 1890s?*

republic, many Americans wondered, becoming an empire like those of Europe? Rarely has the country experienced at one time so many debates over both the meaning and boundaries of freedom.

THE POPULIST CHALLENGE

The Farmers' Revolt

Lead-up to the Farmer's Alliance

Even as labor unrest crested, a different kind of uprising was ripening in the South and the trans-Mississippi West, a response to falling agricultural prices and growing economic dependency in rural areas. In the South, the sharecropping system, discussed in Chapter 15, locked millions of tenant farmers, white and black, into perpetual poverty. The interruption of cotton exports during the Civil War had led to the rapid expansion of production in India, Egypt, and Brazil. The glut of cotton on the world market when southern production resumed led to declining prices, throwing millions of small farmers deep into debt and threatening them with the loss of their land. In the West, farmers who had mortgaged their property to purchase seed, fertilizer, and equipment faced the prospect of losing their farms when unable to repay their bank loans. Farmers increasingly believed that their plight derived from the high freight rates charged by railroad companies, excessive interest rates for loans from merchants and bankers, and the fiscal policies of the federal government (discussed in the previous chapter) that reduced the supply of money and helped to push down farm prices.

Through the Farmers' Alliance, the largest citizens' movement of the nineteenth century, farmers sought to remedy their condition. Founded in Texas in the late 1870s, the Alliance spread to forty-three states by 1890. The Alliance proposed that the federal government establish warehouses where farmers could store their crops until they were sold. Using the crops as collateral, the government would then issue loans to farmers at low interest rates, thereby ending their dependence on bankers and merchants. Since it would have to be enacted by Congress, the "subtreasury plan," as this proposal was called, led the Alliance into politics.

In the most violent encounter of the Homestead strike of 1892, strikers took part in a day-long battle with 300 private policemen from the Pinkerton Detective Agency, eventually setting fire to the agents' barge. The Pinkertons surrendered, but Andrew Carnegie succeeded in crushing the strikers and their union, the Amalgamated Association.

The People's Party

In the early 1890s, the Alliance evolved into the People's Party (or **Populists**), the era's greatest political insurgency. Attempting to speak for all "producing classes," the party did not just appeal to farmers. It achieved some of its greatest successes in states like Colorado and Idaho, where it won the support of miners and industrial workers. But its major base lay in the cotton and wheat belts of the South and West.

Populist organizing

The Populists embarked on a remarkable effort of community organization and education. To spread their message they published numerous pamphlets on political and economic questions, established more than 1,000 local newspapers, and sent traveling speakers throughout rural America. At great gatherings on the western plains, similar in some ways to religious revival meetings, and in small-town southern country stores, one observer wrote, "people commenced to think who had never thought before, and people talked who had seldom spoken." Here was the last great political expression of the nineteenth-century vision of America as a commonwealth of small producers whose freedom rested on the ownership of productive property and respect for the dignity of labor.

The Populist message

But although the Populists used the familiar language of nineteenth-century radicalism, they were hardly a backward-looking movement. They embraced the modern technologies that made large-scale cooperative enterprise possible—the railroad, the telegraph, and the national market—while looking to the federal government to regulate those technologies in the public interest. They promoted agricultural education and believed farmers should adopt modern scientific methods of cultivation.

The Populist Platform

The Populist platform of 1892, adopted at the party's Omaha convention, remains a classic document of American reform. Written by Ignatius Donnelly, a Minnesota editor, it spoke of a nation "brought to the verge of moral, political, and material ruin" by political corruption and economic inequality. The platform put forth a long list of proposals to restore democracy and economic opportunity, many of which would be adopted during the next half-century: the direct election of U.S. senators, government control of the currency, a graduated income tax, a system of low-cost public financing to enable farmers to market their crops, and recognition of the right of workers to form labor unions. In addition, Populists called for public ownership of the railroads to guarantee farmers inexpensive access to

A group of Kansas Populists, perhaps on their way to a political gathering, in a photograph from the 1890s.

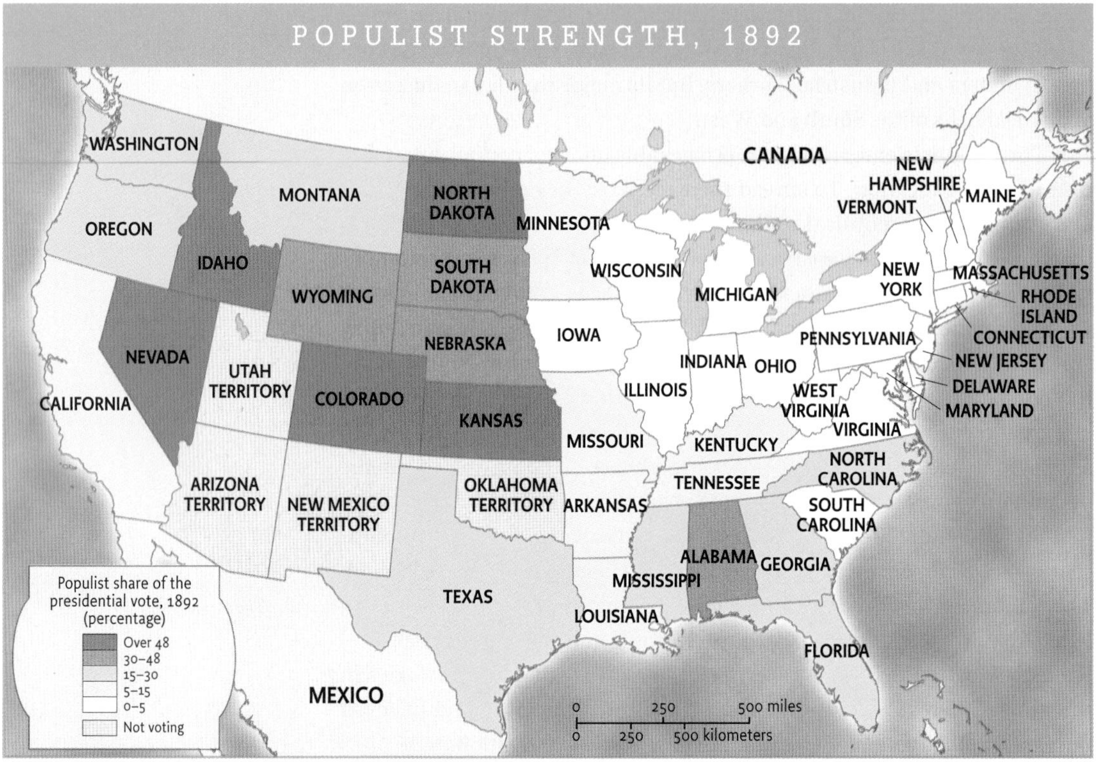

markets. A generation would pass before a major party offered so sweeping a plan for political action to create the social conditions of freedom.

The Populist Coalition

Populism and race

In some southern states, the Populists made remarkable efforts to unite black and white small farmers on a common political and economic program. In general, southern white Populists' racial attitudes did not differ significantly from those of their non-Populist neighbors. Nonetheless, recognizing the need for allies to break the Democratic Party's stranglehold on power in the South, some white Populists insisted that black and white farmers shared common grievances and could unite for common goals. Tom Watson, Georgia's leading Populist, worked the hardest to forge a black-white alliance. "You are kept apart," he told interracial audiences, "that you may be separately fleeced of your earnings." While many blacks refused to abandon the party of Lincoln, others were attracted by the Populist appeal. In most of the South, however, Democrats fended off the Populist challenge by resorting to the tactics they had used to retain power since the 1870s—mobilizing whites with warnings about "Negro supremacy," intimidating black voters, and stuffing ballot boxes on election day.

The Populist movement also engaged the energies of thousands of reform-minded women from farm and labor backgrounds. Some, like Mary Elizabeth Lease, a former homesteader and one of the first female lawyers in Kansas, became prominent organizers, campaigners, and strategists. During the 1890s, referendums in Colorado and Idaho approved extending the vote to women, whereas in Kansas and California the proposal went down in defeat. Populists in all these states endorsed woman suffrage.

Populist presidential candidate James Weaver received more than 1 million votes in 1892. The party carried five western states. In his inaugural address in 1893, Lorenzo Lewelling, the new Populist governor of Kansas, anticipated a phrase made famous seventy years later by Martin Luther King Jr.: "I have a dream. . . . A time is foreshadowed when . . . liberty, equality, and justice shall have permanent abiding places in the republic."

Most Populists in the West supported woman suffrage. In this cartoon published in a Colorado Populist newspaper on July 4, 1894, a man and a woman celebrate the passage of a referendum giving women the right to vote in that state.

The Government and Labor

Were the Populists on the verge of replacing one of the two major parties? The severe depression that began in 1893 led to increased conflict between capital and labor and seemed to create an opportunity for expanding the Populist vote. Time and again, employers brought state or federal authority to bear to protect their own economic power or put down threats to public order. In May 1894, the federal government deployed soldiers to disperse **Coxey's Army**—a band of several hundred unemployed men led by Ohio businessman Jacob Coxey, who marched to Washington demanding economic relief.

The Pullman Strike

Also in 1894, workers in the company-owned town of Pullman, Illinois, where railroad sleeping cars were manufactured, called a strike to protest a reduction in wages. The American Railway Union announced that its members would refuse to handle trains with Pullman cars. When the boycott crippled national rail service, President Grover Cleveland's attorney general, Richard Olney (himself on the board of several railroad companies), obtained a federal court injunction ordering the strikers back to work. Federal troops and U.S. marshals soon occupied railroad centers like Chicago and Sacramento.

Eugene Debs

The strike collapsed when the union's leaders, including its charismatic president, Eugene V. Debs, were jailed for contempt of court for violating the judicial order. In the case of *In re Debs*, the Supreme Court unanimously confirmed the sentences and approved the use of injunctions against striking labor unions. On his release from prison in November 1895, more than 100,000 persons greeted Debs at a Chicago railroad depot.

Federal troops pose atop a railroad engine after being sent to Chicago to help suppress the Pullman Strike of 1894.

Populism and Labor

In 1894, Populists made determined efforts to appeal to industrial workers. Governor Davis Waite of Colorado, who had edited a labor newspaper before his election, sent the militia to protect striking miners against company police. In the state and congressional elections of that year, as the economic depression deepened, voters by the millions abandoned the Democratic Party of President Cleveland.

Labor votes

In rural areas, the Populist vote increased in 1894. But urban workers did not rally to the Populists, whose core issues—the subtreasury plan and lower mortgage interest rates—had little meaning for them. Urban working-class voters instead shifted en masse to the Republicans, who claimed that raising tariff rates (which Democrats had recently reduced) would restore prosperity by protecting manufacturers and industrial workers from the competition of imported goods and cheap foreign labor. In one of the most decisive shifts in congressional power in American history, the Republicans gained 117 seats in the House of Representatives.

Bryan and Free Silver

"Cross of gold" speech

In 1896, Democrats and Populists joined to support William Jennings Bryan for the presidency. A thirty-six-year-old congressman from Nebraska, Bryan won the Democratic nomination after delivering to the national convention an electrifying speech that crystallized the farmers' pride and grievances. "Burn down your cities and leave our farms," Bryan proclaimed, "and your cities will spring up again as if by magic; but destroy our farms and grass will grow in the streets of every city in the country." Bryan called for the "free coinage" of silver—the unrestricted minting of silver money. In language ringing with biblical imagery, Bryan condemned the gold standard: "You shall not crucify mankind upon a cross of gold."

Bryan's demand for "free silver" was the latest expression of the view that increasing the amount of currency in circulation would raise the prices farmers received for their crops and make it easier to pay off their debts. His nomination wrested control of the Democratic Party from long-dominant leaders like President Grover Cleveland who were closely tied to eastern businessmen.

There was more to Bryan's appeal, however, than simply free silver. A devoutly religious man, he was strongly influenced by the Social Gospel movement (discussed in the previous chapter). He championed a vision of the government helping ordinary Americans that anticipated provisions of the New Deal of the 1930s, including a progressive income tax, banking regulation, and the right of workers to form unions. Bryan also broke with tradition and embarked on a nationwide speaking tour, seeking to rally farmers and workers to his cause.

A cartoon from the magazine *Judge*, September 14, 1896, condemns William Jennings Bryan and his "cross of gold" speech for defiling the symbols of Christianity. Bryan tramples on the Bible while holding his golden cross; a vandalized church is visible in the background.

The Campaign of 1896

Republicans met the silverite challenge head on, insisting that gold was the only "honest" currency. Abandoning the gold standard, they insisted, would destroy business confidence and prevent recovery from the depression by making creditors unwilling to extend loans, because they could not be certain of the value of the money in which they would be repaid. The party nominated for president Ohio governor William McKinley, who as a congressman in 1890 had shepherded to passage the strongly protectionist McKinley Tariff.

The election of 1896 is sometimes called the first modern presidential campaign because of the amount of money spent by the Republicans and the efficiency of their national organization. Eastern bankers and industrialists, thoroughly alarmed by Bryan's call for monetary inflation and his fiery speeches denouncing corporate arrogance, poured millions of dollars into Republican coffers. (McKinley's campaign raised some $10 million; Bryan's around $300,000.) While McKinley remained at his Ohio home, his political manager Mark Hanna created a powerful national machine that flooded the country with pamphlets, posters, and campaign buttons.

Campaign financing

The results revealed a nation as divided along regional lines as in 1860. Bryan carried the South and West and received 6.5 million

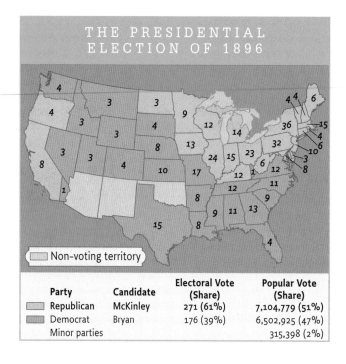

THE PRESIDENTIAL ELECTION OF 1896

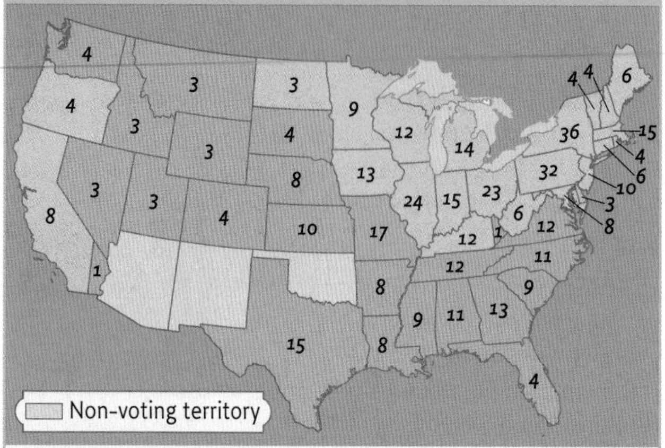

Party	Candidate	Electoral Vote (Share)	Popular Vote (Share)
Republican	McKinley	271 (61%)	7,104,779 (51%)
Democrat	Bryan	176 (39%)	6,502,925 (47%)
Minor parties			315,398 (2%)

votes. McKinley swept the more populous industrial states of the Northeast and Midwest, attracting 7.1 million. Industrial America, from financiers and managers to workers, now voted solidly Republican, a loyalty reinforced when prosperity returned after 1897.

McKinley's victory shattered the political stalemate that had persisted since 1876 and created one of the most enduring political majorities in American history. During McKinley's presidency, Republicans placed their stamp on economic policy by passing the Dingley Tariff of 1897, raising rates to the highest level in history, and the Gold Standard Act of 1900. Not until 1932, in the midst of another economic depression, would the Democrats become the nation's majority party.

THE SEGREGATED SOUTH

The Redeemers in Power

Undoing Reconstruction

The failure of Populism in the South opened the door for the full imposition of a new racial order. The coalition of merchants, planters, and business entrepreneurs who dominated the region's politics after 1877, who called themselves Redeemers, had moved to undo as much as possible of Reconstruction. Hardest hit were the new public school systems. Louisiana spent so little on education that it became the only state in the Union in which the percentage of whites unable to read and write actually increased between 1880 and 1900. Black schools, however, suffered the most, as the gap between expenditures for black and white pupils widened steadily.

Convict labor

New laws authorized the arrest of virtually any person without employment and greatly increased the penalties for petty crimes. As the South's prison population rose, the renting out of convicts became a profitable business. Every southern state placed at least a portion of its convicted criminals, the majority of them blacks imprisoned for minor offenses, in the hands of private businessmen. Railroads, mines, and lumber companies competed for this new form of cheap, involuntary labor. Conditions in labor camps were often barbaric, with disease rife and the death rates high. "One dies, get another" was the motto of the system's architects.

A group of Florida convict laborers. Southern states notoriously used convicts for public labor or leased them out to work in dire conditions for private employers.

The Failure of the New South Dream

During the 1880s, Atlanta editor Henry Grady tirelessly promoted the promise of a **New South**, an era of prosperity based on industrial expansion and agricultural diversification. In fact, while planters, merchants, and industrialists prospered, the region as a whole sank deeper and deeper into poverty. Some industry did develop, such as new upcountry cotton factories that offered jobs to entire families of poor whites from the surrounding countryside. But since the main attractions for investors were the South's low wages and taxes and the availability of convict labor, these enterprises made little contribution to regional economic development. With the exception of Birmingham, Alabama, which by 1900 had developed into an important center for the manufacture of iron and steel, southern cities were mainly export centers for cotton, tobacco, and rice, with little industry or skilled labor. Overall, the region remained dependent on the North for capital and manufactured goods. As late as the 1930s, President Franklin D. Roosevelt would declare the South the nation's "number one" economic problem.

Black Life in the South

As the most disadvantaged rural southerners, black farmers suffered the most from the region's condition. In the Upper South, economic development offered some opportunities—mines, iron furnaces, and tobacco factories employed black laborers, and a good number of black farmers managed to acquire land. In the rice kingdom of coastal South Carolina and Georgia, most of the great plantations had fallen to pieces by the turn of the century, and many blacks acquired land and took up self-sufficient farming. In most of the Lower South, however, African-Americans owned a smaller percentage of land in 1900 than they had at the end of Reconstruction.

In southern cities, the network of institutions created after the Civil War—schools and colleges, churches, businesses, women's clubs, and the like—served as the foundation for increasingly diverse black urban communities. They supported the growth of a black middle class, mostly professionals like teachers and physicians,

Coal miners, in a photograph by Lewis Hine. Mining was one occupation in which blacks and whites often worked side by side.

or businessmen like undertakers and shopkeepers serving the needs of black customers. But the labor market was rigidly divided along racial lines. Black men were excluded from supervisory positions in factories and workshops and white-collar jobs such as clerks in offices. A higher percentage of black women than white worked for wages, but mainly as domestic servants. In most occupations, the few unions that existed in the South excluded blacks, forming yet another barrier to their economic advancement.

The Kansas Exodus

Emigration from the South

Trapped at the bottom of a stagnant economy, some blacks sought a way out through emigration from the South. In 1879 and 1880, an estimated 40,000 to 60,000 African-Americans migrated to Kansas, seeking political equality, freedom from violence, access to education, and economic opportunity. Those promoting the **Kansas Exodus**, including former fugitive slave Benjamin "Pap" Singleton, the organizer of a real estate company, distributed flyers and lithographs picturing Kansas as an idyllic land of rural plenty. Lacking the capital to take up farming, however, most black migrants ended up as unskilled laborers in towns and cities. But few chose to return to the South. In the words of one minister active in the movement, "We had rather suffer and be free."

Despite deteriorating prospects in the South, most African-Americans had little alternative but to stay in the region. The real expansion of job opportunities was taking place in northern cities. But most northern employers refused to offer jobs to blacks in the expanding industrial economy, preferring to hire white migrants from rural areas and immigrants from Europe.

A photograph of townspeople in Nicodemus, a community established by members of the 1879–1880 "Exodus" of southern African-Americans to Kansas.

The Transformation of Black Politics

Neither black voting nor black officeholding came to an abrupt end in 1877. A few blacks even served in Congress in the 1880s and 1890s. Nonetheless, political opportunities became more and more restricted. Not until the 1990s would the number of black legislators in the South approach the level seen during Reconstruction.

With black men of talent and ambition turning away from politics, the banner of political leadership passed to black women activists. The National Association of Colored Women, founded in 1896, brought together local and regional women's clubs to press for both women's rights and racial uplift. They aided poor families, offered lessons in home life and childrearing, and battled gambling and drinking in black communities. By insisting on the right of black women to be considered as "respectable" as their white counterparts, the women reformers challenged the racial ideology that consigned all blacks to the status of degraded second-class citizens.

Booker T. Washington, advocate of industrial education and economic self-help.

The Emergence of Booker T. Washington

The changing currents of black politics were symbolized by the juxtaposition, in 1895, of the death of Frederick Douglass with Booker T. Washington's widely praised speech, titled the "**Atlanta Compromise**," at the Atlanta Cotton Exposition that urged blacks to abandon agitation for civil and political rights. Born a slave in 1856, Washington had studied as a young man at Hampton Institute, Virginia. He adopted the outlook of Hampton's founder, General Samuel Armstrong, who emphasized that obtaining farms or skilled jobs was far more important to African-Americans emerging from slavery than the rights of citizenship. Washington put this view into practice when he became head of Tuskegee Institute in Alabama, a center for vocational education (education focused on training for a job rather than broad learning).

Tuskegee Institute

In his Atlanta speech, Washington repudiated the abolitionist tradition that stressed ceaseless agitation for full equality. He urged blacks not to try to combat segregation: "In all the things that are purely social we can be as separate as the fingers, yet one as the hand in all things essential to mutual progress." Washington advised his people to seek the assistance of white employers who, in a land racked by labor turmoil, would prefer a docile, dependable black labor force to unionized whites. Washington's ascendancy rested in large part on his success in channeling aid from wealthy northern whites to Tuskegee and to black politicians and newspapers who backed his program. But his support in the black community also arose from a widespread sense that in the world of the late nineteenth century, frontal assaults on white power were impossible and that blacks should concentrate on building up their segregated communities.

Washington's Atlanta speech

The Elimination of Black Voting

For nearly a generation after the end of Reconstruction, despite fraud and violence, black southerners continued to cast ballots in large numbers. In some states, such as Virginia, Tennessee, Arkansas, and North Carolina, the Republican Party remained competitive and formed biracial political coalitions that challenged Democratic Party rule. Despite the limits of these alliances, especially those involving the Populists, the threat of a biracial political insurgency frightened the ruling Democrats and contributed greatly to the disenfranchisement movement.

Between 1890 and 1906, every southern state enacted laws or constitutional provisions meant to eliminate the black vote. Since the Fifteenth Amendment prohibited the use of race as a qualification for the suffrage, how were such measures even possible? Southern legislatures drafted laws that on paper appeared color-blind but that were actually designed to end black voting. The most popular devices were the poll tax (a fee that each citizen had to pay in order to retain the right to vote), literacy tests, and the requirement that a prospective voter demonstrate to election officials an "understanding" of the state constitution. Six southern states also adopted a **grandfather clause**, exempting from the new requirements descendants of persons eligible to vote before the Civil War (when only whites, of course, could cast ballots in the South). The racial intent of the grandfather clause was so clear that the Supreme Court in 1915 invalidated such laws for violating the Fifteenth Amendment. The other methods of limiting black voting, however, remained on the books.

Poll tax

Although election officials often allowed whites who did not meet the new qualifications to register, numerous poor and illiterate whites also lost the right to vote, a result welcomed by many planters and urban reformers. Louisiana, for example, reduced the number of blacks registered to vote from 130,000 in 1894 to 1,342 a decade later. But 80,000 white voters also lost the right. **Disenfranchisement** led directly to the rise of a generation of southern demagogues, who mobilized white voters by extreme appeals to racism.

Scope of disenfranchisement

As late as 1940, only 3 percent of adult black southerners were registered to vote. The elimination of black and many white voters, which reversed the nineteenth-century trend toward more inclusive suffrage, could not have been accomplished without the acquiescence of the North and the Supreme Court, both of which gave their approval to disenfranchisement laws, in clear violation of the Fifteenth Amendment. As a result, southern congressmen wielded far greater power on the national scene than their tiny electorates warranted.

The Supreme Court's approval of disenfranchisement

The Law of Segregation

Along with disenfranchisement, the 1890s saw the widespread imposition of segregation in the South. Laws and local customs requiring the separation of the races had numerous precedents. They had existed in many parts of the pre–Civil War North. Southern schools and many other institutions had been segregated during Reconstruction. In the 1880s, however, southern race relations remained unsettled. Some railroads, theaters, and hotels admitted blacks and whites on an equal basis while others separated them by race or excluded blacks altogether.

The black educator Mary McLeod Bethune with girls from the school she established in Florida in a photograph from around 1905.

In 1883, in the *Civil Rights Cases*, the Supreme Court invalidated the Civil Rights Act of 1875, which had outlawed racial discrimination by hotels, theaters, railroads, and other public facilities. In 1896, in the landmark decision in ***Plessy v. Ferguson***, the Court gave its approval to state laws requiring separate facilities for blacks and whites. The case arose in Louisiana, where the legislature had required railroad companies to maintain a separate car or section for black passengers. In a 7–1 decision, the Court upheld the Louisiana law, arguing that segregated facilities did not discriminate so long as they were "**separate but equal**." The lone dissenter, John Marshall Harlan, reprimanded the majority with an oft-quoted comment: "Our constitution is color-blind." Segregation, he insisted, violated the principle of equal liberty. To Harlan, freedom for the former slaves meant the right to participate fully and equally in American society.

As Harlan predicted, states reacted to the *Plessy* decision by passing laws mandating racial segregation in every aspect of southern life, from schools to hospitals, waiting rooms, toilets, and cemeteries. Some states forbade taxi drivers to carry members of different races at the same time.

In *Plessy v. Ferguson* (1896), the U.S. Supreme Court ruled that laws establishing racial segregation did not violate the equal protection clause of the Fourteenth Amendment so long as facilities were "separate but equal." In fact, this was almost never the case, as illustrated by these photographs of the elementary schools for black and white children in South Boston, Virginia, in the early twentieth century.

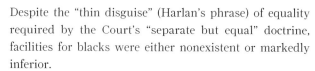

TABLE 17.1 States with Over 200 Lynchings, 1889–1918

STATE	NUMBER OF LYNCHINGS
Georgia	386
Mississippi	373
Texas	335
Louisiana	313
Alabama	276
Arkansas	214

Despite the "thin disguise" (Harlan's phrase) of equality required by the Court's "separate but equal" doctrine, facilities for blacks were either nonexistent or markedly inferior.

More than a form of racial separation, segregation was one part of an all-encompassing system of white domination, in which each component—disenfranchisement, unequal economic status, inferior education—reinforced the others.

Segregation affected other groups as well as blacks. In some parts of Mississippi where Chinese laborers had been brought in to work the fields after the Civil War, three separate school systems—white, black, and Chinese—were established. In California, black, Hispanic, and American Indian children were frequently educated alongside whites, but state law required separate schools for those of "mongolian or Chinese descent." In Texas and California, although Mexicans were legally considered "white," they found themselves barred from many restaurants, places of entertainment, and other public facilities.

The Rise of Lynching

Those blacks who sought to challenge the system faced not only overwhelming political and legal power but also the threat of violent reprisal. In every year between 1883 and 1905, more than fifty persons, the vast majority of them black men, were lynched in the South—that is, murdered by a mob. **Lynching** continued well into the twentieth century. By mid-century, the total number of victims since 1880 had reached over 4,000. Some lynchings occurred secretly at night; others were advertised in advance and attracted large crowds of onlookers. Mobs engaged in activities that shocked the civilized world. In 1899, Sam Hose, a plantation laborer who killed his employer in self-defense, was brutally murdered near Newman, Georgia, before 2,000 onlookers, some of whom arrived on a special excursion train from Atlanta. A crowd including young children watched as his executioners cut off Hose's ears, fingers, and genitals, burned him alive, and then fought over pieces of his bones as souvenirs.

Like many victims of lynchings, Hose was accused after his death of having raped a white woman. Yet in nearly all cases, as activist Ida B. Wells argued in a newspaper editorial after a Memphis lynching in 1892, the charge of rape was a "bare lie." Born a slave in Mississippi

A crowd at the aftermath of the lynching of Laura Nelson and her teenage son L. D. Nelson, African-American residents of Okemah, Oklahoma, in 1911. They were accused of shooting to death a deputy sheriff who had come to the Nelson home to investigate the theft of livestock. A week after being lodged in jail, they were removed by a mob and taken to the bridge. Members of the mob raped Mrs. Nelson before the lynching. The photograph was reproduced as a postcard and sold at local stores. As in most lynchings, no one was prosecuted for the crime.

in 1862, Wells had become a schoolteacher and editor. Her essay condemning the lynching of three black men in Memphis led a mob to destroy her newspaper, the *Memphis Free Press*, while she was out of the city. Wells moved to the North, where she became the nation's leading antilynching crusader. She bluntly insisted that given the conditions of southern blacks, the United States had no right to call itself the "land of the free."

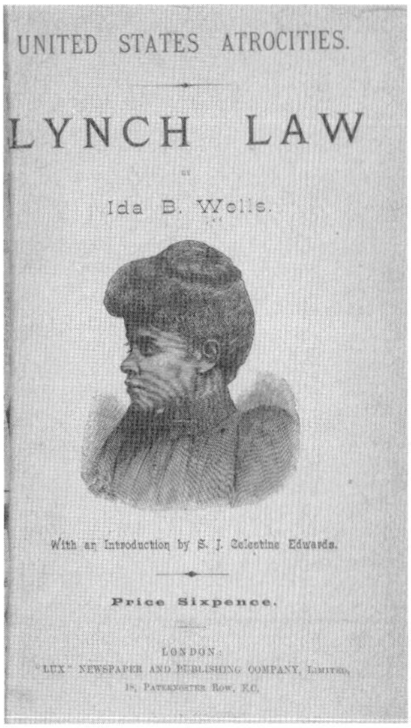
UNITED STATES ATROCITIES.

LYNCH LAW

BY

Ida B. Wells.

With an Introduction by S. J. Celestine Edwards.

Price Sixpence.

LONDON:
"LUX" NEWSPAPER AND PUBLISHING COMPANY, LIMITED,
PATERNOSTER ROW, E.C.

The title page of *Lynch Law*, in which the journalist and lecturer Ida B. Wells exposed the horror of lynching and demonstrated that the justification for murders conducted by southern white mobs—that the black male victims had sexually assaulted white women—was a myth.

Politics, Religion, and Memory

As the white North and South moved toward reconciliation in the 1880s and 1890s, one cost was the abandonment of the dream of racial equality written into the laws and Constitution during Reconstruction. In popular literature and memoirs by participants, at veterans' reunions and in public memorials, the Civil War came to be remembered as a tragic family quarrel among white Americans in which blacks had played no significant part. It was a war of "brother against brother" in which both sides fought gallantly for noble causes—local rights on the part of the South, preservation of the Union for the North. Slavery increasingly came to be viewed as a minor issue, not the war's fundamental cause, and Reconstruction as a regrettable period of "Negro rule."

At the same time as they reduced blacks to second-class citizenship, southern governments erected monuments to **the Lost Cause**, a romanticized version of slavery, the Old South, and the Confederate experience. Religion offered a way for white southerners to come to terms with defeat in the Civil War without abandoning white supremacy. The death of the Confederacy, in many sermons, was equated with the death of Christ, who gave his life for the sins of mankind. Southern churches played a key role in keeping the values of the Old South alive by refusing to reunite with northern counterparts. In the 1840s, the Methodist and Baptist churches had divided into northern and southern branches. Methodists would not reunite until well into the twentieth century; Baptists have yet to do so.

This carving by an unknown southerner from around 1875 juxtaposes Robert E. Lee and the crucified Christ, illustrating the strong religious overtones in the ideology of the Lost Cause.

REDRAWING THE BOUNDARIES

As the nineteenth century drew to a close, American society seemed to be fracturing along lines of both class and race. The result, commented economist Simon Patten, was a widespread obsession with redrawing the boundary of freedom by identifying and excluding those unworthy of the blessings of liberty. "The South," he wrote, "has its negro, the city has its

VOICES OF FREEDOM

From Ida B. Wells, "Lynch Law in All Its Phases" (1893)

After being driven from Memphis because of her outspoken opposition to lynching, Ida B. Wells campaigned to awaken the public to racial terrorism. This is an excerpt from a speech she delivered in Boston in 1893.

I am before the American people today through no inclination of my own, but because of a deep-seated conviction that the country at large does not know the extent to which lynch law prevails in parts of the republic. . . .

Although the impression has gone abroad that most of the lynchings take place because of assaults on white women only one-third of the number lynched in the past ten years have been charged with that offense, to say nothing of those who were not guilty of the charge. . . . But the unsupported word of any white person for any cause is sufficient to cause a lynching. . . . Governors of states and officers of the law stand by and see the work well done.

And yet this Christian nation, the flower of the nineteenth century civilization, says it can do nothing to stop this inhuman slaughter. The general government is willingly powerless to send troops to protect the lives of its black citizens. . . . The lawlessness which has been here described is like unto that which prevailed under slavery. The very same forces are at work now as then. [They] can be traced to the very first year Lee's conquered veterans marched from Appomattox to their homes in the southland. They were conquered in war, but not in spirit. They believed as firmly as ever that it was their right to rule black men and dictate to the national government. . . . All their laws are shaped to this end—school laws, railroad car regulations . . . every device is adopted to make slaves of free men—The rule of the mob is absolute. . . .

Do you ask the remedy? A public sentiment strong against lawlessness must be aroused [to demand] that equal and exact justice be accorded to every citizen of whatever race, who finds a home within the borders of the land of the free and the home of the brave.

From W. E. B. Du Bois, *The Souls of Black Folk* (1903)

Like Wells, the black educator and activist W. E. B. Du Bois demanded equal treatment for black Americans. In *The Souls of Black Folk*, he sought to revive the tradition of agitation for basic civil, political, and educational rights, and for recognition of blacks as full members of American society.

The silently growing assumption of this age is that . . . the backward races of to-day are of proven inefficiency and not worth the saving. Such an assumption is the arrogance of peoples irreverent toward time and ignorant of the deeds of men. A thousand years ago such an assumption, easily possible, would have made it difficult for the Teuton to prove his right to life. Two thousand years ago such dogmatism, readily welcome, would have [refuted] the idea of blond races ever leading civilization. . . .

Your country? How came it yours? Before the Pilgrims landed we were here. Here we have brought our three gifts and mingled them with yours: a gift of story and song—soft, stirring melody in an ill-harmonized and unmelodious land; the gift of sweat and brawn to beat back the wilderness, conquer the soil, and lay the foundations of this vast economic empire two hundred years earlier than your weak hands could have done it; the third, a gift of the Spirit. Around us the history of the land has centered for thrice a hundred years. . . . Actively we have woven ourselves with the very warp and woof of this nation,—we fought their battles, shared their sorrow, mingled our blood with theirs, and generation after generation have pleaded with a headstrong, careless people to despise not Justice, Mercy, and Truth, lest the nation be smitten with a curse. Our song, our toil, our cheer, and warning have been given to this nation in blood-brotherhood. Are not these gifts worth the giving? Is not this work and striving? Would America have been America without her Negro people?

QUESTIONS

1. *Whom does Wells blame for lynching?*
2. *In what ways does Du Bois criticize and in what ways does he seem to embrace the idea of inborn racial characteristics and abilities?*
3. *How do Wells and Du Bois appeal to history to bolster their claims?*

slums. . . . The friends of American institutions fear the ignorant immigrant, and the workingman dislikes the Chinese."

The New Immigration and the New Nativism

Southern and eastern Europe

The 1890s witnessed a major shift in the sources of immigration to the United States. Despite the prolonged depression, 3.5 million newcomers entered the United States during the decade, seeking jobs in the industrial centers of the North and Midwest. Over half arrived not from Ireland, England, Germany, and Scandinavia, the traditional sources of immigration, but from southern and eastern Europe, especially Italy and the Russian and Austro-Hungarian empires. The **new immigrants** were widely described by native-born Americans as members of distinct "races," whose lower level of civilization explained everything from their willingness to work for substandard wages to their supposed inborn tendency toward criminal behavior.

Immigration Restriction

The new immigration helped to trigger a resurgence of racial nationalism in the United States and elsewhere in the world. Talk of "race suicide" abounded as critics of immigration warned about the declining birth rate among native-born "Anglo-Saxon" women. Many Americans who felt aggrieved because of economic changes sought to re-create a sense of belonging, juxtaposing "our" identity against people deemed "other" because of color, religion, political views, or some other characteristic. Restricting immigration was widely seen as a way to determine who was fit to be an American and thus to upgrade the "quality" of the population.

A cartoon from the magazine *Judge*, entitled *The High Tide*, illustrates anti-immigrant sentiment. A tide of newcomers representing the criminal element of other countries washes up on American shores, to the consternation of Uncle Sam. The words on their hats list undesirable immigrants, including criminals, paupers, and anarchists.

Founded in 1894 by a group of Boston professionals, the **Immigration Restriction League** spread rapidly across the country. It made a sharp distinction between "old" and "new" immigrants and, echoing the Know-Nothings of the 1850s, blamed the latter for problems ranging from urban crime and poverty to mass unemployment. The League insisted that newcomers from southern and eastern Europe were incapable of taking part intelligently in democratic politics, and called for reducing immigration by barring the illiterate from entering the United States. Such a measure was adopted by

Congress early in 1897 but vetoed by President Grover Cleveland shortly before he left office. A law of 1903 did bar a long list of persons from entering the United States, among them "idiots, insane persons, epileptics, . . . [and] paupers," as well as anarchists, the first time those holding a specific political viewpoint view were denied the right to immigrate. And with the enactment of measures to exclude the Chinese, the United States pioneered the development of a racialized immigration policy.

A cartoon from *Puck*, March 29, 1882, shortly before President Chester A. Arthur signed the Chinese Exclusion Act, shows European immigrants and blacks constructing a wall to keep out the Chinese. They are motivated by racism, jealousy, and fear of labor competition. In the background, American ships, demanding an "open door" for U.S. goods exported to China, have breached that country's wall restricting commerce. Nearly a century and a half later, President Donald Trump's effort to build an actual wall along the U.S.–Mexico border would inspire bitter debate.

Northern and western states, like those in the South, experimented with ways to eliminate "undesirable" voters. Nearly all the states during the 1890s adopted the secret or "Australian" ballot, meant both to protect voters' privacy and to limit the participation of illiterates (who could no longer receive help from party officials at polling places). Several states ended the practice of allowing immigrants to vote before becoming citizens, and adopted stringent new residency and literacy requirements. None of these measures approached the scope of black disenfranchisement in the South, or the continued denial of voting rights to women in nearly all the states. But throughout the country, suffrage was increasingly becoming a privilege, not a right.

Chinese Exclusion and Chinese Rights

The boundaries of nationhood, expanded so dramatically in the aftermath of the Civil War, slowly contracted. Leaders of both parties expressed vicious opinions regarding immigrants from China—they were "odious, abominable, dangerous, revolting," declared Republican leader James G. Blaine.

Beginning in 1882 with the **Chinese Exclusion Act**, Congress temporarily excluded all immigrants from China from entering the country. Although non-whites had long been barred from becoming naturalized citizens, this was the first time that race had been used to exclude from the country an entire group of people. Congress renewed the restriction ten years later and made it permanent in 1902. Chinese in the United States were required to register with the government and carry identification papers or face deportation. Indeed, the use of photographs for personal identification first came into widespread use as a means of enforcing Chinese exclusion. One Chinese activist complained that the photos, which bore a striking resemblance

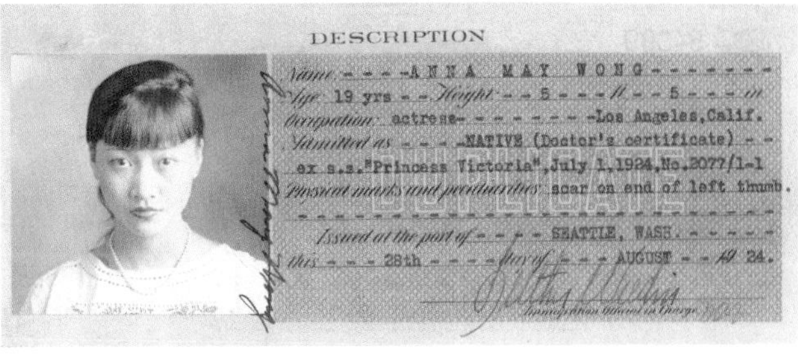

Beginning in 1909, as part of the enforcement of Chinese exclusion, all Chinese in the United States were required to carry a government-issued certificate, the first widespread use of photographs as proof of identity. This certificate, issued in 1924, belonged to Anna May Wong, an American-born movie star.

A group of Chinese-Americans in Golden Gate Park, San Francisco, in a photograph taken in the 1890s.

to "mug shots" of persons under arrest, criminalized people "innocent of any crime" and created a "national rogues' gallery" of Chinese residents. In 2012, Congress passed a Resolution of Regret apologizing for the exclusion laws and acknowledging their role in exacerbating racial discrimination. It was sponsored by Judy Chu, a Chinese-American member of the House of Representatives from California.

By 1930, because of exclusion, the number of Chinese had declined to 75,000. On the West Coast, the Chinese suffered intense discrimination and periodic mob violence. In the late-nineteenth-century West, thousands of Chinese immigrants were expelled from towns and mining camps, and mobs assaulted Chinese residences and businesses. Between 1871 and 1885, San Francisco provided no public education for Chinese children. In 1885, the California Supreme Court, in *Tape v. Hurley*, ordered the city to admit Chinese students to public schools. The state legislature responded by passing a law authorizing segregated education. But Joseph and Mary Tape, who had lived in the United States since the 1860s, insisted that their daughter be allowed to attend her neighborhood school like other children. "Is it a disgrace to be born a Chinese?" Mary Tape wrote. "Didn't God make us all!" But her protest failed. Not until 1947 did California repeal the law authorizing separate schools for the Chinese.

The U.S. Supreme Court also considered the legal status of Chinese-Americans. In *United States v. Wong Kim Ark* (1898), the Court ruled that the Fourteenth Amendment awarded citizenship to children of Chinese immigrants born on American soil. Yet the justices also affirmed the right of Congress to set racial restrictions on immigration. And in its decision in *Fong Yue Ting v. United States* (1893), the Court authorized the federal government to expel Chinese aliens without due process of law. In his dissent, Justice David J. Brewer acknowledged that the power was now directed against a people many Americans found "obnoxious." But "who shall say," he continued, "it will not be exercised tomorrow against other classes and other people?" Brewer proved to be an accurate prophet.

Result of an anti-Chinese riot in Seattle, Washington.

In 1904, the Court cited *Fong Yue Ting* in upholding the law barring anarchists from entering the United States, demonstrating how restrictions on the rights of one group can become a precedent for infringing on the rights of others.

The Rise of the AFL

The social movements that had helped to expand the nineteenth-century boundaries of freedom now redefined their objectives so that they might be realized within the new economic and intellectual framework.

Limited labor movement

Within the labor movement, the demise of the Knights of Labor and the ascendancy of the **American Federation of Labor** (AFL) during the 1890s reflected this shift away from a broadly reformist past to more limited goals. As the Homestead and Pullman strikes demonstrated, direct confrontations with the large corporations were likely to prove suicidal. Unions, declared Samuel Gompers, the AFL's founder and longtime president, should not pursue the Knights' utopian dream of creating a "cooperative commonwealth." Rather, the labor movement should devote itself to negotiating with employers for higher wages and better working conditions for its members. Like Booker T. Washington, Gompers spoke the language of the era's business culture. Indeed, the AFL policies he pioneered were known as "business unionism."

During the 1890s, union membership rebounded from its decline in the late 1880s. But at the same time, the labor movement became less and less inclusive. Abandoning the Knights' ideal of labor solidarity, the AFL restricted membership to skilled workers—a small minority of the labor force—effectively excluding the vast majority of unskilled workers and, therefore, nearly all blacks, women, and new European immigrants. AFL membership centered on sectors of the economy like printing and building construction that were dominated by small competitive businesses. AFL unions had little presence in basic industries like steel and rubber, or in the large-scale factories that now dominated the economy.

The New South, a cartoon in *Puck*, October 23, 1895, depicts sectional and racial reconciliation. African-Americans and Union and Confederate veterans pass a statue of Abraham Lincoln as they stream toward the Atlanta Cotton States Exposition. On the left, a figure representing "Free Labor" stands amid the tools of work. The promise of the New South, however, was never fulfilled.

The Women's Era

Changes in the women's movement reflected the same combination of expanding activities and narrowing boundaries. The 1890s launched what would later be

WHO IS AN AMERICAN?

From William Birney, "Deporting Mohammedans" (1897)

Long before current debates over limiting Muslim immigration to the United States, federal officials excluded a group of Muslims from entering the country. William Birney, an ardent abolitionist and a Union general in the Civil War, protested the action in a letter to the *Washington Post*.

Five men and a lad of fifteen, immigrants from Turkey, passengers on the *Caledonia*, have been held in custody at New York since last Monday and are to be deported, by order of the United States Supervisors of Immigration. The cause of this imprisonment and banishment is that the newcomers, on being questioned by a subordinate official, admitted they were Mohammedans. . . .

Where is this sort of thing to end?. . . If the principle should be approved, it may be applied to any persons whose opinions the officials of the time may think dangerous, to Jews, Catholics, Mormons, Cubans, Spaniards, and even to bankers and bosses. It would be risky for [political bosses] Croker or Platt or Hanna or [J. P.] Morgan to leave the country; he might not get back again.

This deportation by order of a board, because of religion, is too absurd to be tolerated by the authorities. It follows close on the president's Thanksgiving proclamation in which he recommended all persons (including, of course, Jews, Mormons, Spiritualists, Mohammedans, and Christian Scientists) to meet "in their respective places of worship" and offer thanks. Congress has no right to legislate for or against any religious sect or to banish any. It is the glory of our country that a man may believe anything but if he injures other people, the law takes hold of him. . . .

There are Mohammedans in the United States. Some of them are missionaries sent to New York to convert the people. If we deport Mohammedans, the Sultan may retort by deporting American missionaries—whom he regards as a demoralizing and dangerous class. If he should, what can we say against it?

If we let Mohammedan immigrants alone, showing ourselves civilized and kind-hearted, they will soon become Americans in feeling and habits.

QUESTIONS

1. *Why does Birney think that the action of the immigration officials sets a dangerous precedent?*
2. *Why does he think that toleration is likely to promote immigrant assimilation?*

called the "women's era"—three decades during which women, although still denied the vote, enjoyed larger opportunities than in the past for economic independence and played a greater and greater role in public life. Nearly 5 million women worked for wages in 1900. Although most were young, unmarried, and concentrated in traditional jobs such as domestic service and the garment industry, a generation of college-educated women was beginning to take its place in better-paying clerical and professional positions.

Women in the workforce

Through a network of women's clubs, temperance associations, and social reform organizations, women exerted a growing influence on public affairs. Founded in 1874, the Woman's Christian Temperance Union (WCTU) grew to become the era's largest female organization, with a membership by 1890 of 150,000. Under the banner of Home Protection, it moved from demanding the prohibition of alcoholic beverages (blamed for leading men to squander their wages on drink and treat their wives abusively) to a comprehensive program of economic and political reform, including the right to vote. Women, insisted Frances Willard, the group's president, must abandon the idea that "weakness" and dependence were their nature and join assertively in movements to change society.

The Woman's Christian Temperance Union

At the same time, the center of gravity of feminism shifted toward an outlook more in keeping with prevailing racial and ethnic norms. The movement continued to argue for women's equality in employment, education, and politics. But with increasing frequency, the native-born, middle-class women who dominated the suffrage movement claimed the vote as educated members of a "superior race."

Immigrants and former slaves had been enfranchised with "ill-advised haste," declared Carrie Chapman Catt, president of the National American Woman Suffrage Association (created in 1890 to reunite the rival suffrage organizations formed after the Civil War). Indeed, Catt suggested, extending the vote to native-born white women would help to counteract the growing power of the "ignorant foreign vote" in the North and the dangerous potential for a second Reconstruction in the South. In 1895, the same year that Booker T. Washington delivered his Atlanta address, the National American Woman Suffrage Association held its annual convention in that segregated city. Like other American institutions, the organized movement for woman suffrage had made its peace with nativism and racism.

A Woman's Liquor Raid, an illustration in the *National Police Gazette* in 1879, depicts a group of temperance crusaders destroying liquor containers in a Frederickstown, Ohio, saloon.

BECOMING A WORLD POWER

The New Imperialism

In world history, the last quarter of the nineteenth century is known as the age of imperialism, when rival European empires carved up large parts of the world among themselves. For most of this period, the United States remained a second-rate power.

The global context

The "new imperialism" that arose after 1870 was dominated by European powers and Japan. Belgium, Great Britain, and France consolidated their hold on colonies in Africa, and newly unified Germany acquired colonies there as well. By the early twentieth century, most of Asia, Africa, the Middle East, and the Pacific had been divided among these empires.

American Expansionism

Territorial expansion, of course, had been a feature of American life from well before independence. But the 1890s marked a major turning point in America's relationship with the rest of the world. Americans were increasingly aware of themselves as an emerging world power. "We are a great imperial Republic destined to exercise a controlling influence upon the actions of mankind and to affect the future of the world," proclaimed Henry Watterson, an influential newspaper editor.

"All Nations Use Singer Sewing Machines," an advertisement from around 1892 that celebrates the company's success in marketing its products abroad.

Until the 1890s, American expansion had taken place on the North American continent. Ever since the Monroe Doctrine of 1823, to be sure, many Americans had considered the Western Hemisphere an American sphere of influence. The last territorial acquisition before the 1890s had been Alaska, purchased from Russia by Secretary of State William H. Seward in 1867.

Most Americans who looked overseas were interested in expanded trade, not territorial possessions. The country's agricultural and industrial production could no longer be absorbed entirely at home. By 1890, companies like Singer Sewing Machines and John D. Rockefeller's Standard Oil Company aggressively marketed their products abroad. Especially during economic downturns, business leaders insisted on the necessity of greater access to foreign customers. Middle-class American women, moreover, were becoming more and more desirous of clothing and food from abroad, and their demand for consumer goods such as

"Oriental" fashions and exotic spices for cooking spurred the economic penetration of the Far East.

The Lure of Empire

One group of Americans who spread the nation's influence overseas were religious missionaries, thousands of whom ventured abroad in the late nineteenth century to spread Christianity, prepare the world for the second coming of Christ, and uplift the poor. Inspired by Dwight Moody, a Methodist evangelist, the Student Volunteer Movement for Foreign Missions sent more than 8,000 missionaries to "bring light to heathen worlds" across the globe.

A small group of late-nineteenth-century thinkers actively promoted American expansionism, warning that the country must not allow itself to be shut out of the scramble for empire. Naval officer Alfred T. Mahan, in *The Influence of Sea Power upon History* (1890), argued that no nation could prosper without a large fleet of ships engaged in international trade, protected by a powerful navy operating from overseas bases. His arguments influenced the outlook of James G. Blaine, who served as secretary of state during Benjamin Harrison's presidency (1889–1893). Blaine urged the president to try to acquire Hawaii, Puerto Rico, and Cuba as strategic naval bases.

Although independent, Hawaii was already closely tied to the United States through treaties that exempted imports of its sugar from tariff duties and provided for the establishment of an American naval base at Pearl Harbor. Hawaii's economy was dominated by American-owned sugar plantations that employed a workforce of native islanders and Chinese, Japanese, and Filipino laborers under long-term contracts. Early in 1893, a group of American planters organized a rebellion that overthrew the Hawaii government of Queen Liliuokalani. On the eve of leaving office, Harrison submitted a treaty of annexation to the Senate. After determining that a majority of Hawaiians did not favor the treaty, Harrison's successor, Grover Cleveland, withdrew it. In July 1898, in the midst of the Spanish-American War, the United States finally annexed the Hawaiian Islands.

The depression that began in 1893 heightened the belief that a more aggressive foreign policy was necessary to stimulate American exports. These were the years when rituals like the Pledge of Allegiance and the practice of standing for the playing of "The Star-Spangled Banner" came into existence. New, mass-circulation newspapers also promoted nationalistic sentiments. By the late 1890s, papers like William Randolph Hearst's *New York Journal*

A cartoon in *Puck*, December 1, 1897, imagines the annexation of Hawaii by the United States as a shotgun wedding. The minister, President McKinley, reads from a book entitled *Annexation Policy*. The Hawaiian bride appears to be looking for a way to escape. Most Hawaiians did not support annexation.

Queen Liliuokalani, the last ruler of Hawaii before it was annexed by the United States.

and Joseph Pulitzer's *New York World*—dubbed the "**yellow press**" by their critics after the color in which Hearst printed a popular comic strip—were selling a million copies each day by mixing sensational accounts of crime and political corruption with aggressive appeals to patriotic sentiments.

The "Splendid Little War"

Cuban struggle for independence

All these factors contributed to America's emergence as a world power in the Spanish-American War of 1898. But the immediate origins of the war lay not at home but in the long Cuban struggle for independence from Spain. Ten years of guerrilla war had followed a Cuban revolt in 1868. The movement for independence resumed in 1895. As reports circulated of widespread suffering caused by the Spanish policy of rounding up civilians and moving them into detention camps, the Cuban struggle won growing support in the United States.

The U.S.S. Maine

Demands for intervention escalated after February 15, 1898, when an explosion—probably accidental, a later investigation concluded—destroyed the American battleship **U.S.S. *Maine*** in Havana harbor, with the loss of nearly 270 lives. After Spain rejected an American demand for a cease-fire on the island and eventual Cuban independence, President McKinley in April asked Congress for a declaration of war. The purpose, declared Senator Henry Teller of Colorado, was to aid Cuban patriots in their struggle for "liberty and freedom." To underscore the government's humanitarian intentions, Congress adopted the Teller Amendment, stating that the United States had no intention of annexing or dominating the island.

The Spanish-American War

Secretary of State John Hay called the Spanish-American conflict a "splendid little war." It lasted only four months and resulted in fewer than 400 American combat deaths. The war's most decisive engagement took place not in Cuba but at Manila Bay, a strategic harbor in the Philippine Islands in the distant Pacific Ocean. Here, on May 1, the American navy under Admiral George Dewey defeated a Spanish fleet. Soon afterward, soldiers went ashore, becoming the first American army units to engage in combat outside the Western Hemisphere. July witnessed another naval victory off Santiago, Cuba, and the landing of American troops on Cuba and Puerto Rico.

Roosevelt at San Juan Hill

Rough Riders

The most highly publicized land battle of the war took place in Cuba. This was the charge up San Juan Hill, outside Santiago, by Theodore Roosevelt's Rough Riders. An ardent expansionist, Roosevelt had long believed that a war would reinvigorate the nation's unity and sense of manhood, which had suffered, he felt, during the 1890s. A few months shy

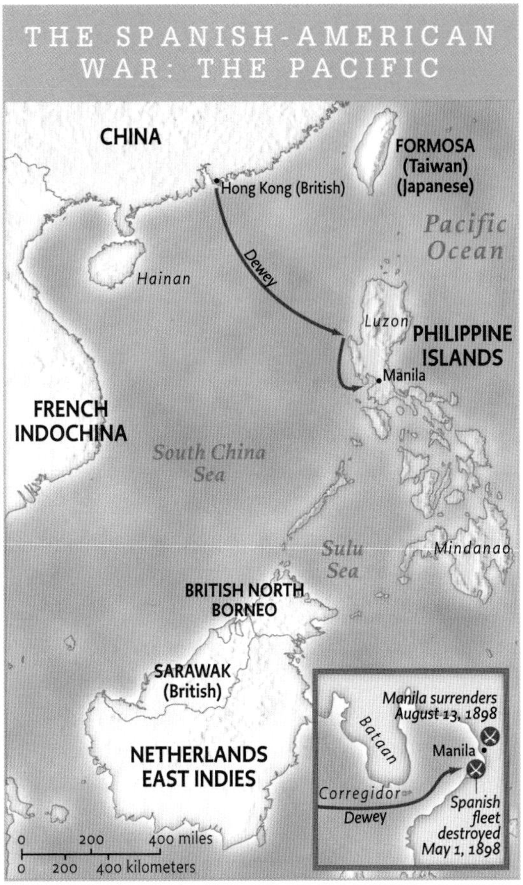

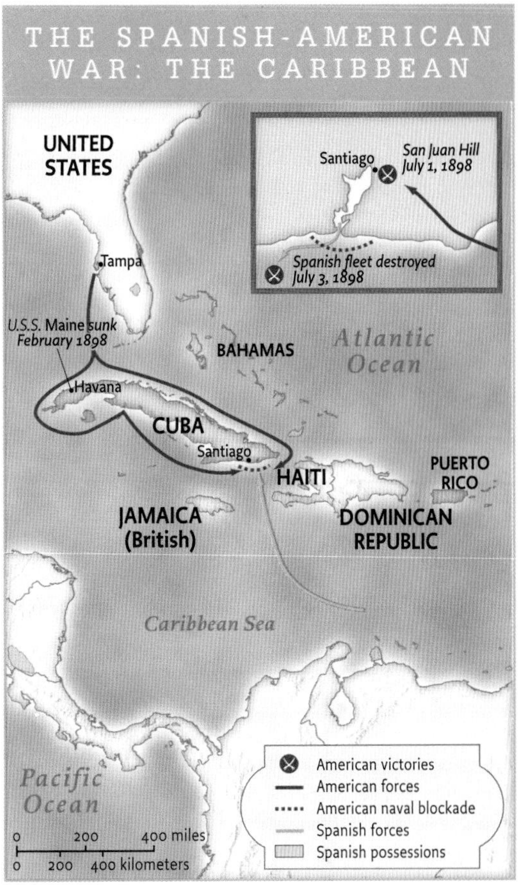

In both the Caribbean and the Pacific, the United States achieved swift victories over Spain in the Spanish-American War.

of his fortieth birthday when war broke out, Roosevelt resigned his post as assistant secretary of the navy to raise a volunteer cavalry unit, which rushed to Cuba to participate in the fighting. His exploits made Roosevelt a national hero. He was elected governor of New York that fall and in 1900 became McKinley's vice president.

An American Empire

With the backing of the yellow press, the war quickly escalated from a crusade to aid the suffering Cubans to an imperial venture that ended with the United States in possession of a small overseas empire. McKinley became convinced that the United States could neither return the Philippines to Spain nor grant them independence, for which he believed the inhabitants unprepared. In an interview with a group of Methodist ministers, the president spoke of receiving a divine revelation that Americans had

Charge of the Rough Riders at San Juan Hill, a painting by Frederic Remington, depicts the celebrated unit, commanded by Theodore Roosevelt, in action in Cuba during the Spanish-American War of 1898. Roosevelt, on horseback, leads the troops. Remington had been sent to the island the previous year by publisher William Randolph Hearst to provide pictures of Spanish atrocities during the Cuban war for independence in the hope of boosting the *New York Journal*'s circulation.

a duty to "uplift and civilize" the Filipino people and to train them for self-government. In the treaty with Spain that ended the war, the United States acquired the Philippines, Puerto Rico, and the Pacific island of Guam. As for Cuba, before recognizing its independence, McKinley forced the island's new government to approve the **Platt Amendment** to the new Cuban constitution (drafted by Senator Orville H. Platt of Connecticut), which authorized the United States to intervene militarily whenever it saw fit. The United States also acquired a permanent lease on naval stations in Cuba, including what is now the facility at Guantánamo Bay.

America's interest in its new possessions had more to do with trade than with gaining wealth from natural resources or large-scale American settlement. Puerto Rico and Cuba were gateways to Latin America, strategic outposts from which American naval and commercial power could be projected throughout the hemisphere. The Philippines, Guam, and Hawaii lay astride shipping routes to the markets of Japan and China. In 1899, soon after the end of the Spanish-American War, Secretary of State John Hay announced the **Open Door Policy**, demanding that European powers that had recently divided China into commercial spheres of influence grant equal access to American exports. The Open Door referred to the free movement of goods and money, not people. Even as the United States banned the immigration of Chinese into this country, it insisted on access to the markets and investment opportunities of Asia.

Hacienda La Fortuna, a sugar plantation, as depicted by the Puerto Rican artist Francisco Oller in 1885. From left to right the buildings are a warehouse, plantation home, and modern steam-powered sugar mill. The acquisition of the island by the United States in the Spanish-American War strengthened the hold of "sugar barons" on the Puerto Rican economy.

The Philippine War

In this cartoon comment on the American effort to suppress the movement for Philippine independence, Uncle Sam tries to subdue a knife-wielding insurgent.

Many Cubans, Filipinos, and Puerto Ricans had welcomed American intervention as a way of breaking Spain's long hold on these colonies. Large planters looked forward to greater access to American markets. Nationalists and labor leaders admired America's democratic ideals and believed that American participation in the destruction of Spanish rule would lead to social reform and political self-government.

But the American determination to exercise continued control, direct or indirect, led to a rapid change in local opinion, nowhere more so than in the Philippines. Filipinos had been fighting a war against Spain since 1896. After Dewey's victory at Manila Bay, their leader, Emilio Aguinaldo, established a provisional government with a constitution modeled on that of the United States. But once McKinley decided to retain possession of the islands, the Filipino movement turned against the United States. The result was a second war, far longer (it lasted from 1899 to 1903) and bloodier (it cost the lives of more than 100,000 Filipinos and 4,200 Americans) than the Spanish-American conflict. Today, the **Philippine War** is perhaps the least remembered of all American wars.

Once in control of the Philippines, the colonial administration took seriously the idea of modernizing the islands. It expanded railroads and harbors, brought in American schoolteachers and public health officials, and sought to modernize agriculture (although efforts to persuade local farmers to substitute corn for rice ran afoul of the Filipino climate and cultural traditions). The United States, said President McKinley, had an obligation to its "little brown brothers." Yet in all the new possessions, American policies tended to serve the interests of land-based local elites—and bequeathed enduring poverty to the majority of the rural population. Under American rule, Puerto Rico, previously an island of diversified small farmers, became a low-wage plantation economy controlled by absentee American corporations. By the 1920s, its residents were among the poorest in the entire Caribbean.

In this illustration from *Puck*, April 6, 1901, a woman representing the United States tries on a hat shaped like a battleship and labeled "World Power." She seems to feel that it fits her well.

Citizens or Subjects?

American rule also brought with it American racial attitudes. In an 1899 poem, the British writer Rudyard Kipling urged the United States to take up the "white man's burden" of imperialism. American proponents of

AMERICAN EMPIRE, 1898

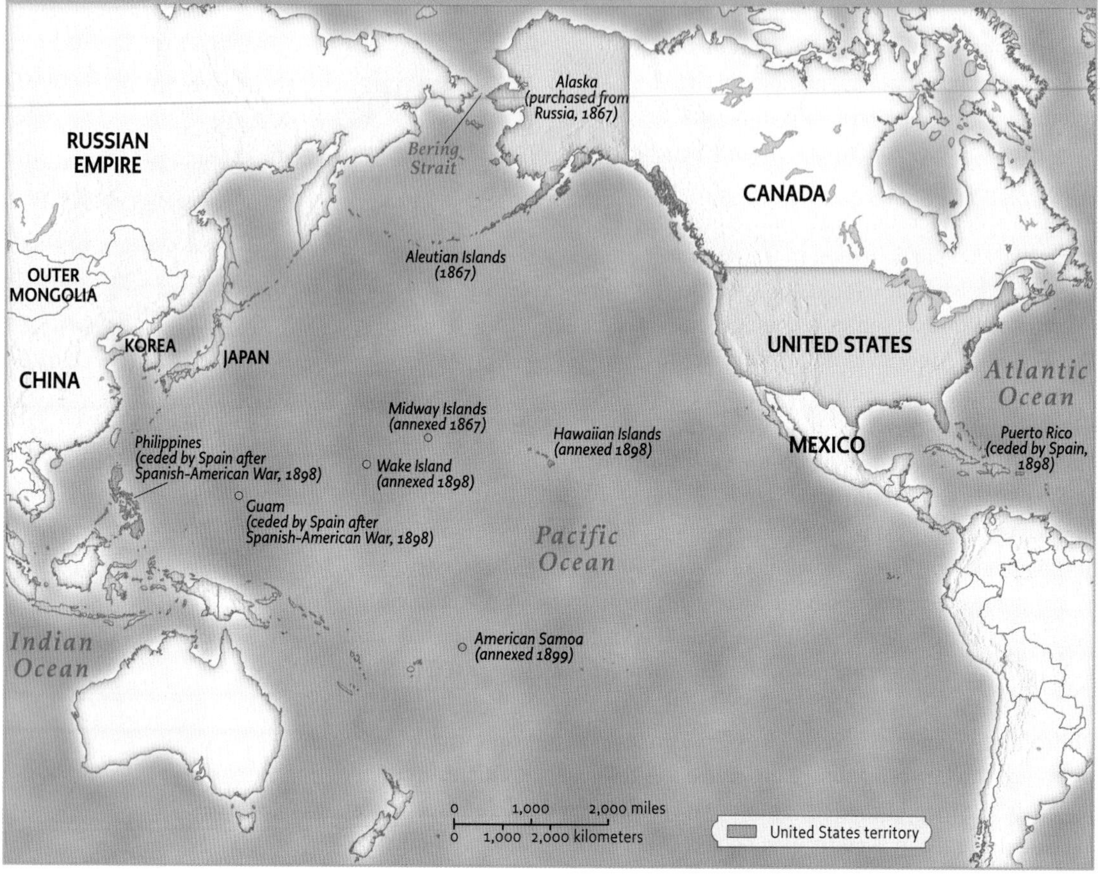

As a result of the Spanish-American War, the United States became the ruler of a far-flung overseas empire.

Colonies in the American framework

empire agreed that the domination of non-white peoples by whites formed part of the progress of civilization.

America's triumphant entry into the ranks of imperial powers sparked an intense debate over the relationship among political democracy, race, and American citizenship. The American system of government had no provision for permanent colonies. The right of every people to self-government was one of the main principles of the Declaration of Independence. The idea of an "empire of liberty" assumed that new territories would eventually be admitted as equal states and their residents would be American citizens. In the aftermath of the Spanish-American War, however, nationalism, democracy, and American freedom emerged more closely identified than ever with notions of Anglo-Saxon superiority.

The Foraker Act of 1900 declared Puerto Rico an "insular territory," different from previous territories in the West. Its 1 million inhabitants were defined as citizens of Puerto Rico, not the United States, and denied a future path to statehood. Filipinos occupied a similar status. In a series of cases decided between 1901 and 1904 and known collectively as the **Insular Cases**, the Supreme Court held that the Constitution did not fully apply to the territories recently acquired by the United States—a significant limitation of the scope of American freedom. Thus, two principles central to American freedom since the War of Independence—no taxation without representation and government based on the consent of the governed—were abandoned when it came to the nation's new possessions.

This propaganda photograph from 1898 depicts the Spanish-American War as a source of national reconciliation in the United States (with Confederate and Union soldiers shaking hands) and of freedom for Cuba (personified by a girl whose arm holds a broken chain).

In the twentieth century, the territories acquired in 1898 would follow different paths. Hawaii, which had a sizable population of American missionaries and planters, became a traditional territory. Its population, except for Asian immigrant laborers, became American citizens, and it was admitted as a state in 1959. After nearly a half-century of American rule, the Philippines achieved independence in 1946. Until 1950, the U.S. Navy administered Guam, which remains today an "unincorporated" territory. As for Puerto Rico, it is sometimes called "the world's oldest colony," because ever since the Spanish conquered the island in 1493 it has lacked full self-government. It elects its own government but lacks a voice in Congress (and in the election of the U.S. president).

Drawing the Global Color Line

"White man's burden"

Just as American ideas about liberty and self-government had circulated around the world in the Age of Revolution, American racial attitudes had a global impact in the age of empire. The turn of the twentieth century was a time of worldwide concern about immigration, race relations, and the "white man's burden," all of which inspired a global sense of fraternity among "Anglo-Saxon" nations. Chinese exclusion in the United States strongly influenced anti-Chinese laws adopted in Canada. The Union of South Africa, inaugurated in 1911, saw its own policy of racial separation—later known as apartheid—as following in the footsteps of segregation in the United States.

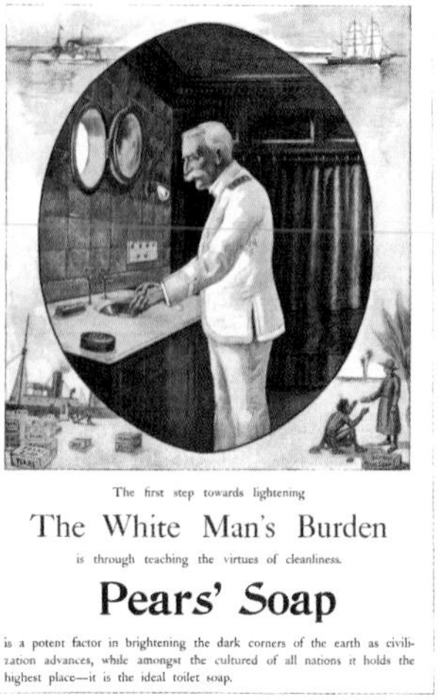

The first step towards lightening
The White Man's Burden
is through teaching the virtues of cleanliness.
Pears' Soap
is a potent factor in brightening the dark corners of the earth as civilization advances, while amongst the cultured of all nations it holds the highest place—it is the ideal toilet soap.

An advertisement employs the idea of a "white man's burden" (borrowed from a poem by Rudyard Kipling) as a way of promoting the virtues of Pears' Soap. Accompanying text claims that Pears' is "the ideal toilet soap" for "the cultured of all nations," and an agent of civilization in "the dark corners of the earth."

"Republic or Empire?"

The emergence of the United States as an imperial power sparked intense debate. Opponents formed the **Anti-Imperialist League**. It united writers and social reformers who believed American energies should be directed at home, businessmen fearful of the cost of maintaining overseas outposts, and racists who did not wish to bring non-white populations into the United States. America's historic mission, the League declared, was to "help the world by an example of successful self-government," not to conquer other peoples.

In 1900, Democrats again nominated William Jennings Bryan to run against McKinley. The Democratic platform opposed the Philippine War for placing the United States in the "un-American" position of "crushing with military force" another people's desire for "liberty and self-government." George S. Boutwell, president of the Anti-Imperialist League, declared that the most pressing question in the election was the nation's future character—"republic or empire?"

But without any sense of contradiction, proponents of an imperial foreign policy also adopted the language of freedom. Riding the wave of patriotic sentiment inspired by the war, and with the economy having recovered from the depression of 1893–1897, McKinley in 1900 repeated his 1896 triumph.

At the dawn of the twentieth century, the United States seemed poised to take its place among the world's great powers. In 1900, many features that would mark American life for much of the twentieth century were already apparent. The United States led the world in industrial production. The political system had stabilized. The white North and South had achieved reconciliation, while rigid lines of racial exclusion—the segregation of blacks, Chinese exclusion, Indian reservations—limited the boundaries of freedom and citizenship.

Yet the questions central to nineteenth-century debates over freedom—the relationship between political and economic liberty, the role of government in creating the conditions of freedom, and the definition of those entitled to enjoy the rights of citizens—had not been permanently answered. Nor had the dilemma of how to reconcile America's role as an empire with traditional ideas of freedom been resolved. These were the challenges bequeathed by the nineteenth century to the first generation of the twentieth.

CHAPTER REVIEW AND ONLINE RESOURCES

REVIEW QUESTIONS

1. *What economic and political issues gave rise to the Populist Party, and what changes did the party advocate?*
2. *How did employers use state and federal forces to protect their own economic interests, and what were the results?*
3. *Who were the Redeemers, and how did they change society and politics in the New South?*
4. *Explain how changes in politics, economics, social factors, and violence interacted to affect the situation of African-Americans in the New South.*
5. *How did religion and the idea of the Lost Cause give support to a new understanding of the Civil War?*
6. *What rights did Chinese immigrants and Chinese-Americans gain in these years, and what limitations did they experience? How did their experiences set the stage for other restrictions on immigration?*
7. *Compare and contrast the goals, strategies, and membership of the American Federation of Labor and the Knights of Labor (you may want to refer back to Chapter 16).*
8. *What ideas and interests motivated the United States to create an empire in the late nineteenth century?*
9. *Compare the arguments for and against U.S. imperialism. Be sure to consider the views of Alfred T. Mahan and Emilio Aguinaldo.*
10. *What was the Immigration Restriction League, and what changes to political participation did it advocate?*

KEY TERMS

Populists (p. 508)
Coxey's Army (p. 511)
New South (p. 515)
Kansas Exodus (p. 516)
Atlanta Compromise (p. 517)
grandfather clause (p. 518)
disenfranchisement (p. 518)
Plessy v. Ferguson (p. 519)
"separate but equal" (p. 519)
lynching (p. 520)
the Lost Cause (p. 521)
new immigrants (p. 524)
Immigration Restriction League (p. 524)
Chinese Exclusion Act (p. 525)
American Federation of Labor (p. 527)
yellow press (p. 532)
U.S.S. *Maine* (p. 532)
Platt Amendment (p. 534)
Open Door Policy (p. 534)
Philippine War (p. 535)
Insular Cases (p. 537)
Anti-Imperialist League (p. 538)

Go to INQUIZITIVE

To see what you know—and learn what you've missed—with personalized feedback along the way.

Visit the ***Give Me Liberty!*** **Student Site** for primary source documents and images, interactive maps, author videos featuring Eric Foner, and more.

1889	Hull House founded
1901	Socialist Party founded in United States
	President McKinley assassinated
1903	Ford Motor Company established
1904	Northern Securities dissolved
1905	Industrial Workers of the World established
1906	Upton Sinclair's *The Jungle*
	Meat Inspection Act
	Pure Food and Drug Act
	Hepburn Act
	John A. Ryan's *A Living Wage*
1908	*Muller v. Oregon*
1911	Triangle Shirtwaist Company fire
	Society of American Indians founded
1912	Theodore Roosevelt organizes the Progressive Party
1913	Sixteenth Amendment
	Seventeenth Amendment
	Federal Reserve established
1914	Federal Trade Commission established
	Clayton Act

CHAPTER 18

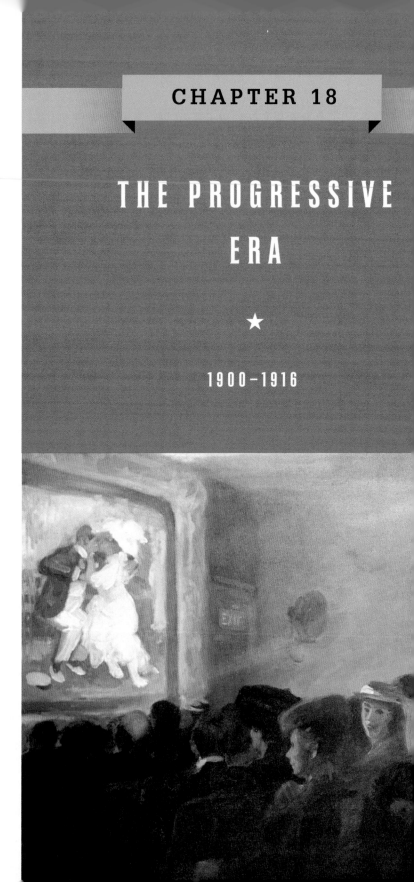

THE PROGRESSIVE ERA

★

1900–1916

Movie, 5 Cents. In this 1907 painting, the artist John Sloan depicts the interior of a movie house. By this time, millions of people each week were flocking to see silent motion pictures. The audience includes different classes and races, as well as couples and women attending alone.

It was late afternoon on March 25, 1911, when fire broke out at the Triangle Shirtwaist Company. The factory occupied the top three floors of a ten-story building in the Greenwich Village neighborhood of New York City. Here some 500 workers, mostly young Jewish and Italian immigrant women, toiled at sewing machines producing ladies' blouses, some earning as little as three dollars per week. Those who tried to escape the blaze discovered that the doors to the stairwell had been locked—the owner's way, it was later charged, of discouraging theft and unauthorized bathroom breaks. The fire department rushed to the scene with high-pressure hoses. But their ladders reached only to the sixth floor. Onlookers watched in horror as girls leaped from the upper stories. By the time the blaze had been put out, 46 bodies lay on the street and 100 more were found inside the building.

Triangle focused attention on the social divisions that plagued American society during the first two decades of the twentieth century, a period known as the Progressive era. These were years when economic expansion produced millions of new jobs and brought an unprecedented array of goods within reach of American consumers. Cities expanded rapidly—by 1920, for the first time, more Americans lived in towns and cities than in rural areas. Yet severe inequality remained the most visible feature of the urban landscape, and persistent labor strife raised anew the question of government's role in combating it.

The word "Progressive" came into common use around 1910 as a way of describing a broad, loosely defined political movement of individuals and groups who hoped to bring about significant change in American social and political life. Progressives included forward-looking businessmen who realized that workers must be accorded a voice in economic decision making, and labor activists bent on empowering industrial workers. Other major contributors to **Progressivism** were members of female reform organizations who hoped to protect women and children from exploitation, social scientists who believed that academic research would help to solve social problems, and members of an anxious middle class who feared that their status was threatened by the rise of big business.

As this and the following chapter discuss, Progressive reformers addressed issues of American freedom in varied, contradictory ways. The era saw the expansion of political and economic freedom through the reinvigoration of the movement for woman suffrage, the use of political power to expand workers' rights, and efforts to improve democratic government by weakening the power of city bosses and giving ordinary citizens more influence on legislation. It witnessed the flowering of understandings of freedom based on individual fulfillment and personal self-determination. At the same time, many Progressives supported efforts to limit the full enjoyment of freedom to those deemed fit to exercise it properly. The new system of

FOCUS QUESTIONS

- *Why was the city such a central element in Progressive America?*
- *How did the labor and women's movements expand the meanings of American freedom?*
- *In what ways did Progressivism include both democratic and antidemocratic impulses?*
- *How did the Progressive presidents foster the rise of the nation-state?*

white supremacy born in the 1890s became fully consolidated in the South. Growing numbers of native-born Americans demanded that immigrants abandon their traditional cultures and become fully "Americanized." And efforts were made at the local and national levels to place political decision making in the hands of experts who did not have to answer to the electorate. The idea of freedom remained as contested as ever in Progressive America.

AN URBAN AGE AND A CONSUMER SOCIETY

Farms and Cities

Economic growth

The Progressive era was a period of explosive economic growth, fueled by increasing industrial production, a rapid rise in population, and the continued expansion of the consumer marketplace. In the first decade of the twentieth century, the economy's total output rose by about 85 percent. For the last time in American history, farms and cities grew together. Farm families poured into the western Great Plains. More than 1 million claims for free government land were filed under the Homestead Act of 1862—more than in the previous forty years. Irrigation transformed the Imperial Valley of California and parts of Arizona into major areas of commercial farming.

But it was the city that became the focus of Progressive politics and of a new mass-consumer society. The United States counted twenty-one cities whose population exceeded 100,000 in 1910, the largest of them New York, with 4.7 million residents. The twenty-three square miles of Manhattan Island were home to over 2 million people, more than lived in thirty-three of the states.

William L. Sonntag was an early twentieth-century painter fascinated by scenes of urban life. In *Bowery at Night*, he depicts a boisterous New York street scene complete with streetcars, private carriages, and crowds of people making their way beneath an elevated railroad.

The stark urban inequalities of the 1890s continued into the Progressive era. Immigrant families in New York's downtown tenements often had no electricity or indoor toilets. Three miles to the north stood the mansions of Fifth Avenue's Millionaire's Row. According to one estimate, J. P. Morgan's financial firm directly or indirectly controlled 40 percent of all financial and industrial capital in the United States.

The Muckrakers

Some observers saw the city as a place where corporate greed undermined traditional American values. At a time when more than 2 million children under the age of fifteen worked for wages, Lewis Hine photographed child laborers to draw attention to persistent social inequality. A new generation of journalists writing for mass-circulation national magazines exposed the ills of industrial and urban life. *The Shame of the Cities* (1904) by Lincoln Steffens showed how party bosses and business leaders profited from political corruption. Theodore Roosevelt disparaged such writing as **muckraking**, the use of journalistic skills to expose the underside of American life.

Major novelists took a similar unsparing approach to social ills. Perhaps the era's most influential novel was Upton Sinclair's *The Jungle* (1906), whose description of unsanitary slaughterhouses and the sale of rotten meat stirred public outrage and led directly to the passage of the Pure Food and Drug Act and the Meat Inspection Act of 1906.

Lewis Hine used his camera to chronicle the plight of child laborers such as this young spinner in a southern cotton factory.

Immigration as a Global Process

If one thing characterized early-twentieth-century cities, it was their immigrant character. The "new immigration" from southern and eastern Europe had begun around 1890 but reached its peak during the Progressive era. Between 1901 and the outbreak of World War I in Europe in 1914, some 13 million immigrants came to the United States, the majority from Italy, Russia, and the Austro-Hungarian empire. Progressive-era immigration formed part of a larger process of worldwide migration set in motion by industrial expansion and the decline of traditional agriculture.

Between 1840 and 1914 (when immigration to the United States would be virtually cut off, first by the outbreak of World War I and then by legislation), perhaps 40 million persons immigrated to the United States and another 20 million to other parts of the Western Hemisphere, including Canada, Argentina, and the Caribbean. Rural southern and eastern Europe and large parts of Asia were regions marked by widespread poverty and illiteracy, burdensome taxation, and declining economies. Political turmoil at home, like the revolution that engulfed Mexico after 1911, also inspired immigration.

Most European immigrants to the United States entered through **Ellis Island**. Located in New York Harbor, this became in 1892 the nation's main facility for processing immigrants. Millions of Americans today trace their ancestry to immigrants who passed through Ellis Island.

TABLE 18.1 Rise of the City, 1880–1920

YEAR	URBAN POPULATION (PERCENTAGE)	NUMBER OF CITIES WITH 100,000+ POPULATION
1880	20%	12
1890	28	15
1900	38	18
1910	50	21
1920	68	26

TABLE 18.2 Immigrants and Their Children as Percentage of Population, Ten Major Cities, 1920

CITY	PERCENTAGE
New York City	76%
Cleveland	72
Boston	72
Chicago	71
Detroit	65
San Francisco	64
Minneapolis	63
Pittsburgh	59
Seattle	55
Los Angeles	45

At the same time, an influx of Asian and Mexican newcomers was taking place in the West. After the exclusion of immigrants from China in the late nineteenth century, approximately 72,000 Japanese arrived, primarily to work as agricultural laborers in California's fruit and vegetable fields and on Hawaii's sugar plantations. Between 1910 and 1940, Angel Island in San Francisco Bay—the "Ellis Island of the West"—served as the main entry point for immigrants from Asia. Far larger was Mexican immigration. Between 1900 and 1930, some 1 million Mexicans (more than 10 percent of that country's population) entered the United States—a number exceeded by only a few European countries.

By 1910, one-seventh of the American population was foreign-born, the highest percentage in the country's history.

The Immigrant Quest for Freedom

Like their nineteenth-century predecessors, the new immigrants arrived imagining the United States as a land of freedom, where all persons enjoyed equality before the law, could worship as they pleased, enjoyed economic opportunity, and had been emancipated from the oppressive social hierarchies of their homelands. "America is a free country," one Polish immigrant wrote home. "You don't have to be a serf to anyone." Agents sent abroad by the American government to investigate the reasons for large-scale immigration reported that the main impetus was a desire to share in the "freedom and prosperity enjoyed by the people of the United States." Although some of the new immigrants, especially Jews fleeing religious persecution in the Russian empire, thought of themselves as permanent emigrants, the majority initially planned to earn enough money to return home and purchase land. Groups like Mexicans and Italians included many "birds of passage," who remained only temporarily in the United States.

The new immigrants clustered in close-knit "ethnic" neighborhoods with their own shops, theaters, and community organizations, and often continued to speak their native tongues. Although most immigrants earned more than was possible in the impoverished regions from which they came, they endured low wages, long hours, and dangerous working conditions. In the mines and factories of Pennsylvania and the Midwest, eastern European immigrants performed low-wage unskilled

A piece of sheet music, published in 1911 and directed at Jewish immigrants, celebrates the United States as the Land of the Free.

labor, whereas native-born workers dominated skilled and supervisory jobs. The vast majority of Mexican immigrants became poorly paid agricultural, mine, and railroad laborers, with little prospect of upward economic mobility. "My people are not in America," remarked one Slavic priest, "they are under it."

Consumer Freedom

Cities, however, were also the birthplace of a mass-consumption society that added new meaning to American freedom. During the Progressive era, large downtown department stores, neighborhood chain stores, and retail mail-order houses made available to consumers throughout the country the vast array of goods now pouring from the nation's factories. By 1910, Americans could purchase, among many other items, electric sewing machines, washing machines, vacuum cleaners, and record players.

Amusement parks, dance halls, and theaters attracted large crowds of city dwellers. By 1910, 25 million Americans per week, mostly working-class urban residents, were attending "nickelodeons"—motion-picture theaters whose five-cent admission charge was far lower than that of vaudeville shows.

One of the numerous advertisements of the early twentieth century that invoked the Statue of Liberty to market consumer goods, in this case a brand of crackers.

The Working Woman

The new visibility of women in urban public places—at work, as shoppers, and in places of entertainment like cinemas and dance halls—indicated that traditional gender roles were changing dramatically in Progressive America. Immigrant women were largely confined to low-paying factory employment. But for native-born white women, the kinds of jobs available expanded enormously. By 1920, around 25 percent of employed women were office workers or telephone operators. Female work was no longer confined to young, unmarried white women and adult black women. In 1920, of 8 million women working for wages, one-quarter were married and living with their husbands. The working woman—immigrant and native, working-class and professional—became a symbol of female emancipation. "We enjoy our independence and freedom" was the assertive statement of the Bachelor Girls Social Club, a group of female mail-order clerks in New York.

The desire to participate in the consumer society produced remarkably similar battles within immigrant families of all nationalities between parents and their self-consciously "free" children, especially daughters. Contemporaries, native and immigrant, noted how "the novelties and frivolities of fashion" appealed to young working women, who spent part of their meager wages on clothing and makeup and at places of entertainment. Daughters considered parents who tried to impose curfews or to prevent them from going out alone to dances or movies as old-fashioned and not sufficiently "American."

The Return from Toil, a drawing by John Sloan for the radical magazine *The Masses*, pictures working women not as downtrodden but as independent-minded, stylish, and self-confident.

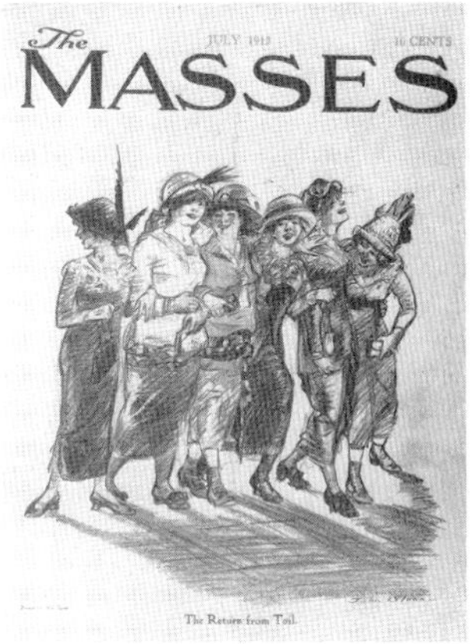

Women at work in a shoe factory, 1908.

TABLE 18.3 Percentage of Women 14 Years and Older in the Labor Force, 1900–1930

YEAR	ALL WOMEN	MARRIED WOMEN	WOMEN AS % OF LABOR FORCE
1900	20.4%	5.6%	18%
1910	25.2	10.7	24
1920	23.3	9.0	24
1930	24.3	11.7	25

The Rise of Fordism

Henry Ford

If any individual exemplified the new consumer society, it was Henry Ford. Ford did not invent the automobile, but he developed the techniques of production and marketing that brought it within the reach of ordinary Americans. In 1905, he established the Ford Motor Company, one of dozens of small automobile manufacturing firms that emerged in these years. Three years later, he introduced the Model T, a simple, light vehicle sturdy enough to navigate the country's poorly maintained roads.

The moving assembly line

In 1913, Ford's factory in Highland Park, Michigan, adopted the method of production known as the moving assembly line, in which car frames were brought to workers on a continuously moving conveyor belt. The process enabled Ford to expand output by greatly reducing the time it took to produce each car. In 1914, he raised wages at his factory to the unheard-of level of five dollars per day (more than double the pay of most industrial workers), enabling him to attract a steady stream of skilled laborers. When other businessmen criticized him for endangering profits by paying high wages, Ford replied that workers must be able to afford the goods being turned out by American factories. Ford's output rose from 34,000 cars, priced at $700 each, in 1910, to 730,000 Model T's that sold at a price of $316 (well within the reach of many workers) in 1916. The economic system based on mass production and mass consumption came to be called **Fordism**.

TABLE 18.4 Sales of Passenger Cars

YEAR	NUMBER OF CARS (IN THOUSANDS)
1900	4.1
1905	24.2
1910	181.0
1915	895.9
1920	1,905.5
1925	3,735.1

Crowds congregate on a New York street in 1896 at the opening of Siegel and Cooper's Department Store, one of numerous emporiums of commerce that reflected the rise of mass consumption as an essential element of the American standard of living.

The Promise of Abundance

As economic production shifted from capital goods (steel, railroad equipment, etc.) to consumer products, the new advertising industry perfected ways of increasing sales, often by linking goods with the idea of freedom. Numerous products took "liberty" as a brand name or used an image of the Statue of Liberty as a sales device. Economic abundance would eventually come to define the "American way of life," in which personal fulfillment was to be found through acquiring material goods.

The maturation of the consumer economy gave rise to concepts—a "living wage" and an **"American standard of living"**—that offered a new language for criticizing the inequalities of wealth and power in Progressive America. Father John A. Ryan's influential book *A Living Wage* (1906) described a decent standard of living (one that enabled a person to participate in the consumer economy) as a "natural and absolute" right of citizenship. For the first time in the nation's history, mass consumption came to occupy a central place in descriptions of American society and its future.

An advertisement for Palmolive soap illustrates how companies marketed goods to consumers by creating anxiety and invoking exotic images. The accompanying text promises "a perfect skin" and includes an imagined image of Cleopatra, claiming that the soap embodies "ancient beauty arts." By 1915, Palmolive was the best-selling soap in the world.

VARIETIES OF PROGRESSIVISM

The immediate task, in the Progressives' view, was to humanize industrial capitalism and find common ground in a society still racked by labor conflict and experiencing massive immigration from abroad. Some

Progressives proposed to return to a competitive marketplace populated by small producers. Others accepted the permanence of the large corporation and looked to the government to reverse the growing concentration of wealth and to ensure social justice. Still others would relocate freedom from the economic and political worlds to a private realm of personal fulfillment and unimpeded self-expression. But nearly all Progressives agreed that freedom must be infused with new meaning to deal with the economic and social conditions of the early twentieth century.

Industrial Freedom

Frederick W. Taylor

In Progressive America, complaints of a loss of freedom came not only from the most poorly paid factory workers but from better-off employees as well. Large firms in the automobile, electrical, steel, and other industries sought to implement greater control over the work process. Efficiency expert Frederick W. Taylor pioneered what he called **scientific management**. Through scientific study, Taylor believed, the "one best way" of producing goods could be determined and implemented. The role of workers was to obey the detailed instructions of supervisors. Not surprisingly, many skilled workers saw the erosion of their traditional influence over the work process as a loss of freedom.

These developments helped to place the ideas of "industrial freedom" and "industrial democracy," which had entered the political vocabulary in the Gilded Age, at the center of political discussion during the Progressive era. Lack of "industrial freedom" was widely believed to lie at the root of the much-discussed "labor problem." Many Progressives believed that the key to increasing industrial freedom lay in empowering workers to participate in economic decision making via strong unions. Louis D. Brandeis, an active ally of the labor movement whom President Woodrow Wilson appointed to the Supreme Court in 1916, maintained that unions embodied an essential principle of freedom—the right of people to govern themselves. The contradiction between "political liberty" and "industrial slavery," Brandeis insisted, was America's foremost social problem.

Roller skaters with socialist leaflets during a New York City strike in 1916. A "scab" is a worker who crosses the picket line during a strike.

The Socialist Presence and Eugene Debs

Economic freedom was also a rallying cry of American socialism, which reached its greatest influence during the Progressive era. Founded in 1901, the **Socialist Party** called for immediate reforms such as free college education, legislation to improve the condition of laborers, and, as an ultimate goal, democratic control over the economy through public ownership of railroads and factories.

SOCIALIST TOWNS AND CITIES, 1900–1920

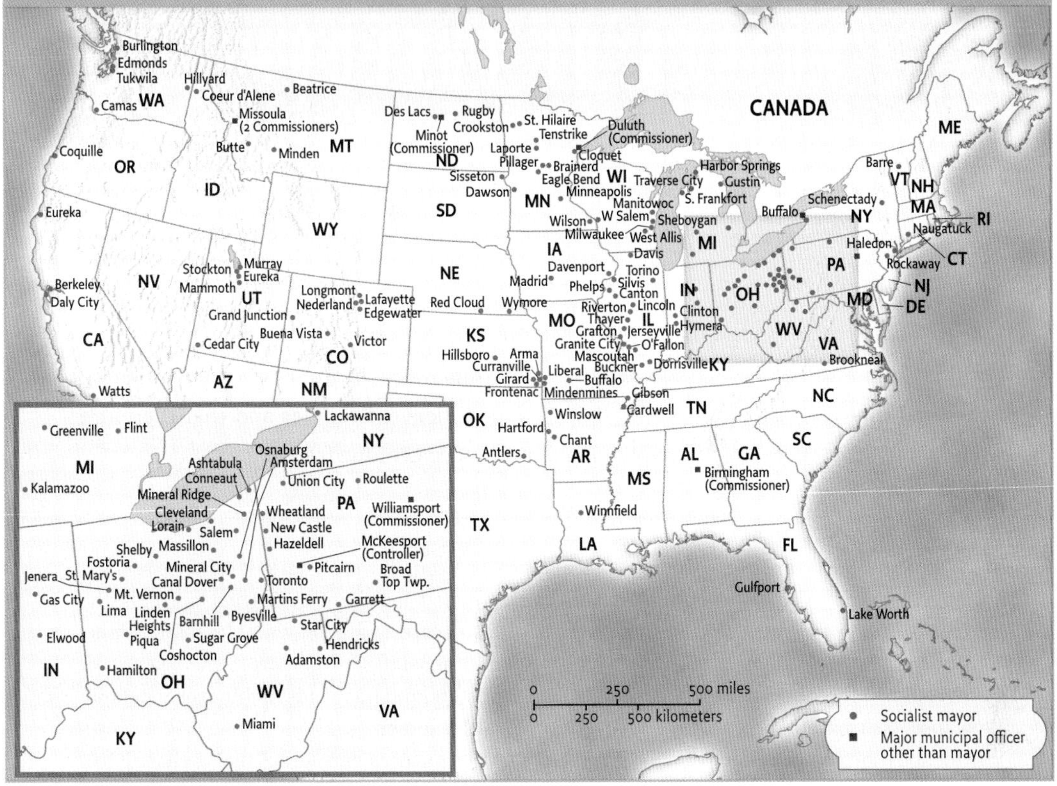

By 1912, the Socialist Party claimed 150,000 dues-paying members, published hundreds of newspapers, enjoyed substantial support in the American Federation of Labor (AFL), and had elected scores of local officials. Socialism flourished in diverse communities throughout the country. On the Lower East Side of New York City, it arose from the economic exploitation of immigrant workers and Judaism's tradition of social reform. Here, a vibrant socialist culture developed, complete with Yiddish-language newspapers and theaters, as well as large public meetings and street demonstrations. In 1914, the district elected socialist Meyer London to Congress. Another center of socialist strength was Milwaukee, where Victor Berger, a German-born teacher and newspaper editor, mobilized local AFL unions into a potent political force. Socialism also made inroads among tenant farmers in old Populist areas like Oklahoma, and in the mining regions of Idaho and Montana.

Although the Socialist Party never won more than 6 percent of the vote nationally, it gained control of numerous small and medium-sized cities between 1900 and 1920.

No one was more important in spreading the socialist gospel or linking it to ideals of equality, self-government, and freedom than Eugene V. Debs,

Eugene V. Debs

VOICES OF FREEDOM

From Charlotte Perkins Gilman, *Women and Economics* (1898)

***Women and Economics*, by the prolific feminist social critic and novelist Charlotte Perkins Gilman, influenced the new generation of women aspiring to greater independence. It insisted that how people earned a living shaped their entire lives and that therefore women must free themselves from the home to achieve genuine freedom.**

It is not motherhood that keeps the housewife on her feet from dawn till dark; it is house service, not child service. Women work longer and harder than most men. . . . A truer spirit is the increasing desire of young girls to be independent, to have a career of their own, at least for a while, and the growing objection of countless wives to the pitiful asking for money, to the beggary of their position. More and more do fathers give their daughters, and husbands their wives, a definite allowance,—a separate bank account,—something . . . all their own.

The spirit of personal independence in the women of today is sure proof that a change has come. . . . The radical change in the economic position of women is advancing upon us. . . . The growing individualization of democratic life brings inevitable change to our daughters as well as to our sons. . . . One of its most noticeable features is the demand in women not only for their own money, but for their own work for the sake of personal expression. Few girls today fail to manifest some signs of this desire for individual expression. . . .

Economic independence for women necessarily involves a change in the home and family relation. But, if that change is for the advantage of individual and race, we need not fear it. It does not involve a change in the marriage relation except in withdrawing the element of economic dependence, nor in the relation of mother to child save to improve it. But it does involve the exercise of human faculty in women, in social service and exchange rather than in domestic service solely. . . . [Today], when our still developing social needs call for an ever-increasing . . . freedom, the woman in marrying becomes the house-servant, or at least the housekeeper, of the man. . . . When women stand free as economic agents, they will [achieve a] much better fulfilment of their duties as wives and mothers and [contribute] to the vast improvement in health and happiness of the human race.

From John Mitchell, "The Workingman's Conception of Industrial Liberty" (1910)

During the Progressive era, the idea of "industrial liberty" moved to the center of political discussion. Progressive reformers and labor leaders like John Mitchell, head of the United Mine Workers, condemned the prevailing idea of liberty of contract in favor of a broader definition of economic freedom.

While the Declaration of Independence established civil and political liberty, it did not, as you all know, establish industrial liberty. . . . Liberty means more than the right to choose the field of one's employment. He is not a free man whose family must buy food today with the money that is earned tomorrow. He is not really free who is forced to work unduly long hours and for wages so low that he can not provide the necessities of life for himself and his family; who must live in a crowded tenement and see his children go to work in the mills, the mines, and the factories before their bodies are developed and their minds trained. To have freedom a man must be free from the harrowing fear of hunger and want; he must be in such a position that by the exercise of reasonable frugality he can provide his family with all of the necessities and the reasonable comforts of life. He must be able to educate his children and to provide against sickness, accident, and old age. . . .

A number of years ago the legislatures of several coal producing States enacted laws requiring employers to pay the wages of their workmen in lawful money of the United States and to cease the practice of paying wages in merchandise. From time immemorial it had been the custom of coal companies to conduct general supply stores, and the workingmen were required, as a condition of employment, to accept products in lieu of money in return for services rendered. This system was a great hardship to the workmen. . . . The question of the constitutionality of this legislation was carried into the courts and by the highest tribunal it was declared to be an invasion of the workman's liberty to deny him the right to accept merchandise in lieu of money as payment of his wages. . . . [This is] typical of hundreds of instances in which laws that have been enacted for the protection of the workingmen have been declared by the courts to be unconstitutional, on the grounds that they invaded the liberty of the working people. . . . Is it not natural that the workingmen should feel that they are being guaranteed the liberties they do not want and denied the liberty that is of real value to them? May they not exclaim, with Madame Roland [of the French Revolution], "O Liberty! Liberty! How many crimes are committed in thy name!"

QUESTIONS

1. *What does Gilman see as the main obstacles to freedom for women?*
2. *What does Mitchell believe will be necessary to establish "industrial liberty"?*
3. *How do the authors differ in their view of the relationship of the family to individual freedom?*

the railroad union leader who, as noted in the previous chapter, had been jailed during the Pullman Strike of 1894. For two decades, Debs crisscrossed the country preaching that control of the economy by a democratic government held out the hope of uniting "political equality and economic freedom." "While there is a lower class," proclaimed Debs, "I am in it. . . . While there is a soul in prison, I am not free."

Throughout the Atlantic world of the early twentieth century, socialism was a rising presence. Debs would receive more than 900,000 votes for president (6 percent of the total) in 1912. In that year, the socialist *Appeal to Reason*, published in Girard, Kansas, with a circulation of 700,000, was the largest weekly newspaper in the country.

AFL and IWW

American Federation of Labor (AFL)

Socialism was only one example of widespread discontent in Progressive America. Having survived the depression of the 1890s, the American Federation of Labor saw its membership triple to 1.6 million between 1900 and 1904. At the same time, its president, Samuel Gompers, sought to forge closer ties with forward-looking corporate leaders willing to deal with unions as a way to stabilize employee relations. Most employers nonetheless continued to view unions as an intolerable interference with their authority and resisted them stubbornly.

Industrial Workers of the World (IWW)

The AFL mainly represented the most privileged American workers—skilled industrial and craft laborers, nearly all of them white, male, and native-born. In 1905, a group of unionists who rejected the AFL's exclusionary policies formed the **Industrial Workers of the World** (IWW). Part trade union, part advocate of a workers' revolution that would seize the means of production and abolish the state, the IWW made solidarity its guiding principle. The organization sought to mobilize those excluded from the AFL—the immigrant factory labor force, migrant timber and agricultural workers, women, blacks, and even the despised Chinese on the West Coast.

The New Immigrants on Strike

The right of collective bargaining

A series of mass strikes among immigrant workers placed labor's demand for the right of **collective bargaining** at the forefront of the reform agenda. These strikes demonstrated that although ethnic divisions among workers impeded labor solidarity, ethnic cohesiveness could also be a basis of unity, so long as strikes were organized on a democratic basis. IWW organizers printed leaflets, posters, and banners in multiple languages and insisted that each nationality enjoy representation on the committee coordinating a walkout. It drew on the sense of solidarity within immigrant communities to persuade local religious leaders, shopkeepers, and officeholders to support the strikes.

The labor conflict that had the greatest impact on public consciousness took place in Lawrence, Massachusetts. The city's huge woolen mills employed 32,000 men, women, and children representing twenty-five nationalities. When the state legislature in January 1912 enacted a fifty-four-hour limit to the workweek, employers reduced the weekly take-home pay of those who had been laboring longer hours. Workers spontaneously went on strike.

Children of Lawrence, Massachusetts, strikers marching in New York City during the epic labor confrontation of 1911.

In February, strikers devised the idea of sending strikers' children out of the city for the duration of the walkout. Socialist families in New York City agreed to take them in. The sight of the children, many of whom appeared pale and half-starved, marching up Fifth Avenue from the train station led to a wave of sympathy for the strikers. The governor of Massachusetts soon intervened, and the strike was settled on the workers' terms. A banner carried by the Lawrence strikers gave a new slogan to the labor movement: "We want bread and roses, too"—a declaration that workers sought not only higher wages but also the opportunity to enjoy the finer things of life.

Labor and Civil Liberties

The fiery organizer Mary "Mother" Jones, who at the age of eighty-three had been jailed after addressing striking Colorado miners, later told a New York audience that the union "had only the Constitution; the other side had the bayonets." Yet the struggle of workers for the right to strike and of labor radicals against restraints on open-air speaking made free speech a significant public issue in the early twentieth century. By and large, the courts rejected their claims. But these battles laid the foundation for the rise of civil liberties as a central component of freedom in twentieth-century America.

The IWW's battle for freedom of expression is a case in point. Lacking union halls, its organizers relied on songs, street theater, impromptu organizing meetings, and street corner gatherings to spread their message and attract support. In response to IWW activities, officials in Los Angeles, Spokane, Denver, and more than a dozen other cities limited or prohibited outdoor meetings. To arouse popular support, the

A 1900 cartoon from *Puck, Divorce the Lesser Evil*. On the left, a quarreling husband and wife are chained to an "unhappy marriage." Justice is about to sever the marriage with her sword, while a minister tries to prevent her. Divorce laws had been liberalized after the Civil War; by the 1890s the United States had the highest divorce rate in the Western world. In the caption, the Church declares divorce an "awful immorality," to which Justice replies, "Divorce is rather an aid to morality."

IWW filled the jails with members who defied local law by speaking in public. In nearly all the free-speech fights, however, the IWW eventually forced local officials to give way. "Whether they agree or disagree with its methods or aims," wrote one journalist, "all lovers of liberty everywhere owe a debt to this organization for . . . [keeping] alight the fires of freedom."

Isadora Duncan brought a new freedom to an old art form.

The New Feminism

During the Progressive era, the word "feminism" first entered the political vocabulary. In 1914, a mass meeting at New York's Cooper Union debated the question "What is Feminism?" Feminism, said one speaker, meant woman's emancipation "both as a human being and a sex-being." Feminism's forthright attack on traditional rules of sexual behavior added a new dimension to the idea of personal freedom.

One symbol of the new era was Isadora Duncan, who brought from California a new, expressive dance based on the free movement of a body liberated from the constraints of traditional technique and costume. "I beheld the dance I had always dreamed of," wrote the novelist Edith Wharton on seeing a Duncan performance, "satisfying every sense as a flower does, or a phrase of Mozart's."

During this era, as journalist William M. Reedy jested, it struck "sex o'clock" in America. Issues of intimate personal relations previously confined to private discussion blazed forth in popular magazines and public debates. For the generation of women who adopted the word "feminism" to express their demand for greater liberty, free sexual expression and reproductive choice emerged as critical definitions of women's emancipation.

The much-beloved and much-feared Emma Goldman, speaking in favor of birth control to an almost entirely male crowd in New York City in 1916.

The Birth-Control Movement

The growing presence of women in the labor market reinforced demands for access to birth control, an issue that gave political expression to changing sexual behavior. Emma Goldman, who had emigrated to the United States from Lithuania at the age of sixteen, toured the country lecturing on subjects from anarchism to the need for more enlightened attitudes toward homosexuality. She regularly included the right to birth control in her speeches and distributed pamphlets with detailed information about various contraceptive devices.

By forthrightly challenging the laws banning contraceptive information and devices, Margaret Sanger, one of eleven children of an Irish-American working-class family, placed the **birth-control movement** at the heart of the new feminism. In 1911, she began a column on sex education,

"What Every Girl Should Know," for *The Call*, a New York socialist newspaper. Postal officials barred one issue, containing a column on venereal disease, from the mails. The next issue of *The Call* included a blank page with the headline: "What Every Girl Should Know—Nothing; by order of the U.S. Post Office."

Margaret Sanger

By 1914, the intrepid Sanger was openly advertising birth-control devices in her own journal, *The Woman Rebel*. "No woman can call herself free," she proclaimed, "who does not own and control her own body [and] can choose consciously whether she will or will not be a mother." In 1916, Sanger opened a clinic in a working-class neighborhood of Brooklyn and began distributing contraceptive devices to poor Jewish and Italian women, an action for which she was sentenced to a month in prison.

Helen Keller

Among the remarkable women involved in the birth-control movement—and radicalism more generally—was Helen Keller. Born in Alabama, she lost her sight and hearing because of a disease at the age of nineteen months. But she learned to read and write in braille and graduated from Radcliffe College in 1904. Keller became known throughout the world as the author of numerous articles and books, especially an autobiography that has been translated into over fifty languages. Later, her story became the subject of a popular play and film, *The Miracle Worker*. Keller became a leading advocate for persons with disabilities. Less well known is that Keller was also an outspoken supporter of socialism, woman suffrage, the rights of laborers, and world peace, and a longtime member of the Industrial Workers of the World.

The careers of Sanger and Keller exemplified how, for a time, the birth-control issue became a crossroads where the paths of labor radicals, cultural modernists, and feminists intersected. The IWW and Socialist Party distributed Sanger's writings. Slowly, laws banning birth control began to change. But since access was determined by individual states, even when some liberalized their laws, birth control remained unavailable in many others.

Native American Progressivism

Many groups participated in the Progressive impulse. Founded in 1911, the **Society of American Indians** was a reform organization typical of the era. It brought together Indian intellectuals to promote discussion of the plight of Native Americans in the hope that public exposure would be the first step toward remedying injustice. It created a pan-Indian public space independent of white control.

Indian intellectuals

Many of these Indian intellectuals were not unsympathetic to the basic goals of federal Indian policy, including the transformation of

Carlos Montezuma

communal landholdings on reservations into family farms. But Carlos Montezuma, a founder of the Society of American Indians, became an outspoken critic. Born in Arizona, he had been captured as a child by members of a neighboring tribe and sold to a traveling photographer, who brought him to Chicago. There Montezuma attended school and eventually obtained a medical degree.

In 1916, Montezuma established a newsletter, *Wassaja* (meaning "signaling"), that called for the abolition of the Bureau of Indian Affairs. Convinced that outsiders exerted too much power over life on the reservations, he insisted that self-determination was the only way for Indians to escape poverty and marginalization. But he also demanded that Indians be granted full citizenship and all the constitutional rights of other Americans. Activists would later rediscover him as a forerunner of Indian radicalism.

THE POLITICS OF PROGRESSIVISM

Effective Freedom

Worldwide Progressivism

Progressivism was an international movement. In the early twentieth century, cities throughout the world experienced similar social strains arising from rapid industrialization and urban growth. Reformers across the globe exchanged ideas and envisioned new social policies. The Chinese leader Sun Yat-Sen, for example, was influenced by the writings of Henry George and Edward Bellamy.

As governments in Britain, France, and Germany instituted old-age pensions, minimum-wage laws, unemployment insurance, and the regulation of workplace safety, American reformers came to believe they had much to learn from the Old World. The term "social legislation," meaning governmental action to address urban problems and the insecurities of working-class life, originated in Germany but soon entered the political vocabulary of the United States.

A photograph from 1910 depicts needy constituents of New York political boss Timothy "Big Tim" Sullivan receiving free pairs of shoes. Each year, Sullivan distributed two thousand pairs on his mother's birthday. Such largesse endeared political bosses to many voters, to the annoyance of municipal reformers.

Progressives sought to reinvigorate the idea of an activist, socially conscious government. Progressives could reject the traditional assumption that powerful government posed a threat to freedom, because their understanding of freedom was itself in flux. "Effective freedom," wrote the philosopher John Dewey, was a positive, not a negative, concept—the "power to do specific things." It sometimes required the government to act on behalf of those with little wealth or power. Thus, freedom in the Progressive era inevitably became a political question.

Pragmatism

Dewey was one of the foremost proponents of a school of philosophy called **pragmatism** that emerged in the late nineteenth century and strongly influenced Progressive thinkers. One of the most important philosophical movements ever to emerge in the United States, pragmatism, as explained in a 1907 book of that title by the philosopher William James (brother of the famous novelist Henry James), insisted that institutions and social policies must be judged by their concrete effects, not their longevity or how well they comport with religious doctrine or traditional political beliefs. Experience, pragmatists insisted, was more important than doctrine.

For Dewey, pragmatism encouraged an experimental approach to social problems characteristic of Progressivism. Given the deep divisions and widespread poverty in American society, ideologies such as Social Darwinism and liberty of contract, judged by the standard of pragmatism, had manifestly failed, and new approaches to social problems were needed. Dewey was a founder of the New School for Social Research in New York City, which stressed the importance of scientifically evaluating public policy. The idea that with proper information social improvement could be achieved was widely shared among American Progressives as well as their counterparts in other countries.

Evaluating public policy

State and Local Reforms

In the United States, with a political structure more decentralized than in European countries, state and local governments enacted most of the era's reform measures. In cities, Progressives worked to reform the structure of government to reduce the power of political bosses, establish public control of "natural monopolies" like gas and water works, and improve public transportation. They raised property taxes in order to spend more money on schools, parks, and other public facilities.

Urban Progressivism

Gilded Age mayors and governors pioneered urban Progressivism. A former factory worker who became a successful shoe manufacturer, Hazen Pingree served as mayor of Detroit from 1889 to 1897. He battled the business interests that had dominated city government, forced gas and telephone companies to lower their rates, and established a municipal power plant.

Progressivism in the West

Although often associated with eastern cities, Progressivism was also a major presence in the West. Former Populists and those who believed in the moral power of the frontier gravitated to Progressive programs to

Nursery children at play at the Italian Industrial School in New York City, one of numerous institutions established in the Progressive era to improve life in urban centers.

regulate the railroads and other large corporations, and to the idea that direct democracy could revitalize corrupt politics. Important Progressive leaders worked for reform in western states and municipalities, including Hiram Johnson of California and Robert La Follette of Wisconsin.

The Oregon System

Oregon stood at the forefront of Progressive reform. The leading figure in that state was William U'Ren, a lawyer who had entered politics as a supporter of Henry George's single-tax program. U'Ren was the founder of the Oregon System, which included the initiative, referendum, and recall. **Initiative**, also known as direct legislation, enabled citizens to propose and vote directly on laws, bypassing state legislatures. **Referendum** similarly provided for popular votes on public policies. **Recall** allowed for the removal of public officials by popular vote. Together with direct primaries, in which voters, rather than party officials, chose candidates for office, all these reforms sought to weaken the power of political bosses and transfer it to ordinary citizens. Using the initiative, Progressives won the vote for women in the state. The Oregon system, studied and emulated in many other states, came into being via an alliance of the urban middle class with reform-minded farmers and workers. But fault lines appeared when labor-oriented Progressives tried to use the initiative and referendum to increase taxes on the well-to-do and require the state to provide jobs for the unemployed. Both measures failed. Moreover, the initiative system quickly became out of control. In the 1912 election, voters in Portland were asked to evaluate forty measures seeking to become law. Nonetheless, between 1910 and 1912, Oregon's West Coast neighbors, Washington and California, also adopted the initiative and referendum and approved woman suffrage.

Public Utilities Act

In California, where a Republican machine closely tied to the Southern Pacific Railroad had dominated politics for decades, Progressives took power under Governor Hiram Johnson, who held office from 1911 to 1917. Having promised to "kick the Southern Pacific [Railroad] out of politics," he secured passage of the Public Utilities Act, one of the country's strongest railroad-regulation measures, as well as laws banning child labor and limiting the working hours of women.

The most influential Progressive administration at the state level was that of Robert M. La Follette, who made Wisconsin a "laboratory

Young boys and girls seek to enter a branch of the New York Public Library in 1910. The original caption reads, "The Children's Room is Already Full, 3:30 pm." Hoping to help uplift and assimilate the new immigrants and their children, libraries expanded rapidly during the Progressive era.

for democracy." After serving as a Republican member of Congress, La Follette became convinced that an alliance of railroad and lumber companies controlled state politics. Elected governor in 1900, he instituted a series of measures known as the Wisconsin Idea, including nominations of candidates for office through primary elections, the taxation of corporate wealth, and state regulation of railroads and public utilities. Other measures created a statewide system of insurance against illness, death, and accident, barred the sale to private companies of land, mineral rights, and other natural resources owned by the state, required safety devices on various forms of machinery, and prohibited child labor. To staff his administration, he drew on nonpartisan faculty members from the University of Wisconsin. Wisconsin offered the most striking merger of the social and political impulses that went under the name of Progressivism.

Progressive Democracy

Civic harmony

Progressives hoped to reinvigorate democracy by restoring political power to the citizenry and civic harmony to a divided society. Alarmed by the upsurge in violent class conflict and the unrestricted power of corporations, they believed that political reforms could help to create a unified "people" devoted to greater democracy and social reconciliation. Yet increasing the responsibilities of government made it all the more important to identify who was entitled to political participation and who was not.

The Progressive era saw a host of changes implemented in the political process, many seemingly contradictory in purpose. The electorate was simultaneously expanded and contracted, empowered and removed from direct influence on many functions of government. Democracy was enhanced by the **Seventeenth Amendment** (1913)—which provided that U.S. senators be chosen by popular vote rather than by state legislatures—by widespread adoption of the popular election of judges, and by the use of primary elections among party members to select candidates for office. The era culminated with a constitutional amendment enfranchising women—the largest expansion of democracy in American history.

Constitutional amendments

Restricting democratic participation

But the Progressive era also witnessed numerous restrictions on democratic participation, most strikingly the disenfranchisement of blacks in the South, as noted in Chapter 17. To make city government more honest and efficient, many localities replaced elected mayors with appointed non-partisan commissions or city managers—a change that insulated officials from machine domination but also from popular control. New literacy tests and residency and registration requirements, common in northern as well as southern states, limited the right to vote among the poor. In the eyes of many Progressives, the "fitness" of voters, not their absolute numbers, defined a functioning democracy.

Government by experts

Most Progressive thinkers were highly uncomfortable with the real world of politics, which seemed to revolve around the pursuit of narrow class, ethnic, and regional interests. Robert M. La Follette's reliance on college professors to staff important posts in his administration reflected a larger Progressive faith in expertise. The government could best exercise intelligent control over society through a democracy run by impartial experts who were in many respects unaccountable to the citizenry. Political freedom was less a matter of direct participation in government than of qualified persons devising the best public policies.

Jane Addams and Hull House

Women reformers and Progressivism

But alongside this elitist politics, Progressivism also included a more democratic vision of the activist state. As much as any other group, organized women reformers spoke for the democratic side of Progressivism. Still barred from voting and from holding office in most states, women nonetheless became central to the political history of the Progressive era. The immediate catalyst was a growing awareness among women reformers of the plight of poor immigrant communities and the emergence of the condition of women and child laborers as a major focus of public concern.

Jane Addams

The era's most prominent female reformer was Jane Addams, who was born in 1860, the daughter of an Illinois businessman. In 1889, she founded Hull House in Chicago, a **settlement house** devoted to improving the lives of the immigrant poor. Unlike previous reformers who had aided the poor from afar, settlement-house workers moved into poor neighborhoods. They built kindergartens and playgrounds for children, established employment bureaus and health clinics, and showed female victims of domestic abuse how to gain legal protection. By 1910, more than 400 settlement houses had been established in cities throughout the country.

Addams was typical of the Progressive era's "new woman." By 1900, there were more than 80,000 college-educated women in the United States. Many found a calling in providing social services, nursing, and education to poor families in the growing cities. The efforts of middle-class women to uplift the poor, and of laboring women to uplift themselves, helped to shift the center of gravity of politics toward activist government. Women like Addams discovered that even well-organized social work was not enough to alleviate the problems of inadequate housing, income, and health. Government action was essential. Hull House inspired an array of reforms in Chicago, soon adopted elsewhere, including stronger building and sanitation codes, shorter working hours and safer labor conditions, and the right of labor to organize.

Mounted on a white horse and wearing a white cape, Inez Milholland evokes the image of Joan of Arc as she waits to lead a suffrage parade in Washington, D.C., in 1913. Three years later, Milholland collapsed and died at the age of thirty while on a suffrage lecture tour in California.

The settlement houses have been called "spearheads for reform." Florence Kelley, a veteran of Hull House, went on to mobilize women's power as consumers as a force for social change. Under Kelley's leadership, the National Consumers' League became the nation's leading advocate of laws governing the working conditions of women and children.

The Campaign for Woman Suffrage

After 1900, the campaign for woman suffrage moved beyond the elitism of the 1890s to engage a broad coalition ranging from middle-class members of women's clubs to unionists, socialists, and settlement-house workers. For the first time, it became a mass movement. Membership in the National American Woman Suffrage Association grew from 13,000 in 1893 to more than 2 million by 1917. By 1900, more than half the states allowed women to vote in local elections dealing with school issues, and Wyoming, Colorado, Idaho, and Utah had adopted full woman suffrage. Between 1910 and 1914, seven more western states enfranchised women. In 1913, Illinois became the first state east of the Mississippi River to allow women to vote in presidential elections.

Mayor Mary W. Howard (center) and the town council of Kanab, Utah. They served from 1912 to 1914, the first all-female municipal government in American history.

These campaigns, which brought women aggressively into the public sphere, were conducted with a new spirit of militancy. They also made effective use of the techniques of advertising, publicity, and mass entertainment characteristic of modern consumer society. California's successful 1911 campaign utilized automobile parades, numerous billboards and electric signs, and countless suffrage buttons and badges. Nonetheless, state campaigns were difficult, expensive, and usually unsuccessful. The movement increasingly focused its attention on securing a national constitutional amendment giving women the right to vote.

Mary Pickford, one of the era's most celebrated movie stars, publicized her support for woman suffrage in this photograph from around 1910.

Maternalist Reform

Ironically, the desire to exalt women's role within the home did much to inspire the reinvigoration of the suffrage movement. Female reformers helped to launch a mass movement for direct government action to improve the living standards of poor mothers and children. Laws providing for mothers' pensions (state aid to mothers of young children who lacked male support) spread rapidly after 1910. These **maternalist reforms** rested on the assumption that the government should encourage women's capacity for bearing and raising children and enable them to be economically independent at the same time. Both feminists and believers in conventional domestic roles supported such measures. The former hoped that these laws would subvert women's dependence on men, the latter that they would strengthen traditional families and the mother-child bond.

Other Progressive legislation recognized that large numbers of women did in fact work outside the home but defined them as a dependent group (like children) in need of state protection in ways male workers were not. In 1908, in the landmark case of ***Muller v. Oregon***, Louis D. Brandeis filed a brief citing scientific and sociological studies to demonstrate that because women had less strength and endurance than men, long hours of labor were dangerous for women, while women's unique ability to bear children gave the government a legitimate interest in their working conditions. Persuaded by Brandeis's argument, the Supreme Court unanimously upheld the constitutionality of an Oregon law setting maximum working hours for women.

Louisine Havemeyer, one of New York City's wealthiest women, was a strong advocate of woman suffrage. Here, in a 1915 photograph, she passes the Torch of Liberty to a group of New Jersey women.

Thus, three years after the notorious *Lochner* decision invalidating a New York law limiting the working hours of male bakers (discussed in Chapter 16), the Court created the first large breach in "liberty of contract" doctrine. But the cost was high: at the very time that women in unprecedented numbers were entering the labor market and earning college degrees, Brandeis's brief and the Court's opinion solidified the view of women workers as weak, dependent, and incapable of enjoying the same economic rights as men. By 1917, thirty states had enacted laws limiting the hours of labor of female workers.

The maternalist agenda that built gender inequality into the early foundations of the welfare state by extension raised the idea that government should better the living and working conditions of men as well. Indeed, Brandeis envisioned the welfare state as one rooted in the notion of universal economic entitlements, including the right to a decent income and protection against unemployment and work-related accidents.

According to this cartoon, giving women the right to vote will clean up political corruption and misgovernment.

This vision, too, enjoyed considerable support in the Progressive era. By 1913, twenty-two states had enacted workmen's compensation laws to benefit workers, male or female, injured on the job. This legislation was the first wedge that opened the way for broader programs of social insurance. But state minimum-wage laws and most laws regulating working hours applied only to women. Women and children may have needed protection, but interference with the freedom of contract of adult male workers was still widely seen as degrading. The establishment of a standard of living and working conditions beneath which no American, male or female, should be allowed to fall would await the coming of the New Deal.

THE PROGRESSIVE PRESIDENTS

Herbert Croly

Despite creative experiments in social policy at the city and state levels, the tradition of localism seemed to most Progressives an impediment to a renewed sense of national purpose. Poverty, economic insecurity, and lack of industrial democracy were national problems that demanded national solutions. *New Republic* editor Herbert Croly proposed a new synthesis of American political traditions. To achieve the "Jeffersonian ends" of democratic self-determination and individual freedom, he insisted, the country needed to employ the "Hamiltonian means" of government intervention in the economy. Each in his own way, the Progressive presidents—Theodore Roosevelt, William Howard Taft, and Woodrow Wilson—tried to address this challenge.

Theodore Roosevelt

In September 1901, the anarchist Leon Czolgosz assassinated William McKinley while the president visited the Pan-American Exposition in Buffalo, New York. At the age of forty-two, Vice President Theodore

President Theodore Roosevelt addressing a crowd in 1902.

Roosevelt became the youngest man ever to hold the office of president. In many ways, he became the model for the twentieth-century president, an official actively and continuously engaged in domestic and foreign affairs. (The foreign policies of the Progressive presidents will be discussed in the next chapter.) He moved aggressively to set the political agenda.

Roosevelt's domestic program, which he called the Square Deal, attempted to confront the problems caused by economic consolidation by distinguishing between "good" and "bad" corporations. The former, among which he included U.S. Steel and Standard Oil, served the public interest. The latter were run by greedy financiers interested only in profit and had no right to exist.

Soon after assuming office, Roosevelt shocked the corporate world by announcing his intention to prosecute under the Sherman Antitrust Act the Northern Securities Company. Created by financier J. P. Morgan, this "holding company" owned the stock and directed the affairs of three major western railroads. It monopolized transportation between the Great Lakes and the Pacific. In 1904, the Supreme Court ordered Northern Securities dissolved, a major victory for the antitrust movement.

Public support for regulation

Reelected that same year, Roosevelt pushed for more direct federal regulation of the economy. He proposed to strengthen the Interstate Commerce Commission (ICC), which the Supreme Court had essentially limited to collecting economic statistics. By this time, journalistic exposés, labor unrest, and the agitation of Progressive reformers had created significant public support for Roosevelt's regulatory program. In 1906, Congress passed the Hepburn Act, giving the ICC the power to examine railroads' business records and to set reasonable rates, a significant step in the development of federal intervention in the corporate economy. That year, as has been noted, also saw passage of the **Pure Food and Drug Act**. Many businessmen supported these measures, recognizing that they would benefit from greater public confidence in the quality and safety of their products. But even they were alarmed by Roosevelt's calls for federal inheritance and income taxes and the regulation of all interstate businesses.

Putting the Screws on Him, a 1904 cartoon, depicts President Theodore Roosevelt squeezing ill-gotten gains out of the trusts.

John Muir and the Spirituality of Nature

If the United States lagged behind Europe in many areas of social policy, it led the way in the conservation of natural resources. The first national park, Yellowstone in Wyoming, was created in 1872, partly to preserve an area of remarkable natural beauty and partly at the urging of the Northern Pacific Railroad, which was anxious to promote western tourism. In the 1890s, the Scottish-born naturalist John Muir organized the Sierra Club to help preserve forests from uncontrolled logging by timber companies.

Muir's love of nature stemmed from deep religious feelings. Nearly blinded in an accident in an Indianapolis machine shop where he worked in his twenties, he found in the restoration of his sight an inspiration to appreciate God's creation. He called forests "God's first temples." In nature, he believed, men could experience directly the presence of God. Muir was inspired by the Transcendentalists of the pre-Civil War era—like Henry David Thoreau, he lamented the intrusions of civilization on the natural environment. But unlike them, Muir developed a broad following. As more and more Americans lived in cities, they came to see nature less as something to conquer and more as a place for recreation and personal growth.

The Old Faithful geyser, the most famous site in Yellowstone, the nation's first national park, in a photograph from the 1880s.

The Conservation Movement

In the 1890s, Congress authorized the president to withdraw "forest reserves" from economic development, a restriction on economic freedom in the name of a greater social good. But it was under Theodore Roosevelt that the **conservation movement** became a concerted federal policy. A dedicated outdoorsman who built a ranch in North Dakota in the 1880s, Roosevelt moved to preserve parts of the natural environment from economic exploitation.

Relying for advice on Gifford Pinchot, the head of the U.S. Forest Service, he ordered that millions of acres be set aside as wildlife preserves and encouraged Congress to create new national parks. In some ways, conservation was a typical Progressive reform. Manned by experts, the government could stand above political and economic battles, serving the public good while preventing "special interests" from causing irreparable damage to the environment. The aim was less to end the economic utilization of natural resources than to develop responsible, scientific plans for their use. Pinchot halted timber companies' reckless assault on the nation's forests. But unlike Muir, he believed that development and conservation could go hand in hand and that logging, mining, and grazing on public lands should be controlled, not eliminated.

Theodore Roosevelt (center) posing with a group in a grove of giant sequoia trees in California in 1903. He called on Americans to protect these "monuments of beauty."

Taft in Office

Having served nearly eight years as president, Roosevelt did not run again in 1908. His chosen successor, William Howard Taft, defeated William Jennings Bryan, making his third unsuccessful race for the White House.

Although temperamentally more conservative than Roosevelt, Taft pursued antitrust policy even more aggressively. He persuaded the Supreme Court in 1911 to declare John D. Rockefeller's Standard Oil Company (one of Roosevelt's "good" trusts) in violation of the Sherman

Antitrust Act and to order its breakup into separate marketing, producing, and refining companies. The government also won a case against American Tobacco, which the Court ordered to end pricing policies that were driving smaller firms out of business.

The income tax

Taft supported the **Sixteenth Amendment** to the Constitution, which authorized Congress to enact a graduated income tax (one whose rate of taxation is higher for wealthier citizens). It was ratified shortly before he left office. A 2 percent tax on incomes over $4,000 had been included in a tariff enacted in 1894 but had been quickly declared unconstitutional by the Supreme Court as a "communistic threat to property." A key step in the modernization of the federal government, the income tax provided a reliable and flexible source of revenue for a national state whose powers, responsibilities, and expenditures were growing rapidly.

Ballinger and Pinchot

Despite these accomplishments, Taft seemed to gravitate toward the more conservative wing of the Republican Party. Taft's rift with Progressives grew deeper when Richard A. Ballinger, the secretary of the interior, concluded that Roosevelt had exceeded his authority in placing land in forest reserves. Ballinger decided to return some of this land to the public domain, where mining and lumber companies would have access to it. Gifford Pinchot accused Ballinger of colluding with business interests and repudiating the environmental goals of the Roosevelt administration. When Taft fired Pinchot in 1910, the breach with party Progressives became irreparable. In 1912, Roosevelt challenged Taft for the Republican nomination. Defeated, Roosevelt launched an independent campaign as the head of the new **Progressive Party**.

The Election of 1912

A key election

All the crosscurrents of Progressive-era thinking came together in the presidential campaign of 1912. The four-way contest between Taft, Roosevelt, Democrat Woodrow Wilson, and Socialist Eugene V. Debs became a national debate on the relationship between political and economic freedom in the age of big business. At one end of the political spectrum stood Taft, who stressed that economic individualism could remain the foundation of the social order so long as government and private entrepreneurs cooperated in addressing social ills. At the other end was Debs. Relatively few Americans supported the Socialist Party's goal of abolishing the "capitalistic system" altogether, but its immediate demands—including public ownership of the railroads and banking system, government aid to the unemployed, and laws establishing shorter working hours and a minimum wage—summarized forward-looking Progressive thought.

But it was the battle between Wilson and Roosevelt over the role of the federal government in securing economic freedom that galvanized public attention in 1912. The two represented competing strands of Progressivism. Both believed government action necessary to preserve individual freedom, but they differed over the dangers of increasing the government's power and the inevitability of economic concentration.

Eugene V. Debs, the Socialist Party candidate, speaking in Chicago during the 1912 presidential campaign.

New Freedom and New Nationalism

Strongly influenced by Louis D. Brandeis, with whom he consulted frequently during the campaign, Wilson insisted that democracy must be reinvigorated by restoring market competition and freeing government from domination by big business. Wilson feared big government as much as he feared the power of the corporations. The **New Freedom**, as he called his program, envisioned the federal government strengthening antitrust laws, protecting the right of workers to unionize, and actively encouraging small businesses—creating, in other words, the conditions for the renewal of economic competition without increasing government regulation of the economy. Wilson warned that corporations were as likely to corrupt government as to be managed by it, a forecast that proved remarkably accurate.

Roosevelt's New Nationalism

To Roosevelt's supporters, Wilson seemed a relic of a bygone era; his program, they argued, served the needs of small businessmen but ignored the inevitability of economic concentration and the interests of professionals, consumers, and labor. Espousing the **New Nationalism**, his program of 1912, Roosevelt insisted that only the "controlling and directing power of the government" could restore "the liberty of the oppressed." He called for heavy taxes on personal and corporate fortunes and federal regulation of industries, including railroads, mining, and oil.

The Progressive Party Platform of 1912

The Progressive Party platform offered numerous proposals to promote social justice. Drafted by a group of settlement-house activists, labor reformers, and social scientists, the platform laid out a blueprint for a modern, democratic welfare state, complete with woman suffrage, federal supervision of corporate enterprise, national labor and health legislation for women and children, an eight-hour day and "living wage" for all workers, and a national system of social insurance covering unemployment, medical care, and old age. Roosevelt's campaign helped to give freedom a modern social and economic content and established an agenda that would define political liberalism for much of the twentieth century.

Roosevelt's Americanism

A redefinition of what it meant to be an American united many strands of Progressive-era thought. Theodore Roosevelt's New Nationalism was one example. Roosevelt wanted immigrants to "Americanize" rather than retaining cultures and customs from their countries of origin. He also believed that fitness for citizenship—or lack thereof—was both inborn and related to past historical experience. Slaves brought from Africa and their descendants, he believed, could not assimilate properly into American culture. Only persons with the capacity for "self-control"—mainly white people—were capable of participating in democracy.

"The right type of good citizenship"

In a 1910 speech in Kansas outlining his New Nationalism, Roosevelt announced that the "prime problem of our nation is to get the right type of good citizenship." Being a proper American required a certain level of material comfort. "No man can be a good citizen," he declared, "unless he has a wage more than sufficient to cover the bare cost of living.... We keep countless men from being good citizens by the conditions of life with which we surround them." Yet the person who lacked the qualities necessary to be "a good man in the home, a good father, a good husband" could also never be a good citizen. Clearly, Roosevelt's idea of citizenship had a strong gender bias. Yet in 1912 he would embrace woman suffrage. Roosevelt's concept of Americanism, although closed to blacks and Asian-Americans, was open to more people than the outlook of his contemporaries who also excluded the "new immigrants" from Europe. But its coercive potential would become starkly evident a few years later, when the United States entered World War I and the government demanded absolute loyalty of all Americans and the immediate assimilation of immigrants.

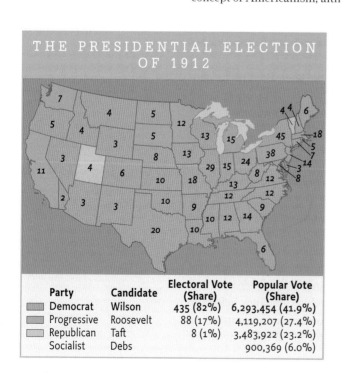

THE PRESIDENTIAL ELECTION OF 1912

Party	Candidate	Electoral Vote (Share)	Popular Vote (Share)
Democrat	Wilson	435 (82%)	6,293,454 (41.9%)
Progressive	Roosevelt	88 (17%)	4,119,207 (27.4%)
Republican	Taft	8 (1%)	3,483,922 (23.2%)
Socialist	Debs		900,369 (6.0%)

Wilson's First Term

The Republican split in 1912 ensured a sweeping victory for Wilson, who won about 42 percent of the popular vote, although Roosevelt humiliated Taft by winning about 27 percent to the president's 23 percent. In office, Wilson proved himself a strong executive leader. He was the first president to hold regular press conferences, and he delivered messages

WHO IS AN AMERICAN?

From Mary Church Terrell, "What it Means to be Colored in the Capital of the United States" (1906)

The daughter of slaves, Mary Church Terrell became one of the nation's most prominent black women. A high school teacher in Washington, D.C., she went on to serve on the city's Board of Education and became a founder of the NAACP. In 1906, Terrell delivered a speech to a women's club in Washington in which she outlined some of the forms of humiliation faced daily by African-Americans in the nation's capital. They were treated, she pointed out, like aliens in their native land.

As a colored woman I might enter Washington any night, a stranger in a strange land, and walk miles without finding a place to lay my head. Unless I happened to know colored people who live here . . . I should be obliged to spend the entire night wandering about. Indians, Chinamen, Filipinos, Japanese and representatives of any other dark race can find hotel accommodations, if they can pay for them. The colored man alone is thrust out of the hotels of the national capital like a leper.

Unless I am willing to engage in a few menial occupations, in which the pay for my services would be very poor, there is no way for me to earn an honest living, if I am not a trained nurse or a dressmaker or can secure a position as teacher in the public schools. . . . If I try to enter many of the numerous vocations in which my white sisters are allowed to engage, the door is shut in my face. . . .

It is impossible for any white person in the United States, no matter how sympathetic and broad, to realize what life would mean to him if his incentive to effort were suddenly snatched away. . . . Surely nowhere in the world do oppression and persecution based solely on the color of the skin appear more hateful and hideous than in the capital of the United States, because the chasm between the principles upon which this Government was founded, in which it still professes to believe, and those which are daily practiced under the protection of the flag, yawn so wide and deep.

QUESTIONS

1. *Why does Terrell compare her situation with that of people from China, Japan, and other countries in Asia?*
2. *Why does she consider prejudice more "hateful" in the United States than in other countries?*

personally to Congress rather than sending them in written form, as had all his predecessors since John Adams.

Wilson's initiatives

With Democrats in control of Congress, Wilson moved aggressively to implement his version of Progressivism. The first significant measure of his presidency was the Underwood Tariff, which substantially reduced duties on imports and, to make up for lost revenue, imposed a graduated income tax on the richest 5 percent of Americans. There followed the Clayton Act of 1914, which exempted labor unions from antitrust laws and barred courts from issuing injunctions curtailing the right to strike. In 1916 came the Keating-Owen Act, outlawing child labor in the manufacture of goods sold in interstate commerce; the Adamson Act, establishing an eight-hour workday on the nation's railroads; and the Warehouse Act, reminiscent of the Populist subtreasury plan, which extended credit to farmers when they stored their crops in federally licensed warehouses.

The Expanding Role of Government

Some of Wilson's policies seemed more in tune with Roosevelt's New Nationalism than the New Freedom of 1912. Wilson presided over the creation of two powerful new public agencies. In 1913, Congress created the Federal Reserve System, consisting of twelve regional banks. They were overseen by a central board appointed by the president and empowered to handle the issuance of currency, aid banks in danger of failing, and influence interest rates so as to promote economic growth.

The Federal Reserve System

A second expansion of national power occurred in 1914, when Congress established the **Federal Trade Commission** (FTC) to investigate and prohibit "unfair" business activities such as price-fixing and monopolistic practices. Both the Federal Reserve and the FTC were welcomed by many business leaders as a means of restoring order to the economic marketplace and warding off more radical measures for curbing corporate power. But they reflected the remarkable expansion of the federal role in the economy during the Progressive era.

A new nation-state

By 1916, the social ferment and political mobilizations of the Progressive era had given birth to a new American state. With new laws, administrative agencies, and independent commissions, government at the local, state, and national levels had assumed the authority to protect and advance "industrial freedom." Government had established rules for labor relations, business behavior, and financial policy, protected citizens from market abuses, and acted as a broker among the groups whose conflicts threatened to destroy social harmony. But a storm was already engulfing Europe that would test the Progressive faith in empowered government as the protector of American freedom.

CHAPTER REVIEW AND ONLINE RESOURCES

REVIEW QUESTIONS

1. *Identify the main groups and ideas that drove the Progressive movement.*
2. *Explain how immigration to the United States in this period was part of a global movement of peoples.*
3. *Describe how Fordism transformed American industrial and consumer society.*
4. *Socialism was a rising force across the globe in the early twentieth century. How successful was the movement in the United States?*
5. *Explain why the Industrial Workers of the World (IWW) grew so rapidly and aroused so much opposition.*
6. *How did pragmatism influence Progressive thinkers like John Dewey?*
7. *How did immigrants adjust to life in America? What institutions or activities became important to their adjustment, and why?*
8. *What did Progressive-era feminists want to change in society, and how did their actions help to spearhead broader reforms?*
9. *How did ideas of women's roles, shared by maternalist reformers, lead to an expansion of activism by and rights for women?*
10. *How did each Progressive-era president view the role of the federal government?*
11. *According to Theodore Roosevelt, what were the qualities that made for "the right type of good citizenship"?*
12. *Pick a Progressive-era reform (a movement, a specific legislation, or an organization) and describe how it shows how Progressives could work for both the expansion of democracy and restrictions on it.*

KEY TERMS

Progressivism (p. 541)
muckraking (p. 543)
Ellis Island (p. 543)
Fordism (p. 546)
"American standard of living" (p. 547)
scientific management (p. 548)
Socialist Party (p. 548)
Industrial Workers of the World (p. 552)
collective bargaining (p. 552)
birth-control movement (p. 554)
Society of American Indians (p. 555)
pragmatism (p. 557)
initiative (p. 558)
referendum (p. 558)
recall (p. 558)
Seventeenth Amendment (p. 559)
settlement house (p. 560)
maternalist reforms (p. 562)
Muller v. Oregon (p. 562)
Pure Food and Drug Act (p. 564)
conservation movement (p. 565)
Sixteenth Amendment (p. 566)
Progressive Party (p. 566)
New Freedom (p. 567)
New Nationalism (p. 567)
Federal Trade Commission (p. 570)

Go to INQUIZITIVE

To see what you know—and learn what you've missed—with personalized feedback along the way.

Visit the ***Give Me Liberty!* Student Site** for primary source documents and images, interactive maps, author videos featuring Eric Foner, and more.

1903	United States secures the Panama Canal Zone
	W. E. B. Du Bois's *The Souls of Black Folk*
1904	Roosevelt Corollary to the Monroe Doctrine
1905	The Niagara movement established
1907	Gentlemen's Agreement with Japan
1909	National Association for the Advancement of Colored People organized
1910	Mexican Revolution begins
1911	*Bailey v. Alabama*
1914	Assassination of Archduke Ferdinand
1914–1919	World War I
1915	D. W. Griffith's *Birth of a Nation* premieres
	Lusitania sinks
1917	Zimmermann Telegram intercepted
	United States enters the war
	Espionage Act passed
	Russian Revolution
1918	Woodrow Wilson's "Fourteen Points" speech
1918–1920	Worldwide flu epidemic
1919	Eighteenth Amendment
	Treaty of Versailles signed
1919–1920	Red Scare
	Senate rejects the Treaty of Versailles
1920	Nineteenth Amendment ratified
1921	Tulsa Riot

CHAPTER 19

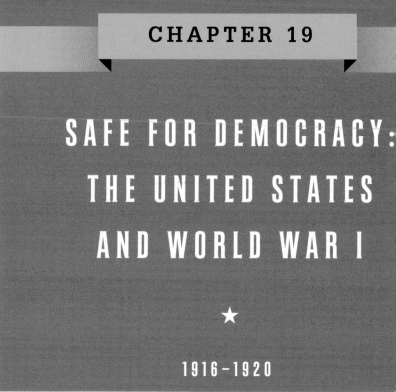

SAFE FOR DEMOCRACY: THE UNITED STATES AND WORLD WAR I

★

1916–1920

American Infantry Advancing with Tanks near Essay, a crayon and charcoal drawing by George Matthews Harding, captures the challenging conditions faced by American soldiers during World War I. An accomplished magazine illustrator, Harding was one of eight official war artists hired by the War Department to record combat scenes. He was particularly intrigued by the new technologies of warfare, including airplanes, trucks, motorcycles, and, as in this work, the armored tank. During World War II he again painted scenes of war, this time in the South Pacific

In 1902, W. T. Stead published a short volume with the arresting title *The Americanization of the World; or, the Trend of the Twentieth Century*, in which he predicted that the United States would soon emerge as "the greatest of world-powers." But what was most striking about his work was that Stead located the source of American power less in the realm of military might or territorial acquisition than in the country's single-minded commitment to the "pursuit of wealth" and the relentless international spread of American culture—art, music, journalism, even ideas about religion and gender relations. He foresaw a future in which the United States promoted its interests and values through an unending involvement in the affairs of other nations. Stead proved to be an accurate prophet.

The Spanish-American War had established the United States as an international empire. Despite the conquest of the Philippines and Puerto Rico, however, the country's overseas holdings remained tiny compared with those of Britain, France, and Germany. And no more were added, except for a strip of land surrounding the Panama Canal, acquired in 1903, and the Virgin Islands, purchased from Denmark in 1917. In 1900, Great Britain ruled over more than 300 million people in possessions scattered across the globe, and France had nearly 50 million subjects in Asia and Africa. Compared with these, the American presence in the world seemed very small. As Stead suggested, America's empire differed significantly from those of European countries—it was economic, cultural, and intellectual, rather than territorial.

The world economy at the dawn of the twentieth century was already highly globalized. An ever-increasing stream of goods, investments, and people flowed from country to country. Although Britain still dominated world banking and the British pound remained the major currency of international trade, the United States had become the leading industrial power. By 1914, it produced more than one-third of the world's manufactured goods. Spearheads of American culture like movies and popular music were not far behind.

Europeans were fascinated by American ingenuity and mass-production techniques. Many feared American products and culture would overwhelm their own. "What are the chief new features of London life?" one British writer asked in 1901. "They are the telephone, the portable camera, the phonograph, the electric street car, the automobile, the typewriter. . . . In every one of these the American maker is supreme."

America's burgeoning connections with the outside world led to increasing military and political involvement. In the two decades after 1900, many of the basic principles that would guide American foreign

FOCUS QUESTIONS

- *In what ways did the Progressive presidents promote the expansion of American power overseas?*
- *How did the United States get involved in World War I?*
- *How did the United States mobilize resources and public opinion for the war effort?*
- *How did the war affect race relations in the United States?*
- *Why was 1919 such a watershed year for the United States and the world?*

policy for the rest of the century were formulated. The "open door"—the free flow of trade, investment, information, and culture—emerged as a key principle of American foreign relations.

Americans in the twentieth century often discussed foreign policy in the language of freedom. A supreme faith in America's historic destiny and in the righteousness of its ideals enabled the country's leaders to think of the United States simultaneously as an emerging great power and as the worldwide embodiment of freedom.

More than any other individual, Woodrow Wilson articulated this vision of America's relationship to the rest of the world. His foreign policy, called by historians **liberal internationalism**, rested on the conviction that economic and political progress went hand in hand. Thus, greater worldwide freedom would follow inevitably from increased American investment and trade abroad. Frequently during the twentieth century, this conviction would serve as a mask for American power and self-interest. It would also inspire sincere efforts to bring freedom to other peoples. In either case, liberal internationalism represented a shift from the nineteenth-century tradition of promoting freedom primarily by example to active intervention to remake the world in the American image.

AN ERA OF INTERVENTION

Just as they expanded the powers of the federal government in domestic affairs, the Progressive presidents were not reluctant to project American power outside the country's borders. At first, they confined their interventions to the Western Hemisphere, whose affairs the United States had claimed a special right to oversee ever since the Monroe Doctrine of 1823.

The Caribbean

Between 1901 and 1920, U.S. marines landed in Caribbean countries more than twenty times. Usually, they were dispatched to create a welcoming economic environment for American companies that wanted stable access to raw materials like bananas and sugar, and for bankers nervous that their loans to local governments might not be repaid.

"I Took the Canal Zone"

Roosevelt's international diplomacy

Theodore Roosevelt became far more active in international diplomacy than most of his predecessors, helping, for example, to negotiate a settlement of the Russo-Japanese War of 1905, a feat for which he was awarded the Nobel Peace Prize. Closer to home, his policies were more aggressive.

THE UNITED STATES IN THE CARIBBEAN, 1898–1941

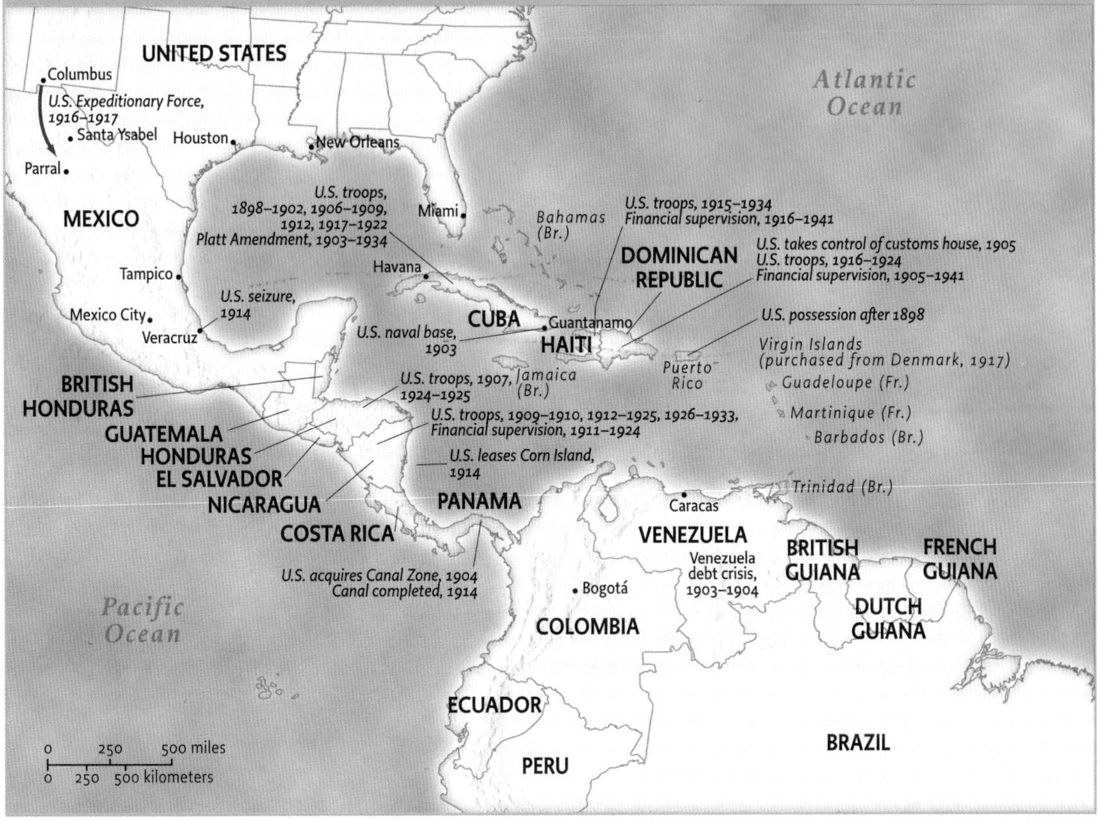

Between 1898 and 1941, the United States intervened militarily numerous times in Caribbean countries, generally to protect the economic interests of American banks and investors.

"I have always been fond of the West African proverb," he wrote, "'Speak softly and carry a big stick.'"

The idea of a canal across the fifty-one-mile-wide Isthmus of Panama had a long history. A longtime proponent of American naval development, Roosevelt was convinced that a canal would facilitate the movement of naval and commercial vessels between the two oceans. In 1903, when Colombia, of which Panama was a part, refused to cede land for the project, Roosevelt helped set in motion an uprising by Panamanian conspirators. An American gunboat prevented the Colombian army from suppressing the rebellion.

The Panama Canal

Upon establishing its independence, Panama signed a treaty giving the United States both the right to construct and operate a canal and sovereignty over the **Panama Canal Zone**, a ten-mile-wide strip of land through which the route would run. A remarkable feat of engineering, the canal was the largest construction project in American history to that date. Like the

Immigrant labor

building of the transcontinental railroad in the 1860s and much construction work today, it involved the widespread use of immigrant labor. Most of the 60,000 workers came from the Caribbean islands of Barbados and Jamaica, but others hailed from Europe, Asia, and the United States. When completed in 1914, the canal reduced the sea voyage between the East and West Coasts of the United States by 8,000 miles. "I took the Canal Zone," Roosevelt exulted. But the manner in which the canal had been initiated, and the continued American rule over the Canal Zone, would long remain a source of tension. In 1977, President Jimmy Carter, as a symbol of a new, noninterventionist U.S. attitude toward Latin America, negotiated treaties that led to turning over the canal's operation and control of the Canal Zone to Panama in the year 2000 (see Chapter 26).

The Roosevelt Corollary

Roosevelt's actions in Panama anticipated the full-fledged implementation of a principle that came to be called the **Roosevelt Corollary** to the Monroe Doctrine. This held that the United States had the right to exercise "an international police power" in the Western Hemisphere—a significant expansion of James Monroe's pledge to defend the hemisphere against European intervention. In 1904, Roosevelt ordered American forces to seize the customs houses of the Dominican Republic to ensure payment of that country's debts to European and American investors. In 1906, he dispatched troops to Cuba to oversee a disputed election; they remained in the country until 1909.

Roosevelt's successor, William Howard Taft, landed marines in Nicaragua to protect a government friendly to American economic interests. In general, however, Taft emphasized economic investment and loans from American banks, rather than direct military intervention, as the best way to spread American influence. As a result, his foreign policy became known as **Dollar Diplomacy**.

The World's Constable, a cartoon commenting on Theodore Roosevelt's "new diplomacy," in *Judge*, January 14, 1905, portrays Roosevelt as an impartial policeman, holding in one hand the threat of force and in the other the promise of the peaceful settlement of disputes. Roosevelt stands between the "undisciplined" non-white peoples of the world and the imperialist powers of Europe and Japan.

Moral Imperialism

The son of a Presbyterian minister, Woodrow Wilson brought to the presidency a missionary zeal and a sense of his own and the nation's moral righteousness. He appointed as secretary of state William Jennings Bryan, a strong anti-imperialist. Wilson promised a new foreign policy that would respect Latin America's independence and free it from foreign economic domination. But Wilson could not abandon the conviction that the United States had a responsibility to teach other peoples the lessons of democracy.

Wilson's **moral imperialism** produced more military interventions in Latin America than those of any president before or since. In 1915, Wilson sent marines to occupy Haiti after the government refused to allow American banks to oversee its financial dealings. In 1916, he established a military government in the Dominican Republic, with the United States controlling the country's customs collections and paying its debts. American soldiers remained in the Dominican Republic until 1924 and in Haiti until 1934. Wilson's foreign policy underscored a paradox of modern American history: the presidents who spoke the most about freedom were likely to intervene most frequently in the affairs of other countries.

Wilson's military interventions in Latin America

Wilson and Mexico

Wilson's major preoccupation in Latin America was Mexico, where in 1911 a revolution led by Francisco Madero overthrew the government of dictator Porfirio Díaz. Two years later, without Wilson's knowledge but with the backing of the U.S. ambassador and of American companies that controlled Mexico's oil and mining industries, military commander Victoriano Huerta assassinated Madero and seized power.

Political turmoil in Mexico

Wilson was appalled. He would "teach" Latin Americans, he added, "to elect good men." When civil war broke out in Mexico, Wilson ordered American troops to land at Vera Cruz to prevent the arrival of weapons meant for Huerta's forces. But to Wilson's surprise, Mexicans greeted the marines as invaders rather than liberators.

Vera Cruz

Huerta resigned in 1914 and fled the country. Meanwhile, various Mexican factions turned on one another. A peasant uprising in the southern part of the country, led by Emiliano Zapata, demanded land reform. The Wilson administration offered support to Venustiano Carranza, a leader devoted to economic modernization. In 1916, several hundred men loyal to Francisco "Pancho" Villa, the leader of another peasant force, raided Columbus, New Mexico, a few miles north of the border, leading to the death of seventeen Americans. With Carranza's approval, Wilson ordered 10,000 troops under the command of General John J. Pershing on an expedition into Mexico that unsuccessfully sought to arrest Villa. Chaos in Mexico continued—within the next few years, Zapata, Carranza,

Pancho Villa

and Villa all fell victim to assassination. Mexico was a warning that it might be difficult to use American might to reorder the internal affairs of other nations.

AMERICA AND THE GREAT WAR

Outbreak of war

In June 1914, a Serbian nationalist assassinated Archduke Franz Ferdinand, heir to the throne of the Austro-Hungarian empire, in Sarajevo. This deed set in motion a chain of events that plunged Europe into the most devastating war the world had ever seen. In the years before 1914, European nations had engaged in a scramble to obtain colonial possessions overseas and had constructed a shifting series of alliances seeking military domination within Europe. Within a little more than a month, because of the European powers' interlocking military alliances, Britain, France, Russia, and Japan (the Allies) found themselves at war with the Central Powers—Germany, Austria-Hungary, and the Ottoman empire, whose holdings included modern-day Turkey and much of the Middle East.

German forces quickly overran Belgium and part of northern France. The war then settled into a prolonged stalemate, with bloody, indecisive battles succeeding one another. New military technologies—submarines, airplanes, machine guns, tanks, and poison gas—produced unprecedented slaughter. In one five-month battle at Verdun, in 1916, 600,000 French and German soldiers died—nearly as many deaths as in the entire American Civil War. By the time the war ended, an estimated 10 million soldiers, and uncounted millions of civilians, had perished.

The Great War, or World War I as it came to be called, dealt a severe blow to the optimism and self-confidence of Western civilization. For decades, philosophers, reformers, and politicians had hailed the triumph

The American painter John Singer Sargent was commissioned by the British government to create a painting depicting World War I and sent to the front lines in France. The result, *Gassed*, completed in 1919 after the war's end, was doubtless not what the authorities had in mind. Revolted by the carnage he had witnessed, Sargent painted a line of soldiers, their eyes bandaged because of exposure to mustard gas, being led off by a medic to receive treatment. More wounded men lie in the foreground. Sargent was one of many artists and intellectuals who concluded that the war had been a ghastly mistake.

of reason and human progress, an outlook hard to reconcile with the mass slaughter of World War I. The conflict was also a shock to European socialist and labor movements. Karl Marx had called on the "workers of the world" to unite against their oppressors. Instead, they marched off to kill each other.

Neutrality and Preparedness

Americans divided

As war engulfed Europe, Americans found themselves sharply divided. British-Americans sided with their nation of origin, as did many other Americans who associated Great Britain with liberty and democracy and Germany with repressive government. On the other hand, German-Americans identified with Germany, and Irish-Americans bitterly opposed any aid to the British. Immigrants from the Russian empire, especially Jews, had no desire to see the United States aid the czar's regime.

When war broke out in 1914, President Wilson proclaimed American neutrality. But naval warfare in Europe reverberated in the United States. Britain declared a naval blockade of Germany and began to stop American merchant vessels. Germany launched submarine warfare against ships entering and leaving British ports. In May 1915, a German submarine sank the British liner ***Lusitania*** (which was carrying a large cache of arms) off the coast of Ireland, causing the deaths of 1,198 passengers, including 124 Americans. Wilson composed a note of protest so strong that Bryan resigned as secretary of state, fearing that the president was laying the foundation for military intervention.

American casualties

The sinking of the *Lusitania* outraged American public opinion and strengthened the hand of those who believed that the United States must prepare for possible entry into the war. Wilson himself had strong pro-British sympathies and viewed Germany as "the natural foe of liberty." By the end of 1915, he had embarked on a policy of "preparedness"—a crash program to expand the American army and navy.

A 1916 Wilson campaign truck (a new development in political campaigning), promising peace, prosperity, and preparedness.

The Road to War

In May 1916, Germany announced the suspension of submarine warfare against noncombatants. Wilson's preparedness program seemed to have succeeded in securing the right of Americans to travel freely on the high seas. "He kept us out of war" became the slogan of his campaign for reelection. With the Republican Party reunited after its split in 1912, the election proved to be one of the closest in American history. Wilson

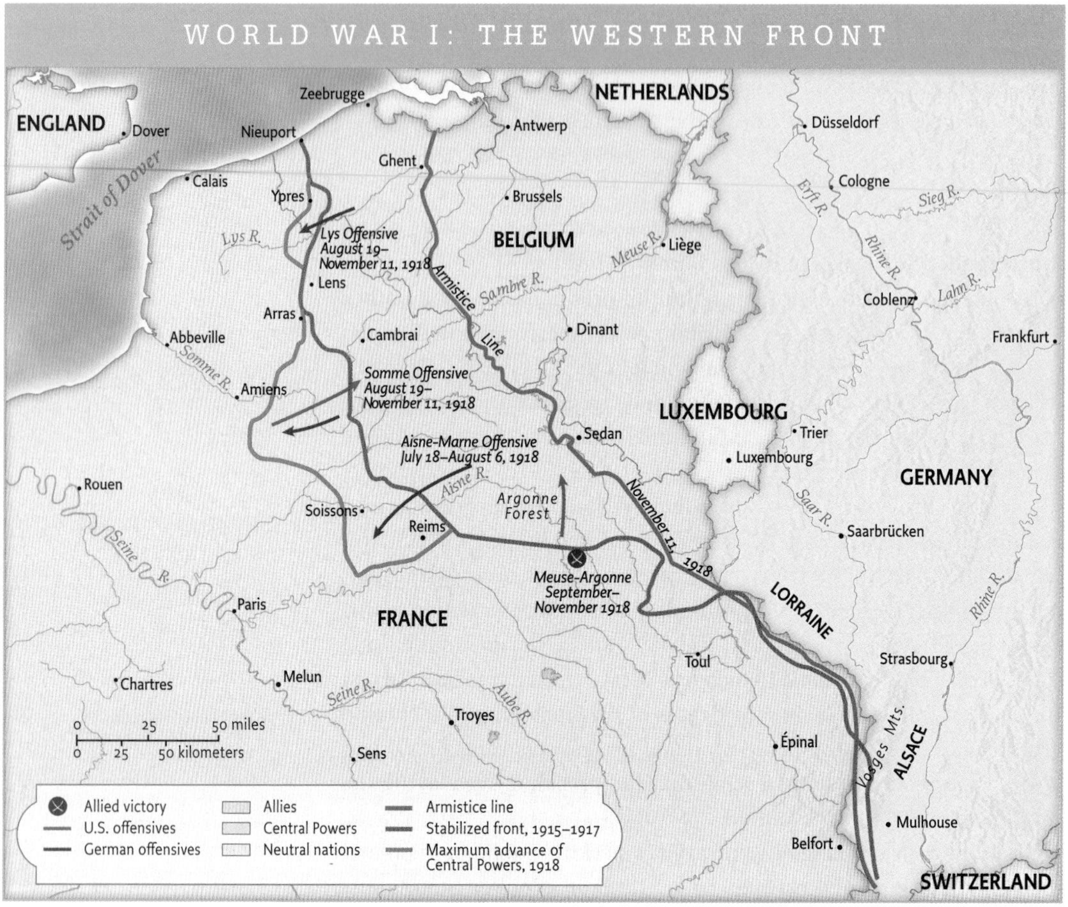

After years of stalemate on the western front in World War I, the arrival of American troops in 1917 and 1918 shifted the balance of power and made possible the Allied victory.

defeated Republican candidate Charles Evans Hughes by only twenty-three electoral votes and about 600,000 popular votes out of more than 18 million cast. Partly because he seemed to promise not to send American soldiers to Europe, Wilson carried ten of the twelve states that had adopted woman suffrage. Without the votes of women, Wilson would not have been reelected.

Almost immediately, however, Germany announced its intention to resume submarine warfare against ships sailing to or from the British Isles, and several American merchant vessels were sunk. In March 1917, British spies intercepted and made public the **Zimmermann Telegram**, a message by German foreign secretary Arthur Zimmermann calling on Mexico to join in a coming war against the United States and promising to help it recover territory lost in the Mexican-American War of 1846–1848. On April 2,

Wilson asked Congress for a declaration of war against Germany. "The world," he proclaimed, "must be made safe for democracy." The war resolution passed the Senate 82–6 and the House 373–50.

"Safe for democracy"

The Fourteen Points

Not until the spring of 1918 did American forces arrive in Europe in large numbers. By then, the world situation had taken a dramatic turn. In November 1917, a communist revolution headed by Vladimir Lenin overthrew the Russian government. Shortly thereafter, Lenin withdrew Russia from the war and published the secret treaties by which the Allies had agreed to divide up conquered territory after the war—an embarrassment for Wilson, who had promised a just peace.

Partly to assure the country that the war was being fought for a moral cause, Wilson in January 1918 issued the **Fourteen Points**, the clearest statement of American war aims and of his vision of a new international order. Among the key principles were self-determination for all peoples, freedom of the seas, free trade, open diplomacy (an end to secret treaties), the readjustment of colonial claims with colonized people given "equal weight" in deciding their futures, and the creation of a "general association of nations" to preserve the peace. Wilson envisioned this last provision, which led to the establishment after the war of the League of Nations, as a kind of global counterpart to the regulatory commissions Progressives had created at home to maintain social harmony. The Fourteen Points established the agenda for the peace conference that followed the war.

League of Nations

The United States threw its economic resources and manpower into the war. When American troops finally arrived in Europe, they turned the tide of battle. In the spring of 1918, they helped repulse a German advance near Paris and by July were participating in a major Allied counteroffensive. In September, in the Meuse-Argonne campaign, American soldiers under the command of General John J. Pershing, fresh from his campaign in Mexico, helped push back the German army. With 1.2 million American soldiers taking part and well over 100,000 dead and wounded, Meuse-Argonne, which lasted a month and a half, was the main American engagement of the war and one of the most significant and deadliest battles in American history. It formed part of a massive Allied offensive involving British, French, and Belgian soldiers and those from overseas European possessions. With his forces in full retreat, the German kaiser abdicated on November 9. Two days later, Germany sued for peace. Over 100,000 Americans had died, a substantial number, but they were only 1 percent of the 10 million soldiers killed in the Great War.

Turning the tide of battle

THE WAR AT HOME

The Progressives' War

For most Progressives, the war offered the possibility of reforming American society along scientific lines, instilling a sense of national unity and self-sacrifice, and expanding social justice. That American power could now disseminate Progressive values around the globe heightened the war's appeal.

Almost without exception, Progressive intellectuals and reformers, joined by prominent labor leaders and native-born socialists, rallied to Wilson's support. The roster included intellectuals like John Dewey, AFL head Samuel Gompers, socialist writers like Upton Sinclair, and prominent reformers including Florence Kelley and Charlotte Perkins Gilman.

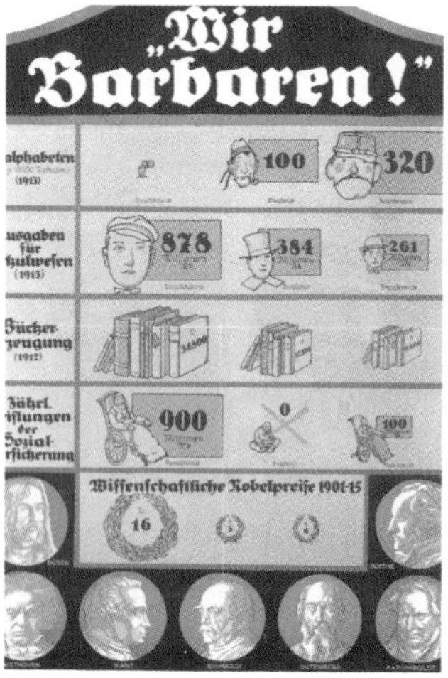

All combatants issued propaganda posters. The American poster, part of a 1917 campaign to sell war bonds, depicts a militarized Statue of Liberty about to take a sword from a kneeling Boy Scout. The German one, satirically entitled *We Are Barbarians*, refutes the charge of barbarism hurled at Germans by the Allies. It relates that Germany outstrips England and France in Nobel Prizes, provision for the elderly, book publication, education, and literacy.

The Wartime State

Like the Civil War, World War I created, albeit temporarily, a national state with unprecedented powers and a sharply increased presence in Americans' everyday lives. Under the **Selective Service Act** of May 1917, 24 million men were required to register with the draft. New federal agencies moved to regulate industry, transportation, labor relations, and agriculture. Headed by Wall Street financier Bernard Baruch, the **War Industries Board** presided over all elements of war production from the distribution of raw materials to the prices of manufactured goods. To spur efficiency, it established standardized specifications for everything from automobile tires to shoe colors (three were permitted—black, brown, and white). The Railroad Administration took control of the nation's transportation system, and the Fuel Agency rationed coal and oil. The Food Administration instructed farmers on modern methods of cultivation and promoted the more efficient preparation of meals.

The War Labor Board, which included representatives of government, industry, and the American Federation of Labor, pressed for the establishment of a minimum wage, an eight-hour workday, and the right to form unions. During the war, wages rose substantially, working conditions in many industries improved, and union membership doubled. To finance the war, corporate and individual income taxes rose enormously. By 1918, the wealthiest Americans were paying 60 percent of their income in taxes. Tens of millions of Americans answered the call to demonstrate their patriotism by purchasing Liberty bonds.

The Propaganda War

During the Civil War, it had been left to private agencies—Union Leagues, the Loyal Publication Society, and others—to mobilize prowar public opinion. But the Wilson administration decided that patriotism was too important to leave to the private sector. Many Americans opposed American participation, notably the Industrial Workers of the World (IWW) and the bulk of the Socialist Party, which in 1917 condemned the declaration of war as "a crime against the people of the United States" and called on "the workers of all countries" to refuse to fight.

In April 1917, the Wilson administration created the Committee on Public Information (CPI) to explain to Americans and the world, as its director, George Creel, put it, "the cause that compelled America to take arms in defense of its liberties and free institutions." The CPI flooded the country with prowar propaganda, using every available medium from pamphlets (of which it issued 75 million) to posters, newspaper advertisements, and motion pictures.

THE NAVY NEEDS YOU!
DON'T READ AMERICAN HISTORY–
MAKE IT!
U·S·NAVY RECRUITING STATION

A navy recruiting poster from World War I. A different outlook was expressed by the Irish writer Oscar Wilde, who once quipped, "Any fool can make history; it takes a genius to write it."

The CPI couched its appeal in the Progressive language of social cooperation and expanded democracy. Abroad, this meant a peace based on the principle of national self-determination. At home, it meant improving "industrial democracy." CPI pamphlets foresaw a postwar society complete with a "universal eight-hour day" and a living wage for all.

While "democracy" served as the key term of wartime mobilization, "freedom" also took on new significance. The war, a CPI advertisement proclaimed, was being fought in "the great cause of freedom." The most common visual image in wartime propaganda was the Statue of Liberty, employed especially to rally support among immigrants. Wilson's speeches cast the United States as a land of liberty fighting alongside a "concert of free people" to secure self-determination for the oppressed peoples of the world. Government propaganda whipped up hatred of the wartime foe by portraying Germany as a nation of barbaric Huns.

Concert of free people

The Coming of Woman Suffrage

The enlistment of "democracy" and "freedom" as ideological war weapons inevitably inspired demands for their expansion at home. In 1916, Wilson had cautiously endorsed votes for women. America's entry into the war threatened to tear the suffrage movement apart, because many advocates had been associated with opposition to American involvement. Indeed, among those who voted against the declaration of war was the first woman member of Congress, the staunch pacifist Jeannette Rankin of Montana. Although defeated in her reelection bid in 1918, Rankin would return to Congress in 1940. She became the only member to oppose the declaration

Jeannette Rankin

A 1915 cartoon showing the western states where women had won the right to vote. Women in the East reach out to a western woman carrying a torch of liberty.

of war against Japan in 1941, which ended her political career. In 1968, at the age of eighty-five, Rankin took part in a giant march on Washington to protest the war in Vietnam.

As during the Civil War, however, most leaders of woman suffrage organizations enthusiastically enlisted in the effort. Women sold war bonds, organized patriotic rallies, and went to work in war production jobs. Some 22,000 served as clerical workers and nurses with American forces in Europe.

At the same time, a new generation of college-educated activists, organized in the National Woman's Party, pressed for the right to vote with militant tactics many older suffrage advocates found scandalous. The party's leader, Alice Paul, had studied in England between 1907 and 1910, when the British suffrage movement adopted a strategy that included arrests, imprisonments, and vigorous denunciations of a male-dominated political system. Paul compared Wilson to the kaiser, and a group of her followers chained themselves to the White House fence, resulting in a seven-month prison sentence. When they began a hunger strike, the prisoners were force-fed.

Alice Paul's hunger strike

The combination of women's patriotic service and widespread outrage over the treatment of Paul and her fellow prisoners pushed the administration toward full-fledged support of woman suffrage. In 1920, the long struggle ended with the ratification of the Nineteenth Amendment, which barred states from using sex as a qualification for the suffrage. The United States became the twenty-seventh country to allow women to vote.

Prohibition

The war gave a powerful impulse to other campaigns that had engaged the energies of many women in the Progressive era. Prohibition, a movement inherited from the nineteenth century that had gained new strength and militancy in Progressive America, finally achieved national success during the war. Employers hoped it would create a more disciplined labor force. Urban reformers believed that it would promote a more orderly city environment and undermine urban political machines, which used saloons as places to organize. Women reformers hoped Prohibition would protect wives and children from husbands who engaged in domestic violence when drunk or who squandered their wages at saloons. Many native-born Protestants saw Prohibition as a way of imposing "American" values on immigrants.

After some success at the state level, Prohibitionists came to see national legislation as their best strategy. The war gave them added ammunition. Many prominent breweries were owned by German-Americans, making beer seem unpatriotic. The Food Administration insisted that grain must be used to produce food, not brewed into beer or distilled into liquor. In December 1917, Congress passed the **Eighteenth Amendment**, prohibiting the manufacture and sale of intoxicating liquor. It was ratified by the states in 1919 and went into effect at the beginning of 1920.

A common patriotic exercise involved massive numbers of soldiers forming images of the Statue of Liberty, the Liberty Bell, or President Woodrow Wilson. Here, in 1918, some 18,000 men about to depart for the war in Europe from Camp Dodge, Iowa, create what contemporaries called a "living photograph."

Liberty in Wartime

World War I raised questions already glimpsed during the Civil War that would trouble the nation again during the McCarthy era and in the aftermath of the terrorist attacks of 2001: What is the balance between security and freedom? Does the Constitution protect citizens' rights during wartime? Should dissent be equated with lack of patriotism?

Despite the administration's idealistic language of democracy and freedom, the war inaugurated the most intense repression of civil liberties the nation has ever known.

The Espionage and Sedition Acts

Restrictions on freedom of speech

For the first time since the Alien and Sedition Acts of 1798, the federal government enacted laws to restrict freedom of speech. The **Espionage Act** of 1917 prohibited not only spying and interfering with the draft but also "false statements" that might impede military success. The postmaster general barred from the mails numerous newspapers and magazines critical of the administration. In 1918, the **Sedition Act** made it a crime to make spoken or printed statements that intended to cast "contempt, scorn, or disrepute" on the "form of government," or that advocated interference with the war effort. The government charged more than 2,000 persons with violating these laws. Over half were convicted. A court sentenced Ohio farmer John White to twenty-one months in prison for saying that the murder of innocent women and children by German soldiers was no worse than what the United States had done in the Philippines in the war of 1899–1903.

The most prominent victim was Eugene V. Debs, convicted in 1918 under

Douglas Fairbanks, one of the era's most celebrated movie stars, addressing a 1918 rally urging people to buy Liberty bonds.

VOICES OF FREEDOM

From Woodrow Wilson, War Message to Congress (1917)

More than any other individual in the early twentieth century, President Woodrow Wilson articulated a new vision of America's relationship to the rest of the world. In his message to a special session of Congress on April 2, 1917, after Germany launched unrestrained submarine warfare against ships, including American ones, in the Atlantic, Wilson asked for a declaration of war. In his most celebrated sentence, Wilson declared, "The world must be made safe for democracy."

Let us be very clear, and make very clear to all the world what our motives and our objects are. . . . Our object . . . is to vindicate the principles of peace and justice in the life of the world as against selfish and autocratic power and to set up amongst the really free and self-governed peoples of the world such a concert of purpose and of action as will henceforth ensure the observance of those principles. . . . The menace to peace and freedom lies in the existence of autocratic governments backed by organized force which is controlled wholly by their will, not by the will of their people.

A steadfast concert for peace can never be maintained except by a partnership of democratic nations. No autocratic government could be trusted to keep faith within it or observe its covenants. . . . Only free peoples can hold their purpose and their honour steady to a common end and prefer the interests of mankind to any narrow interest of their own. . . .

We are now about to accept gage of battle with this natural foe to liberty and shall, if necessary, spend the whole force of the nation to check and nullify its pretensions and its power. We are glad, now that we see the facts with no veil of false pretense about them, to fight thus for the ultimate peace of the world and for the liberation of its peoples, the German peoples included: for the rights of nations great and small and the privilege of men everywhere to choose their way of life and of obedience. The world must be made safe for democracy. Its peace must be planted upon the tested foundations of political liberty. We have no selfish ends to serve. We desire no conquest, no dominion. . . . If there should be disloyalty, it will be dealt with with a firm hand of stern repression. . . .

It is a fearful thing to lead this great peaceful people into war, into the most terrible and disastrous of all wars, civilization itself seeming to be in the balance. But the right is more precious than peace, and we shall fight for the things which we have always carried nearest our hearts—for democracy, . . . for the rights and liberties of small nations, for a universal dominion of right by such a concert of free peoples as shall bring peace and safety to all nations and make the world itself at last free.

From Eugene V. Debs, Speech to the Jury before Sentencing under the Espionage Act (1918)

Socialist leader Eugene V. Debs was arrested for delivering an antiwar speech and convicted of violating the Espionage Act. In his speech to the jury, he defended the right of dissent in wartime.

Gentlemen, you have heard the report of my speech at Canton [Ohio] on June 16, and I submit that there is not a word in that speech to warrant the charges set out in the indictment. . . . In what I had to say there my purpose was to have the people understand something about the social system in which we live and to prepare them to change this system by perfectly peaceable and orderly means into what I, as a Socialist, conceive to be a real democracy. . . . I have never advocated violence in any form. I have always believed in education, in intelligence, in enlightenment; and I have always made my appeal to the reason and to the conscience of the people.

In every age there have been a few heroic souls who have been in advance of their time, who have been misunderstood, maligned, persecuted, sometimes put to death. . . . Washington, Jefferson, Franklin, Paine, and their compeers were the rebels of their day. . . . But they had the moral courage to be true to their convictions. . . .

William Lloyd Garrison, Wendell Phillips, Elizabeth Cady Stanton . . . and other leaders of the abolition movement who were regarded as public enemies and treated accordingly, were true to their faith and stood their ground. . . . You are now teaching your children to revere their memories, while all of their detractors are in oblivion. . . .

The war of 1812 was opposed and condemned by some of the most influential citizens; the Mexican War was vehemently opposed and bitterly denounced, even after the war had been declared and was in progress, by Abraham Lincoln, Charles Sumner, Daniel Webster. . . . They were not indicted; they were not charged with treason. . . .

Isn't it strange that we Socialists stand almost alone today in upholding and defending the Constitution of the United States? The revolutionary fathers . . . understood that free speech, a free press and the right of free assemblage by the people were fundamental principles in democratic government. . . . I believe in the right of free speech, in war as well as in peace.

QUESTIONS

1. *What does Wilson think is the greatest threat to freedom in the world?*
2. *Why does Debs relate the history of wartime dissent in the United States?*
3. *Does anything in Wilson's speech offer a harbinger of the extreme repression of free speech that occurred during World War I?*

the Espionage Act for delivering an antiwar speech. Germany sent a socialist leader to prison for four years for opposing the war; in the United States, Debs's sentence was ten years. After the war's end, Wilson rejected the advice of his attorney general that he commute Debs's sentence. Debs ran for president while still in prison in 1920 and received 900,000 votes. It was left to Wilson's successor, Warren G. Harding, to release Debs from prison in 1921.

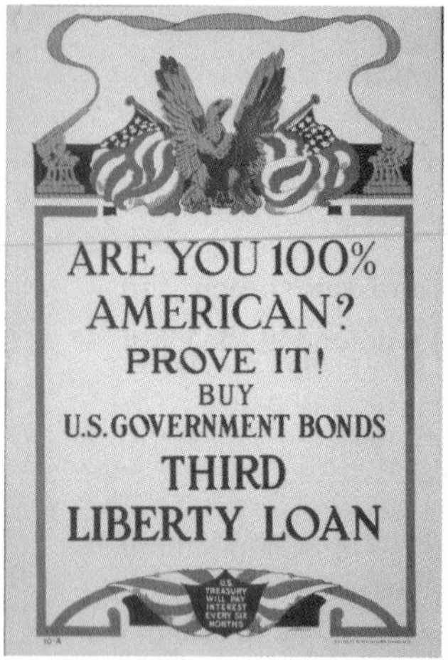
ARE YOU 100%
AMERICAN?
PROVE IT!
BUY
U.S. GOVERNMENT BONDS
THIRD
LIBERTY LOAN

A poster demands that citizens prove they are "100% American" by purchasing war bonds.

Florine Stettheimer's *New York/Liberty*, painted in 1918, depicts the Statue of Liberty, warships, and airplanes in an exuberant tribute to New York City and to the idea of freedom in the wake of World War I.

LIBERTY

Coercive Patriotism

Even more extreme repression took place at the hands of state governments and private groups. During the war, thirty-three states outlawed the possession or display of red or black flags (symbols, respectively, of communism and anarchism), and twenty-three outlawed a newly created offense, "criminal syndicalism," the advocacy of unlawful acts to accomplish political change or "a change in industrial ownership."

"Who is the real patriot?" Emma Goldman asked when the United States entered the war. She answered, those who "love America with open eyes," who were not blind to "the wrongs committed in the name of patriotism." But from the federal government to local authorities and private groups, patriotism came to be equated with support for the government, the war, and the American economic system. Throughout the country, schools revised their course offerings to ensure their patriotism and required teachers to sign loyalty oaths.

The 250,000 members of the newly formed American Protective League (APL) helped the Justice Department identify radicals and critics of the war by spying on their neighbors and carrying out "slacker raids" in which thousands of men were stopped on the streets of major cities and required to produce draft registration cards. Employers cooperated with the government in crushing the Industrial Workers of the World (IWW), a move long demanded by business interests. In September 1917, operating under one of the broadest warrants in American history, federal agents swooped down on IWW offices throughout the country, arresting hundreds of leaders and seizing files and publications.

Although some Progressives protested individual excesses, most failed to speak out against the broad suppression of freedom of expression. Civil liberties, by and large, had never been a major concern of Progressives, who had always viewed the national state as the embodiment of democratic purpose and insisted that freedom flowed from participating in the life of society, not standing in opposition. Strong believers in the use of national power to improve social conditions, Progressives found themselves ill prepared to develop a defense of minority rights against majority or governmental tyranny.

WHO IS AN AMERICAN?

The "Race Problem"

Even before American participation in World War I, what contemporaries called the "race problem"—the tensions that arose from the country's increasing ethnic diversity—had become a major subject of public concern. "Race" referred to far more than black-white relations. The *Dictionary of Races of Peoples,* published in 1911 by the U.S. Immigration Commission, listed no fewer than forty-five immigrant "races," each supposedly with its own inborn characteristics. They ranged from Anglo-Saxons at the top down to Hebrews, Northern Italians, and, lowest of all, Southern Italians—supposedly violent, undisciplined, and incapable of assimilation.

Immigrant "races"

The "Science" of Eugenics

The emergence of eugenics, which studied the alleged mental characteristics of different groups of people, gave an air of scientific expertise to anti-immigrant sentiment. Racial "purity" became an obsession of eugenicists. John Harvey Kellogg (the inventor of the breakfast cereal Corn Flakes) in 1906 founded the Race Betterment Foundation, aimed at promoting the "purity of the gene pool." The foundation tried to discourage people with the "wrong" racial pedigree from having children, and sponsored eugenics fairs throughout the country. The Eugenic Records Office, headquartered in New York State, issued certificates to people who could demonstrate their "Nordic purity."

Racial "purity"

The war accelerated other efforts to "improve" the quality of the American people. Indiana in 1907 passed a law authorizing doctors to sterilize insane and "feeble-minded" inmates in mental institutions so they would not pass their "defective" genes on to children. During and after World War I, numerous other states followed suit. In *Buck v. Bell* (1927), the Supreme Court upheld the constitutionality of these laws. Carrie Buck, an eighteen-year-old inmate at a Virginia mental institution, sued to prevent her sterilization by the state on the grounds that it violated her right to the equal protection of the laws, guaranteed by the Fourteenth Amendment. Justice Oliver Wendell Holmes's opinion rejecting her plea included the widely publicized statement, "Society can prevent those who are manifestly unfit from continuing their kind. . . . Three generations of imbeciles are enough." By the time the practice ended in the 1960s, some 63,000 persons had been involuntarily sterilized. American eugenics policies for manipulating the character of the population were carefully studied in Nazi Germany.

Buck v. Bell

WHO IS AN AMERICAN?

From Randolph S. Bourne, "Trans-National America" (1916)

Probably the most penetrating rejection of the Americanization model issued from the pen of the social critic Randolph Bourne. In an article in *The Atlantic*, Bourne envisioned a democratic, cosmopolitan society in which immigrants and natives alike retained their group identities while at the same time embracing a new "trans-national" culture.

No reverberatory effect of the great war has caused American public opinion more solicitude than the failure of the "melting-pot." The discovery of diverse nationalistic feelings among our great alien population has come to most people as an intense shock. . . . We have had to listen to publicists who . . . insist that the alien shall be forcibly assimilated to that Anglo-Saxon tradition which they unquestionably label "American."... We act as if we wanted Americanization to take place only on our own terms, and not by the consent of the governed....

The Anglo-Saxon was merely the first immigrant.... Colonials from the other nations have come and settled down beside him. They found no definite native culture . . . and consequently they looked back to their mother-country, as the earlier Anglo-Saxon immigrant was looking back to his....

There is no distinctively American culture. It is apparently our lot rather to be a federation of cultures. This we have been for half a century, and the war has made it ever more evident that this is what we are destined to remain. . . . What we have achieved has been rather a cosmopolitan federation of national colonies, of foreign cultures, from whom the sting of devastating competition has been removed. America is already the world-federation in miniature, the continent where for the first time in history has been achieved that miracle of hope, the peaceful living side by side, with character substantially preserved, of the most heterogeneous peoples under the sun. . . . America is coming to be, not a nationality but a trans-nationality, a weaving back and forth, with the other lands, of many threads of all sizes and colors. Any movement which attempts to thwart this weaving, or to dye the fabric any one color, or disentangle the threads of the strands, is false to this cosmopolitan vision.

QUESTIONS

1. *Why does Bourne believe that the "melting pot" has failed?*
2. *What does he mean by describing America as a "trans-nationality?"*

Demands for Americanization

Somehow, the very nationalization of politics and economic life served to heighten awareness of ethnic and racial difference and spurred demands for "Americanization"—the creation of a more homogeneous national culture. A 1908 play by the Jewish immigrant writer Israel Zangwill, *The Melting Pot,* gave a popular name to the process by which newcomers were supposed to merge their identity into existing American nationality. Public and private groups of all kinds—including educators, employers, labor leaders, social reformers, and public officials—took up the task of Americanizing new immigrants. Public schools paid great attention to Americanizing immigrants' children. The federal and state governments demanded that immigrants demonstrate their unwavering devotion to the United States.

The Anti-German Crusade

German culture in America

German-Americans bore the brunt of forced Americanization. The first wave of German immigrants had arrived before the Civil War. By 1914, German-Americans numbered nearly 9 million, including immigrants and persons of German parentage. They had created thriving ethnic institutions including clubs, sports associations, schools, and theaters. On the eve of the war, many Americans admired German traditions in literature, music, and philosophy, and one-quarter of all the high school students in the country studied the German language. But after American entry into the war, the use of German and expressions of German culture became a target of prowar organizations.

Restricting the teaching of foreign languages

By 1919, the vast majority of the states had enacted laws restricting the teaching of foreign languages. Popular words of German origin were changed: "hamburger" became "liberty sandwich," and "sauerkraut" "liberty cabbage." The government jailed Karl Muck, the director of the Boston Symphony and a Swiss citizen, as an enemy alien after he insisted on including the works of German composers like Beethoven in his concerts.

Even as Americanization programs sought to assimilate immigrants into American society, the war strengthened the conviction that certain kinds of undesirable persons ought to be excluded altogether. The new immigrants, one advocate of restriction declared, appreciated the values of democracy and freedom far less than "the Anglo-Saxon." Stanford University psychologist Lewis Terman introduced the term "IQ" (intelligence quotient) in 1916, claiming that this single number could measure an individual's mental capacity. Intelligence tests administered to recruits by the army seemed to confirm scientifically that blacks and the new immigrants stood far below native white Protestants on the IQ scale, further spurring demands for immigration restriction.

A 1919 cartoon, *Close the Gate*, warns that unrestricted immigration allows dangerous radicals to enter the United States.

Groups Apart: Mexicans and Asian-Americans

No matter how coercive, Americanization programs assumed that European immigrants and especially their children could eventually adjust to the conditions of American life, embrace American ideals, and become productive citizens enjoying the full blessings of American freedom. This assumption did not apply to non-white immigrants or to blacks.

Mexicans in the Southwest

The war led to further growth of the Southwest's Mexican population. Wartime demand for labor from the area's mine owners and large farmers led the government to exempt Mexicans temporarily from the literacy test enacted in 1917. Segregation, by law and custom, was common in schools, hospitals, theaters, and other institutions in states with significant Mexican populations. By 1920, nearly all Mexican children in California and the Southwest were educated in their own schools or classrooms. Phoenix, Arizona, established separate public schools for Indians, Mexicans, blacks, and whites. Although in far smaller numbers than blacks, Mexican-Americans also suffered lynchings—over 200 between 1880 and 1930. Discrimination led to the formation of La Grán Liga Mexicanista de Beneficencia y Protección, which aimed to improve the conditions of Mexicans in the United States and "to strike back at the hatred of some bad sons of Uncle Sam who believe themselves better than the Mexicans."

The Gentlemen's Agreement

Even more restrictive were policies toward Asian-Americans. In 1906, the San Francisco school board ordered all Asian students confined to a single public school. When the Japanese government protested, President Theodore Roosevelt persuaded the city to rescind the order. He then negotiated the Gentlemen's Agreement of 1907, whereby Japan agreed to end migration to the United States except for the wives and children of men already in the country. In 1913, California barred all aliens incapable of becoming naturalized citizens (that is, all Asians) from owning or leasing land.

The Color Line

Exclusion of blacks

By far the largest non-white group, African-Americans were excluded from nearly every Progressive definition of freedom described in Chapter 18. After their disenfranchisement in the South, few could participate in American democracy. Barred from joining most unions and from skilled employment, black workers had little access to "industrial freedom." Nor could blacks, the majority desperately poor, participate fully in the emerging consumer economy, either as employees in the new department stores (except as janitors and cleaning women) or as purchasers of the consumer goods now flooding the marketplace.

Progressive intellectuals, social scientists, labor reformers, and suffrage advocates displayed a remarkable indifference to the black condition.

Most settlement-house reformers accepted segregation as natural and equitable. White leaders of the woman suffrage movement said little about black disenfranchisement. The amendment that achieved woman suffrage left the states free to limit voting by poll taxes and literacy tests. Living in the South, the vast majority of the country's black women still could not vote.

A poster advertising the 1915 film *The Birth of a Nation*, which had its premiere at Woodrow Wilson's White House. The movie glorified the Ku Klux Klan and depicted blacks during Reconstruction as unworthy of participation in government and a danger to white womanhood.

Roosevelt, Wilson, and Race

The Progressive presidents shared prevailing attitudes concerning blacks. Theodore Roosevelt shocked white opinion by inviting Booker T. Washington to dine with him in the White House and by appointing a number of blacks to federal offices. But in 1906, when a small group of black soldiers shot off their guns in Brownsville, Texas, killing one resident, and none of their fellows would name them, Roosevelt ordered the dishonorable discharge of three black companies—156 men in all, including six winners of the Congressional Medal of Honor.

Woodrow Wilson, a native of Virginia, could speak without irony of the South's "genuine representative government" and its exalted "standards of liberty." His administration imposed racial segregation in federal departments in Washington, D.C., and dismissed numerous black federal employees. Wilson allowed D. W. Griffith's film *The Birth of a Nation*, which glorified the Ku Klux Klan as the defender of white civilization during Reconstruction, to have its premiere at the White House in 1915.

In one of hundreds of lynchings during the Progressive era, a white mob in Springfield, Missouri, in 1906 falsely accused three black men of rape, hanged them from an electric light pole, and burned their bodies in a public orgy of violence. Atop the pole stood a replica of the Statue of Liberty.

A cartoon from the *St. Louis Post-Dispatch*, April 17, 1906, commenting on the lynching of three black men in Springfield, Missouri. The shadow cast by the Statue of Liberty forms a gallows on the ground.

W. E. B. Du Bois and the Revival of Black Protest

Black leaders struggled to find a strategy to rekindle the national commitment to equality that had flickered brightly, if briefly, during Reconstruction. No one thought more deeply, or over so long a period, about the black condition and the challenge it posed to American democracy than the scholar and activist W. E. B. Du Bois. Born in 1868, and educated at Fisk and Harvard universities, Du Bois lived to his ninety-fifth year. The unifying theme of Du Bois's career was his effort to reconcile the contradiction between what he called "American freedom for whites and the continuing subjection of Negroes." His book *The Souls of Black Folk* (1903) issued a clarion call for blacks dissatisfied with the accommodationist policies of Booker T. Washington to press for equal rights. Du Bois believed that educated African-Americans like himself—the "talented

The "talented tenth"

tenth" of the black community—must use their education and training to challenge inequality.

In some ways, Du Bois was a typical Progressive who believed that investigation, exposure, and education would lead to solutions for social problems. But he also understood the necessity of political action. In 1905, Du Bois gathered a group of black leaders at Niagara Falls (meeting on the Canadian side because no American hotel would provide accommodations) and organized the Niagara movement, which sought to reinvigorate the abolitionist tradition. "We claim for ourselves," Du Bois wrote in the group's manifesto, "every single right that belongs to a freeborn American." Four years later, Du Bois joined with a group of mostly white reformers, shocked by a lynching in Springfield, Illinois (Lincoln's adult home), to create the **National Association for the Advancement of Colored People**. The NAACP, as it was known, launched a long struggle for the enforcement of the Fourteenth and Fifteenth Amendments.

The Niagara movement

The NAACP's legal strategy won a few victories. In *Bailey v. Alabama* (1911), the Supreme Court overturned southern "peonage" laws that made it a crime for sharecroppers to break their labor contracts. Six years later, it ruled unconstitutional a Louisville zoning regulation excluding blacks from living in certain parts of the city (primarily because it interfered with whites' right to sell their property as they saw fit). Overall, however, the Progressive era witnessed virtually no progress toward racial justice.

The men who founded the Niagara movement at a 1905 meeting on the Canadian side of Niagara Falls. W. E. B. Du Bois is in the second row, second from the right, in a white hat. They pledged to renew the struggle for "every single right that belongs to a freeborn American." By the time of the second meeting, a year later, women had become part of the movement.

Closing Ranks

Among black Americans, the wartime language of freedom inspired hopes for a radical change in the country's racial system. The black press rallied to the war. Du Bois himself, in a widely reprinted editorial in the NAACP's monthly magazine, *The Crisis*, called on African-Americans to "close ranks" and enlist in the army, to help "make our own America a real land of the free."

Black participation in the Civil War had helped to secure the destruction of slavery and the achievement of citizenship. But during World War I, closing ranks did not bring significant gains. The navy barred blacks entirely, and the segregated army confined most of the 400,000 blacks who served in the war to supply units rather than combat. Contact with African colonial soldiers fighting alongside the British and French did widen the horizons of black American soldiers. But although colonial troops marched in the victory parade in Paris, the Wilson administration did not allow black Americans to participate.

The Great Migration

Nonetheless, the war unleashed social changes that altered the contours of American race relations. The combination of increased wartime production and a drastic falloff in immigration from Europe opened thousands of industrial jobs to black laborers for the first time, inspiring a large-scale migration from South to North. On the eve of World War I, 90 percent of the African-American population still lived in the South. But between 1910 and 1920, half a million blacks left the South. The black population of Chicago more than doubled, New York City's rose 66 percent, and smaller industrial cities like Akron, Buffalo, and Trenton showed similar gains. Many motives sustained the **Great Migration**—higher wages in northern factories than were available in the South (even if blacks remained confined to menial and unskilled positions), opportunities for educating their children, escape from the threat of lynching, and the prospect of exercising the right to vote.

The black migrants, mostly young men and women, carried with them "a new vision of opportunity, of social and economic freedom," as Alain Locke explained in the preface to his influential book *The New Negro* (1925). Yet the migrants encountered vast disappointments—severely restricted employment opportunities, exclusion from unions, rigid housing segregation, and outbreaks of violence that made it clear that no region

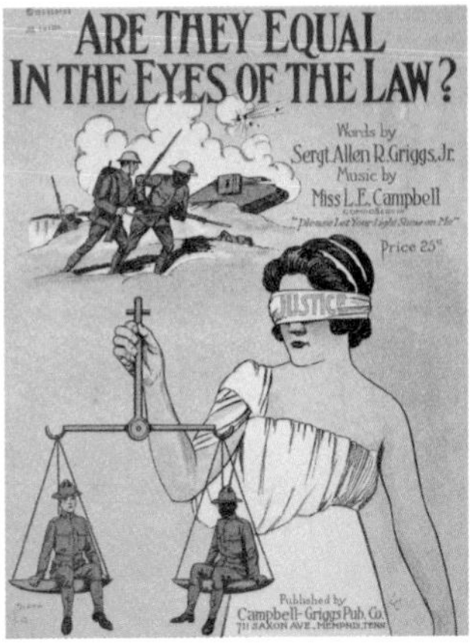

A piece of sheet music from 1919. The cover illustration suggests that because they fought side by side with white soldiers in World War I (although in fact the army was racially segregated), black soldiers deserved legal equality on their return to the United States. Unfortunately, they did not receive it.

TABLE 19.1 The Great Migration

CITY	BLACK POPULATION, 1910	BLACK POPULATION, 1920	PERCENT INCREASE
New York	91,709	152,467	66.3%
Philadelphia	84,459	134,229	58.9
Chicago	44,103	109,458	148.2
St. Louis	43,960	69,854	58.9
Detroit	5,741	40,838	611.3
Pittsburgh	25,623	37,725	47.2
Cleveland	8,448	34,451	307.8

One of a series of paintings by the black artist Jacob Lawrence called *The Migration Series*, inspired by the massive movement of African-Americans to the North during and after World War I. For each, Lawrence composed a brief title, in this case, "In the North the Negro had better educational facilities."

of the country was free from racial hostility. The new black presence, coupled with demands for change inspired by the war, created a racial tinderbox that needed only an incident to trigger an explosion.

Racial Violence, North and South

Dozens of blacks were killed during a 1917 riot in East St. Louis, Illinois, where employers had recruited black workers in an attempt to weaken unions (most of which excluded blacks from membership). In 1919, more than 250 persons died in riots in the urban North. Most notable was the violence in Chicago, touched off by the drowning by white bathers of a black teenager who accidentally crossed the unofficial dividing line between black and white beaches on Lake Michigan. By the time the National Guard restored order, 38 persons had been killed and more than 500 injured.

Violence was not confined to the North. In the year after the war ended, seventy-six persons were lynched in the South, including several returning black veterans wearing their uniforms. The **Tulsa riot**, the worst race riot in American history, occurred in Tulsa, Oklahoma, in 1921 when more than 300 blacks were killed and over 10,000 left homeless after a white mob, including police and National Guardsmen, burned an all-black section of the city to the ground.

The Rise of Garveyism

World War I kindled a new spirit of militancy. The East St. Louis riot of 1917 inspired a widely publicized Silent Protest Parade on New York's Fifth Avenue in which 10,000 blacks silently carried placards reading, "Mr. President, Why Not Make America Safe for Democracy?" In the new densely populated black ghettos of the North, widespread support emerged for the Universal Negro Improvement Association, a movement for African independence and black self-reliance launched by **Marcus Garvey**, a recent immigrant from Jamaica. To Garveyites, freedom meant national self-determination. Blacks,

Buildings in Tulsa, Oklahoma, burn during the city's riot of June 1921. An estimated 300 people died when white mobs destroyed the city's black neighborhood in the worst outbreak of racial violence in American history.

they insisted, should enjoy the same internationally recognized identity enjoyed by other peoples in the aftermath of the war. Du Bois and other established black leaders viewed Garvey as little more than a demagogue. They applauded when the government deported him after a conviction for mail fraud. But the massive following his movement achieved testified to the sense of betrayal that had been kindled in black communities during and after the war.

Marcus Garvey, leader of the largest black movement of the World War I era.

1919

A Worldwide Upsurge

The combination of militant hopes for social change and disappointment with the war's outcome was evident far beyond the black community. In the Union of Soviet Socialist Republics (or Soviet Union), as Russia had been renamed after the revolution, Lenin's government had nationalized landholdings, banks, and factories and proclaimed the socialist dream of a workers' government. The Russian Revolution and the democratic aspirations unleashed by World War I sent tremors of hope and fear throughout the world. General strikes demanding the fulfillment of wartime promises of "industrial democracy" took place in Belfast, Glasgow, and Winnipeg. In Spain, anarchist peasants began seizing land. Crowds in India challenged British rule, and nationalist movements in other colonies demanded independence.

Survival of the Soviet Union

The worldwide revolutionary upsurge produced a countervailing mobilization by opponents of radical change. Despite Allied attempts to overturn its government, the Soviet regime survived, but in the rest of the world the tide of change receded. By the fall, the mass strikes had been suppressed and conservative governments had been installed in central Europe.

Upheaval in America

The flu epidemic

In the United States, 1919 also brought unprecedented turmoil. It seemed all the more disorienting for occurring in the midst of a worldwide flu epidemic that killed over 20 million persons, including nearly 700,000 Americans. Racial violence, as noted above, was widespread. In June, bombs exploded at the homes of prominent Americans, including the attorney general, A. Mitchell Palmer, who escaped uninjured. Among aggrieved American workers, wartime language linking patriotism with democracy and freedom inspired hopes that an era of social justice and economic empowerment was at hand. In 1917, Wilson had told the AFL,

"While we are fighting for freedom, we must see to it among other things that labor is free." Labor took him seriously—more seriously, it seems, than Wilson intended.

In 1919, more than 4 million workers engaged in strikes—the greatest wave of labor unrest in American history. There were walkouts, among many others, by textile workers, telephone operators, and Broadway actors. They were met by an unprecedented mobilization of employers, government, and private patriotic organizations.

The 1919 steel strike

The wartime rhetoric of economic democracy and freedom helped to inspire the era's greatest labor uprising, the 1919 steel strike. Centered in Chicago, it united some 365,000 mostly immigrant workers in demands for union recognition, higher wages, and an eight-hour workday. Before 1917, the steel mills were little autocracies where managers arbitrarily established wages and working conditions and suppressed all efforts at union organizing. During the war, workers won an eight-hour day. "For why this war?" asked one Polish immigrant steelworker at a union meeting. "For why we buy Liberty bonds? For the mills? No, for freedom and America—for everybody."

Middle-class opinion turns against the labor movement

In response to the strike, steel magnates launched a concerted counterattack. Employers appealed to anti-immigrant sentiment among native-born workers, many of whom returned to work, and conducted a propaganda campaign that associated the strikers with the IWW, communism, and disloyalty. With middle-class opinion having turned against the labor movement and the police assaulting workers on the streets, the strike collapsed in early 1920.

The Red Scare

The Palmer Raids

Wartime repression of dissent reached its peak with the **Red Scare of 1919–1920**, a short-lived but intense period of political intolerance inspired by the postwar strike wave and the social tensions and fears generated by the Russian Revolution. Convinced that episodes like the steel strike were part of a worldwide communist conspiracy, Attorney General A. Mitchell Palmer in November 1919 and January 1920 dispatched federal agents to raid the offices of radical and labor organizations throughout the country. More than 5,000 persons were arrested, most of them without warrants, and held for months without charge. The government deported hundreds of immigrant radicals, including Emma Goldman.

The abuse of civil liberties in early 1920 was so severe that Palmer came under heavy criticism from Congress and much of the press. Even the explosion of a bomb outside the New York Stock Exchange in September 1920, which killed forty persons, failed to rekindle the repression of the Red Scare.

(The perpetrators of this terrorist explosion, the worst on American soil until the Oklahoma City bombing of 1995, were never identified.)

The reaction to the Palmer Raids planted the seeds for a new appreciation of the importance of civil liberties that would begin to flourish during the 1920s. But in their immediate impact, the events of 1919 and 1920 dealt a devastating setback to radical and labor organizations of all kinds and kindled an intense identification of patriotic Americanism with support for the political and economic status quo. The IWW had been effectively destroyed, and many moderate unions lay in disarray. The Socialist Party crumbled under the weight of governmental repression (the New York legislature expelled five Socialist members, and Congress denied Victor Berger the seat to which he had been elected from Wisconsin) and internal differences over the Russian Revolution.

Local police with literature seized from a Communist Party office in Cambridge, Massachusetts, November 1919.

Wilson at Versailles

The beating back of demands for fundamental social change was a severe rebuke to the hopes with which so many Progressives had enlisted in the war effort. Wilson's inability to achieve a just peace based on the Fourteen Points compounded the sense of failure. Late in 1918, the president traveled to France to attend the Versailles peace conference. But he proved a less adept negotiator than his British and French counterparts, David Lloyd George and Georges Clemenceau.

Although the Fourteen Points had called for "open covenants openly arrived at," the negotiations were conducted in secret. The resulting **Versailles Treaty** did accomplish some of Wilson's goals. It established the **League of Nations**, the body central to his vision of a new international order. It applied the principle of self-determination to eastern Europe and redrew the map of that region. From the ruins of the Austro-Hungarian empire and parts of Germany and czarist Russia, new European nations emerged from the war—Finland, Poland, Czechoslovakia, Austria, Hungary, Latvia, Lithuania, Estonia, and Yugoslavia. Some enjoyed ethno-linguistic unity, whereas others comprised unstable combinations of diverse nationalities.

Despite Wilson's pledge of a peace without territorial acquisitions or vengeance, the Versailles Treaty was a harsh

Part of the crowd that greeted President Woodrow Wilson in November 1918 when he traveled to Paris to take part in the peace conference. An electric sign proclaims "Long Live Wilson."

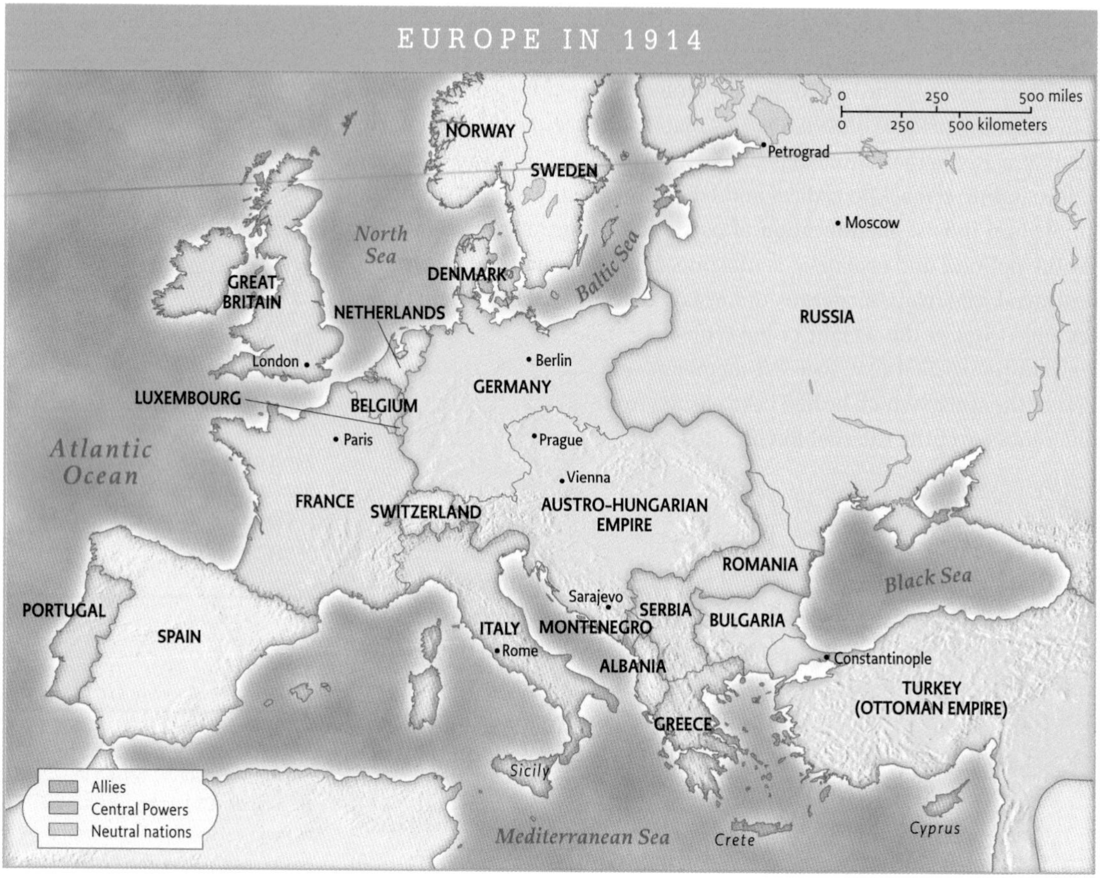

World War I and the Versailles Treaty redrew the map of Europe and the Middle East. The Austro-Hungarian and Ottoman empires ceased to exist, and Germany and Russia were reduced in size. A group of new states emerged in eastern Europe, embodying the principle of self-determination, one of Woodrow Wilson's Fourteen Points.

document that all but guaranteed future conflict in Europe. Lloyd George persuaded Wilson to agree to a clause declaring Germany morally responsible for the war and setting astronomical reparations payments (they were variously estimated at between $33 billion and $56 billion), which crippled the German economy.

The Wilsonian Moment

Like the ideals of the American Revolution, the Wilsonian rhetoric of self-determination reverberated across the globe, especially among colonial peoples seeking independence. In fact, they took Wilson's rhetoric more seriously than he did. Despite his belief in self-determination, he believed that colonial peoples required a long period of tutelage before they were ready for independence.

Spread of Wilsonian ideals

Nonetheless, Wilsonian ideals quickly spread around the globe. In eastern Europe, whose people sought to carve new, independent nations

EUROPE IN 1919

from the ruins of the Austro-Hungarian and Ottoman empires, many considered Wilson a "popular saint." The leading Arabic newspaper, *Al-Ahram*, published in Egypt, then under British rule, gave extensive coverage to Wilson's speech asking Congress to declare war in the name of democracy, and to the Fourteen Points. In Beijing, students demanding that China free itself of foreign domination gathered at the American embassy shouting, "Long live Wilson." Japan proposed to include in the charter of the new League of Nations a clause recognizing the equality of all people, regardless of race.

Self-determination

Outside of Europe, however, the idea of "self-determination" was stillborn. When the Paris peace conference opened, Secretary of State Robert Lansing warned that the phrase was "loaded with dynamite" and would "raise hopes which can never be realized." As Lansing anticipated, advocates of colonial independence descended on Paris to lobby the peace negotiators. Arabs demanded that a unified independent state be carved from the old Ottoman empire in the Middle East. Nguyen That Thanh, a young Vietnamese patriot working in Paris, appealed unsuccessfully to Wilson to help bring an end to French rule in Vietnam. W. E. B. Du Bois organized a Pan-African Congress in Paris that put forward the idea of a self-governing nation to be carved out of Germany's African colonies. Koreans, Indians, Irish, and others also pressed claims for self-determination.

Imperial interests

The British and French, however, had no intention of applying this principle to their own empires. During the war, the British had encouraged Arab nationalism as a weapon against the Ottoman empire and had also pledged to create a homeland in Palestine for the persecuted Jews of Europe. In fact, the victors of World War I divided Ottoman territory into a series of new territories, including Syria, Lebanon, Iraq, and Palestine, controlled by the victorious Allies under League of Nations "mandates." South Africa, Australia, and Japan acquired former German colonies in Africa and Asia. Nor did Ireland achieve its independence at Versailles. Only at the end of 1921 did Britain finally agree to the creation of the Irish Free State while continuing to rule the northeastern corner of the island. As for the Japanese proposal to establish the principle of racial equality, Wilson, with the support of Great Britain and Australia, engineered its defeat.

Interrupting the Ceremony, a 1918 cartoon from the *Chicago Tribune*, depicts Senate opponents of the Versailles Treaty arriving just in time to prevent the United States from becoming permanently ensnared in "foreign entanglements" through the League of Nations.

The Seeds of Wars to Come

Disappointment at the failure to apply the Fourteen Points to the non-European world created a pervasive cynicism about Western use of the language of freedom and democracy. Wilson's apparent willingness to accede to the demands of the imperial powers helped to spark a series of popular protest movements across the Middle East and Asia and the rise of a new anti-Western nationalism. Some leaders, like Nguyen That Thanh, who took the name Ho Chi Minh, turned to communism, in whose name he would lead Vietnam's long and bloody struggle for independence. With the collapse of the Wilsonian moment, Lenin's reputation in the colonial world began to eclipse that of the American president. But whether communist or not, these movements announced the emergence of anticolonial nationalism as a major force in world affairs, which it would remain for the rest of the twentieth century.

"Your liberalness," one Egyptian leader remarked, speaking of Britain and America, "is only for yourselves." Yet ironically, when colonial peoples demanded to be recognized as independent members of the international community, they would invoke the heritage of the American Revolution—the first colonial struggle that produced an independent nation.

Brewing resentment and violence

World War I sowed the seeds not of a lasting peace but of wars to come. German resentment over the peace terms would help to fuel the rise of Adolf Hitler and the coming of World War II. In the breakup of Czechoslovakia and Yugoslavia, violence over the status of Northern Ireland, and seemingly unending conflicts in the Middle East, the world of the late twentieth century was still haunted by the ghost of Versailles.

The Treaty Debate

Fear of international involvement

One final disappointment awaited Wilson on his return from Europe. He viewed the new League of Nations as the war's finest legacy. But many Americans feared that membership in the League would commit the United States to an open-ended involvement in the affairs of other countries.

Refusal to negotiate

A considerable majority of senators would have accepted the treaty with "reservations" ensuring that the obligation to assist League members against attack did not supersede the power of Congress to declare war. Convinced, however, that the treaty reflected "the hand of God," Wilson refused to negotiate with congressional leaders. In October 1919, in the midst of the League debate, Wilson suffered a serious stroke. Although the extent of his illness was kept secret, he remained incapacitated for the rest of his presidency. In effect, his wife, Edith, headed the government for the next seventeen months. In November 1919 and again in March 1920, the Senate rejected the Versailles Treaty.

The enduring impact of Wilsonian policy

American involvement in World War I lasted barely nineteen months, but it cast a long shadow over the following decade—and, indeed, the rest of the century. In its immediate aftermath, the country retreated from international involvements. But in the long run, Wilson's combination of idealism and power politics had an enduring impact. His appeals to democracy, open markets, and a special American mission to instruct the world in freedom, coupled with a willingness to intervene abroad militarily to promote American interests and values, would create the model for twentieth-century American international relations.

"Return to normalcy"

On its own terms, the war to make the world safe for democracy failed. It also led to the eclipse of Progressivism. Republican candidate Warren G. Harding, who had no connection with the party's Progressive wing, swept to victory in the presidential election of 1920. Harding's campaign centered on a "return to normalcy" and a repudiation of what he called "Wilsonism." He received 60 percent of the popular vote. Begun with idealistic goals and grand hopes for social change, American involvement in the Great War laid the foundation for one of the most conservative decades in the nation's history.

CHAPTER REVIEW AND ONLINE RESOURCES

REVIEW QUESTIONS

1. *Explain the role of the United States in the global economy by 1920.*
2. *What were the assumptions underlying the Roosevelt Corollary? How did the doctrine affect our relations with European nations and those in the Western Hemisphere?*
3. *What did President Wilson mean by "moral imperialism," and what measures were taken to apply this to Latin America?*
4. *How did the ratification of the Eighteenth and Nineteenth Amendments show the restrictive and democratizing nature of Progressivism?*
5. *Why did Progressives see in the expansion of governmental powers in wartime an opportunity to reform American society?*
6. *What were the goals and methods of the Committee on Public Information during World War I?*
7. *What are governmental and private examples of coercive patriotism during the war? What were the effects of those efforts?*
8. *How did the "science" of eugenics fuel anti-immigrant sentiment?*
9. *How did World War I and its aftermath provide African-Americans with opportunities?*
10. *What were the major causes—both real and imaginary—of the Red Scare?*
11. *Identify the goals of those pressing for global change in 1919, and of those who opposed them.*

KEY TERMS

liberal internationalism (p. 574)
Panama Canal Zone (p. 575)
Roosevelt Corollary (p. 576)
Dollar Diplomacy (p. 576)
moral imperialism (p. 577)
Lusitania (p. 579)
Zimmermann Telegram (p. 580)
Fourteen Points (p. 581)
Selective Service Act (p. 582)
War Industries Board (p. 582)
Eighteenth Amendment (p. 585)
Espionage Act (p. 585)
Sedition Act (p. 585)
National Association for the Advancement of Colored People (p. 594)
Great Migration (p. 595)
Tulsa riot (p. 596)
Marcus Garvey (p. 596)
Red Scare of 1919–1920 (p. 598)
Versailles Treaty (p. 599)
League of Nations (p. 599)

Go to INQUIZITIVE

To see what you know—and learn what you've missed—with personalized feedback along the way.

Visit the ***Give Me Liberty!* Student Site** for primary source documents and images, interactive maps, author videos featuring Eric Foner, and more.

1915	Reemergence of the Ku Klux Klan
1919	*Schenck v. United States*
	Claude McKay's "If We Must Die"
1920	American Civil Liberties Union established
1921	Trial of Sacco and Vanzetti
1922	Washington Naval Arms Conference
	Hollywood adopts the Hays code
	Herbert Hoover's *American Individualism*
	Meyer v. Nebraska
1924	Immigration Act of 1924
1925	Scopes trial
1927	Charles Lindbergh flies nonstop over the Atlantic
	Sacco and Vanzetti executed
1929	Robert and Helen Lynd's *Middletown*
	Sheppard-Towner Act repealed
	Stock market crashes
1930	Smoot-Hawley Tariff
1932	Reconstruction Finance Corporation established
	Bonus march on Washington

CHAPTER 20

FROM BUSINESS CULTURE TO GREAT DEPRESSION

★

THE TWENTIES, 1920–1932

One of a series of murals painted in 1930 and 1931 by Thomas Hart Benton under the overall title *America Today*. *Changing West* depicts some of the transformations occurring in that region including oil exploration, factory development, and air travel.

In May 1920, at the height of the postwar Red Scare, police arrested two Italian immigrants accused of participating in a robbery at a South Braintree, Massachusetts, factory in which a security guard was killed. Nicola Sacco, a shoemaker, and Bartolomeo Vanzetti, an itinerant unskilled laborer, were anarchists who dreamed of a society in which government, churches, and private property would be abolished. They saw violence as an appropriate weapon of class warfare. But very little evidence linked them to this particular crime. In the atmosphere of anti-radical and anti-immigrant fervor, however, their conviction was a certainty.

Although their 1921 trial aroused little public interest outside the Italian-American community, the case of Sacco and Vanzetti attracted considerable attention during the lengthy appeals that followed. There were mass protests in Europe against their impending execution. On August 23, 1927, Sacco and Vanzetti died in the electric chair.

The **Sacco-Vanzetti case** laid bare some of the fault lines beneath the surface of American society during the 1920s. To many native-born Americans, the two men symbolized an alien threat to their way of life. To Italian-Americans, including respectable middle-class organizations like the Sons of Italy that raised money for the defense, the outcome symbolized the nativist prejudices and stereotypes that haunted immigrant communities.

In popular memory, the decade that followed World War I is recalled as the Jazz Age or the Roaring Twenties. With its flappers (young, sexually liberated women), speakeasies (nightclubs that sold liquor in violation of Prohibition), and a soaring stock market fueled by easy credit

FOCUS QUESTIONS

- *Who benefited and who suffered in the new consumer society of the 1920s?*
- *In what ways did the government promote business interests in the 1920s?*
- *Why did the protection of civil liberties gain importance in the 1920s?*
- *What were the major flash points between fundamentalism and pluralism in the 1920s?*
- *What were the causes of the Great Depression, and how effective were the government's responses by 1932?*

A 1927 photograph shows Nicola Sacco, center right, and Bartolomeo Vanzetti outside the courthouse in Dedham, Massachusetts, surrounded by security agents and onlookers. They are about to enter the courthouse, where the judge will pronounce their death sentences.

and a get-rich-quick outlook, it was a time of revolt against moral rules inherited from the nineteenth century. Observers from Europe, where class divisions were starkly visible in work, politics, and social relations, marveled at the uniformity of American life. Factories poured out standardized consumer goods, their sale promoted by national advertising campaigns. Conservatism dominated a political system from which radical alternatives seemed to have been purged. Radio and the movies spread mass culture throughout the nation.

Many Americans, however, did not welcome the new secular, commercial culture. They resented and feared the ethnic and racial diversity of America's cities and what they considered the lax moral standards of urban life. The 1920s was a decade of profound social tensions—between rural and urban Americans, traditional and "modern" Christianity, participants in the burgeoning consumer culture and those who did not fully share in the new prosperity.

THE BUSINESS OF AMERICA

A Decade of Prosperity

"The chief business of the American people," said Calvin Coolidge, who became president after Warren G. Harding's sudden death from a heart attack in 1923, "is business." Rarely in American history had economic growth seemed more dramatic, cooperation between business and government so close, and business values so widely shared. Productivity and economic output rose dramatically as new industries—chemicals, aviation, electronics—flourished and older ones like food processing and the manufacture of household appliances adopted Henry Ford's moving assembly line. Annual automobile production tripled during the 1920s, from 1.5 to 4.8 million, stimulating steel, rubber, and oil production, and other sectors of the economy. By 1929, half of all Americans owned a car.

Industrial growth

During the 1920s, American multinational corporations extended their sway throughout the world. With Europe still recovering from the Great War, American investment overseas far exceeded that of other countries. The dollar replaced the British pound as the most important currency of international trade. American companies produced 85 percent of the world's cars and 40 percent of its manufactured goods. General Electric and International Telephone and Telegraph bought up companies in other countries. International Business Machines (IBM) was the world's leader in office supplies. American companies took control of raw materials abroad, from rubber in Liberia to oil in Venezuela.

Multinational corporations

A New Society

During the 1920s, consumer goods of all kinds proliferated, marketed by salesmen and advertisers who promoted them as ways of satisfying Americans' psychological desires and everyday needs. Frequently purchased on credit through new installment buying plans, they rapidly altered daily life. Telephones made communication easier. Vacuum cleaners, washing machines, and refrigerators transformed work in the home and reduced the demand for domestic servants. Boosted by Prohibition and an aggressive advertising campaign that, according to the company's sales director, made it "impossible for the consumer to *escape*" the product, Coca-Cola became a symbol of American life.

Leisure activities

Americans spent more and more of their income on leisure activities like vacations, movies, and sporting events. By 1929, weekly movie attendance had reached 80 million, double the figure of 1922. Radios and phonographs brought mass entertainment into American living rooms. The number of radios in American homes rose from 190,000 in 1923 to just under 5 million in 1929. These developments helped create and spread a new celebrity culture, in which recording, film, and sports stars moved to the top of the list of American heroes. During the 1920s, more than 100 million records were sold each year. RCA Victor sold so many recordings of the great opera tenor Enrico Caruso that he is sometimes called the first modern celebrity. He was soon joined by the film actor Charlie Chaplin, baseball player Babe Ruth, and boxer Jack Dempsey. Perhaps the decade's greatest celebrity, in terms of intensive press coverage, was the aviator Charles Lindbergh, who in 1927 made the first solo nonstop flight across the Atlantic.

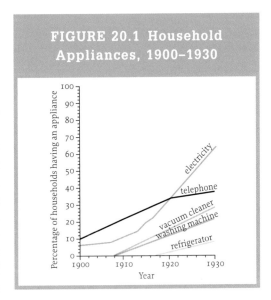

FIGURE 20.1 Household Appliances, 1900–1930

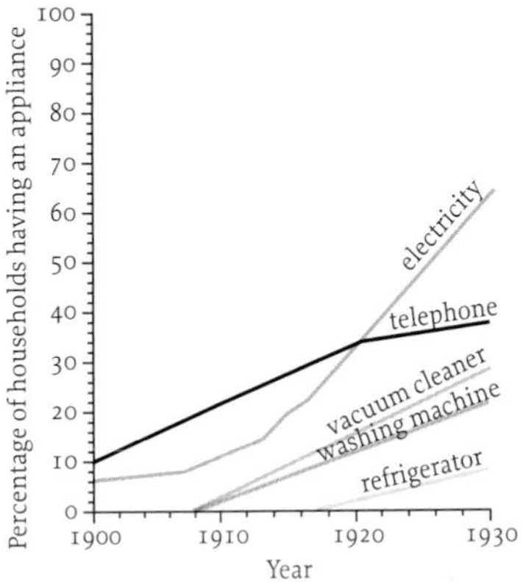

The Limits of Prosperity

But signs of future trouble could be seen beneath the prosperity of the 1920s. The fruits of increased production were very unequally distributed. Real wages for industrial workers (wages adjusted to take account of inflation) rose by one-quarter between 1922 and 1929, but corporate profits rose at more than twice that rate. The process of economic concentration continued unabated. A handful of firms dominated numerous sectors of the economy. In 1929, 1 percent of the nation's banks controlled half of its financial resources. Most of the small auto companies that had existed earlier in the century had fallen by the wayside. General Motors, Ford, and Chrysler now controlled four-fifths of the industry.

Economic weakness

At the beginning of 1929, a majority of families had no savings, and an estimated 40 percent of the population remained in poverty, unable to participate in the flourishing consumer economy. Improved productivity meant that goods could be produced with fewer workers. During the 1920s, more Americans worked in the professions, retailing, finance, and education, but the number of manufacturing workers declined by 5 percent, the first such drop in the nation's history. Parts of New England were already experiencing the chronic unemployment caused by deindustrialization. Many of the region's textile companies failed in the face of low-wage competition from southern factories or shifted production to take advantage of the South's cheap labor.

The Farmers' Plight

Nor did farmers share in the decade's prosperity. The "golden age" of American farming had reached its peak during World War I, when the need to feed war-torn Europe and government efforts to maintain high farm prices had raised farmers' incomes and promoted the purchase of more land on credit. Thanks to mechanization and the increased use of fertilizer and insecticides, agricultural production continued to rise even when government subsidies ended and world demand stagnated. As a result, the price of farm products fell, farm incomes in the 1920s declined steadily, and banks foreclosed tens of thousands of farms.

Facing dire conditions, some 3 million persons migrated out of rural areas. Many headed for southern California, whose rapidly growing economy needed new labor. The population of Los Angeles, the West's leading industrial center—a producer of oil, automobiles, aircraft, and, of course, Hollywood movies—rose from 575,000 to 2.2 million during the decade, largely because of an influx of displaced farmers from the Midwest. Well before the 1930s, rural America was in an economic depression.

Kansas agricultural workers breaking new ground with disk plows, which eased the task of readying the sod of the Great Plains for planting and encouraged the emergence of larger farms. Simon Fishman, a Jewish farmer known as the "wheat king," in jacket and tie, is on the last tractor.

The 1920s, however, was not simply a period of decline on the farm but of significant technological change. New inventions came into widespread use on the Great Plains, especially the steam tractor and the disk plow, which killed weeds, chopped up the sod, and left the surface layer much easier to plant. Mechanization encouraged an increase in the scale of agriculture. From farms growing wheat to California orange groves, the western states became home to modern "factory farms" employing large numbers of migrant laborers. Massive irrigation projects completed in the previous decades made the Far West much more suitable for farming. Farm output boomed in previously arid parts of California, Arizona, New Mexico, and Texas. With immigration from Asia barred and blacks unwanted, agribusinesses recruited workers from across the southern border, and immigrants from Mexico came to make up the vast majority of the West's low-wage farm migrants.

Farmers, such as this family of potato growers in rural Minnesota, did not share in the prosperity of the 1920s.

The Image of Business

America's image

Despite America's underlying economic problems, businessmen like Henry Ford and engineers like Herbert Hoover were cultural heroes. Photographers such as Lewis Hine and Margaret Bourke-White and painters like Charles Sheeler celebrated the beauty of machines and factories.

Numerous firms established public relations departments to justify corporate practices to the public and counteract its long-standing distrust of big business. They even succeeded in changing popular attitudes toward Wall Street.

Rise of the stock market

In the 1920s, as the steadily rising price of stocks made front-page news, the market attracted more investors. Many assumed that stock values would keep rising forever. By 1928, an estimated 1.5 million Americans owned stock—still a small minority of the country's 28 million families, but far more than in the past.

The Decline of Labor

Welfare Capitalism

With the defeat of the labor upsurge of 1919 and the dismantling of the wartime regulatory state, business appropriated the rhetoric of Americanism and "industrial freedom" as weapons against labor unions. Some corporations during the 1920s implemented a new style of management. They provided their employees with private pensions and medical insurance plans, job security, and greater workplace safety. They spoke of "welfare

Charles Sheeler's photograph of the interior of Henry Ford's River Rouge auto factory and his painting of one part of the industrial complex exemplify the "machine-age" aesthetic of the 1920s. Sheeler found artistic beauty in the giant plant, which employed 75,000 workers. Only one, however, is visible here and he is dwarfed by the giant stamping press. What interests Sheeler is machinery, not man. The painting's title, *Classic Landscape*, seems slightly ironic, as landscapes traditionally emphasized scenes of the natural environment.

capitalism," a more socially conscious kind of business leadership, and trumpeted the fact that they now paid more attention to the "human factor" in employment.

At the same time, however, employers in the 1920s embraced the American Plan, at whose core stood the open shop—a workplace free of both government regulation and unions, except, in some cases, "company unions" created and controlled by management. Even the most forward-looking companies continued to employ strikebreakers, private detectives, and the blacklisting of union organizers to prevent or defeat strikes.

During the 1920s, organized labor lost more than 2 million members, and unions agreed to demand after demand by employers in an effort to stave off complete elimination. Uprisings by the most downtrodden workers did occur sporadically throughout the decade. Southern textile mills witnessed desperate strikes by workers who charged employers with "making slaves out of the men and women" who labored there. Facing the combined opposition of business, local politicians, and the courts, as well as the threat of violence, such strikes were doomed to defeat.

The Equal Rights Amendment

Like the labor movement, feminists struggled to adapt to the new political situation. The achievement of suffrage in 1920 eliminated the bond of unity among various activists, each "struggling for her own conception of freedom," in the words of labor reformer Juliet Stuart Poyntz. Black feminists insisted that the movement must now demand enforcement of the

Fifteenth Amendment in the South, but they won little support from their white counterparts.

Debate over the ERA

The long-standing division between two competing conceptions of woman's freedom—one based on motherhood, the other on individual autonomy and the right to work—now crystallized in the debate over an **Equal Rights Amendment** (ERA) to the Constitution promoted by Alice Paul and the National Woman's Party. This amendment proposed to eliminate all legal distinctions "on account of sex." In Paul's opinion, the ERA followed logically from winning the right to vote. Having gained political equality, she insisted, women no longer required special legal protection—they needed equal access to employment, education, and all the other opportunities of citizens. To supporters of mothers' pensions and laws limiting women's hours of labor, which the ERA would sweep away, the proposal represented a giant step backward. Apart from the National Woman's Party, every major female organization opposed the ERA.

The ERA campaign failed, and only six states ratified a proposed constitutional amendment giving Congress the power to prohibit child labor, which farm groups and business organizations opposed. In 1929, Congress repealed the Sheppard-Towner Act of 1921, a major achievement of the maternalist reformers that had provided federal assistance to programs for infant and child health.

Women's Freedom

If political feminism faded, the prewar feminist demand for personal freedom survived in the vast consumer marketplace and in the actual behavior of the decade's much-publicized liberated young women. No longer one element in a broader program of social reform, sexual freedom now meant individual autonomy or personal rebellion. With her bobbed hair, short skirts, public smoking and drinking, and unapologetic use of birth-control methods such as the diaphragm, the young, single **flapper** epitomized the change in standards of sexual behavior, at least in large cities. She frequented dance halls and attended sexually charged Hollywood films featuring stars like Clara Bow, the provocative "'It' Girl," and Rudolph Valentino, the original on-screen "Latin Lover."

Women's self-conscious pursuit of personal pleasure became a device to market goods from automobiles to cigarettes. In 1904, a woman had been arrested for smoking in public in New York City. Two decades later, Edward Bernays, the "father" of modern public relations, masterminded a campaign to persuade women to smoke, dubbing cigarettes women's "torches of freedom." The new freedom, however, was available only during one phase of a woman's life. Marriage, according to one advertisement,

Tipsy, a 1930 painting by the Japanese artist Kobayakawa Kiyoshi, illustrates the global appeal of the "new woman" of the 1920s. The subject, a *moga* ("modern girl" in Japanese), sits alone in a nightclub wearing Western clothing, makeup, and hairstyle and enjoying a cigarette and a martini. The title of the work suggests that Kiyoshi does not entirely approve of her behavior, but he presents her as self-confident and alluring. Japanese police took a dim view of "modern" women, arresting those who applied makeup in public.

(*Left*) Advertisers marketed cigarettes to women as symbols of female independence. The August 27, 1925 cover of *Life* magazine shows a young man and a young woman dressed identically at the beach in revealing bathing suits (by 1920s standards), both enjoying cigarettes. (*Right*) An ad for a washing machine promises to liberate women from the "slavery" of everyday laundering at home.

remained "the one pursuit that stands foremost in the mind of every girl and woman." Having found husbands, women were expected to seek freedom within the confines of the home.

BUSINESS AND GOVERNMENT

Robert and Helen Lynd, Middletown

In 1929, the sociologists Robert and Helen Lynd published *Middletown*, a classic study of life in Muncie, Indiana, a typical community in the American heartland. The Lynds found that new leisure activities and a new emphasis on consumption had replaced politics as the focus of public concern. Elections were no longer "lively centers" of public attention as in the nineteenth century, and voter participation had fallen dramatically. National statistics bore out their point; the turnout of eligible voters, over 80 percent in 1896, dropped to less than 50 percent in 1924. Many factors helped to explain this decline, including the consolidation of one-party politics in the South, the long period of Republican dominance in national elections, and the enfranchisement of women, who for many years voted in lower numbers than men. But the shift from public to private concerns also played a part. "The American citizen's first importance to his country," declared a Muncie newspaper, "is no longer that of a citizen but that of a consumer."

Falling voter participation

The Republican Era

Government policies reflected the pro-business ethos of the 1920s. Business lobbyists dominated Republican national conventions. They called on the federal government to lower taxes on personal incomes and business profits, maintain high tariffs, and support employers' continuing campaign against unions. The administrations of Warren G. Harding and Calvin Coolidge obliged. Under William Howard Taft, appointed chief justice in 1921, the Supreme Court remained strongly conservative. A resurgence of laissez-faire jurisprudence eclipsed the Progressive ideal of a socially active national state. The Court struck down a federal law that barred goods produced by child labor from interstate commerce. It even repudiated *Muller v. Oregon* (see Chapter 18) in a 1923 decision (***Adkins v. Children's Hospital***) overturning a minimum wage law for women in Washington, D.C. Now that women enjoyed the vote, the justices declared, they were entitled to the same workplace freedom as men.

Corruption in Government

Harding administration

Warren G. Harding took office as president in 1921 promising a "return to normalcy" after an era of Progressive reform and world war. Reflecting the prevailing get-rich-quick ethos, his administration quickly became one of the most corrupt in American history. Although his cabinet included men of integrity and talent, like Secretary of State Charles Evans Hughes and Secretary of Commerce Herbert Hoover, Harding also surrounded himself with cronies who used their offices for private gain. Attorney General Harry Daugherty accepted payments not to prosecute accused criminals. The most notorious scandal involved Secretary of the Interior Albert Fall, who accepted nearly $500,000 from private businessmen to whom he leased government oil reserves at **Teapot Dome**, Wyoming. Fall became the first cabinet member in history to be convicted of a felony.

Teapot Dome

A 1924 cartoon commenting on the scandals of the Harding administration. The White House, Capitol, and Washington Monument have been sold to the highest bidder.

The Election of 1924

Harding's successor, Calvin Coolidge, who as governor of Massachusetts had won national fame for using state troops against striking Boston policemen in 1919, was a dour man of few words. But in contrast to his predecessor he seemed to exemplify Yankee honesty. In 1924, Coolidge was elected in a landslide, defeating John W. Davis, a Wall Street lawyer nominated on the 103rd ballot by a badly divided Democratic convention. (This was when the comedian Will Rogers made the quip, often repeated in future years, "I am a member of no organized political party; I am a Democrat.")

One-sixth of the electorate in 1924 voted for Robert La Follette, running as the candidate of a new Progressive Party, which called for greater taxation of wealth, the conservation of natural resources, public ownership of the railroads, farm relief, and the end of child labor. La Follette carried only his native Wisconsin. But his candidacy demonstrated the survival of some currents of dissent in a highly conservative decade.

Augusto Sandino, who led a rebellion against the U.S. military occupation of Nicaragua in the late 1920s. He was assassinated in 1934 by General Anastasio Somoza, who became dictator and established a family dynasty that ruled Nicaragua until overthrown in 1979.

Economic Diplomacy

Foreign affairs also reflected the close working relationship between business and government. The 1920s marked a retreat from Wilson's goal of internationalism in favor of unilateral American actions mainly designed to increase exports and investment opportunities overseas. Indeed, what is sometimes called the "isolationism" of the 1920s represented a reaction against the disappointing results of Wilson's military and diplomatic pursuit of freedom and democracy abroad. The United States did play host to the Washington Naval Arms Conference of 1922, which negotiated reductions in the navies of Britain, France, Japan, Italy, and the United States. But the country remained outside the League of Nations. Even as American diplomats continued to press for access to markets overseas, the Fordney-McCumber Tariff of 1922 raised taxes on imported goods to their highest levels in history, a repudiation of Wilson's principle of promoting free trade.

As before World War I, the government dispatched soldiers when a change in government in the Caribbean threatened American economic interests. Having been stationed in Nicaragua since 1912, American marines withdrew in 1925. But the troops soon returned in an effort to suppress a nationalist revolt headed by General Augusto César Sandino. Having created a National Guard headed by General Anastasio Somoza, the marines finally departed in 1933. A year later, Somoza assassinated Sandino and seized power. For the next forty-five years, he and his family ruled and plundered Nicaragua. Somoza's son was overthrown in 1979 by a popular movement calling itself the Sandinistas (see Chapter 26).

THE BIRTH OF CIVIL LIBERTIES

Among the casualties of World War I and the 1920s was Progressivism's faith that an active federal government embodied the national purpose and enhanced the enjoyment of freedom. Wartime and postwar repression, Prohibition, and the pro-business policies of the 1920s all illustrated, in the eyes of many Progressives, how public power could go grievously wrong.

This lesson opened the door to a new appreciation of civil liberties—rights an individual may assert even against democratic majorities—as essential elements of American freedom. In the name of a "new freedom for the individual," the 1920s saw the birth of a coherent concept of civil liberties and the beginnings of significant legal protection for freedom of speech against the government.

Censorship

Wartime repression continued into the 1920s. Artistic works with sexual themes were subjected to rigorous censorship. The Postal Service removed from the mails books it deemed obscene. The Customs Service barred works by the sixteenth-century French satirist Rabelais, the modern novelist James Joyce, and many others from entering the country. A local crusade against indecency made the phrase "Banned in Boston" a term of ridicule among upholders of artistic freedom. Boston's Watch and Ward Committee excluded sixty-five books from the city's bookstores, including works by the novelists Upton Sinclair, Theodore Dreiser, and Ernest Hemingway. In 1930, the film industry adopted the Hays code, a sporadically enforced set of guidelines that prohibited movies from depicting nudity, long kisses, and adultery, and barred scripts that portrayed clergymen in a negative light or criminals sympathetically.

The Lost Generation

Disillusionment with the conservatism of American politics and the materialism of the culture inspired some American artists and writers to emigrate to Paris. The Lost Generation of cultural exiles included novelists and poets like Ernest Hemingway, Gertrude Stein, and F. Scott Fitzgerald. Europe, they felt, valued art and culture, and appreciated unrestrained freedom of expression (and, of course, allowed individuals to drink legally).

VOICES OF FREEDOM

From Lucian W. Parrish, Speech in Congress on Immigration (1921)

In the immediate aftermath of World War I, fears of foreign radicalism sparked by labor upheavals, and the increased concern with Americanizing immigrants, greatly strengthened demands to curtail immigration. During a debate in the House of Representatives in April 1921, Lucian W. Parrish, a Democrat from Texas, laid out the case for immigration restriction.

We should stop immigration entirely until such a time as we can amend our immigration laws and so write them that hereafter no one shall be admitted except he be in full sympathy with our Constitution and laws, willing to declare himself obedient to our flag, and willing to release himself from any obligations he may owe to the flag of the country from which he came.

It is time that we act now, because within a few short years the damage will have been done. The endless tide of immigration will have filled our country with a foreign and unsympathetic element. Those who are out of sympathy with our Constitution and the spirit of our Government will be here in large numbers, and the true spirit of Americanism left us by our fathers will gradually become poisoned by this uncertain element.

The time once was when we welcomed to our shores the oppressed and downtrodden people from all the world, but they came to us because of oppression at home and with the sincere purpose of making true and loyal American citizens, and in truth and in fact they did adapt themselves to our ways of thinking and contributed in a substantial sense to the progress and development that our civilization has made. But that time has passed now; new and strange conditions have arisen in the countries over there; new and strange doctrines are being taught. The governments of the Orient are being overturned and destroyed, and anarchy and bolshevism are threatening the very foundation of many of them and no one can foretell what the future will bring to many of those countries of the Old World now struggling with these problems.

Our country is a self-sustaining country. It has taught the principles of real democracy to all the nations of the earth; its flag has been the synonym of progress, prosperity, and the preservation of the rights of the individual, and there can be nothing so dangerous as for us to allow the undesirable foreign element to poison our civilization and thereby threaten the safety of the institutions that our forefathers have established for us. . . .

We must hold this country true to the American thought and the American ideals.

From Majority Opinion, Justice James C. McReynolds, in *Meyer v. Nebraska* (1923)

A landmark in the development of civil liberties, the Supreme Court's decision in *Meyer v. Nebraska* rebuked the coercive Americanization impulse of World War I, overturning a Nebraska law that required all school instruction to take place in English.

The problem for our determination is whether the statute [prohibiting instruction in a language other than English] as construed and applied unreasonably infringes the liberty guaranteed . . . by the Fourteenth Amendment. . . .

The American people have always regarded education and acquisition of knowledge as matters of supreme importance which should be diligently promoted. . . . The calling always has been regarded as useful and honorable, essential, indeed, to the public welfare. Mere knowledge of the German language cannot reasonably be regarded as harmful. Heretofore it has been commonly looked upon as helpful and desirable. [Meyer] taught this language in school as part of his occupation. His right to teach and the right of parents to engage him so to instruct their children, we think, are within the liberty of the Amendment.

It is said the purpose of the legislation was to promote civil development by inhibiting training and education of the immature in foreign tongues and ideals before they could learn English and acquire American ideals. . . . It is also affirmed that the foreign born population is very large, that certain communities commonly use foreign words, follow foreign leaders, move in a foreign atmosphere, and that the children are therefore hindered from becoming citizens of the most useful type and the public safety is impaired.

That the State may do much, go very far, indeed, in order to improve the quality of its citizens, physically, mentally, and morally, is clear; but the individual has certain fundamental rights which must be respected. The protection of the Constitution extends to all, to those who speak other languages as well as to those born with English on the tongue. Perhaps it would be highly advantageous if all had ready understanding of our ordinary speech, but this cannot be coerced by methods which conflict with the Constitution. . . . No emergency has arisen which rendered knowledge by a child of some language other than English so clearly harmful as to justify its inhibition with the consequent infringement of rights long freely enjoyed.

QUESTIONS

1. *Why does Parrish consider continued immigration dangerous?*
2. *How does the decision in* Meyer v. Nebraska *expand the definition of liberty protected by the Fourteenth Amendment?*
3. *How do the two excerpts reflect deep divisions over the nature of American society during the 1920s?*

A "Clear and Present Danger"

The American Civil Liberties Union

The arrest of antiwar dissenters under the Espionage and Sedition Acts inspired the formation in 1917 of the Civil Liberties Bureau, which in 1920 became the **American Civil Liberties Union** (ACLU). For the rest of the century, the ACLU would take part in most of the landmark cases that helped to bring about a "rights revolution." Its efforts helped to give meaning to traditional civil liberties like freedom of speech and invented new ones, like the right to privacy. When it began, however, the ACLU was a small, beleaguered organization.

Prior to World War I, the Supreme Court had done almost nothing to protect the rights of unpopular minorities. Now, it was forced to address the question of the permissible limits on political and economic dissent. In 1919, the Court upheld the constitutionality of the Espionage Act and the conviction of Charles T. Schenck, a socialist who had distributed antidraft leaflets through the mails. Speaking for the Court, Justice Oliver Wendell Holmes declared that the First Amendment did not prevent Congress from prohibiting speech that presented a "clear and present danger" of inspiring illegal actions. A week after ***Schenck v. United States***, the Court unanimously upheld the conviction of Eugene V. Debs for a speech condemning the war.

The Court and Civil Liberties

Also in 1919, the Court upheld the conviction of Jacob Abrams and five other men for distributing pamphlets critical of American intervention in Russia after the Russian Revolution. This time, however, Holmes and Louis Brandeis dissented, marking the emergence of a court minority committed to a broader defense of free speech.

Defendants in *U.S. v. Abrams*, on the day of their deportation to Russia in 1921. Jacob Abrams is on the right. They were convicted under the Espionage Act of 1918 for impeding the war effort by distributing pamphlets critical of the American intervention in Russia after the Russian Revolution.

The tide of civil-liberties decision making slowly began to turn. By the end of the 1920s, the Supreme Court had voided a Kansas law that made it a crime to advocate unlawful acts to change the political or economic system and one from Minnesota authorizing censorship of the press. The new regard for free speech went beyond political expression. In 1933, a federal court overturned the Customs Service's ban on James Joyce's novel *Ulysses*, a turning point in the battle against the censorship of works of literature.

A judicial foundation for civil liberties was slowly being born. As Brandeis insisted, "Those who won our independence believed . . . that freedom to think as you will and to speak as you think are indispensable to the discovery and spread of political truth. . . . The greatest menace to freedom is an inert people."

THE CULTURE WARS

The Fundamentalist Revolt

Although many Americans embraced modern urban culture with its religious and ethnic pluralism, mass entertainment, and liberated sexual rules, others found it alarming. Many evangelical Protestants felt threatened by the decline of traditional values and the increased visibility of Catholicism and Judaism because of immigration. They also resented the growing presence within mainstream Protestant denominations of "modernists" who sought to integrate science and religion and adapt Christianity to the new secular culture.

Evangelical Protestants

Convinced that the literal truth of the Bible formed the basis of Christian belief, fundamentalists launched a campaign to rid Protestant denominations of modernism and to combat the new individual freedoms that seemed to contradict traditional morality. Their most flamboyant apostle was Billy Sunday, a talented professional baseball player who became a revivalist preacher. Between 1900 and 1930, Sunday drew huge crowds with a highly theatrical preaching style and a message denouncing sins ranging from Darwinism to alcohol. **Fundamentalism** remained an important strain of 1920s culture and politics. Prohibition, which fundamentalists strongly supported, succeeded in reducing the consumption of alcohol as well as public drunkenness and drink-related diseases.

Billy Sunday

A 1923 lithograph by George Bellows captures the dynamic style of the most prominent evangelical preacher of the 1920s, Billy Sunday.

Often portrayed (especially in Hollywood movies) as a glamorous episode of gangland battles and drinkers easily outwitting the police, Prohibition in fact was effectively enforced, albeit selectively. While wealthy Americans continued to enjoy access to liquor, many poor, black, and immigrant communities suffered large-scale arrests and jailings, often accompanied by police violence. Later deemed to have had no lasting effects, Prohibition in fact led to the building of new federal prisons and laid the foundation for powerful national action against crime and immorality, a precursor to the more recent federal war on drugs.

Federal agents with confiscated liquor in Colorado in 1920, shortly after the advent of Prohibition.

Prohibition, however, remained deeply divisive. The greatest expansion of national authority since Reconstruction, it raised major questions of local rights, individual freedom, and the wisdom of attempting to impose religious and moral values on the entire society through legislation. It divided the Democratic Party into "wet" and "dry" wings, leading to bitter internal battles at the party's 1924 and 1928 national conventions.

Too many Americans deemed Prohibition a violation of individual freedom for the flow of illegal liquor to stop. In urban areas, Prohibition led to large profits for the owners of illegal speakeasies and the "bootleggers" who supplied them. It produced widespread corruption as police and public officials accepted bribes to turn a blind eye to violations of the law.

A scene on the Canadian side of the border with the state of Washington. One hundred feet into Canada, billboards welcome Americans to a country where it is still legal to consume alcohol.

The Scopes Trial

Because of extreme heat, some sessions of the Scopes trial were held outdoors, in front of the courthouse in Dayton, Tennessee. A photographer snapped this picture of the trial's climactic moment, when Clarence Darrow (standing at the center) questioned William Jennings Bryan (seated) about his interpretation of the Bible.

In 1925, a trial in Tennessee threw into sharp relief the division between traditional values and modern, secular culture. John Scopes, a teacher in a Tennessee public school, was arrested for violating a state law that prohibited the teaching of Charles Darwin's theory of evolution. His trial became a national sensation.

The **Scopes trial** reflected the enduring tension between two American definitions of freedom. Fundamentalist Christians clung to the traditional idea of "moral" liberty—voluntary adherence to time-honored religious beliefs. The theory that man had evolved over millions of years from ancestors like apes contradicted the biblical account of creation. To Scopes's defenders, including the American Civil Liberties Union, freedom meant above all the right to independent thought and individual self-expression. To them, the Tennessee law offered a lesson in the dangers of religious intolerance and the merger of church and state.

The renowned labor lawyer Clarence Darrow defended Scopes. The trial's highlight came when Darrow called William Jennings Bryan to the stand as an "expert witness" on the Bible. Bryan revealed an almost complete ignorance of modern science and proved unable to respond effectively to Darrow's sarcastic questioning. Asked whether God had actually created the world in six days, Bryan replied that these should be understood as ages, "not six days of twenty-four hours"—thus opening the door to the very nonliteral interpretation of the Bible that the fundamentalists rejected.

The jury found Scopes guilty, although the Tennessee Supreme Court later overturned the decision on a technicality. Fundamentalists retreated for many years from battles over public education, preferring to build their own schools and colleges where teaching could be done as they saw fit. The battle would be rejoined, however, toward the end of the twentieth century.

In 1926, members of the Ku Klux Klan, in full regalia, paraded in front of the Capitol in Washington, D.C. Unlike the Klan of the Reconstruction era, the second Klan was more powerful in the North and West than in the South.

The Second Klan

Few features of urban life seemed more alien to rural and small-town native-born Protestants than their

A scene from a series of murals painted in 1933 by Thomas Hart Benton for Chicago's "Century of Progress" exposition—now displayed at Indiana University—shows scenes of Americans at work and at play. Benton's inclusion, at the center, of a Ku Klux Klan rally hints at the darker side of the politics and culture of the 1920s. The newspaperman at his typewriter symbolizes the role of the press in exposing the Klan's nefarious deeds.

immigrant populations and cultures. The wartime obsession with "100 percent Americanism" continued into the 1920s. In 1922, Oregon became the only state ever to require all students to attend public schools—a measure aimed, said the state's attorney general, at abolishing parochial education and preventing "bolshevists, syndicalists and communists" from organizing their own schools.

Perhaps the most menacing expression of the idea that enjoyment of American freedom should be limited on religious and ethnic grounds was the resurgence of the Ku Klux Klan. The Klan had been reborn in Atlanta in 1915 after the lynching of Leo Frank, a Jewish factory manager accused of killing a teenage girl. By the mid-1920s, it claimed more than 5 million members, nearly all white, native-born Protestants, many of whom held respected positions in their communities. Unlike the Klan of Reconstruction, the organization now sank deep roots in parts of the North and West. It became the largest private organization in Indiana and for a time controlled the state Republican Party. American civilization, the new Klan insisted, was endangered not only by blacks but also by immigrants (especially Jews and Catholics) and all the forces (feminism, unions, immorality, even, on occasion, the giant corporations) that endangered "individual liberty."

Closing the Golden Door

The Klan's influence faded after 1925, when its leader in Indiana was convicted of assaulting a young woman. But the Klan's attacks on modern secular culture and political radicalism and its demand that control of the nation be returned to "citizens of the old stock" reflected sentiments widely shared in the 1920s.

The 1920s produced a fundamental change in immigration policy. Prior to World War I virtually all the white persons who wished to pass through the "golden door" into the United States and become citizens were able to do so. During the 1920s, however, the pressure for wholesale immigration restriction became irresistible.

In 1921, a temporary measure restricted immigration from Europe to 357,000 per year (one-third of the annual average before the war). Three years later, Congress permanently limited European immigration to 150,000 per year, distributed according to a series of national quotas that severely restricted the numbers from southern and eastern Europe. The immigration law also barred the entry of all those ineligible for naturalized citizenship—that is, the entire population of Asia, even though Japan had fought on the American side in World War I.

The law of 1924 established, in effect, for the first time a new category—the **illegal alien**. With it came a new enforcement mechanism, the Border Patrol, charged with policing the land boundaries of the United States and empowered to arrest and deport persons who entered the country in violation of the new nationality quotas or other restrictions. A term later associated almost exclusively with Latinos, "illegal aliens" at first referred mainly to southern and eastern Europeans who tried to sneak across the border from Mexico or Canada.

The immigration law of 1924 established the Border Patrol to stop those barred from entry from sneaking into the United States from Mexico. At first, the patrol was a modest operation. Here, two officers police the border in California.

Race and the Law

The new immigration law reflected the heightened emphasis on "race" as a determinant of public policy. By the early 1920s, political leaders of both North and South agreed on the relegation of blacks to second-class citizenship. But "race policy" meant far more than black-white relations. When President Coolidge signed the new law, his secretary of labor, James J. Davis, commented that immigration policy must now rest on a biological definition of the ideal population. Although enacted by a highly conservative Congress strongly influenced by nativism, the 1924 immigration law also reflected the Progressive desire to improve the "quality" of democratic citizenship and to employ scientific methods to set public policy. It revealed how these aims were overlaid with pseudo-scientific assumptions about the superiority and inferiority of particular "races."

"Race policy"

A "biologically ideal" population

But the entire concept of race as a basis for public policy lacked any rational foundation. The Supreme Court admitted as much in 1923 when it rejected the claim of Bhagat Singh Thind, an Indian-born World War I veteran, who asserted that as a "pure Aryan," he was actually white and could therefore become an American citizen. "White," the Court declared, was not a scientific concept at all, but part of "common speech, to be interpreted with the understanding of the common man" (a forthright statement of what later scholars would call the "social construction" of race).

WHO IS AN AMERICAN?

Immigration Quotas under the Johnson-Reed Act (1924)

In 1921, Congress imposed temporary country-by-country immigration quotas, based on the number of persons counted from each nation in the 1910 census. Three years later it revised the quotas to further limit the number allowed to enter the country, and changed the base date to 1890, before the arrival of most of the "new immigrants" from southern and eastern Europe. Countries in the Western Hemisphere, including Canada and Mexico, were not subject to quota limitations. The largest reductions applied to Italy (from which 283,000 immigrants had arrived in 1914) and Russia (255,000 in that year).

COUNTRY OR AREA OF BIRTH	IMMIGRATION QUOTA
Africa (total of various countries)	1,100
Albania	100
Arabian Peninsula	100
Asia (total of various countries)	0
Bulgaria	100
Denmark	2,789
Germany	51,227
Great Britain	34,007
Greece	100
Hungary	473
Ireland	28,567
Italy	3,845
Latvia	142
Norway	6,453
Poland	5,982
Russia	2,248
San Marino	100
Spain	131
Sweden	9,561
Turkey	100

QUESTIONS

1. *What do the numbers tell us about which immigrants Congress considered most and least desirable?*
2. *Why do you think no quotas were established for the Western Hemisphere?*

Promoting Tolerance

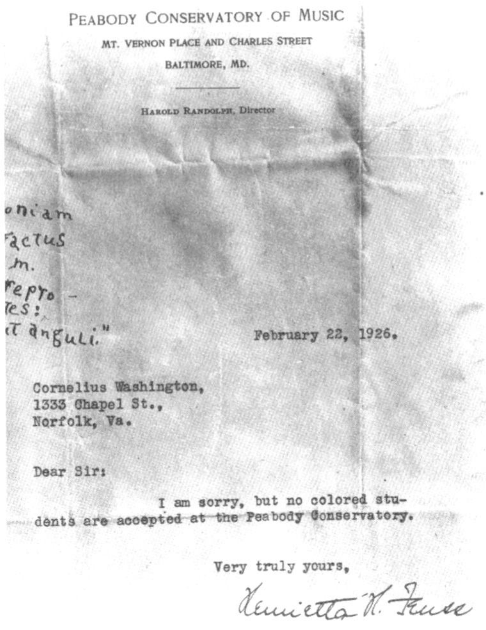
PEABODY CONSERVATORY OF MUSIC
MT. VERNON PLACE AND CHARLES STREET
BALTIMORE, MD.

HAROLD RANDOLPH, Director

February 22, 1926.

Cornelius Washington,
1333 Chapel St.,
Norfolk, Va.

Dear Sir:

I am sorry, but no colored students are accepted at the Peabody Conservatory.

Very truly yours,

Racism severely limited the opportunities open to black Americans. Here, the internationally renowned Peabody Conservatory of Music informs a black applicant that he cannot pursue his musical education there.

In the face of immigration restriction, Prohibition, a revived Ku Klux Klan, and widespread anti-Semitism and anti-Catholicism, immigrant groups asserted the validity of cultural diversity and identified toleration of difference—religious, cultural, and individual—as the essence of American freedom. In effect, they reinvented themselves as "ethnic" Americans, claiming an equal share in the nation's life but, in addition, the right to remain in many respects culturally distinct. The Roman Catholic Church urged immigrants to learn English and embrace "American principles," but it continued to maintain separate schools and other institutions. Throughout the country, organizations like the Anti-Defamation League of B'nai B'rith (founded in 1916 to combat anti-Semitism) and the National Catholic Welfare Council lobbied, in the name of "personal liberty," for laws prohibiting discrimination against immigrants by employers, colleges, and government agencies.

The efforts of immigrant communities to resist coerced Americanization and of the Catholic Church to defend its school system broadened the definition of liberty for all Americans. In landmark decisions, the Supreme Court struck down Oregon's law, mentioned earlier, requiring all students to attend public schools and Nebraska's law prohibiting teaching in a language other than English—one of the anti-German measures of World War I. The *Meyer v. Nebraska* (1923) decision expanded the freedom of all immigrant groups. In its aftermath, federal courts overturned various Hawaii laws imposing special taxes and regulations on private Japanese-language schools. In these cases, the Court also interpreted the Fourteenth Amendment's guarantee of equal liberty to include the right to "marry, establish a home and bring up children" and to practice religion as one chose, "without interference from the state." The decisions gave pluralism a constitutional foundation.

A foundation for pluralism

The Emergence of Harlem

The 1920s also witnessed an upsurge of self-consciousness among black Americans, especially in the North's urban ghettos. With European immigration all but halted, the Great Migration of World War I continued apace as nearly 1 million blacks left the South during the decade. New York's Harlem gained an international reputation as the "capital" of black America, a mecca for migrants from the South and immigrants from the West Indies, 150,000 of whom entered the United States between

Caribbean immigrants

A black family arriving in Chicago in 1922, as part of the Great Migration from the rural South.

1900 and 1930. Unlike the southern newcomers, most of whom had been agricultural workers, the West Indians included a large number of well-educated professional and white-collar workers. Their encounter with American racism appalled them. "I had heard of prejudice in America," wrote the poet and novelist Claude McKay, who emigrated from Jamaica in 1912, "but never dreamed of it being so intensely bitter."

"Slumming"

The 1920s became famous for "slumming," as groups of whites visited Harlem's dance halls, jazz clubs, and speakeasies in search of exotic adventure. The Harlem of the white imagination was a place of primitive passions, free from the puritanical restraints of mainstream American culture. The real Harlem was a community of widespread poverty, its residents confined to low-wage jobs and, because housing discrimination barred them from other neighborhoods, forced to pay exorbitant rents.

The Harlem Renaissance

Vibrant culture

But Harlem also was home to a vibrant black cultural community that established links with New York's artistic mainstream. Poets and novelists such as Countee Cullen, Langston Hughes, and Claude McKay were befriended and sponsored by white intellectuals and published by white presses. Broadway for the first time presented black actors in serious dramatic roles, as well as shows such as *Dixie to Broadway* and *Blackbirds* that featured great entertainers including the singers Florence Mills and Ethel Waters and the tap dancer Bill Robinson.

The "New Negro"

The term "**New Negro**," associated in politics with pan-Africanism and the militancy of the Garvey movement, in art meant the rejection of established stereotypes and a search for black values to put in their place. This quest led the writers of what came to be called the **Harlem Renaissance** to the roots of the black experience—Africa, the rural South's folk traditions, and the life of the urban ghetto. Harlem Renaissance writings also contained a strong element of protest. This mood was exemplified by McKay's poem "If We Must Die," a response to the race riots of 1919. The poem affirmed that blacks would no longer allow themselves to be murdered defenselessly by whites:

Claude McKay

> If we must die, let it not be like hogs
> Hunted and penned in an inglorious spot,
> While round us bark the mad and hungry dogs,
> Making their mock at our accursed lot. . . .
> Like men we'll face the murderous, cowardly pack,
> Pressed to the wall, dying, but fighting back!

Winston Churchill would invoke McKay's words to inspire the British public during World War II.

THE GREAT DEPRESSION

The Election of 1928

Few men elected to the presidency have seemed destined for a more successful term in office than Herbert Hoover. Born in Iowa in 1874, Hoover accumulated a fortune as a mining engineer working for firms in Asia, Africa, and Europe. During and immediately after World War I, he gained international fame by coordinating overseas food relief. In 1922, while serving as secretary of commerce, he published *American Individualism*, which condemned government regulation as an interference with the economic opportunities of ordinary Americans but also insisted that self-interest should be subordinated to public service. Hoover considered himself a Progressive, although he preferred what he called "associational action," in which private agencies directed regulatory and welfare policies, to government intervention in the economy.

A 1928 campaign poster for the Republican ticket of Herbert Hoover and Charles Curtis.

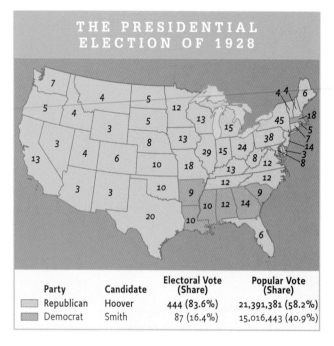

THE PRESIDENTIAL ELECTION OF 1928

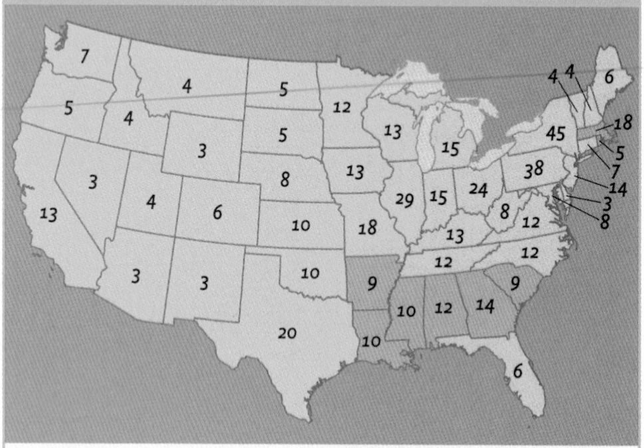

Party	Candidate	Electoral Vote (Share)	Popular Vote (Share)
Republican	Hoover	444 (83.6%)	21,391,381 (58.2%)
Democrat	Smith	87 (16.4%)	15,016,443 (40.9%)

After "silent Cal" Coolidge in 1927 handed a piece of paper to a group of reporters that stated, "I do not choose to run for president in 1928," Hoover quickly emerged as his successor. Accepting the Republican nomination, Hoover celebrated the decade's prosperity and promised that poverty would "soon be banished from this earth." His Democratic opponent was Alfred E. Smith, the first Catholic to be nominated by a major party. Although he had no family connection with the new immigrants from southern and eastern Europe (his grandparents had emigrated from Ireland), Smith became their symbolic spokesman. He served three terms as governor of New York, securing passage of laws limiting the hours of working women and children and establishing widows' pensions. Smith denounced the Red Scare and called for the repeal of Prohibition.

Smith's Catholicism became the focus of the race. Many Protestant ministers and religious publications denounced him for his faith. For the first time since Reconstruction, Republicans carried several southern states, reflecting the strength of anti-Catholicism and nativism among religious fundamentalists. On the other hand, Smith carried the nation's twelve largest cities and won significant support in economically struggling farm areas. With more than 58 percent of the vote, Hoover was elected by a landslide. But Smith's campaign helped to lay the foundation for the triumphant Democratic coalition of the 1930s, based on urban ethnic voters, farmers, and the South.

President Herbert Hoover (front row, right), at the opening day baseball game in Washington, D.C., April 17, 1929.

The Coming of the Depression

On October 21, 1929, President Hoover traveled to Michigan to take part in the Golden Anniversary of the Festival of Light, organized by Henry Ford to commemorate the invention of the lightbulb by Thomas Edison fifty years earlier. Eight days later, on Black Tuesday, the stock market crashed. As panic selling set in, more than $10 billion in market value (equivalent to more than ten times that amount in today's money) vanished in five hours. Soon, the United States and, indeed, the entire world found themselves in the grip of the **Great Depression**, the greatest economic disaster in modern history.

The **stock market crash** did not, by itself, cause the Depression. Even before 1929, signs of economic trouble had become evident. Southern

California and Florida experienced frenzied real-estate speculation and then spectacular busts, with banks failing, land remaining undeveloped, and mortgages foreclosed. The highly unequal distribution of income and the prolonged depression in farm regions reduced American purchasing power. Sales of new autos and household consumer goods stagnated after 1926. European demand for American goods also declined, partly because industry there had recovered from wartime destruction.

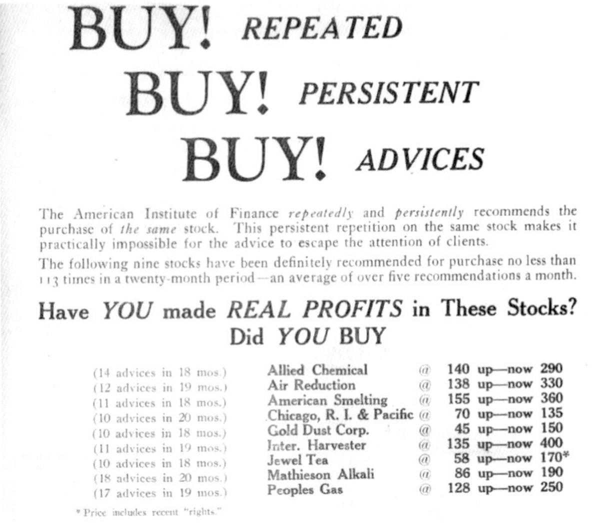
BUY! REPEATED
BUY! PERSISTENT
BUY! ADVICES
The American Institute of Finance repeatedly and persistently recommends the purchase of the same stock. This persistent repetition on the same stock makes it practically impossible for the advice to escape the attention of clients.
The following nine stocks have been definitely recommended for purchase no less than 113 times in a twenty-month period—an average of over five recommendations a month.
Have YOU made REAL PROFITS in These Stocks?
Did YOU BUY
(14 advices in 18 mos.) Allied Chemical @ 140 up—now 290
(12 advices in 19 mos.) Air Reduction @ 138 up—now 330
(11 advices in 18 mos.) American Smelting @ 155 up—now 360
(10 advices in 20 mos.) Chicago, R. I. & Pacific @ 70 up—now 135
(10 advices in 18 mos.) Gold Dust Corp. @ 45 up—now 150
(11 advices in 19 mos.) Inter. Harvester @ 135 up—now 400
(10 advices in 18 mos.) Jewel Tea @ 58 up—now 170*
(18 advices in 20 mos.) Mathieson Alkali @ 86 up—now 190
(17 advices in 19 mos.) Peoples Gas @ 128 up—now 250
* Price includes recent "rights."

Three months before the stock market crash, *The Magazine of Wall Street* was avidly encouraging readers to purchase stocks.

A fall in the bloated stock market, driven ever higher during the 1920s by speculators, was inevitable. But it came with such severity that it destroyed many of the investment companies that had been created to buy and sell stock, wiping out thousands of investors, and it greatly reduced business and consumer confidence.

The global financial system was ill equipped to deal with the downturn. Germany defaulted on reparations payments to France and Britain, leading these governments to stop repaying debts to American banks. Throughout the industrial world, banks failed as depositors withdrew money, fearful that they could no longer count on the promise to redeem paper money in gold. Millions of families lost their life savings.

Stocks' steady decline

Although stocks recovered somewhat in 1930, they soon resumed their relentless downward slide. Between 1929 and 1932, the price of a share of U.S. Steel fell from $262 to $22, and General Motors from $73 to $8. Four-fifths of the Rockefeller family fortune disappeared. In 1932, the economy hit rock bottom. Since 1929, the gross national product (the value of all the goods and services in the country) had fallen by one-third, prices by nearly 40 percent, and more than 11 million Americans—25 percent of the labor force—could not find work. U.S. Steel, which had employed 225,000 full-time workers in 1929, had none at the end of 1932. Those who retained their jobs confronted reduced hours and dramatically reduced wages. Every industrial economy suffered, but the United States, which had led the way in prosperity in the 1920s, was hit hardest of all.

Americans and the Depression

The Depression transformed American life. Hundreds of thousands of people took to the road in search of work. Hungry men and women lined the streets of major cities. In Detroit, 4,000 children stood in

Unemployed men lined up outside a Chicago soup kitchen in 1931. Charitable institutions like this one were overwhelmed by the advent of the Great Depression.

bread lines each day seeking food. Thousands of families, evicted from their homes, moved into ramshackle shantytowns, dubbed Hoovervilles, that sprang up in parks and on abandoned land. In Chicago, where half the working population was unemployed at the beginning of 1932, Mayor Anton Cermak telephoned people individually, begging them to pay their taxes. When the Soviet Union advertised its need for skilled workers, it received more than 100,000 applications from the United States.

Deurbanization

The Depression actually reversed the long-standing movement of population from farms to cities. Many Americans left cities to try to grow food for their families. In 1935, 33 million people lived on farms—more than at any previous point in American history. But rural areas, already poor, saw families reduce the number of meals per day and children go barefoot. With the future shrouded in uncertainty, the American suicide rate rose to the highest level in the nation's history, and the birthrate fell to the lowest.

A Hooverville—a shantytown created by homeless squatters—outside Seattle, Washington, in 1933.

The image of big business, carefully cultivated during the 1920s, collapsed as congressional investigations revealed massive irregularities committed by bankers and stockbrokers. Banks had knowingly sold worthless bonds. Prominent Wall Streeters had unloaded their own portfolios while advising small investors to maintain their holdings. Richard Whitney, the president of the New York Stock

Exchange, was convicted of stealing from customers, including from a fund to aid widows and orphans. He ended up in jail.

Resignation and Protest

Many Americans reacted to the Depression with resignation or blamed themselves for economic misfortune. Others responded with protests that were at first spontaneous and uncoordinated, since unions, socialist organizations, and other groups that might have provided disciplined leadership had been decimated during the 1920s. In the spring of 1932, 20,000 unemployed World War I veterans descended on Washington to demand early payment of a bonus due in 1945, only to be driven away by federal soldiers. That summer, led by the charismatic Milo Reno, a former Iowa Populist, the National Farmers' Holiday Association protested low prices by temporarily blocking roads in the Midwest to prevent farm goods from getting to market.

"Bonus marchers"

Only the minuscule Communist Party seemed able to give a political focus to the anger and despair. One labor leader later recalled that the Communists "brought misery out of hiding," forming unemployed councils, sponsoring marches and demonstrations for public assistance, and protesting the eviction of unemployed families from their homes.

Communist Party headquarters in New York City, 1932. The banners illustrate the variety of activities the party organized in the early 1930s.

Hoover's Response

In the eyes of many Americans, President Hoover's response to the Depression seemed inadequate and uncaring. Leading advisers, including Andrew Mellon, the wealthy secretary of the treasury, told Hoover that economic downturns were a normal part of capitalism, which weeded out unproductive firms and encouraged moral virtue among the less fortunate. Businessmen strongly opposed federal aid to the unemployed, and many publications called for individual "belt-tightening" as the road to recovery.

The federal government had never faced an economic crisis as severe as the Great Depression. Few political leaders understood how important consumer spending had become in the American economy. In 1931, Hoover quoted former president Grover Cleveland from four decades earlier: "The Government should not support the people. . . . Federal aid . . . weakens the sturdiness of our national character."

Cameramen at the White House during the presidency of Herbert Hoover. Hoover never became comfortable dealing with the mass media.

Strongly opposed on principle to direct federal intervention in the economy, Hoover remained committed to "associational action." He put his faith in voluntary steps by business to maintain investment and employment—something few found it possible to do—and efforts by local charity organizations to assist needy neighbors. He attempted to restore public confidence, making frequent public statements that "the tide had turned." But these made him increasingly seem out of touch with reality. About the unemployed men who appeared on city streets offering apples at five cents apiece, Hoover would later write, "Many persons left their jobs for the more profitable one of selling apples."

The Worsening Economic Outlook

Some administration remedies, like the **Smoot-Hawley Tariff**, which Hoover signed with some reluctance in 1930, made the economic situation worse. Raising the already high taxes on imported goods, it inspired similar increases abroad, further reducing international trade.

Government action

By 1932, Hoover had to admit that voluntary action had failed to stem the Depression. He signed laws creating the **Reconstruction Finance Corporation**, which loaned money to failing banks, railroads, and other businesses, and the Federal Home Loan Bank System, which offered aid to homeowners threatened with foreclosure. Having vetoed previous bills to create employment through public-works projects like road and bridge construction, he now approved a measure appropriating nearly $2 billion for such initiatives and helping to fund local relief efforts. These were dramatic departures from previous federal economic policy. But he adamantly opposed offering direct relief to the unemployed.

Freedom in the Modern World

Assessing freedom in the 1920s

In 1927, the New School for Social Research in New York City organized a series of lectures on the theme of freedom in the modern world. The lectures painted a depressing portrait of American freedom on the eve of the Great Depression. The "sacred dogmas of patriotism and Big Business," said the educator Horace Kallen, dominated teaching, the press, and public debate. A definition of freedom reigned supreme that celebrated the unimpeded reign of economic enterprise yet tolerated the surveillance of private life and individual conscience.

The prosperity of the 1920s had reinforced this definition of freedom. With the economic crash, compounded by the ineffectiveness of the Hoover administration's response, it would be discredited. By 1932, the seeds had already been planted for a new conception of freedom that combined two different elements in a sometimes uneasy synthesis. One was the Progressive belief in a socially conscious state making constructive changes in economic arrangements. The other, which arose in the 1920s, centered on respect for civil liberties and cultural pluralism and declared that realms of life like group identity, personal behavior, and the free expression of ideas lay outside legitimate state concern. These two principles would become the hallmarks of modern liberalism, which during the 1930s would redefine American freedom.

An unemployed man and woman selling apples on a city street during the Great Depression.

CHAPTER REVIEW AND ONLINE RESOURCES

REVIEW QUESTIONS

1. *How did consumerism and the idea of the "American way of life" affect people's understanding of American values, including the meaning of freedom, in the 1920s?*
2. *Which groups did not share in the prosperity of the 1920s and why?*
3. *How did business practices and policies lead to a decline in union membership in the 1920s?*
4. *President Calvin Coolidge said, "The chief business of the American people is business." How did the federal government's policies and practices in the 1920s reflect this understanding of the importance of business interests?*
5. *Who supported restricting immigration in the 1920s and why? Why were they more successful in gaining federal legislation to limit immigration in these years?*
6. *Did U.S. society in the 1920s reflect the concept of cultural pluralism as explained by Horace Kallen? Why or why not?*
7. *Identify the causes of the Great Depression.*
8. *What principles guided President Hoover's response to the Great Depression, and how did this restrict his ability to help the American people?*
9. *What issues were of particular concern to fundamentalists in these years and why?*
10. *In what ways did the ideas about (and the reality of) proper roles for women change in these years?*

KEY TERMS

Sacco-Vanzetti case (p. 607)
Equal Rights Amendment (p. 613)
flapper (p. 613)
Adkins v. Children's Hospital (p. 615)
Teapot Dome (p. 615)
American Civil Liberties Union (p. 620)
Schenck v. United States (p. 620)
fundamentalism (p. 621)
Scopes trial (p. 623)
illegal alien (p. 625)
New Negro (p. 629)
Harlem Renaissance (p. 629)
Great Depression (p. 630)
stock market crash (p. 630)
Smoot-Hawley Tariff (p. 634)
Reconstruction Finance Corporation (p. 634)

Go to INQUIZITIVE

To see what you know—and learn what you've missed—with personalized feedback along the way.

Visit the ***Give Me Liberty!* Student Site** for primary source documents and images, interactive maps, author videos featuring Eric Foner, and more.

CHAPTER 21

THE NEW DEAL

★

1932–1940

1931	Scottsboro case
1933	FDR inaugurated
	Bank holiday
	The Hundred Days and the First New Deal
	Twenty-first Amendment ratified
1934	Huey Long launches the Share Our Wealth movement
1934–1940	Height of the Dust Bowl
1935	Second New Deal launched
	Social Security Act
	Supreme Court rules the National Recovery Administration unconstitutional
	John L. Lewis organizes the Congress of Industrial Organizations
1936	Supreme Court rules the Agricultural Adjustment Act unconstitutional
	New Deal coalition leads to Democratic landslide
	John Maynard Keynes's *The General Theory of Employment, Interest, and Money*
1936–1937	United Auto Workers sit-down strike
1938	Fair Labor Standards Act passed
	House Un-American Activities Committee established

A campaign poster from 1936 for the American Labor Party, a left-wing party created by labor unions in New York State that supported Franklin D. Roosevelt and his New Deal. The placards illustrate some of labor's demands at the height of the union upsurge of the mid-1930s.

FOCUS QUESTIONS

- *What were the major policy initiatives of the New Deal in the Hundred Days?*
- *Who were the main proponents of economic justice in the 1930s, and what measures did they advocate?*
- *What were the major initiatives of the Second New Deal?*
- *How did the New Deal recast the meaning of American freedom?*
- *How did New Deal benefits apply to women and minorities?*
- *How did the Popular Front influence American culture in the 1930s?*

The Columbia River winds its way on a 1,200-mile course from Canada through Washington and Oregon to the Pacific Ocean. Because of its steep descent from uplands to sea level, it produces an immense amount of energy. Residents of the economically underdeveloped Pacific Northwest had long dreamed of tapping this unused energy for electricity and irrigation. But not until the 1930s did the federal government launch the program of dam construction that transformed the region. The project created thousands of jobs for the unemployed, and the network of dams produced abundant cheap power.

When the Grand Coulee Dam went into operation in 1941, it was the largest man-made structure in world history. It eventually produced more than 40 percent of the nation's hydroelectric power. The project also had less appealing consequences. From time immemorial, the Columbia River had been filled with salmon. But the Grand Coulee Dam made no provision for the passage of fish, and the salmon all but vanished. This caused little concern during the Depression but became a source of controversy later in the century as Americans became more attuned to preserving the natural environment.

The Columbia River project reflected broader changes in American life and thought during the **New Deal** of the 1930s. Franklin D. Roosevelt believed regional economic development like that in the Northwest would promote economic growth, ease the domestic and working lives of ordinary Americans, and keep control of key natural resources in public rather than private hands. The early Roosevelt administration spent far more money on building roads, dams, airports, bridges, and housing than on any other activity.

Roosevelt also oversaw the transformation of the Democratic Party into a coalition of farmers, industrial workers, the reform-minded urban middle class, liberal intellectuals, northern African-Americans, and, somewhat incongruously, the white supremacist South, united by the belief that the federal government must provide Americans with protection against the dislocations caused by modern capitalism. "Liberalism," traditionally understood as limited government and free-market economics, took on its modern meaning. Thanks to the New Deal, it now referred to active efforts by the national government to uplift less fortunate members of society.

Freedom, too, underwent a transformation during the 1930s. The New Deal elevated a public guarantee of economic security to the forefront of American discussions of freedom. Regional economic planning reflected this understanding of freedom. So did other New Deal measures, including the Social Security Act, which offered aid to the unemployed and aged, and the Fair Labor Standards Act, which established a national minimum wage.

Yet although the New Deal significantly expanded the meaning of freedom, it did not erase freedom's boundaries. Its benefits flowed to industrial workers but not tenant farmers, to men far more fully than women, and to white Americans more than blacks, who, in the South, still were deprived of the basic rights of citizenship.

THE FIRST NEW DEAL

FDR and the Election of 1932

Franklin Delano Roosevelt

FDR, as he liked to be called, was born in 1882, a fifth cousin of Theodore Roosevelt. After serving as undersecretary of the navy during World War I, he ran for vice president on the ill-fated Democratic ticket of 1920 headed by James M. Cox. In 1921, he contracted polio and lost the use of his legs, a fact carefully concealed from the public in that pre-television era. Very few Americans realized that the president who projected an image of vigorous leadership during the 1930s and World War II was confined to a wheelchair.

In his speech accepting the Democratic nomination for president in 1932, Roosevelt promised a "new deal" for the American people. But his campaign offered only vague hints of what this might entail. He advocated a balanced federal budget and criticized his opponent, President Hoover, for excessive government spending. The biggest difference between the parties during the campaign was the Democrats' call for the repeal of Prohibition, although Roosevelt certainly suggested a greater awareness of the plight of ordinary Americans. Battered by the economic crisis, Americans in 1932 were desperate for new leadership, and Roosevelt won a resounding victory. He received 57 percent of the popular vote, and Democrats swept to a commanding majority in Congress.

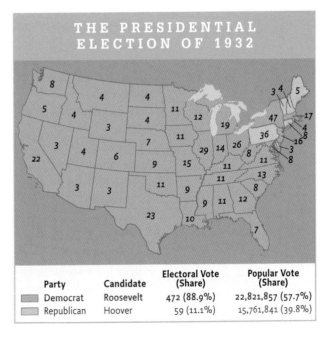

THE PRESIDENTIAL ELECTION OF 1932

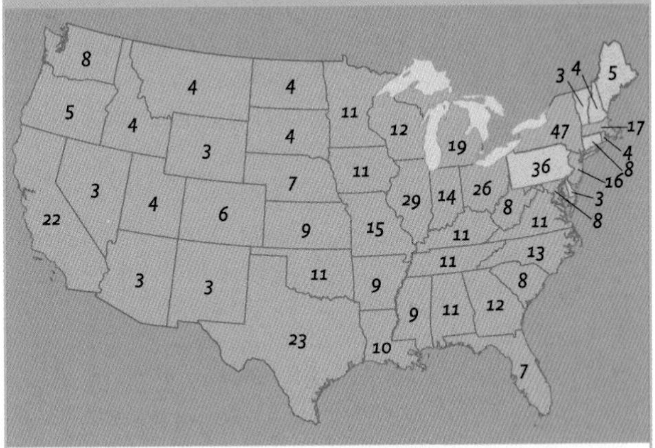

Party	Candidate	Electoral Vote (Share)	Popular Vote (Share)
Democrat	Roosevelt	472 (88.9%)	22,821,857 (57.7%)
Republican	Hoover	59 (11.1%)	15,761,841 (39.8%)

The Coming of the New Deal

Roosevelt conceived of the New Deal as an alternative to socialism on the left, Nazism on the right, and the inaction favored by upholders of unregulated capitalism. He

A photograph of the giant Bonneville Dam on the Columbia River in Oregon as it neared completion in 1936. This was one of numerous New Deal projects that expanded the nation's infrastructure and provided employment to victims of the Depression.

hoped to reconcile democracy, individual liberty, and economic recovery and development. He did not, however, enter office with a blueprint for dealing with the Depression. At first, he relied heavily for advice on a group of intellectuals and social workers who took up key positions in his administration. They included Secretary of Labor Frances Perkins, a veteran of Hull House and the New York Consumers' League; Harry Hopkins, who had headed emergency relief efforts during Roosevelt's term as governor of New York; Secretary of the Interior Harold Ickes, a veteran of Theodore Roosevelt's Progressive campaign of 1912; and Louis Brandeis, who had advised Woodrow Wilson during the 1912 campaign and now offered political advice to FDR while serving on the Supreme Court.

Brandeis believed that large corporations not only wielded excessive power but also had contributed to the Depression by keeping prices artificially high and failing to increase workers' purchasing power. They should be broken up, he insisted, not regulated. But the "brains trust"—a group of academics that included a number of Columbia University professors—saw bigness as inevitable in a modern economy. Large firms needed to be managed and directed by the government, not dismantled. Their view prevailed during what came to be called the First New Deal.

The Banking Crisis

Banking suspended

"This nation asks for action and action now," Roosevelt announced on taking office on March 4, 1933. The new president confronted a banking system on the verge of collapse. As bank funds invested in the stock market lost their value and panicked depositors withdrew their savings, bank after bank closed its doors. By March 1933, banking had been suspended in a majority of the states—that is, people could not gain access to money in their bank accounts. Roosevelt declared a "bank holiday," temporarily halting all bank operations, and called Congress into special session. On March 9, it rushed to pass the **Emergency Banking Act**, which provided funds to shore up threatened institutions.

Further measures soon followed that transformed the American financial system. The Glass-Steagall Act barred commercial banks from becoming involved in the buying and selling of stocks. Until its repeal in the 1990s, the law prevented many of the irresponsible practices that had contributed to the stock market crash. The same law established the Federal Deposit Insurance Corporation (FDIC), a government system that insured the accounts of individual depositors. Together, these measures rescued the financial system and greatly increased the government's power over it.

Presidents Herbert Hoover and Franklin D. Roosevelt on their way to the latter's inauguration on March 4, 1933. The two men strongly disliked one another. They barely spoke during the ride and never saw each other again after that day.

The NRA

The Emergency Banking Act was the first of an unprecedented flurry of legislation during the first three months of Roosevelt's administration, a period known as the **Hundred Days**. Seizing on the sense of crisis and the momentum of his electoral victory, Roosevelt won rapid passage of laws he hoped would promote economic recovery. He persuaded Congress to create a host of new agencies, whose initials soon became part of the language of politics—NRA, AAA, CCC.

The centerpiece of Roosevelt's plan for combating the Depression, the **National Industrial Recovery Act**, was to a large extent modeled on the government-business partnership established by the War Industries Board of World War I. The act established the **National Recovery Administration** (NRA), which would work with groups of business leaders to establish industry codes that set standards for output, prices, and working conditions.

In effect, FDR had repudiated the older idea of liberty based on the idea that the best way to encourage economic activity and ensure a fair distribution of wealth was to allow market competition to operate, unrestrained by the government. And to win support from labor, section 7a of the new law recognized the workers' right to organize unions—a departure from the "open shop" policies of the 1920s and a step toward government support for what workers called "industrial freedom."

A "run" on a bank: crowds of people wait outside a New York City bank, hoping to withdraw their money.

A Civilian Conservation Corps workforce in Yosemite National Park, 1935.

Headed by Hugh S. Johnson, a retired general and businessman, the NRA quickly established codes that set standards for production, prices, and wages in the textile, steel, mining, and auto industries. But the NRA became mired in controversy. Large companies dominated the code-writing process. They used the NRA to drive up prices, limit production, lay off workers, and divide markets among themselves at the expense of smaller competitors. The NRA produced neither economic recovery nor peace between employers and workers. It did, however, combat the pervasive sense that the government was doing nothing to deal with the economic crisis.

Government Jobs

Relief

The Hundred Days also brought the government into providing relief to those in need. Roosevelt and most of his advisers shared the widespread fear that direct government payments to the unemployed would undermine individual self-reliance. But with nearly a quarter of the workforce unemployed, spending on relief was unavoidable. In May 1933, Congress created the Federal Emergency Relief Administration, to make grants to local agencies that aided those impoverished by the Depression. FDR, however, much preferred to create temporary jobs, thereby combating unemployment while improving the nation's infrastructure of roads, bridges, public buildings, and parks.

Creating federal jobs

In March 1933, Congress established the **Civilian Conservation Corps** (CCC), which set unemployed young men to work on projects like forest preservation, flood control, and the improvement of national parks and wildlife preserves. By the time the program ended in 1942, more than 3 million persons had passed through CCC camps, where they received government wages of $30 per month. The CCC made a major contribution to the enhancement of the American environment.

Public-Works Projects

One section of the National Industrial Recovery Act created the **Public Works Administration** (PWA), with an appropriation of $3.3 billion. Directed by Secretary of the Interior Harold Ickes, it built roads, schools,

A map published by the Public Works Administration in 1935 depicts some of the numerous infrastructure projects funded by the New Deal. Among the most famous public-works projects are the Triborough Bridge in New York City, the Overseas Highway in Florida, and the Grand Coulee Dam in Washington. Overall, the New Deal spent $250 billion (in today's money) to construct, among other things, 40,000 public buildings, 72,000 schools, 80,000 bridges, and 8,000 parks.

hospitals, and other public facilities, including New York City's Triborough (now Robert F. Kennedy) Bridge and the Overseas Highway between Miami and Key West, Florida. In November 1933, yet another agency, the Civil Works Administration (CWA), was launched. By January 1934, it employed more than 4 million persons in the construction of highways, tunnels, courthouses, and airports. But as the cost spiraled upward and complaints multiplied that the New Deal was creating a class of Americans permanently dependent on government jobs, Roosevelt ordered the CWA dissolved.

The **Tennessee Valley Authority** (TVA), another product of the Hundred Days, built a series of dams to prevent floods and deforestation along the Tennessee River and to provide cheap electric power for homes and factories in a seven-state region where many families still lived in isolated log cabins. The TVA put the federal government, for the first time, in the business of selling electricity in competition with private companies.

The New Deal and Agriculture

Another policy initiative of the Hundred Days addressed the disastrous plight of American farmers. The **Agricultural Adjustment Act** (AAA) authorized the federal government to set production quotas for major crops

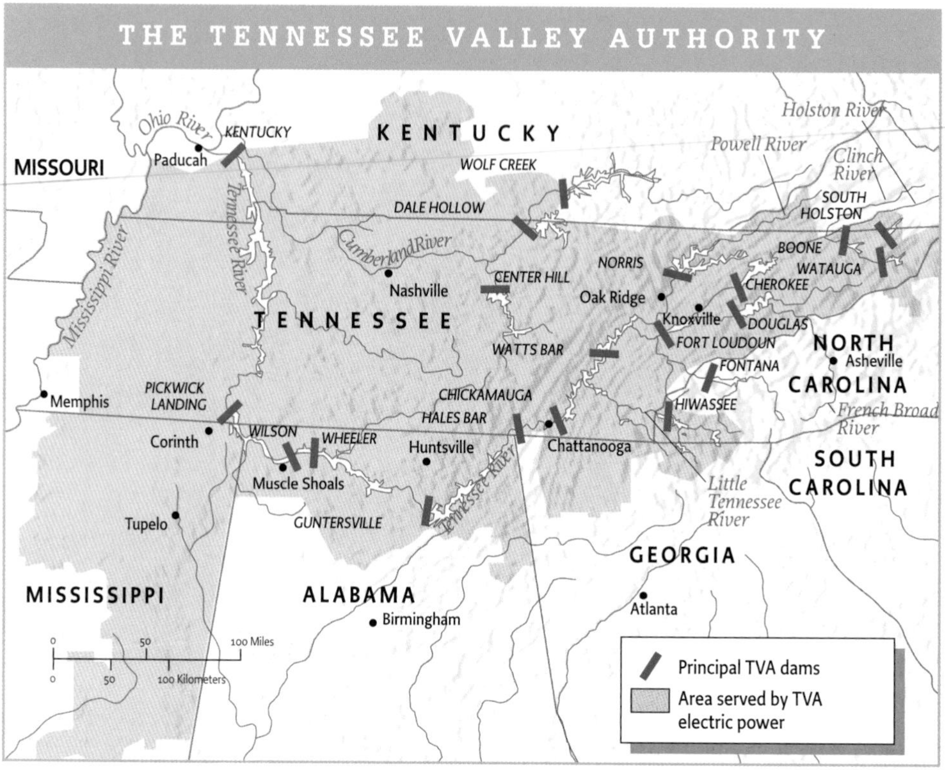

A map showing the reach of the Tennessee Valley Authority, covering all or parts of seven southeastern states.

and pay farmers to plant less in an attempt to raise farm prices. Many crops already in the field were destroyed. In 1933, the government ordered more than 6 million pigs slaughtered as part of the policy, a step critics found strange at a time of widespread hunger.

The AAA succeeded in significantly raising farm prices and incomes. But not all farmers benefited. Money flowed to property-owning farmers, ignoring the large number who worked on land owned by others. The AAA policy of paying landowning farmers not to grow crops encouraged the eviction of thousands of poor tenants and sharecroppers. Many joined the rural exodus to cities or to the farms of the West Coast.

The Dust Bowl

The onset in 1930 of a period of unusually dry weather in the nation's heartland worsened the Depression's impact on rural America. By mid-decade, the region suffered from the century's most severe drought. Mechanized agriculture in this semi-arid region had pulverized the topsoil and killed native grasses that prevented erosion. Winds now blew much of the soil away, creating the **Dust Bowl**, as the affected areas of Oklahoma, Texas, Kansas, and Colorado were called. The drought and dust storms displaced more than 1 million farmers.

The New Deal and Housing

A giant dust storm engulfs a town in western Kansas on April 14, 1935, known as Black Sunday in the American West.

The Depression devastated the American housing industry. The construction of new residences all but ceased, and banks and savings and loan associations that had financed home ownership collapsed or, to remain afloat, foreclosed on many homes (a quarter of a million in 1932 alone). Millions of Americans lived in overcrowded, unhealthy urban slums or in ramshackle rural dwellings. Private enterprise alone, it seemed clear, was unlikely to solve the nation's housing crisis.

Roosevelt spoke of "the security of the home" as a fundamental right. In 1933 and 1934, his administration moved energetically to protect home owners from foreclosure and to stimulate new construction. The Home Owners Loan Corporation and **Federal Housing Administration** (FHA) insured millions of long-term mortgages issued by private banks. At the same time, the federal government itself built thousands of units of low-rent housing. Thanks to the FHA and, later, the Veterans' Administration, home ownership came within the reach of tens of millions of families. It became cheaper for most Americans to buy single-family homes than to rent apartments.

Other important measures of Roosevelt's first two years in office included the ratification of the Twenty-first Amendment to the Constitution, which repealed Prohibition; the establishment of the Federal Communications Commission to oversee the nation's broadcast airwaves and telephone communications; and the creation of the Securities and Exchange Commission to regulate the stock and bond markets.

Taken together, the First New Deal was a series of experiments, some of which succeeded and some of which did not. They transformed the role of the federal government, constructed numerous public facilities, and provided relief to millions of needy persons. Public employment rescued millions of Americans from the ravages of the Depression. But while the economy improved somewhat, sustained recovery had not been achieved. Some 10 million Americans—more than 20 percent of the workforce—remained unemployed when 1934 came to an end.

As it did in other sectors of the economy, the Great Depression led to a collapse in the construction industry.

FIGURE 21.1 The Building Boom and Its Collapse, 1919–1939

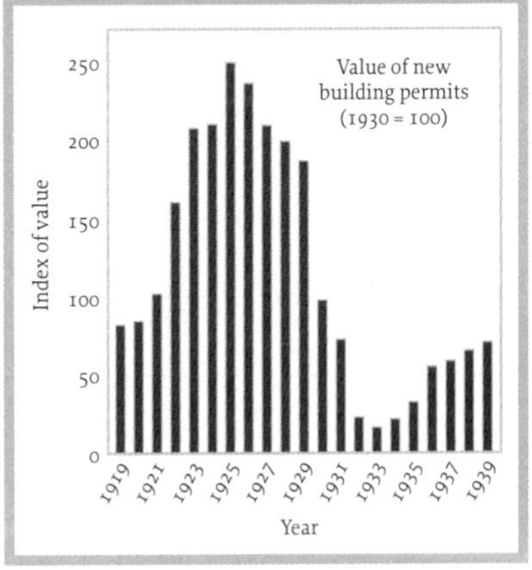

The Court and the New Deal

In 1935, the Supreme Court, still controlled by conservative Republican judges who held to the nineteenth-century understanding of freedom as liberty of contract, began to invalidate key New Deal laws. First came the NRA, declared unconstitutional in May in a case brought by the Schechter Poultry Company of Brooklyn, which had been charged with violating the code adopted by the chicken industry. In a unanimous decision, the Court declared the NRA unlawful because in its codes and other regulations it delegated legislative powers to the president and attempted to regulate local businesses that did not engage in interstate commerce. In January 1936, the AAA fell in *United States v. Butler*, which declared it an unconstitutional exercise of congressional power over local economic activities.

Having failed to end the Depression or win judicial approval, the First New Deal ground to a halt. Meanwhile, pressures were mounting outside Washington that propelled the administration toward more radical departures in policy.

A MULE AND A PLOW
RESETTLEMENT ADMINISTRATION
Small Loans Give Farmers a New Start

The artist Bernarda Shahn, wife of the more famous painter Ben Shahn, created this lithograph in the mid-1930s for the Resettlement Administration, a New Deal agency that relocated rural and urban families—especially victims of the Dust Bowl—to planned communities.

THE GRASSROOTS REVOLT

Labor's Great Upheaval

The most striking development of the mid-1930s was the mobilization of millions of workers in mass-production industries that had successfully resisted unionization. "Labor's great upheaval," as this era of unprecedented militancy was called, came as a great surprise. Unlike in the past, however, the federal government now seemed to be on the side of labor. American-born children of the new immigrants now dominated the industrial labor force, and organizers no longer had to distribute materials in numerous languages as the IWW had done. And a cadre of militant labor leaders, many of them socialists and communists, had survived the repression of the 1920s. They provided leadership to the labor upsurge.

American factories at the outset of the New Deal were miniature dictatorships in which unions were rare, workers could be beaten by supervisors and fired at will, and management determined the length of the workday and speed of the assembly line. Workers' demands during the 1930s went beyond better wages. They included an end to employers' arbitrary power in the workplace, and basic civil liberties for workers, including the right to picket, distribute literature, and meet to discuss their grievances. All these goals required union recognition.

The Illegal Act, a cartoon critical of the Supreme Court's decision declaring the NRA unconstitutional. FDR tells a drowning Uncle Sam, "I'm sorry, but the Supreme Court says I must chuck you back in."

Roosevelt's inauguration unleashed a flood of poignant letters to the federal government describing what a Louisiana sugar laborer called the "terrible and inhuman condition" of many workers. Labor organizers spread the message that the "political liberty for which our forefathers fought" had been "made meaningless by economic inequality" and "industrial despotism."

A year of strikes

Labor's great upheaval exploded in 1934, a year that witnessed no fewer than 2,000 strikes. Many produced violent confrontations between workers and the local police. San Francisco experienced the country's first general strike since 1919. It began with a walkout of dockworkers led by the fiery communist Harry Bridges. Workers demanded recognition of the International Longshoremen's Association and an end to the hated "shape up" system in which they had to gather en masse each day to wait for work assignments. The year 1934 also witnessed a strike of 400,000 textile workers in states from New England to the Lower South, demanding recognition of the United Textile Workers. Many of these walkouts won at least some of the workers' demands. But the textile strike failed.

The Rise of the CIO

The labor upheaval posed a challenge to the American Federation of Labor's traditional policy of organizing workers by craft rather than seeking to mobilize all the workers in a given industry, such as steel manufacturing. In 1934, thirty AFL leaders called for the creation of unions of industrial workers. When the AFL convention of 1935 refused, the head of the United Mine Workers, John L. Lewis, led a walkout that produced a new labor organization, the **Congress of Industrial Organizations** (CIO). It aimed, said Lewis, at nothing less than to secure "economic freedom and industrial democracy" for American workers—a fair share in the wealth produced by their labor, and a voice in determining the conditions under which they worked.

John L. Lewis

In December 1936, unions, most notably the United Auto Workers (UAW), a fledgling CIO union, unveiled the **sit-down strike**, a remarkably effective tactic that the IWW had pioneered three decades earlier. Rather than walking out of the Fisher Auto Body plant in Cleveland, thus enabling management to bring in strikebreakers, workers halted production but remained inside. Sit-downs soon spread to General Motors factories in Flint, Michigan, the nerve center of automobile production. Demonstrating a remarkable spirit of unity, the strikers cleaned the plant, oiled the idle machinery, and settled disputes among themselves. Workers' wives shuttled food into the plant. On February 11, General Motors agreed to negotiate with the UAW. By the end of 1937, the UAW claimed 400,000 members.

The UAW's sit-down strike

Sit-down strike at a General Motors factory in Flint, Michigan, 1937.

The victory in the auto industry reverberated throughout industrial America. Steelworkers had suffered memorable defeats in the struggle for unionization, notably at Homestead in 1892 and in the Great Steel Strike of 1919. But in March 1937, fearing a sit-down campaign and aware that it could no longer count on the aid of state and federal authorities, U.S. Steel, the country's single most important business firm, agreed to recognize the Steel Workers Organizing Committee (forerunner of the United Steelworkers of America). Smaller steel firms, however, refused to follow suit.

Union membership reached 9 million by 1940, more than double the number in 1930. Workers gained new grievance procedures and seniority systems governing hiring, firing, and promotions. The CIO unions helped to stabilize a chaotic employment situation and offered members a sense of dignity and freedom.

Labor and Politics

Federal action

Throughout the industrial heartland, the labor upsurge altered the balance of economic power and propelled to the forefront of politics labor's goal of a fairer, freer, more equal America. The CIO put forward an ambitious program for federal action to shield Americans from economic and social insecurity, including public housing, universal health care, and unemployment and old age insurance.

Building on the idea, so prominent in the 1920s, that the key to prosperity lay in an American standard of living based on mass consumption, CIO leaders explained the Depression as the result of an imbalance of wealth and income. The pathbreaking 1937 agreement between the UAW and General Motors spoke of a "rate of pay commensurate with an American standard of living." By mid-decade, many New Dealers accepted the "underconsumptionist" explanation of the Depression, which saw lack of sufficient consumer demand as its underlying cause.

Voices of Protest

Police break up a gathering along the San Francisco waterfront on the eve of the general strike involving over 200,000 workers in May 1934.

Other popular movements of the mid-1930s also placed the question of economic justice on the political agenda. In California, the novelist Upton Sinclair won the Democratic nomination for governor in 1934 as the head of the End Poverty in California movement. Sinclair called for the state to use idle factories and land in cooperative ventures that would provide jobs for the unemployed. He lost the election after being subjected to one of the first modern "negative" media campaigns. Sinclair's opponents circulated false newsreels showing armies of unemployed men marching to California to support his candidacy and a fake endorsement from the Communist Party.

The rise to national prominence of Huey Long offered another sign of popular dissatisfaction with the slow pace of economic recovery. Driven by intense ambition and the desire to help uplift Louisiana's "common people," Long won election as governor in 1928 and in 1930 took a seat in the U.S. Senate. From Washington, he dominated every branch of state government. He used his dictatorial power to build roads, schools, and hospitals and to increase the tax burden on Louisiana's oil companies.

In 1934, Long launched the **Share Our Wealth movement**, with the slogan "Every Man a King." He called for the confiscation of most of the wealth of the richest Americans in order to finance an immediate grant of $5,000 and a guaranteed job and annual income for all citizens. He was on the verge of announcing a run for president when the son of a defeated political rival assassinated him in 1935.

Dr. Francis Townsend, a California physician, meanwhile won wide support for a plan by which the government would make a monthly payment of $200 to older Americans, with the requirement that they spend it immediately. This, he argued, would boost the economy. Along with the rise of the CIO, these signs of popular discontent helped spark the Second New Deal.

Huey Long, the "Kingfish" of Louisiana politics, in full rhetorical flight. This photo was probably taken in 1934, when Long was in the U.S. Senate but still running the state government.

Religion on the Radio

Also in the mid-1930s, the "radio priest," Father Charles E. Coughlin, attracted millions of listeners with weekly broadcasts attacking Wall Street bankers and greedy capitalists, and calling for government ownership of key

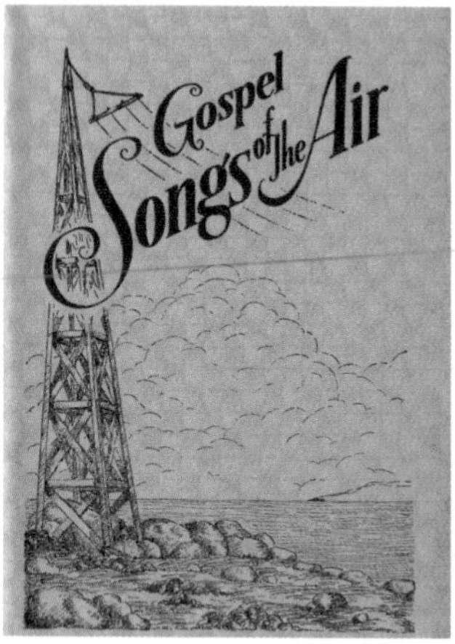

The cover of a songbook to accompany a radio broadcast from the Chicago Gospel Tabernacle. A radio tower dominates the image.

industries as a way of combating the Depression. Initially a strong supporter of FDR, Coughlin became increasingly critical of the president for what he considered the failure of the New Deal to promote social justice. His crusade would later shift to anti-Semitism and support for European fascism.

Other religious leaders of various denominations took advantage of the mass media to spread their beliefs. Ironically, many fundamentalists used the most modern techniques of communication, including the radio and popular entertainment, to promote their anti-modernist message. They found in the radio a way to bypass established churches and their leaders. Aimee Semple McPherson, a Los Angeles revivalist, had her own radio station, which broadcast sermons from the International Church of the Foursquare Gospel she had founded.

THE SECOND NEW DEAL

Buoyed by Democratic gains in the midterm elections of 1934, Roosevelt in 1935 launched the Second New Deal. The first had focused on economic recovery. The emphasis of the second was economic security—a guarantee that Americans would be protected against unemployment and poverty.

The idea that lack of consumer demand caused the Depression had been popularized by Huey Long, Francis Townsend, and the CIO. More and more New Dealers concluded that the government should no longer try to plan business recovery but should try to redistribute the national income so as to sustain mass purchasing power in the consumer economy. A series of measures in 1935 attacked head-on the problem of weak demand and economic inequality. Congress levied a highly publicized tax on large fortunes and corporate profits—a direct response to the popularity of Huey Long's Share Our Wealth campaign. It created the Rural Electrification Agency (REA) to bring electric power to homes that lacked it—80 percent of farms were still without electricity in 1934—in part to enable more Americans to purchase household appliances.

By 1950, 90 percent of the nation's farms had been wired for electricity, and almost all now possessed radios, electric stoves,

This photograph of Wilder, Tennessee, in 1942 illustrates the achievements and limits of the New Deal in rural America. The Tennessee Valley Authority has brought electricity to this section of the small town, but the outdoor pump is still residents' sole source of water.

refrigerators, and mechanical equipment to milk cows. In addition, the federal government under the Second New Deal tried to promote soil conservation and family farming. This effort resulted from the belief that the country would never achieve prosperity so long as farmers' standard of living lagged well behind that of city dwellers, and that rural poverty resulted mainly from the poor use of natural resources. Thus, farmers received federal assistance in reducing soil loss in their fields. These measures (like those of the AAA) mainly benefited landowners, not sharecroppers, tenants, or migrant workers. In the long run, the Second New Deal failed to arrest the trend toward larger farms and fewer farmers.

A poster by the artist Vera Bock for the Federal Art Project of the Works Progress Administration depicts farmers and laborers joining hands to produce prosperity.

The WPA and the Wagner Act

In 1934, Roosevelt had severely curtailed federal employment for those in need. Now, he approved the establishment of the **Works Progress Administration** (WPA), which hired some 3 million Americans, in virtually every walk of life, each year until it ended in 1943. It constructed thousands of public buildings and bridges, more than 500,000 miles of roads, and 600 airports. It built stadiums, swimming pools, and sewage treatment plants. Unlike previous work relief programs, the WPA employed many out-of-work white-collar workers and professionals, even doctors and dentists.

Perhaps the most famous WPA projects were in the arts. The WPA set hundreds of artists to work decorating public buildings with murals. It hired writers to produce local histories and guidebooks to the forty-eight states and to record the recollections of ordinary Americans, including hundreds of former slaves. Thanks to the WPA, audiences across the country enjoyed their first glimpse of live musical and theatrical performances and their first opportunity to view exhibitions of American art.

In 1935, under the auspices of the Works Progress Administration, the New York Jewish Theatre Unit put on a production based on Sinclair Lewis's novel *It Can't Happen Here*. In the drama, a demagogue who is elected president by promising economic change and a return to traditional values proceeds to establish an authoritarian regime akin to Hitler's Germany.

Another major initiative of the Second New Deal, the **Wagner Act**, brought democracy into the American workplace by empowering the National Labor Relations Board to supervise elections in which employees voted on union representation. It also outlawed "unfair labor practices," including the firing and blacklisting of union organizers.

A 1935 poster promoting the new Social Security system.

The American Welfare State: Social Security

The centerpiece of the Second New Deal was the **Social Security Act** of 1935. It embodied Roosevelt's conviction that the national government had a responsibility to ensure the material well-being of ordinary Americans. It created a system of unemployment insurance, old age pensions, and aid to the disabled, the elderly poor, and families with dependent children.

None of these were original ideas. The Progressive platform of 1912 had called for old age pensions. Assistance to poor families with dependent children descended from the mothers' pensions promoted by maternalist reformers. Many European countries had already adopted national unemployment insurance plans. What was new, however, was that in the name of economic security, the American government would now supervise not simply temporary relief but a permanent system of social insurance.

Limits of the American Welfare State

The Social Security Act launched the American version of the **welfare state**—a term that originated in Britain during World War II to refer to a system of income assistance, health coverage, and social services for all citizens. Compared with similar programs in Europe, the American welfare state has always been far more decentralized, involved lower levels of public spending, and covered fewer citizens. The original Social Security bill, for example, envisioned a national system of health insurance. But Congress dropped this after ferocious opposition from the American Medical Association, which feared government regulation of doctors' activities and incomes. And the fact that domestic and agricultural workers were not covered by unemployment and old age benefits meant that Social Security at first excluded large numbers of Americans, especially unmarried women and non-whites.

Government intervention

Nonetheless, Social Security represented a dramatic departure from the traditional functions of government. The Second New Deal transformed the relationship between the federal government and American citizens. Before the 1930s, national political debate often revolved around the question of *whether* the federal government should intervene in the economy. After the New Deal, debate rested on *how* it should intervene. In addition, the government assumed a responsibility, which it has never wholly relinquished, for guaranteeing Americans a living wage and protecting them against economic and personal misfortune.

A RECKONING WITH LIBERTY

The Depression made inevitable, in the words of one writer, a "reckoning with liberty." For too many Americans, Roosevelt proclaimed, "life was no longer free, liberty no longer real, men could no longer follow the pursuit of happiness."

Along with being a superb politician, Roosevelt was a master of political communication. At a time when his political opponents controlled most newspapers, he harnessed radio's power to bring his message directly into American homes. By the mid-1930s, more than two-thirds of American families owned radios. They listened avidly to Roosevelt's radio addresses, known as "fireside chats."

FDR's "fireside chats"

Roosevelt adeptly appealed to traditional values in support of new policies. He gave the term "liberalism" its modern meaning. As we have seen, in the nineteenth century, liberalism had been a shorthand for limited government and free-market economics. Roosevelt consciously chose to employ it to describe a large, active, socially conscious state. He reclaimed the word "freedom" from conservatives and made it a rallying cry for the New Deal. In his second fireside chat, Roosevelt juxtaposed his own definition of liberty as "greater security for the average man" to the older notion of liberty of contract, which served the interests of "the privileged few." Henceforth, he would consistently link freedom with economic security and identify entrenched economic inequality as its greatest enemy. "The liberty of a democracy," he declared in 1938, was not safe if citizens could not "sustain an acceptable standard of living."

FDR delivering one of his "fireside chats." Roosevelt was the first president to make effective use of the radio to promote his policies.

Even as Roosevelt invoked the word to uphold the New Deal, "liberty"—in the sense of freedom from powerful government—became the fighting slogan of his opponents. When conservative businessmen and politicians in 1934 formed an organization to mobilize opposition to Roosevelt's policies, they called it the American Liberty League.

The Election of 1936

By 1936, with working-class voters providing massive majorities for the Democratic Party and businesses large and small bitterly estranged from the New Deal, politics

VOICES OF FREEDOM

From Franklin D. Roosevelt, "Fireside Chat" (1934)

President Roosevelt pioneered the use of the new mass medium of radio to speak directly to Americans in their homes. He used his "fireside chats" to mobilize support for New Deal programs, link them with American traditions, and outline his definition of freedom.

To those who say that our expenditures for public works and other means for recovery are a waste that we cannot afford, I answer that no country, however rich, can afford the waste of its human resources. Demoralization caused by vast unemployment is our greatest extravagance. Morally, it is the greatest menace to our social order. Some people try to tell me that we must make up our minds that in the future we shall permanently have millions of unemployed just as other countries have had them for over a decade. What may be necessary for those countries is not my responsibility to determine. But as for this country, I stand or fall by my refusal to accept as a necessary condition of our future a permanent army of unemployed. . . .

In our efforts for recovery we have avoided, on the one hand, the theory that business should and must be taken over into an all-embracing Government. We have avoided, on the other hand, the equally untenable theory that it is an interference with liberty to offer reasonable help when private enterprise is in need of help. The course we have followed fits the American practice of Government, a practice of taking action step by step, of regulating only to meet concrete needs, a practice of courageous recognition of change. I believe with Abraham Lincoln, that "the legitimate object of Government is to do for a community of people whatever they need to have done but cannot do at all or cannot do so well for themselves in their separate and individual capacities."

I am not for a return to that definition of liberty under which for many years a free people were being gradually regimented into the service of the privileged few. I prefer and I am sure you prefer that broader definition of liberty under which we are moving forward to greater freedom, to greater security for the average man than he has ever known before in the history of America.

From John Steinbeck, *The Harvest Gypsies: On the Road to the Grapes of Wrath* (1938)

John Steinbeck's popular novel *The Grapes of Wrath* (1939), and the film version that followed shortly thereafter, focused national attention on the plight of homeless migrants displaced from their farms as a result of the Great Depression. Before that book appeared, Steinbeck had published a series of newspaper articles based on eyewitness accounts of the migrants, which became the basis for his novel.

In California, we find a curious attitude toward a group that makes our agriculture successful. The migrants are needed, and they are hated. . . . The migrants are hated for the following reasons, that they are ignorant and dirty people, that they are carriers of disease, that they increase the necessity for police and the tax bill for schooling in a community, and that if they are allowed to organize they can, simply by refusing to work, wipe out the season's crops. . . .

Let us see what kind of people they are, where they come from, and the routes of their wanderings. In the past they have been of several races, encouraged to come and often imported as cheap labor. Chinese in the early period, then Filipinos, Japanese and Mexicans. These were foreigners, and as such they were ostracized and segregated and herded about. . . . But in recent years the foreign migrants have begun to organize, and at this danger they have been deported in great numbers, for there was a new reservoir from which a great quantity of cheap labor could be obtained.

The drought in the middle west has driven the agricultural populations of Oklahoma, Nebraska and parts of Kansas and Texas westward. . . . Thousands of them are crossing the borders in ancient rattling automobiles, destitute and hungry and homeless, ready to accept any pay so that they may eat and feed their children. . . .

The earlier foreign migrants have invariably been drawn from a peon class. This is not the case with the new migrants. They are small farmers who have lost their farms, or farm hands who have lived with the family in the old American way. . . . They have come from the little farm districts where democracy was not only possible but inevitable, where popular government, whether practiced in the Grange, in church organization or in local government, was the responsibility of every man. And they have come into the country where, because of the movement necessary to make a living, they are not allowed any vote whatever, but are rather considered a properly unprivileged class. . . .

As one little boy in a squatter's camp said, "When they need us they call us migrants, and when we've picked their crop, we're bums and we got to get out."

QUESTIONS

1. *What does Roosevelt mean by the difference between the definition of liberty that has existed in the past and his own "broader definition of liberty"?*
2. *According to Steinbeck, how do Depression-era migrant workers differ from those in earlier periods?*
3. *Do the migrant workers described by Steinbeck enjoy liberty as Roosevelt understands it?*

Politics and class divisions

reflected class divisions more completely than at any other time in American history. Conceptions of freedom divided sharply as well.

A fight for the possession of "the ideal of freedom," reported the *New York Times*, emerged as the central issue of the presidential campaign of 1936. In his speech accepting renomination, Roosevelt launched a blistering attack against "economic royalists" who, he charged, sought to establish a new tyranny over the "average man." Economic rights, he went on, were the precondition of liberty—poor men "are not free men."

Economic freedom

Throughout the campaign, FDR would insist that the threat posed to economic freedom by the "new despotism" of large corporations was the main issue of the election.

As Roosevelt's opponent, Republicans chose Kansas governor Alfred Landon, a former Theodore Roosevelt Progressive. Landon denounced Social Security and other measures as threats to individual liberty. Opposition to the New Deal planted the seeds for the later flowering of an antigovernment conservatism bent on upholding the free market and dismantling the welfare state. But in 1936 Roosevelt won a landslide reelection, with more than 60 percent of the popular vote. His success stemmed from strong backing from organized labor and his ability to unite southern white and northern black voters, Protestant farmers and urban Catholic and Jewish ethnics, industrial workers and middle-class home owners.

The New Deal coalition

These groups made up the so-called New Deal coalition, which would dominate American politics for nearly half a century.

Fall In!, a cartoon commenting on Roosevelt's proposal to "pack" the Supreme Court, from the *Richmond Times-Dispatch*, January 8, 1937.

The Court Fight

Roosevelt's second inaugural address was the first to be delivered on January 20. In order to shorten a newly elected president's wait before taking office, the recently ratified Twentieth Amendment had moved inauguration day from March 4. The Depression, he admitted, had not been conquered: "I see one-third of a nation ill-housed, ill-clad, and ill-nourished." Emboldened by his electoral triumph, Roosevelt now made what many considered a serious political miscalculation. On the pretext that several members of the Supreme Court were too old to perform their duties, he proposed that the president be allowed to appoint a new justice for each one who remained on the Court past age seventy (which six of the nine had already passed). FDR's aim, of course, was to change the balance of power on a Court that, he feared, might well invalidate Social Security, the Wagner Act, and other measures of the Second New Deal.

Congress rejected the **Court packing** plan. But Roosevelt accomplished his underlying purpose. Coming soon after Roosevelt's landslide victory of 1936, the threat of "Court packing" inspired an astonishing about-face by key justices. Beginning in March 1937, the Court suddenly revealed a new willingness to support economic regulation by both the federal government and the states. It turned aside challenges to Social Security and the Wagner Act. In subsequent cases, the Court affirmed federal power to regulate wages, hours, child labor, agricultural production, and numerous other aspects of economic life.

The about-face for the Court

The Court's new attitude marked a permanent change in judicial policy. Having declared dozens of economic laws unconstitutional in the decades leading up to 1937, the justices have rarely done so since.

The End of the Second New Deal

Even as the Court made its peace with Roosevelt's policies, the momentum of the Second New Deal slowed. The landmark United States Housing Act did pass in 1937, initiating the first major national effort to build homes for the poorest Americans. But the Fair Labor Standards bill failed to reach the floor for over a year. When it finally passed in 1938, it banned goods produced by child labor from interstate commerce, set forty cents as the hourly minimum wage, and required overtime pay for hours of work exceeding forty per week. This last major piece of New Deal legislation established the practice of federal regulation of wages and working conditions, another radical departure from pre-Depression policies.

The year 1937 also witnessed a sharp downturn of the economy. With economic conditions improving in 1936, Roosevelt had reduced federal funding for farm subsidies and WPA work relief. The result was disastrous. Unemployment, still 14 percent at the beginning of 1937, rose to nearly 20 percent by year's end.

In 1936, in *The General Theory of Employment, Interest, and Money*, John Maynard Keynes had challenged economists' traditional belief in the sanctity of balanced budgets. Large-scale government spending, he insisted, was necessary to sustain purchasing power and stimulate economic activity during downturns. Such spending should be enacted even at the cost of a budget deficit (a situation in which the government spends more money than it takes in). By 1938, Roosevelt was ready to follow this prescription, which would later be known as Keynesian economics. In April, he asked Congress for billions more for work relief and farm aid. The events of 1937–1938 marked a major shift in New Deal philosophy. Public spending would now be the government's major tool for combating unemployment and stimulating economic growth. The Second New Deal had come to an end.

The New Deal did not really solve the problem of unemployment, which fell below 10 percent only in 1941, as the United States prepared to enter World War II.

FIGURE 21.2 Unemployment, 1925–1945

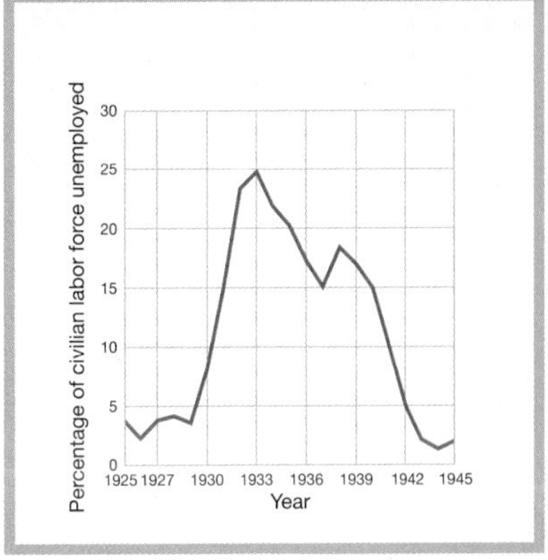

THE LIMITS OF CHANGE

Roosevelt conceived of the Second New Deal, and especially Social Security, as expanding the meaning of freedom by extending assistance to broad groups of needy Americans—the unemployed, elderly, and dependent—as a right of citizenship, not charity or special privilege. But political realities, especially the power of inherited ideas about gender and black disenfranchisement in the South, powerfully affected the drafting of legislation. Different groups of Americans experienced the New Deal in radically different ways.

The New Deal and American Women

Eleanor Roosevelt

The New Deal brought more women into government than ever before in American history. A number of talented women, including Secretary of Labor Frances Perkins, advised the president and shaped public policy. Most prominent of all was Eleanor Roosevelt, FDR's distant cousin, whom he married in 1905. She transformed the role of First Lady, turning a position with no formal responsibilities into a base for political action. She traveled widely, spoke out on public issues, wrote a regular newspaper column, and worked to enlarge the scope of the New Deal in areas like civil rights, labor legislation, and work relief.

But even as the New Deal increased women's visibility in national politics, organized feminism, already in disarray during the 1920s, disappeared as a political force. Indeed, the Depression inspired widespread demands for women to remove themselves from the labor market to make room for unemployed men. Because the Depression hit industrial employment harder than low-wage clerical and service jobs where women predominated, the proportion of the workforce made up of women rose. The government tried to reverse this trend. In its waning days, the Hoover administration prohibited both members of a married couple from holding federal jobs. Until the repeal of that provision in 1937, it led to the dismissal of numerous female civil service employees whose husbands worked for the government. Employers from banks to public school systems barred married women from jobs.

Eleanor Roosevelt transformed the role of First Lady by taking an active and visible part in public life. Here she visits a West Virginia coal mine in 1933.

Most New Deal programs did not exclude women from benefits (although the CCC restricted its camps to men). But the

This photograph from 1933 depicts a march in New York City organized by the Association of Unemployed Single Women. Many men believed that public-works jobs and governmental relief should not go to women, who, the logic went, could be supported by their husbands or fathers.

ideal of the male-headed household powerfully shaped social policy. Since paying taxes on one's wages made one eligible for the most generous Social Security programs—old age pensions and unemployment insurance—they left most women uncovered, because they did not work outside the home. The program excluded the 3 million mostly female domestic workers altogether.

The Southern Veto

Roosevelt made the federal government the symbolic representative of all the people, including racial and ethnic groups generally ignored by previous administrations. Yet the power of the Solid South helped to mold the New Deal welfare state into an entitlement of white Americans. After the South's blacks lost the right to vote around the turn of the century, Democrats enjoyed a political monopoly in the region. Democratic members of Congress were elected again and again. Committee chairmanships in Congress rest on seniority—how many years a member has served in office. Thus, beginning in 1933, when Democrats took control of Congress, southerners assumed the key leadership positions. At their insistence, the Social Security law excluded agricultural and domestic workers, the largest categories of black employment.

Political monopoly in the South

Students from Howard University outside the National Crime Conference in Washington, D.C., in 1934. They wore nooses and the names of victims to protest the conference's failure to include the subject of lynching in its program.

A 1936 photograph shows a black farmer, with his son, repaying a loan from the Farm Security Administration, which sought to improve the conditions of poor land-owning farmers and sharecroppers. The client wears what is probably his nicest attire to meet with the government official.

Black organizations like the Urban League and the NAACP lobbied strenuously for a system that enabled agricultural and domestic workers to receive unemployment and old age benefits and that established national relief standards. The Social Security Act, however, complained the *Pittsburgh Courier*, a black newspaper, reflected the power of "reactionary elements in the South who cannot bear the thought of Negroes getting pensions and compensations" and who feared that the inclusion of black workers would disrupt the region's low-wage, racially divided labor system.

The Stigma of Welfare

Because of the "southern veto," the majority of black workers found themselves confined to the least generous and most vulnerable wing of the new welfare state. The public assistance programs established by Social Security, notably aid to dependent children and to the poor elderly, were open to all Americans who could demonstrate financial need. But they set benefits at extremely low levels and authorized the states to determine eligibility standards, including "moral" behavior as defined by local authorities. As a result, public assistance programs allowed for widespread discrimination in the distribution of benefits. Recipients came to bear the humiliating stigma of dependency on government handouts, which would soon come to be known as "welfare."

The situation seemed certain to identify blacks as recipients of unearned government assistance, and welfare as a program for minorities, thus dooming it forever to inadequate "standards of aid." Over time, this is precisely what happened, until the federal government abolished its responsibility for welfare entirely in 1996, during the presidency of Bill Clinton.

The Indian New Deal

Changes in Indian policy

Overall, the Depression and New Deal had a contradictory impact on America's racial minorities. Under Commissioner of Indian Affairs John Collier, the administration launched an **Indian New Deal**. Collier ended the policy of forced assimilation and allowed Indians unprecedented cultural autonomy. He replaced boarding schools meant to eradicate the tribal heritage of Indian children with schools on reservations, and dramatically increased spending on Indian health. He secured passage of the Indian Reorganization Act of 1934, ending the policy, dating back to the Dawes Act of 1887, of dividing Indian lands into small plots for individual families and selling off the rest. Federal authorities once again recognized Indians' right to govern their own affairs.

The New Deal marked the most radical shift in Indian policy in the nation's history. But living conditions on the desperately poor reservations did not significantly improve.

The Farm Security Administration hired noted photographers to document American life. This image by Dorothea Lange, from 1938, shows Hispanic women packing apricots in Brentwood, California.

The New Deal and Mexican-Americans

For Mexican-Americans, the Depression was a wrenching experience. With demand for their labor plummeting, more than 400,000 (one-fifth of the population of Mexican origin) returned to Mexico, often at the strong urging of local authorities in the Southwest. A majority of those coerced into leaving the country were recent immigrants, but they included perhaps 200,000 Mexican-American children who had been born in the United States and were therefore citizens. Those who remained mostly worked in grim conditions in California's vegetable and fruit fields, whose corporate farms benefited enormously from New Deal dam construction that provided them with cheap electricity and water for irrigation. The Wagner and Social Security acts did not apply to agricultural laborers.

La raza

Mexican-American leaders struggled to develop a consistent strategy for their people. They sought greater rights by claiming to be white Americans—in order to avoid the same discrimination as African-Americans—but also sought the backing of the Mexican government and promoted a mystical sense of pride and identification with Mexican heritage later given the name *la raza*.

Mexican-Americans were not the only group encouraged to leave the United States. In 1935, Congress passed the Filipino Repatriation Act, offering free transportation to those born in the Philippines and willing to return there. Persons who did leave would only be able to return by applying under the Philippines' annual immigration quota of fifty. Given the lack of economic opportunity in the Philippines and fear about being permanently unable to return to the United States, of the 45,000 Filipinos in the country, only around 2,000 accepted the offer.

Last Hired, First Fired

As the "last hired and first fired," African-Americans were hit hardest by the Depression. Even those who retained their jobs now faced competition from unemployed whites who had previously considered positions like

Future congressman Adam Clayton Powell Jr. (at center with billboard), taking part in a "Don't Buy Where You Can't Work" demonstration in Harlem during the Depression. The campaign targeted stores that served black customers but refused to hire black employees. Photograph © Morgan and Marvin Smith.

Unemployment for blacks

waiter and porter beneath them. With an unemployment rate double that of whites, blacks benefited disproportionately from direct government relief and, especially in northern cities, jobs on New Deal public-works projects. Half of the families in Harlem received public assistance during the 1930s. Demonstrations in Harlem demanded jobs in the neighborhood's white-owned stores, with the slogan "Don't Buy Where You Can't Work."

Race in federal government

Although Roosevelt seems to have had little personal interest in race relations or civil rights, he appointed Mary McLeod Bethune, a prominent black educator, as a special adviser on minority affairs and a number of other blacks to important federal positions. Key members of his administration, including his wife, Eleanor, and Secretary of the Interior Harold Ickes, a former president of the Chicago chapter of the NAACP, directed national attention to the injustices of segregation, disenfranchisement, and lynching. In 1939, Eleanor Roosevelt resigned from the Daughters of the American Revolution when the organization refused to allow the black singer Marian Anderson to present a concert at Constitution Hall in Washington. The president's wife arranged for Anderson to sing on the steps of the Lincoln Memorial and for the concert to be broadcast nationally on the radio.

Shift in the black vote

The decade witnessed a historic shift in black voting patterns. In the North and West, where they enjoyed the right to vote, blacks in 1934 and 1936 abandoned their allegiance to the party of Lincoln and emancipation in favor of Democrats and the New Deal. But despite a massive lobbying campaign, southern congressmen prevented passage of a federal antilynching law. FDR offered little support. Because of the exclusion of agricultural and domestic workers, Social Security's old age pensions and unemployment benefits and the minimum wages established by the Fair Labor Standards Act left uncovered 60 percent of all employed blacks and 85 percent of black women.

Federal Discrimination

Federal housing policy, which powerfully reinforced residential segregation, revealed the limits of New Deal freedom. As in the case of Social Security, local officials put national housing policy into practice in a way that reinforced existing racial boundaries. Nearly all municipalities, North as well as South, insisted that housing built or financially aided by the federal government be racially segregated. The Federal Housing Administration, moreover, had no hesitation about insuring mortgages that contained clauses barring future sales to non-white buyers, and it refused to channel money into integrated neighborhoods. Along with discriminatory practices by private banks and real estate companies, federal policy became a major factor in further entrenching housing segregation in the United States.

Federal employment practices also discriminated on the basis of race. As late as 1940, of the 150,000 blacks holding federal jobs, only 2 percent occupied positions other than clerk or custodian. In the South, many New Deal construction projects refused to hire blacks at all. The New Deal began the process of modernizing southern agriculture, but tenants, black and white, footed much of the bill. Tens of thousands of sharecroppers, as noted earlier, were driven off the land as a result of the AAA policy of raising crop prices by paying landowners to reduce cotton acreage.

Not until the Great Society of the 1960s would those left out of Social Security and other New Deal programs—racial minorities, many women, migrants, and other less privileged workers—win inclusion in the American welfare state.

A map of Philadelphia prepared by the Home Owners' Loan Corporation illustrates how federal agencies engaged in "redlining" of neighborhoods containing blue-collar and black residents. The result was to strongly reinforce housing segregation. The colors correspond to the agency's perception of an area's real-estate prospects. Wealthy neighborhoods, colored green and given the best credit ratings, were expected to be racially and ethnically homogeneous. White-collar districts, in blue, were second best. Red districts, the worst, had an "undesirable population." The Corporation prepared maps like this for many cities and shared them with private lenders and the Federal Housing Administration, resulting in massive disinvestment in "red" neighborhoods, whose residents found it almost impossible to obtain housing loans.

A NEW CONCEPTION OF AMERICA

But if the New Deal failed to dismantle the barriers that barred non-whites from full participation in American life, the 1930s witnessed the absorption of other groups into the social mainstream. With Catholics and

During the 1930s, the South remained rigidly segregated. This 1939 photograph by Dorothea Lange depicts a "colored" movie theater in the Mississippi Delta.

Jews occupying prominent posts in the Roosevelt administration and new immigrant voters forming an important part of its electoral support, the New Deal made ethnic pluralism a living reality in American politics.

Thanks to the virtual cutoff of southern and eastern European immigration in 1924; the increasing penetration of movies, chain stores, and mass advertising into ethnic communities; and the common experience of economic crisis, the 1930s witnessed an acceleration of cultural assimilation. For the children of the new immigrants, labor and political activism became agents of a new kind of Americanization. "Unionism is Americanism" became a CIO rallying cry.

The Heyday of American Communism

In the mid-1930s, for the first time in American history, the left—an umbrella term for socialists, communists, labor radicals, and many New Deal liberals—enjoyed a shaping influence on the nation's politics and culture. The CIO and Communist Party became focal points for a broad social and intellectual impulse that helped to redraw the boundaries of American freedom. An obscure, faction-ridden organization when the Depression began, the Communist Party experienced remarkable growth during the 1930s. The party's membership never exceeded 100,000, but several times that number passed through its ranks.

Growth of the Communist Party

It was not so much the party's ideology as its vitality—its involvement in a mind-boggling array of activities, including demonstrations by the unemployed, struggles for industrial unionism, and a renewed movement for black civil rights—that for a time made it the center of gravity for a broad democratic upsurge. At the height of the **Popular Front**—a period during the mid-1930s when the Communist Party sought to ally itself with socialists and New Dealers in movements for social change, urging reform of the capitalist system rather than revolution—Communists gained an unprecedented respectability.

Respectability for Communists

Redefining the People

In theater, film, and dance, the Popular Front vision of American society sank deep roots and survived much longer than the political moment from which it sprang. In this broad left-wing culture, social and economic radicalism, not support for the status quo, defined true Americanism. Ethnic and racial diversity was the glory of American society, and the "American way of life" meant unionism and social citizenship, not the unbridled pursuit of wealth.

History of Southern Illinois, a mural sponsored by the Illinois Federal Art Project, illustrates the widespread fascination during the 1930s with American traditions and the lives of ordinary Americans. On the left, a man strums a guitar, while workers labor on the waterfront.

Popular Front culture

During the 1930s, artists and writers who strove to create socially meaningful works eagerly took up the task of depicting the daily lives of ordinary farmers and city dwellers. Art about the people—such as Dorothea Lange's photographs of migrant workers and sharecroppers—and art created by the people—such as black spirituals—came to be seen as expressions of genuine Americanism. Films celebrated populist figures who challenged and defeated corrupt businessmen and politicians, as in *Mr. Deeds Goes to Town* (1936) and *Mr. Smith Goes to Washington* (1939). Earl Robinson's song "Ballad for Americans," a typical expression of Popular Front culture that celebrated the religious, racial, and ethnic diversity of American society, became a national hit and was performed in 1940 at the Republican national convention.

Challenging the Color Line

Promoting racial tolerance

It was fitting that "Ballad for Americans" reached the top of the charts in a version performed by the magnificent black singer Paul Robeson. Popular Front culture moved well beyond New Deal liberalism in condemning racism as incompatible with true Americanism. In the 1930s, groups like the American Jewish Committee and the National Conference of Christians and Jews actively promoted ethnic and religious tolerance, defining pluralism as "the American way." But whether in Harlem or East Los Angeles, the Communist Party was the era's only predominantly white organization to make fighting racism a top priority. Communist influence spread even to the South. The Communist-dominated International Labor Defense mobilized popular support for black defendants victimized by a racist criminal justice system. It helped to make the **Scottsboro case** an international

The "Scottsboro boys"

cause célèbre. The case revolved around nine young black men arrested for the rape of two white women in Alabama in 1931. Despite the weakness of the evidence against the "Scottsboro boys" and the fact that one of the two accusers recanted, Alabama authorities three times put them on trial and three times won convictions. Landmark Supreme Court decisions overturned the first two verdicts and established legal principles that greatly expanded the definition of civil liberties—that defendants have a constitutional right to effective legal representation and that states cannot systematically exclude blacks from juries. But the Court allowed the third set of convictions to stand, which led to prison sentences for five of the defendants.

The CIO brought large numbers of black industrial workers into the labor movement for the first time and ran extensive educational campaigns to persuade white workers to recognize the interests they shared with their black counterparts. Black workers, many of them traditionally hostile to unions because of their long experience of exclusion, responded with enthusiasm to CIO organizing efforts.

Labor and Civil Liberties

The "Scottsboro boys," flanked by two prison guards, with their lawyer, Samuel Liebowitz.

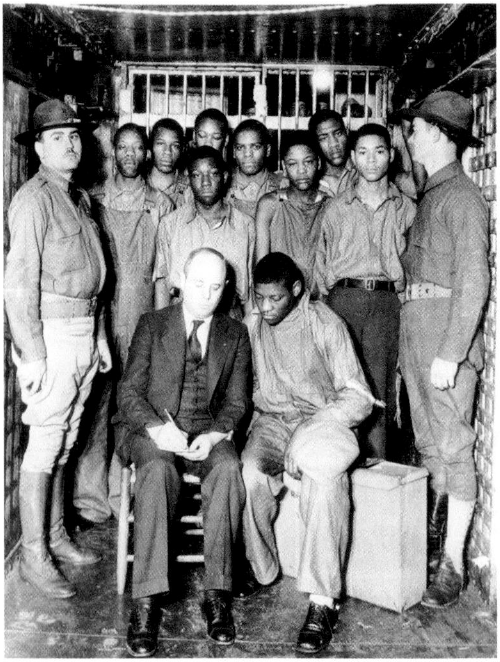

Another central element of Popular Front public culture was its mobilization for civil liberties, especially the right of labor to organize. The struggle to launch industrial unions encountered sweeping local restrictions on freedom of speech as well as repression by private and public police forces.

Labor militancy helped to produce an important shift in the understanding of civil liberties. Previously conceived of as individual rights that must be protected against infringement by the government, the concept now expanded to include violations of free speech and assembly by powerful private groups. As a result, just as the federal government emerged as a guarantor of economic security, it also became a protector of freedom of expression.

By the eve of World War II, civil liberties had assumed a central place in the New Deal understanding of freedom. In 1939, Attorney General Frank Murphy established a Civil Liberties Unit in the Department of Justice. Meanwhile, the same Supreme Court that in 1937 relinquished its role as a judge of economic legislation moved to expand its authority over civil liberties. The justices insisted that constitutional guarantees of free thought and expression were essential to "nearly

A May Day parade in New York City in 1935 includes a placard celebrating the Bill of Rights.

every other form of freedom" and therefore deserved special protection by the courts. Since 1937, the large majority of state and national laws overturned by the courts have been those that infringe on civil liberties, not the property rights of business.

The new appreciation of free expression was hardly universal. In 1938, the House of Representatives established the **House Un-American Activities Committee** to investigate disloyalty. Its expansive definition of "un-American" included communists, labor radicals, and the left of the Democratic Party, and its hearings led to the dismissal of dozens of federal employees on charges of subversion. Two years later, Congress enacted the Smith Act, which made it a federal crime to "teach, advocate, or encourage" the overthrow of the government.

Expansive definition of "un-American"

The End of the New Deal

By then the New Deal, as an era of far-reaching social reform, had already begun to recede. One reason was that more and more southern Democrats were finding themselves at odds with Roosevelt's policies. In 1938, the administration released a "Report on Economic Conditions in the South," along with a letter by the president referring to the region as "the nation's No. 1 economic problem." The document revealed that the South lagged far behind other parts of the country in industrialization and investment in education and public health. Also in 1938, a new generation of home-grown radicals—southern New Dealers, black activists, labor leaders, communists, even a few elected officials—founded the Southern Conference for Human Welfare to work for unionization, unemployment relief, and racial justice.

Southern leaders and the New Deal

Southern business and political leaders feared that continuing federal intervention in their region would encourage unionization and upset race relations. Roosevelt concluded that the enactment of future New Deal measures required a liberalization of the southern Democratic Party. In 1938, he tried to persuade the region's voters to replace conservative congressmen with ones who would support his policies. The South's small electorate dealt him a stinging rebuke.

Political stalemate

A period of political stalemate followed the congressional election of 1938. For many years, a conservative coalition of southern Democrats and northern Republicans dominated Congress. Further reform initiatives became almost impossible, and Congress moved to abolish existing ones. It repealed an earlier tax on corporate profits and rejected a proposed program of national medical insurance. The administration, moreover, increasingly focused its attention on the storm gathering in Europe. Even before December 1941, when the United States entered World War II, "Dr. Win the War," as Roosevelt put it, had replaced "Dr. New Deal."

The New Deal in American History

Failures and accomplishments of the New Deal

Given the scope of the economic calamity it tried to counter, the New Deal seems in many ways limited. Compared with later European welfare states, Social Security remained restricted in scope and modest in cost. The New Deal failed to address the problem of racial inequality, which in some ways it actually worsened.

Yet even as the New Deal receded, its substantial accomplishments remained. It greatly expanded the federal government's role in the American economy and made it an independent force in relations between industry and labor. The government influenced what farmers could and could not plant, required employers to deal with unions, insured bank deposits, regulated the stock market, loaned money to home owners, and provided payments to a majority of the elderly and unemployed. It transformed the physical environment through hydroelectric dams, reforestation projects, rural electrification, and the construction of innumerable public facilities. It restored faith in democracy and made the government an institution directly experienced in Americans' daily lives and directly concerned with their welfare. It redrew the map of American politics. It helped to inspire, and was powerfully influenced by, a popular upsurge that recast the idea of freedom to include a public guarantee of economic security for ordinary citizens and that identified economic inequality as the greatest threat to American freedom.

The New Deal certainly improved economic conditions in the United States. But more than 15 percent of the workforce remained unemployed in 1940. Only the mobilization of the nation's resources to fight World War II would finally end the Great Depression.

CHAPTER REVIEW AND ONLINE RESOURCES

REVIEW QUESTIONS

1. *Discuss how regional development such as the Tennessee Valley Authority and the Columbia River project reflected broader changes in American life during the New Deal.*
2. *What actions did President Roosevelt and Congress take to help the banking system recover as well as to reform how it operated in the long run?*
3. *How did the actions of the AAA benefit many farmers, injure others, and provoke attacks by conservatives?*
4. *Explain what labor did in the 1930s to secure "economic freedom and industrial democracy" for American workers.*
5. *How did the emphasis of the Second New Deal differ from that of the First New Deal?*
6. *How did the entrenched power of southern white conservatives limit African-Americans' ability to enjoy the full benefits of the New Deal and eliminate racial violence and discrimination? Why did African-Americans still support the Democratic Party?*
7. *Analyze the effects of the Indian Reorganization Act of 1934 on Native Americans.*
8. *Explain how New Deal programs contributed to the stigma of blacks as welfare-dependent.*
9. *What were the political forces that informed the Filipino Repatriation Act?*
10. *How did the New Deal build on traditional ideas about the importance of home ownership to Americans, and how did it change Americans' ability to own their own homes?*
11. *What were the major characteristics of liberalism by 1939?*

KEY TERMS

New Deal (p. 638)
Emergency Banking Act (p. 640)
Hundred Days (p. 641)
National Industrial Recovery Act (p. 641)
National Recovery Administration (p. 641)
Civilian Conservation Corps (p. 642)
Public Works Administration (p. 642)
Tennessee Valley Authority (p. 643)
Agricultural Adjustment Act (p. 643)
Dust Bowl (p. 644)
Federal Housing Administration (p. 645)
Congress of Industrial Organizations (p. 647)
sit-down strike (p. 647)
Share Our Wealth movement (p. 649)
Works Progress Administration (p. 651)
Wagner Act (p. 652)
Social Security Act (p. 652)
welfare state (p. 652)
Court packing (p. 656)
Indian New Deal (p. 660)
Popular Front (p. 664)
Scottsboro case (p. 665)
House Un-American Activities Committee (p. 667)

Go to INQUIZITIVE

To see what you know—and learn what you've missed—with personalized feedback along the way.

Visit the ***Give Me Liberty!* Student Site** for primary source documents and images, interactive maps, author videos featuring Eric Foner, and more.

1931	Japan invades Manchuria
1933	U.S. recognizes Soviet Union
1935–1939	Congress passes Neutrality Acts
1937	Sino-Japanese War begins
1938	Munich agreement
1939	Germany invades Poland
1940	Draft established
1941	Four Freedoms speech
	Henry Luce's *The American Century*
	Executive Order 8802
	Lend-Lease Act
	Pearl Harbor attacked
1942	Executive Order 9066
	Battle of Midway Island
	Congress of Racial Equality (CORE) formed
1943	Zoot suit riots
	Detroit race riot
	Congress lifts Chinese Exclusion Act
1944	*Smith v. Allwright*
	D-Day
	GI Bill of Rights
	Bretton Woods conference
	Korematsu v. United States
	Battle of the Bulge
1945	Yalta conference
	Roosevelt dies; Harry Truman becomes president
	V-E Day (May)
	Atomic bombs dropped on Japan
	End of war in Pacific

CHAPTER 22

FIGHTING FOR THE FOUR FREEDOMS: WORLD WAR II

★

1941–1945

Part of a sheet of fifty miniature reproductions of World War II posters. The themes include invocations of freedom, depictions of the enemy, calls for disciplined labor, and warnings against inadvertently revealing military secrets. Artists for Victory, an organization founded in 1942, sponsored a national poster competition to encourage artists to use their talents to promote the Allied war effort.

By far the most popular works of art produced during World War II were paintings of the **Four Freedoms** by the magazine illustrator Norman Rockwell. In his State of the Union Address, delivered before Congress on January 6, 1941, President Roosevelt spoke eloquently of a future world order founded on the "essential human freedoms": freedom of speech, freedom of worship, freedom from want, and freedom from fear. The Four Freedoms became Roosevelt's favorite statement of Allied aims. They embodied, Roosevelt declared in a 1942 radio address, the "rights of men of every creed and every race, wherever they live," and made clear "the crucial difference between ourselves and the enemies we face today."

Rockwell's paintings succeeded in linking the Four Freedoms with the defense of traditional American values. Drawing on the lives of his Vermont neighbors, Rockwell translated the Four Freedoms into images of real people situated in small-town America. Each of the paintings focuses on an instantly recognizable situation. An ordinary citizen rises to speak at a town meeting; members of different religious groups are seen at prayer; a family enjoys a Thanksgiving dinner; a mother and father stand over sleeping children.

Even as Rockwell invoked images of small-town life to rally Americans to the war effort, however, the country experienced changes as deep as at any time in its history. As during World War I, but on a far larger scale, wartime mobilization expanded the size and scope of government and energized the economy. The gross national product more than doubled, and unemployment disappeared as war production finally conquered the Depression. The demand for labor drew millions of women into the workforce and sent a tide of migrants from rural America to the industrial cities of the North and West, permanently altering the nation's social geography.

World War II gave the country a new and lasting international role and greatly strengthened the idea that American security was global in scope and could be protected only by the worldwide triumph of core American values. Government military spending sparked the economic development of the South and West, laying the foundation for the rise of the modern Sunbelt. The war created a close link between big business and a militarized federal government—a "military-industrial complex," as President Dwight D. Eisenhower would later call it—that long survived the end of fighting.

World War II also redrew the boundaries of American nationality. In contrast to World War I, the government recognized the "new immigrants" of the early twentieth century and their children as loyal Americans. Black Americans' second-class status assumed, for the first

FOCUS QUESTIONS

- *What steps led to American participation in World War II?*
- *How did the United States mobilize economic resources and promote popular support for the war effort?*
- *What visions of America's postwar role began to emerge during the war?*
- *How did American minorities face threats to their freedom at home and abroad during World War II?*
- *How did the end of the war begin to shape the postwar world?*

time since Reconstruction, a prominent place on the nation's political agenda. But toleration had its limits. With the United States at war with Japan, the federal government removed more than 110,000 Japanese-Americans, the majority of them American citizens, from their homes and confined them to internment camps.

As a means of generating support for the struggle, the Four Freedoms provided a crucial language of national unity. But this unity obscured underlying divisions concerning freedom. Although some Americans looked forward to a worldwide New Deal, others envisioned "free enterprise" replacing government intervention in the economy. The movement of women into the labor force challenged traditional gender relations, but most men and not a few women longed for the restoration of family life with a male breadwinner and a wife responsible for the home.

FIGHTING WORLD WAR II

The immensely popular Office of War Information poster reproducing Norman Rockwell's paintings of the Four Freedoms, President Franklin D. Roosevelt's shorthand for American purposes in World War II. ("Four Freedoms" illustrations © SEPS licensed by Curtis Licensing, IN.)

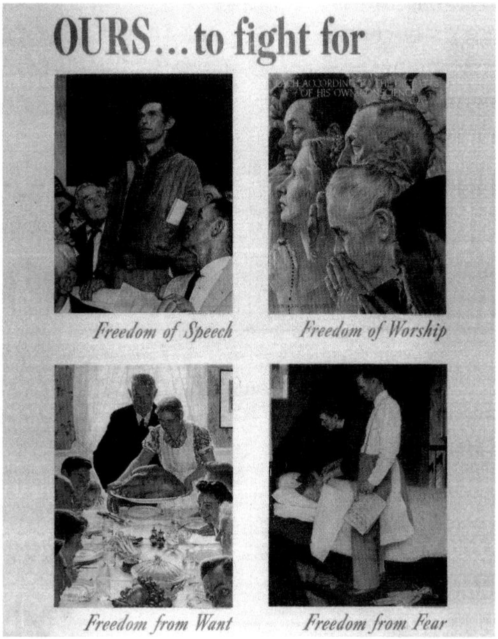
OURS... to fight for
Freedom of Speech
Freedom of Worship
Freedom from Want
Freedom from Fear

Good Neighbors

During the 1930s, with Americans preoccupied by the economic crisis, international relations played only a minor role in public affairs. From the outset of his administration, nonetheless, FDR embarked on a number of departures in foreign policy. In 1933, hoping to stimulate American trade, he exchanged ambassadors with the Soviet Union, whose government his Republican predecessors had stubbornly refused to recognize.

Roosevelt also formalized a policy initiated by Herbert Hoover by which the United States repudiated the right to intervene militarily in the internal affairs of Latin American countries. This **Good Neighbor Policy**, as it was called, offered a belated recognition of the sovereignty of America's neighbors. But the United States lent its support to dictators like Anastasio Somoza in Nicaragua, Rafael Trujillo Molina in the Dominican Republic, and Fulgencio Batista in Cuba. "He may be a son of a bitch, but he's *our* son of a bitch," FDR said of Somoza.

The Road to War

Ominous developments in Asia and Europe quickly overshadowed events in Latin America. By the mid-1930s, it seemed clear that the rule of law was disintegrating in international relations and that war was on the horizon. In 1931, seeking to expand its military and economic power in Asia, Japan invaded Manchuria, a province of northern China. Six years later, its troops moved farther into China. When the Japanese overran the city of Nanjing, they massacred an estimated 300,000 Chinese prisoners of war and civilians.

An aggressive power threatened Europe as well. After brutally consolidating his rule in Germany, Adolf Hitler embarked on a campaign to control the entire continent. In 1936, he sent troops to occupy the Rhineland, a demilitarized zone between France and Germany established after World War I. The failure of Britain, France, and the United States to oppose this action convinced Hitler that the democracies could not muster the will to halt his aggressive plans. The Italian leader Benito Mussolini, the founder of fascism, a movement similar to Hitler's Nazism, invaded and conquered Ethiopia. As part of a campaign to unite all Europeans of German origin in a single empire, Hitler in 1938 annexed Austria and the Sudetenland, an ethnically German part of Czechoslovakia. Shortly thereafter, he gobbled up all of that country.

Adolf Hitler

As the 1930s progressed, Roosevelt became more and more alarmed at Hitler's aggression as well as his accelerating campaign against Germany's Jews, whom the Nazis stripped of citizenship and property and began to deport to concentration camps. But Roosevelt had little choice but to follow the policy of "appeasement" adopted by Britain and France, which hoped that agreeing to Hitler's demands would prevent war.

In a 1940 cartoon, war clouds engulf Europe, while Uncle Sam observes that the Atlantic Ocean no longer seems to shield the United States from involvement.

Isolationism

To most Americans, the threat arising from Japanese and German aggression seemed very distant. Moreover, Hitler had more than a few admirers in the United States. Obsessed with the threat of communism, some Americans approved of his expansion of German power as a counterweight to the Soviet Union. Businessmen did not wish to give up profitable overseas markets. Henry Ford did business with Nazi Germany throughout the 1930s. Trade with Japan also continued, including shipments of American trucks and aircraft and considerable amounts of oil.

Many Americans remained convinced that involvement in World War I had been a mistake. Ethnic allegiances reinforced Americans' traditional reluctance to enter foreign conflicts. Many Americans of German and Italian descent celebrated the expansion of national power in their countries of origin, even as they disdained their dictatorial governments. Irish-Americans remained strongly anti-British.

The Neutrality Acts

Isolationism—the 1930s version of Americans' long-standing desire to avoid foreign entanglements—dominated Congress. Beginning in 1935, lawmakers passed a series of **Neutrality Acts** that banned travel on belligerents' ships and the sale of arms to countries at war. These policies, Congress hoped, would allow the United States to avoid the conflicts over freedom of the seas that had contributed to involvement in World War I.

The War in Europe

In the Munich agreement of 1938, Britain and France had caved in to Hitler's aggression. In 1939, the Soviet Union proposed an international agreement to oppose further German demands for territory. Britain and France, who distrusted Stalin and saw Germany as a bulwark against the spread of communist influence in Europe, refused. Stalin then astonished the world by signing a nonaggression pact with Hitler, his former sworn enemy. On September 1, 1939, immediately after the signing of the Nazi–Soviet pact, Germany invaded Poland. This time, Britain and France, which had pledged to protect Poland against aggression, declared war. But Germany appeared unstoppable. Within a year, the Nazi *blitzkrieg* (lightning war) had overrun Poland and much of Scandinavia, Belgium, and the Netherlands. On June 14, 1940, German troops occupied Paris. Hitler now dominated nearly all of Europe, as well as North Africa. In September 1940, Germany, Italy, and Japan created a military alliance known as the Axis.

For one critical year, Britain stood virtually alone in fighting Germany. In the Battle of Britain of 1940–1941, German planes launched devastating attacks on London and other cities. The Royal Air Force eventually turned back the air assault.

A newsreel theater in New York's Times Square announces Hitler's *blitzkrieg* in Europe in the spring of 1940.

Toward Intervention

Roosevelt viewed Hitler as a mad gangster whose victories posed a direct threat to the United States. But most Americans remained desperate to stay out of the conflict. After a tumultuous debate, Congress in 1940 agreed to allow the sale of arms to Britain on a "cash and carry" basis—that is, they had to be paid for in cash and transported in British ships. It also approved plans for military rearmament. But with a presidential election looming,

Roosevelt was reluctant to go further. Opponents of involvement in Europe organized the America First Committee, with hundreds of thousands of members and a leadership that included such well-known figures as Henry Ford, Father Coughlin, and Charles A. Lindbergh.

A third term

In 1940, breaking with a tradition that dated back to George Washington, Roosevelt announced his candidacy for a third term as president. The international situation was too dangerous and domestic recovery too fragile, he insisted, for him to leave office. Republicans chose as his opponent a political amateur, Wall Street businessman and lawyer Wendell Willkie. Willkie, who endorsed New Deal social legislation, captured more votes than Roosevelt's previous opponents. But FDR still emerged with a decisive victory. Soon after his victory, in a fireside chat in December 1940, Roosevelt announced that the United States would become the "arsenal of democracy," providing Britain and China with military supplies in their fight against Germany and Japan.

Financial support

During 1941, the United States became more and more closely allied with those fighting Germany and Japan. At Roosevelt's urging, Congress passed the **Lend-Lease Act**, which authorized military aid so long as countries promised somehow to return it all after the war. Under the law's provisions, the United States funneled billions of dollars' worth of arms to Britain and China, as well as the Soviet Union, after Hitler renounced his nonaggression pact and invaded that country in June 1941. FDR also froze Japanese assets in the United States, halting virtually all trade between the countries, including the sale of oil vital to Japan.

Pearl Harbor

December 7, 1941

Until November 1941, the administration's attention focused on Europe. But at the end of that month, intercepted Japanese messages revealed that an assault in the Pacific was imminent. No one, however, knew where it would come. On December 7, 1941, Japanese planes, launched from aircraft carriers, bombed the naval base at Pearl Harbor in Hawaii, the first attack by a foreign power on American soil since the War of 1812. Japan launched the attack in the hope of crippling American naval power in the Pacific. With a free hand in its campaign of conquest in East Asia, Japan would gain access to supplies of oil and other resources it could no longer obtain from the United States. It hoped that destroying the American fleet would establish Japan for years to come as the dominant power in the region.

Pearl Harbor was a complete and devastating surprise. In a few hours, more than 2,000 American servicemen were killed, and 187 aircraft and 18 naval vessels, including 8 battleships, had been destroyed or damaged.

Secretary of Labor Frances Perkins, who saw the president after the attack, remarked that he seemed calm—"his terrible moral problem had been resolved." Terming December 7 "a date which will live in infamy," Roosevelt asked Congress for a declaration of war against Japan. The combined vote in Congress was 477 in favor and 1 against—pacifist Jeanette Rankin of Montana, who had also voted against American entry into World War I. The next day, Germany declared war on the United States. America had finally joined the largest war in human history.

Declaration of war

The War in the Pacific

World War II has been called a "gross national product war," meaning that its outcome turned on which coalition of combatants could outproduce the other. In retrospect, it appears inevitable that the entry of the United States, with its superior industrial might, would ensure the defeat of the **Axis powers**. But the first few months of American involvement witnessed an unbroken string of military disasters. Japan in early 1942 conquered Burma (Myanmar) and Siam (Thailand). Japan also took control of the Dutch East Indies (Indonesia), whose extensive oil fields could replace supplies from the United States. And it occupied Guam, the Philippines, and other Pacific islands. At Bataan, in the Philippines, the Japanese forced 78,000 American and Filipino troops to lay down their arms—the largest surrender in American military history. Thousands perished on the ensuing "death march" to a prisoner-of-war camp. At the same time, German submarines sank hundreds of Allied merchant and naval vessels during the Battle of the Atlantic.

Military disasters

American army reinforcements wading ashore on Saipan, one of the Mariana Islands, during one of the bloodiest battles in the "island hopping" campaign in the Pacific theater of World War II.

Soon, however, the tide of battle began to turn. In May 1942, in the Battle of the Coral Sea, the American navy turned back a Japanese fleet intent on attacking Australia. The following month, it inflicted devastating losses on the Japanese navy in the Battle of Midway Island. American codebreakers had managed to decipher the Japanese communications code, so the navy was forewarned about the timing of the assault at Midway and prepared an ambush for the attacking fleet. In the battle, four Japanese aircraft carriers, along with other vessels, were destroyed. Midway was the turning point of the Pacific naval war. The victories there and in the Coral Sea allowed

WORLD WAR II IN THE PACIFIC, 1941–1945

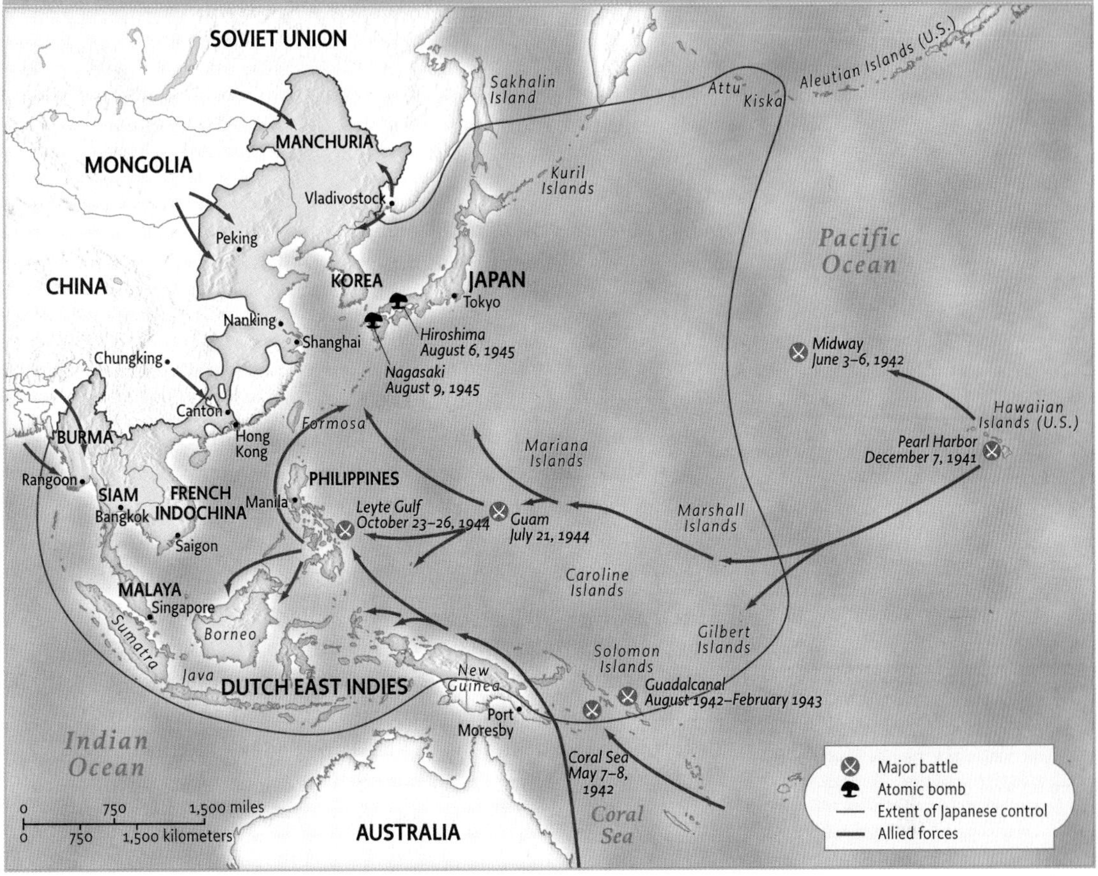

Although the Japanese navy never fully recovered from its defeats at the Coral Sea and Midway in 1942, it took three more years for American forces to near the Japanese homeland.

American forces to launch the bloody campaigns that one by one drove the Japanese from fortified islands like Guadalcanal and the Solomons in the western Pacific and brought American troops ever closer to Japan.

The War in Europe

The "Grand Alliance" of World War II in Europe brought together the United States, Great Britain, and the Soviet Union, each led by an iron-willed, larger-than-life figure: Roosevelt, Winston Churchill, and Joseph Stalin. United in their determination to defeat Nazi Germany, they differed not only in terms of the societies they represented but also in their long-range goals. Stalin was set on establishing enough control over eastern Europe that his country would never again be invaded from the west. Churchill hoped to ensure that the British Empire emerged intact from the war. Roosevelt, like Woodrow Wilson before him, hoped to establish a new international order so that world wars would never again take place.

Facing wars in two hemispheres, Roosevelt had to determine how best to deploy American manpower and resources. Bearing the brunt of the fighting after Hitler invaded the Soviet Union in 1941, Stalin demanded an early Allied attack across the English Channel to confront German forces in occupied France and relieve pressure on his beleaguered army. Churchill's strategy was to attack the "soft underbelly" of Axis power through Allied operations in the Mediterranean, starting with an invasion of North Africa. Churchill's approach prevailed, and the cross-Channel invasion did not come until 1944.

Allied victories

By the spring of 1943, the Allies also gained the upper hand in the Atlantic, as British and American destroyers and planes devastated the German submarine fleet. In July 1943, American and British forces invaded Sicily, beginning the liberation of Italy. A popular uprising in Rome overthrew the Mussolini government, whereupon Germany occupied most of the country. Fighting there raged throughout 1944.

The major involvement of American troops in Europe did not begin until June 6, 1944. On that date, known as **D-Day**, nearly 200,000 American, British, and Canadian soldiers under the command of General Dwight D. Eisenhower landed in Normandy in northwestern France. More than a million troops followed them ashore in the next few weeks, in the most massive sea-land operation in history. After fierce fighting, German armies retreated eastward. By August, Paris had been liberated.

The crucial fighting in Europe, however, took place on the eastern front, the scene of an epic struggle between Germany and the Soviet Union. More than 3 million German soldiers took part in the 1941 invasion. After sweeping through western Russia, German armies in August 1942 launched a siege of Stalingrad, a city located deep inside Russia on the Volga River. This proved to be a catastrophic mistake. Bolstered by an influx of military supplies from the United States, the Russians surrounded the German troops and forced them to surrender in January 1943. Stalingrad marked the turning point of the European war.

Of 13.6 million German casualties in World War II, 10 million came on the Russian front. They were only part of the war's vast toll in human lives. Millions of Poles and at least 20 million Russians, probably many more,

German prisoners of war guarded by an American soldier shortly after D-Day in June 1944. By this time, the Germans were drafting very young men into their armies.

Most of the land fighting in Europe during World War II took place on the eastern front between the German and Soviet armies.

perished—not only soldiers but civilian victims of starvation, disease, and massacres by German soldiers. After his armies had penetrated eastern Europe in 1941, moreover, Hitler embarked on the "final solution"—the mass extermination of "undesirable" peoples—Slavs, gypsies, gay men and women, and, above all, Jews. By 1945, 6 million Jewish men, women, and children had died in Nazi death camps. What came to be called the **Holocaust** was the horrifying culmination of the Nazi belief that Germans constituted a "master race" destined to rule the world.

Hitler's "final solution"

THE HOME FRONT

Mobilizing for War

By the end of World War II, some 50 million men had registered for the draft and 10 million had been inducted into the military. The army exemplified how the war united American society in new ways. Military service threw together Americans from every region and walk of life, and almost every racial and ethnic background (African-Americans continued to serve in segregated units). It brought into contact young men who would never have encountered each other in peacetime. Many were the children of immigrants who now emerged from urban ethnic communities to fight alongside Americans from rural regions with very different cultures and outlooks. The federal government ended voluntary enlistment in 1942, relying entirely on the draft for manpower. This ensured that wartime sacrifice was widely shared throughout American society. By contrast, in the decades following the Vietnam War, the armed forces have been composed entirely of volunteers and the military today includes few men and women from middle- and upper-class backgrounds.

Military diversity

War-related production essentially ended the Great Depression. In this photograph from 1942, workers wait to be paid at a Maryland shipyard.

World War II also transformed the role of the national government. FDR created federal agencies like the War Production Board, the War Manpower Commission, and the Office of Price Administration to regulate the allocation of labor, control the shipping industry, establish manufacturing quotas, and fix wages, prices, and rents. The number of federal workers rose from 1 million to 4 million, helping to push the unemployment rate down from 14 percent in 1940 to 2 percent three years later.

The government built housing for war workers and forced civilian industries to retool for war production. Michigan's auto factories now turned out trucks, tanks, and jeeps for the army. The gross national product rose from $91 billion to $214 billion during the war, and the federal government's expenditures amounted to twice the combined total of the previous 150 years. The government marketed billions of dollars' worth of war bonds, increased taxes, and began the practice of withholding income tax directly from weekly paychecks.

Bombers being manufactured at Ford's Willow Run factory, "the greatest single manufacturing plant the world has ever seen," according to the *Washington Post*. During the war, Ford, General Motors, and other automakers produced tanks, armored vehicles, and airplanes for the armed forces rather than cars for consumers.

Business and the War

Americans marveled at the achievements of wartime manufacturing. Thousands of aircraft, 100,000 armored vehicles, and 2.5 million trucks rolled off American assembly lines, and entirely new products like synthetic rubber replaced natural resources now controlled by Japan. Government-sponsored scientific research perfected inventions like radar, jet engines, and early computers that helped to win the war and would have a large impact on postwar life. These accomplishments not only made it possible to win a two-front war but also helped to restore the reputation of business and businessmen, which had reached a low point during the Depression.

West Coast military manufacturing

Federal funds reinvigorated established manufacturing areas and created entirely new industrial centers. World War II saw the West Coast emerge as a focus of military-industrial production. The government invested billions of dollars in the shipyards of Seattle, Portland, and San Francisco and in the steel plants and aircraft factories of southern California. By the war's end, California had received one-tenth of all federal spending. Nearly 2 million Americans moved to California for jobs in defense-related industries, and millions more passed through for military training and embarkation to the Pacific war.

In the South, the combination of rural out-migration and government investment in military-related factories and shipyards hastened a shift from agricultural to industrial employment. The South remained very poor when the war ended. Much of its rural population still lived in small wooden shacks with no indoor plumbing.

Labor in Wartime

During the war, labor entered a three-sided arrangement with government and business that allowed union membership to soar to unprecedented levels. In order to secure industrial peace and stabilize war production, the federal government forced reluctant employers to recognize unions. In 1944, when Montgomery Ward, the large mail-order company, defied a pro-union order, the army seized its headquarters and physically evicted its president. For their part, union leaders agreed not to strike.

By 1945, union membership stood at nearly 15 million, one-third of the non-farm labor force and the highest proportion in American history. But if labor became a partner in government, it was very much a junior partner. Congress continued to be dominated by a conservative alliance of Republicans and southern Democrats. Despite the "no-strike" pledge, 1943 and 1944 witnessed numerous brief walkouts in which workers protested the increasing speed of assembly-line production and the disparity between wages frozen by government order and expanding corporate profits.

TABLE 22.1 Labor Union Membership

YEAR	NUMBER OF MEMBERS
1933	2,857,000
1934	3,728,000
1935	3,753,000
1936	4,107,000
1937	5,780,000
1938	8,265,000
1939	8,980,000
1940	8,944,000
1941	10,489,000
1942	10,762,000
1943	13,642,000
1944	14,621,000
1945	14,796,000

Fighting for the Four Freedoms

Previous conflicts, including the Mexican War and World War I, had deeply divided American society. In contrast, World War II came to be remembered as the Good War, a time of national unity in pursuit of indisputably noble goals. But all wars require the mobilization of patriotic public opinion. "To sell *goods*, we must sell *words*" had become a motto of advertisers. Foremost among the words that helped to "sell" World War II was "freedom."

Talk of freedom pervaded wartime America. In 1941, the administration celebrated with considerable fanfare the 150th anniversary of the Bill of Rights (the first ten amendments to the Constitution). FDR described their protections against tyrannical government as defining characteristics of American life, central to the rights of "free men and free women."

The "most ambiguous" of the Four Freedoms, *Fortune* magazine remarked, was freedom from want. Yet this "great inspiring phrase," as a Pennsylvania steelworker put it in a letter to the president, seemed to strike the deepest chord in a nation just emerging from the Depression. Roosevelt initially meant it to refer to the elimination of barriers to international trade. But he quickly came to link freedom from want to an economic goal more relevant to the average citizen—protecting the future "standard of living of the American worker and farmer" by guaranteeing that the Depression would not resume after the war. This, he declared, would bring "real freedom for the common man."

In this recruitment poster for the Boy Scouts, a svelte Miss Liberty prominently displays the Bill of Rights, widely celebrated during World War II as the centerpiece of American freedom.

In this advertisement by the Liberty Motors and Engineering Corporation, published in the February 1944 issue of *Fortune*, Uncle Sam offers the Fifth Freedom—"free enterprise"—to war-devastated Europe. To spread its message, the company offered free enlargements of its ad.

The Fifth Freedom

Under the watchful eye of the War Advertising Council, private companies joined in the campaign to promote wartime patriotism, while positioning themselves and their brand names for the postwar world. Alongside advertisements urging Americans to purchase war bonds, guard against revealing military secrets, and grow "victory gardens" to allow food to be sent to the army, the war witnessed a burst of messages marketing advertisers' definition of freedom. Without directly criticizing Roosevelt, they repeatedly suggested that he had overlooked a fifth freedom. The National Association of Manufacturers and individual companies bombarded Americans with press releases, radio programs, and advertisements attributing the amazing feats of wartime production to "free enterprise."

With the memory of the Depression still very much alive, businessmen predicted a postwar world filled with consumer goods, with "freedom of choice" among abundant possibilities assured if only private enterprise were liberated from government controls.

Women workers during their lunch break at the roundhouse of the Chicago and Northwestern Railroad in Clinton, Iowa, in 1943.

Women at Work

During the war, the nation engaged in an unprecedented mobilization of "womanpower" to fill

This photograph captures the enthusiasm of three "fly girls"—female pilots employed by the air force to deliver cargo and passengers and test military aircraft. Known as WASPs (Women Airforce Service Pilots), they eventually numbered over 1,000 aviators, who trained at an all-female base at Avenger Field in Sweetwater, Texas. They did not take part in combat, but thirty-eight died in service.

industrial jobs vacated by men. Hollywood films glorified the independent woman, and private advertising celebrated the achievements of female industrial laborers. With 15 million men in the armed forces, women in 1944 made up more than one-third of the civilian labor force, and 350,000 served in auxiliary military units.

Even though most women workers still labored in clerical and service jobs, new opportunities suddenly opened in industrial, professional, and government positions previously restricted to men. On the West Coast, one-third of the workers in aircraft manufacturing and shipbuilding were women. For the first time in history, married women in their thirties outnumbered the young and single among female workers. Women forced unions like the United Auto Workers to confront issues like equal pay for equal work, maternity leave, and child-care facilities for working mothers. Having enjoyed what one wartime worker called "a taste of freedom"—doing "men's" jobs for men's wages and, sometimes, engaging in sexual activity while unmarried—many women hoped to remain in the labor force once peace returned.

"We as a nation," proclaimed one magazine article, "must change our basic attitude toward the work of women." But change proved difficult. The government, employers, and unions depicted work as a temporary necessity, not an expansion of women's freedom. When the war ended, most female war workers, especially those in better-paying industrial employment, did indeed lose their jobs.

Despite the upsurge in the number of working women, the advertisers' "world of tomorrow" rested on a vision of family-centered prosperity. Advertisements portrayed working women dreaming of their boyfriends in the army and emphasized that with the proper makeup, women could labor in a factory and remain attractive to men. Men in the army seem to have assumed that they would return home to resume traditional family life.

VISIONS OF POSTWAR FREEDOM

Toward an American Century

The prospect of an affluent future provided a point of unity between New Dealers and conservatives, business and labor. And the promise of prosperity to some extent united two of the most celebrated blueprints for the postwar world. One was *The American Century*, the publisher Henry Luce's 1941 effort to mobilize the American people both for the coming war and for an era of postwar world leadership. Americans, Luce's book insisted, must embrace the role history had thrust on them as the "dominant power in the world." After the war, American power and American values would underpin a previously unimaginable prosperity—"the abundant life," Luce called it—produced by "free economic enterprise."

Luce's essay anticipated important aspects of the postwar world. But its bombastic rhetoric and a title easily interpreted as a call for an American imperialism aroused immediate opposition among liberals and the left. Henry Wallace offered their response in "The Price of Free World Victory," an address delivered in May 1942 to the Free World Association. Wallace, secretary of agriculture during the 1930s, had replaced Vice President John Nance Garner as Roosevelt's running mate in 1940. In contrast to Luce's American Century, a world of business dominance no less than of American power, Wallace predicted that the war would usher in a "century of the common man." Governments acting to "humanize" capitalism and redistribute economic resources would eliminate hunger, illiteracy, and poverty.

Luce and Wallace had one thing in common—a new conception of America's role in the world, tied to continued international involvement, the promise of economic abundance, and the idea that the American experience should serve as a model for all other nations.

This is America...
...where the family is a sacred institution. Where children love, honor and respect their parents ...where a man's home is his castle ★ This is your America
...Keep it Free!

Despite the new independence enjoyed by millions of women, propaganda posters during World War II emphasized the male-dominated family as an essential element of American freedom.

"The Way of Life of Free Men"

Even as Congress moved to dismantle parts of the New Deal, liberal Democrats and their left-wing allies unveiled plans for a postwar economic policy that would allow all Americans to enjoy freedom from want. In 1942 and 1943, the reports of the National Resources Planning Board (NRPB) offered a blueprint for a peacetime economy based on full employment, an expanded welfare state, and a widely shared American standard of living. The board called for a "new bill of rights" that would include all Americans in an expanded Social Security system and guarantee access to education, health care, adequate housing, and jobs for able-bodied adults. The NRPB's plan for a "full-employment economy" with a "fair distribution of income," said *The Nation*, embodied "the way of life of free men."

This pamphlet, produced by the Office for Emergency Management for Labor Day in 1942, invoked the nineteenth-century ideal of free labor to describe the battle against the Axis powers.

Mindful that public-opinion polls showed a large majority of Americans favoring a guarantee of employment for those who could not find work, the president in 1944 called for an "Economic Bill of Rights." The original Bill of Rights restricted the power of government in the name of liberty. FDR proposed to expand its power in order to secure full employment, an adequate income, medical care, education, and a decent home for all Americans.

An Economic Bill of Rights

The replacement of Vice President Henry Wallace by Harry S. Truman, then a little-known senator from Missouri, however, suggested that the president did not intend to do battle with Congress over social policy. Congress did not enact the Economic Bill of Rights. But in 1944, it extended to the millions of returning veterans an array of benefits, including unemployment pay, scholarships for further education, low-cost mortgage loans, pensions, and job training. The Servicemen's Readjustment Act, or **GI Bill of Rights**, was one of the farthest-reaching pieces of social legislation in American history. Aimed at rewarding members of the armed forces for their service and preventing the widespread unemployment and economic disruption that had followed World War I, it profoundly shaped postwar society. By 1946, more than 1 million veterans were attending college under its provisions, making up half of total college enrollment. Almost 4 million would receive home mortgages, spurring the postwar suburban housing boom.

GI Bill

The Road to Serfdom

The Road to Serfdom (1944), a surprise best-seller by Friedrich A. Hayek, a previously obscure Austrian-born economist, claimed that even the best-intentioned government efforts to direct the economy posed a threat to individual liberty. Coming at a time when the miracles of war production had reinvigorated belief in the virtues of capitalism, and with the confrontation with Nazism highlighting the danger of merging economic and political power, Hayek offered a new intellectual justification for opponents of active government. In a complex economy, he insisted, no single person or group of experts could possibly possess enough knowledge to direct economic activity intelligently. A free market, he wrote, mobilizes the fragmented and partial knowledge scattered throughout society far more effectively than a planned economy.

Friedrich A. Hayek and laissez-faire economics

By equating fascism, socialism, and the New Deal and by identifying economic planning with a loss of freedom, Hayek helped lay the foundation for the rise of modern conservatism and a revival of laissez-faire economic thought. As the war drew to a close, the stage was set for a renewed battle over the government's proper role in society and the economy, and the social conditions of American freedom.

THE AMERICAN DILEMMA

A poster issued by the Fair Employment Practices Commission, created in 1941 to combat discrimination in military-related jobs. The workers building a tank represent numerous European ethnic groups but not non-whites, even though the Commission was created to forestall a planned march on Washington organized by black leaders.

The unprecedented attention to freedom as the defining characteristic of American life had implications that went far beyond wartime mobilization. The struggle against Nazi tyranny and its theory of a master race discredited ethnic and racial inequality. A pluralist vision of American society now became part of official rhetoric. What set the United States apart from its wartime foes, the government insisted, was not only dedication to the ideals of the Four Freedoms but also the principle that Americans of all races, religions, and national origins could enjoy those freedoms equally. Racism was the enemy's philosophy; Americanism rested on toleration of diversity and equality for all. By the end of the war, the new immigrant groups had been fully accepted as loyal ethnic Americans, rather than members of distinct and inferior "races." And the contradiction between the principle of equal freedom and the actual status of blacks had come to the forefront of national life.

Patriotic Assimilation

Among other things, World War II created a vast melting pot, especially for European immigrants and their children. Millions of Americans moved out of urban ethnic neighborhoods and isolated rural enclaves and into the army and industrial plants, where they came into contact with people of very different backgrounds. What one historian has called their "patriotic assimilation" differed sharply from the forced Americanization of World War I.

Horrified by the uses to which the Nazis put the idea of inborn racial difference, biological and social scientists abandoned belief in a link among race, culture, and intelligence, an idea only recently central to their disciplines. Ruth Benedict's *Races and Racism* (1942) described racism as "a travesty of scientific knowledge." By the war's end, racism and nativism had been stripped of intellectual respectability, at least outside the South, and were viewed as psychological disorders.

Intolerance, of course, hardly disappeared from American life. Many business and government circles still excluded Jews. Along with the fact that early reports of the Holocaust were too terrible to be believed,

In this patriotic war poster the words of Abraham Lincoln are linked to the struggle against Nazi tyranny.

"THIS WORLD CANNOT EXIST HALF SLAVE AND HALF FREE"
FIGHT FOR FREEDOM!

This is America..
. . . where every boy can dream of being President. Where free schools, free opportunity, free enterprise, have built the most decent nation on earth. A nation built upon the rights of all men • This is your America
... Keep it Free!
Another *This Is America* propaganda poster emphasizes the American dream of equal opportunity for all. All the children in the classroom, however, are white boys, and the poster seems to limit the American dream to males.

One series of posters issued by the Office of War Information to mobilize support for the war effort emphasized respect for the country's racial and ethnic diversity. This one, directed at Hispanics, suggests that there is no contradiction between pride in ethnic heritage and loyalty to the United States.

AMERICANOS TODOS
LUCHAMOS POR LA VICTORIA
AMERICANS ALL
LET'S FIGHT FOR VICTORY

anti-Semitism contributed to the government's unwillingness to allow more than a handful of European Jews (21,000 during the course of the war) to find refuge in the United States. Roosevelt himself learned during the war of the extent of Hitler's "final solution" to the Jewish presence in Europe. But he failed to authorize air strikes that might have destroyed German death camps.

The *Bracero* Program

The war had a far more ambiguous meaning for non-white groups than for whites. On the eve of Pearl Harbor, racial barriers remained deeply entrenched in American life. Southern blacks were still trapped in a rigid system of segregation. Asians could not immigrate to the United States or become naturalized citizens. Most American Indians still lived on reservations in dismal poverty.

The war set in motion changes that would reverberate in the postwar years. Under the ***bracero* program** agreed to by the Mexican and American governments in 1942 (the name derives from *brazo*, the Spanish word for arm), tens of thousands of contract laborers crossed into the United States to take up jobs as domestic and agricultural workers. Initially designed as a temporary response to the wartime labor shortage, the program lasted until 1964. During that period, more than 4.5 million Mexicans entered the United States under labor contracts (while a slightly larger number were arrested for illegal entry by the Border Patrol).

Although the *bracero* program reinforced the status of immigrants from Mexico as an unskilled labor force, wartime employment opened new opportunities for second-generation Mexican-Americans. Hundreds of thousands of men and women emerged from ethnic neighborhoods, or *barrios*, to work in defense industries and serve in the army (where, unlike blacks, they fought alongside whites). For Mexican-American women in particular, the war afforded new opportunities for public participation and higher incomes. Government publications and newspaper accounts celebrated their role as patriotic mothers who encouraged their sons to enlist in the army and offered moral support while they were away at war. Contact with other groups led many to learn English and sparked a rise in interethnic marriages.

The **zoot suit riots** of 1943, in which club-wielding sailors and policemen attacked Mexican-American youths wearing flamboyant clothing on the streets of Los Angeles, illustrated the limits of wartime tolerance. But the contrast between the war's rhetoric of freedom and pluralism and the reality of continued discrimination inspired a heightened consciousness of civil rights. Mexican-Americans brought complaints of discrimination before the Fair Employment Practices Commission (FEPC) to fight the practice in the Southwest of confining them to the lowest-paid work or paying them lower wages than white workers doing the same jobs. Perhaps half a million Mexican-American men and women served in the armed forces.

Indians during the War

The war also brought many American Indians closer to the mainstream of American life. Some 25,000 served in the army (including the famous Navajo "code-talkers," who transmitted messages in their complex native language, which the Japanese could not decipher). Insisting that the United States lacked the authority to draft Indian men into the army, the Iroquois issued their own declaration of war against the Axis powers. Tens of thousands of Indians left reservations for jobs in war industries. Exposed for the first time to urban life and industrial society, many chose not to return to the reservations after the war ended. (Indeed, the reservations did not share in wartime prosperity.) Some Indian veterans took advantage of the GI Bill to attend college after the war, an opportunity that had been available to very few Indians previously.

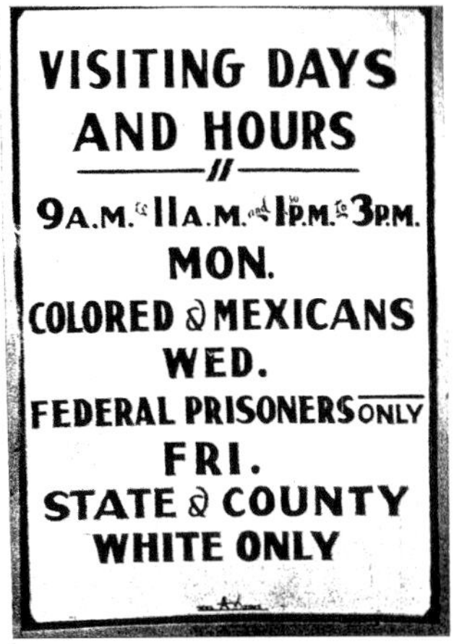

A sign on the Tarrant County Courthouse in Fort Worth, Texas, in 1942. Racial segregation extended to prison visiting hours.

Asian-Americans in Wartime

Asian-Americans' war experience was paradoxical. More than 50,000—the children and grandchildren of immigrants from China, Japan, Korea, and the Philippines—fought in the army, mostly in all-Asian units. With China an ally in the Pacific war, Congress in 1943 ended decades of complete exclusion by establishing a nationality quota for Chinese immigrants. The annual limit of 105 hardly suggested a desire for a large-scale influx. But the image of the Chinese as gallant fighters defending their country against Japanese aggression called into question long-standing racial stereotypes.

The experience of Japanese-Americans was far different. Both sides saw the Pacific war as a race war. Japanese propaganda depicted Americans as a self-indulgent people contaminated by ethnic and racial diversity as opposed to the racially "pure" Japanese. In the United States, long-standing prejudices and the shocking attack on Pearl Harbor combined to produce an unprecedented hatred of Japan. Government propaganda and war films portrayed the Japanese as rats, dogs, gorillas, and snakes—bestial and subhuman. They blamed Japanese aggression on a violent racial or national character, not, as in the case of Germany and Italy, on tyrannical rulers.

Wartime propaganda in the United States sought to inspire hatred against the Pacific foe. This poster, issued by the U.S. Army, recalls the Bataan death march in the Philippines.

VOICES OF FREEDOM

From League of United Latin American Citizens, "World War II and Mexican Americans" (1945)

Founded in 1929, the League of United Latin American Citizens (LULAC) campaigned for equal treatment for Americans of Latino descent and their full integration into American life. Soon after the war ended, an editorial in its publication *LULAC News* condemned continuing discrimination, reflecting how the war sparked a rising demand for equal rights among many minority groups.

"We do not serve Mexicans here." "You will have to get out as no Mexicans are allowed." "Your uniform and service ribbons mean nothing here. We still do not allow Mexicans."

These, and many other stronger-worded ones, are the embarrassing and humiliating retorts given our returning veterans of Latin American descent and their families. They may all be worded differently, and whereas some are toned with hate and loathness while others are toned with sympathy and remorse, still the implication remains that these so-called "Mexicans" are considered unworthy of equality, regardless of birthright or service. . . .

Why this hate, this prejudice, this tendency to discriminate against a people whose only fault seems to be that they are heirs of a culture older than any known "American Culture," to find themselves a part of a land and people they have helped to build and to defend, to find themselves a part of a minority group whose acquired passive nature keeps them from boldly demanding those rights and privileges which are rightfully theirs? Can it be the result of difference in race, nationality, language, loyalty, or ability?

There is no difference in race. Latin Americans, or so-called "Mexicans," are Caucasian or white. . . . There is no difference in nationality. These "Mexicans" were born and bred in this country and are just as American as Jones or Smith. . . . Difference in language? No, these "Mexicans" speak English. Accented, perhaps, in some cases, but English all over the United States seems to be accented. . . . Difference in loyalty? How can that be when all revere the same stars and stripes, when they don the same service uniforms for the same principles? Difference in intelligence and ability? Impossible. . . .

This condition is not a case of difference; it is a case of ignorance. . . . An ignorance of the cultural contributions of Americans of Latin American descent to the still young American Culture; . . . an ignorance of a sense of appreciation for a long, profitable, and loyal association with a group of Americans whose voice cries out in desperate supplication: "We have proved ourselves true and loyal Americans . . . now give us social, political, and economic equality."

From Charles H. Wesley, "The Negro Has Always Wanted the Four Freedoms," in *What the Negro Wants* (1944)

In 1944, the University of North Carolina Press published *What the Negro Wants*, a book of essays by fourteen prominent black leaders. Virtually every contributor called for the right to vote in the South, the dismantling of segregation, and access to the "American standard of living." Several essays also linked the black struggle for racial justice with movements against European imperialism in Africa and Asia. When he read the manuscript, W. T. Couch, the director of the press, was stunned. "If this is what the Negro wants," he told the book's editor, "nothing could be clearer than what he needs, and needs most urgently, is to revise his wants." In this excerpt, the historian Charles H. Wesley explains that blacks are denied each of the Four Freedoms and also illustrates how the war strengthened black internationalism.

[Negroes] have wanted what other citizens of the United States have wanted. They have wanted freedom and opportunity. They have wanted the pursuit of the life vouchsafed to all citizens of the United States by our own liberty documents. They have wanted freedom of speech, [but] they were supposed to be silently acquiescent in all aspects of their life. . . . They have wanted freedom of religion, for they had been compelled to "steal away to Jesus" . . . in order to worship God as they desired. . . . They have wanted freedom from want. . . . However, the Negro has remained a marginal worker and the competition with white workers has left him in want in many localities of an economically sufficient nation. They have wanted freedom from fear. They have been cowed, browbeaten or beaten, as they have marched through the years of American life. . . .

The Negro wants democracy to begin at home. . . . The future of our democratic life is insecure so long as the hatred, disdain and disparagement of Americans of African ancestry exist. . . .

The Negro wants not only to win the war but also to win the peace. . . . He wants the peace to be free of race and color restrictions, of imperialism and exploitation, and inclusive of the participation of minorities all over the world in their own governments. When it is said that we are fighting for freedom, the Negro asks, "Whose freedom?" Is it the freedom of a peace to exploit, suppress, exclude, debase and restrict colored peoples in India, China, Africa, Malaya in the usual ways? . . . Will Great Britain and the United States specifically omit from the Four Freedoms their minorities and subject peoples? The Negro does not want such a peace.

QUESTIONS

1. *What evidence does the editorial offer that Latinos are deserving of equality?*
2. *Why does Wesley believe that black Americans are denied the Four Freedoms?*
3. *What differences and what commonalities exist between these two claims for greater rights in American society?*

The entrance to a grocery store in Oakland, California, in a photograph by Dorothea Lange in March 1942. The owner, Tatsuro Masuda, a graduate of the University of California, Berkeley, had the sign painted the day after the Japanese attack on Pearl Harbor as an expression of loyalty to the nation. Like other Japanese-Americans, he and his family were interned.

About 70 percent of Japanese-Americans in the continental United States lived in California, where they dominated vegetable farming in the Los Angeles area. One-third were first-generation immigrants, or *issei*, but a substantial majority were *nisei*—American-born, and therefore citizens. Many of the latter spoke only English, had never been to Japan, and had tried to assimilate despite prevailing prejudice. The government bent over backward to include German-Americans and Italian-Americans in the war effort. It ordered the arrest of only a handful of the more than 800,000 German and Italian nationals in the United States when the war began. But it viewed every person of Japanese ethnicity as a potential spy.

Japanese-American Internment

Inspired by exaggerated fears of a Japanese invasion of the West Coast and pressured by whites who saw an opportunity to gain possession of Japanese-American property, the military persuaded FDR to issue Executive Order 9066. Promulgated in February 1942, this ordered the relocation of all persons of Japanese descent from the West Coast. That spring and summer, authorities removed more than 110,000 men, women, and children—nearly two-thirds of them American citizens—to camps far from their homes. The order did not apply to persons of Japanese descent living in Hawaii, where they made up nearly 40 percent of the population. Despite Hawaii's vulnerability, its economy could not function without Japanese-American labor.

Fumiko Hayashida holds her thirteen-month-old daughter while waiting for relocation to an internment camp. Both wear baggage tags, as if they were pieces of luggage. This photo, taken by a journalist for the *Seattle Post-Intelligencer*, came to symbolize the entire internment experience. Ms. Hayashida died in 2014 at the age of 103.

The internees were subjected to a quasi-military discipline in the camps. Living in former horse stables, makeshift shacks, or barracks behind barbed-wire fences, they were awakened for roll call at 6:45 each morning and ate their meals (which rarely involved the Japanese cooking to which they were accustomed) in giant mess halls. Nonetheless, the internees did their best to create an atmosphere of home, decorating their accommodations with pictures, flowers, and curtains, planting vegetable gardens, and setting up activities like sports clubs and art classes for themselves.

Japanese-American internment revealed how easily war can undermine basic freedoms. There were no court hearings, no due process, and no writs of habeas corpus. One searches the wartime record in vain for public protests among non-Japanese against the gravest violation of civil liberties since the end of slavery.

The courts refused to intervene. In 1944, in ***Korematsu v. United States***, the Supreme Court denied the appeal of Fred Korematsu, a Japanese-American citizen who had been arrested for refusing to present

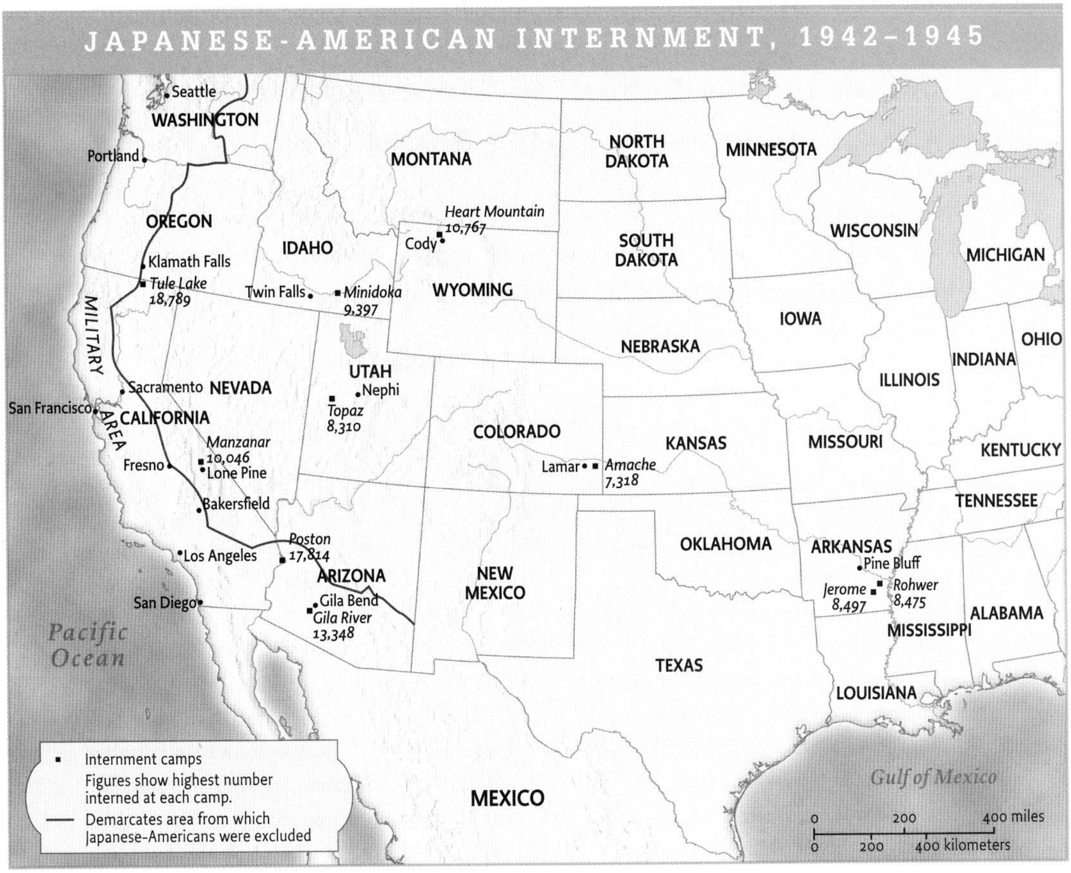

More than 100,000 Japanese-Americans—the majority American citizens—were forcibly moved from their homes to internment camps during World War II.

himself for internment. Speaking for a 6-3 majority, Justice Hugo Black, usually an avid defender of civil liberties, upheld the legality of the internment policy, insisting that an order applying only to persons of Japanese descent was not based on race. In 2018, in a case involving President Trump's order banning travel to the United States by citizens of several Muslim-majority countries, the Supreme Court, as an aside, declared that the *Korematsu* decision was "gravely wrong" and had no legal standing.

Apology and restitution

The government established a loyalty oath program, expecting Japanese-Americans to swear allegiance to the government that had imprisoned them and to enlist in the army. Some young men refused, and about 200 were sent to prison for resisting the draft. But 20,000 Japanese-Americans joined the armed forces from the camps, along with another 13,000 from Hawaii. A long campaign for acknowledgment of the injustice done to Japanese-Americans followed the end of the war. In 1988, Congress apologized for internment and provided $20,000 in compensation to each surviving victim.

WHO IS AN AMERICAN?

From Justice Robert A. Jackson, dissent in *Korematsu v. United States* (1944)

The decision upholding the order interning Japanese-Americans during World War II is one of the most infamous in the Supreme Court's history. Justice Jackson's dissent has often been cited as a powerful warning against government-sponsored racism. In 2018, the Court repudiated the *Korematsu* decision.

Korematsu was born on our soil, of parents born in Japan. The Constitution makes him a citizen of the United States by nativity, and a citizen of California by residence. No claim is made that he is not loyal to this country. . . .

Now, if any fundamental assumption underlies our system, it is that guilt is personal and not inheritable. Even if all of one's antecedents had been convicted of treason, the Constitution forbids its penalties to be visited upon him. . . . But here is an attempt to make an otherwise innocent act a crime merely because this prisoner is the son of parents as to whom he had no choice, and belongs to a race from which there is no way to resign. . . .

In the very nature of things, military decisions are not susceptible of intelligent judicial appraisal. . . . Courts can never have any real alternative to accepting the mere declaration of the authority that issued the order that it was reasonably necessary from a military viewpoint.

Much is said of the danger to liberty from the Army program for deporting and detaining these citizens of Japanese extraction. But a judicial construction of the due process clause that will sustain this order is a far more subtle blow to liberty than the promulgation of the order itself. A military order, however unconstitutional, is not apt to last longer than the military emergency. Even during that period, a succeeding commander may revoke it all. But once a judicial opinion rationalizes such an order to show that it conforms to the Constitution, or rather rationalizes the Constitution to show that the Constitution sanctions such an order, the Court for all time has validated the principle of racial discrimination in criminal procedure and of transplanting American citizens. The principle then lies about like a loaded weapon, ready for the hand of any authority that can bring forward a plausible claim of an urgent need.

QUESTIONS

1. *Why does Justice Jackson believe that even though military authorities have the power to violate constitutional protections in time of war, the courts should not approve their actions?*
2. *What does he mean by likening the Court's decision to "a loaded weapon"?*

Blacks and the War

Although the treatment of Japanese-Americans revealed the stubborn hold of racism in American life, the wartime message of freedom portended a major transformation in the status of blacks. Nazi Germany cited American practices as proof of its own race policies. Washington remained a rigidly segregated city, and the Red Cross refused to mix blood from blacks and whites in its blood banks (thereby, critics charged, in effect accepting Nazi race theories). Charles Drew, the black scientist who pioneered the techniques of storing and shipping blood plasma—a development of immense importance to the treatment of wounded soldiers—protested bitterly against this policy, pointing out that it had no scientific basis.

Segregation during wartime

The war spurred a movement of black population from the rural South to the cities of the North and West that dwarfed the Great Migration of World War I and the 1920s. In the **second Great Migration**, about 700,000 black migrants poured out of the South on what they called "liberty trains," seeking jobs in the industrial heartland. They encountered sometimes violent hostility. In 1943, a fight at a Detroit city park spiraled into a race riot that left thirty-four persons dead, and a "hate strike" of 20,000 workers protested the upgrading of black employees in a plant manufacturing aircraft engines.

Second Great Migration

Blacks and Military Service

When World War II began, the air force and marines had no black members. The army restricted the number of black enlistees and contained only five black officers, three of them chaplains. The navy accepted blacks only as waiters and cooks.

During the war, more than 1 million blacks served in the armed forces. They did so in segregated units, largely confined to construction, transport, and other noncombat tasks. Black soldiers sometimes had to give up their seats on railroad cars to accommodate Nazi prisoners of war.

Segregation in the armed forces

When southern black veterans returned home and sought benefits through the GI Bill, they encountered even more evidence of racial discrimination. On the surface, the GI Bill contained no racial differentiation in offering benefits like health care, college tuition assistance, job training, and loans to start a business or purchase a farm. But local authorities who administered its provisions allowed southern black veterans to use its education benefits only at segregated colleges, limited their job training to unskilled work and low-wage service jobs, and restricted loans for farm purchase to white veterans.

Postwar segregation

Birth of the Civil Rights Movement

The war years witnessed the birth of the modern civil rights movement. Angered by the almost complete exclusion of African-Americans from jobs in the rapidly expanding war industries (of 100,000 aircraft workers in 1940, fewer than 300 were blacks), the black labor leader A. Philip Randolph in July 1941 called for a March on Washington. His demands included access to defense employment, an end to segregation, and a national antilynching law.

Randolph's March on Washington

The prospect of thousands of angry blacks descending on Washington, remarked one official, "scared the government half to death." To persuade Randolph to call off the march, Roosevelt issued Executive Order 8802, which banned discrimination in defense jobs and established a Fair Employment Practices Commission (FEPC) to monitor compliance. The first federal agency since Reconstruction to campaign for equal opportunity for black Americans, the FEPC played an important role in obtaining jobs for black workers in industrial plants and shipyards. By 1944, more than 1 million blacks, 300,000 of them women, held manufacturing jobs. ("My sister always said that Hitler was the one that got us out of the white folks' kitchen," recalled one black woman.)

FEPC

The Double-V

During the war, NAACP membership grew from 50,000 to nearly 500,000. The Congress of Racial Equality (CORE), founded by an interracial group of pacifists in 1942, held sit-ins in northern cities to integrate restaurants and theaters. In February of that year, the *Pittsburgh Courier* coined the phrase that came to symbolize black attitudes during the war—the **double-V**.

CORE

Black servicemen in Brooklyn, New York, flash the "double-V" sign, symbolizing the dual battle against Nazism abroad and racism at home.

Victory over Germany and Japan, it insisted, must be accompanied by victory over segregation at home. Whereas the Roosevelt administration and the white press saw the war as an expression of American ideals, black newspapers pointed to the gap between those ideals and reality.

Surveying wartime public opinion, a political scientist concluded that "symbols of national solidarity" had very different meanings to white and black Americans. To blacks, freedom from fear meant, among other things, an end to lynching, and freedom from want included doing away with "discrimination in getting jobs." If, in whites' eyes, freedom was a "possession to be defended," he observed, to blacks and other racial minorities it remained a "goal to be achieved."

This is the Enemy, a 1942 poster by Victor Ancona and Karl Koehler, suggests a connection between Nazism abroad and lynching at home.

The War and Race

During the war, a broad political coalition centered on the left but reaching well beyond it called for an end to racial inequality in America. The NAACP and American Jewish Congress cooperated closely in advocating laws to ban discrimination in employment and housing. Despite considerable resistance from rank-and-file white workers, CIO unions, especially those with strong left-liberal and communist influence, made significant efforts to organize black workers and win them access to skilled positions.

The new black militancy alarmed southern politicians. The "war emergency," insisted Governor Frank Dixon of Alabama, "should not be used as a pretext to bring about the abolition of the color line." Even as the war gave birth to the modern civil rights movement, it also planted the seeds for the South's "massive resistance" to desegregation during the 1950s.

Although progress was slow, it was measurable. The National War Labor Board banned racial wage differentials. In *Smith v. Allwright* (1944), the Supreme Court outlawed all-white primaries, one of the mechanisms by which southern states deprived blacks of political rights. The government also ordered that soldiers be allowed to vote without paying a poll tax, enabling thousands of black men to cast ballots for the first time. In 1944, the navy began assigning small numbers of black sailors to previously all-white ships. In the final months of the war, it ended segregation altogether, and the army established a few combat units that included black and white soldiers.

A sign displayed opposite a Detroit housing project in 1942 symbolizes one aspect of what Gunnar Myrdal called "the American Dilemma"—the persistence of racism in the midst of a worldwide struggle for freedom.

An American Dilemma

No event reflected the new concern with the status of black Americans more than the publication in 1944 of *An American Dilemma*, a sprawling account of the country's

Paul Robeson, the black actor, singer, and battler for civil rights, leading Oakland dockworkers in singing the national anthem in 1942. World War II gave a significant boost to the vision, shared by Robeson and others on the left, of an America based on genuine equality.

racial past, present, and future written by the Swedish social scientist Gunnar Myrdal. The book offered an uncompromising portrait of how deeply racism was entrenched in law, politics, economics, and social behavior. But Myrdal combined this sobering analysis with admiration for what he called the American Creed—belief in equality, justice, equal opportunity, and freedom. He concluded that "there is bound to be a redefinition of the Negro's status as a result of this War."

Myrdal's notion of a conflict between American values and American racial policies was hardly new—Frederick Douglass and W. E. B. Du Bois had said much the same thing. But in the context of a worldwide struggle against Nazism and rising black demands for equality at home, his book struck a chord. It identified a serious national problem and seemed to offer an almost painless path to peaceful change, in which the federal government would take the lead in outlawing discrimination.

Black Internationalism

A picket line of black workers in Chicago evokes the memory of slavery in protesting low wages in 1941.

In the nineteenth century, black radicals like David Walker and Martin Delany had sought to link the fate of African-Americans with that of peoples of African descent in other parts of the world, especially the Caribbean and Africa. In the first decades of the twentieth century, this kind of international consciousness was reinvigorated. At the home of George Padmore, a West Indian labor organizer and editor living in London, black American leaders like W. E. B. Du Bois and Paul Robeson came into contact with future leaders of African independence movements such as Jomo Kenyatta (Kenya), Kwame Nkrumah (Ghana), and Nnamdi Azikiwe (Nigeria).

Through these gatherings, Du Bois, Robeson, and others developed an outlook that linked the plight of black Americans with that of people of color worldwide. Freeing Africa from colonial rule, they came to believe, would encourage greater equality at home. World War II stimulated among African-Americans an even greater awareness of the links between racism in the United States and colonialism abroad.

THE END OF THE WAR

As 1945 opened, Allied victory was assured. In December 1944, in a desperate gamble, Hitler launched a surprise counterattack in France that pushed Allied forces back fifty miles, creating a large bulge in their lines. The largest single battle ever fought by the U.S. Army, the Battle of the Bulge produced more than 70,000 American casualties. But by early 1945 the assault had failed.

In March, American troops crossed the Rhine River and entered the industrial heartland of Germany. Hitler took his own life, and shortly afterward Soviet forces occupied Berlin. On May 8, 1945, known as **V-E Day** (for victory in Europe), came the formal end to the war against Germany. In the Pacific, American forces moved ever closer to Japan.

V-E Day

"The Most Terrible Weapon"

Franklin D. Roosevelt defeated Republican nominee Thomas E. Dewey, the governor of New York, to win an unprecedented fourth term in 1944. But FDR did not live to see the Allied victory. He succumbed to a stroke on April 12, 1945. To his successor, Harry S. Truman, fell one of the most momentous decisions ever confronted by an American president—whether to use the atomic bomb against Japan. Truman did not know about the bomb until after he became president. Then, Secretary of War Henry L. Stimson informed him that the United States had secretly developed "the most terrible weapon ever known in human history."

Truman and the atomic bomb

The bomb was a practical realization of the theory of relativity, a rethinking of the laws of physics developed early in the twentieth century by the German scientist Albert Einstein. Energy and matter, Einstein showed, were two forms of the same phenomenon. By using certain forms of uranium, or the man-made element plutonium, scientists could create an atomic reaction that transformed part of the mass into energy. This energy could be harnessed to provide a form of controlled power—or it could be unleashed in a tremendous explosion.

Albert Einstein

In 1940, FDR authorized what came to be known as the **Manhattan Project**, a top-secret program in which American scientists developed an atomic bomb during World War II. The weapon was tested successfully in the New Mexico desert in July 1945.

The Manhattan Project

"Fat Man," the atomic bomb dropped on Nagasaki, Japan, on August 9, 1945.

The Dawn of the Atomic Age

On August 6, 1945, an American plane dropped an atomic bomb that detonated over Hiroshima, Japan—a target chosen because almost alone among major Japanese cities, it had not yet suffered damage. In an instant, nearly every building in the city was destroyed. Of the city's population of 280,000 civilians and 40,000 soldiers, approximately 70,000 died immediately. Because atomic bombs release deadly radiation, the death toll kept rising in the months that followed. By the end of the year, it reached at least 140,000. On August 9, the United States exploded a second bomb over Nagasaki, killing 70,000 persons. On the same day, the Soviet Union declared war on Japan. Within a week, Japan surrendered.

A controversial choice

Because of the enormous cost in civilian lives—more than twice America's military fatalities in the entire Pacific war—the use of the bomb remains controversial. An American invasion of Japan, some advisers warned Truman, might cost as many as 250,000 American lives. No such invasion was planned to begin, however, until the following year, and considerable evidence had accumulated that Japan was nearing surrender. Japan's economy had been crippled and its fleet destroyed, and it would

After the dropping of the atomic bomb on Hiroshima, Japan, the federal government restricted the circulation of images of destruction. But soon after the end of the war, it dispatched photographers to compile a Strategic Bombing Survey to assess the bomb's impact. This photograph, which long remained classified, shows the remains of an elementary school.

now have to fight the Soviet Union as well as the United States. Some of the scientists who had worked on the bomb urged Truman to demonstrate its power to international observers. But Truman did not hesitate. The bomb was a weapon, he reasoned, and weapons are created to be used.

The Nature of the War

The war and civilian populations

The dropping of the atomic bombs was the logical culmination of the way World War II had been fought. All wars inflict suffering on noncombatants. But never before had civilian populations been so ruthlessly targeted. Of the estimated 50 million persons who perished during World War II (including 400,000 American soldiers), perhaps 20 million were civilians. Germany had killed millions of members of "inferior races." The Allies carried out deadly air assaults on civilian populations. Early in 1945, the firebombing of Dresden killed some 100,000 people, mostly women, children, and elderly men. On March 9, nearly the same number died in an inferno caused by the bombing of Tokyo.

Hersey's Hiroshima

Four years of war propaganda had dehumanized the Japanese in Americans' eyes, and few persons criticized Truman's decision in 1945. But public doubts began to surface, especially after John Hersey published *Hiroshima* (1946), a graphic account of the horrors suffered by the civilian population. General Dwight D. Eisenhower, who thought the use of the bomb unnecessary, later wrote, "I hated to see our country be the first to use such a weapon."

Planning the Postwar World

The "Big Three" conferences

Even as the war raged, a series of meetings between Allied leaders formulated plans for the postwar world. Churchill, Roosevelt, and Soviet chief Joseph Stalin met at Tehran, Iran, in 1943, and at Yalta, in the southern Soviet Union, early in 1945, to hammer out agreements. The final "Big Three" conference took place at Potsdam, near Berlin, in July 1945. It involved Stalin, Truman, and Churchill (replaced midway in the talks by Clement Attlee, who became prime minister when his Labour Party swept the British elections). At the **Potsdam conference**, the Allied leaders established a military administration for Germany and agreed to place top Nazi leaders on trial for war crimes.

Relations among the three Allies were often uneasy, as each maneuvered to maximize its postwar power. Neither Britain nor the United States trusted Stalin. But since Stalin's troops had won the war on the eastern front, it was difficult to resist his demand that eastern Europe become a Soviet sphere of influence (a region whose governments can be counted on to do a great power's bidding).

The Big Three—Stalin, Roosevelt, and Churchill—at their first meeting, in Tehran, Iran, in 1943, where they discussed the opening of a second front against Germany in western Europe.

Yalta and Bretton Woods

At the **Yalta conference**, Roosevelt and Churchill entered only a mild protest against Soviet plans to retain control of the Baltic states (Estonia, Latvia, and Lithuania) and a large part of eastern Poland, in effect restoring Russia's pre-World War I western borders. Stalin agreed to enter the war against Japan later in 1945 and to allow "free and unfettered elections" in Poland, but he was intent on establishing communism in eastern Europe. Yalta saw the high-water mark of wartime American-Soviet cooperation. But it planted seeds of conflict, since the participants soon disagreed over the fate of eastern Europe.

Tension also existed between Britain and the United States. Churchill rejected American pressure to place India and other British colonies on the road to independence. He concluded private deals with Stalin to divide southern and eastern Europe into British and Soviet spheres of influence.

Shaping the postwar economic order

Britain also resisted, unsuccessfully, American efforts to reshape and dominate the postwar economic order. A meeting of representatives of forty-five nations at Bretton Woods, New Hampshire, in July 1944 replaced the British pound with the dollar as the main currency for international transactions. The **Bretton Woods conference** also created two American-dominated financial institutions. The World Bank would provide money to developing countries and to help rebuild Europe. The International Monetary Fund would work to prevent governments from devaluing their currencies to gain an advantage in international trade, as many had done during the Depression. Both of these institutions, American leaders believed, would encourage free trade and the growth of the world economy, an emphasis that until the presidency of Donald Trump remained central to American foreign policy.

The United Nations

Early in the war, the Allies also agreed to establish a successor to the League of Nations. In a 1944 conference at Dumbarton Oaks, near Washington, D.C., they developed the structure of the **United Nations** (UN).

There would be a General Assembly—essentially a forum for discussion where each member enjoyed an equal voice—and a Security Council responsible for maintaining world peace. Along with six rotating members, the Council would have five permanent ones—Britain, China, France, the Soviet Union, and the United States—each with the power to veto resolutions. In June 1945, representatives of fifty-one countries met in San Francisco to adopt the UN Charter, which outlawed force or the threat of force as a means of settling international disputes. In July, the U.S. Senate endorsed the charter. In contrast to the bitter dispute over membership in the League of Nations after World War I, only two senators voted against joining the UN.

The UN Charter

Peace, but Not Harmony

World power redistributed

World War II produced a radical redistribution of world power. Japan and Germany, the two dominant military powers in their regions before the war, were utterly defeated. Britain and France, though victorious, were substantially weakened. Only the United States and the Soviet Union remained able to project significant influence beyond their national borders.

Overall, however, the United States was clearly the dominant world power. But peace did not usher in an era of international harmony. The Soviet occupation of eastern Europe created a division soon to be solidified in the Cold War. The dropping of the atomic bombs left a worldwide legacy of fear.

The Four Freedoms speech had been intended primarily to highlight the differences between Anglo-American ideals and Nazism. Nonetheless, it had unanticipated consequences. As one of Roosevelt's speechwriters remarked, "when you state a moral principle, you are stuck with it, no matter how many fingers you have kept crossed at the moment." The language with which World War II was fought helped to lay the foundation for postwar ideals of human rights that extend to all mankind.

Postwar ideals of human rights

During the war, Mahatma Gandhi, the Indian nationalist leader, wrote to Roosevelt that the idea "that the Allies are fighting to make the world safe for freedom of the individual and for democracy seems hollow, so long as India, and for that matter, Africa, are exploited by Great Britain, and America has the Negro problem in her own home." Allied victory saved mankind from a living nightmare—a worldwide system of dictatorial rule and slave labor in which peoples deemed inferior suffered the fate of European Jews and the victims of Japanese outrages in Asia. But disputes over the freedom of colonial peoples overseas and non-whites in the United States foretold wars and social upheavals to come.

CHAPTER REVIEW AND ONLINE RESOURCES

REVIEW QUESTIONS

1. *Why did most Americans support isolationism in the 1930s?*
2. *What factors after 1939 led to U.S. involvement in World War II?*
3. *How did government, business, and labor work together to promote wartime production? How did the war affect each group?*
4. *How did different groups understand or experience the Four Freedoms differently?*
5. *Explain how conservatives in Congress and business used the war effort to attack the goals and legacy of the New Deal.*
6. *How did the war alter the lives of women on the home front, and what did different groups think would happen after the war?*
7. *How did a war fought to bring "essential human freedoms" to the world fail to protect the home front liberties of blacks, Indians, Japanese-Americans, and Mexican-Americans?*
8. *Explain how World War II promoted an awareness of the links between racism in the United States and colonialism around the world.*
9. *What was the impact of the GI Bill of Rights on American society, including minorities?*
10. *Describe how the decisions made at the Bretton Woods conference in 1944 created the framework for postwar U.S. economic and foreign policy.*

KEY TERMS

Four Freedoms (p. 671)
Good Neighbor Policy (p. 672)
isolationism (p. 674)
Neutrality Acts (p. 674)
Lend-Lease Act (p. 675)
Axis powers (p. 676)
D-Day (p. 678)
Holocaust (p. 680)
GI Bill of Rights (p. 686)
bracero program (p. 688)
zoot suit riots (p. 688)
Japanese-American internment (p. 692)
Korematsu v. United States (p. 692)
second Great Migration (p. 695)
double-V (p. 696)
V-E Day (p. 699)
Manhattan Project (p. 699)
Potsdam conference (p. 701)
Yalta conference (p. 702)
Bretton Woods conference (p. 702)
United Nations (p. 702)

Go to INQUIZITIVE

To see what you know—and learn what you've missed—with personalized feedback along the way.

Visit the ***Give Me Liberty!* Student Site** for primary source documents and images, interactive maps, author videos featuring Eric Foner, and more.

CHAPTER 23

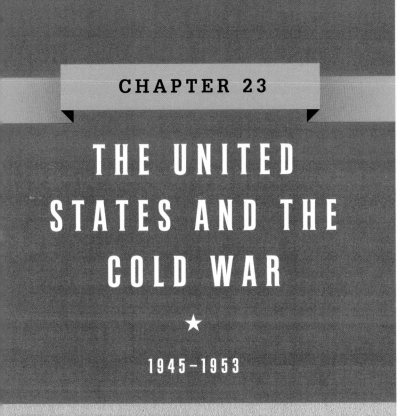

THE UNITED STATES AND THE COLD WAR

★

1945–1953

TREASURE CHEST
S IS THE VOICE OF YOUR COMMUNIST VERNMENT SPEAKING. TODAY, COMMUNIST RCES HAVE COMPLETED THE OCCUPATION YOUR COUNTRY. THE UNITED STATES LONGER EXISTS. IT IS NOW THE UNION SOVIET STATES OF AMERICA! LONG LIVE THE U.S.S.A.!!

1947	Truman Doctrine
	Federal Employee Loyalty program
	Jackie Robinson integrates major league baseball
	Marshall Plan
	Taft-Hartley Act
	Freedom Train exhibition
	House Un-American Activities Committee investigates Hollywood
1948	UN adopts Universal Declaration of Human Rights
	Truman desegregates military
1948–1949	Berlin blockade and airlift
1949	North Atlantic Treaty Organization established
	Soviet Union tests atomic bomb
	People's Republic of China established
1950	McCarthy's Wheeling, W.V., speech
	NSC-68 issued
	McCarran Internal Security Act
1950–1953	Korean War
1953	Julius and Ethel Rosenberg executed for spying
1954	Army-McCarthy hearings
1955	Warsaw Pact organized

The Cold War led to widespread fears of a communist takeover in the United States (a task far beyond the capacity of the minuscule American Communist Party or the Soviet Union). This image is from the first page of *This Godless Communism*, an issue of a comic book series called *Treasure Chest* published from 1946 to 1972. The issue warned of the danger that communists might overthrow the government, and detailed the horrors of life in a communist America, including the arrest and jailing of priests and ministers. It was circulated to parochial schools by the Roman Catholic Church and contained an introduction by J. Edgar Hoover, head of the Federal Bureau of Investigation.

FOCUS QUESTIONS

- *What series of events and ideological conflicts prompted the Cold War?*
- *How did the Cold War reshape ideas of American freedom?*
- *What major domestic policy initiatives did Truman undertake?*
- *What effects did the anticommunism of the Cold War have on American politics and culture?*

On September 16, 1947, the 160th anniversary of the signing of the Constitution, the Freedom Train opened to the public in Philadelphia. A traveling exhibition of 133 historical documents, the train, bedecked in red, white, and blue, soon embarked on a sixteen-month tour that took it to more than 300 American cities. Never before or since have so many cherished pieces of Americana—among them the Mayflower Compact, the Declaration of Independence, and the Gettysburg Address—been assembled in one place.

The idea for the Freedom Train originated in 1946 with the Department of Justice. President Harry S. Truman endorsed it as a way of contrasting American freedom with "the destruction of liberty by the Hitler tyranny." Since direct government funding raised fears of propaganda, however, the administration turned the project over to a nonprofit group, the American Heritage Foundation.

By any measure, the Freedom Train was an enormous success. Behind the scenes, however, the Freedom Train demonstrated that the meaning of freedom remained as controversial as ever.

The liberal staff members at the National Archives who proposed the initial list of documents had included the Wagner Act of 1935, which guaranteed workers the right to form unions, as well as President Roosevelt's Four Freedoms speech of 1941, with its promise to fight "freedom from want." The more conservative American Heritage Foundation removed these documents. They also deleted from the original list the Fourteenth and Fifteenth Amendments, which had established the principle of equal civil and political rights regardless of race after the Civil War. In the end, nothing on the train referred to organized labor or any twentieth-century social legislation. The only documents relating to African-Americans were the Emancipation Proclamation, the Thirteenth Amendment, and a 1776 letter by South Carolina patriot Henry Laurens criticizing slavery.

On the eve of the train's unveiling, the poet Langston Hughes wondered whether there would be "Jim Crow on the Freedom Train." "When it stops in Mississippi," Hughes asked, "will it be made plain / Everybody's got a right to board the Freedom Train?" In fact, with the Truman administration about to make civil rights a major priority, the train's organizers announced that they would not permit segregated viewing. In an unprecedented move, the American Heritage Foundation canceled visits to Memphis, Tennessee, and Birmingham, Alabama, when local authorities insisted on separating visitors by race. The Freedom Train visited forty-seven other southern cities without incident.

Even as the Freedom Train reflected a new sense of national unease about expressions of racial inequality, its journey also revealed the growing impact of the **Cold War**. In the spring of 1947, a few months before the train was dedicated, President Truman committed the United States to the worldwide **containment** of Soviet power and inaugurated a program to root out "disloyal" persons from government employment. The Freedom Train revealed how the Cold War helped to reshape freedom's meaning, identifying it ever more closely with anticommunism, "free enterprise," and the defense of the social and economic status quo.

Visitors viewing historic documents aboard the Freedom Train in 1948.

ORIGINS OF THE COLD WAR

The Two Powers

The United States emerged from World War II as by far the world's greatest power. The United States accounted for half the world's manufacturing capacity. It alone possessed the atomic bomb. American leaders believed that the nation's security depended on the security of Europe and Asia, and that American prosperity required global economic reconstruction.

The only power that in any way could rival the United States was the Soviet Union, whose armies now occupied most of eastern Europe, including the eastern part of Germany. Its crucial role in defeating Hitler and its claim that communism had wrested a vast backward nation into modernity gave the Soviet Union considerable prestige in Europe and among colonial peoples struggling for independence. Having lost more than 20 million dead and suffered immense devastation during the war, however, Stalin's government was in no position to embark on new military adventures. But the Soviet government remained determined to establish a sphere of influence in eastern Europe, through which Germany had twice invaded Russia in the past thirty years.

The Roots of Containment

Alliance unraveled

In retrospect, it seems all but inevitable that the two major powers to emerge from the war would come into conflict. Born of a common foe rather than common long-term interests, values, or history, the wartime alliance between the United States and the Soviet Union began to unravel almost from the day that peace was declared.

The Cold War in the Middle East

The first confrontation of the Cold War took place in the Middle East. At the end of World War II, Soviet troops had occupied parts of northern Iran, hoping to pressure that country to grant it access to its rich oil fields. Under British and American pressure, Stalin quickly withdrew Soviet forces. At the same time, however, the Soviets installed procommunist governments in Poland, Romania, and Bulgaria, a step they claimed was no different from American domination of Latin America or Britain's determination to maintain its own empire.

George Kennan

Early in 1946, in his famous **Long Telegram** from Moscow, American diplomat George Kennan advised the Truman administration that the Soviets could not be dealt with as a normal government. Communist ideology drove them to try to expand their power throughout the world, he claimed, and only the United States had the ability to stop them. His telegram laid the foundation for what became known as the policy of "containment," according to which the United States committed itself to preventing any further expansion of Soviet power.

Churchill's speech

Shortly afterward, in a speech at Fulton, Missouri, Britain's former wartime prime minister Winston Churchill declared that an **iron curtain** had descended across Europe, partitioning the free West from the communist East. But not until March 1947, in a speech announcing what came to be known as the **Truman Doctrine**, did the president officially embrace the Cold War as the foundation of American foreign policy and describe it as a worldwide struggle over the future of freedom.

The Truman Doctrine

Harry S. Truman never expected to become president. When he assumed the presidency after Roosevelt's death in April 1945, Truman found himself forced to decide foreign policy debates in which he had previously played virtually no role.

Convinced that Stalin could not be trusted and that the United States had a responsibility to provide leadership to a world that he tended to view in stark, black-and-white terms, Truman soon determined to put the policy of containment into effect. The immediate occasion for this epochal decision came early in 1947 when Britain informed the United States that because its economy had been shattered by the war, it had no choice but to end military and financial aid to two crucial governments—Greece, a monarchy threatened by a communist-led rebellion, and Turkey, from which the Soviets were demanding joint control of the straits linking the Black Sea and the Mediterranean. Britain asked the United States to fill the vacuum.

Britain's step back

The Soviet Union had little to do with the internal problems of Greece and Turkey, where opposition to corrupt, undemocratic regimes was largely homegrown. But the two countries occupied strategically important sites at the gateway to southeastern Europe and the oil-rich Middle East. Truman had been told by Senate leader Arthur Vandenberg that the only way a

President Harry S. Truman delivering his Truman Doctrine speech before Congress on March 12, 1947.

reluctant public and Congress would support aid to these governments was for the president to "scare hell" out of the American people. Truman rolled out the heaviest weapon in his rhetorical arsenal—the defense of freedom. As the leader of the "free world," the United States must now shoulder the responsibility of supporting "freedom-loving peoples" wherever communism threatened them. Twenty-four times in the eighteen-minute speech, Truman used the words "free" and "freedom."

Truman succeeded in persuading both Republicans and Democrats in Congress to support his policy, beginning a long period of bipartisan support for the containment of communism. As Truman's speech to Congress suggested, the Cold War was, in part, an ideological conflict. Both sides claimed to be promoting freedom and social justice while defending their own security, and each offered its social system as a model the rest of the world should follow.

American assistance to anticommunist regimes

Truman's rhetoric suggested that the United States had assumed a permanent global responsibility. The speech set a precedent for American assistance to anticommunist regimes throughout the world, no matter how undemocratic, and for the creation of a set of global military alliances directed against the Soviet Union. There soon followed the creation of new national security bodies immune from democratic oversight, such as the Atomic Energy Commission, National Security Council, and Central Intelligence Agency (CIA), the last established in 1947 to gather intelligence and conduct secret military operations abroad.

The Marshall Plan

Postwar foreign aid to Europe

The threat of American military action overseas formed only one pillar of containment. Secretary of State George C. Marshall spelled out the other in a speech at Harvard University in June 1947. Marshall pledged the United States to contribute billions of dollars to finance the economic recovery of Europe. Two years after the end of the war, much of the continent still lay in ruins with widespread food shortages and rampant inflation. The economic chaos had strengthened the communist parties of France and Italy. American policymakers feared that these countries might fall into the Soviet orbit.

The **Marshall Plan** offered a positive vision to go along with containment. Avoiding Truman's language of a world divided between free and unfree blocs, Marshall insisted, "Our policy is directed not against any

Bales of American cotton in a warehouse at the French port of Le Havre, 1949. Part of the Marshall Plan aid program, the shipment helped to revive the French cotton textile industry.

country or doctrine, but against hunger, poverty, desperation, and chaos."

The Marshall Plan proved to be one of the most successful foreign aid programs in history. By 1950, western European production exceeded pre-war levels and the region was poised to follow the United States down the road to a mass-consumption society. Because the Soviet Union refused to participate, fearing American control over the economies of eastern Europe, the Marshall Plan further solidified the division of the continent. At the same time, the United States worked out with twenty-three other Western nations the General Agreement on Tariffs and Trade (GATT), which proposed to stimulate freer trade among the participants, creating an enormous market for American goods and investment.

The Reconstruction of Japan

A democratic constitution

Under the guidance of General Douglas MacArthur, the "supreme commander" in Japan until 1948, that country adopted a new, democratic constitution. Thanks to American insistence, and against the wishes of most Japanese leaders, the new constitution gave women the right to vote for the first time in Japan's history. Furthermore, Article 9 of the new constitution stated that Japan would renounce forever the policy of war and armed aggression, and would maintain only a modest self-defense force.

Japan's recovery

The United States also oversaw the economic reconstruction of Japan. Initially, the United States proposed to dissolve Japan's giant industrial corporations, which had contributed so much to the nation's war effort. But this plan was abandoned in 1948 in favor of an effort to rebuild Japan's industrial base as a bastion of anticommunist strength in Asia. By the 1950s, thanks to American economic assistance, the adoption of new technologies, and low spending on the military, Japan's economic recovery was in full swing.

The Berlin Blockade and NATO

Meanwhile, the Cold War intensified and, despite the Marshall Plan, increasingly took a militaristic turn. At the end of World War II, each

Occupation of Germany

of the four victorious powers assumed control of a section of occupied Germany, and of Berlin, located deep in the Soviet zone. In June 1948, the United States, Britain, and France introduced a separate currency in their zones, a prelude to the creation of a new West German government that would be aligned with them in the Cold War. In response, the Soviets cut off road and rail traffic from the American, British, and French zones of occupied Germany to Berlin.

Airlift

An eleven-month airlift followed, with Western planes supplying fuel and food to their zones of the city. When Stalin lifted the blockade in May 1949, the Truman administration had won a major victory. Soon, two new nations emerged, East and West Germany, each allied with a side in the Cold War. Berlin itself remained divided. Not until 1991 would Germany be reunified.

Also in 1949, the Soviet Union tested its first atomic bomb, ending the American monopoly of that weapon. In the same year, the United States, Canada, and ten western European nations established the **North Atlantic Treaty Organization** (NATO), pledging mutual defense against any future Soviet attack. Soon, West Germany became a crucial part of NATO. The North Atlantic Treaty was the first long-term military alliance between the United States and Europe since the Treaty of Amity and Commerce with France during the American Revolution. The Soviets formalized their own eastern European alliance, the Warsaw Pact, in 1955.

The Growing Communist Challenge

In 1949, communists led by Mao Zedong emerged victorious in the long Chinese civil war—a serious setback for the policy of containment. Assailed by Republicans for having "lost" China (which, of course, the United States never "had" in the first place), the Truman administration refused to recognize the new government—the People's Republic of China—and blocked it from occupying China's seat at the United Nations. Until the 1970s, the United States insisted that the ousted regime, which had been forced into exile on the island of Taiwan, remained the legitimate government of China.

In the wake of Soviet-American confrontations in Europe, the communist victory in China, and Soviet success in developing an atomic bomb, the National Security Council approved a call for a permanent military buildup to enable the United States to pursue a global crusade against communism. Known as **NSC-68**, this 1950 manifesto described the Cold War as an epic struggle between "the idea of freedom" and the "idea of slavery under the grim oligarchy of the Kremlin."

A poster issued by the Defense Department's Office of Public Information in 1950 seeks to drum up popular support for the Korean War. An armed, determined Uncle Sam stands before an idealized rural landscape, an embodiment of "all the things we have" that needed to be defended by war, even though by this time most Americans lived in cities or suburbs.

COLD WAR EUROPE, 1956

The division of Europe between communist and noncommunist nations, solidified by the early 1950s, would last for nearly forty years.

The Korean War

In the shadow of the Eiffel Tower in Paris in 1955, NATO delegates vote to admit West Germany to membership, symbolizing the political and military integration of western Europe.

Initially, American postwar policy focused on Europe. But it was in Asia that the Cold War suddenly turned hot. Occupied by Japan during World War II, Korea had been divided in 1945 into Soviet and American zones. These zones soon evolved into two governments: communist North Korea and anticommunist South Korea, undemocratic but aligned with the United States. In June 1950, the North Korean army invaded the south, hoping to reunify the country under communist control. North Korean soldiers soon occupied most of the peninsula. The Truman administration persuaded the United Nations Security Council to authorize the use of force to repel the invasion. (The Soviets, who could have vetoed the resolution, were boycotting Security Council meetings to protest the refusal to seat communist China.)

American troops did the bulk of the fighting on this first battlefield of the Cold War. In September 1950, General Douglas MacArthur launched a daring counterattack at Inchon, behind North Korean lines. MacArthur's army soon occupied most of North Korea. Truman now hoped to unite Korea under a pro-American government. But in October 1950, when UN forces neared the Chinese border, hundreds of thousands of Chinese troops intervened, driving them back in bloody fighting. MacArthur demanded the right to push north again and possibly even invade China and use nuclear weapons against it. But Truman, fearing an all-out war on the Asian mainland, refused. MacArthur did not fully accept the principle of civilian control of the military. When he went public with criticism of the president, Truman removed him from command. The war then settled into a stalemate around the thirty-eighth parallel, the original boundary between the two Koreas. Not until 1953 was an armistice agreed to, essentially restoring the prewar status quo. There has never been a formal peace treaty ending the **Korean War**.

A photograph of a street battle in Seoul, South Korea, during the Korean War illustrates the ferocity of the fighting.

More than 33,000 Americans died in Korea. The Asian death toll reached an estimated 1 million Korean soldiers and 2 million civilians, along with hundreds of

THE KOREAN WAR, 1950–1953

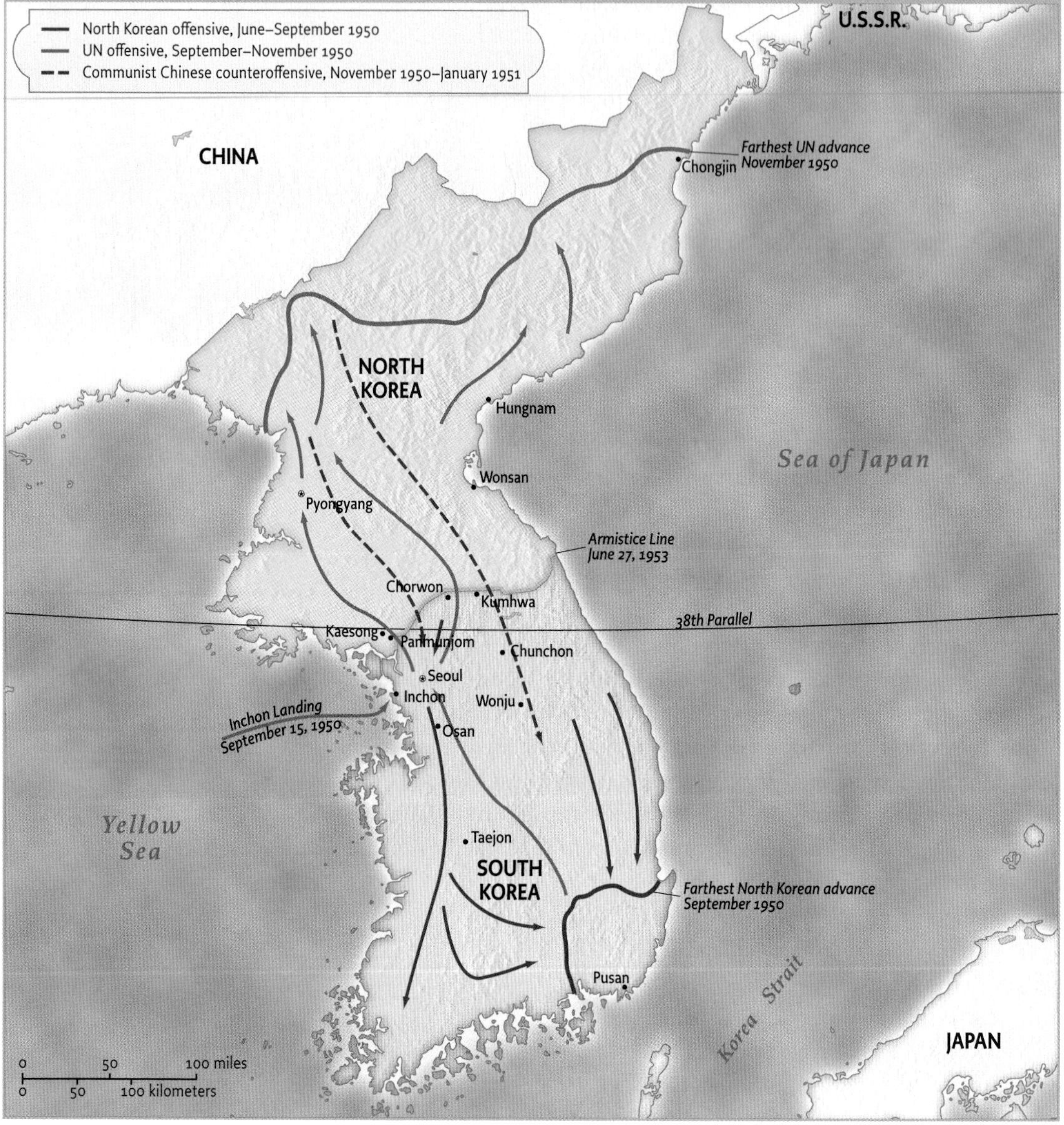

As this map indicates, when General Douglas MacArthur launched his surprise landing at Inchon, North Korean forces controlled nearly the entire Korean peninsula.

thousands of Chinese troops. Korea made it clear that the Cold War, which began in Europe, had become a global conflict.

Cold War Critics

Stalin's brutal dictatorship

In the Soviet Union, Stalin had consolidated a brutal dictatorship that jailed or murdered millions of Soviet citizens. With its one-party rule, stringent state control of the arts and intellectual life, and government-controlled economy, the Soviet Union presented a stark opposite of democracy and "free enterprise." As a number of contemporary critics, few of them sympathetic to Soviet communism, pointed out, however, casting the Cold War in terms of a worldwide battle between freedom and slavery had unfortunate consequences.

Walter Lippmann

In a penetrating critique of Truman's policies, Walter Lippmann, one of the nation's most prominent journalists, objected to turning foreign policy into an "ideological crusade." To view every challenge to the status quo as part of a contest with the Soviet Union, Lippmann correctly predicted, would require the United States to recruit and subsidize an "array of satellites, clients, dependents and puppets." It would have to intervene continuously in the affairs of nations whose political problems did not arise from Moscow and could not be easily understood in terms of the battle between freedom and slavery. World War II, he went on, had shaken the foundations of European empires. In the tide of revolutionary nationalism now sweeping the world, communists were certain to play an important role.

Imperialism and Decolonization

Awareness of imperialism

World War II had increased American awareness of the problem of imperialism. Many movements for colonial independence borrowed the language of the American Declaration of Independence in demanding the right to self-government. Liberal Democrats and black leaders urged the Truman administration to take the lead in promoting worldwide **decolonization**, insisting that a Free World worthy of the name should not include colonies and empires. But as the Cold War developed, the United States backed away from pressuring its European allies to grant self-government to colonies like French Indochina, the Dutch East Indies, and British possessions like the Gold Coast and Nigeria in Africa and Malaya in Asia.

The Free World

No matter how repressive to its own people, if a nation joined the worldwide anticommunist alliance led by the United States, it was counted as a member of the Free World. The Republic of South Africa, for example, was considered a part of the Free World even though its white minority had deprived the black population of nearly all their rights.

THE COLD WAR AND THE IDEA OF FREEDOM

Among other things, the Cold War was a battle, in a popular phrase of the 1950s, for the "hearts and minds" of people throughout the world. During the 1950s, freedom became an inescapable theme of academic research, popular journalism, mass culture, and official pronouncements.

One of the more unusual Cold War battlefields involved American culture. National security agencies encouraged Hollywood to produce anticommunist movies, such as *The Red Menace* (1949) and *I Married a Communist* (1950), and urged that film scripts be changed to remove references to less-than-praiseworthy aspects of American history, such as Indian removal and racial discrimination.

A poster for *The Red Menace*, one of numerous anticommunist films produced by Hollywood during the 1950s.

To counteract the widespread European view of the United States as a cultural backwater, the CIA secretly funded an array of overseas publications, conferences, publishing houses, concerts, and art exhibits. And to try to improve the international image of American race relations, the government sent jazz musicians and other black performers abroad, especially to Africa and Asia.

Freedom and Totalitarianism

Along with freedom, the Cold War's other great mobilizing concept was **totalitarianism**. The term originated in Europe between the world wars to describe fascist Italy and Nazi Germany—aggressive, ideologically driven states that sought to subdue all of civil society, including churches, unions, and other voluntary associations, to their control. By the 1950s, the term had become shorthand for describing those on the Soviet side in the Cold War. As the eventual collapse of communist governments in eastern Europe and the Soviet Union would demonstrate, the idea of totalitarianism greatly exaggerated the totality of government control of private life and thought in these countries.

Just as the conflict over slavery redefined American freedom in the nineteenth century and the confrontation with the Nazis shaped understandings of freedom during World War II, the Cold War reshaped them once again. Whatever Moscow stood for was by definition the opposite of freedom, including anything to which the word "socialized" could be attached. In the largest public relations campaign in American history, the American Medical Association raised the specter of "socialized medicine" to defeat Truman's proposal for national health insurance.

The Rise of Human Rights

Mark Rothko was a painter whose works seemed to exemplify American artists' freedom from the constraints of European traditions. The painting has no subject other than color itself, with the different shades of red meant to evoke what Rothko called "the basic human emotions—tragedy, ecstasy, and doom."

The Cold War also affected the emerging concept of human rights. The atrocities committed during World War II, as well as the global language of the Four Freedoms, forcefully raised the issue of human rights in the postwar world. After the war, the victorious Allies put numerous German officials on trial before special courts at Nuremberg for crimes against humanity. For the first time, individuals were held directly accountable to the international community for violations of human rights. The trials resulted in prison terms for many Nazi officials and the execution of ten leaders.

In 1948, the UN General Assembly approved the Universal Declaration of Human Rights, drafted by a committee chaired by Eleanor Roosevelt. It identified a broad range of rights to be enjoyed by people everywhere, including freedom of speech, religious toleration, and protection against arbitrary government, as well as social and economic entitlements like the right to an adequate standard of living and access to housing, education, and medical care. The document had no enforcement mechanism. Some considered it an exercise in empty rhetoric. But the core principle—that a nation's treatment of its own citizens should be subject to outside evaluation—slowly became part of the language in which freedom was discussed.

Ambiguities of Human Rights

Human rights in world affairs

One reason for the lack of an enforcement mechanism in the Universal Declaration of Human Rights was that both the United States and the Soviet Union refused to accept outside interference in their internal affairs. In 1947, the NAACP did file a petition with the United Nations asking it to investigate racism in the United States as a violation of human rights. But the UN decided that it lacked jurisdiction. Nonetheless, since the end of World War II, the enjoyment of human rights has increasingly taken its place in definitions of freedom across the globe.

After the Cold War ended, the idea of human rights would play an increasingly prominent role in world affairs. But during the 1950s, Cold War imperatives shaped the concept. Neither the United States nor the Soviet Union could resist emphasizing certain provisions of the Universal Declaration while ignoring others. The Soviets claimed to provide all citizens with social and economic rights, but violated democratic rights and civil liberties. Many Americans condemned these nonpolitical rights as a path to socialism.

THE TRUMAN PRESIDENCY

The Fair Deal

Economic transition

With the end of World War II, President Truman's first domestic task was to preside over the transition from a wartime to a peacetime economy. More than 12 million men remained in uniform in August 1945. Most wanted nothing more than to return home to their families. Some returning soldiers found the adjustment to civilian life difficult. The divorce rate in 1945 rose to double its prewar level. Others took advantage of the GI Bill of Rights (discussed in the previous chapter) to obtain home mortgages, set up small businesses, and embark on college educations. The majority of returning soldiers entered the labor force—one reason why more than 2 million women workers lost their jobs. The government abolished wartime agencies that regulated industrial production and labor relations, and it dismantled wartime price controls, leading to a sharp rise in prices.

Raising the standard of living

In the immediate aftermath of World War II, President Truman, backed by party liberals and organized labor, moved to revive the stalled momentum of the New Deal. Truman's program, which he announced in September 1945 and would later call the **Fair Deal**, focused on improving the social safety net and raising the standard of living of ordinary Americans. He called on Congress to increase the minimum wage, enact a program of national health insurance, and expand public housing, Social Security, and aid to education.

The Postwar Strike Wave

A few of the numerous World War II veterans who attended college after the war, thanks to the GI Bill.

In 1946, a new wave of labor militancy swept the country. The AFL and CIO launched **Operation Dixie**, a campaign to bring unionization to the South and, by so doing, shatter the hold of anti-labor conservatives on the region's politics. More than 200 labor organizers entered the region, seeking support especially in the southern textile industry, the steel industry in the Birmingham region, and agriculture. As inflation soared following the removal of price controls, the resulting drop in workers' real income sparked the largest strike wave in American history. Nearly 5 million workers—including those in the steel, auto, coal, and other key industries—walked off their jobs, demanding wage increases. The strike of

750,000 steelworkers represented the largest single walkout in American history to that date.

An NAACP youth march against racial segregation in Houston, Texas, in 1947 illustrates the civil rights upsurge of the years immediately following the end of World War II.

The Republican Resurgence

In the congressional elections of 1946, large numbers of middle-class voters, alarmed by the labor turmoil, voted Republican. For the first time since the 1920s, Republicans swept to control of both houses of Congress. Meanwhile, in the face of vigorous opposition from southern employers and public officials and the reluctance of many white workers to join interracial labor unions, Operation Dixie failed to unionize the South or dent the political control of conservative Democrats in the region. The election of 1946 ensured that a conservative coalition of Republicans and southern Democrats would continue to dominate Congress.

Congress turned aside Truman's Fair Deal program. It enacted tax cuts for wealthy Americans and, over the president's veto, in 1947 passed the **Taft-Hartley Act**, which sought to reverse some of the gains made by organized labor in the past decade. The measure authorized the president to suspend strikes by ordering an eighty-day "cooling-off period," and it banned sympathy strikes and secondary boycotts (labor actions directed not at an employer but at those who did business with him). It outlawed the closed shop, which required a worker to be a union member when taking up a job, and authorized states to pass "right-to-work" laws, prohibiting other forms of compulsory union membership. It also forced union officials to swear that they were not communists. Over time, as population and capital investment shifted to states with "right-to-work" laws like Texas, Florida, and North Carolina, Taft-Hartley contributed to the decline of organized labor's share of the nation's workforce.

Jackie Robinson sliding into third base, 1949.

Postwar Civil Rights

During his first term, Truman reached out in unprecedented ways to the nation's black community. In the years immediately following World War II, the status of black Americans enjoyed a prominence in national affairs unmatched since Reconstruction.

Part of a series of giant murals painted between 1941 and 1948 for the lobby of the Rincon Center (formerly a post office, now a shopping mall in San Francisco), this work by the artist Anton Refregier links the Four Freedoms of World War II to a multicultural vision of American society. (In Norman Rockwell's celebrated paintings, shown in Chapter 22, nearly all the figures depicted are white.)

Between 1945 and 1951, eleven states from New York to New Mexico established fair employment practices commissions, and numerous cities passed laws against discrimination in access to jobs and public accommodations. A broad civil rights coalition involving labor, religious groups, and black organizations supported these measures. By 1952, 20 percent of black southerners were registered to vote, nearly a sevenfold increase since 1940. (Most of the gains took place in the Upper South—in Alabama and Mississippi, the heartland of white supremacy, the numbers barely budged.) Also in 1952, for the first time since record keeping began seventy years earlier, no lynchings took place in the United States. In 1946, the Superman radio show devoted several episodes to the man of steel fighting the Ku Klux Klan, a sign of changing race relations in the wake of World War II.

In another indication that race relations were in flux, the Brooklyn Dodgers in 1947 challenged the long-standing exclusion of black players from major league baseball by adding Jackie Robinson to their team. Robinson, who possessed both remarkable athletic ability and a passion for equality, had been tried and acquitted for insubordination in 1944 when he refused to move to the back of a bus at Fort Hood, Texas, while serving in the army. But he promised Dodger owner Branch Rickey that he would not retaliate when subjected to racist taunts by opposing fans and players. His dignity in the face of constant verbal abuse won Robinson nationwide respect, and his baseball prowess earned him the Rookie of the Year award. His success opened the door to the integration of baseball and led to the demise of the Negro Leagues, to which black players had previously been confined.

To Secure These Rights

In October 1947, a Commission on Civil Rights appointed by the president issued *To Secure These Rights*, one of the most devastating indictments ever published of racial inequality in America. It called on the federal government to assume the responsibility for abolishing segregation and ensuring equal treatment in housing, employment, education, and the criminal justice system.

In February 1948, Truman presented an ambitious civil rights program to Congress, calling for a permanent federal civil rights commission, national laws against lynching and the poll tax, and action to ensure equal access to jobs and education. Congress, as Truman anticipated, approved none of his proposals. But in July 1948, just as the presidential campaign was getting under way, Truman issued an executive order desegregating the armed forces. The armed services became the first large institution in American life to promote racial integration actively and to attempt to root out long-standing racist practices. The Korean War would be the first American conflict fought by an integrated army since the War of Independence.

Desegregating the armed forces

The Democratic platform of 1948 was the most progressive in the party's history. Led by Hubert Humphrey, the young mayor of Minneapolis, party liberals overcame southern resistance and added a strong civil rights plank to the platform.

The Dixiecrat and Wallace Revolts

"I say the time has come," Humphrey told the Democratic national convention, "to walk out of the shadow of states' rights and into the sunlight of human rights." Whereupon numerous southern delegates—dubbed **Dixiecrats** by the press—walked out of the gathering. They soon formed the States' Rights Democratic Party and nominated for president Governor Strom Thurmond of South Carolina. His platform called for the "complete segregation of the races," and his campaign drew most of its support from those alarmed by Truman's civil rights initiatives.

Also in 1948, a group of left-wing critics of Truman's foreign policy formed the Progressive Party and nominated former vice president Henry A. Wallace for president. Wallace advocated an expansion of social welfare programs at home and denounced racial segregation even more vigorously than Truman. When he campaigned in the South, angry white crowds attacked him. But his real difference with the president concerned the Cold War. Wallace called for international control of nuclear

Blacks, led by A. Philip Randolph (*left*), picketing at the 1948 Democratic national convention. The delegates' adoption of a strong civil rights plank led representatives of several southern states to withdraw and nominate their own candidate for president, Strom Thurmond.

THE PRESIDENTIAL ELECTION OF 1948

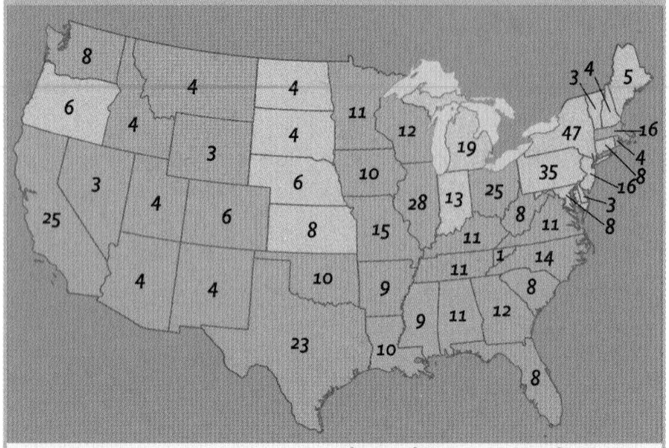

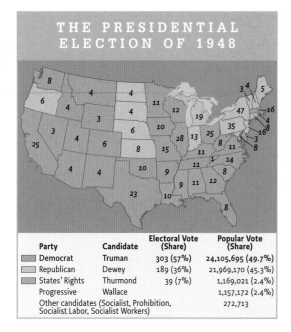

Party	Candidate	Electoral Vote (Share)	Popular Vote (Share)
Democrat	Truman	303 (57%)	24,105,695 (49.7%)
Republican	Dewey	189 (36%)	21,969,170 (45.3%)
States' Rights	Thurmond	39 (7%)	1,169,021 (2.4%)
Progressive	Wallace		1,157,172 (2.4%)
Other candidates (Socialist, Prohibition, Socialist Labor, Socialist Workers)			272,713

weapons and a renewed effort to develop a relationship with the Soviet Union based on economic co-operation rather than military confrontation. The influence of the now much-reduced Communist Party in Wallace's campaign led to an exodus of New Deal liberals and severe attacks on his candidacy. A vote for Wallace, Truman declared, was in effect a vote for Stalin.

Wallace threatened to draw votes from Truman on the left, and Thurmond to undermine the president's support in the South, where whites had voted solidly for the Democrats throughout the twentieth century. But Truman's main opponent, fortunately for the president, was the colorless Republican Thomas A. Dewey. Certain of victory and an ineffective speaker and campaigner, Dewey seemed unwilling to commit himself on controversial issues. Truman, by contrast, ran an aggressive campaign. He crisscrossed the country by train, delivering fiery attacks on the Republican-controlled "do-nothing Congress."

Virtually every public-opinion poll and newspaper report predicted a Dewey victory. Truman's success—by 303 to 189 electoral votes—represented one of the greatest upsets in American political history. For the first time since 1868, blacks (in the North, where they enjoyed the right to vote) played a decisive role in the outcome.

Thurmond carried four Lower South states, demonstrating that the race issue, couched in terms of individual freedom, had the potential to lead traditionally Democratic white voters to desert their party. In retrospect, the States' Rights campaign offered a preview of the political transformation that by the end of the twentieth century would leave every southern state in the Republican column. As for Wallace, he suffered the humiliation of polling fewer popular votes than Thurmond.

THE ANTICOMMUNIST CRUSADE

For nearly half a century, the Cold War profoundly affected American life. There would be no return to "normalcy" as after World War I. The military-industrial establishment created during World War II would become permanent, not temporary. National security became the stated reason for a host of government projects, including aid to higher education and the building of a new national highway system (justified by the need to

National security and government projects

A postcard promoting tourism to Las Vegas highlights as one attraction the city's proximity to a nuclear test site. Witnessing nearby atomic explosions became a popular pastime in the city. The government failed to issue warnings of the dangers of nuclear fallout, and only years later did it admit that many onlookers had contracted diseases from radiation.

speed the evacuation of major cities in the event of nuclear war). The Cold War encouraged a culture of secrecy and dishonesty. American nuclear tests, conducted on Pacific islands and in Nevada, exposed thousands of civilians to radiation that caused cancer and birth defects.

Cold War military spending helped to fuel economic growth and support scientific research that not only perfected weaponry but also led to improved aircraft, computers, medicines, and other products with a large impact on civilian life. The Cold War reshaped immigration policy, with refugees from communism being allowed to enter the United States regardless of national-origin quotas. The international embarrassment caused by American racial policies contributed to the dismantling of segregation. And like other wars, the Cold War encouraged the drawing of a sharp line between patriotic Americans and those accused of being disloyal. At precisely the moment when the United States celebrated freedom as the foundation of American life, the right to dissent came under attack.

Loyalty, Disloyalty, and American Identity

The fear inspired by communism became a catalyst for reconsidering American identity in the mid-twentieth century. This led to some paradoxical outcomes. In public opinion polls, many Americans expressed devotion to civil liberties while also favoring depriving communists and other nonconformists of their jobs or even citizenship. Accusations of communist activity were often framed as assertions that an individual had betrayed or abandoned his or her American identity. Much of the clampdown on communism fell disproportionately against people already seen as outside the American mainstream, including Jews and other immigrants and gay persons. As the historian Henry Steele Commager argued in a 1947 magazine article, the anticommunist crusade promoted a new definition of American loyalty and identity: conformity. Anything other than "uncritical and unquestioning acceptance of

In 1952, a quota was established allowing some Japanese immigrants to become American citizens. Here, in the following year, hundreds take part in a naturalization ceremony in Seattle.

A group of Mexican immigrants who lacked work permits being taken from police headquarters in San Fernando, California, for deportation to Mexico in 1954 during "Operation Wetback."

America as it is," he wrote, could now be labeled unpatriotic.

The relationship between communism and citizenship was codified in the **McCarran-Walter Act** of 1952, which made it possible to revoke the citizenship and deport an American born abroad if he or she refused to testify about "subversive" activity, joined a subversive organization, or voted in a foreign election. The first major piece of immigration legislation since 1924, it passed over Truman's veto. Truman had appointed a Commission on Immigration, whose report, *Whom Shall We Welcome?*, called for replacing the quotas based on national origins with a more flexible system taking into account family reunion, labor needs, and political asylum. But the McCarran-Walter Act kept the quotas in place. They would remain the basis of immigration law until 1965.

The renewed fear of immigrants sparked by the anticommunist crusade went far beyond communists. In 1954, the federal government launched a program that employed the military to invade Mexican-American neighborhoods and round up and deport undocumented aliens. It was called Operation Wetback, utilizing an insulting term sometimes directed at Mexican immigrants. Within a year, some 1 million Mexicans had been deported.

An immigration official questions a farm worker in the fields near San Ysidro, California, in 1954.

Dividing the world between liberty and slavery automatically made those who could be linked to communism enemies of freedom. Although the assault on civil liberties came to be known as **McCarthyism**, it began before Senator Joseph R. McCarthy of Wisconsin burst onto the national scene in 1950. In 1947, less than two weeks after announcing the Truman Doctrine, the president established a loyalty review system that required government employees to demonstrate their patriotism without being allowed to confront accusers or, in some cases, knowing the charges against them. Along with persons suspected of disloyalty, the new national security system also targeted gay men and lesbians who worked for the government. Gay men were deemed particularly susceptible to blackmail by Soviet agents as well as supposedly lacking the "manly" qualities needed to maintain the country's resolve in the fight against communism. The loyalty program failed to uncover any cases of espionage. But the federal government dismissed several hundred gay men and lesbians from their jobs.

From Oscar Handlin, "The Immigration Fight Has Only Begun" (1952)

Published shortly after passage of the McCarran-Walter Act, an article by Harvard historian Oscar Handlin, himself the son of Russian-Jewish immigrants, became a rallying cry for those attacking the law and demanding a new immigration policy. As was common at the time, Handlin's language had an unspoken gender dimension, using "man" to encompass both men and women.

Not since the Alien and Sedition Acts of 1798 has an act of Congress come so close to subverting the underlying assumption on which the conception of citizenship in the United States rests: the assumption that there are no degrees of citizenship, that all Americans are completely equal in rights whatever their place of birth.... Retaining the rigid national quotas, it [also] curtails severely the civil liberties of immigrants and resident aliens....

The [immigration] laws are bad because they rest on the racist assumption that mankind is divided into fixed breeds, biologically and culturally separated from each other, and because, within that framework, they assume that Americans are Anglo-Saxons by origin and ought to remain so. To all other peoples, the laws say that the United States ranks them in terms of their racial proximity to our own "superior" stock; and upon the many, many millions of Americans not descended from the Anglo-Saxons, the laws cast a distinct imputation of inferiority.

More recent defenders of the quota system, unwilling to endorse the open racism that gave it birth, have urged that the differentiations it establishes be regarded as cultural rather than racial. The South Italian or the Syrian, it is argued, is culturally less capable of adjusting to American life than the Englishman or the German.... There is no evidence to support that contention. . . . Allowed to settle in peace, every variety of man has been able to make a place for himself in American life, to his own profit and to the enrichment of the society that has accepted him. The dreaded "riff-raff" of 1910—Greeks, Armenians, Magyars, Slovaks, Polish Jews—are the respected parents of respected citizens today....

The Americans of the 19th century had confidence enough in their own society and in their own institutions to believe any man could become an American. More than ever do we now need to reaffirm that faith.

QUESTIONS

1. *Why does Handlin believe that basic premises of the immigration quota system have been disproven?*
2. *How does he invoke history to bolster his arguments?*

Movie stars, led by actors Humphrey Bogart and Lauren Bacall, on their way to attend the 1947 hearings of the House Un-American Activities Committee, in a demonstration of support for those called to testify about alleged communist influence in Hollywood.

Also in 1947, the House Un-American Activities Committee (HUAC) launched a series of hearings about communist influence in Hollywood. Calling well-known screenwriters, directors, and actors to appear before the committee ensured a wave of national publicity, which its members relished. Celebrities like producer Walt Disney and actors Gary Cooper and Ronald Reagan testified that the movie industry harbored numerous communists. But ten "unfriendly witnesses" refused to answer the committee's questions about their political beliefs or to "name names" (identify individual communists) on the grounds that the hearings violated the First Amendment's guarantees of freedom of speech and political association. The committee charged the **Hollywood Ten** with contempt of Congress, and they served jail terms of six months to a year. Hollywood studios blacklisted them (denied them employment), along with more than 200 others who were accused of communist sympathies or who refused to name names.

The Spy Trials

A series of highly publicized legal cases followed, which fueled the growing anticommunist hysteria. Whittaker Chambers, an editor at *Time* magazine, testified before HUAC that during the 1930s, Alger Hiss, a high-ranking State Department official, had given him secret government documents to pass to agents of the Soviet Union. Hiss vehemently denied the charge, but a jury convicted him of perjury and he served five years in prison. A young congressman from California and a member of HUAC, Richard Nixon, achieved national prominence because of his dogged pursuit of Hiss.

The trial of Julius and Ethel Rosenberg

The most sensational trial involved Julius and Ethel Rosenberg, a working-class Jewish communist couple from New York City (quite different from Hiss, a member of the eastern Protestant "establishment"). In 1951, a jury convicted the Rosenbergs of conspiracy to pass secrets concerning the atomic bomb to Soviet agents during World War II (when the Soviets were American allies). Their chief accuser was David Greenglass, Ethel Rosenberg's brother, who had worked at the Los Alamos nuclear research center.

Senator Joseph R. McCarthy at the Army-McCarthy hearings of 1954. McCarthy points to a map detailing charges about the alleged extent of the communist menace, while the army's lawyer, Joseph Welch, listens in disgust.

The case against Julius Rosenberg rested on highly secret documents that could not be revealed in court. (When they were released many years later, the scientific information they contained seemed too crude to justify the government's charge that Julius had passed along the "secret of the atomic bomb," although he may have helped the Soviets speed up their atomic program.) The government had almost no evidence against Ethel Rosenberg, and Greenglass later admitted that he had lied in some of his testimony about her. Indeed, prosecutors seem to have indicted her in the hope of pressuring Julius to confess and implicate others. But in the atmosphere of hysteria, their conviction was certain. Even though they had been convicted of conspiracy, a far weaker charge than spying or treason, Judge Irving Kaufman called their crime "worse than murder." Despite an international outcry, their death sentences were carried out in 1953.

McCarthy and McCarthyism

In this atmosphere, a little-known senator from Wisconsin suddenly emerged as the chief national pursuer of subversives and gave a new name to the anticommunist crusade. Joseph R. McCarthy had won election to the Senate in 1946, partly on the basis of a fictional war record (he falsely claimed to have flown combat missions in the Pacific). In a speech in Wheeling, West Virginia, in February 1950, McCarthy announced that he had a list of 205 communists working for the State Department. The charge was preposterous, the numbers constantly changed, and McCarthy never identified a single person guilty of genuine disloyalty. But with a genius for self-promotion, McCarthy used the Senate subcommittee he chaired to hold hearings and level wild charges against numerous individuals as well as the Defense Department, the Voice of America, and other government agencies.

Few political figures had the courage to speak up against McCarthy's crusade. One who did was Margaret Chase Smith of Maine, the Senate's only woman member. On June 1, 1950, soon after McCarthy's Wheeling speech, Smith addressed the Senate with what she called a "declaration of conscience." She did not name McCarthy, but few could mistake the target of her condemnation of a "campaign of hate and character assassination." Most of her colleagues, however, remained silent.

"Fire!" The cartoonist Herbert Block, known as "Herblock," offered this comment in 1949 on the danger to American freedom posed by the anticommunist crusade.

VOICES OF FREEDOM

From Joseph R. McCarthy, Speech at Wheeling (1950)

During the 1950s, the demagogic pursuit of supposed communists in government and other places of influence became known as McCarthyism, after Senator Joseph R. McCarthy, Republican of Wisconsin. In a speech in West Virginia in February 1950, McCarthy claimed to have a list of 205 communists working for the State Department. When he entered the speech into the Congressional Record a few days later, he reduced the number to fifty-seven. He never named any of them.

Today we are engaged in a final, all-out battle between communistic atheism and Christianity. The modern champions of communism have selected this as the time. And, ladies and gentlemen, the chips are down—they are truly down.

Six years ago, at the time of the first conference to map out peace . . . there was within the Soviet orbit 180 million people. Lined up on the antitotalitarian side there were in the world at that time roughly 1.625 billion people. Today, only six years later, there are 800 million people under the absolute domination of Soviet Russia—an increase of over 400 percent. On our side, the figure has shrunk to around 500 million. . . .

The reason why we find ourselves in a position of impotency is not because our only powerful, potential enemy has sent men to invade our shores, but rather because of the traitorous actions of those who have been treated so well by this nation. It has not been the less fortunate or members of minority groups who have been selling this nation out, but rather those who have had all the benefits that the wealthiest nation on earth has had to offer—the finest homes, the finest college education, and the finest jobs in government we can give.

This is glaringly true in the State Department. There the bright young men who are born with silver spoons in their mouths are the ones who have been worst. . . . In my opinion the State Department, which is one of the most important government departments, is thoroughly infested with communists.

I have in my hand 57 cases of individuals who would appear to be either card carrying members or certainly loyal to the Communist Party, but who nevertheless are still helping to shape our foreign policy. . . . One thing to remember in discussing the communists in our government is that we are not dealing with spies who get 30 pieces of silver to steal the blueprints of new weapons. We are dealing with a far more sinister type of activity because it permits the enemy to guide and shape our policy.

From Margaret Chase Smith, Speech in the Senate (1950)

Most of McCarthy's colleagues were cowed by his tactics. One who was not was Margaret Chase Smith of Maine, the Senate's only female member. On June 1, she delivered a brief speech, along with a Declaration of Conscience, signed by six other Republican senators.

The United States Senate has long enjoyed worldwide respect as the greatest deliberative body in the world. But recently that deliberative character has too often been debased to the level of a forum of hate and character assassination sheltered by the shield of congressional immunity. . . .

I think that it is high time for the United States Senate and its members to do some soul searching—for us to weigh our consciences—on the manner in which we are performing our duty to the people of America—on the manner in which we are using or abusing our individual powers and privileges. . . . I think that it is high time that we remembered; that the Constitution, as amended, speaks not only of the freedom of speech but also of trial by jury instead of trial by accusation.

Those of us who shout the loudest about Americanism in making character assassinations are all too frequently those who, by our own words and acts, ignore some of the basic principles of Americanism—

The right to criticize; The right to hold unpopular beliefs; The right to protest; The right of independent thought.

The exercise of these rights should not cost one single American citizen his reputation or his right to a livelihood nor should he be in danger of losing his reputation or livelihood merely because he happens to know some one who holds unpopular beliefs. Who of us doesn't? Otherwise none of us could call our souls our own. Otherwise thought control would have set in.

The American people are sick and tired of being afraid to speak their minds lest they be politically smeared as "Communists" or "Fascists" by their opponents. Freedom of speech is not what it used to be in America. It has been so abused by some that it is not exercised by others. The American people are sick and tired of seeing innocent people smeared and guilty people whitewashed.

The nation sorely needs a Republican victory. But I don't want to see the Republican Party ride to political victory on the Four Horsemen of Calumny—Fear, Ignorance, Bigotry and Smear. . . .

As a United States Senator, I am not proud of the way in which the Senate has been made a publicity platform for irresponsible sensationalism.

QUESTIONS

1. *What kind of social resentments are evident in McCarthy's speech?*
2. *What does Smith believe is the essence of freedom of speech?*
3. *What do these documents suggest about how the Cold War affected discussions of freedom in the early 1950s?*

McCarthy's downfall came in 1954, when a Senate committee investigated his charges that the army had harbored and "coddled" communists. The nationally televised **Army-McCarthy hearings** revealed McCarthy as a bully who browbeat witnesses and made sweeping accusations with no basis in fact. The dramatic high point came when McCarthy attacked the loyalty of a young attorney in the firm of Joseph Welch, the army's chief lawyer. "Let us not assassinate this lad further," Welch pleaded. "You have done enough. Have you no sense of decency, sir?" After the hearings ended, the Republican-controlled Senate voted to "condemn" McCarthy for his behavior. But the word "McCarthyism" had entered the political vocabulary, a shorthand for character assassination, guilt by association, and abuse of power in the name of anticommunism.

"McCarthyism" enters the lexicon

An Atmosphere of Fear

State and local actions

States created their own committees, modeled on HUAC, that investigated suspected communists and other dissenters. States and localities required loyalty oaths of teachers, pharmacists, and members of other professions, and they banned communists from fishing, holding a driver's license, and, in Indiana, working as professional wrestlers. Throughout the country in the late 1940s and 1950s, those who failed to testify about their past and present political beliefs and to inform on possible communists frequently lost their jobs.

Local anticommunist groups forced public libraries to remove from their shelves "un-American" books like the tales of Robin Hood, who took from the rich to give to the poor. Universities refused to allow left-wing speakers to appear on campus and fired teachers who refused to sign loyalty oaths or to testify against others.

The Uses of Anticommunism

There undoubtedly were Soviet spies in the United States. Yet the tiny U.S. Communist Party hardly posed a threat to American security. And the vast majority of those jailed or deprived of their livelihoods during the McCarthy era were guilty of nothing more than holding unpopular beliefs and engaging in lawful political activities.

Anticommunist groups and goals

Anticommunism had many faces and purposes. A popular mass movement, it grew especially strong among ethnic groups like Polish-Americans, with roots in eastern European countries now dominated by the Soviet Union, and among American Catholics in general, who resented and feared communists' hostility to religion. Government agencies like the Federal Bureau of Investigation (FBI) used anticommunism to expand their power. Under director J. Edgar Hoover, the FBI developed files on thousands of American citizens, including political dissenters, gay men and lesbians, and others, most of whom had no connection to communism. For business, anticommunism became part of a campaign to identify labor unions and government intervention in the economy with socialism. White supremacists employed anticommunism as a weapon against black civil rights. Upholders of sexual morality and traditional gender roles raised the cry of subversion against feminists and gay persons, both supposedly responsible for eroding the country's fighting spirit.

Anticommunist Politics

At its height, from the late 1940s to around 1960, the anticommunist crusade powerfully structured American politics and culture. After launching the government's loyalty program in 1947, Truman had become increasingly alarmed at the excesses of the anticommunist crusade. He vetoed the McCarran Internal Security Act of 1950, which required "subversive" groups to register with the government, allowed the denial of passports to their members, and authorized their deportation or detention on presidential order. But Congress quickly gave the measure the two-thirds majority necessary for it to become law.

McCarran Internal Security Act of 1950

Truman did secure passage of a 1950 law that added previously excluded self-employed and domestic workers to Social Security. Otherwise, however, the idea of expanding the New Deal faded. In its place, private welfare arrangements proliferated. The labor contracts of unionized workers established health insurance plans, automatic cost-of-living wage increases, paid vacations, and pension plans that supplemented Social Security. Western European governments provided these benefits to all citizens. In the United States, union members in major industries enjoyed them, but not the nonunionized majority of the population, a situation that created increasing inequality among laboring Americans.

The privatization of social benefits

Organized labor emerged as a major supporter of the foreign policy of the Cold War. Internal battles over the role of communists and their allies led to the purging of some of the most militant union leaders, often the ones most committed to advancing equal rights to women and racial minorities in the workplace.

Purging militant union leaders

Cold War Civil Rights

The civil rights movement also underwent a transformation. Although a few prominent black leaders, notably the singer and actor Paul Robeson and the veteran crusader for equality W. E. B. Du Bois, became outspoken

Black organizations and the Cold War

critics of the Cold War, most felt they had no choice but to go along. The NAACP purged communists from local branches. When the government deprived Robeson of his passport and indicted Du Bois for failing to register as an agent of the Soviet Union, few prominent Americans, white or black, protested. (The charge against Du Bois was so absurd that even at the height of McCarthyism, the judge dismissed it.)

American image abroad

Black organizations embraced the language of the Cold War and used it for their own purposes. They insisted that by damaging the American image abroad, racial inequality played into the Russians' hands. Thus, they helped to cement Cold War ideology as the foundation of the political culture, while complicating the idea of American freedom.

President Truman, as noted above, had called for greater attention to civil rights in part to improve the American image abroad. All in all, however, the height of the Cold War was an unfavorable time to raise questions about the imperfections of American society. In 1947, two months after the Truman Doctrine speech, Undersecretary of State Dean Acheson delivered a major address defending the president's pledge to aid "free peoples" seeking to preserve their "democratic institutions." Acheson chose as his audience the Delta Council, an organization of Mississippi planters, bankers, and merchants. He seemed unaware that to make the case for the Cold War, he had ventured into what one historian has called the "American Siberia," a place of grinding poverty whose black population (70 percent of the total) enjoyed neither genuine freedom nor democracy. Most of the Delta's citizens were denied the very liberties supposedly endangered by communism.

The waning civil rights impulse

By 1948, the Truman administration's civil rights flurry had subsided. In 1952, the Democrats showed how quickly the issue had faded by nominating for president Adlai Stevenson of Illinois, a candidate with little interest in civil rights, with southern segregationist John Sparkman as his running mate.

Time would reveal that the waning of the civil rights impulse was only temporary. Yet it came at a crucial moment—the late 1940s and early 1950s, when the United States experienced the greatest economic boom in its history. The rise of an "affluent society" transformed American life, opening new opportunities for tens of millions of white Americans in rapidly expanding suburbs. But it left blacks trapped in the declining rural areas of the South and urban ghettos of the North. The contrast between new opportunities and widespread prosperity for whites and continued discrimination for blacks would soon inspire a civil rights revolution and, with it, yet another redefinition of American freedom.

Rising affluence

CHAPTER REVIEW AND ONLINE RESOURCES

REVIEW QUESTIONS

1. *What major ideological conflicts, security interests, and events brought about the Cold War?*
2. *President Truman referred to the Truman Doctrine and the Marshall Plan as "two halves of the same walnut." Explain the similarities and differences between these two aspects of containment.*
3. *How did the tendency of both the United States and the Soviet Union to see all international events through the lens of the Cold War lessen each country's ability to understand what was happening in various countries around the world?*
4. *Why did the United States not support movements for colonial independence around the world?*
5. *How did the government attempt to shape public opinion during the Cold War?*
6. *Explain the differences between the United States' and the Soviet Union's application of the UN Universal Declaration of Human Rights.*
7. *How did the anticommunist crusade affect organized labor in the postwar period?*
8. *What accounts for the Republican resurgence in these years?*
9. *What were the major components of Truman's Fair Deal? Which ones were implemented, and which ones were not?*
10. *How did the Cold War affect civil liberties in the United States?*
11. *How did the McCarran-Walter Act codify the relationship between communism and citizenship? Why did the clampdown on communism fall disproportionately on those regarded as outside the American mainstream?*

KEY TERMS

Cold War (p. 707)
containment (p. 707)
Long Telegram (p. 708)
iron curtain (p. 708)
Truman Doctrine (p. 708)
Marshall Plan (p. 709)
North Atlantic Treaty Organization (p. 711)
NSC-68 (p. 711)
Korean War (p. 713)
decolonization (p. 715)
totalitarianism (p. 716)
Fair Deal (p. 718)
Operation Dixie (p. 718)
Taft-Hartley Act (p. 719)
Dixiecrats (p. 721)
McCarran-Walter Act (p. 724)
McCarthyism (p. 724)
Hollywood Ten (p. 726)
Army-McCarthy hearings (p. 730)

Go to INQUIZITIVE

To see what you know—and learn what you've missed—with personalized feedback along the way.

Visit the ***Give Me Liberty!* Student Site** for primary source documents and images, interactive maps, author videos featuring Eric Foner, and more.

1946	*Mendez v. Westminster*
1947	Levittown development starts
1950	David Riesman's *The Lonely Crowd*
1952	United States detonates first hydrogen bomb
1953	Soviet Union detonates hydrogen bomb
1954	*Brown v. Board of Education*
	CIA-led Guatemalan coup
	Geneva Accords for Vietnam
1955	AFL and CIO merge
	Allen Ginsberg's *Howl*
1955–1956	Montgomery bus boycott
1956	"Southern Manifesto"
	Start of interstate highway system
1957	Southern Christian Leadership Conference organized
	Integration of Little Rock's Central High School
	Sputnik launched
1958	National Defense Education Act
1959	Nixon-Khrushchev "kitchen debate"
1960	John F. Kennedy elected president

CHAPTER 24

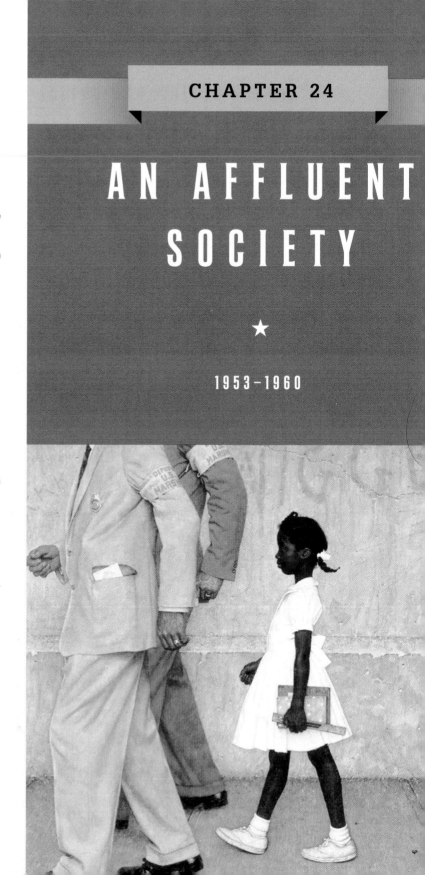

AN AFFLUENT SOCIETY

★

1953–1960

The Problem We All Live With. This 1964 painting by Norman Rockwell depicts federal marshals escorting six-year-old Ruby Bridges to kindergarten in New Orleans in 1960 in accordance with a court order to integrate the city's schools. Rockwell, intent on focusing on the child, presents the mob of angry onlookers only through their graffiti and tomatoes thrown against the wall, and does not show the faces of the marshals. Because of the decision to send her to the formerly white school, Bridges's father lost his job, and her grandparents, sharecroppers in Mississippi, were evicted from their land. In 2001, President Bill Clinton presented her with the Presidential Citizens Medal.

In 1958, during a "thaw" in the Cold War, the United States and the Soviet Union agreed to exchange national exhibitions in order to allow citizens of each "superpower" to become acquainted with life in the other. The Soviet Exhibition, unveiled in New York City in June 1959, featured factory machinery, scientific advances, and other illustrations of how communism had modernized a backward country. The following month, the American National Exhibition opened in Moscow. A showcase of consumer goods and leisure equipment, complete with stereo sets, a movie theater, home appliances, and twenty-two different cars, the exhibit, *Newsweek* observed, hoped to demonstrate the superiority of "modern capitalism with its ideology of political and economic freedom." Yet the exhibit's real message was not freedom but consumption—or, to be more precise, the equating of the two. Vice President Richard Nixon opened the exhibit with an address entitled "What Freedom Means to Us." He spoke of the "extraordinarily high standard of living" in the United States, with its 56 million cars and 50 million television sets.

The Moscow exhibition became the site of a classic Cold War confrontation over the meaning of freedom—the "kitchen debate" between Nixon and Soviet premier Nikita Khrushchev. Nixon and Khrushchev engaged in unscripted debate, first in the kitchen of a model suburban ranch house, then in a futuristic "miracle kitchen" complete with a mobile robot that swept the floors. Supposedly the home of an average steelworker, the ranch house represented, Nixon declared, the mass enjoyment of American freedom within a suburban setting—freedom of choice among products, colors, styles, and prices. It also implied a

FOCUS QUESTIONS

- *What were the main characteristics of the affluent society of the 1950s?*
- *How were the 1950s a period of consensus in both domestic policies and foreign affairs?*
- *What were the major thrusts of the civil rights movement in this period?*
- *What was the significance of the presidential election of 1960?*

Vice President Richard Nixon, with hands folded, and Soviet premier Nikita Khrushchev during the "kitchen debate," a discussion, among other things, of the meaning of freedom, which took place in 1959 at the American National Exposition in Moscow. Khrushchev makes a point while a woman demonstrates a washing machine.

particular role for women. Throughout his exchanges with Khrushchev, Nixon used the words "women" and "housewives" interchangeably. His stance reflected the triumph during the 1950s of a conception of freedom centered on economic abundance and consumer choice within the context of traditional family life—a vision that seemed to offer far more opportunities for the "pursuit of happiness" to men than to women.

THE GOLDEN AGE

The end of World War II was followed by what one scholar has called the "golden age" of capitalism, a period of economic expansion, stable prices, low unemployment, and rising standards of living that continued until 1973. Between 1946 and 1960, the American gross national product more than doubled. Much of the benefit flowed to ordinary citizens in rising wages. In every measurable way—diet, housing, income, education, recreation—most Americans lived better than their parents and grandparents had. The official poverty rate, 30 percent of all families in 1950, had declined to 22 percent a decade later (still, to be sure, representing more than one in five Americans).

Economic growth

Numerous innovations came into widespread use in these years, transforming Americans' daily lives. They included television, home air-conditioning, automatic dishwashers, inexpensive long-distance telephone calls, and jet air travel.

Between 1950 and 1973, the average real wages of manufacturing workers doubled. Wages rose faster for low-income than high-income Americans, lessening economic inequality. The reduction of income inequality stemmed from many causes, among them the federal government's progressive income tax policy, according to which wealthy Americans paid a far higher rate of taxation than others. During the 1950s, 1960s, and 1970s, the tax rate for the richest Americans never fell below 70 percent. (Today, it is 43 percent, although because of numerous tax loopholes for the wealthy, few actually pay that rate.) At

FIGURE 24.1 Real Gross Domestic Product per Capita, 1790–2014

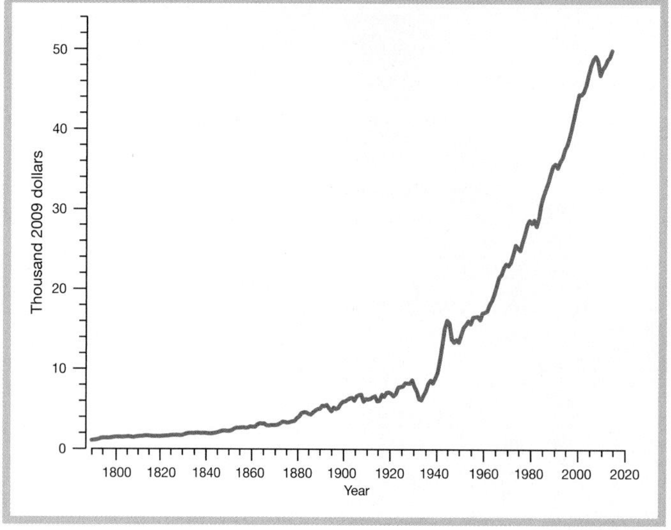

the time, widespread affluence and the narrowing gap between rich and poor seemed to have become a permanent feature of American society, a model for other countries to follow. History would show that this was, in fact, an exceptional moment, made possible by government policies, a strong union movement, and the country's global economic dominance in the wake of World War II. When the long postwar boom ended in 1973, it would be succeeded by an even longer period of stagnant incomes for most Americans and increasing inequality.

A Changing Economy

Like other wars, the Cold War fueled U.S. industrial production and promoted a redistribution of the nation's population and economic resources. The West, especially the Seattle area, southern California, and the Rocky Mountain states, benefited enormously from government contracts for aircraft, guided missiles, and radar systems. The South became the home of numerous military bases and government-funded shipyards.

Industrial strength

In retrospect, the 1950s appear as the last decade of the industrial age in the United States. Since then, the American economy has shifted rapidly toward services, education, information, finance, and entertainment, while employment in manufacturing has declined. Unions' very success in raising wages inspired employers to mechanize more and more elements of manufacturing in order to reduce labor costs. In 1956, for the first time in American history, white-collar workers outnumbered blue-collar factory and manual laborers.

The decade witnessed an acceleration of the transformation of southern life that had begun during World War II. New tractors and harvesting machinery and a continuing shift from cotton production to less labor-intensive soybean and poultry raising reduced the need for farm workers. More than 3 million black and white hired hands and sharecroppers migrated out of the region. The large corporate farms of California, worked by Latino and Filipino migrant laborers, poured forth an endless supply of fruits and vegetables for the domestic and world markets. Items like oranges and orange juice, once luxuries, became an essential part of the American diet.

Corporate farms

A Suburban Nation

The main engines of economic growth during the 1950s, however, were residential construction and spending on consumer goods. The postwar baby boom (discussed later) and the shift of population from cities to suburbs created an enormous demand for housing, television sets, home appliances, and cars.

Consumer demand

THE INTERSTATE HIGHWAY SYSTEM

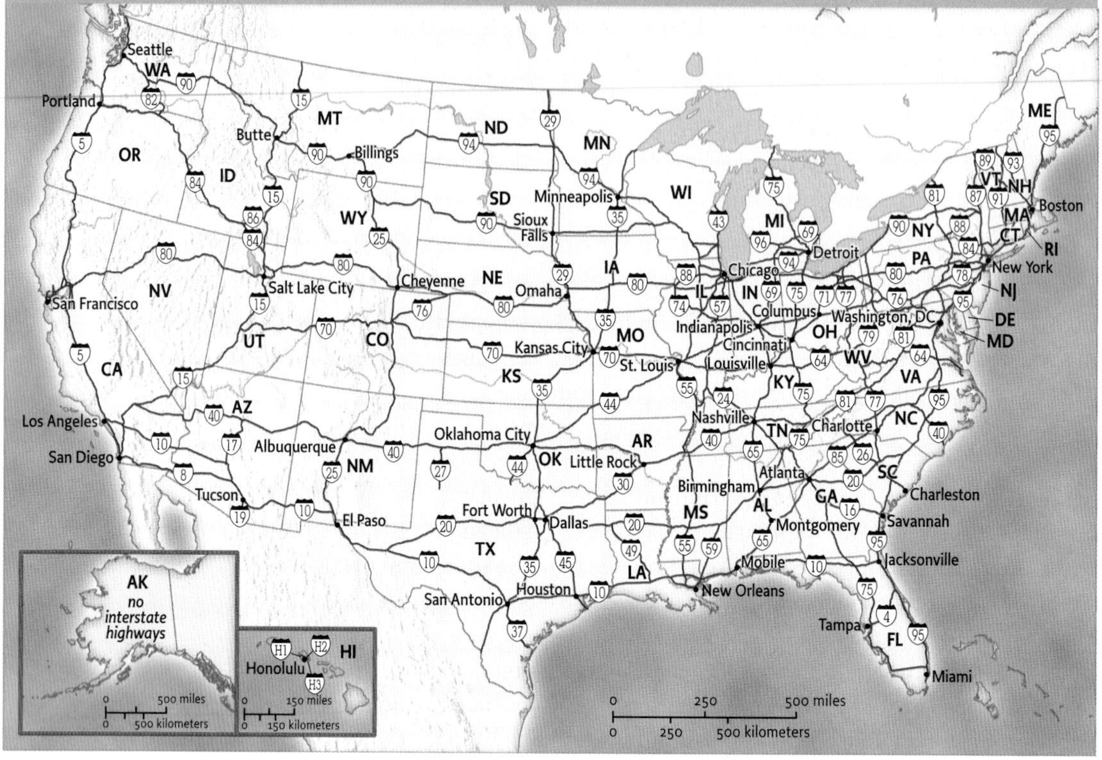

Begun in 1956 and completed in 1993, the interstate highway system dramatically altered the American landscape and Americans' daily lives. It made possible more rapid travel by car and stimulated the growth of suburbs along its many routes.

During the 1950s, the number of houses in the United States doubled, nearly all of them built in the suburbs that sprang up across the landscape. William and Alfred Levitt, who shortly after the war built the first **Levittown** on 1,200 acres of potato fields on Long Island near New York City, became the most famous suburban developers. Levittown's more than 10,000 houses were assembled quickly from prefabricated parts and priced well within the reach of most Americans. Levittown was soon home to 40,000 people. At the same time, suburbs required a new form of shopping center—the mall—to which people drove in their cars.

Suburbs and the automobile

The automobile, the pivot on which suburban life turned, transformed the nation's daily life, just as the interstate highway system (discussed later) transformed Americans' travel habits, making possible long-distance vacationing by car and commuting to work from ever-increasing distances. The result was an altered American landscape, leading to the construction of motels, drive-in movie theaters, and roadside eating establishments. The first McDonald's fast food restaurant opened in Illinois in 1954.

McDonald's

A portrait of affluence: In this photograph by Alex Henderson, Steve Czekalinski, an employee of the DuPont Corporation, poses with his family and the food they consumed in a single year, 1951. The family spent $1,300 (around $12,000 in today's money) on food, including 699 bottles of milk, 578 pounds of meat, and 131 dozen eggs. Nowhere else in the world was food so available and inexpensive.

Within ten years, having been franchised by the California businessman Ray Kroc, approximately 700 McDonald's stands had been built, which had sold over 400 million hamburgers. The car symbolized the identification of freedom with individual mobility and private choice. Americans could imagine themselves as modern versions of western pioneers, able to leave behind urban crowds and workplace pressures for the "open road."

The Growth of the West

The modern West emerged in the postwar years. Unlike the 1930s, when most migrants to the West came from the South and the Dust Bowl states, all parts of the country now contributed to the region's growth. Federal spending on dams, highways, and military installations helped to fuel the flow of people. So did the pleasant climate of many parts of the region, and the diffusion of air-conditioning in warmer places such as Arizona and southern California. The rapid expansion of oil production (a result of the tremendous increase in automobile ownership) led to the explosive growth of urban centers connected to the oil industry such as Denver, Dallas, and Houston.

Indeed, it was California that became the most prominent symbol of the postwar suburban boom. Between World War II and 1975, more than 30 million Americans moved west of the

Ernst Haas's 1969 photograph of Albuquerque, New Mexico, could have been taken in any one of scores of American communities. As cities spread out, "strips," consisting of motels, gas stations, and nationally franchised businesses, became common. Meanwhile, older downtown business sections stagnated.

A family watching television, photographed by Jack Gould in 1948. Television quickly surpassed movies and live theater as the country's major form of entertainment.

Mississippi River. In 1963, California surpassed New York to become the nation's most populous state.

"Centerless" western cities like Houston, Phoenix, and Los Angeles differed greatly from traditional urban centers in the East. Rather than consisting of downtown business districts linked to residential neighborhoods by public transportation, western cities were decentralized clusters of single-family homes and businesses united by a web of highway. Life centered around the car; people drove to and from work and did their shopping at malls reachable only by driving. The spread of suburban homes created millions of new lawns. Today, more land is cultivated in grass than any agricultural crop in the United States.

The TV World

TV journalism and entertainment

Thanks to television, images of middle-class life and advertisements for consumer goods blanketed the country. By the end of the 1950s, nearly nine of ten American families owned a TV set. Television replaced newspapers as the most common source of information about public events, and TV watching became the nation's leading leisure activity. Television changed Americans' eating habits (the frozen TV dinner, heated and eaten while diners watched a program, went on sale in 1954).

With a few exceptions, like the Army-McCarthy hearings mentioned in the previous chapter, TV avoided controversy and projected a bland image of middle-class life. The dominant programs were quiz shows, westerns, and comedies set in suburban homes, like *Leave It to Beaver* and *The Adventures of Ozzie and Harriet*.

FIGURE 24.2 Average Daily Television Viewing, 1950–1970

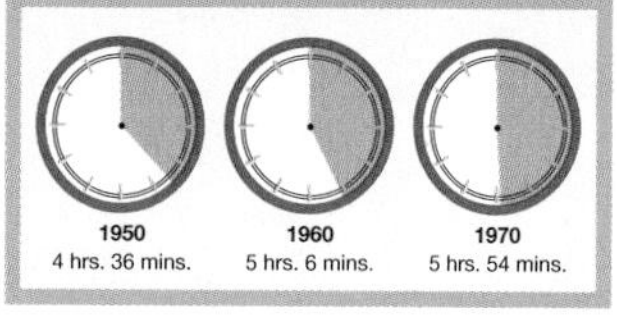

Women at Work and at Home

The emergence of suburbia placed pressure on the family—and especially on women—to live up to freedom's promise. After a sharp postwar drop in female employment, the number of women at work soon began to rise. By 1955, it exceeded the level during World War II. But the nature and aims of women's work had changed. The modern woman worked part-time to help support the family's middle-class lifestyle, not to help pull it out of poverty or to pursue personal fulfillment or an independent career.

Working women in 1960 earned, on average, only 60 percent of the income of men.

Despite the increasing numbers of wage-earning women, the suburban family's breadwinner was assumed to be male, while the wife remained at home. Films, TV shows, and advertisements portrayed marriage as the most important goal of American women. And during the 1950s, men and women married younger (at an average age of twenty-two for men and twenty for women), divorced less frequently than in the past, and had more children (3.2 per family). A **baby boom** that lasted into the mid-1960s followed the end of the war. At a time of low immigration, the American population rose by nearly 30 million (almost 20 percent) during the 1950s.

Like other forms of dissent, feminism seemed to have disappeared from American life or was widely dismissed as evidence of mental disorder. Prominent psychologists insisted that the unhappiness of individual women or even the desire to work for wages stemmed from a failure to accept the "maternal instinct."

Advertisers during the 1950s sought to convey the idea that women would find happiness in their roles as suburban homemakers, as in this ad for a Maytag washer and dryer.

A Segregated Landscape

For millions of city dwellers, the suburban utopia fulfilled the dream, postponed by depression and war, of home ownership and middle-class incomes. The move to the suburbs also promoted Americanization, cutting residents off from urban ethnic communities and bringing them fully into the world of mass consumption. But if the suburbs offered a new site for the enjoyment of American freedom, they retained at least one familiar characteristic—rigid racial boundaries.

Suburbia has never been as uniform as either its celebrants or its critics claimed. There are upper-class suburbs, working-class suburbs, industrial suburbs, and "suburban" neighborhoods within city limits. But suburbia's racial uniformity was all too real. As late as the 1990s, nearly 90 percent of suburban whites lived in communities with non-white populations of less than 1 percent—the legacy of decisions by government, real-estate developers, banks, and residents.

During the postwar suburban boom, federal agencies continued to insure mortgages that barred resale of houses to non-whites, thereby financing housing segregation. Even after the Supreme Court in 1948 declared such provisions legally unenforceable, banks and private developers barred non-whites from the suburbs. The government refused to subsidize their mortgages, except in segregated enclaves. The vast new

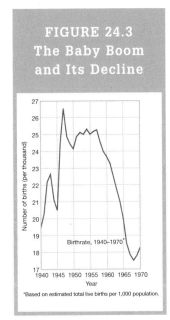

FIGURE 24.3 The Baby Boom and Its Decline

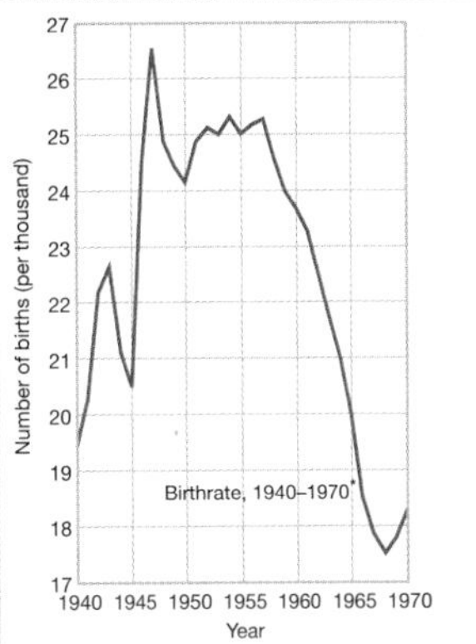

*Based on estimated total live births per 1,000 population.

Students at an East Harlem elementary school in 1947. Most have recently migrated from Puerto Rico to the mainland with their families, although some are probably children of the area's older Italian-American community.

communities built by the Levitts refused to allow blacks, including army veterans, to rent or purchase homes. A lawsuit forced Levitt to begin selling to non-whites in the 1960s, but by 1990, his Long Island community, with a population of 53,000, included only 127 black residents.

At the same time, under programs of **urban renewal**, cities demolished poor neighborhoods in city centers that occupied potentially valuable real estate. In their place, developers constructed retail centers and all-white middle-income housing complexes, and states built urban public universities like Wayne State in Detroit and the University of Illinois at Chicago. White residents displaced by urban renewal often moved to the suburbs. Non-whites, unable to do so, found housing in run-down city neighborhoods.

The Divided Society

Suburbanization hardened the racial lines of division in American life. Between 1950 and 1970, about 7 million white Americans left cities for the suburbs. Meanwhile, nearly 3 million blacks moved from the South to the North, greatly increasing the size of existing urban ghettos and creating entirely new ones. And half a million Puerto Ricans, mostly small coffee and tobacco farmers and agricultural laborers forced off the land when American sugar companies expanded their landholdings on the island, moved to the mainland.

The process of racial exclusion became self-reinforcing. Non-whites remained concentrated in manual and unskilled jobs, the result of employment discrimination and their virtual exclusion from educational opportunities at public and private universities, including those outside the South. As the white population and industrial jobs fled the old city centers for the suburbs, poorer blacks and Latinos remained trapped in urban ghettos, seen by many whites as places of crime, poverty, and welfare.

Suburban builders sometimes openly advertised the fact that their communities excluded minorities. This photograph was taken in southern California in 1948.

Religion and Anticommunism

Both Protestant and Roman Catholic religious leaders played crucial roles in the spread of anticommunism and Cold War culture. Official American values celebrated the nation's religiosity as opposed to "godless" communism. During the 1950s, a majority of Americans—the highest percentage in the nation's history—were affiliated with a church or synagogue. In 1954, to "strengthen our national resistance to communism," Congress added the words "under God" to the Pledge of Allegiance. In 1957, "**In God We Trust**" was included on paper money. Big-budget Hollywood films like *The Ten Commandments* and *Ben Hur* celebrated early Judaism and Christianity. Leading clerics like Bishop Fulton J. Sheen of the Catholic Church and Protestant evangelist Billy Graham used radio and television to spread to millions a religious message heavily imbued with anticommunism. Communism, Graham declared, was not only an economic and political outlook but also a religion—one "inspired, directed and motivated by the Devil himself."

An image from a booklet issued by the American Economic Foundation illustrates the linkage of anticommunism and religious faith during the Cold War. The hairy hand in the bottom half of the drawing represents the communist threat, which endangers religious freedom in the United States. Most of the booklet, however, dealt with the superiority of free enterprise to communism.

Selling Free Enterprise

The economic content of Cold War freedom increasingly came to focus on consumer capitalism, or, as it was now universally known, "free enterprise." More than political democracy or freedom of speech, which many allies of the United States outside western Europe lacked, an economic system resting on private ownership united the nations of the Free World.

Free enterprise seemed an odd way of describing an economy in which a few large corporations dominated key sectors. Until well into the twentieth century, most ordinary Americans had been deeply suspicious of big business, associating it with images of robber barons who manipulated politics, suppressed economic competition, and treated their workers unfairly.

In 1953, 4.5 million Americans—only slightly more than in 1928—owned shares of stock. By the mid-1960s, the number had grown to 25 million. In the face of widespread abundance, who could deny that the capitalist marketplace embodied individual freedom or that poverty would soon be a thing of the past? "It was American Freedom," proclaimed *Life* magazine, "by which and through which this amazing achievement of wealth and power was fashioned."

The Libertarian Conservatives and the New Conservatives

During the 1950s, a group of thinkers began the task of reviving conservatism and reclaiming the idea of freedom from liberals. Although largely ignored outside their own immediate circle, they developed ideas that

Opposition to strong national government

would define conservative thought for the next half-century. One was opposition to a strong national government, an outlook that had been given new political life in conservatives' bitter reaction against the New Deal. To these "libertarian" conservatives, freedom meant individual autonomy, limited government, and unregulated capitalism. These ideas had great appeal to conservative entrepreneurs, especially in the rapidly growing South and West, who desired to pursue their economic fortunes free of government regulation, high taxes, and labor unions.

A second strand of thought became increasingly prominent in the 1950s. Convinced that the Free World needed to arm itself morally and intellectually, not just militarily, for the battle against communism, "new conservatives" insisted that toleration of difference—a central belief of modern liberalism—offered no substitute for the search for absolute truth. The West, they warned, was suffering from moral decay, and they called for a return to a civilization based on values grounded in the Christian tradition and in timeless notions of good and evil. The "new conservatives" understood freedom as first and foremost a moral condition. It required a decision by independent men and women to lead virtuous lives or governmental action to force them to do so.

Freedom and morality

Division in conservatism

Here lay the origins of a division in conservative ranks that would persist into the twenty-first century. Unrestrained individual choice and moral virtue are radically different starting points from which to discuss freedom. Was the purpose of conservatism, one writer wondered, to create the "free man" or the "good man"? Libertarian conservatives spoke the language of progress and personal autonomy; the "new conservatives" emphasized tradition, community, and moral commitment. The former believed that too many barriers existed to the pursuit of individual liberty. The latter condemned an excess of individualism and a breakdown of common values.

Fortunately for conservatives, political unity often depends less on intellectual coherence than on the existence of a common foe. And two powerful enemies became focal points for the conservative revival—the Soviet Union abroad and the federal government at home. Republican control of the presidency did not lessen conservatives' hostility to the federal government, partly because they did not consider President Eisenhower one of their own.

THE EISENHOWER ERA

Ike and Nixon

Dwight D. Eisenhower

Dwight D. Eisenhower, or "Ike," as he was affectionately called, emerged from World War II as the military leader with the greatest political appeal, partly because his public image of fatherly warmth set him apart from other successful generals like the arrogant Douglas MacArthur. Eisenhower became convinced that Senator Robert A. Taft of Ohio, a leading contender for the Republican nomination, would lead the United States back toward isolationism. Eisenhower entered the contest and won the Republican nomination.

For his running mate, Eisenhower chose Richard Nixon of California, a World War II veteran who had made a name for himself with his vigorous anticommunism. Nixon won election to the U.S. Senate in 1950 in a campaign in which he suggested that the Democratic candidate, Congresswoman Helen Gahagan Douglas, had communist sympathies.

Dwight D. Eisenhower's popularity was evident at this appearance in Baltimore during the 1952 presidential campaign.

These tactics gave Nixon a lifelong reputation for opportunism and dishonesty. But Nixon was also a shrewd politician who pioneered efforts to transform the Republican Party's image from defender of business to champion of the "forgotten man"—the hardworking citizen burdened by heavy taxation and unresponsive government bureaucracies. In using populist language to promote free market economics, Nixon helped to lay the foundation for the triumph of conservatism a generation later.

The 1952 Campaign

Television was beginning to transform politics by allowing candidates to bring carefully crafted images directly into Americans' living rooms. The 1952 campaign became the first to make extensive use of TV ads. Parties, one observer complained, were "selling the president like toothpaste."

More important to the election's outcome, however, was Eisenhower's popularity (invoked in the Republican campaign slogan "I Like Ike") and the public's weariness with the Korean War. Ike's pledge to "go to Korea" in search of peace signaled his intention to bring the conflict to an end. He won a resounding victory over the Democratic candidate, Adlai Stevenson. Four years later, Eisenhower again defeated Stevenson by an even wider margin. His popularity, however, did not extend to his party. Republicans won a razor-thin majority in Congress in 1952, but Democrats regained control in 1954 and retained it for the rest of the decade. In 1956,

A poster for Adlai Stevenson, Democratic candidate for president in 1952. The party's main argument, it seems, was that Republican victory would usher in a return of the Great Depression. Stevenson was soundly defeated by Dwight D. Eisenhower.

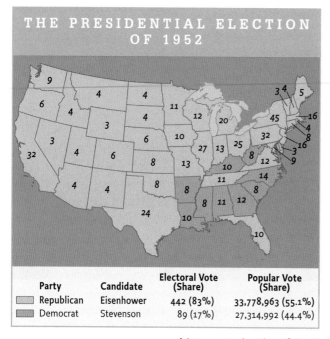

THE PRESIDENTIAL ELECTION OF 1952

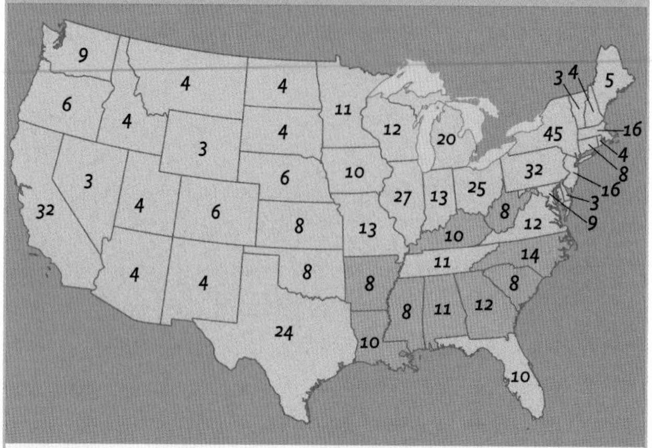

	Party	Candidate	Electoral Vote (Share)	Popular Vote (Share)
▭	Republican	Eisenhower	442 (83%)	33,778,963 (55.1%)
▬	Democrat	Stevenson	89 (17%)	27,314,992 (44.4%)

Eisenhower became the first president to be elected without his party controlling either house of Congress.

During the 1950s, voters at home and abroad seemed to find reassurance in selecting familiar, elderly leaders to govern them. At age sixty-two, Eisenhower was one of the oldest men ever elected president. But he seemed positively youthful compared with Winston Churchill, who returned to office as prime minister of Great Britain at age seventy-seven; Charles De Gaulle, who assumed the presidency of France at sixty-eight; and Konrad Adenauer, who served as chancellor of West Germany from age seventy-three until well into his eighties. In retrospect, Eisenhower's presidency seems almost uneventful, at least in domestic affairs—an interlude between the bitter party battles of the Truman administration and the social upheavals of the 1960s.

Modern Republicanism

With a Republican serving as president for the first time in twenty years, the tone in Washington changed. Wealthy businessmen dominated Eisenhower's cabinet. Defense Secretary Charles Wilson, the former president of General Motors, made the widely publicized statement: "What is good for the country is good for General Motors, and vice versa." A champion of the business community and a fiscal conservative, Ike worked to scale back government spending, including the military budget. But although right-wing Republicans saw his victory as an invitation to roll back the New Deal, Eisenhower realized that such a course would be disastrous. "Should any political party attempt to abolish Social Security, unemployment insurance, and eliminate labor laws and farm programs," he declared, "you would not hear of that party again in our political history."

Scaling back government spending

Eisenhower called his domestic agenda Modern Republicanism. It aimed to sever his party's identification in the minds of many Americans with the Great Depression. The core New Deal programs not only remained in place but expanded.

Accepting the New Deal

Eisenhower presided over the largest public-works enterprise in American history, the building of the 41,000-mile **interstate highway system**.

Public works

As noted in the previous chapter, Cold War arguments—especially the need to provide rapid exit routes from cities in the event of nuclear war—justified this multibillion-dollar project. But automobile manufacturers, oil companies, suburban builders, and construction unions had very practical reasons for supporting highway construction regardless of any Soviet threat. When the Soviets launched ***Sputnik***, the first artificial earth satellite, in 1957, the administration responded with the **National Defense Education Act**, which for the first time offered direct federal funding to higher education.

Legitimizing the New Deal

All in all, rather than dismantling the New Deal, Eisenhower's Modern Republicanism consolidated and legitimized it. By accepting its basic premises, he ensured that its continuation no longer depended on Democratic control of the presidency.

The Social Contract

The 1950s also witnessed an easing of the labor conflict of the two previous decades. The passage of the Taft-Hartley Act in 1947 (discussed in the previous chapter) had reduced labor militancy. In 1955, the AFL and CIO merged to form a single organization representing 35 percent of all nonagricultural workers. In leading industries, labor and management hammered out what has been called a new **social contract**. Unions signed long-term agreements that left decisions regarding capital investment, plant location, and output in management's hands. Employers stopped trying to eliminate existing unions and granted wage increases and fringe benefits such as private pension plans, health insurance, and automatic cost-of-living adjustments to pay.

Labor and management cooperation

Unionized workers shared fully in 1950s prosperity. Although the social contract did not apply to the majority of workers, who did not belong to unions, it did bring benefits to those who labored in nonunion jobs. For example, trade unions in the 1950s and 1960s were able to use their political power to win a steady increase in the minimum wage, which was earned mostly by nonunion workers at the bottom of the employment pyramid. But the majority of workers did not enjoy anything close to the wages, benefits, and job security of unionized workers in such industries as automobiles and steel.

Nonunion workers

By the end of the 1950s, the social contract was weakening. In 1959, the steel industry sought to tighten work rules and limit wage increases in an attempt to boost profits battered by a recession that hit two years earlier. The plan sparked a strike of 500,000 steelworkers, which successfully beat back the proposed changes.

Massive Retaliation

Soon after he entered office, Eisenhower approved an armistice that ended fighting in Korea. But this failed to ease international tensions. Ike took office at a time when the Cold War had entered an extremely dangerous

The hydrogen bomb

phase. In 1952, the United States exploded the first hydrogen bomb—a weapon far more powerful than those that had devastated Hiroshima and Nagasaki. The following year, the Soviets matched this achievement. Both sides feverishly developed long-range bombers capable of delivering weapons of mass destruction around the world.

John Foster Dulles

A professional soldier, Ike hated war, which he viewed as a tragic waste. "Every gun that is made," he said in 1953, "every warship launched . . . signifies a theft from those who hunger and are not fed." But his secretary of state, John Foster Dulles, was a grim Cold Warrior. In 1954, Dulles announced an updated version of the doctrine of containment. **Massive retaliation**, as it was called, declared that any Soviet attack on an American ally would be countered by a nuclear assault on the Soviet Union itself.

Fear of MAD

Massive retaliation ran the risk that any small conflict, or even a miscalculation, could escalate into a war that would destroy both the United States and the Soviet Union. The reality that all-out war would result in "mutual assured destruction" (or MAD, in military shorthand) did succeed in making both great powers cautious in their direct dealings with one another. But it also inspired widespread fear of impending nuclear war. Government programs encouraging Americans to build bomb shelters in their backyards and school drills that trained children to hide under their desks in the event of an atomic attack aimed to convince Americans that nuclear war was survivable.

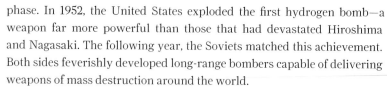

Ike and the Russians

The end of the Korean War and the death of Stalin, both of which occurred in 1953, convinced Eisenhower that rather than being blind zealots, the Soviets were reasonable and could be dealt with in conventional diplomatic terms. In 1955, Ike met in Geneva, Switzerland, with Nikita Khrushchev, the new Soviet leader, at the first "summit" conference since Potsdam a decade earlier. The following year, Khrushchev delivered a speech to the Communist Party Congress in Moscow that detailed Stalin's crimes, including purges of political opponents numbering in the millions.

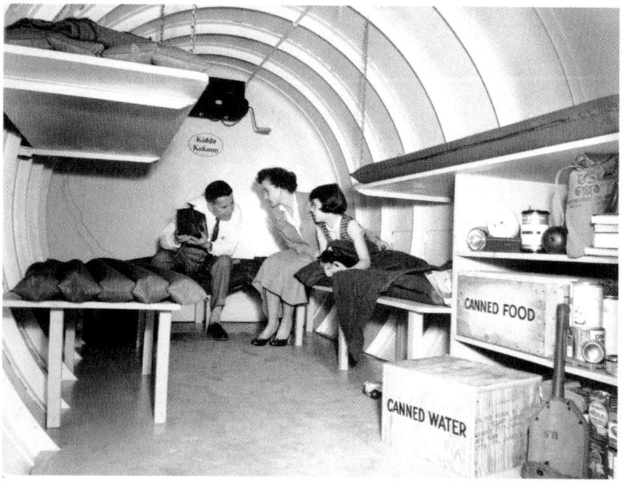

H-Bomb Hideaway, a photograph taken in 1955, shows a family in their underground bomb shelter, where—the manufacturer claimed—the occupants could survive for five days after a nuclear war.

Khrushchev's call in the same 1956 speech for "peaceful coexistence" with the United States raised the possibility of an easing of the Cold War. The "thaw" was abruptly shaken that fall, however, when Soviet troops put down an anticommunist uprising in Hungary. Eisenhower refused to extend aid to the Hungarian rebels, an indication that he believed it impossible to "roll back" Soviet domination of eastern Europe.

In 1958, the two superpowers agreed to a voluntary halt to the testing of nuclear weapons. The pause lasted until 1961. It had been demanded by the National Committee for a Sane Nuclear Policy, which publicized the danger to public health posed by radioactive fallout from nuclear tests. But the spirit of cooperation ended abruptly in 1960, when the Soviets shot down an American U-2 spy plane over their territory. Eisenhower first denied that the plane had been involved in espionage and refused to apologize even after the Russians produced the captured pilot. The incident torpedoed another planned summit meeting.

National Committee for a Sane Nuclear Policy

The Emergence of the Third World

Even as Europe, where the Cold War began, settled into what appeared to be a permanent division between a communist East and a capitalist West, an intense rivalry, which sometimes took a military form, persisted in what came to be called the Third World. The term was invented to describe developing countries aligned with neither of the two Cold War powers and desirous of finding their own model of development between Soviet centralized economic planning and free market capitalism.

Nonaligned developing countries

The post–World War II era witnessed the crumbling of European empires. Decolonization began when India and Pakistan (the latter carved out of India to give Muslims their own nation) achieved independence in 1947. Ten years later, Britain's Gold Coast colony in West Africa emerged as the independent nation of Ghana. Other new nations—including Indonesia, Malaysia, Nigeria, Kenya, and Tanzania—soon followed.

Decolonization begins

The Soviet Union strongly supported the dissolution of Europe's overseas empires, and communists participated in movements for colonial independence. Most of the new Third World nations resisted alignment with either major power bloc, hoping to remain neutral in the Cold War.

By the end of the 1950s, much of the focus of the Cold War shifted to the Third World. The policy of containment easily slid over into opposition to any government, whether communist or not, that seemed to threaten American strategic or economic interests. Jacobo Arbenz Guzmán in Guatemala and Mohammed Mossadegh in Iran were elected, homegrown nationalists, not agents of Moscow. But they were determined to reduce foreign corporations' control over their countries' economies. Arbenz embarked on a sweeping land-reform policy that threatened the domination of Guatemala's economy by the American-owned United

Containment

The military junta installed in Guatemala by the CIA in 1954 enters Guatemala City in a Jeep driven by CIA agent Carlos Castillo Armas. Although hailed by the Eisenhower administration as a triumph for freedom, the new government suppressed democracy in Guatemala and embarked on a murderous campaign to stamp out opposition.

Fruit Company. Mossadegh nationalized the Anglo-Iranian Oil Company, whose refinery in Iran was Britain's largest remaining overseas asset. In 1953 and 1954, the Central Intelligence Agency organized the ouster of both governments—a clear violation of the UN Charter, which barred a member state from taking military action against another except in self-defense.

In 1956, Israel, France, and Britain—without prior consultation with the United States—invaded Egypt after the country's nationalist leader, Gamal Abdel Nasser, nationalized the Suez Canal, jointly owned by Britain and France. A furious Eisenhower forced them to abandon the invasion. After the Suez fiasco, the United States moved to replace Britain as the major Western power in the Middle East.

Origins of the Vietnam War

In Vietnam, the expulsion of the Japanese in 1945 led not to independence but to a French military effort to preserve France's Asian empire against Ho Chi Minh's nationalist forces. Anticommunism led the United States into deeper and deeper involvement. Following a policy initiated by Truman, the Eisenhower administration funneled billions of dollars in aid to bolster French efforts. By the early 1950s, the United States was paying four-fifths of the cost of the war. Wary of becoming bogged down in another land war in Asia immediately after Korea, however, Ike declined to send in American troops when France requested them to avert defeat in 1954, leaving France no alternative but to agree to Vietnamese independence.

Geneva agreements

Issued from a peace conference in 1954, the **Geneva Accords** divided Vietnam temporarily into northern and southern districts, with elections scheduled for 1956 to unify the country. But the staunchly anticommunist southern leader Ngo Dinh Diem, urged on by the United States, refused to hold elections, which would almost certainly have resulted in a victory for Ho Chi Minh's communists. American aid poured into South Vietnam in order to bolster the Diem regime. By the time Eisenhower left office in 1961, Diem nevertheless faced a full-scale guerrilla revolt by the communist-led National Liberation Front.

Little by little, the United States was becoming accustomed to intervention, both open and secret, in far-flung corners of the world. Despite the Cold War rhetoric of freedom, American leaders seemed more comfortable dealing with reliable military regimes than democratic governments. A series of military governments succeeded Arbenz in Guatemala. The shah of Iran replaced Mossadegh and remained in office until 1979 as one of the world's most tyrannical rulers, until his overthrow in a revolution led by the fiercely anti-American radical Islamist Ayatollah Khomeini. In Vietnam, the American decision to prop up Diem's regime laid the groundwork for what would soon become the most disastrous military involvement in American history.

American intervention

Mass Society and Its Critics

The fatherly Eisenhower seemed the perfect leader for the placid society of the 1950s. Consensus was the dominant ideal in an era in which McCarthyism had defined criticism of the social and economic order as disloyalty and most Americans located the enjoyment of freedom in private pleasures rather than the public sphere. Even *Life* magazine commented that American freedom might be in greater danger from "disuse" than from communist subversion.

Dissenting voices could be heard. The sociologist C. Wright Mills wrote of a "power elite"—an interlocking directorate of corporate leaders, politicians, and military men whose domination of government and society had made political democracy obsolete. Freedom, Mills insisted, rested on the ability "to formulate the available choices," and this most Americans were effectively denied.

C. Wright Mills and the "power elite"

Rebels without a cause. Teenage members of a youth gang, photographed at Coney Island, Brooklyn, in the late 1950s.

Elvis Presley's gyrating hips appealed to teenagers but alarmed many adults during the 1950s.

Other writers worried that modern mass society inevitably produced loneliness and anxiety, causing mankind to yearn for stability and authority, not freedom. In *The Lonely Crowd* (1950), the decade's most influential work of social analysis, the sociologist David Riesman described Americans as "other-directed" conformists who lacked the inner resources to lead truly independent lives. Other social critics charged that corporate bureaucracies had transformed employees into "organization men" incapable of independent thought.

William Whyte's *The Organization Man* (1956) and Vance Packard's *The Hidden Persuaders* (1957), which criticized the monotony of modern work, the emptiness of suburban life, and the pervasive influence of advertising, created the vocabulary for an assault on the nation's social values that lay just over the horizon.

Rebels without a Cause

The social critics did not offer a political alternative or have any real impact on the parties or government. Nor did other stirrings of dissent. With teenagers a growing part of the population thanks to the baby boom, the rise of a popular culture geared to the emerging youth market suggested that significant generational tensions lay beneath the bland surface of 1950s life. The 1955 films *Blackboard Jungle* and *Rebel without a Cause* (the latter starring James Dean as an aimlessly rebellious youth) highlighted the alienation of at least some young people from the world of adult respectability. These works helped to spur a mid-1950s panic about juvenile delinquency.

Cultural life during the 1950s seemed far more daring than politics. Teenagers wore leather jackets and danced to rock-and-roll music that

A poetry meeting at a Beat coffeehouse in New York City, photographed in 1959, where poets, artists, and others who rejected 1950s mainstream culture gathered.

brought the hard-driving rhythms and sexually provocative movements of black musicians and dancers to enthusiastic young white audiences. They made Elvis Presley, a rock-and-roll singer with an openly sexual performance style, an immensely popular entertainment celebrity.

In New York City and San Francisco, as well as college towns like Madison, Wisconsin, and Ann Arbor, Michigan, **the Beats**, a small group of poets and writers, railed against mainstream culture. "I saw the best minds of my generation destroyed by madness, starving hysterical naked," wrote the Beat poet Allen Ginsberg in *Howl* (1955), a brilliant protest against materialism and conformism written while the author was under the influence of hallucinogenic drugs. Ginsberg became nationally known when San Francisco police in 1956 confiscated his book and arrested bookstore owners for selling an obscene work. (A judge later overturned the ban on the grounds that *Howl* possessed redeeming social value.) Rejecting the work ethic, the "desperate materialism" of the suburban middle class, and the militarization of American life by the Cold War, the Beats celebrated impulsive action, immediate pleasure (often enhanced by drugs), and sexual experimentation. Despite Cold War slogans, they insisted, personal and political repression, not freedom, were the hallmarks of American society.

Allen Ginsberg

Rejecting repressive society

THE FREEDOM MOVEMENT

Not until the 1960s would young white rebels find their cause, as the seeds of dissent planted by the social critics and Beats flowered in an outpouring of political activism, new attitudes toward sexuality, and a full-fledged generational rebellion. A more immediate challenge to the complacency of the 1950s arose from the twentieth century's greatest citizens' movement—the black struggle for equality.

Origins of the Movement

Today, with the birthday of Martin Luther King Jr. a national holiday and the struggles of Montgomery, Little Rock, Birmingham, and Selma celebrated as heroic episodes in the history of freedom, it is easy to forget that at the time, the civil rights revolution came as a great surprise. Few predicted the emergence of the southern mass movement for civil rights.

With blacks' traditional allies on the left decimated by McCarthyism, most union leaders unwilling to challenge racial inequalities within their own ranks, and the NAACP concentrating on court battles, new constituencies and new tactics were sorely needed. The movement found in the southern black church the organizing power for a militant, nonviolent assault on segregation.

The southern black church

The persistence of *Jim Crow*

The United States in the 1950s was still a segregated, unequal society. Half of the nation's black families lived in poverty. In the South, evidence of Jim Crow abounded—in separate public institutions and the signs "white" and "colored" at entrances to buildings, train carriages, drinking fountains, restrooms, and the like. In the North and West, the law did not require segregation, but custom barred blacks from many colleges, hotels, and restaurants, and from most suburban housing. Las Vegas, Nevada, for example, was as strictly segregated as any southern city. Hotels and casinos did not admit blacks except in the most menial jobs. Lena Horne, Sammy Davis Jr., Louis Armstrong, and other black entertainers played the hotel-casinos on the "strip" but could not stay as guests where they performed.

Segregation in schools

In 1950, seventeen southern and border states and Washington, D.C., had laws requiring the racial segregation of public schools, and several others permitted local districts to impose it. In northern communities housing patterns and school district lines created de facto segregation—separation in fact if not in law. Few white Americans felt any urgency about confronting racial inequality.

The Legal Assault on Segregation

LULAC and Mendez v. Westminster

With the Eisenhower administration reluctant to address the issue, it fell to the courts to confront the problem of racial segregation. In the Southwest, the **League of United Latin American Citizens** (LULAC), the counterpart of the NAACP, challenged restrictive housing, employment discrimination, and the segregation of Latino students. It won an important victory in 1946 in the case of *Mendez v. Westminster*, when a federal court ordered the schools of Orange County, California, desegregated. In response, the state legislature repealed all school laws requiring racial segregation. The governor who signed the measure, Earl Warren, had presided over the internment of Japanese-Americans during World War II as the state's attorney general. After the war, he became convinced that racial inequality had no place in American life. When Chief Justice Fred Vinson died in 1953, Eisenhower appointed Earl Warren to replace him on the U.S. Supreme Court.

A segregated school in West Memphis, Arkansas, photographed for *Life* magazine in 1949. Education in the South was separate but hardly equal.

For years, the NAACP, under the leadership of attorneys Charles Hamilton Houston and Thurgood

Marshall, had pressed legal challenges to the "separate but equal" doctrine laid down by the Court in 1896 in *Plessy v. Ferguson* (see Chapter 17). At first, the NAACP sought to gain admission to white institutions of higher learning for which no black equivalent existed. In 1938, the Supreme Court ordered the University of Missouri Law School to admit Lloyd Gaines, a black student, because the state had no such school for blacks. Missouri responded by setting up a segregated law school, satisfying the courts. But in 1950, the Supreme Court unanimously ordered Heman Sweatt admitted to the University of Texas Law School even though the state had established a "school" for him in a basement containing three classrooms and no library.

The *Brown* Case

Thurgood Marshall and the NAACP

Marshall now launched a frontal assault on segregation itself. He brought the NAACP's support to local cases that had arisen when black parents challenged unfair school policies. For parents to do so required remarkable courage. In Clarendon County, South Carolina, Levi Pearson, a black farmer who brought a lawsuit on behalf of his children, saw his house burned to the ground. The Clarendon case attacked not segregation itself but the unequal funding of schools. Black children attended class in buildings with no running water or indoor toilets and were not provided with buses to transport them to classes. Five such cases from four states and the District of Columbia were combined in a single appeal that reached the Supreme Court late in 1952.

When cases are united, they are listed alphabetically and the first case gives the entire decision its name. In this instance, the first case alphabetically was one brought by Harry Briggs of South Carolina. But since the new chief justice, Earl Warren, did not want to seem to be singling out the states of the old Confederacy, the Court consolidated the cases under the name of a case from the Midwest, ***Brown v. Board of Education of Topeka, Kansas.*** Oliver Brown went to court because his daughter, a third grader, was forced to walk across dangerous railroad tracks each morning rather than being allowed to attend a nearby school restricted to whites.

Thurgood Marshall decided that the time had come to attack the "separate but equal" doctrine itself. Even with the same funding and facilities, he insisted, segregation was inherently unequal because it stigmatized one group of citizens as unfit to associate with others. In its legal brief, the Eisenhower administration did not directly support Marshall's position, but it urged the justices to consider "the problem of racial discrimination . . . in the context of the present world struggle between freedom and tyranny." Other peoples, it noted, "cannot understand how such a practice

Linda Brown's parents sued the school board of Topeka, Kansas, demanding that it admit their daughter to a school near her home restricted to whites, rather than requiring her to walk across dangerous railroad tracks each day, as in this photograph, to attend a black school. The result was the Supreme Court's landmark *Brown* decision outlawing school segregation.

can exist in a country which professes to be a staunch supporter of freedom, justice, and democracy."

Chief Justice Warren managed to create unanimity on a divided Court, some of whose members disliked segregation but feared that a decision to outlaw it would spark widespread violence. On May 17, 1954, Warren himself read aloud the decision, only eleven pages long. Segregation in public education, he concluded, violated the equal protection of the laws guaranteed by the Fourteenth Amendment. "In the field of education, the doctrine of 'separate but equal' has no place. Separate educational facilities are inherently unequal."

The Warren Court

The decision did not order immediate implementation but instead called for hearings as to how segregated schooling should be dismantled. But *Brown* marked the emergence of the Warren Court as an active agent of social change. And it inspired a wave of optimism that discrimination would soon disappear.

The Montgomery Bus Boycott

Brown did not cause the modern civil rights movement, which, as noted in the previous two chapters, began during World War II and continued in cities like New York after the war. But the decision did ensure that when the movement resumed after waning in the early 1950s, it would have the backing of the federal courts. Mass action against Jim Crow soon reappeared. On December 1, 1955, Rosa Parks, a black tailor's assistant who had just completed her day's work in a Montgomery, Alabama, department store, refused to surrender her seat on a city bus to a white rider, as required by local law. Parks's arrest sparked a yearlong **Montgomery bus boycott**, the beginning of the mass phase of the civil rights movement in the South. In 2000, *Time* magazine named Rosa Parks one of the 100 most significant persons of the twentieth century.

The mug shot of Rosa Parks taken in December 1955 at a Montgomery, Alabama, police station after she was arrested for refusing to give up her seat on a city bus to a white passenger.

Parks is widely remembered today as a "seamstress with tired feet," a symbol of ordinary blacks' determination to resist the daily injustices and indignities of the Jim Crow South. In fact, her life makes clear that the civil rights revolution built on earlier struggles. Parks was a veteran of black politics. During the 1930s, she took part in meetings protesting the conviction of the Scottsboro Boys. She served for many years as secretary to E. D. Nixon, the local leader of the NAACP. In 1943, she tried to register to vote, only to be turned away because she supposedly failed a literacy test. After two more attempts, Parks succeeded in becoming one of the few blacks in Montgomery able to cast a ballot.

Response to Parks's arrest

When news of Parks's arrest spread, hundreds of blacks gathered in a local church and vowed to refuse to ride the buses until accorded equal treatment. For 381 days, despite legal harassment and occasional violence, black maids, janitors, teachers, and students walked to their destinations or rode an informal network of taxis. Finally, in November 1956, the Supreme Court ruled segregation in public transportation unconstitutional. The boycott ended in triumph.

The Daybreak of Freedom

The rise of Martin Luther King Jr.

The Montgomery bus boycott marked a turning point in postwar American history. It launched the movement for racial justice as a nonviolent crusade based in the black churches of the South. It gained the support of northern liberals and focused unprecedented and unwelcome international attention on the country's racial policies. And it marked the emergence of the twenty-six-year-old Martin Luther King Jr., who had recently arrived in Montgomery to become pastor of a Baptist church, as the movement's national symbol. On the night of the first protest meeting, King's call to action electrified the audience: "We, the disinherited of this land, we who have been oppressed so long, are tired of going through the long night of captivity. And now we are reaching out for the daybreak of freedom and justice and equality."

From the beginning, the language of freedom pervaded the black movement. It resonated in the speeches of civil rights leaders and in the hand-lettered placards of the struggle's foot soldiers. During the summer of 1964, when civil rights activists established "freedom schools" for black children across Mississippi, lessons began with students being asked to define the word. Some gave specific answers ("going to public libraries"), some more abstract ("standing up for your rights"). Some insisted that freedom meant legal equality, others saw it as liberation from years of deference to and fear of whites. "Freedom of the mind," wrote one, was the greatest freedom of all.

The movement and freedom

For adults as well, freedom had many meanings. It meant enjoying the political rights and economic opportunities taken for granted by whites. It required eradicating historic wrongs such as segregation, disenfranchisement, confinement to low-wage jobs, and the ever-present threat of violence. It meant the right to be served at lunch counters and downtown department stores, central locations in the consumer culture, and to be addressed as "Mr.," "Miss," and "Mrs.," rather than "boy" and "auntie."

The Leadership of King

"I Have a Dream"

In King's soaring oratory, the protesters' understandings of freedom fused into a coherent whole. His most celebrated oration, the "I Have a Dream" speech of 1963, began by invoking the unfulfilled promise of emancipation ("one hundred years later, the Negro still is not free") and closed with a cry borrowed from a black spiritual: "Free at last! Free at last! Thank God Almighty, we are free at last!"

Peaceful civil disobedience

King presented the case for black rights in a vocabulary that merged the black experience with that of the nation. Having studied the writings of Henry David Thoreau and Mahatma Gandhi on peaceful civil disobedience, King outlined a philosophy of struggle in which evil must be met with good, hate with Christian love, and violence with peaceful demands for change. Echoing Christian themes derived from his training in the black church, King's speeches resonated deeply in both black communities and the broader culture. He repeatedly invoked the Bible to preach justice and forgiveness. Like Frederick Douglass before him, King appealed to white America by stressing the protesters' love of country and devotion to national values. If Africa was gaining its freedom, he asked, why must black America lag behind?

Massive Resistance

Southern Christian Leadership Conference

Buoyed by success in Montgomery, King in 1956 took the lead in forming the **Southern Christian Leadership Conference**, a coalition of black ministers and civil rights activists, to press for desegregation. But despite

A pro-segregation rally at the Arkansas Capitol in Little Rock in 1959.

the movement's success in popular mobilization, the fact that Montgomery's city fathers agreed to the boycott's demands only after a Supreme Court ruling indicated that without national backing, local action might not be enough to overturn Jim Crow. The white South's refusal to accept the *Brown* decision reinforced the conviction that black citizens could not gain their constitutional rights without Washington's intervention. This was not immediately forthcoming. When the Supreme Court finally issued its implementation ruling in 1955, the justices declared that desegregation should proceed "with all deliberate speed." This vague formulation unintentionally encouraged a campaign of "massive resistance" that paralyzed civil rights progress in much of the South.

A door in a San Antonio, Texas, restaurant in 1958.

Ninety-six of 106 southern congressmen—and every southern senator except Lyndon B. Johnson of Texas and Albert Gore and Estes Kefauver of Tennessee—signed a **Southern Manifesto** in 1956, denouncing the *Brown* decision as a "clear abuse of judicial power," and calling for resistance to "forced integration" by "any lawful means." State after state passed laws to block desegregation. Virginia pioneered the strategy of closing any public schools ordered to desegregate and offering funds to enable white pupils, but not black, to attend private institutions. Prince Edward County, Virginia, shut its schools entirely in 1959; not until 1964 did the Supreme Court order them reopened.

Eisenhower and Civil Rights

The federal government tried to remain aloof from the black struggle. Thanks to the efforts of Senate majority leader Lyndon B. Johnson, who hoped to win liberal support for a run for president in 1960, Congress in 1957 passed the first national civil rights law since Reconstruction. It targeted the denial of black voting rights in the South, but with weak enforcement provisions it added few voters to the rolls. President Eisenhower failed to provide moral leadership. He called for Americans to abide by the law, but he made it clear that he found the whole civil rights issue distasteful.

Federal troops escort black children to Little Rock Central High School, enforcing a court order for integration in 1957.

In 1957, however, after Governor Orval Faubus of Arkansas used the National Guard to prevent the court-ordered integration of Little Rock's

VOICES OF FREEDOM

From Martin Luther King Jr., Speech at Montgomery, Alabama (December 5, 1955)

A few days after Rosa Parks's arrest for refusing to give up her seat on a Montgomery bus to a white passenger, a mass rally of local African-Americans decided to boycott city buses in protest. In his speech to the gathering, the young Baptist minister Martin Luther King Jr. invoked Christian and American ideals of justice and democracy—themes he would strike again and again during his career as the leading national symbol of the civil rights struggle.

We are here this evening . . . because first and foremost we are American citizens, and we are determined to apply our citizenship to the fullness of its means. We are here also because of our love for democracy. . . . Just the other day . . . one of the finest citizens in Montgomery—not one of the finest Negro citizens but one of the finest citizens in Montgomery—was taken from a bus and carried to jail and arrested because she refused to give her seat to a white person. . . .

Mrs. Rosa Parks is a fine person. And since it had to happen I'm happy that it happened to a person like Mrs. Parks, for nobody can doubt the boundless outreach of her integrity! Nobody can doubt the height of her character, nobody can doubt that depth of her Christian commitment and devotion to the teachings of Jesus. And I'm happy since it had to happen, it happened to a person that nobody can call a disturbing factor in the community. Mrs. Parks is a fine Christian person, unassuming, and yet there is integrity and character there. And just because she refused to get up, she was arrested.

I want to say, that we are not here advocating violence. We have never done that. . . . We believe in the teachings of Jesus. The only weapon that we have in our hands this evening is the weapon of protest. . . . There will be no white persons pulled out of their homes and taken out to some distant road and lynched. . . .

We are not wrong in what we are doing. If we are wrong, then the Supreme Court of this nation is wrong. If we are wrong, the Constitution of the United States is wrong. If we are wrong, God Almighty is wrong. . . . If we are wrong, justice is a lie. . . .

We, the disinherited of this land, we who have been oppressed so long, are tired of going through the long night of captivity. And now we are reaching out for the daybreak of freedom and justice and equality. . . . Right here in Montgomery when the history books are written in the future, somebody will have to say, "There lived a race of people, a black people, . . . a people who had the moral courage to stand up for their rights. And thereby they injected a new meaning into the veins of history and of civilization."

From The Southern Manifesto (1956)

Drawn up early in 1956 and signed by ninety-six southern members of the Senate and House of Representatives, the Southern Manifesto repudiated the Supreme Court decision in *Brown v. Board of Education* and offered support to the campaign of resistance in the South.

The unwarranted decision of the Supreme Court in the public school cases is now bearing the fruit always produced when men substitute naked power for established law. . . .

We regard the decisions of the Supreme Court in the school cases as a clear abuse of judicial power. It climaxes a trend in the Federal Judiciary undertaking to legislate, in derogation [violation] of the authority of Congress, and to encroach upon the reserved rights of the States and the people.

The original Constitution does not mention education. Neither does the 14th Amendment nor any other amendment. The debates preceding the submission of the 14th Amendment clearly show that there was no intent that it should affect the system of education maintained by the States.

In the case of *Plessy v. Ferguson* in 1896 the Supreme Court expressly declared that under the 14th Amendment no person was denied any of his rights if the States provided separate but equal facilities. This decision . . . restated time and again, became a part of the life of the people of many of the States and confirmed their habits, traditions, and way of life. It is founded on elemental humanity and commonsense, for parents should not be deprived by Government of the right to direct the lives and education of their own children.

Though there has been no constitutional amendment or act of Congress changing this established legal principle almost a century old, the Supreme Court of the United States, with no legal basis for such action, undertook to exercise their naked judicial power and substituted their personal political and social ideas for the established law of the land.

This unwarranted exercise of power by the Court, contrary to the Constitution, is creating chaos and confusion in the States principally affected. It is destroying the amicable relations between the white and Negro races that have been created through 90 years of patient effort by the good people of both races. It has planted hatred and suspicion where there has been heretofore friendship and understanding.

With the gravest concern for the explosive and dangerous condition created by this decision and inflamed by outside meddlers: . . . we commend the motives of those States which have declared the intention to resist forced integration by any lawful means. . . .

QUESTIONS

1. *How do religious convictions shape King's definition of freedom?*
2. *Why does the Southern Manifesto claim that the Supreme Court decision is a threat to constitutional government?*
3. *How do these documents illustrate contrasting understandings of freedom at the dawn of the civil rights movement?*

A photograph by Gordon Parks shows black children peering wistfully into a whites-only playground in Mobile, Alabama, in 1956.

Central High School, Eisenhower dispatched federal troops to the city. In the face of a howling mob, soldiers of the 101st Airborne Division escorted nine black children into the school. Events in Little Rock showed that in the last instance, the federal government would not allow the flagrant violation of court orders. But because of massive resistance, the pace of the movement slowed in the final years of the 1950s. When Eisenhower left office, fewer than 2 percent of black students attended desegregated schools in the states of the old Confederacy.

Ever since the beginning of the Cold War, American leaders had worried about the impact of segregation on the country's international reputation. Foreign nations and colonies paid close attention to the unfolding of the American civil rights movement. The global reaction to the *Brown* decision was overwhelmingly positive. But the slow pace of change led to criticism that embarrassed American diplomats seeking to win the loyalty of people in the non-white world.

THE ELECTION OF 1960

Kennedy and Nixon

JFK

The presidential campaign of 1960 turned out to be one of the closest in American history. Republicans chose Vice President Richard Nixon as their candidate to succeed Eisenhower. Democrats nominated John F. Kennedy, a senator from Massachusetts and a Roman Catholic, whose father, a millionaire Irish-American businessman, had served as ambassador to Great Britain during the 1930s. Kennedy's chief rivals for the nomination were Hubert Humphrey, leader of the party's liberal wing, and Lyndon B. Johnson of Texas, who accepted Kennedy's offer to run for vice president.

Kennedy's Catholicism

The atmosphere of tolerance promoted by World War II had weakened traditional anti-Catholicism. But many Protestants remained reluctant to vote for a Catholic, fearing that Kennedy would be required to support church doctrine on controversial public issues or, in a more extreme version, take orders from the pope. Kennedy addressed the question directly. "I do not speak for my church on public matters," he insisted,

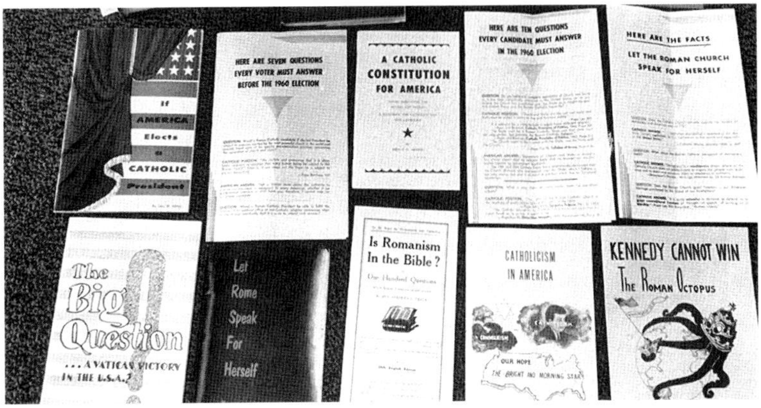

The 1960 presidential campaign produced a flood of anti-Catholic propaganda. Kennedy's victory, the first for an American Catholic, was a major step in the decline of this long-standing prejudice.

and "the church does not speak for me." At age forty-three, Kennedy became the youngest major-party nominee for president in the nation's history.

Both Kennedy and Nixon were ardent Cold Warriors. But Kennedy claimed that the United States had lost the sense of national purpose necessary to fight the Cold War. He warned that Republicans had allowed a **missile gap** to develop in which the Soviets had achieved technological and military superiority over the United States. In fact, as both Kennedy and Nixon well knew, American economic and military capacity far exceeded that of the Soviets. But the charge persuaded many Americans that the time had come for new leadership. The stylishness of Kennedy's wife, Jacqueline, reinforced the impression that Kennedy would conduct a more youthful, vigorous presidency.

In the first televised debate between presidential candidates, judging by viewer response, the handsome Kennedy bested Nixon, who was suffering from a cold and appeared tired and nervous. Those who heard the encounter on the radio thought Nixon had won, but, on TV, image counted for more than substance. In November, Kennedy eked out a narrow victory, winning the popular vote by only 120,000 out of 69 million votes cast (and, Republicans charged, benefiting from a fraudulent vote count by the notoriously corrupt Chicago Democratic machine).

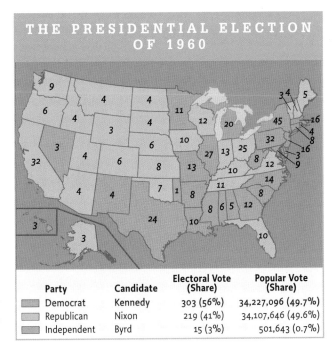

THE PRESIDENTIAL ELECTION OF 1960

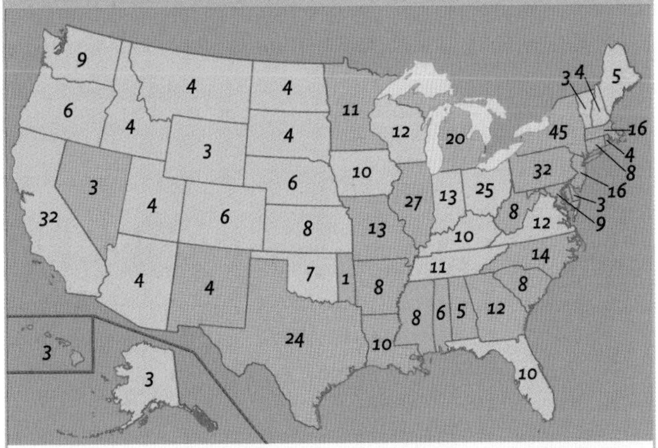

Party	Candidate	Electoral Vote (Share)	Popular Vote (Share)
Democrat	Kennedy	303 (56%)	34,227,096 (49.7%)
Republican	Nixon	219 (41%)	34,107,646 (49.6%)
Independent	Byrd	15 (3%)	501,643 (0.7%)

The End of the 1950s

A photograph of John F. Kennedy and his wife, Jacqueline, strolling along the pier at Hyannis Port, Massachusetts, illustrates their youthful appeal.

In January 1961, shortly before leaving office, Eisenhower delivered a televised Farewell Address, modeled to some extent on George Washington's address of 1796. Knowing that the missile gap was a myth, Ike warned against the drumbeat of calls for a new military buildup. He urged Americans to think about the dangerous power of what he called the **military-industrial complex**—the conjunction of "an immense military establishment" with a "permanent arms industry"—with an influence felt in "every office" in the land. "We must never let the weight of this combination," he advised his countrymen, "endanger our liberties or democratic processes." Few Americans shared Ike's concern—far more saw the alliance of the Defense Department and private industry as a source of jobs and national security rather than a threat to democracy. A few years later, however, with the United States locked in an increasingly unpopular war in Vietnam, Eisenhower's warning would come to seem prophetic.

By then, other underpinnings of 1950s life were also in disarray. The tens of millions of cars that made suburban life possible were spewing toxic lead, an additive to make gasoline more efficient, into the atmosphere. Penned in to the east by mountains that kept automobile emissions from being dispersed by the wind, Los Angeles had become synonymous with smog, a type of air pollution produced by cars. The chemical insecticides that enabled agricultural conglomerates to produce the country's remarkable abundance of food were poisoning farm workers, consumers, and the water supply. Housewives were rebelling against a life centered in suburban dream houses. Blacks were increasingly impatient with the slow progress of racial change. The United States, in other words, had entered that most turbulent of decades, the 1960s.

CHAPTER REVIEW AND ONLINE RESOURCES

REVIEW QUESTIONS

1. *Explain the meaning of the "American standard of living" during the 1950s.*
2. *Describe how the automobile transformed American communities and culture in the 1950s.*
3. *Identify the prescribed roles and aspirations for women during the social conformity of the 1950s.*
4. *What are some ways in which mass consumption was promoted as a patriotic act?*
5. *How did governmental policies, business practices, and individual choices contribute to racially segregated suburbs?*
6. *Explain the ideological rifts among conservatives in the 1950s. Why did many view President Eisenhower as "not one of them"?*
7. *What was the new "social contract" between labor and management, and how did it benefit both sides as well as the nation as a whole?*
8. *How did the United States and Soviet Union shift the focus of the Cold War to the Third World?*
9. *What were the most significant factors that contributed to the growing momentum of the civil rights movement in the 1950s?*
10. *How did many southern whites, led by their elected officials, resist desegregation and civil rights in the name of "freedom"?*
11. *How and why did the federal government's concern with U.S. relations overseas shape its involvement with the* Brown v. Board of Education *case?*

KEY TERMS

Levittown (p. 738)
baby boom (p. 741)
urban renewal (p. 742)
"In God We Trust" (p. 743)
interstate highway system (p. 746)
Sputnik (p. 747)
National Defense Education Act (p. 747)
social contract (p. 747)
massive retaliation (p. 748)
Geneva Accords (p. 750)
the Beats (p. 753)
League of United Latin American Citizens (p. 754)
Brown v. Board of Education (p. 755)
Montgomery bus boycott (p. 756)
Southern Christian Leadership Conference (p. 758)
Southern Manifesto (p. 759)
missile gap (p. 763)
military-industrial complex (p. 764)

Go to INQUIZITIVE

To see what you know—and learn what you've missed—with personalized feedback along the way.

Visit the ***Give Me Liberty!*** **Student Site** for primary source documents and images, interactive maps, author videos featuring Eric Foner, and more.

1960	Greensboro, NC, sit-in
	Young Americans for Freedom founded
1961	Bay of Pigs
	Freedom Rides
	Berlin Wall constructed
1962	Port Huron Statement
	University of Mississippi desegregated
	Rachel Carson's *Silent Spring*
	Cuban missile crisis
1963	Betty Friedan's *The Feminine Mystique*
	King's "Letter from Birmingham Jail"
	March on Washington
	Kennedy assassinated
1964	Freedom Summer
	Civil Rights Act passed
	Gulf of Tonkin resolution
1965–1967	Great Society
1965	Voting Rights Act
	Watts riots
	Hart-Celler Act
1966	National Organization for Women organized
1968	Tet offensive
	Martin Luther King Jr. assassinated
	American Indian movement founded
	Richard Nixon elected
1969	Police raid on Stonewall Inn
	Woodstock festival
1973	*Roe v. Wade*

CHAPTER 25

THE SIXTIES

★

1960–1968

An antiwar demonstrator offers a flower to military police stationed outside the Pentagon at a 1967 rally against the Vietnam War. Some 100,000 protesters took part in this demonstration.

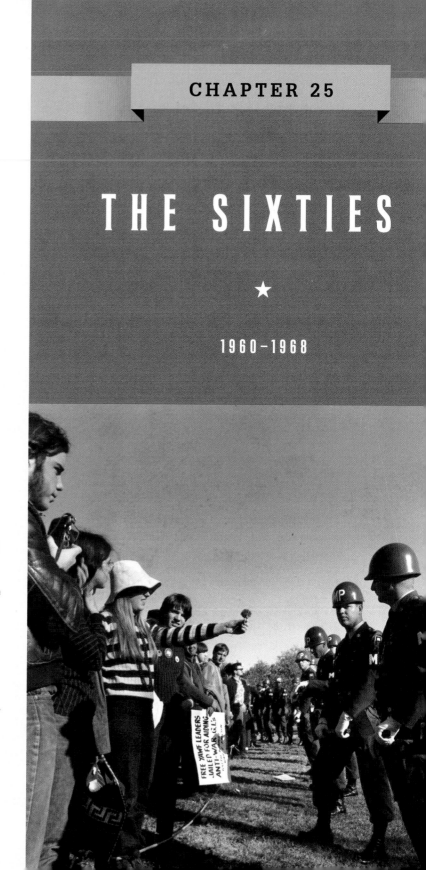

On the afternoon of February 1, 1960, four students from North Carolina Agricultural and Technical State University, a black college in Greensboro, North Carolina, entered the local Woolworth's department store. After making a few purchases, they sat down at the lunch counter, an area reserved for whites. Told that they could not be served, they remained in their seats until the store closed. They returned the next morning and the next. After resisting for five months, Woolworth's in July agreed to serve black customers at its lunch counters.

More than any other event, the Greensboro **sit-in** launched the 1960s: a decade of political activism and social change. Similar demonstrations soon took place throughout the South as activists demanded the integration not only of lunch counters but of parks, pools, restaurants, bowling alleys, libraries, and other facilities as well. By the end of 1960, some 70,000 demonstrators had taken part in sit-ins. Angry whites often assaulted them. But having been trained in nonviolent resistance, the protesters did not strike back.

Even more than elevating blacks to full citizenship, declared the writer James Baldwin, the civil rights movement challenged the United States to rethink "what it really means by freedom"—including whether freedom applied to all Americans or only to part of the population. With their freedom rides, freedom schools, freedom marches, and the insistent cry "Freedom now," black Americans and their white allies risked physical and economic retribution to lay claim to freedom. Their courage inspired a host of other challenges to the status quo, including a student movement known as the New Left, the "second wave" of feminism, and activism among other minorities.

FOCUS QUESTIONS

- *What were the major events in the civil rights movement of the early 1960s?*
- *What were the major crises and policy initiatives of the Kennedy presidency?*
- *What were the purposes and strategies of Johnson's Great Society programs?*
- *How did the civil rights movement change in the mid-1960s?*
- *How did the Vietnam War transform American politics and culture?*
- *What were the sources and significance of the rights revolution of the late 1960s?*
- *In what ways was 1968 a climactic year for the Sixties?*

Participants in a sit-in in Raleigh, North Carolina, in 1960. The protesters, students from a local college, brought books and newspapers to emphasize the seriousness of their intentions and their commitment to nonviolence. Two waitresses declined to serve them.

By the time the decade ended, these movements had challenged the 1950s' understanding of freedom linked to the Cold War abroad and consumer choice at home. They made American society confront the fact that certain groups, including students, women, members of racial minorities, and gay persons, felt themselves excluded from full enjoyment of American freedom.

Reflecting back years later on the struggles of the 1960s, one black organizer in Memphis remarked, "All I wanted to do was to live in a free country." Of the movement's accomplishments, he added, "You had to fight for every inch of it. Nobody gave you anything. Nothing."

Civil rights demonstrators in Orangeburg, South Carolina, in 1960.

THE CIVIL RIGHTS REVOLUTION

The Rising Tide of Protest

Student Nonviolent Coordinating Committee (SNCC)

With the sit-ins, college students for the first time stepped onto the stage of American history as the leading force for social change. In April 1960, Ella Baker, a longtime civil rights organizer, called a meeting of young activists in Raleigh, North Carolina. Out of the gathering came the **Student Nonviolent Coordinating Committee** (SNCC), dedicated to replacing the culture of segregation with a "beloved community" of racial justice and to empowering ordinary blacks to take control of the decisions that affected their lives.

Freedom Rides

In 1961, the Congress of Racial Equality (CORE) launched the **Freedom Rides**. Integrated groups traveled by bus into the Lower South to test compliance with court orders banning segregation on interstate buses and trains and in terminal facilities. Violent mobs assaulted them. Near Anniston, Alabama, a firebomb was thrown into the vehicle and the passengers beaten as they escaped. In Birmingham, Klansmen attacked riders with bats and chains while police refused to intervene. But the Interstate Commerce Commission ordered buses and terminals desegregated.

As protests escalated, so did the resistance of local authorities. In September 1962, a court ordered the University of Mississippi to admit James Meredith, a black student. The state police stood aside as a mob, encouraged by Governor Ross Barnett, rampaged through the streets of Oxford, where the university is located. Two bystanders lost their lives in the riot. President Kennedy was forced to dispatch the army to restore order.

Birmingham

The high point of protest came in the spring of 1963, when demonstrations took place in towns and cities across the South. In one week in June, there were more than 15,000 arrests in 186 cities. The dramatic culmination came in Birmingham, Alabama, a citadel of segregation. Even for the Lower South, Birmingham was a violent city—there had been over fifty bombings of black homes and institutions since World War II.

With the movement flagging, some of its leaders invited Martin Luther King Jr. to come to Birmingham. While serving a nine-day prison term in April 1963 for violating a ban on demonstrations, King composed one of his most eloquent pleas for racial justice, the "Letter from Birmingham Jail." Responding to local clergymen who counseled patience, King related the litany of abuses faced by black southerners, from police brutality to the daily humiliation of having to explain to their children why they could not enter amusement parks or public swimming pools. The "white moderate," King declared, must put aside fear of disorder and commit himself to racial justice.

During the climactic demonstrations in Birmingham, firemen assaulted young African-Americans with high-pressure hoses. Broadcast on television, such pictures posed a serious problem for the United States in its battle for the "hearts and minds" of people around the world and forced the Kennedy administration to confront the contradiction between the rhetoric of freedom and the reality of racism.

In May, King made the bold decision to send black schoolchildren into the streets of Birmingham. Police chief Eugene "Bull" Connor unleashed his forces against the thousands of young marchers. The images, broadcast on television, of children being assaulted with nightsticks, high-pressure fire hoses, and attack dogs produced a wave of revulsion throughout the world. It led President Kennedy, as will be related later, to endorse the movement's goals. Leading businessmen, fearing that the city was becoming an international symbol of brutality, brokered an end to the demonstrations that desegregated downtown stores and restaurants and promised that black salespeople would be hired.

In June 1963, a sniper killed Medgar Evers, field secretary of the NAACP in Mississippi. In September, a bomb exploded at a black Baptist church in Birmingham, killing four young girls. (Not until 2002 was the last of those who committed this act of domestic terrorism tried and convicted.)

Three participants in the 1963 March on Washington stand in front of the White House with signs invoking freedom and the memory of slavery.

The March on Washington

On August 28, 1963, two weeks before the Birmingham church bombing, 250,000 black and white Americans converged on the nation's capital for the **March on Washington**, often considered the high point of the nonviolent civil rights movement. Calls for the passage of a civil rights bill pending before Congress took center stage. But the march's goals also included a public-works program to reduce unemployment, an increase in the minimum wage, and a law barring discrimination in employment. These demands, and the marchers' slogan, "Jobs and Freedom," revealed how the black movement had, for the moment, forged an alliance with white liberal groups. On the steps of the Lincoln Memorial, King delivered his most famous speech, including the words, "I have a dream that one day this nation will rise up and live out the true meaning of its creed: 'We hold these truths to be self-evident, that all men are created equal.'"

Tensions within the civil rights movement

The movement was not without internal tensions. March organizers ordered SNCC leader John Lewis (later a congressman from Georgia) to tone down his speech, the original text of which called on blacks to "free ourselves of the chains of political and economic slavery" and march "through the heart of Dixie the way Sherman did . . . and burn Jim Crow to the ground." Lewis's rhetoric forecast the more militant turn many in the movement would soon be taking.

Placing hope in the federal government

Civil rights activists also resurrected the Civil War–era vision of national authority as the custodian of American freedom. Despite the fact that the federal government had for many decades promoted segregation, blacks' historical experience suggested that they had more hope for justice from national power than from local governments or civic institutions—home owners' associations, businesses, private clubs—still riddled with racism. It remained unclear whether the federal government would take up this responsibility.

THE KENNEDY YEARS

John F. Kennedy served as president for less than three years and, in domestic affairs, had few tangible accomplishments. But his administration is widely viewed today as a moment of youthful glamour, soaring hopes, and dynamic leadership at home and abroad.

"The torch has been passed"

Kennedy's inaugural address of January 1961 announced a watershed in American politics: "The torch has been passed," he declared, "to a new generation of Americans" who would "pay any price, bear any burden," to "assure the survival and success of liberty." But although the sit-ins were by now a year old, the speech said nothing about segregation or race. At the outset of his presidency, Kennedy regarded civil rights as a distraction from his main concern—vigorous conduct of the Cold War.

Kennedy and the World

Kennedy's agenda envisioned new initiatives aimed at countering communist influence in the world. One of his first acts was to establish the Peace Corps, which sent young Americans abroad to aid in the economic and educational progress of developing countries and to improve the image of the United States there. When the Soviets in April 1961 launched a satellite carrying the first man into orbit around the earth, Kennedy announced that the United States would mobilize its resources to land a man on the moon by the end of the decade. The goal seemed almost impossible when announced, but it was stunningly accomplished in 1969.

The Peace Corps

Like his predecessors, Kennedy viewed the entire world through the lens of the Cold War. This outlook shaped his dealings with Fidel Castro, who led a revolution that in 1959 ousted Cuban dictator Fulgencio Batista. Until Castro took power, Cuba was an economic dependency of the United States. When his government began nationalizing American landholdings and other investments and signed an agreement to sell sugar to the Soviet Union, the Eisenhower administration suspended trade and diplomatic relations with the island. The CIA began training anti-Castro exiles for an invasion of Cuba.

Kennedy as Cold Warrior

In April 1961, Kennedy allowed the CIA to launch its invasion at a site known as the Bay of Pigs. But the **Bay of Pigs invasion** proved to be a total failure and only strengthened Cuba's ties to the Soviet Union. The Kennedy administration tried other methods, including assassination attempts, to get rid of Castro's government.

Bay of Pigs

President Kennedy and his wife, Jacqueline, arriving at Love Field in Dallas, Texas, on the day of his assassination.

The Missile Crisis

Meanwhile, relations between the two "superpowers" deteriorated. In August 1961, in order to stem a growing tide of emigrants fleeing from East to West Berlin, the Soviets constructed a wall separating the two parts of the city. Until its demolition in 1989, the Berlin Wall would stand as a tangible symbol of the Cold War and the division of Europe.

The most dangerous crisis of the Kennedy administration, and in many ways of the entire Cold War, came in October 1962, when American spy planes discovered that the Soviet Union was installing missiles in Cuba capable of reaching the United States with nuclear weapons. Rejecting advice from military leaders that he authorize an attack on Cuba, which would almost certainly have triggered a Soviet response in Berlin and perhaps a nuclear war, Kennedy imposed a blockade, or "quarantine," of the island and demanded the missiles' removal. After tense behind-the-scenes negotiations, Soviet premier Nikita Khrushchev agreed to

James Meredith, the first black student to attend the University of Mississippi, in a classroom where white classmates refused to sit near him.

withdraw the missiles. Kennedy pledged that the United States would not invade Cuba and secretly agreed to remove American Jupiter missiles from Turkey, from which they could reach the Soviet Union.

The **Cuban missile crisis** seems to have lessened Kennedy's passion for the Cold War. Indeed, he appears to have been shocked by the casual way military leaders spoke of "winning" a nuclear exchange in which tens of millions of Americans and Russians were certain to die. In 1963, he called for greater cooperation with the Soviets. That summer, the two countries agreed to a treaty banning the testing of nuclear weapons in the atmosphere and in space. In announcing the agreement, Kennedy paid tribute to the small movement against nuclear weapons that had been urging such a ban for several years.

New York City train passengers reading the news of President Kennedy's assassination, November 22, 1963.

Kennedy and Civil Rights

In his first two years in office, Kennedy was preoccupied with foreign policy. But in 1963, the crisis over civil rights eclipsed other concerns. Until then, Kennedy had been reluctant to take a forceful stand on black demands. He used federal force when obstruction of civil rights law became acute, as at the University of Mississippi. But he failed to protect activists from violence, insisting that law enforcement was a local matter.

Events in Birmingham in May 1963 forced Kennedy's hand. In June, he went on national television to call for the passage of a law banning discrimination in all places of public accommodation, a major goal of the civil rights movement. The nation, he asserted, faced a moral crisis: "We preach freedom around the world, . . . but are we to say to the world, and much more importantly, to each other, that this is a land of the free except for Negroes?"

Kennedy did not live to see his civil rights bill enacted. On November 22, 1963, while riding in a motorcade through Dallas, Texas, he was shot and killed. Most likely, the assassin was Lee Harvey Oswald, a troubled former marine. Partly because Oswald was murdered two days later by a local nightclub owner while in police custody, speculation about a possible conspiracy continues to this day. In any event, Kennedy's death brought an abrupt and utterly unexpected end to his presidency. It fell to his successor, Lyndon B. Johnson, to secure passage of the civil rights bill and to launch a program of domestic liberalism far more ambitious than anything Kennedy had envisioned.

Kennedy assassination

LYNDON JOHNSON'S PRESIDENCY

Unlike John F. Kennedy, raised in a wealthy and powerful family, Lyndon Johnson grew up in one of the poorest parts of the United States, the central Texas hill country. Johnson never forgot the poor Mexican and white children he had taught in a Texas school in the early 1930s. Far more interested than Kennedy in domestic reform, he continued to hold the New Deal view that government had an obligation to assist less fortunate members of society.

The Civil Rights Act of 1964

Just five days after Kennedy's assassination, Johnson called on Congress to enact the civil rights bill as the most fitting memorial to his slain predecessor.

In 1964, Congress passed the **Civil Rights Act**, which prohibited racial discrimination in employment, institutions like hospitals and schools, and privately owned public accommodations such as restaurants, hotels, and theaters. It also banned discrimination on the grounds of sex—a provision added by opponents of civil rights in an effort to derail the entire bill and embraced by liberal and female members of Congress as a way to broaden its scope. Johnson knew that many whites opposed the new law. An aide

Civil Rights Act of 1964

later claimed that after signing the bill, Johnson remarked, "I think we delivered the South to the Republican Party."

Two students at a Freedom School in Mississippi, photographed in 1964.

Freedom Summer

The 1964 law did not address a major concern of the civil rights movement—the right to vote in the South. That summer, a coalition of civil rights groups launched a voter registration drive in Mississippi. Hundreds of white college students from the North traveled to the state to take part in Freedom Summer. An outpouring of violence greeted the campaign, including thirty-five bombings and numerous beatings of civil rights workers. In June, three young activists—Michael Schwerner and Andrew Goodman, white students from the North, and James Chaney, a local black youth—were kidnapped by a group headed by a deputy sheriff and murdered near Philadelphia, Mississippi. Although many black lives had been lost in the movement, the deaths of the two white students now focused unprecedented attention on Mississippi and on the apparent inability of the federal government to protect citizens seeking to exercise their constitutional rights.

The MFDP

Freedom Summer led directly to one of the most dramatic confrontations of the civil rights era—the campaign by the Mississippi Freedom Democratic Party (MFDP) to take the seats of the state's all-white official party at the 1964 Democratic national convention in Atlantic City, New Jersey. The civil rights movement in Mississippi had created the MFDP, open to all residents of the state. At televised hearings before the credentials committee, Fannie Lou Hamer of the MFDP held a national audience spellbound with her account of growing up in poverty in the Yazoo-Mississippi Delta and of the savage beatings she had endured at the hands of police. Party liberals, including Johnson's running mate, Hubert Humphrey, pressed for a compromise in which two black delegates would be granted seats. But the MFDP rejected the proposal.

Fannie Lou Hamer

The 1964 Election

The events at Atlantic City severely weakened black activists' faith in the responsiveness of the political system and forecast the impending breakup of the coalition between the civil rights movement and the liberal wing of the Democratic Party. For the moment, however, the movement rallied behind Johnson's campaign for reelection. Johnson's opponent, Senator Barry Goldwater of Arizona, demanded a more aggressive conduct of the Cold War. But Goldwater directed most of his critique against "internal" dangers to freedom, especially the New Deal welfare state, which he believed stifled individual initiative and independence. He voted against the Civil Rights Act of 1964. His acceptance speech at the Republican national convention contained the explosive statement, "Extremism in the defense of liberty is no vice."

A billboard for Senator Barry Goldwater's 1964 presidential campaign appealed to voters who were reluctant to support Goldwater's candidacy openly but secretly agreed with his conservatism. An opponent added a comment at the bottom.

Stigmatized by the Democrats as an extremist who would repeal Social Security and risk nuclear war, Goldwater went down to a disastrous defeat. Johnson received almost 43 million votes to Goldwater's 27 million. Democrats swept to two-to-one majorities in both houses of Congress. But Goldwater's message enabled him to carry five Lower South states, and segregationist governor George Wallace of Alabama showed in several Democratic primaries that politicians could strike electoral gold by appealing to white opposition to the civil rights movement. Although few realized it, the 1964 campaign marked a milestone in the resurgence of American conservatism.

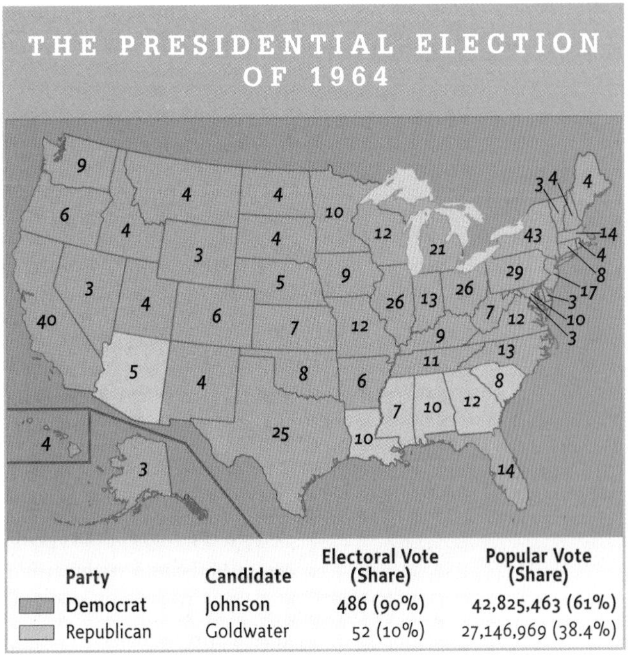

THE PRESIDENTIAL ELECTION OF 1964
Party | Candidate | Electoral Vote (Share) | Popular Vote (Share)
Democrat | Johnson | 486 (90%) | 42,825,463 (61%)
Republican | Goldwater | 52 (10%) | 27,146,969 (38.4%)

The Conservative Sixties

The 1960s, today recalled as a decade of radicalism, clearly had a conservative side as well. With the founding in 1960 of Young Americans for Freedom (YAF), conservative students emerged as a force in politics. There were striking parallels between the Sharon Statement, issued by ninety young people who gathered at the estate of conservative intellectual William F. Buckley in Sharon, Connecticut, to establish YAF, and the Port Huron Statement of

Segregationists wave Confederate battle flags at a 1960 protest against school integration in New Orleans, an example of "white backlash" that enabled Barry Goldwater to carry the state in 1964.

SDS of 1962 (discussed later in this chapter). Both manifestos portrayed youth as the cutting edge of a new radicalism, and both claimed to offer a route to greater freedom. The Sharon Statement summarized beliefs that had circulated among conservatives during the past decade—the free market underpinned "personal freedom," government must be strictly limited, and "international communism," the gravest threat to liberty, must be destroyed.

Goldwater also brought new constituencies to the conservative cause. His campaign aroused enthusiasm in the rapidly expanding suburbs of southern California and the Southwest. Orange County, California, many of whose residents had recently arrived from the East and Midwest and worked in defense-related industries, became a nationally known center of grassroots conservative activism. And by carrying five states of the Lower South, Goldwater showed that the civil rights revolution had redrawn the nation's political map, opening the door to a "southern strategy" that would eventually lead the entire region into the Republican Party.

Strom Thurmond

Well before the rise of Black Power, a reaction against civil rights gains offered conservatives new opportunities and threatened the stability of the Democratic coalition. In 1962, YAF bestowed its Freedom Award on Senator Strom Thurmond of South Carolina, one of the country's most prominent segregationists. During the 1960s, most conservatives abandoned talk of racial superiority and inferiority. But conservative appeals to law and order, "freedom of association," and the evils of welfare often had strong racial overtones. Racial divisions would prove to be a political gold mine for conservatives.

The Voting Rights Act

Selma, Alabama

One last legislative triumph, however, lay ahead for the civil rights movement. In January 1965, King launched a voting rights campaign in Selma, Alabama, a city where only 355 of 15,000 black residents had been allowed to register to vote. In March, defying a ban by Governor Wallace, King attempted to lead a march from Selma to the state capital, Montgomery. When the marchers reached the bridge leading out of the city, state police assaulted them with cattle prods, whips, and tear gas.

Once again, violence against nonviolent demonstrators flashed across television screens throughout the world. Calling Selma a milestone in "man's unending search for freedom," Johnson asked Congress to enact a law securing the right to vote. He closed his speech by quoting the demonstrators' song, "We Shall Overcome." Never before had the movement received so powerful an endorsement from the federal government. Congress quickly passed the **Voting Rights Act** of 1965, which allowed federal officials to register voters. In addition, the Twenty-fourth Amendment to the Constitution outlawed the poll tax, which had long prevented poor blacks (and some whites) from voting in the South.

LBJ's support

Immigration Reform

By 1965, the civil rights movement had succeeded in eradicating the legal bases of second-class citizenship. The belief that racism should no longer serve as a foundation of public policy spilled over into other realms. In 1965, the **Hart-Celler Act** abandoned the national-origins quota system of immigration, which had excluded Asians and severely restricted southern and eastern Europeans. The law established new, racially neutral criteria for immigration, notably family reunification and possession of skills in demand in the United States. On the other hand, because of growing hostility in the Southwest to Mexican immigration, the law established the first limit, 120,000, on newcomers from the Western Hemisphere.

Abandoning the national-origins quota system

The immigration law opened the country's borders in significant ways compared with the restrictive quotas in existence since 1924. As Oscar Handlin made plain in the "Who Is an American?" document in Chapter 23, immigrants and their descendants believed that the 1924 quotas suggested that they were not truly welcome in American society. They demanded to be seen as equal members.

The new law had many unexpected results. At the time, immigrants represented only 5 percent of the American population—the lowest proportion since the 1830s. No one anticipated that the new quotas not only would lead to an explosive rise in immigration but also would spark a dramatic shift in which newcomers from Latin America, the Caribbean, and Asia came to outnumber those from Europe. Taken together, the civil rights revolution and immigration reform marked the triumph of a pluralist conception of Americanism. By 1976, 85 percent of respondents to a public-opinion survey agreed with the statement, "The United States was meant to be . . . a country made up of many races, religions, and nationalities."

A sharecropper's shack alongside Jefferson Davis Highway, the route followed from Selma to Montgomery, Alabama, in 1965, by marchers demanding voting rights. The photograph, by James "Spider" Martin, who chronicled the march, suggests the deep-seated inequalities that persisted a century after the end of the Civil War.

Seated near the Statue of Liberty, with New York's skyline in the background, President Johnson signs the Hart-Celler Act of 1965.

The Great Society

Expanding social programs

Expansion of federal government

After his landslide victory of 1964, Johnson outlined the most sweeping proposal for governmental action to promote the general welfare since the New Deal. Johnson's initiatives of 1965–1967, known collectively as the **Great Society**, provided health services to the poor and elderly in the new Medicaid and Medicare programs and poured federal funds into education and urban development. New agencies, such as the Equal Employment Opportunity Commission, the National Endowments for the Humanities and for the Arts, and a national public broadcasting network, were created. These measures greatly expanded the powers of the federal government, and they completed and extended the social agenda (with the exception of national health insurance) that had been stalled in Congress since 1938.

Unlike the New Deal, the Great Society was a response to prosperity, not depression. The mid-1960s was a time of rapid economic expansion, fueled by increased government spending and a tax cut on individuals and businesses initially proposed by Kennedy and enacted in 1964. Johnson and Democratic liberals believed that economic growth made it possible to fund ambitious new government programs and to improve the quality of life.

The War on Poverty

The centerpiece of the Great Society, however, was the crusade to eradicate poverty, launched by Johnson early in 1964. Michael Harrington's 1962 book *The Other America* revealed that 40 to 50 million Americans lived in poverty.

During the 1930s, Democrats had attributed poverty to an imbalance of economic power and flawed economic institutions. In the 1960s, the administration attributed it to an absence of skills and a lack of proper attitudes and work habits. Thus, the **War on Poverty** did not address the economic changes that were reducing the number of well-paid manufacturing jobs and leaving poor families in rural areas like Appalachia and decaying urban ghettos with little hope of economic advancement.

One of the Great Society's most popular and successful components, food stamps, offered direct aid to the poor. But, in general, the War on Poverty concentrated on equipping the poor with skills and rebuilding their spirit and motivation. It provided Head Start (an early childhood education program), job training, legal services, and scholarships for poor college students. It also created VISTA, a domestic version of the Peace Corps for the inner cities. The War on Poverty required that poor people play a leading part in the design and implementation of local policies, a recipe for continuing conflict with local political leaders accustomed to controlling the flow of federal dollars. The grassroots War on Poverty contributed to an upsurge of local radical activism.

As part of his War on Poverty, President Lyndon Johnson visited Appalachia, one of the poorest places in the United States.

Freedom and Equality

Recognizing that black poverty was fundamentally different from white, because its roots lay in "past injustice and present prejudice," Johnson sought to redefine the relationship between freedom and equality. Economic liberty, he insisted, meant more than equal opportunity: "You do not wipe away the scars of centuries by saying: Now you are free to go where you want, do as you desire, and choose the leaders you please. . . . We seek . . . not just equality as a right and a theory, but equality as a fact and as a result."

Johnson's Great Society may not have achieved equality "as a fact." But it represented the most expansive effort in the nation's history to mobilize the powers of the national government to address the needs of the least-advantaged Americans.

Coupled with the decade's high rate of economic growth, the War on Poverty succeeded in reducing the incidence of poverty from 22 percent to 13 percent of American families during the 1960s. It has fluctuated around the latter figure ever since. By the 1990s, thanks to the civil rights movement and the Great Society, the historic gap between whites and blacks in education, income, and access to skilled employment narrowed considerably. But one-third of all black children still live in poverty.

During the 1960s, an expanding economy and government programs assisting the poor produced a steady decrease in the percentage of Americans living in poverty.

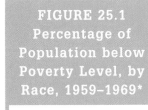

FIGURE 25.1 Percentage of Population below Poverty Level, by Race, 1959–1969*

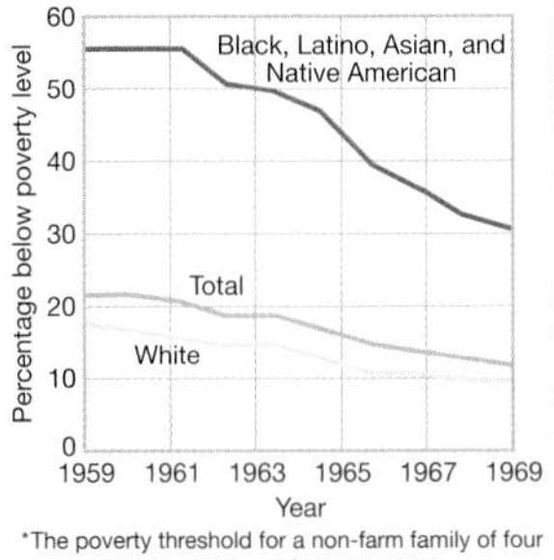

*The poverty threshold for a non-farm family of four was $3,743 in 1969 and $2,973 in 1959.

THE CHANGING BLACK MOVEMENT

In the mid-1960s, economic issues rose to the forefront of the civil rights agenda. Violent outbreaks in black ghettos outside the South drew attention to the national scope of racial injustice and to inequalities in jobs, education, and housing that the dismantling of legal segregation left intact.

The Urban Uprisings

Riots

The first riots—really, battles between angry blacks and the predominantly white police (widely seen by many residents as an occupying army)—erupted in Harlem in 1964. Far larger was the Watts uprising of 1965, which took place in the black ghetto of Los Angeles only days after Johnson signed the Voting Rights Act. An estimated 50,000 persons took part in this "rebellion," attacking police and firemen, looting white-owned businesses, and burning buildings. It required 15,000 police and National Guardsmen to restore order, by which time thirty-five people lay dead, 900 were injured, and $30 million worth of property had been destroyed.

By the summer of 1967, urban uprisings left twenty-three dead in Newark and forty-three in Detroit, where entire blocks went up in flames and property damage ran into the hundreds of millions of dollars. The vio-

A semblance of normal life resumes amid the rubble of the Watts uprising of August 1965.

lence led Johnson to appoint a commission headed by Illinois governor Otto Kerner to study the causes of urban rioting. Released in 1968, the Kerner Report blamed the violence on "segregation and poverty" and offered a powerful indictment of "white racism." But the report failed to offer any clear proposals for change.

With black unemployment twice that of whites and the average black family income little more than half the white norm, the movement looked for ways to "make freedom real" for black Americans. In 1964, King called for a "Bill of Rights for the Disadvantaged" to mobilize the nation's resources to abolish economic deprivation. His proposal was directed against poverty in general, but King also insisted that after "doing something special *against* the Negro for hundreds of years," the United States had an obligation to "do something special *for* him now"—an early call for what would come to be known as "affirmative action."

Early affirmative action

In 1966, King launched the Chicago Freedom Movement, with demands quite different from its predecessors in the South—an end to discrimination by employers and unions, equal access to mortgages, the integration of public housing, and the construction of low-income housing scattered throughout the region. Confronting the entrenched power of Mayor Richard J. Daley's political machine and the ferocious opposition of white home owners, the movement failed.

Chicago Freedom Movement

Malcolm X

The civil rights movement's first phase had produced a clear set of objectives, far-reaching accomplishments, and a series of coherent if sometimes competitive organizations. The second witnessed political fragmentation and few significant victories. Even during the heyday of the integration struggle, the fiery orator Malcolm X had insisted that blacks must control the political and economic resources of their communities and rely on their own efforts rather than working with whites. Malcolm Little dropped his "slave surname" in favor of "X," symbolizing blacks' separation from their African ancestry. He became a spokesman for the Nation of Islam, or Black Muslims, and a sharp critic of the ideas of integration and nonviolence.

The Nation of Islam

On a 1964 trip to Mecca, Saudi Arabia, Islam's spiritual home, Malcolm X witnessed harmony among Muslims of all races. He now began to speak of the possibility of interracial cooperation for radical change in the United States. But when members of the Nation of Islam assassinated him in February 1965 after he had formed his own Organization of Afro-American Unity, Malcolm X left neither a consistent ideology nor a coherent movement. However, his call for blacks to

Legacy of Malcolm X

rely on their own resources struck a chord among the urban poor and younger civil rights activists.

The Rise of Black Power

Malcolm X was the intellectual father of **Black Power**, a slogan that came to national attention in 1966 when SNCC leader Stokely Carmichael used it during a civil rights march in Mississippi.

African-American pride

A highly imprecise idea, Black Power suggested everything from the election of more black officials (hardly a radical notion) to the belief that black Americans were a colonized people whose freedom could be won only through a revolutionary struggle for self-determination. In many communities where black parents felt that the local public education system failed to educate their children adequately, it inspired the establishment of black-operated local schools that combined traditional learning with an emphasis on pride in African-American history and identity. But however employed, the idea reflected the radicalization of young civil rights activists and sparked an explosion of racial self-assertion, reflected in the slogan "Black Is Beautiful." The abandonment of the word "Negro" in favor of "Afro-American" as well as the popularity of African styles of dress and the "natural," or "Afro," hairdo among both men and women reflected a new sense of racial pride and a rejection of white norms.

The Black Panther Party

Inspired by the idea of black self-determination, SNCC and CORE repudiated their previous interracialism, and new militant groups sprang into existence. Most prominent of the new groups, in terms of publicity, if not numbers, was the Black Panther Party. Founded in Oakland, California, in 1966, it became notorious for advocating armed self-defense in response to police brutality. The party's youthful members alarmed whites by wearing military garb, although they also ran health clinics, schools, and children's breakfast programs. But internal disputes and a campaign against the Black Panthers by police and the FBI, which left several leaders dead in shootouts, destroyed the organization. A number of former members successfully made the transition to electoral politics, including Bobby Rush, a long-serving member of Congress from Chicago; Charles Barron, a city councilman in New York; and Marion Barry, mayor of Washington.

Social crisis

By 1967, with the escalation of U.S. military involvement in Vietnam, the War on Poverty ground to a halt. By then, with uprisings punctuating the urban landscape, the antiwar movement assuming massive proportions, and millions of young people ostentatiously rejecting mainstream values, American society faced its greatest crisis since the Depression.

VIETNAM AND THE NEW LEFT

Old and New Lefts

To most Americans, the rise of a protest movement among white youth came as a complete surprise. If blacks' grievances appeared self-evident, those of white college students were difficult to understand. What persuaded large numbers of children of affluence to reject the values and institutions of their society? In part, the answer lay in a redefinition of the meaning of freedom by what came to be called the **New Left**.

The New Left

The New Left challenged not only mainstream America but also what it dismissively called the Old Left. Unlike the Communist Party, it did not take the Soviet Union as a model or see the working class as the main agent of social change. Instead of economic equality, the language of New Deal liberals, the New Left spoke of loneliness, isolation, and alienation, of powerlessness in the face of bureaucratic institutions and a hunger for authenticity that affluence could not provide. By 1968, thanks to the coming of age of the baby-boom generation and the growing number of jobs that required post–high school skills, more than 7 million students attended college, more than the number of farmers or steelworkers.

Rising college attendance

The New Left's greatest inspiration was the black freedom movement. More than any other event, the sit-ins catalyzed white student activism. Here was the unlikely combination that created the upheaval known as the Sixties—the convergence of society's most excluded members demanding full access to all its benefits, with the children of the middle class rejecting the social mainstream.

Members of Students for a Democratic Society (SDS) at the University of Delaware in their yearbook photo. Despite their raised fists, they appear eminently respectable compared to radicals who emerged later in the decade. The group is entirely white.

The Fading Consensus

The years 1962 and 1963 witnessed the appearance of several pathbreaking books that challenged one or another aspect of the 1950s consensus. James Baldwin's *The Fire Next Time* gave angry voice to the black revolution. Rachel Carson's *Silent Spring* exposed the environmental costs of economic growth. Michael Harrington's *The Other America* revealed the persistence of poverty amid plenty. *The Death and Life of Great American Cities*, by Jane Jacobs, criticized urban renewal, the removal of the poor from city centers, and the destruction of neighborhoods to build highways.

Yet in some ways the most influential critique of all arose in 1962 from **Students for a Democratic Society** (SDS), an offshoot of the socialist League for Industrial Democracy. Meeting at Port Huron, Michigan, some sixty college students adopted a document that captured the mood and summarized the beliefs of this generation of student protesters.

The Port Huron Statement

The **Port Huron Statement** offered a new vision of social change. "We seek the establishment," it proclaimed, of "a democracy of individual participation, [in which] the individual shares in those social decisions determining the quality and direction of his life." Freedom, for the New Left, meant "participatory democracy." Although rarely defined with precision, this became a standard by which students judged existing social arrangements—workplaces, schools, government—and found them wanting.

University of California at Berkeley

In 1964, events at the University of California, Berkeley, revealed the possibility for a mobilization of students in the name of participatory democracy. Berkeley was an immense, impersonal institution where enrollments in many classes approached 1,000 students. The spark that set student protests alight was a new rule prohibiting political groups from using a central area of the campus to spread their ideas. Students responded by creating the Free Speech movement.

Thousands of Berkeley students became involved in the protests in the months that followed. Their program moved from demanding a repeal of the new rule to a critique of the entire structure of the university and of an education geared toward preparing graduates for corporate jobs. The university gave in on the speech ban early in 1965.

America and Vietnam

Vietnam and anticommunism

By 1965 the black movement and the emergence of the New Left had shattered the climate of consensus of the 1950s. But what transformed protest into a full-fledged generational rebellion was the war in Vietnam. The war tragically revealed the danger that Walter Lippmann had warned of at the outset of the Cold War—viewing the entire world and every local situation within it through the either-or lens of an anticommunist crusade. A Vietnam specialist in the State Department who attended a policy meeting in August 1963 later recalled "the abysmal ignorance around the table of the particular facts of Vietnam. . . . They [believed] that we could manipulate other states and build nations; that we knew all the answers."

Commitment to South Vietnam

As noted in the previous chapter, the Truman and Eisenhower administrations cast their lot with French colonialism in the region. After the French defeat, they financed the creation of a pro-American South Vietnamese government. By the 1960s, the United States was committed to the survival of this corrupt regime.

A photograph, date unknown, of members of the National Liberation Front, which fought the United States in Vietnam. Women made up a substantial part of the NLF.

Fear that voters would not forgive them for "losing" Vietnam made it impossible for presidents Kennedy and Johnson to remove the United States from an increasingly untenable situation. Kennedy's foreign policy advisers saw Vietnam as a test of whether the United States could, through "counterinsurgency"—intervention to counter internal uprisings in non-communist countries—halt the spread of Third World revolutions. South Vietnamese leader Ngo Dinh Diem resisted American advice to broaden his government's base of support. In October 1963, after large Buddhist demonstrations against his regime, the United States approved a military coup that led to Diem's death. When Kennedy was assassinated the following month, there were 17,000 American military advisers in South Vietnam.

"Counterinsurgency"

Lyndon Johnson's War

Lyndon B. Johnson came to the presidency with little experience in foreign relations. But he was an adept politician and knew that Republicans had used the "loss" of China as a weapon against Truman.

In August 1964, North Vietnamese vessels encountered an American ship on a spy mission off its coast. When North Vietnamese patrol boats fired on the American vessel, Johnson proclaimed that the United States was a victim of "aggression." In response, Congress passed the **Gulf of Tonkin resolution**, authorizing the president to take "all necessary measures to repel armed attack" in Vietnam. Only two members—senators Ernest Gruening of Alaska and Wayne Morse of Oregon—voted against giving Johnson this blank check.

Authorizing military action

VOICES OF FREEDOM

From Barry Goldwater, Speech at Republican National Convention (1964)

In his speech accepting the Republican nomination for president in 1964, Senator Barry Goldwater of Arizona outlined a political vision rooted in the conservatism of the Southwest and California. Charged with being an extremist, Goldwater responded, "Extremism in the defense of liberty is no vice," an explosive statement that enabled President Lyndon Johnson to portray him as a dangerous radical.

My fellow Americans, the tide has been running against freedom. Our people have followed false prophets. We must, and we shall, return to proven ways—not because they are old, but because they are true. We must, and we shall, set the tide running again in the cause of freedom. And this party, with its every action, every word, every breath, and every heartbeat, has but a single resolve, and that is freedom—freedom made orderly for this Nation by our constitutional government; freedom under a government limited by laws of nature and of nature's God; freedom—balanced so that liberty lacking order will not become the slavery of the prison cell; balanced so that liberty lacking order will not become the license of the mob and of the jungle.

Now, we Americans understand freedom. We have earned it, we have lived for it, and we have died for it. This Nation and its people are freedom's model in a searching world. We can be freedom's missionaries in a doubting world. But, ladies and gentlemen, first we must renew freedom's mission in our own hearts and in our own homes. . . .

Tonight there is violence in our streets, corruption in our highest offices, aimlessness among our youth, anxiety among our elders and there is a virtual despair among the many who look beyond material success for the inner meaning of their lives. . . .

We Republicans seek a government that attends to its inherent responsibilities of maintaining a stable monetary and fiscal climate, encouraging a free and a competitive economy and enforcing law and order. . . .

Our towns and our cities, then our counties, then our states, then our regional contacts and only then, the national government. That, let me remind you, is the ladder of liberty, built by decentralized power. On it also we must have balance between the branches of government at every level. . . .

I would remind you that extremism in the defense of liberty is no vice. And let me remind you also that moderation in the pursuit of justice is no virtue.

From Statement of Purpose, National Organization for Women (1966)

Founded in 1966, the National Organization for Women (NOW) gave voice to the movement for equality for women known as the "second wave" of feminism. Written by Betty Friedan and adopted at the group's organizing meeting in Washington, D.C., the statement of purpose outlined a wide range of areas, public and private, where women continued to be denied full freedom.

The time has come for a new movement toward true equality for all women in America, and toward a fully equal partnership of the sexes, as part of the world-wide revolution of human rights now taking place within and beyond our national borders.

The purpose of NOW is to take action to bring women into full participation in the mainstream of American society now, exercising all the privileges and responsibilities thereof in truly equal partnership with men. . . .

The actual position of women in the United States has declined, and is declining, to an alarming degree throughout the 1950's and '60s. . . . Working women are becoming increasingly—not less—concentrated on the bottom of the job ladder. . . . Today, women earn only one in three of the B.A.'s and M.A.'s granted, and one in ten of the Ph.D.'s. In all the professions considered of importance to society, and in the executive ranks of industry and government, women are losing ground. Where they are present it is only a token handful. Women comprise less than 1% of federal judges; less than 4% of all lawyers; 7% of doctors. . . .

We do not accept the traditional assumption that a woman has to choose between marriage and motherhood, on the one hand, and serious participation in industry or the professions on the other. . . . True equality of opportunity and freedom of choice for women requires such practical, and possible innovations as a nationwide network of child-care centers, which will make it unnecessary for women to retire completely from society until their children are grown. . . .

We believe that a true partnership between the sexes demands a different concept of marriage, and equitable sharing of the responsibilities of home and children and of the economic burdens of their support. We believe that proper recognition should be given to the economic and social value of homemaking and child-care.

QUESTIONS

1. *Why does Goldwater stress the interconnection of order and liberty?*
2. *What social changes does NOW believe necessary to enable women to enjoy equality and freedom?*
3. *How do the two documents differ in assessing the dangers to American freedom?*

THE VIETNAM WAR, 1964–1975

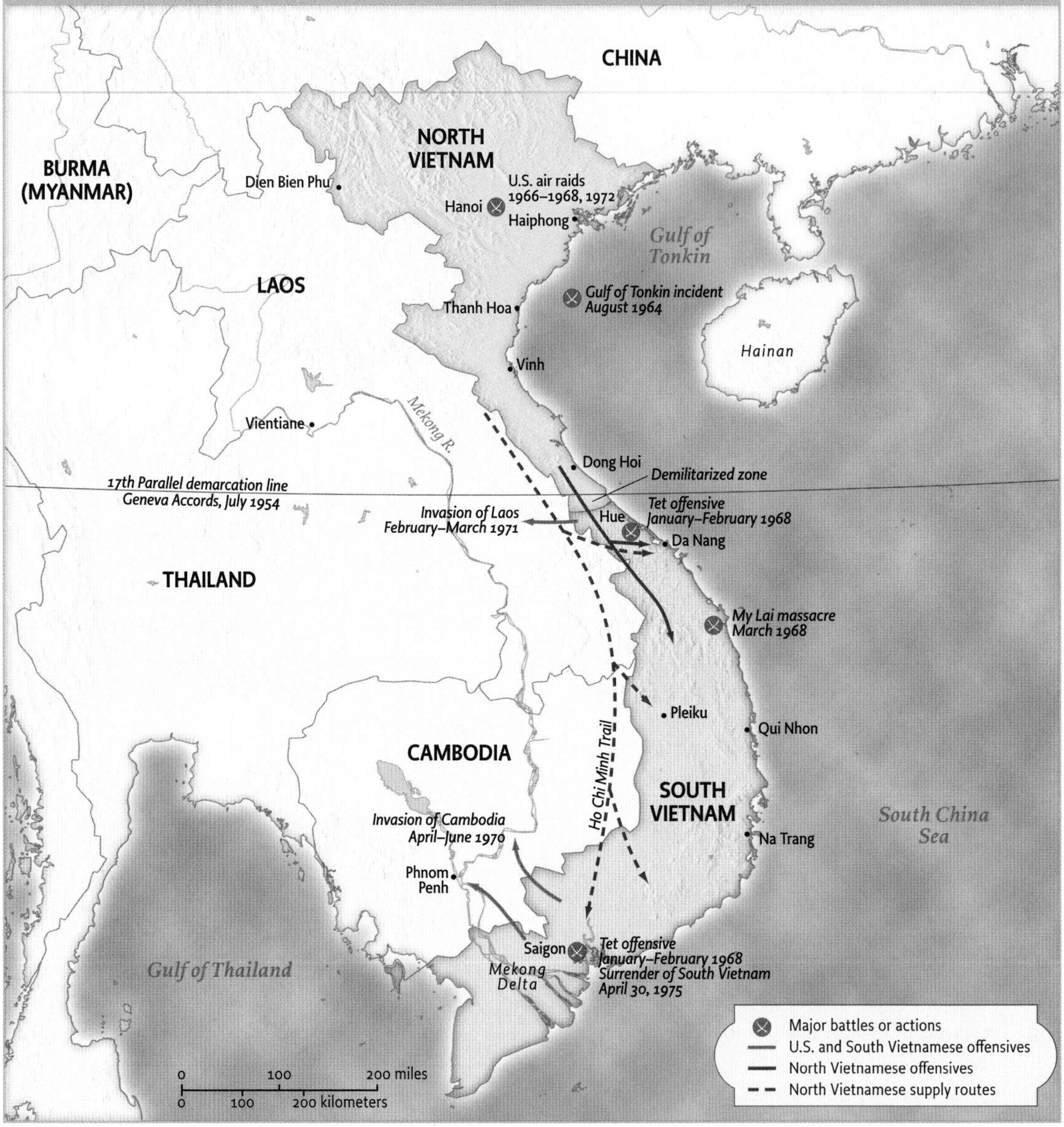

A war of aerial bombing and small guerrilla skirmishes rather than fixed land battles, Vietnam was among the longest wars in American history and the only one the United States has lost.

Immediately after Johnson's 1964 election, the National Security Council recommended that the United States begin air strikes against North Vietnam and introduce American ground troops in the south. Johnson put the plan into effect. At almost the same time, he intervened in the Dominican Republic. Here, military leaders in 1963 had overthrown the left-wing but noncommunist Juan Bosch, the country's first elected president since 1924. In April 1965, another group of military men attempted to restore Bosch to power but were defeated by the ruling junta. Fearing the unrest would lead to "another Cuba," Johnson dispatched 22,000 American troops. The operation's success seemed to bolster Johnson's determination in Vietnam.

Escalation in Vietnam

By 1968, the number of American troops in Vietnam exceeded half a million, and the conduct of the war had become more and more brutal. The North Vietnamese mistreated American prisoners of war held in a camp known sardonically by the inmates as the Hanoi Hilton. American planes dropped more tons of bombs on the small countries of North and South Vietnam than both sides had used in all of World War II. They spread chemicals that destroyed forests to deprive the Viet Cong of hiding places and dropped incendiary bombs filled with napalm, a gelatinous form of gasoline that clings to the skin of anyone exposed to it as it burns.

The Antiwar Movement

As casualties mounted and American bombs poured down on North and South Vietnam, the Cold War foreign policy consensus began to unravel. By 1968, the war had sidetracked much of the Great Society and had torn families, universities, and the Democratic Party apart.

Opposition to the war became the organizing theme that united people with all kinds of doubts and discontents. With college students exempted from the draft, the burden of fighting fell on the working class and the poor. In 1967, Martin Luther King Jr. condemned the administration's Vietnam policy as an unconscionable use of violence and for draining resources from needs at home. At this point, King was the most prominent American to speak out against the war.

Secretary of Defense Robert McNamara, on the left, and his deputy, Cyrus Vance, at a May 1965 meeting at the White House where the war in Vietnam was discussed. A bust of President Kennedy stands in the background. McNamara later wrote in his memoirs that his misgivings only grew as the war progressed.

A poster listing some of the performers who took part in the Woodstock festival in 1969. A dove of peace sits on the guitar, symbolizing the overlap between the antiwar movement and counterculture.

As for SDS, the war seemed the opposite of participatory democracy, since American involvement had come through secret commitments and decisions made by political elites, with no real public debate. In April 1965, SDS invited opponents of American policy in Vietnam to assemble in Washington, D.C. The turnout of 25,000 amazed the organizers, offering the first hint that the antiwar movement would soon enjoy a mass constituency.

By 1967, young men were burning their draft cards or fleeing to Canada to avoid fighting in what they considered an unjust war. In October of that year, 100,000 antiwar protesters assembled at the Lincoln Memorial in Washington, D.C. Many marched across the Potomac River to the Pentagon, where photographers captured them placing flowers in the rifle barrels of soldiers guarding the nerve center of the American military.

The Counterculture

The New Left's definition of freedom initially centered on participatory democracy, a political concept. But as the 1960s progressed, young Americans' understanding of freedom increasingly expanded to include cultural freedom as well. By the late 1960s, millions of young people openly rejected the values and behavior of their elders. For the first time in American history, the flamboyant rejection of respectable norms in clothing, language, sexual behavior, and drug use, previously confined to artists and bohemians, became the basis of a mass movement. Its rallying cry was "liberation."

"Your sons and your daughters are beyond your command," Bob Dylan's song "The Times They Are A-Changin' " bluntly informed mainstream America. To be sure, the **counterculture** in some ways represented not rebellion but the fulfillment of the consumer marketplace. It extended into every realm of life the definition of freedom as the right to individual choice. Self-indulgence and self-destructive behavior were built into the counterculture.

Personal Liberation and the Free Individual

New forms of radical action

But there was far more to the counterculture than new consumer styles or the famed trio of sex, drugs, and rock and roll. To young dissenters, personal liberation meant a search for a way of life in which friendship and pleasure eclipsed the single-minded pursuit of wealth. It also encouraged new forms of radical action. "Underground" newspapers pioneered a personal and politically committed style of journalism. The Youth

A gathering of "Jesus People," one of the religious groups that sprang up in the 1960s.

International Party, or "yippies," introduced humor and theatricality as elements of protest. From the visitors' gallery of the New York Stock Exchange, yippie founder Abbie Hoffman showered dollar bills onto the floor, bringing trading to a halt as brokers scrambled to retrieve the money.

Woodstock

Rock festivals, like Woodstock in upstate New York in 1969, brought together hundreds of thousands of young people to celebrate their alternative lifestyle and independence from adult authority. The opening song at Woodstock, performed by Richie Havens, began with eight repetitions of the single word "freedom."

Faith and the Counterculture

Religious conviction, as has been noted, helped to inspire the civil rights movement. A different religious development, the sweeping reforms initiated in Roman Catholic practice (such as the delivery of the Mass in local languages, not Latin) by the Second Vatican Council of 1962–1965, led many priests, nuns, and lay Catholics to become involved in social justice movements, producing a growing split in the church between liberals and conservatives. Many members of the New Left were motivated by a quest for a new sense of brotherhood and social responsibility, which often sprang from Christian roots. Many young people came to believe that a commitment to social change was a fulfillment of Christian values.

Among the religious developments of the 1960s was the spread of interest in eastern religions and religious practices. The cover of *Yoga Journal* illustrates how one practice entered the mainstream of American life.

The quest for personal authenticity, a feature of the counterculture, led to a flowering of religious and spiritual creativity and experimentation. The Jesus People (called by their detractors Jesus Freaks) saw the hippy lifestyle, with its long hair, unconventional attire, and quest for universal love, as an authentic expression of the outlook of the early church. The

Eastern religions and the counter culture

Sixties also witnessed a burgeoning interest in eastern religions. The Beats of the 1950s had been attracted to Buddhism as a religion that rejected violence and materialism, which they saw as key features of American society. Now, Buddhist practices like yoga and meditation became popular with members of the counterculture and even in the suburban mainstream as a way of promoting spiritual and physical well-being. Some Americans traveled to Tibet and India to seek spiritual guidance from "gurus" (religious leaders) there.

THE NEW MOVEMENTS AND THE RIGHTS REVOLUTION

The civil rights revolution, soon followed by the rise of the New Left, inspired other Americans to voice their grievances and claim their rights. By the late 1960s, new social movements dotted the political landscape.

The counterculture's notion of liberation centered on the free individual. Starting in 1960, the mass marketing of birth-control pills made possible what "free lovers" had long demanded—the separation of sex from procreation. By the late 1960s, sexual freedom had become as much an element of the youth rebellion as long hair and drugs. The sexual revolution was central to another mass movement that emerged in the 1960s—the "second wave" of feminism.

"Second wave" feminism

The Feminine Mystique

During the 1950s, some commentators had worried that the country was wasting its "woman power," a potential weapon in the Cold War. But the public reawakening of feminist consciousness did not get its start until the publication in 1963 of Betty Friedan's ***The Feminine Mystique***. Friedan had written pioneering articles during the 1940s on pay discrimination against women workers and racism in the workplace for the newspaper of the United Electrical Workers' union. But, like other social critics, she now took as her themes the emptiness of consumer culture and the discontents of the middle class. Her opening chapter, "The Problem That Has No Name," painted a devastating picture of talented, educated women trapped in a world that viewed marriage and motherhood as their primary goals.

Betty Friedan

Few books have had the impact of *The Feminine Mystique*. Friedan was deluged by desperate letters from female readers relating how the suburban dream had become a nightmare.

The law slowly began to address feminist concerns. In 1963, Congress passed the Equal Pay Act, barring sex discrimination among holders of the same jobs. The Civil Rights Act of 1964, as noted earlier, prohibited inequalities based on sex as well as race. Deluged with complaints of discrimination from working women, the Equal Employment Opportunity Commission established by the law became a major force in breaking down barriers to female employment. In 1966 the **National Organization for Women** (NOW) was formed, with Friedan as president. Modeled on civil rights organizations, it demanded equal opportunity in jobs, education, and political participation and attacked the "false image of women" spread by the mass media.

In 1967, in a celebrated incident arising from the new feminism, a race official tried to eject Kathrine Switzer from the Boston Marathon, only to be pushed aside by other runners. Considered too fragile for the marathon (whose course covers more than twenty-six miles), women were prohibited from running. Switzer completed the race, and today hundreds of thousands of women around the world compete in marathons each year.

Women's Liberation

A different female revolt was brewing within the civil rights and student movements. Young women who had embraced an ideology of social equality and personal freedom and learned methods of political organizing encountered inequality and sexual exploitation in organizations like SNCC and SDS. Many women in the movement found themselves relegated to typing, cooking, and cleaning for male coworkers.

By 1967, women throughout the country were establishing "consciousness-raising" groups to discuss the sources of their discontent. The new feminism burst onto the national scene at the Miss America beauty pageant of 1968, when protesters filled a "freedom trash can" with objects of "oppression"—girdles, brassieres, high-heeled shoes, and copies of *Playboy* and *Cosmopolitan*. (Contrary to legend, they did not set the contents on fire, but the media invented a new label for radical women—"bra burners.") Inside the hall, demonstrators unfurled banners carrying the slogans "Freedom for Women" and "Women's Liberation."

Personal Freedom

The women's liberation movement inspired a major expansion of the idea of freedom by insisting that it should be applied to the most intimate realms of life. It contended that sexual relations, conditions of marriage, and standards of beauty were as much "political" questions as the war, civil rights, and the class tensions that had traditionally inspired the Left to action. The idea that family life is not off limits to considerations of power and justice repudiated the family-oriented public culture of the 1950s, and it permanently changed Americans' definition of freedom.

Radical feminists' first public campaign demanded the repeal of state laws that underscored women's lack of self-determination by banning abortions or leaving it up to physicians to decide whether a pregnancy could be terminated. In 1969, a group of feminists disrupted legislative hearings on New York's law banning abortions, where the

A 1970 poster urging gay men and lesbians to join the Gay Liberation Front, one of the numerous movements that sprang to life in the late 1960s.

experts scheduled to testify consisted of fourteen men and a Roman Catholic nun.

By this time, feminist ideas had entered the mainstream. In 1962, a poll showed that two-thirds of American women did not feel themselves to be victims of discrimination. By 1974, two-thirds did.

Gay Liberation

In a decade full of surprises, perhaps the greatest of all was the emergence of the movement for gay liberation. Gay men and lesbians had long been stigmatized as sinful or mentally disordered. Most states made homosexual acts illegal, and police regularly harassed the gay subcultures that existed in major cities like San Francisco and New York. Although gay persons had achieved considerable success in many fields, especially the arts and fashion, most kept their sexual orientation secret, or "in the closet."

If one moment marked the advent of "gay liberation," it was a 1969 police raid on the **Stonewall Inn** in New York's Greenwich Village, a gathering place for the gay and lesbian community. Rather than bowing to police harassment, as in the past, gays fought back. Five days of rioting followed, and a militant movement was born. Gay men and lesbians stepped out of the "closet" to insist that sexual orientation is a matter of rights, power, and identity. Prejudice against them persisted. But within a few years, "gay pride" marches were being held in numerous cities.

Latino Activism

As in the case of blacks, a movement for legal rights had long flourished among Mexican-Americans. But the mid-1960s saw the flowering of a new militancy challenging the group's second-class economic status. Like Black Power advocates, the movement emphasized pride in both the Mexican past and the new Chicano culture that had arisen in the United States. Unlike the Black Power movement and SDS, it was closely linked to labor struggles. Beginning in 1965, César Chávez, the son of migrant farm workers and a disciple of King, and Dolores Huerta, a longtime labor activist whose father was a migrant worker and whose mother owned a restaurant and hotel that catered to low-wage farm laborers, led a series of nonviolent pro-

Union activist Dolores Huerta (*center*) and Senator Robert F. Kennedy (*on the far right*) at a demonstration marking the end of César Chávez's twenty-five-day hunger strike in support of striking workers in California's grape fields.

tests, including marches, fasts, and a national boycott of California grapes, to pressure growers to agree to labor contracts with the United Farm Workers union (UFW). The UFW was as much a mass movement for civil rights as a campaign for economic betterment. The boycott mobilized Latino communities throughout the Southwest and drew national attention to the pitifully low wages and oppressive working conditions of migrant laborers. In 1970, the major growers agreed to contracts with the UFW.

An unknown artist transformed the familiar image of a Native American on the nickel into a symbol of militancy.

Red Power

The 1960s also witnessed an upsurge of Native American militancy. The Truman and Eisenhower administrations had sought to dismantle the reservation system and integrate Indians into the American mainstream—a policy known as "termination," since it meant ending recognition of the remaining elements of Indian sovereignty. Many Indian leaders protested vigorously against this policy, and it was abandoned by President Kennedy. Johnson's War on Poverty channeled increased federal funds to reservations. But like other minority groups, Indian activists demanded not simply economic aid but self-determination.

Founded in 1968, the **American Indian Movement** staged protests demanding greater tribal self-government and the restoration of economic resources guaranteed in treaties. In 1969, a group calling itself "Indians of All Tribes" occupied (or, from their point of view, re-occupied) Alcatraz Island in San Francisco Bay, claiming that it had been illegally seized from its original inhabitants. In the years that followed, many Indian tribes would win greater control over education and economic development on the reservations. Indian activists would bring land claims suits, demanding and receiving monetary settlements for past dispossession. In an atmosphere of rising Native American pride, the number of Americans identifying themselves as Indians doubled between 1970 and 1990.

The occupation of Alcatraz Island in San Francisco Bay in 1969 by "Indians of All Tribes" symbolized the emergence of a new militancy among Native Americans.

Environmentalism and the Consumer Movement

Another movement, environmentalism, called into question different pillars of American life—the equation of progress with endless increases in consumption and the faith that science, technology, and economic growth would advance social welfare. In keeping with the spirit of

Environmentalism advanced through affluence

the Sixties, the new environmentalism reflected the very affluence celebrated by proponents of the American Way. As the "quality of life"—including physical fitness, health, and opportunities to enjoy leisure activities—occupied a greater role in the lives of middle-class Americans, the environmental consequences of economic growth received increased attention.

Rachel Carson

The publication in 1962 of ***Silent Spring*** by the marine biologist Rachel Carson brought home to millions of readers the effects of DDT, an insecticide widely used by home owners and farmers against mosquitoes, gypsy moths, and other insects. In chilling detail, Carson related how DDT killed birds and animals and caused sickness among humans.

Carson's work launched the modern environmental movement. The Sierra Club, founded in the 1890s to preserve forests, saw its membership more than triple, and other groups sprang into existence to alert the country to the dangers of water contamination, air pollution, lead in paint, and the extinction of animal species. Nearly every state quickly banned the use of DDT.

Bipartisan support

Despite vigorous opposition from business groups that considered its proposals a violation of property rights, environmentalism attracted the broadest bipartisan support of any of the new social movements. Under Republican president Richard Nixon, Congress during the late 1960s and early 1970s passed a series of measures to protect the environment, including the Clean Air and Clean Water Acts and the Endangered Species Act. On April 22, 1970, the first Earth Day, some 20 million people, most of them under the age of thirty, participated in rallies, concerts, and teach-ins.

Consumer activism

Closely related to environmentalism was the consumer movement, spearheaded by the lawyer Ralph Nader. His book *Unsafe at Any Speed* (1965) exposed how auto manufacturers produced highly dangerous vehicles. General Motors, whose Chevrolet Corvair Nader singled out for its tendency to roll over in certain driving situations, hired private investigators to discredit him.

Consumer protection laws

Nader's campaigns laid the groundwork for the numerous new consumer protection laws and regulations of the 1970s. Unlike 1960s movements that emphasized personal liberation, environmentalism and the consumer movement called for limiting some kinds of freedom—especially the right to use private property in any way the owner desired—in the name of a greater common good.

The Rights Revolution

It is one of the more striking ironies of the 1960s that although the "rights revolution" began in the streets, it achieved constitutional legitimacy through the Supreme Court, historically the most conservative branch of government. Under the guidance of Chief Justice Earl Warren, the Court vastly expanded the rights enjoyed by all Americans and placed them beyond the reach of legislative and local majorities.

Karl Hubenthal's December 8, 1976, cartoon for the *Los Angeles Herald-Examiner* celebrates the rights revolution as an expansion of American liberty.

The Court moved to rein in the anticommunist crusade. The justices overturned convictions of individuals for advocating the overthrow of the government, failing to answer questions before the House Un-American Activities Committee, and refusing to disclose their political beliefs to state officials. By the time Warren retired in 1969, the Court had reaffirmed the right of even the most unpopular viewpoints to First Amendment protection.

The landmark ruling in *New York Times v. Sullivan* (1964) overturned a libel judgment by an Alabama jury against the nation's leading newspaper for carrying an advertisement critical of how local officials treated civil rights demonstrators. Before the 1960s, few Supreme Court cases had dealt with newspaper publishing. *Sullivan* created the modern constitutional law of freedom of the press.

The Court in the 1960s continued the push toward racial equality, overturning numerous local Jim Crow laws. In *Loving v. Virginia* (1967), it declared unconstitutional the laws still on the books in sixteen states that prohibited interracial marriage. This aptly named case arose from the interracial marriage of Richard and Mildred Loving. Barred by Virginia law from marrying, they did so in Washington, D.C., and later returned to their home state. Two weeks after their arrival, the local sheriff entered their home in the middle of the night, roused the couple from bed, and arrested them.

The Court simultaneously pushed forward the process of imposing on the states the obligation to respect the liberties outlined in the Bill of Rights. Among the most important of these decisions was the 5-4 ruling in *Miranda v. Arizona* (1966). This held that an individual in police custody must be informed of the rights to remain silent and to confer with a lawyer before answering questions and must be told that any statements might be used in court. The decision made "Miranda warnings" standard police practice.

The Court also assumed the power to oversee the fairness of democratic procedures at the state and local levels. *Baker v. Carr* (1962) established the principle that districts electing members of state legislatures and Congress must be equal in population. This "one man, one

Richard and Mildred Loving with their children in a 1965 photograph by Grey Villet. Their desire to live in Virginia as husband and wife led to a Supreme Court decision declaring unconstitutional state laws that barred interracial marriages.

"WHAT DO THEY EXPECT US TO DO — LISTEN TO THE KIDS PRAY AT HOME?"
SUPREME COURT RULING
HERBLOCK
THE WASHINGTON POST

The cartoonist Herbert Block's comment on critics of the Supreme Court's decision barring prayer in public schools.

vote" principle overturned apportionment systems in numerous states that had allowed individuals in sparsely inhabited rural areas to enjoy the same representation as residents of populous city districts.

The justices also moved to reinforce the "wall of separation" between church and state. In *Engel v. Vitale,* they decreed that prayers and Bible readings in public schools violated the First Amendment. These rulings proved to be the most unpopular of all the Warren Court's decisions.

The Right to Privacy

The Warren Court not only expanded existing liberties but also outlined entirely new rights in response to the rapidly changing contours of American society. Most dramatic was its assertion of a constitutional right to privacy in ***Griswold v. Connecticut*** (1965), which overturned a state law prohibiting the use of contraceptives. Justice William O. Douglas, who wrote the decision, had once declared, "The right to be let alone is the beginning of all freedom."

Griswold linked privacy to the sanctity of marriage. But the Court soon transformed it into a right of individuals. It extended access to birth control to unmarried adults and ultimately to minors—an admission by the Court that law could not reverse the sexual revolution. These decisions led directly to the most controversial decision that built on the rulings of the Warren Court (even though it occurred in 1973, four years after Warren's retirement). This was ***Roe v. Wade,*** which created a constitutional right to terminate a pregnancy. *Roe* provoked vigorous opposition that has continued to this day.

The rights revolution completed the transformation of American freedom from a set of entitlements enjoyed mainly by white men into an open-ended claim to equality, recognition, and self-determination.

Striking sanitation workers in Memphis, Tennessee. As their signs suggest, they demanded respect as well as higher wages. Having traveled to Memphis to support the strikers, Martin Luther King Jr. was assassinated on April 4, 1968.

I AM A MAN

1968

A Year of Turmoil

The Sixties reached their climax in 1968, a year when momentous events succeeded each other so rapidly that the foundations of society seemed to be dissolving. Late January 1968 saw the **Tet offensive,** in which Viet Cong and North Vietnamese troops launched well-organized uprisings in cities throughout South Vietnam, completely surprising American military leaders. The intensity of the fighting, brought into America's homes on television, shattered public confidence in the Johnson administration, which had repeatedly proclaimed victory to be "just around the corner." Eugene McCarthy, an antiwar senator from Minnesota, announced that he would seek the Democratic nomination for president. Aided by a small army of student volunteers, McCarthy received more than 40 percent of the vote in the New Hampshire primary. Johnson then stunned the nation by announcing that he had decided not to seek reelection.

Meanwhile, Martin Luther King Jr. was organizing a Poor People's March, hoping to bring thousands of demonstrators to Washington to demand increased anti-poverty efforts. On April 4, having traveled to Memphis to support a strike of the city's grossly underpaid black garbage collectors, King was killed by a white assassin. The greatest outbreak of urban violence in the nation's history followed in black neighborhoods across the country. Washington, D.C., had to be occupied by soldiers before order was restored.

In June, a young Palestinian nationalist assassinated Robert F. Kennedy, who was seeking the Democratic nomination as an opponent of the war. In August, tens of thousands of antiwar activists descended on Chicago for protests at the Democratic national convention, where the delegates nominated Vice President Hubert Humphrey as their presidential candidate. The city's police, never known for restraint, assaulted the marchers with nightsticks, producing hundreds of injuries outside the convention hall and pandemonium inside it.

In one of the most widely publicized acts of nonviolent protest of the 1960s, American athletes Tommie Smith (*center*) and John Carlos raised their fists in a Black Power salute at the medal ceremony for the 200-meter dash at the 1968 Mexico City Olympics. The third athlete is silver medalist Peter Norman of Australia. Avery Brundage, the international Olympic president who had removed Jewish athletes from the American team to avoid offending Adolph Hitler at the 1936 Berlin games, denounced the two for "politicizing" the Olympics, and the U.S. Olympic Committee expelled them. Nearly fifty years later, in 2016, thirteen members of the 1968 U.S. Olympic rowing team, all of them white, unsuccessfully asked the Olympic Committee to apologize for its action.

The Global 1968

Like 1848 and 1919, 1968 was a year of worldwide upheaval. In many countries, young radicals challenged existing power structures, often borrowing language and strategies from the decade's social movements in the United States and adapting them to their own circumstances.

Massive antiwar demonstrations took place in London, Rome, Paris, Munich, and Tokyo, leading to clashes with police and scores of injuries. In Paris, a nationwide student uprising began in May 1968 that echoed American demands for educational reform and personal liberation. Unlike in the United States, millions of French workers soon joined the protest, adding their own demands for higher wages and greater democracy in the workplace. The result was a general strike that paralyzed the country. In communist Czechoslovakia, leaders bent on reform came to power by

A mural in Belfast, Northern Ireland, depicts the black American abolitionist Frederick Douglass, illustrating how the movement for Catholic civil rights associated itself with the struggle for racial justice in the United States. The text points out that Douglass lectured in Ireland in the 1840s on abolitionism, women's rights, and Irish independence.

promising to institute "socialism with a human face," only to be ousted by a Soviet invasion. Soldiers fired on students demonstrating for greater democracy on the eve of the opening of the Olympic Games in Mexico City, leading to more than 500 deaths. In Northern Ireland, which remained part of Great Britain after the rest of Ireland achieved independence, the police attacked a peaceful march of Catholics demanding an end to religious discrimination who were inspired by the American civil rights movement. This event marked the beginning of the Troubles, a period of both peaceful protest and violent conflict in the region that did not end until the turn of the twenty-first century.

Nixon's Comeback

White "backlash"

In the United States, instead of radical change, the year's events opened the door for a conservative reaction. Turmoil in the streets produced a demand for public order. Black militancy produced white "backlash."

In August, Richard Nixon capped a remarkable political comeback by winning the Republican nomination. He called for a renewed commitment to "law and order." With 43 percent of the vote, Nixon had only a razor-thin margin over his Democratic rival. But George Wallace, running as an independent and appealing to resentments against blacks' gains, Great Society programs, and the Warren Court, received an additional 13 percent. Taken together, the Nixon and Wallace totals indicated that four years after Johnson's landslide election ushered in the Great Society, liberalism was on the defensive.

The Legacy of the Sixties

The 1960s transformed American life in ways unimaginable when the decade began. It produced new rights and new understandings of freedom. It made possible the entrance of numerous members of racial minorities into the mainstream of American life, while leaving unsolved the problem of urban poverty. It set in motion a transformation of the status of women.

As the country became more conservative, the Sixties would be blamed for every imaginable social ill, from crime and drug abuse to a decline of respect for authority. Yet during the 1960s, the United States became a more open, more tolerant—in a word, a freer—country.

CHAPTER REVIEW AND ONLINE RESOURCES

REVIEW QUESTIONS

1. *How did the idea of a "zone of privacy" build on or change earlier notions of rights and freedom?*
2. *In what ways were President Kennedy's foreign policy decisions shaped by Cold War ideology?*
3. *How did immigration policies change in these years, and what were the consequences for the makeup of the population in the United States?*
4. *Explain why many blacks, especially in the North, did not believe that civil rights legislation went far enough in promoting black freedom.*
5. *What were the effects of President Johnson's Great Society and War on Poverty programs?*
6. *In what ways was the New Left not as new as it claimed?*
7. *How did the goals and actions of the United States in Vietnam cause controversy at home and abroad?*
8. *Discuss the impact of the civil rights movement on at least two other movements for social change in the 1960s.*
9. *Identify the origins, goals, and composition of the feminist, or women's liberation, movement.*
10. *Describe how the social movements of the 1960s in the United States became part of global movements for change by 1968. How did those connections affect the United States' position in the world?*
11. *How did the counterculture expand the meaning of freedom in these years?*

KEY TERMS

sit-in (p. 767)
Student Nonviolent Coordinating Committee (p. 768)
Freedom Rides (p. 768)
March on Washington (p. 769)
Bay of Pigs invasion (p. 771)
Cuban missile crisis (p. 772)
Civil Rights Act (p. 773)
Voting Rights Act (p. 777)
Hart-Celler Act (p. 777)
Great Society (p. 778)
War on Poverty (p. 779)
Black Power (p. 782)
New Left (p. 783)
Students for a Democratic Society (p. 784)
Port Huron Statement (p. 784)
Gulf of Tonkin resolution (p. 785)
counterculture (p. 790)
The Feminine Mystique (p. 792)
National Organization for Women (p. 793)
Stonewall Inn (p. 794)
American Indian Movement (p. 795)
Silent Spring (p. 796)
Griswold v. Connecticut (p. 798)
Roe v. Wade (p. 798)
Tet offensive (p. 798)

Go to INQUIZITIVE

To see what you know—and learn what you've missed—with personalized feedback along the way.

Visit the ***Give Me Liberty!* Student Site** for primary source documents and images, interactive maps, author videos featuring Eric Foner, and more.

CHAPTER 26

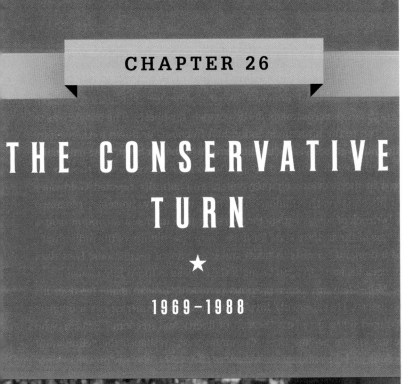

THE CONSERVATIVE TURN

★

1969–1988

1968	My Lai massacre
1970	United States invades Cambodia
1971	Pentagon Papers published
	United States goes off the gold standard
1972	Nixon travels to the People's Republic of China
	Congress passes the Equal Rights Amendment for ratification
	SALT is signed
	Congress approves Title IX
1973	War Powers Act
	CIA-aided Chilean coup
	Paris Peace Accords end U.S. involvement in Vietnam War
1974	Nixon resigns in Watergate scandal
1975	Collapse of South Vietnamese government
1976	Jimmy Carter elected
1978	*Regents of the University of California v. Bakke*
	Camp David Accords signed between Israel and Egypt
1979	Three Mile Island accident
	Sagebrush Rebellion
	Fifty-three Americans taken hostage in Iran
1980	Ronald Reagan elected
1981	Air traffic controllers strike
1983	Strategic Defense Initiative
1985–1987	Iran-Contra affair
1986	*Bowers v. Hardwick*

Ronald Reagan addressing the Republican national convention of 1980, which nominated him for president. His election that fall brought modern conservatism to the White House and launched the Reagan Revolution.

FOCUS QUESTIONS

- *What were the major policies of the Nixon administration on social and economic issues?*
- *How did Vietnam and the Watergate scandal affect popular trust in the government?*
- *In what ways did the opportunities of most Americans diminish in the 1970s?*
- *What were the roots of the rise of conservatism in the 1970s?*
- *How did the Reagan presidency affect American aims at home and abroad?*

On October 27, 1964, Ronald Reagan, a well-known movie star, stood before a Los Angeles audience to campaign for Republican presidential nominee Barry Goldwater. The nation, Reagan warned, faced a crossroads in the struggle for liberty. The choice was to move "up to the ultimate in individual freedom" or down to the welfare state and, eventually, the "totalitarianism of the ant heap." The nationally televised speech launched Reagan's political career, even though, as noted in the previous chapter, voters emphatically rejected Goldwater and his conservative philosophy. That philosophy, however, remained the bedrock of conservatism for years to come: intense anticommunism, a critique of the welfare state for destroying "the dignity of the individual," and a demand for cuts in taxes and government regulations. Less than two decades later, Reagan brought these ideas to the White House.

More than any other previous president, Reagan made freedom his watchword. He repeatedly invoked the idea that America has a divinely appointed mission to be a "beacon of liberty and freedom." Reagan, who became known as "the Great Communicator," reshaped the definition of freedom, and the national agenda, more effectively than any president since Franklin D. Roosevelt. Like Roosevelt, Reagan promised to free government from control by "special interests," but these were racial minorities, unionists, and others hoping to use Washington's power to attack social inequalities, not businessmen seeking political favors, the traditional target of liberals.

The second half of the 1960s and the 1970s witnessed pivotal developments that reshaped American politics—the breakup of the political coalition forged by Franklin D. Roosevelt; an economic crisis that traditional liberal remedies seemed unable to solve; a shift of population and economic resources to conservative strongholds in the Sunbelt of the South and West; the growth of an activist, conservative Christianity increasingly aligned with the Republican Party; and a series of setbacks for the United States overseas. Together, they led to growing popularity for conservatives' ideas, including their understanding of freedom.

PRESIDENT NIXON

Richard Nixon's presidency bridged the eras of liberalism under Kennedy and Johnson and the conservatism of the Reagan era. Nixon was the first president from California, and his victory signaled the growing power of the conservative Sunbelt in national politics. From the vantage point of the early twenty-first century, it is difficult to recall how marginal conservatism seemed at the end of World War II. Associated in many minds with conspiracy theories, anti-Semitism, and preference for social hierarchy over democracy and equality, conservatism seemed a relic of a discredited past.

Nonetheless, as noted in the previous two chapters, the 1950s and 1960s witnessed a conservative rebirth. And in 1968, a "backlash" among formerly Democratic voters against both black assertiveness and antiwar demonstrations helped to propel Richard Nixon into the White House. But conservatives found Nixon no more to their liking than his predecessors. In office, he expanded the welfare state and moved to improve American relations with the Soviet Union and China. During his presidency, the social changes set in motion by the 1960s—seen by conservatives as forces of moral decay—continued apace.

Nixon's Domestic Policies

Having won the presidency by a very narrow margin, Nixon moved toward the political center on many issues. A shrewd politician, he worked to solidify his support among Republicans while reaching out to disaffected elements of the Democratic coalition. Mostly interested in foreign policy, he had no desire to battle Congress, still under Democratic control, on domestic issues. Just as Eisenhower had helped to institutionalize the New Deal, Nixon accepted and even expanded many elements of the Great Society.

Nixon's New Federalism

Conservatives applauded Nixon's New Federalism, which offered federal "block grants" to the states to spend as they saw fit, rather than for specific purposes dictated by Washington. On the other hand, the Nixon administration created a host of new federal agencies. The Environmental Protection Agency oversaw programs to combat water and air pollution, cleaned up hazardous wastes, and required "environmental impact" statements from any project that received federal funding. The Occupational Safety and Health Administration sent inspectors into the nation's workplaces. The National Transportation Safety Board instructed automobile makers on how to make their cars safer.

Environmental Protection Agency

Nixon also signed measures that expanded the food stamp program and made Social Security benefits adjust automatically to the rising cost of living. His environmental initiatives included the Endangered Species Act and the Clean Air Act, which set air quality standards for carbon monoxide and other chemicals released by cars and factories.

Nixon and Welfare

Family Assistance Plan

Perhaps Nixon's most startling initiative was his proposal for a Family Assistance Plan, or "negative income tax," that would replace Aid to Families with Dependent Children (AFDC) by having the federal

Richard Nixon (on the right) and former Alabama governor George Wallace at an "Honor America" celebration in February 1974. Nixon's "southern strategy" sought to woo Wallace's supporters into the Republican Party.

government guarantee a minimum income for all Americans. Originally a New Deal program that mainly served the white poor, welfare had come to be associated with blacks, who by 1970 accounted for nearly half the recipients. The AFDC rolls expanded rapidly during the 1960s. This arose from an increase in births to unmarried women, which produced a sharp rise in the number of poor female-headed households, and from an aggressive campaign by welfare rights groups to encourage people to apply for benefits. Conservative politicians now attacked recipients of welfare as people who preferred to live at the expense of honest taxpayers rather than by working. A striking example of Nixon's willingness to break the political mold, his plan to replace welfare with a guaranteed annual income failed to win approval by Congress.

Nixon and Race

Nixon's racial policies offered a similarly mixed picture. To consolidate support in the white South, he nominated to the Supreme Court two conservative southern jurists with records of support for segregation. Both were rejected by the Senate. On the other hand, in Nixon's first three years in office, the proportion of southern black students attending integrated schools rose from 32 percent to 77 percent. His administration opened the Office of Minority Business Enterprise to fund black capitalist initiatives, calling on blacks to embrace self-help strategies to "get a piece of the action." He even courted some black power advocates, providing former civil rights leader Floyd McKissick with $14 million to establish Soul City, a town in North Carolina. (The project did not succeed.)

Even as he pursued his southern strategy, President Nixon courted black support. Here he meets with three African-Americans in the White House, including football legend and actor Jim Brown (dressed in white).

For a time, the Nixon administration also pursued **affirmative action** programs to upgrade minority employment. The Philadelphia Plan required that construction contractors on federal projects hire specific numbers of minority workers. Secretary of Labor George Shultz, who initiated the idea, sincerely hoped to open more jobs for black workers. Nixon seems to have viewed the plan mainly as a way of fighting inflation by weakening the power of the building trades unions. Their control over the labor market, he believed, pushed wages to unreasonably high levels, raising the cost of construction.

Trade union opposition

Trade unions of skilled workers like plumbers and electricians, which had virtually no black members, strongly opposed the Philadelphia Plan. After a widely publicized incident in May 1970, when a group of construction workers assaulted antiwar demonstrators in New York City, Nixon suddenly decided that he might be able to woo blue-collar workers in preparation for his 1972 reelection campaign. He abandoned the Philadelphia Plan in favor of an ineffective one that stressed voluntary local efforts toward minority hiring instead of federal requirements.

The Burger Court and Busing

When Earl Warren retired as chief justice in 1969, Nixon appointed Warren Burger, a federal court-of-appeals judge, to succeed him.

Busing

In 1971, in *Swann v. Charlotte-Mecklenburg Board of Education*, which arose from North Carolina, the justices unanimously approved a lower court's plan that required the extensive transportation of students to achieve school integration. The decision led to hundreds of cases in which judges throughout the country ordered the use of **busing** as a tool to achieve integration. With many white parents determined to keep their children in neighborhood schools and others willing to move to the suburbs or enroll them in private academies to avoid integration, busing became a lightning rod for protests. One of the most bitter fights took place in Boston in the mid-1970s. Residents of the tightly knit Irish-American community of South Boston demonstrated vociferously and sometimes violently against a busing plan decreed by a local judge. The protesters adopted the language and strategies associated with the progressive social movements of the 1960s, calling for a restoration of their "rights" and "freedom." The busing issue helped to consolidate white hostility to "too powerful government," a position that would eventually benefit conservatives.

Milliken v. Bradley

The Supreme Court soon abandoned the idea of overturning local control of schools or moving students great distances to achieve integration. In *Milliken v. Bradley* (1974), the justices overturned a lower court order that required Detroit's predominantly white suburbs to enter into a regional desegregation plan with the city's heavily minority school system. By absolving suburban districts of responsibility for assisting in integrating urban schools, the decision guaranteed that housing segregation would be mirrored in public education. Indeed, by the 1990s, public schools in the North were considerably more segregated than those in the South.

Opposition to affirmative action

Many whites came to view affirmative action programs as a form of **reverse discrimination**. Even as such programs quickly spread from blacks to encompass women, Latinos, Asian-Americans, and Native Americans, conservatives demanded that the Supreme Court invalidate them all.

The justices proved increasingly hostile to governmental affirmative action policies. In *Regents of the University of California v. Bakke* (1978), the Court overturned an admissions program of the University of California at Davis, a public university, which set aside 16 of 100 places in the entering medical school class for minority students. Justice Lewis F. Powell, a Nixon appointee who cast the deciding vote in the 5-4 decision, rejected the idea of fixed affirmative action quotas. He added, however, that race could be used as one factor among many in admissions decisions, so affirmative action continued at most colleges and universities. *Bakke* continues to be the standard by which affirmative action programs are judged today.

The Rights of the Disabled

As noted in the previous chapter, the social activism associated with the 1960s continued in the following decade. Both right and left took part in grassroots movements, ranging from campaigns against nuclear weapons and nuclear power plants and struggles to aid migrant workers to battles to stop the court-ordered busing of public school children and movements against abortion rights. Some movements inspired by the 1960s achieved support across the political spectrum. Increased activism demanding equal opportunities and treatment for people with disabilities resulted in passage—unanimously in both houses of Congress—of the Rehabilitation Act of 1973, which prohibited discrimination on the basis of disability in programs conducted by federal agencies or receiving federal financial assistance, and in employment practices of federal contractors. The act represented a dramatic repudiation of the "science" of eugenics, discussed in Chapter 19, which encouraged government action to "improve" the American population, and of the practice of involuntary sterilization of the "less fit" practiced by state governments well into the twentieth century.

Rehabilitation Act of 1973

Disability activism

Further efforts to enable persons with disabilities to participate fully in society followed. In 1977, disability activists organized a sit-in at offices of the Department of Health, Education, and Welfare, forcing the department to issue regulations to put the law into effect. Over time, public and private buildings ranging from apartment houses to train stations to sites of business have been redesigned to improve access for persons with physical disabilities. A major inspiration for these changes came in the Americans with Disabilities Act, passed in 1990. Modeled on civil rights legislation of the 1960s, it extended the ban on discrimination against persons with disabilities to state and local governments and private employers and required public accommodations such as restaurants to take steps to ensure that they were fully accessible to those with impaired mobility.

FIGURE 26.1 Median Age at First Marriage, 1947–1981

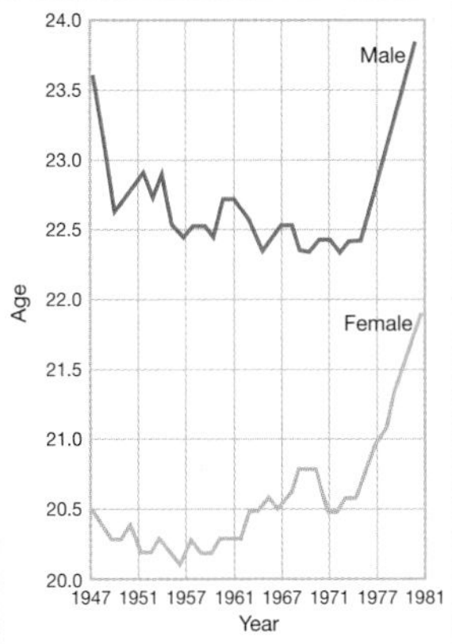

The Continuing Sexual Revolution

But the most profound changes in American life arose from the continuing sexual revolution. To the alarm of conservatives, during the 1970s the sexual revolution passed from the counterculture into the social mainstream. The number of divorces soared, reaching more than 1 million in 1975, double the number ten years earlier. The age at which both men and women married rose dramatically. As a result of women's changing aspirations and the availability of birth control and legal abortions, the American birthrate declined dramatically. By 1976, the average woman was bearing 1.7 children during her lifetime, less than half the figure of 1957 and below the level at which a population reproduces itself. A 1971 survey of the last five graduating classes at Bryn Mawr, an elite women's college, reported the birth of more than seventy children. A similar survey covering the classes of 1971 through 1975 found that only three had been born. (Of course, many of these women eventually did marry and have children. But unlike their mothers of the "baby-boom" generation, they postponed these decisions to pursue careers.)

Title IX

During the Nixon years, women made inroads into areas from which they had long been excluded. In 1972, Congress approved **Title IX**, which banned gender discrimination in higher education. The giant corporation American Telephone and Telegraph (AT&T) entered into a landmark agreement in which it paid millions of dollars to workers who had suffered gender discrimination and to upgrade employment opportunities for women. The number of women at work continued its upward climb. Working women were motivated by varied aims. Some sought careers in professions and skilled jobs previously open only to men. Others, spurred by the need to bolster family income as the economy faltered, flooded into the traditional, low-wage, "pink-collar" sector, working as cashiers, secretaries, and telephone operators.

Expansion of gay and lesbian movement

In addition, the gay and lesbian movement, born at the end of the 1960s, expanded greatly during the 1970s and became a major concern of the right. In 1969, there had been about fifty local gay rights groups in the United States; ten years later, their numbers reached into the thousands. They began to elect local officials, persuaded many states to decriminalize same-sex relations, and succeeded in convincing cities with large gay populations to pass antidiscrimination laws. They actively encouraged gay men and lesbians to "come out of the closet"—that is, to reveal their sexual orientation.

Nixon and Détente

"Soft" approach to communism

Just as many of his domestic policies and social trends under Nixon disappointed conservatives, they viewed his foreign policy as dangerously "soft" on communism. To be sure, Nixon and Henry Kissinger, his national security adviser and secretary of state, continued their predecessors' policy of attempting to undermine Third World governments deemed dangerous to American strategic or economic interests. Nixon funneled arms to dictatorial pro-American regimes in Iran, the Philippines, and South Africa. After Chile in 1970 elected socialist Salvador Allende as president, the CIA worked with his domestic opponents to destabilize the regime. On September 11, 1973, Allende was overthrown and killed in a military coup, which installed a bloody dictatorship under General Augusto Pinochet. Thousands of Allende backers, including a few Americans then in Chile, were tortured and murdered, and many others fled the country. The Nixon administration continued to back Pinochet despite his brutal policies. Democracy did not return to Chile until the end of the 1980s.

The Allende affair

Nixon and Kissinger's "realist" foreign policy

In his relations with the major communist powers, however, Nixon fundamentally altered Cold War policies. In the language of foreign relations, he and Kissinger were "realists." They had more interest in power than ideology and preferred international stability to relentless conflict. Nixon also hoped that if relations with the Soviet Union improved, the Russians would influence North Vietnam to agree to an end to the Vietnam War on terms acceptable to the United States.

Nixon realized that far from being part of a unified communist bloc, China had its own interests, different from those of the Soviet Union, and was destined to play a major role on the world stage. The policy of refusing to recognize China's communist government had reached a dead end. In 1971, Kissinger flew secretly to China, paving the way for Nixon's own astonishing public visit of February 1972. The trip led to the Beijing government's taking up China's seat at the United Nations, previously occupied by the exiled regime on Taiwan.

Richard Nixon at a banquet celebrating his visit to China in February 1972. To his right is Premier Zhou Enlai.

Three months after his trip to Beijing, Nixon became the first Cold War American president to visit the Soviet Union, where he engaged in intense negotiations with his Soviet counterpart, Leonid Brezhnev. Out of this summit meeting came agreements for increased trade and two landmark arms-control treaties. SALT (named for the **Strategic Arms Limitation Talks** under way since 1969) froze each country's arsenal of intercontinental missiles capable of carrying nuclear warheads. The Anti-Ballistic Missile Treaty banned the development of systems designed to intercept incoming missiles, so that neither side would be tempted to attack the other without fearing devastating retaliation. Nixon and Brezhnev proclaimed a new era of "peaceful coexistence," in which **détente** (cooperation) would replace the hostility of the Cold War.

Tear gas envelops the campus as members of the Ohio National Guard prepare to fire on student demonstrators at Kent State University. Shortly after this photo was taken, four students lay dead.

VIETNAM AND WATERGATE

Nixon and Vietnam

Despite Nixon's foreign policy triumphs, one issue would not go away—Vietnam. On taking office, he announced a new policy, Vietnamization. Under this plan, American troops would gradually be withdrawn while South Vietnamese soldiers, backed by continued American bombing, did more and more of the fighting. But Vietnamization neither limited the war nor ended the antiwar movement. Hoping to cut North Vietnamese supply lines, Nixon in 1970 ordered American troops into neutral Cambodia. The invasion did not achieve its military goals, but it destabilized the Cambodian government and set in motion a chain of events that eventually brought to power the Khmer Rouge. Before being ousted by a Vietnamese invasion in 1979, this local communist movement attempted to force virtually all Cambodians into rural communes and committed widespread massacres in that unfortunate country.

As the war escalated, protests again spread on college campuses, partly because the policy of exempting students from the draft had ended. In the wake of the killing of four antiwar protesters at Kent State University by the Ohio National Guard and two by police at Jackson State University in Mississippi, the student movement reached its high-water mark. In the spring of 1970, more than 350 colleges and universities experienced strikes, and troops occupied 21 campuses. The protests at Kent State, a public university with a largely working-class student body, and Jackson State, a black institution, demonstrated how antiwar sentiment had spread far beyond elite campuses.

The same social changes sweeping the home front were evident among troops in Vietnam. Soldiers experimented with drugs, openly wore peace and Black-Power symbols, refused orders, and even assaulted unpopular officers. In 1971, thousands deserted the army, while at home Vietnam veterans held antiwar demonstrations.

Students peer from a residence hall window—pockmarked by bullet holes—at Jackson State, a historically black university in Mississippi. Two students were killed when police opened fire on the building, claiming they were returning sniper fire. The event took place eleven days after the tragedy at Kent State University, but received much less attention.

The decline of discipline within the army convinced increasing numbers of high-ranking officers that the United States must extricate itself from Vietnam.

Eroding public support for the war

Public support for the war was rapidly waning. In 1969, the *New York Times* published details of the **My Lai massacre** of 1968, in which a company of American troops killed some 350 South Vietnamese civilians. After a military investigation, one soldier, Lieutenant William Calley, was found guilty of directing the atrocity. (The courts released him from prison in 1974.) While hardly typical of the behavior of most servicemen, My Lai further undermined public support for the war. In 1971, the *Times* began publishing the **Pentagon Papers**, a classified report prepared by the Defense Department that traced American involvement in Vietnam back to World War II and revealed how successive presidents had misled the American people about it. In a landmark freedom-of-the-press decision, the Supreme Court rejected Nixon's request for an injunction to halt publication. In 1973, Congress passed the **War Powers Act**. The most vigorous assertion of congressional control over foreign policy in the nation's history, it required the president to seek congressional approval for the commitment of American troops overseas.

The Pentagon Papers

A campaign poster from the 1972 election does not even name Richard Nixon, referring to him only as "the president." It includes images of some of his accomplishments, including pursuing détente with China (bottom) and the Soviet Union (above and to the left).

The End of the Vietnam War

Early in 1973, Nixon achieved what had eluded his predecessors—a negotiated settlement in Vietnam. The Paris peace agreement, the result of five years of talks, made possible the final withdrawal of American troops. The compromise left in place the government of South Vietnam, but it also left North Vietnamese and Viet Cong soldiers in control of parts of the South. The U.S. military draft came to an end. Henceforth, volunteers would make up the armed forces. But in the spring of 1975, the North Vietnamese launched a final military offensive. The government of South Vietnam collapsed. The United States did not intervene except to evacuate the American embassy, and Vietnam was reunified under communist rule.

The only war the United States has ever lost, Vietnam was a military, political, and social disaster. By the time it ended, 58,000 Americans had been killed, along with 3 million to 4 million Vietnamese. Vietnam undermined Americans' confidence in their own institutions and challenged long-standing beliefs about the country and its purposes.

Two decades after the war ended, former secretary of defense Robert McNamara published a memoir in which he admitted that the policy he had helped to shape had been "terribly wrong." Ignorance of the history and culture of Vietnam and a misguided belief that every communist movement in the world was a puppet of Moscow, he wrote, had led the country into a war that he now profoundly regretted. The political establishment had supported the war for most of its duration. For far too long, the press and political leaders had accepted its basic premise—that the United States had the right to decide the fate of a faraway people about whom it knew almost nothing.

Beat poet Allen Ginsberg and feminist leader Bella Abzug (later elected to Congress from New York City) at the 1972 Democratic national convention in Miami Beach. Their presence illustrated the growing role of the counterculture and new social movements in the party, to the dismay of its traditional leaders.

The 1972 Election

To run against Nixon in 1972, Democrats chose Senator George McGovern, a liberal from South Dakota. New rules established in the wake of Hubert Humphrey's nomination in 1968 brought increased diversity to the party's ranks, but also opened new rifts. In the primaries, Shirley Chisholm, a member of Congress from Brooklyn, became the first black woman to seek the presidency. George Wallace rallied the party's southern and blue-collar base with a racial and populist appeal. McGovern, a strong opponent of the Vietnam War, won the nomination, to the discomfort of the broad Democratic middle. Many Democratic voters stayed home or voted for Nixon, who won in a landslide. McGovern carried only Massachusetts. The loyalty of white southerners and northern white working-class voters to the party of FDR could no longer be taken for granted.

Watergate

Nixon's landslide victory contained the seeds of his downfall. Nixon was obsessed with secrecy. He viewed every critic as a threat to national security and developed an "enemies list" that included reporters, politicians, and celebrities unfriendly to the administration. In June 1972, five former employees of Nixon's reelection committee took part in a break-in at Democratic Party headquarters in the **Watergate** apartment complex in Washington, D.C. A security guard called police, who arrested the intruders.

The break-in

No one knows precisely what the Watergate burglars were looking for (perhaps they intended to install listening devices), and the botched robbery played little role in the 1972 presidential campaign. But in 1973, Judge John J. Sirica, before whom the burglars were tried, determined to find out who had sponsored the break-in. A pair of *Washington Post* journalists began publishing investigative stories that made it clear that persons close to the president had ordered the burglary and then tried to cover up White House involvement. Congressional hearings followed that revealed

The Watergate hearings

a wider pattern of wiretapping, break-ins, and attempts to sabotage political opposition. When it became known that Nixon had made tape recordings of conversations in his office, Archibald Cox, a special prosecutor the president had reluctantly appointed to investigate the Watergate affair, demanded the tapes. In October 1973, Nixon proposed to allow Senator John C. Stennis of Mississippi to review the tapes, rather than release them. When Cox refused, Nixon fired him, whereupon Attorney General Elliot Richardson and his deputy resigned in protest. These events, known as the Saturday Night Massacre, further undermined Nixon's standing. The Supreme Court unanimously ordered Nixon to provide the tapes—a decision that reaffirmed the principle that the president is not above the law.

Nixon's Fall

Week after week, revelations about the scandal unfolded. By mid-1974, it had become clear that whether or not Nixon knew in advance of the Watergate break-in, he had become involved immediately afterward in authorizing payments to the burglars to remain silent or commit perjury, and he had ordered the FBI to halt its investigation of the crime. In August 1974, the House Judiciary Committee voted to recommend that Nixon be impeached for conspiracy to obstruct justice. His political support having evaporated, Nixon became the only president in history to resign.

Nixon's resignation

Nixon's presidency remains a classic example of the abuse of political power. In 1973, his vice president, Spiro T. Agnew, resigned after revelations that he had accepted bribes from construction firms while serving as governor of Maryland. Nixon's attorney general, John Mitchell, and White House aides H. R. Haldeman and John Ehrlichman, were convicted of obstruction of justice in the Watergate affair and went to jail. As for the president, he insisted that he had done nothing wrong.

The aftermath of Watergate

His departure from office was followed by Senate hearings headed by Frank Church of Idaho that laid bare a history of abusive actions involving every administration since the beginning of the Cold War. In violation of the law, the FBI had spied on millions of Americans and had tried to disrupt the civil rights movement. The CIA had conducted secret operations to overthrow foreign governments and had tried to assassinate foreign leaders. Abuses of power, in other words, went far beyond the misdeeds of a single president.

Freedom of Information Act

The Church Committee revelations led Congress to enact new restrictions on the power of the FBI and CIA to spy on American citizens or conduct operations abroad without the knowledge of lawmakers. Congress also strengthened the Freedom of Information Act (FOIA), initially enacted in 1966. Since 1974, the FOIA has allowed scholars, journalists, and ordinary citizens to gain access to millions of pages of records of federal agencies.

Liberals, who had despised Nixon throughout his career, celebrated his downfall. Nixon's fall and the revelations of years of governmental misconduct helped to convince many Americans that conservatives were correct when they argued that to protect liberty it was necessary to limit Washington's power over Americans' lives.

The impact of Watergate

THE END OF THE GOLDEN AGE

The Decline of Manufacturing

During the 1970s, the long period of postwar economic expansion and consumer prosperity came to an end, succeeded by slow growth and high inflation. For the only time in the twentieth century, other than the 1930s, the average American ended the 1970s poorer than when the decade began. There were many reasons for the end of capitalism's "golden age." With American prosperity seemingly unassailable and the military-industrial complex thriving, successive administrations had devoted little attention to the less positive economic consequences of the Cold War. To strengthen its anticommunist allies, the United States promoted the industrial reconstruction of Japan and Germany and the emergence of new centers of manufacturing in places like South Korea and Taiwan. It

Economic weakness

TABLE 26.1 The Misery Index, 1970–1980

YEAR	RATE OF INFLATION (%)	RATE OF UNEMPLOYMENT (%)	MISERY INDEX (%)
1970	5.9	4.9	10.8
1971	4.3	5.9	10.2
1972	3.3	5.6	8.9
1973	6.2	4.9	11.1
1974	11.0	5.6	16.6
1975	9.1	8.5	17.6
1976	5.8	7.7	13.5
1977	6.5	7.1	13.6
1978	7.7	6.1	13.8
1979	11.3	5.8	17.1
1980	13.5	7.1	20.6

encouraged American companies to invest in overseas plants. The strong dollar, linked to gold by the Bretton Woods agreement of 1944, made it harder to sell American goods overseas (discussed in Chapter 22).

Trade deficit

In 1971, for the first time in the twentieth century, the United States experienced a merchandise trade deficit—that is, it imported more goods than it exported. By 1980, nearly three-quarters of goods produced in the United States were competing with foreign-made products, and the number of manufacturing workers, 38 percent of the American workforce in 1960, had fallen to 28 percent.

Currency values and trade

In 1971, Nixon announced the most radical change in economic policy since the Great Depression. He took the United States off the gold standard, ending the Bretton Woods agreement that fixed the value of the dollar and other currencies in terms of gold. Henceforth, the world's currencies would "float" in relation to one another, their worth determined not by treaty but by international currency markets. Nixon hoped that lowering the dollar's value in terms of the German mark and Japanese yen would promote exports by making American goods cheaper overseas and reduce imports, because foreign products would be more expensive in the United States. But the end of fixed currency rates injected a new element of instability into the world economy. Nixon also ordered wages and prices frozen for ninety days.

Stagflation

Nixon's policies temporarily curtailed inflation and reduced imports. But in 1973, a brief war broke out between Israel and its neighbors Egypt and

Drivers lining up to purchase gas in San Jose, California, during the gas shortage of early 1974. One man hopes to fill up his lawn mower.

Syria. Middle Eastern Arab states retaliated against Western support of Israel by quadrupling the price of oil and suspending the export of oil to the United States for several months. During the **oil embargo**, long lines of cars appeared at American gas stations, which either ran out of fuel or limited how much a customer could buy. A second "oil shock" occurred in 1979 as a result of the revolution that overthrew the shah of Iran, discussed later.

Rising oil prices rippled through the world economy, contributing to the combination of stagnant economic growth and high inflation known as **stagflation**. Between 1973 and 1981, the rate of inflation in developed countries was 10 percent per year and the rate of economic growth only 2.4 percent, a sharp deterioration from the economic conditions of the 1960s. The so-called misery index—the sum of the unemployment and inflation rates—stood at 10.8 percent when the decade began. By 1980, it had almost doubled. As oil prices rose, many Americans shifted from large, domestically produced cars, known for high gasoline consumption, to smaller, more fuel-efficient imports. By the end of the decade, Japan had become the world's leading automobile producer, and imports accounted for nearly 25 percent of car sales in the United States.

The World Trade Center under construction in New York City in the 1970s.

The Beleaguered Social Compact

The economic crisis contributed to a breakdown of the postwar social compact. Faced with declining profits and rising overseas competition, corporations stepped up the trend, already under way before 1970, toward eliminating well-paid manufacturing jobs through automation and shifting production to low-wage areas of the United States and overseas. By 1980, **deindustrialization** in Detroit and Chicago included the loss of more than half the manufacturing jobs in existence three decades earlier.

In some manufacturing centers, political and economic leaders welcomed the opportunity to remake their cities as finance, information, and entertainment hubs. In New York, the construction of the World Trade Center, completed in 1977, symbolized this shift in the economy. Until destroyed by terrorists twenty-four years later, the 110-story "twin towers" stood as a symbol of New York's grandeur. But to make way for the World Trade Center, the city displaced hundreds of small electronics, printing, and other firms, causing the loss of thousands of manufacturing jobs.

Increasingly, jobs, investment, and population flowed to the nonunion, low-wage states of the **Sunbelt**, a term that came into widespread use to describe the growing economic and political influence of this conservative region. Ninety-six percent of population growth in metropolitan areas during the 1970s occurred in the South and West. Booming Sunbelt cities pursued a different model of development and spatial growth than the older urban centers of the North and Midwest. Businesses and new housing developments

Because of economic dislocations and deindustrialization, Americans' real wages (wages adjusted to take account of inflation) peaked in the early 1970s and then began a sharp, prolonged decline.

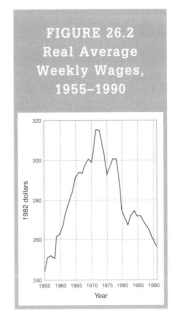

FIGURE 26.2 Real Average Weekly Wages, 1955–1990

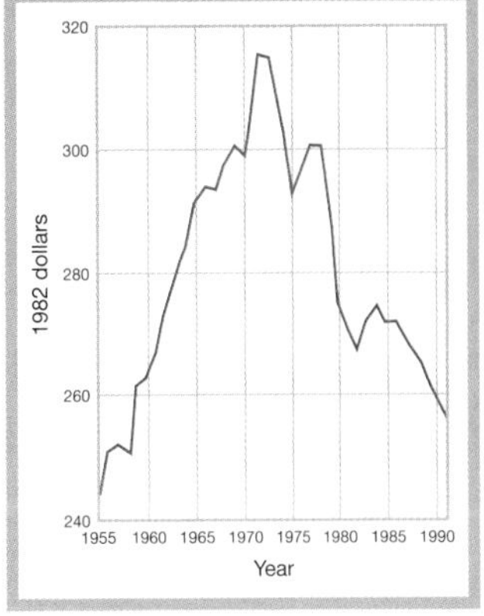

sprang up along highways, with cities like Houston, Dallas, and Los Angeles reaching to the horizon. Gated communities became a popular project for developers, promoting a style of life that emphasized security and privacy, and that relied on cars, not public transport, to get around.

Labor movement weakens

Always a junior partner in the Democratic coalition, the labor movement found itself forced onto the defensive. It has remained there ever since.

The weakening of unions and the continuation of the economy's long-term shift from manufacturing to service employment had an adverse impact on ordinary Americans. Between 1953 and 1973, median family income had doubled. But in 1973, real wages began to fall.

The Ford and Carter Administrations

Economic problems dogged the presidencies of Nixon's successors. Gerald Ford, who had been appointed to replace Vice President Agnew, succeeded to the White House when Nixon resigned. Ford named Nelson Rockefeller of New York as his own vice president. Thus, for the only time in American history, both offices were occupied by persons for whom no one had actually voted. Among his first acts as president, Ford pardoned Nixon, shielding him from prosecution for obstruction of justice. Ford claimed that he wanted the country to put the Watergate scandal behind it, a decision that proved to be widely unpopular.

In domestic policy, Ford's brief presidency lacked significant accomplishment. To combat inflation, Ford urged Americans to shop wisely, reduce expenditures, and wear WIN buttons (for "Whip Inflation Now"). Although inflation fell, joblessness continued to rise. During the steep recession of 1974–1975 unemployment exceeded 9 percent, the highest level since the Depression.

President Gerald Ford tried to enlist Americans in his "Whip Inflation Now" program. It did not succeed.

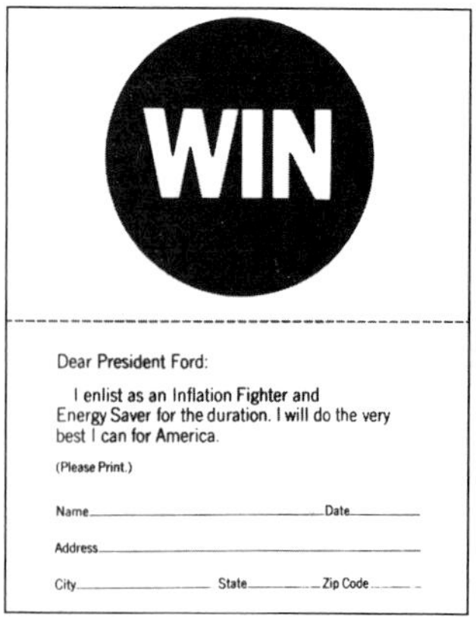

In the international arena, 1975 witnessed the major achievement of Ford's presidency. In a continuation of Nixon's policy of détente, the United States and Soviet Union signed an agreement at Helsinki, Finland, that recognized the permanence of Europe's post–World War II boundaries (including the division of Germany). In addition, both superpowers agreed to respect the basic liberties of their citizens. Over time, the **Helsinki Accords** inspired movements for greater freedom within the communist countries of eastern Europe.

In the presidential election of 1976, Jimmy Carter, a former governor of Georgia, narrowly defeated Ford. A graduate of the U.S. Naval Academy who later became a peanut farmer, Carter was virtually unknown outside his state when he launched his campaign for the Democratic nomination. But realizing that Watergate and Vietnam had produced a crisis in confidence in the federal government, he turned his obscurity into an advantage. Carter ran for president as an "outsider," making a virtue of the fact that he had never held federal office. A devout "born-again" Baptist, he spoke openly of his religious convictions. His promise, "I'll never lie to you," resonated with an electorate tired of official dishonesty.

Carter and race

Carter had much in common with Progressives of the early twentieth century. His passions were making government more efficient, protecting the environment, and raising the moral tone of politics. Unlike the Progressives, however, he embraced the aspirations of black Americans. As president, Carter appointed an unprecedented number of blacks to important positions, including Andrew Young, a former lieutenant of Martin Luther King Jr., as ambassador to the United Nations.

Carter and the Economic Crisis

The New Democrats

The Democratic Party found itself ill-equipped to deal with the economic crisis. The social upheavals of the 1960s had led to the emergence of politicians known collectively as the New Democrats. Representing affluent urban and suburban districts, they viewed issues like race relations, gender equality, the environment, and improving the political process as more central than traditional economic matters. Although his party controlled both houses, Carter often found himself at odds with Congress. He viewed inflation, not unemployment, as the country's main economic problem, and to combat it he promoted cuts in spending on domestic programs. In the hope that increased competition would reduce prices, his administration enacted **deregulation** in the airline and trucking industries. In 1980, with Carter's approval, Congress repealed usury laws—laws that limit how much interest lenders can charge—allowing credit card companies to push their interest rates up to 20 percent or even higher.

Carter also believed that expanded use of nuclear energy could help reduce dependence on imported oil. For years, proponents of nuclear power had hailed it as an inexpensive way of meeting the country's energy needs. By the time Carter took office, more than 200 nuclear plants were operating or on order. But in 1979 the industry suffered a near-fatal blow when an accident at the **Three Mile Island** plant in Pennsylvania released a large amount of radioactive steam into the atmosphere. The Three Mile Island mishap reinforced fears about the environmental hazards associated with nuclear energy and put a halt to the industry's expansion.

The deregulation of the airline industry brought lower fares but also a drastic decline in service. Before deregulation, with prices fixed, airlines sought to attract customers by providing good service. Today, fares may be lower, but passengers are jammed in like sardines and have to pay for checked baggage, onboard meals, and other amenities.

VOICES OF FREEDOM

From Barry Commoner, *The Closing Circle* (1971)

Environmentalism, a movement born in the 1960s, expanded rapidly in the following decade. In *The Closing Circle*, Barry Commoner, a biologist later called the Paul Revere of the movement, warned that technological development and the pursuit of economic growth regardless of consequences were creating an environmental crisis. He called on Americans to alter their lifestyles to bring them into harmony with the "ecosphere"—the natural environment within which people live.

The environment has just been rediscovered by the people who live in it. In the United States the event was celebrated in April 1970, during Earth Week. It was a sudden, noisy awakening. School children cleaned up rubbish; college students organized new demonstrations; determined citizens recaptured the streets from the automobile, at least for a day. Everyone seemed to be aroused to the environmental danger and eager to do something about it.

They were offered lots of advice. Almost every writer, almost every speaker, on the college campuses, in the streets and on television and radio broadcasts, was ready to fix the blame and pronounce a cure for the environmental crisis.

Some blamed pollution on the rising population. . . . Some blamed man's innate aggressiveness. . . . Having spent some years in the effort simply to detect and describe the growing list of environmental problems—radioactive fallout, air and water pollution, the deterioration of the soil—and in tracing some of their links to social and political processes, the identification of a single cause and cure seemed a rather bold step. . . .

Any living thing that hopes to live on the earth must fit into the ecosphere or perish. The environmental crisis is a sign that the finely sculpted fit between life and its surroundings has begun to corrode. As the links between one living thing and another, and between all of them and their surroundings, begin to break down, the dynamic interactions that sustain the whole have begun to falter and, in some places, stop. . . .

We have broken out of the circle of life, converting its endless cycles into man-made, linear events; oil is taken from the ground, distilled into fuel, burned in an engine, converted thereby into noxious fumes, which are emitted into the air. At the end of the line is smog. Other man-made breaks in the ecosphere's cycle spew out toxic chemicals, sewage, heaps of rubbish—the testimony to our power to tear the ecological fabric that has, for millions of years, sustained the planet's life.

From Richard E. Blakemore, Report on the Sagebrush Rebellion (1979)

The rapid growth of the environmentalist movement sparked a conservative reaction, especially in the western states. What came to be called the Sagebrush Rebellion denounced federal control of large areas of western land as well as new environmental regulations that, the "rebels" claimed, threatened energy production and long-standing grazing rights. Richard E. Blakemore, a member of the Nevada state senate, offered this explanation of the outlook of many westerners.

The "sagebrush rebellion" is a catchy but somewhat misleading term used to describe the western states' demands for a greater role in determining the future of the west. Unlike the dictionary definition, in this rebellion there is no armed or unlawful resistance to government. Neither is western land desolate or worthless as the term "sagebrush" connoted. Moreover, if much of the land in the west ever was considered of little worth, the need for energy has changed that.

Statistics show that much of the west is controlled by the federal government. . . . On average, the federal government controls 52.6 percent of the land in the 12 western states. . . . For many years, the public domain was open to ranching, mining, and outdoor recreation. But a number of federal acts, passed to protect and conserve the environment, have closed great parts of the public domain to traditional uses. . . .

The west today is at the confluence of two major movements—that for protection of the environment and that for production of energy. To a great extent, the success of the attempt for U.S. energy independence depends on resources of the west. In addition, the west is looked to for increased agricultural production and for its reserves of minerals necessary to modern industry. The environmental movement prompted the passage of federal legislation aimed at protecting the environment and maintaining great portions of the country in a natural state. Among the major environmental acts of the past 15 years are the Wilderness Act, the National Environmental Protection Act, the Federal Land Policy Management Act, the Wild and Scenic Rivers Act, and the National Forest Management Act.

The genesis of the sagebrush rebellion can be found in the conflict between the desires to protect and preserve the environment and the demands for food, minerals, and energy from the west. . . .

QUESTIONS

1. *How and why does Commoner ask Americans to rethink their definition of freedom?*
2. *What elements of environmental policy does Blakemore see as a threat to "our freedoms"?*
3. *How do the two writers differ in their visions of the future of American society?*

Since the New Deal, Democrats had presented themselves as the party of affluence and economic growth. But Carter seemed to be presiding over a period of national decline. It did not help his popularity when, in a speech in 1979, he spoke of a national "crisis of confidence" and seemed to blame it on the American people themselves and their "mistaken idea of freedom" as "self-indulgence and consumption."

The Emergence of Human Rights Politics

Carter's human rights foreign policy

Under Carter, a commitment to promoting human rights became a centerpiece of American foreign policy for the first time. He was influenced by the proliferation of information about global denials of human rights that was spread by nongovernmental agencies like Amnesty International. Its reports marked a significant break with dominant ideas about international affairs since World War II, which had viewed the basic division in the world as between communist and noncommunist countries. Such reports, along with congressional hearings, exposed misdeeds not only by communist countries but also by American allies, especially the death squads of Latin American dictatorships.

In 1978, Carter cut off aid to the brutal military dictatorship governing Argentina, which in the name of anticommunism had launched a "dirty war" against its own citizens, kidnapping off the streets and secretly murdering an estimated 10,000 to 30,000 persons. Carter's action was a dramatic gesture, as Argentina was one of the most important powers in Latin America, and previous American administrations had turned a blind eye to human rights abuses by Cold War allies. By the end of his presidency, the phrase "human rights" had acquired political potency.

President Jimmy Carter (*center*), Egyptian president Anwar Sadat (*left*), and Israeli prime minister Menachem Begin (*right*) celebrating the signing of the 1979 peace treaty between Israel and Egypt.

Carter believed that in the post-Vietnam era, promoting human rights should take priority over what he called "the inordinate fear of communism that once led us to embrace any dictator who joined us in that fear." In one of his first acts as president, he offered an unconditional pardon to Vietnam-era draft resisters.

Carter's emphasis on pursuing peaceful solutions to international problems and his willingness to think outside the Cold War framework yielded important results. In 1979, he brought the leaders of Egypt and

Israel to the presidential retreat at Camp David and brokered a historic peace agreement, the **Camp David Accords**, between the two countries. He improved American relations with Latin America by agreeing to a treaty, ratified by the Senate in 1978, that provided for the transfer of the Panama Canal to local control by the year 2000. Carter attempted to curb the murderous violence of death squads allied to the right-wing government of El Salvador, and in 1980 he suspended military aid after the murder of four American nuns by members of the country's army.

Camp David

Both conservative Cold Warriors and foreign policy "realists" criticized Carter's emphasis on human rights. He himself found it difficult to translate rhetoric into action. He criticized American arms sales to the rest of the world. But with thousands of jobs and billions of dollars in corporate profits at stake, he did nothing to curtail them. The United States continued its support of allies with serious human rights violations such as the governments of Guatemala, the Philippines, South Korea, and Iran. Indeed, the American connection with the shah of Iran, whose secret police regularly jailed and tortured political opponents, proved to be Carter's undoing.

Carter's effectiveness

The Iran Crisis and Afghanistan

Occupying a strategic location on the southern border of the Soviet Union, Iran was a major supplier of oil and an importer of American military equipment. At the end of 1977, Carter traveled there to help celebrate the shah's rule, causing the internal opposition to become more and more anti-American. Early in 1979, a popular revolution inspired by the exiled Muslim cleric Ayatollah Khomeini overthrew the shah and declared Iran an Islamic republic.

When Carter in November 1979 allowed the deposed shah to seek medical treatment in the United States, Khomeini's followers invaded the American embassy in Tehran and seized sixty-six hostages. They did not regain their freedom until January 1981, on the day Carter's term as president ended. Events in Iran made Carter seem helpless and inept and led to a rapid fall in his popularity.

Another crisis that began in 1979 undermined American relations with Moscow. At the end of that year, the Soviet Union sent thousands of troops into Afghanistan to support a friendly government threatened by an Islamic rebellion. In the long run, Afghanistan became the Soviet Vietnam,

American hostages being paraded by their Iranian captors on the first day of the occupation of the American embassy in Tehran in 1979. Television gave extensive coverage to the plight of the hostages, leading many Americans to view the Carter administration as weak and inept.

an unwinnable conflict whose mounting casualties seriously weakened the government at home. Initially, however, it seemed another example of declining American power.

Declaring the invasion the greatest crisis since World War II (a considerable exaggeration), the president announced the Carter Doctrine, declaring that the United States would use military force, if necessary, to protect its interests in the Persian Gulf. He organized a Western boycott of the 1980 Olympics, which took place in Moscow, and dramatically increased American military spending. In a reversion to the Cold War principle that any opponent of the Soviet Union deserved American support, the United States funneled aid to fundamentalist Muslims in Afghanistan who fought a decade-long guerrilla war against the Soviets. The alliance had unforeseen consequences. A faction of Islamic fundamentalists known as the Taliban eventually came to power in Afghanistan. Tragically, they would prove as hostile to the United States as to Moscow.

Actions in Afghanistan

THE RISING TIDE OF CONSERVATISM

The combination of domestic and international dislocations during the 1970s created a widespread sense of anxiety among Americans and offered conservatives new political opportunities. Economic problems heightened the appeal of lower taxes, reduced government regulation, and cuts in social spending to spur business investment. Fears about a decline of American power in the world led to calls for a renewal of the Cold War. The civil rights and sexual revolutions produced resentments that undermined the Democratic coalition. Rising urban crime rates reinforced demands for law and order and attacks on courts considered too lenient toward criminals. These issues brought new converts to the conservative cause.

Issues for conservatives

As the 1970s went on, conservatives abandoned overt opposition to the black struggle for racial justice. The fiery rhetoric and direct confrontation tactics of Bull Connor, George Wallace, and other proponents of massive resistance were succeeded by appeals to freedom of association, local control, and resistance to the power of the federal government. This language of individual freedom resonated throughout the country, appealing especially to the growing, predominantly white, suburban population that was fleeing the cities and their urban problems. The suburbs would become one of the bastions of modern conservatism.

Conservatives and freedom

One set of recruits was the **neoconservatives**, a group of intellectuals who charged that the 1960s had produced a decline in moral standards and respect for authority. Once supporters of liberalism, they had come to believe that even well-intentioned government social programs did more

Neoconservatives

harm than good. Conservative "think tanks" created during the 1970s, like the Heritage Foundation and the American Enterprise Institute, refined and spread these ideas.

The Religious Right

The rise of religious fundamentalism during the 1970s expanded conservatism's popular base. Even as membership in mainstream denominations like Episcopalianism and Presbyterianism declined, evangelical Protestantism flourished. Some observers spoke of a Third Great Awakening (like those of the 1740s and early nineteenth century). The election of Carter, the first "born-again" Christian to become president, highlighted the growing influence of evangelical religion. But unlike Carter, most fundamentalists who entered politics did so as conservatives.

Evangelical religion

Evangelical Christians had become more and more alienated from a culture that seemed to them to trivialize religion and promote immorality. Although it spoke of restoring traditional values, the Religious Right proved remarkably adept at using modern technology, including mass mailings and televised religious programming, to raise funds for its crusade and spread its message. In 1979, Jerry Falwell, a Virginia minister, founded the self-styled Moral Majority, devoted to waging a "war against sin" and electing "pro-life, pro-family, pro-America" candidates to office.

Conservatism and the evangelicals

Christian conservatives seemed most agitated by the ongoing sexual revolution, which they saw as undermining the traditional family and promoting immorality. As a result of the 1960s, they believed, American freedom was out of control.

The Battle over the Equal Rights Amendment

During the 1970s, "family values" moved to the center of conservative politics, nowhere more so than in the battle over the Equal Rights Amendment (ERA). Originally proposed during the 1920s by Alice Paul and the Women's Party, the ERA had been revived by second-wave feminists. In the wake of the rights revolution, the amendment's affirmation that "equality of rights under the law" could not be abridged "on account of sex" hardly seemed controversial. In 1972, with little opposition, Congress approved the ERA and sent it to the states for ratification. Designed to eliminate obstacles to the full participation of women in public life, it aroused unexpected protest from those who claimed it would discredit the role of wife and homemaker.

Division among women

The ERA debate reflected a division among women as much as a battle of the sexes. To its supporters, the amendment offered a guarantee of

WHO IS AN AMERICAN?

Brochure on the Equal Rights Amendment (1970s)

First proposed in the 1920s, the Equal Rights Amendment (ERA) to the Constitution was resurrected in the 1970s as an outgrowth of the second wave of feminism. Its language was brief: "Equality of rights under the law shall not be denied or abridged by the United States or by any State on account of sex." But its implications were anything but simple. It quickly won approval by Congress, but as states debated ratification, it aroused a storm of protest from conservatives who claimed it would undermine women's traditional roles as mothers, wives, and homemakers. The amendment failed to gain ratification by the required number of states. In this brochure, the Philadelphia chapter of the National Organization for Women (NOW) details the gender inequalities that persisted long after women gained the right to vote and outlined what it hoped the ERA would accomplish.

Did You Know . . .

Under the U.S. Constitution corporations are considered legal persons but women are not.

Women earn on an average 41% less than men. . . .

A husband controls his wife's use of "his" credit cards; a wife cannot establish credit in her own name. . . .

During probate, a joint bank account is considered to be solely the property of the husband. . . .

Unemployment is twice as high for women as for men.

There are over 1,795 laws which discriminate against women.

The ERA will . . .

Declare women full persons under the law.

Outlaw discrimination on the basis of sex, establishing constitutionally the legal right of "equal pay for equal work." . . .

Give married women the right to establish credit, own businesses, buy and control property, and sign contracts. . . .

Strike down laws which restrict rights. If a law protects rights, it will be extended to the other sex.

QUESTIONS

1. *What kinds of inequality seem to concern NOW the most?*
2. *What does the brochure see as necessary for women to take part fully in American life?*

A women's liberation march in Detroit in 1970 highlights the issue of equal pay for equal work. At the time, women earned less than men in virtually every category of employment.

women's freedom in the public sphere. To its foes, freedom for women still resided in the divinely appointed roles of wife and mother. They claimed that the ERA would let men "off the hook" by denying their responsibility to provide for their wives and children. Polls consistently showed that a majority of Americans, male and female, favored the ERA. But thanks to the mobilization of conservative women, the amendment failed to achieve ratification by the required thirty-eight states.

The Abortion Controversy

An even more acrimonious battle emerged in the 1970s over abortion rights, another example, to conservatives, of how liberals in office promoted sexual immorality at the expense of moral values. The movement to reverse the 1973 *Roe v. Wade* decision began among Roman Catholics, whose church condemned abortion under any circumstances. But it soon enlisted evangelical Protestants and social conservatives more generally. Life, the movement insisted, begins at conception, and abortion is nothing less than murder. Between this position and the feminist insistence that a woman's right to control her body includes the right to a safe, legal abortion, compromise was impossible.

The abortion issue drew a bitter, sometimes violent line through American politics. It affected battles over nominees to judicial positions and led to demonstrations at family-planning and abortion clinics. The anti-abortion movement won its first victory in 1976 when Congress, over President Ford's veto, ended federal funding for abortions for poor women through the Medicaid program. By the 1990s, a few fringe anti-abortion activists were placing bombs at medical clinics and murdering doctors who terminated pregnancies.

Demonstrators at a rally supporting abortion rights.

A 1979 anti-abortion rally in Washington, D.C., on the sixth anniversary of the Supreme Court's decision in *Roe v. Wade*, which barred states from limiting a woman's right to terminate a pregnancy.

The Tax Revolt

With liberals unable to devise an effective policy to counteract deindustrialization and declining real wages, economic anxieties also created a growing constituency for conservative economics. Unlike during the Great Depression, economic distress inspired a critique of government rather than of business. New environmental regulations led to calls for less government intervention in the economy. The descent from affluence to "stagflation" increased the appeal of the conservative argument that government regulation raised business costs and eliminated jobs.

Demands for lower taxes

Economic decline also broadened the constituency receptive to demands for lower taxes. To conservatives, tax reductions served the dual purposes of enhancing business profits and reducing the resources available to government, thus making new social programs financially impossible.

Conservatism in the West

The West has always both reflected and contributed to national political trends. In the 1970s and 1980s it offered fertile soil for various strands of conservatism. The population movements of previous decades stimulated this development. Many southerners had left their homes for southern California, bringing with them their distinctive form of evangelical Christianity. Increasingly alienated from a Democratic Party that embraced the rights revolution and with it, evangelicals felt, the decline of traditional values, they gravitated to the California Republican Party, from which emerged national Republican leaders such as Richard Nixon

California conservatives

and Ronald Reagan. California conservatives also embraced the new anti-tax mood.

California's Proposition 13

In 1978, conservatives sponsored and California voters approved Proposition 13, a ban on further increases in property taxes. The vote demonstrated that the level of taxation could be a powerful political issue. Proposition 13 proved to be a windfall for businesses and home owners while reducing funds available for schools, libraries, and other public services. Many voters, however, proved willing to accept this result of lower taxes. As anti-tax sentiment flourished throughout the country, many states followed California's lead.

Sagebrush Rebellion

There have always been voices in the West insisting that the region has a colonial relationship with the rest of the country. They point to federal ownership of large swaths of western land, and the dependence of western development on investment from the East. In the late nineteenth century, this view helped give rise to western Populism, when the targets of protest were eastern banks and railroad companies, as well as a national economic policy that favored these corporations. Nearly a century later it became associated with a conservative upsurge known as the Sagebrush Rebellion (the name given to a bill passed by the Nevada legislature in 1979) directed at the federal government. The roots of this "rebellion" lie as far back as the 1920s, when the U.S. Forest Service announced plans to increase grazing fees and mineral rights in national forests and other public lands. Nevada's ranchers went to court to block these fees but were rebuffed by the Supreme Court. In the 1970s, new environmental regulations won fresh recruits to the movement. The Clean Air Act alarmed western coal operators. Westerners who believed the environmental policies of the Carter administration were closing the public domain to exploitation eagerly supported Ronald Reagan's presidential candidacy.

The Election of 1980

By 1980, Carter's approval rating had fallen to 21 percent—lower than Nixon's at the time of his resignation. Ronald Reagan's 1980 campaign for the presidency brought together the many strands of 1970s conservatism. He pledged to end stagflation and restore the country's dominant role in the

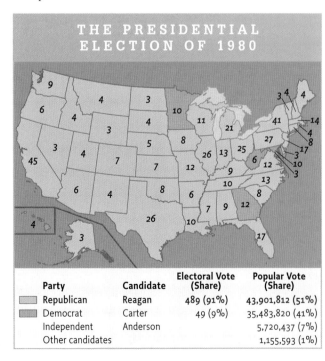

THE PRESIDENTIAL ELECTION OF 1980

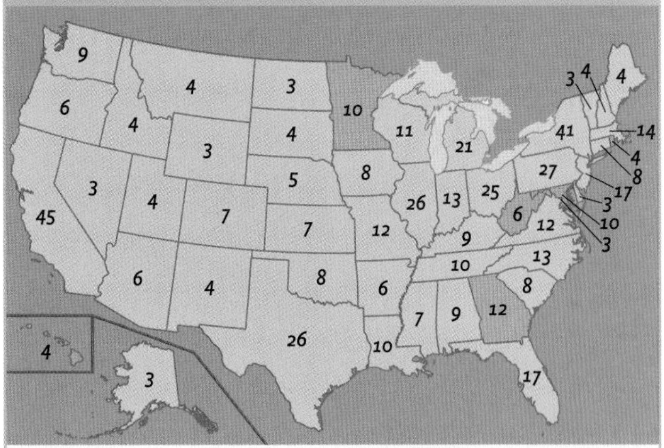

Party	Candidate	Electoral Vote (Share)	Popular Vote (Share)
Republican	Reagan	489 (91%)	43,901,812 (51%)
Democrat	Carter	49 (9%)	35,483,820 (41%)
Independent	Anderson		5,720,437 (7%)
Other candidates			1,155,593 (1%)

Before entering politics, Ronald Reagan was a prominent actor and a spokesperson for General Electric. In this 1958 photograph, he demonstrates the use of a GE oven.

world and its confidence in itself. "Let's make America great again," he proclaimed. "The era of self-doubt is over."

Reagan also appealed skillfully to "white backlash." He kicked off his campaign in Philadelphia, Mississippi, where three civil rights workers had been murdered in 1964, with a speech emphasizing his belief in states' rights. Many white southerners understood this doctrine as including opposition to federal intervention on behalf of civil rights. During the campaign, Reagan repeatedly condemned welfare "cheats," school busing, and affirmative action. The Republican platform reversed the party's long-standing support for the Equal Rights Amendment and condemned moral permissiveness. Although not personally religious and the first divorced man to run for president, Reagan won the support of the Religious Right and conservative upholders of "family values."

Riding a wave of dissatisfaction with the country's condition, Reagan swept into the White House. Carter received 41 percent of the popular vote, a humiliating defeat for a sitting president.

The election of 1980 launched the **Reagan Revolution**, which completed the transformation of freedom from the rallying cry of the left to a possession of the right.

THE REAGAN REVOLUTION

A delegate to the Republican national convention of 1980 wears a hat festooned with the flags of the United States and Texas and a button with a picture of her hero, Ronald Reagan.

Ronald Reagan followed a most unusual path to the presidency. Originally a New Deal Democrat and head of the Screen Actors Guild (he was the only union leader ever to reach the White House), he emerged in the 1950s as a spokesman for the General Electric Corporation, preaching the virtues of unregulated capitalism. His speech for Barry Goldwater in 1964 (mentioned earlier) brought Reagan to national attention. Two years later, California voters elected Reagan as governor. His victory in 1980 brought to power a diverse coalition of old and new conservatives: Sunbelt suburbanites and urban working-class ethnics, antigovernment crusaders and advocates of a more aggressive foreign policy, libertarians who believed in freeing the individual from restraint, and the Christian Right, which sought to restore what they considered traditional moral values to American life.

Reagan and American Freedom

Reagan's opponents often underestimated him. Unlike most modern presidents, he was content to outline broad policy themes and leave their implementation to others. Reagan, however, was hardly a political novice. He was an excellent public speaker, and his optimism and affability appealed to large numbers of Americans. Reagan made conservatism seem progressive, rather than an attempt to turn back the tide of progress.

On issues ranging from taxes to government spending, national security, crime, welfare, and "traditional values," Reagan put Democrats on the defensive. But he also proved to be a pragmatist, recognizing when to compromise so as not to fragment his diverse coalition of supporters.

Reagan as leader

Reagan's Economic Policies

In 1981, Reagan persuaded Congress to reduce the top tax rate from 70 percent to 50 percent and to index tax brackets to take inflation into account. Five years later, the Tax Reform Act reduced the rate on the wealthiest Americans to 28 percent. These measures marked a sharp retreat from the principle of progressivity (the idea that the wealthy should pay a higher percentage of their income in taxes than other citizens), one of the ways twentieth-century societies tried to address the unequal distribution of wealth. Reagan also appointed conservative heads of regulatory agencies, who cut back on environmental protection and workplace safety rules, about which business had complained for years.

Tax reform

Since the New Deal, liberals had tried to promote economic growth by using the power of the government to bolster ordinary Americans' purchasing power. Reagan's economic program, known as "supply-side economics" by proponents and "trickle-down economics" by critics, relied on high interest rates to curb inflation and lower tax rates, especially for businesses and high-income Americans, to stimulate private investment. The policy assumed that cutting taxes would inspire Americans at all income levels to work harder, because they would keep more of the money they earned.

Supply-side economics

Reagan and Labor

Reagan inaugurated an era of hostility between the federal government and organized labor. In August 1981, when 13,000 members of PATCO, the union of air traffic controllers, began a strike in violation of federal law, Reagan fired them all. He used the military to oversee the nation's air traffic system until new controllers could be trained. Reagan's action inspired many private employers to launch anti-union offensives. The hiring of workers to replace permanently those who had gone

Striking air traffic controllers on a picket line at an air traffic control center in upstate New York. President Reagan's firing of over 10,000 strikers launched a new anti-union offensive by both government and private employers.

This photograph of the remains of the Bethlehem Steel plant in Lackawanna, New York, which closed in 1982, depicts the aftermath of deindustrialization. Today, the site is a wind farm, with eight windmills helping to provide electricity for the city.

on strike, a rare occurrence before 1980, became widespread. Manufacturing employment, where union membership was concentrated, meanwhile continued its long-term decline. By the mid-1990s, the steel industry employed only 170,000 persons—down from 600,000 in 1973.

Reaganomics, as critics dubbed the administration's policies, initially produced the most severe recession since the 1930s. A long period of economic expansion, however, followed the downturn of 1981–1982. As companies "downsized" their workforces, shifted production overseas, and took advantage of new technologies such as satellite communications, they became more profitable. At the same time, the rate of inflation, 13.5 percent at the beginning of 1981, declined to 3.5 percent in 1988, partly because a period of expanded oil production that drove down prices succeeded the shortages of the 1970s. By the end of Reagan's presidency in 1989, the real gross domestic product had risen by 25 percent and unemployment was down to 5.5 percent. These were significant accomplishments.

The Problem of Inequality

40 percent of nation's wealth owned by richest 1 percent

Together, Reagan's policies, rising stock prices, and deindustrialization resulted in a considerable rise in economic inequality. By the mid-1990s, the richest 1 percent of Americans owned 40 percent of the nation's wealth, twice their share twenty years earlier. Most spent their income not on productive investments and charity as supply-side economists had promised, but on luxury goods, real-estate speculation, and corporate buyouts that often led to plant closings as operations were consolidated. The income of middle-class families, especially those with a wife who did not work outside the home, stagnated while that of the poorest one-fifth of the population declined.

During the 1970s, Jim Crow had finally ended in many workplaces and unions. But just as decades of painful efforts to obtain better jobs bore fruit, hundreds of thousands of black workers lost their jobs when factories closed their doors. In South Gate, a working-class suburb of Los Angeles, for example, the giant Firestone tire factory shut down in 1980, only a few years after black and Latino workers made their first breakthroughs in employment. When the national unemployment rate reached 8.9 percent at the end of 1981, the figure for blacks exceeded 20 percent.

The Second Gilded Age

In retrospect, the 1980s, like the 1890s, would be widely remembered as a decade of misplaced values. Buying out companies generated more profits than running them; making deals, not making products, became the way to get rich. The merger of Nabisco and R. J. Reynolds Tobacco Company in 1988 produced close to $1 billion in fees for lawyers, economic advisers, and stockbrokers. "Greed is healthy," declared Wall Street financier Ivan Boesky (who ended up in prison for insider stock trading). "Yuppie"—the young urban professional who earned a high income working in a bank or stock-brokerage firm and spent lavishly on designer clothing and other trappings of the good life—became a household word.

Taxpayers footed the bill for some of the consequences. The deregulation of savings and loan associations—banks that had generally confined themselves to financing home mortgages—allowed those institutions to invest in unsound real-estate ventures and corporate mergers. Losses piled up, and the Federal Savings and Loan Insurance Corporation, which insured depositors' accounts, faced bankruptcy. After Reagan left office, the federal government bailed out the savings and loan institutions at a cost to taxpayers estimated at $250 billion.

Supply-side advocates insisted that lowering taxes would enlarge government revenue by stimulating economic activity. But spurred by large increases in funds for the military, federal spending far outstripped income, producing large budget deficits, despite assurances by supply-siders that this would not happen. During Reagan's presidency, the national debt tripled to $2.7 trillion.

Nonetheless, Reagan remained immensely popular. He won a triumphant reelection in 1984. His opponent, Walter Mondale (best remembered for choosing Congresswoman Geraldine Ferraro of New York as his running mate, the first woman candidate on a major-party presidential ticket), carried only his home state of Minnesota and the District of Columbia.

FIGURE 26.3 Changes in Families' Real Income, 1980–1990

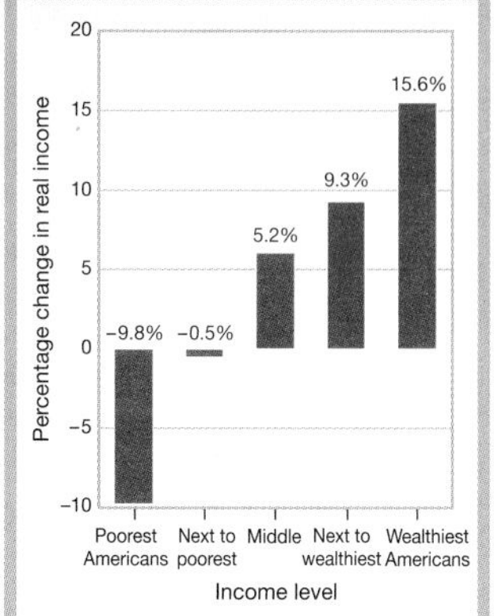

The wealthiest American families benefited the most from economic expansion during the 1980s, whereas the poorest 40 percent of the population saw their real incomes decline. (Real income indicates income adjusted to take account of inflation.)

A homeless St. Louis mother and her children, forced to live in their car, photographed in 1987.

Reagan and Immigration Reform

Under Reagan, Congress passed the most significant reform of immigration policy since 1965. Large numbers of immigrants had entered the country from Mexico without authorization—the so-called illegals. These newcomers were drawn by strong demand for low-wage labor, which far exceeded the annual legal quotas established under the Hart-Celler Act (discussed in the previous chapter). Calls to stem the flow of undocumented

First lady Nancy Reagan promoting her "Just Say No" campaign against the use of drugs, in a photo from 1986.

immigrants grew. Reagan viewed immigration as crucial to the country's economic strength. He promised to "continue America's tradition as a land that welcomes people," even as the nation regained control of its borders. The Immigration Reform and Control Act of 1986 provided amnesty and a path to citizenship for nearly 3 million undocumented immigrants who had put down roots in the country, but penalized employers who knowingly hired them. But unauthorized immigration continued.

Conservatives and Reagan

Although he implemented their economic policies, Reagan in some ways disappointed ardent conservatives. The administration left intact core elements of the welfare state, such as Social Security, Medicare, and Medicaid, which many conservatives wished to curtail significantly or repeal. The Reagan era did little to advance the social agenda of the Christian Right. Abortion remained legal, women continued to enter the labor force in unprecedented numbers, and Reagan even appointed the first female member of the Supreme Court, Sandra Day O'Connor. In 1986, in *Bowers v. Hardwick*, in a rare victory for cultural conservatives, the Supreme Court did uphold the constitutionality of state laws outlawing homosexual acts. (In 2003, the justices would reverse the *Bowers* decision, declaring such laws unconstitutional.)

The Wars on Crime and Drugs

"Freedom from fear"

If Reagan weakened the federal government's power to regulate business, he strengthened its role in crime control. He championed a strand of thought about freedom favored by social conservatives that emphasized law and order to secure "freedom from fear." Reagan built on initiatives begun during the Nixon administration. With reported crime rising sharply and cities gripped by riots, Nixon had called for increased spending on policing and law enforcement, and an expansion of the nation's prisons. Although the number of prisoners had remained low and stable for years, Nixon anticipated a large increase as part of a crackdown on the growing use, in cities, in suburbs, and on college campuses, of marijuana and heroin. In 1973, Nixon declared an "all-out war on the global drug menace," but with little result.

Reagan expanded on Nixon's "tough on crime" approach. The Comprehensive Crime Control Act of 1984 reinstated the federal death penalty, abolished the federal parole system, and instituted harsh sentencing guidelines for judges to implement. Public fears about the spread of crack in urban areas contributed to support for these punitive policies. Reagan brought national spending on criminal justice to a record high of nearly $3.5 billion. In 1986, the Anti-Drug Abuse Act led to a surge in arrests, and a rapidly expanding prison population. In 1980 there were 50,000 Americans in prison for nonviolent drug violations; by 1997 the number had reached 400,000, most of them blacks and Hispanics, who were disproportionately targeted by police. But the war on drugs failed to seriously disrupt global supply chains or the domestic demand for drugs.

People of color disproportionately targeted

Reagan and the Cold War

In foreign policy, Reagan resumed vigorous denunciation of the Soviet Union—calling it an "evil empire"—and sponsored the largest military buildup in American history, including new long-range bombers and missiles. In 1983, he proposed an entirely new strategy, the Strategic Defense Initiative, which would develop a space-based system to intercept and destroy enemy missiles. The idea was not remotely feasible technologically, and, if deployed, it would violate the Anti-Ballistic Missile Treaty of 1972. But it appealed to Reagan's desire to reassert America's worldwide power.

Reasserting America as a military power

Reagan came into office determined to overturn the "**Vietnam Syndrome**"—as widespread public reluctance to commit American forces overseas was called. He sent American troops to the Caribbean island of Grenada to oust a pro-Cuban government. In 1982, Reagan dispatched marines as a peacekeeping force to Lebanon, where a civil war raged between the Christian government, supported by Israeli forces, and Muslim insurgents. But he quickly withdrew them after a bomb exploded at their barracks, killing 241 Americans. The public, Reagan realized, would support minor operations like Grenada but remained unwilling to sustain heavy casualties abroad.

Hollywood joined enthusiastically in the revived Cold War. The 1984 film *Red Dawn* depicted a Soviet invasion of the United States.

Abandoning the Carter administration's emphasis on human rights, Reagan embraced the idea, advanced in 1979 by neoconservative writer Jeane Kirkpatrick, that the United States should oppose "totalitarian" communists but assist "authoritarian" noncommunist regimes. The United States stepped up its alliances with Third World anticommunist dictatorships like the governments of Chile and South Africa. The administration poured in funds to combat insurgencies against the governments of El Salvador and Guatemala,

THE UNITED STATES IN THE CARIBBEAN AND CENTRAL AMERICA, 1954–2004

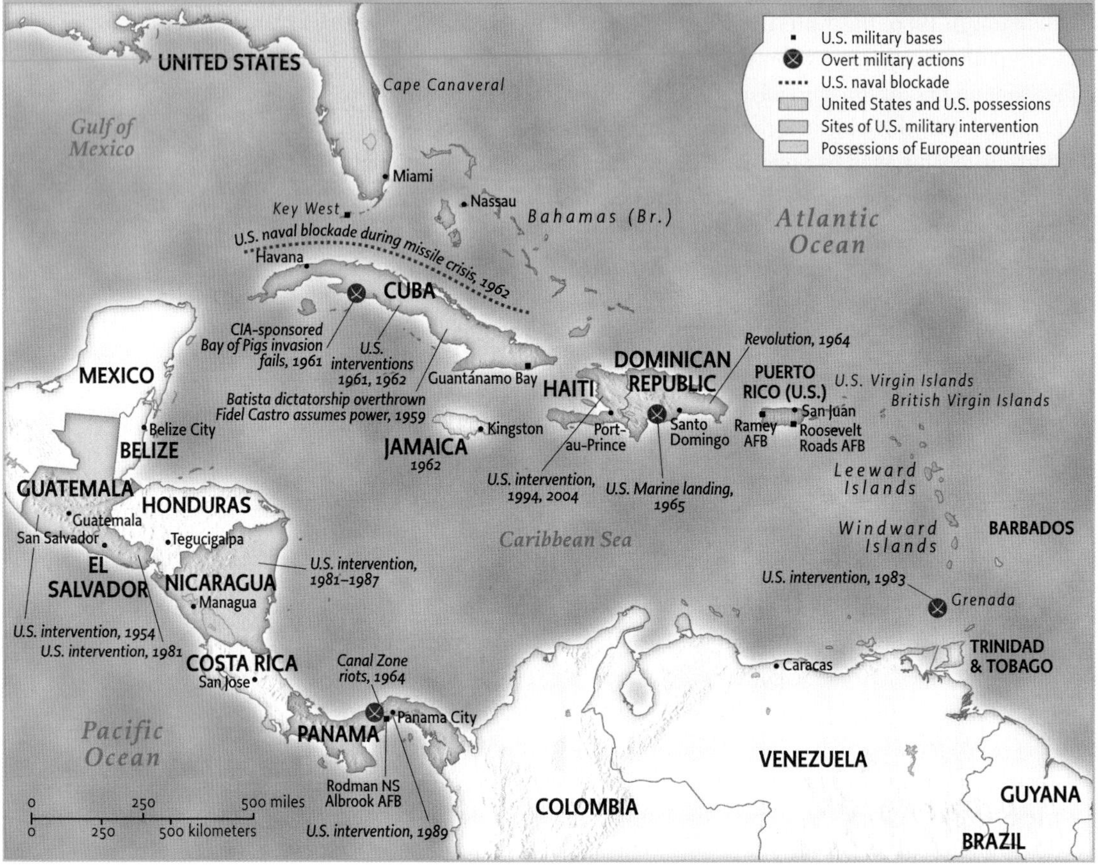

As in the first part of the twentieth century, the United States intervened frequently in Caribbean and Central American countries during and immediately after the Cold War.

whose armies and associated death squads committed flagrant abuses against their own citizens. When El Salvador's army massacred hundreds of civilians in the town of El Mozote in 1981, the State Department denied that the event, widely reported in the press, had taken place.

The Iran-Contra Affair

Arms for hostages

American involvement in Central America produced the greatest scandal of Reagan's presidency, the **Iran-Contra affair**. In 1984, Congress banned military aid to the Contras (derived from the Spanish word for "against") fighting the Sandinista government of Nicaragua, which had ousted the American-backed dictator Anastasio Somoza in 1979. In 1985, Reagan secretly authorized the sale of arms to Iran—now involved in a war with its neighbor, Iraq—in order to secure the release of a number of American hostages held by Islamic groups in the Middle East. CIA director William Casey and Lieutenant Colonel Oliver North of the National Security Council set up a system that diverted some of the proceeds to buy military supplies for the Contras in defiance of the congressional ban. The scheme continued for nearly two years.

In 1987, after a Middle Eastern newspaper leaked the story, Congress held televised hearings that revealed a pattern of official duplicity and violation of the law reminiscent of the Nixon era. Eleven members of the administration eventually were convicted of perjury or destroying documents, or pleaded guilty before being tried. Reagan denied knowledge of the illegal proceedings, but the Iran-Contra affair undermined confidence that he controlled his own administration.

President Reagan visited Moscow in 1988, cementing his close relationship with Soviet leader Mikhail Gorbachev. They were photographed in Red Square.

Reagan and Gorbachev

In his second term, to the surprise of both his foes and his supporters, Reagan softened his anticommunist rhetoric and established good relations with Soviet premier Mikhail Gorbachev. Gorbachev had come to power in 1985, bent on reforming the Soviet Union's repressive political system and reinvigorating its economy. Gorbachev inaugurated policies known as *glasnost* (political openness) and *perestroika* (economic reform).

Arms control agreements

Gorbachev realized that significant change would be impossible without reducing his country's military budget. Reagan was ready to negotiate. A series of talks between 1985 and 1987 yielded more progress on arms control than in the entire postwar period to that point, including an agreement to eliminate intermediate- and short-range nuclear missiles in Europe. In 1988, Gorbachev began pulling Soviet troops out of Afghanistan. Having entered office as an ardent Cold Warrior, Reagan left with hostilities between the superpowers much diminished. He even repudiated his earlier comment that the Soviet Union was an "evil empire," saying that it referred to "another era."

Reagan's Legacy

Social and economic repurcussions

Reagan's presidency revealed the contradictions at the heart of modern conservatism. In some ways, the Reagan Revolution undermined the very values and institutions conservatives held dear. Intended to discourage reliance on government handouts by rewarding honest work and business initiative, Reagan's policies inspired a speculative frenzy that enriched architects of corporate takeovers and investors in the stock market while leaving in their wake plant closings, job losses, and devastated communities. Nothing proved more threatening to local traditions or family stability than deindustrialization, insecurity about employment, and the relentless downward pressure on wages.

Reagan's impact

Nonetheless, few figures have so successfully changed the landscape and language of politics. Reagan's vice president, George H. W. Bush, defeated Michael Dukakis, the governor of Massachusetts, in the 1988 election partly because Dukakis could not respond effectively to the charge that he was a "liberal"—now a term of political abuse. Conservative assumptions about the virtues of the free market and the evils of "big government" dominated the mass media and political debates. During the 1990s, these and other conservative ideas would be embraced almost as fully by President Bill Clinton, a Democrat, as by Reagan and the Republicans.

The Election of 1988

The 1988 election seemed to show politics sinking to new lows. Television advertisements and media exposés now dominated political campaigns. The race for the Democratic nomination had hardly begun before the front-runner, Senator Gary Hart of Colorado, withdrew after a newspaper reported that he had spent the night at his Washington town house with a woman other than his wife. Democrats ridiculed the Republican vice presidential nominee, Senator Dan Quayle of Indiana, for factual and linguistic mistakes. Republicans spread unfounded rumors that Michael Dukakis's wife had burned an American flag during the 1960s. The low point of the campaign came in a Republican television ad depicting the threatening image of Willie Horton, a black murderer and rapist who had been furloughed from prison during Dukakis's term as governor of Massachusetts. Rarely in the modern era had a major party appealed so blatantly to racial fears.

A dismal campaign

Bush achieved a substantial majority, winning 54 percent of the popular vote. Democratic success in retaining control of Congress suggested that an electoral base existed for a comeback. But this would only occur if the party fashioned a new appeal to replace traditional liberalism, which had been eclipsed by the triumph of conservatism.

CHAPTER REVIEW AND ONLINE RESOURCES

REVIEW QUESTIONS

1. *Why were social issues associated with the sexual revolution so contested by all sides?*
2. *What were continuing challenges to the cohesiveness of the Democratic (New Deal) coalition? What were the consequences of those divisions?*
3. *What were the main features of Nixon's policy of "realism" in dealing with China and the Soviet Union?*
4. *Describe the basic events and the larger significance of the Watergate scandal.*
5. *What were the major causes for the decline of the U.S. economy during the 1970s?*
6. *What were the causes and consequences of the public's disillusionment with the federal government in the 1970s and 1980s?*
7. *Identify the groups and their agendas that combined to create the new conservative base in the 1970s and 1980s.*
8. *What impact did Ronald Reagan have on the American political scene?*
9. *Why was there growth in economic inequality in the 1980s?*
10. *How did various groups see the relationship between women's rights and freedom differently?*

KEY TERMS

affirmative action (p. 806)
busing (p. 807)
reverse discrimination (p. 808)
Title IX (p. 809)
Strategic Arms Limitation Talks (p. 810)
détente (p. 811)
My Lai massacre (p. 812)
Pentagon Papers (p. 812)
War Powers Act (p. 812)
Watergate (p. 813)
oil embargo (p. 817)
stagflation (p. 817)
deindustrialization (p. 817)
Sunbelt (p. 817)
Helsinki Accords (p. 818)
deregulation (p. 819)
Three Mile Island (p. 819)
Camp David Accords (p. 823)
neoconservatives (p. 824)
Reagan Revolution (p. 830)
Reaganomics (p. 832)
Vietnam Syndrome (p. 835)
Iran-Contra affair (p. 836)

Go to INQUIZITIVE

To see what you know—and learn what you've missed—with personalized feedback along the way.

Visit the ***Give Me Liberty!* Student Site** for primary source documents and images, interactive maps, author videos featuring Eric Foner, and more.

1989	Communism falls in eastern Europe
1991	Gulf War
	Dissolution of the Soviet Union
1992	Los Angeles riots
	Casey v. Planned Parenthood of Pennsylvania
	William Jefferson Clinton elected president
1993	North American Free Trade Agreement approved
1994	Republicans win in Congress; Contract with America
1995	Oklahoma City federal building bombed
1996	Clinton eliminates Aid to Families with Dependent Children
1998–1999	Clinton impeachment proceedings
1999	Protests in Seattle against the World Trade Organization
	Glass-Steagall Act repealed
2000	*Bush v. Gore*
2001	9/11 attacks
2001	United States enters war in Afghanistan
	USA Patriot Act
2002	Bush identifies "axis of evil"
	Department of Homeland Security established
2003	Iraq War begins

CHAPTER 27

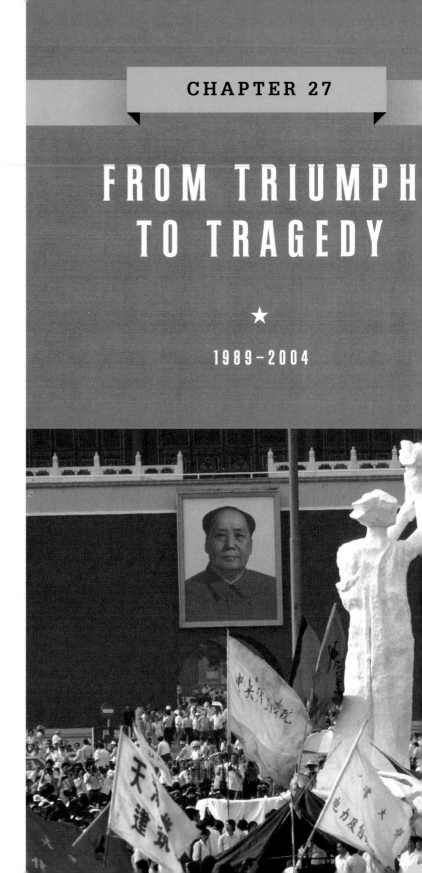

FROM TRIUMPH TO TRAGEDY

★

1989–2004

The Goddess of Democracy and Freedom, a statue reminiscent of the Statue of Liberty, was displayed by pro-democracy advocates during the 1989 demonstrations in Beijing's Tiananmen Square. After allowing it to continue for two months, the Chinese government sent troops to crush the peaceful occupation of the square.

The year 1989 was one of the most momentous of the twentieth century. In April, tens of thousands of student demonstrators occupied Tiananmen Square in the heart of Beijing, demanding greater democracy in China. The students erected a figure reminiscent of the Statue of Liberty, calling it "The Goddess of Democracy and Freedom." In June, Chinese troops crushed the protest, killing an unknown number of people, possibly thousands.

In the fall of 1989, pro-democracy demonstrations spread across eastern Europe. Soviet leader Mikhail Gorbachev made it clear that unlike in the past, the Soviet Union would not intervene. The climactic event took place on November 9 when crowds breached the Berlin Wall, which since 1961 had stood as the Cold War's most prominent symbol. One by one, the region's communist governments agreed to give up power. In 1990, a reunified German nation absorbed East Germany. The remarkably swift and almost entirely peaceful collapse of communism in eastern Europe became known as the "velvet revolution."

Meanwhile, the Soviet Union itself slipped deeper and deeper into crisis. One after another, the republics of the Soviet Union declared themselves sovereign states. By the end of 1991, the Soviet Union ceased to exist; in its place were fifteen new independent nations.

The sudden and unexpected collapse of communism marked the end of the Cold War and a stunning triumph for the United States and its allies. For the first time since 1917, there existed a truly worldwide capitalist system. Even China, though remaining under Communist Party rule, had already embarked on market reforms and rushed to attract foreign investment. Other events suggested that the 1990s would be a "decade

Demonstrators dancing atop the Berlin Wall on November 10, 1989. The next day, crowds began dismantling it, in the most dramatic moment of the collapse of communist rule in eastern Europe.

FOCUS QUESTIONS

- *How did Bush and Clinton transform America's world role?*
- *What forces drove the economic resurgence of the 1990s?*
- *What cultural conflicts emerged in the 1990s?*
- *How did a divisive political partisanship affect the election of 2000?*
- *Why did Al Qaeda attack the United States on September 11, 2001?*
- *What were the major policy elements of the war on terror in the wake of 9/11?*
- *How did the war in Iraq unfold in the wake of 9/11?*
- *How did the war on terror affect the economy and American liberties?*

EASTERN EUROPE AFTER THE COLD WAR

The end of the Cold War and breakup of the Soviet Union, Czechoslovakia, and Yugoslavia redrew the map of eastern Europe (compare this map with the map of Cold War Europe in Chapter 23). Two additional nations that emerged from the Soviet Union lie to the east and are not indicated here: Kyrgyzstan and Tajikistan.

of democracy." In 1990, South Africa released Nelson Mandela, head of the African National Congress, from prison. Four years later, as a result of the first democratic elections in the country's history, Mandela became president, ending the system of state-sponsored racial inequality, known as "apartheid," and white minority government. The sudden shift from a bipolar world to one of unquestioned American predominance promised to redefine the country's global role. President George H. W. Bush spoke of the coming of a **new world order**. But no one knew what its characteristics would be and what new challenges to American power might arise.

THE POST–COLD WAR WORLD

Bush's first major foreign policy action was a throwback to the days of American interventionism in the Western Hemisphere. At the end of 1989, he dispatched troops to Panama to overthrow the government of General Manuel Antonio Noriega, a former ally of the United States who had become involved in the international drug trade.

U.S. soldiers seated under a portrait of Iraqi ruler Saddam Hussein at the border between Iraq and Kuwait during the Gulf War of 1991.

The Gulf War

A far more serious crisis arose in 1990 when Iraq invaded and annexed Kuwait, an oil-rich sheikdom on the Persian Gulf. Fearing that Iraqi dictator Saddam Hussein might next attack Saudi Arabia, a longtime ally that supplied more oil to the United States than any other country, Bush rushed troops to defend Kuwait and warned Iraq to withdraw from the country or face war.

Operation Desert Storm

In February 1991, the United States launched Operation Desert Storm, which quickly drove the Iraqi army from Kuwait. The United Nations ordered Iraq to disarm and imposed economic sanctions that produced widespread civilian suffering for the rest of the decade. But Hussein remained in place. So did a large American military establishment in Saudi Arabia, to the outrage of Islamic fundamentalists who deemed its presence an affront to their faith. In the **Gulf War's** immediate aftermath, Bush's public approval rating rose to an unprecedented 89 percent.

Public approval

The Election of Clinton

Had a presidential election been held early in 1991, Bush would undoubtedly have been victorious. But later that year, the economy slipped into recession. Despite victory in the Cold War and the Gulf, more and more Americans believed the country was on the wrong track. No one seized more effectively on this widespread sense of unease than Bill Clinton, a former governor of Arkansas. In 1992, Clinton won the Democratic nomination by combining social liberalism (he supported abortion rights, gay rights, and

Bill Clinton's appeal

affirmative action for racial minorities) with elements of conservatism (he pledged to reduce government bureaucracy and, borrowing a page from Republicans, promised to "end welfare as we know it").

Bush's weakness

A charismatic campaigner, Clinton conveyed sincere concern for voters' economic anxieties. Bush, by contrast, seemed out of touch with the day-to-day lives of ordinary Americans. He was further weakened when conservative leader Pat Buchanan delivered a fiery televised speech at the Republican national convention that declared cultural war against gays, feminists, and supporters of abortion rights. This rhetoric seemed to confirm the Democratic portrait of Republicans as intolerant and divisive.

A third candidate, the eccentric Texas billionaire Ross Perot, also entered the fray. He attacked Bush and Clinton as lacking the economic know-how to deal with the recession and the ever-increasing national debt. That millions of Americans considered Perot a credible candidate—at one point, polls showed him leading both Clinton and Bush—testified to widespread dissatisfaction with the major parties. Perot's support faded, but he still received 19 percent of the popular vote, the best result for a third-party candidate since Theodore Roosevelt in 1912. Clinton won by a substantial margin, a humiliating outcome for Bush, given his earlier popularity.

Clinton in Office

Clinton's domestic policy

In his first two years in office, Clinton turned away from some of the social and economic policies of the Reagan and Bush years. He appointed several blacks and women to his cabinet, including Janet Reno, the first female attorney general, and named two supporters of abortion rights, Ruth Bader Ginsburg and Stephen Breyer, to the Supreme Court. He modified the military's strict ban on gay soldiers, instituting a "**Don't ask, don't tell**" policy by which officers would not seek out gays for dismissal from the armed forces. His first budget raised taxes on the wealthy and significantly expanded the Earned Income Tax Credit (EITC)—a cash payment for low-income workers begun during the Ford administration. The most effective antipoverty policy since the Great Society, the EITC raised more than 4 million Americans, half of them children, above the poverty line during Clinton's presidency.

Earned Income Tax Credit

Clinton shared his predecessor's passion for free trade. Despite strong opposition from unions and environmentalists, he obtained congressional approval in 1993 of the **North American Free Trade Agreement (NAFTA),** a treaty negotiated by Bush that created a free-trade zone consisting of Canada, Mexico, and the United States.

Free-trade zone

The major policy initiative of Clinton's first term was a plan devised by a panel headed by his wife, Hillary, to address the rising cost of health care and the increasing number of Americans who lacked health insurance. In Canada and western Europe, governments provided universal medical coverage. The United States had the world's most advanced medical technology but a woefully incomplete system of health insurance. Tens of millions of Americans lacked any coverage at all. Too complex to be easily understood by most voters, however, and vulnerable to criticism for further expanding the unpopular federal bureaucracy, the Clinton plan died in 1994.

The "Freedom Revolution"

With the economy recovering slowly from the recession and Clinton's first two years in office seemingly lacking in significant accomplishments, voters in 1994 turned against the administration. For the first time since the 1950s, Republicans won control of both houses of Congress. They proclaimed their triumph the "Freedom Revolution." Newt Gingrich, a conservative congressman from Georgia who became the new Speaker of the House, masterminded their campaign. Gingrich had devised a platform called the **Contract with America**, which promised to curtail the scope of government, cut back on taxes and economic and environmental regulations, overhaul the welfare system, and end affirmative action.

Republican control

Republicans moved swiftly to implement its provisions. The House approved deep cuts in social, educational, and environmental programs, including the popular Medicare system. With the president and Congress unable to reach agreement on a budget, the government in December 1995 shut down all nonessential operations, including Washington, D.C., museums and national parks. Most Americans blamed Republicans for the impasse, however, and Congress soon retreated.

Clinton's Political Strategy

Like Truman after the Republican sweep of 1946, Clinton rebuilt his popularity by campaigning against a radical Congress. He opposed the most extreme parts of his opponents' program, while adopting others. In his State of the Union address of January 1996, he announced that "the era of big government is over," in effect turning his back on the tradition of Democratic Party liberalism and embracing the antigovernment outlook associated with Republicans.

Ending AFDC

Also in 1996, ignoring the protests of most Democrats, Clinton signed into law a Republican bill that abolished the program of Aid to Families with Dependent Children (AFDC), commonly known as "welfare." Grants of money to the states, with strict limits on how long recipients could receive payments, replaced it. At the time of its abolition, AFDC assisted

VOICES OF FREEDOM

From Bill Clinton, Speech on Signing of NAFTA (1993)

The North American Free Trade Agreement was signed by President Bill Clinton early in his first term. It created a free-trade zone (an area where goods can travel freely without import duties) composed of Canada, the United States, and Mexico. Clinton asked Americans to accept economic globalization as an inevitable form of progress and the path to future prosperity. "There will be no job loss," he promised. Things did not entirely work out that way.

As President, it is my duty to speak frankly to the American people about the world in which we now live. Fifty years ago, at the end of World War II, an unchallenged America was protected by the oceans and by our technological superiority and, very frankly, by the economic devastation of the people who could otherwise have been our competitors. We chose then to try to help rebuild our former enemies and to create a world of free trade supported by institutions which would facilitate it. . . . As a result, jobs were created, and opportunity thrived all across the world. . . .

For the last 20 years, in all the wealthy countries of the world—because of changes in the global environment, because of the growth of technology, because of increasing competition—the middle class that was created and enlarged by the wise policies of expanding trade at the end of World War II has been under severe stress. Most Americans are working harder for less. They are vulnerable to the fear tactics and the averseness to change that are behind much of the opposition to NAFTA. But I want to say to my fellow Americans: When you live in a time of change, the only way to recover your security and to broaden your horizons is to adapt to the change—to embrace, to move forward. . . . The only way we can recover the fortunes of the middle class in this country so that people who work harder and smarter can, at least, prosper more, the only way we can pass on the American dream of the last 40 years to our children and their children for the next 40, is to adapt to the changes which are occurring.

In a fundamental sense, this debate about NAFTA is a debate about whether we will embrace these changes and create the jobs of tomorrow or try to resist these changes, hoping we can preserve the economic structures of yesterday. . . . I believe that NAFTA will create 1 million jobs in the first 5 years of its impact. . . . NAFTA will generate these jobs by fostering an export boom to Mexico by tearing down tariff walls. . . . There will be no job loss.

From Global Exchange, Seattle, Declaration for Global Democracy (December 1999)

The demonstrations that disrupted the December 1999 meeting of the World Trade Organization in Seattle brought to public attention a widespread dissatisfaction with the effects of economic globalization. In this declaration, organizers of the protest offered their critique.

As citizens of global society, recognizing that the World Trade Organization is unjustly dominated by corporate interests and run for the enrichment of the few at the expense of all others, we demand:

Representatives from all sectors of society must be included in all levels of trade policy formulations. All global citizens must be democratically represented in the formulation, implementation, and evaluation of all global social and economic policies.

Global trade and investment must not be ends in themselves, but rather the instruments for achieving equitable and sustainable development including protection for workers and the environment.

Global trade agreements must not undermine the ability of each nation-state or local community to meet its citizens' social, environmental, cultural or economic needs.

The World Trade Organization must be replaced by a democratic and transparent body accountable to citizens—not to corporations.

No globalization without representation!

QUESTIONS

1. *Why does Clinton feel that free trade is necessary to American prosperity?*
2. *Why do the Seattle protesters feel that the World Trade Organization is a threat to democracy?*
3. *How do these documents reflect contradictory arguments about the impact of globalization in the United States?*

14 million individuals, 9 million of them children. Thanks to stringent new eligibility requirements imposed by the states and the economic boom of the late 1990s, welfare rolls plummeted. But the number of children living in poverty remained essentially unchanged.

The presidential election of 1996

Clinton's strategy enabled him to neutralize Republican claims that Democrats were the party of high taxes and lavish spending on persons who preferred dependency to honest labor. Clinton's passion for free trade alienated many working-class Democrats but convinced much of the middle class that the party was not beholden to the unions. Clinton easily defeated Republican Bob Dole in the presidential contest of 1996, becoming the first Democrat elected to two terms since FDR. Clinton accomplished for Reaganism what Eisenhower had done for the New Deal and Nixon for the Great Society—consolidating a basic shift in American politics by accepting many of the premises of his opponents.

Clinton and World Affairs

Like Jimmy Carter before him, Clinton took steps to encourage the settlement of long-standing international conflicts and tried to elevate support for human rights to a central place in international relations. He achieved only mixed success.

Like Carter, Clinton found it difficult to balance concern for human rights with strategic and economic interests and to formulate clear guidelines for humanitarian interventions overseas. For example, the United States did nothing in 1994 when tribal massacres racked Rwanda, in central Africa. More than 800,000 people were slaughtered in the **Rwandan genocide**, and 2 million refugees fled the country.

The most complex foreign policy crisis of the Clinton years arose from the disintegration of Yugoslavia, a multi-ethnic state in southeastern Europe that had been carved from the old Austro-Hungarian empire after World War I. As in the rest of eastern Europe, the communist government that had ruled Yugoslavia since the 1940s collapsed in 1989. Within a few years, the country's six provinces dissolved into five new states. During the ensuing **Balkan crisis**, ethnic conflict plagued several of these new nations. **Ethnic cleansing**—a terrible new term meaning the forcible expulsion of a particular ethnic group—now entered the international vocabulary.

Serbian refugees fleeing a Croat offensive during the 1990s. By the fall of 1995, the wars that followed the breakup of Yugoslavia and accompanying "ethnic cleansing" had displaced over 3 million people.

With the Cold War over, protection of human rights in the Balkans gave NATO a new purpose. In 1998, Yugoslavian troops and local Serbs conducted ethnic cleansing against the Albanian population of Kosovo, a province of Serbia. More than 800,000 Albanians fled the region. To halt the bloodshed, NATO launched a two-month war in 1999 against Yugoslavia that led to the deployment of American and UN forces in Kosovo.

Human Rights

During Clinton's presidency, human rights played an increasingly important role in international affairs. Hundreds of nongovernmental agencies throughout the world defined themselves as protectors of human rights. During the 1990s, the agenda of international human rights organizations expanded to include access to health care, women's rights, and the rights of indigenous peoples like the Aborigines of Australia and the descendants of the original inhabitants of the Americas. The United States dispatched the military to distant parts of the world to assist in international missions to protect civilians. It remained to be seen whether these initiatives would grow into an effective international system of protecting human rights across national boundaries.

An expanding agenda

GLOBALIZATION AND ITS DISCONTENTS

In December 1999, delegates from around the world gathered in Seattle for a meeting of the World Trade Organization (WTO), a 135-nation group created five years earlier to reduce barriers to international commerce and settle trade disputes. To the astonishment of residents of the city, more than 30,000 persons gathered to protest the meeting. Their marches and rallies brought together factory workers, who claimed that global free trade encouraged corporations to shift production to low-wage centers overseas, and "tree-huggers," as some reporters called environmentalists, who complained about the impact on the earth's ecology of unregulated economic development.

Once a center of labor radicalism, the Seattle area in 1999 was best known as the home of Microsoft, developer of the Windows operating system used in most of the world's computers. The company's worldwide reach symbolized **globalization**, the process by which people, investment, goods, information, and culture increasingly flow across national boundaries.

Globalization in action: workers in a factory at the Foxconn campus in China. With 300,000 employees, this is the world's largest industrial complex, where iPhones are assembled for sale around the world.

Protesters dressed as sea turtles, an endangered species, at the demonstrations against the World Trade Organization in Seattle, December 1999.

Globalization, of course, was hardly a new phenomenon. The internationalization of commerce and culture and the reshuffling of the world's peoples have been going on since the explorations of the fifteenth century. But the scale and scope of late-twentieth-century globalization were unprecedented. Thanks to satellites and the Internet, information and popular culture flowed instantaneously to every corner of the world. Manufacturers and financial institutions scoured the world for profitable investment opportunities.

Perhaps most important, the collapse of communism between 1989 and 1991 opened almost the entire world to the spread of market capitalism and to the idea that government should interfere as little as possible with economic activity. American politicians and social commentators increasingly criticized the regulation of wages and working conditions, assistance to the less fortunate, and environmental protections as burdens on international competitiveness. During the 1990s, presidents Bush, a Republican, and Clinton, a Democrat, both spoke of an American mission to create a single global free market as the path to rising living standards, the spread of democracy, and greater worldwide freedom.

Gap between haves and have-nots

The media called the loose coalition of groups who organized the Seattle protests and others like it the "antiglobalization" movement. In fact, they challenged not globalization itself but its social consequences. Globalization, the demonstrators claimed, accelerated the worldwide creation of wealth but widened gaps between rich and poor countries and between haves and have-nots within societies. Decisions affecting the day-to-day lives of millions of people were made by institutions—the World Trade Organization, International Monetary Fund, World Bank, and multinational corporations—that operated without any democratic input. Demonstrators demanded the establishment of international standards for wages, labor conditions, and the environment, and greater investment in health and education in poor countries.

The Battle of Seattle placed on the national and international agendas a question that reverberated into the twenty-first century—the relationship between globalization, economic justice, and freedom.

Economic growth

The economy's performance in the 1990s at first seemed to justify the claims of globalization's advocates. Clinton's popularity rested in part on the American economy's remarkable performance in the mid- and late 1990s. After recovery from the recession of 1990–1991, economic expansion continued for the rest of the decade. By 2000, unemployment stood below 4 percent, a figure not seen since the 1960s. Because Reagan and Bush had left behind massive budget deficits, Clinton worked hard to balance the federal budget—a goal traditionally associated with fiscal conservatives. Because economic growth produced rising tax revenues, Clinton during his second term not only balanced the budget but actually produced budget surpluses.

Economic growth

The Computer Revolution

Many commentators spoke of the 1990s as the dawn of a "new economy," in which computers and the Internet would produce vast new efficiencies and the production and sale of information would occupy the central place once held by the manufacture of goods. Computers had first been developed during and after World War II to solve scientific problems and do calculations involving enormous amounts of data. The early ones were extremely large, expensive, and, by modern standards, slow. Research for the space program of the 1960s spurred the development of the microchip, on which circuits could be imprinted.

Origins of computers

Microchips made possible the development of entirely new consumer products. Video cassette recorders, handheld video games, cellular phones, and digital cameras were mass produced at affordable prices during the 1990s, mostly in Asia and Latin America rather than the United States. But it was the computer that transformed American life. As computers became smaller, faster, and less expensive, they found a place in businesses of every kind. They also changed private life. By the year 2000, nearly half of all American households owned a personal computer, used for entertainment, shopping, and sending and receiving electronic mail. Centers of computer technology, such as Silicon Valley south of San Francisco, the Seattle and Austin metropolitan areas, and lower Manhattan, boomed during the 1990s.

The Internet, first developed as a high-speed military communications network, was simplified and opened to commercial and individual use through personal computers. The Internet expanded the flow of information and communications more radically than any invention since the printing press. The fact that anyone with a computer could post his or her ideas for worldwide circulation led "netizens" ("citizens" of the Internet) to hail the advent of a new, democratic public

Two architects of the computer revolution, Steve Jobs (on the left), the head of Apple Computer, and Bill Gates, founder of Microsoft, which makes the operating system used in most of the world's computers.

sphere in cyberspace. Unfortunately, it also offered cranks, conspiracy theorists, and racists an easy way to spread their views.

The Stock Market Boom and Bust

Economic growth and talk of a new economy sparked a frenzied boom in the stock market that was reminiscent of the 1920s. Investors, large and small, poured funds into stocks, spurred by the rise of discount and online firms that advertised aggressively and charged lower fees than traditional brokers.

Investors were especially attracted to the new "dot coms"—companies that conducted business via the Internet and seemed to symbolize the promise of the new economy. Many of these "high-tech" companies never turned a profit. But economic journalists and stockbrokers explained that the new economy had so revolutionized business that traditional methods of assessing a company's value no longer applied. Inevitably, the bubble burst. On April 14, 2000, stocks suffered their largest one-day point drop in history. For the first time since the Depression, stock prices declined for three successive years (2000–2002), wiping out billions of dollars in Americans' net worth and pension funds. The value of NASDAQ stocks fell by nearly 80 percent between 2000 and 2002. By 2001, the American economy had fallen into a recession. Talk of a new economy, it appeared, had been premature.

Dot-com bubble bursts

Only after the market dropped did it become apparent that the stock boom of the 1990s had been fueled in part by fraud. Enron, a Houston-based energy company that epitomized the new economy—it bought and sold electricity rather than actually producing it—reported as profits billions of dollars in operating losses.

Cartoonist David Jacobson's comment on the Enron scandal.

"Let's say I was Enron, how would you do my taxes?"

Fruits of Deregulation

At the height of the 1990s boom, with globalization in full swing, stocks rising, and the economy expanding, the economic model of free trade and deregulation appeared unassailable. But the retreat from government economic regulation, a policy embraced by both the Republican Congress and President Clinton, left no one to represent the public interest. The sectors of the economy most affected by the scandals—energy, telecommunications, and stock trading—had all been subjects of deregulation.

Many stock frauds stemmed from the repeal in 1999 of the Glass-Steagall Act, a New Deal measure that separated commercial banks, which accept deposits and make loans, from investment banks, which invest in stocks and real estate and take larger risks. Banks took their new freedom as an invitation to engage in all sorts of misdeeds, knowing that they had become so big that if disaster struck, the federal government would have no choice but to rescue them. They poured money into risky mortgages. When the housing bubble collapsed in 2008, the banks suffered losses that threatened to bring down the entire financial system. The George W. Bush and Obama administrations felt they had no choice but to expend hundreds of billions of dollars of taxpayer money to save the banks from their own misconduct.

Barbie's Liberty, a satirical work by the artist Hans Haacke, recasts the Barbie doll, one of America's most successful toys, in the image of the Statue of Liberty to comment on the loss of manufacturing jobs to low-wage areas overseas.

Rising Inequality

The boom that began in 1995 benefited nearly all Americans. For the first time since the early 1970s, average real wages and family incomes began to grow significantly. Economic expansion at a time of low unemployment brought rapid increases in wages for families at all income levels. Yet, despite these gains, in the last two decades of the twentieth century, the poor and the middle class became worse off while the rich became significantly richer. The wealth of the richest Americans exploded during the 1990s. Sales of luxury goods like yachts and mansions boomed. Bill Gates, head of Microsoft and the country's richest person, owned as much wealth as the bottom 40 percent of the American population put together.

Companies continued to shift manufacturing jobs overseas. Thanks to NAFTA, which eliminated barriers to imports from Mexico, a thriving industrial zone emerged just across the southern border of the United States, where American manufacturers built plants to take advantage of cheap labor and weak environmental and safety regulations. Despite low unemployment, companies' threats to shut down and move exerted downward pressure on American wages. Business, moreover, increasingly relied on financial operations for profits rather than making things. The financial sector of the economy accounted for around 10 percent of total profits in 1950; by 2000 the figure

This graph illustrates the steady decline of manufacturing as a component of the American economy since 1970. The number of workers employed in manufacturing has fallen from about 33 percent at the beginning of World War II to under 10 percent today.

FIGURE 27.1 Share of U.S. Workers Employed in the Manufacturing Sector, 1970–2012

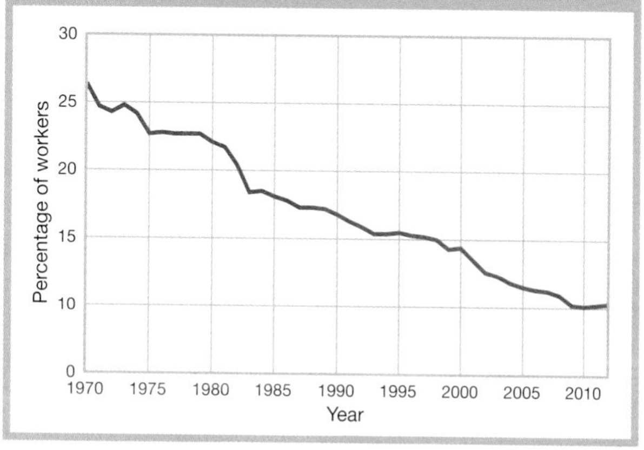

was up to 40 percent. Companies like Ford and General Electric made more money from interest on loans to customers and other financial operations than from selling their products.

Huge companies and little job growth

In 1970, General Motors had been the country's largest corporate employer. In the early twenty-first century, it was replaced by Wal-Mart, a giant discount retail chain that paid most of its 1.6 million workers slightly more than the minimum wage. Wal-Mart aggressively opposed efforts at collective bargaining. Not a single one of its employees belonged to a union. Overall, between 1990 and 2008, companies that did business in global markets contributed almost nothing to job growth in the United States.

CULTURE WARS

A "rebellion of particularisms"

The end of the Cold War ushered in hopes for a new era of global harmony. Instead, what one observer called a "rebellion of particularisms"—renewed emphasis on group identity and insistent demands for group recognition and power—has racked the international arena. The declining power of nation-states arising from globalization seemed to unleash long-simmering ethnic and religious antagonisms. Partly in reaction to the global spread of a secular culture based on consumption and mass entertainment, intense religious movements attracted increasing numbers of followers—Hindu nationalism in India, orthodox Judaism in Israel, Islamic fundamentalism in much of the Muslim world, and evangelical Christianity in the United States. Like other nations, although in a far less extreme way and with little accompanying violence, the United States has experienced divisions arising from the intensification of ethnic and racial identities and religious fundamentalism.

The Newest Immigrants

Because of shifts in immigration, cultural and racial diversity have become increasingly visible in the United States. Until the immigration law of 1965, the vast majority of twentieth-century newcomers hailed from Europe. Between 1965 and 2010, nearly 38 million immigrants entered the United States, substantially more than the 27 million during the peak period of immigration between 1880 and 1924. About 50 percent came from Latin America and the Caribbean, 35 percent from Asia, and smaller numbers from the Middle East and Africa. Only 10 percent arrived from Europe, mostly from the war-torn Balkans and the former Soviet Union.

The immigrant influx changed the country's religious and racial map. By 2010, more than 4 million Muslims resided in the United States, and the combined population of Buddhists and Hindus exceeded 1 million.

Erected on U.S. 5, an interstate highway running from the Mexican to Canadian borders along the Pacific Coast, this sign warns motorists to be on the lookout for people (i.e., undocumented immigrant families) crossing the road on foot. The sign's placement north of San Diego, about thirty miles north of Mexico, illustrates how the "border" had become an entire region, not simply a geographical boundary.

Unlike in the past, rather than being concentrated in one or two parts of city centers, immigrants quickly moved into outlying neighborhoods and older suburbs. By the turn of the century, more than half of all Latinos lived in suburbs. Immigrants brought cultural and racial diversity to once-homogeneous communities in the American heartland.

Post-1965 immigration formed part of the worldwide uprooting of labor arising from globalization. Those who migrated to the United States included poor, illiterate refugees from places of economic and political crisis—Central Americans escaping the region's civil wars and poverty, Haitians and Cambodians fleeing repressive governments. But many immigrants were well-educated professionals from countries like India and South Korea, where the availability of skilled jobs had not kept pace with the spread of higher education. In the year 2000, more than 40 percent of all immigrants to the United States had a college education.

For the first time in American history, women made up the majority of newcomers, reflecting the decline of manufacturing jobs that had previously absorbed immigrant men, as well as the spread of employment

FIGURE 27.2 Persons Obtaining Legal Permanent Residency, 1820–2015

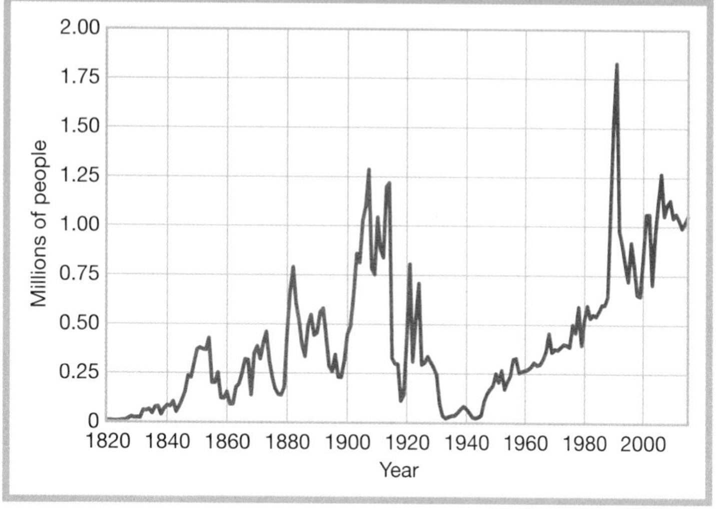

A graph depicting the number of persons from abroad who obtained lawful permanent residence status, from before the Civil War to the present. Almost none did so from the imposition of nationality quotas in 1924 to the end of the 1940s. The spike in the mid-1980s reflects the passage of a law granting amnesty and a path to citizenship for undocumented immigrants.

Recent immigrants at a naturalization ceremony held at Fenway Park, Boston, in 2008. Over 3,000 people became U.S. citizens at this event.

IMMIGRANT POPULATIONS IN CITIES AND STATES, 1900 AND 2010

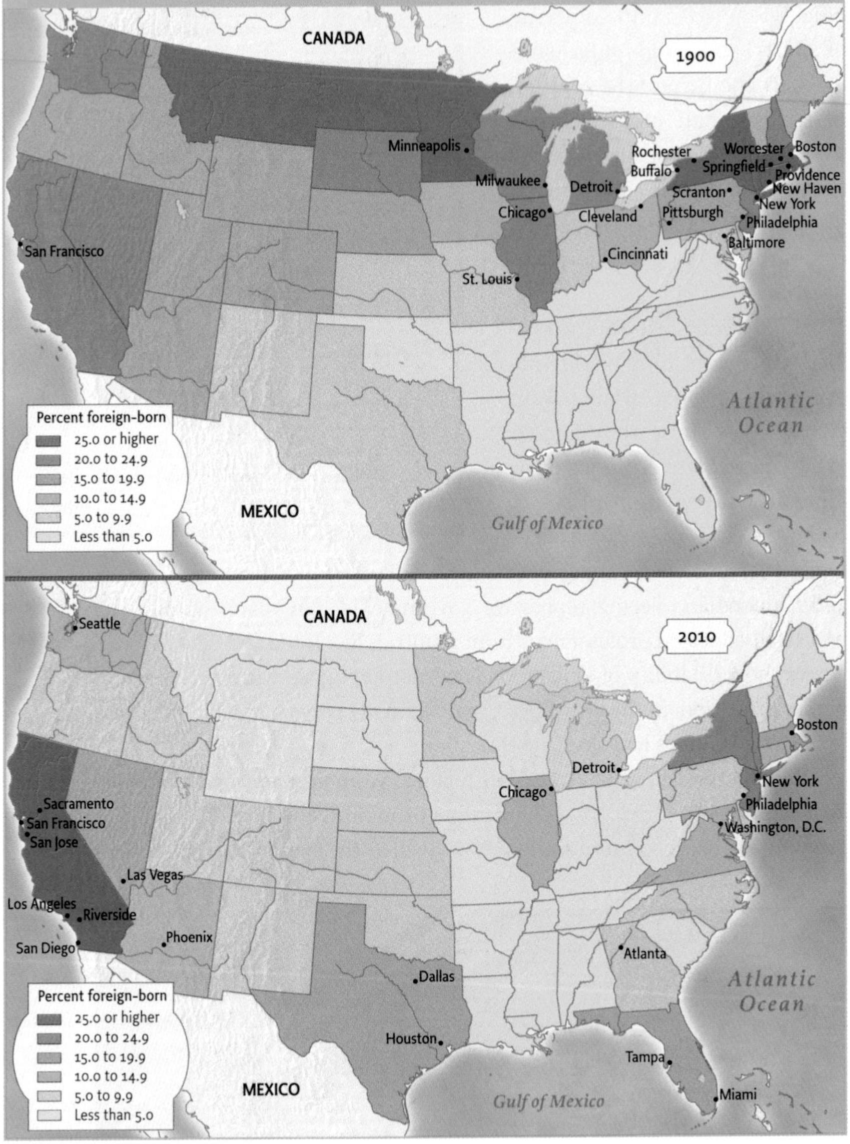

Maps illustrating states' foreign-born populations and the twenty metropolitan areas with the most immigrants in 1900 and 2010. In 1900 nearly all went to the Northeast and Upper Midwest, the heartland of the industrial economy. In 2010 the largest number headed for cities in the South and West, especially California, although major cities of the Northeast also attracted many newcomers.

Los Tigres del Norte, "Juala de Oro" (1984)

Having sunk roots and established families in the United States, but unable to visit Mexico for fear of not being able to return, many undocumented immigrants suffered a crisis of identity. They felt trapped in a "cage of gold" ("juala de oro") and alienated from their Americanized children. The Mexican-American group *Los Tigres del Norte* developed these themes in a popular song.

I am established here
In the United States
Many years have passed
Since I crossed as a wetback
With no papers
I'm still an illegal

I have my wife and kids
That I brought so young
And they've already forgotten
My dear Mexico
Which I will never forget
And cannot return to

What use is money
If I'm like a prisoner
In this great nation
When I'm reminded, I cry
Although this cage is made of gold
It's still a prison

Listen son,
Would you like to go back and live in Mexico?
"Whatcha talkin' about dad?
I don't want to go back to Mexico,
No way, dad."

My kids don't talk to me
They have learned another language
And they've forgotten Spanish
They think like Americans
Deny that they're Mexicans
Even though they have my complexion

From my work to my home
I don't know what's wrong with me
Even though I'm man of the house
I barely go outside
Since I'm afraid that they'll catch me
And deport me

What use is money
If I'm like a prisoner
In this great nation
When I'm reminded, I cry
Although this cage is made of gold
It's still a prison

QUESTIONS

1. *What elements of Mexican culture are disappearing in immigrant households, according to the song?*
2. *How do you think the experience of the narrator compares with that of members of previous immigrant groups?*

opportunities in traditionally female fields like care of children and the elderly and retail sales. Thanks to cheap global communications and jet travel, modern-day immigrants retain strong ties with their countries of origin, frequently phoning and visiting home.

The New Diversity

Latino immigrants

Latinos formed the largest single immigrant group. The term "Latino" was invented in the United States and includes people of quite different origins—Mexicans, Central and South Americans, and migrants from Spanish-speaking Caribbean island nations such as Cuba, the Dominican Republic, and Puerto Rico (although the last group, of course, are American citizens, not immigrants). With 95 million people, Mexico in 2000 had become the world's largest Spanish-speaking nation. Its poverty, high birthrate, and proximity to the United States made it a source of massive legal and illegal immigration. Almost every state witnessed an influx of Mexican immigrants. In 1930, 90 percent of the Mexican population of the United States lived in states that had once been part of Mexico. Today, there is a significant Mexican-American presence in almost every state, including such places as Kansas, Minnesota, and Georgia, with very little experience, until recently, with ethnic diversity.

Numbering around 50 million in 2010, Latinos had become the largest minority group in the United States. Latinos were highly visible in entertainment, sports, and politics. Indeed, the Hispanic presence transformed American life. José was now the most common name for baby boys in Texas and the third most popular in California. Smith remained the most common American surname, but Garcia, Rodriguez, Gonzales, and other Hispanic names were all in the top fifty.

Latino communities remained far poorer than the rest of the country. The influx of legal and undocumented immigrants swelled the ranks of low-wage urban workers and agricultural laborers. Latinos lagged far behind other Americans in education. In 2010, their poverty rate stood at nearly double the national figure of 15 percent. Living and working conditions among predominantly Latino farm workers in the West fell back to levels as dire as when César Chavez established the United Farm Workers union in the 1960s.

Latina nannies pushing baby carriages in Beverly Hills, California, in the 1990s. For the first time in American history, female immigrants outnumbered male immigrants.

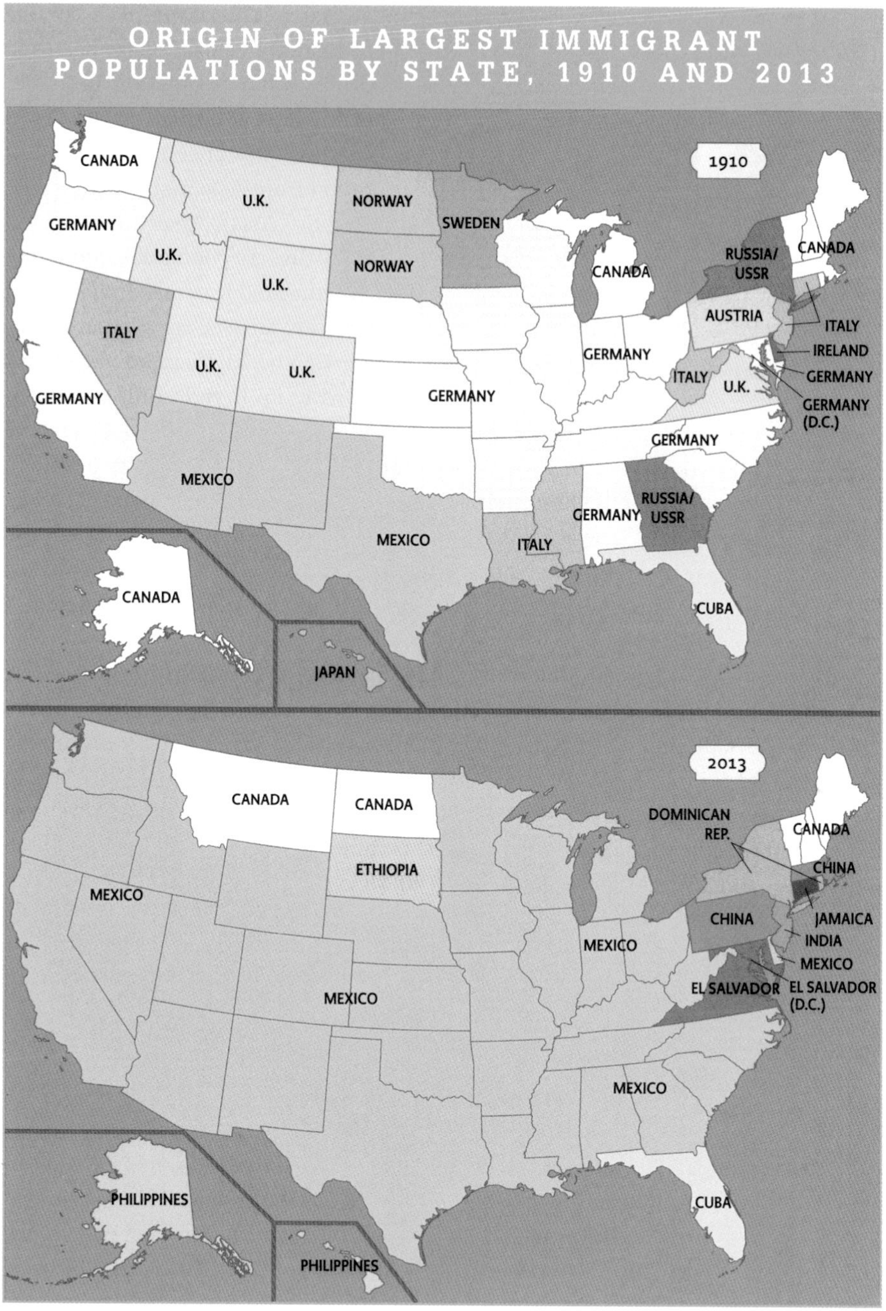

Maps depicting the birthplace of each state's largest immigrant population in 1910 and 2013. A century ago, most immigrants hailed from Europe, and the leading country of origin varied among the states. Today, in almost every state outside the Northeast, those born in Mexico constitute the largest number of immigrants.

Young Korean girls rehearsing a dance at the Veterans Administration Medical Center in Columbia, South Carolina, an illustration of the growing diversity of American society.

FIGURE 27.3 The Projected Non-White Majority: Racial and Ethnic Breakdown

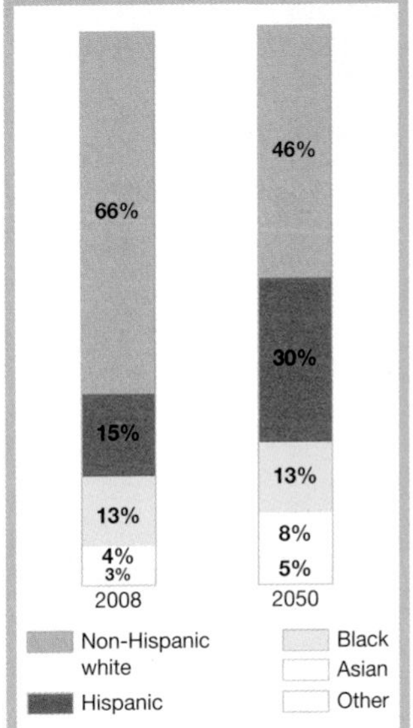

Asian-Americans also became increasingly visible. There had long been a small population of Asian ancestry in California and New York City, but only after 1965 did immigration from Asia assume large proportions. Asian-Americans were a highly diverse population, including well-educated Koreans, Indians, and Japanese, as well as poor refugees from Cambodia, Vietnam, and China. Growing up in tight-knit communities that placed great emphasis on education, young Asian-Americans poured into American colleges and universities. Once subjected to harsh discrimination, Asian-Americans now achieved remarkable success. White Americans hailed them as a "model minority." By 2007, the median family income of Asian-Americans, $66,000, surpassed that of whites. But more than any other group, Asian-Americans clustered at opposite ends of the income spectrum.

The United States, of course, had long been a multiracial society. But for centuries race relations had been shaped by the black-white divide and the experience of slavery and segregation. The growing visibility of Latinos and Asians suggested that a two-race system no longer adequately described American life. Interracial marriage, at one time banned in forty-two states, became more common and acceptable. Among Asian-Americans, half of all marriages involved a non-Asian partner. The figure for Latinos was 30 percent. Because the birthrate of racial minorities is higher than that of whites, the Census Bureau projected that by 2050, less than 50 percent of the American population would be white.

The Changing Face of Black America

Compared with the situation in 1900 or 1950, the most dramatic change in American life at the turn of the century was the absence of legal segregation and the presence of blacks in areas of American life from which they had once been almost entirely excluded. Thanks to the decline in overt discrimination and the effectiveness of many affirmative action programs, blacks now worked in unprecedented numbers alongside whites in corporate board rooms, offices, and factories.

One major change in black life was the growing visibility of Africans among the nation's immigrants. Between 1970 and 2010, more than twice as many Africans immigrated to the United States as had entered during the entire period of the Atlantic slave trade. For the first time, all the elements of the African diaspora—natives of Africa, the Caribbean, Central and South Americans of African descent, Europeans with African roots—could be found in the United States alongside the descendants of American slaves. More than half the African newcomers had college educations, the highest percentage for any immigrant group.

TABLE 27.1 Home Ownership Rates by Group, 1970–2000

	1970	1980	1990	2000
Whites	65.0%	67.8%	68.2%	73.8%
Blacks	41.6	44.4	43.4	47.2
Latinos	43.7	43.4	42.4	46.3
All families	62.9	64.4	64.2	67.4

Most African-Americans, nonetheless, remained in a more precarious situation than whites or many recent immigrants. In the early twenty-first century, half of all black children lived in poverty, two-thirds were born out of wedlock, and in every index of social well-being from health to quality of housing, blacks continued to lag. Housing segregation remained pervasive.

Housing patterns and school segregation

Despite the nation's growing racial diversity, school segregation—now resulting from housing patterns and the divide between urban and suburban school districts rather than laws requiring racial separation—was on the rise. Most city public school systems consisted overwhelmingly of minority students, large numbers of whom failed to receive an adequate education. Since school funding rested on property taxes, poor communities continued to have less to spend on education than wealthy ones.

The Spread of Imprisonment

During the 1960s, the nation's prison population declined. But in the 1970s, as noted in the previous chapter, with urban crime rates rising, politicians of both parties sought to convey the image of being "tough on crime." They treated drug addiction as a violation of the law rather than as a disease. As a result, the number of Americans in prison rose dramatically, most of them incarcerated for nonviolent drug offenses.

22 million inmates in 2016

During the 1990s, thanks to the waning of the crack epidemic and more effective urban police tactics, crime rates dropped dramatically across the country. But this did nothing to stem the increase of the prison population. In 2016, it reached 2.2 million. Ten times the figure of 1970 and one-fourth of the entire world's inmates, this number represented one-quarter of the entire world's inmates and far exceeded the number in any

A private, for-profit, maximum-security prison under construction in 1999 in California City, in the Mohave Desert, illustrates the expansion of the "prison-industrial complex."

other country. Several million more Americans were on parole, on probation, or under some other kind of criminal supervision.

Racial minorities and incarceration

Members of racial minorities experienced most strongly the paradox of growing islands of unfreedom in a nation that prided itself on liberty. In 1950, whites accounted for 70 percent of the nation's prison population and non-whites 30 percent. By 2016, these figures had almost been reversed. One reason was that severe penalties faced those convicted of using or selling crack, a particularly potent form of cocaine concentrated among the urban poor, whereas the use of powder cocaine, the drug of choice in suburban America, led to far lighter sentences.

This graph vividly displays the extreme disparity between the incarceration rate for black and white Americans since the advent of the "wars" on crime and drugs.

The percentage of the black population in prison stood five times higher than the proportion of white Americans. More than one-quarter of all black men could expect to serve time in prison at some time during their lives. Partly because so many young men were in prison, blacks have a significantly lower rate of marriage than other Americans. And thanks to state laws disfranchising persons with a felony conviction, as of 2018, around 5 million Americans, mostly black men, could not vote. In 2018, however, Florida voters approved a measure to restore this right to nearly all felons after they have served their prison terms—a total of 1.4 million persons.

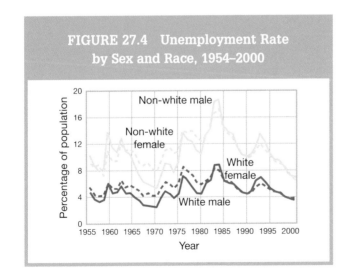

FIGURE 27.4 Unemployment Rate by Sex and Race, 1954–2000

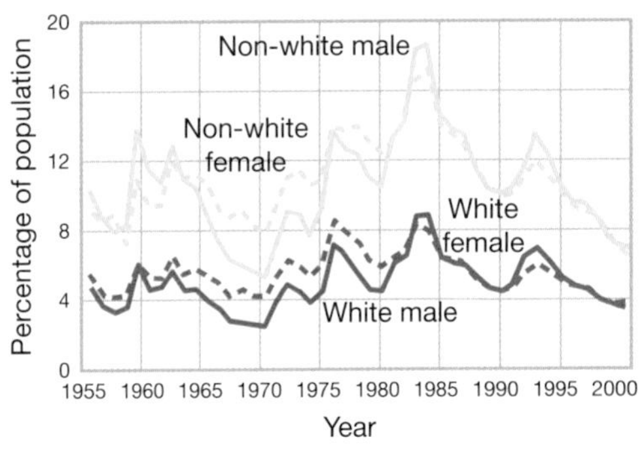

The continuing frustration of urban blacks exploded in 1992 when an all-white suburban jury found four Los Angeles police officers not guilty in the beating of black motorist Rodney King, even though an onlooker had captured their assault on videotape. The deadliest urban uprising since the New York draft riots of 1863 followed. Some fifty-two people died, and property damage approached $1 billion. Many Latino youths, who shared blacks' resentment over mistreatment by the police, joined in the violence. The uprising suggested that despite the civil rights revolution, the nation had failed to address the plight of the urban poor.

The Continuing Rights Revolution

Reflecting the continued power of the rights revolution, in 1990, disabled Americans won passage of the **Americans with Disabilities Act**. This far-reaching measure prohibited discrimination in hiring and promotion against persons with disabilities and required that entrances to public buildings be redesigned so as to ensure access for the disabled.

Some movements that were descended from the late 1960s achieved great visibility in the 1990s. Prominent among these was the campaign for gay rights, which turned its attention to combating acquired immunodeficiency syndrome (AIDS), a fatal disease spread by sexual contact, drug use, and transfusions of contaminated blood. AIDS first emerged in the early 1980s. It quickly became epidemic among gay men. The gay movement mobilized to promote "safe sex" and press the federal government to devote greater resources to fighting the disease. The Gay Men's Health Crisis organized educational programs and assistance to those affected by the disease, and demanded that drug companies put AZT, a drug with some success in treating AIDS, on the market. A more radical group, ACT UP, disrupted a mass at New York's St. Patrick's Cathedral to protest what it called the Catholic Church's prejudices against gays. By 2000, even though more than 400,000 Americans had died of AIDS, its spread among gays had been sharply curtailed.

Gay groups also played an increasing role in politics. In cities with large gay populations, such as New York and San Francisco, politicians vied to attract their votes. Overall, the growth of public tolerance of gay men and lesbians was a striking change in social attitudes. In the second decade of the twenty-first century, this would lead to the remarkably rapid acceptance of the right of gay Americans to form legal marriages.

The AIDS quilt, each square of which represents a person who died of AIDS, on display in Washington, D.C. The quilt was exhibited throughout the country, heightening public awareness of the AIDS epidemic.

Native Americans in the New Century

Another social movement spawned by the 1960s that continued to flourish was the American Indian movement. The Indian population reached over 5 million (including people choosing more than one race) in the 2010 census—a sign not only of population growth but also of a renewed sense of pride that led many Indians for the first time to identify themselves as such to census enumerators.

The legal position of Indians as American citizens who enjoy a kind of quasi-sovereignty still survives in some cases. Notable examples are the lucrative Indian casinos now operating in states that otherwise prohibit gambling. In 2011, Indian casinos took in over $27 billion, making some tribes rich.

Continued economic hardship

Although some tribes have reinvested casino profits in improved housing and health care and college scholarships for Native American students, most Indian casinos are marginal operations whose low-wage jobs as cashiers, waitresses, and the like have done little to relieve Indian poverty. Native Americans continue to occupy the lowest rung on the economic ladder.

At the beginning of the twenty-first century, less than one-quarter of American households consisted of a "traditional" family—a married couple living with their children.

FIGURE 27.5 Change in Family Structure, 1970–2010*

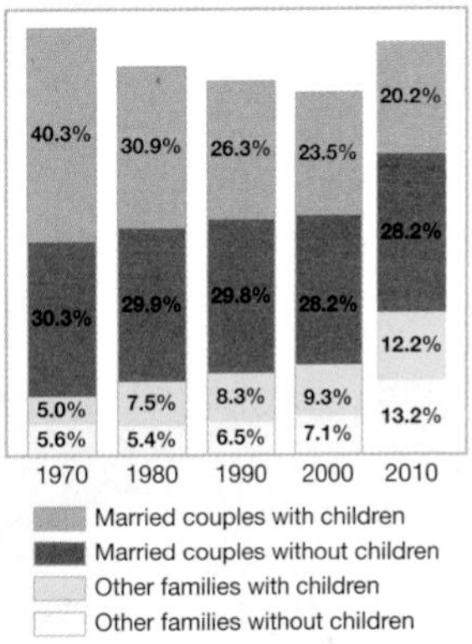

*Not shown are single people living alone and nonrelated people living together. "Children" are a family's own children under age eighteen living at home.

The Identity Debate

Among some Americans, the heightened visibility of immigrants, racial minorities, and inheritors of the sexual revolution inspired not celebration of pluralism and **multiculturalism** but alarm over perceived cultural fragmentation.

Increased cultural diversity and changes in educational policy inspired harsh debates over whether further immigration should be discouraged. These issues entered politics most dramatically in California, whose voters in 1994 approved Proposition 187, which denied undocumented immigrants and their children access to welfare, education, and most health services. (How denying health care to ill people would make others safer was not explained.) A federal judge soon barred implementation of the measure on the grounds that control over immigration policy rests with the federal government. Proposition 187 sparked an enormous mobilization among Latinos and others, helping to make the state solidly Democratic. In 2016, Hillary Clinton defeated Donald Trump in California by over 4 million votes. Yet it also laid the groundwork for the anti-immigrant politics that, in other states, helped propel Trump into the White House.

Immigration occupied only one front in what came to be called the **Culture Wars**—battles over moral values that raged throughout the 1990s. The Christian Coalition, founded by evangelical minister Pat Robertson, launched crusades against gay rights, abortion, secularism in public schools, and government aid to the arts.

It sometimes appeared during the 1990s that the country was refighting old battles between traditional religion and modern secular culture. In an echo of the 1920s, a number of localities required the teaching of creationism, a religious alternative to Darwin's theory of evolution. Many conservatives railed against the erosion of the nuclear family, the changing racial landscape produced by immigration, and what they considered a general decline of traditional values.

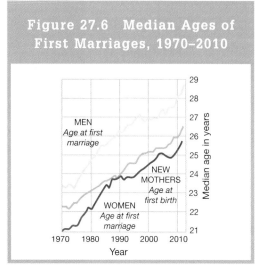

Figure 27.6 Median Ages of First Marriages, 1970–2010

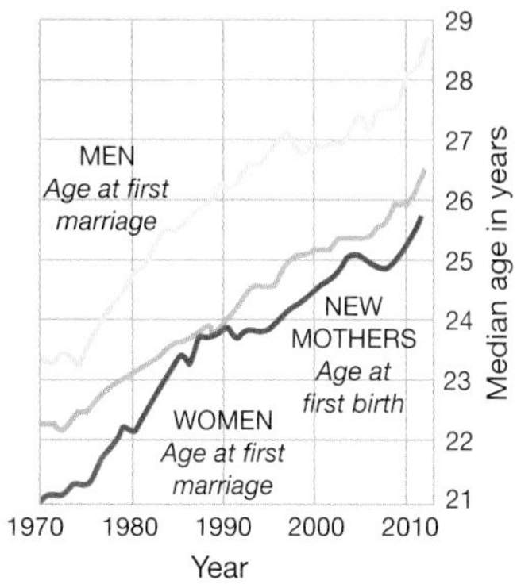

Both men and women are getting married later, shifting marriage to an act of later adulthood and increasing the number of births to unmarried parents.

Family Values in Retreat

The censuses of 2000 and 2010 showed **family values** increasingly in disarray. Half of all marriages ended in divorce (70 percent on the West Coast). In 2010, over 40 percent of births were to unmarried women, not only sexually active teenagers but growing numbers of professional women in their thirties and forties as well. For the first time, less than half of all households consisted of married couples, and only one-fifth were "traditional" families—a wife, husband, and their children. Two-thirds of married women worked outside the home. The pay gap between men and women, although narrowing, persisted. In 2010, the weekly earnings of women with full-time jobs stood at 82 percent of those of men—up from

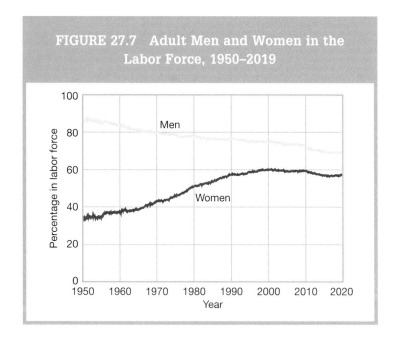

FIGURE 27.7 Adult Men and Women in the Labor Force, 1950–2019

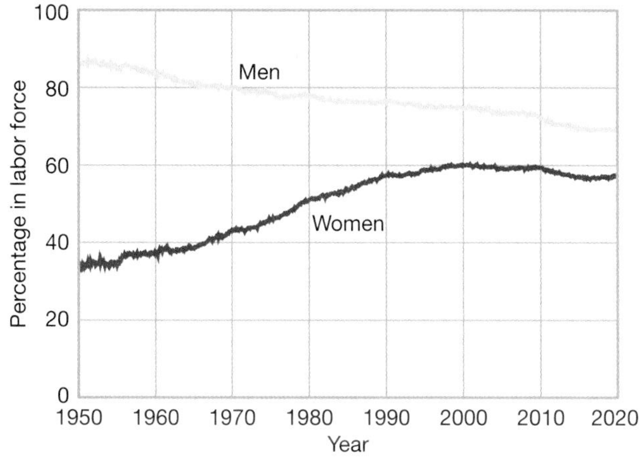

The percentage of adult men and women in the labor force has declined since the beginning of the Great Recession in 2008. The decline for men is part of a long-term trend sparked by deindustrialization. The decline for women, reversing a process that had gathered strength since 1950, was partly caused by low wages and the difficulty of finding affordable day care.

Rescue workers sifting the wreckage of a federal office building in Oklahoma City after it was heavily damaged by a bomb in 1995, the worst act of terrorism in the United States during the twentieth century.

63 percent in 1980. In only two occupational categories did women earn more than men: postal service clerks and special education teachers.

Casey v. Planned Parenthood of Pennsylvania

Although dominated by conservatives, the Supreme Court, in *Casey v. Planned Parenthood of Pennsylvania* (1992), reaffirmed a woman's right to terminate a pregnancy. The decision overturned a requirement that the husband be notified before the procedure was undertaken. "At the heart of liberty," said the Court, "is the right to . . . make the most intimate and personal choices" without outside interference.

The Antigovernment Extreme

Private militias

At the radical fringe of conservatism, the belief that the federal government posed a threat to American freedom led to the creation of private militias who armed themselves to fend off oppressive authority. Groups like Aryan Nation, Posse Comitatus, and other self-proclaimed "Christian patriots" spread a mixture of racist, anti-Semitic, and antigovernment ideas.

Although such organizations had been growing for years, they burst into the national spotlight in 1995 when Timothy McVeigh, a member of the militant antigovernment movement, exploded a bomb at a federal office building in Oklahoma City. The blast killed 168 persons, including numerous children at a day-care center. McVeigh was captured, convicted, and executed. The bombing alerted the nation to the danger of violent antigovernment right-wing groups.

IMPEACHMENT AND THE ELECTION OF 2000

The unusually intense partisanship of the 1990s seemed ironic, given Clinton's move toward the political center. Republicans' strong dislike of Clinton could be explained only by the fact that he seemed to symbolize everything conservatives hated about the 1960s. As a college student, the president had smoked marijuana and participated in antiwar demonstrations. He had married a feminist, made a point of leading a multicultural administration, and supported gay rights. Clinton's popularity puzzled and frustrated conservatives, reinforcing their conviction that something was deeply amiss in American life. From the very outset of his administration, Clinton's political opponents and a scandal-hungry media stood ready to pounce. Clinton himself provided the ammunition.

The Impeachment of Clinton

In 1998, it became known that Clinton had carried on an affair with Monica Lewinsky, a White House intern. Kenneth Starr, the special counsel who had been appointed to investigate a previous scandal, shifted his focus to Lewinsky. He issued a lengthy report containing details of Clinton's sexual acts with the young woman. In December 1998, the Republican-controlled House of Representatives voted to impeach Clinton for perjury and obstruction of justice. He became the second president to be tried before the Senate. Early in 1999, the vote took place. Neither charge mustered a simple majority, much less than the two-thirds required to remove Clinton from office.

Monica Lewinsky

Herbert Block's 1998 cartoon comments humorously on Clinton's talent for political survival.

Polls suggested that the obsession of Kenneth Starr and members of Congress with Clinton's sexual acts appalled Americans far more than the president's irresponsible behavior. Clinton's continuing popularity throughout the impeachment controversy demonstrated how profoundly traditional attitudes toward sexual morality had changed.

The Disputed Election

Had Clinton been eligible to run for reelection in 2000, he would probably have won. But after the death of FDR, the Constitution had been amended to limit presidents to two terms in office. Democrats nominated Vice President Al Gore to succeed Clinton (pairing him with Senator Joseph Lieberman of Connecticut, the first Jewish vice presidential nominee).

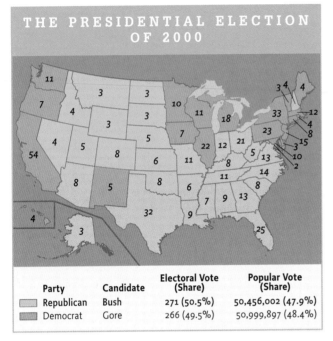

THE PRESIDENTIAL ELECTION OF 2000

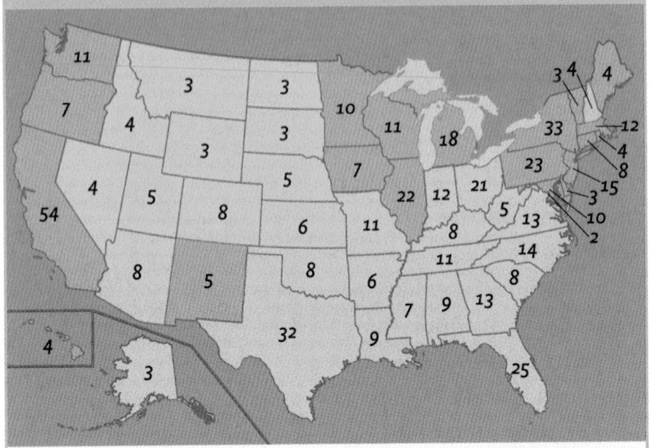

Party	Candidate	Electoral Vote (Share)	Popular Vote (Share)
Republican	Bush	271 (50.5%)	50,456,002 (47.9%)
Democrat	Gore	266 (49.5%)	50,999,897 (48.4%)

Republicans chose George W. Bush, the governor of Texas and son of Clinton's predecessor, as their candidate, with former secretary of defense Dick Cheney as his running mate.

The election proved to be one of the closest in the nation's history. The outcome remained uncertain until a month after the ballots had been cast. Gore won the popular vote by a tiny margin—540,000 votes of 100 million cast, or one-half of 1 percent. Victory in the electoral college hinged on which candidate had carried Florida. There, amid widespread confusion at the polls and claims of irregularities in counting the ballots, Bush claimed a margin of a few hundred votes.

It fell to Supreme Court justices to decide the outcome. On December 12, 2000, by a 5-4 vote, the Court ordered a halt to the recounting of Florida ballots, allowing the state's governor Jeb Bush (George W. Bush's brother) to certify that the Republican candidate had carried the state and had therefore won the presidency.

The decision in ***Bush v. Gore*** was one of the oddest in Supreme Court history. The majority justified their decision by insisting that the "equal protection" clause of the Fourteenth Amendment required that all ballots within a state be counted in accordance with a single standard, something impossible given the wide variety of machines and paper ballots used in Florida. Perhaps recognizing that this new constitutional principle threatened to throw into question results throughout the country—since many states had voting systems as complex as Florida's—the Court added that it applied only in this single case.

A member of a Florida election board trying to determine a voter's intent during the recount of presidential ballots in November 2000. The U.S. Supreme Court eventually ordered the recount halted.

A Challenged Democracy

Coming at the end of the "decade of democracy," the 2000 election revealed troubling features of the American political system. The electoral college, devised by the founders to enable the country's prominent men rather than ordinary voters to choose the president, gave the White House to a candidate who did not receive the most votes, an odd result in a political democracy. A country that prided itself on modern technology had a voting system in which citizens' choices could not be reliably determined.

Counting both congressional and presidential races, the campaign cost more than $1.5 billion, mostly raised from wealthy individuals and corporate donors. This amount reinforced the widespread belief that money dominated the political system.

Political disengagement

Evidence abounded of a broad disengagement from public life. More people watched the televised Nixon-Kennedy debates of 1960 than the Bush-Gore debates of 2000, even though the population had risen by 100 million. Major issues like health care, race relations, and economic inequality went virtually unmentioned during the campaign. And no one discussed the issue that would soon come to dominate Bush's presidency—the threat of international terrorism.

THE ATTACKS OF SEPTEMBER 11

September 11, 2001, a beautiful late-summer morning, began with the sun rising over the East Coast of the United States in a crystal-clear sky. But September 11 soon became one of the most tragic dates in American history.

Around 8 AM, hijackers seized control of four jet airliners filled with passengers. They crashed two into the World Trade Center in New York City, igniting infernos that soon caused these buildings, which dominated the lower Manhattan skyline, to collapse. A third plane hit a wing of the Pentagon, the country's military headquarters, in Washington, D.C. On the fourth aircraft, passengers who had learned of these events via their cell phones overpowered the hijackers. The plane crashed in a field near Pittsburgh, killing all aboard. Counting the nineteen hijackers, the more than 200 passengers, pilots, and flight attendants, and the victims on the ground, around 3,000 people died on September 11. The victims included nearly 400 police and firefighters who had rushed to the World Trade Center in a rescue effort.

The twin towers of the World Trade Center after being struck by hijacked airplanes on September 11, 2001. Shortly after this photograph was taken, the towers collapsed.

The administration of George W. Bush quickly blamed Al Qaeda, a shadowy terrorist organization headed by Osama bin Laden, for the attacks. A wealthy Islamic fundamentalist from Saudi Arabia, bin Laden had joined the fight against the Soviet occupation of Afghanistan in the 1980s. He had developed a relationship with the Central Intelligence Agency and received American funds to help build his mountain bases. But after the Gulf War of 1991, his anger increasingly turned against the United States. Bin Laden was especially outraged by the presence of American military bases in Saudi Arabia and by American support for Israel in its ongoing conflict with the Palestinians.

Two bystanders gaze at some of the missing-persons posters with photographs of those who died on September 11.

Terrorists associated with Al Qaeda exploded a truck bomb at the World Trade Center in 1993, killing six persons, and set off blasts in 1998 at two American embassies in Africa, killing over 200 persons. Nonetheless, the attack of September 11 came as a complete surprise. With the end of the Cold War in 1991, most Americans felt more secure, especially within their own borders, than they had for decades.

The attacks of September 11, 2001, lent new urgency to questions that had recurred many times in American history: Should the United States act in the world as a republic or an empire? What is the proper balance between liberty and security? Who deserves the full enjoyment of American freedom? Suddenly, the Bush administration had to face these questions.

THE WAR ON TERRORISM

"They Hate Freedom"

Patriotism and increased trust in government

September 11 transformed the international situation, the domestic political environment, and the Bush presidency. An outpouring of popular patriotism followed the attacks, all the more impressive because it was spontaneous, not orchestrated by the government or private organizations. Throughout the country, people demonstrated their sense of resolve and their sympathy for the victims by displaying the American flag. Public trust in government rose dramatically, and public servants like firemen and policemen became national heroes. After two decades in which the dominant language of American politics centered on deregulation and individualism, the country experienced a renewed feeling of common social purpose.

Bush seized the opportunity to give his administration a new direction and purpose. Like presidents before him, he made freedom the rallying cry for a nation at war. On September 20, 2001, Bush addressed a joint session of Congress and a national television audience. His speech echoed the words of FDR, Truman, and Reagan: "Freedom and fear are at war. The advance of human freedom . . . now depends on us." The country's antagonists, Bush went on, "hate our freedoms, our freedom of religion, our freedom of speech, our freedom to assemble and disagree with each other." In later speeches, he repeated this theme. Why did terrorists attack the United States, the president repeatedly asked. His answer: "Because we love freedom, that's why. And they hate freedom."

The Bush Doctrine

Bush's speech announced a new foreign policy principle, which quickly became known as the **Bush Doctrine**. The United States would launch a **war on terrorism**. Unlike previous wars, this one had a vaguely defined enemy—terrorist groups around the world that might threaten the United States or its allies—and no predictable timetable for victory. The American administration would recognize no middle ground in the new war: "Either you are with us, or you are with the terrorists." Bush demanded that Afghanistan, ruled by a group of Islamic fundamentalists called the Taliban, surrender Osama bin Laden, the architect of the 9/11 attacks, who had established a base in the country. When the Taliban refused, the United States on October 7, 2001, launched air strikes against its strongholds.

"Enduring Freedom"

Bush gave the **war in Afghanistan** the name "Enduring Freedom." By the end of the year, the combination of American bombing and ground combat by the Northern Alliance (Afghans who had been fighting the Taliban for years) had driven the regime from power. A new government, friendly to and dependent on the United States, took its place. It found it difficult to establish full control over the country. U.S. forces would remain in Afghanistan at least into 2019, making the war the longest in American history.

Supporters of the Bush administration who turned out in Washington, D.C., late in 2001 to confront demonstrators opposed to the war in Afghanistan.

The "Axis of Evil"

The toppling of the Taliban, Bush repeatedly insisted, marked only the beginning of the war on terrorism. In his State of the Union address of January 2002, the president accused Iraq, Iran, and North Korea of harboring terrorists and developing "weapons of mass destruction"—nuclear, chemical, and biological—that posed a potential threat to the United States. He called the three countries an "axis of evil," even though no evidence connected them with the attacks of September 11 and they had never cooperated with one another (Iraq and Iran, in fact, had fought a long and bloody war in the 1980s).

AN AMERICAN EMPIRE?

The "axis of evil" speech and National Security Strategy sent shock waves around the world. In the immediate aftermath of September 11, a wave of sympathy for the United States had swept across the globe. Most of the world supported the war in Afghanistan as a legitimate response to the terrorist attacks. By late 2002, however, many persons overseas feared that the United States was claiming the right to act as a world policeman in violation of international law.

A global empire

Charges quickly arose that the United States was bent on establishing itself as a new global empire. Indeed, September 11 and its aftermath highlighted not only the vulnerability of the United States but also its overwhelming strength. In every index of power—military, economic, cultural—the United States far outpaced the rest of the world. The United States was the only country that maintained military bases throughout the world and deployed its navy on every ocean. It was not surprising that in such circumstances many American policymakers felt that the country had a responsibility to impose order in a dangerous world.

Steve Benson's 2003 cartoon, which alters a renowned World War II photograph of soldiers raising an American flag, illustrates widespread skepticism about American motivations in the Iraq War.

Confronting Iraq

These tensions became starkly evident in the Bush administration's next initiative. From the outset of the Bush administration, a group of conservative policymakers including Vice President Dick Cheney, Secretary of Defense Donald Rumsfeld, and Deputy Defense Secretary Paul D. Wolfowitz were determined to oust Iraqi dictator Saddam Hussein from power. They insisted that the oppressed Iraqi people would welcome an American army as liberators and quickly establish a democratic government, allowing for the early departure of American soldiers. This group seized on the opportunity presented by the attacks of September 11 to press their case, and President Bush adopted their outlook. Secretary of State Colin Powell, who believed the conquest and stabilization of Iraq would require hundreds of thousands of American soldiers and should not be undertaken without the support of America's allies, found himself marginalized in the administration.

Even though no known evidence linked the Hussein to the terrorist attacks of September 11, the Bush administration in 2002 announced a goal of "regime change" in Iraq. Hussein, administration spokesmen insisted, must be ousted from power because he had developed an arsenal of chemical and bacterial "weapons of mass destruction" and was seeking to acquire nuclear arms. American newspaper and television journalists repeated these claims with almost no independent investigation. Early in 2003, despite his original misgivings, Secretary of State Powell delivered a speech before the United Nations outlining the administration's case. He claimed that Hussein possessed a mobile chemical weapons laboratory, had hidden weapons of mass destruction in his many palaces, and was seeking to acquire uranium in Africa to build nuclear weapons. (Every one of these assertions later turned out to be false.)

The Iraq War

Foreign policy "realists," including members of previous Republican administrations like Brent Scowcroft, the national security adviser under the first President Bush, warned that the United States could not unilaterally transform the Middle East into a bastion of democracy, as the administration claimed was its long-term aim. The decision to begin the **Iraq War** split the Western alliance and inspired a massive antiwar movement throughout the world. In February 2003, between 10 million and 15 million people across the globe demonstrated against the impending war.

Part of the massive crowd that gathered in New York City on February 15, 2003, a day of worldwide demonstrations against the impending war against Iraq.

Both traditional foes of the United States like Russia and China and traditional allies like Germany and France refused to support a "preemptive" strike against Iraq. Unable to obtain approval from the United Nations for attacking Iraq, the United States went to war anyway in March 2003, with Great Britain as its sole significant ally. President Bush called the war "Operation Iraqi Freedom." Its purpose, he declared, was to "defend our freedom" and "bring freedom to others." The Hussein regime proved no match for the American armed forces, with their precision bombing, satellite-guided missiles, and well-trained soldiers. Within a month, American troops occupied Baghdad. After hiding out for several months, Hussein was captured by American forces and subsequently put on trial before an Iraqi court. Late in 2006, he was found guilty of ordering the killing of many Iraqis during his reign, and was sentenced to death and executed.

President Bush standing on the deck of the aircraft carrier *Abraham Lincoln* on May 10, 2003, announcing the end of combat operations in Iraq. A banner proclaims, "Mission Accomplished." Unfortunately, the war was not in fact over.

Another Vietnam?

Soon after the fall of Baghdad, a triumphant President Bush appeared on the deck of an aircraft carrier beneath a banner reading "Mission Accomplished." But then everything seemed to go wrong. Rather than parades welcoming American liberators, looting and chaos followed the fall of the Iraqi regime. An insurgency quickly developed that targeted American soldiers and Iraqis cooperating with them. Sectarian violence soon swept throughout Iraq, with militias of Shiite and Sunni Muslims fighting each other. (Under Hussein, Sunnis, a minority of Iraq's population, had dominated the government and army; now, the Shiite majority sought to exercise power and exact revenge.) As in Vietnam, American policy was made by officials who had little or no knowledge of the countries to which they were sending troops.

The war marked a new departure in American foreign policy. While the United States had exerted enormous influence in the Middle East since World War II, never before had it occupied a nation in the center of the world's most volatile region. Rarely in its history had the United States found itself so isolated from world public opinion. Initially, the war in Iraq proved to be popular in the United States. But the realization that in fact Hussein had no weapons of mass destruction discredited the administration's rationale for the war. By early 2007, polls showed that a large majority of Americans considered the invasion of Iraq a mistake, and the war a lost cause.

THE AFTERMATH OF SEPTEMBER 11 AT HOME

Security and Liberty

The USA Patriot Act

Like earlier wars, the war on terrorism raised anew the problem of balancing security and liberty. In the immediate aftermath of the attacks, Congress rushed to pass the **USA Patriot Act**, a mammoth bill (it ran to more than 300 pages) that few members of the House or Senate had actually read. It conferred unprecedented powers on law-enforcement agencies charged with preventing the new, vaguely defined crime of "domestic terrorism," including the power to wiretap, spy on citizens, open letters, read e-mail, and obtain personal records from third parties like universities and libraries without the knowledge of a suspect. At least 5,000 foreigners with Middle Eastern connections were rounded up, and more than 1,200 arrested. Many with no link to terrorism were held for months, without either a formal charge or a public notice of their fate. The administration also set up a detention camp at the U.S. naval base at **Guantánamo Bay**, Cuba, for persons captured in Afghanistan or otherwise accused of terrorism. More than 700 persons, the nationals of many foreign countries, were detained there.

Before the Cuban Revolution of 1959, Guantánamo Bay was mostly known as an American naval base where the families of servicemen enjoyed a slice of suburban life, as in this photograph from the 1950s. Today, Guantánamo is famous as the site of the world's most notorious prison.

In November 2001, the Bush administration issued an executive order authorizing the holding of secret military tribunals for noncitizens deemed to have assisted terrorism. In such trials, traditional constitutional protections, such as the right of the accused to choose a lawyer and see all the evidence, would not apply. A few months later, the Justice Department declared that American citizens could be held indefinitely without charge and not allowed to see a lawyer, if the government declared them to be "enemy combatants."

The Power of the President

In the new atmosphere of heightened security, numerous court orders and regulations of the 1970s, inspired by abuses of the CIA, FBI, and local police forces, were rescinded, allowing these agencies to resume surveillance of Americans without evidence that a crime had been committed. Soon after September 11, President Bush authorized the National Security Agency (NSA) to eavesdrop on Americans' telephone conversations without a court warrant, a clear violation of a law limiting the NSA to foreign intelligence gathering.

War and civil liberties

The majority of Americans seemed willing to accept the administration's contention that restraints on time-honored liberties were necessary to fight terrorism. Others recalled previous times when wars produced limitations on civil liberties and public officials equated political dissent with lack of patriotism: the Alien and Sedition Acts during the "quasi-war" with France in 1798, the suspension of the writ of habeas corpus during the Civil War, the severe repression of free speech and persecution of German-Americans during World War I, Japanese-American internment in World

U.S. PRESENCE IN THE MIDDLE EAST, 1947–2019

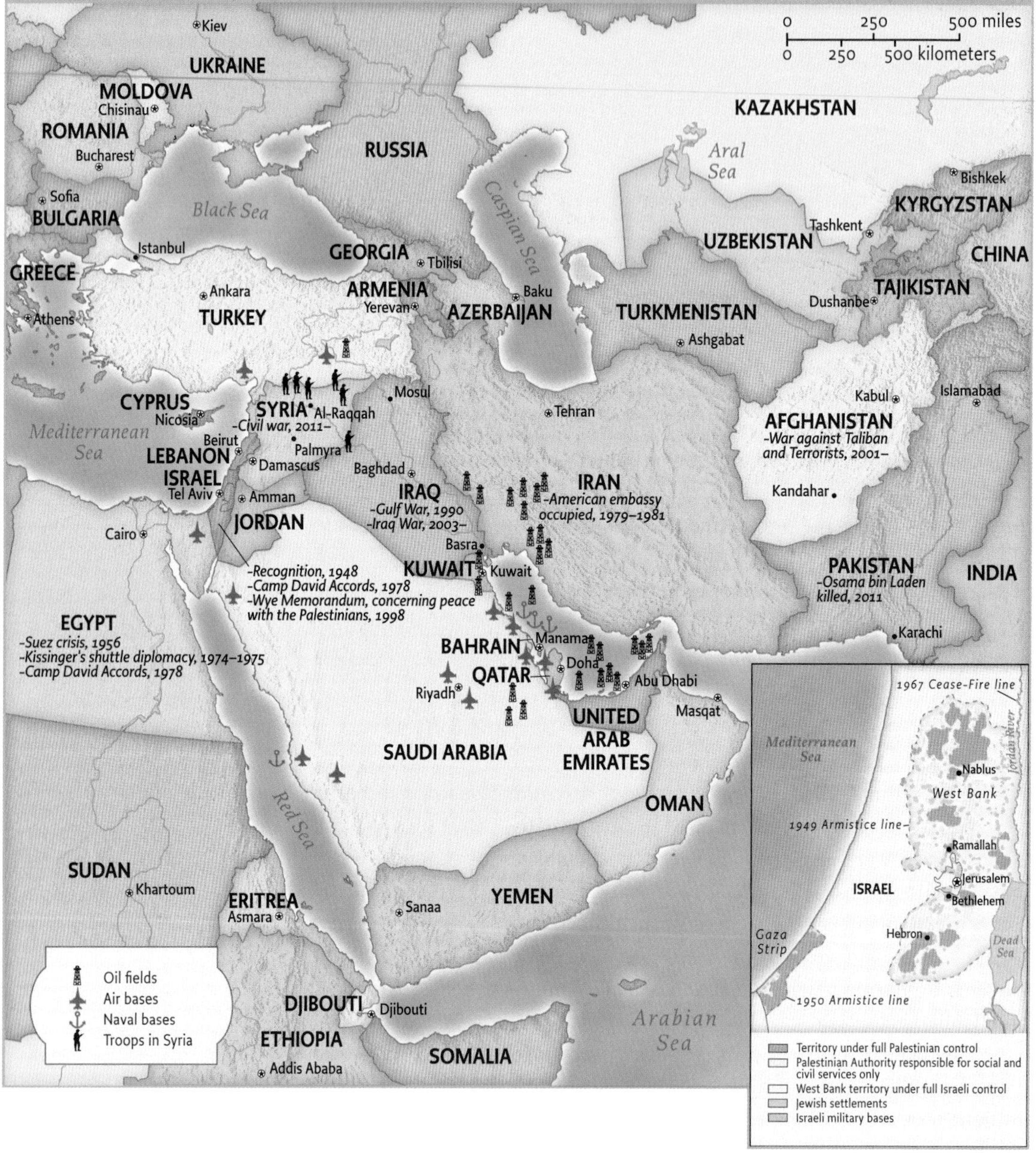

Since World War II, the United States has become more and more deeply involved in the affairs of the Middle East, whose countries are together the world's largest exporter of oil. Note that the positions of U.S. troops in Syria shown here are as of April 2018.

War II, and McCarthyism during the Cold War. The debate over liberty and security seemed certain to last as long as the war on terrorism itself.

Based on an infamous photograph, circulated around the world, of an Iraqi prisoner abused while in American custody, this 2004 cartoon suggests how such mistreatment damaged the image of the United States.

The Torture Controversy

Officials of the Bush administration also insisted in the aftermath of September 11 that the United States need not be bound by international law in pursuing the war on terrorism. They were especially eager to sidestep the Geneva Conventions and the International Convention against Torture, which regulate the treatment of prisoners of war and prohibit torture and other forms of physical and mental coercion.

Amid strong protests from Secretary of State Powell and senior military officers who feared retaliatory mistreatment of American prisoners of war, in April 2003 the president prohibited the use of torture except where special permission had been granted. Nonetheless, the Defense Department approved methods of interrogation that most observers considered torture. In addition, the CIA set up a series of jails in foreign countries outside the traditional chain of military command and took part in the "rendition" of suspects—that is, kidnapping them and spiriting them to prisons in Egypt, Yemen, Syria, and former communist states of eastern Europe, where torture is practiced.

Abu Ghraib

In this atmosphere and lacking clear rules of behavior, some military personnel—in Afghanistan, at Abu Ghraib prison in Iraq, and at Guantánamo—beat prisoners who were being held for interrogation, subjected them to electric shocks, let them be attacked by dogs, and forced them to strip naked and lie atop other prisoners. Photographs of the maltreatment of prisoners, circulated by e-mail, became public. Their exposure around the world in newspapers, on television, and on the Internet undermined the reputation of the United States as a country that adheres to standards of civilized behavior and the rule of law.

The full extent of the torture policy did not become known until 2014, when a Senate committee released a scathing report stemming from a long investigation. It revealed a pattern of brutality and deception, while concluding that no useful information had been obtained from tortured prisoners. Torture, it concluded, did not arise from the actions of a few "bad apples" but was systematically employed at secret U.S. prisons around the world.

The Court and the President

The Supreme Court did not prove receptive to President Bush's claim of authority to disregard laws and treaties and to suspend constitutional protections of individual liberties. In a series of decisions, the Court reaffirmed the rule of law both for American citizens and for foreigners held prisoner by the United States.

The rights of detainees

In *Hamdi v. Rumsfeld,* in 2004, the Court considered the lawsuit of Yasir Hamdi, an American citizen who had moved to Saudi Arabia and been captured in Afghanistan. Hamdi was imprisoned in a military jail in South Carolina without charge or the right to see a lawyer. The Court ruled that he had a right to a judicial hearing. "A state of war," wrote Sandra Day O'Connor for the 8-1 majority, "is not a blank check for the president when it comes to the rights of the nation's citizens."

Hamdan v. Rumsfeld

By the time the next significant case, *Hamdan v. Rumsfeld,* came before the Court in 2006, President Bush had appointed two new justices—Chief Justice John Roberts, to replace William Rehnquist, who died in 2005, and Samuel Alito Jr., who succeeded the retiring Sandra Day O'Connor. The Court was clearly becoming more conservative. But in June 2006, by a 5-3 margin (with Roberts not participating because he had ruled on the case while serving on an appeals court), the justices offered a stinging rebuke to the key presumptions of the Bush administration—that the Geneva Conventions do not apply to prisoners captured in the war on terrorism, and that the president can unilaterally set up secret military tribunals in which defendants have very few if any rights. The protections were afforded to prisoners of war by the Geneva Conventions, which, the Court declared, was the law of the land.

In June 2008, the Supreme Court rebuffed the Bush administration's strategy of denying detainees at Guantánamo Bay the normal protections guaranteed by the Constitution. Written by Justice Anthony Kennedy, the 5-4 decision in *Boumediene v. Bush* affirmed the detainees' right to challenge their detention in U.S. courts. "The laws and Constitution are designed," Kennedy wrote, "to survive, and remain in force, in extraordinary times." Security, he added, consists not simply in military might, but "in fidelity to freedom's first principles," including freedom from arbitrary arrest and the right of a person to go to court to challenge his or her imprisonment. The decision was a powerful affirmation that constitutional rights remain intact during wartime. But the question of how to find the proper balance between liberty and security was certain to persist in the twenty-first century.

Boumediene v. Bush

CHAPTER REVIEW AND ONLINE RESOURCES

REVIEW QUESTIONS

1. *Why was the year 1989 one of the most momentous in the twentieth century?*
2. *Describe the different visions of the U.S. role in the post-Cold War world as identified by President George H. W. Bush and President Clinton.*
3. *Identify the factors that, in the midst of 1990s prosperity, increased the levels of inequality in the United States.*
4. *What are the similarities and differences between immigration patterns of the 1990s and earlier?*
5. *Assess the role of the Supreme Court in the presidential election of 2000.*
6. *What is globalization, and how did it affect the United States in the 1990s?*
7. *How did the foreign policy initiatives of the George W. Bush administration depart from the policies of other presidents since World War II?*
8. *How did the September 11 attacks transform Americans' understanding of their security? How did the response compare with that after Pearl Harbor?*
9. *What are the similarities and differences between America's involvement in Afghanistan and Iraq since 2001?*
10. *In what ways did American leaders and citizens draw lessons from Vietnam when considering U.S. involvement in Iraq?*
11. *What does the war on terrorism suggest about the tension between freedom and security as priorities of the United States?*
12. *How did Supreme Court decisions since 2001 indicate that the rights revolution was here to stay?*

KEY TERMS

new world order (p. 842)
Gulf War (p. 843)
"Don't ask, don't tell" (p. 844)
North American Free Trade Agreement (NAFTA) (p. 844)
Contract with America (p. 845)
Rwandan genocide (p. 848)
Balkan crisis (p. 848)
ethnic cleansing (p. 848)
globalization (p. 849)
Americans with Disabilities Act (p. 863)
multiculturalism (p. 864)
Culture Wars (p. 864)
family values (p. 865)
Bush v. Gore (p. 868)
Bush Doctrine (p. 871)
war on terrorism (p. 871)
war in Afghanistan (p. 871)
Iraq War (p. 873)
USA Patriot Act (p. 874)
Guatánamo Bay (p. 875)

Go to INQUIZITIVE

To see what you know—and learn what you've missed—with personalized feedback along the way.

Visit the ***Give Me Liberty!* Student Site** for primary source documents and images, interactive maps, author videos featuring Eric Foner, and more.

2005	Hurricane Katrina hits the Gulf Coast
2007	Great Recession begins
2008	Federal bailout of banks and companies
	Barack Obama elected
2009	Sonia Sotomayor named to Supreme Court
	Federal stimulus package
	Tea Party movement develops
2010	Affordable Care Act
2011	Arab Spring
	Osama bin Laden killed
	Occupy Wall Street movement
2012	Obama reelected
2013	Edward Snowden revelations
2015	Supreme Court declares constitutional right to gay marriage
	United States reestablishes relations with Cuba
2016	Election of Donald Trump
2018	Democrats win control of House of Representatives

CHAPTER 28

A DIVIDED NATION

★

Newly naturalized citizens recite the Oath of Allegiance at the Brooklyn Federal Courthouse in 2016. The portraits on the walls depict former federal judges.

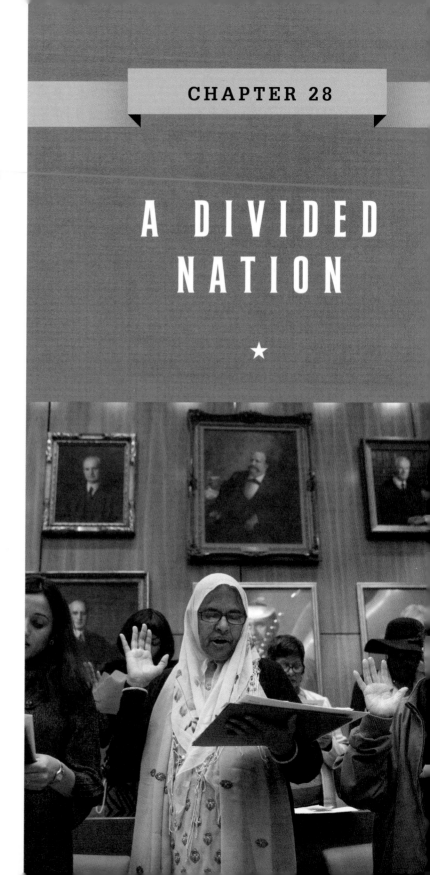

The years following the attacks of September 11, 2001 produced great political surprises. Having been reelected in 2004, George W. Bush saw his public approval plummet as the Iraq War settled into a frustrating stalemate, and, late in his presidency, the country experienced the worst economic crisis since the Great Depression. Widespread dissatisfaction with established political leadership enabled relative newcomers to national politics to reach the White House in the presidential elections of 2008 and 2016—Barack Obama, a first-term U.S. senator from Illinois and the first African-American to win a major party's presidential nomination, and Donald Trump, a New York real estate developer and television personality with no political experience at all.

The two men's campaigns had much in common. Both appealed successfully to a desire for new political leadership and to a sense that the country was moving in the wrong direction. Both made effective use of the Internet and new social media to spread their messages. Both inspired rapturous enthusiasm from supporters but deep resentment from opponents. In their political philosophies, personal demeanor, and sources of electoral support, however, Obama and Trump could not have been more different. Whether either represented the long-term future of American politics remained to be seen. What was certain was that Americans were as deeply divided in their social and political outlooks as at any point since the Civil War.

Whatever one's opinion of Obama's policies, there is no question that in view of the nation's racial history, the election and reelection of the first African-American president marked an important turning point. Yet the election of Trump to succeed him with a campaign that forthrightly appealed to voters hostile to immigration and resentful that a black man occupied the White House suggested that issues as old as the republic—who is an American, who is entitled to full freedom and equality—remained as contested as ever.

FOCUS QUESTIONS

- *What events eroded support for President Bush's policies during his second term?*
- *What were the economic practices that contributed to the crisis of 2008?*
- *What kinds of change did voters hope for when they elected Barack Obama?*
- *What were the major challenges of Obama's first term?*
- *What was divisive about Donald Trump's campaign and early presidency?*
- *What were the prevailing ideas of American freedom at the beginning of the 21st century?*

THE WINDS OF CHANGE

The 2004 Election

With President Bush's popularity sliding because of the Iraq War and a widespread sense that many Americans were not benefiting from economic growth, Democrats in 2004 sensed a golden opportunity to retake the White House. They nominated as their candidate John Kerry, a senator from Massachusetts and the first Catholic to run for president since John F.

Kennedy in 1960. A decorated combat veteran in Vietnam, Kerry had joined the antiwar movement after leaving the army.

John Kerry

Kerry proved a surprisingly ineffective candidate. An aloof man who lacked the common touch, he failed to generate the same degree of enthusiasm among his supporters as Bush did among his. The Bush campaign consistently and successfully appealed to fear, with continuous reminders of September 11 and warnings of future attacks.

Bush won a narrow victory, with a margin of 2 percent of the popular vote and thirty-four electoral votes. The results revealed a remarkable electoral stability. Both sides spent tens of millions of dollars in advertising and mobilized new voters—nearly 20 million since 2000. But in the end, only three states voted differently from four years earlier—New Hampshire, which Kerry carried, and Iowa and New Mexico, which swung to Bush.

Bush's Second Term

A more conciliatory tone

In his second inaugural address, in January 2005, Bush outlined a new American goal—"ending tyranny in the world." Striking a more conciliatory tone than during his first administration, he promised that the United States would not try to impose "our style of government" on others and that it would in the future seek the advice of allies. He said nothing specific about Iraq but tried to shore up falling support for the war by invoking the ideal of freedom. In his first inaugural, in January 2001, Bush had used the words "freedom," "free," or "liberty" seven times. In his second, they appeared forty-nine times. But the ongoing chaos in Iraq, coupled with a spate of corruption scandals surrounding Republicans in Congress and the White House, eroded Bush's standing.

Domestic scandals

Hurricane Katrina

Disasters, natural and man-made

A further blow to the Bush administration's standing came in August 2005, when **Hurricane Katrina** slammed ashore near New Orleans. Situated below sea level between the Mississippi River and Lake Pontchartrain and protected by levees, New Orleans has always been vulnerable to flooding. For years, scientists had predicted a catastrophe if a hurricane hit the city. When the storm hit on August 29, the levees broke. Nearly the entire city, with a population of half a million, was inundated. Nearby areas of the Louisiana and Mississippi Gulf Coast were also hard hit.

The natural disaster quickly became a man-made one, with ineptitude evident from local government to the White House. The mayor of New Orleans had been slow to order an evacuation, fearing it would damage the city's tourist trade. The Federal Emergency Management Agency (FEMA) had made almost no preparations. If the Bush administration had prided itself on anything, it was competence in dealing with disaster. Katrina shattered that image.

For days, vast numbers of people, most of them poor African-Americans, remained abandoned amid the floodwaters. Bodies floated in the streets, and people died in city hospitals and nursing homes. By the time aid began to arrive, damage stood at $80 billion, the death toll was around 1,500, and two-thirds of the city's population had been displaced. The televised images of misery in the streets of New Orleans shocked the world and shamed the country.

Hurricane Katrina also shone a bright light on the heroic side of American life. Where government failed, individual citizens stepped into the breach. People with boats rescued countless survivors from rooftops and attics, private donations flowed in to aid the victims, and neighboring states like Texas opened their doors to thousands of refugees.

Residents of New Orleans, stranded on a rooftop days after flood waters engulfed the city, frantically attempt to attract the attention of rescue helicopters.

Battle over the Border

The attacks of September 11 and subsequent war on terrorism threw into sharp relief the status of American borders and borderlands, especially in the Southwest. The existence of the borderland embracing parts of the United States and Mexico, with people enjoying well-developed connections with communities in both countries, has always been a source of tension and insecurity in the eyes of many Americans. Fears of terrorists crossing the border merged with older worries about undocumented immigration and the growth of Hispanic culture in the Southwest.

The Bush and Obama administrations greatly accelerated efforts to police the border. By 2013, the number of U.S. Border Patrol officers stood at 20,000, making it the nation's second-largest police force after the New York City Police Department, and 400,000 undocumented immigrants were being deported annually, far more than in the past. Latino communities experienced the southwestern borderlands as increasingly militarized, since the "border" stretched far inland and persons accused of having entered the country illegally—almost all of them from Mexico, Guatemala, Honduras, and El Salvador—could be apprehended many miles north of Mexico. Nonetheless, some

In 2015, the artist JR took photographs of immigrants and affixed them to the walls of New York City buildings and to other public places. This image is of Kamola Akilova, from Uzbekistan. The purpose, according to the artist, is to take immigrants out of the shadows and make people aware of their presence in the city.

Members of the Texas Minutemen patrolling the U.S.-Mexico border. Claiming that the federal government was failing to prevent undocumented immigrants from entering the United States, vigilantes tried to do so on their own.

Americans in the region, claiming that the federal government was not doing enough to enforce the border's status as a dividing line, set up unofficial militias to police the area.

In the spring of 2006, the immigration issue suddenly burst again onto the center stage of politics. Alongside legal immigrants, millions of undocumented newcomers had made their way to the United States, mostly from Mexico. Economists disagree about their impact. It seems clear that the presence of large numbers of uneducated, low-skilled workers pushes down wages at the bottom of the economic ladder, especially affecting African-Americans. On the other hand, immigrants both legal and undocumented receive regular paychecks, spend money, and pay taxes. They fill jobs for which American workers seem to be unavailable because the wages are so low. It is estimated that more than one-fifth of construction workers, domestic workers, and agricultural workers are in the United States illegally.

In 2006, with many Americans convinced that the United States had lost control of its borders and that immigration was in part responsible for the stagnation of real wages, the House of Representatives approved a bill making it a felony to be in the country illegally and a crime to offer aid to undocumented immigrants. The response was utterly unexpected: a series of massive demonstrations in the spring of 2006 by immigrants—legal and undocumented—and their supporters, demanding the right to remain in the country as citizens. In cities from New York to Chicago, Los Angeles, Phoenix, and Dallas, hundreds of thousands of protesters took to the streets. Congress, however, could not agree on a response. The immigration issue was at a stalemate.

The U.S.-Canada boundary, which stretches for over 3,000 miles, has long been called the world's "longest undefended border." With borders becoming more contested lately, however, it has seen increased restrictions on crossing (but, as yet, no armed patrols, unlike the Mexican border).

WARNING!
If you are entering the United States
without presenting yourself to an Immigration Officer,
YOU MAY BE ARRESTED AND PROSECUTED
for violating U.S. Immigration and Customs Laws.

Islam, America, and the "Clash of Civilizations"

The events of September 11, 2001, placed new pressures on religious liberty. Even before the terrorist attacks, the political scientist Samuel P. Huntington had published a widely noted book, *The Clash of Civilizations and the Remaking of the World Order* (1996), which argued that with the Cold War over, a new global conflict impended between Western and Islamic "civilizations."

In April 2006, millions of people demonstrated for immigrant rights. This photograph shows part of the immense crowd in Chicago, bearing the flags of many nations.

Many readers, including politicians, interpreted Huntington, not entirely correctly, as reducing politics and culture to a single characteristic—in this case, religion—that remains forever static, divorced from historical development. "Islam," in fact, consists of well over a billion people, in very different countries ranging from South Asia to the Middle East, Africa, Europe, and the Americas. Nonetheless, in the aftermath of 9/11, the formula that pitted a freedom-loving United States against militant, authoritarian Muslims became popular as a way of making sense of the terrorist attacks.

What did this mean for the nearly 5 million Americans who practiced the Muslim religion? President Bush insisted that the war on terror was not a war against Islam. But many Americans found it difficult to separate the two, even though most American Muslims were as appalled by the terrorist attacks as their fellow countrymen. Some critics claimed that Islam was fundamentally incompatible with American life—a position reminiscent of prejudice in the nineteenth century against Catholics and Mormons. In a number of states, politicians appealed for votes by opposing the construction of new mosques and raising the nonexistent threat that courts would impose "sharia law"—the religious rules laid down in the Koran—on all Americans.

The Constitution and Liberty

Two significant Supreme Court decisions in June 2003 revealed how the largely conservative justices had come to accept that the social revolution that began during the 1960s could not be undone.

Revisiting the Bakke *case*

In two cases arising from challenges to the admissions policies of the University of Michigan, the Supreme Court issued its most important rulings on affirmative action since the *Bakke* case twenty-five years earlier. A 5-4 majority upheld the right of colleges and universities to take race into account in admissions decisions. Writing for the majority, Justice Sandra Day O'Connor argued that such institutions have a legitimate interest in creating a "diverse" student body to enhance education.

Lawrence v. Texas

In the second decision, in *Lawrence v. Texas*, a 6-3 majority declared unconstitutional a Texas law making sexual acts between persons of the same gender a crime. The *Lawrence* decision paved the way for an even more momentous Supreme Court ruling in 2015 in ***Obergefell v. Hodges***, which overturned state laws barring marriages for same-sex couples. Public opinion on this question had evolved with remarkable rapidity, especially among younger Americans. In 2003, two-thirds of Americans opposed legalizing such marriages; by the time of the 2015 ruling, over 60 percent were in favor.

Marriage for same-sex couples

Both decisions relating to gay Americans, written by Justice Anthony Kennedy, repudiated the conservative view that constitutional interpretation must rest either on the "original intent" of the founders and authors of constitutional amendments or on a narrow reading of the text. Instead, Kennedy, generally a conservative, reaffirmed the liberal view of the Constitution as a living document whose protections expand as society changes. "The nature of injustice is such," he wrote in *Obergefell*, "that we may not always see it in our own times. The generations that wrote and ratified the Bill of Rights and the Fourteenth Amendment did not presume to know the extent of freedom in all of its dimensions, and so they entrusted to future generations a charter protecting the right of all persons to enjoy liberty as we learn its meaning."

The Constitution as a living document

The Midterm Elections of 2006

With President Bush's popularity having plummeted because of the Iraq War and the Hurricane Katrina disaster, Congress beset by scandal after scandal, and public-opinion polls revealing that a majority of Americans believed the country to be "on the wrong track," Democrats expected to reap major gains in the congressional elections of 2006. They were not disappointed. In a sweeping repudiation of the administration, voters gave Democrats control of both houses of Congress for the first time since 1994. In January 2007, Democrat Nancy Pelosi of California became the first female Speaker of the House in American history.

Democratic majorities in Congress

In January 2009, as Bush's presidency came to an end, only 22 percent of Americans approved of his performance in office—the lowest figure since such polls began in the mid-twentieth century. Indeed, it was difficult to think of many substantive achievements during Bush's eight years in office. His foreign policy alienated most of the world, leaving the United States militarily weakened and diplomatically isolated. Because of tax cuts for the wealthy that he pushed through Congress during his first term, as well as the cost of the wars in Iraq and Afghanistan, the large budget surplus he had inherited was transformed into an immense deficit. And in his final year in office, Bush had to confront the most severe economic crisis since the Great Depression.

George W. Bush's legacy

THE GREAT RECESSION

The Housing Bubble

At one point in his administration, Bush might have pointed to the economic recovery that began in 2001 as a major success. But late in 2007, the economy entered a recession. And in 2008, the American banking system suddenly found itself on the brink of collapse.

The economy in crisis

The roots of the crisis of 2008 lay in a combination of public and private policies that favored economic speculation, free-wheeling spending, and get-rich-quick schemes over more traditional avenues to economic growth and personal advancement. For years, the Federal Reserve Bank kept interest rates at unprecedented low levels, first to help the economy recover from the bursting of the technology bubble in 2000 and then to enable more Americans to borrow money to purchase homes. Housing prices rose rapidly. Consumer indebtedness also rose dramatically as people who owned houses took out second mortgages or simply spent to the limits on their credit cards. In mid-2008, when the median family income was around $50,000, the average American family owed an $84,000 home mortgage, $14,000 in auto and student loans, $8,500 to credit card companies, and $10,000 in home equity loans.

All this borrowing fueled increased spending. An immense influx of cheap goods from China accelerated the loss of manufacturing jobs in the United States but also enabled Americans to keep buying, even though for most, household income stagnated during the Bush years. Indeed, China helped to finance the American spending spree by buying up hundreds of billions of dollars' worth of federal bonds—in effect loaning money to the United States so that it could purchase Chinese-made goods. Banks and other lending institutions issued more and more "subprime" mortgages—risky loans to people who lacked the income to meet their monthly payments.

An Arizona house left unfinished when the housing bubble collapsed. When prices were at their peak, housing developers rushed to build new residences; many were abandoned when prices plunged.

Wall Street bankers developed complex new ways of repackaging and selling these mortgages to investors. Insurance companies, including the world's largest, American International Group (AIG), insured these new financial products against future default. Credit-rating agencies gave these securities their highest

FIGURE 28.1
Portrait of a Recession

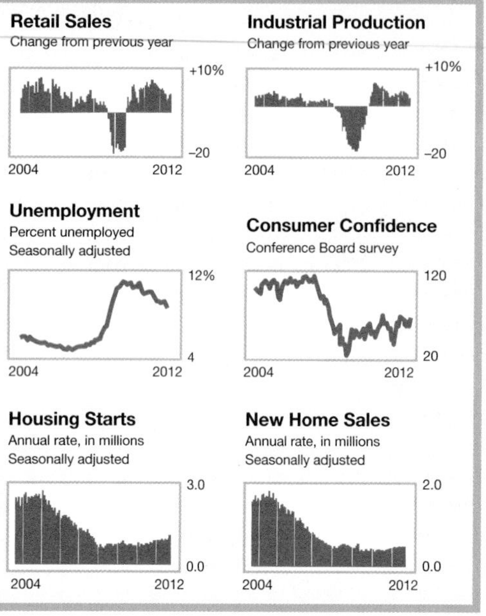

These graphs offer a vivid visual illustration of the steep decline in the American economy in 2008 and the first part of 2009, and the slow recovery to 2012.

ratings, even though they were based on loans that clearly would never be repaid. Believing that the market must be left to regulate itself, the Federal Reserve Bank and other regulatory agencies did nothing to slow the speculative frenzy. Banks and investment firms reported billions of dollars in profits and rewarded their executives with unheard-of bonuses.

The Bubble Bursts

In 2006 and 2007, overbuilding had reached the point where home prices began to fall. More and more home owners found themselves owing more money than their homes were worth. As mortgage rates reset, increasing numbers of borrowers defaulted—that is, they could no longer meet their monthly mortgage payments. Banks suddenly found themselves with billions of dollars of worthless investments on their books. In 2008, the situation became a full-fledged crisis, as banks stopped making loans, business dried up, and the stock market collapsed. Once above 14,000, the Dow Jones Industrial Average plunged to around 8,000—the worst percentage decline since 1931. Lehman Brothers, a venerable investment house, recorded a $2.3 billion loss and went out of existence in history's biggest bankruptcy. Leading banks seemed to be on the verge of failure.

With the value of their homes and stock market accounts in free fall, Americans cut back on spending, leading to business failures and a rapid rise in unemployment. By the end of 2008, 2.5 million jobs had been lost—the most in any year since the end of World War II. Unemployment was concentrated in manufacturing and construction, sectors dominated by men. As a result, by mid-2009, for the first time in history, more women than men in the United States held paying jobs.

The Great Recession

Even worse than the economic meltdown was the meltdown of confidence as millions of Americans lost their jobs and/or their homes and saw their retirement savings and pensions, if invested in the stock market, disappear. In April 2009, the recession that began in December 2007 known as the **Great Recession** became the longest since the Great Depression.

"A Conspiracy against the Public"

In *The Wealth of Nations* (1776), Adam Smith wrote: "People of the same trade seldom meet together, even for merriment and diversion, but the conversation ends in a conspiracy against the public." This certainly seemed

This cartoon suggests that the near-collapse of the financial system in 2008 indicates the need for "a little more regulation."

an apt description of the behavior of leading bankers and investment houses whose greed helped bring down the American economy.

Amid mounting revelations of corporate misdeeds, the reputation of stockbrokers and bankers fell to lows last seen during the Great Depression. One poll showed that of various social groups, bankers ranked third from the bottom in public esteem—just above prostitutes and convicted felons. Resentment was fueled by the fact that Wall Street had long since abandoned the idea that pay should be linked to results. By the end of 2008, the worst year for the stock market since the Depression, Wall Street firms had fired 240,000 employees. But they also paid out $20 billion in bonuses to top executives.

In 2010, Goldman Sachs, the Wall Street banking and investment firm, paid a fine of half a billion dollars to settle charges that it had knowingly marketed to clients mortgage-based securities it knew were bound to fail and then in effect bet on their failure. (This was like a real-estate agency selling an unsuspecting customer a house with faulty wiring and then taking out insurance so that the agency would be paid when the house burned down.)

Waived penalties for banks

Overall, during the next few years, an incredible litany of malfeasance by the world's largest banks became public. Between 2009 and 2016, major banks, American and foreign, were forced by their respective governments to pay fines totaling in excess of $100 billion for such actions as facilitating tax evasion by wealthy clients, fixing foreign currency exchange rates and international interest rates to boost their own profits, often at the expense of their customers, and misleading regulators about their activities. Yet bank profits are so large that the institutions accepted these fines as simply a minor cost of doing business. Even when J. P. Morgan Chase and Citibank pleaded guilty to felony conspiracy charges, no meaningful punishment followed. No individual executive was charged with a crime, and the Securities and Exchange Commission granted waivers from penalties that are supposed to punish criminal behavior, such as being barred from certain kinds of financial transactions.

It was also revealed in 2010 that Bernard Madoff, a Wall Street investor who claimed to have made enormous profits for his clients, had in fact run a Ponzi scheme in which investors who wanted to retrieve their money were paid with funds from new participants. Madoff sent fictitious monthly financial statements to his clients, but he never actually made stock purchases for them. When the scheme collapsed, Madoff's investors suffered losses amounting to around $50 billion. The crisis exposed the dark side of market fundamentalism—the ethos of deregulation that had dominated world affairs for the preceding thirty years.

The Bernard Madoff scandal

Every president from Ronald Reagan onward had lectured the rest of the world on the need to adopt the American model of unregulated economic competition and berated countries like Japan and Germany for assisting failing businesses. Now, the American model lay in ruins and a new role for government in regulating economic activity seemed inevitable.

Bush and the Crisis

In the fall of 2008, with the presidential election campaign in full swing, the Bush administration seemed unable to come up with a response to the crisis. In keeping with the free market ethos, it allowed Lehman Brothers to fail. But this immediately created a domino effect, with the stock prices of other banks and investment houses collapsing, and the administration quickly reversed course. It persuaded a reluctant Congress to appropriate $700 billion dollars to bail out other floundering firms. Insurance companies like AIG, banks like Citigroup and Bank of America, and giant financial companies like the Federal Home Loan Mortgage Corporation (popularly known as Freddie Mac) and the Federal National Mortgage Association (Fannie Mae), which insured most mortgages in the country, were deemed "too big to fail"—that is, they were so interconnected with other institutions that their collapse would drive the economy into a full-fledged depression. Through the federal bailout, taxpayers in effect took temporary ownership of these companies, absorbing the massive losses created by the companies' previous malfeasance. But despite the bailout, the health of the banking system remained fragile.

The bailout

"Too big to fail"

The crisis also revealed the limits of the American social "safety net" compared with those of other industrialized countries. In western Europe, workers who lose their jobs typically receive many months of unemployment insurance amounting to a significant percentage of their lost wages. In the United States, only one-third of out-of-work persons even qualify for unemployment insurance, and it runs out after a few months. The abolition of "welfare" (the national obligation to assist the neediest Americans) during the Clinton administration left the American safety net a patchwork of a few national programs such as food stamps supplemented by locally administered aid. The poor were dependent on aid from the states, which found their budgets collapsing as revenues from property and sales taxes dried up.

The limits of the American social safety net

In 2012, fifty-seven years after the arrest of Rosa Parks for failing to give up her seat to a white passenger, Barack Obama, the first African-American president, took a seat on the very same bus, now at the Henry Ford Museum in Dearborn, Michigan.

The Emergence of Barack Obama

A little-known forty-seven-year-old senator from Illinois when the campaign of 2008 began, Barack Obama owed his success both to his own exceptional skills as a speaker and campaigner and to the evolution of American politics and society during his lifetime.

Obama's life story

Obama's life story exemplified the enormous changes the United States had undergone since 1960. Without the civil rights movement, his election would have been inconceivable. He was the product of an interracial marriage, which ended in divorce when he was two years old, between a Kenyan immigrant and a white American woman. When Obama was born in 1961, their marriage was still illegal in many states. He attended Harvard Law School and worked in Chicago as a community organizer before going into politics. He also wrote two best-selling books about his upbringing in Indonesia (where his mother worked as an anthropologist) and Hawaii (where his maternal grandparents helped to raise him) and his search for a sense of identity given his complex background. Obama was elected to the U.S. Senate in 2004 and first gained national attention with an eloquent speech at the Democratic national convention that year. His early opposition to the Iraq War won the support of the Democratic Party's large antiwar element, his race galvanized the support of black voters, and his promise of change appealed to the young.

The 2008 Campaign

John McCain and Sarah Palin

In 2008, Obama faced Senator John McCain, the Republican nominee, in the general election. At age seventy-two, McCain was the oldest man ever to run for president. He surprised virtually everyone by choosing as his

Barack Obama and his family greet enthusiastic supporters at an outdoor celebration in Chicago on the night of his election as president on November 4, 2008.

running mate Sarah Palin, the little-known governor of Alaska, in part as an attempt to woo Democratic women disappointed at their party's rejection of Hillary Clinton, who had sought the Democratic nomination. Palin proved extremely popular with the Republican Party's conservative base. But her performances in speeches and interviews soon made it clear that she lacked familiarity with many of the domestic and foreign issues a new administration would confront.

But the main obstacles for the McCain campaign were President Bush's low popularity and the financial crisis that reached bottom in September and October. Obama's promise of change seemed more appealing than ever. On election day, he swept to victory with 53 percent of the popular vote and a large majority in the electoral college. His election redrew the nation's political map. Obama carried not only Democratic strongholds in New England, the mid-Atlantic states, the industrial Midwest, and the West Coast but also states that had been reliably Republican for years. He cracked the solid South, winning Virginia, North Carolina, and Florida. He did extremely well in suburbs throughout the country. He even carried Indiana, where Bush had garnered 60 percent of the vote in 2004 but which now was hard hit by unemployment. He did exceptionally well among young voters. Obama carried every age group except persons over sixty-five. Thus, he was elected even though he received only 43 percent of the nation's white vote.

Obama's First Inauguration

Obama's first inaugural address

Few presidents have come into office facing as serious a set of problems as did Barack Obama. The economy was in crisis and the country involved in two wars. But Americans, including many who had not voted for him, viewed Obama's election as a cause for optimism. On January 20, 2009, a day after the Martin Luther King Jr. holiday and more than forty-five years after King's "I Have a Dream" speech, Obama was inaugurated as president. More than 1 million people traveled to Washington to view the historic event. In his inaugural address Obama offered a stark rebuke to eight years of Bush policies and, more broadly, to the premises that had shaped government policy since the election of Reagan. He promised a foreign policy based on diplomacy rather than unilateral force, pledged to protect the environment, spoke of the need to combat income inequality and lack of access to health care, and blamed a culture of "greed and irresponsibility" for helping to bring on the economic crisis. He promised to renew respect for the Constitution. Instead of freedom, he spoke of community and responsibility. His address harked back to the revolutionary-era ideal of putting the common good before individual self-interest.

Community and responsibility

OBAMA IN OFFICE

In many ways, Obama's first policy initiatives lived up to the promise of change. In his first three months, he barred the use of torture, launched a diplomatic initiative to repair relations with the Muslim world, reversed the previous administration's executive orders limiting women's reproductive rights, and abandoned Bush's rhetoric about a God-given American mission to spread freedom throughout the world. When Supreme Court justice David Souter announced his retirement, Obama named **Sonia Sotomayor**, the first Hispanic and third woman in the Court's history, to replace him. In 2010, Obama appointed a second woman, Elena Kagan, to the Court.

Sonia Sotomayor

Obama's first budget recalled the New Deal and Great Society. Breaking with the Reagan-era motto, "Government is the problem, not the solution," it anticipated active government support for health-care reform, clean energy, and public education, paid for in part by allowing Bush's tax cuts for the wealthy to expire in 2010. He pushed through Congress a "stimulus" package amounting to nearly $800 billion in new government spending—for construction projects, the extension of unemployment benefits, and aid to the states to enable them to balance their budgets. The largest single spending

The "stimulus" package

This photograph, taken in 2010, depicts the four women who have served on the Supreme Court. From left to right, are Sandra Day O'Connor, the first female justice, (appointed in 1981); Sonia Sotomayor (2009); Ruth Bader Ginsburg (1993), and Elena Kagan (2010).

In the spring of 2009, Republicans and independents opposed to President Obama's "stimulus" plan held "tea parties" around the country, seeking to invoke the tradition of the Boston Tea Party and its opposition to taxation. In this demonstration in Austin, Texas, some participants wore hats reminiscent of the revolutionary era. One participant carries a sign urging the state to secede from the Union.

appropriation in American history, the bill was meant to pump money into the economy in order to save and create jobs and to ignite a resumption of economic activity.

The Health-Care Debate

For most of Obama's first year in office, congressional debate revolved around a plan to restructure the nation's health-care system so as to provide insurance coverage to the millions of Americans who lacked it, and to end abusive practices by insurance companies, such as their refusal to cover patients with existing illnesses. After months of increasingly bitter debate, in March 2010, Congress passed the Affordable Care Act, a sweeping health-care measure that required all Americans to purchase health insurance and most businesses to provide it to their employees. It also offered subsidies to persons of modest incomes so they could afford insurance and required insurance companies to accept all applicants. The legislation aroused strong partisan opposition. Claiming that it amounted to a "government takeover" of the health-care industry, every Republican in Congress voted against the bill.

Throughout Obama's presidency, Republicans remained bitterly opposed to the new law, and vowed to repeal it when they could. Indeed, in October 2013, in an effort to get the president to abandon the health-care law, the Republican-dominated Congress shut down the federal government—a tactic that, as during the Clinton administration, backfired. By 2015, what came to be known as Obamacare proved to be a remarkably successful policy. Sixteen million uninsured Americans had obtained medical coverage under its provisions, most of them less affluent Americans who received some sort of government subsidy. Despite a conservative majority on the Supreme Court, the justices twice rejected challenges to the constitutionality of Obamacare.

Financial Reform

Another significant measure, enacted in July 2010, was a financial regulatory reform law that sought to place under increased federal oversight many of the transactions that had helped create the economic crisis. Although the details remained to be worked out through specific regulations, the law represented a reversal of the policies of the past fifty years that had given banks a free hand in their operations. But it did not require a breakup of banks deemed "too big to fail," and left open the possibility of future taxpayer bailouts of these institutions. Moreover, officials responsible for issuing new regulations watered them down when banks complained.

Taken together, the measures of Obama's first year and a half in office saw the most dramatic domestic reform legislation since the Great Society of the 1960s. "Change"—the slogan of his election campaign—was significant but did not go far enough for many of his supporters. The health-care bill failed to include a "public option," in which the government itself would offer medical insurance to those who desired it (much like Medicare for elderly Americans). Obama chose his economic advisers from Wall Street, who underestimated the depth of the crisis, and continued the Bush administration policy of pouring taxpayer money into the banks. Little was done to help home owners facing foreclosure. Deindustrialization continued.

Not enough change for supporters

The Problem of Inequality

In 2014, the economic recovery finally gathered momentum. Consumer spending and confidence were on the rise, unemployment was falling, home sales were rising, and the stock market reached record highs. The one exception to these favorable trends, however, was a significant one—Americans' wages remained stagnant. In fact, because of the growing number of low-paid jobs, the continuing decline in the power of unions, and the rising value of stocks, owned primarily by upper-income Americans, virtually the entire benefit of the recovery went to the top 1 percent of earners, while the real incomes of most families declined, deepening the long-term trend toward greater and greater economic inequality. In 2013, the top 10 percent of Americans received nearly half the total income. Meanwhile, the percentage of families in the middle class continued to shrink while that of those living in poverty continued to grow.

At the bottom of the social scale, Americans employed by some of the country's largest corporations, including McDonald's and Wal-Mart, received pitiably low wages, at or just slightly above the federal minimum wage of $7.25 per hour (a figure lower, in income adjusted for inflation, than fifty years before). Nearly three-quarters of people helped by programs designed for the poor, such as food stamps and Medicaid, include a working member, so in effect taxpayers are subsidizing the low-wage policies

A chart showing how much of the nation's total income has been enjoyed by the top 10 percent of families from 1910 to 2015. This is an index of income inequality. There was a sharp drop during World War II, which persisted until 1980, when the share began to rise. Today, income inequality is near historic highs.

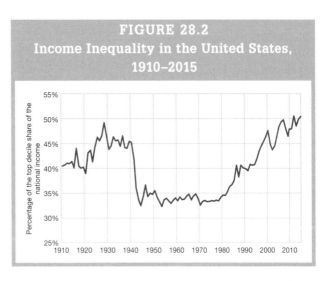

FIGURE 28.2
Income Inequality in the United States, 1910–2015

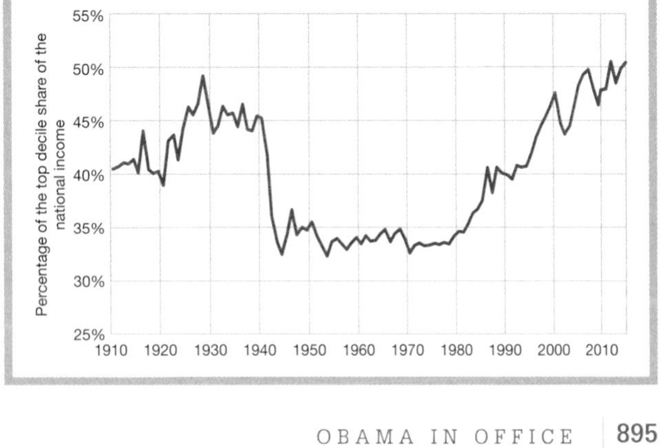

VOICES OF FREEDOM

From Opinion of the Court in *Obergefell v. Hodges* (2015)

In 2015, in a 5-4 decision, the Supreme Court ruled that the Constitution's Fourteenth Amendment establishes a constitutional right to marriage for gay Americans. The ruling reflected a remarkably rapid shift in public opinion regarding gay marriage in the previous few years. Written by Justice Anthony Kennedy, the majority opinion included a powerful exposition of the meaning of freedom in the early twenty-first century.

The history of marriage is one of both continuity and change. That institution—even as confined to opposite-sex relations—has evolved over time. For example, marriage was once viewed as an arrangement by the couple's parents based on political, religious, and financial concerns; but by the time of the Nation's founding it was understood to be a voluntary contract between a man and a woman. . . . As the role and status of women changed, the institution further evolved. Under the centuries-old doctrine of coverture, a married man and woman were treated by the State as a single, male-dominated legal entity. As women gained legal, political, and property rights, and as society began to understand that women have their own equal dignity, the law of coverture was abandoned. . . .

New dimensions of freedom become apparent to new generations, often through perspectives that begin in pleas or protests. . . .

The identification and protection of fundamental rights is an enduring part of the judicial duty to interpret the Constitution. . . . The nature of injustice is such that we may not always see it in our own times. The generations that wrote and ratified the Bill of Rights and the Fourteenth Amendment did not presume to know the extent of freedom in all of its dimensions, and so they entrusted to future generations a charter protecting the right of all persons to enjoy liberty as we learn its meaning. When new insight reveals discord between the Constitution's central protections and a received legal structure, a claim to liberty must be addressed. . . .

The right to marry is a fundamental right inherent in the liberty of the person, and . . . couples of the same sex may not be deprived of that right and that liberty.

From Barack Obama, Eulogy at Emanuel African Methodist Episcopal Church (2015)

In the summer of 2015, the nation was shocked by the murder of nine black parishioners in a black church in Charleston by a white supremacist gunman. President Obama traveled to the city to deliver a eulogy for one of the victims, Clementa Pinckney, the church's pastor and a member of the South Carolina Senate. His speech reflected on the history of race relations and the condition of black America fifty years after the height of the civil rights revolution.

The church is and always has been the center of African American life . . . a place to call our own in a too-often hostile world, a sanctuary from so many hardships. . . .

There's no better example of this tradition than Mother Emanuel, . . . a church built by blacks seeking liberty, burned to the ground because its founders sought to end slavery only to rise up again, a phoenix from these ashes. . . .

We do not know whether the killer of Reverend Pinckney and eight others knew all of this history, but he surely sensed the meaning of his violent act. It was an act that drew on a long history of bombs and arson and shots fired at churches, not random but as a means of control, a way to terrorize and oppress. . . .

For too long, we've been blind to the way past injustices continue to shape the present. Perhaps we see that now. Perhaps this tragedy causes us to ask some tough questions about how we can permit so many of our children to languish in poverty . . . or attend dilapidated schools or grow up without prospects for a job or for a career. Perhaps it causes us to examine what we're doing to cause some of our children to hate. Perhaps it softens hearts towards those lost young men, tens and tens of thousands caught up in the criminal-justice system and leads us to make sure that that system's not infected with bias. . . .

None of us can or should expect a transformation in race relations overnight. . . . Whatever solutions we find will necessarily be incomplete. But it would be a betrayal of everything Reverend Pinckney stood for, I believe, if we allow ourselves to slip into a comfortable silence again. . . .

QUESTIONS

1. *How does Justice Kennedy believe we should understand the meaning of freedom?*
2. *Why does President Obama believe that the freedom of some Americans is interconnected with the freedom of others?*
3. *What do these documents suggest about how much has changed in American life in the past half-century and how much has not changed?*

of highly profitable corporations by enabling their employees to survive. McDonald's had a helpful website to assist its workers in making ends meet. It urged them to try to have two full-time jobs, spend no more than twenty dollars per month on health insurance, and break food into small pieces so that it would seem to go further.

An Occupy Wall Street demonstrator expresses her concern about rising economic inequality.

The Occupy Movement

The problem of inequality burst into public discussion in 2011. On September 17, a few dozen young protesters unrolled sleeping bags in Zuccotti Park, in the heart of New York City's financial district. They vowed to remain—to **Occupy Wall Street** as they put it—as a protest against growing economic inequality, declining opportunity, and the banks' malfeasance.

Over the next few weeks, hundreds of people camped out in the park, and thousands took part in rallies organized by the Occupy movement. Similar encampments sprang up in cities across the country. Using social media and the Internet, the Occupy movement spread its message far and wide. In the spring of 2012, public authorities began to evict the protesters. But the Occupy movement's language, especially the charge that "the 1 percent" (the very richest Americans) dominated political and economic life, had entered the political vocabulary. And it spurred a movement among low-paid workers, especially in fast-food establishments, demanding a rise in the hourly minimum wage. States and cities are allowed to establish higher minimum-wage rates than the federal government and many do so, although some large states, including Texas, Florida, and Pennsylvania, make no such provision. In 2014, Seattle and Los Angeles raised their minimums to $15 per hour. New York State followed in 2015 by announcing a $15 minimum for workers in fast-food restaurants. What began as a quixotic movement of the least empowered workers against some of the country's most prominent corporations had achieved some remarkable successes.

Demand for higher minimum wage

The United States was by far the world's most unequal developed economy. In a variety of social statistics, it was falling further and further behind other advanced countries. More than one-fifth of American children lived in poverty in 2015, the highest figure in the industrialized world. In 1980, the United States ranked thirteenth among advanced countries in life expectancy at birth; in 2015 it ranked twenty-ninth. In a reversal of the historic pattern, the size of the American middle class continued to shrink, average family income and the number of low-income students graduating from college trailed that of several other countries, and social mobility—the opportunity for people to move up the economic ladder—stood at a lower level in the United States than in western Europe.

Shrinking middle class

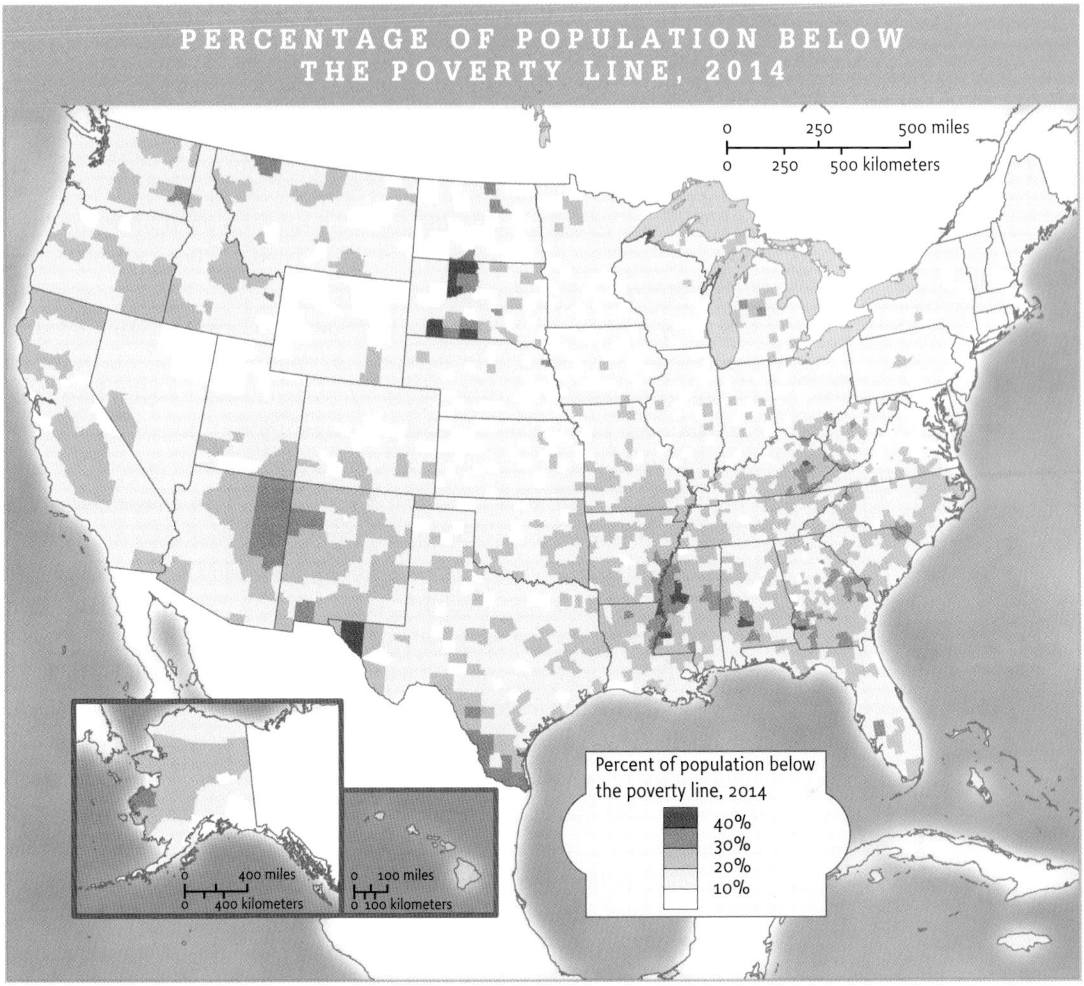

A map showing the distribution of poverty in the United States. The darker the color, the higher the percentage of families living below the poverty line. Areas with concentrations of African-Americans, Latinos, and Native Americans, along with portions of Appalachia inhabited by whites, have the highest poverty rates.

THE OBAMA PRESIDENCY

Postracial America?

African-Americans and the recession

Ironically, under the nation's first black president, African-Americans suffered most severely from the recession. A far higher proportion of blacks' family wealth was in their homes compared with whites, so the collapse of the housing bubble devastated their economic status. In 2016, the median family wealth of white families was $171,000, that of blacks only $17,600, and for Hispanics, $20,700.

Despite this grim reality, Obama's election spurred discussions among political commentators and ordinary Americans that the nation had finally put the legacy of racial inequality behind it. Talk proliferated of a new, "postracial" America, in which racial differences no longer affected public policy or private attitudes. In 2013, the Supreme Court employed this very logic in a 5-4 decision that invalidated the heart of the Voting Rights Act of 1965, a milestone of the civil rights era. Since states identified in the law, most of them in the Old South, no longer discriminated on the basis of race, the majority declared, they should no longer be required to gain permission from the Justice Department before changing their election laws. The decision, in *Shelby County v. Holden*, unleashed a flood of laws in Republican-controlled states, such as limits on early voting and requiring voters to possess state-issued identification. These measures were intended to limit the right to vote for poor people of all races, many of whom do not possess driver's licenses or other official IDs.

Voting Rights

Police killings of unarmed African-Americans

A series of events involving the deaths of unarmed black men at the hands of police or other authorities also suggested that self-congratulation about the end of racial inequality was premature. In 2012, Trayvon Martin, a black teenager walking through a Florida neighborhood to visit his father, was accosted by George Zimmerman, a white member of the "neighborhood watch." An altercation followed in which Zimmerman shot and killed Martin. Subsequently, a jury acquitted Zimmerman of all charges related to the incident. In 2014, Eric Garner, a forty-four-year-old black man selling cigarettes on the street in Staten Island, a borough of New York City, died after being wrestled to the ground and choked by police. Although "choke holds" were illegal, a grand jury declined to bring charges. In ensuing months other such incidents followed including the death of a twenty-five-year-old black man in Baltimore while in a police van after being arrested for carrying a small knife (legal in Maryland). In Ferguson, Missouri, a suburb of St. Louis, Michael Brown, an unarmed black eighteen-year-old, was shot in disputed circumstances by a white police officer, whom a grand jury subsequently cleared of potential charges. In Baltimore, by contrast, the local district attorney moved to indict the police implicated in these cities' deaths.

Michael Brown

Black Lives Matter movement

This cascade of events spurred the emergence of a national movement, **Black Lives Matter**, which demanded that police practices be changed and officers who used excessive force be held accountable. It gave public voice to the countless African-Americans who had experienced disrespect, harassment, or violence at the hands of police. The movement used social media and current technology to organize protests and disseminate videos of encounters between black persons and the police. The Black Lives Matter movement was less an articulation of specific policy demands than a broad claim to black humanity. In this sense, it had historical precedents in abolitionism, with its slogan "Am I Not a Man and a Brother?," and in "I Am a Man," the defiant claim of Memphis sanitation workers during their 1968 strike, where Martin Luther King Jr. was assassinated.

Heavily armed police confront a resident of Ferguson, Missouri, during demonstrations there.

In Ferguson, Missouri, Brown's death inspired weeks of sometimes violent street demonstrations. These led to the deployment of state police and National Guardsmen dressed in battle gear and armed with assault rifles and armored personnel carriers, as if equipped for a war zone overseas—a sign of how policing had become militarized since the 1960s. In Ferguson, investigations after the death of Michael Brown revealed that the almost entirely white police, city government, and local judiciary regularly preyed on black residents, seeing them not as citizens to be served and protected but as a source of revenue to balance the local budget. Blacks were hauled into court to pay fines for nonexistent driving violations, jaywalking, or even walking on the sidewalks too close to the street. Nationally, public reaction to the Black Lives Matter movement revealed a sharp divide between white and black Americans. In public opinion polls, over 80 percent of blacks but just 30 percent of whites agreed with the statement that blacks are victims of discriminatory treatment by the police.

Obama and the World

End of Iraq War

The most dramatic achievement of Obama's presidency in foreign affairs was fulfillment of his campaign promise to end American involvement in the Iraq War. At the end of 2011, the last American soldiers came home. Nearly 5,000 Americans and, according to the estimates of U.S. and Iraqi analysts, hundreds of thousands of Iraqis, most of them civilians, had died during this eight-year conflict. The war had cost the United States nearly $2 trillion, an almost unimaginable sum. Whether it would produce a stable, democratic Iraq remained to be seen.

At the same time, Obama continued many of the policies of the Bush administration. He dramatically increased the American troop presence in Afghanistan, while pledging to withdraw American forces by the end of 2014, although he failed to meet this deadline. Polls showed that a large majority of Americans felt the war was a mistake and wanted it to end.

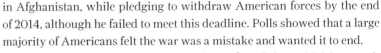

Like many of his predecessors, Obama found that criticizing presidential power from outside is one thing, dismantling it another. He reversed his previous promise to abolish the military tribunals Bush had established and to close the military prison at Guantánamo, Cuba. And in 2011 he signed a four-year extension of key provisions of the USA Patriot Act originally passed under Bush. In May 2011, to wide acclaim in the United States, Obama authorized an armed raid into Pakistan that resulted in the death of Osama bin Laden, who had been hiding there for years. And in 2011 Obama sent the air force to participate in a NATO campaign that assisted rebels who overthrew Libyan dictator Muammar Gadhafi. But a seemingly endless civil war followed, not the restoration of democracy. Obama did not seek congressional approval of the action.

Fighting terrorism

In 2014, Obama abandoned the half-century-old policy of isolating Cuba and moved to resume diplomatic relations with the island nation. The policy of isolation had long outlived its Cold War origins and had made the United States seem petty and vindictive in the eyes of Latin Americans. In the following year, the administration, in conjunction with the European Union, Russia, and China, worked out an arrangement with Iran to ensure that that nation's nuclear energy program was confined to peaceful purposes and did not lead to the manufacture of nuclear weapons. This was a remarkable achievement in view of the decades of hostility between the United States and Iran dating back to the hostage crisis of 1979–1981. Also in 2015, the United States played a major role in forging the Paris Agreement, which committed every country in the world to reduce emissions (notably from the burning of coal and oil) that contributed to global warming.

International diplomacy

Events overseas presented new challenges and opportunities for the Obama administration. To the surprise of almost everyone, beginning in 2011 popular revolts swept the Middle East. Uprisings brought millions of people into the streets, toppling long-serving dictators in Tunisia, Egypt, and Libya. Freedom emerged as the rallying cry of those challenging autocratic governments. "I'm in Tahrir Square," one demonstrator yelled into his cell phone while standing at the epicenter of the Egyptian revolution. "In freedom, in freedom, in freedom." Once again, the tension between the ideals of freedom and democracy and American strategic interests posed a difficult challenge for policymakers. After some hesitation, the United

President Barack Obama, Vice President Joe Biden, Secretary of State Hillary Clinton, and other members of Obama's national security team receiving an update on the mission against Osama bin Laden at the White House on May 1, 2011.

States sided with those seeking the ouster of Egyptian dictator Hosni Mubarak, a staunch American ally. It then stood on the sidelines throughout 2011 and 2012 as Egypt lurched from popular uprising to military rule to electoral victory by the Muslim Brotherhood, a previously illegal Islamic group, to a military coup in 2013, with the final outcome of the revolution always in doubt. When a military coup in 2013 ousted the elected president and instituted a regime even more repressive than Mubarak's, the Obama administration suspended shipments of military equipment to Egypt, but soon resumed them. In general, like his predecessors during the Cold War, Obama used "human rights" as a political weapon, condemning abuses by adversaries like China while remaining largely silent in the face of serious abuses by allies in the "war on terror" such as Pakistan, Ethiopia, and Saudi Arabia.

This photograph depicts a drone, an unmanned armed aircraft controlled electronically from the ground, sometimes from thousands of miles away. Drones have been widely used for U.S. air raids in Afghanistan, Syria, and other countries, targeting enemy forces and individuals accused of terrorism without endangering American pilots. Targets on the ground are often mistaken by those controlling the planes, leading to widespread civilian casualties.

In his second term, Obama faced a new crisis when the self-proclaimed Islamic State took control of parts of Iraq, Syria, and Libya. **ISIS**, as it was called, conducted campaigns of exceptional brutality, beheading prisoners of war and driving religious minorities out of territory it conquered. The videos of these acts posted by ISIS on social media horrified most of the world but also attracted recruits to the organization. ISIS also sponsored terror attacks outside the Middle East. In 2015 over 100 persons were killed in a series of coordinated attacks in Paris. A few weeks later, two followers of ISIS in the United States killed fourteen people in San Bernardino, California. By 2018, in the face of counterattacks by the United States and its allies, ISIS was on the defensive throughout the Middle East, having surrendered the territory it had occupied.

A cartoon in the magazine the *New Yorker* inspired by revelations that the National Security Agency has been spying on the phone conversations and e-mails of millions of Americans.

"Get me everything on everybody."

Another area in which Obama continued the policies initiated during the Bush administration's war on terror was governmental surveillance, both domestic and overseas. The extent of such activity became known in 2013 when **Edward Snowden**, a former employee of the National Security Agency, released documents online that detailed NSA programs that monitored virtually all telephone, instant messaging, and e-mail traffic in the United States, tracked the location of numerous American cell phones, and spied on the private communications of world leaders, including close allies of the United States such as Chancellor Angela Merkel of Germany and French president François Hollande. The government also secretly worked with major Internet and communications companies like AT&T and Verizon to gain access to the private data of their users. Of course, the overwhelming majority of the people subject to government surveillance had no connection to terrorism or to any crime at all. To avoid prosecution, Snowden took up residence in Russia. But his revelations rekindled the age-old debate over the balance between national security and Americans' civil liberties and offered another example of how, whichever party is in power, the balance always seems to shift in favor of security. In 2015, Congress approved a measure curtailing the government's sweeping surveillance of phone records. But much of the government's prying into Americans' communications continued.

The Republican Resurgence

In nearly all midterm elections in American history the party in power has lost seats in Congress. But Democrats faced more serious difficulties than usual in the midterm elections of 2010. Grassroots Republicans were energized by hostility to Obama's sweeping legislative enactments. The **Tea Party**, named for the Boston Tea Party of the 1770s and inspired by its opposition to taxation by a faraway government, mobilized grassroots opposition to the administration.

Grassroots support

With their opponents energized and their own supporters demoralized by the slow pace of economic recovery, Democrats suffered a severe reversal. Republicans swept to control of the House of Representatives and substantially reduced the Democratic majority in the Senate. The result was political gridlock that lasted for the remainder of Obama's presidency.

The immigration issue

Tea Party–inspired conservative gains at the state level in 2010 unleashed a rash of new legislation. Several states moved to curtail abortion rights. New conservative legislatures also took aim at undocumented immigrants. Alabama, which has no land border with a foreign country and a small population of immigrants, enacted the harshest measure, making it a crime for undocumented immigrants to apply for a job and for anyone to transport them, even to a church or hospital. During the contest for the Republican presidential nomination in early 2012, candidates vied with each other to demonstrate their determination to drive undocumented immigrants from the country. Oddly, all this took place at a time when undocumented immigration from Mexico, the largest source of undocumented workers, had ceased almost completely because of stricter controls at the border and the drying up of available jobs because of the recession. These measures associated the Republican Party with intense nativism.

The 2012 Campaign

Despite the continuing economic crisis, sociocultural issues played a major role in the campaign for the Republican presidential nomination in 2012, as candidates vied to win the support of the evangelical Christians who formed a major part of the party's base. The front-runner was Mitt Romney, the former governor of Massachusetts. But the party's powerful conservative wing disliked Romney because of his moderate record (as governor he had instituted a state health-care plan remarkably similar to Obama's 2010 legislation) and a distrust of his Mormon faith among many evangelical Christians.

Mitt Romney

Eventually, using his personal fortune to outspend his rivals by an enormous amount, Romney emerged as the Republican candidate, the first Mormon to win a major party's nomination—a significant moment in the history of religious toleration in the United States. He chose as his running mate Congressman Paul D. Ryan of Wisconsin, a favorite of the Tea Party and a Roman Catholic. For the first time in its history, the Republican Party's ticket did not contain a traditional Protestant.

President Obama began the 2012 campaign with numerous liabilities. The enthusiasm that greeted his election had long since faded as the worst economic slump since the Great Depression dragged on, and voters became fed up with both the president and Congress because of the intensity of partisanship and legislative gridlock. The war in Afghanistan was increasingly unpopular, and his signature health-care law was under ferocious assault by Republicans.

Obama's re-election

Nonetheless, after a heated campaign, Obama emerged victorious, winning 332 electoral votes to Romney's 206, and 51 percent of the popular vote to his opponent's 47 percent. At the same time, while Democrats gained a few seats in the House and Senate, the balance of power in Washington remained unchanged. This set the stage for continued partisan infighting and political gridlock during Obama's second term.

Continued party tensions

Obama's victory stemmed from many causes, including an extremely efficient get-out-the-vote organization on election day and Romney's weaknesses as a campaigner. Romney never managed to shed the image of a millionaire who used loopholes to avoid paying taxes (his federal tax rate of 14 percent was lower than that of most working-class Americans). Many people believed he held ordinary people in contempt, particularly after he was videotaped making an off-the-cuff remark that 47 percent of the people would not vote for him because they were "victims" dependent on government payments like Medicare and Social Security. But more important, as in 2008, the result reflected the new diversity of the American population in the twenty-first century. Romney won 60 percent of the white vote, which in previous elections would have guaranteed victory. But Obama carried over 90 percent of the black vote and over 70 percent of Asians and Hispanics.

Twenty-first century diversity

The 2012 election reflected the new diversity in other ways as well. Hawaii elected Tulsi Gabbard, the first Hindu to serve in the House of Representatives, and the first Buddhist, Mazie K. Hirono, to the Senate. But perhaps the most striking feature of the election was the unprecedented amount of money spent on the campaign. In 2010, in *Citizens United v. Federal Elections Commission*, the conservative majority on the Supreme Court had overturned federal restrictions on political contributions by corporations. At the same time, political action committees were allowed to spend as much money as they wished supporting or denigrating candidates for office so long as they did not coordinate their activities with the candidates' campaigns. Meanwhile, the Romney and Obama campaigns themselves raised and spent hundreds of millions of dollars from individual donors. All this resulted in an election that cost, for presidential and congressional races combined, some $6 billion.

Campaign finance

PRESIDENT TRUMP

The Candidates in 2016

As the election year 2016 began, all signs pointed to a victory for Hillary Clinton. Most Democrats seemed to feel that she deserved the nomination that Obama had wrested from her eight years earlier. She had long political experience as a senator and secretary of state, and many women were galvanized by the prospect of the nation's first female president.

Clinton, however, faced a surprisingly robust challenge for the nomination from Senator Bernie Sanders of Vermont, a self-proclaimed "democratic socialist." By this he meant strengthening and expanding the regulatory policies and social safety net of the New Deal and Great Society through such measures as universal health insurance and limits on corporations' political spending. But beyond specific issues, Sanders spoke to widespread discontent with a society in which those who had plunged the country into economic crisis walked away scot-free while taxpayers were left to pick up the pieces. Adopting themes enunciated by the Occupy Wall Street movement, Sanders accused Clinton of being part of a political establishment whose policies had widened the gap between the 1 percent at the top of the American economy and everyone else. Like Eugene McCarthy in 1968, Sanders inspired a small army of young people to campaign for him as a challenge to the political and economic status quo.

Bernie Sanders

One of the remarkable accomplishments of his campaign was to put the word "socialism"—long banished because of the Cold War—back into the vocabulary of American politics.

Hillary Clinton at a campaign rally in North Carolina a few days before the 2016 election.

With the united support of the Democratic party establishment, Clinton secured the nomination. Meanwhile, Republicans fractured. Seventeen candidates, including governors, senators, and business leaders, presented themselves. Assuming that Donald Trump, a New York real estate developer and television celebrity, could never be nominated, they tended to ignore him while turning their fire on each other. The result was to weaken each conventional candidate without denting Trump. He shocked the country and the world by winning the Republican nomination.

The Election of Trump

Trump's campaign played on both racial and gender resentments spawned by the growing diversity of American society and the rapid changes in gender roles, as well as the widespread sense, especially in areas suffering from the decline of manufacturing, that millions of ordinary Americans had been left behind by the recovery from the Great Recession.

"Make America Great Again"

Trump did not speak much about freedom. He preferred to invoke slogans suggesting military and economic power, such as Make America Great Again, and America First. He explicitly rejected the idea that the United States should seek to remake other countries in its own image, or pay attention to their behavior concerning human rights. He cast doubt on traditional alliances such as NATO. Trump's policies marked a significant change in the national sense of purpose, inspired, in part, by weariness with the seemingly endless wars in Iraq and Afghanistan. No longer would the United States see itself as a global policeman with a mission to uphold freedom across the globe. It would now be one nation—a powerful one to be sure—among many, each pursuing national self-interest. Spreading ideals such as freedom and democracy had no place in his vision of the world.

Trump's political outlook had a strong racial component. In 1989, he had taken out newspaper ads to demand the death penalty for a group

Donald Trump at a rally in West Virginia during his campaign for the 2016 Republican presidential nomination. He wears a hard hat as part of his appeal for support from the state's coal miners and, more broadly, blue-collar workers suffering from the impact of deindustrialization.

of black and Latino youths accused of the rape of a female jogger. DNA evidence later established that they did not commit the crime, but Trump continued to insist on their guilt. He was a major spokesman for the "birther" movement, which claimed that Obama had been born in Africa and was ineligible to serve as president. (Actually, Obama's birthplace was Hawaii.) When he announced his candidacy, Trump condemned immigrants from Mexico as murderers and rapists and galvanized supporters by promising to build a wall along the long border with Mexico to stop people from entering the country.

Trump ran an unusual campaign. He did not have a conventional campaign organization, spent little on television ads, and did not seek newspaper endorsements. He spread his views via social media and through large rallies where he whipped his supporters into a frenzy with chants such as "Build That Wall" and "Lock Her Up"—the latter a reference to charges that as secretary of state, Hillary Clinton had illegally used a private server for email. While presidential campaigns have always included scurrilous charges, never before had a major party candidate claimed that his predecessor was not an American citizen, or promised to jail his opponent. Allegations that the three-times-married Trump had conducted numerous affairs, and the release of a video that showed him making lewd remarks about women and boasting about sexually harassing them, which would have destroyed the prospects of a more conventional candidate, did little to dent his support.

Anxiety over globalization and immigration

Despite her long political experience, Clinton failed to address effectively widespread anxiety about the economic and cultural effects of globalization and large-scale immigration. Trump understood that these were the issues of most concern to voters, not his personal foibles and prejudices. He rode this insight to the White House. Trump appealed successfully to nostalgia for a time when people of color and women knew their "place" and American manufacturing dominated the world economy.

Trump was an unusual candidate, but he did not come out of nowhere. The Tea Party had recently shown that hostility to immigrants could pay electoral dividends. Ross Perot in 1992 had run as a businessman whose lack of political experience was a plus, and had denounced free trade agreements for costing millions of Americans their jobs. George Wallace

In the summer of 2016, a group of activists placed an ice sculpture, *The American Dream*, near the Republican and Democratic national conventions. During the gatherings, the sculpture melted away, symbolizing the widespread sense of declining economic opportunity.

in 1968 and 1972 had appealed to white workers' resentments over racial and economic change, and Richard Nixon's "southern strategy" had won many Wallace voters to the Republican fold.

Trump realized that social media had transformed American politics, allowing him to communicate inexpensively with millions of followers via Facebook and, especially, Twitter. He also understood that on social media, insults, bragging, and even expressions of hatred garnered the most attention. Clinton issued long documents outlining her policies on various issues. But at a time when many Americans were dissatisfied with the way the country was headed, political experience such as that possessed by Clinton turned out to be an electoral liability. Like Obama in 2008, Trump promised change to a country unhappy with the status quo. Clinton seemed to represent more of the same.

Sharp divisions in America

Throughout 2018, public opinion polls showed Clinton almost certain to be elected. But Trump triumphed, in possibly the biggest upset in American political history. To be sure, he trailed Clinton by around 3 million popular votes. But by carrying key "swing" states such as Ohio and Florida and by winning Pennsylvania, Michigan, and Wisconsin, where disgruntled white working-class voters who had supported Obama either stayed home or shifted to the Republicans, he gained victory in the electoral college. Overall, the results revealed a sharp divide between rural and small-town America, predominantly white in population and suffering economic decline, which Trump carried with large majorities, and economically thriving, multicultural large metropolitan areas, which went overwhelmingly for Clinton. Trump won 58 percent of white voters but only one-third of Hispanics and 8 percent of blacks. Clinton carried 54 percent of women voters, but in a humiliating rebuff, a majority of white women voted for Trump.

WHO IS AN AMERICAN?

From Khizr Khan, Speech at the Democratic National Convention (2016)

Donald Trump's incessant attacks on immigrants and association of Muslims with terrorism appealed to many Americans but alienated many others. In a powerful speech at the Democratic convention that nominated Hillary Clinton, with his wife standing at his side, the Pakistani-American father of an American soldier killed during the Iraq War responded to Trump's nativist pronouncements. The Khans had moved to the United States in 1980; Khizr Khan graduated from Harvard Law School in 1986, the same year the couple became American citizens.

First, our thoughts and prayers are with our veterans and those who serve today. Tonight, we are honored to stand here as the parents of Capt. Humayun Khan, and as patriotic American Muslims with undivided loyalty to our country.

Like many immigrants, we came to this country empty-handed. We believed in American democracy—that with hard work and the goodness of this country, we could share in and contribute to its blessings. We were blessed to raise our three sons in a nation where they were free to be themselves and follow their dreams. Our son, Humayun, had dreams of being a military lawyer. But he put those dreams aside the day he sacrificed his life to save his fellow soldiers. . . .

If it was up to Donald Trump, he never would have been in America. Donald Trump consistently smears the character of Muslims. He disrespects other minorities—women, judges, even his own party leadership. He vows to build walls and ban us from this country.

Donald Trump . . . let me ask you: Have you even read the U.S. Constitution? I will gladly lend you my copy. In this document, look for the words "liberty" and "equal protection of law." Have you ever been to Arlington Cemetery? Go look at the graves of the brave patriots who died defending America—you will see all faiths, genders, and ethnicities.

We can't solve our problems by building walls and sowing division. We are stronger together.

QUESTIONS

1. *Why does Khan refer to the U.S. Constitution?*
2. *What evidence does he offer of the patriotism of immigrants?*

Trump's victory was part of a global voter revolt against a political establishment many people blamed for job losses, stagnant wages, and large-scale immigration, all elements of globalization. Throughout the world, strongmen who showed a willingness to dispense with democratic norms and stir up hatreds rooted in national or tribal identity consolidated their authority. Whether elected, chosen by a ruling party, or seizing power in a coup d'état, they enjoyed wide popularity—rulers such as Abdel Fattah el-Sisi in Egypt, Vladimir Putin in Russia, Viktor Orban in Hungary, and Rodrigo Duterte in the Philippines. Trump expressed admiration for all these men. In disorienting times, it seemed, many people wanted strong authority figures at the helm of their nation and a secure sense of belonging and national identity.

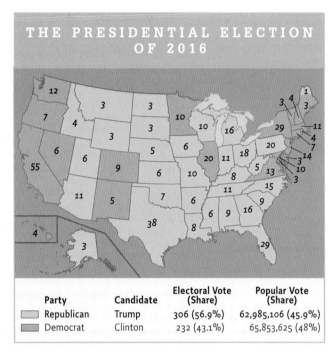

THE PRESIDENTIAL ELECTION OF 2016

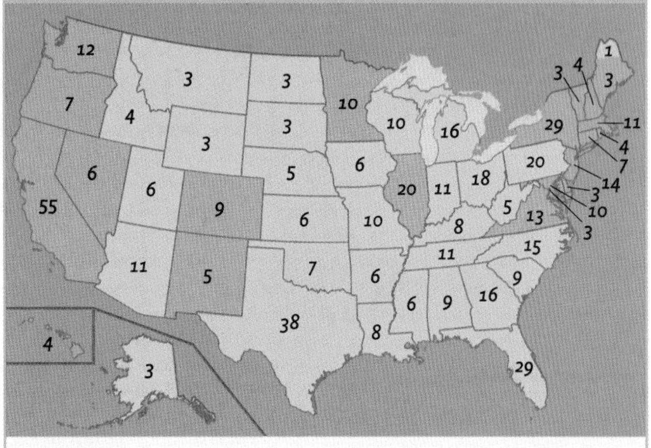

Party	Candidate	Electoral Vote (Share)	Popular Vote (Share)
Republican	Trump	306 (56.9%)	62,985,106 (45.9%)
Democrat	Clinton	232 (43.1%)	65,853,625 (48%)

Trump in Office

Despite his promise to upend the political system, many of Trump's policies as president, including increased military spending, opposition to women's reproductive rights, deregulation of the economy, and opposition to measures to protect the environment, were standard conservative Republican fare. He and the Republican majority in Congress made strenuous attempts to repeal the Affordable Care Act (Obamacare), but, with nothing to put in its place, their efforts failed. Trump's main legislative achievement during his first two years in office was a massive tax cut. In keeping with the "supply-side" economic outlook embraced by his party since Ronald Reagan's presidency, most of the benefits were directed toward corporations and the wealthiest Americans, on the theory that they would invest the money they saved in economically productive activities and higher wages.

The economy

Given a boost by the tax cuts, the economic recovery of the Obama administration continued, with unemployment falling to under 4 percent during 2018. But many corporations used their tax windfall not for productive purposes but to buy back their own stock, enriching investors and corporate executives. Wage increases continued to lag behind inflation so that most Americans saw no economic gain. The typical worker in 2018 earned $44,500 a year, virtually the same as in 1979 when adjusted for inflation. Nearly 80 percent lived paycheck to paycheck, with little economic cushion in case of an emergency. With 560,000 employees, Amazon, the online company that sold every conceivable product, had become, after Wal-Mart, the second largest employer in the United States. Most were low-wage men and women who worked in the company's giant warehouses. Their median pay was $28,000 per year.

Raising traiffs

Trump did, however, break with Republican free trade orthodoxy by raising tariffs on goods imported from China, Canada, other countries, and the European Union in the hope of promoting American manufacturing. He negotiated a few changes in NAFTA, the free trade agreement with Canada and Mexico that Clinton had worked out in the 1990s. Those with a sense of history noted that he was returning to the Republican Party's protectionist economic outlook of the late nineteenth and early twentieth centuries. The results of what he called his "trade war" remained to be seen.

In both foreign and domestic affairs, Trump seemed determined to erase as much of Obama's legacy as possible. He withdrew the United States from the multinational agreement that limited Iran's ability to develop nuclear weapons, preferring to pressure that country with economic sanctions and threats of war. Despite his party's majorities in both houses of Congress, Trump relied on executive orders, not legislation, to erase many of Obama's initiatives, from banking regulations that sought to prevent a repeat of the 2008 financial crisis to rules protecting workers from unsafe conditions, and communities from air and water pollution. These and other regulations, Trump declared, were impediments to economic growth.

Early in Trump's presidency, evidence accumulated that the Russian government had interfered in the 2016 election by spreading disinformation on social media and hacking into the email servers of the Democratic National Committee. Russian president Putin seems to have promoted Trump's campaign in the hope that Trump would remove some of the economic sanctions the United States and other countries had instituted after Russia invaded and annexed Crimea, a part of the nation of Ukraine. The Justice Department appointed a special prosecutor, Robert Mueller, to determine whether illegal collusion had occurred between Trump's campaign and Russian officials. As time went on, Mueller expanded his investigation to include other forms of campaign malfeasance, such as secret payments shortly before the election that purchased the silence of two women who claimed to have had affairs with Trump. A number of persons close to the president, including Paul Manafort, his campaign manager; his personal lawyer Michael Cohen; and Michael Flynn, his national security adviser, pleaded guilty to crimes such as tax evasion and lying to the FBI, or were convicted of doing so. Mueller's final report, however, found no evidence that Trump had personally conspired with the Russians.

Mueller investigation

Trump and Immigration

President Trump's travel ban barring persons from several Muslim-majority countries from entering the United States led to widespread protests, in which images of the Statue of Liberty were prominently displayed. This one was in Seattle on January 20, 2018.

As president, Trump kept up his rhetorical attacks on Mexicans, Muslims, and immigrants more generally, but during 2017 and 2018, when his party controlled both houses of Congress, failed to convince lawmakers to authorize the building of his border wall, or to legislate at all on immigration. Trump had demanded a complete "shutdown" of Muslim immigration to the United States during the campaign, and one of his first acts as president was to ban travel to the United States from a number of Muslim-majority countries. Federal courts blocked the ban as a form of religious discrimination; eventually, the Supreme Court allowed a watered-down version to go into effect. In the summer of 2018, the administration began removing young children from the custody of parents who had come to the southern border with their families seeking asylum in the United States. The pictures of young children, even toddlers, separated from their parents and held in cage-like structures on abandoned army bases caused an uproar, and a judge ordered the administration to reunite the families.

Misinformation abounded in the continuing debate over immigration. Trump repeatedly blamed undocumented immigrants for urban crime, even though their crime rate, and that of newcomers legally in the United States, was far lower than that of native-born Americans. About 12 percent of the country's population in 2018 was born abroad, but when asked about the number in polls, Americans gave an average response of 35 percent.

At the end of 2018, the Trump administration inspired an international uproar when it began separating families seeking to enter the United States from Mexico, holding the children in cage-like structures. The courts ordered that the families be reunited.

Trump and the Environment

One area in which Trump turned his back not only on Obama's policies but also on the rest of the world was his administration's response to the problem of global warming—a slow rise in the earth's temperature that scientists warn could have disastrous effects on the climate and human life more broadly. Global warming is caused when carbon dioxide released by burning fossil fuels such as oil and coal remains in the upper atmosphere, trapping

A work by the artist Dennis Hallinan offers a warning about climate change, one of whose consequences in coming decades will be a rise in sea levels, flooding many low-lying coastal communities.

heat reflected from the earth. Evidence of this development surfaced in the 1980s and 1990s, when scientists studying layers of ice in Greenland concluded that the earth's temperature had risen significantly during the past century.

Today, most scientists consider global warming a serious situation. Climate change threatens to disrupt long-established patterns of agriculture and lead to a large expansion of the size of the world's deserts. The melting of glaciers and polar ice caps because of rising temperatures will eventually raise ocean levels, flooding coastal cities. Global warming exacerbates the destructiveness of hurricanes, wildfires, and other natural disasters. But while this was not originally a partisan issue, during the 1990s more and more Republicans came to reject the scientific consensus that human activity causes climate change, and they opposed efforts to promote sources of energy—solar and wind power, for example—that would reduce dependency on oil and coal.

In 2017, Trump withdrew from the **Paris Agreement** on climate change of 2015, making the United States the only country in the world not to commit itself to take steps to reduce emissions that cause climate change. He promised to revive the American coal industry, which was suffering a long decline because of competition from less expensive natural gas as well as from worries about coal's effects on the climate, by weakening restrictions on how much pollution coal-burning power plants spewed into the air. Trump appointed Scott Pruitt of Oklahoma, a close ally of the oil industry who considered global warming a hoax, to head the Environmental Protection Agency. The agency proposed to weaken fuel efficiency standards for automobiles. This would result in cars burning more gasoline and producing more emissions, harming the environment but further enriching oil companies. Late in 2018, government scientists issued a report predicting dire consequences—from widespread flooding to ever more intense storms and wildfires and serious crop failures—if climate change is not addressed. But President Trump declared, "I don't believe it," and the administration continued its efforts to reduce regulations aimed at combating global warming.

Consequences of climate change

A Polarized Nation

Trump's unprecedented conduct as a candidate continued in office. He held virtually no press conferences (and, indeed, denounced the mainstream media as "enemies of the people" who spread "fake news"). Instead, he issued a daily barrage of tweets that promoted his ideas and insulted political opponents, critics, and even political allies such as his attorney general Jeff Sessions. Often, his tweets had a racial component. He declared basketball great LeBron James and Maxine Waters, a black member of Congress, lacking in intelligence. The tone set by the president helped to produce a coarsening of public discourse, empowering Trump supporters young and old to vent their prejudices on social media, in schools and colleges, and at political rallies.

Trump's presidency exacerbated the intense polarization that had been a feature of politics since Clinton's presidency. His supporters, who represented, according to polls, around 40 percent of Americans, remained steadfastly loyal. Those who disliked Trump's policies or were offended by his behavior were galvanized to express their opposition. Many people were deeply offended by his derogatory remarks about women. On the day after his inauguration, a **Women's March** on Washington brought hundreds of thousands of people to the nation's capital to express their support for women's rights, immigration reform, racial equality, and protection of the environment.

On January 21, 2017, the day after the inauguration of President Trump, over 3 million people participated in Women's Marches throughout the country, including one that brought half a million to the nation's capital. They called for protection of women's and immigrant rights, but also protested the crude language Trump employed about women and his boasts about committing acts of sexual harassment.

Another expression of women's activism, the **Me Too movement,** brought to light evidence of rampant sexual harassment by entertainment moguls, business leaders, public officials, and other powerful men. Prominent women, including members of Congress and leading actresses, and ordinary ones publicized their experiences in workplaces, universities, and social gatherings, and demanded the punishment of offenders. Charges of sexual misconduct led to the firing or resignation of figures as diverse as Minnesota senator Al Franken, TV personality Charlie Rose, and movie producer Harvey Weinstein.

The Elections of 2018

With the economic recovery that had begun under Obama still underway and unemployment at a historic low, a conventional politician would have emphasized economic issues in the midterm elections of 2018. Not Trump. In the last weeks of the campaign he traveled the country, holding rallies where he whipped up fear of immigrants, warning of a coming "invasion" of people bringing crime, disease, and terrorism. These appeals consolidated his political base but alienated more moderate voters. With Democrats, and many independents, galvanized by opposition to Trump's policies and behavior, the elections of 2018 in part reversed the verdict of two years earlier. Democrats replaced Republicans in forty seats in the House of Representatives, regaining control of that body. Trump's policies and demeaning comments regarding women produced a giant gender gap in voting. Women supported Democratic candidates by 59 to 40 percent. The gap was even wider among young voters; those below age thirty voted Democratic by 35 percentage points. On the other hand, Republicans increased their majority in the Senate.

Electoral divides

The 2018 elections revealed other deep divides—between rural areas, strongly Republican, and cities and suburbs dominated by Democrats; and between Republicans' almost entirely white and largely male support and the diversity of Democrats. Republicans won 54 percent of white voters but only 29 percent of Hispanics and 9 percent of blacks. These patterns were reflected in the new House of Representatives. Over 100 women were elected to the body, the most in American history. Of the forty-two new women members, thirty-eight were Democrats; of twenty-three new people of color elected to Congress, only one was a Republican. The new members of Congress included the first two Native American women (Sharice Davids of Kansas and Deb Haaland of New Mexico, both Democrats) and the first two Muslim women (Ilhan Omar of Minnesota and Rashida Tlaib of Michigan, also Democrats). The year 2018 also saw the election of the first openly gay governor, Democrat Jared Polis of Colorado.

Representation in Congress

Thus, two visions of America clashed, one based on exclusion and whiteness, the other welcoming and diverse. Both were deeply rooted in the American experience.

FREEDOM IN THE TWENTY-FIRST CENTURY

The century that ended in 2000 witnessed vast human progress and unimaginable human tragedy. It saw the decolonization of Asia and Africa, the emergence of women into full citizenship in most parts of the world, and amazing advances in science, medicine, and technology. Thanks to the spread of new products, available at ever-cheaper prices, it brought more improvement in the daily conditions of life to more human beings than any other century in history. But the twentieth century also witnessed the death of uncounted millions in wars and genocides and the widespread degradation of the natural environment, the underside of progress.

Exceptional America

America from 1900 to 2013

In the early twenty-first century, people in the United States lived longer and healthier lives compared with previous generations, and they enjoyed a level of material comfort unimagined a century before. In

1900, the typical American had no indoor plumbing, had no telephone or car, and had not graduated from high school. As late as 1940, one-third of American households did not have running water. In 2017, health conditions had improved so much that the average life expectancy for men had risen to seventy-seven and for women to eighty-one (from forty-six and forty-eight in 1900). On the other hand, poverty, income inequality, and infant mortality in the United States considerably exceeded that of other economically advanced countries, and fewer than 10 percent of workers in private firms belonged to unions, a figure not seen since the nineteenth century.

A lock-down drill in Belle Plaine, Minnesota, trains an eighth-grade class how to respond in the event of a school shooting.

Many of the changes affecting American life have taken place in all economically advanced societies. In other ways, however, the United States at the dawn of the twenty-first century differed sharply from other developed countries. Prevailing ideas of freedom in the United States seemed more attuned to individual advancement than to broad social welfare. The United States was a far more religious country. Sixty percent of Americans agreed with the statement, "Religion plays a very important part in my life," whereas the comparable figure was 32 percent in Britain, 26 percent in Italy, and only 11 percent in France.

Gun violence

Other forms of **American exceptionalism** had a darker side. Among advanced countries, the United States has by far the highest rate of murder using guns. Over 40 percent of the world's guns in private hands, from pistols to hunting weapons to assault rifles, are owned in the United States. Americans are far more likely to be killed by guns than are residents of other developed countries. In 2012, there were 9,146 murders with guns in the United States, as opposed to 158 in Germany, 173 in Canada, and 11 in Japan. The year 2017 saw nearly 40,000 deaths from firearms in the country, including murders, suicides, and accidents, the highest number in half a century. Only fifty-eight Americans died from acts classified as terrorism.

Indeed, in the last years of the twentieth century and the beginning of the twenty-first, the United States was the scene of a horrifying number of mass murders, often committed at schools. In 1999, two students killed twelve students and a teacher at Columbine High School in Colorado. In 2007, a student at Virginia Tech University shot and killed thirty-two people. Five years later, a lone gunman killed twenty children aged five and six and seven adults at Sandy Hook Elementary School in Newtown, Connecticut. In the 1950s, schools across the country had conducted drills to enable students to survive a nuclear attack. Now they trained pupils in seeking shelter if a gunman entered the building. There were also mass killings at a movie theater in Aurora, Colorado, and at the Washington Navy Yard. In 2015, a gunman influenced by racist Internet sites murdered nine black participants in a Bible study group, including the minister, at Emanuel African Methodist Episcopal Church in Charleston, South Carolina. Around sixty people were killed by a gunman firing from a hotel window on a crowd gathered for a country and western music festival in Las Vegas in November 2017. Other countries also experienced instances of mass violence, but not with the frequency of the United States.

March for Our Lives

In March 2018, hundreds of thousands of young people took part in demonstrations across the country for gun control, under the slogan **March for Our Lives**. The movement was organized by students at a high school in Parkland, Florida, after a shooting there that left seventeen pupils and teachers dead. But the strong commitment of many Americans to the Second Amendment's guarantee of the right to bear arms, coupled with the remarkable power of the National Rifle Association, one of the country's most influential lobbies, ensured that no new regulations were enacted.

Lag in social rights

The United States continued to lag behind other countries in providing social rights to its citizens. In Europe, workers are guaranteed by law a paid vacation each year and a number of paid sick days. American employers are not required to offer either to their workers. Only three countries in the world have no national provision for paid maternity leave after a woman gives birth to a child: Papua New Guinea, Suriname, and the United States. And as noted in the previous chapter, the United States has by far the world's highest rate of imprisonment.

It was an irony of early-twenty-first-century life that Americans enjoyed more personal freedom than ever before but less of what earlier generations called "industrial freedom." The sustained recovery from the recession of the early 1990s did not entirely relieve a widespread sense of economic insecurity. Globalization—which treated workers at home and abroad as interchangeable factors of production, capable of being uprooted or dismissed without warning—seemed to render individual and even national sovereignty all but meaningless. Because economic liberty has long been associated with economic security, and rights have historically been linked to democratic participation and membership in a nation-state, these processes had ominous implications for traditional understandings of freedom. It remained to be seen whether a conception of freedom grounded in access to the consumer marketplace and the glorification of individual self-fulfillment unrestrained by government, social citizenship, or a common public culture could provide an adequate way to comprehend the world of the twenty-first century.

Battles over History

In a politically polarized nation, history itself has become a battleground. Debates proliferate over the fate of public monuments to the Confederacy and its leaders. Some see these statues as harmless expressions of southern civic heritage; to others, they represent the glorification of slavery and racism.

Some statues have recently been taken down, including those of Confederate president Jefferson Davis at the University of Texas and Chief Justice Roger B. Taney, author of the infamous Dred Scott decision, in Baltimore. New Orleans mayor Mitch Landrieu ordered four removed from public property—statues of Davis, Confederate generals P. G. T. Beauregard and Robert E. Lee, and a monument to the Battle of Liberty Place of 1874, when the White League attempted to violently overthrow Louisiana's biracial Reconstruction government. The inscription on this monument celebrated the league's insurrection as an effort to restore "white supremacy." Landrieu explained his city's decision: "In the second decade of the 21st century, asking African Americans—or anyone else—to drive by property that they own; occupied by reverential statues of men who fought to destroy the country and deny that person's humanity seems perverse and absurd."

The monuments controversy took a deadly turn in August 2017, when a group of white supremacists and neo-Nazis marched in Charlottesville, Virginia, chanting anti-Semitic and racist slogans, to demand that a statue of Robert E. Lee remain in place. They were confronted by opposing demonstrators. Violent clashes ensued, leading to the death of a woman mowed down when a marcher ran his car into the anti-racist crowd. To the dismay of many Americans, including leaders of his own party, President Trump refused to apportion blame, insisting that there were "very fine people" on both sides of the confrontation. He also sent out a tweet lamenting the removal of Confederate statues, claiming such actions tear apart "the history and culture of our great country."

Inadvertently, the president had raised the perennial question, Who is an American? "Our" history and culture are far more complex and diverse than he appeared to realize. Existing monuments and statues, however, mostly celebrate only one piece of the American story. There are innumerable statues of Confederate generals, for example, but virtually none of black Civil War soldiers or leaders of Reconstruction. A step toward a more inclusive public presentation of history came in 2018 with the opening of the National Memorial for Peace and Justice and Legacy Museum in Montgomery, Alabama. This site commemorates the over 4,000 victims of lynching between 1880 and the 1950s. They, too, are part of "our" history.

In 2017 the artist Hank William Thomas and photographer Emily Shur reimagined Norman Rockwell's famous 1943 painting *Freedom from Want* (see Chapter 22) to depict today's more diverse American society. The work also brings to mind the post–Civil War engraving *Uncle Sam's Thanksgiving Dinner* (Chapter 15).

Neo-Nazis and white supremacists marching through the campus of the University of Virginia in August 2017 to protest plans to remove a statue of Confederate general Robert E. Lee. A violent altercation with counterdemonstrators followed.

Learning from History

Across the globe, debates are taking place about how public monuments should represent the darker aspects of countries' histories. This sculpture, *Sin Titolo* (Without Title) by Robert Aizenberg, is part of Remembrance Park in Buenos Aires, which commemorates the thousands of Argentines who "disappeared" (almost all of them murdered) at the hands of the military government that ruled the country in the 1970s and early 1980s. The three figures represent the kidnapped children of Aizenberg's partner. The voids remind us of their absence but the silhouettes perpetuate their memory.

"The owl of Minerva takes flight at dusk." Minerva was the Roman goddess of wisdom, and this saying suggests that the meaning of events only becomes clear once they are over.

As of the end of 2018, the world seemed far more unstable than anyone could have predicted when the Cold War ended. The future of Iraq, Afghanistan, and indeed the entire Middle East remained uncertain. No settlement of the long-standing conflict between Israel and its Arab neighbors seemed in sight.

Other regions of the world also presented daunting problems for American policymakers. China's rapidly growing economic power posed a challenge to American predominance. Relations with Russia, which was supporting a separatist movement in eastern Ukraine, were at their lowest point since the end of the Cold War even though President Trump made a point of his admiration for Russian president Putin.

No one could predict how any of these crises, or others yet unimagined, would be resolved.

What *is* clear is that as in the past, freedom is central to Americans' sense of themselves as individuals and as a nation. Americans continue to debate contemporary issues in a political landscape shaped by ideas of freedom. Indeed, freedom remains, as it has always been, an evolving concept, its definition open to disagreement, its boundaries never fixed or final. Freedom is neither self-enforcing nor self-correcting. It cannot be taken for granted, and its preservation requires eternal vigilance, especially in times of crisis.

More than half a century ago, the African-American poet Langston Hughes urged Americans both to celebrate the freedoms they enjoy and to remember that freedom has always been incomplete:

There are words like *Freedom*
Sweet and wonderful to say.
On my heartstrings freedom sings
All day everyday.

There are words like *Liberty*
That almost make me cry.
If you had known what I know
You would know why.

Seeking the lessons of history: a young visitor at the Civil Rights Memorial in Montgomery, Alabama.

CHAPTER REVIEW AND ONLINE RESOURCES

REVIEW QUESTIONS

1. *What were the political and social effects of Hurricane Katrina? Which were lasting?*
2. *In what ways did the Obama administration diverge from the policies of other recent administrations? In what ways was it similar?*
3. *How did the 2012 election reveal changes in American political and social practices? How did it represent continuities?*
4. *What is meant by American exceptionalism? In what ways is the United States different from the rest of the world, and how is it similar?*
5. *What did Obama's and Trump's presidential campaigns have in common? In what ways did Trump run an unusual presidential campaign?*
6. *How was Trump's victory part of a larger global voter revolt against the political establishment?*
7. *Describe the basic events of the investigation into the Russian government's interference in the 2016 election.*
8. *What are some of the consequences of Trump's withdrawal from the 2015 Paris Agreement on climate change?*
9. *What are some similarities and differences between the Black Lives Matter movement and the Me Too movement?*
10. *How did the elections of 2018 reflect a divided America?*
11. *How did national debates over Confederate monuments illuminate the complexity of representing history? How did they once again raise the question of who is an American?*

KEY TERMS

Hurricane Katrina (p. 882)
Obergefell v. Hodges (p. 886)
Great Recession (p. 888)
Sonia Sotomayor (p. 893)
Occupy Wall Street (p. 898)
Black Lives Matter (p. 900)
ISIS (p. 903)
Edward Snowden (p. 903)
Tea Party (p. 904)
Paris Agreement (p.914)
Women's March (p.915)
Me Too movement (p.915)
American exceptionalism (p. 917)
March for Our Lives (p. 918)

Go to INQUIZITIVE

To see what you know—and learn what you've missed—with personalized feedback along the way.

Visit the ***Give Me Liberty!* Student Site** for primary source documents and images, interactive maps, author videos featuring Eric Foner, and more.

APPENDIX

THE DECLARATION OF INDEPENDENCE (1776)

When in the course of human events, it becomes necessary for one people to dissolve the political bands which have connected them with another, and to assume among the Powers of the earth, the separate and equal station to which the Laws of Nature and of Nature's God entitle them, a decent respect to the opinions of mankind requires that they should declare the causes which impel them to the separation.

We hold these truths to be self-evident, that all men are created equal, that they are endowed by their Creator with certain unalienable rights, that among these are Life, Liberty, and the pursuit of Happiness. That to secure these rights, Governments are instituted among Men, deriving their just powers from the consent of the governed. That whenever any Form of Government becomes destructive of these ends, it is the Right of the People to alter or to abolish it, and to institute new Government, laying its foundation on such principles and organizing its powers in such form, as to them shall seem most likely to effect their Safety and Happiness. Prudence, indeed, will dictate that Governments long established should not be changed for light and transient causes; and accordingly all experience hath shown, that mankind are more disposed to suffer, while evils are sufferable, than to right themselves by abolishing the forms to which they are accustomed. But when a long train of abuses and usurpations, pursuing invariably the same Object evinces a design to reduce them under absolute Despotism, it is their right, it is their duty, to throw off such Government, and to provide new Guards for their future security.—Such has been the patient sufferance of these Colonies; and such is now the necessity which constrains them to alter their former Systems of Government. The history of the present King of Great Britain is a history of repeated injuries and usurpations, all having in direct object the establishment of an absolute Tyranny over these States. To prove this, let Facts be submitted to a candid world.

He has refused his Assent to Laws, the most wholesome and necessary for the public good.

He has forbidden his Governors to pass Laws of immediate and pressing importance, unless suspended in their operation till his Assent should be obtained; and when so suspended, he has utterly neglected to attend to them.

He has refused to pass other Laws for the accommodation of large districts of people, unless those people would relinquish the right of Representation in the Legislature, a right inestimable to them and formidable to tyrants only.

He has called together legislative bodies at places unusual, uncomfortable, and distant from the depository of their public Records, for the sole purpose of fatiguing them into compliance with his measures.

He has dissolved Representative Houses repeatedly, for opposing with manly firmness his invasions on the rights of the people.

He has refused for a long time, after such dissolutions, to cause others to be elected; whereby the Legislative powers, incapable of Annihilation, have returned to the People at large for their exercise; the State remaining in the mean time exposed to all dangers of invasion from without, and convulsions within.

He has endeavoured to prevent the population of these States; for that purpose obstructing the Laws of Naturalization of Foreigners; refusing to pass others to encourage their migrations hither, and raising the conditions of new Appropriations of Lands.

He has obstructed the Administration of Justice, by refusing his Assent to Laws for establishing Judiciary powers.

He has made Judges dependent on his Will alone, for the tenure of their offices, and the amount and payment of their salaries.

He has erected a multitude of New Offices, and sent hither swarms of Officers to harass our People, and eat out their substance.

He has kept among us, in times of peace, Standing Armies without the Consent of our legislatures.

He has affected to render the Military independent of and superior to the Civil Power.

He has combined with others to subject us to a jurisdiction foreign to our constitution, and unacknowledged by our laws; giving his Assent to their Acts of pretended Legislation:

For quartering large bodies of armed troops among us:

For protecting them, by a mock Trial, from Punishment for any Murders which they should commit on the Inhabitants of these States:

For cutting off our Trade with all parts of the world:

For imposing taxes on us without our Consent:

For depriving us of many cases, of the benefits of Trial by jury:

For transporting us beyond Seas to be tried for pretended offences:

For abolishing the free System of English Laws in a neighbouring Province, establishing therein an Arbitrary government, and enlarging its Boundaries so as to render it at once an example and fit instrument for introducing the same absolute rule into these Colonies:

For taking away our Charters, abolishing our most valuable Laws, and altering fundamentally the Forms of our Governments:

For suspending our own Legislatures, and declaring themselves invested with Power to legislate for us in all cases whatsoever.

He has abdicated Government here, by declaring us out of his Protection and waging War against us.

He has plundered our seas, ravaged our Coasts, burnt our towns, and destroyed the lives of our people.

He is at this time transporting large armies of foreign mercenaries to compleat the works of death, desolation, and tyranny, already begun with circumstances of Cruelty & perfidy scarcely paralleled in the most barbarous ages, and totally unworthy the Head of a civilized nation.

He has constrained our fellow Citizens taken Captive on the high Seas to bear Arms against their Country, to become the executioners of their friends and Brethren, or to fall themselves by their Hands.

He has excited domestic insurrections amongst us, and has endeavoured to bring on the inhabitants of our frontiers, the merciless Indian Savages, whose known rule of warfare, is an undistinguished destruction of all ages, sexes, and conditions.

In every stage of these Oppressions We have Petitioned for Redress in the most humble terms: Our repeated Petitions have been answered only by repeated injury. A Prince, whose character is thus marked by every act which may define a Tyrant, is unfit to be the ruler of a free people.

Nor have We been wanting in attention to our British brethren. We have warned them from time to time of attempts by their legislature to extend an unwarrantable jurisdiction over us. We have reminded them of the circumstances of our emigration and settlement here. We have appealed to their native justice and magnanimity, and we have conjured them by the ties of our common kindred to disavow these usurpations, which, would inevitably interrupt our connections and correspondence. They too must have been deaf to the voice of justice and of consanguinity. We must, therefore, acquiesce in the necessity, which denounces our Separation, and hold them, as we hold the rest of mankind, Enemies in War, in Peace Friends.

WE, THEREFORE, the Representatives of the UNITED STATES OF AMERICA, in General Congress, Assembled, appealing to the Supreme Judge of the world for the rectitude of our intentions, do, in the Name, and by Authority of the good People of these Colonies, solemnly publish and declare, That these United Colonies are, and of Right ought to be FREE AND INDEPENDENT STATES; that they are Absolved from all Allegiance to the British Crown, and that all political connection between them and the State of Great Britain, is and ought to be totally dissolved; and that as Free and Independent States, they have full Power to levy War, conclude Peace, contract Alliances, establish Commerce, and to do all other Acts and Things which Independent States may of right do. And for the support of this Declaration, with a firm reliance on the Protection of Divine Providence, we mutually pledge to each other our Lives, our Fortunes, and our sacred Honor.

The foregoing Declaration was, by order of Congress, engrossed, and signed by the following members:

John Hancock

NEW HAMPSHIRE
Josiah Bartlett
William Whipple
Matthew Thornton

MASSACHUSETTS BAY
Samuel Adams
John Adams
Robert Treat Paine
Elbridge Gerry

RHODE ISLAND
Stephen Hopkins
William Ellery

CONNECTICUT
Roger Sherman
Samuel Huntington
William Williams
Oliver Wolcott

NEW YORK
William Floyd
Philip Livingston
Francis Lewis
Lewis Morris

NEW JERSEY
Richard Stockton
John Witherspoon
Francis Hopkinson
John Hart
Abraham Clark

PENNSYLVANIA
Robert Morris
Benjamin Rush
Benjamin Franklin
John Morton
George Clymer
James Smith
George Taylor
James Wilson
George Ross

DELAWARE
Caesar Rodney
George Read
Thomas M'Kean

MARYLAND
Samuel Chase
William Paca
Thomas Stone
Charles Carroll, of Carrollton

VIRGINIA
George Wythe
Richard Henry Lee
Thomas Jefferson
Benjamin Harrison
Thomas Nelson, Jr.
Francis Lightfoot Lee
Carter Braxton

NORTH CAROLINA
William Hooper
Joseph Hewes
John Penn

SOUTH CAROLINA
Edward Rutledge
Thomas Heyward, Jr.
Thomas Lynch, Jr.
Arthur Middleton

GEORGIA
Button Gwinnett
Lyman Hall
George Walton

Resolved, That copies of the Declaration be sent to the several assemblies, conventions, and committees, or councils of safety, and to the several commanding officers of the continental troops; that it be proclaimed in each of the United States, at the head of the army.

THE CONSTITUTION OF THE UNITED STATES (1787)

We the People of the United States, in order to form a more perfect Union, establish Justice, insure domestic Tranquility, provide for the common defence, promote the general Welfare, and secure the Blessings of Liberty to ourselves and our Posterity, do ordain and establish this Constitution for the United States of America.

ARTICLE. I.

Section. 1. All legislative Powers herein granted shall be vested in a Congress of the United States, which shall consist of a Senate and House of Representatives.

Section. 2. The House of Representatives shall be composed of Members chosen every second Year by the People of the several States, and the Electors in each State shall have the Qualifications requisite for Electors of the most numerous Branch of the State Legislature.

No Person shall be a Representative who shall not have attained to the Age of twenty five Years, and been seven Years a Citizen of the United States, and who shall not, when elected, be an Inhabitant of that State in which he shall be chosen.

Representatives and direct Taxes shall be apportioned among the several States which may be included within this Union, according to their respective Numbers, which shall be determined by adding to the whole Number of free Persons, including those bound to Service for a Term of Years, and excluding Indians not taxed, three fifths of all other Persons. The actual Enumeration shall be made within three Years after the first Meeting of the Congress of the United States, and within every subsequent Term of ten Years, in such Manner as they shall by Law direct. The Number of Representatives shall not exceed one for every thirty Thousand, but each State shall have at Least one Representative; and until such enumeration shall be made, the State of New Hampshire shall be entitled to chuse three, Massachusetts eight, Rhode-Island and Providence Plantations one, Connecticut five, New York six, New Jersey four, Pennsylvania eight, Delaware one, Maryland six, Virginia ten, North Carolina five, South Carolina five, and Georgia three.

When vacancies happen in the Representation from any state, the Executive Authority thereof shall issue Writs of Election to fill such Vacancies.

The House of Representatives shall chuse their Speaker and other Officers; and shall have the sole Power of Impeachment.

Section. 3. The Senate of the United States shall be composed of two Senators from each State, chosen by the legislature thereof, for six Years; and each Senator shall have one Vote.

Immediately after they shall be assembled in Consequence of the first Election, they shall be divided as equally as may be into three Classes. The Seats of the Senators of the first Class shall be vacated at the Expiration of the second Year, of the second Class at the Expiration of the fourth Year, and of the third Class at the Expiration of the sixth Year, so that one third may be chosen every second Year; and if Vacancies happen by Resignation, or otherwise, during the Recess of the Legislature of any State, the Executive thereof may make temporary Appointments until the next Meeting of the Legislature, which shall then fill such Vacancies.

No Person shall be a Senator who shall not have attained to the Age of thirty Years, and been nine Years a Citizen of the United States, and who shall not, when elected, be an Inhabitant of that State for which he shall be chosen.

The Vice President of the United States shall be President of the Senate, but shall have no Vote, unless they be equally divided.

The Senate shall chuse their other Officers, and also a President pro tempore, in the Absence of the Vice President, or when he shall exercise the Office of President of the United States.

The Senate shall have the sole Power to try all Impeachments. When sitting for that Purpose, they shall be on Oath or Affirmation. When the President of the United States is tried, the Chief Justice shall preside: And no Person shall be convicted without the Concurrence of two thirds of the Members present.

Judgment in Cases of Impeachment shall not extend further than to removal from Office, and disqualification to hold and enjoy any Office of honor, Trust or Profit under the United States: but the Party convicted shall nevertheless be liable and subject to Indictment, Trial, Judgment and Punishment, according to Law.

Section. 4. The Times, Places and Manner of holding Elections for Senators and Representatives, shall be prescribed in each State by the Legislature thereof; but the Congress may at any time by Law make or alter such Regulations, except as to the Places of chusing Senators.

The Congress shall assemble at least once in every Year, and such Meeting shall be on the first Monday in December, unless they shall by Law appoint a different Day.

Section. 5. Each House shall be the Judge of the Elections, Returns and Qualifications of its own Members, and a Majority of each shall constitute a Quorum to do Business; but a smaller Number may adjourn from day to day, and may be authorized to compel the Attendance of absent Members, in such Manner, and under such Penalties as each House may provide.

Each House may determine the Rules of its Proceedings, punish its Members for disorderly Behaviour, and, with the Concurrence of two thirds, expel a Member.

Each House shall keep a Journal of its Proceedings, and from time to time publish the same, excepting such Parts as may in their Judgment require Secrecy; and the Yeas and Nays of the Members of either House on any question shall, at the Desire of one fifth of those Present, be entered on the Journal.

Neither House, during the Session of Congress, shall, without the Consent of the other, adjourn for more than three days, nor to any other Place than that in which the two Houses shall be sitting.

Section. 6. The Senators and Representatives shall receive a Compensation for their Services, to be ascertained by Law, and paid out of the Treasury of the United States. They shall in all Cases, except Treason, Felony and Breach of the Peace, be privileged from Arrest during their Attendance at the Session of their respective Houses, and in going to and returning from the same; and for any Speech or Debate in either House, they shall not be questioned in any other Place.

No Senator or Representative shall, during the Time for which he was elected, be appointed to any civil Office under the Authority of the United States, which shall have been created, or the Emoluments whereof shall have been encreased during such time; and no Person holding any Office under the United States, shall be a Member of either House during his Continuance in Office.

Section. 7. All Bills for raising Revenue shall originate in the House of Representatives; but the Senate may propose or concur with Amendments as on other Bills.

Every Bill which shall have passed the House of Representatives and the Senate shall, before it become a Law, be presented to the President of the United States; If he approve he shall sign it, but if not he shall return it, with his Objections to that House in which it shall have originated, who shall enter the Objections at large on their Journal, and proceed to reconsider it. If after such Reconsideration two thirds of that House shall agree to pass the Bill, it shall be sent, together with the Objections, to the other House, by which it shall likewise be reconsidered, and if approved by two thirds of that House, it shall become a Law. But in all such Cases the Votes of both Houses shall be determined by Yeas and Nays, and the Names of the Persons voting for and against the Bill shall be entered on the Journal of each House respectively. If any Bill shall not be returned by the President within ten Days (Sundays excepted) after it shall have been presented to him, the Same shall be a Law, in like Manner as if he had signed it, unless the

Congress by their Adjournment prevent its Return, in which Case it shall not be a Law.

Every Order, Resolution, or Vote to which the Concurrence of the Senate and House of Representatives may be necessary (except on a question of Adjournment) shall be presented to the President of the United States; and before the Same shall take Effect, shall be approved by him, or being disapproved by him, shall be repassed by two thirds of the Senate and House of Representatives, according to the Rules and Limitations prescribed in the Case of a Bill.

Section. 8. The Congress shall have Power To lay and collect Taxes, Duties, Imposts and Excises, to pay the Debts and provide for the common Defence and general Welfare of the United States; but all Duties, Imposts and Excises shall be uniform throughout the United States;

To borrow Money on the credit of the United States;

To regulate Commerce with foreign Nations, and among the several States, and with the Indian Tribes;

To establish an uniform Rule of Naturalization, and uniform Laws on the subject of Bankruptcies throughout the United States;

To coin Money, regulate the Value thereof, and of foreign Coin, and fix the Standard of Weights and Measures;

To provide for the Punishment of counterfeiting the Securities and current Coin of the United States;

To establish Post Offices and Post Roads;

To promote the Progress of Science and useful Arts, by securing for limited Times to Authors and Inventors the exclusive Right to their respective Writings and Discoveries;

To constitute Tribunals inferior to the supreme Court;

To define and punish Piracies and Felonies committed on the high Seas, and Offences against the Law of Nations;

To declare War, grant Letters of Marque and Reprisal, and make Rules concerning Captures on Land and Water;

To raise and support Armies, but no Appropriation of Money to that Use shall be for a longer Term than two Years;

To provide and maintain a Navy;

To make Rules for the Government and Regulation of the land and naval Forces;

To provide for calling forth the Militia to execute the Laws of the Union, suppress Insurrections and repel Invasions;

To provide for organizing, arming, and disciplining, the Militia, and for governing such Part of them as may be employed in the Service of the United States, reserving to the States respectively, the Appointment of the Officers, and the Authority of training the Militia according to the discipline prescribed by Congress;

To exercise exclusive Legislation in all Cases whatsoever, over such District (not exceeding ten Miles square) as may, by Cession of Particular States, and the Acceptance of Congress, become the Seat of the Government of the United States, and to exercise like Authority over all Places purchased by the Consent of the Legislature of the State in which the Same shall be, for the Erection of Forts, Magazines, Arsenals, dock-Yards, and other needful Buildings;—And

To make all Laws which shall be necessary and proper for carrying into Execution the foregoing Powers, and all other Powers vested by this Constitution in the Government of the United States, or in any Department or Officer thereof.

Section. 9. The Migration or Importation of such Persons as any of the States now existing shall think proper to admit, shall not be prohibited by the Congress prior to the Year one thousand eight hundred and eight, but a Tax or duty may be imposed on such Importation, not exceeding ten dollars for each Person.

The Privilege of the Writ of Habeas Corpus shall not be suspended, unless when in Cases of Rebellion or Invasion the public Safety may require it.

No Bill of Attainder or ex post facto Law shall be passed.

No Capitation, or other direct, Tax shall be laid, unless in Proportion to the Census or Enumeration herein before directed to be taken.

No Tax or Duty shall be laid on Articles exported from any State.

No Preference shall be given by any Regulation of Commerce or Revenue to the Ports of one State over those of another: nor shall Vessels bound to, or from, one State, be obliged to enter, clear, or pay Duties in another.

No Money shall be drawn from the Treasury, but in Consequence of Appropriations made by Law; and a regular Statement and Account of the Receipts and Expenditures of all public Money shall be published from time to time.

No Title of Nobility shall be granted by the United States: And no Person holding any Office of Profit or Trust under them, shall, without the Consent of the Congress, accept of any present, Emolument, Office, or Title, of any kind whatever, from any King, Prince, or foreign State.

Section. 10. No State shall enter into any Treaty, Alliance, or Confederation; grant Letters of Marque and Reprisal; coin Money; emit Bills of Credit; make any Thing but gold and silver Coin a Tender in Payment of Debts; pass any Bill of Attainder, ex post facto Law, or Law impairing the Obligation of Contracts, or grant any Title of Nobility.

No State shall, without the Consent of the Congress, lay any Imposts or Duties on Imports or Exports, except what may be absolutely necessary for executing its inspection Laws: and the net Produce of all Duties and Imposts, laid by any State on Imports or Exports, shall be for the Use of the Treasury of the United States; and all such Laws shall be subject to the Revision and Controul of the Congress.

No State shall, without the Consent of Congress, lay any Duty of Tonnage, keep Troops, or Ships of War in time of Peace, enter into any Agreement or Compact with another State, or with a foreign Power, or engage in War, unless actually invaded, or in such imminent Danger as will not admit of delay.

ARTICLE. II.

Section. 1. The executive Power shall be vested in a President of the United States of America. He shall hold his Office during the term of four Years, and, together with the Vice President, chosen for the same Term, be elected, as follows:

Each State shall appoint, in such Manner as the Legislature thereof may direct, a Number of Electors, equal to the whole Number of Senators and Representatives to which the State may be entitled in the Congress: but no Senator or Representative, or Person holding an Office of Trust or Profit under the United States, shall be appointed an Elector.

The Electors shall meet in their respective States, and vote by Ballot for two Persons, of whom one at least shall not be an Inhabitant of the same State with themselves. And they shall make a List of all the Persons voted for, and of the Number of Votes for each; which List they shall sign and certify, and transmit sealed to the Seat of the Government of the United States, directed to the President of the Senate. The President of the Senate shall, in the Presence of the Senate and House of Representatives, open all the Certificates, and the Votes shall then be counted. The Person having the greatest Number of Votes shall be the President, if such Number be a Majority of the whole Number of Electors appointed; and if there be more than one who have such Majority, and have an equal Number of Votes, then the House of Representatives shall immediately chuse by Ballot one of them for President; and if no Person have a Majority, then from the five highest on the List the said House shall in like Manner chuse the President. But in chusing the President, the Votes shall be taken by States, the Representation from each State having one Vote; A quorum for this Purpose shall consist of a Member or Members from two thirds of the States, and a Majority of all the States shall be necessary to a Choice. In every Case, after the Choice of the President, the Person having the greatest Number of Votes of the Electors shall be the Vice President. But if there should remain two or more who have equal Votes, the Senate shall chuse from them by Ballot the Vice President.

The Congress may determine the Time of chusing the Electors, and the Day on which they shall give their Votes; which Day shall be the same throughout the United States.

No Person except a natural born Citizen, or a Citizen of the United States, at the time of the Adoption of this Constitution, shall be eligible to the Office of President; neither shall any Person be eligible to that Office who shall not have attained to the Age of thirty five Years, and been fourteen Years a Resident within the United States.

In Case of the Removal of the President from Office, or of his Death, Resignation, or Inability to discharge the Powers and Duties of the said Office, the Same shall devolve on the Vice President, and the Congress may by Law provide for the Case of Removal, Death, Resignation or Inability, both of the President ~~and Vice President, declaring~~ what Officer shall then act as President, and such Officer shall act accordingly, until the Disability be removed, or a President shall be elected.

The President shall, at stated Times, receive for his Services, a Compensation, which shall neither be encreased or diminished during the Period for which he shall have been elected, and he shall not receive within that Period any other Emolument from the United States, or any of them.

Before he enters on the Execution of his Office, he shall take the following Oath or Affirmation:—"I do solemnly swear (or affirm) that I will faithfully execute the Office of President of the United States, and will to the best of my Ability, preserve, protect and defend the Constitution of the United States."

Section. 2. The President shall be Commander in Chief of the Army and Navy of the United States, and of the Militia of the several States, when called into the actual Service of the United States; he may require the Opinion, in writing, of the principal Officer in each of the executive Departments, upon any Subject relating to the Duties of their respective Offices, and he shall have Power to grant Reprieves and Pardons for Offences against the United States, except in Cases of Impeachment.

He shall have Power, by and with the Advice and Consent of the Senate, to make Treaties, provided two thirds of the Senators present concur; and he shall nominate, and by and with the Advice and Consent of the Senate, shall appoint Ambassadors, other public Ministers and Consuls, Judges of the supreme Court, and all other Officers of the United States, whose Appointments are not herein otherwise provided for, and which shall be established by Law; but the Congress may by Law vest the Appointment of such inferior Officers, as they think proper, in the President alone, in the Courts of Law, or in the Heads of Departments.

The President shall have Power to fill up all Vacancies that may happen during the Recess of the Senate, by granting Commissions which shall expire at the End of their next Session.

Section. 3. He shall from time to time give to the Congress Information of the State of the Union, and recommend to their Consideration such Measures as he shall judge necessary and expedient; he may, on extraordinary Occasions, convene both Houses, or either of them, and in Case of Disagreement between them, with Respect to the Time of Adjournment, he may adjourn them to such Time as he shall think proper; he shall receive Ambassadors and other public Ministers; he shall take Care that the Laws be faithfully executed, and shall Commission all the Officers of the United States.

Section. 4. The President, Vice President and all civil Officers of the United States, shall be removed from Office on Impeachment for, and Conviction of, Treason, Bribery, or other high Crimes and Misdemeanors.

ARTICLE. III.

Section. 1. The judicial Power of the United States, shall be vested in one supreme Court, and in such inferior Courts as the Congress may from time to time ordain and establish. The Judges, both of the supreme and inferior Courts, shall hold their Offices during good Behavior, and shall, at stated Times, receive for their Services, a Compensation, which shall not be diminished during their Continuance in Office.

Section. 2. The judicial Power shall extend to all Cases, in Law and Equity, arising under this Constitution, the Laws of the United States, and Treaties made, or which shall be made, under their Authority;—to all Cases affecting Ambassadors, other public Ministers and Consuls;—to all Cases of admiralty and maritime Jurisdiction;—the Controversies to which the United States shall be a Party;—to Controversies between two or more States;—between a State and Citizens of another State;—between Citizens of different States;—

between Citizens of the same State claiming Lands under Grants of different States, and between a State, or the Citizens thereof, and foreign States, Citizens or Subjects.

In all cases affecting Ambassadors, other public Ministers and Consuls, and those in which a State shall be Party, the supreme Court shall have original Jurisdiction. In all the other Cases before mentioned, the supreme Court shall have appellate Jurisdiction, both as to Law and Fact, with such Exceptions, and under such Regulations as the Congress shall make.

The Trial of all Crimes, except in Cases of Impeachment, shall be by Jury; and such Trial shall be held in the State where the said Crimes shall have been committed; but when not committed within any State, the Trial shall be at such Place or Places as the Congress may by Law have directed.

Section. 3. Treason against the United States, shall consist only in levying War against them, or in adhering to their Enemies, giving them Aid and Comfort. No Person shall be convicted of Treason unless on the Testimony of two Witnesses to the same overt Act, or on Confession in open Court.

The Congress shall have Power to declare the Punishment of Treason, but no Attainder of Treason shall work Corruption of Blood, or Forfeiture except during the Life of the Person attainted.

ARTICLE. IV.

Section. 1. Full Faith and Credit shall be given in each State to the public Acts, Records, and judicial Proceedings of every other State. And the Congress may by general Laws prescribe the Manner in which such Acts, Records and Proceedings shall be proved, and the Effect thereof.

Section. 2. The Citizens of each State shall be entitled to all Privileges and Immunities of Citizens in the several States.

A Person charged in any State with Treason, Felony, or other Crime, who shall flee from Justice, and be found in another State, shall on Demand of the executive Authority of the State from which he fled, be delivered up, to be removed to the State having Jurisdiction of the Crime.

No Person held to Service or Labour in one State, under the Laws thereof, escaping into another, shall, in Consequence of any Law or Regulation therein, be discharged from such Service or Labour, but shall be delivered up on Claim of the Party to whom such Service or Labour may be due.

Section. 3. New States may be admitted by the Congress into this Union; but no new State shall be formed or erected within the Jurisdiction of any other State; nor any State be formed by the Junction of two or more States, or Parts of States, without the consent of the Legislatures of the States concerned as well as of the Congress.

The Congress shall have Power to dispose of and make all needful Rules and Regulations respecting the Territory or other Property belonging to the United States; and nothing in this Constitution shall be so construed as to Prejudice any Claims of the United States, or of any particular States.

Section. 4. The United States shall guarantee to every State in this Union a Republican Form of Government, and shall protect each of them against Invasion; and on Application of the Legislature, or of the Executive (when the Legislature cannot be convened) against domestic Violence.

ARTICLE. V.

The Congress, whenever two thirds of both Houses shall deem it necessary, shall propose Amendments to this Constitution, or, on the Application of the Legislatures of two thirds of the several States, shall call a Convention for proposing Amendments, which, in either Case, shall be valid to all Intents and Purposes, as Part of this Constitution, when ratified by the Legislatures of three fourths of the several States, or by Conventions in three fourths thereof, as the one or the other Mode of Ratification may be proposed by the Congress; Provided that no Amendment which may be made prior to the Year One thousand eight hundred and eight shall in any Manner affect the first and fourth Clauses in the Ninth Section of the first Article; and that no State, without its Consent, shall be deprived of its equal Suffrage in the Senate.

ARTICLE. VI.

All Debts contracted and Engagements entered into, before the Adoption of this Constitution, shall be as valid against the United States under this Constitution, as under the Confederation.

This Constitution, and the Laws of the United States which shall be made in Pursuance thereof; and all Treaties made, or which shall be made, under the Authority of the United States, shall be the supreme Law of the Land; and the Judges in every State shall be bound thereby, any Thing in the Constitution or Laws of any State to the Contrary notwithstanding.

The Senators and Representatives before mentioned, and the Members of the several State Legislatures, and all executive and judicial Officers, both of the United States and of the several States, shall be bound by Oath or Affirmation, to support this Constitution; but no religious Test shall ever be required as a Qualification to any Office or public Trust under the United States.

ARTICLE. VII.

The Ratification of the Conventions of nine States, shall be sufficient for the Establishment of this Constitution between the States so ratifying the Same.

Done in Convention by the Unanimous Consent of the States present the Seventeenth Day of September in the Year of our Lord one thousand seven hundred and Eighty seven and of the Independence of the United States of America the Twelfth. In witness thereof We have hereunto subscribed our Names,

G^{o}. WASHINGTON—Presd^{t}.
and deputy from Virginia

NEW HAMPSHIRE
John Langdon
Nicholas Gilman

MASSACHUSETTS
Nathaniel Gorham
Rufus King

CONNECTICUT
Wm Saml Johnson
Roger Sherman

NEW YORK
Alexander Hamilton

NEW JERSEY
Wil: Livingston
David A. Brearley
Wm Paterson
Jona: Dayton

PENNSYLVANIA
B Franklin
Thomas Mifflin
Robt Morris
Geo. Clymer
Thos FitzSimons
Jared Ingersoll
James Wilson
Gouv Morris

DELAWARE
Geo: Read
Gunning Bedford jun
John Dickinson
Richard Bassett
Jaco: Broom

MARYLAND
James McHenry
Dan of St Thos Jenifer
Danl Carroll

VIRGINIA
John Blair—
James Madison Jr.

NORTH CAROLINA
Wm Blount
Richd Dobbs Spaight
Hu Williamson

SOUTH CAROLINA
J. Rutledge
Charles Cotesworth Pinckney
Charles Pinckney
Pierce Butler

GEORGIA
William Few
Abr Baldwin

AMENDMENTS TO THE CONSTITUTION

Articles in addition to, and Amendment of the Constitution of the United States of America, proposed by Congress, and ratified by the Legislatures of the several States, pursuant to the fifth Article of the original Constitution.

AMENDMENT I.*

Congress shall make no law respecting an establishment of religion, or prohibiting the free exercise thereof; or abridging the freedom of speech, or of the press; or the right of the people peaceably to assemble, and to petition the Government for a redress of grievances.

AMENDMENT II.

A well regulated Militia, being necessary to the security of a free State, the right of the people to keep and bear Arms, shall not be infringed.

AMENDMENT III.

No Soldier shall, in time of peace be quartered in any house, without the consent of the Owner, nor in time of war, but in a manner to be prescribed by law.

AMENDMENT IV.

The right of the people to be secure in their persons, houses, papers, and effects, against unreasonable searches and seizures, shall not be violated, and no Warrants shall issue, but upon probable cause, supported by Oath or affirmation, and particularly describing the place to be searched, and the persons or things to be seized.

AMENDMENT V.

No person shall be held to answer for a capital, or otherwise infamous crime, unless on a presentment or indictment of a Grand Jury, except in cases arising in the land or naval forces, or in the Militia, when in actual service in time of War or public danger; nor shall any person be subject for the same offence to be twice put in jeopardy of life or limb; nor shall be compelled in any criminal case to be a witness against himself, nor be deprived of life, liberty, or property, without due process of law; nor shall private property be taken for public use, without just compensation.

AMENDMENT VI.

In all criminal prosecutions, the accused shall enjoy the right to a speedy and public trial, by an impartial jury of the State and district wherein the crime shall have been committed, which district shall have been previously ascertained by law, and to be informed of the nature and cause of the accusation; to be confronted with the witnesses against him; to have compulsory process for obtaining witnesses in his favor, and to have the Assistance of Counsel for his defence.

AMENDMENT VII.

In Suits at common law, where the value in controversy shall exceed twenty dollars, the right of trial by jury shall be preserved, and no fact tried by a jury, shall be otherwise re-examined in any Court of the United States, than according to the rules of the common law.

AMENDMENT VIII.

Excessive bail shall not be required, nor excessive fines imposed, nor cruel and unusual punishments inflicted.

AMENDMENT IX.

The enumeration in the Constitution, of certain rights, shall not be construed to deny or disparage others retained by the people.

AMENDMENT X.

The powers not delegated to the United States by the Constitution, nor prohibited by it to the States, are reserved to the States respectively, or to the people.

AMENDMENT XI.

The Judicial power of the United States shall not be construed to extend to any suit in law or equity, commenced or prosecuted against one of the United States by Citizens of another State, or by Citizens or Subjects of any Foreign State. [January 8, 1798]

*The first ten Amendments (the Bill of Rights) were ratified in 1791.

AMENDMENT XII.

The Electors shall meet in their respective states, and vote by ballot for President and Vice-President, one of whom, at least, shall not be an inhabitant of the same state with themselves; they shall name in their ballots the person voted for as President, and in distinct ballots the person voted for as Vice-President, and they shall make distinct lists of all persons voted for as President, and of all persons voted for as Vice President, and of the number of votes for each, which lists they shall sign and certify, and transmit sealed to the seat of the government of the United States, directed to the President of the Senate;—The President of the Senate shall, in the presence of the Senate and House of Representatives, open all the certificates and the votes shall then be counted;—The person having the greatest number of votes for President, shall be the President, if such number be a majority of the whole number of Electors appointed; and if no person have such majority, then from the persons having the highest numbers not exceeding three on the list of those voted for as President, the House of Representatives shall choose immediately, by ballot, the President. But in choosing the President, the votes shall be taken by states, the representation from each state having one vote; a quorum for this purpose shall consist of a member or members from two-thirds of the states, and a majority of all the states shall be necessary to a choice. And if the House of Representatives shall not choose a President whenever the right of choice shall devolve upon them, before the fourth day of March next following, then the Vice-President shall act as President, as in the case of the death or other constitutional disability of the President.—The person having the greatest number of votes as Vice-President, shall be the Vice-President, if such number be a majority of the whole number of Electors appointed, and if no person have a majority, then from the two highest numbers on the list, the Senate shall choose the Vice-President; a quorum for the purpose shall consist of two-thirds of the whole number of Senators, and a majority of the whole number shall be necessary to a choice. But no person constitutionally ineligible to the office of President shall be eligible to that of Vice-President of the United States. [September 25, 1804]

AMENDMENT XIII.

Section 1. Neither slavery nor involuntary servitude, except as a punishment for crime whereof the party shall have been duly convicted, shall exist within the United States, or any place subject to their jurisdiction.

Section 2. Congress shall have power to enforce this article by appropriate legislation. [December 18, 1865]

AMENDMENT XIV.

Section 1. All persons born or naturalized in the United States, and subject to the jurisdiction thereof, are citizens of the United States and of the State wherein they reside. No State shall make or enforce any law which shall abridge the privileges or immunities of citizens of the United States; nor shall any State deprive any person of life, liberty, or property, without due process of law; nor deny to any person within its jurisdiction the equal protection of the laws.

Section 2. Representatives shall be apportioned among the several States according to their respective numbers, counting the whole number of persons in each State, excluding Indians not taxed. But when the right to vote at any election for the choice of electors for President and Vice President of the United States, Representatives in Congress, the Executive and Judicial officers of a State, or the members of the Legislature thereof, is denied to any of the male inhabitants of such State, being twenty-one years of age, and citizens of the United States, or in any way abridged, except for participation in rebellion, or other crime, the basis of representation therein shall be reduced in the proportion which the number of such male citizens shall bear to the whole number of male citizens twenty-one years of age in such State.

Section 3. No person shall be a Senator or Representative in Congress, or elector of President and Vice President, or hold any office, civil or military, under the United States, or under any State, who, having previously taken an oath, as a member of Congress, or as an officer of the United States, or as a member of any State legislature, or as an executive or judicial officer of any State, to support the Constitution of the United

States, shall have engaged in insurrection or rebellion against the same, or given aid or comfort to the enemies thereof. But Congress may by a vote of two-thirds of each House, remove such disability.

Section 4. The validity of the public debt of the United States, authorized by law, including debts incurred for payment of pensions and bounties for services in suppressing insurrection or rebellion, shall not be questioned. But neither the United States nor any State shall assume or pay any debt or obligation incurred in aid of insurrection or rebellion against the United States, or any claim for the loss or emancipation of any slave; but all such debts, obligations and claims shall be held illegal and void.

Section 5. The Congress shall have power to enforce, by appropriate legislation, the provisions of this article. [July 28, 1868]

AMENDMENT XV.

Section 1. The right of citizens of the United States to vote shall not be denied or abridged by the United States or by any State on account of race, color, or previous condition of servitude—

Section 2. The Congress shall have power to enforce this article by appropriate legislation. [March 30, 1870]

AMENDMENT XVI.

The Congress shall have power to lay and collect taxes on incomes, from whatever source derived, without apportionment among the several States, and without regard to any census or enumeration. [February 25, 1913]

AMENDMENT XVII.

The Senate of the United States shall be composed of two senators from each State, elected by the people thereof, for six years; and each Senator shall have one vote. The electors in each State shall have the qualifications requisite for electors of the most numerous branch of the State legislatures.

When vacancies happen in the representation of any State in the Senate, the executive authority of such State shall issue writs of election to fill such vacancies: *Provided,* That the legislature of any State may empower the executive thereof to make temporary appointments until the people fill the vacancies by election as the legislature may direct.

This amendment shall not be so construed as to affect the election or term of any senator chosen before it becomes valid as part of the Constitution. [May 31, 1913]

AMENDMENT XVIII.

After one year from the ratification of this article, the manufacture, sale, or transportation of intoxicating liquors within, the importation thereof into, or the exportation thereof from the United States and all territory subject to the jurisdiction thereof for beverage purposes is hereby prohibited.

The Congress and the several States shall have concurrent power to enforce this article by appropriate legislation.

This article shall be inoperative unless it shall have been ratified as an amendment to the Constitution by the legislatures of the several States, as provided in the Constitution, within seven years from the date of the submission thereof to the States by Congress. [January 29, 1919]

AMENDMENT XIX.

The right of citizens of the United States to vote shall not be denied or abridged by the United States or by any State on account of sex.

The Congress shall have power by appropriate legislation to enforce the provisions of this article. [August 26, 1920]

AMENDMENT XX.

Section 1. The terms of the President and Vice-President shall end at noon on the twentieth day of January, and the terms of Senators and Representatives at noon on the third day of January, of the years in which such terms would have ended if this article had not been ratified; and the terms of their successors shall then begin.

Section 2. The Congress shall assemble at least once in every year, and such meeting shall begin at noon on the third day of January, unless they shall by law appoint a different day.

Section 3. If, at the time fixed for the beginning of the term of the President, the President-elect shall have died, the Vice-President-elect shall become President. If a President shall not have been chosen before the time fixed for the beginning of his term, or if the President-elect shall have failed to qualify, then the Vice-President-elect shall act as President until a President shall have qualified; and the Congress may by law provide for the case wherein neither a President-elect nor a Vice-President-elect shall have qualified, declaring who shall then act as President, or the manner in which one who is to act shall be selected, and such person shall act accordingly until a President or Vice-President shall have qualified.

Section 4. The Congress may by law provide for the case of the death of any of the persons from whom the House of Representatives may choose a President whenever the right of choice shall have devolved upon them, and for the case of the death of any of the persons from whom the Senate may choose a Vice-President whenever the right of choice shall have devolved upon them.

Section 5. Sections 1 and 2 shall take effect on the 15th day of October following the ratification of this article.

Section 6. This article shall be inoperative unless it shall have been ratified as an amendment to the Constitution by the legislatures of three-fourths of the several States within seven years from the date of its submission. [February 6, 1933]

AMENDMENT XXI.

Section 1. The eighteenth article of amendment to the Constitution of the United States is hereby repealed.

Section 2. The transportation or importation into any State, Territory or possession of the United States for delivery or use therein of intoxicating liquors, in violation of the laws thereof, is hereby prohibited.

Section 3. This article shall be inoperative unless it shall have been ratified as an amendment to the Constitution by convention in the several States, as provided in the Constitution, within seven years from the date of the submission thereof to the States by the Congress. [December 5, 1933]

AMENDMENT XXII.

Section 1. No person shall be elected to the office of the President more than twice, and no person who has held the office of President, or acted as President, for more than two years of a term to which some other person was elected President shall be elected to the office of the President more than once. But this Article shall not apply to any person holding the office of President when this Article was proposed by the Congress, and shall not prevent any person who may be holding the office of President, or acting as President, during the term within which this Article becomes operative from holding the office of President or acting as President during the remainder of such term.

Section 2. This article shall be inoperative unless it shall have been ratified as an amendment to the Constitution by the legislatures of three-fourths of the several States within seven years from the date of its submission to the States by the Congress. [February 27, 1951]

AMENDMENT XXIII.

Section 1. The District constituting the seat of government of the United States shall appoint in such manner as the Congress may direct:

A number of electors of President and Vice-President equal to the whole number of Senators and Representatives in Congress to which the District would be entitled if it were a State, but in no event more than the least populous State; they shall be in addition to those appointed by the States, but they shall be considered, for the purposes of the election of President and Vice-President, to be electors appointed by a State; and they shall meet in the District and perform such duties as provided by the twelfth article of amendment.

Section 2. The Congress shall have the power to enforce this article by appropriate legislation. [March 29, 1961]

AMENDMENT XXIV.

Section 1. The right of citizens of the United States to vote in any primary or other election for President or Vice President, for electors for President or Vice President, or for Senator or Representative in Congress, shall not be denied or abridged by the United States or any State by reason of failure to pay any poll tax or other tax.

Section 2. The Congress shall have power to enforce this article by appropriate legislation. [January 23, 1964]

AMENDMENT XXV.

Section 1. In case of the removal of the President from office or of his death or resignation, the Vice President shall become President.

Section 2. Whenever there is a vacancy in the office of Vice President, the President shall nominate a Vice President who shall take office upon confirmation by a majority vote of both Houses of Congress.

Section 3. Whenever the President transmits to the President pro tempore of the Senate and the Speaker of the House of Representatives his written declaration that he is unable to discharge the powers and duties of his office, and until he transmits to them a written declaration to the contrary, such powers and duties shall be discharged by the Vice President as Acting President.

Section 4. Whenever the Vice President and a majority of either the principal officers of the executive departments or of such other body as Congress may by law provide, transmit to the President pro tempore of the Senate and the Speaker of the House of Representatives their written declaration that the President is unable to discharge the powers and duties of his office, the Vice President shall immediately assume the powers and duties of the office as Acting President.

Thereafter, when the President transmits to the President pro tempore of the Senate and the Speaker of the House of Representatives his written declaration that no inability exists, he shall resume the powers and duties of his office unless the Vice President and a majority of either the principal officers of the executive departments or of such other body as Congress may by law provide, transmit within four days to the President pro tempore of the Senate and the Speaker of the House of Representatives their written declaration that the President is unable to discharge the powers and duties of his office. Thereupon Congress shall decide the issue, assembling within forty-eight hours for that purpose if not in session. If the Congress, within twenty-one days after receipt of the latter written declaration, or, if Congress is not in session, within twenty-one days after Congress is required to assemble, determines by two-thirds vote of both Houses that the President is unable to discharge the powers and duties of his office, the Vice-President shall continue to discharge the same as Acting President; otherwise, the President shall resume the powers and duties of his office. [February 10, 1967]

AMENDMENT XXVI.

Section 1. The right of citizens of the United States, who are eighteen years of age or older, to vote shall not be denied or abridged by the United States or by any State on account of age.

Section 2. The Congress shall have power to enforce this article by appropriate legislation. [June 30, 1971]

AMENDMENT XXVII.

No law, varying the compensation for the services of the Senators and Representatives shall take effect, until an election of Representatives shall have intervened. [May 8, 1992]

SUGGESTED READING

CHAPTER 1: A NEW WORLD

Books

Bender, Thomas. *A Nation among Nations: America's Place in World History* (2006). Attempts to place American history in an international context; the opening chapters offer a global portrait of the age of exploration and conquest.

Crosby, Alfred J. *The Columbian Exchange: Biological and Cultural Consequences of 1492* (1972). Examines the flow of goods and diseases across the Atlantic and their consequences.

Fernández-Armesto, Felipe. *Pathfinders: A Global History of Exploration* (2006). A history of explorations throughout the centuries, including those of the fifteenth and sixteenth centuries.

Fischer, David H. *Champlain's Dream* (2008). A lively account of Samuel de Champlain's effort to build a French colony in North America based on toleration and mutual respect between settlers and Native Americans.

Gutiérrez, Ramón A. *When Jesus Came, the Corn Mothers Went Away: Marriage, Sexuality, and Power in New Mexico, 1500–1846* (1991). Discusses the changes in Indian life in New Mexico as a result of Spanish colonization.

Haefeli, Evan. *New Netherland and the Dutch Origins of American Religious Liberty* (2012). Explores the complex conditions of religious life in New Netherland.

Knaut, Andrew L. *The Pueblo Revolt of 1680: Conquest and Resistance in Seventeenth-Century New Mexico* (1997). A recent account of the largest revolt of native peoples.

Mann, Charles C. *1491: New Revelations of the Americas before Columbus* (2005). A comprehensive portrait of life in the Western Hemisphere before the arrival of Europeans.

Richter, Daniel K. *Facing East from Indian Country* (2001). Examines the era of exploration and settlement as viewed through the experience of Native Americans.

Rodriguez, Jaime E. *Political Culture in Spanish America, 1500–1830* (2017). Political ideas and practices from colonization through Spanish-American independence.

Witgen, Michael. *An Infinity of Nations: How the Native New World Shaped Early North America* (2012). An imaginative account of how native peoples and Europeans interacted in the Great Lakes region.

Websites

Archive of Early American Images: www.brown.edu/academics/libraries/john-carter-brown/jcb-online/image-collections/archive-early-american-images

Cahokia Mounds: http://cahokiamounds.org

Exploring the Early Americas: www.loc.gov/exhibits/earlyamericas/

France in America: http://international.loc.gov/intldl/fiahtml

Jamestown, Quebec, Santa Fe: Three North American Beginnings: http://americanhistory.si.edu/jamestown-quebec-santafe/en/introduction

CHAPTER 2: BEGINNINGS OF ENGLISH AMERICA, 1607–1660

Books

Anderson, Virginia. *Creatures of Empire: How Domestic Animals Transformed Early America* (2006). Shows how livestock brought by English settlers helped to transform the colonial landscape and provoked conflict with Native Americans.

Banner, Stuart. *How the Indians Lost Their Land: Law and Power on the Frontier* (2005). Argues that most Indian land came into settlers' hands by legal processes rather than conquest.

Brown, Kathleen. *Good Wives, Nasty Wenches, and Anxious Patriarchs: Gender, Race, and Power in Colonial Virginia* (1996). A pioneering study of gender relations and their impact on Virginia society.

Cronon, William. *Changes in the Land: Colonists and the Ecology of New England* (1983). A pathbreaking examination of how English colonization affected the natural environment in New England.

Gaskill, Malcolm. *Between Two Worlds: How the English Became Americans* (2014). Traces the slow development of a distinctive American identity in the mainland British colonies.

Gleach, Frederic W. *Powhatan's World and Colonial Virginia: A Conflict of Cultures* (1997). A study of Indian culture and the impact of European colonization upon it.

Noll, Mark. *The Old Religion in a New World: The History of North American Christianity* (2001). Relates how the transplantation of European religions to America changed religious institutions and practices.

Norton, Mary Beth. *Founding Mothers and Fathers: Gendered Power and the Forming of American Society* (2011). An examination of legal cases that illuminate the power relations involving colonial women and men.

Pestana, Carla G. *The English Atlantic in an Age of Revolution, 1640–1661* (2001). Analyzes how the English Civil War reverberated in the American colonies.

Philbrick, Nathaniel. *Mayflower* (2006). An account of one of the most celebrated voyages of the colonial era and the early history of the Plymouth colony.

Price, David A. *Love and Hate in Jamestown: John Smith, Pocahontas, and the Start of a New Nation* (2003). Presents the legend and reality of John Smith, Pocahontas, and early Virginia.

Rees, John. *The Leveller Revolution: Radical Political Organization in England, 1640–1650* (2017). The most recent study of history's first democratic popular movement.

Taylor, Alan. *American Colonies* (2001). A comprehensive survey of the history of North American colonies from their beginnings to 1763.

Websites

The Plymouth Colony Archive Project: www.histarch.illinois.edu/plymouth

Virtual Jamestown: www.virtualjamestown.org

CHAPTER 3: CREATING ANGLO-AMERICA, 1660–1750

Books

Bailyn, Bernard. *The Peopling of British North America* (1986). A brief survey of the movement of peoples across the Atlantic.

Berlin, Ira. *Many Thousands Gone: The First Two Centuries of Slavery in North America* (1998). The most extensive study of the origins and development of colonial slavery.

Bushman, Richard. *The Refinement of America: Persons, Houses, Cities* (1992). A study of how a more "refined" lifestyle emerged in the eighteenth-century colonies.

Dayton, Cornelia H. *Women before the Bar: Gender, Law, and Society in Connecticut, 1639–1789* (1995). Examines the changing legal status of women in one American colony.

Kidd, Thomas S. *The Great Awakening* (2007). An account of the religious movement that swept the American colonies in the eighteenth century.

Lipman, Andrew. *The Saltwater Frontier: Indians and the Contest for the American Coast* (2015). Explores how the sea was an area of conflict between Native American fishermen and merchants and European colonizers.

Morgan, Edmund S. *American Slavery, American Freedom: The Ordeal of Colonial Virginia* (1975). An influential study of the slow development of slavery in seventeenth-century Virginia.

Norton, Mary Beth. *In the Devil's Snare: The Salem Witchcraft Crisis of 1692* (2002). A study of the witch trials that places them in the context of anxieties over Indian warfare on the Massachusetts frontier.

Pestana, Carla G. *Protestant Empire: Religion and the Making of the British Atlantic World* (2009). Discusses the role of Protestantism in inspiring and justifying British overseas expansion.

Silver, Peter. *Our Savage Neighbors: How Indian War Transformed Early America* (2008). Argues that hostility to Indians provided a way of unifying the diverse population of European origin that made up colonial America.

Website

Afro-Louisiana History and Genealogy: www.ibiblio.org/laslave/

CHAPTER 4: SLAVERY, FREEDOM, AND THE STRUGGLE FOR EMPIRE, TO 1763

Books

Anderson, Fred. *Crucible of War: The Seven Years' War and the Fate of Empire in British North America, 1754–1766* (2000). A general history of the Seven Years' War and its consequences.

Beeman, Richard R. *Varieties of Political Experience in Eighteenth-Century America* (2004). Explores how political life differed from colony to colony and what characteristics they had in common.

Calloway, Colin G. *The Scratch of a Pen: 1763 and the Transformation of North America* (2006). Examines the impact of the Peace of Paris on North America, especially the Native American population.

Colley, Linda. *Britons: Forging the Nation, 1707–1837* (1992). An influential study of the rise of a sense of national identity in Great Britain, relevant also for the American colonies.

Newman, Simon P. *A New World of Labor: The Development of Plantation Slavery in the British Atlantic* (2013). The most recent account of how slavery emerged and was consolidated in the British empire.

Noll, Mark. *The Rise of Evangelicalism: The Age of Edwards, Whitefield, and the Wesleys* (2004). Explores the Great Awakening on both sides of the Atlantic and its impact on religious life.

Rediker, Marcus. *The Slave Ship: A Human History* (2007). A fascinating and disturbing account of the Atlantic slave trade that focuses on the captains, sailors, and slaves aboard the slave ships.

Reséndez, Andrés. *The Other Slavery: The Uncovered Story of Indian Enslavement in America* (2016). A careful analysis of the development and extent of Indian slavery in the early colonies.

Rucker, Walter C. *The River Flows On: Black Resistance, Culture, and Identity Formation in Early America* (2006). Traces the emergence of a new African-American identity and how it affected modes of slave resistance.

Smith, Barbara Clark. *The Freedoms We Lost: Consent and Resistance in Revolutionary America* (2010). Examines the ways colonial Americans participated in public life and sought to defend their concepts of freedom.

Valerio-Jiménez, Omar S. *River of Hope: Forging Identity and Nation in the Rio Grande Borderlands* (2013). Traces the processes of cultural interaction and the establishment of national power in a major borderlands region.

White, Richard. *The Middle Ground: Indians, Empires, and Republics in the Great Lakes Region, 1650–1815* (1991). The book that developed the idea of a middle ground where Europeans and Indians both exercised authority.

Websites

Africans in America: www.pbs.org/wgbh/aia/

Web de Anza: http://anza.uoregon.edu

CHAPTER 5: THE AMERICAN REVOLUTION, 1763–1783

Books

Armitage, David. *The Declaration of Independence: A Global History* (2007). Traces the international impact of the Declaration of Independence in the years since it was written.

Bailyn, Bernard. *The Ideological Origins of the American Revolution* (1967; 2nd ed., 1992). A classic study of the ideas that shaped the movement for independence.

Bloch, Ruth. *Visionary Republic: Millennial Themes in American Thought, 1756–1800* (1988). Explores how the religious vision of a more perfect society contributed to the coming of the Revolution.

Breen, T. H. *Marketplace of Revolution: How Consumer Politics Shaped American Independence* (2004). An examination of how the colonists' very dependence on British consumer goods led them to resent interference with trade.

Countryman, Edward. *The American Revolution* (rev. ed., 2002). A brief summary of the Revolution's causes, conduct, and consequences.

Foner, Eric. *Tom Paine and Revolutionary America* (1976). Examines the ideas of the era's greatest pamphleteer of revolution and how they contributed to the struggle for independence.

Maier, Pauline. *American Scripture: Making the Declaration of Independence* (1997). The most detailed study of the writing of the Declaration and of previous calls for independence within the colonies.

Nash, Gary. *The Urban Crucible: Social Change, Political Consciousness, and the Origins of the American Revolution* (1979). Explores how the social history of American cities contributed to the coming of the Revolution.

Neimeyer, Charles. *America Goes to War: A Social History of the Continental Army* (1995). A history of Washington's army that stresses the role of nonelite Americans in the fighting and the impact of military service on the soldiers.

Polansky, Janet. *Revolutions without Borders: The Call to Liberty in the Atlantic World* (2015). Explores both the revolutions of the late eighteenth century and the kinds of sources historians use to study them.

Raphael, Ray. *A People's History of the American Revolution* (2001). A study of grassroots resistance to Britain before and during the War of Independence.

Saunt, Claudio. *West of the Revolution: An Uncommon History of 1776* (2014). An account of events in North America among Indians, Spanish colonists, and others in the year of the Declaration of Independence.

Taylor, Alan. *American Revolutions: A Continental History, 1750–1804* (2015). An excellent history of the Revolution as a continental event.

Websites

The American Revolution and Its Era: Maps and Charts of North America and the West Indies: http://memory.loc.gov/ammem/gmdhtml/armhtml/armhome.html

The Coming of the American Revolution: www.masshist.org/revolution/

CHAPTER 6: THE REVOLUTION WITHIN

Books

Berkin, Carol. *Revolutionary Mothers: Women in the Struggle for American Independence* (2005). Presents profiles of women who took part in the movement for independence.

Boulton, Terry. *Taming Democracy: "The People," the Founders, and the Troubled Ending of the American Revolution* (2007). Argues that the democratic impulse unleashed by the War of Independence was to some extent reversed by the events of the 1780s.

Calloway, Colin. *The American Revolution in Indian Country* (1995). Examines how the Revolution affected Indians in each region of the United States.

Davis, David Brion. *The Problem of Slavery in the Age of Revolution* (1975). An influential study of the emergence of slavery as a major public issue in the Atlantic world.

DuVal, Kathleen. *Independence Lost: Lives on the Edge of the American Revolution* (2015). A study of the Revolution as a borderlands conflict on the Gulf Coast, in which European empires and Native Americans fought for their own ideas of power and liberty.

Frey, Sylvia R. *Water from the Rock: Black Resistance in a Revolutionary Age* (1991). A study of the many ways blacks sought to gain freedom for themselves during the Revolution.

Hatch, Nathan O. *The Democratization of American Christianity* (1989). A comprehensive account of the Revolution's impact on religion, and its aftermath.

Jasanoff, Maya. *Liberty's Exiles: American Loyalists in the Revolutionary World* (2011). A study of Americans who remained loyal to Great Britain during the War of Independence.

Kruman, Marc. *Between Authority and Liberty: State Constitution Making in Revolutionary America* (1997). The most detailed account of how state constitutions were changed during the era.

Parkinson, Robert G. *The Common Cause: Creating Race and Nation in the American Revolution* (2016). How hostility to Native Americans and slaves helped to create a sense of shared identity among white patriots fighting for American independence.

Taylor, Alan. *The Divided Ground: Indians, Settlers, and the Northern Borderland of the American Revolution* (2006). Examines the Revolution and its consequence in the Iroquois region of upstate New York.

Wood, Gordon. *The Radicalism of the American Revolution* (1992). An influential work that sees the Revolution as transforming a hierarchical society into a democratic one.

Websites

Creating the United States: www.loc.gov/exhibits/creating-the-united-states

The Geography of Slavery in Virginia: www2.vcdh.virginia.edu/gos/

CHAPTER 7: FOUNDING A NATION, 1783–1791

Books

Cornell, Saul. *The Other Founders: Anti-Federalism and the Dissenting Tradition in America, 1788–1828* (1999). A careful examination of the ideas of those who opposed ratification of the Constitution.

Dowd, Gregory E. *A Spirited Resistance: The North American Indian Struggle for Unity, 1745–1815* (1992). Contains an important discussion of the place of Indians in the new American nation.

Dunbar, Eric Armstrong. *Never Caught: The Washingtons' Relentless Pursuit of Their Runaway Slave Ona Judge* (2017). Uses the fascinating story of one of George and Martha Washington's slaves to illuminate the dilemma of slavery and freedom in the early republic.

Holton, Woody. *Unruly Americans and the Origins of the Constitution* (2007). Argues that the political activities of ordinary Americans helped to shape the Constitution.

Kettner, James T. *The Development of American Citizenship, 1608–1870* (1978). Traces the development of the definition of American citizenship from early colonization to the aftermath of the Civil War.

Klarman, Michael. *The Framers' Coup: The Making of the United States Constitution* (2016). Unlike many other books on the Constitutional Convention, emphasizes the deep divides among the delegates rather than eventual consensus.

Levy, Leonard. *The Establishment Clause: Religion and the First Amendment* (1994). A historical account of one of the key components of the Bill of Rights.

Maier, Pauline. *Ratification: The People Debate the Constitution, 1787–1788* (2010). The most complete account of the state-by-state debates over ratification of the Constitution.

Nash, Gary. *The Forgotten Fifth: African Americans in the Age of Revolution* (2006). A comprehensive survey of the Revolution's impact on blacks, slave and free.

Rakove, Jack. *Original Meanings: Politics and Ideas in the Making of the Constitution* (1996). An influential interpretation of the ideas that went into the drafting of the Constitution.

Wilentz, Sean. *No Property in Man: Slavery and Antislavery at the Nation's Founding* (2018). Emphasizes the long-term consequences of the framers' refusal to include a direct national acknowledgment of property in man in the Constitution.

Websites

Creating the United States: www.loc.gov/exhibits/creating-the-united-states

Explore the Constitution: http://constitutioncenter.org

The Presidency: http://americanhistory.si.edu/presidency/home.html

CHAPTER 8: SECURING THE REPUBLIC, 1791–1815

Books

Egerton, Douglas R. *Gabriel's Rebellion: The Virginia Slave Conspiracies of 1800 and 1802* (1993). The most comprehensive account of one of the most important slave conspiracies in American history.

Elkins, Stanley, and Eric L. McKitrick. *The Age of Federalism* (1993). A detailed account of the politics of the 1790s.

Kerber, Linda K. *Women of the Republic: Intellect and Ideology in Revolutionary America* (1980). A study of prevailing ideas about women's place in the new republic.

Lambert, Frank. *The Barbary Wars: American Independence in the Atlantic World* (2005). An account of the first foreign military conflict conducted by the newly independent United States.

McCoy, Drew. *The Elusive Republic: Political Economy in Jeffersonian America* (1980). An influential study of the economic and political outlooks and policies of Federalists and Jeffersonians.

Perl-Rosenthal, Nathan. *Citizen Sailors: Becoming American in the Age of Revolution* (2015). How sailors, white and black, asserted their rights as American citizens in the decades after the Revolution.

Ronda, James P. *Lewis and Clark among the Indians* (1984). An account of the most famous exploring party in American history.

Rothman, Adam. *Slave Country: American Expansion and the Origins of the Deep South* (2005). A pioneering study of how the United States secured control of what are now the Gulf states, opening the door for the expansion of slavery.

Taylor, Alan. *The Civil War of 1812* (2010). An account of the War of 1812 that stresses how divided Americans were during the conflict.

Waldstreicher, David. *In the Midst of Perpetual Fetes: The Making of American Nationalism, 1776–1820* (1997). Explores how Americans celebrated and thought about their nation's independence in the years of the early republic.

Websites

Rivers, Edens, Empires: Lewis and Clark and the Revealing of America: www.loc.gov/exhibits/lewisandclark/lewisandclark.html

CHAPTER 9: THE MARKET REVOLUTION, 1800–1840

Books

Bergmann, William H. *The American National State and the Early West* (2014). Demonstrates how governmental action was crucial to early western development.

Boydston, Jeanne. *Home and Work: Housework, Wages, and the Ideology of Work in the Early Republic* (1990). Examines how the market revolution affected ideas relating to women's work.

Deyle, Steven. *Carry Me Back: The Domestic Slave Trade in American Life* (2005). The most comprehensive history of the internal slave trade, by which millions of slaves were transported to the Lower South.

Harris, Leslie. *In the Shadow of Slavery: African-Americans in New York City, 1626–1863* (2003). A study that emphasizes the exclusion of African-Americans from the economic opportunities offered by the market revolution.

Haselby, Sam. *The Origins of American Religious Nationalism* (2015). Explores how the battle between frontier evangelists and more traditional New England ministers shaped religion and politics in the early republic.

Howe, Daniel W. *What Hath God Wrought: The Transformation of America, 1815–1848* (2007). A comprehensive account of social and political changes in this era, emphasizing the significance of the communications revolution.

Johnson, Paul E. *A Shopkeeper's Millennium: Society and Revivals in Rochester, New York, 1815–1837* (1978). Explores the impact of religious revivals on a key city of upstate New York.

Larson, John L. *The Market Revolution in America: Liberty, Ambition, and the Eclipse of the Common Good* (2010). The most recent account of the market revolution and its impact on American society and values.

Miller, Kerby A. *Exiles and Emigrants: Ireland and the Irish Exodus to North America* (1985). An examination of Irish immigration over the course of American history.

Ryan, Mary P. *Cradle of the Middle Class: The Family in Oneida County, New York, 1790–1865* (1981). Examines how economic change helped to produce a new kind of middle-class family structure centered on women's dominance of the household.

Wilentz, Sean. *Chants Democratic: New York City and the Rise of the American Working Class, 1788–1850* (1984). A study of the early labor movement in one of its key centers in antebellum America.

Zakim, Michael. *Accounting for Capitalism: The World the Clerks Made* (2018). How a new generation of clerks arose in the early nineteenth century and how they personified and helped to shape the market revolution.

Websites

American Transcendentalism: www.vcu.edu/engweb/transcendentalism/

Women in America, 1820–1842: http://xroads.virginia.edu/~hyper/detoc/fem/home.htm

CHAPTER 10: DEMOCRACY IN AMERICA, 1815–1840

Books

Balogh, Brian. *A Government Out of Sight: The Mystery of National Authority in Nineteenth-Century America* (2009). Examines the paradox of widespread belief in limited government yet frequent energetic use of federal authority.

Fitz, Caitlin. *Our Sister Republics: The United States in an Age of American Revolutions* (2016). Traces changes in responses in the United States to the Latin American Wars of Independence, from initial enthusiasm to skepticism as the new nations moved to end slavery.

Forbes, Robert. *The Missouri Compromise and Its Aftermath: Slavery and the Meaning of America* (2007). Places the Missouri controversy in the context of the long national debate over slavery.

Guyatt, Nicholas. *Bind Us Apart: How Enlightened Americans Invented Racial Segregation* (2016). Compares the movements for Indian removal and colonization of African-Americans outside the country as precursors to later racial segregation laws.

Howe, Daniel W. *The Political Culture of the American Whigs* (1979). Illuminates the key ideas that held the Whig Party together.

Keyssar, Alexander. *The Right to Vote: The Contested History of Democracy in the United States* (2000). The most up-to-date history of the right to vote in America from the colonial era to the present.

Schlesinger, Arthur M., Jr. *The Age of Jackson* (1945). An influential account of Jacksonian ideas and politics, which shaped debate among a generation of historians.

Starr, Paul. *Creation of the Media: Political Origins of Modern Communications* (2004). Contains an illuminating account of the "information revolution" in Jacksonian America.

Wallace, Anthony. *The Long, Bitter Trail: Andrew Jackson and the Indians* (1993). A brief history of Jackson's Indian policies, especially Indian Removal in the southern states.

Watson, Harry. *Liberty and Power: The Politics of Jacksonian America* (1990). A valuable brief account of the politics of the 1820s and 1830s.

Wilentz, Sean. *The Rise of American Democracy: Jefferson to Lincoln* (2005). A comprehensive history of democratic ideas and politics from the American Revolution to the Civil War.

Websites

Democracy in America, Alexis de Tocqueville: http://xroads.virginia.edu/~hyper/detoc/home.html

Legacy: Spain and the United States in the Age of Independence, 1763–1848: http://latino.si.edu/SpainLegacy/Archive/index.html

CHAPTER 11: THE PECULIAR INSTITUTION

Books

Beckert, Sven. *The Empire of Cotton* (2014). A history of one of the world's most important commodities, placing the Old South in an international context.

Berlin, Ira. *Slaves without Masters: The Free Negro in the Antebellum South* (1974). A careful study of the status of free blacks, stressing differences between the Upper and Lower South.

Breen, Patrick H. *The Land Shall Be Deluged in Blood: A New History of the Nat Turner Revolt* (2016). The most recent account of the most famous slave rebellion in American history.

Davis, David Brion. *Inhuman Bondage: The Rise and Fall of Slavery in the New World* (2006). Places the history of slavery in the United States firmly in a hemispheric context.

Foner, Eric. *Gateway to Freedom: The Hidden History of the Underground Railroad* (2015). A study of the operations of the Underground Railroad, focusing on New York City, and of the fugitives it assisted.

Genovese, Eugene D. *Roll, Jordan, Roll: The World the Slaves Made* (1974). A classic study of the paternalist ethos and the culture that developed under slavery.

Gutman, Herbert G. *The Black Family in Slavery and Freedom* (1976). A pioneering examination of how slaves created and sustained families under the harsh conditions of slavery.

Johnson, Walter. *Soul by Soul: Life inside the Antebellum Slave Market* (1999). Considers the operations of the New Orleans slave market as a window into slavery as a whole.

Karp, Matthew. *This Vast Southern Empire: Slaveholders at the Helm of American Foreign Policy* (2016). Explores how slaveholders tried to use the power of the federal government to protect slavery in the United States and the rest of the Western Hemisphere.

Kaye, Anthony E. *Joining Places: Slave Neighborhoods in the Old South* (2007). Emphasizes the importance of the local networks established by slaves in Mississippi.

Kolchin, Peter. *American Slavery, 1619–1877* (rev. ed., 2003). A careful, up-to-date survey of the history of slavery in North America from its beginning through emancipation.

McCurry, Stephanie. *Masters of Small Worlds: Yeoman Households, Gender Relations, and the Political Culture of Antebellum South Carolina* (1995). Studies the lives of men and women in non-slaveholding families to explore their links with the planter class.

Stevenson, Brenda. *Life in Black and White: Family and Community in the Slave South* (1996). Focusing on Virginia, an examination of how slaves adapted to the rise of the interstate slave trade.

Websites

Born in Slavery: Slave Narratives from the Federal Writers' Project: http://lcweb2.loc.gov/ammem/snhtml/snhome.html

Documenting the American South: http://docsouth.unc.edu

Slaves and the Courts, 1740–1860: http://memory.loc.gov/ammem/sthtml/sthome.html

CHAPTER 12: AN AGE OF REFORM, 1820–1840

Books

Bestor, Arthur E. *Backwoods Utopias: The Sectarian and Owenite Phases of Communitarian Socialism in America* (1948). An account of some of the numerous communitarian experiments in pre–Civil War America.

Boylan, Anne M. *The Origins of Women's Activism: New York and Boston, 1797–1840* (2002). Considers how middle-class urban women organized numerous associations for social improvement and thereby gained a place in the public sphere.

Goodman, Paul. *Of One Blood: Abolitionists and the Origins of Racial Equality* (1998). Explores the origins of racial egalitarianism in the movement against slavery.

Jeffrey, Julie R. *The Great Silent Army of Abolitionism: Ordinary Women in the Antislavery Movement* (1998). The role of women as the grassroots foot soldiers of the abolitionist movement.

Jones, Martha S. *Birthright Citizens: A History of Race and Rights in Antebellum America* (2018). Examines how free black activists before the Civil War struggled to gain recognition as American citizens in the face of legal inequality and demands that they be "colonized" outside the country.

Kantrowitz, Stephen. *More Than Freedom: Fighting for Black Citizenship in a White Republic, 1829–1889* (2012). A study of the black abolitionists of Boston and their struggle for an expansive understanding of freedom.

McGreevy, John T. *Catholicism and American Freedom* (2003). Contains an illuminating discussion of how

Catholics responded to Protestant-based reform movements.

Sinha, Manisha. *The Slave's Cause: A History of Abolition* (2016). A comprehensive history of the antislavery movement from the colonial era through the Civil War.

Tyrrell, Ian. *Sobering Up: From Temperance to Prohibition in Antebellum America, 1800–1860* (1979). Traces the movement against the sale and use of liquor and how it changed in the first part of the nineteenth century.

Zboray, Ronald J., and Mary Zboray. *Voices without Votes: Women and Politics in Antebellum New England* (2010). Shows how women took part in Jacksonian-era politics in ways other than voting.

Websites

Samuel J. May Anti-Slavery Collection: http://dlxs.library.cornell.edu/m/mayantislavery/

Women and Social Movements in the United States, 1600–2000: http://asp6new.alexanderstreet.com/wam2/wam2.index.map.aspx

CHAPTER 13: A HOUSE DIVIDED, 1840–1861

Books

Cronon, William. *Nature's Metropolis: Chicago and the Great West* (1992). An influential account of the rise of Chicago and the city's relationship to its agricultural hinterland.

Dean, Adam W. *An Agrarian Republic: Farming, Antislavery Politics, and Nature Parks in the Civil War Era* (2015). Challenges the idea of the coming of the Civil War as a clash between an agricultural South and an industrialized North by stressing the agrarian origins of political antislavery.

DeLay, Brian. *War of a Thousand Deserts: Indian Raids and the U.S.-Mexican War* (2008). A history of the Mexican war that emphasizes its impact on Native Americans.

Foner, Eric. *Free Soil, Free Labor, Free Men: The Ideology of the Republican Party before the Civil War* (1970). A discussion of the basic ideas that united Republicans in the 1850s, especially their "free labor ideology."

Freeman, Joanne B. *The Field of Blood: Violence in Congress and the Road to Civil War* (2018). How fistfights, assaults, and other violence among members of Congress (of which the assault on Charles Sumner was the most prominent example, but by no means the only one) reflected and contributed to the growing divide between the sections.

Haas, Lisbeth. *Conquests and Historical Identities in California, 1769–1936* (1995). Contains a detailed description of how California's acquisition by the United States affected the state's diverse population groups.

Levine, Bruce. *Half Slave and Half Free: The Roots of the Civil War* (1992). A survey of the coming of the Civil War, stressing irreconcilable differences between North and South.

Maizlish, Stephen E. *A Strife of Tongues: The Compromise of 1850 and the Ideological Foundations of the American Civil War* (2018). A careful account of the long congressional debate over the Compromise of 1850, showing how it revealed the hardening of sectional ideologies.

Montejano, David. *Anglos and Mexicans in the Making of Texas* (1987). A history of cultural relations among the varied populations of Texas.

Potter, David M. *The Impending Crisis, 1848–1861* (1976). Still the standard account of the nation's history in the years before the Civil War.

Sinha, Manisha. *The Counterrevolution of Slavery: Politics and Ideology in Antebellum South Carolina* (2002). A detailed study of how a vigorous defense of slavery developed in South Carolina, which justified the decision for secession.

Stephanson, Anders. *Manifest Destiny: American Expansionism and the Empire of Right* (1995). Considers how the idea of an American mission to spread freedom and democracy has affected American foreign policy throughout the country's history.

Websites

Gold Rush!: www.museumca.org/goldrush/

The Mexican-American War and the Media, 1845–1858: www.history.vt.edu/MxAmWar/Index.htm

The Oregon Trail: http://oregontrail101.com

Record of Fugitives: https://exhibitions.cul.columbia.edu/exhibits/show/fugitives/record_fugitives

Uncle Tom's Cabin and American Culture: http://jefferson.village.virginia.edu/utc/

CHAPTER 14: A NEW BIRTH OF FREEDOM: THE CIVIL WAR, 1861–1865

Books

Ayers, Edward L. *In the Presence of Mine Enemies: War in the Heart of America, 1859–1863* (2003), and *The Thin Light of Freedom: The Civil War and Emancipation in the Heart of America* (2017). A two-volume study of the experiences of Americans in two counties—one in

Pennsylvania, one in Virginia—in the early years of the Civil War.

Foner, Eric. *The Fiery Trial: Abraham Lincoln and American Slavery* (2010). A study of the evolution of Lincoln's ideas and policies relating to slavery over the course of his life.

Glatthaar, Joseph T. *Forged in Battle: The Civil War Alliance of Black Soldiers and White Officers* (1990). Relates the complex experience of black Civil War soldiers and their officers.

Lawson, Melinda. *Patriot Fires: Forging a New Nationalism in the Civil War North* (2002). Considers how both public and private groups, in order to mobilize support for the war effort, promoted a new idea of American nationalism.

McCurry, Stephanie. *Confederate Reckoning: Power and Politics in the Civil War South* (2010). A pioneering study of the political mobilization of poorer white women and slaves in the Confederacy.

McPherson, James M. *Battle Cry of Freedom: The Civil War Era* (1988). The standard account of the coming of the war, its conduct, and its consequences.

Mitchell, Reid. *Civil War Soldiers* (1988). A look at the Civil War from the point of view of the experience of ordinary soldiers.

Neely, Mark E. *The Fate of Liberty: Abraham Lincoln and Civil Liberties* (1991). Explores how the Lincoln administration did and did not meet the challenge of preserving civil liberties while fighting the war.

Oakes, James. *Freedom National: The Destruction of Slavery in the United States* (2012). A careful account of the complex path to emancipation.

Richardson, Heather C. *Greatest Nation of the Earth: Republican Economic Policies during the Civil War* (1997). Considers the far-reaching impact of the economic measures adopted by the Union during the war.

Silber, Nina. *Daughters of the Union: Northern Women Fight the Civil War* (2005). Examines the participation of northern women in the war effort and how this did and did not alter their lives.

Websites

Civil War Photographs: http://memory.loc.gov/ammem/cwphtml/cwphome.html

A House Divided: America in the Age of Lincoln: www.digitalhistory.uh.edu/exhibits/ahd/index.html

The Valley of the Shadow: Two Communities in the American Civil War: http://valley.vcdh.virginia.edu

CHAPTER 15: "WHAT IS FREEDOM?": RECONSTRUCTION, 1865–1877

Books

Bottoms, D. Michael. *An Aristocracy of Color: Race and Reconstruction in California and the West, 1850–1890* (2013). A study of changing race relations, and definitions of race, in the western states.

Butchart, Ronald E. *Schooling the Freed People: Teaching, Learning, and the Struggle for Black Freedom* (2010). Relates the efforts of black and white teachers to educate the former slaves and some of the conflicts that arose over the purposes of such education.

Downs, Gregory. *Declarations of Dependence: The Long Reconstruction of Popular Politics in the South, 1861–1908* (2011). Traces the changing ways black and white southerners sought aid and protection from the government during and after the Civil War and Reconstruction.

Downs, James. *Sick from Freedom: The Deadly Consequences of Emancipation* (2012). How disease shaped the experience of freedom and how the Freedmen's Bureau and other agencies sought to cope with widespread illness among former slaves.

DuBois, Ellen C. *Feminism and Suffrage: The Emergence of an Independent Women's Movement in America, 1848–1869* (1978). Explores how the split over the exclusion of women from the Fourteenth and Fifteenth Amendments gave rise to a movement for woman suffrage no longer tied to the abolitionist tradition.

Edwards, Laura. *A Nation of Rights: A Legal History of the Civil War and Reconstruction* (2015). A careful analysis of how this era changed American law and the Constitution.

Fields, Barbara J. *Slavery and Freedom on the Middle Ground: Maryland during the Nineteenth Century* (1985). A study of slavery and emancipation in a key border state.

Foner, Eric. *Nothing but Freedom: Emancipation and Its Legacy* (1983). Includes a comparison of the emancipation experience in different parts of the Western Hemisphere.

Foner, Eric. *Reconstruction: America's Unfinished Revolution, 1863–1877* (1988). A comprehensive account of the Reconstruction era.

Hahn, Steven. *A Nation under Our Feet: Black Political Struggles in the Rural South from Slavery to the Great Migration* (2003). A detailed study of black political activism, stressing nationalist consciousness and emigration movements.

Hahn, Steven. *A Nation without Borders: The United States and Its World in an Age of Civil Wars, 1830–1910* (2016). The chapters on Reconstruction emphasize the role of the West during that period.

Litwack, Leon F. *Been in the Storm So Long: The Aftermath of Slavery* (1979). A detailed look at the immediate aftermath of the end of slavery and the variety of black and white responses to emancipation.

Parsons, Elaine F. *Ku-Klux: The Birth of the Klan during Reconstruction* (2016). Emphasizes both the Klan's terrorism and how discourse about it helped to shape politics and culture, North and South.

Rodrigue, John C. *Reconstruction in the Cane Fields: From Slavery to Free Labor in Louisiana's Sugar Parishes, 1862–1880* (2001). A study of how an often-neglected part of the South experienced the aftermath of slavery.

Websites

America's Reconstruction: People and Politics after the Civil War: www.digitalhistory.uh.edu/exhibits/reconstruction/index.html

Freedmen and Southern Society Project: www.history.umd.edu/Freedmen/

Freedmen's Bureau Online: http://www.freedmensbureau.com/

CHAPTER 16: AMERICA'S GILDED AGE, 1870–1890

Books

Bensel, Richard F. *The Political Economy of American Industrialization, 1877–1900* (2000). A study of the policies and political divisions that contributed to and resulted from the second industrial revolution.

Deutsch, Sarah. *No Separate Refuge: Culture, Class, and Gender on the Anglo-Hispanic Frontier in the American Southwest, 1880–1940* (1987). A careful analysis of the changing experience of people of Hispanic origin in the Southwest during these years.

Fink, Leon. *Workingmen's Democracy: The Knights of Labor and American Politics* (1983). Examines the rise of the Knights of Labor and their forays into local politics in the mid-1880s.

Foster, Gaines. *Moral Reconstruction: Christian Lobbyists and the Federal Legislation of Morality, 1865–1920* (2002). Traces the rise of efforts to use the federal government to promote Protestant notions of moral behavior.

Freeberg, Ernest. *The Age of Edison: Electric Light and the Invention of Modern America* (2013). Explores the numerous ways electricity altered Americans' lives.

Hamalainen, Pekka. *The Comanche Empire* (2008). The rise and fall of Comanche domination over much of the southwestern United States.

Jeffrey, Julie R. *Frontier Women: "Civilizing" the West? 1840–1880* (rev. ed., 1998). A study, based on letters and diaries, of the experience of women on the western frontier.

Kasson, Joy S. *Buffalo Bill's Wild West: Celebrity, Memory, and Popular History* (2000). An account of the popular theatrical production that helped to fix an image of the Wild West in the American imagination.

Maggor, Noam. *Brahmin Capitalism: Frontiers of Wealth and Populism in America's First Gilded Age* (2017). Explores how Boston capitalists helped to finance the spread of railroads, mining, and other enterprises in the West, and the conflicts over how the fruits of economic development should be distributed.

Ostler, Jeffrey. *The Plains Sioux and U.S. Colonialism from Lewis and Clark to Wounded Knee* (2004). Covering nearly the entire nineteenth century, traces the complex relationship between the federal government and the Sioux Indians.

Thomas, John L. *Alternative Americas: Henry George, Edward Bellamy, Henry Demarest Lloyd and the Adversary Tradition* (1983). A thorough exposition of the thought of three critics of Gilded Age society.

White, Richard. *The Republic for Which It Stands: The United States during Reconstruction and the Gilded Age* (2017). A comprehensive account of the social, economic, and political history of this transformative era.

Websites

First-hand Accounts of California 1849–1900: http://memory.loc.gov/ammem/cbhtml/cbhome.html

Indian Peoples of the Northern Great Plains: http://arc.lib.montana.edu/indian-great-plains

CHAPTER 17: FREEDOM'S BOUNDARIES, AT HOME AND ABROAD, 1890–1900

Books

Aleinikoff, Alexander. *Semblances of Sovereignty: The Constitution, the State, and American Citizenship* (2002). Includes a careful discussion of the citizenship status of American minorities and residents of overseas possessions.

Blight, David. *Race and Reunion: The Civil War in American Memory* (2001). Examines how a memory of the Civil War that downplayed the issue of slavery played a part in sectional reconciliation and the rise of segregation.

Blum, Edward. *Reforging the White Republic: Race, Religion, and American Nationalism, 1865–1898* (2005). Explores the development of a shared religious culture that united northern and southern Protestants in support of white supremacy and overseas expansion.

Factor, Robert L. *The Black Response to America: Men, Ideals, and Organization from Frederick Douglass to the NAACP* (1970). Discusses black social and political thought, including that of Booker T. Washington and his critics.

Goodwyn, Lawrence. *The Populist Moment: A Short History of the Agrarian Revolt in America* (1978). A sympathetic account of the rise and fall of Populism.

Higginbotham, Evelyn. *Righteous Discontent: The Women's Movement in the Black Baptist Church, 1880–1920* (1993). Explains how black women developed ways of exerting their influence in public life even as black men were losing the right to vote.

Hoganson, Kristin L. *Consumers' Imperium: The Global Production of American Domesticity, 1865–1920* (2007). Shows how the consumer desires of middle-class women helped to spur the consolidation of an American empire.

Hsu, Madeline. *Dreaming of Gold, Dreaming of Home: Transnationalism and Migration between the United States and South China, 1882–1934* (2000). Examines the enduring connections between Chinese immigrants in the United States and their home communities.

Krause, Paul. *The Battle for Homestead, 1880–1892: Politics, Culture, and Steel* (1992). An account of the era's most celebrated conflict between capital and labor.

LaFeber, Walter. *The New Empire: An Interpretation of American Expansion, 1860–1898* (1963). A classic examination of the forces that led the United States to acquire an overseas empire.

Lake, Marilyn, and Henry Reynolds. *Drawing the Global Color Line* (2008). Traces the global transmission of ideas about white supremacy in the late nineteenth century.

Linn, Brian M. *The Philippine War, 1899–1902* (2000). A detailed history of America's "forgotten war."

McClain, Charles J. *In Search of Equality: The Chinese Struggle against Discrimination in Nineteenth-Century America* (1994). Explores how Chinese-Americans worked to combat the discrimination to which they were subjected and to assert their rights.

McMillen, Neil R. *Dark Journey: Black Mississippians in the Age of Jim Crow* (1989). A powerful account of black life in the segregation era and the boundaries within which it operated.

Perez, Louis A. *The War of 1898: The United States and Cuba in History and Historiography* (1998). Presents the Cuban side of the Spanish-American War, including a detailed discussion of the Cuban movement for independence and how American intervention affected it.

Postel, Charles. *The Populist Vision* (2007). A history of the Populist movement that stresses how it anticipated many public policies of the twentieth century.

Sanders, Elizabeth. *Roots of Reform: Farmers, Workers, and the American State, 1877–1917* (1999). Emphasizes the role of farmers' movements in putting forth many of the proposals associated with political reform in the late nineteenth and early twentieth centuries.

Wong, Eddie J. *Racial Reconstruction: Black Inclusion, Chinese Exclusion, and the Fictions of Citizenship* (2015). Juxtaposes policies regarding these two groups in the late nineteenth century.

Websites

1896: The Presidential Campaign: http://projects.vassar.edu/1896/1896home.html

The Rise and Fall of Jim Crow: www.pbs.org/wnet/jimcrow

The World of 1898: The Spanish-American War: www.loc.gov/rr/hispanic/1898

CHAPTER 18: THE PROGRESSIVE ERA, 1900–1916

Books

Bodnar, John. *The Transplanted: A History of Immigrants in Urban America* (1985). A comprehensive account of American immigration.

Cott, Nancy F. *The Grounding of Modern Feminism* (1987). A careful study of feminist ideas in the Progressive era.

Dawley, Alan. *Struggles for Justice: Social Responsibility and the Liberal State* (1991). Examines the varieties of Progressive reform and various efforts to use the power of government for social betterment.

Diner, Steven. *A Very Different Age: Americans of the Progressive Era* (1998). A survey of the main trends of the Progressive period.

Glickman, Lawrence B. *A Living Wage: Workers and the Making of American Consumer Society* (1997). Traces the origins and development of the idea that workers are entitled to a "living wage."

Hofstadter, Richard. *The Age of Reform: From Bryan to F.D.R.* (1955). A classic account of the ideas of reformers from Populism to the New Deal.

Johnston, Robert D. *The Radical Middle Class: Populist Democracy and the Question of Capitalism in Progressive Era Portland* (2003). Analyzes how Progressivism operated in one important city.

Lears, Jackson. *Rebirth of a Nation: The Making of Modern America, 1877–1920* (2009). A comprehensive history of the Gilded Age and Progressive era, stressing the extent of social and cultural change.

Menand, Louis. *The Metaphysical Club: A Story of Ideas in America* (2001). A study of the life and ideas of the thinkers who created the philosophy of pragmatism.

Montgomery, David. *The Fall of the House of Labor: The Workplace, the State, and American Labor Activism, 1865–1925* (1987). An account of the labor battles of the era and the gradual decline of labor's power, especially at the workplace.

Orsi, Robert A. *The Madonna of 115th Street: Faith and Community in Italian Harlem, 1880–1950* (1985). An influential study of a single immigrant community and the role of religion in binding it together.

Recchiuti, John L. *Civic Engagement: Social Science and Progressive-Era Reform in New York City* (2006). Examines the influence of a group of reform-minded scholars on the politics of the Progressive era.

Rodgers, Daniel T. *Atlantic Crossings: Social Politics in a Progressive Age* (1998). A comprehensive study of the flow of Progressive ideas and policies back and forth across the Atlantic.

Stansell, Christine. *American Moderns: Bohemian New York and the Creation of a New Century* (2000). A colorful account of the Greenwich Village radicals who expanded the idea of personal freedom in the Progressive era.

Stromquist, Shelton. *Re-Inventing "The People": The Progressive Movement, the Class Problem, and the Origins of Modern Liberalism* (2006). Discusses how the desire to re-create social harmony in an age of labor conflict shaped Progressivism.

Tichi, Cecelia. *Civic Passions: Seven Who Launched Progressive America* (2009). An exploration of the careers of some of the most prominent leaders of Progressive reform.

Websites

Evolution of the Conservation Movement, 1860–1920: http://lcweb2.loc.gov/ammem/amrvhtml/conshome.html

Immigration to the United States, 1789–1930: http://ocp.hul.harvard.edu/immigration/

Triangle Shirtwaist Factory Fire: www.ilr.cornell.edu/trianglefire/

Urban Experience in Chicago: Hull House and Its Neighborhoods: http://hullhouse.uic.edu/hull/urbanexp

Votes for Women: http://memory.loc.gov/ammem/naw/nawshome.html

CHAPTER 19: SAFE FOR DEMOCRACY: THE UNITED STATES AND WORLD WAR I, 1916–1920

Books

Bederman, Gail. *Manliness and Civilization: A Cultural History of Race and Gender in the United States, 1880–1917* (1995). Explores how ideas concerning civilization and gender affected American foreign policy.

Capozzola, Christopher. *Uncle Sam Wants You: World War I and the Making of the Modern American Citizen* (2008). A careful study of public and private efforts to enforce patriotic ideas and actions during World War I.

Dawley, Alan. *Changing the World: American Progressives in War and Revolution* (2003). Presents the war as a fulfillment and betrayal of the Progressive impulse.

Gilmore, Glenda E. *Gender and Jim Crow: Women and the Politics of White Supremacy in North Carolina, 1896–1920* (1996). A careful study of how black and white women negotiated the boundaries of segregation in a southern state.

Green, Elna C. *Southern Strategies: Southern Women and the Woman Suffrage Question* (1997). Describes how southern women campaigned for the vote without challenging the subordinate status of African-Americans.

Greene, Julie. *The Canal Builders: Making American Empire at the Panama Canal* (2009). Tells the story of the construction of the Panama Canal and the tens of thousands of workers who did the work.

Grossman, James R. *Land of Hope: Chicago, Black Southerners, and the Great Migration* (1989). An in-depth study of the migration of blacks to one American city.

Healy, David. *Drive to Hegemony: The United States in the Caribbean, 1898–1917* (1988). Examines American foreign policy in the Caribbean from McKinley to Wilson.

Jensen, Kimberly. *Mobilizing Minerva: American Women in the First World War* (2008). Examines the participation of women in the war effort and its impact on gender relations.

Kennedy, David M. *Over Here: The First World War and American Society* (1980). A comprehensive account of how the war affected domestic life in the United States.

Ladd-Taylor, Molly. *Fixing the Poor: Eugenic Sterilization and Child Welfare in the Twentieth Century* (2017). A harrowing account of the eugenics movement and the social policies it helped to inspire.

Manela, Erez. *The Wilsonian Moment* (2007). Details how the Wilsonian ideal of self-determination was received around the world, with results Wilson did not anticipate.

Meier, August. *Negro Thought in America, 1880–1915* (1966). A pioneering study of the ideas of black leaders, including W. E. B. Du Bois.

Mitchell, David J. *1919: Red Mirage* (1970). A global account of the upheavals of 1919.

Preston, William, Jr. *Aliens and Dissenters: Federal Suppression of Radicals, 1903–1933* (1963). An influential study of the federal government's efforts to suppress dissenting ideas, especially during and immediately after World War I.

Renda, Mary A. *Taking Haiti: Military Occupation and the Culture of U.S. Imperialism, 1915–1940* (2001). Examines the causes and consequences of the American occupation of Haiti.

Stein, Judith. *The World of Marcus Garvey: Race and Class in Modern Society* (1986). Places the Garvey movement in an Atlantic perspective linking Africa, the United States, and the West Indies.

Sullivan, Patricia. *Lift Every Voice: The NAACP and the Making of the Civil Rights Movement* (2009). A sweeping history of the country's preeminent civil rights organization, from its founding to the 1950s.

Websites

The Bisbee Deportation of 1917: www.library.arizona.edu/exhibits/bisbee/

The U.S.A. and Latin America: www.casahistoria.net/uslatam.htm

CHAPTER 20: FROM BUSINESS CULTURE TO GREAT DEPRESSION: THE TWENTIES, 1920–1932

Books

Boyle, Kevin. *Arc of Justice: A Saga of Race, Civil Rights, and Murder in the Jazz Age* (2004). A history of the Sweet case, placing it in the context of postwar Detroit and the nation.

Dumenil, Lynn. *The Modern Temper: America in the Twenties* (1995). A brief survey of the main political and cultural trends of the decade.

Garraty, John A. *The Great Depression* (1986). Places the Depression in a global context and compares various governments' responses to it.

Gerstle, Gary. *American Crucible: Race and Nation in the Twentieth Century* (2002). A sweeping survey of how changing ideas of race have affected the concept of American nationality, with a strong account of the debates of the 1920s.

Gordon, Linda. *The Second Coming of the KKK: The Ku Klux Klan of the 1920s and the American Political Tradition* (2017). Illuminates the reasons for the Klan's surprising revival in the 1920s.

Larson, Edward. *Summer for the Gods: The Scopes Trial and America's Continuing Debate over Science and Religion* (1998). A history of the famous trial and the enduring debate over evolution.

Lewis, David L. *When Harlem Was in Vogue* (1981). A lively account of the Harlem Renaissance of the 1920s.

Marchand, Roland. *Advertising the American Dream: Making Way for Modernity, 1920–1940* (1985). Examines how advertisers responded to and helped to shape changes in American life between the two world wars.

McGirr, Lisa. *The War on Alcohol: Prohibition and the Rise of the American State* (2015). A penetrating analysis of Prohibition's impact on American society and government.

Murphy, Paul L. *World War I and the Origin of Civil Liberties in the United States* (1979). An analysis of how the repression of free speech during World War I paved the way for a heightened awareness of the importance of civil liberties.

Ngai, Mae. *Impossible Subjects: Illegal Aliens and the Making of Modern America* (2004). An influential examination of immigration policy toward Mexicans and Asians, and the development of the legal category of "illegal alien."

Ross, William G. *Forging New Freedoms: Nativism, Education, and the Constitution, 1917–1927* (1994). Discusses battles over cultural pluralism in the 1920s and how they laid the groundwork for an expanded definition of personal liberty.

Websites

Chicago and the Great Migration: www.loc.gov/exhibits/african/afam011.html

Emergence of Advertising in America: http://library.duke.edu/digitalcollections/eaa/

Prosperity and Thrift: The Coolidge Era and the Consumer Economy: http://memory.loc.gov/ammem/coolhtml/coolhome.html

Scopes Trial: http://law2.umkc.edu/faculty/projects/ftrials/scopes/scopes.htm

CHAPTER 21: THE NEW DEAL, 1932–1940

Books

Blackwelder, Julia Kirk. *Women of the Depression* (1998). Examines how female members of three communities—Anglo, Mexican-American, and black—coped with the Great Depression.

Cohen, Lizabeth. *Making a New Deal: Industrial Workers in Chicago, 1919–1939* (1990). Describes how the assimilation of immigrants and their children paved the way for the creation of the New Deal political coalition.

Denning, Michael. *The Cultural Front: The Laboring of American Culture in the Twentieth Century* (1996). A comprehensive account of the rise of cultural activity associated with the political left and the New Deal.

Egan, Timothy. *The Worst Hard Time* (2006). A social history of the Dust Bowl during the Depression, including the stories of victims and survivors.

Katznelson, Ira. *Fear Itself: The New Deal and the Origins of Our Time* (2013). Examines the shaping of New Deal policy and especially the compromises Roosevelt had to make to get measures through a Congress dominated by segregationist members from the South.

Kessler-Harris, Alice. *In Pursuit of Equity: Men, Women, and the Quest for Economic Citizenship in 20th-Century America* (2001). Explores how assumptions regarding the proper roles of men and women helped to shape New Deal measures such as Social Security.

Leuchtenberg, William E. *Franklin D. Roosevelt and the New Deal, 1932–1940* (1963). Still the standard one-volume account of Roosevelt's first two terms as president.

Patel, Kiran Klaus. *The New Deal: A Global History* (2016). A comparative account of how different countries, including the United States, Italy, Germany, and the Soviet Union, responded to the Great Depression.

Phillips, Sarah T. *The Land, This Nation: Conservation, Rural America, and the New Deal* (2007). Examines New Deal policies regarding agricultural development, rural conservation, and land use, and its attempt to modernize and uplift rural life.

Sanchez, George. *Becoming Mexican American: Ethnicity, Culture, and Identity in Chicano Los Angeles, 1900–1945* (1995). A careful study of Mexican-Americans in Los Angeles, including their participation in the social unrest of the 1930s and the movement for deporting them during that decade.

Smith, Jason B. *Building New Deal Liberalism: The Political Economy of Public Works* (2006). Places the great construction projects of the 1930s at the center of New Deal economic policy.

Sullivan, Patricia. *Days of Hope: Race and Democracy in the New Deal Era* (1996). Analyzes how the New Deal inspired the emergence of a biracial movement for civil rights in the South.

Williams, Mason B. *City of Ambition: FDR, La Guardia, and the Making of Modern New York* (2014). An illuminating study of the most prominent "little New Deal" and its long-term results.

Websites

America from the Great Depression to World War II: http://memory.loc.gov/ammem/fsowhome.html

FDR Cartoon Archive: www.nisk.k12.ny.us/fdr/FDRcartoons.html

Flint Sit-Down Strike: www.historicalvoices.org/flint/

CHAPTER 22: FIGHTING FOR THE FOUR FREEDOMS: WORLD WAR II, 1941–1945

Books

Anderson, Karen. *Wartime Women: Sex Roles, Family Relations, and the Status of Women during World War II* (1981). Explores how the experience of World War II opened new opportunities for women and challenged existing gender conventions.

Borgwardt, Elizabeth. *A New Deal for the World: America's Vision for Human Rights* (2005). The emergence during the war of the idea of human rights as an international entitlement.

Brinkley, Alan. *The End of Reform: New Deal Liberalism in Recession and War* (1995). Describes how liberals' ideas and policies moved away, during the late New Deal and the war, from combating inequalities of economic power.

Daniels, Roger. *Prisoners without Trial: Japanese Americans in World War II* (1993). A brief history of the internment of Japanese-Americans during the war.

Dower, John W. *War without Mercy: Race and Power in the Pacific War* (1986). Explores how racial fears and antagonisms motivated both sides in the Pacific theater.

Escobedo, Elizabeth R. *From Coveralls to Zoot Suits: The Lives of Mexican American Women on the World War II Home Front* (2013). Examines how the rise of racial liberalism during World War II and the opening of new jobs affected Mexican-American women.

Kennedy, David M. *Freedom from Fear: The American People in Depression and War, 1929–1945* (1999). A detailed and lively account of American history from the Great Depression through the end of World War II.

Rhodes, Richard. *The Making of the Atomic Bomb* (1986). A dramatic account of how the atomic bomb was created.

Von Eschen, Penny. *Race against Empire: Black Americans and Anticolonialism, 1937–1957* (1997). Examines how black Americans responded to the rise of movements for colonial independence overseas during and after World War II.

Websites

Bittersweet Harvest: The Bracero Program 1942–1964: http://americanhistory.si.edu/exhibitions/bittersweet-harvest-bracero-program-1942-1964

A More Perfect Union: Japanese Americans and the U.S. Constitution: http://amhistory.si.edu/perfectunion/experience/

A People at War: www.archives.gov/exhibits/a_people_at_war/a_people_at_war.html

Remembering Nagasaki: www.exploratorium.edu/nagasaki/

CHAPTER 23: THE UNITED STATES AND THE COLD WAR, 1945–1953

Books

Biondi, Martha. *To Stand and Fight: The Struggle for Civil Rights in Postwar New York City* (2003). A comprehensive account of the broad coalition that battled for racial justice in New York City, in areas such as jobs, education, and housing.

Canaday, Margot. *The Straight State: Sexuality and Citizenship in Twentieth-Century America* (2009). Details the federal government's efforts to stigmatize and punish homosexuality.

Donovan, Robert. *Conflict and Crisis: The Presidency of Harry S. Truman, 1945–1948* (1977). A careful account of Truman's first administration and his surprising election victory in 1948.

Dudziak, Mary L. *Cold War Civil Rights: Race and the Image of American Democracy* (2000). Analyzes how the Cold War influenced and in some ways encouraged the civil rights movement at home.

Glendon, Mary Ann. *A World Made New: Eleanor Roosevelt and the Universal Declaration of Human Rights* (2001). Relates the drafting of the Universal Declaration of Human Rights and the response of governments around the world, including the United States.

Hajimu, Masuda. *Cold War Crucible: The Korean Conflict and the Postwar World* (2015). A history of the Korean War that combines global and local perspectives and emphasizes how it laid the foundation for a large standing army in the United States and military bases around the world.

Hunt, Michael. *Ideology and U.S. Foreign Policy* (1987). Discusses how ideas, including the idea of freedom, have shaped America's interactions with the rest of the world.

Johnson, David K. *The Lavender Scare: The Cold War Persecution of Gays and Lesbians in the Federal Government* (2004). A study of the persecution of gay men and lesbians during the Cold War, including a view of the gay culture that thrived in Washington.

Saunders, Frances S. *The Cultural Cold War: The CIA and the World of Arts and Letters* (2000). Describes how the CIA and other government agencies secretly funded artists and writers as part of the larger Cold War.

Schrecker, Ellen. *Many Are the Crimes: McCarthyism in America* (1998). A full account of the anticommunist crusade at home and its impact on American intellectual and social life.

Sugrue, Thomas. *Origins of the Urban Crisis: Race and Inequality in Postwar Detroit* (1996). Explores race relations in a key industrial city after World War II and how they set the stage for the upheavals of the 1960s.

Westad, Odd Arne. *The Cold War: A World History* (2017). A comprehensive account of the Cold War emphasizing how the conflict played out in Asia and Africa.

Websites

Cold War International History Project: www.wilsoncenter.org/program/cold-war-international-history-project

The Korean War and Its Origins, 1945–1953: www.trumanlibrary.org/korea/

CHAPTER 24: AN AFFLUENT SOCIETY, 1953–1960

Books

Freeman, Joshua B. *Working-Class New York: Life and Labor since World War II* (2000). An account of the lives of laborers in the nation's largest city, tracing the rise and decline of the labor movement.

Inboden, William. *Religion and American Foreign Policy, 1945–1960: The Soul of Containment* (2008). How religious groups influenced American diplomacy at the height of the Cold War.

Jackson, Kenneth T. *Crabgrass Frontier: The Suburbanization of America* (1985). The standard account of the development of American suburbia.

Jacobs, Meg. *Pocketbook Politics: Economic Citizenship in Twentieth-Century America* (2005). Discusses how consumer freedom became central to Americans' national identity after World War II.

Klarman, Michael J. *From Jim Crow to Civil Rights: The Supreme Court and the Struggle for Racial Equality* (2004). A full study of Supreme Court cases dealing with civil rights, and how they both reflected and helped to stimulate social change.

Klein, Jennifer. *For All These Rights: Business, Labor, and the Shaping of America's Public-Private Welfare State* (2003). Examines the development of the "social contract" of the 1950s whereby many workers received social benefits from their employers rather than the government.

Nicolaides, Becky M. *My Blue Heaven: Life and Politics in the Working-Class Suburbs of Los Angeles, 1920–1965* (2002). Traces the transformation of Southgate, an industrial neighborhood of Los Angeles, into an all-white suburb, and the political results.

Phillips-Fein, Kim. *Invisible Hands: The Making of the Conservative Movement from the New Deal to Reagan* (2009). Relates how a group of economic thinkers and businessmen worked to fashion a conservative movement in an attempt to reverse many of the policies of the New Deal.

Rothstein, Richard. *The Color of Law: A Forgotten History of How Our Government Segregated America* (2017). How actions by federal, state, and local governments, reinforced by banks and real estate developers, promoted housing segregation.

Wall, Wendy L. *Inventing the "American Way": The Politics of Consensus from the New Deal to the Civil Rights Movement* (2008). A careful examination of the political and ideological world of the Cold War era.

Websites

Brown v. Board of Education: www.lib.umich.edu/brown-versus-board-education/

Herblock's History: Political Cartoons from the Crash to the Millennium: www.loc.gov/rr/print/swann/herblock/

CHAPTER 25: THE SIXTIES, 1960–1968

Books

Anderson, John A., III. *The Other Side of the Sixties: Young Americans for Freedom and the Rise of Conservative Politics* (1997). Considers conservative students of the 1960s and how they laid the groundwork for the later growth of their movement.

Brick, Howard. *Age of Contradiction: American Thought and Culture in the 1960s* (1998). A careful examination of the complex currents of thought that circulated during the decade.

Dittmer, John. *Local People: The Struggle for Civil Rights in Mississippi* (1994). Traces the civil rights movement in one state, looked at from the experience of grassroots activists.

Horwitz, Morton J. *The Warren Court and the Pursuit of Justice* (1998). Analyzes how the Supreme Court redefined the rights of Americans under Chief Justice Earl Warren.

Isserman, Maurice, and Michael Kazin. *America Divided: The Civil War of the 1960s* (2000). A comprehensive account of the social movements and political debates of the 1960s.

Logevall, Frederik. *Embers of War: The Fall of an Empire and the Making of America's Vietnam* (2012). An international account of the origins of American military intervention in Vietnam.

Rosen, Ruth. *The World Split Open: How the Modern Women's Movement Changed America* (2000). Considers how the "second wave" of feminism transformed the lives of American women and men.

Sale, Kirkpatrick. *The Green Revolution: The American Environmental Movement, 1962–1992* (1993). A brief history of one of the most significant movements to emerge from the 1960s.

Sugrue, Thomas. *Sweet Land of Liberty: The Forgotten Struggle for Civil Rights in the North* (2015). A broad history of civil rights struggles outside the South, emphasizing regional differences within the movement.

Zelizer, Julian. *The Fierce Urgency of Now: Lyndon Johnson, Congress, and the Battle for the Great Society* (2015). Shows how Johnson's leadership, the mass mobilization of the civil rights movement, and the election of liberal Democrats to Congress in 1964 made possible the enactment of measures that had been stalled since the New Deal.

Websites

Free Speech Movement Digital Archive: http://bancroft.berkeley.edu/FSM/

Freedom Now!: http://cds.library.brown.edu/projects/FreedomNow

A Visual Journey: Photographs by Lisa Law, 1965–1971: http://americanhistory.si.edu/lisalaw/1.htm

CHAPTER 26: THE CONSERVATIVE TURN, 1969–1988

Books

Borstelman, Thomas. *The 1970s: A New Global History from Civil Rights to Economic Inequality* (2012). Shows how developments in the United States, from economic crisis to greater cultural inclusiveness, played out in other countries as well.

Busch, Andrew E. *Ronald Reagan and the Politics of Freedom* (2001). Discusses how Ronald Reagan interpreted the idea of freedom and how it influenced his presidency.

Cowie, Jefferson. *Stayin' Alive: The 1970s and the Last Days of the Working Class* (2016). Traces the decline of manufacturing employment and union power in the 1970s and how these affected the lives of individual workers.

Erickson, Ansley T. *Making the Unequal Metropolis: School Desegregation and Its Limits* (2016). With Nashville as its focus, shows how a combination of federal and local policies, and the actions of real estate developers, thwarted efforts at school desegregation.

Foley, Michael S. *Front Porch Politics: The Forgotten Heyday of American Activism in the 1970s and 1980s* (2013). A lively account of the grassroots movements, of both left and right, that followed the 1960s.

Jacobs, Meg. *Panic at the Pump: The Energy Crisis and the Transformation of American Politics in the 1970s* (2016). Examines the effects of the energy crisis, including strengthening conservative efforts to reduce the role of government in the economy.

Kruse, Kevin. *White Flight: Atlanta and the Making of Modern Conservatism* (2005). Explores how conservative politics took root in the predominantly white suburbs of Atlanta, with implications for similar communities across the country.

Luker, Kristin. *Abortion and the Politics of Motherhood* (1984). Describes how the abortion issue affected American politics and the ideas about gender relations that lay behind the debate.

McGirr, Lisa. *Suburban Warriors: The Origins of the New American Right* (2001). An influential study of the rise of conservatism in Orange County, California, once one of its more powerful centers.

Minian, Ana Raquel. *Undocumented Lives: The Untold Story of Mexican Migration* (2018). Traces government policies toward migration in Mexico and the United States in the 1960s and 1970s, and the experiences of individual immigrants.

Moreton, Bethany. *To Serve God and Wal-Mart: The Making of Christian Free Enterprise* (2009). Explores how the nation's largest employer drew on evangelical Christianity to justify its often-criticized labor policies.

Nielsen, Kim E. *A Disability History of the United States* (2013). A comprehensive history of the experiences of people with disabilities over the course of American history, including the rise of disability rights activism in the 1970s.

Spruill, Marjorie J. *Divided We Stand: The Battle over Women's Rights and Family Values That Polarized American Politics* (2017). How the growth of feminism in the 1970s sparked the emergence of an antifeminist movement led by women committed to traditional definitions of women's role in society.

Stein, Judith. *Pivotal Decade: How the United States Traded Factories for Finance in the Seventies* (2010). A careful analysis of the economic transformations of the 1970s.

Wilentz, Sean. *The Age of Reagan: A History, 1974–2008* (2008). Explores how Ronald Reagan set the terms of public debate during and after his presidency.

Websites

National Security Archive: http://nsarchive.gwu.edu

Watergate: http://watergate.info/

CHAPTER 27: FROM TRIUMPH TO TRAGEDY, 1989–2004

Books

Bacevich, Andrew J. *American Empire: The Realities and Consequences of U.S. Diplomacy* (2003). Examines how the idea of an American empire reemerged after September 11, and some of the results.

Cole, David. *Terrorism and the Constitution: Sacrificing Civil Liberties in the Name of National Security* (2006). Explores the constitutional issues raised by the war on terrorism.

Gardner, Lloyd C. *The Long Road to Baghdad: A History of U.S. Foreign Policy from the 1970s to the Present* (2008). A careful study of recent American foreign policy and the origins of the Iraq War.

Hartman, Andrew. *A War for the Soul of America: A History of the Culture Wars* (2015). An account of the numerous social and cultural cleavages spawned by immigration and the social movements of the 1960s.

Hinton, Elizabeth. *From the War on Poverty to the War on Crime: The Making of Mass Incarceration in America* (2016). Traces the evolution of policies, from Johnson through Reagan, that gave rise to mass incarceration.

Hsu, Madeline Y. *The Good Immigrants: How the Yellow Peril Became the Model Minority* (2015). Examines the history of attitudes toward Asian immigrants and the decline of prejudice against them.

Levitas, Daniel. *The Terrorist Next Door: The Militia Movement and the Radical Right* (2003). A careful study of right-wing extremism of the 1990s.

Lichtenstein, Nelson. *The Retail Revolution: How Wal-Mart Created a Brave New World of Business* (2009). How Wal-Mart became the largest employer in the United States and one of the most profitable.

Phillips, Kevin. *Wealth and Democracy* (2002). A critique of the influence of money on American politics.

Power, Samantha. *A Problem from Hell: America and the Age of Genocide* (2002). Discusses genocides of the 1990s and the problem of the appropriate American response.

Smelser, Neil J., and Jeffrey C. Alexander. *Diversity and Its Discontents: Cultural Conflict and Common Ground in Contemporary American Society* (1999). Describes the new social diversity of the 1990s and the cultural and political tensions arising from it.

Websites

The AIDS Crisis: http://americanhistory.si.edu/exhibitions/hiv-and-aids-thirty-years-ago

Global Exchange: www.globalexchange.org

Making the Macintosh: Technology and Culture in Silicon Valley: http://library.stanford.edu/mac/

September 11 Digital Archive: http://911digitalarchive.org

CHAPTER 28: A DIVIDED NATION

Books

Appiah, Anthony. *The Lies That Bind: Rethinking Identity* (2018). A critique of contemporary ideas of identity based on nation, religion, and race, arguing that they sow divisions within societies and are often based on historical misconceptions.

Brinkley, Douglas. *The Great Deluge: Hurricane Katrina, New Orleans, and the Mississippi Gulf Coast* (2006). A scathing account of how government at all levels failed the people of New Orleans.

Cherlin, Andrew J. *Labor's Love Lost: The Rise and Fall of the Working-Class Family in America* (2015). Studies how class differences affect family life and opportunities for social mobility in today's America.

Fraser, Steve. *The Age of Acquiescence* (2015). A comparison of the late nineteenth century with the current era, exploring why protest against inequality was stronger in the former.

Hyman, Louis. *Temp: How American Work, American Business, and the American Dream Became Temporary* (2018). Explores the reasons for the rise of temporary jobs as the norm and the impact of prospects for workers moving into the middle class.

Lakoff, George. *Whose Freedom? The Battle over America's Most Important Idea* (2006). Describes how conservatives and liberals continue to interpret freedom in very different ways.

Lansley, Stewart. *Divided We Stand: Why Inequality Keeps Rising* (2011). A prominent economist explains the reasons for rising economic inequality.

Mounk, Yascha. *The People vs. Democracy: Why Our Freedom Is in Danger and How to Save It* (2018). Sees the 2016 election as endangering democratic institutions and respect for the rights of minorities in the United States.

Tooze, Adam. *Crashed: How a Decade of Financial Crises Changed the World* (2018). Examines the causes of the financial crisis of 2008, its global implications, and why governments did so little to assist its victims.

Turk, Katherine. *Equality on Trial: Gender and Rights in the Modern American Workplace* (2015). An examination of the persistence of gender inequality in offices, factories, and other sites of work.

Weisser, Michael. *From My Cold Dead Hands: Why Americans Won't Give Up Their Guns* (2018). A judicious examination of the debate over gun control.

Zakaria, Fareed. *The Future of Freedom: Illiberal Democracy at Home and Abroad* (2003). A foreign policy analyst discusses how the United States should respond to threats to freedom in the world.

Websites

The White House: www.whitehouse.gov

GLOSSARY

abolition Social movement of the pre–Civil War era that advocated the immediate emancipation of the slaves and their incorporation into American society as equal citizens.

Act Concerning Religion (or Maryland Toleration Act) 1649 law that granted free exercise of religion to all Christian denominations in colonial Maryland.

Adkins v. Children's Hospital 1923 Supreme Court case that reversed *Muller v. Oregon,* the 1908 case that permitted states to set maximum hours to protect working women. Justices ruled in *Adkins* that women no longer deserved special treatment because they could vote.

affirmative action Policy efforts to promote greater employment opportunities for minorities.

Agricultural Adjustment Act New Deal legislation passed in 1933 that established the Agricultural Adjustment Administration (AAA) to improve agricultural prices by limiting market supplies; declared unconstitutional in *United States v. Butler* (1936).

Albany Plan of Union A failed 1754 proposal by the seven northern colonies in anticipation of the French and Indian War, urging the unification of the colonies under one crown-appointed president.

Alien and Sedition Acts Four measures passed in 1798 during the undeclared war with France that limited the freedoms of speech and press and restricted the liberty of noncitizens.

American Anti-Slavery Society Founded in 1833, the organization that sought an immediate end to slavery and the establishment of equality for black Americans. It split in 1840 after disputes about the role of women within the organization and other issues.

American Civil Liberties Union Organization founded during World War I to protest the suppression of freedom of expression in wartime; played a major role in court cases that achieved judicial recognition of Americans' civil liberties.

American Colonization Society Organized in 1816 to encourage colonization of free blacks to Africa; West African nation of Liberia founded in 1822 to serve as a homeland for them.

American exceptionalism The belief that the United States has a special mission to serve as a refuge from tyranny, a symbol of freedom, and a model for the rest of the world.

American Federation of Labor A federation of trade unions founded in 1881, composed mostly of skilled, white, native-born workers; its long-term president was Samuel Gompers.

American Indian Movement (AIM) Movement founded in 1963 by Native Americans who were fed up with the poor conditions on Indian reservations and the federal government's unwillingness to help. In 1973, AIM led 200 Sioux in the occupation of Wounded Knee. After a ten-week standoff with the federal authorities, the government agreed to reexamine Indian treaty rights and the occupation ended.

"American standard of living" The Progressive-era idea that American workers were entitled to a wage high enough to allow them full participation in the nation's mass consumption economy.

American System Program of internal improvements and protective tariffs promoted by Speaker of the House Henry Clay in his presidential campaign of 1824; his proposals formed the core of Whig ideology in the 1830s and 1840s.

American system of manufactures A system of production that relied on the mass production of interchangeable parts that could be rapidly assembled into standardized finished products. First perfected in Connecticut by clockmaker Eli Terry and by small-arms producer Eli Whitney in the 1840s and 1850s.

Americans with Disabilities Act 1990 law that prohibited the discrimination against persons with disabilities in both hiring and promotion. It also mandated accessible entrances for public buildings.

the *Amistad* Ship that transported slaves from one port in Cuba to another, seized by the slaves in 1839. They made their way northward to the United States, where the status of the slaves became the subject of a celebrated court case; eventually most were able to return to Africa.

Anglican Church The established state church of England, formed by Henry VIII after the pope refused to annul his marriage to Catherine of Aragon.

annuity system System of yearly payments to Native American tribes by which the federal government justified and institutionalized its interference in Indian tribal affairs.

Antietam, Battle of One of the bloodiest battles of the Civil War, fought to a standoff on September 17, 1862, in western Maryland.

Anti-Federalists Opponents of the Constitution who saw it as a limitation on individual and states' rights; their demands led to the addition of a Bill of Rights to the document.

Anti-Imperialist League Coalition of anti-imperialist groups united in 1899 to protest American territorial expansion, especially in the Philippine Islands; its membership included prominent politicians, industrialists, labor leaders, and social reformers.

Appomattox Courthouse, Virginia Site of the surrender of Confederate general Robert E. Lee to Union general Ulysses S. Grant on April 9, 1865, marking the end of the Civil War.

Army-McCarthy hearings Televised U.S. Senate hearings in 1954 on Senator Joseph McCarthy's charges of disloyalty in the army; his tactics contributed to his censure by the Senate.

Arnold, Benedict A traitorous American commander who planned to sell out the American garrison at West Point to the British. His plot was discovered before it could be executed, and he joined the British army.

Articles of Confederation First frame of government for the United States; in effect from 1781 to 1788, it provided for a weak central authority and was soon replaced by the Constitution.

Atlanta Compromise Speech to the Cotton States and International Exposition in 1895 by educator Booker T. Washington, the leading black spokesman of the day; black scholar W. E. B. Du Bois gave the speech its derisive name and criticized Washington for encouraging blacks to accommodate segregation and disenfranchisement.

Atlantic slave trade The systematic importation of African slaves from their native continent across the Atlantic Ocean to the New World, largely fueled by rising demand for sugar, rice, coffee, and tobacco.

Attucks, Crispus During the Boston Massacre, the individual who was supposedly at the head of the crowd of hecklers and who baited the British troops. He was killed when the British troops fired on the crowd.

Axis powers In World War II, the nations of Germany, Italy, and Japan.

Aztec Mesoamerican people who were conquered by the Spanish under Hernan Cortes, 1519–1528.

baby boom Markedly higher birthrate in the years following World War II; led to the biggest demographic "bubble" in American history.

backcountry In colonial America, the area stretching from central Pennsylvania southward through the Shenandoah Valley of Virginia and into upland North and South Carolina.

Bacon's Rebellion Unsuccessful 1676 revolt led by planter Nathaniel Bacon against Virginia governor William Berkeley's administration because of governmental corruption and because Berkeley had failed to protect settlers from Indian raids and did not allow them to occupy Indian lands.

Balkan crisis A series of ethnic and political crises that arose following the dissolution of Yugoslavia in the 1990s. Many atrocities were committed during the conflict, and NATO, the United Nations, and the United States intervened several times.

Bank of the United States Proposed by the first secretary of the treasury, Alexander Hamilton, the bank that opened in 1791 and operated until 1811 to issue a uniform currency, make business loans, and collect tax monies. The Second Bank of the United States was chartered in 1816 but President Andrew Jackson vetoed the recharter bill in 1832.

Bank War Political struggle in the early 1830s between President Jackson and financier Nicholas Biddle over the renewing of the Second Bank's charter.

Barbary Wars The first wars fought by the United States, and the nation's first encounter with the Islamic world. The wars were fought from 1801 to 1805 against plundering pirates off the Mediterranean coast of Africa after President Thomas Jefferson's refusal to pay them tribute to protect American ships.

Bargain of 1877 Deal made by a Republican and Democratic special congressional commission to resolve the disputed presidential election of 1876; Republican Rutherford B. Hayes, who had lost the popular vote, was declared the winner in exchange for the withdrawal of federal troops from involvement in politics in the South, marking the end of Reconstruction.

Bay of Pigs Invasion U.S. mission in which the CIA, hoping to inspire a revolt against Fidel Castro, sent 1,500 Cuban exiles to invade their homeland on April 17, 1961; the mission was a spectacular failure.

the Beats A term coined by Jack Kerouac for a small group of poets and writers who railed against 1950s mainstream culture.

Bill for Establishing Religious Freedom A Virginia law, drafted by Thomas Jefferson in 1777 and enacted in 1786, that guarantees freedom of, and from, religion.

Bill of Rights First ten amendments to the U.S. Constitution, adopted in 1791 to guarantee individual rights against infringement by the federal government.

birth-control movement An offshoot of the early twentieth-century feminist movement that saw access to birth control and "voluntary motherhood" as essential to women's freedom. The birth-control movement was led by Margaret Sanger.

Black Codes Laws passed from 1865 to 1866 in southern states to restrict the rights of former slaves; to nullify the codes, Congress passed the Civil Rights Act of 1866 and the Fourteenth Amendment.

Black Legend Idea that the Spanish New World empire was more oppressive toward the Indians than other European empires; was used as a justification for English imperial expansion.

Black Lives Matter Civil rights movement sparked by a series of incidents of police brutality and lethal force against people of color.

Black Power Post-1966 rallying cry of a more militant civil rights movement.

"Bleeding Kansas" Violence between pro- and antislavery settlers in the Kansas Territory, 1856.

bonanza farms Large farms that covered thousands of acres and employed hundreds of wage laborers in the West in the late nineteenth century.

borderland A place between or near recognized borders where no group of people has complete political control or cultural dominance.

Boston Massacre Clash between British soldiers and a Boston mob, March 5, 1770, in which five colonists were killed.

Boston Tea Party The incident on December 16, 1773, in which the Sons of Liberty, dressed as Indians, dumped hundreds of chests of tea into Boston Harbor to protest the Tea Act of 1773. Under the Tea Act, the British exported to the colonies millions of pounds of cheap—but still taxed—tea, thereby undercutting the price of smuggled tea and forcing payment of the tea duty.

***bracero* program** System agreed to by Mexican and American governments in 1942 under which tens of thousands of Mexicans entered the United States to work temporarily in agricultural jobs in the Southwest; lasted until 1964 and inhibited labor organization among farm workers since *braceros* could be deported at any time.

Bretton Woods conference International meeting held in the town of Bretton Woods, New Hampshire, in 1944 in which participants agreed that the American dollar would replace the British pound as the most important international currency. The conference also created the World Bank and International Monetary Fund to promote rebuilding after World War II and to ensure that countries did not devalue their currencies.

Brown v. Board of Education 1954 U.S. Supreme Court decision that struck down racial segregation in public education and declared "separate but equal" unconstitutional.

Bull Run, first Battle of The first land engagement of the Civil War, which took place on July 21, 1861, at Manassas Junction, Virginia, and at which Union troops quickly retreated.

Bull Run, second Battle of Civil War engagement that took place one year after the first Battle of Bull Run, on August 29–30, during which Confederates captured the federal supply depot at Manassas Junction, Virginia, and forced Union troops back to Washington.

Bunker Hill, Battle of First major battle of the Revolutionary War; it actually took place at nearby Breed's Hill, Massachusetts, on June 17, 1775.

Bush Doctrine President George W. Bush's foreign policy principle wherein the United States would launch a war on terrorism.

Bush v. Gore U.S. Supreme Court case that determined the winner of the disputed 2000 presidential election.

busing The means of transporting students via buses to achieve school integration in the 1970s.

Camp David Accords Peace agreement between the leaders of Israel and Egypt, brokered by President Jimmy Carter in 1978.

captivity narratives Accounts written by colonists after their time in Indian captivity, often stressing the captive's religious convictions.

caravel A fifteenth-century European ship capable of long-distance travel.

carpetbaggers Derisive term for northern emigrants who participated in the Republican governments of the Reconstruction South.

checks and balances A systematic balance to prevent any one branch of the national government from dominating the other two.

Chinese Exclusion Act 1882 law that halted Chinese immigration to the United States.

Church of Jesus Christ of Latter-Day Saints Religious sect founded in 1830 by Joseph Smith; it was a product of the intense revivalism of the "burned-over district" of New York. Smith's successor Brigham Young led 15,000 followers to Utah in 1847 to escape persecution.

Civil Rights Act (1964) Law that outlawed discrimination in public accommodations and employment.

Civil Rights Act of 1875 The last piece of Reconstruction legislation, which outlawed racial discrimination in places of public accommodation such as hotels and theaters. Many parts of it were ruled unconstitutional by the Supreme Court in 1883.

Civil Rights Bill of 1866 Along with the Fourteenth Amendment, legislation that guaranteed the rights of citizenship to former slaves.

Civil Service Act of 1883 Law that established the Civil Service Commission and marked the end of the spoils system.

Civilian Conservation Corps (CCC) 1933 New Deal public work relief program that provided outdoor manual work for unemployed men, rebuilding infrastructure and implementing conservation programs. The program cut the unemployment rate, particularly among young men.

Cold War Term for tensions, 1945–1989, between the Soviet Union and the United States, the two major world powers after World War II.

collective bargaining The process of negotiations between an employer and a group of employees to regulate working conditions.

Columbian Exchange The transatlantic flow of goods and people that began with Columbus's voyages in 1492.

Committee of Correspondence Group organized by Samuel Adams in retaliation for the *Gaspée* incident to address American grievances, assert American rights, and form a network of rebellion.

common school Tax-supported state schools of the early nineteenth century open to all children.

Common Sense A pamphlet anonymously written by Thomas Paine in January 1776 that attacked the English principles of hereditary rule and monarchical government.

communitarianism Social reform movement of the nineteenth century driven by the belief that by establishing small communities based on common ownership of property, a less competitive and less individualistic society could be developed.

Compromise of 1850 Complex compromise devised by Senator Henry Clay that admitted California as a free state, included a stronger fugitive slave law, and delayed determination of the slave status of the New Mexico and Utah territories.

Congress of Industrial Organizations Umbrella organization of semiskilled industrial unions, formed in 1935 as the Committee for Industrial Organization and renamed in 1938.

conquistadores Spanish term for "conquerors," applied to Spanish and Portuguese soldiers who conquered lands held by indigenous peoples in central and southern America as well as the current states of Texas, New Mexico, Arizona, and California.

conservation movement A progressive reform movement focused on the preservation and sustainable management of the nation's natural resources.

Constitutional Convention Meeting in Philadelphia, May 25–September 17, 1787, of representatives from twelve colonies—excepting Rhode Island—to revise the existing Articles of Confederation; the convention soon resolved to produce an entirely new constitution.

containment General U.S. strategy in the Cold War that called for containing Soviet expansion; originally devised by U.S. diplomat George F. Kennan.

Continental army Army authorized by the Continental Congress in 1775 to fight the British; commanded by General George Washington.

Continental Congress First meeting of representatives of the colonies, held in Philadelphia in 1774 to formulate actions against British policies; in the Second Continental Congress (1775–1789), the colonial representatives conducted the war and adopted the Declaration of Independence and the Articles of Confederation.

"the contrabands" Slaves who sought refuge in Union military camps or who lived in areas of the Confederacy under Union control.

Contract with America A list of conservatives' promises in response to the supposed liberalism of the Clinton administration, that was drafted by Speaker of the House Newt Gingrich and other congressional Republicans as the GOP platform for the 1994 midterm elections. It was more a campaign tactic than a practical program; few of its proposed items ever became law.

cotton gin Invented by Eli Whitney in 1793, the machine that separated cotton seed from cotton fiber, speeding cotton processing and making profitable the cultivation of the more hardy, but difficult to clean, short-staple cotton; led directly to the dramatic nineteenth-century expansion of slavery in the South.

"Cotton is king" Phrase from Senator James Henry Hammond's speech extolling the virtues of cotton, and, implicitly, the slave system of production that led to its bounty for the South. "King Cotton" became a shorthand for Southern political and economic power.

Cotton Kingdom Cotton-producing region, relying predominantly on slave labor, that spanned from North Carolina west to Louisiana and reached as far north as southern Illinois.

counterculture "Hippie" youth culture of the 1960s, which rejected the values of the dominant culture in favor of illicit drugs, communes, free sex, and rock music.

Court packing President Franklin D. Roosevelt's failed 1937 attempt to increase the number of U.S. Supreme Court justices from nine to fifteen in order to save his Second New Deal programs from constitutional challenges.

Covenant Chain Alliance formed in the 1670s between the English and the Iroquois nations.

coverture Principle in English and American law that a married woman lost her legal identity, which became "covered" by that of her husband, who therefore controlled her person and the family's economic resources.

Coxey's Army A march on Washington organized by Jacob Coxey, an Ohio member of the People's Party. Coxey believed in abandoning the gold standard and printing enough legal tender to reinvigorate the economy. The marchers demanded that Congress create jobs and pay workers in paper currency not backed by gold.

creoles Persons born in the New World of European ancestry.

crop lien Credit extended by merchants to tenants based on their future crops; under this system, high interest rates and the uncertainties of farming often led to inescapable debts.

Cuban missile crisis Tense confrontation caused when the United States discovered Soviet offensive missile sites in Cuba in October 1962; the U.S.-Soviet confrontation was the Cold War's closest brush with nuclear war.

cult of domesticity The nineteenth-century ideology of "virtue" and "modesty" as the qualities that were essential to proper womanhood.

Culture Wars Battles over moral values that occurred throughout the 1990s. The Culture Wars touched many areas of American life—from popular culture to academia. Flashpoints included the future of the nuclear family and the teaching of evolution.

Dartmouth College v. Woodward 1819 U.S. Supreme Court case in which the Court upheld the original charter of the college against New Hampshire's attempt to alter the board of trustees; set the precedent of support of contracts against state interference.

Dawes Act Law passed in 1887 meant to encourage adoption of white norms among Indians; broke up tribal holdings into small farms for Indian families, with the remainder sold to white purchasers.

D-Day June 6, 1944, when an Allied amphibious assault landed on the Normandy coast and established a foothold in Europe, leading to the liberation of France from German occupation.

Declaration of Independence Document adopted on July 4, 1776, that made the break with Britain official; drafted by a committee of the Second Continental Congress, including principal writer Thomas Jefferson.

decolonization The process by which African and Asian colonies of European empires became independent in the years following World War II.

deindustrialization Term describing decline of manufacturing in old industrial areas in the late twentieth century as companies shifted production to low-wage centers in the South and West or in other countries.

Deism Enlightenment thought applied to religion; emphasized reason, morality, and natural law.

Democracy in America Two works, published in 1835 and 1840, by the French thinker Alexis de Tocqueville on the subject of American democracy. Tocqueville stressed the cultural nature of American democracy, and the importance and prevalence of equality in American life.

Democratic-Republican societies Organizations created in the mid-1790s by opponents of the policies of the Washington administration and supporters of the French Revolution.

Denmark Vesey's conspiracy An 1822 failed slave uprising in Charleston, South Carolina, purported to have been led by Denmark Vesey, a free black man.

deregulation Legislation of the Reagan-Clinton era that removed regulations on many industries, including finance and air travel.

détente Period of improving relations between the United States and Communist nations, particularly China and the Soviet Union, during the Nixon administration.

disenfranchisement Depriving a person or persons of the right to vote; in the United States, exclusionary policies were used to deny groups, especially African-Americans and women, their voting rights.

Dissenters Protestants who belonged to denominations outside of the established Anglican Church.

division of powers The division of political power between the state and federal governments under the U.S. Constitution (also known as federalism).

Dix, Dorothea An important figure in increasing the public's awareness of the plight of the mentally ill. After a two-year investigation of the treatment of the mentally ill in Massachusetts, she presented her findings and won the support of leading reformers. She eventually convinced twenty states to reform their treatment of the mentally ill.

Dixiecrats Lower South delegates who walked out of the 1948 Democratic national convention in protest of the party's support for civil rights legislation and later formed the States' Rights Democratic (Dixiecrat) Party, which nominated Strom Thurmond of South Carolina for president.

Dollar Diplomacy A foreign policy initiative under President William Howard Taft that promoted the spread of American influence through loans and economic investments from American banks.

Dominion of New England Consolidation into a single colony of the New England colonies—and later New York and New Jersey—by royal governor Edmund Andros in 1686; dominion reverted to individual colonial governments three years later.

"Don't ask, don't tell" President Clinton's compromise measure that allowed gay people to serve in the military incognito, as officers could no longer seek them out for dismissal but they could not openly express their identity. "Don't ask, don't tell" was ended under the Obama administration, when gay military service was allowed.

the Dorr War A movement in Rhode Island against property qualifications for voting. The movement formed an extralegal constitutional convention for the state and elected Thomas Dorr as a governor, but was quashed by federal troops dispatched by President John Tyler.

double-V Led by *the Pittsburgh Courier*, the movement that pressed for victory over fascism abroad and over racism at home. It argued that since African-Americans were risking their lives abroad, they should receive full civil rights at home.

dower rights In colonial America, the right of a widowed woman to inherit one-third of her deceased husband's property.

Dred Scott v. Sandford 1857 U.S. Supreme Court decision in which Chief Justice Roger B. Taney ruled that Congress could not prohibit slavery in the territories, on the grounds that such a prohibition would violate the Fifth Amendment rights of slaveholders, and that no black person could be a citizen of the United States.

Dust Bowl Great Plains counties where millions of tons of topsoil were blown away from parched farmland in the 1930s; massive migration of farm families followed.

Eighteenth Amendment Prohibition amendment passed in 1919 that made illegal the manufacture, sale, or transportation of alcoholic beverages; repealed in 1933.

Ellis Island Reception center in New York Harbor through which most European immigrants to America were processed from 1892 to 1954.

Emancipation Proclamation Declaration issued by President Abraham Lincoln; the preliminary proclamation on September 22, 1862, freed the slaves in areas under Confederate control as of January 1, 1863, the date of the final proclamation, which also authorized the enrollment of black soldiers into the Union army.

Embargo Act Attempt in 1807 to exert economic pressure by prohibiting all exports from the United States, instead of waging war in reaction to continued British impressment of American sailors; smugglers easily circumvented the embargo, and it was repealed two years later.

Emergency Banking Act Passed in 1933, the First New Deal measure that provided for reopening the banks under strict conditions and took the United States off the gold standard.

empire of liberty The idea, expressed by Jefferson, that the United States would not rule its new territories as colonies, but rather would eventually admit them as full member states.

enclosure movement A legal process that divided large farm fields in England that were previously collectively owned by groups of peasants into smaller, individually owned plots. The enclosure movement took place over several centuries, and resulted in eviction for many peasants.

Enforcement Acts Three laws passed in 1870 and 1871 that tried to eliminate the Ku Klux Klan by outlawing it and other such terrorist societies; the laws allowed the president to deploy the army for that purpose.

English Bill of Rights A series of laws enacted in 1689 that inscribed the rights of Englishmen into law and enumerated parliamentary powers such as taxation.

English liberty The idea that English people were entitled to certain liberties, including trial by jury, habeas corpus, and the right to face one's accuser in court. These rights meant that even the English king was subject to the rule of law.

English Toleration Act A 1690 act of Parliament that allowed all English Protestants to worship freely.

Enlightenment Revolution in thought in the eighteenth century that emphasized reason and science over the authority of traditional religion.

Equal Rights Amendment Amendment to guarantee equal rights for women, introduced in 1923 but not passed by Congress until 1972; it failed to be ratified by the states.

Era of Good Feelings Contemporary characterization of the administration of popular Republican president James Monroe, 1817–1825.

Erie Canal Most important and profitable of the canals of the 1820s and 1830s; stretched from Buffalo to Albany, New York, connecting the Great Lakes to the East Coast and making New York City the nation's largest port.

Espionage Act 1917 law that prohibited spying and interfering with the draft as well as making "false statements" that hurt the war effort.

ethnic cleansing The systematic removal of an ethnic group from a territory through violence or intimidation in order to create a homogeneous society; the term was popularized by the Yugoslav policy brutally targeting Albanian Muslims in Kosovo.

Ex parte Milligan 1866 Supreme Court case that declared it unconstitutional to bring accused persons before military tribunals where civil courts were operating.

Exposition and Protest Document written in 1828 by Vice President John C. Calhoun of South Carolina to protest the so-called Tariff of Abominations, which seemed to favor northern industry; introduced the concept of state interposition and became the basis for South Carolina's Nullification Doctrine of 1833.

Fair Deal Domestic reform proposals of the Truman administration; included civil rights legislation, national health insurance, and repeal of the Taft-Hartley Act, but only extensions of some New Deal programs were enacted.

family values Set of beliefs usually associated with conservatism that stressed the superiority of nuclear family, heterosexual marriage, and traditional gender roles.

family wage Idea that male workers should earn a wage sufficient to enable them to support their entire family without their wives having to work outside the home.

Federal Housing Administration (FHA) A government agency created during the New Deal to guarantee mortgages, allowing lenders to offer long-term (usually thirty-year) loans with low down payments (usually 10 percent of the asking price). The FHA seldom underwrote loans in racially mixed or minority neighborhoods.

Federal Trade Commission (FTC) Independent agency created by the Wilson administration that replaced the Bureau of Corporations as an even more powerful tool to combat unfair trade practices and monopolies.

federalism A system of government in which power is divided between the central government and the states.

The Federalist Collection of eighty-five essays that appeared in the New York press in 1787–1788 in support of the Constitution; written by Alexander Hamilton, James Madison, and John Jay and published under the pseudonym "Publius."

Federalists and Republicans The two increasingly coherent political parties that appeared in Congress by the mid-1790s. The Federalists, led by George Washington, John Adams, and Alexander Hamilton, favored a strong central government. The Republicans, first identified during the early nineteenth century, supported a strict interpretation of the Constitution, which they believed would safeguard individual freedoms and states' rights from the threats posed by a strong central government.

The Feminine Mystique The book widely credited with sparking second-wave feminism in the United States. Author Betty Friedan focused on college-educated women, arguing that they would find fulfillment by engaging in paid labor outside the home.

feminism Term that entered the lexicon in the early twentieth century to describe the movement for full equality for women, in political, social, and personal life.

Fifteenth Amendment Constitutional amendment ratified in 1870, which prohibited states from discriminating in voting privileges on the basis of race.

flappers Young women of the 1920s whose rebellion against prewar standards of femininity included wearing shorter dresses, bobbing their hair, dancing to jazz music, driving cars, smoking cigarettes, and indulging in illegal drinking and gambling.

Force Act 1833 legislation, sparked by the nullification crisis in South Carolina, that authorized the president's use of the army to compel states to comply with federal law.

Fordism Early twentieth-century term describing the economic system pioneered by Ford Motor Company based on high wages and mass consumption.

Fort McHenry Fort in Baltimore Harbor unsuccessfully bombarded by the British in September 1814; Francis Scott Key, a witness to the battle, was moved to write the words to "The Star-Spangled Banner."

Fort Sumter First battle of the Civil War, in which the federal fort in Charleston (South Carolina) Harbor was captured by the Confederates on April 14, 1861, after two days of shelling.

Four Freedoms Freedom of speech, freedom of worship, freedom from want, and freedom from fear, as described by President Franklin D. Roosevelt during his January 6, 1941, State of the Union address.

Fourteen Points President Woodrow Wilson's 1918 plan for peace after World War I; at the Versailles peace conference, however, he failed to incorporate all of the points into the treaty.

Fourteenth Amendment 1868 constitutional amendment that guaranteed rights of citizenship to former slaves, in words similar to those of the Civil Rights Act of 1866.

franchise The right to vote.

free blacks African-American persons not held in slavery; immediately before the Civil War, there were nearly a half million in the United States, split almost evenly between North and South.

Free Soil Party Political organization formed in 1848 to oppose slavery in the territory acquired in the Mexican War; nominated Martin Van Buren for president in 1848. By 1854 most of the party's members had joined the Republican Party.

free trade The belief that economic development arises from the exchange of goods between different countries without governmental interference.

the Freedmen's Bureau Reconstruction agency established in 1865 to protect the legal rights of former slaves and to assist with their education, jobs, health care, and landowning.

freedom petitions Arguments for liberty presented to New England's courts and legislatures in the early 1770s by enslaved African-Americans.

Freedom Rides Bus journeys challenging racial segregation in the South in 1961.

French and Indian War The last—and most important—of four colonial wars fought between England and France for control of North America east of the Mississippi River.

Fugitive Slave Act 1850 law that gave the federal government authority in cases involving runaway slaves; aroused considerable opposition in the North.

fugitive slaves Slaves who escaped from their owners.

fundamentalism Anti-modernist Protestant movement started in the early twentieth century that proclaimed the literal truth of the Bible; the name came from *The Fundamentals*, published by conservative leaders.

Gabriel's Rebellion An 1800 uprising planned by Virginian slaves to gain their freedom. The plot was led by a blacksmith named Gabriel, but was discovered and quashed.

gag rule Rule adopted by the House of Representatives in 1836 prohibiting consideration of abolitionist petitions; opposition, led by former president John Quincy Adams, succeeded in having it repealed in 1844.

Garvey, Marcus The leading spokesman for Negro Nationalism, which exalted blackness, black cultural expression, and black exclusiveness. He called upon African-Americans to liberate themselves from the surrounding white culture and create their own businesses, cultural centers, and newspapers. He was also the founder of the Universal Negro Improvement Association.

Geneva Accords A 1954 document that had promised elections to unify Vietnam and established the Seventeenth Parallel demarcation line that divided North and South Vietnam.

"gentlemen of property and standing" Well-to-do merchants who often had commercial ties to the South and resisted abolitionism, occasionally inciting violence against its adherents.

Gettysburg, Battle of Battle fought in southern Pennsylvania, July 1–3, 1863; the Confederate defeat and the simultaneous loss at Vicksburg marked the military turning point of the Civil War.

Ghost Dance A spiritual and political movement among Native Americans whose followers performed a ceremonial "ghost dance" intended to connect the living with the dead and make the Indians bulletproof in battles intended to restore their homelands.

GI Bill of Rights The 1944 legislation that provided money for education and other benefits to military personnel returning from World War II.

Gibbons v. Ogden 1824 U.S. Supreme Court decision reinforcing the "commerce clause" (the federal government's right to regulate interstate commerce) of the Constitution; Chief Justice John Marshall ruled against the State of New York's granting of steamboat monopolies.

the Gilded Age The popular but derogatory name for the period from the end of the Civil War to the turn of the century, after the title of the 1873 novel by Mark Twain and Charles Dudley Warner.

globalization Term that became prominent in the 1990s to describe the rapid acceleration of international flows of commerce, financial resources, labor, and cultural products.

Glorious Revolution A coup in 1688 engineered by a small group of aristocrats that led to William of Orange taking the British throne in place of James II.

gold rush The massive migration of Americans into California territory in the late 1840s and 1850s in pursuit of gold, which was discovered there in 1848.

gold standard Policy at various points in American history by which the value of a dollar is set at a fixed price in terms of gold (in the post–World War II era, for example, $35 per ounce of gold).

Good Neighbor Policy Policy proclaimed by President Franklin D. Roosevelt in his first inaugural address in 1933 that sought improved diplomatic relations between the United States and its Latin American neighbors.

gradual emancipation A series of acts passed in state legislatures throughout the North in the years following the Revolution that freed slaves after they reached a certain age, following lengthy "apprenticeships."

grandfather clause Loophole created by southern disenfranchising legislatures of the 1890s for illiterate white males whose grandfathers had been eligible to vote before the Civil War.

Great Awakening Fervent religious revival movement in the 1720s through the 1740s that was spread throughout the colonies by ministers like New England Congregationalist Jonathan Edwards and English revivalist George Whitefield.

Great Depression Worst economic depression in American history; it was spurred by the stock market crash of 1929 and lasted until World War II.

Great League of Peace An alliance of the Iroquois tribes, originally formed sometime between 1450 and 1600, that used their combined strength to pressure Europeans to work with them in the fur trade and to wage war across what is today eastern North America.

Great Migration Large-scale migration of southern blacks during and after World War I to the North, where jobs had become available during the labor shortage of the war years.

Great Migration (1630s) The migration of approximately 21,000 English Puritans to the Massachusetts Bay Colony.

Great Railroad Strike A series of demonstrations, some violent, held nationwide in support of striking railroad workers in Martinsburg, West Virginia, who refused to work due to wage cuts.

Great Recession A period of major economic stagnation across the United States and western Europe, characterized by rising unemployment and inflation and a 37 percent decline in the stock market between March and December 1974.

Great Society Term coined by President Lyndon B. Johnson in his 1965 State of the Union address, in which he proposed legislation to address problems of voting rights, poverty, diseases, education, immigration, and the environment.

Griswold v. Connecticut Supreme Court decision that, in overturning Connecticut law prohibiting the use of contraceptives, established a constitutional right to privacy.

Guantánamo Bay A detention center at the American naval base at Guantánamo Bay, Cuba, where beginning in 2002 suspected terrorists and war prisoners were held indefinitely and tried by extrajudicial military tribunals. During his 2008 presidential campaign, Senator Barack Obama pledged to close the prison, but as of 2015 it remained open.

Gulf of Tonkin resolution Legislation passed by Congress in 1964 in reaction to supposedly unprovoked attacks on American warships off the coast of North Vietnam; it gave the president unlimited authority to defend U.S. forces and members of the Southeast Asia Treaty Organization (SEATO).

Gulf War Military action in 1991 in which an international coalition led by the United States drove Iraq from Kuwait, which it had occupied the previous year.

hacienda Large-scale farm in the Spanish New World empire worked by Indian laborers.

Haitian Revolution A slave uprising that led to the establishment of Haiti as an independent country in 1804.

Half-Way Covenant A 1662 religious compromise that allowed baptism and partial church membership to colonial New Englanders whose parents were not among the Puritan elect.

Harlem Renaissance African-American literary and artistic movement of the 1920s centered in New York City's Harlem neighborhood; writers Langston Hughes, Jean Toomer, Zora Neale Hurston, and Countee Cullen were among those active in the movement.

Harpers Ferry, Virginia Site of abolitionist John Brown's failed raid on the federal arsenal, October 16–17, 1859; Brown became a martyr to his cause after his capture and execution.

Hart-Celler Act 1965 law that eliminated the national origins quota system for immigration established by laws in 1921 and 1924; led to radical change in the origins of immigrants to the United States, with Asians and Latin Americans outnumbering Europeans.

Hartford Convention Meeting of New England Federalists on December 15, 1814, to protest the War of 1812; proposed seven constitutional amendments (limiting embargoes and changing requirements for officeholding, declaration of war, and admission of new states), but the war ended before Congress could respond.

Haymarket Affair Violence during an anarchist protest at Haymarket Square in Chicago on May 4, 1886; the deaths of eight, including seven policemen, led to the trial of eight anarchist leaders for conspiracy to commit murder.

Haynes, Lemuel A black member of the Massachusetts militia and celebrated minister who urged that Americans extend their conception of freedom to enslaved Africans during the Revolutionary era.

headright system A land-grant policy that promised fifty acres to any colonist who could afford passage to Virginia, as well as fifty more for any accompanying servants. The headright policy was eventually expanded to include any colonists—and was also adopted in other colonies.

Helsinki Accords 1975 agreement between the USSR and the United States that recognized the post–World War II boundaries of Europe and guaranteed the basic liberties of each nation's citizens.

Hessians German soldiers, most from Hesse-Cassel principality (hence, the name), paid to fight for the British in the Revolutionary War.

Hollywood Ten A group called before the House Un-American Activities Committee who refused to speak about their political leanings or "name names"—that is, identify communists in Hollywood. Some were imprisoned as a result.

Holocaust Systematic racist attempt by the Nazis to exterminate the Jews of Europe, resulting in the murder of over 6 million Jews and more than a million other "undesirables."

Homestead Act 1862 law that authorized Congress to grant 160 acres of public land to a western settler, who had to live on the land for five years to establish title.

horizontal expansion The process by which a corporation acquires or merges with its competitors.

House of Burgesses The first elected assembly in colonial America, established in 1619 in Virginia. Only wealthy landowners could vote in its elections.

House Un-American Activities Committee (HUAC) Committee formed in 1938 to investigate subversives in the government and holders of radical ideas more generally; best-known investigations were of Hollywood notables and of former State Department official Alger Hiss, who was accused in 1948 of espionage and Communist Party membership. Abolished in 1975.

Hundred Days Extraordinarily productive first three months of President Franklin D. Roosevelt's administration in which a special session of Congress enacted fifteen of his New Deal proposals.

Hurricane Katrina 2005 hurricane that devastated much of the Gulf Coast, especially New Orleans. The Bush administration's response was widely criticized as inadequate.

illegal alien A new category established by the Immigration Act of 1924 that referred to immigrants crossing U.S. borders in excess of the new immigration quotas.

Immigration Restriction League A political organization founded in 1894 that called for reducing immigration to the United States by requiring a literacy test for immigrants.

impeachment Bringing charges against a public official; for example, the House of Representatives can impeach a president for "treason, bribery, or other high crimes and misdemeanors" by majority vote, and after the trial the Senate can remove the president by a vote of two-thirds. Two presidents, Andrew Johnson and Bill Clinton, have been impeached and tried before the Senate; neither was convicted.

impressment The British navy's practice of using press-gangs to kidnap men in British and colonial ports who were then forced to serve in the British navy.

"In God We Trust" Phrase placed on all new U.S. currency as of 1954.

indentured servants Settlers who signed on for a temporary period of servitude to a master in exchange for passage to the New World; Virginia and Pennsylvania were largely peopled in the seventeenth and eighteenth centuries by English and German indentured servants.

Indian New Deal Phrase that refers to the reforms implemented for Native Americans during the New Deal era. John Collier, the commissioner of the Bureau of Indian Affairs (BIA), increased the access Native Americans had to relief programs and employed more Native Americans at the BIA. He worked to pass the Indian Reorganization Act. However, the version of the act passed by Congress was a much diluted version of Collier's original proposal and did not greatly improve the lives of Native Americans.

Indian Removal Act 1830 law signed by President Andrew Jackson that permitted the negotiation of treaties to obtain the Indians' lands in exchange for their relocation to what would become Oklahoma.

individualism Term that entered the language in the 1820s to describe the increasing emphasis on the pursuit of personal advancement and private fulfillment free of outside interference.

Industrial Workers of the World Radical union organized in Chicago in 1905 and nicknamed the Wobblies; its opposition to World War I led to its destruction by the federal government under the Espionage Act.

inflation An economic condition in which prices rise continuously.

initiative A Progressive-era reform that allowed citizens to propose and vote on laws, bypassing state legislatures.

Insular Cases Series of cases between 1901 and 1904 in which the Supreme Court ruled that constitutional protection of individual rights did not fully apply to residents of "insular" territories acquired by the United States in the Spanish-American War, such as Puerto Rico and the Philippines.

Interstate Commerce Commission Organization established by Congress, in reaction to the U.S. Supreme Court's ruling in *Wabash Railroad v. Illinois* (1886), in order to curb abuses in the railroad industry by regulating rates.

interstate highway system National network of interstate superhighways; its construction began in the late 1950s for the purpose of commerce and defense. The interstate highways would enable the rapid movement of military convoys and the evacuation of cities after a nuclear attack.

Intolerable Acts Four parliamentary measures in reaction to the Boston Tea Party that forced payment for the tea, disallowed colonial trials of British soldiers, forced their quartering in private homes, and reduced the number of elected officials in Massachusetts.

Iran-Contra Affair Scandal of the second Reagan administration involving sales of arms to Iran in partial exchange for release of hostages in Lebanon and use of the arms money to aid the Contras in Nicaragua, which had been expressly forbidden by Congress.

Iraq War Military campaign in 2003 in which the United States, unable to gain approval by the United Nations, unilaterally occupied Iraq and removed dictator Saddam Hussein from power.

iron curtain Term coined by Winston Churchill to describe the Cold War divide between western Europe and the Soviet Union's eastern European satellites.

ISIS An insurgency that emerged from the sectarian civil wars that destabilized Syria and post–Saddam Hussein Iraq. Beginning in 2014, ISIS forces attacked towns and cities in Iraq, Syria, and Libya, systematically murdering members of ethnic and religious minorities.

isolationism The desire to avoid foreign entanglements that dominated the U.S. Congress in the 1930s; beginning in 1935, lawmakers passed a series of Neutrality Acts that banned travel on belligerents' ships and the sale of arms to countries at war.

Japanese-American internment Policy adopted by the Roosevelt administration in 1942 under which 110,000 persons of Japanese descent, most of them American citizens, were removed from the West Coast and forced to spend most of World War II in internment camps; it was the largest violation of American civil liberties in the twentieth century.

Jay's Treaty Treaty with Britain negotiated in 1794 by Chief Justice John Jay; Britain agreed to vacate forts in the Northwest Territories, and festering disagreements (border with Canada, prewar debts, shipping claims) would be settled by commission.

Kansas Exodus A migration in 1879 and 1880 by some 40,000–60,000 blacks to Kansas to escape the oppressive environment of the New South.

Kansas-Nebraska Act 1854 law sponsored by Illinois senator Stephen A. Douglas to allow settlers in newly organized territories north of the Missouri border to decide the slavery issue for themselves; fury over the resulting repeal of the Missouri Compromise of 1820 led to violence in Kansas and to the formation of the Republican Party.

"King Cotton diplomacy" An attempt during the Civil War by the South to encourage British intervention by banning cotton exports.

King Philip's War A multiyear conflict that began in 1675 with an Indian uprising against white colonists. Its end result was broadened freedoms for white New Englanders and the dispossession of the region's Indians.

Knights of Labor Founded in 1869, the first national union; lasted, under the leadership of Terence V. Powderly, only into the 1890s; supplanted by the American Federation of Labor.

Know-Nothing Party Nativist, anti-Catholic third party organized in 1854 in reaction to large-scale German and Irish immigration; the party's only presidential candidate was Millard Fillmore in 1856.

Korean War Conflict touched off in 1950 when Communist North Korea invaded South Korea; fighting, largely by U.S. forces, continued until 1953.

Korematsu v. United States 1944 Supreme Court case that found Executive Order 9066 to be constitutional. Fred Korematsu, an American-born citizen of Japanese descent, defied the military order that banned all persons of Japanese ancestry from designated western coastal areas. The Court upheld Korematsu's arrest and internment.

Ku Klux Klan Group organized in Pulaski, Tennessee, in 1866 to terrorize former slaves who voted and held political offices during Reconstruction; a revived organization in the 1910s and 1920s that stressed white, Anglo-Saxon, fundamentalist Protestant supremacy; revived a third time to fight the civil rights movement of the 1950s and 1960s in the South.

Las Casas, Bartolomé de A Catholic missionary who renounced the Spanish practice of coercively converting Indians and advocated their better treatment. In 1552, he wrote *A Brief Relation of the Destruction of the Indies*, which described the Spanish's cruel treatment of the Indians.

League of Nations Organization of nations to mediate disputes and avoid war, established after World War I as part of the Treaty of Versailles; President Woodrow Wilson's "Fourteen Points" speech to Congress in 1918 proposed the formation of the league, which the United States never joined.

League of United Latin American Citizens Often called LULAC, an organization that challenged restrictive housing, employment discrimination, and other inequalities faced by Latino Americans.

Lend-Lease Act 1941 law that permitted the United States to lend or lease arms and other supplies to the Allies, signifying increasing likelihood of American involvement in World War II.

Levittown Low-cost, mass-produced developments of suburban tract housing built by William Levitt after World War II on Long Island and elsewhere.

Lewis and Clark expedition Led by Meriwether Lewis and William Clark, a mission to the Pacific coast commissioned for the purposes of scientific and geographical exploration.

Lexington and Concord, Battles of The first shots fired in the Revolutionary War, on April 19, 1775, near Boston; approximately 100 minutemen and 250 British soldiers were killed.

liberal internationalism Woodrow Wilson's foreign policy theory, which rested on the idea that economic and political freedom went hand in hand, and encouraged American intervention abroad in order to secure these freedoms globally.

liberalism Originally, political philosophy that emphasized the protection of liberty by limiting the power of government to interfere with the natural rights of citizens; in the twentieth century, belief in an activist government promoting greater social and economic equality.

liberty of contract A judicial concept of the late nineteenth and early twentieth centuries whereby the courts overturned laws regulating labor conditions as violations of the economic freedom of both employers and employees.

Liberty Party Abolitionist political party that nominated James G. Birney for president in 1840 and 1844; merged with the Free Soil Party in 1848.

Lincoln-Douglas debates Series of senatorial campaign debates in 1858 focusing on the issue of slavery in the territories; held in Illinois between Republican Abraham Lincoln, who made a national reputation for himself, and incumbent Democratic senator Stephen A. Douglas, who managed to hold on to his seat.

the Little Bighorn, Battle of Most famous battle of the Great Sioux War; took place in 1876 in the Montana Territory; combined Sioux and Cheyenne warriors massacred a vastly outnumbered U.S. Cavalry commanded by Lieutenant Colonel George Armstrong Custer.

Long Telegram A telegram by American diplomat George Kennan in 1946 outlining his views of the Soviet Union that eventually inspired the policy of containment.

Lord Dunmore's proclamation A proclamation issued in 1775 by the earl of Dunmore, the British governor of Virginia, that offered freedom to any slave who fought for the king against the rebelling colonists.

Lords of Trade An English regulatory board established to oversee colonial affairs in 1675.

the Lost Cause A romanticized view of slavery, the Old South, and the Confederacy that arose in the decades following the Civil War.

Louisiana Purchase President Thomas Jefferson's 1803 purchase from France of the important port of New Orleans and 828,000 square miles west of the Mississippi River to the Rocky Mountains; it more than doubled the territory of the United States at a cost of only $15 million.

Loyalists Colonists who remained loyal to Great Britain during the War of Independence.

Lusitania British passenger liner sunk by a German U-boat, May 7, 1915, creating a diplomatic crisis and public outrage at the loss of 128 Americans (roughly 10 percent of the total aboard); Germany agreed to pay reparations, and the United States waited two more years to enter World War I.

lynching Practice, particularly widespread in the South between 1890 and 1940, in which persons (usually black) accused of a crime were murdered by mobs before standing trial. Lynchings often took place before large crowds, with law enforcement authorities not intervening.

Manhattan Project Secret American program during World War II to develop an atomic bomb; J. Robert Oppenheimer led the team of physicists at Los Alamos, New Mexico.

manifest destiny Phrase first used in 1845 to urge annexation of Texas; used thereafter to encourage American settlement of European colonial and Indian lands in the Great Plains and the West and, more generally, as a justification for American empire.

Marbury v. Madison First U.S. Supreme Court decision to declare a federal law—the Judiciary Act of 1801—unconstitutional.

March for Our Lives Student-led protest on March 24, 2018, against gun violence and for gun control legislation in the United States.

March on Washington Civil rights demonstration on August 28, 1963, where the Reverend Martin Luther King Jr. gave his "I Have a Dream" speech on the steps of the Lincoln Memorial.

Marshall Plan U.S. program for the reconstruction of post–World War II Europe through massive aid to former enemy nations as well as allies; proposed by General George C. Marshall in 1947.

massive retaliation Strategy that used the threat of nuclear warfare as a means of combating the global spread of communism.

maternalist reforms Progressive-era reforms that sought to encourage women's child-bearing and -rearing abilities and to promote their economic independence.

Mayflower Compact Document signed in 1620 aboard the *Mayflower* before the Pilgrims landed at Plymouth; the document committed the group to majority-rule government.

McCarran-Walter Act Immigration legislation passed in 1952 that allowed the government to deport immigrants who had been identified as communists, regardless of whether they were citizens.

McCarthyism Post–World War II Red Scare focused on the fear of Communists in U.S. government positions; peaked during the Korean War; most closely associated with Joseph McCarthy, a major instigator of the hysteria.

McCulloch v. Maryland 1819 U.S. Supreme Court decision in which Chief Justice John Marshall, holding that Maryland could not tax the Second Bank of the United States, supported the authority of the federal government versus the states.

mercantilism Policy of Great Britain and other imperial powers of regulating the economies of colonies to benefit the mother country.

mestizos Spanish word for persons of mixed Native American and European ancestry.

Metacom The chief of the Wampanoags, whom the colonists called King Philip. He resented English efforts to convert Indians to Christianity and waged a war against the English colonists, one in which he was killed.

métis Children of marriages between Indian women and French traders and officials.

Me Too movement Social movement founded in 2006 by Tarana Burke to help survivors of sexual violence and oppose sexual harassment and assault, particularly in the workplace. In October 2017 it spread virally on social media with the hashtag #MeToo.

Mexican War Controversial war with Mexico for control of California and New Mexico, 1846–1848; the Treaty of Guadalupe Hidalgo fixed the border at the Rio Grande and extended the United States to the Pacific coast, annexing more than a half-million square miles of Mexican territory.

middle ground A borderland between European empires and Indian sovereignty where various native peoples and Europeans lived side by side in relative harmony.

Middle Passage The hellish and often deadly middle leg of the transatlantic "Triangular Trade" in which European ships carried manufactured goods to Africa, then transported enslaved Africans to the Americas and the Caribbean, and finally conveyed American agricultural products back to Europe; from the late sixteenth to the early nineteenth century, some 12 million Africans were transported via the Middle Passage, unknown millions more dying en route.

military-industrial complex The concept of "an immense military establishment" combined with a "permanent arms industry," which President Eisenhower warned against in his 1961 Farewell Address.

mill girls Women who worked at textile mills during the Industrial Revolution who enjoyed new freedoms and independence not seen before.

missile gap The claim, raised by John F. Kennedy during his campaign for president in 1960, that the Soviet Union had developed a technological and military advantage during Eisenhower's presidency.

Missouri Compromise Deal proposed by Kentucky senator Henry Clay in 1820 to resolve the slave/free imbalance in Congress that would result from Missouri's admission as a slave state; Maine's admission as a free state offset Missouri, and slavery was prohibited in the remainder of the Louisiana Territory north of the southern border of Missouri.

Monroe Doctrine President James Monroe's declaration to Congress on December 2, 1823, that the American continents would be thenceforth closed to European colonization, and that the United States would not interfere in European affairs.

Montgomery bus boycott Sparked by Rosa Parks's arrest on December 1, 1955, for refusing to surrender her seat to a white passenger, a successful yearlong boycott protesting segregation on city buses; led by the Reverend Martin Luther King Jr.

moral imperialism The Wilsonian belief that U.S. foreign policy should be guided by morality, and should teach other peoples about democracy. Wilson used this belief to both repudiate Dollar Diplomacy and justify frequent military interventions in Latin America.

moral suasion The abolitionist strategy that sought to end slavery by persuading both slaveowners and complicit northerners that the institution was evil.

muckraking Writing that exposed corruption and abuses in politics, business, meatpacking, child labor, and more, primarily in the first decade of the twentieth century; included popular books and magazine articles that spurred public interest in reform.

Muller v. Oregon 1908 Supreme Court decision that held that state interest in protecting women could override liberty of contract. Louis D. Brandeis, with help from his sister-in-law Josephine Goldmark of the National Consumers League, filed a brief in *Muller* that used statistics about women's health to argue for their protection.

multiculturalism Term that became prominent in the 1990s to describe a growing emphasis on group racial and ethnic identity and demands that jobs, education, and politics reflect the increasingly diverse nature of American society.

Murray, Judith Sargent A writer and early feminist thinker prominent in the years following the American Revolution.

My Lai massacre Massacre of 347 Vietnamese civilians in the village of My Lai by Lieutenant William Calley and troops under his command. U.S. army officers covered up the massacre for a year until an investigation uncovered the events. Eventually twenty-five army officers were charged with complicity in the massacre and its cover-up, but only Calley was convicted. He served little time for his crimes.

Nat Turner's Rebellion Most important slave uprising in nineteenth-century America, led by a slave preacher who, with his followers, killed about sixty white persons in Southampton County, Virginia, in 1831.

National Association for the Advancement of Colored People Founded in 1910, the civil rights organization that brought lawsuits against discriminatory practices and published *The Crisis*, a journal edited by African-American scholar W. E. B. Du Bois.

National Defense Education Act 1958 law passed in reaction to America's perceived inferiority in the space race; encouraged education in science and modern languages through student loans, university research grants, and aid to public schools.

National Industrial Recovery Act 1933 law passed on the last of the Hundred Days; it created public-works jobs through the Federal Emergency Relief Administration and established a system of self-regulation for industry through the National Recovery Administration, which was ruled unconstitutional in 1935.

National Organization for Women Organization founded in 1966 by writer Betty Friedan and other feminists; it pushed for abortion rights, nondiscrimination in the workplace, and other forms of equality for women.

National Recovery Administration (NRA) Controversial federal agency created in 1933 that brought together business and labor leaders to create "codes of fair competition" and "fair labor" policies, including a national minimum wage.

nativism Anti-immigrant and anti-Catholic feeling especially prominent from the 1830s through the 1850s; the largest group of its proponents was New York's Order of the Star-Spangled Banner, which expanded into the American (Know-Nothing) Party in 1854.

Navajo's Long Walk The forced removal of 8,000 Navajos from their lands by Union forces to a reservation in the 1860s.

Navigation Act Law passed by the English Parliament to control colonial trade and bolster the mercantile system, 1650–1775; enforcement of the act led to growing resentment by colonists.

neoconservatives The leaders of the conservative insurgency of the early 1980s. Their brand of conservatism was personified in Ronald Reagan, who believed in less government, supply-side economics, and "family values."

Neolin A Native American religious prophet who, by preaching pan-Indian unity and rejection of European technology and commerce, helped inspire Pontiac's Rebellion.

Neutrality Acts Series of laws passed between 1935 and 1939 to keep the United States from becoming involved in war by prohibiting American trade and travel to warring nations.

New Deal Franklin D. Roosevelt's campaign promise, in his speech to the Democratic National Convention of 1932, to combat the Great Depression with a "new deal for the American people"; the phrase became a catchword for his ambitious plan of economic programs.

new feminism A new aspect of the women's rights movement that arose in the early part of the twentieth century. New feminism added a focus on individual and sexual freedom to the movement, and introduced the word "feminism" into American life.

New Freedom Democrat Woodrow Wilson's political slogan in the presidential campaign of 1912; Wilson wanted to improve the banking system, lower tariffs, and, by breaking up monopolies, give small businesses freedom to compete.

New Harmony Community founded in Indiana by British industrialist Robert Owen in 1825; the short-lived New Harmony Community of Equality was one of the few nineteenth-century communal experiments not based on religious ideology.

new immigrants Wave of newcomers from southern and eastern Europe, including many Jews, who became a majority among immigrants to America after 1890.

New Jersey Plan New Jersey's delegation to the Constitutional Convention's plan for one legislative body with equal representation for each state.

New Left Radical youth protest movement of the 1960s, named by leader Tom Hayden to distinguish it from the Old (Marxist-Leninist) Left of the 1930s.

New Nationalism Platform of the Progressive Party and slogan of former president Theodore Roosevelt in the presidential campaign of 1912; stressed government activism, including regulation of trusts, conservation, and recall of state court decisions that had nullified progressive programs.

New Negro Term used in the 1920s, in reference to a slow and steady growth of black political influence that occurred in northern cities, where African-Americans were freer to speak and act. This political activity created a spirit of protest that expressed itself culturally in the Harlem Renaissance and politically in "new Negro" nationalism.

New Orleans, Battle of Last battle of the War of 1812, fought on January 8, 1815, weeks after the peace treaty was signed but prior to the news' reaching America; General Andrew Jackson led the victorious American troops.

New South *Atlanta Constitution* editor Henry W. Grady's 1886 term for the prosperous post–Civil War South he envisioned: democratic, industrial, urban, and free of nostalgia for the defeated plantation South.

new world order President George H. W. Bush's term for the post–Cold War world.

Ninety-Five Theses The list of moral grievances against the Catholic Church by Martin Luther, a German priest, in 1517.

"No taxation without representation" The rallying cry of opponents to the 1765 Stamp Act. The slogan decried the colonists' lack of representation in Parliament.

North American Free Trade Agreement (NAFTA) Approved in 1993, the agreement with Canada and Mexico that allowed goods to travel across their borders free of tariffs. Critics of the agreement argued that American workers would lose their jobs to cheaper Mexican labor.

North Atlantic Treaty Organization (NATO) Alliance founded in 1949 by ten western European nations, the United States, and Canada to deter Soviet expansion in Europe.

Northwest Ordinance of 1787 Law that created the Northwest Territory (area north of the Ohio River and west of Pennsylvania), established conditions for self-government and statehood, included a Bill of Rights, and permanently prohibited slavery.

Notes on the State of Virginia Thomas Jefferson's 1785 book that claimed, among other things, that black people were incapable of becoming citizens and living in harmony alongside white people due to the legacy of slavery and what Jefferson believed were the "real distinctions that nature has made" between races.

NSC-68 Top-secret policy paper approved by President Truman in 1950 that outlined a militaristic approach to combating the spread of global communism.

nullification crisis The 1832 attempt by the State of South Carolina to nullify, or invalidate within its borders, the 1832 federal tariff law. President Jackson responded with the Force Act of 1833.

Obergefell v. Hodges 2015 Supreme Court decision that allowed same-sex couples to marry throughout the United States.

Occupy Wall Street A grassroots movement in 2011 against growing economic inequality, declining opportunity, and the depredations of Wall Street banks.

oil embargo Prohibition on trade in oil declared by the Organization of Petroleum Exporting Countries, dominated by Middle Eastern producers, in October 1973 in response to U.S. and western European support for Israel in the 1973 Yom Kippur War. The rise in gas prices and fuel shortages resulted in a global economic recession and profoundly affected the American economy.

Oneida Utopian community founded in 1848; the Perfectionist religious group practiced "complex marriage" under leader John Humphrey Noyes.

Open Door Policy Demand in 1899 by Secretary of State John Hay, in hopes of protecting the Chinese market for U.S. exports, that Chinese trade be open to all nations.

Operation Dixie CIO's largely ineffective post–World War II campaign to unionize southern workers.

Ordinance of 1784 A law drafted by Thomas Jefferson that regulated land ownership and defined the terms by which western land would be marketed and settled; it established stages of self-government for the West. First Congress would govern a territory; then the territory would be admitted to the Union as a full state.

Ordinance of 1785 A law that regulated land sales in the Old Northwest. The land surveyed was divided into 640-acre plots and sold at $1 per acre.

Panama Canal Zone The small strip of land on either side of the Panama Canal. The Canal Zone was under U.S. control from 1903 to 1979 as a result of Theodore Roosevelt's assistance in engineering a coup in Colombia that established Panama's independence.

Panic of 1819 Financial collapse brought on by sharply falling cotton prices, declining demand for American exports, and reckless western land speculation.

Panic of 1837 Beginning of major economic depression lasting about six years; touched off by a British financial crisis and made worse by falling cotton prices, credit and currency problems, and speculation in land, canals, and railroads.

Paris Agreement 2016 agreement within the United Nations Framework Convention on Climate Change, concerned with mitigating greenhouse gas emissions.

paternalism A moral position developed during the first half of the nineteenth century that claimed that slaves were deprived of liberty for their own "good." Such a rationalization was adopted by some slaveowners to justify slavery.

the "peculiar institution" A phrase used by whites in the antebellum South to refer to slavery without using the word "slavery."

Pentagon Papers Informal name for the Defense Department's secret history of the Vietnam conflict; leaked to the press by former official Daniel Ellsberg and published in the *New York Times* in 1971.

Pequot War An armed conflict in 1637 that led to the destruction of one of New England's most powerful Indian groups.

perfectionism The idea that social ills once considered incurable could in fact be eliminated, popularized by the religious revivalism of the nineteenth century.

Perry, Commodore Matthew U.S. naval officer who negotiated the Treaty of Kanagawa in 1854. That treaty was the first step in starting a political and commercial relationship between the United States and Japan.

pet banks Local banks that received deposits while the charter of the Bank of the United States was about to expire in 1836. The choice of these banks was influenced by political and personal connections.

Philippine War American military campaign that suppressed the movement for Philippine independence after the Spanish-American War; America's death toll was over 4,000, and the Philippines' was far higher.

Pilgrims Puritan separatists who broke completely with the Church of England and sailed to the New World aboard the *Mayflower*, founding Plymouth Colony on Cape Cod in 1620.

plantation An early word for a colony, a settlement "planted" from abroad among an alien population in Ireland or the New World. Later, a large agricultural enterprise that used unfree labor to produce a crop for the world market.

Platt Amendment 1901 amendment to the Cuban constitution that reserved the United States' right to intervene in Cuban affairs and forced newly independent Cuba to host American naval bases on the island.

Plessy v. Ferguson U.S. Supreme Court decision supporting the legality of Jim Crow laws that permitted or required "separate but equal" facilities for blacks and whites.

Pontiac's Rebellion An Indian attack on British forts and settlements after France ceded to the British its territory east of the Mississippi River, as part of the Treaty of Paris in 1763, without consulting France's Indian allies.

Popular Front A period during the mid-1930s when the Communist Party sought to ally itself with socialists and New Dealers in movements for social change, urging reform of the capitalist system rather than revolution.

popular sovereignty Program that allowed settlers in a disputed territory to decide the slavery issue for themselves; most closely associated with Senator Stephen A. Douglas of Illinois.

Populists Founded in 1892, a group that advocated a variety of reform issues, including free coinage of silver, income tax, postal savings, regulation of railroads, and direct election of U.S. senators.

Porkopolis Nickname of Cincinnati, coined in the mid-nineteenth century, after its numerous slaughter houses.

Port Huron Statement A manifesto by Students for a Democratic Society that criticized institutions ranging from political parties to corporations, unions, and the military-industrial complex, while offering a new vision of social change.

Potsdam conference Last meeting of the major Allied powers; the conference that took place outside Berlin from July 17 to August 2, 1945, at which U.S. president Harry Truman, Soviet dictator Joseph Stalin, and British prime minister Clement Attlee finalized plans begun at Yalta.

Proclamation of 1763 Royal directive issued after the French and Indian War prohibiting settlement, surveys, and land grants west of the Appalachian Mountains; caused considerable resentment among colonists hoping to move west.

Progressive Party Political party created when former president Theodore Roosevelt broke away from the Republican Party to run for president again in 1912; the party supported progressive reforms similar to those of the Democrats but stopped short of seeking to eliminate trusts. Also the name of the party backing Robert La Follette for president in 1924.

Progressivism Broad-based reform movement, 1900–1917, that sought governmental action in solving problems in many areas of American life, including education, public health, the economy, the environment, labor, transportation, and politics.

proslavery argument The series of arguments defending the institution of slavery in the South as a positive good, not a necessary evil. The arguments included the racist belief that black people were inherently inferior to white people, as well as the belief that slavery, in creating a permanent underclass of laborers, made freedom possible for whites. Other elements of the argument included biblical citations.

Public Works Administration A New Deal agency that contracted with private construction companies to build roads, bridges, schools, hospitals, and other public facilities.

Pueblo Revolt Uprising in 1680 in which Pueblo Indians temporarily drove Spanish colonists out of modern-day New Mexico.

Pure Food and Drug Act Passed in 1906, the first law to regulate manufacturing of food and medicines; prohibited dangerous additives and inaccurate labeling.

Puritans English religious group that sought to purify the Church of England; founded the Massachusetts Bay Colony under John Winthrop in 1630.

Radical Republicans Group within the Republican Party in the 1850s and 1860s that advocated strong resistance to the expansion of slavery, opposition to compromise with the South in the secession crisis of 1860–1861, emancipation and arming of black soldiers during the Civil War, and equal civil and political rights for blacks during Reconstruction.

Reagan Revolution The rightward turn of American politics following the 1980 election of Ronald Reagan. The Reagan Revolution made individual "freedom" a rallying cry for the right.

Reaganomics Popular name for President Ronald Reagan's philosophy of "supply side" economics, which combined tax cuts with an unregulated marketplace.

recall A Progressive-era reform that allowed the removal of public officials by popular vote.

reconquista The "reconquest" of Spain from the Moors completed by King Ferdinand and Queen Isabella in 1492.

Reconstruction Act 1867 law that established temporary military governments in ten Confederate states—excepting Tennessee—and required that the states ratify the Fourteenth Amendment and permit freedmen to vote.

Reconstruction Finance Corporation Federal program established in 1932 under President Herbert Hoover to loan money to banks and other institutions to help them avert bankruptcy.

Red Scare of 1919–1920 Fear among many Americans after World War I of Communists in particular and noncitizens in general, a reaction to the Russian Revolution, mail bombs, strikes, and riots.

Redeemers Post–Civil War Democratic leaders who supposedly saved the South from Yankee domination and preserved the primarily rural economy.

redemptioners Indentured families or persons who received passage to the New World in exchange for a promise to work off their debt in America.

referendum A Progressive-era reform that allowed public policies to be submitted to popular vote.

Regulators Groups of backcountry Carolina settlers who protested colonial policies.

***repartimiento* system** Spanish labor system under which Indians were legally free and able to earn wages but were also required to perform a fixed amount of labor yearly. Replaced the *encomienda* system.

republic Representative political system in which citizens govern themselves by electing representatives, or legislators, to make key decisions on the citizens' behalf.

republican motherhood The ideology that emerged as a result of American independence where women played an indispensable role by training future citizens.

republicanism Political theory in eighteenth-century England and America that celebrated active participation in public life by economically independent citizens as central to freedom.

reverse discrimination Belief that affirmative action programs discriminate against white people.

Revolution of 1800 First time that an American political party surrendered power to the opposition party; Jefferson, a Republican, had defeated incumbent Adams, a Federalist, for president.

Roanoke colony English expedition of 117 settlers, including Virginia Dare, the first English child born in the New World; the colony disappeared from Roanoke Island in the Outer Banks sometime between 1587 and 1590.

robber barons Also known as "captains of industry"; Gilded-Age industrial figures who inspired both admiration, for their economic leadership and innovation, and hostility and fear, due to their unscrupulous business methods, repressive labor practices, and unprecedented economic control over entire industries.

Roe v. Wade 1973 U.S. Supreme Court decision requiring states to permit first-trimester abortions.

Roosevelt Corollary 1904 announcement by President Theodore Roosevelt, essentially a corollary to the Monroe Doctrine, that the United States could intervene militarily to prevent interference from European powers in the Western Hemisphere.

Rwandan genocide 1994 genocide conducted by the Hutu ethnic group upon the Tutsi minority in Rwanda.

Sacco-Vanzetti case A case held during the 1920s in which two Italian-American anarchists were found guilty and executed for a crime in which there was very little evidence linking them to the particular crime.

Salem witch trials A crisis of trials and executions in Salem, Massachusetts, in 1692 that resulted from anxiety over witchcraft.

salutary neglect Informal British policy during the first half of the eighteenth century that allowed the American colonies considerable freedom to pursue their economic and political interests in exchange for colonial obedience.

Sanitary Fairs Fund-raising bazaars led by women on behalf of Civil War soldiers. The fairs offered items such as uniforms and banners, as well as other emblems of war.

Santa Anna, Antonio López de The military leader who, in 1834, seized political power in Mexico and became a dictator. In 1835, Texans rebelled against him, and he led his army to Texas to crush their rebellion. He captured the missionary called the Alamo and killed all of its defenders, which inspired Texans to continue their resistance and Americans to volunteer to fight for Texas. The Texans captured Santa Anna during a surprise attack, and he bought his freedom by signing a treaty recognizing Texas's independence.

Saratoga, Battle of Major defeat of British general John Burgoyne and more than 5,000 British troops at Saratoga, New York, on October 17, 1777.

scalawags Southern white Republicans—some former Unionists—who supported Reconstruction governments.

Schenck v. United States 1919 U.S. Supreme Court decision upholding the wartime Espionage and Sedition Acts; in the opinion he wrote for the case, Justice Oliver Wendell Holmes set the now-familiar "clear and present danger" standard.

scientific management Management campaign to improve worker efficiency using measurements like "time and motion" studies to achieve greater productivity; introduced by Frederick Winslow Taylor in 1911.

Scopes trial 1925 trial of John Scopes, Tennessee teacher accused of violating state law prohibiting teaching of the theory of evolution; it became a nationally celebrated confrontation between religious fundamentalism and civil liberties.

Scottsboro case Case in which nine black youths were convicted of raping two white women; in overturning the verdicts of this case, the Court established precedents in *Powell v. Alabama* (1932) that adequate counsel must be appointed in capital cases, and in *Norris v. Alabama* (1935) that African-Americans cannot be excluded from juries.

Sea Islands experiment The 1861 pre-Reconstruction social experiment that involved converting slave plantations into places where former slaves could work for wages or own land. Former slaves also received education and access to improved shelter and food.

Second American Revolution The transformation of American government and society brought about by the Civil War.

Second Great Awakening Religious revival movement of the early decades of the nineteenth century, in reaction to the growth of secularism and rationalist religion; began the predominance of the Baptist and Methodist Churches.

second Great Migration The movement of black migrants from the rural South to the cities of the North and West, which occurred from 1941 through World War II, that dwarfed the Great Migration of World War I.

Second Middle Passage The massive trade of slaves from the upper South (Virginia and the Chesapeake) to the lower South (the Gulf states) that took place between 1820 and 1860.

Sedition Act 1918 law that made it a crime to make spoken or printed statements that criticized the U.S. government or encouraged interference with the war effort.

Selective Service Act Law passed in 1917 to quickly increase enlistment in the army for the United States' entry into World War I; required men to register with the draft.

"separate but equal" Principle underlying legal racial segregation, upheld in *Plessy v. Ferguson* (1896) and struck down in *Brown v. Board of Education* (1954).

separation of powers Feature of the U.S. Constitution, sometimes called "checks and balances," in which power is divided between executive, legislative, and judicial branches of the national government so that no one can dominate the other two and endanger citizens' liberties.

Serra, Father Junípero Missionary who began and directed the California mission system in the 1770s and 1780s. Serra presided over the conversion of many Indians to Christianity, but also engaged them in forced labor.

settlement house Late-nineteenth-century movement to offer a broad array of social services in urban immigrant neighborhoods; Chicago's Hull House was one of hundreds of settlement houses that operated by the early twentieth century.

Seven Years' War The last—and most important—of four colonial wars fought between England and France for control of North America east of the Mississippi River.

Seventeenth Amendment Progressive reform passed in 1913 that required U.S. senators to be elected directly by voters; previously, senators were chosen by state legislatures.

Shakers Religious sect founded by Mother Ann Lee in England. The United Society of Believers in Christ's Second Appearing settled in Watervliet, New York, in 1774, and subsequently established eighteen additional communes in the Northeast, Indiana, and Kentucky.

Share Our Wealth movement Program offered by Huey Long as an alternative to the New Deal. The program proposed to confiscate large personal fortunes, which would be used to guarantee every poor family a cash grant of $5,000 and every worker an annual income of $2,500. It also promised to provide pensions, reduce working hours, and pay veterans' bonuses and ensured a college education to every qualified student.

sharecropping Type of farm tenancy that developed after the Civil War in which landless workers—often former slaves—farmed land in exchange for farm supplies and a share of the crop.

Shays's Rebellion Attempt by Massachusetts farmer Daniel Shays and 1,200 compatriots, seeking debt relief through issuance of paper currency and lower taxes, to prevent courts from seizing property from indebted farmers.

Sherman Antitrust Act Passed in 1890, first law to restrict monopolistic trusts and business combinations; extended by the Clayton Antitrust Act of 1914.

Silent Spring A 1962 book by biologist Rachel Carson about the destructive impact of the widely used insecticide DDT that launched the modern environmentalist movement.

single tax Concept of taxing only landowners as a remedy for poverty, promulgated by Henry George in *Progress and Poverty* (1879).

sit-down strike Tactic adopted by labor unions in the mid- and late 1930s, whereby striking workers refused to leave factories, making production impossible; proved highly effective in the organizing drive of the Congress of Industrial Organizations.

sit-in Tactic adopted by young civil rights activists, beginning in 1960, of demanding service at lunch counters or public accommodations and refusing to leave if denied access; marked the beginning of the most militant phase of the civil rights struggle.

Sixteenth Amendment Constitutional amendment passed in 1913 that legalized the federal income tax.

Smith, John A swashbuckling soldier of fortune with rare powers of leadership and self-promotion who was appointed to the resident council to manage Jamestown.

Smoot-Hawley Tariff 1930 act that raised tariffs to an unprecedented level and worsened the Great Depression by raising prices and discouraging foreign trade.

Snowden, Edward An NSA contractor turned whistleblower, who released classified information relating to the United States' intelligence gathering both at home and abroad.

social contract Agreement hammered out between labor and management in leading industries; called a new "social contract." Unions signed long-term agreements that left decisions regarding capital investment, plant location, and output in management's hands, and they agreed to try to prevent unauthorized "wildcat" strikes.

Social Darwinism Application of Charles Darwin's theory of natural selection to society; used the concept of the "survival of the fittest" to justify class distinctions and to explain poverty.

Social Gospel Ideals preached by liberal Protestant clergymen in the late nineteenth and early twentieth centuries; advocated the application of Christian principles to social problems generated by industrialization.

Social Security Act 1935 law that created the Social Security system with provisions for a retirement pension, unemployment insurance, disability insurance, and public assistance (welfare).

Socialist Party Political party demanding public ownership of major economic enterprises in the United States as well as reforms like recognition of labor unions and woman suffrage; reached peak of influence in 1912 when presidential candidate Eugene V. Debs received over 900,000 votes.

Society of American Indians Organization founded in 1911 that brought together Native American intellectuals of many tribal backgrounds to promote discussion of the plight of Indian peoples.

Society of Friends (Quakers) Religious group in England and America whose members believed all persons possessed the "inner light" or spirit of God; they were early proponents of abolition of slavery and equal rights for women.

soft money and hard money In the 1830s, "soft money" referred to paper currency issued by banks. "Hard money" referred to gold and silver currency—also called specie.

Sons of Liberty Organization formed by Samuel Adams, John Hancock, and other radicals in response to the Stamp Act.

Sotomayor, Sonia First Supreme Court Justice of Hispanic descent. Justice Sotomayor was appointed by President Barack Obama in 2009.

Southern Christian Leadership Conference (SCLC) Civil rights organization founded in 1957 by the Reverend Martin Luther King Jr. and other civil rights leaders.

Southern Manifesto A document written in 1956 that repudiated the Supreme Court decision in *Brown v. Board of Education* and supported the campaign against racial integration in public places.

spoils system The term meaning the filling of federal government jobs with persons loyal to the party of the president; originated in Andrew Jackson's first term.

Sputnik First artificial satellite to orbit the earth; launched October 4, 1957, by the Soviet Union.

stagflation A combination of stagnant economic growth and high inflation present during the 1970s.

Stamp Act Parliament's 1765 requirement that revenue stamps be affixed to all colonial printed matter, documents, and playing cards; the Stamp Act Congress met to formulate a response, and the act was repealed the following year.

staple crops Important cash crops;—for example, cotton or tobacco.

steamboats Paddlewheelers that could travel both up- and down-river in deep or shallow waters; they became commercially viable early in the nineteenth century and soon developed into America's first inland freight and passenger service network.

stock market crash Also known as Black Tuesday, a stock market panic in 1929 that resulted in the loss of more than $10 billion in market value (worth approximately ten times more today). One among many causes of the Great Depression.

Stonewall Inn A gathering place for New York's gay community, the site of the 1969 police raids and resulting riots that launched the modern gay rights movement.

Stono Rebellion A slave uprising in 1739 in South Carolina that led to a severe tightening of the slave code and the temporary imposition of a prohibitive tax on imported slaves.

Strategic Arms Limitation Talks 1972 talks between President Nixon and Secretary Brezhnev that resulted in the Strategic Arms Limitation Treaty (or SALT), which limited the quantity of nuclear warheads each nation could possess, and prohibited the development of missile defense systems.

Student Nonviolent Coordinating Committee (SNCC) Organization founded in 1960 to coordinate civil rights sit-ins and other forms of grassroots protest.

Students for a Democratic Society (SDS) Major organization of the New Left, founded at the University of Michigan in 1960 by Tom Hayden and Al Haber.

suffrage The right to vote.

Sugar Act 1764 decision by Parliament to tax refined sugar and many other colonial products.

Sunbelt The label for an arc that stretched from the Carolinas to California. During the postwar era, much of the urban population growth occurred in this area.

Taft-Hartley Act 1947 law passed over President Harry Truman's veto; the law contained a number of provisions to weaken labor unions, including the banning of closed shops.

tariff of abominations Tariff passed in 1828 by Parliament that taxed imported goods at a very high rate; it aroused strong opposition in the South.

tariff of 1816 First true protective tariff, intended to protect certain American goods against foreign competition.

Tea Party A grassroots Republican movement that emerged in 2009 named for the Boston Tea Party of the 1770s. The Tea Party opposed the Obama administration's sweeping legislative enactments and advocated for a more stringent immigration policy.

Teapot Dome Harding administration scandal in which Secretary of the Interior Albert B. Fall profited from secret leasing to private oil companies of government oil reserves at Teapot Dome, Wyoming, and Elk Hills, California.

Tecumseh and Tenskwatawa Tecumseh—a leader of the Shawnee tribe who tried to unite all Indians into a confederation to resist white encroachment on their lands. His beliefs and leadership made him seem dangerous to the American government. He was killed at the Battle of the Thames. His brother, Tenskwatawa—a religious prophet who called for complete separation from whites, the revival of traditional Indian culture, and resistance to federal policies.

Tejanos Texas settlers of Spanish or Mexican descent.

temperance movement A widespread reform movement, led by militant Christians, focused on reducing the use of alcoholic beverages.

Tennessee Valley Authority Administrative body created in 1933 to control flooding in the Tennessee River valley, provide work for the region's unemployed, and produce inexpensive electric power for the region.

Tenochtitlán The capital city of the Aztec Empire. The city was built on marshy islands on the western side of Lake Tetzcoco, which is the site of present-day Mexico City.

Ten-Percent Plan of Reconstruction President Lincoln's proposal for reconstruction, issued in 1863, in which southern states would rejoin the Union if 10 percent of the 1860 electorate signed loyalty pledges, accepted emancipation, and had received presidential pardons.

Tenure of Office Act 1867 law that required the president to obtain Senate approval to remove any official whose appointment had also required Senate approval; President Andrew Johnson's violation of the law by firing Secretary of War Edwin Stanton led to Johnson's impeachment.

Tet offensive Surprise attack by the Viet Cong and North Vietnamese during the Vietnamese New Year of 1968; turned American public opinion strongly against the war in Vietnam.

Texas revolt The 1830s rebellion of residents of the territory of Texas—many of them American emigrants—against Mexican control of the region.

Thirteenth Amendment Constitutional amendment adopted in 1865 that irrevocably abolished slavery throughout the United States.

Three Mile Island Nuclear power plant near Harrisburg, Pennsylvania, site of a 1979 accident that released radioactive steam into the air; public reaction ended the nuclear power industry's expansion.

three-fifths clause A provision signed into the Constitution in 1787 that three-fifths of the slave population would be counted in determining each state's representation in the House of Representatives and its electoral votes for president.

Title IX Part of the Educational Amendments Act of 1972 that banned gender discrimination in higher education.

totalitarianism The term that describes aggressive, ideologically driven states that seek to subdue all of civil society to their control, thus leaving no room for individual rights or alternative values.

Townshend Acts 1767 parliamentary measures (named for the chancellor of the Exchequer) that taxed tea and other commodities, and established a Board of Customs Commissioners and colonial vice-admiralty courts.

Trail of Tears Cherokees' own term for their forced removal, 1838–1839, from the Southeast to Indian lands (later Oklahoma); of 15,000 forced to march, 4,000 died on the way.

transcendentalists Philosophy of a small group of mid-nineteenth-century New England writers and thinkers, including Ralph Waldo Emerson, Henry David Thoreau, and Margaret Fuller; they stressed personal and intellectual self-reliance.

transcontinental railroad First line across the continent from Omaha, Nebraska, to Sacramento, California, established in 1869 with the linkage of the Union Pacific and Central Pacific railroads at Promontory, Utah.

Treaty of Greenville 1795 treaty under which twelve Indian tribes ceded most of Ohio and Indiana to the federal government, and that also established the "annuity" system.

Treaty of Paris Signed on September 3, 1783, the treaty that ended the Revolutionary War, recognized American independence from Britain, established the border between Canada and the United States, fixed the western border at the Mississippi River, and ceded Florida to Spain.

Truman Doctrine President Harry S. Truman's program announced in 1947 of aid to European countries—particularly Greece and Turkey—threatened by communism.

trusts Companies combined to limit competition.

Tubman, Harriet Abolitionist who was born a slave, escaped to the North, and then returned to the South nineteen times and guided 300 slaves to freedom.

Tulsa riot A race riot in 1921—the worst in American history—that occurred in Tulsa, Oklahoma, after a group of black veterans tried to prevent a lynching. Over 300 African-Americans were killed, and 10,000 lost their homes in fires set by white mobs.

Uncle Tom's Cabin Harriet Beecher Stowe's 1852 antislavery novel that popularized the abolitionist position.

Underground Railroad Operating in the decades before the Civil War, a clandestine system of routes and safehouses through which slaves were led to freedom in the North.

United Nations Organization of nations to maintain world peace, established in 1945 and headquartered in New York.

Uprising of 1622 Unsuccessful uprising of Virginia Native Americans that wiped out one-quarter of the settler population, but ultimately led to the settlers' gaining supremacy.

urban renewal A series of policies supported by all levels of government that allowed local governments and housing authorities to demolish so-called blighted areas in urban centers to replace them with more valuable real estate usually reserved for white people.

USA Patriot Act A 2001 mammoth bill that conferred unprecedented powers on law-enforcement agencies charged with preventing domestic terrorism, including the power to wiretap, read private messages, and spy on citizens.

U.S.S. *Maine* Battleship that exploded in Havana Harbor on February 15, 1898, resulting in 266 deaths; the American public, assuming that the Spanish had mined the ship, clamored for war, and the Spanish-American War was declared two months later.

utopian communities Ideal communities that offered innovative social and economic relationships to those who were interested in achieving salvation.

V-E Day May 8, 1945, the day World War II officially ended in Europe.

Versailles Treaty The treaty signed at the Versailles peace conference after World War I that established President Woodrow Wilson's vision of an international regulating body, redrew parts of Europe and the Middle East, and assigned economically crippling war reparations to Germany, but failed to incorporate all of Wilson's Fourteen Points.

vertical integration Company's avoidance of middlemen by producing its own supplies and providing for distribution of its product.

Vicksburg, Battle of The fall of Vicksburg, Mississippi, to General Ulysses S. Grant's army on July 4, 1863, after two months of siege; a turning point in the war because it gave the Union control of the Mississippi River.

Vietnam Syndrome The belief that the United States should be extremely cautious in deploying its military forces overseas that emerged after the end of the Vietnam War.

Virginia and Kentucky resolutions Legislation passed in 1798 and 1799 by the Virginia and the Kentucky legislatures; written by James Madison and Thomas Jefferson in response to the Alien and Sedition Acts, the resolutions advanced the state-compact theory of the Constitution. Virginia's resolution called on the federal courts to protect free speech. Jefferson's draft for Kentucky stated that a state could nullify federal law, but this was deleted.

Virginia Company A joint-stock enterprise that King James I chartered in 1606. The company was to spread Christianity in the New World as well as find ways to make a profit in it.

Virginia Plan Virginia's delegation to the Constitutional Convention's plan for a strong central government and a two-house legislature apportioned by population.

virtual representation The idea that the American colonies, although they had no actual representative in Parliament, were "virtually" represented by all members of Parliament.

Voting Rights Act Law passed in the wake of Martin Luther King Jr.'s Selma-to-Montgomery March in 1965; it authorized federal protection of the right to vote and permitted federal enforcement of minority voting rights in individual counties, mostly in the South.

Wade-Davis Bill Radical Republicans' 1864 plan for reconstruction that required loyalty oaths, abolition of slavery, repudiation of war debts, and denial of political rights to high-ranking Confederate officials; President Lincoln refused to sign the bill.

Wagner Act Law that established the National Labor Relations Board and facilitated unionization by regulating employment and bargaining practices.

Walking Purchase An infamous 1737 purchase of Indian land in which Pennsylvanian colonists tricked the

Lenni Lanape Indians. The Lanape agreed to cede land equivalent to the distance a man could walk in thirty-six hours, but the colonists marked out an area using a team of runners.

war in Afghanistan War fought against the Taliban and Al Qaeda in Afghanistan following the attacks of September 11, 2001. It remains the longest war in American history.

War Industries Board Board run by financier Bernard Baruch that planned production and allocation of war materiel, supervised purchasing, and fixed prices, 1917–1919.

War of 1812 War fought with Britain, 1812–1814, over issues that included impressment of American sailors, interference with shipping, and collusion with Northwest Territory Indians; settled by the Treaty of Ghent in 1814.

War on Poverty Plan announced by President Lyndon B. Johnson in his 1964 State of the Union address; under the Economic Opportunity Bill signed later that year, Head Start, VISTA, and the Jobs Corps were created, and programs were created for students, farmers, and businesses in efforts to eliminate poverty.

war on terrorism Global crusade to root out anti-American, anti-Western Islamist terrorist cells; launched by President George W. Bush as a response to the 9/11 attacks.

War Powers Act Law passed in 1973, reflecting growing opposition to American involvement in the Vietnam War; it required congressional approval before the president sent troops abroad.

Watergate Washington office and apartment complex that lent its name to the 1972–1974 scandal of the Nixon administration; when his knowledge of the break-in at the Watergate and subsequent cover-up were revealed, Nixon resigned the presidency under threat of impeachment.

The Wealth of Nations The 1776 work by economist Adam Smith that argued that the "invisible hand" of the free market directed economic life more effectively and fairly than governmental intervention.

Webster-Hayne debate U.S. Senate debate of January 1830 between Daniel Webster of Massachusetts and Robert Hayne of South Carolina over nullification and states' rights.

welfare state A term that originated in Britain during World War II to refer to a system of income assistance, health coverage, and social services for all citizens.

Whiskey Rebellion Violent protest by western Pennsylvania farmers against the federal excise tax on whiskey, 1794.

Wilmot Proviso Proposal to prohibit slavery in any land acquired in the Mexican War; it was defeated by southern senators, led by John C. Calhoun of South Carolina, in 1846 and 1847.

Winthrop, John Puritan leader and governor of the Massachusetts Bay Colony who resolved to use the colony as a refuge for persecuted Puritans and as an instrument of building a "wilderness Zion" in America.

woman suffrage Movement to give women the right to vote through a constitutional amendment, spearheaded by Susan B. Anthony and Elizabeth Cady Stanton's National Woman Suffrage Association.

Women's March International protest on January 21, 2017 for women's rights, LGBT rights, gender equality, and racial equality following the inauguration of President Donald Trump, and the biggest single-day protest in U.S. history.

Worcester v. Georgia 1832 Supreme Court case that held that the Indian nations were distinct peoples who could not be dealt with by the states—instead, only the federal government could negotiate with them. President Jackson refused to enforce the ruling.

Works Progress Administration (WPA) Part of the Second New Deal; it provided jobs for millions of the unemployed on construction and arts projects.

Wounded Knee massacre Last incident of the Indian Wars; it took place in 1890 in the Dakota Territory, where the U.S. Cavalry killed over 200 Sioux men, women, and children.

writs of assistance One of the colonies' main complaints against Britain; the writs allowed unlimited search warrants without cause to look for evidence of smuggling.

XYZ affair Affair in which French foreign minister Talleyrand's three anonymous agents demanded payments to stop French plundering of American ships in 1797; refusal to pay the bribe was followed by two years of undeclared sea war with France (1798–1800).

Yalta conference Meeting of Franklin D. Roosevelt, Winston Churchill, and Joseph Stalin at a Crimean resort to discuss the postwar world on February 4–11, 1945; Joseph Stalin claimed large areas in eastern Europe for Soviet domination.

Yamasee uprising Revolt of Yamasee and Creek Indians, aggravated by rising debts and slave traders' raids, against Carolina settlers. It resulted in the expulsion of many Indians to Florida.

yellow press Sensationalism in newspaper publishing that reached a peak in the circulation war between Joseph Pulitzer's *New York World* and William Randolph Hearst's *New York Journal* in the 1890s; the papers' accounts of events in Havana Harbor in 1898 led directly to the Spanish-American War.

yeoman farmers Small landowners (the majority of white families in the Old South) who farmed their own land and usually did not own slaves.

Yorktown, Battle of Last battle of the Revolutionary War; General Lord Charles Cornwallis along with over 7,000 British troops surrendered at Yorktown, Virginia, on October 17, 1781.

Zimmermann Telegram Telegram from the German foreign secretary to the German minister in Mexico, February 1917, instructing the minister to offer to recover Texas, New Mexico, and Arizona for Mexico if it would fight the United States to divert attention from Germany in the event that the United States joined the war.

zoot suit riots 1943 riots in which sailors on leave attacked Mexican-American youths.

CREDITS

PHOTOS

Front Matter: In order of appearance: Library of Congress; **(top left and right):** Granger Collection; **(bottom left):** Museum of the City of New York / Bridgeman Images; **(bottom right):** Dorothea Lange / National Archives; Photo by Erin Silber; Art Collection 4 / Alamy Stock Photo; Collection of the New-York Historical Society / Bridgeman Images; Archivart / Alamy Stock Photo; Abby Aldrich Rockefeller Folk Art Museum, museum purchase of the Friends of Colonial Williamsburg Collections Fund; Huntington Library and Art Gallery, San Marino, CA / © The Huntington Library, Art Collections & Botanical Gardens / Bridgeman Images; Collection of the New-York Historical Society / Bridgeman Images; Smithsonian American Art Museum, Washington, DC / Art Resource, NY; Gift of Constance Fuller Threinen, great-granddaughter of Margaret Fuller's brother, the Rev. Arthur Buckminster Fuller, who was a Unitarian minister in Boston, a chaplain in the Civil War, and was killed at the Battle of Fredericksburg in 1862. National Portrait Gallery, Smithsonian; Wisconsin Historical Society, WHS- 6909; Chicago History Museum, ICHi-022125; Library of Congress; Hulton Archive / Getty Images; later, R. P. Niagara Movement founders, 1905, 1905. W. E. B. Du Bois Papers (MS 312). Special Collections and University Archives, University of Massachusetts Amherst Libraries; The Stapleton Collection / Bridgeman Images; Densho: The Japanese American Legacy Project; AP Photo / File; Richard Nixon Presidential Library and Museum, NARA; Ron Sachs / Shutterstock; Mark Dixon Blue Lens; Granger Collection. **Chapter 1: Page 1**: Art Collection 4 / Alamy Stock Photo; **p. 5:** Cahokia Mounds State Historic Site, painting by William R. Iseminger; **p. 6:** Georg Gerster / Science Source; **p. 7:** Bridgeman Images; **p. 9:** Library of Congress; **p. 10:** Courtesy of the John Carter Brown Library at Brown University; **p. 11 (top):** Library of Congress; **(bottom):** Courtesy Lilly Library, Indiana University, Bloomington, IN; **p. 16:** Granger Collection; **p. 17:** Granger Collection; **p. 20:** Unknown artist, Young Woman With a Harpsichord, 1735–50. Denver Art Museum: Gift of the Collection of Frederick and Jan Mayer, 2014.209. Photo courtesy of Denver Art Museum; **p. 21:** DeA Picture Library / Art Resource, NY; **p. 23:** Library of Congress; **p. 27:** National Museum of American History, Smithsonian Institution, Behring Center; **p. 33 (top):** Bettmann / Corbis / Getty Images; **(bottom):** Bibliotheque Nationale, Paris / Bridgeman Images; **p. 35:** Granger Collection; **p. 36:** Collection of the New-York Historical Society / Bridgeman Images. **Chapter 2: Page 38:** © The Trustees of the British Museum / Art Resource, NY; **p. 40:** The London Art Archive / Alamy; **p. 41:** Woburn Abbey, Bedfordshire, UK / The Bridgeman Art Library; **p. 45:** Museum of Art, Rhode Island School of Design. Gift of Robert Winthrop. Photography by Erik Gould; **p. 46:** The Picture Art Collection / Alamy Stock Photo; **p. 48 (top):** Granger Collection; **(bottom):** National Portrait Gallery, Smithsonian Institution; transfer from the National Gallery of Art; gift of the A.W. Mellon Educational and Charitable Trust, 1942; **p. 50:** The New York Public Library / Art Resource, NY; **p. 51:** MPI / Getty Images; **p. 54:** Courtesy of the John Carter Brown Library at Brown University; **p. 55:** Courtesy of the Massachusetts Archives; **p. 56:** Worcester Art Museum, Worcester, Massachusetts, Gift of William A. Savage / Bridgeman Images; **p. 57:** Massachusetts Historical Society; **p. 60:** The New York Public Library / Art Resource, NY; **p. 64:** Annenberg Rare Book and Manuscript Library, Van Pelt-Dietrich Library Center, U Penn; **p. 65:** Library of Congress; **p. 66:** Mrs. Elizabeth Freake and Baby Mary, unknown artist, 1963.134, Worcester Art Museum / Bridgeman Images; **p. 67:** Private Collection / Bridgeman Images; **p. 68:** British Library Board / Robana / Art Resource, NY. **Chapter 3: Page 72:** Emmet Collection, Miriam and Ira D. Wallach Division of Art, Prints and Photographs, The New York Public Library; **p. 76:** Library of Congress; **p. 78:** Unidentified artist, British, 18th century or first quarter 19th century; Quaker Meeting; Oil on canvas; 64.1 x 76.2cm (25 1/4 x 30in.); Museum of Fine Arts, Boston; Bequest of Maxim Karolik; 64.456; **p. 80:** Free Women of Color with Their Children and Servants in a Landscape, 1770–1796 (oil on canvas), Brunias, Agostino (1728–96) / Brooklyn Museum of Art, New York, USA / Gift of Mrs. Carl H. de Silver in memory of her husband, by exchange and gift of George S. Hellman, by exchange / Bridgeman Images; **p. 81:** © British Library Board. All Rights Reserved / The Bridgeman Art Library; **p. 83:** © National Maritime Museum, Greenwich, London; **p. 87:** Courtesy of the John Carter Brown Library at Brown University; **p. 90:** The New York Public Library / Art Resource, NY; **p. 95:** Library of Congress; **p. 96:** Eileen Tweedy / REX / Shutterstock; **p. 98:** Collection of the New-York Historical Society / Bridgeman Images; **p. 99:** National Portrait Gallery, Smithsonian Institution; **p. 100:** Private Collection. Photograph by Alex Jamison, courtesy the National Portrait Gallery, Smithsonian Institution; **p. 101:** Gift of Edgar William and Bernice Chrysler Garbisch, Image © 2006 Board of Trustees, National Gallery of Art, Washington. **Chapter 4: Page 104**: Barry Lawrence Ruderman Antique Maps Inc. www.raremaps.com; **p. 106:** Library of Congress; **p. 109:** Chateau des ducs de Bretagne, Musee d'histoire de Nantes; **p. 112:** Jamestown-Yorktown Foundation; **p. 113:** The Colonial Williamsburg Foundation. Gift of Abby Aldrich Rockefeller; **p. 114:** Image copyright © The Metropolitan Museum of Art. Image source: Art Resource, NY; **p. 115:** Schomburg Center for Research in Black Culture, Photographs and Prints Division, The New York Public Library; **p. 116:** Chicago History Museum, ICHi-032162; **p. 117:** Library of Congress; **p. 119:** The Library Company of Philadelphia; **p. 122:** Archivart / Alamy Stock Photo; **p. 124:** National Portrait Gallery,

London; **p. 125:** Library of Congress; **p. 126:** Granger Collection; **p. 127:** Album / Alamy Stock Photo; **p. 129:** Library of Congress; **p. 130:** Library of Congress. **Chapter 5: Page 138:** Library of Congress; **p. 140:** Library of Congress; **p. 142:** The Colonial Williamsburg Foundation. Museum Purchase; **p. 146:** Library of Congress; **p. 147:** Library of Congress; **p. 149:** Chicago History Museum, ICHi-076663; **p. 151:** American Philosophical Society; **p. 153:** Courtesy, American Antiquarian Society; **p. 156:** © The Trustees of the British Museum / Art Resource, NY; **p. 157:** Anne S.K. Brown Military Collection, Brown University; **p. 158:** The New York Public Library / Art Resource, NY; **p. 160:** Image Courtesy of the Museum of the American Revolution; **p. 163:** Library of Congress. **Chapter 6: Page 167:** Library Company of Philadelphia. Gift of the artist, 1792; **p. 169:** National Gallery of Art, Washington, Gift of Mrs. Robert Homans; **p. 170:** Courtesy, Winterthur Museum, Mug by William Will, 1750–1780, Philadelphia, PA, Pewter, bequest of Henry Francis du Pont, 1967.1369; **p. 171:** Historical Society of Pennsylvania; **p. 172:** Collection of the New-York Historical Society; **p. 173:** York County Historical Society, America, USA / The Bridgeman Art Library; **p. 175:** Courtesy, American Antiquarian Society; **p. 176**: Library of Congress; **p. 178:** The Library Company of Philadelphia; **p. 179:** Library of Congress; **p. 181:** Corbis/Getty Images; **p. 182:** Collection of the New-York Historical Society; **p. 183:** Library of Congress; **p. 184:** Abby Aldrich Rockefeller Folk Art Museum, museum purchase of the Friends of Colonial Williamsburg Collections Fund; **p. 185:** The New York Public Library Digital Collections; **p. 188 (top):** Collection of The New-York Historical Society;(bottom): MPI/Getty Images; **p. 189 (top):** The Philadelphia Museum of Art / Art Resource, NY; **(bottom):** Courtesy, Winterthur Museum, Graphic: Keep Within Compass, 1785–1805, England, Ink, Laid Paper, Gift of Henry Francis du Pont, 1954.93.1; **p. 190:** AB Historic / Alamy Stock Photo. **Chapter 7: Page 192: Granger** Collection; **p. 195:** National Archives; **p. 199:** Print Collection, Miriam and Ira D. Wallach Division of Art, Prints, and Photographs, The New York Public Library; Astor, Lenox, and Tilden Foundations. Art Resource, NY; **p. 200 (top):** Library of Congress; **(bottom):** The Metropolitan Museum of Art / Art Resource; **p. 202:** Huntington Library and Art Gallery, San Marino, CA, / © The Huntington Library, Art Collections & Botanical Gardens / Bridgeman Images; **p. 203:** The Library of Virginia; **p. 205:** MPI / Getty Images; **p. 206:** Library of Congress; **p. 207:** Granger Collection; **p. 209:** Collection of the New-York Historical Society / Bridgeman Art Library; **p. 216:** Chicago History Museum, ICHi-064806; **p. 219 (top):** Collection of the New-York Historical Society / Bridgeman Images; **(bottom):** Library of Congress. **Chapter 8: Page 221:** Chicago History Museum, ICHi-066154, J. L. Boqueta de Woieseri, artist; **p. 223:** Fenimore Art Museum, Cooperstown, New York, gift of Stephen C. Clark, Elie & Viola Spiess Flannery Nadelman Collection. N0535.1948. Photograph by Richard Walker; **p. 225:** Division of Home and Community Life, National Museum of American History, Smithsonian Institution; **p. 226 (top):** Courtesy, Winterthur Museum, Painting: General George Washington Reviewing the Western Army by Frederick Kemelmeyer, 1794–1800, Baltimore, Maryland, Oil paint, Paper, Masonite, Bequest of Hery F. duPont; **(bottom):** Library of Congress; **p. 227 (top):** Print Collection, Miriam and Ira D. Wallach Division of Art, Prints, and Photographs, The New York Public Library; Astor, Lenox, and Tilden Foundations. Art Resource, NY; **(bottom):** American Folk Art Museum / Art Resource, NY; **p. 230 (top):** Chicago History Museum, ICHi-032137; p. 233: Division of Political History, National Museum of American History, Smithsonian Institution; **p. 234:** Photos 12 / Alamy; **p. 236:** National Portrait Gallery, Smithsonian Institution; **p. 238:** Missouri Historical Society, St. Louis; **p. 241:** Royal Ontario Museum; **p. 243 (top):** National Portrait Gallery, Smithsonian Institution; **(bottom):** Library of Congress; **p. 246:** Photography by Erik Arneson © Nicholas S. West. **Chapter 9: Page 249**: Collection of the New-York Historical Society / Bridgeman Images; **p. 251:** I.N. Phelps Stokes Collection, Miriam and Ira D. Wallach Division of Art, Prints and Photographs, The New York Public Library, Astor, Lenox and Tilden Foundations. Art Resource, NY; p. 252: Chicago History Museum, ICHi-022129; **p. 254:** Historical Society of Pennsylvania; **p. 255:** © Collection of the New-York Historical Society / Bridgeman Images; **p. 260:** Courtesy, the Winterthur Library: Joseph Downs Collection of Manuscripts and Printed Ephemera; **p. 261 (top):** Cincinnati Museum Center / Getty Images; **(bottom):** Granger Collection; **p. 262:** Barfoot, American, Progress of Cotton, Reeding or Drawing In, No. 9, Mabel Brady Garvan Collection, Yale University Art Gallery; **p. 266:** Library of Congress; **p. 267:** Historical Society of Pennsylvania; **p. 268:** Library of Congress; **p. 269:** The New York Public Library / Art Resource, NY; **p. 270:** Library of Congress; **p. 272:** Church Archives of The Church of Jesus-Christ of Latter-day Saints; **p. 273:** John Neagle, American, 1796-1865; Pat Lyon at the Forge, 1826–27; Oil on canvas; 238.12 x 172.72 cm (93 3/4 x 68 in.); Museum of Fine Arts, Boston; Henry H. and Zoe Oliver Sherman Fund; 1975.806. Photograph © 2013 Museum of Fine Arts, Boston; **p. 275:** Unidentified maker, Spinning Woman, ca. 1850–1875. Carved and painted wood and metal, 25 1/2 x 20 x 11 in. Collection of Shelburne Museum, museum purchase, 1953, acquired from Edith Halpert, The Downtown Gallery. 1961-1.179; **p. 276:** Collection of the New-York Historical Society / Bridgeman Images; **p. 277:** Library of Congress. **Chapter 10: Page 279:** Courtesy of the Pennsylvania Academy of the Fine Arts, Philadelphia. Bequest of Henry C. Carey (The Carey Collection); **p. 281:** Library of Congress; **p. 282:** Fenimore Art Museum, Cooperstown, New York, gift of Stephen C. Clark. N0411.1955. Photograph by Richard Walker; **p. 284:** Granger Collection; **p. 285:** Library of Congress; **p. 286:** Granger Collection; **p. 290:** Bettmann / Corbis / Getty Images; **p. 294:** Pook & Pook; **p. 298:** National Portrait Gallery, Smithsonian Institution; **p. 301: (top):** Library of Congress; **(bottom):** Smithsonian American Art Museum, Washington, DC / Art Resource, NY; **p. 302:** Collection of the New-York Historical Society / Bridgeman Images; **p. 303:** Library of Congress; **p. 305:** Library of Congress; **p. 306:** Library of Congress**. Chapter 11: Page 308:** Private Collection / © Michael Graham-Stewart / Bridgeman Images; **p. 310:** Newberry Library, Chicago, Edward E. Ayer Digital Collection; **p. 311 (both):** The Historic New Orleans Collection / Bridgeman Images; **p. 313 (top):** Hulton Archive / Getty Images; **(bottom):** Library of Congress; **p. 314:** Missouri Historical Society; **p. 315:** Library of Congress; **p. 317:** Merseyside Maritime Museum, Liverpool; **p. 318:** Granger Collection; **p. 319:** Courtesy of the South Carolina Library, University of South Carolina, Columbia, SC; **p. 320 (both):** Library of Congress; **p. 321 (both):** Library of Congress; **p. 323 (top):** The Historic New Orleans Collection / Bridgeman Images **(bottom):** Chicago History Museum, ICHi-022003; **p. 324 (top):** Abby Aldrich Rockefeller Folk Art Museum, Colonial Williamsburg Foundation, Williamsburg, VA; **(bottom):** GL Archive / Alamy Stock Photo; p. **328:** GLC07238 $2,500 Reward! Mississippi Co., Missouri broadside advertising runaway slaves, August 23, 1852 / Courtesy of The Gilder Lehrman Institute of American History; **p. 329: (top):** New Haven Museum; **(bottom):** The Library Company of Philadelphia; **p. 332:** Library of Congress. **Chapter 12: Page 334:** Collection of Dr. and Mrs. John Livingston and Mrs. Elizabeth Livingston Jaeger, Photo: Hearts and Hands Media Arts. Photography courtesy of Hearts & Hands Media Arts, from the book and film "Hearts and Hands: A Social History of 19th Century Women and their Quilts" (New Day Films); **p. 336:** Granger Collection; **p. 337:** Library of Congress; **p. 339:** Bibliotheque Nationale, Paris, France / Archives Charmet / The Bridgeman Art Library; **p. 340:** Library of Congress; **p. 343:** Massachusetts Historical Society. Banner, William Lloyd Garrison (1805-1879) "Proclaim Liberty Throughout all the Land unto all the inhabitants thereof." MHS image #332; **p. 344:** Collection of the New-York Historical Society / Purchase, The Louis Durr Fund / Bridgeman Images; **p. 345:** Boston Athenaeum; **p. 346:** Library of Congress; **p. 348 (top):** Chicago History Museum; **(bottom):** Samuel J. Miller, Frederick Douglass, 1847–52, cased half-plate daguerreotype, plate: 14 x 10.6 cm, Major Acquisitions Centennial Endowment, The Art Institute of Chicago; **p. 349:** The Library Company of Philadelphia; **p. 350:** Library of Congress; **p. 353:** Gift of Constance Fuller Threinen, great-granddaughter of Margaret Fuller's brother, the Rev. Arthur Buckminster Fuller, who was a Unitarian minister in Boston, a chaplain in the Civil War, and was killed at the Battle of Fredericksburg in 1862. National Portrait Gallery, Smithsonian; **p. 356:** Bettmann / Corbis / Getty Images; **p. 358:** Library of Congress. **Chapter 13: Page 360:** Courtesy of the Maryland Historical Society; **p. 361 (left):** Library of Congress; **(right):** Architect of the Capitol; p. 362: A65.43 Alfred Sully, Monterey, California Rancho Scene, circa 1849. Watercolor on paper, 15.25 x 18 in. Collection of the Oakland Museum of California. The Oakland Museum of California Kahn Collection; **p. 364:** Bettmann / Corbis / Getty Images; **p. 365 (top):** Collection of the New-York Historical Society / Gift of George K. Higgins / Bridgeman Images; **(bottom):** Sarah Ann Lillie Hardinge (1824–1913) View on the Guadalupe, Seguin, Texas 1853, transparent and opaque watercolor over graphite on paper, 4 3/4 x 7 1/2 in. Amon Carter Museum of American Art, Fort Worth, Texas, Gift of Natalie K. Shastid, 1984.3.14; **p. 367:** Granger Collection; **p. 370:** The Bancroft Library, University of California, Berkeley; **p. 371:** Image copyright (c) The Metropolitan Museum of Art / Art Resource, NY; **p. 374 (top):** © The Metropolitan Museum of Art / Art Resource, NY; **(bottom):** Library of Congress; **p. 375:** Fugitive slave law . . . Hamlet in chains. National anti-slavery standard. Vol. 21 (Oct. 17, 1850), page 82, Rare Book & Manuscript Library, Columbia University in the City of New York; **p. 379:** Library of Congress; **p. 381:** Bettmann / Corbis / Getty Images; **p. 382:** Collection of the New-York Historical Society / Bridgeman Images; **p. 384:** Bettmann / Corbis / Getty Images; **p. 385 (top):** Chicago History Museum, ICHi-022206; Christopher S. German, photographer; **(bottom):** George Eastman House / Getty Images; **p. 386:** Collection of the New-York Historical Society / Bridgeman Images; **p. 391:** Library of Congress; **p. 39:** Greenville County Museum of Art, Greenville, SC. **Chapter 14: Page 395:** Museum of Fine Arts, Boston / M. and M. Karolik Collection of American Watercolors and / Drawings, 1800–75 / The Bridgeman Art Library; **p. 398 (both):** Library of Congress; **p. 399 (top):** Library of Congress; **(bottom):** Newark Museum / Art Resource, NY; **p. 403:** Artist/maker unknown, American, Fourth Pennsylvania Cavalry After 1861 Oil on canvas. The Collection of Edgar William and Bernice Chrysler Garbisch, 1968 1968-222-3 Philadelphia Museum of Art; **p. 405 (both):** Library of Congress; **p. 406:** Granger Collection; **p. 408:** The Print Collector / Alamy Stock Photo; **p. 409 (top):** Smithsonian Institution, Photographic History Collection, Division of Information Technology; **(bottom):** Library of Congress; **p. 410 (top):** Library of Congress; **(bottom):** GLC00968 Unknown (Civil War Songbook). November 24, 1862 / Courtesy of The Gilder Lehrman Institute of American History; **p. 411:** David Bustill Bowser. Untitled (Lincoln and the Female Slave) 1863. Oil on canvas 1987.1.83. Simpson Collection, The Amistad Center for Art & Culture. Photo: John Groo / The Amistad Center for Art & Culture; **p. 412 (top):** Courtesy, Daughters of Charity, Province of St. Louise, St. Louis, MO; **(bottom):** Library of Congress; **p. 413 (top):** Chicago History Museum, ICHi-016764; **(bottom):** Chicago History Museum, ICHi-027442; **p. 414:** Wisconsin Historical Society, WHS- 6909; **p. 415:** Granger Collection; **p. 418 (top):** Library of Congress; **(bottom):** Collection of the New-York Historical Society / Bridgeman Images; **p. 419 (top):** Chicago History Museum, ICHi-068078; **(bottom):** The New York Public Library Digital Collections; **p. 421 (both):** Louisiana State University Special Collections From the U.S. Civil War Center exhibit Beyond Face Value, courtesy of Jules d'Hemecourt; **p. 424:** provided courtesy (c) HarpWeek., LLC; **p. 425:** William Washington (1831–1870), The Burial of Latané, 1864, oil on canvas, 38 x 48 inches. The Johnson Collection, Spartanburg, South Carolina; **p. 426 (both):** Library of Congress; **p. 428 (both):** Library of Congress; **p. 429:** Library of Congress; **p. 430:** National Archives; **p. 432 (top):** provided courtesy © HarpWeek LLC; **p. 433 (top):** Library of Congress; **(bottom):** © The Metropolitan Museum of Art / Art Resource, NY. **Chapter 15: Page 435:** Chicago History Museum, ICHi-022125; **p. 437:** Pictures Now / Alamy Stock Photo; **p. 438:** Library of Congress; **(bottom):** Photographic History Collection, Division of Information Technology and Communications, National Museum of American History, Smithsonian Institution; **p. 439:** Granger Collection; **p. 441:** Smithsonian American Art Museum, Washington, DC / Art Resource, NY; **p. 442:** Library of Congress; **p. 443:** The Valentine; **p. 447:** Niday Picture Library / Alamy Stock Photo; **p. 449 (both):** Library of Congress; **p. 450:** Library of Congress; **p. 451:** Museum of Political Life, University of Hartford; **p. 452:** Library of Congress; **p. 453:** Library of Congress; **p. 457:** Library of Congress; **p. 458 (both):** Library of Congress; **p. 459 (both):** Library of Congress; **p. 460:** Granger Collection; **p. 461:** Clements Library Collection, University of Michigan; **p. 462:** Granger Collection; **p. 463:** Wikimedia, public domain; **p. 464 (top both):** Library of Congress; **(bottom):** National Archives; p. 466: Library of

Congress; **p. 467:** Library of Congress. **Chapter 16: Page 469:** Iris & B. Gerald Cantor Center for Visual Arts at Stanford University; Stanford Family Collections. Conservation of this work was made possible by a generous gift from Honorable "Bill" and Jean Lane; **p. 472 (top):** © The Metropolitan Museum of Art. Image source: Art Resource, NY; **(bottom):** Museum of the City of New York / Bridgeman Images; **p. 474:** Library of Congress; **p. 475:** Granger Collection; **p. 476:** Library of Congress; **p. 477 (top):** Benjamin Paquette / Dreamstime; **(bottom):** Museum of the City of New York / Bridgeman Images; **p. 478 (top):** Museum of the City of New York, The Jacob Riis Collection (#108); **(bottom):** Bettmann / Getty Images; **p. 482 (top):** Scribner's Magazine, July 1895, public domain; **(bottom):** Bettmann / Corbis / Getty Images; **p. 483 (top):** National Portrait Gallery, Smithsonian Institution; **(bottom):** Bettmann / Corbis / Getty Images; **p. 486:** Wisconsin Historical Society, WHS-47662; **p. 487:** Newberry Library, Chicago; **p. 488:** Solomon Butcher Collection. History Nebraska, Nebraska State Historical Society; **p. 489:** Granger Collection; **p. 490 (top):** Courtesy of the Braun Research Library Collection, Autry National Museum, Los Angeles; Photo # P.13250; **(bottom):** Library of Congress; **p. 492:** Image copyright © The Metropolitan Museum of Art / Art Resource, NY; **p. 493:** Image copyright © The Metropolitan Museum of Art. Image source: Art Resource, NY; **p. 494:** Adoc-photos / Art Resource, NY; **p. 495:** Library of Congress; **p. 496 (top):** Missouri History Museum, St. Louis; **(bottom):** Courtesy of the Museum of the South Dakota State Historical Society, Pierre SD; **p. 497:** Library of Congress; **p. 503:** The Ohio State University Billy Ireland Cartoon Library & Museum. **Chapter 17: Page 506:** Disembarkation of the American at Ponce, Puerto Rico, 27th July 1898 (oil on canvas), Cuyàs Agulló, Manuel (19th century) / Private Collection / Photo © Christie's Images / Bridgeman Images; **p. 508:** Granger Collection; **p. 509:** Fotosearch / Getty Images; **p. 511:** The Denver Public Library, Western History Collection, WH2129RMN; **p. 512:** Bettmann / Corbis / Getty Images; **p. 513:** Library of Congress; **p. 515 (top):** Florida State Archives; **(bottom):** Library of Congress; **p. 516:** Library of Congress; **p. 517 (both):** Library of Congress; **p. 519 (top):** Mary McLeod Bethune with a line of girls from the school. ca 1905. Black & white photonegative. State Archives of Florida, Florida Memory. Accessed 28 Dec. 2018.https://www.floridamemory.com/items/show/149519; (bottom, both): Library of Congress; **p. 520:** Research Division of the Oklahoma Historical Society; **p. 521 (top):** Schomburg Center, NYPL / Art Resource, NY; **(bottom):** Courtesy of the Tennessee State Museum; **p. 524:** Judge Magazine, August 22, 1903; **p. 525 (top):** Library of Congress; **(bottom):** National Archives; **p. 526 (top):** Roy D. Graves pictorial collection, Bancroft Library, UC Berkeley; **(bottom):** University of Washington Libraries, Special Collections, #UW1678; **p. 527:** Library of Congress; **p. 529:** Library of Congress; **p. 530**: Library of Congress; **p. 531 (top):** Library of Congress; **(bottom):** Courtesy of the Hawaii State Archives, Queen Liliuokalani, Photograph Exhibition: Liliuokalani, Withdrawn Photos, PPWD-16-4-019; **p. 534 (top):** Courtesy Frederic Remington Art Museum, Ogdensburg, New York; **(bottom):** Hacienda La Fortuna, 1885 (oil on canvas) , Oller, Francisco (1833–1917) / Brooklyn Museum of Art, New York, USA / Gift of Lilla Brown in memory of her husband John W. Brown, by exchange / Bridgeman Images; **p. 535 (top):** Granger Collection; **(bottom):** Library of Congress; **p. 537:** Library of Congress; **p. 538:** North Wind Picture Archives / Alamy. **Chapter 18: Page 540:** John Sloan © 2013 Delaware Art Museum / Artists Rights Society (ARS), New York. Granger Collection; **p. 542:** Museum of the City of New York / Bridgeman Images; **p. 543:** Library of Congress; **p. 544:** Library of Congress; **p. 545 (top):** Library of Congress; **(bottom):** Courtesy of the author; **p. 546:** Library of Congress; **p. 547 (top):** Museum of the City of New York / Bridgeman Images; **(bottom):** Image Courtesy of The Advertising Archives; **p. 548:** Library of Congress; **p. 553 (top):** Library of Congress; **(bottom):** General Research Division, The New York Public Library; **p. 554 (top):** Library of Congress; **(bottom):** Bettmann / Corbis / Getty Images; **p. 556:** Library of Congress; **p. 558:** Collection of the New-York Historical Society / Bridgeman Images**; p. 559:** The New York Public Library; **p. 561 (top):** Library of Congress; **(bottom):** Utah State Historical Society; **p. 562 (top):** Hulton Archive / Getty Images; **(bottom):** archive.org. pd; **p. 563:** Courtesy of the Bancroft Library. University of California, Berkeley; **p. 564 (top):** Roosevelt 560.51 1902-156, Houghton Library, Harvard University; **(bottom):** provided courtesy © HarpWeek LLC; **p. 565 (top):** Frank Jay Haynes. Old Faithful Geyser, Yellowstone, 1885 (printed 1887) Albumen print, 21 5/8 x 16 5/8" The Frances Lehman Loeb Art Center, Vassar College, Poughkeepsie, New York Purchase, Jim and Carol Kautz, class of 1955, in honor of Richard and Ronay Menschel, 2002.6.2; **(bottom):**Roosevelt 560.51 1903-115, Houghton Library, Harvard University; **p. 567:** Fotosearch / Getty Images. **Chapter 19: Page 573:** Division of Political and Military History, National Museum of American History, Smithsonian Institution; **p. 577:** Everett Collection Inc / Alamy Stock Photo; **p. 578:** Christie's Images / Bridgeman Images; **p. 579:** Bettmann / Corbis / Getty Images; **p. 583 (top):** Gift of Mrs. Ernest Weidhaas, 1975, Collection of the Hudson River Museum, Yonkers, NY; **(bottom):** bpk Bildagentur / Kunstbibliothek, Staatliche Museen /Dietmar Katz / Art Resource, NY; **p. 584:** Library of Congress; **p. 585:** Library of Congress; **p. 586 (top):** Universal History Archive / UIG / Bridgeman Images; **(bottom):** National Archives; **p. 589 (top):** Library of Congress; **(bottom):** Jerry L. Thompson / Art Resource, NY; **p. 592:** Wikimedia, public domain; **p. 594 (top):** Paris Pierce / Alamy Stock Photo; **(bottom):** St. Louis Post-Dispatch, 1906, public domain; **p. 595:** later, R. P. Niagara Movement founders, 1905, 1905. W. E. B. Du Bois Papers (MS 312). Special Collections and University Archives, University of Massachusetts Amherst Libraries; **p. 596:** Library of Congress; **p. 597 (top):** ©2019 The Jacob and Gwendolyn Knight Lawrence Foundation, Seattle / Artist Rights Society (ARS), NY. Digital Image © The Museum of Modern Art / Licensed by SCALA / Art Resource, NY; **(bottom):** Courtesy of Tulsa Historical Society & Museum; **p. 598:** Library of Congress; **p. 600 (top):** Bettmann / Corbis / Getty Images; **(bottom):** National Archives; **p. 603:** Granger Collection. **Chapter 20: Page 606:** © 2019 T. H. and R. P. Benton Testamentary Trusts / UMB Bank Trustee/ Licensed by VAGA at Artists Rights Society (ARS), NY. Image copyright © The Metropolitan Museum of Art. Image source: Art Resource, NY; **p. 607:** Library of Congress; **p. 610:** kansasmemory.org, Kansas State Historical Society, Copy and Reuse Restrictions Apply; **p. 611:** Minnesota Historical Society;

p. 612 (left): The Lane Collection, Museum of Fine Arts, Boston; **(right):** National Gallery of Art, Washington, D.C., collection of Barney A. Ebsworth; **p. 613:** Honolulu Academy of Arts: Gift of Philip H. Roach, Jr., 2001; **p. 614 (both):** Granger Collection; **p. 615:** Granger Collection; **p. 616:** Bettmann / Corbis / Getty Images; **p. 620:** Library of Congress; **p. 621:** San Diego Museum of Art / Bridgeman Images; **p. 622 (top):** The Denver Public Library, Western History Collection, Rh-1158; **(bottom):** City of Vancouver Archives, Image AM54-S4-I-: CVA 20-2; **p. 623 (top):** Smithsonian Institution Archives #2005-26202; **(bottom):** Library of Congress **p. 624:** Indiana University Campus Art Collection, THB X, Thomas Hart Benton, Indiana Murals: Parks, the Circus, the Klan, the Press. Photograph by Michael Cavanagh and Kevin Montague, Eskenazi Museum of Art at Indiana University; **p. 625:** National Border Patrol Museum, El Paso, Texas; **p. 627:** Library of Congress; **p. 628:** Schomburg Center / The New York Public Library / Art Resource, NY; **p. 629:** Collection of David J. And Janice L. Frent; **p. 630:** Library of Congress; **p. 631:** Courtesy of the author; p. 632 **(top):** National Archives; **(bottom):** Granger Collection; **p. 633:** John Tresilian / NY Daily News Archive via Getty Images; **p. 634:** Buyenlarge / Getty Images; **p. 635:** AP Photo. **Chapter 21: Page 637:** The Stapleton Collection / Bridgeman Images; **p. 640:** National Archives; **p. 641: (top):** Granger Collection; **(bottom):** Bettmann / Corbis / Getty Images; **p. 642:** National Archives; **p. 643:** David Rumsey Map Collection; **p. 645:** kansasmemory.org, Kansas State Historical Society; **p. 646 (top):** Library of Congress; **(bottom):** Punch Limited / Top Foto; **p. 648:** Bettmann / Corbis / Getty Images; **p. 649 (top):** Underwood Archives/Getty Images; **(bottom):** Library of Congress; **p. 650 (top):** Billy Graham Center Archives, Wheaton College, Wheaton, IL; **(bottom):** FDR Library Photo Collection, National Archives; **p. 651 (top):** Library of Congress; **(bottom):** National Archives; **p. 652:** Library of Congress; **p. 653:** Bettmann / Getty Images; **p. 656:** Franklin D. Roosevelt Library; **p. 658:** Bettmann / Corbis / Getty Images; **p. 659 (top):** Library of Congress; **(bottom):** Bettmann / Getty Images; **p. 660:** Library of Congress; **p. 661:** Library of Congress; **p. 662:** Photograph © Morgan and Marvin Smith; **p. 663:** HOLC Residential Security Map, Federal Home Loan Bank Board, Records of the City Survey Program," RG 195, 450/68/03/02, National Archives II, College Park, MD; **p. 664:** Library of Congress; **p. 665:** Franklin D. Roosevelt Presidential Library; **p. 666:** Bettmann / Corbis / Getty Images; **p. 667:** © 2019 Estate of Ben Shahn / Licensed by VAGA at Artists Rights Society (ARS), NY. Harvard Art Museum / Art Resource, NY. **Chapter 22: Page 670:** Published with the permission of The Wolfsonian - Florida International University (Miami, Florida); **p. 672:** "Four Freedoms" illustrations (c) SEPS licensed by Curtis Licensing Indianapolis, IN. Printed by permission of the Norman Rockwell Family Agency © Copyright 1943 the Norman Rockwell Family Entities; **p. 673:** Washington Star; **p. 674:** Andreas Feninger / George Eastman House / Getty Images; **p. 676:** National Archives; **p. 678:** Bettmann / Corbis/Getty Images; **p. 680:** Mariners' Museum and Park; **p. 681:** PhotoQuest / Getty Images; **p. 682:** Library of Congress; **p. 683 (both):** Library of Congress; **p. 684:** Image Courtesy of The WASP Archive, The TWU Libraries Woman's Collection, Texas Woman's University, Denton, Texas; **p. 685 (top):** war posters / Alamy Stock Photo; **(bottom):** National Archives; **p. 687**: **(top):**Prisma by Dukas Presseagentur GmbH / Alamy Stock Photo; **(bottom):** Courtesy Northwestern University Library; **p. 688 (top):** National Archives; **p. 692 (top):** Dorothea Lange / National Archives; **(bottom):** Library of Congress/ Getty Images; **p. 696**: Collection of the Smithsonian National Museum of African American History and Culture, Gift of Joe Schwartz and Family, © Joe Schwartz; **p. 697 (both):** Library of Congress; **p. 698 (top):** National Archives; **(bottom):** Library of Congress; **p. 700 (top):** Los Alamos Scientific Laboratory, Courtesy of Harry S. Truman Library; **(bottom):** Unidentified Photographer, (Interior damage to steel frame of Honkawa Grammar School Auditorium, Hiroshima), November 8, 1945 International Center Of Photography, Purchase, with funds provided by the ICP Acquisitions Committee, 2006; **p. 702:** Library of Congress. **Chapter 23: Page 705:** American Catholic History Research Center and University Archives, Catholic University of America; **p. 707:** National Archives; **p. 709:** Bettmann / Corbis / Getty Images; **p. 710:** Bettmann / Corbis / Getty Images; **p. 711**: PhotoQuest / Getty Images; **p. 713 (top):** Bettmann / Corbis / Getty Images; **(bottom):** AP Photo; **p. 716:** Photofest; **p. 717:** © 1998 Kate Rothko Prizel & Christopher Rothko / Artist Rights Society (ARS), New York; **p. 718:** Bettmann / Corbis / Getty Images; **p. 719 (top):** Library of Congress; **(bottom):** Hy Peskin's SL & WH, www .HyPeskin.com; **p. 720:** The Jon B. Lovelace Collection of California Photographs in Carol M. Highsmith's America Project, Library of Congress; **p. 721:** Bettmann / Corbis / Getty Images; **p. 723 (top):** Lake County Illinois Discovery Museum, Curt Teich Postcard Archives; **(bottom):** Densho: The Japanese American Legacy Project; **p. 724 (top):** Los Angeles Public Library Photo Collection; **(bottom):** San Diego History Center; **p. 726:** Bettmann / Corbis / Getty Images; **p. 727 (top):** Betttmann / Corbis / Getty Images; **(bottom):** A 1949 Herblock Cartoon, © The Herb Block Foundation. **Chapter 24: Page 734:** Artwork courtesy of the Norman Rockwell Family Agency; **p. 735:** Howard Sochurek / Time Life Pictures / Getty Images; p. 739 **(top):** Hagley Museum & Library, Wilmington, Delaware / Bridgeman Images; **(bottom):** Hulton Archive / Getty Images; **p. 740:** Harvard Art Museums / Fogg Museum, Transfer from the Carpenter Center for the Visual Arts, American Professional Photographers Collection. © President and Fellows of Harvard College; **p. 741:** The Advertising Archives; **p. 742 (top):** Bettmann / Corbis / Getty Images; **(bottom):** Fotosearch / Getty Images; **p. 743:** American Economic Foundation, "Man's Belief in God is Personal," CU Libraries Exhibitions , accessed February 22, 2013, https://exhibitions.cul.columbia.edu/items/show/2829; **p. 745 (top):** Dwight D. Eisenhower Presidential Library; **(bottom):** Library of Congress; **p. 748:** Bettmann / Corbis / Getty Images; **p. 750:** AP Photo; **p. 751:** Bruce Davidson / Magnum Photos; **p. 752 (top):** Album / Art Resource, NY; **(bottom):** Burt Glinn / Magnum Photos; **p. 754:** Ed Clark / Time Life Pictures / Getty Images; **p. 755:** Carl / Wasaki / Time Life Pictures / Getty Images; **p. 756:** AP Photo; **p. 758:** Library of Congress; **p. 759 (top):** Lexey Swall / The New York Times/Redux; **(bottom):** Bettmann / Corbis / Getty Images; **p. 762:** Photograph by Gordon Parks, Courtesy of © The Gordon Parks Foundation; **p. 763:** Time & Life Pictures / Getty Images; **p. 764:** Corbis / Getty Images. **Chapter 25: Page 766:** National Archives; **p. 767:** Bettmann / Getty Images; **p. 768:** © Cecil Williams;

p. 769 (top): © Bob Adelman Estate; **(bottom):** © Walter P. Reuther Library, Wayne State University; **p. 771:** Art Rickerby / The LIFE Picture Collection / Getty Images; p. 772 **(top):** Meek Collection / University of Mississippi; **(bottom):** Photo by Carl Mydans / Time Life Pictures/Getty Image**; p. 774:** Photo, by Ken Thompson. Used by permission of © The General Board of Global Ministries of the United Methodist Church, Inc; **p. 775:** Bettmann / Getty Images; **p. 776:** Bettmann / Getty Images; **p. 777:** © 1965 Spider Martin; **p. 778:** LBJ Library photo by Yoichi Okamoto; **p. 779:** LBJ Library photo by Cecil Stoughton; **p. 780:** Bettmann / Corbis / Getty Images; **p. 783:** University of Delaware Archives; **p. 785:** CPA Media / Pictures From History; **p. 789:** Photograph by Yoichi Okamoto, courtesy of the Lyndon Baines Johnson Library; **p. 790:** Getty Images; **p. 791 (top):** Courtesy of Special Collections, Buswell Library; **(bottom):** Ralph Crane / Time Life Pictures / Getty Images; **p. 793:** Boston Globe via Getty Images; **p. 794 (top):** © 1987 The Peter Hujar Archive LLC. Courtesy Pace / MacGil Gallery, New York and Fraenkel Gallery, San Francisco. Alexander Turbull Library, New Zealand; **(bottom):** Photo: Dick Darby. Walter P. Reuther Library, Archives of Labor and Urban Affairs, Wayne State University; **p. 795 (top):** Arthur Rice, Red Power. Courtesy of The Merrill C. Berman Collection; **(bottom):** AP Photo; **p. 797 (top):** Estate of Karl Hubenthal; **(bottom):** © Grey Villet; **p. 798 (top):** A 1963 Herblock Cartoon, © The Herb Block Foundation; **(bottom):** © Dr. Ernest C. Withers, Sr. courtesy of the WITHERS Family TRUST; **p. 799:** AP Photo / File; **p. 800:** Frederick Douglass mural on the 'Solidarity Wall', Falls Road, Belfast; http://en.wikipedia.org/wiki/GNU_Free_Documentation_License. **Chapter 26: Page 807:** Courtesy Ronald Reagan Library; **p. 810 (top):** National Archives; **(bottom):** Richard Nixon Presidential Library and Museum, NARA; **p. 814:** NARA / Alamy Stock Photo; **p. 815 (top):** May 4 Collection. Kent State University Libraries. Special Collections and Archives; **(bottom):** AP Photo / Jack Thorne; **p. 816:** Library of Congress; **p. 817:** Copyright © Diana Mara Henry / www.dianamarahenry.com; **p. 820:** AP Photo; **p. 821:** AP Photo; **p. 822:** Courtesy Gerald R. Ford Library; **p. 823:** Fox Photos / Getty Images; **p. 826:** AP Photo; **p. 827:** Bettmann / Corbis / Getty Images; **p. 831 (both):** Bettmann / Corbis / Getty Images; **p. 832:** Bettmann / Corbis / Getty Images; **p. 834 (top):** Los Angeles Examiner Collection, USC Libraries Special Collections; **(bottom):** Time Life Pictures / Getty Images; **p. 835:** AP Photo / David Handschuh; **p. 836:** Library of Congress; **p. 837:** © Eli Reed / Magnum Photos; **p. 838:** Ronald Reagan Presidential Library; **p. 839:** Photofest; **p. 841:** AP Photo / Ira Schwartz. **Chapter 27: Page 844:** Peter Charlesworth / LightRocket via Getty Images; **p. 847:** Peter Turnley / Corbis / VCG via Getty Images; **p. 845:** AP Photo / Thomas Kienzle; **p. 852:** Peter Turnley / Corbis / VCG via Getty Images; **p. 853:** Tony Law/Redux; p. 854: © Patrick Hagerty; **p. 855:** Photo by Joi Ito; http://creativecommons.org/licenses/by/2.0/deed.en; **p. 856:** Reprinted with permission of David Jacobson; **p. 857:** © Hans Haacke / Artists Rights Society [ARS], New York / VG Bild-Kunst, Bonn; **p. 858:** AP Photo / Damian Dovarganes; **p. 859:** AP Photo/Steven Senne; **p. 862:** © Catherine Karnow; **p. 864:** Takaaki Iwabu KRT / Newscom; **p. 866:** AP Photo; **p. 867:** Vanessa Vick / Science Source; **p. 870:** Ralf-Finn Hestoft / Corbis / Getty Images; **p. 871:** A 1998 Herblock Cartoon, © The Herb Block Foundation; **p. 872:** Colin Braley / REUTERS / Newscom; **p. 873:** Steve Ludlum / The New York Times / Redux; **p. 874**: Edward Keating / The New York Times / Redux; **p. 875:** Serge J-F. Levy; **p. 876:** Steve Benson / Creators Syndicate; **p. 877:** Mario Tama / Getty Images; **p. 878**: AP Photo; **p. 879**: Hank Walker / Getty Images; **p. 881:** Michael Ramirez / Creators Syndicate. **Chapter 28: Page 884:** Victor J. Blue / The New York Times / Redux; **p. 887: (top):** AP Photo; **(bottom):** jr-art.net; **p. 888 (top):** AP Photo / Kampha Bouaphanh; **(bottom):** Wikipedia, public domain; **p. 889:** AP Photo; **p. 891:** Joshua Lott / The New York Times / Redux; **p. 893:** AUTH © 2009 The Philadelphia Inquirer. Reprinted with permission of UNIVERSAL UCLICK. All rights reserved; **p. 896:** Ron Sachs / Shutterstock; **p. 895:** White House Photo / Alamy Stock Photo; **p. 897**: Steve Petteway / USSC via CNP/Newscom; p. 898: AP Photo; **p. 902:** Spencer Platt / Getty Images; **p. 905**: Whitney Curtis, The New York Times, Redux; **p. 906**: Official White House Photo by Pete Souza; **p. 907 (top):** U.S. Air Force photo / Lt. Col. Leslie Pratt; **(bottom):** David Sipress The New Yorker Collection / The Cartoon Bank; **p. 911**: Win McNamee / Getty Images; **p. 912**: Mark Lyons / Getty Images; **p. 913:** The American Dream Project, Democratic Convention, Independence Mall, Philadelphia, July 25, 2016. LigoranoReese, photo credit; **p. 917 (top):** Richard Theis / Alamy Stock Photo; **(bottom):** U.S. Customs and Border Protection via Getty Images; **p. 918:** Dennis Hallinan / Alamy Stock Photo; **p. 919:** Mark Dixon Blue Lens; **p. 921:** Alec Soth / Magnum Photos; **p. 923 (top):** Hank Willis Thomas and Emily Shur, Freedom From Want, 2018. Copyright For Freedoms; **(bottom):** Shay Horse / NurPhoto via Getty Images; **p. 924 (top):** Bjanka Kadic / Alamy Stock Photo ; **(bottom):** Eli Reed / Magnum Photos.

TEXT

Chapter 1: Bartolomé de las Casas: "History of the Indies [1528]", excerpt from *History of the Indies*, translated and edited by Andrée Collard (New York: Harper & Row, 1971), pp. 82, 112–115. Copyright © 1971 by Andrée M. Collard, renewed © 1999 by Joyce J. Contrucci. Reprinted by permission of Joyce J. Contrucci. **Chapter 2: Thomas Hutchinson**: "The Examination of Mrs. Ann Hutchinson at the court of Newtown." Reprinted by permission of the publisher from *The History of the Colony and Province of Massachusetts Bay, Vol. II* by Thomas Hutchinson, edited by Lawrence Shaw Mayo, pp. 366–391, Cambridge, Mass.: Harvard University Press, Copyright © 1963 by the President and Fellows of Harvard College. Copyright © renewed 1964 by Lawrence Shaw Mayo. **Chapter 6: Abigail Adams**: "Abigail Adams to John Adams, 31 March 1776." Reprinted by permission of the publisher from *The Adams Papers: Adams Family Correspondence, Volume I and II: December 1761–March 1778*, edited by L. H. Butterfield, Cambridge, Mass.: The Belknap Press of Harvard University Press, Copyright © 1963 by the Massachusetts Historical Society. **Chapter 8: Democratic-Republican Society of Pennsylvania**: Excerpt from minutes of The Democratic Society of Pennsylvania, December 18, 1794. The Historical Society of Pennsylvania (HSP), Collection # Am. 315/3150. Reprinted with permission. **Chapter 9: Margaret McCarthy**: "Letter of Margaret McCarthy to Her Family (1850") From "State-Aided Emigration Schemes from Crown Estates in Ireland c. 1850" by Eilish Ellis. *Analecta Hibernica 22* (1960), pp. 390–393. Reprinted by permission of the estate of Eilish Ellis.

Chapter 11: Joseph Taper: Excerpt from "Letter from Joseph Taper to Joseph Long, November 11, 1840" in the Joseph Long Papers located in the Rare Book, Manuscript, and Special Collections Library, Duke University. **Chapter 19: Woodrow Wilson**: President Wilson's Declaration of War Message to Congress, April 2, 1917. From Link, Arthur S.: *The Papers of Woodrow Wilson, 1912.* Vol. 25, © 1978, Princeton University Press. Reprinted by permission of Princeton University Press. **John Steinbeck**: Excerpt from *The Harvest Gypsies* by John Steinbeck. Copyright © 1936 by *The San Francisco News.* Reprinted by permission of Heyday Books, Berkeley, California. **Chapter 22: LULAC News**: "Editorial on World War II and Mexican-Americans (1945)" from *LULAC News*, Volume 12, October 1945. Reprinted by permission of LULAC News. **Charles H. Wesley**: "The Negro Has Always Wanted the Four Freedoms," from *What the Negro Wants* edited by Rayford W. Logan. Copyright © 1944 by the University of North Carolina Press, renewed 1972 by Rayford W. Logan. Used by permission of the publisher. www.uncpress.org **Chapter 23: Oscar Handlin**: "The Immigration Fight Has Only Begun" by Oscar Handlin. Originally published in *Commentary*, July 1952. Reprinted by permission of the Oscar Handlin estate. **Chapter 24: Martin Luther King Jr.**: "Meeting at Holt Street Church", Reprinted by arrangement with The Heirs to the Estate of Martin Luther King Jr., c/o Writers house as agent for the proprietor, New York, NY. Copyright © 1963 Martin Luther King Jr.; Copyright © renewed 1991 Coretta Scott King. **Chapter 25: Barry Goldwater**: "Acceptance Speech to the Republican National Convention (1964)", from the Barry M. Goldwater Papers, Arizona Historical Foundation Collection, Arizona State University Libraries. Reprinted by permission. **National Organization for Women**: Excerpts from "The National Organization for Women's 1966 Statement of Purpose," by Betty Friedan. Reprinted with permission of National Organization for Women. This is a historical document and may not reflect the current language or priorities of the organization. **Chapter 26: Barry Commoner**: Excerpts from "Chapter 1: The Environmental Crisis" from *The Closing Circle: Nature, Man, and Technology* by Barry Commoner. Copyright © 1971 by Barry Commoner. Reprinted by permission of Lisa Feiner. **Philadelphia Chapter of the National Organization for Women:** Brochure on the Equal Rights Amendment, National Organization for Women, Philadelphia Chapter records [2054], Historical Society of Pennsylvania. **Chapter 27: Global Exchange**: "Declaration for Global Democracy," from Global Exchange, Seattle, December 1999. Reprinted by permission. **Los Tigres del Norte:** *Jaula de Oro.* Fonovisa, 1984. Lyrics by Enrique Franco. Translated by Alana Graffam. Reprinted with permission of TN Ediciones Musicales. **Chapter 28: Khizr Khan:** Excerpt(s) from AN AMERICAN Family: A MEMOIR OF HOPE AND SACRIFICE by Khizr Khan, copyright © 2017 by Khizr Khan. Used by permission of Random House, an imprint and division of Penguin Random House LLC. All rights reserved.

LINE ART

M27.3: Map 1 from "Contemporary Immigrant Gateways in Historical Perspective," by Audrey Singer. *Daedalus*, Summer 2013, Vol. 142, No. 3: 76–91. Reprinted by permission of the author. **F28.3**: Figure: Income Inequality in the United States, 1910–2010, From *Capital in the Twenty-First Century* by Thomas Piketty. Reprinted by permission of the author.

INDEX

Page numbers in *italics* refer to illustrations.